Nineteenth-Century Literature Criticism

Guide to Thomson Gale Literary Criticism Series

For criticism on	Consult these Thomson Gale series
Authors now living or who died after December 31, 1999	*CONTEMPORARY LITERARY CRITICISM (CLC)*
Authors who died between 1900 and 1999	*TWENTIETH-CENTURY LITERARY CRITICISM (TCLC)*
Authors who died between 1800 and 1899	*NINETEENTH-CENTURY LITERATURE CRITICISM (NCLC)*
Authors who died between 1400 and 1799	*LITERATURE CRITICISM FROM 1400 TO 1800 (LC)* *SHAKESPEAREAN CRITICISM (SC)*
Authors who died before 1400	*CLASSICAL AND MEDIEVAL LITERATURE CRITICISM (CMLC)*
Authors of books for children and young adults	*CHILDREN'S LITERATURE REVIEW (CLR)*
Dramatists	*DRAMA CRITICISM (DC)*
Poets	*POETRY CRITICISM (PC)*
Short story writers	*SHORT STORY CRITICISM (SSC)*
Literary topics and movements	*HARLEM RENAISSANCE: A GALE CRITICAL COMPANION (HR)* *THE BEAT GENERATION: A GALE CRITICAL COMPANION (BG)* *FEMINISM IN LITERATURE: A GALE CRITICAL COMPANION (FL)* *GOTHIC LITERATURE: A GALE CRITICAL COMPANION (GL)*
Asian American writers of the last two hundred years	*ASIAN AMERICAN LITERATURE (AAL)*
Black writers of the past two hundred years	*BLACK LITERATURE CRITICISM (BLC)* *BLACK LITERATURE CRITICISM SUPPLEMENT (BLCS)*
Hispanic writers of the late nineteenth and twentieth centuries	*HISPANIC LITERATURE CRITICISM (HLC)* *HISPANIC LITERATURE CRITICISM SUPPLEMENT (HLCS)*
Native North American writers and orators of the eighteenth, nineteenth, and twentieth centuries	*NATIVE NORTH AMERICAN LITERATURE (NNAL)*
Major authors from the Renaissance to the present	*WORLD LITERATURE CRITICISM, 1500 TO THE PRESENT (WLC)* *WORLD LITERATURE CRITICISM SUPPLEMENT (WLCS)*

ISSN 0732-1864

Volume 177

Nineteenth-Century Literature Criticism

Criticism of the
Works of Novelists, Philosophers, and Other
Creative Writers Who Died between 1800
and 1899, from the First Published Critical
Appraisals to Current Evaluations

Kathy D. Darrow
Russel Whitaker
Project Editors

THOMSON

GALE

Detroit • New York • San Francisco • New Haven, Conn. • Waterville, Maine • London

THOMSON

GALE™

Nineteenth-Century Literature Criticism, Vol. 177

Project Editors
Kathy Darrow and Russel Whitaker

Editorial
Jeffrey W. Hunter, Jelena O. Krstović, Michelle Lee, Thomas J. Schoenberg, Noah Schusterbauer, Lawrence J. Trudeau

Data Capture
Frances Monroe, Gwen Tucker

Indexing Services
Factiva, Inc.

Rights and Acquisitions
Edna Hedblad, Emma Hull, Sue Rudolph

Imaging and Multimedia
Randy Bassett, Lezlie Light, Mike Logusz, Dan Newell, Christine O'Bryan

Composition and Electronic Capture
Tracey L. Matthews

Manufacturing
Rhonda Dover

Associate Product Manager
Marc Cormier

LIBRARY OF CONGRESS CATALOG CARD NUMBER 84-643008

ISBN-13: 978-0-7876-9848-5
ISBN-10: 0-7876-9848-2
ISSN 0732-1864

Printed in the United States of America
10 9 8 7 6 5 4 3 2 1

Contents

Preface

Since its inception in 1981, *Nineteenth-Century Literature Criticism* (*NCLC*) has been a valuable resource for students and librarians seeking critical commentary on writers of this transitional period in world history. Designated an "Outstanding Reference Source" by the American Library Association with the publication of is first volume, *NCLC* has since been purchased by over 6,000 school, public, and university libraries. The series has covered more than 500 authors representing 38 nationalities and over 28,000 titles. No other reference source has surveyed the critical reaction to nineteenth-century authors and literature as thoroughly as *NCLC*.

Scope of the Series

NCLC is designed to introduce students and advanced readers to the authors of the nineteenth century and to the most significant interpretations of these authors' works. The great poets, novelists, short story writers, playwrights, and philosophers of this period are frequently studied in high school and college literature courses. By organizing and reprinting commentary written on these authors, *NCLC* helps students develop valuable insight into literary history, promotes a better understanding of the texts, and sparks ideas for papers and assignments. Each entry in *NCLC* presents a comprehensive survey of an author's career or an individual work of literature and provides the user with a multiplicity of interpretations and assessments. Such variety allows students to pursue their own interests; furthermore, it fosters an awareness that literature is dynamic and responsive to many different opinions.

Every fourth volume of *NCLC* is devoted to literary topics that cannot be covered under the author approach used in the rest of the series. Such topics include literary movements, prominent themes in nineteenth-century literature, literary reaction to political and historical events, significant eras in literary history, prominent literary anniversaries, and the literatures of cultures that are often overlooked by English-speaking readers.

NCLC continues the survey of criticism of world literature begun by Thomson Gale's *Contemporary Literary Criticism* (*CLC*) and *Twentieth-Century Literary Criticism* (*TCLC*).

Organization of the Book

An *NCLC* entry consists of the following elements:

- The **Author Heading** cites the name under which the author most commonly wrote, followed by birth and death dates. Also located here are any name variations under which an author wrote, including transliterated forms for authors whose native languages use nonroman alphabets. If the author wrote consistently under a pseudonym, the pseudonym will be listed in the author heading and the author's actual name given in parenthesis on the first line of the biographical and critical information. Uncertain birth or death dates are indicated by question marks. Single-work entries are preceded by a heading that consists of the most common form of the title in English translation (if applicable) and the original date of composition.

- The **Introduction** contains background information that introduces the reader to the author, work, or topic that is the subject of the entry.

- The list of **Principal Works** is ordered chronologically by date of first publication and lists the most important works by the author. The genre and publication date of each work is given. In the case of foreign authors whose works have been translated into English, the list will focus primarily on twentieth-century translations, selecting those works most commonly considered the best by critics. Unless otherwise indicated, dramas are dated by first performance, not first publication. Lists of **Representative Works** by different authors appear with topic entries.

- Reprinted **Criticism** is arranged chronologically in each entry to provide a useful perspective on changes in critical evaluation over time. The critic's name and the date of composition or publication of the critical work are given at the beginning of each piece of criticism. Unsigned criticism is preceded by the title of the source in which it appeared. All titles by the author featured in the text are printed in boldface type. Footnotes are reprinted at the end of each essay or excerpt. In the case of excerpted criticism, only those footnotes that pertain to the excerpted texts are included. Criticism in topic entries is arranged chronologically under a variety of subheadings to facilitate the study of different aspects of the topic.

- A complete **Bibliographical Citation** of the original essay or book precedes each piece of criticism.

- Critical essays are prefaced by brief **Annotations** explicating each piece.

- An annotated bibliography of **Further Reading** appears at the end of each entry and suggests resources for additional study. In some cases, significant essays for which the editors could not obtain reprint rights are included here. Boxed material following the further reading list provides references to other biographical and critical sources on the author in series published by Thomson Gale.

Indexes

Each volume of *NCLC* contains a **Cumulative Author Index** listing all authors who have appeared in a wide variety of reference sources published by Thomson Gale, including *NCLC*. A complete list of these sources is found facing the first page of the Author Index. The index also includes birth and death dates and cross references between pseudonyms and actual names.

A **Cumulative Nationality Index** lists all authors featured in *NCLC* by nationality, followed by the number of the *NCLC* volume in which their entry appears.

A **Cumulative Topic Index** lists the literary themes and topics treated in the series as well as in *Classical and Medieval Literature Criticism, Literature Criticism from 1400 to 1800, Twentieth-Century Literary Criticism,* and the *Contemporary Literary Criticism* Yearbook, which was discontinued in 1998.

An alphabetical **Title Index** accompanies each volume of *NCLC*, with the exception of the Topics volumes. Listings of titles by authors covered in the given volume are followed by the author's name and the corresponding page numbers where the titles are discussed. English translations of foreign titles and variations of titles are cross-referenced to the title under which a work was originally published. Titles of novels, dramas, nonfiction books, and poetry, short story, or essay collections are printed in italics, while individual poems, short stories, and essays are printed in roman type within quotation marks.

In response to numerous suggestions from librarians, Thomson Gale also produces an annual paperbound edition of the *NCLC* cumulative title index. This annual cumulation, which alphabetically lists all titles reviewed in the series, is available to all customers. Additional copies of this index are available upon request. Librarians and patrons will welcome this separate index; it saves shelf space, is easy to use, and is recyclable upon receipt of the next edition.

Citing *Nineteenth-Century Literature Criticism*

When citing criticism reprinted in the Literary Criticism Series, students should provide complete bibliographic information so that the cited essay can be located in the original print or electronic source. Students who quote directly from reprinted criticism may use any accepted bibliographic format, such as University of Chicago Press style or Modern Language Association style.

The examples below follow recommendations for preparing a bibliography set forth in *The Chicago Manual of Style,* 14th ed. (Chicago: The University of Chicago Press, 1993); the first example pertains to material drawn from periodicals, the second to material reprinted from books:

Franklin, J. Jeffrey. "The Victorian Discourse of Gambling: Speculations on *Middlemarch* and *The Duke's Children*." *ELH* 61, no. 4 (winter 1994): 899-921. Reprinted in *Nineteenth-Century Literature Criticism*. Vol. 168, edited by Jessica Bomarito and Russel Whitaker, 39-51. Detroit: Thomson Gale, 2006.

Frank, Joseph. "*The Gambler*: A Study in Ethnopsychology." In *Freedom and Responsibility in Russian Literature: Essays in Honor of Robert Louis Jackson,* edited by Elizabeth Cheresh Allen and Gary Saul Morson, 69-85. Evanston, Ill.: Northwestern University Press, 1995. Reprinted in *Nineteenth-Century Literature Criticism*. Vol. 168, edited by Jessica Bomarito and Russel Whitaker, 75-84. Detroit: Thomson Gale, 2006.

The examples below follow recommendations for preparing a works cited list set forth in the *MLA Handbook for Writers of Research Papers,* 6th ed. (New York: The Modern Language Association of America, 2003); the first example pertains to material drawn from periodicals, the second to material reprinted from books:

Franklin, J. Jeffrey. "The Victorian Discourse of Gambling: Speculations on *Middlemarch* and *The Duke's Children*." *ELH* 61.4 (Winter 1994): 899-921. Reprinted in *Nineteenth-Century Literature Criticism*. Eds. Jessica Bomarito and Russel Whitaker. Vol. 168. Detroit: Thomson Gale, 2006. 39-51.

Frank, Joseph. "*The Gambler*: A Study in Ethnopsychology." *Freedom and Responsibility in Russian Literature: Essays in Honor of Robert Louis Jackson.* Eds. Elizabeth Cheresh Allen and Gary Saul Morson. Evanston, Ill.: Northwestern University Press, 1995. 69-85. Reprinted in *Nineteenth-Century Literature Criticism*. Eds. Jessica Bomarito and Russel Whitaker. Vol. 168. Detroit: Thomson Gale, 2006. 75-84.

Suggestions are Welcome

Readers who wish to suggest new features, topics, or authors to appear in future volumes, or who have other suggestions or comments are cordially invited to call, write, or fax the Associate Product Manager:

Associate Product Manager, Literary Criticism Series
Thomson Gale
27500 Drake Road
Farmington Hills, MI 48331-3535
1-800-347-4253 (GALE)
Fax: 248-699-8054

Acknowledgments

The editors wish to thank the copyright holders of the criticism included in this volume and the permissions managers of many book and magazine publishing companies for assisting us in securing reproduction rights. Following is a list of the copyright holders who have granted us permission to reproduce material in this volume of *NCLC*. Every effort has been made to trace copyright, but if omissions have been made, please let us know.

COPYRIGHTED MATERIAL IN *NCLC,* VOLUME 177, WAS REPRODUCED FROM THE FOLLOWING PERIODICALS:

American Quarterly, v. xv, fall, 1963. Copyright © 1963 The Johns Hopkins University Press. Reproduced by permission.—*American Studies,* v. 35, fall, 1994. Copyright © Mid-America American Studies Association, 1978. Reproduced by permission of the publisher.—*ELH,* v. 57, winter, 1990. Copyright © 1990 The Johns Hopkins University Press. Reproduced by permission.—*English Language Notes,* v. xxii, September, 1984. Copyright © 1984, Regents of the University of Colorado. All rights reserved. Reproduced by permission.—*English Studies,* v. 52, June, 1971; v. 61, April, 1980. Copyright © 1971, 1980 Swets & Zeitlinger. Both reproduced by permission.—*European Romantic Review,* v. 4, summer, 1993 for "Dramatic Form, 'Double Voice,' and 'Carnivalization' in 'Christabel'" by Avery F. Gaskins. Reproduced by permission of Taylor & Francis, Ltd., http//:www.tandf.co.uk/journals and the author.—*The German Quarterly,* v. xli, May, 1968; v. 61, summer, 1988. Copyright © 1968, 1988 by the American Association of Teachers of German. Both reproduced by permission.—*German Studies Review,* v. iv, May, 1981. Copyright © 1981 by the Western Association for German Studies. All rights reserved. Reproduced by permission.—*The Germanic Review,* v. lv, spring, 1980 for "C. M. Wieland's Narrators, Heroes and Readers" by Charlotte C. Prather; v. lxx, spring, 1995 for "Christoph Martin Wieland and the German Making of Greece" by James M. van der Laan. Both reproduced by permission of the respective authors.—*Journal of Southern History,* v. LVI, November, 1990 for "A Sadder Simon Suggs: Freedom and Slavery in the Humor of Johnson Hooper" by Johanna Nicol Shields. Copyright © 1990 by the Southern Historical Association. Reprinted by permission of the Managing Editor and the author.—*Journal of English and Germanic Philology,* v. 102, October, 2003. Copyright © 2003 by the Board of Trustees of the University of Illinois. Used with permission of the University of Illinois Press.—*Lessing Yearbook,* v. viii, 1976 for "Wieland as Essayist" by John A. McCarthy. Copyright, 1976 Wayne State University Press. Reproduced by permission of Wallstein Verlag GmbH.—*MLN,* v. 95, April, 1980. Copyright © 1980 The Johns Hopkins University Press. Reproduced by permission.—*Neophilologus,* v. lxxxviii, January, 2004 for "'Nenne doch, o Muse, den Sitz der kleinen Kolonie': Wieland's Portrayals of Nature Utopias in Verse and Prose" by Florian Gelzer. Copyright © 2004 Kluwer Academic Publishers. Reproduced with kind permission from Springer Science and Business Media and the author.—*Romanticism Past & Present,* v. 10, winter, 1986 for "Christabel's 'Wandering Mother' and the Discourse of the Self: A Lacanian Reading of Repressed Narration" by Charles J. Rzepka. Copyright © 1986 Northeastern University. Reproduced by permission of the author.—*Studies in English Literature, 1500-1900,* v. 4, autumn, 1964; v. 37, autumn, 1997; v. 42, autumn, 2002. Copyright © 1964, 1997, 2002 The Johns Hopkins University Press. All reproduced by permission.—*Studies in Romanticism,* v. 19, fall, 1980; v. 23, winter, 1984. Copyright 1980, 1984 by the Trustees of Boston University. Reproduced by permission.—*Women's Studies: An Interdisciplinary Journal,* v. 21, 1992. Copyright © 1992 Gordon and Breach, Science Publishers SA. All rights reserved. Reproduced by permission of Taylor & Francis Group, LLC, http://www.taylorandfrancis.com.—*The Wordsworth Circle,* v. 32, spring, 2001. Copyright © 2001 Marilyn Gaull. Reproduced by permission of the editor.

COPYRIGHTED MATERIAL IN *NCLC,* VOLUME 177, WAS REPRODUCED FROM THE FOLLOWING BOOKS:

Baldwin, Claire. From *The Emergence of the Modern German Novel: Christoph Martin Wieland, Sophie von La Roche, and Maria Anna Sagar.* Camden House, 2002. Copyright © 2002 Claire Baldwin. All rights reserved. Reproduced by permission.—Blair, Walter, and Hamlin Hill. From *America's Humor: From Poor Richard to Doonesbury.* Oxford University Press, 1978. Copyright © 1978 by Oxford University Press. Used by permission of Oxford University Press, Inc.—Cooper, Andrew M. From "Doubt and Identity," in *Romantic Poetry.* Yale University Press, 1988. Copyright © 1988 by Yale University. All rights reserved. Reproduced by permission.—Durham, Margery. From "The Mother Tongue: 'Christabel' and the Language of Love," in *The (M)other Tongue: Essays in Feminist Psychoanalytic Interpretation.* Edited by Shirley Nelson Garner, Claire Kahane, and Madelon Sprengnether. Cornell University Press, 1985. Copyright © 1985 by Cornell

Thomson Gale Literature Product Advisory Board

"Christabel"

Samuel Taylor Coleridge

English poet, playwright, and essayist.

The following entry presents critical discussion of Coleridge's 1816 poem "Christabel." For information on Coleridge's complete career, see *NCLC*, Volume 9; for critical discussion of the poem "The Rime of the Ancient Mariner" (1798), see *NCLC*, Volume 54; for discussion of the poem "Kubla Khan" (1816), see *NCLC*, Volume 99; and for discussion of the poetry collection *Lyrical Ballads* (1798), see *NCLC*, Volume 111.

INTRODUCTION

Coleridge's two-part fragment "Christabel" is one of the landmark poems of the Romantic period. Originally composed between 1797 and 1800—Coleridge's most fertile years as a poet—the work embodies the full breadth of his intellectual and creative powers. Although the poem was never completed, many modern scholars consider it a triumph of Coleridge's imaginative genius. "Christabel" is known primarily for its use of gothic images, as well as by its ambiguity of meaning, a quality that its incompleteness further accentuates. The poem is also remarkable for its highly suggestive, though enigmatic and oblique, depictions of sexuality, as embodied in the unsettling relationship between the heroine, Christabel, and the mysterious figure of Geraldine.

While widely regarded as a masterpiece today, "Christabel" proved too unusual for the tastes many of Coleridge's contemporaries, and even Coleridge's good friend and collaborator William Wordsworth refused to include an early draft of the poem in the second edition of their *Lyrical Ballads* (1800). Soon after completing the first two parts of the poem, Coleridge slipped into a profound depression, his emotional distress exacerbated by prolonged opium addiction. While he eventually recovered from this self-described "state of suspended animation" to revise and publish these two parts, Coleridge never fulfilled his promise to add three additional sections to the work, and it remained unchanged after its publication in 1816. A number of contemporary reviews of "Christabel" expressed bewilderment, and in some cases outrage, and the work was largely dismissed throughout the nineteenth and early twentieth centuries.

Only in recent decades have scholars truly begun to appreciate the poem's rich symbolic framework, its psychological complexity, and its lyric beauty. Moreover, many modern commentators regard the poem as ahead of its time, both for its highly original, sometimes surreal imagery and for its powerful erotic undertones. Experts cannot agree on a single reading of Coleridge's poem, however, and the work has inspired a broad range of interpretations over the years—arguably the most revealing testament of its complexity and resonance.

PLOT AND MAJOR CHARACTERS

Part one of the poem opens at midnight in the landscape surrounding the estate of Sir Leoline, a wealthy baron. The scene is vaguely menacing; owls cry, the cock crows, and Sir Leoline's mastiff bitch howls (according to local superstition) at the "shroud" of Leoline's dead wife. Although it is April, the narrator confides that "the Spring comes slowly up this way," and the night is "chilly." Into this setting the figure of Leoline's daughter, the virtuous Christabel, emerges, venturing silently away from the house through the "midnight wood." The narrator introduces her nocturnal wanderings in the form of a question—"What makes her in the wood so late / A furlong from the castle gate?"—further imbuing the scene with a sense of foreboding. Christabel's mood is clearly melancholy, almost sorrowful, as she wanders into the woods to pray for the safety of her "betrothed knight," who is far from home. As she kneels beside an oak tree, however, Christabel hears a faint moaning from a place nearby. After overcoming her fright, she circles the "huge, broad-breasted" oak to discover a woman, weary and in "sore distress." The woman's noble stature is immediately evident: she is "richly clad, with a "stately neck" and "gems entangled in her hair." When Christabel rushes to her aid, the woman introduces herself as Geraldine and begins to recount how she was abducted by "five warriors" and left "scarce alive" beneath the tree. Expressing dread at the prospect of the men's return, Geraldine implores Christabel to help her escape. Christabel readily agrees, offering the full assistance of her father to help transport Geraldine safely to her home. The two women make their way toward the castle, Christabel praising "the Virgin all divine" for delivering Geraldine from harm. Geraldine responds, simply, that she "cannot speak for weariness." As they steal quietly through the darkened castle, the sleeping mastiff bitch emits an "angry moan"; the "dying" lights that line the dim castle hall suddenly burst into a "fit of flame" as Geraldine passes.

When the women have settled into Christabel's chamber for the night, Christabel offers Geraldine a glass of wine "of virtuous powers," which, she explains, was made by her mother. Geraldine asks Christabel if her mother will take pity on a "maiden most forlorn," to which Christabel sadly replies that her mother died years before, in childbirth. At first Geraldine expresses her sympathy, but with "altered voice" she promptly adds, "'Off, wandering mother! Peak and pine! / I have power to bid thee flee.'" Taking Geraldine's strange utterance to be the result of her "wildered" state, Christabel kneels to comfort her, and Geraldine immediately resumes her normal voice. She praises Christabel, calling her beloved by "All they, who live in the upper sky." She then tells Christabel to disrobe and get into bed, which Christabel does. Lying naked, Christabel watches as Geraldine, seemingly in pain, slowly undresses. As Geraldine removes her garment, she reveals to Christabel her breast, described by the narrator simply as "a sight to dream of, not to tell!" Christabel looks on in silent fear, while Geraldine, assuming a look of "scorn and pride," takes Christabel in her arms and puts her into a trance. Declaring that strange powers lie "in the touch of this bosom," which she further describes as the mark of her "shame" and "sorrow," Geraldine tells Christabel that, while she will know Geraldine's horrible secret, she will be powerless to reveal it to anyone. In the "Conclusion to Part I," Coleridge describes the frightened Christabel emerging from her trance and the two woman lying down together for the night "as a mother with her child."

Part two of the poem introduces the character of Sir Leoline, a man in a state of permanent mourning over his wife's death. Indeed, the entire landscape is colored by Leoline's somber mood; at dawn each day, a "heavy bell" tolls forty-five times, a "warning knell" of the inevitability of death that "not a soul can choose but hear" throughout the surrounding countryside. In this atmosphere of gloom, the narrator describes Christabel and Geraldine awakening from a deep sleep. Christabel is vaguely troubled by the events of the preceding night, exclaiming "Sure I have sinned!" and praying that her innocent, safe existence will be restored. Saying little, Christabel prays, gets dressed, and brings Geraldine to meet her father. Upon listening to Geraldine's story, Leoline realizes that she is the daughter of one of his oldest friends, Lord Roland, with whom he had had a painful falling out years earlier. The sight of Geraldine's regal beauty, however, combined with the harrowing story of her abduction, resurrects Leoline's former feelings of loyalty toward Lord Roland, and he vows to

avenge her dishonor. As Leoline, moved to tears, embraces Geraldine, the silent Christabel experiences a "vision of fear," as she recollects the sight of Geraldine's "bosom old" and the touch of her "bosom cold." Although the sound of Christabel's "hissing" breath alarms her father, she is powerless to reveal anything to him, and when he turns to look at her, he finds her on her knees praying, "his own sweet maid."

Reassured by Christabel's assertion that "'All will yet be well,'" Leoline again turns his attention to Geraldine's predicament. He calls his servant, Bracy the bard, and instructs him to summon Lord Roland to come retrieve his daughter and to make amends with his old friend. Bracy replies that Leoline's words are "sweeter than my harp can tell," and he proceeds to recount his dream from the previous night. He describes a scene reminiscent of Christabel's encounter with Geraldine in the woods the night before, in which a dove named Christabel is "uttering fearful moan / Among the green herbs in the forest alone"; upon closer inspection, Bracy finds a "bright green snake / Coiled around its wings and neck." Bracy tells Leoline that he awoke that morning troubled by his dream and intent on inspecting the surrounding forest for signs of trouble. Leoline immediately interprets Bracy's dream to represent Geraldine's ordeal from the night before, and he once again assures Geraldine that he will bring her assailants to justice. As the grateful Geraldine, "with blushing cheek and courtesy fine," turns away from Leoline, she casts a terrifying look at Christabel, who once again slips into a trance. Unable to reveal the source of her distress, Christabel falls to the ground and begs Leoline to send Geraldine away. Leoline, however, feels "dishonoured" by Christabel's insulting behavior and ignores her. After once again bidding Bracy to set out for Roland's estate, he leads Geraldine out of the room. The second part of the poem also ends with a brief "Conclusion," in which Coleridge meditates on the strong emotions that underlie a father's love for his daughter, suggesting that they are sometimes so powerful that he "Must needs express his love's excess / With words of unmeant bitterness."

MAJOR THEMES

The tension between the opposing forces of fantasy and reality lies at the core of "Christabel." The tone at the beginning of the poem is one of religious piety and medieval chivalry: Christabel, the devoted daughter of Sir Leoline, wanders into the woods to pray for the safety of her "betrothed knight"; although it is midnight, Christabel walks through the darkness with confidence, secure in the protection of "Jesu" and "Mary mother." While the mood and imagery are decidedly gothic, the scene seems firmly rooted in the world of the familiar. As the narrative of Geraldine's mysterious appearance unfolds, however, Coleridge subverts this underlying sense of order. The story of Geraldine's abduction by "five warriors" is disturbing in its vivid evocation of violence and terror, and her sudden shifts in personality, from a "weary weight" seeking the "pity" of Christabel's mother to a demonic figure with an "unsettled eye" and "hollow voice," introduce a distinctly supernatural element into the poem. As Geraldine makes her way through the castle, Sir Leoline's realm becomes transformed into a type of dream state, one rendered all the more unsettling by its vagueness; Christabel's bedroom is "carved with figures strange and sweet / All made out of the carver's brain," while Geraldine's bosom is described merely as a condition "to dream of, not to tell," its terrifying aspects made evident only by the narrator's plea to "shield sweet Christabel" from the sight of it. Even after Geraldine has taken possession of Christabel's power to speak, her motives remain indeterminate; while many scholars have argued that this mysterious quality is due to the fact that Coleridge never completed the poem, the overall effect of the mystery is still disturbing. Indeed, the enigmatic quality of Geraldine's character continually undermines any clear sense of the direction of the poem, and the vacillations in her voice, appearance, and attitude leave the reader uncertain about what she is supposed to represent. Equally unsettling is the illicit sensuality that characterizes the interaction between Geraldine and Christabel. Christabel's helpless obedience to Geraldine's power has decidedly erotic undertones, and Geraldine's conquest of the young maiden's will resembles a form of seduction. By drawing parallels between Geraldine and Christabel's dead mother, Coleridge also introduces an element of incest into their relationship, heightening the sense of sexual taboo that pervades the poem.

CRITICAL RECEPTION

While most contemporary responses to "Christabel" were negative, a few early reviewers found considerable merit in the work. An anonymous review in the *London Times*, believed by some modern scholars to have been written by essayist and critic Charles Lamb, claimed that the poem's publication could not "be an indifferent circumstance to any true lover of poetry." The reviewer lauded the "picturesqueness" of Coleridge's imagery, as well as the "peculiar richness and variety" of the poem's meter. Writing in the *European Magazine* in November 1816, G. F. Mathew defended the work against the harsh responses of other critics, calling its language "sweet, simple, and appropriate." The majority of critics, however, greeted the publication of the first two parts of "Christabel" with disdain, even mockery. In his review of the poem, literary critic William Hazlitt complained of Coleridge's failure to bring "Christabel" to a satisfying conclusion, describing the work as "more like a dream than a reality," while

also finding "something disgusting at the bottom of his subject." The poem prompted Hazlitt to level a more general criticism at Coleridge as a poet, arguing that he stood "suspended between poetry and prose, truth and falsehood, and an infinity of other things." Reviewing "Christabel" in the *Anti-Jacobin,* an anonymous commentator declared that "so wretched a performance is beneath the dignity of criticism" and described the poem as evoking "nothing but astonishment and disgust." Throughout the nineteenth and early twentieth centuries, "Christabel" inspired several parodies, as well as a number of satirical sequels and conclusions.

In more recent times scholars have begun to examine the importance of the poem within the context of the Romantic Movement, finding in its ambiguity and strangeness a decidedly modern sensibility. A number of commentators analyze the stylistic innovations of "Christabel," paying particular attention to Coleridge's inventive use of meter in the poem, while others focus on the work's unusual depictions of profound psychological states. While several scholars examine the fragmentary quality of the work, Jane Nelson argues that in spite of Coleridge's plan to add three more sections, the poem represents a complete text. Nelson further asserts that critical interpretations of the work must eschew speculations concerning Coleridge's intentions for the conclusion of the work. Other recent criticism focuses on issues of gender and sexuality in the poem, with some arguing that the work's enigmatic qualities reflect the inherent inexpressibility of human desire.

PRINCIPAL WORKS

*The Fall of Robespierre [with Robert Southey] (play) 1794

Poems on Various Subjects (poetry) 1796; revised as *Poems,* 1797

Ode on the Departing Year (poetry) 1797

†*Osorio* (play) 1797; revised as *Remorse,* 1813

Fears in Solitude, Written in 1798, During the Alarm of an Invasion. To Which are Added, France, an Ode; and Frost at Midnight (poetry) 1798

‡*Lyrical Ballads, with a few Other Poems* [with William Wordsworth] (poetry) 1798; revised and enlarged, 1800; revised, 1802

#*The Friend* (essays) 1812; revised and enlarged, 1818

Christabel. Kubla Khan: A Vision. The Pains of Sleep (poetry) 1816

Statesman's Manual; or the Bible the Best Guide to Political Skill and Foresight (prose) 1816

Biographia Literaria; or, Biographical Sketches of My Literary Life and Opinions. 2 vols. (essays) 1817

Sibylline Leaves (poetry) 1817

Aids to Reflection in the Formation of a Manly Character on the Several Grounds of Prudence, Morality, and Religion: Illustrated by Select Passages from Our Elder Divines, Especially from Archbishop Leighton (prose) 1825

Specimens of the Table Talk of the Late Samuel Taylor Coleridge. 2 vols. (prose) 1835

The Literary Remains of Samuel Taylor Coleridge. 4 vols. (poetry and prose) 1836-39

Hints towards the Formation of a More Comprehensive Theory of Life (prose) 1848

#*Essays on His Own Times; Forming a Second Series of* The Friend. 3 vols. (essays) 1850

The Complete Works of Samuel Taylor Coleridge. 7 vols. (poetry, plays, and essays) 1853

Anima Poetae. From the Unpublished Note-Books of Samuel Taylor Coleridge (prose) 1895

Christabel by Samuel Taylor Coleridge, Illustrated by a Facsimile of the Manuscript and by Textual and Other Notes (poetry) 1907

The Complete Poetical Works of Samuel Taylor Coleridge. 2 vols. (poetry) 1912

Collected Letters of Samuel Taylor Coleridge. 6 vols. (letters) 1956-71

The Notebooks of Samuel Taylor Coleridge. 4 vols. (journal) 1957-90

Poems (poetry) 1963; revised edition, 1974; revised edition, 1993

The Collected Works of Samuel Taylor Coleridge. 16 vols. (poetry and prose) 1971-2001

*First publication.

†First staged in 1813, as *Remorse*.

‡Includes the poem "The Rime of the Ancient Mariner."

#The essays in these collections originally appeared in periodicals.

CRITICISM

Samuel Taylor Coleridge (preface date 1816)

SOURCE: Coleridge, Samuel Taylor. "'Christabel': Preface to the Edition of 1816." In *Table Talk of Samuel Taylor Coleridge, and The Rime of the Ancient Mariner, Christabel, &c.,* p. 287. London: George Routledge and Sons, 1884.

[*In the following preface, originally published in 1816, Coleridge describes the circumstances surrounding composition of "Christabel." Coleridge asserts his intention to finish the work nearly two decades after he started it, while at the same time lamenting his "own indolence" for not completing it sooner. Coleridge also offers a brief explanation of the poem's unique approach to meter.*]

The first part of the following poem ["**Christabel**"] was written in the year 1797, at Stowey, in the county of Somerset. The second part, after my return from Germany, in the year 1800, at Keswick, Cumberland. Since the latter date, my poetic powers have been, till very lately, in a state of suspended animation. But as in my very first conception of the tale I had the whole present to my mind, with the wholeness no less than with the liveliness of a vision, I trust that I shall be able to embody in verse the three parts yet to come, in the course of the present year. It is probable, that if the poem had been finished at either of the former periods, or if even the first and second part had been published in the year 1800, the impression of its originality would have been much greater than I dare at present expect. But for this, I have only my own indolence to blame. The dates are mentioned for the exclusive purpose of precluding charges of plagiarism or servile imitation from myself. For there is amongst us a set of critics, who seem to hold, that every possible thought and image is traditional; who have no notion that there are such things as fountains in the world, small as well as great; and who would therefore charitably derive every rill they behold flowing, from a perforation made in some other man's tank. I am confident, however, that as far as the present poem is concerned, the celebrated poets whose writings I might be suspected of having imitated, either in particular passages, or in the tone and the spirit of the whole, would be among the first to vindicate me from the charge, and who, on any striking coincidence, would permit me to address them in this doggrel version of two monkish Latin hexameters:—

> 'Tis mine and it is likewise yours;
> But an if this will not do;
> Let it be mine, good friend! for I
> Am the poorer of the two.

I have only to add, that the metre of the **"Christabel"** is not, properly speaking, irregular, though it may seem so from its being founded on a new principle: namely, that of counting in each line the accents, not the syllables. Though the latter may vary from seven to twelve, yet in each line the accents will be found to be only four. Nevertheless this occasional variation in the number of syllables is not introduced wantonly, or for the mere ends of convenience, but in correspondence with some transition, in the nature of the imagery or passion.

London Times (review date 20 May 1816)

SOURCE: Review of "Christabel," by Samuel Taylor Coleridge. *London Times* (20 May 1816): 3-7.

[*In the following review, the unsigned critic praises the "fragmental beauty" of "Christabel" and lauds its unorthodox use of meter. The reviewer expresses excite-*

ment over Coleridge's intention to finish the poem, but also voices some misgivings, fearing that the work's ambiguity might be diminished with its completion.]

It is not often that we venture to notice the poetical compositions of the day: they have their appropriate sphere of criticism, which, indeed, is for the most part very debatable: but when a work appears of indisputable originality, forming almost a class by itself—attractive no less by its beauty than by its singularity, we may be pardoned for deviating a little from our customary track. The publication of **Christabel** cannot be an indifferent circumstance to any true lover of poetry; and its publication in its present imperfect state may not improbably give an additional zest to public curiosity. Like the "half-told" tale of Cambuscan, it might excite a wish to call up him who left it thus abrupt, even if he quitted this earthly scene: but the poet lives. He tells us, that his poetic powers, which have been for some years "in a state of suspended animation," have very lately revived. The two parts, therefore, which he presents to us, may, beside their intrinsic merits, be thought valuable with reference to three others yet to come, and which, he says, he hopes to embody in verse in the course of the present year. We own we scarcely venture to indulge such an expectation. It is well known to many of Mr. Coleridge's friends, that **Christabel,** as it now stands, has remained, with scarcely the variation of a line, ever since the year 1800, a singular monument of genius—shall we add, of indolence, or of those wayward negligences by which genius is often characterized? Mr. Coleridge will, therefore, excuse us if, without at all adverting to any possible additions which his tale may or may not hereafter receive, we confine our remarks altogether to its present form. For our own part, indeed, we know not whether the fragmental beauty that it now possesses can be advantageously exchanged for the wholeness of a finished narrative. In its present form it lays irresistible hold of the imagination. It interests, if we may so speak, more by what it leaves untold, than even by what it tells. We should, in all probability, think less of Chaucer's "wondrous horse of brass," if we possessed an exact catalogue of his aerial journeys; and in like manner, if we hereafter learn more of the birth, parentage, and education of Lady Geraldine, though we may respect or detest her more, we shall certainly not look on her with the same thought-suspending awe.

Hitherto we have been speaking of this poem as if it were well known to our readers, which we have no doubt, if it be not already the case, will soon be so. We shall, however, now proceed to give some slight account of it. The story is, like a dream of lovely forms, mixed with strange and indescribable terrors. The scene, the personages, are those of old, romantic superstition; but we feel intimate with them, as if they were of our own day, and of our own neighbourhood. It is impos-

sible not to suppose that we have known "sweet Christabel" from the time when she was "a fairy thing, with red round cheeks," till she had grown up, through all the engaging prettinesses of childhood and budding charms of youth, to be the pure and dignified creature which we find her at the opening of the poem. The scene is laid, at midnight, in the yet leafless wood, a furlong from the castle-gate of the rich baron Sir Leoline, whose daughter, "the lovely Lady Christabel," has come, in consequence of a vow, to pray, at the old oak tree, "for the weal of her lover, that's far away." In the midst of her orisons she is suddenly alarmed by a moaning near her, which turns out to be the complaint of the Lady Geraldine, who had been carried off by warriors and brought to this wild wood, where they had left her with intent quickly to return. Geraldine's story easily obtains credence from the unsuspecting Christabel, who conducts her privately to a chamber in the castle. There the mild and beautiful Geraldine seems transformed in language and appearance to a foul sorceress, contending with the spirit of Christabel's deceased mother for the mastery over her daughter; but Christabel's lips are sealed by a spell. What she knows she cannot utter; and scarcely can she herself believe that she knows it. On the return of morning, Geraldine, in all her pristine beauty, accompanies her innocent but perplexed hostess to the presence-room of the baron, who is soon delighted to learn that she is the daughter of his once-loved friend, Lord Rowland De Vaux of Triermaine.

We shall not pursue the distresses of Christabel, the mysterious warnings of Bracy the bard, the assumed sorrow of Geraldine, or the indignation of Sir Leoline at his daughter's seemingly causeless jealousy—what we have principally to remark, with respect to the tale, is, that wild, and romantic, and visionary as it is, it has a truth of its own, which seizes on and masters the imagination, from the beginning to the end. In this respect we know of nothing so like it, in modern composition, as Burns's *Tom* [sic] *o' Shanter.* In both instances, the preternatural occurrences are not merely surprising—they possess a peculiar interest, as befalling individuals, for whom our affections have, from other causes, been kindled. True it is, that the partiality which we feel for the drunken rustic is totally different, in kind, from that which we indulge for the noble virgin. It is, however, (speaking from our own feelings) much the same in degree. In the one case, to borrow the powerful language of a poetical critic, "the poet fears not to tell the reader in the outset, that his hero was a desperate and sottish drunkard, whose excesses were frequent as his opportunities. This reprobate sits down to his cups while the storm is roaring, and heaven and earth are in confusion—the night is driven on by song and tumultuous noise—laughter and jest thicken as the beverage improves upon the palate—conjugal fidelity archly bends to the service of general benevolence—selfishness is not absent, but wearing the mask of social cordiality:" yet are "these various elements of humanity blended into one proud and happy composition of elated spirits;" and "the poet, penetrating the unsightly and disgusting surfaces of things, unveils, with exquisite skill, the finer ties of imagination and feeling," by which they are linked to the human heart. The elements of our sensibility, to all that concerns fair Christabel, are of a purer texture: they are not formally announced in a set description; but they accompany and mark her every moment through the piece—*Incessu patuit Dea.*[1] She is the support of her noble father's declining age—sanctified by the blessing of her departed mother—the beloved of a valorous and absent knight—the delight and admiration of an inspired bard—she is a being made up of tenderness, affection, sweetness, piety! There is a fine discrimination, in the descriptions of Christabel and Geraldine, between the lovely and merely beautiful. There is a moral sensitiveness about Christabel which none but a true poet could seize. It would be difficult to find a more delicate touch of this kind, in any writer, than her anxious exclamation, when in passing the hall with Geraldine a gleam bursts from the dying embers.

Next in point of merit to the power which Mr. Coleridge has displayed in interesting us by the moral beauty of his heroine, comes the skill with which he has wrought up the feelings and fictions of superstition into shape. The witchlike Geraldine lying down by the side of Christabel, and uttering the spell over her, makes the reader thrill with undefinable horror.

Another striking excellence of the poem is its *picturesqueness,* by which we mean a quality, not indeed essential to poetry, (for the most sublime poets often soar far above it), but one which powerfully affects every reader, by placing, as it were, before his eyes a distinct picture of the events narrated, with all their appendages of sight and sound—the dim forest—the massive castlegate—the angry moan of the sleeping mastiff bitch—the sudden flash of the dying embers—the echoing hall—the carved chamber, with its curiously elegant lamp—in short, all that enriches and adorns this tale, with a luxuriance of imagination seldom equalled. Of the higher requisites of poetry, extracts will seldom enable a person to form an adequate judgment: but descriptive passages may often be selected from a poem without much injury to their effect. We shall, therefore, indulge ourselves in extracting the two following pictures, leaving it to the painter to determine whether they would not furnish most exquisite subjects for his art:

> It was a lovely sight to see
> The Lady Christabel, when she
> Was praying at the old oak-tree.
>   Amid the jagged shadows
>   Of mossy, leafless boughs,
>   Kneeling in the moonlight,
>   To pay her gentle vows:

> Her slender palms together prest,
> Heaving sometimes on her breast;
> Her face resign'd to bliss or bale—
> Her face!—oh, call it fair, not pale—
> And both blue eyes, more bright than clear.
> Each about to have a tear.

> [I.279-291.]

> —Geraldine, in maiden wise,
> Casting down her large bright eyes—
> With blushing cheek, and courtesy fine,
> She turn'd her from Sir Leoline,
> Softly gath'ring up her train,
> That o'er her right arm fell again;
> And folded her arms across her chest,
> And couched her head upon her breast—

> [II.573-580.]

We break off here, because the transition from this graceful picture to the "look of dull and treacherous hate" which she casts askance on Christabel, falls not within the sphere of the painter's art; inasmuch as time, which is a necessary element of all change, defies the descriptive power of the pencil; and, consequently, the picture of the lady's shrunken, serpent eye, would convey no idea of those large bright orbs which had just before formed so striking a feature in Geraldine's countenance.

We had intended to notice, at some length, the peculiar richness and variety which the metre of this poem displays; but time will not allow us to enter fully into this topic. With great apparent irregularity, there are no harsh transitions, no real deviations from the scene of aptitude and proportion which is the basis of all the pleasure of rhythm. Mr. Coleridge, however, is wrong in calling the principle of scanning by accents, rather than by syllables, a new one. At this time of day new principles of composition would be rather to be suspected than desired. The truth is, that our oldest balladwriters were guided by no other principle. It exists in the genius of our language, and owes its efficacy to habits which have originated in a very remote antiquity, and grown up with every one of us from infancy. This, indeed, is a point with which the readers of the poem have little concern. Whatever may be their opinion of Mr. Coleridge's theory, they will not deny him the praise of very high practical excellence; and they will not be much inclined to ask whether they are affected by accents or syllables, while they enjoy the gratification of perusing and reperusing so sweet a poem as Christabel.

Note

1. Virgil's *Aeneid,* I. 405: "The goddess was revealed in her step."

William Hazlitt (review date 2 June 1816)

SOURCE: Hazlitt, William. "Mr. Coleridge's 'Christabel.'" In *The Complete Works of William Hazlitt.* Vol. 19, edited by P. P. Howe, pp. 32-4. London: J. M. Dent and Sons, 1933.

[*In the following review, originally published in the* Examiner *on June 2, 1816, Hazlitt criticizes the obscurity of "Christabel," while taking Coleridge to task for failing to complete the poem.*]

The fault of Mr. Coleridge is, that he comes to no conclusion. He is a man of that universality of genius, that his mind hangs suspended between poetry and prose, truth and falsehood, and an infinity of other things, and from an excess of capacity, he does little or nothing. Here are two unfinished poems, and a fragment. *Christabel,* which has been much read and admired in manuscript, is now for the first time confided to the public. The *Vision of Kubla Khan* still remains a profound secret; for only a few lines of it ever were written.

The poem of *Christabel* sets out in the following manner:

'Tis the middle of night by the castle clock,
And the owls have awaken'd the crowing cock;
Tu—whit! Tu—whoo!
And hark, again! the crowing cock,
How drowsily it crew.
Sir Leoline, the Baron rich,
Hath a toothless mastiff bitch;
From her kennel beneath the rock
She makes answer to the clock,
Four for the quarters and twelve for the hour;
Ever and aye, moonshine or shower,
Sixteen short howls, not over loud;
Some say, she sees my lady's shroud.

We wonder that Mr. Murray, who has an eye for things, should suffer this 'mastiff bitch' to come into his shop. Is she a sort of Cerberus to fright away the critics? But—gentlemen, she is toothless.

There is a dishonesty as well as affectation in all this. The secret of this pretended contempt for the opinion of the public, is that it is a sorry subterfuge for our self-love. The poet, uncertain of the approbation of his readers, thinks he shews his superiority to it by shocking their feelings at the outset, as a clown, who is at a loss how to behave himself, begins by affronting the company. This is what is called *throwing a crust to the critics.* If the beauties of *Christabel* should not be sufficiently admired, Mr. Coleridge may lay it all to two lines which he had too much manliness to omit in complaisance to the bad taste of his contemporaries.

We the rather wonder at this bold proceeding in the author, as his courage has cooled in the course of the publication, and he has omitted, from mere delicacy, a line

which is absolutely necessary to the understanding the whole story. The Lady Christabel, wandering in the forest by moonlight, meets a lady in apparently great distress, to whom she offers her assistance and protection, and takes her home with her to her own chamber. This woman,

——beautiful to see,
Like a lady of a far countree,

is a witch. Who she is else, what her business is with Christabel, upon what motives, to what end her sorceries are to work, does not appear at present; but this much we know, that she is a witch, and that Christabel's dread of her arises from her discovering this circumstance, which is told in a single line, which line, from an exquisite refinement in efficiency, is here omitted. When the unknown lady gets to Christabel's chamber, and is going to undress, it is said—

Then drawing in her breath aloud
Like one that shuddered, she unbound
The cincture from beneath her breast:
Her silken robe and inner vest
Dropt to her feet, and full in view
Behold! her bosom and half her side—
A sight to dream of, not to tell!
And she is to sleep by Christabel!

The manuscript runs thus, or nearly thus:—

Behold her bosom and half her side—
Hideous, deformed, and pale of hue.

This line is necessary to make common sense of the first and second part. 'It is the keystone that makes up the arch.' For that reason Mr. Coleridge left it out. Now this is a greater psychological curiosity than even the fragment of *Kubla Khan.*

In parts of *Christabel* there is a great deal of beauty, both of thought, imagery, and versification; but the effect of the general story is dim, obscure, and visionary. It is more like a dream than a reality. The mind, in reading it, is spell-bound. The sorceress seems to act without power—Christabel to yield without resistance. The faculties are thrown into a state of metaphysical suspense and theoretical imbecility. The poet, like the witch in Spenser, is evidently

Busied about some wicked gin.—

But we do not foresee what he will make of it. There is something disgusting at the bottom of his subject, which is but ill glossed over by a veil of Della Cruscan sentiment and fine writing—like moon-beams playing on a charnel-house, or flowers strewed on a dead body. Mr. Coleridge's style is essentially superficial, pretty, ornamental, and he has forced it into the service of a story which is petrific. In the midst of moon-light, and fluttering ringlets, and flitting clouds, and enchanted echoes, and airy abstractions of all sorts, there is one genuine outburst of humanity, worthy of the author, when no dream oppresses him, no spell binds him. We give the passage entire:—

> But when he heard the lady's tale,
> And when she told her father's name,
> Why waxed Sir Leoline so pale,
> Murmuring o'er the name again,
> Lord Roland de Vaux of Tryermaine?
>
> Alas! they had been friends in youth;
> But whispering tongues can poison truth;
> And constancy lives in realms above;
> And life is thorny; and youth is vain;
> And to be wroth with one we love
> Doth work like madness in the brain.
> And thus it chanced, as I divine,
> With Roland and Sir Leoline.
> Each spake words of high disdain
> And insult to his heart's best brother:
> They parted—ne'er to meet again!
> But never either found another
> To free the hollow heart from paining—
> They stood aloof, the scars remaining,
> Like cliffs which had been rent asunder;
> A dreary sea now flows between.
> But neither heat, nor frost, nor thunder,
> Shall wholly do away, I ween,
> The marks of that which once hath been.
>
> Sir Leoline, a moment's space,
> Stood gazing in the damsel's face:
> And the youthful Lord of Tryermaine
> Came back upon his heart again.

Why does not Mr. Coleridge always write in this manner, that we might always read him? The description of the Dream of Bracy the bard is also very beautiful and full of power.

The conclusion of the second part of **Christabel,** about 'the little limber elf,' is to us absolutely incomprehensible. *Kubla Khan,* we think, only shews that Mr. Coleridge can write better *nonsense* verses than any man in England. It is not a poem, but a musical composition.

> A damsel with a dulcimer
> In a vision once I saw:
> It was an Abyssinian maid,
> And on her dulcimer she play'd,
> Singing of Mount Abora.

We could repeat these lines to ourselves not the less often for not knowing the meaning of them.

Anti-Jacobin (review date 16 July 1816)

SOURCE: Review of "Christabel," by Samuel Taylor Coleridge. *Anti-Jacobin* 1 (16 July 1816): 632-36.

[*In the following review, the unsigned author presents a scathing critique of the poem, concluding with the as-sertion that "to discuss so wretched a performance is beneath the dignity of criticism."*]

These verses have been ushered into the world by a new species of *puff direct*; under the auspices of Lord Byron, who, as the newspapers informed the public, had read them in manuscript, and, in a letter to the author, had called **'Christabel'**, it seems, a 'singularly wild and beautiful Poem'. The artifice has succeeded so far as to force it into a second edition! for what woman of fashion would not purchase a book recommended by Lord Byron? For our part, we confess, that the perusal of it has excited in our minds, nothing but astonishment and disgust; we have discovered in it, wildness enough to confound common-sense, but, not having the acuteness of the noble bard, the *beauty* of the composition has wholly eluded our observation.

As any attempt to characterize such versification would be vain, the only mode by which any thing like an adequate idea of its *wildness* and its *beauty* can be conveyed, is by laying a specimen of the composition before our readers. And that we may not be suspected of unfair dealing towards the poet, we shall extract the very first lines.

> 'Tis the middle of the night by the castle clock,
> And the owls have waken'd the crowing cock;
> Tu—whit!——Tu—whoo!
> And hark, again! the crowing cock,
> How drowsily it crew.
>
> Sir Leoline, the Baron rich,
> Hath a toothless mastiff bitch;
> From her kennel beneath the rock,
> She makes answer to the clock,
> Four for the quarters, and twelve for the hour;
> Ever and aye, moonshine or shower,
> Sixteen short howls, not overloud;
> Some says she sees my lady's shroud.

Whoever has taste enough to relish this introduction, may peruse the tale, or vision, or reverie, or whatever it may be called; when he will learn how my Lady Christabel, the daughter of this 'Baron rich', had strayed out, one chilly, but not dark, night, into a neighbouring wood,

> The night is chill, the cloud is grey,
> 'Tis a month before the month of May,
> And the spring comes slowly up this way—

in order to pray for her absent lover. The only reason assigned for the strange preference given to the wood over her own chamber, as the scene of her evening orisons, is, that she had had some strange dreams the night before.

> Dreams, that made her moan and *leap*,
> As on her bed she lay in sleep.

Behind an oak tree, Christabel discovers

> A damsel bright,
> Drest in a silken robe of white;
> Her neck, her feet, her arms were bare,
> And the jewels disordered in her hair.
> I guess, 'twas frightful there to see
> A lady so richly clad as she—
> Beautiful exceedingly!

Frightful, indeed, to see a handsome girl, half naked, exposed to the chill damps of an April night! The lady tells Christabel that her name is Geraldine, that her father is Lord Roland de Vaux, of Tryermaine, that she had been forced from home by five Knights, who were strangers to her, but who had left her in the wood, and promised to return. Christabel, moved by this tale of distress, conducts the lady to her father's castle. The Baron and his family had all retired to rest, it seems, while Miss Christabel had been employed in saying her prayers in the wood. But she had taken the prudent precaution to put the key in her pocket.

> and Christabel
> Took the key that fitted well;
> A little door she opened strait,
> All in the middle of the gate;
> The gate that was ironed within and without,
> Where an army in battle-array had marched out.

The lady was extremely fatigued, and requested to go to bed without delay; which request appears to have produced a very extraordinary effect on the mastiff-bitch, who was introduced to our notice, at the opening of the poem.

> Outside her kennel, the mastiff old
> Lay fast asleep, in moonshine cold.
> The mastiff old did not awake,
> Yet she an angry moan did make!
> And what can ail the mastiff bitch?
> Never till now she utter'd yell
> Beneath the eye of Christabel.
> Perhaps it is the owlet's scritch;
> For what can ail the mastiff bitch?

They reached, however, fair Christabel's chamber in safety; when Christabel trimmed her lamp—and gave her guest some wine.

> Again the wild-flower wine she drank:
> Her fair large eyes gave glitter bright,
> And from the floor whereon she sank
> The lofty lady stood upright!
> She was most beautiful to see,
> Like a lady of far countree.!!!!!!

Geraldine requests Christabel to get into bed before her, which she does; but, not being inclined to sleep, she rose in her bed, and laying her cheek on her hand, looked through the curtains at her destined bed-fellow; when,

> full in view,
> Behold! her bosom and half her side—
> A sight to dream of, not to tell!
> And she's to sleep by Christabel.

She got into bed, took Christabel in her arms, and said,

> In the touch of this bosom there worketh a spell
> Which is Lord of thy utterance, Christabel!

We suppose, it is meant, by this, to inform us that Christabel is bewitched!

In the morning Christabel introduced her guest to her father, who was infinitely pleased with her, and resolved to espouse her cause, and, like a *preux chevalier,* to avenge the insult that had been offered her. While, she appeared all beauty to Sir Leoline, she appeared all deformity to Christabel.

> A snake's small eye blinks dull and shy,
> And the lady's eyes they shrunk in her head,
> Each shrunk up to a serpent's eye,
> And with somewhat of malice, and more of dread,
> At Christabel she look'd askance!—
> One moment—and the sight was fled!
> But Christabel in dizzy trance,
> Stumbling on the unsteady ground—
> Shuddered aloud, with a hissing sound.

When Christabel recovered from the kind of trance into which she had been thrown, she earnestly besought her father to send the woman away; but being, by the spell it is supposed, prevented from stating her reasons for such request, her father expressed his displeasure, paid greater attention to Geraldine, and dispatched a messenger to her father, to inform him where his daughter had taken shelter—and thus ends 'this singularly wild and beautiful poem'—that is, all of it that is, at present, printed. But, in his preface, the author threatens us with *three more parts.* It is to be hoped, however, that he will think better of it, and not attempt to put his threats in execution. Had we not known Mr. Coleridge to be a man of genius and of talents, we should really, from the present production, have been tempted to pronounce him wholly destitute of both. In truth, a more senseless, absurd, and stupid, composition, has scarcely, of late years, issued from the press. Yet is it not, we are surprised to learn, a *hasty* composition; the first part of it having been written nineteen years, and the second, eight years, ago! That a man, at a time when he had not his sober senses about him, might commit such balderdash to paper, is conceivable; but that, after it had been thrown by for so many years, he should calmly look over it, and deliberately resolve to give it to the public, is scarcely credible! Mr. Coleridge might have spared himself the trouble of anticipating the charge 'of plagiarism or of servile imitation'—it is a perfectly original composition, and the like of it is not to be found in the English language. The metre of this poem, the author gravely tells the public, 'is not, properly speaking, irregular, though it may seem so for its being founded on a new *principle,* namely, that of counting in each line the accents, not the syllables'. If we were called upon seriously to investigate this new principle, we could soon show the folly of it—but really, gravely to discuss so wretched a performance is beneath the dignity of criticism.

G. F. Mathew (review date November 1816)

SOURCE: Mathew, G. F. Review of "Christabel," by Samuel Taylor Coleridge. *European Magazine* 70 (November 1816): 434-37.

[In the following review, Mathew finds "Christabel" beautiful and original. While Mathew concedes that the poem's meaning is difficult to decipher, he argues that its evocative imagery and innovative language still make it a pleasure to read.]

Mr. Coleridge's last publication, containing the fragment of **'Christabel'**, &c., &c. has already passed into a second edition; it has been read, it has been talked of, and it is at least not blighted by the cold overhanging atmosphere of neglect, however harshly it may have been visited by the rude breezes of disapprobation, trampled upon by the cold-blooded critic by profession and ill-spoken of in many a motley circle.

Every poet is not a Homer; nor, it may be retorted, is every critic an Aristotle; nor indeed, is it at all times that every reader is capable of encountering either the one or the other.

Surely however some merit, some considerable merit, ought not to be denied the individual who possesses the ability to sustain us throughout those hours of indolence and weariness which we all so frequently experience—in that midway of imagination which, though it be below the mountain heights of reason, is nevertheless above the depths of sensuality and corruption: and however numerous at the present day this class of authors may be, there are few, the beauty of whose descriptions, the delicacy of whose characters, the simplicity of whose sentiments, and the morality of whose pages, may be placed in competition with these qualities in Coleridge.

In days of Gothic severity, when the convent and the castle were the temples of Virtue and of Beauty; when virgins were more loved, because they were more retired; when they were more sought after, because they were more backward to be found: when the simplicity of their lives and their ignorance of the world, were equalled only by the purity of their manners and the sincerity of their hearts, the mild, the tender-hearted, the virtuous, the amiable Christabel 'shone upon the dark earth'.

Motherless from her birth, whether she possessed so much of the spirit of her deceased parent as to be formed in character and in shape after so excellent a model, or who she had for her companion and her patron, is not upon record; this however appears: she is charitable, religious, beautiful, and tender; and Mr. Coleridge has, with the taste and delicacy of an able artist, pourtrayed his heroine in the sweetest and most interesting colours.

It has been said of poetry, as of music and of painting, that dark shades and discordant passages seem absolutely necessary to the exposition of the bright and the harmonious. But it may also be contended that, for the setting forth of beauty, however necessary may be the introduction of deformity; however suitable to the exaltation of what is good may be the combination of that which is bad; however Virtue may appear more amiable in distress, and Vice more contemptible in power: it does not follow that, because a poet is harmonious he should be discordant; or, because he is manly, that he should be also puerile, in other words, discordant in the language of that whose essence is harmonious, and puerile in the conception of that whose character is heroism. Such weaknesses of style, and such puerilities of thought, are not under these pretensions to be reconciled either to our approbation or endurance; but who will condemn the lily because it has not the colour of tulip, or discard the unassuming primrose because it bears not upon its stem the glory of the sunflower.

This Poem, as we have before observed, is not heroic, neither is there any thing of Dryden or of Goldsmith in it's composition: little also (though what it does contain includes the *worst* parts of both) either of Scott or Southey. It is, as Lord Byron says of it, *'wildly original'*: his lordship might have added, in some places, 'incoherently unintelligible'; it is not, therefore, to be judged of by comparison, but by those effects which it produces upon the hearts and imaginations of its readers. Its greatest peculiarity exists in the contrariety of its combinations, its descriptions, its incidents, are almost all of them made more imposing by the power of contrasted circumstances:

> Perhaps 'tis pretty to force together
> Thoughts so all unlike each other

And:

> At each wild word to feel within
> A sweet recoil of love and pity!

We ourselves know several ladies who, in the act of caressing their children, make use of the most singular and *outré* expressions: this is eminently characteristic of the peculiarities of **'Christabel'**, and Coleridge has not forgotten it:

A little child, a limber elf,
Singing, dancing, to itself,
A fairy thing with red round cheeks
That always finds, and never seeks,
Makes such a vision to the sight
As fills a father's eyes with light:
And pleasures flow in so thick and fast
Upon his heart, that he at last
Must needs express his love's excess
With words of unmeant bitterness.

Christabel having been disturbed during the previous night by dreams of terror and ill-forboding visions of her lover, in the depth of melancholy wanders into the forest alone and late: and here the feminine beauty and helplessness of Christabel, together with her sincerity and pious spirit, are *admirably contrasted* with the depression which her unfortunate dreams had occasioned, and the wintry desolation and the gloomy silence of the surrounding scene:

It was a lovely sight to see
The lady Christabel, when she
Was kneeling at the old oak tree.
    Amid the jagged shadows
    Of mossy leafless boughs,
    Kneeling in the moonlight,
    To make her gentle vows;
Her slender palms together prest,
Heaving sometimes on her breast;
Her face resign'd to bliss or bale—
Her face, oh call it fair, not pale,
And both blue eyes more bright than clear,
    Each about to have a tear.

But the terrors of Christabel become more lively at the melancholy and plaintive sounds which proceed from the other side of the oak:

It moan'd as near as near could be,
But what it is, she cannot tell.
. . . .
She folded her arms beneath her cloak,
And stole to the other side of the oak.
    What sees she there?

She discovers a strange and beautiful lady, elegantly attired, but in a most pitiable situation, having been ruthlessly seized by two unknown warriors, conveyed from her father's hall, and left alone, and without assistance, in this wild and desolate spot.

The name of this lady is Geraldine, the daughter of Baron Roland de Vaux, formerly the friend of Christabel's father; but, in consequence of a violent dispute which had arisen between them, former friendship only served to heighten their present animosity.

Bold and beautiful is the image by which Coleridge illustrates this circumstance, and we shall transcribe the passage which contains it:

Alas! they had been friends in youth:
But whisp'ring tongues can poison truth;
And constancy lives in realms above;
And life is thorny; and youth is vain;
And to be wroth with one we love,
Doth work like madness in the brain.
And thus it chanced, as I divine,
With Roland and Sir Leoline.
Each spake words of high disdain
And insult to his heart's best brother:
They parted—ne'er to meet again!
But never either found another
To free the hollow heart from paining—
They stood aloof, the scars remaining,
Like cliffs which had been rent asunder;
A dreary sea now flows between;
But neither heat, nor frost, nor thunder,
Shall wholly do away, I ween,
The marks of that which once hath been.

But, to return to our story: Christabel speaks words of comfort to her distress, with the assurances of the service of Sir Leoline in her behalf; she must however be contented with the shelter and protection of the castle for the night; and the domestics having all retired to rest, she must sleep with Christabel:

So up they rose, and forth they pass'd.
With *hurrying steps,* yet *nothing fast*:

Rather, by the way, an Irish mode of proceeding.

They cross'd the moat, and Christabel
Took the key that fitted well;
A little door she opened straight,
All in the middle of the gate;
The gate that was iron'd within and without,
Where an army in battle array had march'd out.

This poem, however romantic, is entirely domestic, and we cannot but esteem the poet who delights to remember, and to dwell upon such delicate and interesting incidents as these:

O softly tread! said Christabel,
My father seldom sleepeth well.
Sweet Christabel her feet she bares,
And they are creeping up the stairs;
Now in glimmer, and now in gloom,
And now they pass the Baron's room
As still as death, with stifled breath!

The following description of the bed-chamber, however minute, is not the tedious account of an upholsterer:

The moon shines dim in the open air,
And not a moonbeam enters here.
But they without its light can see
The chamber carv'd so curiously,
Carv'd with figures strange and sweet,
All made out of the carver's brain;
For a lady's chamber meet:
The lamp with twofold silver chain
Is fasten'd to an angel's feet.

Christabel lost her mother the hour that she was born; but from her father and from her friends, as well as also from the domestics, she must have continually heard those little tales which Memory, in love and admiration of her qualities, took pleasure in repeating. Christabel loved her mother, and she would dwell upon the remembrance of many instances of her domestic providence with peculiar fondness; she does not forget, therefore, what to her was an additional recommendation of it, when offering the wild flower wine to the weary lady, who had sunk down upon the floor through weakness, to inform her that her mother made it:

> O weary lady, Geraldine,
> I pray you drink this cordial wine!
> It is a wine of virtuous powers;
> My mother made it of wild flowers.

It has been observed, that '"Christabel" is not so censurable in itself, as it is in consideration of the source from which it sprang'. We must honestly confess we do not understand this: it is assuredly the legitimate offspring of Coleridge's imagination; its relationship to his other compositions is strongly marked in all the more important features of it: it is, indeed, the twin-sister of his **Remorse**. Besides, supposing it to be of quite a different character and complexion: is Hogarth's 'Sigismunda' more censurable on its author's account comparatively, than upon it's own intrinsically? If it had been equal to his works of humour in execution, however different in character, it had called forth equal approbation from the connoisseur; nay, would not the painter have attained to higher glory because of the versatility of his genius? And shall it be considered unlawful for Coleridge to pay his addresses to more than one muse? or for the children of his imagination to be not only sons, but daughters? and shall the offspring of that muse, whose coral mansion is the human heart, wherein she sings so wildly and so sweetly, be condemned because it is not so sublime, or because it is not so terrific as it might have been?

The Lady Geraldine is a very mysterious character, and there seems to be something preternatural both in her power and her appearance. The poet describes her as having a withered side—a mark of shame upon her—of fearful shuddering effect to the beholder; but from whom the touch of which takes away the power of expressing the abhorrence which it excites. All this Christabel sees and experiences on the fearful night of her charity to the bewildered lady, when she divides with her the pillow of her repose: at this sight the terrors of Christabel are excited; by this spell the tongue of Christabel is enchained. The fine eye of this strange lady also now and then assumes to the shuddering observation of Christabel, the size, the colour, the treacherous and malignant spirit of the serpent's orb of vision. These circumstances affect the imagination not more on their own account, than in dependence upon the style in which they are narrated, and upon the gentle spirit by which their horrors are experienced. These preternatural peculiarities the sequel of the poem must elucidate; till its appearance, we must look upon them as strong figures, indicative of the quality of the lady's disposition, or of the result of her introduction at the castle: we may imagine that she affects the happiness of Christabel, by an unfortunate attachment to her lover; or, by alienating from his own sweet maid the affection of her father; or, by introducing a chain of unhappy circumstances in the re-union of the two long-sundered friends.

These appearances, which disturb the peace of Christabel so evidently, are not visible to Sir Leoline, and the portion of the poem which is now before the public is concluded by the catastrophe which this occasions.

The morning after the silent introduction of Lady Geraldine at the castle, Christabel presents her to Sir Leoline: he receives her with a courteous surprise, learns the circumstances of her distress, remembers his former friendship with Sir Roland, is anxious for a reconciliation, is warm and knightly in his professions to the lady, and all this in the presence of his daughter: before whom, in the mean time, passes in the person of this creature, a repetition of these frightful and abhorred appearances. Affected thus in spirit, but without the power of expressing herself any further in explanation to Sir Leoline, she says:

> By my mother's soul I do entreat
> That you this woman send away!

Highly offensive is this apparent jealousy, on the part of Christabel, to Sir Leoline, at that instant warmly attached to the interests of the fair stranger—the child of his early friend—beautiful in person—honourable in birth—grateful, timid, and lowly in demeanor. Highly offensive, therefore, to Sir Leoline was this apparently ungenerous breach of hospitality on the part of Christabel; hospitality which he was then violently expressing; but which, to make the mortification more exquisite, it should be remembered Christabel herself had been the first tenderly to practice.

Again he caresses the lady Geraldine; who, in consequence of the conduct of Christabel, seemed for her sake to be embarrassed and distressed. Angrily he dismisses the bard Bracy from his presence, who had been relating a vision of parallel mystery with all that Christabel had suffered; and, leading forth the lady, he leaves his daughter alone to the melancholy wandering of her thoughts, and the acute vibration of her feelings.

Among the descriptions which, as they have not immediately fallen into our relation of the tale we have hitherto omitted, we cannot deny ourselves the pleasure of transcribing the following:

The night is chill, the forest bare;
Is it the wind that moaneth bleak?
There is not wind enough in the air
To move away the ringlet curl
From the lovely lady's cheek—
There is not wind enough to twirl
The one red leaf, the last of its clan,
That dances as often as dance it can,
Hanging so light, and hanging so high,
On the topmost twig that looks up at the sky.

The larger and more imposing appearances of nature are generally made use of in description; but although the '*one red leaf* on the topmost twig', be minute on the one hand, it is on the other too new, too natural, and too obvious not to be considerably effective; and this one passage may atone for many of the inconsistencies of '**Christabel**'. We shall close our quotations from the poem by this pathetic appeal to Sir Leoline, in behalf of his daughter:

Why is thy cheek so wan and wild,
Sir Leoline? Thy only child
Lies at thy feet, thy joy, thy pride,
So fair, so innocent, so mild;
The same for whom thy Lady died!
O by the pangs of thy dear mother
Think thou no evil of thy child!
For her, and thee, and for no other,
She pray'd the moment ere she died:
Pray'd that the babe for whom she died,
Might prove her dear lord's joy and pride.
That prayer her deadly pangs beguil'd,
        Sir Leoline!
And would'st thou wrong thy only child,
        Her child and thine?

In fine, '**Christabel**' is a composition which may be read often, and in every instance with increase of pleasure; it is neither calculated to relax the morals nor to degenerate the feelings; the ideas and incidents are for the most part natural and affecting; the language and versification, sweet, simple, and appropriate. In our opinion, it carries with it the peculiarity of Sterne's writings, it is hard of imitation; the attempt published in the *Poetic Mirror* is a burlesque, without similar combination of circumstances, and without a suitable application of style: we here allude to the 'Isabell', of that volume; the 'Cherub' is more successful, shining forth with beautiful conceptions, though in point of style too tame, too diffuse.

There are hours when the mind is so fitted for the reception of such a work as '**Christabel**', that, could the pictures, the images, the incidents, containing all the spirit and all the novelty of this specimen, be so extensively diversified, were it continued to the completion of four and twenty cantos:

Itself should save, above the critic's breath,
Its leaves from mould, ring and its fame from death!

Quarterly Review (review date August and November 1834)

SOURCE: Review of *The Poetical Works of S. T. Coleridge,* by Samuel Taylor Coleridge. *Quarterly Review* 52, no. 103 (August and November 1834): 1-37.

[*In the following excerpt, the unsigned critic compares "Christabel" favorably to Coleridge's other long poem from the period, "The Rime of the Ancient Mariner." The reviewer argues that the former's aesthetic power lies in its incompleteness.*]

The '**Ancient Mariner**' ['**The Rime of the Ancient Mariner**'] displays Mr. Coleridge's peculiar mastery over the wild and preternatural in a brilliant manner; but in his next poem, '**Christabel,**' the exercise of his power in this line is still more skilful and singular. The thing attempted in '**Christabel**' is the most difficult of execution in the whole field of romance—witchery by daylight; and the success is complete. Geraldine, so far as she goes, is perfect. She is *sui generis*. The reader feels the same terror and perplexity that Christabel in vain struggles to express, and the same spell that fascinates her eyes. Who and what is Geraldine—whence come, whither going, and what designing? What did the poet mean to make of her? What could he have made of her? Could he have gone on much farther without having had recourse to some of the ordinary shifts of witch tales? Was she really the daughter of Roland de Vaux, and would the friends have met again and embraced?—

Alas! they had been friends in youth;
But whispering tongues can poison truth;
And constancy lives in realms above;
And life is thorny—and youth is vain—
And to be wroth with one we love
Doth work like madness in the brain.
And thus it chanced, as I divine,
With Roland and Sir Leoline.
Each spake words of high disdain
And insult to his heart's best brother:
They parted—ne'er to meet again!
But never either found another
To free the hollow heart from paining;—
They stood aloof, the scars remaining,
Like cliffs which had been rent asunder:—
A dreary sea now flows between:
But neither heat, nor frost, nor thunder,
Shall wholly do away, I ween,
The marks of that which once has been.

—vol. ii. p. 45

We are not amongst those who wish to have '**Christabel**' finished. It cannot be finished. The poet has spun all he could without snapping. The theme is too fine and subtle to bear much extension. It is better as it is, imperfect as a story, but complete as an exquisite production of the imagination, differing in form and colour from the 'Ancient Mariner,' yet differing in effect from it only so as the same powerful faculty is directed to the feudal or the mundane phases of the preternatural.

Littell's Living Age (essay date 16 December 1871)

SOURCE: "A Century of Great Poets, from 1750 Downwards, No. IV: Samuel Taylor Coleridge." *Littell's Living Age* 111, no. 1436 (16 December 1871): 643-61.

[*In the following excerpt from an article originally published the same year in* Blackwood's Magazine, *the unsigned critic praises the subtlety and ambiguity of* "Christabel," *arguing that the poem suggests far more to the imagination because it is unfinished. The reviewer also interprets the poem as a religious allegory, comparing the character of Christabel to a Christian saint.*]

[T]he same period which produced the **"Ancient Mariner"** [**"The Rime of the Ancient Mariner"**] brought into being at least the first part of the never-completed tale of **"Christabel."** This wonderful poem has a more distinct character than its predecessor. The first was, as it were, introductory—the uplifting of the veil, the revelation of a vast unseen world, full of struggles and mysteries. The second is the distinct identification of a mystery of evil, an unseen harm and bane, working secretly in the dark places of the earth against white innocence, purity, and truth. The poet does not stop to tell us why this should be. Philosopher as he is to the depth of his soul, he is yet so much more poet as to see that any theory of spiritual hate against the happiness of earth would confuse the unity of his strain, and probably transfer, as it has done in *Paradise Lost,* our interest to the despairing demon, whose envy and enmity arise out of that hopeless majesty of wretchedness, great enough to be sublime, which devours his own soul. Coleridge has avoided this danger. He has assigned no cause for the hideous and terrible persecution of which his lovely lady Christabel, symbolical even in name, is the object. The poem is a romance of Christianity, a legend of sainthood. The heroine is not only the lovely but the holy Christabel. For no fault of hers, but rather for her virtues, are the powers of evil raised against her; and one of the most subtle and wonderful touches of truth in the tale is the ignorance of her innocence—her want of any knowledge or experience which can explain to her what the evil is, or how to deal with it. The witch Geraldine has all the foul wisdom of her wickedness to help her—her sorceries, her supernatural knowledge, her spells and cunning. But Christabel has nothing but her purity, and stands defenceless as a lamb, not even knowing where the danger is to come from; exposed at every point in her simplicity, and paralyzed, not instructed, by the first gleam of bewildering acquaintance with evil. Never was there a higher or more beautiful conception. It is finer in its indefiniteness than even the contrast of Una and Duessa—the pure and impure, the false and true of a more elaborate allegory. Spenser, who lived in a more downright age, keeps himself within a narrower circle, and is compelled by his story to direct action; but his very distinctness limits his power. The sorceress or lovely demon of Coleridge does not attempt to ruin her victim in such an uncompromising way. What she does is to throw boundless confusion into the gentle soul, to fill its limpid depths with fear and horror, and distrust of all fair appearances, and of itself—a still more appalling doubt; to undermine the secret foundations of all that love and honour in which Christabel's very name is enshrined; and to establish herself a subtle enemy, an antagonist power of evil, at the pure creature's side, turning all her existence into chaos. Una is a foully-slandered and innocent maid; but Christabel is a martyr-soul, suffering for her race without knowing it—struggling in a dumb consternation, yet resistance, against the evil that holds her spell-bound. And all the more pathetic, all the more enthralling, is the picture, that the Christ-maiden is entirely human—too young, too childlike, too simple even to understand the high mission which has dropped upon her from the skies. She knows nothing, neither her own wonderful position—a sight for angels to watch—nor all that depends upon her steadfast adherence to her white banner of religious faith and purity; but her antagonist knows everything, and has an armoury of subtle perilous weapons at her disposal. "Jesu, Maria, shield her well!" for she is at fearful odds.

And once again, the poet fits all his accessories, all his scenery, into accordance with the soul of his meaning. The clock strikes in the middle of the night, a mysterious life in the stillness. The owls awake the crowing cock; the mastiff bays in answer to the chimes. There is nothing audible except this thrill of unrest among the dumb creatures, who are bound from all human communication by chains of nature. Why do they stir and make a movement in the silence? because the very air is full of harm unseen. They are aware of evil approaching with that subtle sense of supernatural danger which the lower creatures (so called) possess in a higher degree than ourselves. The very "thin grey cloud," which covers but does not hide the sky; the moon, which though at the full, looks "both small and dull,"—betray the same consciousness. All creation feels it with a pang of suppressed fear and pain, unable to warn or aid the only being who is unconscious, the innocent and fearless sufferer. All but she have an instinctive knowledge of her election to endure for them, to stand their spiritual representative in the mysterious conflict. And the dumb inexpressible support of the material world—which in some silent awful way is affected, we know not how, by every struggle for the mastery between good and evil—is with her; and the minstrel's instinctive adherence, and the listener's confused and aching sympathy—these and no more. Such is the picture the poet sets before us, painting the scene, the struggle, and the beautiful fated creature who is the centre of the whole, with such a tender and exquisite touch, and with such mysterious reality, that we catch our very breath as we gaze. Christabel is no allegorical martyr, and yet she is something other than a bewitched maiden. The very world seems to hang with a suspense beyond words upon the issue of her fiery trial.

And the very vagueness of the horror helps its supreme effect. Had we known what the fatal mark was which she saw on Geraldine's side, half our consternation and dismay would have been dissipated. And then, too, the incompleteness of the tale, that broken thread of story which has tantalized so many readers, increases the power of the poem. Completion could scarcely have failed to lessen its reality, for the reader could not have endured, neither could the poet's own theory have endured, the sacrifice of Christabel, the triumph of evil over good; and had she triumphed, there is a vulgar well-being in victory which has nothing to do with such a strain. It was indolence, no doubt, that left the tale half told—indolence and misery—and a poetic instinct higher than all the better impulses of industry and virtuous gain. The subject by its very nature was incomplete; it had to be left, a lovely, weird suggestion—a vision for every eye that could see. . . .

Such is the unfinished and unfinishable tale of Christabel—a poem which, despite its broken notes and over-brevity, has raised its author to the highest rank of poets, and which in itself is at once one of the sweetest, loftiest, most spiritual utterances that has ever been framed in English words. We know of no existing poem in any language to which we can compare it. It stands by itself, exquisite, celestial, ethereal—a song of the spheres—yet full of such pathos and tenderness and sorrowful beauty as only humanity can give.

William Rose Benét (poem date 8 February 1935)

SOURCE: Benét, William Rose. "The End of 'Christabel.'" *Commonweal* 21, no. 15 (8 February 1935): 424.

[*In the following poem, Benét offers a comic rendering of Coleridge's efforts to complete "Christabel," while parodying several of the work's gothic themes.*]

> *I desisted with a deeper dejection than I am willing to remember.*
>
> —*Coleridge*

Along the mountain, moving through a cloud
Less tenebrous than that upon his mind,

Went Coleridge; and the wind was loud behind,
Ahead and overhead the wind was loud.

Incessantly it blustered, to prevail
Against all effort of the marvelous brain,
Dissolving aery edifice as vain:
The wind from Skiddaw and from Borrowdale.

Searching within his double cloud a sign
For new pursuit of his mysterious theme,
And hearing only requiem to his dream,
And muttering "Accursèd 'Wallenstein'!"

At length, by rectory firelight, filled and warm
And deep in wine, anew began to burn
The dream, the brilliant faculty return
As in a lull of inner and outer storm.

So all the following day the driven pen
Ran on and on, as deep in trance he wrought
The spell-bound chronicle that thralled his thought,
The like of which was never known again.

Such verse as Purchas and an anodyne
From treasuries of Time had stolen in dream,
"Images on the surface of a stream
Scattered to naught"—line on mesmeric line!

Till, in a "giddiness of heart and brain,"
He reached the last whereat the pen was dropt;
The vision vanished and the music stopped;
And, staring up beyond the dismal pane,

He heard again the wind that seemed to be
Destiny, as it triumphed down the vale,
The wind from Skiddaw and from Borrowdale
Blowing his requiem through eternity;

The sound that seemed forever in his ears,
The drone of Time that mocked his works and ways,
The imminent desertion of the days,
The faint inexorable horn one hears

Far off in youth—against the last resort
Of words, a clarion—till we clearly see
The shrouded figure by the shadowy tree,
Dim though our eyes; and know he blows the mort.

So Coleridge listened in his gloom; and yet,
Forgot by haggard eye and tightened lip,
In port already stood the phantom ship
That means the wreck of art if men forget.

More than the mariner's curse it had to tell,
Significant of splendor through the gloom,
Whose burning seraphs filled the twilit room
That marked the unending end of "Christabel"!

Charles Tomlinson (essay date 1955)

SOURCE: Tomlinson, Charles. "Coleridge: 'Christabel.'" In *Interpretations: Essays on Twelve English Poems*, edited by John Wain, pp. 103-12. London: Routledge and Kegan Paul, 1955.

[*In the following essay, Tomlinson describes "Christabel" as a "tale of terror," examining the poem's formal qualities, as well as its psychological insights, within the framework of the terror genre.*]

1. THE CONTEXT

Christabel is a tale of terror. It was written, that is to say, within a certain literary convention. Although this convention was not, artistically, a particularly successful one, its nature has some bearing on our reading of the poem. The genre was a European phenomenon. It expressed, or tried to express, a contemporary state of mind reacting to profound social changes and it did so, not by dealing with them directly, but by appearing to ignore these changes. Walpole said that he wrote *Otranto* 'glad to think of anything rather than politics'. But the politics, or rather the feelings which the external events gave rise, reappeared on the plane of fantasy in the combined expression of nostalgia for, yet fear of, the past.

One modern writer, M. André Breton, in his essay 'Limits not Frontiers of Surrealism',[1] has traced the significance, in this light, of the ubiquitous ruins, the inevitable ghost and the subterranean passages of the convention and suggests even that 'in the stormy night can be heard the incessant roar of cannon'. Be this as it may, one can agree with M. Breton's formulation of the basic conflict which is played out against this turbulent background, a background 'chosen', as he says, 'for the appearance of beings of pure temptation, combining in the highest degree the struggle between the instinct of death on the one hand . . . and, on the other, Eros who exacts after each human hecatomb, the glorious restoration of life'.

In the fragmentary **Christabel** there is no 'glorious restoration of life' as, for example, in the business of the long-lost child of *Otranto* who is found at last and rules in the tyrant's stead. All the other elements of the tale of terror, however, are present—elements which Coleridge had admired in Mrs. Radcliffe (see his review of *Udolpho* of 1794[2]) and was to guy later on when he sent to Wordsworth a satirical 'recipe'[3] on the subject of Scott's 'Lady of the Lake'. His list of requirements (too lengthy for quotation here) is present, almost in its entirety, in **Christabel**. The surprising thing is that **Christabel,** though a minor work, is an entirely successful one within its particular limits.

We have in **Christabel** perhaps the only tale of terror which expresses with any real subtlety the basic pattern of the genre, the struggle between the instinct of death and Eros. This struggle centres on the relationship of Geraldine, the 'fatal woman' (one of M. Breton's 'beings of pure temptation'), with Christabel herself, 'the maid devoid of guile and sin'. Geraldine does not appear among Dr. Mario Praz's fatal women in his *The Romantic Agony* and one feels that she provides a far more compelling example than many of those we find there. She clearly belongs under Dr. Praz's heading of 'La Belle Dame Sans Merci' (the genesis of Keats's poem of this title Dr. Praz traces to Coleridge's ballad **'Love'**), her characteristics being those of the fated and fatal men and women of Romantic literature, characteristics which are primarily the dramatization of an inner disturbance such as we find commented on by M. Breton. This condition, as Dr. Praz shows, finds expression either in the inflicting of, or the passive submission to, pain. Both attitudes of mind are present in **Christabel.**

2. THE TEXT

In **Christabel** the struggle of evil and innocence is examined, although within the framework of the typical tale of terror, for the purposes of moral realization of the manner in which evil works upon and transforms innocence. Coleridge's success in achieving this realization by poetic means is due to a dramatic tension building up to a final, irrevocable climax and skilfully regulated by its background of symbols from the natural world.

As far as the poem goes (it is a 'fragment') it is complete.[4] The climax of,

> And turning from his own sweet maid
> The aged knight, Sir Leoline,
> Led forth the Lady Geraldine.

leaves Christabel in that condition of pathological isolation which the Mariner also feels and which Coleridge must himself have known. It follows upon the carefully ordered series of psychological shocks to which Christabel has been subjected and beneath which her innocence is crushed. Mr. Humphry House says of the poem in his excellent book on Coleridge that it is 'fragmentary and finally unsatisfying' and that its mystery remains both incomplete and clueless. If one feels a certain incompleteness about the poem it is because we are left with Christabel's pathological isolation which is never, unlike that of the Ancient Mariner, to be resolved. (Indeed, of the Mariner's, it would perhaps be more true to say that it is only partially resolved.) The 'story', of course, was never completed and the elements concerning the broken friendship between Sir Leoline and the father of Geraldine, relevant as they are to the poem's theme of the division of the inmost being and of the most intimate relationships, were never knit up into a more organic significance. **Christabel** offers, however, despite its abrupt conclusion in psychological stasis, a completeness concerning what *does* happen, if only we pay attention to the premonitory nature of the symbols at the opening and see the poetic interest as centering on the uncertain balance which is represented here between health and disease, good and evil, and the end as a tragedy in which neurosis, not death, strikes the final blow. One has in *Christabel,* in allegorical form, that same concern which tormented the self-analyst of the notebooks and the reader of John Webster's Folio on *The Displaying of Supposed Witchcraft*: 'the mind's failure to guide the Will'. For Christabel, bewitched, suffers simultaneously with the disintegration of personality the disintegration of the will.

Let us begin with the first important symbolical passage of the poem:

> The thin grey cloud is spread on high,
> It covers but not hides the sky.
> The moon is behind and at the full
> And yet she looks both small and dull.

Everything hangs in this state of precarious uncertainty, of incipient disease. The cloud threatens the sky, but the sky still shows through, and to counterpoint this, the moon has achieved its most fruitful phase yet remains without the bright appearance of a full moon. Coleridge thus reinforces the idea of potentialities in Nature which are never finally to be realized in the story:

> 'Tis a month before the month of May,
> And the Spring comes slowly up this way.

The light of the moon is 'cold' and where it falls, it illumines a further symbol of decay, the toothless mastiff. In Christabel's room 'not a moonbeam enters here' and here she—ironically enough—feels safe.

Behind the moon in *The Ancient Mariner* [*The Rime of the Ancient Mariner*] there is the association of the Queen of Heaven, 'the holy Mother' as Coleridge calls her. In *Christabel* the diseased condition of the moon links suggestively with the inability of Christabel's dead mother, her guardian spirit, to operate in her defence. This symbolical use of the moon to reinforce the presentation of a psychological condition is characteristic of Coleridge's natural effects. 'In looking at objects of Nature', as he writes in *Anima Poetae* (Ed. E. H. Coleridge, 1895, p. 136), 'I seem rather to be seeking, as it were asking for, a symbolical language for something within me that already and forever exists, than observing anything new'. The sky—again, symbolically, a potential which remains frustrate—should offer Christabel the feeling of freedom and of free will:

> All they who live in the upper sky
> Do love you, holy Christabel

says Geraldine; and Christabel herself knows

> in joys and woes
> That saints will aid if men will call:
> For the blue sky bends over all.

But the sky is not blue during the time of the action of the poem: its sphere no longer operates upon that of the world below although, 'covered but not hidden', one can see it. Its presence adds to our appreciation of Christabel's growing feelings of helplessness and isolation. The diseased moon prepares us for her transition from a condition of organic innocence to one of complete division. What is the nature of this division and how is its appearance developed in the poem? The development, it should be noticed, takes place through instances of what happens *to* Christabel rather than what she does. Evil works upon her and by the time she feels *possessed* by it and, 'with forced unconscious sympathy' perhaps even becoming evil herself, she has lost her own free will.

It is worth while here to bear in mind Coleridge's interest in psychological phenomena, in Mesmerism, and also in witchcraft, where a powerful idea working upon the human psyche produces the feeling of guilt followed by mental deterioration. An interesting and relevant indication of Coleridge's interests as a psychologist occurs in the preface to his unsuccessful poem **'The Three Graves'**. After the inevitable Coleridgean apologia for the subject, the metre and the fragmentary nature of the piece, he goes on to tell us that at the time of its composition he 'had been reading Bryan Edward's account of the effect of the Oby witchcraft on the Negroes in the West Indies, and Hearne's deeply interesting anecdotes of similar workings on the imagination of the Copper Indians'. In settling on a story of psychological obsession brought about by a blasphemous curse (a story Coleridge says is 'positive fact, and of no very distant date') he had wanted to show 'the possible effect on the imagination from an Idea violently and suddenly impressed on it'. 'I conceived the design', he says, 'of showing that instances of this kind are not peculiar to savage or barbarous tribes, and of illustrating the mode in which the mind is affected in these cases, and the progress and symptoms of the morbid action on the fancy from the beginning'. All three protagonists in the poem are reduced to a condition of morbid introversion and their minds possessed by the image of the woman who has delivered the curse. Coleridge, despite a certain psychological acuteness, handles the affair somewhat clumsily as poetic material and we must return to Geraldine's onslaught upon Christabel to see what he is really capable of in dealing with this kind of subject.

To begin with, Christabel finds herself alone. Her lover is absent, her mother dead, her father sick:

> Each matin bell, the Baron saith,
> Knells us back to a world of death
>
> . . . .
> These words Sir Leoline will say
> Many a morn to his dying day.

Here is the position of the typical persecuted woman of the tale of terror, defenceless and vulnerable, her isolation being intensified by its juxtaposition with the fine image of 'the one red leaf, the last of its clan',

That dances as often as dance it can,
Hanging so light, and hanging so high,
On the topmost twig that looks up at the sky.

In this condition Christabel finds the Lady Geraldine who, according to her own story, has been abducted, then abandoned, and takes her into the castle. Coleridge conveys Geraldine's character of fatal woman in a cumulative series of startling touches. At the outset he gives no hint of the evil in her nature and Christabel sees her as 'Beautiful exceedingly'. The first hint—and it is scarcely even that until we re-read the poem—comes with her unwillingness to join in Christabel's prayer:

Praise we the Virgin all divine
Who hath rescued thee from thy distress!
Alas, alas! said Geraldine,
I cannot speak for weariness.

Christabel's first disquiet occurs as they go into the castle and past the sleeping mastiff:

The mastiff old did not awake
Yet she an angry moan did make . . .

But even this disquiet seems connected rather with the circumstances of the night than with the actual character of Geraldine. The third stroke is more direct. It takes up the motif of Geraldine's eye which is to be dramatically reintroduced at the climax of the poem. As they are passing the almost extinguished hall fire,

. . . when the lady passed, there came
A tongue of light, a fit of flame;
And Christabel saw the lady's eye,
And nothing else she saw thereby.

The fourth leaves us in no doubt. Geraldine, fearing the spirit of Christabel's dead mother, the young girl's guardian spirit, bursts out in a tirade against its presence. Coleridge gives the situation an added uncertainty by withholding from us as yet Geraldine's exact intentions. Indeed, whatever they may be, the fatal woman, aware of her own fatality, seems half to regret what she is about to do—

Even I in my degree will try,
Fair maiden, to requite you well.—

and as she undresses,

Beneath the lamp the lady bowed
And slowly rolled her eyes around . . .

As she lies down to sleep beside Christabel, she has put by all her scruples:

In the touch of this bosom there worketh a spell,
Which is lord of thy utterance, Christabel.

They sleep and the suggestions crystallize into a final irony:

. . . lo, the worker of these harms,
That holds the maiden in her arms,
Seems to slumber still and mild
As a mother with her child.

—Christabel has lost her natural father and has found an unnatural mother: the guardian spirit has been worsted. The important final image of this passage of the sleeping mother embracing her child comes to mind once more, as we shall see, when we hear Bracy's dream of the same night.

In Part One the ground has been prepared: in Part Two the evil of Geraldine begins to operate within Christabel herself. Geraldine, 'nothing doubting of her spell / Awakens the lady Christabel'. Christabel has, on the level of the conscious mind, reassured herself and sees her tormentor as 'fairer yet! and yet more fair!', but her unconscious fears become conscious once more as her father embraces Geraldine and the latter prolongs the embrace 'with joyous look':

Which when she viewed a vision fell
Upon the soul of Christabel,
The vision of fear, the touch and pain!
She shrunk and shuddered, and saw again
. . . .
Again she saw that bosom old,
Again she saw that bosom cold
And drew in her breath with a hissing sound.

It is the hissing of a horrified intake of breath, but its significance becomes deepened when Bracy the Bard tells his story and with what follows. During the night he has dreamed that he saw the tame dove which bears Christabel's name

Fluttering, and uttering fearful moan
. . . .
I stopped, methought the dove to take,
When lo! I saw a bright green snake
Coiled around its wings and neck
. . . .
And with the dove it heaves and stirs,
Swelling its neck as she swells hers!

This moment is one of the most startling and suggestive touches in the poem. We are recalled by the image to that of the two sleeping together; we see in the movement of the snake an attempt to *imitate* that of the bird as well as to prevent its flight; we remember that the sound Christabel herself made resembled that of a snake. Just as the full moon that is dulled, holds in a frightful balance the image of health with the image of disease, the latter overpowering the former, so now there is a further frightful balance: we are on the brink of the suggestion that the identity of Christabel is coveted by Geraldine and that Christabel has unconsciously assumed something of the evil identity of the other. We come now to the most important dramatic climax of the whole, when Geraldine is kissed by Sir Leoline and the significance of Bracy's dream jestingly ignored by the Knight:

Geraldine looks askance at Christabel:

> A snake's small eye blinks dull and shy,
> And the lady's eyes they shrunk in her head,
> Each shrunk up to a serpent's eye
> . . . .
> One moment and the sight was fled!

Our worst suspicion is now confirmed by what follows:

> But Christabel in dizzy trance,
> Stumbling on the unsteady ground—
> Shuddered aloud, with a hissing sound.

She shudders with horror still, but she emits the sound a snake would make. Her imagination is so overpowered by 'those shrunken serpent eyes',

> That all her features were resigned
> To this sole image in her mind . . .

And not only does she see the image, she feels herself *becoming* the image:

> . . . And passively did *imitate*
> That look of dull and treacherous hate,
> And thus she stood, in dizzy trance;
> Still picturing that look askance
> With *forced unconscious sympathy* . . .

The idea has rooted itself in her mind. Despite this fact, she still fights against Geraldine's spell by asking her father to send her tormenter away, instead of which he 'leads forth the Lady Geraldine', symbolically rejecting his own daughter. There is an extremely dramatic propriety about this incident as Sickness and Evil move off together. It completes the psychological fable with a succinctness in juxtaposition with which Coleridge's tacked-on conclusion to the second part sticks out uncomfortably from the rest.

One might note finally that Coleridge makes use of the old and familiar material of folk tale: the ageing ruler ignores his wise counsellor, rejects his 'natural' daughter and prefers his unnatural. None of the protagonists in Coleridge's narrative is in him- or herself complex: all are stock figures and therefore near to allegory and to what J. F. Danby, speaking of *King Lear* where Shakespeare uses the same fable, calls 'the unambiguous Morality statement' (*Shakespeare's Doctrine of Nature*). One is compelled to see the characters as symbols relating to Everyman's condition of inner psychological tension—the evil preying on the good, the sick undermining the healthy—which brings one back to M. Breton's statement of the symbolical conflict of the tale of terror, and to the fact that Coleridge's poem, limited though it is by its inability to resolve the conflict, presents an extremely individual variant on this basic pattern.

Notes

1. In *Surrealism* edited by Herbert Read (Faber and Faber [1936]).

2. In the Nonesuch *Coleridge,* p. 203.

3. In *Selected Letters,* edited by Kathleen Raine [(Gray Walls Press, 1952)], p. 172.

4. On Coleridge's insistence that 'in my very first conception of the tale I had the whole present to my mind, with the wholeness, no less than the loveliness, of a vision', we have Wordsworth's comment: 'I am sure that he never formed a plan or knew what was to be the end of *Christabel,* and that he merely deceived himself when he thought, as he says, that he had the idea quite clear in his mind'. (Recorded in Crabb Robinson's Diary, Feb. 1st., 1836.)

Richard Harter Fogle (essay date 1962)

SOURCE: Fogle, Richard Harter. "'Christabel.'" In *The Idea of Coleridge's Criticism,* pp. 130-59. Berkeley: University of California Press, 1962.

[*In the following essay, Fogle presents a detailed examination of the central themes of "Christabel," employing Coleridge's own dialectical approach to literary criticism. In Fogle's reading, the poem provides a valuable illustration of Coleridge's core intellectual and philosophical beliefs.*]

A large body of modern literary interpretation, particularly in the United States, has followed the dialectic method of Coleridge's Shakespearean criticism, applying it not only to the drama but to lyric poetry as well, and latterly to the short story and the novel. Such critiques treat all types of literature as dramatic imitations of conflict, thematically stated, developed, and finally resolved. The method has its weaknesses and its dangers: incautiously handled, it confuses genres and makes inappropriate demands; of itself the only value it can state is dramatic appropriateness of function; employing a logical structure, it may see in its object only a logical argument, and instead of an organic development a linear and mechanical progression toward a predetermined end. Well employed, however, it has the advantage of focusing the problem with which as movement any literary work must deal, and of offering an evolving pattern in which the work's relationships may be studied.

The interpretation of **Christabel** in this chapter is an illustration, but does not presume to be an example, of this general method. It attempts a Coleridgean reconciliation of induction with principles. The requirement is sufficient system to permit of intelligible, communicable conclusions, combined with sufficient flexibility of approach. The approach, indeed, must be determined by the poem, so that the critique is a relatively abstract, discursive imitation of it, intended to expound the vital relationships that may be intuitively grasped but without exposition cannot be firmly possessed. My hope in commencing is that this task will be accomplished without mutilating or destroying the vitality the critique proposes to celebrate.

One might question the propriety, of which I myself am yet fully convinced, of using an early work such as *Christabel* to illuminate Coleridge's mature critical method and thought. Yet fundamentally Coleridge's poetry and thought, his early and his later literary life, are one and the same. This is not to blink Coleridge's apparent shifts, such as his great swing from Hartley to idealism; but I affirm here the basic consistency and continuity of Coleridge's development, considering that in his philosophy "distinction is not division," that in his mind as in his dialectic he struggled to synthesize oppositions into organic unity, with Wordsworthian confidence that nothing need finally be discarded as irrelevant or irreconcilable.

* * *

The theme of Coleridge's *Christabel* is the problem of innocence; or, framed as an opposition, it is the beauty of innocence, represented by the heroine, against the beauty of evil in the enchantress Geraldine.[1] Christabel is lovely, holy, and sheltered; the insidious Geraldine is the first evil thing in her experience. From this point of view *Christabel* might be taken for an "initiation" story, concentrating upon that crucial moment between childhood and maturity which decides the direction of the individual's further growth. Freudian and Jungian critics would find material in *Christabel,* and the methods of their depth psychology could also be applied to it. From their close relationship Christabel and Geraldine may be taken as different aspects of the same person. Thus Christabel could be interpreted as the conscious opposed to Geraldine the unconscious mind, the ego or superego to her id; or if the heroine's mother were added to the scheme as superego the scheme could be made triadic, with the mother as reconciler of the opposition or, more simply, as a means of escape or evasion.

In a kindred mythical pattern this opposition could be represented in the Uranian and the Pandemonian Aphrodite, sacred versus profane love; or, correspondingly, Agape versus Eros, or Apollo versus Dionysus. If we view Geraldine in herself, the variety of her shifts and disguises suggests the displacements and transferences of the Freudian theory of dream imagery, which would have some warrant from Coleridge's own experience. Geraldine bears some occult relation to Christabel's

mother, who died in giving her birth; her proximity occasions ambiguous dreams; she may or may not be the daughter of a family friend, Lord Roland de Vaux of Tryermaine; and in Dr. Gilman's account of Coleridge's plan for finishing the poem Geraldine is to appear in the false guise of Christabel's lover. This protean quality of Geraldine's is interesting as a version of the one and the many, a single identity persisting under various forms, as Coleridge called Shakespeare the single divinity, "the one Proteus of fire and flood." This analogy is arbitrary and tenuous, but Coleridge was unquestionably preoccupied with the basic relationship that suggests the connection.

If one considers Geraldine in her influence upon Christabel, her ambiguity has symbolic import. Evil can attack the spirit in many forms, and it may be unintended by the agent in whom it is lodged. There may be evil for us in mother, friend, or lover, ambiguous but real, unwilled but inherent in being itself. This notion would serve to explain Geraldine's strange reluctance to carry out her mission, which many critics have pointed out. Although the agent she is also a victim of evil, controlled by forces she would willingly escape. It has been suggested that she is a victim of demonic possession, an idea that would make her beauty and goodness not merely apparent but real, and render her an unfortunate case of split personality. This idea is the connecting link of Mr. Nethercot's studies in vampire, lamia, and demon lore; like the vampire and the lamia Geraldine is a victim as well as a villain, and like the demon she is an unwilling emissary of unknown powers and destinies.[2]

These various possibilities are sparkles cast off by *Christabel* as one turns it in the light, and it is significant of the poem's complexity that it can evoke them. Each, however, illuminates only a single facet, and all are imposed from without, assuming structures of belief and relationship for which the poem gives no real warrant. If Geraldine, for example, is specifically a vampire, lamia, demon, or witch, Coleridge has kept his own counsel in the matter. We know that she is an evil being in the form of a beautiful woman, and the specification of her rank and regiment in the armies of darkness can only lessen her power upon imagination. Of the crucial revelation, "A sight to dream of, not to tell," E. H. Coleridge remarks that the poet's omission of detail is "on the principle of 'omne ignotum pro MYSTERIO,'"[3] and Coleridge's references to the supernatural bear this out.

If it were necessary to find a source for the supernatural elements in *Christabel,* Book I of Spenser's *Faerie Queene* would be the most interesting candidate for the honor.[4] In *Christabel* the discrepancy between appearance and reality is vitally important, for evil cannot triumph directly. It must resort for its weapons to confusion and disguise. Thus in the heroine Christabel, appearance and reality are one—Una; but in Geraldine they are two, as in the false witch Duessa, who disguises herself as the maid Fidessa. Like Una, Christabel is "holy," and we recall that Holiness is the theme of Spenser's Book I.

In *The Faerie Queene* evil must always resort to duplicity, for in direct encounters good is stronger, and is aided not only by its spiritual powers but also by the force of chivalry and arms. The enchanter Archimago disguises himself as the Red Cross Knight, but his armor is no more than a hollow shell. Entrapped by circumstances into an open fight, he is unhorsed at the first onset by the Paynim Sansloy, in one of the many instances of mistaken identity with which *The Faerie Queene* abounds (Book I, Canto 3, 34-39). Archimago on other occasions succeeds in deceiving St. George, the Red Cross Knight, by a variety of disguises, as Geraldine deceives Christabel and Sir Leoline. He works also through false dreams, which are calculated to destroy the integrity of the dreamer whom they attack. Such are Christabel's dreams as she lies imprisoned in the arms of Geraldine. They are literally true, for she is

> Fearfully dreaming, yet, I wis,
> Dreaming that alone which is . . . ,

but in the last analysis they are delusions. *The Faerie Queene* shows the same mingling of dream and reality as *Christabel* when St. George, who has been dreaming of Una, awakes to find the apparition of Una standing by his side (Canto 1, 45-49). There is a difference, for the seeming Una is only an invention of Archimago's, whereas Christabel is awakened by the real Geraldine. Yet the resemblance remains, for Geraldine as we know her in the poem is false to begin with.

The resemblances between *The Faerie Queene* and *Christabel,* however, point to an essential distinction. Spenser's disguises and delusions are merely physical and temporary. He is careful to present before us his evil creatures as they really are, for the reader is not to share the confusions of the characters. In Coleridge the problem is deep-seated, like the ambiguity of James's "The Turn of the Screw," or of Hawthorne's "Rappaccini's Daughter," in which only heaven can separate the tangled strands of good and evil. It is clearly Coleridge's intention to provide a happy ending—

> But this she knows, in joys and woes,
> That saints will aid if men will call:
> For the blue sky bends over all!—

yet, on the other hand, Geraldine's spell, like the spell on the Ancient Mariner, is woven for the precise purpose of making Christabel unable to call for aid. Doubtless, as in *The Ancient Mariner* [*The Rime of the Ancient Mariner*], the spell was to be broken—"Sure my kind saint had pity on me!"—but the poem actually leaves Christabel completely entangled.

This complexity is reflected in Geraldine herself, alike agent and victim. Whereas Spenser's characters are allegorical representations of qualities, and in themselves lifeless, Geraldine is an individual as well as an emissary, with her own self-conflicts, her revulsions as well as her unhallowed pride. On occasions she counterfeits goodness and reality so successfully that we hardly know what to think, as when, upon arising,

> . . . her looks, her air
> Such gentle thankfulness declare
> That (so it seemed) her girded vests
> Grew tight beneath her heaving breasts.

One explanation, of course, is simply that Coleridge is inordinately skillful in working up suspense, but the problem goes beyond the technical requirements of the genre.

For Coleridge the poem of the supernatural is comparable within its kind to the "Romantic drama," and shares with it the ultimate purpose of enlivening our perceptions, awakening our affections, and increasing our ability to imagine reality.[5] It must defeat the prejudices and prepossessions of the understanding, which is bounded by the senses and the abstract logic derived from them. This victory is to be won, however, not by literally taking leave of the senses but by limiting them to their proper sphere. The poem of the supernatural is, like other works of the imagination, a reconciliation of understanding and reason, though with a greater than usual freedom from the bounds of time and space in accordance with its emphasis and function. It intends to endow with provisional reality a supersensuous world, through the concrete, sensuous medium of art.

Correspondingly the illusion that is the immediate artistic end of the poem of the supernatural is a mean between delusion and literal reality. Here it is necessary to distinguish with extreme care, in order to convey the precise nuance of meaning in the famous phrase, "the willing suspension of disbelief." The formula provides a way of distinguishing poetry, the discourse of imagination, from religion, science, and philosophy, by avoiding the terms of truth and belief in connection with it. Religion, philosophy, science, history all try to equip us to deal directly with reality, and in order to do so they abstract from it, whereas poetry as an imitation proposes to help us grasp as much reality as we can in the imagination. Reality is the imagination of God, whereas poetry and art are the imagination of man. We cannot possibly imagine too much, so that after its kind the poem of the supernatural is the truest realism, which enlarges our minds to a true vision of the infinite creation. Only we must not confuse imaginative creation with literal belief, when we are confronted with matters beyond our literal knowledge. Supernatural beings are by definition beyond us.

Thus Coleridge believes in supernatural powers, and infers from all he knows of the natural world a supernatural hierarchy between ourselves and God. But he cannot present the figures of imagination as figures of literal truth. Ideas, in his sense of the term, are always indefinite, and can be comprehended only when embodied in symbols, not when fixed, as in allegory, to represent something already determined and known. A supernatural character such as Geraldine is a symbol of spiritual conflict and evil, and in that sense she is real; but we do not learn of her real form, which remains ambiguous, and we are not entitled to draw up a system of supernatural Mammalia in which she can be accurately classified as vampire, lamia, or witch-woman. She is not, on the other hand, merely a means of expressing psychological conflicts,[6] such as Coleridge's own inner stresses at the time of writing, although these as well as his knowledge of demon lore may very well have entered into her total composition. Coleridge's psychology should never be divorced from his cosmos of nature and spirit; he is always looking outward and upward as well as inside. The mental faculties of his psychological vocabulary belong to his philosophy and to his criticism as well, and even to his theology; they are organs of knowledge, not merely peepholes for watching the mind's behavior.

E. H. Coleridge comments finely upon the beginning of **Christabel,** that crucial sector of the poem of the supernatural where acquiescence and sympathy must primarily be won:

> Perhaps the most wonderful quality or characteristic of this First Part . . . is that the action is not that of a drama which is *ex hypothesi* a representative of fact;— nor are we persuaded to reproduce it for ourselves as by a tale that is told, but we behold it, scene after scene, episode by episode, as in a mirror, as the Lady of Shalott saw the knights ride by. If we stay to think of Christabel "praying beneath the huge oak tree" or of Geraldine and Christabel crossing the moat and passing through the hall, and stealing their way from stair to stair, our minds make pictures, but we do not stay to think or reflect on their fears or their rejoicings. We "see, we see it all," and now in glimmer and now in gloom we "live o'er again" that midnight hour. It is not a tale that is told, it is a personal experience. The mechanism which shifts the scenes is worked by nature and not by art. The necessity of their connexion is not logical, but in the strictest sense of the word, accidental. It happened, and it was so.[7]

E. H. C. [E. H. Coleridge] catches the effect of **Christabel** admirably, and he goes on to praise its artistry. His account is, however, metaphorical, and perhaps occasionally misleading. Do we see the scenes of Part I "as in a mirror"? Perhaps, if the mirror is an idealizing and selective medium like the dim moonlight that picks out the early scenes; otherwise, the figure might be thought ill-chosen. It would be better to say that they appear before us suddenly as if by magic, with the magician sometimes visibly directing our attention from close by, and sometimes orally expressing them in broken exclamations or lulling musical cadences. And in what sense we see the scenes is questionable, as indeed E. H. C. appears to hint. It may be idiosyncrasy, but I do not really visualize the "huge, broad-breasted, old oak tree," or Christabel, or Geraldine, nor am I prompted to do so. I imagine outlines, a vague silhouette of the tree, and attitudes, like Christabel praying, or Christabel and Geraldine stealing toward the castle; I catch the shadowy gleam of Geraldine's robe, and the glitter of the jewels in her hair. By his skillful use of a few particulars, Coleridge convinces us that the scene exists and could be described if it were desirable to do so; and this is enough to secure the suspension of our disbelief and render us receptive, to convince us that here is a mystery worth straining to illumine. We recall that Coleridge was skeptical about detailed description in poetry, and relegated it to the fancy. It is a law of the imagination to create living wholes out of parts, if the parts have the potentiality of life.

The effect of immediacy so necessary to the supernatural is also attained by a kind of hypnotism. The poet acts as an Ancient Mariner to the reader's Wedding Guest. This hypnotic quality is partly suggested by the subject matter. To talk of trances, dreams, spells, and of the hypnotic power of the eye, is a step toward inducing their effects, and Coleridge accompanies the narrative with the equivalent of dramatic gesture and recitation in his meter and melody. Like the rhapsode Ion he intends, although more subtly, to raise up absent things as though they were present. He makes use of emotional notations both direct and indirect, as in the sudden, ostensibly involuntary exclamation, "O shield her! shield sweet Christabel!" or the quieter comment on Geraldine,

> She was most beautiful to see
> Like a lady of a far countrie.

The poet has a steady sense of his audience, and an eye for both his matter and his manner. To win us he must himself be captivated ("himself that great Sublime he draws"), and also be able to infect us with his feelings by his power of projecting them upon us. To achieve his effect, however, he needs to make use of variety. In a poem of any length it is impossible to maintain an even intensity throughout, or to keep precisely equidistant from one's material. Thus Coleridge steadily alternates, for example, between the present as his narrative tense and the somewhat more distant past, not with mechanical regularity but so constantly that the usage must have been intended. By itself the historical present would after a certain point be mannered and unnatural; the variation tempers it while it supports its effect.

The supernatural poem must assert, not argue. It presents a necessity without logic, and it would be fatal to protest too much. Therefore its opening is characteristically swift:

> 'Tis the middle of night by the castle clock,
> And the owls have awakened the crowing cock;
> Tu—whit!——Tu—whoo!
> And hark, again! the crowing cock,
> How drowsily it crew.

It is worthwhile noting for its bearing upon Coleridge's method in *Christabel* that line 3 is direct dramatic presentation, with stage directions added in lines 4-5, and to some degree in the spelling and punctuation. The single and double dashes and the extra *o* indicate extraordinary duration, as does the same usage in lines 306-310, dramatically appropriate in its context:

> By tairn and rill,
> The night-birds all that hour were still.
> But now they are jubilant anew,
> From cliff and tower, tu—whoo! tu—whoo!
> Tu—whoo! tu—whoo! from wood and fell!

The continued repetitions suggest that echoes and reverberations fill all the interspaces and intensify until the point of danger at which one's ear begins to rebel.

Coleridge's description reconciles particularity with sparseness. It is precise without being in the least luxuriant. The poet is exact almost to grotesqueness (possibly as an antidote to the danger of bathos) in the "Sixteen short howls, not over loud" (l. 12) of the mastiff, in the observation that "The night is chilly, but not dark" (l. 15), and in the statement that

> The thin gray cloud is spread on high,
> It covers but not hides the sky.

> [Ll. 16-17]

The old oak tree is bare save for "moss and rarest mistletoe" (l. 34) and the famous "one red leaf, the last of its clan" (l. 49). Most striking, perhaps, is the effect of the cloud covering upon the moon:

> The moon is behind, and at the full;
> And yet she looks both small and dull.

> [Ll. 18-19]

More incidentally, it might be remarked that the two daring rhetorical questions ("Is the night chilly and dark?" and "Is it the wind that moaneth bleak?") on the one hand focus and project the scene toward the foreground, and on the other modify the impression of it by their incantatory quality, which tends to formalize it.

The imagery of Part I, then, endows the scenes with a life of their own. Sparse as it is, it possesses the mingled delicacy and fullness that are characteristic of Coleridge's sensibility. Everything is modulated. The cock that is awakened by the owls crows drowsily, the howls of the mastiff are not overloud, the night is chilly but not dark, and "The moon shines dim in the open air" (l. 175). These touches serve the genre of the supernatural, with a vitality added from Coleridge's own nature. A good deal remains to be said, however, of the bearing of the imagery upon the themes and motifs of *Christabel,* and in turn of their functions in the service of the meaning as a whole.

The technical function of the references to trance and dream has been mentioned. They help to establish the suspension of everyday judgment which is common both to dream and to the atmosphere of the poem of the supernatural. Dreams and trance states, however, as expressions of the inner, subterranean reality of the unconscious mind, also raise a crucial problem of meaning. Where is truth to be found, in the dream or in the waking? "Fled is that music,—do I wake or sleep?" asks Keats, and does not answer. And what is the relationship between the two? For there are waking dreams in *Christabel,* and it is not easy to keep the two states clearly separate. Dreams seem to be both good and evil, too: Christabel's prayer beneath the oak tree is a kind of dreaming in its concentrated devotion, associated with dreams "Of her own betrothed knight," and this impression is reinforced by the reprise at the conclusion to Part I:

> Kneeling in the moonlight
> To make her gentle vows;
> Her slender palms together prest,
> Heaving sometimes on her breast;
> Her face resigned to bliss or bale.

> [Ll. 284-288]

The conclusion goes on to make an explicit contrast with another waking dream, this time of evil:

> With open eyes (ah woe is me!)
> Asleep, and dreaming fearfully,
> Fearfully dreaming, yet, I wis,
> Dreaming that alone, which is—
> O sorrow and shame! Can this be she,
> The lady, who knelt at the old oak tree?

> [Ll. 292-297]

Meanwhile, in a strange reversal of values,

> And lo! the worker of these harms,
> That holds the maiden in her arms,
> Seems to slumber still and mild,
> As a mother with her child.

> [Ll. 298-301]

The juxtaposition of Geraldine and the mother is horrible and perverse, yet in Christabel's dream the two must somehow be united, for the image of mother and child merges with another dream, this time beneficent. Christabel "Gathers herself from out her trance," and

> Her limbs relax, her countenance
> Grows sad and soft; the smooth thin lids
> Close o'er her eyes; and tears she sheds—
> Large tears that leave the lashes bright!
> And oft the while she seems to smile
> As infants at a sudden light!
>
> [Ll. 312-318]

The effect is to add to the complexity of the situation. In some occult sense the enchantress Geraldine and Christabel's mother, "her guardian spirit," are one and the same.

In Part II Christabel is again cast into a trance at the sight of Geraldine, once more beautiful after the terrible revelations of the night just passed, in the welcoming embrace of her father Sir Leoline. She is overwhelmed by the ironic contrast:

> Which when she viewed, a vision fell
> Upon the soul of Christabel,
> The vision of fear, the touch and pain!
> She shrunk, and shuddered, and saw again—
> (Ah, woe is me! Was it for thee,
> Thou gentle maid! such sights to see?)
> Again she saw that bosom old,
> Again she felt that bosom cold,
> And drew in her breath with a hissing sound:
> Whereat the Knight turned wildly round,
> And nothing saw, but his own sweet maid
> With eyes upraised, as one that prayed.
>
> [Ll. 451-462]

Again the vision of evil passes swiftly into its opposite, the "vision Blest" of the mother, and again the connection between the mother and Geraldine is placed before us, supported by the remark that Geraldine is in outward appearance "a thing divine." From a different point of view this remark is merely one link in the chain of ironies in which Christabel is helplessly bound throughout the poem, beginning from the moment she innocently places herself within the power of evil; and from this point of view the reference to Geraldine's divinity serves to heighten the contrast between appearance and reality. Yet the possibility remains that the mother and Geraldine are, for Christabel, somehow one.

Bard Bracy's dream vision, which follows, symbolizes the plight of Christabel as a dove coiled about by a snake:

> So strange a dream hath come to me,
> That I had vowed with music loud
> To clear yon wood from thing unblest,
> Warned by a vision in my rest!
>
> [Ll. 527-530]

Then Christabel undergoes the same trance experience as before, narrated in terms of the snake image suggested by Bracy's account of his dream. This time, however, she undergoes not the shock of ironic contrast, as before, but the direct shock of Geraldine's malice and power:[8]

> At Christabel she looked askance!—
> One moment—and the sight was fled!
> But Christabel in dizzy trance
> Stumbling on the unsteady ground
> Shuddered aloud, with a hissing sound;
> And Geraldine again turned round,
> And like a thing, that sought relief,
> Full of wonder and full of grief,
> She rolled her large bright eyes divine
> Wildly on Sir Leoline.
>
> [Ll. 587-596]

Once again Geraldine becomes almost instantly a thing divine. At this penultimate moment of the poem, however, Christabel is terribly isolated and estranged from her entire moral and social world, as if by the trance that has torn her away. She reflects the evil that has come upon her in a "look of dull and treacherous hate." The trance passes, and she regains a measure of self-possession, but what she can reveal is fatally misunderstood, as it is in a literal sense fatally liable to misunderstanding:

> And when the trance was o'er the maid
> Paused awhile, and inly prayed:
> Then falling at the Baron's feet,
> "By my mother's soul do I entreat
> That thou this woman send away!"
> She said: and more she could not say:
> For what she knew she could not tell,
> O'er-mastered by the mighty spell.
>
> [Ll. 613-620]

The prayer "By my mother's soul," however, once more links Geraldine and the mother in an ambiguous association.

Imagery of bareness enters into the dream-and-trance theme, as a question of reality. As **Christabel** is a drama of concealment, revelation is a matter of some importance. What is revealed is of course ugly and fearsome, and one has some ominous hint of a hidden death that lies at the root of things. Coleridge has chosen a cold and bare forest for his opening scene, with no life except the parasite moss and mistletoe, and no movement except the weird dance of "The one red leaf, the last of its clan." It is in this setting of chill and death, half-lighted by a dull moon, that the evil thing comes forth. Christabel bares her feet (l. 166) in an ironic effect of concealment, as she and her dangerous guest steal silently through the castle; and Geraldine bids her to "unrobe yourself" (l. 233) under the pretext that she in the meantime must pray. But Christabel lies down "in her loveliness," having nothing to hide; what she is and what she pretends to be are the same. The central event of the poem is of course the revelation of Geraldine— "Behold! her bosom and half her side"⁹—as she, with a strange reluctance, unbinds "The cincture from beneath her breast," and allows her gown to drop to the floor. What she unbares is evidently ugly and shameful to herself as well as to the horrified beholder, but the only concrete hint of its nature has to be learned retrospectively from the unhappy trance vision of Christabel in Part II:

> Again she saw that bosom old,
> Again she felt that bosom cold. . . .
>
> [Ll. 457-458]

When she dresses herself in the morning Geraldine apparently puts on youth, beauty, and goodness with her gown:

> Puts on her silken vestments white,
> And tricks her hair in lovely plight
>
> . . . .
>
> And while she spake, her looks, her air
> Such gentle thankfulness declare,
> That (so it seemed) her girded vests
> Grew tight beneath her heaving breasts.
>
> [Ll. 364-365, 377-380]

A little earlier in this discussion I raised the question: Might not this goodness and beauty in a sense be genuine? It is not the prerogative of the critic to answer, and hardly within the power of the poet.

Images of the eye and of the serpent in *Christabel* are closely linked with the themes of dream and of revelation, and they are inevitably joined to each other by the notion of the snake's hypnotic eye. The small, dull moon of the opening scene comes, we know, from observation, on the evidence of Dorothy Wordsworth's journal; but it takes on symbolic meaning as an ominous eye when we compare it with later indications in the poem. The mastiff, which "Lay fast asleep in moonshine cold," moans angrily as Christabel and Geraldine pass by her, and it is said pointedly that

> Never till now she uttered yell
> Beneath the eye of Christabel.
>
> [Ll. 150-151]

Beneath the eye of Christabel, no; but another eye is to be considered. Shortly after, in the midst of the mounting series of premonitory warnings that an evil spirit is present, a sudden tongue of light from the fire flares up,

> And Christabel saw the lady's eye,
> And nothing else saw she thereby,
> Save the boss of the shield of Sir Leoline tall,
> Which hung in a murky old niche in the wall.
>
> [Ll. 160-163]

The boss of the shield is another eye, a silent evidence that the castle is somehow awake and watchful. If one observes the several uses of the word "shield" throughout the poem, this detail deepens in meaning.

Geraldine's eyes receive special attention, and their aspect as Geraldine is serpent or beautiful woman is directly in contrast; the blue eyes of Christabel are also contrasted with them. The enchantress stares "with unsettled eye" (l. 208) when by a false step she has evoked the presence of her victim's guardian spirit, whereas Christabel in astonished sympathy

> . . . knelt by the lady's side
> And raised to heaven her eyes so blue.
>
> [Ll. 214-215]

Recovering herself, in one of the many alternations of the poem, Geraldine rises, and "Her fair large eyes 'gan glitter bright" (l. 221). The "glitter" is an echo of the glitter of her jewels in the moonlight (l. 64), which glitter *wildly*. Geraldine's eyes are unnaturally large, bright, and wild, in direct contrast with their smallness and dullness in her other aspect. Excess in one direction prepares us for excess in the other, according to Coleridge's dictum that "extremes meet." Thus during the central episodes of the eye in Part II Geraldine's eyes are the eyes of a snake, and she is a serpent in physical attitude, whereas both before and afterward her eyes are large and bright, and she is a stately and beautiful woman who looks in appeal to the Baron:

> And Geraldine in maiden wise
> Casting down her large bright eyes,
> With blushing cheek and courtesy fine
> She turned her from Sir Leoline;
> Softly gathering up her train,
> That o'er her right arm fell again;
> And folded her arms across her chest,
> And couched her head upon her breast,
> And looked askance at Christabel—
> Jesu, Maria, shield her well!
>
> A snake's small eye blinks dull and shy
> And the lady's eyes they shrunk in her head,
> Each shrunk up to a serpent's eye,
> And with somewhat of malice, and more of dread,
> At Christabel she looked askance!—
> One moment—and the sight was fled!
> But Christabel in dizzy trance
> Stumbling on the unsteady ground
> Shuddered aloud, with a hissing sound;
> And Geraldine again turned round,
> And like a thing, that sought relief,
> Full of wonder and full of grief,
> She rolled her large bright eyes divine
> Wildly on Sir Leoline.
>
> [Ll. 573-596]

There is perhaps more appropriateness in the familiar anecdote of Shelley and *Christabel* than we ordinarily consider. It will be recalled that he imagined Geraldine with eyes where nipples should have been.

Christabel's blue eyes are heavenly, akin to the blue sky that "bends over all." During her prayer beneath the oak they are "more bright than clear" with unshed tears of devotion (ll. 290-291). They are fearfully open in her enthrallment to Geraldine; when she is recovered and naturally asleep, her lids close (perhaps an oblique allusion to the serpent's lidless eyes), and she weeps and smiles at once (ll. 314-318). Sir Leoline's eyes are also expressive, although they always express a misunderstanding of the meaning of what is going on; the boss of his shield, in fact, shows insight superior to his. His first vision of Geraldine fills them with "cheerful wonder" (l. 399); "his eye in lightning rolls" (l. 444) at her supposed wrongs; later they are "made up of wonder and love" (l. 567) in admiration of her; "his eyes were wild" (l. 641) at Christabel's apparent breach of hospitality to their guest; and finally "He rolled his eye with stern regard" (l. 648) upon Bracy, as he orders him away from the unhappy scene.

The serpent motif, intermingled as it is with the other themes, appears by itself in Bracy's dream vision of the dove and the snake:

> I stooped, methought, the dove to take,
> When lo! I saw a bright green snake
> Coiled around its wings and neck.
> Green as the herbs on which it couched,
> Close by the dove's its head it crouched;
> And with the dove it heaves and stirs,
> Swelling its neck as she swelled hers!

[Ll. 548-554]

Like Geraldine the snake disguises itself, taking on the coloration of its background, and like Geraldine it holds its victim in physical embrace. Color is used sparingly in *Christabel,* with a lightly stressed symbolic value. Green, the color of universal nature, occurs only unnaturally, in parasitic moss and mistletoe among the bare forest trees, until Bracy's vision, where it is modified into the "bright lady" Geraldine. Its suggestions are therefore perverse. In the snake-Geraldine conjunction the serpent's bright green is analogous to her shining white robe and her dazzling skin, which counterfeit the holiness of Christabel and her mother and her guardian saint. The color for Christabel, partly no doubt through a principle of emphasis and variety which would deny to her the use of white, is the heavenly but warmer and less assuming blue, proper to the sky and to the Virgin Mary. To return to the snake theme, Geraldine's voice is reported as "faint and sweet" (ll. 72, 76) in preparation for the contrast of the "hissing sound" (ll. 459, 591) that the unfortunate Christabel under her influence twice utters involuntarily. Another such irony occurs in Sir Leoline's promise to Geraldine (l. 571) that "Thy sire and I will crush the snake!"

The snake theme must stand in the center of any interpretation of *Christabel.* In a sense interpretation is impossible—matter-of-factly, because the poem is un-

finished, and more fundamentally, because no abstraction can comprise within itself the poem's potentialities of meaning. Coleridge has refrained from attempting to say what he means, and his doctrine of symbol should warn us to leave his meanings embedded in their substance, inseparable from its life and being. One may, however, legitimately discuss his symbols' capability to suggest. It is almost certain, as Nethercot declares, that there is something of the lamia in Geraldine, but perhaps a more orthodox snake, "the old serpent"[10] of the Garden of Eden, will provide a more interesting background for her. One thinks especially of the Satan of *Paradise Lost,* that bright and ruined archangel, with his disguises as serpent and toad; and also of the universal hiss as Satan and his peers receive the reward of their triumph in Pandemonium.

Christabel is, indeed, after its kind a story of the Fall of Man. It is not the story of the original Fall, with its problems of predestination and free will, but of the consequences of the Fall for every mortal. Christabel does not sin, but she is liable for her human debt. In this regard *Christabel* is more like Blake's *Book of Thel* than like *Paradise Lost.* It is the first encounter of innocence with a fallen world, an event that is inevitable. Blake's attitude is of course quite different from Coleridge's: Thel has her choice of actions, and flees once more into the safe valleys of Har. In any rational sense Christabel ("The maid, devoid of guile and sin") is sinless. She is like Melville's Handsome Sailor, Billy Budd, who falls only because of the slight stammer, a symbol of the inarticulateness that is his single mortal blemish. *Christabel* is a story of the spiritual estrangement that every human being must undergo, and which swallows some of us forever. Geraldine, who so artfully insinuates herself into the castle and into the hearts of its inmates, is simply that which in one form or another must come to us all. It would be interesting to ask, concerning *Christabel,* to what extent the carelessness of innocence itself invites the evil within its doors, assuming that evil cannot initiate action. Undoubtedly, however, the conclusion Coleridge envisaged would have supposed a guardian of genuine innocence as inevitable as the evil that besets it, in the person of the dead mother. The presence of Geraldine, indeed, almost immediately evokes the mother's presence as well (ll. 202-213).

One might speculate that Coleridge was dealing, in the character of Christabel, especially with the problem of a child. Some of the images in the poem are related to observations on Hartley Coleridge in notebooks and letters, and Coleridge's feeling for young children was always strong. A child is peculiarly innocent and vulnerable, and helplessly incapable of expressing his real feelings to his elders. There are vast gulfs of misunderstanding yawning between the child and the adult, and these are perhaps invisible to the parties on either side of them. The advent of Geraldine with her "mighty spell" could be taken as a projection of the feelings of a child, suddenly and mysteriously estranged from his safe, familiar surroundings and his intimates, with no power of putting an end to his misery, and no conception that it is other than endless in itself. Every effort to escape only increases the involvement.

Christabel is of course a young woman, old enough to be married, so that such an interpretation is admittedly partial. But she is set before us as the child of her mother and Sir Leoline, and the emphasis upon her childhood seems too steady to be accidental. Geraldine holds her in her arms "As a mother with her child" (ll. 299-301) during the fatal hour of the spell. The spell relaxed, Christabel "seems to smile / As infants at a sudden light"—a reminiscence of Hartley. Sir Leoline thinks of Geraldine primarily as "the child of his friend" (l. 446), Lord Roland de Vaux of Tryermaine. The vision of the guardian saint spreads "smiles like light" upon Christabel's lips and eyes, and the Baron enquires, "What ails then my beloved child?" (Ll. 463-470.) Sir Leoline is besought repeatedly to think no evil of his child (ll. 622, 627, 634); he is especially wounded, on the other hand, to find "his only child" dishonoring him with gross inhospitality to the distressed daughter of his friend.

In *Christabel* the background of the child is a chivalric order. This setting is doubtless a "Gothic" convention— the supernatural melodrama laid in an isolated castle, at some unspecified but picturesque time in the past—but it is not merely a convention or a device of atmosphere. The strong castle and the knightly order are meant to be taken seriously, as a solid framework of values. Christabel, the holy maid, is supported by a combination of spiritual, temporal, and even (in Bracy) bardic powers, in a single cohesive society, symbolically focused in the castle, which is comparable to the encircling walls and towers of *Kubla Khan,* and the harbor, kirk, and "steady weathercock" of *The Ancient Mariner.* She is shielded by "Jesu, Maria," her guardian spirit, her baronial father, and all the forces at his command. Sir Leoline and the absent but ringingly denominated Lord Roland de Vaux of Tryermaine[11] are evidently towers of strength.

Within the walls of the castle Christabel, we imagine, is safe, but inevitably she must at some time emerge from them and take her chances as an individual in this dark and confusing world. Her purpose in venturing forth is worthy, and it is in keeping with chivalry and her society, for she intends to pray for the welfare of "her own betrothed knight." But the question is asked,

> What makes her in the wood so late,
> A furlong from the castle gate?
>
> [Ll. 26-27]

With the implication that she has ventured outside the pale and is appropriately exposed to the evil awaiting her on the other side of the great oak, itself a symbol of

strength and refuge. Threatened, her first utterance is significantly, "Mary, mother, save me now!" And Geraldine effectively disguises herself in the ceremonial robes of chivalry, as a lady outraged by wanton violation of the laws of knighthood in the persons of the mysterious "Five warriors."

Christabel comforts the supposed daughter of a noble line by offering her the service of her father Sir Leoline and "our stout chivalry." In passing the formidable entrance to the castle with the purpose of penetrating to its innermost sanctum, the bedroom of Christabel, in triumphant desecration, Geraldine has to be helped by someone from within the stronghold. Inside, the shield sternly acknowledges her presence; and Sir Leoline, as the center of the castle's power, must be evaded by stealth, although literally the furtiveness of the movement comes from consideration for his sleep. Sir Leoline's response to Geraldine's story is thoroughly chivalric:

> He swore by the wounds in Jesu's side
> He would proclaim it far and wide,
> With trump and solemn heraldry,
> That they, who thus had wronged the dame,
> Were base as spotted infamy!
> "And if they dare deny the same,
> My herald shall appoint a week,
> And let the recreant traitors seek
> My tourney court—that there and then
> I may dislodge their reptile souls
> From the bodies and the forms of men!"
>
> [Ll. 433-443]

There is a touch of irony in "reptile souls"; the worthy Baron is doomed to look for his snakes in the wrong places. Thus, after planning on a grand scale a chivalric meeting with his friend and Geraldine's supposed father Sir Roland de Vaux, at which both nobles are to appear "with all their numerous array," he asserts confidently that

> With arms more strong than harp or song,
> Thy sire and I will crush the snake!
>
> [Ll. 570-571]

One is tempted to speculate on the place of "harp and song" in this close-knit feudal order. Bard Bracy clearly has an integral and honorable part in it; the solemn ceremonial visit to Lord Roland is entrusted to him (ll. 483-504) as ambassador. His position is subordinate, however; his advice is disregarded and his superior insight remains unused. He alone in his dream vision has detected the evil that has crept within, although it could be pointed out that he has seen it in strictly poetic—that is, figurative and symbolic—guise: not, indeed, the tale of a cock and a bull, as the Baron evidently thinks it, but of a snake and a bird. The relation between poetry and action is fated to be indirect. Nevertheless, his powers seem almost vatic. His "music strong and saintly song" is capable of exorcising the evil thing, if the Baron would permit him to employ it for the purpose. It would be possible to take Bracy as a symbol of the romantic poet.

The meaning of *Christabel* is inseparable from its unique metrical effects. In his Preface to the poem Coleridge said that

> the metre of Christabel is not properly speaking, irregular, though it may seem so from its being founded on a new principle: namely, that of counting in each line the accents, not the syllables. Though the latter may vary from seven to twelve, yet in each line the accents will be found to be only four. Nevertheless, this occasional variation in number of syllables is not introduced wantonly, or for the mere ends of convenience, but in correspondence with some transition in the nature of the imagery or passion.

Whether the principle of *Christabel*'s versification is absolutely new it would be useless, in fact mischievous, to inquire;[12] but it is highly original and entirely organic to the poem. It is evident enough that Coleridge, as his last sentence implies, was seeking after a more intimate interpenetration of meter and meaning than he believed had been hitherto accomplished.

In so doing he was also in search of variety and flexibility, to the end of dramatic expressiveness or propriety, in a complex narrative poem in which constant shifts of feeling or "passion" were to be the rule. If, however, dramatic propriety had been his only consideration he might well have chosen blank verse for his measure. There would be a number of more or less obvious reasons against such a choice. First, the genre of the supernatural presumably calls for something different; its special illusion, and the range of feeling natural to it, narrower yet more intense than in drama, would demand a more concentrated, a denser texture of metric and sound. Drama, too, has spectacle to complete it, for which the narrative poet must substitute an equivalent attraction in the verse itself. A poem, said Coleridge, should offer as much pleasure in each part as is consonant with our pleasure in it as a whole; and the poem's part-whole relationship is unique.

Thus the meter of a poem like *Christabel* exists more completely for and in itself than would the meter of any poetic drama. The meter of *Christabel* also exists more intensely in its own right than, say, that of a narrative poem by Scott or Byron, both of whom owed a debt to *Christabel* for metrical suggestions. Yet it is at the same time more organic and less arbitrary than the meters of Scott or Byron; it is more thoroughly entwined in the total meaning and the movement of the poem. It illustrates and substantiates, indeed, what Coleridge meant by the principle of individuation in his theory of life

and organic unity: that, organic life being presupposed, intense individuality in a part is not only reconcilable with but essential to a corresponding intensity of the whole. The greatest variety is also the greatest unity, in the presence of a sufficient creative agency. *Christabel* cannot be termed an organic unity in the sense of a complete correspondence of idea and execution, or of a perfect reconciliation of part and whole, but its potentialities toward unity are magnificent.

The intensity of its parts is too great for its proportions. *Christabel* is Coleridge's chief poetic trial of strength, in which his strength was inadequate to the delicacy, the elaboration, and the density of texture required in the execution. The more austere among our critics have sometimes treated the author of *Christabel* as if he had been a lazy schoolboy who failed to complete his assignment in English composition. The task, however, was self-assigned, and almost impossibly exacting.

Christabel was evidently to be a poem in which the parts would be uniquely self-significant and consummately wrought, each part a whole in itself and yet contributing to the larger whole. If one considers first the metrical lines as the basic units, and the poetic vitality that has been lavished upon them; then the verse paragraphs, each of which is a whole, elaborated and rounded, individual and self-justifying as a stanza need not be, for no two paragraphs are exactly alike; then the conclusions to the parts, which recapitulate yet advance the argument (the conclusion to Part I is its capstone, a triadic reconciliation of opposites);[13] then the relation of Parts I and II, maintaining the same illusion and atmosphere under different conditions, one cannot wonder that Coleridge failed in his gigantic effort at infusing an unprecedented intensity of life at once into each part and into a highly complex totality. In the latter years of his life he maintained that he still had and always had had the idea of *Christabel* in mind.[14]

Coleridge apparently intended in the meter of *Christabel* a new blend of variety with unity, of flexibility with regularity. His principle of accentuation does not seem to be absolute and exclusive, as indeed we should not expect from his general habit of thought. He was too well trained in classical metrics to write lines that could not be scanned into feet, and too naturally melodious to dally with deliberate harshness or with any radical experiments in counterpoint. His meter may be analyzed as a basic iambic tetrameter with an unprecedented number of exceptions, consisting of inversions of stress or accent, and of three-syllable feet with their characteristic swiftness of movement.

Time or duration plays a large part, however. We may assume that lines with less than the average number of syllables in *Christabel* usually take more than the average time per syllable, so that they roughly equal other lines in their length. This, however, though substantially true, is not literally and arithmetically true.[15] The most important consideration is the melody. There seems to be little doubt that Coleridge intends a very wide variation in the length of time a syllable can be held; that his accents are like musical beats;[16] that his sound effects include differences of pitch and intensity or volume; and that in general he seeks freedom and variety more usual in music than in verse, as one might indicate in notations like allegro, or legato, or andante.

The verse of *Christabel* sings and, in its use of repetition, dances as well, in a ritual celebration of design which goes beyond the bounds of dramatic propriety, unless we interpret very broadly what is proper to the illusion of the supernatural. Coleridge does not of course violate propriety, which is indeed his first consideration, but he characteristically endows his meter with qualities of its own, and his parts with their own vitality. Thus there is the dance of the leaf:

> There is not wind enough to twirl
> The one red leaf, the last of its clan,
> That dances as often as dance it can,
> Hanging so light, and hanging so high
> On the topmost twig that looks up at the sky.
>
> [Ll. 48-52]

The image functions in its context to suggest the dead bareness of the forest trees, and, by an interesting contrast, to convey the stillness of the air. But the passage also stands by itself as a *danse macabre,* at once wailing and exultant in singing and dancing. The song, one might say, commences with the lilting ripple from the extra syllable of "The one red leaf, the last of its clan"; the dance begins in the words and the beat of the following line, and there is a movement of vertiginous swinging in the parallelism of "Hanging so light, and hanging so high," with height, distance, and piercing melancholy and joy combined, from the interfusion of the vowel quality in *light* and *high* with the movement of the line and the meanings of the words.

A semihypnotic incantation is no doubt the principal effect, as in Geraldine's "In the touch of this bosom there worketh a spell . . ." (ll. 267-278), and in Sir Leoline's orders to the Bard, which he imagines executed even while uttering

> (And when he has crossed the Irthing flood,
> My merry bard! he hastes, he hastes . . .),

so that they seem to be accompanied by the movements of an actor. In each instance, however, there is a self-delighting power of pure aesthetic design which goes beyond the function of meaning in even its broadest sense: in the excursions and the returns of the balladlike repetitions and refrains, and in the variations of couplets, the more fluid cross rhyming, and the occasional

mounting triplets. Repetition, on the order of the Miltonic turn, is a characteristic of *Christabel.*[17] It occurs in sound, or in syllable, as in internal rhyme, in words and phrases, and more elaborately in complete sentences. It is a device of vital progression which is basic to Coleridge and peculiarly typical of *Christabel's* elaborate technique, a single configuration of the winding filaments of growth, the never-ceasing play of associations that represent Coleridge's idea of organic unity.[18]

Notes

1. "The antithesis of the beauty of innocence to the beauty of sin" (E. H. Coleridge, ed., *Christabel* [London, Henry Frowde, 1907], p. 15).

2. Arthur H. Nethercot, *The Road to Tryermaine* (Chicago, University of Chicago Press, 1939), pp. 59-139. See also E. H. Coleridge, *op. cit.,* pp. 6-15.

3. *Op. cit.,* p. 76.

4. See E. H. Coleridge, *op. cit.,* pp. 12-15; Nethercot, *op. cit.,* pp. 122-124.

5. See above, pp. 115-116.

6. I am forced to disagree with Kathleen Coburn's conclusions in her interesting essay on "Coleridge and Wordsworth and 'the Supernatural,'" *University of Toronto Quarterly,* XXV (1956), 121-130. Edward E. Bostetter in "Christabel: The Vision of Fear," *Philological Quarterly,* XXXVI (1957), 183-194, emphasizes parallels with Coleridge's own state of mind.

7. *Op. cit.,* pp. 15-16.

8. This description might be taxed with inaccuracy in two particulars: that Geraldine looked *askance* at Christabel, and that the look possessed "somewhat of malice, *and more of dread*" (l. 586). It has seemed best nevertheless to let the statement stand as true in context, rather than to modify it. The malice of Geraldine's glance suggests an interesting comparison with Herman Melville's *Billy Budd,* in a scene where the almost sinless Billy is confronted with the depraved Claggart, who is seeking to swear his life away: "Claggart deliberately advanced within short range of Billy, and mesmerically looking him in the eye, briefly recapitulated the accusation.

"Not at first did Billy take it in. When he did the rose-tan of his cheek looked struck as by white leprosy. He stood like one impaled and gagged. Meanwhile the accuser's eyes removing not as yet from the blue dilated ones, underwent a phenomenal change, their wonted rich violet color blurring into a muddy purple. Those lights of human intelligence losing human expression, gelidly protruding like the alien eyes of certain uncatalogued creatures of the deep. The first mesmeric glance was one of surprised fascination; the last was as the hungry lurch of the torpedo-fish."

9. After this line, the line "Are lean and old and foul of hue" immediately followed in a number of manuscripts.

10. Cf. ll. 457-459:

> Again she saw that bosom old,
> Again she felt that bosom cold,
> And drew in her breath with a hissing sound.

11. E. H. Coleridge's account (*op. cit.,* pp. 23-27) of the history of the de Vaux family testifies interestingly to the solidity of the chivalric framework in *Christabel.*

12. Among discussions of the meter of *Christabel* see *ibid.,* pp. 58-59n.; Ada L. F. Snell, "The Meter of Christabel," in *Fred Newton Scott Anniversary Papers* (Chicago, University of Chicago Press, 1929); Karl Shapiro, "English Prosody and Modern Poetry," *ELH,* XIV (1947), 77-92; Sir Herbert Read, *The True Voice of Feeling* (New York, Pantheon Books, 1953), pp. 27-28. See also George Whalley, "Coleridge on Classical Prosody: An Unidentified Review of 1797," *Review of English Studies,* II (1951), 248-249; Charles I. Patterson, "An Unidentified Criticism by Coleridge Related to *Christabel,*" *Publications of the Modern Language Association,* LXVII (1952), 973-988.

13. The conclusion to Part II seems to bear an intelligible relationship to what has gone before, whatever the immediate circumstances of its composition. Part II ends with a father's harshness to his child, the result of a tragic misunderstanding. The conclusion, which Coleridge had called a "very metaphysical account of fathers calling their children rogues, rascals, and little varlets," presents a pretended and humorous harshness, and accounts for it by the tentative hypothesis that in this fallen world most strong passions are evil and in consequence the passion of love must borrow its vocabulary from its opposite:

> Perhaps 'tis pretty to force together
> Thoughts so all unlike each other;
> To mutter and mock a broken charm
> To dally with wrong that does no harm:
> Perhaps 'tis tender too and pretty
> At each wild word to feel within
> A sweet recoil of love and pity!
> And what, if in a world of sin
> (O sorrow and shame should this be true!)
> Such giddiness of heart and brain
> Comes seldom save from rage and pain,
> So talks as it's most used to do?

Coleridge seems about to go on, "But what if the father's rage and pain should be genuine, as is Sir Leoline's; as may happen in a world of sin whose fatal influence can bring about such estrangement as this? That would indeed be sorrow and shame." In other words, the conclusion would have reëmphasized the tragic breach in the father-child relationship. This interpretation is strengthened by the earlier use of "sorrow and shame" to describe Christabel's fallen state: Geraldine avows to her that

> Thou knowest to-night, and will know tomorrow,
> This mark of my shame, this seal of my sorrow;

and the conclusion to Part I laments,

> O sorrow and shame! Can this be she,
> The lady, who knelt at the old oak tree?

14. "Good music never tires me, nor sends me to sleep. I feel physically refreshed and strengthened by it, as Milton says he did.

"I could write as good verse now as ever I did, if I were perfectly free from vexations, and were in the *ad libitum* hearing of fine music, which has a sensible effect in harmonizing my thoughts, and in animating, and, as it were, lubricating my inventive faculty. The reason of my not finishing *Christabel* is not that I don't know how to do it— for I have, as I always had, the whole plan entire from beginning to end in my mind; but I fear I could not carry on with equal success the execution of the idea, an extremely subtle and difficult one" (*Table Talk,* July 6, 1833). The association of music with *Christabel* is significant. In fact, the topic of *Christabel* seems to have arisen in connection with music, which Coleridge had previously been discussing, and from which he had gotten to Milton, then to his own poetry, and finally to *Christabel* specifically. See the entire entry for this date.

15. See Read, *op. cit.,* pp. 27-28. In keeping with his customary exhilarating view of Coleridge and romanticism, Sir Herbert emphasizes irregularity in *Christabel:* "An examination of this measure shows that it is even more irregular than Coleridge had forewarned us in his Preface. At least, if we take lines like:

> Of the huge, broad-breasted, old oak tree

or

> On the topmost twig that looks up at the sky

it is difficult to scan them without allowing, in the first case six, in the second five, accents. In other cases it is difficult to discover more than three:

> My sire is of a noble line

or

> Is the night chilly and dark."

I am predisposed to argue against this interpretation as giving too little heed to the base of unity or regularity which Coleridge used as his point of departure. Read seems to be assuming a principle of absolute, invariable accentuation not intended by the poet. The lines may be scanned as follows to show a much higher degree of regularity, if it is assumed that accent does not depend upon quantity or upon ordinary stress entirely, but rather upon interrelationships within the line or possibly within the period. That is, a syllable that would ordinarily be accented may yield to a stronger accent in its vicinity:

> Of the *huge*/broad-*breast*/ed *old*/oak *tree*
> On the *top*/most *twig*/that looks *up*/at the *sky*
> My *sire*/is *of*/a *no*/ble *line*
> Is the *night*//*chil*ly/and *dark?*

Thus interpreted, each line has four accents.

16. See Shapiro, *op. cit.*

17. The extent of repetition in *Christabel,* too great to represent in the text of this essay, can hardly be recognized without wearisome listing. Without attempting to be definitive, I have noted ninety-nine instances of significant repetition. The count is a listing of the lines in which repetition occurs, and does not include repetition within single lines or repetition, such as internal rhyme, alliteration, assonance, or consonance, in elements smaller than a word.

18. The following statements on meter bear upon Coleridge's presumed practice in *Christabel:* "To read Dryden, Pope, &c., you need only count syllables; but to read Donne you must measure *Time,* and discover the *Time* of each word by the sense of Passion" (*Coleridge on the Seventeenth Century,* ed. R. F. Brinkley [Durham, N.C., Duke University Press, 1955], pp. 519-520).

"In the Iambic Pentameter of the *Paradise Lost,* I assume fifteen breves as the total quantity of each line—this isochrony being the identity or element of sameness, the varying quality of the isochronous feet constituting the difference; and from that harmony or fine balance of the two opposite (N.B. *not* contrary) forces, viz., identity and difference, results the likeness; and again, this likeness (*quicquid simile est, non est idem*) [is] reducible to a law or principle and therefore anticipable, and, in fact, though perhaps unconsciously expected by the reader, or auditor, constitutes poetic metre. Each line is a metre—ex. gr., we should not say, that an hexameter is a line of six metres, but that it is a metre of six feet. But the harmonious relation of the metres to each other, the fine medium between division and continuity, distinction without disjunction, which a good reader expresses by a pause without a cadence, constitutes rhythm. And it is this harmonious opposition and balance of metre and rhythm, super-added to the former balance of the same in quantity with the difference in quality, the one belonging to the lines, the other to the paragraphs, that makes the peculiar charm, the *excellency,* of the Miltonic poesy. The Greek epic poets left rhythm to the orators. The metre all but precluded rhythm. But the ancients *sang* their poetry. Now for a nation who, like the English, have substituted *reading,* impassioned and tuneful reading, I grant, but still *reading,* for *recitative,* this counter-action, this interpenetration, as it were, of metre and rhythm is the dictate of a sound judgment and like all other excellencies in the fine arts, a postulate of common sense fulfilled by genius . . ." (*ibid.,* p. 580). Coleridge's assumption of a uniform quantity to each line, balanced by variety in the metrical feet, and the further balance of meter in the line with rhythm in the verse paragraph, has a strong likeness to what he said of the meter of *Christabel* in his Preface, to which the poem's system of paragraphs adds a further similarity.

Of Beaumont and Fletcher he remarks, "It is true that *Quantity,* an almost iron Law with the Greek, is in our language rather a subject for a peculiarly fine ear, than any law or even rule; but then we, instead of it have first, accent; 2ndly, emphasis; and lastly, retardation & acceleration of the Times of Syllables according to the meaning of the words, the passion that accompanies them, and even the character of the Person that uses them" (*Coleridge's Miscellaneous Criticism,* ed. T. M. Raysor [Cambridge, Harvard University Press, 1936], pp. 66-67). Of Massinger he writes: ". . . the rhythm and metre are incomparably good, and form the very model of dramatic versification, flexible and seeming to arise out of the passions, so that whenever a line sounds immetrical, the speaker may be certain he has recited it amiss, either that he has misplaced or misproportioned the emphasis, or neglected the acceleration or retardation of the voice in the pauses . . ." (Brinkley, *op. cit.,* p. 676).

Virginia L. Radley (essay date autumn 1964)

SOURCE: Radley, Virginia L. "'Christabel': Directions Old and New." *Studies in English Literature, 1500-1900* 4, no. 4 (autumn 1964): 531-41.

[*In the following essay, Radley examines the tendency of many scholars and critics to attribute the complexity of "Christabel" to the fact that it is incomplete. Radley argues that such an approach ignores the poem's more vital stylistic innovations and imaginative ambiguities.*]

Few would contend that Samuel Taylor Coleridge's poem **Christabel** is a simple poem; but many would contend that the reasons for its complexity lie in the fact that it was never completed. This latter point of view seems to epitomize the essential weakness manifest in all critiques of the poem. Admittedly, *Christabel* is complex and, I would propose, infinitely so. I would certainly not contend that the understanding of a poem is facilitated by its being unfinished. But I would say that *Christabel* critiques suffer on the whole from oversimplification of approach and from inattention on the part of its critics to the multitudinous intricacies which characterize the poem. This paper does not purport to do any more than suggest directions the critic might take in order to establish a basis for a more valid criticism and to provide, by so doing, a larger frame of reference within which to order the component parts of the poem.

First of all, there is the matter of the date of composition to be considered. Although the poem was first published in 1816, the discrepancies in ascribing a date of composition are many. Nethercot believes that the materials for *Christabel* were being gathered from 1795 to 1798 and that the first book and one-half of the second were finished in 1797.[1] He cites Coleridge in a letter to Byron as having said this (p. 4), and also Dorothy Wordsworth's mention of the poem in her Journal dated 1798. Nethercot also quotes Coleridge as having said that the poem ran to 1300 lines, of which there now remain 677 (p. 12). Most critics seem to accept this evidence. Nonetheless, interest in witches, in love, in religion certainly occupied Coleridge's mind in 1801 as Professor Coburn's admirable edition of the *Notebooks* [*Notebooks of Samuel Taylor Coleridge*] illustrates,[2] and this material most assuredly combined to shape *Christabel.* An intensive study of the Coburn edition (projected to eight volumes) might well yield further information on the date of composition.

Turning to the readings of the poem, I found more problems accruing. The vicissitudes in *Christabel* interpretation seem to me to redact to two, the *logical* and the *psychological.* By far the more "respectable," though by no means the more reliable, is that supported by Professor Nethercot and advanced, I would wager, in most college classrooms throughout the Anglo-American world. This interpretation is the *logical*; it holds that the evil is a supernatural evil typically seen in the medieval romance, one which can be explained logically in terms of the machinery of demonology, demonolatry, and like trappings, that Geraldine is an enchantress, a witch, a lamia, that she has been commissioned by sources external to man to bring about the fall of innocence, to pervert, to corrupt good incarnate in the persons of Christabel and perhaps also Sir Leoline. We are on safe ground here, for textual support abounds for this reading of the poem: the dark gothic forest, the moonlight,

the dog that moans when he senses the presence of evil, the spirits who watch over Christabel, the devil's mark—that "sight to dream of, not to tell," in fact an almost limitless number of references which can be interpreted in the light of witchcraft. In support of this reading, there are again the *Notebooks* with their many references manifesting interest in this subject. In the same source are Coleridge's references to his nightmares involving strange ladies vaguely reminiscent of the genus Geraldine. He dreams, for example, that "a frightful pale woman" wanted to kiss him, that her breath was lethal (p. 1252). In an earlier nightmare, he describes a woman of darkness who is wrenching at his right eye; he screams in pain; Wordsworth calls to him three times before he is able to awaken him; upon awakening, Coleridge finds his right eyelid is swollen and sore (pp. 848-849). The internal evidence in *Kubla Khan* and *The Rime of the Ancient Mariner,* of "woman wailing for her demon-lover," of "The Nightmare LIFE IN DEATH," have been alluded to many times in sundry critiques of *Christabel.* All combine to support the reading that supernatural causes motivate the ensuing action. Nonetheless, despite the evidence in support of this logical interpretation, the reading is inadequate to the task of promoting complete understanding. In my experience, this reading of the poem bereft of the alternative, the *psychological* reading, merely serves to make students of the poem react as if Hepzibah Pyncheon were instructing the class. While I think the logical reading is essential to an understanding of the poem, it seems to me that the modern scholar can no more ignore the alternate reading than could many of those who encountered the poem first-hand upon its publication in 1816.

The second reading, the psychological, attempts to interpret the poem in terms of a psycho-sexual evil. Admittedly, innocence falls (as it does in the former reading) but the causes are natural and not supernatural; that is, they are found within the mind and psyche of man and do not redound upon man from external sources. Geraldine is again a "witch" but in the modern sense of the word. She is evil, but her particular brand of evil finds its source in her own inner self, a self twisted, perverted, intensely sensual. She seduces Christabel in the well-known passage:

> In the touch of this bosom there worketh a spell,
> Which is lord of thy utterance, Christabel!
> Thou knowest to-night, and wilt know to-morrow,
> This mark of my shame, this seal of my sorrow;[3]

Whether the seduction involves a mental recapitulation, a physical, or a combination of the two, depends upon the individual critic's approach. In recent times, G. Wilson Knight spoke of the evil as specifically sexual.[4] This theme was developed more fully by R. P. Basler first in an article[5] and then a reprint of the same with introductory commentary prefixed.[6]

The text of the poem underwent explication in the above terms in an article published in 1951 by Edgar Jones entitled, "A New Reading of *Christabel*." New reading it was not. The article does explore, however, this theme with some thoroughness and raises some very interesting points. For example, the statement, "The embrace of the snake and the dove in Bracy's dream accords perfectly with the sexual nature of Geraldine's embrace of Christabel in the fact."[7] Here Mr. Jones quite nicely refutes Nethercot's interpretation that the snake is a snake: "There is no evidence that Geraldine is a snake *qua snake,* as Nethercot suggests, a hazardous complication. The episode is wholly symbolic" (p. 106).

Far from being a "new" reading, Mr. Jones's point of view has a long history of commitment. Charges of obscenity greeted the poem almost immediately upon publication. Professor Nethercot covers the history of this down to 1939. Among those who were aware of these charges were the unknown reviewers who wrote the articles in *Blackwood's Magazine* (4th edition, London, 1818) and in the *Edinburgh Review* (June, 1819) and Gillman, Hazlitt, P. G. Patmore, and Rossetti, to mention but a few of those who knew.[8]

No one, however, seems to be particularly interested in determining whether or not Coleridge was knowledgeable in matters of sexual perversion. Basler does mention Coleridge's knowledge of the sexual implications in witchcraft,[9] but what of Coleridge's knowledge of human behavior in this respect? I would suggest that the critic who intends to support the psycho-sexual interpretation give some attention to the *Notebooks* for some light on this matter. In an examination of them, I found two or three references which might be pertinent. In particular were the various allusions to the Greek poet, Sappho, whose *modus operandi* is no secret to the modern scholar. I do not believe that Coleridge exuded sophistication in matters of sexual perversion, but I have no doubt that he had some awareness of such matters and that this awareness extended beyond the area circumscribed by witchcraft and demonology.[10] The following passage interests me for many reasons, but the allusion to Sappho in the context of love is relevant to the point in question here: "To write a series of Love Poems—truly Sapphic, save that they shall have a large Interfusion of moral Sentiment [and] calm Imagery on Love in all the moods of the mind—Philosophic, fantastic, in moods of high enthusiasm, of Simple Feeling, of mysticism, of Religion—comprise in it all the practice [and] all the philosophy of love" (p. 1064). Professor Coburn sets the date of this entry as December 1801, scarcely too late to be relevant in a consideration of the

meaning of *Christabel*. If I interpret the passage correctly, Coleridge had in mind a plan to show love in its many facets and was projecting a "series of love Poems." They would be Sapphic (here I think he was alluding not to the mechanics of versification but to the *intensity* implicit in the word) but with one significant difference. These poems would have "a large Interfusion of moral Sentiment." We know, for example, that Coleridge broke into the writing of *Christabel* to write the poem **"Love,"** and that **"Love"** raised some of the same questions as does *Christabel*.[11] Coleridge knew of Sappho, apparently both of her life and of her poetry.[12] Coleridge intended to write a series of love poems; how long this had been in his mind, I could not ascertain. Such comprises the evidence I could find which might be used to bolster the psychological explication of *Christabel*. Certainly without some kind of external evidence in support of this reading, it is small wonder that scholars look askance at this approach. A systematic examination of such evidence might therefore prove fruitful and thus provide another direction in which the critic could proceed.[13]

So much for the two significant readings of the poem, the *logical* and the *psychological*. There remains but one tangent which might be used in support of the latter and thus provide the critic with a byway. This direction leads to a consideration of the really real as Coleridge conceived it. What is real? Are witches real? Are ghosts real? Apparently for Coleridge dreams may be real (as he implies in his comment concerning the swollen eyelid resulting from his nightmare encounter with the woman of darkness) but ghosts are not:

> There is a great difference in the credibility to be attached to stories of dreams and stories of ghosts. Dreams have nothing in them which are absurd and nonsensical; and though most of the coincidences may be readily explained by the diseased system of the dreamer, and the great and surprising power of association, yet it is impossible to say whether an inner sense does not really exist in the mind, seldom developed, indeed, but which may have a power of presentiment. All the external objects have their correspondents in the mind; the eye can see the object before it is distinctly apprehended—why may there not be a corresponding power in the soul? The power of prophecy might have been merely a spiritual excitation of this dormant faculty. . . . But ghost stories are absurd.[14]

In a note to this passage, John Taylor Coleridge is quoted as saying that Samuel Taylor Coleridge felt that it was ". . . impossible that you should really see with bodily eye what was impalpable unless it were a shadow . . ." (pp. 44-45). Thus Coleridge's believing in dreams while disbelieving in ghosts makes the dream of Bard Bracy in *Christabel* take on a great deal more significance than Professor Nethercot accords it; as a result, the lamia-witch motif fades into background coloring. The dream then seems, once again, correctly interpreted by Mr. Jones as an episode "wholly symbolic" and therefore achieving a verisimilitude that the witch-motif never achieves. To be interested in witches and their machinery is one thing; we know Coleridge was interested. To be convinced of their reality and to try to make an entire poem depend upon this conviction, is quite another. Coleridge never oversimplifies; thus the world of dreams may be a significant world while the world of ghosts and witches is not.[15] This biographical information would tend to support the psychological interpretation of *Christabel* and, therefore, to draw the poem away from the logical reading of it.

I hope it has been made clear to the reader that I am not attempting to dismiss either reading of *Christabel* as worthless. Both are essential to an understanding of the poem, but neither may be accepted exclusive of the other. What is needed is a new frame of reference within which to order the two readings. Some direction to this end has been indicated: that is, the biographical information found notably in the *Notebooks* and in *Table Talk* [*The Table Talk of Samuel Taylor Coleridge*]. I should now like to explore one possible structure for this frame of reference.

If Coleridge really was contemplating writing a series of poems reflective of all aspects of love, then this fact might well provide the frame of reference which would yield the most valid reading of the poem. Providing this intention on the part of Coleridge was already being realized in the writing of *Christabel* and "Love," then neither the logical nor the psychological (defined as psycho-sexual by Basler) will suffice. The frames are, as it were, too small. The larger frame would be not only a synthesis of the two, but also an inclusion of all pertinent external data. If the poem is more than a study of the nature of evil, its effect upon innocence, and I think it is; if the poem has a great deal to do with love-relationships, and I think it does; then the critic must depart from the well-worn paths made by the two readings discussed above in this paper.

Certainly Coleridge was no stranger to love. His ill-fated loves for Mary Evans and Sarah Hutchinson, his ill-fated marriage to Sarah Fricker, made him peculiarly aware of the alienating and isolating qualities of love. Nor was Coleridge any stranger to the ambivalence to which love often falls heir. Students of the Romantic Mind find themselves increasingly aware of the attraction and repulsion which exist concomitantly inherent within the nature of intense love, providing the condition for ambivalence. To my mind, *Christabel* is a study in ambivalent love-relationships; therefore, in the main, a psychological study in the broadest sense of the term. Although the psycho-sexual elements are quite apparent, they form but one of the many kinds of love-relationships manifest in the poem. To enumerate, there is the "love," which might be classified as infatuation,

between Christabel and the lovely lady, Geraldine; there is the love of Christabel for her dead mother; that held for her lover who is "far away"; and that she holds for her father, Sir Leoline, (at first a reciprocal love). Then, subsidiary to these loves, but by no means inconsequential, is the love of Sir Leoline for Lord Roland de Vaux of Tryermaine. In no less than three of these loves, and possibly four, ambivalence distinguishes the relationship: Christabel for Geraldine; Leoline for Christabel; Leoline for Lord Roland; and, less obvious but still manifest, Geraldine for Christabel.

Turning to an examination of this characteristic, clearly ambivalence marks the meeting of Christabel with Geraldine in the forest. Geraldine, strangely beautiful, "Beautiful exceedingly" (line 68), come upon in this lonely setting evokes in Christabel mixed feelings: she is afraid and she prays, "Mary mother, save me now!" (line 71). And still she sympathizes and is initially attracted. These latter feelings take precedence over, yet do not obliterate, the fear, to the end that Christabel takes Geraldine into the castle, into her own bedroom, and it is here that one of the major scenes in the poem takes place. Although Christabel loves her mother, she seeks an excuse for Geraldine's wild ravings against the spirit of the mother who appears in the bedroom scene: "Alas, said she, [Christabel] this ghastly ride / Dear lady! it hath wildered you!" (lines 216-217), thus attributing Geraldine's hostile behavior to her unfortunate experiences prior to having been found in the forest. The upshot of this suspension of fear on Christabel's part, results in an acceptance of the "demon lover," Geraldine, and the seduction is a fact. Mr. Jones shows quite conclusively that the seduction is both mental and physical. The point I would emphasize is that neither kind lasts. Christabel's ambivalent feelings arise once again in the following episode when Geraldine, having been introduced to the father, Sir Leoline, begins to work her charms on him:

> And fondly in his arms he took
> Fair Geraldine, who met the embrace,
> Pro-longing it with joyous look.
> Which when she viewed, a vision fell
> Upon the soul of Christabel,
> The vision of fear, the touch and pain!

> (ll. 448-453)

Undoubtedly, Christabel recalls here her nefarious activities of the night before but, in addition, Christabel is also harkening back to her initial fear felt when she first heard Geraldine in the forest; the significant ambivalence, it seems probable, arises again upon seeing the lovely lady embraced so enthusiastically by her own beloved father. Overcome by a feeling not alien to jealousy (though of which one raises a moot question), Christabel draws in "her breath with a hissing sound," and startles Sir Leoline.

From here on, Sir Leoline manifests ambivalence in his reactions to his daughter. Once wholly beloved, she now seems bent (in his eyes) on causing an affront to the lady Geraldine, and thus providing an affront to his baronial hospitality. He is, therefore, hurt, puzzled, angry, his mind embroiled in ambivalence.

> Why is thy cheek so wan and wild,
> Sir Leoline? Thy only child
> Lies at thy feet, thy joy, thy pride,
> So fair, so innocent, so mild;
>
> (ll. 621-624)

> Within the Baron's heart and brain
> If thoughts, like these, had any share,
> They only swelled his rage and pain,
> And did but work confusion there.
> His heart was cleft with pain and rage . . .
>
> (ll. 636-640)

Directly after this passage, the baron rejects Christabel and leads forth the lady Geraldine. Thus the second part of the poem draws to a close, culminating in the conclusion which has baffled readers since the publication of the poem. Looked at in the light that *Christabel* is a poem of ambivalent love-relationships, however, the conclusion ceases to baffle, for it now becomes consistent with the rest of the poem. The lines quoted below obviously refer to the shifting relationship between father and daughter. Quite obviously, they are neither psycho-sexual, nor witch-ridden. They do explore the question of rising ambivalence experienced by Sir Leoline in his feelings toward his daughter:

> A little child, a limber elf,
> Singing, dancing to itself,
> A fairy thing with red round cheeks,
> That always finds, and never seeks,
> Makes such a vision to the sight
> As fills a father's eyes with light;
> And pleasures flow in so thick and fast
> Upon his heart, that he at last
> Must needs express his love's excess
> With words of unmeant bitterness.
> Perhaps 'tis pretty to force together
> Thoughts so all unlike each other;
> To mutter and mock a broken charm,
> To dally with wrong that does no harm.
> Perhaps 'tis tender too and pretty
> At each wild word to feel within
> A sweet recoil of love and pity.
> And what, if in a world of sin
> (O sorrow and shame should this be true!)
> Such giddiness of heart and brain
> Comes seldom save from rage and pain,
> So talks as it's most used to do.
>
> (ll. 656-677)

Herein it seems that Coleridge suggests that ambivalent feelings toward the loved one is the natural condition of intense love. Certainly, within Sir Leoline's nature ambivalence runs strong, serving to increase his capacity for passion, for hatred, for love.

Support for this point can be found in an examination of the relationship between Sir Leoline and Lord Roland de Vaux of Tryermaine. In their youth, these two had been the closest of friends, veritable soul-mates. They had quarrelled, parted, never again to meet. But the love they had for each other is constant, though unadmittedly so. The entire relationship seems characterized by a mixture of antithetical feelings:

> Alas! they had been friends in youth;
> But whispering tongues can poison truth;
> And constancy lives in realms above;
> And life is thorny; and youth is vain;
> And to be wroth with one we love
> Doth work like madness in the brain.
>
> (ll. 408-413)

They part in wrath; but, upon hearing Geraldine's story and gazing on her face, the "youthful Lord of Tryermaine" comes back upon Sir Leoline's heart. The pendulum of emotion swings from one point of emotion to its antithesis, reflecting a deep-seated ambivalence.

The fourth relationship of this type is by no means so clear-cut in nature as the three previously discussed. The relationship of Geraldine to Christabel, never as fully delineated as that of Christabel to Geraldine, nevertheless reflects a mixture of feelings within the heart (and she does seem to have one!) of Geraldine. She has obviously been commissioned to pervert the goodness of Christabel, and to that end she bends her major efforts. In one passage, however, she clearly states that she will endeavor to convey good will to Christabel:

> All they who live in the upper sky,
> Do love you, holy Christabel!
> And you love them, and for their sake
> And for the good which me befel,
> Even I in my degree will try,
> Fair maiden, to requite you well.
>
> (ll. 227-232)

Were Geraldine's feeling totally malevolent, she would scarcely speak as she does above nor as she acts in the following passage, which occurs just before she and Christabel get into bed together:

> Yet Geraldine nor speaks nor stirs;
> Ah! what a stricken look was hers!
> Deep from within she seems half-way
> To lift some weight with sick assay,
> And eyes the maid and seeks delay;
>
> (ll. 255-259)

Granting that Keats's Lamia had a mixed nature, and that such is not an uncommon phenomenon in the genus-witch, still not only has Geraldine a mixed nature within, but she also demonstrates considerable ambivalence in her attitude toward Christabel. This characteristic tends to extract her from the witch role per se and thus to humanize her, to make her a creature capable of love as well as of evil.

The poem is unfinished. If we consider Dr. James Gillman's account of Coleridge's plan to complete **Christabel** as one in keeping with the poet's intent, then the poem becomes even more involved with love and its ensuing ambivalence.[16] In the Gillman account, Geraldine finds it necessary to leave Sir Leoline's court. This is a temporary departure, for she soon returns disguised as Christabel's lover who was, at the opening of the poem, far away. Christabel, who has formerly prayed for the weal of this lover, cannot understand why she is now repelled by "his" advances. The action is resolved by the appearance of the true lover at which point the fake lover, Geraldine in disguise, disappears. The ambivalent feelings of Christabel toward this interloper are in keeping with the marked ambivalence seen in the other four relationships.

Within this larger frame of reference, **Christabel** becomes, to my mind, a poem of infinite complexity and great intricacy of movement. The poem begs further study. It is my hope that some of the points raised here and some of the directions indicated may be of help to others interested in **Christabel**.

Notes

1. Arthur Nethercot, *The Road to Tryermaine* (Chicago, 1939), p. 4.

2. *The Notebooks of Samuel Taylor Coleridge,* ed. Kathleen Coburn, I (New York, 1957), 940, 942, 1000, 1064—hereafter cited as *Notebooks.*

3. *The Poems of Samuel Taylor Coleridge,* ed. Ernest Hartley Coleridge (New York, 1945), pp. 224-225, lines 267-270; this edition was first published in 1912. Hereafter references to poems will be by lines only, the text taken from this edition.

4. G. Wilson Knight, *The Starlit Dome* (London, 1959), pp. 83-84; this edition first published in 1941.

5. Roy P. Basler, "Christabel," *The Sewanee Review,* LI (1943), 74-94.

6. Basler, *Sex, Symbolism, and Psychology in Literature* (New Brunswick, 1948), pp. 3-51.

7. Edgar Jones, "A New Reading of *Christabel,*" *The Cambridge Journal,* (November, 1951), 106.

8. Nethercot, pp. 34 and 94, for more concerning this.

9. Basler, *Sex, Symbolism and Psychology,* p. 26.

10. I am indebted to Professor Frederick L. Beaty for pointing out the references to Bathyllus and Alexis in Chapter XIV of the *Biographia Literaria* which certainly substantiate this contention.

11. Nethercot, p. 35.

12. *Notebooks,* pp. 373, 1064, 1803.

13. The following statement is taken from *The Table Talk of Samuel Taylor Coleridge,* ed. H. N. Coleridge (London, 1835): "I [Coleridge] believe it possible that a man may, under certain states of the moral feeling, entertain something deserving the name of love towards a male object—an affection beyond friendship, and wholly aloof from appetite," p. 206; the phrase "wholly aloof from appetite" would scarcely apply to Geraldine as Mr. Jones describes her.

14. *Table Talk,* p. 43.

15. Basler apparently guessed this to be true but shows no evidence in support (*Sex, Symbolism and Psychology,* p. 25).

16. James Gillman, *Life of Samuel Taylor Coleridge,* I (London, 1838), 301-302.

Paul Edwards and MacDonald Emslie (essay date June 1971)

SOURCE: Edwards, Paul, and MacDonald Emslie. "'Thoughts So All Unlike Each Other': The Paradoxical in 'Christabel.'" *English Studies* 52, no. 3 (June 1971): 236-46.

[In the following essay, Edwards and Emslie explore Coleridge's depictions of complex psychological states in "Christabel."]

In her article 'Coleridge and Wordsworth and "the Supernatural"',[1] Miss Kathleen Coburn argues that despite a famous passage in **Biographia Literaria**,[2] neither **The Ancient Mariner** [*The Rime of the Ancient Mariner*] nor **Christabel** can properly be called poems of the supernatural at all. Supernatural events are appropriate enough to a cruder Gothic world, but in the case of Coleridge similar events might better be described as psychological:

> The crude use of the supernatural was always recognized and abhorred by Coleridge, as his early reviews of Monk Lewis and Mrs Radcliffe show. The **Biographia** passage is an endeavour to make clear his interest in its psychological and imaginative possibilities and to describe his attempt in poetry to realize the familiar in the strange.

However, Miss Coburn goes on rather to hobble her argument by restricting the psychology of **Christabel** largely to Coleridge's own immediate nervous problems, drawing the conclusion that 'Geraldine is a malignity out of Coleridge's dreams'. This seems to us to beg the question of Geraldine's malignancy, ignoring as it does such evidence as Derwent Coleridge's curious account of the projected ending of the poem, and moments in the poem when Geraldine appears to be far from simply malignant.

Because it is a fragment, *Christabel* confronts the reader with special difficulties, and these are aggravated by the apparent lack of consistency between the three hypothetical conclusions, two given by Gillman and the third (already mentioned) by Derwent.[3] Each of these conclusions might give some support to a reading of the poem as Gothic, along the lines of Scott's 'Bridal of Triermain'; on the other hand, both the second account of Gillman and Derwent's version point towards something more complex and disturbing. In any case, as Miss Coburn says, it is unlikely that Coleridge intended *Christabel* to develop in any simple Gothic way in view of his strictures on Lewis and Mrs Radcliffe.[4] And if we are to see Geraldine as acting, in Derwent's puzzling words, 'with the best good will', the unnerving atmosphere so brilliantly established, particularly in Part I of the poem, would be no more than the sensational sleight of hand that Coleridge criticised as mere stage effect in 'Monk' Lewis's *Castle Spectre*. Once she is seen as an innocent agent, then subtly sinister effects such as the disturbing repetition of

> So free from danger, free from fear,
> They crossed the court: right glad they were,
>
> (135-44)[5]

begin to degenerate into hollow tricks. But on the other hand if Geraldine is to be seen as simply malevolent (as in Gillman's second account), and the poem an uncomplicated battle between good and evil, what are we to make of the sense we are given, again particularly in Part I, of Geraldine's duality, her own reluctance and suffering as she goes about the task she must perform?

> Yet Geraldine nor speaks nor stirs;
> Ah! what a stricken look was hers!
> Deep from within she seems half-way
> To lift some weight with sick assay,
> And eyes the maid and seeks delay;
> Then suddenly, as one defied,
> Collects herself with scorn and pride,
> And lay down by the Maiden's side!—
>
> (255-62)

This is the very quality in Geraldine that gives support to the statement of Derwent that she was intended to be 'no witch or goblin, or malignant being of any kind, but a spirit, executing her appointed task with the best good will'.

It is usually assumed that the Gillman versions and that of Derwent are incompatible, and that consequently one or the other must be dismissed. But the inconsistency

between the second Gillman and the Derwent accounts could be resolved if it were recognised (and this is what we wish to demonstrate) that 'the power of evil' (Gillman) might in some perplexing way turn out to be 'her appointed task' (Derwent); and indeed something very much like this is taking place in a poem which Coleridge said was 'ever present to my mind whilst writing the second part of *Christable*; if, indeed, by some subtle process of the mind [it] did not suggest the first thought of the whole poem'[6]—Crashaw's 'Hymn to St Teresa'.[7] But this point will be dealt with later in our argument.

It may also be possible to find help in these difficulties by looking closely at the description of the 'little child' in the Conclusion to Part II of *Christabel,* the child 'That always *finds* and never *seeks*' (the two words are underlined in the first ms. version, a letter to Southey).[8] The particular quality of the child's discoveries stressed here is that they come as sensation, as a confrontation with life, perhaps even as a shock; the child does not know what he seeks, only what he finds, an open state clearly approved of in these opening lines of the Conclusion, and one constantly explored too by Wordsworth and Blake. The last dozen lines are perplexed and perplexing:

> Perhaps 'tis pretty to force together
> Thoughts so all unlike each other;
> To mutter and mock a broken charm,
> To dally with wrong that does no harm.
> Perhaps 'tis tender too and pretty
> At each wild word to feel within
> A sweet recoil of love and pity.
> And what if in a world of sin
> (O sorrow and shame should this be true!)
> Such giddiness of heart and brain
> Comes seldom save from rage and pain,
> So talks as it's most used to do.
>
> (666-77)

A realistic recognition of the complexities of love and hate are combined here with a Christian acknowledgement of 'a world of sin'. Rage and pain may be the way we sometimes realise our human condition: we may only be able to know love and pity through our knowledge of pain and rage. Earlier, Sir Leoline has had two opportunities to gain this kind of awareness, but his rage is essentially stereotyped, conventionally 'gothic' even, not an adequate response to an adult human situation:

> Within the Baron's heart and brain
> If thoughts, like these, had any share,
> They only swelled his pain and rage,
> And did but work confusion there.
> His heart was cleft with pain and rage,
> His cheeks they quivered, his eyes were wild,
> Dishonoured thus in his old age;
> Dishonoured by his only child,

And all his hospitality
To the wronged daughter of his friend
By more than woman's jealousy
Brought thus to a disgraceful end—

(636-47)

Like Christabel in Part I, the Baron in Part II is seen to have an over-simple view of the world, though the differences between the two views are marked by the differences of language in the two parts, the first principally recording Christabel's naive voice, which takes on malevolent overtones in the reader's imagination—'For what can ail the mastiff bitch?' or 'So free from sorrow, free from fear, They crossed the court: right glad they were'; the second, the Baron's voice, in which the language of Gothic sensationalism and the romantic-heroic posture are used to indicate his unawareness of what is really going on.

Some of the words in the Conclusion to Part II strike us as odd. *Pretty, sweet,* perhaps even *giddiness* appear too trivial for the disturbing matters they describe. Yet the fact that we feel them to be odd is important, in that the use of these words results in a nervous disturbance in the reader, recreating the shock of sudden perplexity that Coleridge is here concerned with, the state of the repeated 'perhaps' of lines 666 and 670, which seek a deliberate effect. The world of Christabel and our own world are brought together in this Conclusion, sinful and imperfect, often not subject to reason, indeed, at times only to be understood by finding, not seeking. The state of 'giddiness' is like an existentialist condition in which we discover ourselves through shock, this being the only means we have of penetrating certain regions of our nature. Thus while we are disturbed by the thought that 'to mock a broken charm, To dally with wrong that does no harm' is not *tender* or *pretty* at all (at this point the words appear to take on an ironic or even malevolent tone), at the same time we may see that this anger sometimes springs from a complex region of love and tenderness. Rage and pain may then be seen to have, at times, their proper function and so may in that sense be 'good':

I was angry with my friend:
I told my wrath, my wrath did end.
I was angry with my foe:
I told it not, my wrath did grow.

(Blake, 'A Poison Tree')

So the 'sweet recoil of love and pity' is a direct consequence of the display of anger—'He who desires but acts not breeds pestilence'.

Christabel may share Blakean features with **Kubla Khan.** Blake's view that 'without contraries is no progression'—that the dark and frightful lower world may be necessary to the formal constructed upper world,

both a threat, and the source of its fertility—is behind **Kubla Khan,** where the ultimate Paradise is to be achieved through a revival of lost harmony between the two worlds, the 'mingled measure, From the fountain and the caves', the 'miracle of rare device, A sunny pleasure-dome with caves of ice'. The two worlds are in balance here, interdependent and complementary, and the designed and ordered world of the garden-paradise only survives because it is sustained by forces from the seemingly chaotic and threatening underworld, out of which the fertilising water rises and to which it returns, 'lifeless', for regeneration. Ancestral voices prophecy war; the stability is not static, but a consequence of continuing change and re-asserted balance in the man-made paradise. The same sort of duality is found in Wordsworth's description of the Simplon Pass, written about the same time as **Kubla Khan** and **Christabel,** where

Tumult and peace, the darkness and the light,
Were all like workings of one mind, the features
Of the same face, blossoms upon one tree.[9]

And it may be some such world as this that Christabel enters when she embraces Geraldine. Far from being a simple evil, Geraldine might be seen as representing something like the seemingly ominous and demonic, but nevertheless necessary forces of life that lie beneath the peace of the Khan's garden. This is not to suggest any sharp equation between Christabel's Langdale and Kubla Khan's pleasure-garden; but they are similar in this, that they both represent a state of threatened stasis and calm, the pleasure-garden an Eden about to be lost, Christabel's castle a state of negative, virtually prenatal innocence.

Many in Coleridge's own time found **Christabel** distinctly uncomfortable reading. One commentator called it 'the most obscene poem in the English language', adding that it sinned 'heinously against purity and decency'.[10] Hazlitt found 'something disgusting at the bottom of the subject . . . like moonbeams playing on a charnel-house, or flowers strewed on a dead body'.[11] Even Wordsworth, despite all the enthusiasm which Coleridge's letters tell us he felt for the poem, decided in the end against including it in the second volume of **Lyrical Ballads,** and was recorded by Alaric Watts as responding ambiguously to it:

He did not dissent from my expressions of admiration of this poem, but rather discomposed me by observing that it was an indelicate poem, a defect which it had never suggested itself to me to associate with it.[12]

This was in 1825-6, and by this time the tradition of **Christabel**'s obscenity was long established. Coleridge himself seems to have taken it that such charges were supported by the notion that Geraldine had a dual sexual rôle:

It seems that Hazlitt from pure malignity had spread about the Report that Geraldine was a man in disguise.[13]

It is curious, all the same, that Gillman's second account of the projected ending should have Geraldine transform herself into the shape of Christabel's lover, and pursue a courtship 'most distressing to Christabel'. It could indeed be argued that the dual function of Geraldine is perverse, that of both mother and lover, in the lines

> And lo! the worker of these harms,
> That holds the maiden in her arms,
> Seems to slumber still and mild,
> As a mother with her child.
>
> A star hath set, a star hath risen,
> O Geraldine! since arms of thine
> Have been the lovely lady's prison.
> O Geraldine! one hour was thine—
> Thou'st had thy will! . . .
>
> (298-306)

Whatever explicit construction we put on these lines, they are, like many more in the poem, suggestive of some sexual initiation, and if we are to believe Gillman's second version, Coleridge was not unaware of this, though he may not have been fully conscious of it at the time of composition. Coleridge would have been the first to admit that certain kinds of poetry, and certainly kinds of his own poetry, need not always be the product of a fully awakened and rational consciousness.

Further indications of this reading might be discovered when we examine Crashaw's 'Hymn to St Teresa', lines from which, according to Allsop, were said by Coleridge to have been 'ever present to my mind whilst writing the second part of Christabel; if, indeed, by some subtle process of the mind they did not suggest the first thought of the whole poem'. The lines he spoke of were those beginning 'Since 'tis not to be had at home, / She'll travel to a martyrdom', down to 'She's for the Moores, and martyrdom'. Humphry House, suggesting that *Christabel* is in some way tied up with sexual matters, refers to four lines coming shortly before those quoted by Coleridge:

> Shee never undertooke to know,
> What death with love should have to doe
> Nor hath shee ere yet understood
> Why to show love, shee should shed blood.
>
> (19-22)

But House does not pursue the subject or discuss the relevance of Crashaw's poem any further. There are nevertheless other sections of it that might throw light on *Christabel*. Immediately before the Crashaw lines said by Coleridge to have been in his mind when writing *Christabel* we read:

> Her weak breast heaves with strong desire,
> Of what shee may with fruitlesse wishes
> Seeke for, amongst her mothers kisses.
>
> (40-2)

Here clearly enough we have the theme of the necessary and painful separation of the child from the mother, the weaning that is prophetic of a later, often equally distressing separation from the home—which, like Thel's grave, may seem to the uninitiated a death, yet be a way to life. A little later in Crashaw's poem:

> Farewell what ever deare may bee,
> Mothers armes, or fathers knee.
> Farewell house, and farewell home:
> Shees for the Moores & Martyrdome.
>
> (61-4)

But the young Teresa is not destined for so simple an end:

> Wise heaven will never have it so.
> Thou art Love's victim, and must dye
> A death more misticall & high.
>
> (74-6)

A state of living death, a 'still surviving funeral', at once painful and joyous, is to be brought Teresa by 'blest Seraphims', 'Fit executioners for thee'.

> The fairest and the first-born sons of fire,
> Blest Seraphims shall leave their quire,
> And turn Love's soldiers, upon thee
> To exercise their Archerie.
> O how oft shalt thou complaine
> Of a sweet and subtile paine?
> Of intollerable joyes?
> Of a death in which who dyes
> Loves his death, and dyes againe,
> And would for ever so be slaine.
>
> (93-102)

Crashaw, as is customary with him, is dealing with religious matters in sexual terms. To Teresa, sufferings are Heaven-sent and to be welcomed as the marks of love and the means to salvation:

> All thy old woes shall now smile on thee,
> All thy pains set bright upon thee . . .
> Even thy deaths shall live, and new
> Dresse the soul, which late they slew.
>
> (146-7, 152-3)

So the poem ends with Teresa's mystic marriage to 'the Lamb thy Lord':

> And where so e're hee sits his white
> Steps, walke with him those wayes of Light.
> Which who in death would live to see,
> Must learne in life to dye like thee.
>
> (180-3)

Clearly this is a different kind of poem from *Christabel,* yet one can see why it should have been in Coleridge's mind when he wrote his poem. Like Christabel, Teresa must go beyond the protection of father and mother (lines 61-4), and encounter sufferings which, far from finding their source in such obvious simple evils as 'the Moores' (or Geraldine's 'three' or 'five warriors', or 'ruffians'—mss. vary) are brought by 'Blest Seraphims'. So one can see why Coleridge should on the one hand have told Gillman that 'The pious and good Christabel suffers and prays for "The weal of her lover that is far away"' and why on the other he should have told Derwent that Geraldine, the source of this suffering, far from being malignant, should be 'a spirit executing her task with the best good will'. Some readers may find that the context of the lines quoted by Gillman contains a further hint of the stirrings of sexuality in innocence:

> She had dreams all yesternight
> Of her own betrothèd knight;
> *Dreams that made her moan and leap*
> *As on her bed she lay in sleep.*
> And she in the midnight wood will pray
> For the weal of her lover that's far away.

(27-30)

(This is the reading of the first edition; in the Hinves copy the italicised lines are erased; they are not found in any ms. nor in later editions.)

Christabel does not set out consciously on her path to martyrdom, and it is nowhere suggested that her sufferings will lead her to anything other than earthly bliss— marriage to her lover, reconciliation with her father. The sufferings of Christabel must be seen as a preparation for life in this world, not the next, while her initiation into suffering is more like that offered to Blake's Thel than that of Crashaw's Teresa. And this is the point to reaffirm the importance of the conclusion to Part II, and its theme of the interrelation of love and hate, rage and tenderness. Towards the end of Part II of *Christabel,* Sir Leoline has responded naively and erroneously to Bracy's dream of the snake and the dove. But the irony is not one of simple reversal—that Geraldine is the snake. In a sense it *is* true that Geraldine is the snake, but Christabel too has acquired snakelike characteristics, and indeed might seem at this point to be a dove in the process of becoming a combination of dove and snake. This is not a world of simple oppositions, as Sir Leoline supposes, in which figures can be defined unambiguously as doves or serpents.[14] The description of the dream is curious:

> . . . I saw a bright green snake
> Coiled around its wings and neck,
> Green as the herbs on which it couched,
> Close by the dove's its head it crouched;

And with the dove it heaves and stirs,
Swelling its neck as she swells hers.

(549-54)

The snake and dove achieve a strange union here, though one is the destroyer, the other the victim.[15] So when Sir Leoline confidently asserts to Geraldine that 'Thy sire and I will crush the snake' (571), not only do we know that he is wrong in identifying Geraldine with the dove,[16] but also that he is unable to see that in the adult human world dove and serpent co-exist, so that in crushing the snake he would probably crush the dove too. This accords with Coleridge's fable; at the end of Part II Sir Leoline's favouring of Geraldine goes along with his anger with Christabel.

In ignorance, he fails to understand the experience of his child; the child revolts against Leoline's seeking to recapture his own youth in a relationship with Geraldine. In the nature of things, parents and children experience loves and aggressions towards each other; but at least at this point the world of Langdale is no longer so drastically simple and inert. In the process of self-affirmation the child will inevitably cause suffering to the parent; in the process of imposing 'will' on the child, the parent helps to create the child's own self-consciousness through aggression. Christabel is on the threshold of adulthood and sexuality, and when the innocence is shattered we need not see it merely as an evil process: indeed, Christabel's bringing Geraldine into the castle effects a necessary disruption there. At last, instead of a wandering spirit-mother, it contains a living woman against whom the growing girl can feel jealousy for 'possessing' the father, the adolescent first-form of the 'lover that's far away'.

Notes

1. *University of Toronto Quarterly,* XXV (1955-6), 121-30. An analysis of *Christabel* supporting our own reading of the poem has appeared in *Essays in Criticism,* XX (1970), 57-70.

2. *Biographia Literaria,* ed. J. Shawcross (Oxford, 1907), II, 5.

3. James Gillman, *The Life of Samuel Coleridge* (1838), I, 283: 'The story of the Christabel is partly founded on the notion, that the virtuous of this world save the wicked. The pious and good Christabel suffers and prays for

   The weal of her lover that is far away,

   exposed to various temptations in a foreign land; and thus she defeats the power of evil represented in the person of Geraldine. This is one main object of the tale'.

   Gillman, *ibid.,* I, 301-2: 'Over the mountains, the Bard, as directed by Sir Leoline, "hastes" with his disciple; but in consequence of one of those inundations supposed to be common to this country, the spot only where the castle once stood is discovered,—the edifice itself being washed away. He determines to return. Geraldine being acquainted with all that is passing, like the Weird Sisters in Macbeth, vanishes. Re-appearing, however, she waits the return of the Bard, exciting in the mean time, by her wily arts, all the anger she could rouse in the Baron's breast, as well as that jealousy of which he is described to have been susceptible. The old Bard and the youth at length arrive, and therefore she can no longer personate the character of Geraldine, the daughter of Lord Roland de Vaux, but changes her appearance to that of the accepted though absent lover of Christabel. Next ensues a courtship most distressing to Christabel, who feels—she knows not why—a great disgust for her once favoured knight. This coldness is very painful to the Baron, who has no more conception than herself of the supernatural transformation. She at last yields to her father's entreaties, and consents to approach the altar with this hated suitor. The real lover returning, enters at this moment, and produces the ring which she had once given him in sign of her betrothment. Thus defeated, the supernatural being Geraldine disappears. As predicted, the castle bell tolls, the mother's voice is heard, and to the exceeding great joy of the parties, the rightful marriage takes place, after which follows a reconciliation and explanation between the father and daughter'.

Derwent Coleridge's account was published in his introductory essay prefixed to Coleridge's *Poems,* eds. Derwent and Sara Coleridge (1868), p. xlii. It can be found in *Christabel,* ed. E. H. Coleridge (1907), p. 52 n.: 'The sufferings of Christabel were to have been represented as vicarious, endured for her "lover far away"; and Geraldine, no witch or goblin, or malignant being of any kind, but a spirit, executing her appointed task with the best good will, as she herself says:—

> All they who live in the upper sky,
> Do love you, holy Christabel, etc.'

(227-32)

4. *Collected Letters of Samuel Taylor Coleridge,* ed. E. L. Griggs (Oxford, 1956-8), I, 318; I, 378-9. The second of these letters, written to Wordsworth in January 1798, criticising Lewis, says that Lewis's *Castle Spectre* contains 'Dreams full of hell, serpents, & skeletons' and goes on to compare the language of Lewis with that of the ballad Sir Cauline, from which Coleridge borrowed the name Christabel (i.e. Christobel).

5. Quotations from Coleridge's poems are from the edition of E. H. Coleridge (Oxford, 1912).

6. *Letters, Conversations and Recollections of S. T. Coleridge,* ed. Thomas Allsop (1836), I, 195-6. T. Ashe, the editor of *Table Talk and Omniana of S. T. Coleridge* (1884), p. 322 n. 2, is wrong in saying that the Crashaw quotation is from the 1646 text, from which Coleridge departs at three points. He appears to be quoting from memory, though memory of the 1646 text.

7. *The Poems . . . of Richard Crashaw,* ed. L. C. Martin (Oxford, 1927), pp. 131-4 for the 1646 text and pp. 315-21 for the 1648 text. Our quotations are from the 1646 text.

8. This first appears in a letter to Southey, 6 May 1801: *Letters,* II, 728-9. Wordsworth thought that the Conclusion to Part II had little to do with the rest of the poem (cf. A. H. Nethercott, *The Road to Tryermaine* [Chicago, 1939], p. 55). But though the original poem to Southey referred to the infant Hartley, Coleridge hardly altered it at all when he added it to *Christabel* many years later, and he had plenty of time to do so had he thought it should be given a more direct bearing on the poem. See also Coleridge's notebook entry of April-June 1803: 'A kindhearted man obliged to give a refusal or the like, that will give great pain, finds relief in doing it roughly & fiercely—explain this, & use it in Christabel'. *The Notebooks of Samuel Taylor Coleridge,* ed. Kathleen Coburn (London, 1957), I, 1392.

9. *Prelude* (1805), Book VI, lines 567-9.

10. Anon., *Hypocrisy Unveiled and Calumny Detected: In a Review in Blackwood's Magazine,* 4th edn. (London, 1818), p. 50.

11. *The Collected Works of Wm. Hazlitt,* ed. A. R. Waller and A. Glover (Dent, 1904), XI, 581.

12. Alaric A. Watts, *Alaric Watts: A Narrative of his Life* (1884), I, 239.

13. Letter to Southey: *Letters* II, 728.

14. [J. B.] Beer, p. 195 is near to this in referring to 'the central problem involved in creating a doctrine of redemption when good and evil are identified with innocence and experience respectively'. We suggest that Christabel was intended to represent an innocent experience, as Geraldine represents a necessary and 'good' evil. Coleridge himself (*Table Talk,* p. 241) said the basic idea of the poem was 'an extremely subtle and difficult one'. Referring to lines 16-19, Beer shows (pp. 183-4) how 'The image of sun or moon veiled by cloud is one which Coleridge uses with great frequency to express his view that apparent evils are really good seen in distortion'; the Gutch notebook's 'Behind the thin / Grey cloud that cover'd but not

hid the sky / The round full moon look'd small' has *dull* added to it in *Christabel,* linking the description with Geraldine's snakelike glance, 'dull and shy', line 583 (*The Notebooks of Samuel Taylor Coleridge,* ed. Kathleen Coburn [1957], I §, 216 [G. 212]). Geraldine's eye, incidentally, was very likely Mrs Inchbald's, in a description which Coleridge later regretted: 'Mrs Inchbald I do not like at all—every time, I recollect her, I like her less. That segment of a *look* at the corner of her eye—O God in heaven! it is so cold and cunning—!' *Letters* I, 589. Later, he called this 'A very foolish sentence or two'. *Letters* II, 744.

15. 'We are recalled by the image to that of the two sleeping together; we see in the movement of the snake an attempt to *imitate* that of the bird as well as to prevent the flight; we remember that the sound Christabel herself made resembled that of a snake . . . We are on the brink of the suggestion that the identity of Christabel is coveted by Geraldine . . . "All her features were resigned / To this sole image in her mind . . .". And not only does she see the image, she feels herself becoming the image: "And passively did *imitate* / That look of dull and treacherous hate . . . With *forced unconscious sympathy*"'. C. Tomlinson in *Interpretations,* ed. J. Wain (1955), pp. 110-11.

16. The mistake is all the more pointed by having Sir Leoline call his favourite dove 'Christabel' (lines 531-3); and *couched* line 551, repeated line 580, associates Geraldine with the snake of Bracy's dream.

Abe Delson (essay date April 1980)

SOURCE: Delson, Abe. "The Function of Geraldine in 'Christabel': A Critical Perspective and Interpretation." *English Studies* 61, no. 2 (April 1980): 130-41.

[*In the following essay, Delson analyzes the relationship between Geraldine and Christabel in the poem.*]

'What is it all about? What is the idea? Is *Lady Geraldine* a sorceress? or a vampire? or a man? or what is she, or he, or it?' So asked an anonymous reviewer of ***Christabel*** in 1816,[1] and so readers continue to ask. And, like the reviewer, they have felt an understanding of the poem dependent on an understanding of the function of Geraldine. She seems to be increasingly malevolent toward Christabel, but, paradoxically, under the control of some providential agent and able to sympathize with whatever physical and psychological distress she inflicts on her (e.g., see 11. 203, 226-232, 247-8, 255-9, 586, 593-6[2]). To further complicate matters, the two well-known versions of Coleridge's recorded intentions concerning Geraldine's characterization, Joseph Gillman's and Derwent Coleridge's, differ fundamentally over whether she is evil or good.[3]

Though in recent criticism there has been a marked tendency to treat ***Christabel*** as embodying a serious theme, in accordance with Coleridge's statements in Chapter XIV of ***Biographia Literaria,***[4] there is no consensus as to what it is. As in the case of the other two mystery poems, the sensibilities of the interpreters have often worked in ways radically different from one another. Perhaps the best way to approach the problem of Geraldine's function is first to inspect the varying critical frames of reference in which she has already been placed. In the following survey, particular attention will be given to how well the interpretation sheds light on the problem of Geraldine's ostensibly ambivalent behavior toward Christabel.

In his elaborate source study, *The Road to Tryermaine,* Arthur Nethercot interpreted Geraldine's function with regard to the supposed sources for her characterization in Coleridge's prior reading. Accordingly, she is a composite vampire-lamia, unwillingly doing the bidding of some supernatural agency in causing Christabel to suffer. Nethercot accepts Derwent Coleridge's account that the theme revolves around the doctrine of vicarious atonement. Like Christ's, Christabel's suffering is for a good purpose, in her case for the 'weal of her lover that's far away' (1. 30).[5] The problem with this reading is that it relies on what is not in the poem. There the sinfulness of Christabel's lover and the idea of vicarious atonement are not developed. Also, the vampire, as Nethercot himself documents the legend, does not appear to be a fit vehicle for the operation of divine ministry.

What is curious about Nethercot's interpretation is his refusal to import into it any of the sexual overtones surrounding the vampire and lamia legends.[6] Geraldine may suck Christabel's blood, but there is no sexual violation. But most readers will probably agree that there seems to be in some way, either literally or symbolically, a sexual dimension to Geraldine's 'hour' that was hers. Recent interpretations have increasingly stressed such a dimension, ranging from conscious focus on Coleridge's part to subconscious and unconscious projection.

As contemporaneous comment and the numerous nineteenth-century parodies illustrate, the sexual element was responded to from the time the poem was published.[7] In this regard, the most obvious reading was that Geraldine is a man in disguise and the poem a hoax. Those who felt Coleridge was using sex in a less obvious way were uneasy about it. William Hazlitt was probably one of these when he wrote: 'There is something disgusting at the bottom of his subject, which is but ill glossed over . . . like moonbeams playing on a charnel-house, or flowers strewn on a dead body'.[8] William Wordsworth is recorded as having objected to the poem's being 'indelicate'.[9]

The history of more recent sexual interpretations begins with G. Wilson Knight's abbreviated commentary in 1941. In calling the poem a nightmare and an exploration of Hell, and in linking the bedroom-scene with the sexual desecration of Christabel, he clearly characterized Geraldine as evil. But Knight was also the first to explicitly associate the serpentine imagery with sex, and he is suggestive, though contradictory, when he states that the way out for Christabel may be for her to embrace spontaneously (like the Mariner) what the snakes represent psychologically.[10] Roy P. Basler in 1943 offered a different type of sexual reading. Drawing on the psychological interpretation of folklore motifs in which demons are often seen as projections of man's suppressed sexual desires, Basler sees Geraldine as 'sexual necessity' that leads Christabel, given her repressed circumstances, to irrational behavior.[11] Gerald Enscoe in his *Eros and the Romantics* (1967) spelled out Basler's interpretation in greater detail and with some variation.[12] Geraldine is not opposed to goodness but to sterility, particularly that of the environment at Langdale with which she is continually contrasted. The signs which have traditionally linked Geraldine with evil are really more fitting as emblematic of the erotic and carnal: her emphasis on touch, her having Christabel carry her across the threshold, the dying brands bursting into flame, her inability to pray to the Virgin, and the ineffectual protest of the sterile 'toothless' mastiff. As the principle of eros, she gives life not only to Christabel but to her father, who becomes infatuated with her. Basler and Enscoe suggest that Coleridge could not complete the poem because he was in conflict over the value of eros he unleashed through Geraldine. This also explains Geraldine's ambivalent nature.

But if Coleridge were writing a poem about the inevitability of man and woman's compulsive sexual drives, given certain circumstances, why should he have complicated an already daring theme by using a Lesbian relationship to embody it? Basler and Enscoe never address themselves to this question, though Basler speaks of Coleridge's being 'on dangerous ground' in this respect and hints that Geraldine has a touch of the 'androgynous' in her make-up.

Contrary to Basler and Enscoe, Jonas Spatz, in a more recent reading published in 1975, did not see any Lesbianism but viewed the poem as the 'final expression of Coleridge's ideas on sex, love, and marriage'.[13] Geraldine is not really a character but a projection of Christabel's ambivalent feelings toward sex, including 'desire, fear, shame, and pleasure'. As a proxy for Christabel's varying sexual attitudes toward herself and her lover,

Geraldine engages in role-playing with Christabel. Geraldine is the submissive female and Christabel the aggressive male lover as she carries Geraldine across the threshold and invites her into her bedroom. Geraldine becomes masculine when she disrobes and embraces Christabel, who is now her feminine self. At this point Christabel is both attracted to and repelled by the 'phallic potency' of Geraldine. Christabel's hissing while Geraldine embraces her father is a dramatization of Christabel's Oedipal conflicts; she recoils from the horrors of her incestuous desires. In sum, 'Geraldine has impersonated Christabel as threatened virgin, ardent lover, resigned bride, mistress, and finally the stepmother as wife and incestuous daughter'. If Coleridge had completed the poem, Spatz believes, he would have shown Geraldine being submerged in Christabel's maturing consciousness as she resolves her sexual conflicts with the appearance of her betrothed. In effect, according to Spatz, Coleridge consciously embodied in the poem present-day psychoanalytic theory and imagery.

Spatz, more than any other interpreter, has stressed the protean quality in Geraldine's characterization, but his reliance on psychoanalytic theory strains his case since Coleridge's response to images in his own nightmares indicating sexual conflicts reveals no such understanding. As recorded in his notebooks and letters, predatory females and other figures repeatedly appeared in Coleridge's dreams threatening him with humiliation, assault, and mutilation. Also, he often behaved in his dreams in ways that made him ashamed. However, he did not associate such images and behavior with post-Freudian awareness.[14] The draft of **'The Pains of Sleep'**, in his letter to Southey dated 11 September 1803, records his typical response.[15] In referring to scenes from his nightmares in which 'Desire with Loathing strangely mixt, / On wild or hateful Objects fixt' and 'To know and loathe, yet wish and do!' Coleridge feels such behavior more appropriate 'To natures deepliest stained with sin'. His reaction is more that of a helpless child than a psychoanalyst:

> . . . O wherefore this on me? . . .
> To be belov'd is all I need,
> And whom I love, I love indeed . . .

More plausibly, psychoanalysis has been used to detect supposed personal conflicts Coleridge projected into the poem unconsciously. The most influential of such interpretations has been by a professional psychoanalyst, Dr. David Beres. After establishing Coleridge as an 'oral' personality who had markedly estranged relations with his mother during the latter years of her life, Beres, through an analysis of the imagery of the mystery poems, diagnosed Coleridge as having a mother-image problem imbedded in his unconscious. The image is that of a 'phallic mother'. Coleridge's revolt at harboring such an image led to murderous desires, reflected imaginatively in Christabel's mother dying in childbirth (as, in *The Ancient Mariner* [*The Rime of the Ancient Mariner*], it is reflected by the absence of conscious motivation for the Mariner's shooting the albatross). The characters and events become a paradigm for Coleridge's unconscious battle with his mother-image. Christabel is Coleridge; Geraldine in her malevolent phase is the mother murdered in his unconscious, seeking revenge; the hour Christabel spends with Geraldine and Bracy's dream, manifestations of Coleridge's incestuous desires; and the spirit of Christabel's mother and Geraldine in her benevolent guise, reflections of his desire to be forgiven by his mother.[16]

Though such a reading does account for the alternating moods of cruelty and love in Geraldine's characterization, it does not show how it squares with whatever conscious design Coleridge had in mind when he wrote the poem. Also, the resorting, in psycho-analytic criticism, to ambivalence and role-playing to resolve cruxes in characterization seems too facile.

In frequency, the most common recent approach has been one that, while avoiding psychoanalytic parlance, has nevertheless relied on Coleridge's psychological and philosophical problems as revealed in his personal and public writings. This approach holds that Coleridge found in Christabel's sufferings a subconscious projection of his own. Kathleen Coburn gave impetus to this view when, in an article published in 1956, she referred to Geraldine as a 'malignity out of Coleridge's own dreams'.[17] The most elaborate interpretation along these lines is E. E. Bostetter's.[18] Interpreting the poem in the light of **'The Pains of Sleep'** (with which it was originally published), he viewed Christabel's suffering as a vehicle for Coleridge's own sense of unwarranted victimization. To Bostetter, the poem is also an expression of Coleridge's philosophic and religious anxieties. He could not complete the poem because he was not able to solve the problem of evil in his own life as demonstrated by his compulsive shameful impulses and nightmares. As an incarnation of sadism, Geraldine is sincere when she says to Christabel that the angels above do love her since their agency, like hers, is for a divinity that is itself sadistic. To a later critic, Geraldine represents 'diseased imagination', an aspect of his psyche that Coleridge found increasingly uncontrollable and that can be traced back to the time he wrote **'The Aeolian Harp'**.[19]

Other interpretations speculate as to the cause of Coleridge's neurotic guilt feelings that found release through Geraldine's victimization of Christabel. Since Part II was written after Coleridge met and fell in love with Sara Hutchinson, one critic suggests that a cause for Christabel's worsening plight was Coleridge's guilt over the circumstances he was placing his children and Sara Hutchinson in because of his love for her. Accord-

ingly, Geraldine's ascendance over Christabel in Part II, on one level, reflects Coleridge's abuse of Hartley as he agonizes over what his domestic situation is doing to his loved ones. Another reading has Sara Hutchinson, curiously enough, becoming Geraldine at this point while Coleridge becomes Sir Leoline as they engage in the author's wish-fulfillment of going off together while abandoning Hartley, now become Christabel. Still another view has Geraldine stand for Wordsworth whom Coleridge supposedly felt smothered by because of his ego and lack of sympathetic appreciation for his friend's talents.[20]

These different speculations on the biographical source, at some stage, for Geraldine—the persecuting figures in Coleridge's nightmares, his diseased imagination, Sara Hutchinson, Wordsworth, and even Coleridge himself—suggest a weakness in the method. While agreeing with Coleridge's theory of the imagination that takes into account the unconscious during the creative act, and while providing an interesting and at times fascinating guessing-game, they do not carry conviction. Focusing on unconscious motivation inevitably shortchanges conscious intent. Also, the evidence for emotional and psychological trauma is not so apparent during the period *Christabel* was written in (particularly Part I) as it is subsequently.

Another interpretation, by Charles Tomlinson, comes to a similar conclusion to Bostetter's but operates from different premises by placing the poem in the context of the Gothic romance, not Coleridge's other writings or personal biography. To Tomlinson, Geraldine is the traditional *femme fatale,* an agent whose symbolic function in the tale of terror is to personify psychological disease in the protagonist, as manifested by sado-masochistic impulses. In Christabel's surrendering to such impulses, she illustrates the 'mind's failure to guide the Will'. The poem is a typical Gothic romance but, in the absence of Christabel's restoration to psychological health, without the traditional happy ending.[21]

A significant commentary by Virginia Radley has suggested that the poem makes a statement about love: 'that ambivalent feelings toward the loved one is a natural condition of intense love'. This ambivalence is shown in the relationships between Geraldine and Christabel, the Baron and Christabel, and the Baron and Lord Roland; and it is reinforced by the father's relationship with his child described in the Conclusion to Part II.[22] While pointing out an essential psychological pattern, this reading does not relate the ambivalence to a fuller thematic statement by exploring the symbolism of Geraldine.

Contrary to viewing Geraldine as inherently evil, what is probably the most important source study since *The Road to Tryermaine* emphasizes her potential goodness.

By examining the history of the vampire and lamia legends as Coleridge was probably aware of them through his reading, Nethercot saw the sources as being mainly in the Gothic tradition. But J. B. Beer in *Coleridge the Visionary* (1959) focused on a different tradition Coleridge was aware of, a pre-Christian Egyptian and neo-Platonic one. To Beer, Coleridge used the imagery of this tradition in his mystery poems to provide an imagistic fabric for visionary experience in this world. The essential imagistic hierogram of the tradition deals with a serpent, a dove, and a winged serpent. (The most famous version is the Isis-Osiris myth). As applied to *Christabel,* the serpent (Geraldine) is not evil but an emblem of love and energy separated from its proper source in the dove (Christabel). Only when separated, does the serpent assume an ostensibly hostile guise. When a proper union takes place between serpent and dove, the image is that of a winged serpent. Beer believes that Coleridge would have ultimately subsumed what Geraldine psychologically represents (love and energy) in Christabel.[23]

Another interpretation, '*Christabel* and the Mystical Tradition' by Thomas R. Preston, has viewed Christabel's experience through mystical lore but in a different way from Beer's. Depending on Coleridge's comment that he had Crashaw's 'Hymn to Saint Teresa' in mind when he wrote the poem, Preston interprets Christabel's encounter with Geraldine as equivalent to Teresa's mystical encounter with the 'Blest Seraphims'. According to Christian mystical tradition, the metaphor of sexual embrace, common to both poems, leads through suffering to God. To Preston, Geraldine is the Christ-like instrumentality of such a union.[24]

Both Beer and Preston tend to read the poem as illustrations of the lore they deal with, instead of using it more circumspectly as part of the imaginative background of the poem. Perhaps their most important contribution is to remind the reader that the snake is not necessarily to be associated with either evil or sex—that to an ancient tradition Coleridge was aware of, kept alive by Christian mystics like Jacob Boehme, the snake when viewed properly is linked with visionary experience.

The most significant change in recent views of Geraldine has come in readings which view her, not as a symptom of mental disease or as evil, but as a beneficent agent. And she is seen not in religious or mystical terms (as Derwent Coleridge, Nethercot, Beer, and Preston did), but in secular and psychological ones.

In relating the poem to Coleridge's theory of the imagination, Richard Harter Fogle has warned against trying to ascertain the specific identity of Geraldine. 'Not precisely witch or angel, but as a symbol mediating between the real and imagined worlds', she is meant to exercise the reader's imagination through her elusive and protean qualities. But at the same time, to Fogle, the poem deals with a type of initiation rite for Christabel essential for her to pass if she is to mature. If Geraldine is evil, it is an evil that should not be avoided but encountered through experience: 'There may be evil in mother, friend or lover, ambiguous but real, unwilled but inherent in being itself'.[25] In two later articles, jointly written by Paul Edwards and MacDonald Emslie, this view is more elaborately worked out. Like Fogle, they compare the controlling idea behind the poem to the one in Blake's *Book of Thel*. Geraldine represents the 'necessary forces of life' and the 'paradoxes of human experience'. Sir Leoline is wrong when he desires to kill the snake after Bard Bracy's dream of one encircling a dove. To a mature vision, the snake and dove are intertwined in the world of experience, and any effort to separate them is doomed. In a novel reading of the Conclusion to Part II, Edwards and Emslie defend the father's unwarranted cruelty inflicted on the child, since it will hopefully assist in the child's maturing self-consciousness.[26] A still more recent reading along these lines construes Geraldine as 'a catalyst for psychological change' not only for Christabel but for the other personae in the poem: the Baron, Bard Bracy, the narrator, and the speaker of the Conclusion to Part II. To all of these, Geraldine brings a deeper level of consciousness more troubled but more satisfying than formerly.[27]

In this review, Geraldine has run the gamut from being interpreted as psychological disease to what is necessary for psychological health, if not religious ecstasy. Cumulatively, the interpretations have shown such an ambivalence to Geraldine's ambiguity that it seems to support the view of a recent critic that 'attempts to resolve it certainly seem unlikely to succeed'.[28] While not disproving this view, a premise of this study is that one should be able to read a work more sensitively after observing how other readers have responded. Also, an inspection of previous responses should indicate some conclusions about the best way to go about a fresh reading. Chief among them may very well be to downplay Coleridge's alleged comments about the continuation of the poem. In view of the contradictory versions (and interpretations based on them), they have acted as a distraction to call attention away from what he actually wrote. Also, in view of the state of psychological and philosophical flux Coleridge was in between 1798-1801, it seems best to de-emphasize the personal and intellectual background at the time of composition. What seems to be called for now is a response that focuses on the work, though a fragment, as a poem, and that attempts to find a thematic pattern not based on external sources, be they biographical, philosophical, or literary.

The best clue to such a pattern seems to be the Conclusion to Part II. It can be construed as a kind of coda (hereafter referred to as such) to what Coleridge completed. We cannot be sure that when Coleridge composed the coda in 1801, he intended it for **Christabel.**[29] But whether he did or not, the important fact is that by 1816 he thought it a fitting close to what he had written, and he never changed his mind. (Nevertheless, some critics have ignored the coda entirely, others have been hard put to see a relationship between it and the rest of the poem, and those that do have not always agreed with one another).

The coda is psychologically oriented. It deals with reflections over a father's gratuitous explosion of verbal abuse directed at his little child. The cause, ostensibly, is not any form of inner resentment or subconscious hostility but an excess of delight in observing the child's carefreeness. And the display of anger causes in the father an almost simultaneous 'sweet' sensation of love and pity toward the son he has abused. The concluding lines

> And what, if in a world of sin
> (O sorrow and shame should this be true!)
> Such giddiness of heart and brain
> Comes seldom save from rage and pain,
> So talks as it's most used to do.

express disapproval though fatalism at the near universality of such an emotional pattern. The psychological instability in human experience illustrating this pattern is called a 'sorrow and shame'.

'Sorrow and shame' is a verbal echo of two earlier uses in Part I. Geraldine, after disrobing in Christabel's bedroom, confides to her what is to take place:

> Thou knowest to-night and wilt know to-morrow,
> This mark of my shame, this seal of my sorrow.

(11. 269-270)

Now the mark and seal, if we are to attach any symbolic importance to Geraldine, and to read the poem beyond the Gothic level, is not only a secret anatomical mark, such as the deformed breast, revealing her to be a witch or vampire. Like the sorrow and shame of the father's emotions in the coda, Geraldine's behavior reveals a psychological deformity. On the most obvious level, Geraldine is confessing that she is not what she seems. Defenseless until she reaches Christabel's chamber, she now becomes dominant and aggressive. (In Part II she appears to be taking almost spiritual possession of Christabel). Up to this point a weak, defenseless stranger, Geraldine now betrays Christabel's hospitality.

The second use of 'sorrow and shame' is the narrator's response, in the Conclusion to Part I, to Christabel in the arms of Geraldine:

> With open eyes (ah woe is me!)
> Asleep and dreaming fearfully,

> Fearfully dreaming, yet, I wis,
> Dreaming that alone, which is—
> O sorrow and shame! Can this be she,
> The lady, who knelt at the old oak tree?

(11. 292-7)

As in the coda, a psychological contrast, in this case applicable to both the narrator and Christabel, is emphasized. The narrator's joy at remembering Christabel devoutly praying for her beloved (described in the preceding stanza) is contrasted with his grief over her horrible mental state at the reality of being in the arms of Geraldine.

The bedroom-scene in which Christabel spends an hour in Geraldine's embrace is at the heart of the poem and of Geraldine's nature. But before exploring it further, other relationships should be examined to see how they may aid in determining Geraldine's function. The father is the third main character, the only one who does not figure in the bedroom-scene. The coda, when commented upon in the past, has usually been taken to underscore the Baron's subsequent remorse after abandoning Christabel, at the end of Part II. This instability in his makeup has been prepared for by the reference to the quarrel with his friend, Lord Roland, over an apparently trivial cause (11. 408-413). Also, his mourning for his dead wife seems obsessive and, in light of the sexual overtones of his later attraction to Geraldine, insincere. That it is insincere is hinted at even before Sir Leoline meets Geraldine by the mocking way the narrator treats the sacristan's ritual of obedience to the Baron's commands. The sacristan says the rosary prayer forty-five times between each toll, only to have the knell answered by 'sinful sextons' ghosts'. And often the devil himself joins in mocking 'the doleful tale / With a merry peal'. Similarly, the Baron's reaction to Bard Bracy's dream seems melodramatic and imperceptive. He refuses to heed the warning the dream contains by deliberately reversing the symbolism of the dove. Bracy states that it had Christabel for its name while Sir Leoline sees it as standing for Geraldine.

Geraldine dispels the Baron's emotional stasis and brings him back to life, though with questionable results. With the arrival of Geraldine, Christabel witnesses her father experience a wide range of feeling and behavior: regret for a friendship that was heedlessly terminated, determination to renew it, gallantry toward a new woman, imperceptive disregard for a warning contained in a dream, and cruelty toward herself. Geraldine is the cause of an education that Christabel receives in regard to her father's make-up. Pride, fickleness, gallantry, obtuseness, and betrayal are some of the traits revealed.

Now let us return to the bedroom-scene. Besides her father, the two most important figures in Christabel's life are her dead mother and her betrothed. Though her mother died in giving birth to her, Christabel almost seems to have memories of her. She has preserved the wine made by her mother and which she now offers to Geraldine as a cordial. She repeats to Geraldine the legend that her mother will appear on Christabel's wedding day. Curiously enough, Geraldine at times has an allusive quality giving her characteristics of Christabel's mother. While casting a spell on Christabel, Geraldine is pictured in maternal imagery:

> And lo! the worker of these harms,
> That holds the maiden in her arms,
> Seems to slumber still and mild,
> As a mother with her child.
>
> (11. 298-301)

When Christabel awakens, she is both saddened and joyful, and the maternal imagery is sustained through her being compared to an infant:

> And oft the while she seems to smile
> As infants at a sudden light.
>
> (11. 317-318)

Her smile is explained as having been caused by a vision of her mother as guardian-spirit.

Though Geraldine is feminine (notice that she does wake up with heaving breasts the following morning), she at times also has an allusive masculine quality. The spirit of Christabel's mother seems to be hovering about as if in fulfillment of the legend that she is to appear the day her daughter marries. In her domination of Christabel, Geraldine's arms are compared to a 'prison'. The sexual resonance of 'O Geraldine, one hour was thine— / Thou'st had thy will' is confirmed by the epithalamium effect of a co-operating and rejoicing nature:

> By tairn and rill,
> The night-birds all that hour were still.
> But now they are jubilant anew,
> From cliff and tower, tu-whoo!
> Tu-whoo! tu whoo! from wood and fell.
>
> (11. 306-310)

And Christabel's combination of tears and smiles when she awakens is suggestive of the loss of innocence in the sense of a post-coital 'after-rest', a word the narrator himself uses (1. 465). Coital associations are also suggested in Bracy's dream of the serpent embracing the dove.

The chief characteristic of Geraldine is her protean quality: good-bad, feminine-masculine, dove-like-ophidian, alluring-repulsive, passive-aggressive. Symbolically, she is the vehicle for Christabel to experience relationships otherwise denied her, and on this level Geraldine lacks specific identity either as female or male. There is no actual sexual violation but, considering Christabel's inexperience, a psychological one. The hour that is Geraldine's is one in which she transmits an awareness about the human condition that includes, but is not restricted to, the sexual. Geraldine's banishment of the protective spirit of Christabel's mother is necessary for Christabel's development and self-reliance in the world of experience. The behavior of Geraldine, as stranger, mother, and betrothed, represents the instability in basic human relationships, an instability only accented by sexual tensions.

The coda emphasizes the instability. Christabel's father illustrates it in his relationship with Lord Roland, and with his daughter when he abandons her. To Christabel, sexual desires, when yearned for and fulfilled, produce a sense of sin. A daughter's sense of gratification over her mother's protectiveness must be joined with a realization that her mother has needs and desires that may exclude her. Both times Christabel hisses follow physical contact between Geraldine and the Baron: the first an embrace, the second a kiss. If Geraldine represents the protean quality of experience with others, Christabel appears traumatized, symbolically through her hissing, at a realization of unexpected sexuality: her father's, her mother's, her lover's, and her own.

The poem, as we have it, does not predict inevitable defeat for Christabel. Though the vampire and lamia myths in which handsome men and beautiful women conceal demonic natures are an appropriate correlative for the instability and treachery in human experience, the way out may be suggested by what happens in Coleridge's other narrative mystery poem. There the Mariner finds at least temporary redemption by blessing the snakes. Christabel must accept what the snakes represent in human nature. Geraldine is sincere when she states that her mission is providential and for Christabel's own good. By experiencing in concentrated form the flux of human relationships, Christabel will be able to transcend the tendency toward it dramatized by her father, the personages represented by Geraldine, and herself.

Unlike St. Teresa's, Christabel's is a secular martyrdom. Her sufferings inflicted by others are to make her more human and, ultimately, a more effective agent for the happiness of others. The pessimism of the coda that makes love and pity dependent on cruelty she will demonstrate need not be so through her own behavior.[30]

Notes

1. *The Champion,* May 26, 1816, p. 166; rpt. *The Romantics Reviewed, Part A: The Lake Poets,* ed. Donald H. Reiman (N.Y., 1972), I, 268.

2. Unless otherwise specified, all line references to *Christabel* are from *The Poems of Samuel Taylor Coleridge,* ed. Ernest Hartley Coleridge (Oxford, 1912), pp. 213-236. Subsequent references to this edition will appear in the text.

3. The versions appear in Arthur H. Nethercot, *The Road to Tryermaine* (1939; rpt. New York, 1962), pp. 41-3.

4. For a discussion of Coleridge's meaning, see Kathleen Coburn, 'Coleridge and Wordsworth and "the Supernatural",' *UTQ* [*University of Toronto Quarterly*], 25 (1955-6), 121-30.

5. Nethercot, pp. 207-14.

6. In his review of past criticism, Nethercot refers to this level of interpretation as 'lurid' and 'scandalous' (p. 28). Similarly, E. H. Coleridge, in the most thorough study of the poem prior to Nethercot's, is emphatic in denying anything sexual in the relationship between Christabel and Geraldine: 'Whatever may be indicated, or symbolized, or adumbrated in *Christabel,* there is no rending of the veil of the *senses.* The passion is psychical, and by no means sensual' (*Christabel by Samuel Taylor Coleridge, Illustrated by a Facsimile of the Manuscript and by Textual and Other Notes,* ed. E. H. Coleridge [London, 1907], p. 11).

7. Nethercot, pp. 28-36.

8. *The Examiner,* June 2, 1816, p. 349; rpt. *The Romantics Reviewed,* II, 531.

9. Alaric A. Watts, *Alaric Watts: A Narrative of His Life* (London, 1884), I, 239. I am indebted for this reference to Paul Edwards and MacDonald Emslie, '"Thoughts so all unlike each other": The Paradoxical in *Christabel'. ES* [*English Studies*], 52 (1971), 241.

10. 'Coleridge's Divine Comedy', *The Starlit Dome* (London); rpt. in *English Romantic Poets: Modern Essays in Criticism,* ed. M. H. Abrams (N.Y., 1975), pp. 202-05.

11. 'Christabel', *Sewanee Review,* 51 (1943), 73-95; rpt. in *Sex, Symbolism, and Psychology in Literature* (New Brunswick, 1948), pp. 25-51.

12. *Eros and the Romantics* (The Hague, 1967), pp. 37-60, 166-7.

13. 'The Mystery of Eros: Sexual Initiation in Coleridge's "Christabel"', *PMLA,* 90 (1975), 107-116.

14. There is a good discussion of this in Norman Fruman, *Coleridge, The Damned Archangel* (New York, 1971), pp. 374-87.

15. *The Collected Letters of Samuel Taylor Coleridge,* ed. Earl Leslie Griggs (Oxford, 1956), II, 983-4.

16. 'A Dream, a Vision, and a Poem', *International Journal of Psychoanalysis,* 32 (1951), 97-116. Later interpreters who read the poem essentially the same way are Douglas Angus, 'The Theme of Love and Guilt in Coleridge's Three Major Poems', *JEGP* [*Journal of English and Germanic Philology*], 59 (1960), 662-3; and Norman Fruman, pp. 402-07. They, however, state the source of Coleridge's mother-image problem as originating in an Oedipal conflict, not a pre-Oedipal one.

17. 'Coleridge and Wordsworth and "the Supernatural"', p. 130.

18. 'Christabel: The Vision of Fear', *PQ* [*Philological Quarterly*], 36 (1957), 183-94.

19. Paul Magnuson, *Coleridge's Nightmare Poetry* (Charlottesville, 1974), p. 102.

20. Patricia M. Adair, *The Waking Dream: A Study of Coleridge's Poetry* (London, 1967), pp. 165-8; Geoffrey Yarlott, *Coleridge and the Abyssinian Maid* (London, 1967), pp. 194-201, 321; Warren Stevenson, 'Christabel: A Reinterpretation', *Alphabet,* No. 4 (June, 1962), 18-35; respectively.

21. *Interpretations: Essays on Twelve English Poems,* ed. John Wain (London, 1955), pp. 103-112.

22. 'Christabel: Directions Old and New', *SEL* [*Studies in English Literature, 1500-1900*], 4 (1964), 536-41.

23. *Coleridge the Visionary* (1959; rpt. New York, 1962), Chapter 6.

24. *Essays and Studies in Language and Literature,* ed. Herbert H. Petit. Duquesne Univ. Philological Series No 5 (Pittsburgh, 1964), pp. 138-157.

25. *The Idea of Coleridge's Criticism* (Berkeley, 1962), pp. 131-154.

26. 'The Limitations of Langdale: A Reading of *Christabel'*, *EIC* [*Essays in Criticism*], 20 (1970), 57-70; '"Thoughts so all unlike each other": The Paradoxical in *Christabel'*, *ES* [*English Studies*], 52 (1971), 236-46.

27. Michael E. Holstein, 'Coleridge's *Christabel* as Psychodrama: Five Perspectives on the Intruder', *The Wordsworth Circle,* 7 (1976), 119-28.

28. David Pirie, *Coleridge's Verse: A Selection,* ed. William Empson and David Pirie (New York, 1973), p. 244.

29. The coda originally appeared in a letter to Southey, dated 6 May 1801 (*Collected Letters,* II, 728).

30. Aside from *The Book of Thel,* a literary analogue with a similar theme is Nathaniel Hawthorne's 'Young Goodman Brown'. There too an innocent becomes traumatized through finding out, via a night journey to the forest and under the auspices of a preternatural agent, a dimension of human

nature and relationships that had been previously concealed. Psychologically, Goodman Brown's 'baptism' can be compared to Geraldine's embrace. (Also, in both narratives mother-figures are depicted as resisting initiation.) Goodman Brown's reaction is one of despair; Christabel's need not have been so.

Jane A. Nelson (essay date fall 1980)

SOURCE: Nelson, Jane A. "Entelechy and Structure in 'Christabel.'" *Studies in Romanticism* 19, no. 3 (fall 1980): 375-93.

[*In the following essay, Nelson examines the fragmentary qualities of "Christabel." Nelson argues that, in spite of Coleridge's stated intention to finish the poem, the work is in its own way complete, and its powerful meaning would inevitably be altered if it had been expanded.*]

For many readers the fragmentary nature of **"Christabel"** is self-evident and incontrovertible although Coleridge's failure to conclude **"Christabel"** is self-evident only in certain traditional contexts that are themselves incomplete and fragmentary. In fact, contemporary developments in the history and theory of genres may eventually isolate a literary context within which closure in the poem will be recognized. Within less traditional but already existing theoretical contexts, moreover, the half-human child figure in The Conclusion to Part II can be identified as an appropriate mediating term for the oppositions developed steadily throughout the poem. In such contexts, I will argue, the function of this figure in **"Christabel"** is precisely that of achieving closure.

Of course the recognition of closure requires that we "read" the poem differently. We must put aside, insofar as possible, habits of response that encourage us to see the poem as a fragment. At present two principal reasons appear to sustain the traditional classification. First, the conviction of Coleridge himself that **"Christabel"** remained unfinished. Second, but perhaps more important, the failure of the poem to meet a number of conditioned expectations in the reader. Since in reading we make conscious and unconscious comparisons of **"Christabel"**'s narration with that of other literary structures it partly resembles, we expect a different conclusion from the one the poem provides. A third possibility—that the poem violates unconscious responses to some narrative grammar still to be isolated and described—cannot, at this time, enter into a consideration of the poem-as-fragment. Unfortunately the first two reasons for reading **"Christabel"** as a fragment are difficult to ignore. Even when we make the attempt, their claims too frequently intrude.

The first reason—Coleridge's own belief that the poem is unfinished—settles the issue too quickly. If we accept this claim unconditionally, we commit ourselves to the familiar but always treacherous assumption that a writer is reliably aware of what he is doing or has done in a work of literature and that what he thinks he is doing is privileged information about the work we have. Certainly the author is aware—he intends.[1] The choice of the name *Christabel* is itself an important example of significant intention. But to establish the extent and nature of an author's intention remains difficult if not impossible. If one accepts (with conditions) the importance of the author's formal intentions, for example, he must also remember that Coleridge attached The Conclusion to Part II to the poem and left it there. Those who consider this conclusion inappropriate seem unwilling to accept intention in this important instance. For that matter, much of the significant commentary on the poem ignores The Conclusion altogether. Of course it does not follow that Coleridge consciously recognized that this section appropriately ended the poem. But given the similar nature of "mediating terms" in other narrative circumstances, that he did so unconsciously is quite likely.[2]

In spite of these difficulties, let us grant for the moment that Coleridge's intentions provide a number of important and useful contexts in terms of which the text develops meanings for us or we develop meanings for the text. Which of his intentions bear on the question of the ending? And how? In the case of **"Christabel,"** for example, the "ideological and creative context" in which the poem was written has been extended by Jonas Spatz to include a theory of human sexuality developed by Coleridge in notebooks, letters, and the poems written from 1797 to 1801.[3] In such a context, Spatz argues, the unwritten ending outlined by Coleridge's physician and biographer, James Gillman, and based apparently on the poet's own detailed suggestions, offers a thematically meaningful conclusion to the narrative elements introduced in the first two parts. Spatz's argument is most convincing if Christabel (as is usually the case in the criticism) is treated as a fully "human" figure.[4] But Coleridge's interest in sexuality enters the poem in other ways, I believe—ways that include other elements in the poem's structures. Moreover, if we focus on the "psychology" of Christabel or on the diachronic possibilities of a story developed around her sexual adventures and marital possibilities, we distort her role in the structure and obscure the various functions of her figure in the poem.

Indeed, other "creative contexts" are relevant to the reading of **"Christabel"** and bear significantly on the question of closure. During the same period in which the poem was written, for example, Coleridge's absorbed but ambivalent interest in his own children and in the "child"—as well as his life-long interest in the problems of opposition (emerging most importantly in his speculations on "polar logic")—undoubtedly provided generative creative and ideological contexts for its writing. Certainly that is the case if we turn our attention from the story of a Christabel we create in human form (as we read) to an attempt to categorize the relationships established among as many of the elements as we can isolate in the system of the poem. Other figures—such as the father—are too frequently ignored or slighted in commentary on the poem-as-fragment, but nevertheless function significantly in this system. Finally, although to pursue intention in a study of **"Christabel"** is a dubious enterprise, if we do examine closure in the contexts of intention, the fact that Coleridge intended to write a longer poem on any specific issue should not commit us in any way to seeing the poem as a fragment nor to "seeing" the figure of Christabel as disproportionately important.

The second principal reason for considering **"Christabel"** a fragment—that it does not correspond to our conscious or unconscious experience of most literary narrative—presents us with greater difficulties. Several attempts to provide suitable and conventional endings for **"Christabel"** (including Coleridge's own suggestions) indicate an operation that may affect all our readings: a normalizing of the poem by generating from its seminal narrative elements more familiar literary structures, even though plot outline, as J. B. Beer pointed out, cannot tell us how the "symbolic structure of the poem might have been resolved."[5] Unfortunately all such attempts to rescue **"Christabel"** from its anomalies will direct our analyses away from the poem's combinations of embryonic narrative elements or even prevent us from recognizing "narrative" itself on a less familiar "level."

To be sure, at the same time we normalize the text by supplying characters and story lines, we acknowledge the generative power of this "fragment" and often point to its similarity to dream and nightmare or to fairy tale and myth, especially in their elemental, non-literary forms. If at this point we were to entertain the arguments of A. J. Greimas that "narrativity" exists prior to its manifestations in linguistic substance or other languages such as those of dream or cinema,[6] we might see emerging in **"Christabel,"** at a more elemental level than that of literary narrative proper, manifestations of narrativity significantly closer to non-literary myth. Furthermore, we could expect to find analogues to the poem's structure (as an arrangement of images) in the "language" of dream, since the figures and actions of the poem so persistently suggest nightmare to its readers. In both instances I believe the focus of analysis should be on the complex relations of oppositions (and their possible resolution) in the poem.

For that matter, the functions of these oppositions in the structuring of **"Christabel"** should not be overlooked nor underestimated in any reading inasmuch as all operations in the poem manifest relationships among oppositions: the "characterization," the "setting" and other spatial representations, the "actions," and the arrangement of parts. These oppositions extend into other systems by which a number of the poem's meanings are established. References to Christ and Abel in the title provide an obvious and first illustration of such extension, evoking as they would for most readers a recognition of the opposites Christ/Satan, Abel/Cain in Christian mythology, and taking the reader both into and out of the poem.[7] "Within" the poem, the concentration—and stylization—of oppositions, as well as the poem's primitive development of both "character" and narrative segment command attention. At this point, Greimas' analyses of narrativity suggest useful and provocative contexts for reading the poem, whether or not the still fragile outlines of his current narrative "grammar" survive. I do not exclude other contexts in which the text could be read and in terms of which closure should be examined. In fact, two of these will be introduced later when the question of a resolution of opposites is discussed.

The first consideration must be "characterization" in **"Christabel"** insofar as that can be isolated for comment. Greimas argues for the development of character from a so-called "deep" structure, prior to language and consisting of a homology of logical or conceptual oppositions. In order for this "taxonomic core" to manifest itself ultimately in narrative, an *anthropomorphizing* of these operations must occur, resulting in what he calls *actants*. When these *actants* are assigned identifiably social or cultural attributes, they are transformed into recognizable fictional *roles* which, upon further individuation, emerge ultimately as "characters" (*acteurs*). The anthropomorphic level (a "surface" narrative grammar, but not narrative manifested in figurative language) is a necessary intermediate level capable of generating—but not identical with—"narrative manifested in a *figurative* form (where human or personified actors would accomplish tasks, undergo trials, reach goals)."[8] The transformations by which such initial logical oppositions develop into narratives are complex and by no means fully sketched. Nor are *actant* and *character*, as described by Greimas, isomorphic and susceptible of a simple one-to-one conversion: a "character" may represent two *actants*, or two "characters" manifest one, for example. Nevertheless, if Greimas is correct, the figures and actions of manifest narrative remain characterized by the initial binary semic oppositions from which they are generated (p. 33).

Do these figures in **"Christabel"** suggest more clearly in their functions the *actants* of Greimas' surface narrative grammar than they do the "characters" of more developed narrative in which the devices of manifest narrative are extensively displayed?[9] Certainly they appear in recognizably "literary" language. (The language of dream, whatever it is, is something else.) They do demonstrate in a considerable number of actions, *but not all,* the characteristics of literary role and even (for many readers) the shadowy lines of "character," although scant textual "evidence" exists for these elaborations which seem to me attempts to normalize and humanize the text. The question cannot be answered finally at this point, but what will be traced is the extent to which the figures (avoiding the term *character*) reveal in their functions the operations of opposition which Greimas sees as essential in the generation of narrative: the transfer of a value (or object) from one *actant* to another (p. 34).

It may be granted that insofar as they appear at almost every moment capable of losing whatever figurative (human) character they possess and resolving themselves into anthropomorphized oppositions, the figures of the poem reveal "actantial" origins more obviously than do many if not most characters of more familiar narrative. This effect—of threatening to resolve into conceptual components—results in part from the abstracting function of point-of-view in the poem: that of an observing and commenting narrator. (In part the "events" appear as the manifestations of the mental operations of an "I.") It also results from the presentation of "character" in a minimal number of discrete encapsulated motifs. Unfortunately, even critics who focus on the "dream" character of the poem "humanize" these figures. Patricia Adair, for example, agrees with Coleridge that poetry is "rationalized dream," but when she speaks of Christabel, her literary prejudice is clearly in favor of "humanized" character:

> It may be intellectually satisfying to say that it [the poem] is about the corruption of the will, so that, in the end, evil is indistinguishable from good, but it means that we lose the humanity of the poem. Christabel has become a symbol and ceased to be a person, but, as we read the poem, no evil really seems to touch her inner essence. Far from feeling her to be sinful, we are tormented with sympathy for her, as her creator surely was. . . .[10]

We might agree that no evil seems to touch her inner essence—not, however, because she is a person who somehow maintains her personality against contagion, but because her inner essence, defined by her functions in the poem and her relationships with Geraldine (and other quasi-human figures) is one of opposition, principally to the figure of Geraldine (in spite of the exchange of natures between the two). The *values* we attach to this term are various and are probably established initially by the manifest "system" of meanings evoked by the title. Christabel's name, it has been noted, has more than Christ in it: she "is" both Christ and Abel, the Son Destroyed. Although Coleridge himself experimented with the forms Christobell/Christabel,[11] the reader who

brings a Judeo-Christian context to the poem cannot escape the value of the term in the poet's final choice.[12] In fact, this dimension of meaning introduces the elaborate play of opposites in the poem since Christ and Abel are defined by (and presuppose) their opposites, Satan and Cain.

In the motifs identifying Christabel and Geraldine in Part I, several bisexual indications introduce oppositions that will be important to later stages of this argument: Christ and Abel appear in female form; Geraldine evokes by her actions, her form, and her name, the powerful suggestions of masculinity. She, like Cain (and other mythological parallels to her figure), bears the "mark" of her shame.[13] It might also be noted at this point that the fatal division between brothers reappears clearly in Part II in the split between Sir Leoline and Lord Roland. But the most extensive demonstration of the operation of opposites in Part I lies in Christabel's complex dialectical relationship with Geraldine, especially as each of these figures functions in generating its opposite. Moreover, the extensive *generation* of opposites in the poem's manifest level argues for the existence in the "logic" of **"Christabel"** of another essential characteristic of the taxonomic core Greimas identifies in his fundamental narrative grammar: the ability of each of the terms of a binary semic category to project "a new term which would be its contradictory" (p. 25).

Before identifying the core "logic" of the narrative, however, the complex of surface oppositions needs tracing. These oppositions in **"Christabel"** appear in a nexus of relationships expressed principally in images of rising and falling, swelling and retracting, dividing and uniting. There are other important categories: inner/outer, above/below, light/dark—to name some of the most obvious. But the important point for our analysis of "character" is that the major figures function as part of this nexus—not as "human" figures placed in a complementary or appropriate "setting." Frequently the images in which they appear clearly indicate the "power" of one opposite to "generate" the other: the rising of Geraldine's powers, for example, occurs at the same moment that a literal "falling" of Christabel (or some other opposite) occurs; this "rising" is countered immediately, until the end of Part I, with an increase in the power of Christabel. And the reverse. Put more abstractly, whenever the power of action of one figure becomes dominant, a "transfer" of power to its opposite occurs. No equilibrium is sustained.

In the representation of such exchanges, we "see" Christabel—the "good" Christ/Abel figure—literally bring an "evil" Geraldine to life, beginning with an exchange in Part I between *inner* and *outer.* Christabel leaves the enclosed "human" environment of the castle—here the sign of "culture"—to enter the open and unformed dark forest world. There she "falls" (kneels) beneath a huge oak tree to pray. (The power of "nature" over "culture" at this moment is apparent.) While still on her knees she hears Geraldine moan. Christabel's very *sinking down* has evoked that response, at the sound of which she *springs up*. On the opposite side of the tree she finds a lady in many ways her counterpart but whose silken robes in that dark world, we already suspect, hide a darker nature. Detail after detail in these passages produces a "play" of opposites: Christabel folds her arms beneath her cloak; Geraldine's stately neck and arms are bare. Geraldine speaks of *white*-mounted horsemen who crossed the "shade of night" to carry her to the wide oak. We are directed from the image of a Christabel below to the oak's last red leaf "Hanging so high / On the topmost twig that looks up at the sky" and "That dances as often as dance it can."[14] (The only other time the color *red* appears in the poem is in the description of the child— the "limber elf" with "red round cheeks," that "fairy thing" who also dances in The Conclusion to Part II.) The night of Christabel's first encounter with Geraldine reminds us of autumn, but the month is April. The steps of the two figures as they move toward the castle "strove to be, and were not, fast" (Pt. I, l. 113; *CPW* [*The Complete Poetical Works of Samuel Taylor Coleridge*], I, 219).

When Christabel first sees Geraldine, she assists her to rise and supports her passage from "outer" to "inner." But the support Christabel provides at this point and the mysterious ebbing and flowing of Geraldine's power (long noticed by critics) belong to that larger system of binary oppositions in which each rise in "power" on the part of one element or figure generates its opposite as inexorably as the owl wakes the cock in the first few lines of the poem or the devil answers the matin bell at the beginning of Part II. Even the "might and main" of Christabel in the initial scene in Part I represents a shift of power to her figure when Geraldine falters at the threshold of exchange between inner and outer:

> The lady sank, belike through pain,
> And Christabel with might and main
> Lifted her up, a weary weight,
> Over the threshold of the gate:
> Then the lady rose again,
> And moved, as she were not in pain.
>
> (Pt. I, ll. 129-34; *CPW*, I, 220)

The introduction of this outsider contaminates the enclosed space of the castle—truly a land of the dead before Geraldine's arrival in spite of its significance as enclosed human space. It now contains the explosive potential of an exchange of power between opposites. More important to a later stage in this argument is the recognition that a new term has been introduced into the relationships represented by Christabel and her father.

Inside the castle, the transfer of power from subject to object, "heroine" to "villain," and back again continues. The moment Christabel praises the Virgin (representative of the powers above and also significant in the fundamental sexual oppositions in the poem), Geraldine's powers fade: "Alas, alas! said Geraldine, / I cannot speak for weariness" (Pt. I, ll. 141-42; *CPW*, I, 221). This invocation of the Virgin increases Christabel's power. But in the next few lines, flames, hidden in the ashes of the fire, flare up as Geraldine passes, suggesting that the fires of Hell have answered this revelation of Heaven's power. In unknowing "response" to these flames of fire, Christabel next trims the "lamp with twofold silver chain . . . fastened to an angel's feet," causing Geraldine once more to sink down "in wretched plight" (Pt. I, ll. 182-83; *CPW*, I, 222). Such rising and falling action in Part I registers clearly the operation of opposites that becomes progressively magnified and obvious in the poem. Indeed, the references in Part I, by evoking early in the poem the apocalyptic and demonic worlds of Heaven and Hell, delineate the cosmological antinomies of Christian mythology.

The *negative* effects of Geraldine's actions have long been studied: an "evil" Geraldine (not without apparently ambivalent motives in the eyes of some critics) invades the very substance of a "good" Christabel, modifying Christabel's behavior, destroying her relationships with her father, and providing her with intuitions of even greater evil to come. But if we attend closely to the interplay of opposites, we are obliged to acknowledge the extent of the *positive* effects of Geraldine's actions, that is, the generating of an opposite "good" from her "evil" acts. Sir Leoline is the principal example. That he is under the influence of an "evil" figure, moreover, and turns against an "innocent," should in no way obscure the positive effect on him of Geraldine's presence in the hall nor the appearance of a new set of terms in hostile opposition: Sir Leoline and Lord Roland, Leoline's "heart's best brother."

Undue emphasis on the "story" of Christabel and Geraldine, in fact, has led readers to slight these significant changes in the figure of Christabel's father. Described as so weak in health in Part I that he cannot be awakened even in the extraordinary circumstances of Geraldine's appearance, he appears so roused in Part II by the tale she tells him that he swells to phallic splendor and vigorous protest. (In this section shrinking and swelling appear as expressions of power or its loss; splitting and reuniting are the most significant relational terms.) Sir Leoline moves to act swiftly—hardly the image of a sick man who himself decreed that each matin bell should knell him back to a world of death. Such a recovery underscores the essential "logic" of his "character"; he is generated as an opposite (active, powerful) to which various values (phallic, parental, moral) may be attached. Clearly, too, Geraldine's tale of her misfortune—an "evil" ruse—has a "positive" effect on Sir Leoline even in the most familiar and shallow of moral contexts.

More abstractly, a transfer of power of action has occurred in the interaction of opposites in this section as in Part I. If we look at Sir Leoline in the various contexts some of the motifs evoke, we must describe this change as salutary. He forgets his age; his "noble" heart "swells high with rage"—directed not against an innocent Christabel at this point, but against what in familiar moral categories would be considered "evil": the forcible abduction of Geraldine. But even more important than the Baron's return to vigor is his vow to mend the rift between himself and the brother-friend of his young manhood. "A dreary sea now flows between" them (Pt. II, l. 423; *CPW*, I, 229). Before Geraldine's appearance, however, the piety and love of a dutiful daughter never worked to restore Sir Leoline to health nor urged him to mend the ancient and "brotherly" rift between himself and Lord Roland. These changes and Sir Leoline's further reactions complicate and climax the interplay of opposites in the poem's system.

The significance of such oppositions for the presentation of "character" in the poem should be recalled at this point. "Characters" (or, preferably, *figures*) in **"Christabel"** play out functions that are positive in some instances, negative in others. While it is true in most contexts that Geraldine's violation of Christabel's innocence appears evil, her effect can be perceived as positive in the contexts we have just described and as regenerative in the "land of the dead" presented as Sir Leoline's castle. Her functions are positive—and work toward *re*-union of *what-once-was-one* by producing Sir Leoline's resolve to mend the rift that divides him from Lord Roland.[15] I will argue later that Geraldine's figure also completes an equation in the poem's narrative structure that is essential to the appearance of the child figure in The Conclusion to Part II. But as "characters" the figures operate variously in the larger system of oppositions the poem develops. The lesser systems of motifs by which each is presented provide foci for this relentless presentation of oppositions and indicate the significant categories of "core" oppositions.

At this point I would argue that the mysterious figures of Geraldine and Christabel, acting in a more-or-less familiar Judeo-Christian cosmology, do more than echo the mythological. The structure of oppositions in which they appear in the poem suggests the operations of myth itself before it has undergone extensive literary elaboration. In fact, **"Christabel"** manifests clearly those characteristics of what Lévi-Strauss calls "mythical thought." Such thinking "always progresses from the awareness of oppositions toward their resolution" ("The Structural Study of Myth," p. 221). Describing mythical "thought" roughly as a kind of process, Lévi-Strauss observes that

this process attempts (not always successfully) to find a "mediating term" between what is perceived by human beings as the irreconcilable opposites of their experience. "Mist," for example, is construed as mediating between sky and earth, or "garments" between "nature" and "culture." Those terms that do not admit of mediation in mythical structures are frequently replaced by those that do; moreover, one may find a "chain" of mediators in a collection of related myths.[16] These mediating terms are anomalous with respect to the categories they mediate—an essential characteristic described by Edmund Leach in his analysis of Genesis:

> In every myth system we will find a persistent sequence of binary discriminations as between human/superhuman, mortal/immortal, male/female, legitimate/illegitimate, good/bad . . . followed by a "mediation" of the paired categories thus distinguished.
>
> "Mediation" (in this sense) is always achieved by introducing a third category which is "abnormal" or "anomalous" in terms of ordinary "rational" categories. Thus myths are full of fabulous monsters, incarnate gods, virgin mothers. This middle ground is abnormal, non-natural, holy. It is typically the focus of all taboo and ritual observance.[17]

"Christabel" is *par excellence* a poem of anomalous terms—as well as of the awareness of oppositions. It is also a poem of "middle," often disturbingly liminal terms whether or not their anomalous character is readily apparent: the middle of the night, the time of the year *just between* winter and spring, the oak green with moss and rarest mistletoe (instead of leaves) that stands *between* Christabel and Geraldine, Geraldine's "half-way" attempt to lift some mysterious weight within as Christabel rises "half-way" in her bed to look at the lofty lady. The list could be continued into Part II where Bracy is half listened to and mist and cloud lie between the castle and the Devil in Borrodale, recalling the "thin gray cloud" of Part I that "covers but not hides the sky." (As a mediating term between earth and sky, the cloud appears here in a familiar mythological function [Leach, p. 14]). The poem is haunted by the monstrous, the holy and unholy, the ritual gesture, the broken charm. But the most important "anomalous" term leading to closure in **"Christabel"** is that of the child in The Conclusion to Part II. This figure alone mediates successfully between the categories of male and female fundamental to the oppositions developed in the poem. It resolves, if only temporarily, the painful contemplation of sexual division and human coupling Coleridge presents. *The re-union of what in this world is divided* is the problem the "logic" of the poem attempts to solve. It is an issue raised explicitly in the lines of the poem and essentially in the structural equations from which the narrative segments are generated. It is also an ancient issue in mythological speculations.

Division, separation, and opposition, we have seen, are everywhere in Part I of **"Christabel."** They are equally significant in Part II and are endlessly inclusive, relentlessly crossing all the categories of human cultural and physical experience Coleridge could have known—male and female, up and down, inner and outer, life and death, Heaven and Hell, night and day, far and near, good and evil. But the focus of division (and opposition) in the relationships among the motifs constituting the major figures is familial and sexual.[18] Male/female, parent/child, brother/brother, "sister"/"sister," brother/"sister"—the terms of the relationships arrange themselves along axes that connect familial or sexual categories of division and opposition. Moreover, each "figure" is representative of several terms in the relationships. The narrative segments that appear in the poem develop from various attempts to replace one term with another in such relationships in order to achieve a union of opposites.

The original perception of fundamental human sexual division and opposition generates all such efforts to achieve union. Even attempts to join brother with brother or sister with sister in order to resolve division and reunite oppositions depend on the introduction of a real or implied sexual relationship. The recognition (and Coleridge's rejection) of the division of the human world into male and female is the principal or "core" binary opposition in the poem, but these terms themselves have undergone division, generating others that are in curious and perhaps unexpected (except from a psychoanalytic perspective) opposition. Such is the division of the male term into *hostile* "brothers." The Abel of Christabel's name first evokes the ancient fratricidal crime that so haunted Coleridge. Even more obvious in the narrative development is the ancient, angry separation of Lord Roland and Sir Leoline to be resolved in Part II by Sir Leoline's promise to restore Geraldine to her father. But the inerasable *identity* of the two male figures is asserted in the analogies drawn:

> They stood aloof, the scars remaining,
> Like cliffs which had been rent asunder;
> A dreary sea now flows between;—
> But neither heat, nor frost, nor thunder,
> Shall wholly do away, I ween,
> The marks of that which once hath been.

(Pt. II, ll. 421-26; *CPW*, I, 229)

It is Geraldine's presence that initiates the attempt to reunite the two although in fact it is not this reunion, but the establishing of a significant relationship between Sir Leoline and Geraldine that actually takes place.

If the division of the male term produces inevitably hostile brothers, the division of the female creates "sisters" in opposition. "Sister," I would argue, is one of the relationships between Christabel and Geraldine: they are sisters in the sense that both are daughters

(given Geraldine's account of her origins) of a two-part male figure, that of Sir Leoline and Lord Roland. The designation also acknowledges the perception of many readers that Christabel and Geraldine are in many ways halves of the same self, or more accurately, polarized manifestations of the same substance.[19] Whether one accepts the designation "sister" or not, it is clear in the poem (and in life) that what was (or is) *one* becomes *two*. We perceive Man endlessly divided into men in his generations, and original oneness lost. The poem attempts to reverse this experience. Can *one* be recreated from *two*? From two of the same *kind*? Are *two* really *one*? How can what was *one* become *two*? And in opposition? The essential mythological divisions of world into light and dark, above and below, of human kind into male and female, of male and female into sisters and brothers—those puzzles which may give rise to the narratives of Genesis and the questions of human familial experience, appear in the divisions and unions of **"Christabel."** The poem attempts to undo the reality of division the mind perceives by restoring an original lost unity—the elusive genesis of our being.

Coleridge's poem has suggested The Book of Genesis to other critics for many different reasons. Beverly Fields, for example, again focusing principally on the figure of Christabel in her analysis, sees Christabel's loss of innocence as the fall from a symbolic Eden, that sheltered home she leaves at the beginning of Part I (p. 77). Actually this Eden is more truly a "land of the dead" in which, significantly, the appropriate sexual partner is missing for *both* Christabel and Sir Leoline. If narrative is frequently precipitated, as Vladimir Propp's analysis of fairy tales suggests, by a *lack*,[20] the figures of the poem form an equation of sexual opposition at this point in which four terms are significant and two of them are lacking:

	Male	*Female*
	Sir Leoline	x (wife)
	x (lover)	Christabel

Not only is the virgin daughter's lover absent, the female parent is dead. In the fallen world of human culture we observe, Eden is already lost, and regeneration cannot occur except incestuously between daughter and father. Only this incestuous union of opposites could restore original oneness in the human terms present at this point in the narrative. (Disguised incestuous relationships that have not gone unnoticed appear inevitably in the working out of the poem's equation.) In fact, the puzzle Coleridge presents cannot avoid an incestuous "solution," as I will argue in a moment. But it is Geraldine, an apparent outsider in Part I, whose serpentine and sexual nature initiates the actions of union and reunion once she is introduced into the "Eden" of the castle. She substitutes, however monstrously, for *both* missing terms, the wife-mother and the lover.

In Part I Geraldine lies with Christabel in circumstances many readers have seen as mysteriously, pervertedly, even incestuously sexual.[21] She appears as a "lofty" lady, commanding Christabel to lie down, and revealing in her undressing a bosom and half a side that are a "sight to dream of, not to tell" (Pt. I, l. 253; *CPW,* I, 224). She hesitates mysteriously, then takes Christabel to what is described in Part II, in Christabel's recollection of the event, as her "bosom old," her "bosom cold" (Pt. II, ll. 457-58; *CPW,* I, 230).[22] The results of this coalescence are several. First, in The Conclusion to Part I, Christabel becomes a "child" and Geraldine a "mother" figure; second, Christabel acquires a serpentine nature and it is as this monstrous product of their union that Christabel functions principally in Part II. In Part II, Geraldine, by this time identified in one set of relationships as a maternal figure, is "led forth" by Sir Leoline.

The passage which shifts Christabel into the role of child (thereby denying her nubility) seems curious indeed after the images in which the apparently unholy coalescence is described, but it is as true to the poem's attempt to solve the problem of the missing term as it is to the ancient anomalous character of sexuality itself in mythical solutions to the problem of original oneness:

> And lo! the worker of these harms,
> That holds the maiden in her arms,
> Seems to slumber still and mild,
> As a mother with her child.
>
> (Conclusion to Pt. I, ll. 298-301; *CPW,* I, 226)

At the end of Part II, moreover, Sir Leoline leads forth the lady Geraldine in a ritual gesture that most readers interpret as a rejection of Christabel, but which most clearly suggests a replacing of the mother figure. True, both attempts to replace the missing terms of the initial homology are anomalous, even monstrous, but their monstrosity results in part from the incestuous nature of the resolution to the original lack. To pursue the issue: Geraldine is by no means a stranger to the familial relationships I have indicated as dominant in the poem, nor is she an outsider except in a special sense.[23] If Geraldine is perceived as a counterpart of Christabel, her role as "mother" in The Conclusion to Part I and subsequent "replacing" of Christabel with Sir Leoline at the end, suggest in fact an incestuous development in attempts to solve the problem of the union of opposites. Geraldine is, as we have seen, "generated" by Christabel. Her appearance, moreover, as Coleridge put the poem together, is necessary for Sir Leoline's recognition that the rift between himself and Lord Roland must be mended. But Geraldine identifies herself as Lord Roland's daughter, that is, she also marks in the "logic" of the poem her issue from the male counterpart of Leoline. Consequently, she bears the relationships of "daughter" and "niece" to Leoline, providing yet another reason for our mixed responses to the implications of his leading forth the "tall lady" Geraldine.

Yet the puzzle cannot be "solved" *except* incestuously (and of course it cannot be "solved," finally, at all). In this respect, a comparison of the poem's structures with those isolated by Leach in his analysis of Genesis, is, I think, helpful. Leach identifies the problem of generation as a constant in myths that deal with rules of incest and exogamy: "How was it in the beginning? If our first parents were persons of two kinds, what was that other kind? But if they were both of our kind, then their relations must have been incestuous and we are all born in sin" (p. 10). Leach also points out the persistence of the conviction in mythologies that unity in Paradise becomes duality in this world, and myth seeks to mediate the dualities developed. The figure of Eve is anomalous to the earlier opposition of Man versus Animal, and hence a mediator between these categories; but as a "final mediation . . . the Serpent, a creeping thing, is anomalous to the opposition Man versus Woman" (p. 14)—a development that explains, Leach believes, the frequent identification of Eve and the Serpent. And in order for procreation to occur, sexuality was introduced into Paradise.

A return to the nonsexual world where all-is-one, the blissful child-world of the psychoanalyst's oral fantasy, is, of course, impossible. In Coleridge's poem, nevertheless, the narrative attempts to find a unifying term that denies the separations and divisions of human experience. At best it can offer only the issue of human sexuality—the one made from two. Hence we have the unstable "fairy" figure of the child that appears in the coda to the poem like those abrupt, apparently unmotivated (in the sense of conventional literary narrative) conclusions to numerous non-literary myths. Later conceptualizing of this problem in Coleridge's writing pursues these issues and demonstrates an important preoccupation with the question of polarities and unity. For the poet-turned-philosopher, the concept of polarity, Owen Barfield argues, is seminal.[24] The duality of opposite forces is for Coleridge "the *manifestation* of prior unity" (p. 35). Coleridge also insisted, as Barfield points out, that "polar opposites" *generate each other*—and are "together generative of a new product" (p. 36). Since Lévi-Strauss's "mythic thinking" could be described as a pre-conceptual thinking-in-images, one is strongly tempted to see in Coleridge's poetry the pre-conceptual "mythic" adumbrations of what he later expresses in "philosophic" terms in his *Treatise on Logic* and elsewhere. This temptation is especially strong when one learns the details of Coleridge's arguments and recognizes that his insistence on thinking as *process,* not as *product* (thought), has affinities with Lévi-Strauss's descriptions of mythic thinking. The analysis I have offered of the relationships between Geraldine and Christabel and the systematic *generation* of aspects of one figure by the other suggests the earlier "mythical" exploration of Coleridge's "generative interpenetration" of polar opposites essential to the reconciliation of opposites.

But this is not the place to pursue Coleridge's complex speculations on polar logic nor on polarity as a universal principle except to indicate his conceptual isolation of the problems raised figuratively in **"Christabel."** Moreover the mediating function of the child figure in The Conclusion to Part II needs further comment. This figure fulfills in several respects the requirements of a mediating term, given the exploration of opposites in the poem that has as its focus a fundamental opposition of male and female, an initial "lack" of suitable sexual partners for the original male and female figures presented, a familial complex of oppositions, and a regenerative sexual component.[25] This conclusion is "true" whether the child is read as a collection of signifying motifs or as a single complex figure. As a figure, it reproduces within itself (and is capable of generating) the antithetical terms confronted by the narrative. Sexless (in the poem), it is the one-from-two that unites temporarily the male and female of the parental opposition, and it is only quasi-human, an elf and fairy in the poem's words:

> A little child, a limber elf,
> Singing, dancing to itself,
> A fairy thing with red round cheeks,
> That always finds, and never seeks.
>
> (Conclusion to Pt. II, ll. 656-59; *CPW*, I, 235)

(Coleridge's *Theory of Life* [*Hints towards the Formation of a More Comprehensive Theory of Life*] argues that on the organic level the "central phenomenon" that reveals the law of polarity is reproduction [Barfield, p. 53].) As a mediating term, the child figure is anticipated in the operations of Part I—in the transformations of the "union" of Geraldine and Christabel into "mother and child." In the ambivalence of parental response and the sexual promise of the child, only temporarily asexual, we find the recognition of the persistence of division in our world.

Such an ending is, of course, abrupt and "unmotivated" in the usual sense of narrative. At first glance its only connection to the text is vaguely thematic, not structural, in spite of the fact that the union of Christabel and Geraldine (so grotesque in conventional terms) results so strikingly in the analogy between a sleeping mother and her child. Yet it is the inevitable "mediating" term for the oppositions presented and indeed the term which suitably results from the narrative operations introduced at the beginning of the poem.

Since an original lost unity is presupposed in Coleridge's (and the Bible's) contemplation of the division of the world into male and female, the ancient incestuous resolution is the inevitable conclusion to the problem to be solved: Adam and Eve are of one kind. All men are "brothers," all women "sisters," all women the daughters of Adam, all men the sons of Eve. Man is divided into men and into fratricidal brothers. (Leach equates Cain's fratricide with Adam's incest.[26]) Reunion of opposites is the problem posed in Parts I and II, but it cannot occur without the introduction of sexuality into the relationships perceived. The serpentine Geraldine, an *apparent* outsider, enables the "resolution" to occur, but only after the problem is confronted twice: once on the level of the "children" (Cain, Abel, Geraldine, Christabel); next on the "parental" level by the substitution of a more acceptable (more "distant," less incestuous) Geraldine for the nubile Christabel. The abrupt "appearance" of a child image in which the opposites unite—temporarily—is the resolution of the puzzle and the conclusion to the poem. The problem haunts Coleridge elsewhere and endlessly, but a continuation of the narrative of **"Christabel"** would not be necessary. The poem is complete.

Notes

1. The question of intention has been reopened in contemporary literary theory. But even Quentin Skinner, who makes a strong case against the "intentional fallacy" and who distinguishes helpfully among different motives and intentions, points out that a claim can still be made that "the writer may have been self-deceiving about recognizing his intentions, or incompetent at stating them. And this seems to be perennially possible in the case of any complex human action" ("Motives, Intentions and the Interpretation of Texts," *New Literary History,* 3 [1972], 405).

2. The "other narrative circumstances" are principally those of myth in which "mediating terms" are introduced in an attempt to resolve oppositions. See Claude Lévi-Strauss, "The Structural Study of Myth," in his *Structural Anthropology,* trans. Claire Jacobsen and Brook Grundfest Schoepf (Garden City: Anchor Books, 1967), pp. 202-28. Beverly Fields, writing from a psychoanalytic perspective, argues that the *narrative* of "Christabel" is incomplete, but that *psychologically* the poem is finished since in it appear the tensions Coleridge could express no other way and that "when he had fully expressed his fantasies, he had also finished with the poem" (*Reality's Dark Dream: Dejection in Coleridge* [Kent, Ohio: The Kent State U. Press, 1967], p. 83).

3. Jonas Spatz, "The Mystery of Eros: Sexual Initiation in Coleridge's 'Christabel,'" *PMLA,* 90 (1975), 107-10.

4. Spatz, pp. 113-15. Spatz recognizes archetypal figures in the poem (the innocent maiden, the step-

mother and others) as well as fairy tale parallels to its structures, but he focuses on Christabel as "human" (she has an unconscious) and on the structures of fairy tales that have undergone considerable literary elaboration.

5. J. B. Beer, *Coleridge the Visionary* (1959; rpt. New York: Collier Books, 1962), p. 199.

6. A. J. Greimas, "Elements of a Narrative Grammar," trans. Catherine Porter, *Diacritics,* 7, No. 1 (1977), 23.

7. Coleridge's interest in the great fratricidal crime of Christian myth is clearly part of the creative context in which "Christabel" was written. He worked on *The Wanderings of Cain* in the same year in which he wrote Part 1 of "Christabel." Norman Fruman sees the name *Christ-Abel* as "embracing the two archetypal victims of man's murderous impulses" and links Coleridge's "murderous rage" against an older brother to the persistent theme of brother-murder in the poet's work (*Coleridge, The Damaged Archangel* [New York: Braziller, 1971], p. 362).

8. Greimas, p. 29. For a discussion of Greimas' contribution to models of character, see Jonathan Culler, *Structuralist Poetics* (Ithaca, N.Y.: Cornell U. Press, 1975), pp. 233-35.

9. Coleridge appears to have been uneasily aware of the paucity of "incident" and "character" in the poem. He apparently recognized that considerable literary elaboration would be necessary in order for the poem to reach a reading public conditioned by certain experiences in literature. See the discussion of this issue in Paul Magnuson, *Coleridge's Nightmare Poetry* (Charlottesville: U. Press of Virginia, 1974), pp. 95-96.

10. Patricia M. Adair, *The Waking Dream: A Study of Coleridge's Poetry* (London: Edward Arnold, Ltd., 1967), p. 163.

11. Arthur H. Nethercot, *The Road to Tryermaine* (New York: Russell, 1962), p. 37.

12. Nethercot ignored the *Abel* in Christabel's name although he made a considerable argument for the significance of the *Christ* (see pp. 207-08). Fruman's identification of the fratricidal theme in the *Abel* motif is closer to a recognition of the relation of opposites in the poem (see n. 7 above).

13. The parallel between Cain and Geraldine, insofar as it is made on the basis of the archetypal "mark" each bore, was early recognized, as was her link with other figures who bore a "definite token of some transgression" (Nethercot, pp. 127-28).

14. *The Complete Poetical Works of Samuel Taylor Coleridge,* ed. Ernest Hartley Coleridge (Oxford:

Oxford U. Press, 1912), I, 217 (Pt. I, ll. 51-52). Further references to this edition appear in the text and are abbreviated *CPW.*

15. The brother-rift is a persistent personal as well as literary concern for Coleridge. His letters and dreams reflect a "bitter hatred" for his brothers. See Fruman, p. 363 and p. 548, n. 26.

16. Lévi-Strauss, "The Structural Study of Myth," p. 222. In the numerous versions of particular myths, "mythical thought" is manifested in a multiplicity and recurrence of themes; according to Lévi-Strauss, it "never develops any theme to completion: there is always something left unfinished. Myths, like rites, are interminable" (*The Raw and the Cooked,* trans. John and Doreen Weightman [1964; New York: Harper and Row, 1969], p. 6). However, when mediation appears, it often closes a particular version of a myth, even if such closure is unstable. This instability is true of the mediating function of the child figure in The Conclusion to Part II, although the term introduced provides "closure" in the sense of presenting an appropriate mediation of the opposites in the poem.

17. Edmund Leach, "Genesis as Myth," in *Genesis as Myth and Other Essays* (1962; rpt. London: Jonathan Cape, 1969), p. 11.

18. The exception is Bracy, although at least one commentator argues that Bracy is a "good father" figure (Fields, p. 70). Bracy's incipient narrative function appears likely to be that of *donor.* See Vladimir Propp, *The Morphology of the Folktale,* 2nd ed., trans. Laurence Scott, rev. and ed. Louis A. Wagner (Austin and London: U. of Texas Press, 1968), p. 39. Bracy also represents an earlier and unsuccessful attempt at mediation.

19. Magnuson believes the presence of good as well as evil in the Geraldine of Part I is explained by recognizing Christabel and Geraldine as "mirror images" (*Coleridge's Nightmare Poetry,* p. 102).

20. Propp, pp. 76-78. See especially his remarks on the function of a *lack* of a suitable marriage partner for the hero of the fairy tale.

21. Homoeroticism is the most obvious of the taboo sexual relationships identified by readers. But the sexual ambiguity of Geraldine's nature leads to complex analyses of the significance of the act performed on Christabel. See, for example, Nethercot's vampirism (*The Road to Tryermaine,* pp. 77-78) and Norman Fruman's exploration in his *The Damaged Archangel* of the relationships between Coleridge's troubled responses to sexuality and his expression of these in his poetry. More schematically, Fields traces the "force of the in-

cest fear" in the scene between Geraldine and Christabel to Coleridge's "actual or fantasied witnessing of the primal scene" (*Reality's Dark Dream,* pp. 79-80).

22. In an earlier version, Coleridge described Geraldine's mark as "lean and old and foul of hue." This sight is recalled, although in different terms, at the very moment Sir Leoline takes Geraldine in his arms and she meets his embrace, "Prolonging it with joyous look" (Pt. I, l. 450; *CPW,* I, 230). The symmetry of these relationships is thereby established as is their ambiguous and taboo sexual character.

23. She comes into the castle from the "outside," and the castle walls are obviously an attempt to exclude the external, "natural" world suggested by the woods and the oak hung with mistletoe. But her link with the essentially human as well as the mysteriously charged pagan and phallic powers of the mistletoe is established by her account of her parentage. Granted, in some literal sense one does not have to "believe" her account, but it is "she" who introduces the familial elaborations into the poem since her "father" is a "brother" figure for Sir Leoline.

24. Owen Barfield, *What Coleridge Thought* (Middletown, Conn.: Wesleyan U. Press, 1971), p. 60.

25. A striking parallel may be found in Jung's analyses of the functions of the child figure in the relationships among mythological motifs in psychopathology and alchemy. This figure may appear in dreams as the dreamer's son or daughter, but its function is to unite "the opposites; [it is] a mediator, bringer of healing, that is, one who makes whole." The child is the "irrational third" term in a conflict situation; out of the collision of opposites "the unconscious psyche always creates a third thing of an irrational nature, which the conscious mind neither expects nor understands." The child is a symbol that contains the opposites, but mediates between them—in effect, a mediating term (*The Archetypes and the Collective Unconscious,* Vol. IX, Part I of *The Collected Works* [New York: Pantheon Books, Inc., 1959], pp. 159-81). Of course Jung's explanation of this phenomenon as part of a psychological process is in other respects quite different. Although his insistence on the "binary" operation of the mind pervades his studies of mythological motifs in psychopathology, it receives less attention than his more rigid formulations. It should be noticed that his "mediating terms" frequently suggest the anomalous categories in myth that have interested structuralists.

26. In this reading Cain's sin is also "incestuous homosexuality" (Leach, p. 15).

Barbara A. Schapiro (essay date 1983)

SOURCE: Schapiro, Barbara A. "Coleridge." In *The Romantic Mother: Narcissistic Patterns in Romantic Poetry,* pp. 61-92. Baltimore: Johns Hopkins University Press, 1983.

[*In the following excerpt, Schapiro considers "Christabel"'s psychological elements.*]

A READING

Although the composition and publication of **Christabel** extended over a four-year period, between 1797 and 1801, and although never completed, the poem can nevertheless be considered unified. Coleridge himself stresses that his conception of the poem had always been whole in his mind: "The reason of my not finishing **Christabel** is not that I don't know how to do it—for I have, as I always had, the whole plan entire from beginning to end in my mind; but I fear I cannot carry on with equal success the execution of the idea, an extremely subtle and difficult one."[1] This "idea," as we shall see, concerns an unconscious conflict that indeed involves subtle and difficult emotions. The danger to the ego of uncovering these threatening emotions perhaps accounts for Coleridge's inability to proceed further with the poem than he did. Regardless of his reasons for not completing it, since he did see the two Parts and the Conclusion as belonging to a single idea, I feel justified in beginning my analysis with the Conclusion. The feelings expressed in this brief last section expose, in a clear and direct manner, the feelings animating the more obscurely complicated drama of the two preceding sections.

The Conclusion opens with the portrait of a child, a vision the poet considers blissfully ideal:

> A little child, a limber elf,
> Singing, dancing to itself,
> A fairy thing with red round cheeks,
> That always finds, and never seeks,
> Makes such a vision to the sight
> As fills a father's eyes with light;

Coleridge significantly highlights the child's complete autonomy and self-sufficiency. It is singing and dancing "to itself," and it "never seeks." In an earlier version, Coleridge emphasizes this feature by italicizing the words *finds* and *seeks.* Apparently, the child is also amply nourished, for it has "red round cheeks." These characteristics of the child curiously oppose those of Christabel in Parts One and Two. Christabel always seeks and never finds; she is always seeking a love that is absent—her absent knight, her absent mother, and, in Part Two, the love of her angry father. Also unlike the child, Christabel is pale and wan, and, by the end, wasted and shrinking. The vision of the child is a vision of an ideally fulfilled self, a condition that the poem as a whole recognizes as impossible. For it is the unfulfilled love and the intense pain and rage it incites that is the real subject of **Christabel** and the subject of the remainder of the Conclusion. Coleridge describes the child's father, whose heart overflows with love for the child, and yet he

> . . . at last
> Must needs express his love's excess
> With words of unmeant bitterness.
>
> . . . .
>
> Perhaps 'tis tender too and pretty
> At each wild word to feel within
> A sweet recoil of love and pity.
> And what, if in a world of sin
> (O sorrow and shame should this be true!)
> Such giddiness of heart and brain
> Comes seldom save from rage and pain,
>
> . . . .

Coleridge here and throughout the poem is deeply troubled by what he recognizes as a mysterious, intimate connection between "love's excess" and a bitter, aggressive rage. It is significantly an *excessive* love that results in the wild and bitter words. The love is most likely felt to be excessive because it is more than can be accepted or reciprocated by the love object; it is a needy and demanding love that causes shame. Coleridge intuitively recognizes that at the source of this "giddiness of heart and brain," this maelstrom of love and hate, is the "rage and pain" of unfulfilled love.

The three main characters in **Christabel**—Geraldine, Christabel, and Sir Leoline—all embody the intensely ambivalent condition described in the Conclusion. In Part Two, "pain and rage" is indeed the most oft-repeated phrase. The fact that Christabel is female, furthermore, may be due not only to an attempted disguise, as Wormhoudt suggests, but also to a closer identification with the loved and hated mother whose presence dominates the poem. As Kernberg and others have shown, a fixation on and identification with the mother imago is a typical response to an early frustration and ambivalence in the mother-child relationship. This internal psychic conflict also bears on the overall form and style of the poem. The ballad form, with its repetitions and simple rocking rhythms, is a good vehicle, as Beverly Fields has pointed out, for unconscious primitive feelings.[2] Being an ancient and traditional form, it also allows the poet to feel safely distanced from the emotionally threatening material. The supernatural mode further enables Coleridge to avoid dealing directly with Nature/mother in his poetry. Yet as Harding observes in his analysis of **The Ancient Mariner [The Rime of the Ancient Mariner]**, the supernatural machinery often does have a real correspondence with inner psychological workings. The mariner's small, impulsive act, for instance, "which presses the supernatural trigger," Harding asserts, "does form an effective parallel to the hidden impulse which has such a devastating meaning for one's irrational, and partly unconscious, private standards."[3] In **Christabel** the supernatural transformations are comparable to the irrational displacements and condensations that occur in dreams. A Gothic tale of terror is ultimately the form most suitable for Coleridge's deepest nightmare.

The first part of **Christabel,** as Knight has noted, is indeed "strangely feminine." The images with which Coleridge introduces the tale have associations that are at once feminine, passive, deathly, and sinister. It is the middle of the night. Whereas the male cock is crowing only "drowsily," the baron's "toothless mastiff bitch" is howling as if "she sees my lady's shroud" (6-13). It is apparent from later revisions that Coleridge troubled over the destructive aggression exposed in these lines, specifically over the offensive connotations of the word *bitch*. He changed the lines "Sir Leoline, the Baron rich, / Hath a toothless mastiff bitch" first to "Sir Leoline, the Baron bold / Hath a toothless mastiff old," and then finally to "Sir Leoline, the Baron rich, / Hath a toothless mastiff which." Wormhoudt believes that *which* can be read as *witch*. If so read, the lines express the same unconscious rage as they do in the original version.

The stanza that immediately follows presents another feminine image in hostile and aggressive shades. Coleridge describes the night as "chilly" but not as completely dark, for "The thin gray cloud is spread on high, / It covers but not hides the sky, / The moon is behind, and at the full; / And yet she looks both small and dull." As in Keats's poetry, the moon is a prominent and heavily loaded image in Coleridge's work; it figures always as an ever-watchful maternal presence. In **The Ancient Mariner,** for instance, the rising of an ominous "horned Moon" heralds the entrance of the Nightmare Life-in-Death. Yet it is by the light of a graciously shining moon that the mariner beholds the water snakes and consequently redeems himself by blessing them, and when the "thick black cloud" subsequently pours down a reparative rain, "The Moon was at its side." (Other aspects of Coleridge's moon image will be discussed later in an analysis of **"Frost at Midnight."**) In **Christabel,** the moon resides in a chilly night and is significantly "small and dull." The moon/mother, in other words, is denying her light/milk; she is cold, withdrawn, and shrunken. This withdrawn and shrunken image forms a recurring motif in the poem—from Geraldine's lean and shrunken bosom to Christabel's "dull" and "shrunken serpent eyes" at the end.

Thus, the angry and destructive feelings toward the mother which are imagistically revealed in the setting preface Christabel's entrance into the woods and affect the action that takes place there. Christabel is going to the woods to pray because "She had dreams all yester-night / Of her own betrothed knight; / And she in the midnight wood will pray / For the weal of her lover that's far away" (27-30). In the first edition of the poem, the agitating and erotic nature of these dreams is emphasized: "Dreams that made her moan and leap, / As on her bed she lay in sleep." Christabel feels that she must pray for the welfare of her absent lover apparently because her dreams have led her to fear him harm. In other words, she is perhaps afraid of the damaging powers revealed in her own disturbingly erotic/destructive dreams. The absent knight, furthermore, is intimately connected with Geraldine, for it is Geraldine who appears to Christabel as a result of her night journey to pray; Geraldine appears indeed as if in answer to the prayer. As we shall see shortly, she is also inextricably connected with Christabel's dead mother. Christabel's prayer, then, like the poet's supplication in **"Pains of Sleep,"** is really addressed to the loved and hated mother. Her praying under a "broad-breasted" oak tree enforces this idea.

Christabel's first vision of Geraldine, as she spies her lying behind the oak, is at once beautiful and terrifying. Coleridge invokes "Jesu, Maria" to "shield her well!"

> There she sees a damsel bright,
> Drest in a silken robe of white,
> That shadowy in the moonlight shone:
> The neck that made that white robe wan,
> Her stately neck, and arms were bare;
> Her blue-veined feet unsandal'd were,
> And wildly glittered here and there
> The gems entangled in her hair.
>
> [58-65]

The aspect of Geraldine's appearance which Coleridge first emphasizes—her "silken robe of white" which shines in the moonlight—associates the "damsel bright" with the white light of the moon itself. Coleridge refers more than once to Geraldine's "vestments white," and throughout the poem she is generally associated with whiteness. She tells Christabel, for instance, of the white steeds of the warriors and of how they tied her to a "palfrey white." Her whiteness suggests not only moon/mother but also breast/milk. The initial portrait of Geraldine hints at qualities that are both erotic and incipiently violent and destructive. Coleridge describes the lady's bare neck and arms and particularly highlights her bare "blue-veined feet." Considering the poet's recurrent nightmare image of being trampled, emphasis on the bared feet is significant; certainly the feet have destructive, perhaps phallic, associations. Finally, the "wildly" glittering gems that are "entangled" in her hair also suggest erotic as well as unbridled and potentially

violent passions. Christabel exclaims that "twas frightful" to see a lady so beautiful and richly clad, and she cries, "Mary mother, save me now!" As Geraldine embodies both the desired and ideal good mother and the feared and vengeful bad mother, so the mother-image is split generally between the good and the bad throughout the poem. Christabel frequently appeals to the image of the idealized good mother to defend her from the bad. She is threatened, not only by the bad mother in Geraldine, but by the bad mother within herself, due to her internalization of and identification with that object of her obsessive desire and terror.

Geraldine indeed allows Christabel the opportunity to act out the mother role herself. The mother-child parts alternate between them throughout the poem. At the beginning, Christabel finds Geraldine in a weak and helpless state, having been seized and abandoned by the wicked warriors. Geraldine's position is thus initially that of a forlorn and abandoned child. Coleridge describes how Christabel "stretched forth her hand, / And comforted fair Geraldine" and promised to "guide and guard" her "safe and free" (104-10). Christabel thus acts the comforting and protecting mother. Coleridge extends this image even further as he describes Christabel and Geraldine crossing the moat:

> They crossed the moat, and Christabel
> Took the key that fitted well;
> A little door she opened straight,
> All in the middle of the gate;
> The gate that was ironed within and without,
> Where an army in battle array had marched out.
> The lady sank, belike through pain,
> And Christabel, with might and main
> Lifted her up, a weary weight,
> Over the threshold of the gate:
> Then the lady rose again,
> And moved, as she were not in pain.
>
> [123-34]

As Beres has pointed out, the passage reveals some unmistakable birth imagery. With a mighty effort, Christabel carries Geraldine over the threshold, delivering her through the portal. Once in the court, Coleridge states, then repeats, that they were now "free from danger, free from fear" (135, 143). The statement is, of course, ironical. It serves perhaps as a defensive denial of the very fear and danger that is always present for Coleridge in the mother-child relationship.

The fearful and dangerous aspect of that relationship is immediately betrayed when Christabel proposes that they "move as if in stealth" (120) so as not to wake the ailing Sir Leoline. In an earlier version the lines read, "So to my room we'll creep in stealth." Certainly the fear of the father has oedipal undertones. Nevertheless, the essential emotional conflict is still preoedipal. Christabel's guilty stealth is due less to a guilty oedipal desire than to a more primitive, greedy desire for the mother's exclusive attention. In Part Two, Christabel's attitude toward her father suggests that she merely redirects this same desire toward him. Sir Leoline himself will be seen to be less a retaliatory oedipal father than, once again, a loved and hated mother-figure. Christabel's feelings of shame and guilt, then, arise from the angry and aggressive nature of her greedy love.

After Christabel and Geraldine cross the court, Christabel's, or Coleridge's, anxiety begins to surface more forcefully. The mastiff bitch, first of all, asleep in the "moonshine cold," awakes and makes an "angry moan." Then as Geraldine passes the hall where the brands lay dying "Amid their own white ashes,"

> . . . there came
> A tongue of light, a fit of flame;
> And Christabel saw the lady's eye,
> And nothing else saw she thereby,
> Save the boss of the shield of Sir Leoline tall,
> Which hung in a murky niche in the wall.
>
> [159-63]

Ocular imagery is prominent throughout the poem, and the connection here among the "lady's eye," the "white ashes," and the "tongue of light" suggests a psychological explanation. In this passage, oral images immediately precede the illumination of Geraldine's eye; white, as discussed, associates in Coleridge's mind with breast/milk, and the "tongue of light" further enforces the oral idea. Voyeurism is rooted in the oral disposition; the desire to get and "drink in" with the eyes is akin to the oral wish. As Wormhoudt explains, "The voyeur uses his eyes to take in forbidden sights just as the lips are used to suck at the breast." Kohut has also written about the oral-visual relationship. If the mother physically and emotionally recoils from the child, if she withholds her body, he says, the visual will become hypercathectic for the child.[4] The oral-eye images in the above passage also project a distinctly ominous light. The dying brands and ashes, the flamed tongue, and the portentous "evil" eye reflect the enraged and ambivalent feelings at the root of the oral experience. That Christabel's only other sight is of the boss of Sir Leoline's shield, which Wormhoudt sees as another breast image, emphasizes the fear of retaliation which accompanies the greedy and destructive oral wish. In the final lines of the stanza, Christabel anxiously reminds Geraldine to "softly tread" for her father "seldom sleepeth well."

Once they reach Christabel's chamber, however, the fear and anxieties only become more urgent, for the threat comes less from the father than from the ambivalent mother. As they enter the room, Coleridge again mentions the "dim" moon. Although its beams cannot enter the room, the chamber is nevertheless provided with its own moon—a "silver lamp" that "burns dead

and dim" (186). Thus, the cold and deathly moon/mother image again appears. The lamp exhibits another forboding feature: a silver chain "fastened to an angel's feet." If we recall the phallic and destructive associations that feet have for Coleridge, the ambivalent nature of the moon image here becomes all the more apparent. It is in the light of this ambivalent mother image that the climactic scene between Geraldine and Christabel unfolds.

Christabel offers Geraldine a drink: "I pray you, drink this cordial wine! / It is a wine of virtuous powers; / My mother made it of wild flowers" (191-93). The drink causes Geraldine's "fair large eyes" to "glitter bright." Although the scene reverses the oral experience, with Christabel again assuming the mother's role, the manifest emotions are still the child's (Christabel's and Coleridge's) fears of and ambivalence toward the mother. The wine, first of all, was made by Christabel's mother. When Geraldine is informed of this, she asks, "And will your mother pity me, / Who am a maiden most forlorn?" The mother, however, is incapable of love and pity for the forlorn child. As Christabel explains, "She died the hour that I was born." The child indeed feels guiltily responsible for the mother's death. In the mother's deathbed prophecy, which Christabel describes to Geraldine, the fear of punishment is evident: "I have heard the grey-haired friar tell / How on her death-bed she did say, / That she would hear the castle-bell / Strike twelve upon my wedding-day" (198-202).

The tolling of the castle bell is associated throughout the poem with death: the mastiff bitch howls in answer to the clock "as if she sees my lady's shroud," and in Part Two, the Baron declares, "Each matin bell . . . Knells us back to a world of death" (332-33). Christabel fears retaliation for her unconscious destruction of her mother. That fear is projected onto Geraldine who now assumes the form of the vengeful, bad mother. In her fear of the bad mother, Christabel again appeals to the image of the good mother—"O mother dear! that thou wert here!"—but Geraldine as the bad mother image prevails. She commands, "'Off, wandering mother! Peak and pine! / I have power to bid thee flee,'" and "with hollow voice," she cries, "Off, woman, off! this hour is mine— / Though thou her guardian spirit be, / Off, woman, off! 'tis given to me.'" (204-13). Geraldine then orders Christabel to unrobe herself and lie beside her. The two recline, but Christabel is restless and succumbs to a desire to rise up and "look at the lady Geraldine." The desire to look, as discussed, is akin to the oral wish to take in. Christabel is thus to be punished for her greedy desire to "look" at Geraldine. The scene that follows vividly expresses the anger and terror associated with the original oral experience:

> Beneath the lamp the lady bowed,
> And slowly rolled her eyes around;

Then drawing in her breath aloud,
Like one that shuddered, she unbound
The cincture from beneath her breast:
Her silken robe, and inner vest,
Dropt to her feet, and full in view,
Behold! her bosom and half her side—
A sight to dream of, not to tell!
O shield her, shield sweet Christabel!

[245-54]

In an earlier version, Coleridge describes the breasts even more explicitly as "lean and old and foul of hue." It is reportedly at this point that Shelley, while attending a reading of the poem, hallucinated eyes in Mary Godwin's nipples and fled the room in terror.[5] The incident is revealing both of Shelley's personality and of the psychological structure of the poem. Clearly it exemplifies the general oral-voyeuristic association. Shelley obviously identified with Christabel and his confused terror simply mirrors that of Christabel herself. Finally, Geraldine proclaims, "In the touch of this bosom there worketh a spell / Which is lord of thy utterance, Christabel!" The bad, denying mother thus takes her revenge.

The Conclusion to Part One serves only to reinforce the presiding power of the good-bad mother image. Coleridge returns to the image of Christabel "Kneeling in the moonlight" at the old oak tree:

It was a lovely sight to see
The lady Christabel, when she
Was praying at the old oak tree.
    Amid the jagged shadows
    Of mossy leafless boughs,
    Kneeling in the moonlight,
    To make her gentle vows;
. . . .

[279-85]

The sight is no longer so "lovely," however, for the shadows are pointedly "jagged" and the boughs "leafless." Neither is the image of Christabel herself so innocent and pleasing as before. She is "Asleep, and dreaming fearfully," as she is at the beginning of the poem, but now she is dreaming "with open eyes (ah woe is me!) . . . Dreaming that alone, which is— / O sorrow and shame! Can this be she, / The lady, who knelt at the old oak tree?" (292-97). Christabel is now confronting with open eyes those destructive and shameful dreams concerning the mother. She only "seems to slumber still and mild" in Geraldine's arms. Moreover, Coleridge explicitly likens the scene to that of "a mother with her child" (300).

The final stanza of the Conclusion to Part One makes one last appeal to the good mother image. Although Christabel's sleep is unquiet and full of fearful dreams, she is yet, Coleridge says, "praying always"—she

"prays in sleep" (322). The restlessness, he continues, "'tis but the blood so free / Comes back and tingles in her feet." The remark, with its allusion to the maiden's feet, only further betrays the unconscious destructive passions that are the real disturbance to sleep. The poet, however, concludes,

What if her guardian spirit 'twere,
What if she knew her mother near?
But this she knows, in joys and woes,
That saints will aid if men will call:
For the blue sky bends over all!

Coleridge thus ends hopefully, with the benevolent maternal image of a blue sky bending attentively and lovingly over all.

Part One was completed in 1797. Three years later Coleridge published Part Two. The unconscious emotional conflicts that shaped Part One nevertheless remained active through the years, and Part Two picks up the threads of the earlier section. The second part, however, does indicate some psychological progress. Whereas Part One concentrates primarily on the terrifying and ambivalent figure of Geraldine, the focus of Part Two is increasingly inward, on the ambivalence, the guilt and shame within Christabel herself. The poem displays Coleridge's developing awareness of the destructive feelings within himself and his growing ability to take responsibility for them.

Part Two opens with a reminder of the mother's death and thus of Christabel's murderous and guilty feelings:

Each matin bell, the Baron saith,
Knells us back to a world of death.
These words Sir Leoline first said,
When he rose and found his lady dead:
These words Sir Leoline will say
Many a morn to his dying day!

Christabel thus associates the father with the mother's revenge. She indeed comes to identify the father with the same loving/vengeful mother. Yet the mother/father figure is less guilty of vengeful feelings than is Christabel herself. Describing Christabel waking beside Geraldine in the morning, Coleridge writes, "And Christabel awoke and spied / The same who lay down by her side— / O rather say, the same whom she / Raised up beneath the old oak tree!" (369-72). Why "rather say" that Christabel "raised up" Geraldine than that Geraldine "lay down by her side"? The altered phrasing, which makes Christabel the active subject, clearly places the responsibility for the previous night's terror with her. She cries, "Sure I have sinn'd!'" and she greets Geraldine "with such perplexity of mind / As dreams too lively leave behind" (381-86). Christabel is troubled and bewildered by her own unconscious violent emotions.

The baron's role in the drama further excites Christabel's confusion and anxiety, and his character again gives expression to the poem's central ambivalent conflict. Sir Leoline discovers that Geraldine is the daughter of Lord Roland, the estranged friend of his youth. Where once Roland had been "his heart's best brother," the two had quarreled and parted, "ne'er to meet again." Coleridge comments, "And to be wroth with one we love / Doth work like madness in the brain." The madness is indeed Christabel's own. The baron only incites that madness by again acting the role of the rejecting parent. Leoline's anger and hatred toward Roland turns easily back to love (the hate being only a product of frustrated love in the first place), and he embraces Geraldine as a long lost child. It is precisely this embrace, however, that Christabel herself covets, and thus the sight of it fills her with a furious envy. Although her jealousy could be interpreted oedipally (Christabel as the disguised Coleridge witnessing the father's embrace of the mother), Leoline's relation to Geraldine as to a child, referring to her always as "the child of his friend," suggests that Christabel's jealousy has a more infantile source.

Christabel's fury toward the denying mother/father figure, however, only turns back on her; she feels guilty for her enraged hostility and fears retaliation. Leoline swears revenge on the warriors who seized Geraldine and vows that he will "dislodge their reptile souls," and as he speaks, Coleridge says, "his eye in lightening rolls!" (442-44). Because of the oral-voyeuristic connection, the child's fear is again expressed in the parent's evil, vengeful eye. Christabel is further threatened by the father's promised revenge in that the reference to the "reptile souls" associates not only with Geraldine, but, as we shall see, with Christabel herself. When Christabel views Leoline and Geraldine's embrace, Coleridge describes:

> Again she saw that bosom old,
> Again she felt that bosom cold,
> And drew in her breath with a hissing sound:
> Whereat the Knight turned wildly round,
> And nothing saw, but his own sweet maid
> With eyes upraised, as one that prayed.
>
> [456-62]

The sight of the embrace stirs up the same enraged envy that the child originally experienced in relation to the mother who withheld all her love, warmth, and milk. In this passage, however, it is not Geraldine who reveals the cold reptilian aspect but Christabel herself, who "drew in her breath with a hissing sound." Christabel, like the mother image, is split between the ideal and the malevolent, divided by her ambivalent feelings. As Coleridge makes increasingly clear, the serpentine, bad mother resides in the heart of the seemingly innocent "sweet maid."

Reptilian imagery is ubiquitous throughout Part Two. The image of the snake, as Sloane observes, has traditionally been associated with ambivalent earth-goddesses. Besides its obvious phallic associations, the snake's curved and sinuous aspect relates it to a woman's body. It is thus a perfect image for the phallic, or ambivalent, woman. Leoline's bard Barcy, who has been instructed to report to Lord Roland that his daughter is "safe and free" (echoing Christabel's ironic words), hesitates because of a strange dream he has had concerning a snake and a dove. He wishes to delay his journey,

> For in my sleep I saw that dove,
> That gentle bird, whom thou dost love,
> And call'st by thy own daughter's name—
> Sir Leoline! I saw the same
> Fluttering, and uttering fearful moan,
> Among the green herbs in the forest alone.
> . . . .
> I stooped, methought, the dove to take,
> When lo! I saw a bright green snake
> Coiled around its wings and neck.
> Green as the herbs on which it couched,
> Close by the dove's head it crouched;
> And with the dove it heaves and stirs,
> Swelling its neck as she swelled hers!
> I woke; it was the midnight hour,
> The clock was echoing in the tower;
> . . . .
>
> [531-36, 548-56]

The clock again tolls as a reminder of the mother's death and thus of Christabel's guilty, destructive feelings. In this passage, Christabel is imaged as the innocent dove who is being destroyed by the phallic mother. In the stanza that follows, however, Leoline addresses Geraldine as "Lord Roland's beauteous dove" and promises to "crush the snake" (569-71). The threat terrifies Christabel and triggers the following fantasy. Coleridge describes how Geraldine "couched her head upon her breast, / And looked askance at Christabel." He again invokes "Jesu, Maria" to "shield" Christabel from the terrible mother:

> A snake's small eye blinks dull and shy;
> And the lady's eyes they shrunk in her head,
> Each shrunk up to a serpent's eye,
> And with somewhat of malice, and more of dread,
> At Christabel she looked askance!—
> One moment—and the sight was fled!
>
> [583-88]

The description combines the "dull" and "shrunken" moon image with that of the serpent, and again the terror is associated with the eyes. The bad mother's glance, however, contains only "somewhat of malice" but "more of dread." She is less terrible than terrified herself. It is Christabel's, or the child's, own violent and destructive feelings that are the real source of dread; she fears most the serpent within herself. Christabel "shuddered aloud, with a hissing sound," and Coleridge describes,

> The maid, alas! her thoughts are gone,
> She nothing sees—no sight but one!
> The maid, devoid of guile and sin,
> I know not how, in fearful wise,
> So deeply has she drunken in
> That look, those shrunken serpent eyes,
> That all her features were resigned
> To this sole image in her mind:
> And passively did imitate
> That look of dull and treacherous hate!
> And thus she stood, in dizzy trance,
> Still picturing that look askance
> With forced unconscious sympathy
> Full before her father's view—
> As far as such a look could be
> In eyes so innocent and blue!

[597-612]

The passage reveals a profound psychological insight. Coleridge intuitively recognizes the internalization and identification with the bad mother imago, the "forced unconscious sympathy," that results from the child's frustrated oral need to take in and possess. Christabel had "so deeply . . . drunken in . . . those shrunken serpent eyes" that she becomes possessed by the hateful, treacherous image—it indeed becomes the "sole image in her mind." The child is thus not simply victim, but is herself deeply culpable.

Finally, Christabel implores the Baron, "'By my mother's soul do I entreat / That thou this woman send away.'" For the sake of the good mother, in other words, he must rid her of the bad. Sir Leoline, however, suffers from the same paralyzing ambivalence as Christabel. "His heart was cleft with pain and rage," his bosom swelled with "confusion," "his eyes were wild," and his cheek "wan and wild" (621-41). The poet himself pleads with the baron:

> Why is thy cheek so wan and wild,
> Sir Leoline? Thy only child
> Lies at thy feet, thy joy, thy pride,
> So fair, so innocent, so mild;
> The same, for whom thy lady died!
> O by the pangs of her dear mother
> Think thou no evil of thy child!

[621-25]

By emphasizing Christabel's alliance with the dead mother here, Coleridge only stresses again the child's ambivalence and guilt. The rest of the stanza further accents this alliance as Coleridge discusses how the mother "Prayed that the babe for whom she died, / Might prove her dear lord's joy and pride!" Coleridge concludes, "And woulds't thou wrong thy only child, / Her child and thine?" (635). By stressing once more the child's association with the mother—it is "Her child" as

well as his—Coleridge again identifies the ambivalent mother with Christabel, who is thus forced to suffer the consequences. The baron feels disgraced and "Dishonoured by his only child." He rolls "his eye with stern regard," orders the bard on his mission, and ultimately rejects and abandons Christabel as he leads the lady Geraldine from the room. Thus Christabel is punished by being made to suffer the same rejection and abandonment, the same traumatizing treatment, that originally excited her ambivalence and guilt. It is ultimately the retribution she expects.

After Christabel receives her due punishment, Coleridge perhaps no longer felt compelled to continue with the poem. Yet even in his proposed ending, which James Gilman reports,[6] the central theme of ambivalent love continues. Coleridge considered ending the poem by having Geraldine leave the court to return disguised as Christabel's lover. Christabel was to be strangely repelled by "his" advances, and the action was finally to be resolved by the appearance of the true lover, at which point Geraldine as the false lover would disappear. The proposed ending thus supports the interpretation of Geraldine as Christabel's ambivalent love object. The beloved is both good and bad, true and false, desired and feared. Coleridge apparently had planned to exorcise the bad mother image. The task evidently proved more difficult than he anticipated.

Notes

1. Samuel Taylor Coleridge, *Table Talk,* July 6, 1833, in *The Collected Works of Samuel Taylor Coleridge.*

2. Beverly Fields, *Reality's Dark Dream.*

3. Harding, "'Ancient Mariner,'" p. 56.

4. Wormhoudt, *The Demon Lover,* p. 11; Heinz Kohut, *The Analysis of the Self,* p. 116.

5. As recounted by Newman Ivey White in *Portrait of Shelley,* p. 203.

6. James Gilman, quoted by Humphry House in *Coleridge,* pp. 301-2.

Bibliography

PRIMARY SOURCES

Coleridge: Poetical Works. Edited by Ernest Hartley Coleridge. London: Oxford University Press, 1967.

The Collected Works of Samuel Taylor Coleridge. 16 vols. Vol. 14. Edited by Kathleen Coburn. Princeton: Princeton University Press, 1978.

PSYCHOANALYTIC SOURCES

Kernberg, Otto. *Borderline Conditions and Pathological Narcissism.* New York: Jason Aronson, 1975.

Kohut, Heinz. *The Analysis of the Self.* New York: International Universities Press, 1971.

CRITICAL SOURCES

Beres, David. "A Dream, a Vision, and a Poem: A Psychoanalytic Study of the Origins of 'The Rime of the Ancient Mariner,'" *International Journal of Psychoanalysis,* no. 32 (1951), pp. 97-116.

Fields, Beverly. *Reality's Dark Dream: Dejection in Coleridge.* Kent, Ohio: Kent State University Press, 1967.

Harding, D. W. "The Theme of the 'Ancient Mariner.'" In *Coleridge: A Collection of Critical Essays,* edited by Kathleen Coburn. Englewood Cliffs: Prentice-Hall, 1967.

House, Humphrey. *Coleridge.* London: Rupert Hart-Davis, 1967.

White, Newman Ivey. *Portrait of Shelley.* New York: Alfred Knopf, 1945.

Wormhoudt, Arthur, *The Demon Lover: A Psychoanalytic Approach to Literature.* 2d ed., 1949; reprint ed., Freeport, New York: Books for Libraries Press, 1968.

Karen Swann (essay date winter 1984)

SOURCE: Swann, Karen. "'Christabel': The Wandering Mother and the Enigma of Form." *Studies in Romanticism* 23, no. 4 (winter 1984): 533-53.

[*In the following essay, Swann examines Coleridge's treatment of gender identity in "Christabel." Swann contends that, while Coleridge's representations of femininity are largely drawn from gothic literature, his apparent ambivalence toward the behavior of his female protagonists, along with his sexually-charged portrayal of the relationship between Geraldine and Christabel, ultimately subvert many of the basic conventions of the genre.*]

The first questions Christabel asks Geraldine [in Coleridge's **"Christabel"**] refer to identity and origins: "who art thou?" and "how camest thou here?" Geraldine's response is oblique; in effect she replies, "I am like you, and my story is like your own":

> My sire is of a noble line,
> And my name is Geraldine:
> Five warriors seized me yestermorn,
> Me, even me, a maid forlorn:
> . . . .
> They spurred amain, their steeds were white:
> And once we crossed the shade of night.
> As sure as Heaven shall rescue me,
> I have no thought what men they be;
> Nor do I know how long it is

> (For I have lain entranced I wis)
> Since one, the tallest of the five,
> Took me from the palfrey's back,
> A weary woman, scarce alive.
> . . . .
> Whither they went I cannot tell—
> I thought I heard, some minutes past,
> Sounds as of a castle bell.
> Stretch forth thy hand (thus ended she),
> And help a wretched maid to flee.

> (ll. 79-104)[1]

Geraldine's tale echoes and anticipates Christabel's. Christabel is also first introduced as the daughter of a "noble" father; she, too, experiences things she "cannot tell," calls on Heaven to rescue her, crosses thresholds and falls into trances. But in contrast to the story **"Christabel,"** often criticized for its ambiguities, Geraldine's tale presents sexual and moral categories as unambiguous and distinct: villainous male force appropriates and silences an innocent female victim. This difference effects a corresponding clarification of genre. Geraldine translates **"Christabel"** into the familiar terms of the tale of terror.

Geraldine's translation would appear to establish the identity of the woman. Ultimately, however, her story complicates the issue of feminine identity by suggesting its entanglement, at the origin, with genre. How one takes Geraldine depends on one's sense of the "line" of representations she comes from. For Christabel, but also, for any absorbed reader of circulating library romances, Geraldine's story of abduction works as a seduction—Christabel recognizes Geraldine as a certain type of heroine and embraces her.[2] More guarded readers appropriate Geraldine as confidently as Christabel does, but they see her quite differently. Charles Tomlinson, for example, reads **"Christabel"** as "a tale of terror," but in contrast to Geraldine's own story casts her in the role of villain, while for Patricia Adair, Geraldine is betrayed by her very conventionality: she tells her story in "rather unconvincing and second-rate verse which was, no doubt, deliberately meant to sound false."[3] Geraldine is "false" because she comes from an ignoble line of Gothic temptresses, or, in the case of other critics, because she can be traced back to the ignoble Duessa and to a host of other predatory figures. Tellingly these sophisticated readers, who employ literary history to read Geraldine as a figure of untruth, are the worst ruffians—they either refuse to hear the woman's story of her own abduction, or assume that her protests are really a come-on.

Geraldine may be Christabel's ghost or projection as many critics have suggested, but only if we acknowledge that Christabel produces herself as a received representation—a feminine character who in turn raises the ghosts of different subtexts, each dictating a reading of her as victim or seductress, good or evil, genuine or affected. I will be arguing in this essay that **"Christabel"** both dramatizes and provokes hysteria. The poem explores the possessing force of certain bodies—Geraldine's, of course, but also bodies of literary convention, which I am calling "genres." Particularly in Coleridge's day, debates on literary decorum allowed the gendering of structure in a way that seemed to assuage anxiety about the subject's relation to cultural forms. Questions involving the subject's autonomy could be framed as an opposition between authentic, contained "manly" speech and "feminine" bodies—the utterly conventional yet licentiously imaginative female characters, readers, and genres of the circulating libraries. In **"Christabel,"** Coleridge both capitalizes on and exposes culture's tactical gendering of formal questions. The poem invites us to link the displacing movement of cultural forms through subjects to the "feminine" malady of hysteria and the "feminine" genres of the circulating library; at the same time, it mockingly and dreamily informs us that hysteria is the condition of all subjects in discourse, and that the attribution of this condition to feminine bodies is a conventional, hysterical response.

I

If Coleridge were thinking of dramatizing hysteria in a poem, he might have turned to Burton's account of "Maids', Nuns', and Widows' Melancholy" in *The Anatomy of Melancholy,* a book he knew well. According to Burton, hysterics "think themselves bewitched":

> Some think they see visions, confer with spirits and devils, they shall surely be damned, are afraid of some treachery, imminent danger, and the like, they will not speak, make answer to any question, but are almost distracted, mad, or stupid for the time, and by fits. . . .[4]

The malady befalls barren or celibate women; among these, Catholic noblewomen who are forced to remain idle are particularly susceptible. Most of the symptoms Burton catalogues are touched on in the passage quoted above. Hysterics have visions and are afraid "by fits"—the "fits of the mother" or womb ("the heart itself beats, is sore grieved, and faints . . . like fits of the mother" [p. 415]). The symptom which most interests Burton, though, is the inability of hysterics to communicate their troubles: they "cannot tell" what ails them. This fact becomes a refrain of his own exposition: "and yet will not, cannot again tell how, where, or what offends them"; "many of them cannot tell how to express themselves in words, or how it holds them, what ails them; you cannot understand them, or well tell what to make of their sayings" (p. 416).

They "cannot tell," and *you* cannot "well tell" what to make of them: the phenomenon of their blocked or incomprehensible speech seems to produce similar effects in the writer. And indeed, Burton's impetuous and fitful prose in many respects resembles the discourse of the

hysteric, into whose point of view he regularly tumbles ("Some *think* they see visions," but "they *shall* surely be damned" [my italics]). Far from resisting this identification, Burton makes narrative capital from the slippage, as here, when he allows himself to become "carried away" by sympathy for the Christabel-like afflicted:

> I do not so much pity them that may otherwise be eased, but those alone that out of a strong temperament, innate constitution, are violently carried away with this torrent of inward humours, and though very modest of themselves, sober, religious, virtuous, and well given (as many so distressed maids are), yet cannot make resistance . . .

and then, as if shaking off a "fit," comically pauses to reflect on his own indecorous "torrents":

> But where am I? Into what subject have I rushed? What have I to do with nuns, maids, virgins, widows? I am a bachelor myself, and lead a monastic life in a college: *nae ego sane ineptus qui haec dixerim,* I confess 'tis an indecorum, and as Pallas, a virgin, blushed when Jupiter by chance spake of love matters in her presence, and turned away her face, *me reprimam*; though my subject necessarily require it, I will say no more.
>
> (p. 417)

Protesting all the while his ignorance of women, the "old bachelor" coyly figures himself as a virgin whose body betrays her when desire takes her unawares. He also takes the part of the apparently more knowing and self-controlled Jupiter, but only to suggest that the latter's fatherly indifference is an act. For whether he is an artful or artless seducer, Jupiter himself appears only to rush into speech "by chance"—the "chance," we suspect, of finding himself in such close proximity to his virginal daughter. The woman whose desire is written on her body is like the man who makes love the "matter" of his discourse: both attempt to disguise desire, and become the more seductive when desire is revealed in the context of their attempts to suppress it.

The story of Pallas and Jupiter is placed at a strategic point in Burton's chapter. It punctuates his resolve to check the torrents of his narrative, a resolve immediately and engagingly broken when, more "by chance" than design, he finds he has to say something more ("And yet I must and will say something more"). This time he is prompted by his commiseration with all distressed women to launch an attack on "them that are in fault,"

> . . . those tyrannizing pseudo-politicians, superstitious orders, rash vows, hard-hearted parents, guardians, unnatural friends, allies (call them how you will), those careless and stupid overseers . . .

those fathers and parental substitutes (particularly the Church), who "suppress the vigour of youth" and ensure the orderly descent of their estates through the enforced celibacy of their daughters (p. 418). An "old bachelor" who leads a monastic life in a college; whose own discourse, like the discourse of the hysteric, seems to be the product of a strained compromise between lawless impulses and the claims of order; who might himself be said to be possessed by spirits and the dead language in which they wrote, ends his discussion of "maids', nuns', and widows' melancholy" by championing those who "cannot tell" against the ungenerous legislators of the world.

There are suggestive correspondences between Burton's chapter on hysteria and **"Christabel."** Christabel is a virtuous Catholic gentlewoman whose lover is away, possibly at the behest of her father, out of whose castle she "steals" at the beginning of the poem. Whether or not he is responsible for blighting love affairs,[5] Sir Leoline has affinities with both of Burton's father-figures: like the "pseudopoliticians" he is intimately linked with repressive law; like Jupiter, his relation to his daughter is somewhat suspect. Moreover, the poem's descriptions of Christabel's experiences—first with the possibly supernatural Geraldine and later, with a traumatic memory or scene which comes over her by fits and bars her from telling—and its insistent references to a "mother" who at one point threatens to block Geraldine's speech ("Off, wandering mother!" [l. 205]), follow Burton's account of the characteristic symptoms of hysteria. But Coleridge may have appreciated most the comic slippages in Burton's narrative between the slightly hysterical scholar whose business it is to "tell" and the women who are the matter of his discourse. When he came to write **"Christabel,"** Coleridge told the story through narrators who are as enigmatic as the women they tell about—we cannot "well tell" if they are one voice or two. More than any detail of the plot, the participation of these narrators in the "feminine" exchanges they describe, and the poem's playful suggestion that hysteria cannot be restricted to *feminine* bodies, marks the kinship of **"Christabel"** and Burton's text.

II

Who is Geraldine and where does she come from? Possibly, from Christabel. In the opening of the poem Christabel has gone into the woods to pray for her absent lover after having had uneasy dreams "all yesternight"—"Dreams, that made her moan and leap, / As on her bed she lay in sleep," we are told in the 1816 version of the poem. In the woods *two* ladies perform the actions of moaning and leaping which, yesternight, *one* lady had performed alone:

> The lady leaps up suddenly,
> The lovely lady, Christabel!
> It moaned as near, as near can be,
> But what it is she cannot tell—

> On the other side it seems to be,
> Of the huge, broad-breasted, old oak tree.

> (1816: ll. 37-42)

For a moment we, too, are in the woods, particularly if, like the poem's "first" readers, we already know something of the plot. Does "the lady" refer to Christabel or Geraldine? Is her leaping up the cause or effect of fright? The next lines supply answers to these questions, and as the scene proceeds "it" resolves into the distinct, articulate character Geraldine. For a moment's space, however, we entertain the notion that an uneasy lady leaped up suddenly and terrified herself.

Burton says of hysterics, "some think they see visions, confer with spirits and devils, they shall surely be damned." Geraldine is such a "vision." She appears in response to what Burton implies and psychoanalysis declares are the wishes of hysterics—to get around patriarchal law, which legislates desire. In the beginning of the poem Christabel "cannot tell" what ails her, but critics have theorized from her sighs that she is suffering from romance, from frustrated love for the "lover that's far away," for the Baron, or even, for the mother.[6] Geraldine, who appears as if in answer to Christabel's prayer, "steals" with her back into the castle, sleeps with her "as a mother with her child," and then meets the Baron's embrace, allows the performance of these wishes. Moreover, like an hysterical symptom, which figures both desire and its repression, Geraldine also fulfills the last clause of Burton's formula: although much is ambiguous *before* she appears, it is not until she appears that Christabel feels "damned," and that we are invited to moralize ambiguity as duplicity, the cause of "sorrow and shame" (ll. 270, 296, 674).

As well as answering *Christabel's* desires, however, Geraldine answers the indeterminacy of the narrative and the reader's expectancy. The wood outside the Baron's castle is not the "natural" world, as is often declared,[7] but a world stocked with cultural artifacts. Before Geraldine ever appears it is haunted by the ghosts of old stories: familiar settings and props function as portents, both for the superstitious and the well-read. The wood and the midnight hour are the "moment's space" where innocence is traditionally put to the test, or when spirits walk abroad; other details—the cock's crow at midnight, the mastiff's unrest, the contracted moon—we know to be art's way of signifying nature's response to human disorder. These so-called "Gothic trappings" ensnare us because they mean nothing ("Tu-whit, tu-whoo") and too much: like the sighs we seize on as evidence of Christabel's inner life, they gesture to an enigma, something as yet hidden from view. Geraldine makes "answer meet" to these suspensions of the narrative, not by providing closure, but by representing indeterminacy:

> There she sees a damsel bright,
> Drest in a silken robe of white,
> That shadowy in the moonlight shone:
> The neck that made that white robe wan,
> Her stately neck, and arms were bare;
> Her blue-veined feet unsandal'd were,
> And wildly glittered here and there
> The gems entangled in her hair.

(ll. 58-65)

Precipitating out of the Gothic atmosphere, Geraldine promises to contain in herself an entrapping play of surfaces and shadows; with her appearance suspense resolves into a familiar sign of ambiguity.

Geraldine is a fantasy, produced by the psychic operations of condensation and displacement. On the one hand, her function is to objectify: she intervenes in moments of interpretive crisis as a legible representation—a "vision," a story, and a plot. At the same time, though, she, the story she tells, and the plot she seems to set in motion are all displacing performances of ambiguities she might at first promise to "answer" more decisively. After she pops up, two women dramatize the implied doubleness of the daughter who "stole" along the forest keeping her thoughts to herself (l. 31). Very little else changes. Prompted by an uneasy dream one women "stole" out of her father's castle; two women return to it "as if in stealth" (l. 120), and by the end of Part I Christabel has simply resumed "fearfully dreaming," at least according to the narrator (l. 294). The spell that becomes "lord of her utterance" (l. 268) that night does no more than render explicit the inhibition of her "telling" already operative in the opening scene of the poem, where her silence was obscurely connected to the brooding, dreaming "lord" of the castle, the father who loved the daughter "so well." By the end of the poem we have simply returned to where we began: Christabel is "inly praying" once again, this time at the "old" Baron's feet, and once again Geraldine is on "the other side" (l. 614).

While it proposes an answer to the question "who art thou?" this reading only makes Christabel's second question to Geraldine more problematic: Geraldine is a fantasy, but she does not seem to "come from" any locatable place. The many source studies of the poem have shown that her origins are as much in literature as in Christabel: she first appears to the latter as a highly aestheticized object, and first speaks, many readers think to her discredit, in a highly encoded discourse. A material, communally available representation, she could have been dreamed up by any of the characters to whom she appears in the course of the poem—by the uneasy dreamer Christabel, but also by the Baron, into whose castle she steals while he is asleep, and, Christabel suggests, dreaming uneasily (l. 165), or by Bracy, whose dream of her seems to "live upon [his] eye" the next

day (l. 559). She could even be part of *our* dream. For in **"Christabel"** as in all of his poems of the supernatural, Coleridge plots to turn us into dreamers—to "procure" our "willing suspension of disbelief," our happy relinquishment of the reality principle. In **"Christabel"** as in dreams there is no version of the negative: questions raise possibilities that are neither confirmed nor wholly dismissed ("Is it the wind . . . ? / There is not wind enough . . ." [ll. 44-45]). Tags drift from one "lady" to another, suggesting the affinity of apparent adversaries; signs are familiar yet unreadable, laden with associations which neither exclude each other nor resolve into univocality.

Geraldine intervenes into these several dreamlike states as a figure of the imaginary itself—a figure whose legibility derives from its status within the symbolic order. She obeys the laws which structure all psychic phenomena, including dreams, jokes, and hysteria, the malady which allowed Freud to "discover" these very laws. The latter, however, do not explain why *particular* representations become collectively privileged. Why, at moments when they brush with the (il-)logic of the unconscious, do subjects automatically, even hysterically, produce certain *gendered* sights and stories?—produce the image of a radically divided woman, or of two women in each other's arms; and produce the story of a woman who seduces, and/or is seduced, abducted, and silenced by a father, a seducer, and/or a ruffian? This story, including all the ambiguities that make it hard to "tell," is of course the story of hysteria as told by Burton, and later, painstakingly reconstructed by Freud from its plural, displacing performances on the bodies of women. Even the common reader would know it, however, for it describes all the permutations of the romance plot—a form largely, but not exclusively, associated with a body of popular, "feminine" literature.

If a body like Geraldine's pops up from behind a tree when all the witnesses are in the woods, it is no accident: everyone thinks feminine forms appropriately represent the dangers and attractions of fantasy life. Coleridge, who dramatized the highly overdetermined romance/hysteria plot in **"Christabel"** and happily flaunted feminine bodies when it suited him, was no exception. But I want to argue, first by looking at his generic play, and then by examining his treatment of the family romance, that in **"Christabel"** he was also mockingly obtruding a conspiracy to view, allowing us to see "feminine" genre and gender alike as cultural fantasy.

III

"Christabel's" narrators are themselves hysterics. The poem's interlocutor and respondent mime the entanglement of Geraldine and Christabel—I call them "they," but it is not clear if we hear two voices or one. Like the women they describe, they are overmastered by "visions." Repeatedly, they abandon an authoritative point of view to fall into the story's present; or they engage in transferential exchanges with the characters whose plot they are narrating. In the opening scene, for example, one of them plunges into the tale to plead to and for Christabel: "Hush, beating heart of Christabel! / Jesu, Maria, shield her well!" As if she hears, a stanza later Christabel cries out, "Mary mother, save me now!" (ll. 53-54, 69). Further on, the sequence is reversed when the speaker seems to take up Christabel's speech. She has just assured Geraldine that Sir Leoline will "guide and guard [her] safe and free" (l. 110); although the narrators generally are not as trusting as Christabel, one seems inspired by her confidence to echo her, twice: "So free from danger, free from fear / They crossed the court: right glad they were" (ll. 135-36, 143-44).

These narrators create the conditions and logic of dream: like them, and because of them, the reader is impotent to decide the poem's ambiguities from a position outside its fictions. Furthermore, the poem's "fictions" seem to be about little else than these formal slippages. The repressed of **"Christabel"**'s dreamwork is almost too visible to be seen—not a particular psychic content but literary conventions themselves, like those which demand that narrators speak from privileged points of view, and important for this argument, bodies of conventions or "genres." **"Christabel"** obtrudes genre to our notice. The Gothic atmosphere of the first stanza, with its enumerations of ominously co-incident bird and clock noises, goes slightly bad in the second—partly because of the very presence of the shocking "mastiff bitch," but also because both mastiff and narrator become heady with coincidence: making answer to the clock, "Four for the quarters, and twelve for the hour . . . Sixteen short howls, not over loud," she becomes an obvious piece of Gothic machinery (ll. 10-13). A similar generic disturbance occurs between Part I, told more or less in the "tale of terror" convention, and its conclusion, which recapitulates the story in a new convention, that of sentimental fiction. Suddenly Christabel "means" "a bourgeois lady of delicate, even saccharine, sensibility": "Her face, oh call it fair not pale, / And both blue eyes more bright than clear, / Each about to have a tear" (ll. 289-91). As suddenly, the narrators are exposed in a desperate act of wielding genre, using convention to force legibility on a sight that won't be explained.

Once we become aware of these instabilities, no stretch of the poem is exempt. In life women might faint, dogs might moan, and fires might flare up without anyone remarking it; if these coincide in story, they mean something. When they coincide in the overloaded, tonally unsettling Part I of **"Christabel"** they simultaneously draw attention to themselves as elements of a code. Although we may think of genres as vessels which suc-

cessive authors infuse with original content, **"Christabel"**'s "originality" is to expose them as the means by which significance is produced and contained.

This analysis raises the issue of the generic status of **"Christabel."** What is its literary genre? But also, what genre of psychic phenomenon does the poem aspire to—is it like a dream, as we first proposed, or like a joke? The latter question may not immediately seem important, since jokes and dreams have so much in common: like hysteria, they work by condensation and displacement to bring the repressed to light.[8] But for the poem's first readers, at least, it clearly mattered which was which. The reviewers of 1816 fiercely protested the poem's "licentious" mixing of joke and dream, categories of psychic phenomena which they translated into literary categories: was **"Christabel"** a bit of "doggrel," a wild, weird tale of terror, or a fantastic combination of the two? (Modern readers, less tuned to genre play, have decided the question by not hearing the jokes.)[9] Coleridge's contemporaries recognized that jokes and dreams demand different attitudes: if one responds to **"Christabel"** as though it were just a wild weird tale, and it turns out to be a joke, then the joke is on oneself. **"Christabel"** frightened its reviewers, not because it was such a successful tale of terror, but because they couldn't decide what sort of tale it was.

"Christabel" made its first readers hysterical because it is not one genre or another but a joke on our desire to decide genre. As such, it turned a "merely" formal question into a matter of one upsmanship. Most of the critics responded by redirecting the joke, giving the impression that it was on the poem and the author. Coleridge, they claimed, mixed the genres of joke and dream, not as a joke, but in a dream. What is telling is their almost universal decision to recast these issues of literary and formal mastery into the more obviously charged and manageable terms of sexual difference. According to them, the poem was, after all, just one of those tales of terror which ladies like to read ("For what woman of fashion would not purchase a book recommended by Lord Byron?" asks the *Anti-Jacobin*[10]); the author, variously described as an "enchanted virgin," an "old nurse," a "dreamer"—by implication, a hysteric—simply could not control the discourses that spoke through him like so many "lords" of his utterance.[11]

Gendering the formal question, the reviewers reenact the scene of Geraldine's first appearance: then, too, a variety of characters responded to indeterminacy by producing a feminine body at once utterly conventional and too full of significance. In critical discourse as in fantasy life, it seems, feminine forms—the derogated genres of the circulating library, the feminized body of the author, or the body of Geraldine—represent the enigma of form itself. Female bodies "naturally" seem to figure an ungraspable truth: that form, habitually viewed as the arbitrary, contingent vessel of more enduring meanings, is yet the source and determinant of all meanings, whether the subject's or the world's.

Displacing what is problematic about form onto the feminine gender ultimately serves the hypothetical authenticity and integrity of masculine gender and "manly" language. Look, for example, at the opening lines of the passage Hazlitt selects as the only "genuine burst of humanity" "worthy of the author" in the whole poem—the only place where "no dream oppresses him, no spell binds him"[12]:

> Alas! they had been friends in youth;
> But whispering tongues can poison truth;
> And constancy lives in realms above;
> And life is thorny; and youth is vain;
> And to be wroth with one we love
> Doth work like madness in the brain.
> And thus it chanced, as I divine,
> With Roland and Sir Leoline.
>
> (ll. 408-15)

Hazlitt was not alone in his approbation: many reviewers of the poem quoted this passage with approval, and Coleridge himself called them "the best & sweetest Lines [he] ever wrote."[13] They are indeed outstanding—the only moment, in this tale about mysterious exchanges among women, when an already-past, already-interpreted, fully-breached male friendship is encountered. For those of us who don't equate "manliness" with universality and authenticity, this unremarked confluence of masculine subject-matter and "genuine" discourse is of course suspicious: it's not *simply* purity of style that made this passage the standard against which all other Christabellian discourse could be measured and found "licentious," "indecorous," "affected"—in short, effeminate.

But here, we are anticipated by the passage itself, which exposes "manliness" as a gendered convention. When the narrator begins this impassioned flight, we assume he speaks from privileged knowledge: why else such drama? Several lines later, though, he betrays that this is all something he has "divined," something that may have chanced. "Chancing" on a situation that really spoke to him—a ruined manly friendship—the narrator has constructed a "divination" based on what he knows—about constancy (it isn't to be found on earth), life (it's thorny), and youth (it's vain). Although he is more caught up in his speech than she, his voice is as "hollow" as Geraldine's. His flight or "genuine burst of humanity" is a fit of the mother, and a mocking treatment of manly discourse on the part of Coleridge, whose later accession to the going opinion was either a private joke or a guilty, revisionary reading of his licentious youth. If this tonal instability was lost on "**Christabel**"'s reviewers, it can only be because, like the narrator himself, they were reading hysterically: a "vision" of autonomous male identities caused them automatically to produce a set of received ideas about manly discourse.

"**Christabel**" exposes the conventionality of manly authenticity and the giddiness of manly decorum; in the same move, it suggests that attributing hysteria to feminine forms is a hysterical response to a more general condition. In the poem as elsewhere, "the feminine" is the locus of erotic and generic license: this can have the exciting charge of perversity or madness, or can seem absolutely conventional, affected. "**Christabel**" contrives to have these alternatives redound on the reader, who continually feels mad or just stupid, unable to "tell" how to characterize the verse at any given point. Here is Christabel "imprisoned" in the arms of Geraldine:

> With open eyes (ah woe is me!)
> Asleep, and dreaming fearfully,
> Fearfully dreaming, yet, I wis,
> Dreaming that alone, which is—
> O sorrow and shame! Can this be she,
> The lady, who knelt at the old oak tree?
> And lo! the worker of these harms,
> That holds the maiden in her arms,
> Seems to slumber still and mild,
> As a mother with her child.
>
> (ll. 292-301)

Geraldine's arms, the scene of the close embrace, and the conclusion as a whole, which recasts part I as a sentimental narrative—all in some sense work to imprison the significances of the text. Yet the scenario only imperfectly traps, and closes not at all, the questions which circulated through part I. Identity is still a matter of debate, and still hangs on a suggestively ambiguous "she" ("Can this be she?"). Even the women's gender identities and roles are undecidable, their single embrace "read" by multiple, superimposed relationships. Geraldine, a "lady" like Christabel, is also sleeping with Christabel; a "worker of harms," a ruffian-like assaultor of unspecified gender, she is also like a "mild," protective mother. If in keeping with the sentimentality of this section of the poem, the mother/child analogy is introduced to clean up the post-coital embrace of the women, it redounds to suggest the eroticism of maternal attention. These ghostly stories, all already raised in the text of Part I, work to create the compellingly charged erotic ambivalence of "**Christabel**"—ambivalence about becoming absorbed into a body which may be "the same" as one's own, or may belong to an adversary, a "worker of harms," and which is associated with, or represented by, the maternal body.

Christabel's situation, including, perhaps her feminine situation, is contagious. The narrator, who seems overmastered by the very spell he is describing, can only direct us to a "sight" ("And lo!"), the significance of which he "cannot tell." His speech breaks down before the woman who is "dreaming fearfully, / Fearfully dreaming," before the form that may conceal "that alone, which is."

The narrator circles round but cannot tell the enigma of form, of the body or sign that is at once meaningless and too full of significance. His own discourse repeats the paradox of the "sight," and becomes a locus of the reader's interpretive breakdown. His lament strikes us as coming from "genuine" distress at the remembrance of Christabel's horrible predicament. But particularly in context, the lines—

> With open eyes (ah woe is me!)
> Asleep and dreaming fearfully,
> Fearfully dreaming, yet, I wis,
> Dreaming that alone which is—

raise the ghost of a sentimental style that as a matter of course suppresses all distressing sights and implications, while coyly directing the reader to what's not being said. To decide the narrator's credibility—is he bewildered or merely "affected," effeminate; could he even be camping it up?—it is necessary to bring genre to bear, to decide whether Gothic or sentimental romance is a determining convention. This is simultaneously to recognize that the voice we have been hearing cannot be authentic—if mad, it speaks in the tale of terror's legislated mad discourse; that genres are constructs which produce meaning for the subject; and that genres, like fantasy, reproduce the indeterminacies they at first appear to limit or control. Our relation to Christabel's narrators is like theirs to Christabel: the enigmatic form of their discourse turns us into hysterical readers, subject to the possessing, conventional bodies that that discourse raises in us.

IV

"Christabel"'s romance plot suggests that our culture's hysterical relation to feminine forms—or its hysterical feminization of form—has its origins in the family romance. The poem invites us to distinguish between paternal and feminine orders of experience. The father's sphere is the Law—a legislative, symbolic order structured according to a divisive logic:

> Each matin bell, the Baron saith,
> Knells us back to a world of death.
> These words Sir Leoline first said,
> When he rose and found his lady dead:
> These words Sir Leoline will say
> Many a morn to his dying day!
>
> And hence the custom and law began
> That still at dawn the sacristan,
> Who duly pulls the heavy bell,
> Five and forty beads must tell

> Between each stroke—a warning knell,
> Which not a soul can choose but hear
> From Bratha Head to Wyndermere.
>
> (ll. 332-44)

The Baron's response to a traumatic event is to commemorate it. Every day, punctually, he relives the loss of "his lady," spacing and controlling the recurrences of his sorrow. By institutionalizing the observance, he turns a private grief into a public ceremony. The compulsive becomes the compulsory: the sacristan "duly" pulls his bell, and "not a soul can choose but hear."

Separation is something of a habit with the Baron. Three other times during the poem he attempts to stabilize his relation to a disturbing person or event by opening out a "space between" (l. 349). In the past, the narrator "divine[s]," Sir Leoline had been "wroth" with Lord Roland (ll. 412-13). Wrath and the threat of madness precipitate a separation which leaves each scarred (ll. 421-22). The speaker "ween[s]" these scars will never go away and seems to guess right, since the Baron's memory of that friendship revives when Geraldine appears on the scene and tells her story:

> Sir Leoline, a moment's space,
> Stood gazing on the damsel's face:
> And the youthful Lord of Tryermaine
> Came back upon his heart again.
>
> (ll. 427-30)

For a second time the Baron experiences maddening confusion, here obscurely related to the striking together of "youthful lord" and "damsel," known and new, past and present, revived love and recognized loss. Once again he becomes wrathful ("His noble heart swelled high with rage" [l. 432]), and introduces a "law" of deathly separation: he will "dislodge" the "reptile souls" of Geraldine's abductors "from the bodies and forms of men" (ll. 442-43). Finally, for a third time the Baron meets "[swelling] rage and pain" (l. 638) and "confusion" (l. 639) with division: in the last stanza of the poem, "turning from his own sweet maid," he leads Geraldine off (l. 653).

The Baron's customs and laws divide and oppose potential "sames" or potentially intermingling parts of "the same." In contrast, femininity bewilders the narrator because one can never tell if identities and differences are constant, "the same": "Can this be she, / The lady, who knelt at the old oak tree?" (ll. 296-97); "And Christabel awoke and spied / The same who lay down by her side— / Oh rather say, the same . . ." (ll. 370-71). Tales, glances, and verbal tags circulate between Christabel and Geraldine throughout the poem: each is a "lady," each makes "answer meet" to the other. These exchanges could be said to obey the law of "the mother." Her function has puzzled some critics, who have found it hard to reconcile her angelic guardianship of Christabel with her likeness to Geraldine.[14] Coleridge, however, intended **"Christabel"**'s mother to be a punning, rather than a stable, character. Referring simultaneously to the malady of hysteria, the womb whose vaporish fantasies were thought to block the hysteric's speech, and the female parent, "the mother" is an exemplarily vagrant sign, whose shifts of meaning obey the very "laws" which determine the characteristic displacements of hysteria.

The mother escapes the Baron's divisive categories. Neither opposites nor "the same," Geraldine and Christabel are identically self-divided, each subject to a "sight" or "weight" whose history and effects she "cannot tell." The Baron might attempt to redress such duplicity by dislodging offending "souls" from the "bodies and forms" they occupy. The "mother," however, is neither spirit nor body. Dying the hour Christabel was born, she inhabits her daughter as an already-dislodged form, or in psychoanalytic terms, as an alien internal entity or fantasy.[15] At times Christabel feels this "weight" as the fully external, "weary weight" of Geraldine (l. 131), at times as an inner "vision" which "falls" on her. Where the Baron imagines parenthood bestowing on him all the privileges of ownership (*"his own* sweet maid"), possession by the "mother" breaks down privilege, including that of an original, controlling term. The "weight" or "sight" is both within and without, both the fantasy that cannot be told and the representation that makes it legible.

The Baron also remembers the mother by a weary weight, but he gets someone else to heft it: every morning his sacristan "duly pulls the heavy bell" which "not a soul can choose but hear." Obviously the organizations we have been calling the father's and the mother's exist in some relation to one another. A feminist reading of this relation might charge the Law with producing hysterics, women who "cannot tell" what ails them because the Law legislates against every voice but its own. The *Baron* stifles the daughter by his oppressive, deathly presence: stealing back into his castle with Geraldine, Christabel passes his room "as still as death / With stifled breath" (l. 171). "The mother"—the malady of hysteria—symptomatically represents the daughter's internalization of patriarchal law. This reading is supported by Burton, who laid the daughter's troubles on the pseudopoliticians, and by Geraldine, who identifies the curse that prevents Christabel from "telling" as masculine prohibition: the sign which seals them both up is a "lord" of utterance and an "overmastering" spell.

A plot as popular as this one, however, is probably overdetermined. **"Christabel"** invites at least two other readings of the relation between hysteria and the law. First, that hysteria produces the Law: repeatedly, the Baron opens out a space between himself and perceived threats in order to "shield" himself from overmastering confusion or madness. Second, that the Law is just one form of hysteria. According to the narrator, the Baron's cutting efforts leave him internally scarred. The space between is also a mark within, from which no "shield" can protect him. Like the hysteric he is always vulnerable to a recurrence of "swelling" confusion, a revival of the already-internalized mark, to which he responds with another legislative cut. The Law resembles hysteria in its defenses and effects: it attempts to decide irresolution by producing something "on the other side," and its cuts leave the legislator subject to recurrences.[16]

"Christabel" invites us to decide there is only one significant "sight"—Geraldine's bosom; and to infer that it is women who can have no discourse within the law. But at the same time it allows us to see hysteria as the coincidence of superimposed fields: as a metaphysical condition of the speaking subject, as a malady historically affecting women who suffer under patriarchal law, and as a fantasy of patriarchal culture—a representation which figures the subject's alienation from the symbolic order on the bodies of women. Christabel and Geraldine, who enter the Baron's castle while he sleeps, enact their 'own' fantasy and his dream.

To account for the power of this dream, we might try tracing it back to the origin. At the moment the Baron is about to cast off his only child, a protesting narrator invokes the mother:

> Why is thy cheek so wan and wild,
> Sir Leoline? Thy only child
> Lies at thy feet, thy joy, thy pride,
> So fair, so innocent, so mild;
> The same, for whom thy lady died!
> O by the pangs of her dear mother
> Think thou no evil of thy child!
> For her, and thee, and for no other,
> She prayed the moment ere she died:
> Prayed that the babe for whom she died,
> Might prove her dear lord's joy and pride!
>   That prayer her deadly pangs beguiled,
>   Sir Leoline!
>   And wouldst thou wrong thy only child,
>   Her child and thine?

(ll. 621-35)

These lines refer us back to the opening of part II, where custom and law were instituted in response to a "lady's" death. This "lady" was also a mother, the narrator reminds us here; her death was simultaneous with a birth, her "pangs"—at once labor and death pangs—were beguiled by prayers, her suffering mingled with joy.

The Baron's law is an interpretive moment: he decides to read the occasion as a death only. His action anticipates his later disavowal of Christabel, which occurs almost as if in response to the narrator's reminder that she is "[thy lady's] child and thine"; and it resonates with Geraldine's response when, diverted from her plot for a moment as love for Christabel and longing for the mother rise up in her, she collects herself by flinging off the latter ("Off, wandering mother!" [l. 205]). In each case, a feminine body comes to represent a threat to the wishfully autonomous self. **"Christabel,"** with its punning allusions to "the mother," invites us to speculate that the "law" of gender, which legislates the systematic exclusion of feminine forms, is connected to the experience of maternal attention. In this view, representations of feminine bodies as sites of non-self-identity all take revenge on the maternal body, which, in its historical role as the first "worker of harms," is the agent through which identity is constituted on a split. The mother "wounds" with her love, constituting the subject as originally, irreducibly divided, marked by the meanings and desires of the Other.

This reading, however, may play into the hands of the patriarchs. Historically, they have used maternity to ground a question of origins; they have used gender to naturalize what is in fact a function of genre—of constructs which are only meaningful within an already-originated cultural order. To suggest that misogyny can be traced to experience of the mother, to attribute it to blind revenge for the subject's condition, is to give it a sort of tragic weight. It's also to forget the tone of **"Christabel."** The urbane ironist and even the apparently less controlled patriarch of that poem suggest that the projects of culture are at once more political and more finessed than what we've just described. The Baron's exclusion and readmission of women amounts to a kind of play. He guards his fantasied autonomy by opening out spaces between—between bodies, genders, generations. He lives in a deathly, "dreary" world, until his "dream" of radically split women reanimates it with desire. With the appearance of Geraldine, the threat of abduction—a threat for every subject in discourse—can be rewritten, flirted with, in dreams of seduction which repeat, at a safe distance, the "confusions" of first love. That night, a fantasized feminine body—single yet double, like the mother's when pregnant with child, or the hysteric's when inhabited by the vaporish conceptions of an origin which is never *her* origin—performs exchanges with another body like her own. These women figure but only imperfectly contain impropriety, allowing its threats and attractions to return to the Baron's world as a taint. Geraldine moves from Christabel's bed to his arms, supplanting the daughter who had supplanted the mother; for a moment, she produces in him the illusion that one can "forget . . . age" (l. 431) and all that has intervened, and recapture the fantasied past, when exchanges traversed the laws of self-identity and even the laws of gender.

V

Coleridge, who capitalizes on the potential of feminine bodies to eroticize masculine discourse, is himself a pseudopolitician; at the same time, like the hysteric he seems to counter the Law. Drawing together matters of form and desire, his discussion of meter in the Preface to **"Christabel"** nicely illustrates this double relation to the symbolic order. On the one hand, the principle the author lays down is strikingly consonant with the Baron's tolling "custom and law":

> I have only to add that the metre of Christabel is not, properly speaking, irregular, though it may seem so from its being founded on a new principle: namely, that of counting in each line the accents, not the syllables. Though the latter may vary from seven to twelve, yet in each line the accents will be found to be only four. Nevertheless, this occasional variation in number of syllables is not introduced wantonly, or for the mere ends of convenience, but in correspondence with some transition in the nature of the imagery or passion.

"Christabel"'s metrics are figured in the poem as the ringing of the Baron's clock and matin bell. Coleridge's "principle," however, is designed to accommodate, not just the Baron, who would institute unvarying repetition, but also the movement of desire, "transition[s] in the nature of the imagery or passion."

Coleridge's meter, or more broadly, his joking treatment of gender and genre, can thus be seen as a compromise between the Law's reificatory strategies and the potentially wanton, disruptive liveliness of passion—a compromise which ultimately benefits the ironist who acquiesces to the laws he also exposes as interested. Yet Coleridge's play, which mocks the law of gender/genre by too faithfully reinscribing its conventions, also opens up the possibility of a more radical collapse between the positions of patriarch, hysteric, and ironist: it exposes the wantonness of the Law, and allows one to discover the laws of desire; it suggests that the Law itself may be inseparable from the operations of desire. When Bracy the Bard hears the Baron's deathly matin bell, he declares, "So let it knell!"—

> There is no lack of such, I ween,
> As well fill up the space between.
> In Langdale Pike and Witch's Lair,
> And Dungeon-ghyll so foully rent,
> With ropes of rock and bells of air
> Three sinful sextons' ghosts are pent,
> Who all give back, one after t'other,
> The death-note to their living brother;
> And oft too, by the knell offended,
> Just as their one! two! three! is ended,
> The devil mocks the doleful tale
> With a merry peal from Borodale.

(ll. 348-59)

NINETEENTH-CENTURY LITERATURE CRITICISM, Vol. 177

Bracy's accession echoes Christabel's words at the end of Part I, when she announces her obedience to Geraldine's request: "So let it be!" (l. 235). Bracy is in league with the hysteric, and Coleridge with them all—and all submit to the Law. When Christabel steals into her father's house with Geraldine, we "cannot tell" if her silence is the absolute solicitude of a dutiful daughter or a sign of subversive intent: does hysteria come from too much or too little respect for the father? In a sense it doesn't matter, since the effects are the same for the Baron and us: her very unreadability draws out and mocks his and our possessing desire to decide meaning. Her strategy resembles Bracy's—apparently without doing anything himself, he simply "lets" the law mock its own voice. It echoes through hollow, rent spaces, which in dutifully returning its knell, elude its efforts to control the significance of an event. "Telling" notes become the occasion of ghostly echoes, which in turn generate Bracy's lively ghost stories; finally, as if by way of commentary, the "devil" makes merry mockery of the whole phenomenon. The passage describes in little the narrative tactics of **"Christabel."** By too-dutiful accession to the laws of gender and genre, **"Christabel"** exposes their strategies to view, letting the Law subvert itself.

Notes

1. Quotations from "Christabel" and its preface are taken from *Coleridge's Poetical Works,* ed. Ernest Hartley Coleridge (1912; rpt. Oxford: Oxford U. Press, 1969).

2. See Susan Luther, "'Christabel' as Dream Reverie," *Romantic Reassessments* 61, ed. Dr. James Hogg (Salzburg: Institut fur Englische Sprache und Literatur, Univ. Salzburg A5020, 1976), for the argument that Christabel is a reader of romances.

3. "'Christabel'" (1955), rpt. in *The Ancient Mariner and Other Poems: A Casebook,* eds. Alun R. Jones and William Tydemann (London and Basingstoke: Macmillan, 1973), p. 235; *The Waking Dream: A Study of Coleridge's Poetry* (London: Edward Arnold, 1967), p. 146.

4. *The Anatomy of Melancholy,* ed. Holbrook Jackson (New York: Random House-Vintage Books, 1977), p. 416. Future references to this edition appear in the text.

5. In "Sir Cauline," the ballad from which Coleridge took the name Christabel, this is the case; that Christabel's lover is dismissed by her father.

6. See for example Roy Basler, *Sex, Symbolism, and Psychology in Literature* (New Brunswick: Rutgers U. Press, 1948), p. 41; Gerald Enscoe, *Eros and the Romantics* (The Hague and Paris: Mou-

ton, 1967), pp. 44-45; Jonas Spatz, "The Mystery of Eros: Sexual Initiation in Coleridge's 'Christabel,'" *PMLA* 90 (1975), 112-13; Barbara A. Schapiro, *The Romantic Mother: Narcissistic Patterns in Romantic Poetry* (Baltimore and London: Johns Hopkins U. Press, 1983), 61-85.

7. See for example Enscoe, p. 43; John Beer, *Coleridge's Poetic Intelligence* (London and Basingstoke: Macmillan, 1977), p. 187; and H. W. Piper, "The Disunity of *Christabel* and the Fall of Nature," *Essays in Criticism* 28 (1978), 216-27.

8. Or so Freud claims in *Jokes and their Relation to the Unconscious,* chapter VI ("Jokes, Dreams, and the Unconscious"), trans. James Strachey (New York: Norton, 1963), pp. 159-80.

9. For examples of the reviews, see *The Romantics Reviewed,* ed. Donald H. Reiman (New York and London: Garland, 1977), II, 666, 239. Modern critics sometimes notice tonal or generic instability as "falls" into Gothic trickery, into caricature of the Gothic, or into sentimentality; see for example Max Schulz, *The Poetic Voices of Coleridge* (Detroit: Wayne State U. Press, 1963), pp. 66-71; and Paul Edwards and MacDonald Emslie, "'Thoughts all so unlike each other': The Paradoxical in *Christabel,*" *English Studies* 52 (1971), 328. The latter suggest these discrepancies are intended to shock.

10. *Romantics Reviewed* I, 23.

11. *Romantics Reviewed* I, 373; II, 866; II, 531. I discuss these reviews more fully in my essay "Literary Gentlemen and Lovely Ladies: The Debate on the Character of 'Christabel,'" forthcoming in *ELH.*

12. *Romantics Reviewed* II, 531.

13. *Collected Letters of Samuel Taylor Coleridge,* ed. Earl Leslie Griggs (Oxford: Clarendon Press, 1956-71), III, 435.

14. See for example Abe Delson, "The Function of Geraldine in *Christabel*: A Critical Perspective and Interpretation," *English Studies* 61 (1980), 130-41; and Enscoe, p. 46.

15. My understanding of fantasy here follows that of Jean Laplanche and J.-B Pontalis in their "Fantasy and the Origins of Sexuality," *International Journal of Psycho-Analysis* 49 (1968), 1-18.

16. My argument here is indebted to Richard Rand's discussion of the ubiquitous "mark" in "Geraldine," *Glyph* 3 (1978), 74-97.

Jane Chambers (essay date September 1984)

SOURCE: Chambers, Jane. "Leoline's Mastiff Bitch: Functions of a Minor Figure in 'Christabel.'" *English Language Notes* 22, no. 1 (September 1984): 38-43.

[*In the following essay, Chambers analyzes the symbolic importance of the mastiff bitch in "Christabel."*]

Since the initial publication of Coleridge's **Christabel** in 1816, critics have generally de-emphasized, or disregarded (if not indeed ridiculed) the minor figure of Sir Leoline's mastiff bitch. William Hazlitt, for example, in his *Examiner* review of June 2, 1816, sarcastically dismissed the dog as "a sort of Cerberus to fright away the critics."[1] Although some modern scholars have noted that the dog can be linked to the poem's larger concerns or its characters, critical attention to the mastiff's role in the poem has been limited and sporadic.[2] Most scholars give the figure of the sleeping dog little more than a passing glance. Many readers probably see the mastiff much as Rosemarie Maier has defined it, as little more than an "ugly," somewhat "comic" animal, whose only important function is merely to betray the presence of Geraldine.[3]

The mastiff is, however, an excellent example of Coleridge's skillful use of imagery in **Christabel.** The two passages depicting the dog (ll. 6-13 and 145-153) effectively function to introduce or to advance major ideas in the poem. To look closely at the role of the mastiff in the poem is in fact to understand more clearly not only aspects of the poem's chief characters and central themes, but also the operation of the symbol in Coleridge's poetry.

The opening lines of **Christabel** introduce a basic question—what is time?—that is a part of the poem's larger question: what is reality? Together with the cock and the owls, the mastiff focuses our attention on these interrelated questions. That these simple creatures tell time by different clocks introduces a central point in the poem: that reality, even on such a seemingly simple level as time, is not only complex and arbitrarily defined, but also, even within an agreed-upon context, subject to misinterpretation. The poem opens with the narrator's apparently simple declaration "'Tis the middle of night," but this statement is complicated in the following phrase, "by the castle clock."[4] To the owls (whose clock is the moon) it is something like "the middle of day." The cock, a domestic bird, exhibits confusion about the time. Awakened by the owls, it begins to crow, as if the time were dawn (the sun is its clock). Momentarily, the cock believes with the owls that it is day, not night. In a minor way, the cock's confusion here anticipates Christabel's confusion later concerning that much more complicated reality, Geraldine, who will appear to be "day" but will in reality be "night."

Sir Leoline's old dog, apparently hearing neither the owls nor the cock, responds in her sleep to the human definition of time, signified by the clock's chiming, and "She maketh answer to the clock" (l. 9) just as the cock has answered the owls. But whereas the cock's statement of time was false, the dog's statement is true. The dog's "Sixteen short howls" (l. 12) declare that it is, by humanity's clock, shortly after midnight when Christabel encounters Geraldine at the oak tree. That the dog is correct about this reality of time in the human context suggests that she will also be right about Geraldine's reality later. The dog's "angry moan" (l. 148) will define Geraldine as a force that humanity defines as evil, thus a threatening intruder.

That the mastiff hears the clock and then "sees" Geraldine while being asleep introduces yet another central idea emphasized in the poem: that reality may be perceived on the unconscious level. The dog's sleeping response to that "lady strange" (l. 71) that Christabel meets in the forest thus anticipates the dream-visions of Christabel and Bard Bracy, more complex yet similarly unconscious ways of knowing the reality that is Geraldine. Thus the "angry moan" passage is more than a bit of Gothic trapping or a mechanical response to the owls. It is the initial instance in the poem of the operation of the unconscious in the process of comprehending reality.

The mastiff is also used to define the world of the poem, which includes both the natural world and the domestic and the inhabitants of this collective environment. Two key adjectives, or their equivalents, define the poem's world: "old" and "cold." Both of these traits are directly or indirectly associated with the dog, who is "toothless" (l. 7), "old" (l. 145), and lies "in moonshine cold" (l. 146). Everything in Christabel's world is old—from the "huge, broad-breasted, old oak tree" (l. 42) to the castle with its "murky old niche in the wall" (l. 163) wherein hangs Leoline's disused shield. And every character present in the poem except Christabel is old. The poem's initial imagery (including the dog) establishes that there is but one world in **Christabel** and that all things in it—animal, human, or vegetative—are or will eventually be old, diseased, enfeebled, or in some sense impotent. The oak has fallen prey to parasitic moss and mistletoe; the mastiff is now a harmless and impotent watchdog; and Sir Leoline is old and "weak in health" (l. 118). Thus the dog is one of several minor images in the early part of the poem that establish Christabel's as "a world of death" (l. 333)—the Fallen world, dominated by disease, decay, confusion, isolation, and helplessness in the face of evil. As Richard H. Fogle says, **Christabel** is "after its kind of story of the Fall of Man . . . not the story of the original Fall, . . . but of the consequences of the Fall for every mortal."[5]

To be old in Christabel's world is to be weak. But there is one exception: Geraldine. Although appearing to be young and vital like Christabel, she too is old and cold, as evidenced by her bosom, which Christabel will recall in a "vision of fear" in Part II:

> Again she saw that bosom old,
> Again she felt that bosom cold.

(ll. 457-458)

Geraldine is apparently not subject to time's ravages in the same way as are the other inhabitants of this world, from oak tree to dog to man. She appears able somehow to defeat, or at least to postpone, age, and perhaps even death, by sapping the vitality of others. By preying upon Christabel (and later, Leoline), she is able to sustain an outward appearance of youth and beauty, the illusion that she is as young and vital as her hostess.

It has been argued that we see the mastiff as symbolically linked with Geraldine,[6] but the differences between the two are much more striking than any supposed similarities, and the one word ("old") which links them applies to all entities in the poem's world except Christabel. It is important to notice that "cold" is associated with both the dog and Geraldine, but that the "moonshine cold" (l. 146) in which the dog lies sleeping apparently enfeebles it, while reviving Geraldine: underscoring the dog's "toothlessness" while "resurrecting" Geraldine. Although Geraldine is barefoot and is wearing only a sleeveless silk robe (whereas Christabel has on a cloak), Geraldine appears perfectly comfortable in this cold atmosphere. That coldness is her natural element (whereas it is for others a source of discomfort) suggests that Geraldine represents that one entity that thrives in the Fallen world: evil.

MacDonald Emslie and Paul Edwards have noted a "pattern of sound-references" in the poem, starting with the dog's howling and the initial presentation of Geraldine "as a sound."[7] They have said these sound-references bind the poem together, but have not explained how, or why. Perhaps the chief point emerging from consideration of these sound references is that sound, like time, is an aspect of reality more complex than it appears to be. Sounds heard must be interpreted and may easily be misunderstood, as demonstrated by the cock's confusion in the poem's opening lines. The poem's narrator speculates about the dog's howling in response to the clock—"Some say, she sees my lady's shroud" (l. 13)—and about the dog's "angry moan" (l. 148), stating "Perhaps it is the owlet's scritch" (l. 152) that causes it. The narrator is seeking a symbolic level of meaning in the dog's "language." The two passages concerning the mastiff therefore serve to introduce yet another problem related to the problem of comprehending reality in *Christabel*: that of comprehending language. The poem's protagonist, Christabel, is soon to be confronted with Geraldine's language, which is fluid, complex, a mixture of the modern and the antique, and

bewildering; and which includes moans and abrupt fluctuations in tone as well as words. For example, in the bedchamber scene to follow, Christabel will have to try to reconcile her initial image of Geraldine as "maiden most forlorn" (l. 195) with Geraldine's "altered" and "hollow" voice (ll. 204 and 210). Christabel's struggle to interpret Geraldine's language is foreshadowed in the narrator's struggle to interpret the dog's language.

Finally, the mastiff bitch serves to introduce the topic of communication of experience, another central idea in the poem. The dog's angry moan as Geraldine and Christabel cross the courtyard is perhaps an attempt to communicate some truth about Geraldine that the dog unconsciously knows. But this attempt fails to reach both the narrator and Christabel. That the dog cannot tell what she knows foreshadows Christabel's dilemma in Part II of the poem, where Christabel (by then aware of Geraldine's true nature) vainly tries to tell Leoline what she knows:

> 'By my mother's soul do I entreat
> That thou this woman send away!'
> She said: and more she could not say:
> For what she knew she could not tell,
> O'er-mastered by the mighty spell.

(ll. 616-621)

Christabel's own "angry moan" in this scene is as badly misunderstood by her father as was the dog's moan misunderstood by the narrator. Thus, just as the mastiff was unable to protect Christabel the night before, Christabel is unable to shield Leoline now. She has herself now been rendered as "toothless" as the watchdog by Geraldine's spell that binds her speech.

Analysis of these functions of Leoline's mastiff bitch shows this minor figure to be more important in the poem than has been recognized previously. The two passages depicting the mastiff help to establish or clarify such central themes as the nature of reality (including time, place, and personage), the role of the unconscious in locating reality, and the problems of interpreting and communicating experience. In *The Statesman's Manual*, in 1816 (the year in which *Christabel* was published), Coleridge wrote about the nature of the literary symbol:

> a Symbol is characterized by a translucence of the Special in the Individual or of the General in the Especial or of the Universal in the General. Above all by the translucence of the Eternal through and in the Temporal. It always partakes of the reality which it renders intelligible; and while it enunciates the whole, abides itself as a living part of that Unity, of which it is the representative.[8]

Leoline's "toothless mastiff bitch" in *Christabel* is precisely the kind of literary symbol that Coleridge was describing here, partaking of "the Reality" explored in the poem, enunciating "the whole," acting as "a living part of that Unity, of which it is the representative." Although a minor figure in the poem, the mastiff is an excellent example of "the Especial" that demonstrates "the Universal" in *Christabel.*

Notes

1. Rev. of *Christabel; Kubla Khan, A Vision: The Pains of Sleep,* by Samuel Taylor Coleridge, in *Coleridge: the Critical Heritage,* ed. J. R. de J. Jackson (London, 1970), p. 206.

2. See, for example, J. B. Beer's *Coleridge the Visionary* (London, 1959), p. 186, and Beverly Fields' *Reality's Dark Dream: Dejection in Coleridge,* Kent Studies in English, 5 (Kent, Ohio, 1967), pp. 68-69. Typically, chapter-length studies of *Christabel* minimize or even ignore the role of the mastiff, and virtually no essay-length studies of this minor figure have been produced.

3. "The Bitch and the Bloodhound: Generic Similarity in 'Christabel' and 'The Eve of St. Agnes,'" *JEGP* [*Journal of English and German Philology*], 70, No. 1 (Jan. 1971), 62-75. Maier's title suggests a closer consideration of the mastiff than is actually given in the article.

4. Lines 1-2. All quotations here from *Christabel* are from the poem as it appears in *Coleridge: Poetical Works,* ed. Ernest Hartley Coleridge (London, 1912; rpt. 1969), pp. 215-236. Subsequent references are given in parenthetical notes.

5. *The Idea of Coleridge's Criticism,* Perspectives in Criticism, 9 (Berkeley, 1962), pp. 149-150.

6. Fields, in *Reality's Dark Dream* (cited above) argues that the dog is "the double for Christabel's dead mother" and thus "the mother of Geraldine," but this argument is based on invalid assumptions and illogical leaps, such as that both the dog and Geraldine communicate with the dead mother of Christabel. The narrator's comment that "Some say" the dog sees the dead mother (l. 13) is no proof that the dog does, anymore than that Geraldine *seems* to address and dismiss the dead mother means that in fact she *does.* In this poem so firmly grounded upon the contrast between reality and appearances, it is important that we make such distinctions.

7. "The Limitations of Langdale: A Reading of *Christabel,*" *Essays in Criticism,* 20, No. 1 (Jan. 1970), pp. 58-61. As I have demonstrated, the motif of sound actually begins in the poem's opening lines, with the references to the owls and the cock.

8. Quoted in *Inquiring Spirit: A New Presentation of Coleridge from His Published and Unpublished Prose Writings,* ed. Kathleen Coburn (Toronto, 1979), p. 104.

Margery Durham (essay date 1985)

SOURCE: Durham, Margery. "The Mother Tongue: 'Christabel' and the Language of Love." In *The (M)other Tongue: Essays in Feminist Psychoanalytic Interpretation,* edited by Shirley Nelson Garner, Claire Kahane, and Madelon Sprengnether, pp. 169-93. Ithaca: Cornell University Press, 1985.

[*In the following essay, Durham offers a psychoanalytical reading of "Christabel," discussing the symbolic importance of female identity in the poem.*]

At the time of its publication a reviewer declared *Christabel* "the most obscene Poem in the English language." Coleridge replied, "I saw an old book in Coleorton in which the Paradise Lost was described as an 'obscene poem,' so I am in good company."[1] In its portrayal of innocence mixed with depravity, *Christabel* draws readers into its gothic atmosphere, and there it leaves them, intrigued and bewildered. Like most readers, I am puzzled by the way in which Coleridge clouds the innocence of his central female figure. The ambivalence he suggests can be understood, I think, by reading the poem in the light of certain passages in the poet's notebooks, where his entries around the time he composed *Christabel* define topics in which he was deeply, even passionately interested. Most relevant to the poem are his speculations about associative thought, as it might function in the origin of both speech and moral choice. In the notebooks Coleridge speculates that language may develop from the physical contact between infant and mother. For Coleridge, culture begins at the breast, and language is indeed the mother tongue.

A considerable body of psychoanalytic theory recognizes the infant's relationship with the mother as the source of symbol formation and therefore of language and culture, and since Coleridge himself is credited with coining the word "psycho-analytical," it seems all the more reasonable to inquire whether any of the current theories can yield insights into his poem.[2] Since the time of Freud and his earliest associates, Melanie Klein and those who have developed the implications of her work have further advanced our understanding of the individual's relationship to culture, and the tensions they describe in this relationship are, I believe, analogous to the ambivalence one finds in *Christabel.* Klein's definition of the alternative ways, which she terms "manic" and "depressive," by which these tensions are resolved also helps us to interpret Coleridge's work. I will therefore compare the poem with both Coleridge's notebook speculations and Klein's more systematically developed theory. Relevant to this comparison is the poem's thematic resemblance, in its consideration of a fall from innocence, to *Paradise Lost,* and this parallel provides a mythic resolution of the dilemmas, logical and psychological, which Coleridge depicts.

We must avoid, however, ascribing to Coleridge any intention of assigning women a significant role in high culture. His idea of women was the conventional one of his time, expressed, for example, in his praise of an acquaintance "married to the woman of his choice, of whose mind his own had been the mould & model."[3] It seems likely that *Christabel*'s analysis of mental processes is primarily a self-examination. Coleridge's notes on his own nightmares describe aspects of the poem, and the confused feelings of both victimization and guilt which these "bad most shocking Dreams" left with him is recorded in his admittedly confessional poem **"The Pains of Sleep,"** first published with *Christabel*:

> Deeds to be hid which were not hid,
> Which all confused I could not know
> Whether I suffered, or I did:
> For all seemed guilt, remorse or woe,
> My own or others still the same
> Life-stifling fear, soul-stifling shame.
> . . . .
> But wherefore, wherefore fall on me?
> To be beloved is all I need,
> And whom I love, I love indeed.[4]

In connecting his personal fear and guilt with the general human condition he chose a female persona, perhaps to emphasize the passivity which he indeed felt, but which in a male hero could have been unacceptable to his readers.

The Problem: Symbolization and Its Discontents

Klein began her work with the common psychoanalytic assumption that all formation of symbols (all fantasy, all conceptualization, and therefore all mental relationship to the outside world) is a projection of the infant's sense of the mother's body. Ernest Jones had pointed out that nonmaternal experience can provide a pleasure similar in quality to that received from the mother. Then, when access to the original pleasure is blocked, the infant can redirect its desire to the analogous experience. Cradling and suckling thus replace the womb. These pleasures can yield to the enjoyment of solid food, and in time to babbling, to speaking, even to writing poetry. From this redirection Klein reasoned not only that the outside world is "the mother's body in an extended sense," but also "that symbolism is the foundation of all sublimation and of every talent, since it is by way of symbolic equation that things, activities and interests become the subject of libidinal phantasies."[5] From the symbolization of infantile conflict and desire in children's play and in art, she developed her theory of reparation, according to which civilization actively remodels the world into a sublimated version of the infant's original pleasure.

Klein also found that the procedure could go wrong, and it is here that her theory first illuminates *Christabel.* If the original source of pleasure fails and no analogous equation has been made, then the former pleasures become equated with potentially analogous ones within a category of unfulfillment and therefore of pain. The child then withdraws from both the painfully tantalizing mother and the analogous outside world, and the result is paranoid delusion and inhibition, including as one extreme form the speech-inhibiting psychosis now termed autism. Putting the matter rather too simply: feeding problems can thus create stuttering and, at last, silence. Most important for our study of *Christabel,* Klein maintains that neurosis and sublimation are inversions of each other and, she adds, "for some time the two follow the same path" from original pleasure to possible alternatives and back—for better or worse—to the child. Emphasizing the necessity for ambivalence toward the mother, Klein wrote, "It is a question of a certain optimum balance of the factors concerned. A sufficient quantity of anxiety [that is, the mother's absence or other failure to satisfy the infant] is the necessary basis for an abundance of symbol-formation and of phantasy; an adequate capacity on the part of the ego to tolerate anxiety is essential if anxiety is to be satisfactorily worked over."[6]

At best, however, poetry, music, politics—all the civilized arts—become the means of creating, on the cultural level, a maternal equivalent. As we reshape the world to our satisfaction, Klein maintained, we try to recreate the life-giving environment that a mother can no longer provide, and our standard of comparison (outside the womb) is our recollection of the earliest moments at the breast. Aesthetic balance may suggest such analogous pleasure, and I shall argue that *Christabel* also symbolizes the conflicts within the reparative struggle.

In Coleridge's own time, David Hartley studied the process by which infantile pleasure may develop into complex, socially integrated action. Although Coleridge was at first enthusiastic, he eventually rejected Hartley's explanation of mental life by the association of ideas, because automatic association seemed to grant human nature only the impoverished innocence of the machine. On March 16, 1801, he wrote to his friend Thomas Poole:

> If I do not greatly delude myself, I have not only completely extricated the notions of Time, and Space; but have overthrown the doctrine of Association, as taught by Hartley, and with it all the irreligious metaphysics of modern Infidels—especially, the doctrine of Necessity.—This I have *done*; but I trust, that I am about to do more—namely, that I shall be able to evolve all the five senses, that is, to deduce them from *one sense,* & to state their growth, & the causes of their difference—& in this evolvement to solve the process of Life & Consciousness. . . . I shall . . . take a Week's respite; & make Christabel ready for the Press.[7]

This letter has been taken to suggest that "to a certain extent" *Christabel* actually provided little if any respite from philosophical speculation, that in Coleridge's mind one task depended on the successful completion of the other, and that the poem might have been finished if a psychology alternative to Hartley's had taken shape.[8] One cannot claim that the poet resolved the problem abstractly; in that regard the triumphant assertion recorded less reality than hope. Nor did Coleridge feel that he had finished *Christabel*; even after its publication in 1816 he had plans for the poem's completion.[9] Nevertheless, it is possible to discern a way in which the poem deals successfully with complex connections among sense, feeling, and moral choice—relationships that Coleridge felt Hartley had failed to account for, and that involve both the symbol formation and the ambivalence described by Klein.

To readers of the poem, Christabel's name might well suggest Christ and his prototype Abel, the victim of Cain, while also presenting the belle as Christ. Of course both connections suggest innocence. While praying outside her father's castle one night, the heroine mysteriously meets the unfortunate Lady Geraldine, with whom she hospitably shares her bed. Here she sees Geraldine's wound, the "mark of . . . shame" and "seal of . . . sorrow"; and the woman's "touch of pain" produces a "vision of fear" in nightmares that disturb Christabel's sleep until they yield to better dreams. Meanwhile Geraldine casts a spell on the girl's speech.[10]

The next morning, although Christabel remembers her "bad most shocking dreams" and their ugly cause, she cannot articulate them. Her father receives Geraldine as the daughter of the estranged companion of his youth, Sir Roland. The spell takes effect; the girl's speech degenerates into a hiss, and her eyes seem to resemble those of a snake. Geraldine now seems likely to replace the girl's dead mother, and as father and "mother" recede, Christabel is left alone, virtually homeless, as Geraldine had been the night before. Part II concludes with a brief meditation on the frequent mixture of "rage and pain" in words of love. This final, apparently irrelevant musing, I believe, actually reminds us of the poem's central tragic idea: the origin of speech and of all achievement in the mother's touch, the rage at not possessing her completely, and the guilt incurred by either remaining with her (rejecting growth and life) or leaving her, which, as I hope to make clear later, is seen as a kind of destruction. Relevant also, I shall argue, is what Klein terms the "manic" evasion of that rage and guilt: despising the mother and by extension all women, and ignoring them.

Coleridge, I suggest, set out to discover poetically how the mind can work by a process of pleasurable association and yet be responsible for good and evil. The poem's solution is to show that this formulation of the problem is, at last, superficial, by placing it within the symbolic pattern of myth. Without evading the significant facts of desire, dependency, separation, anxiety, and rage, the poem places them in a perspective within which such apparently irreconcilable terms as "association" and "free will" or "responsibility" become irrelevant. By changing from the prose of his notebooks to the language of poetry, Coleridge develops his thought successfully, concentrating on the phenomenon of separation, first from the mother, then from both parents, and at last from life itself. If we read the poem and the notebooks together, we can see that he is concerned with separation at four stages: first in weaning; then in the development of speech with its awareness of separate yet related speaker and hearer; third, in sexual maturity and the assumption of responsibility for one's own and the next generation; and finally in death, the inevitable consequence of individuality. The dilemmas that this process involves are tragically resolved, I believe, by the myth into which the poem emerges, and it is thus that Coleridge discovers for himself what he later describes as the nature and function of poetry: the portrayal of paradox, which we feel emotionally as ambivalence. In doing so, he seems also to discover another function of art: the refinement of simple, instinctual drives into mentally nourishing symbols, in this case literary ones. The poet's notebooks introduce us to his speculations, which, while they help us to interpret the poem, nevertheless find their own resolution only in poetic form.

THE NOTEBOOKS: ABSTRACT LANGUAGE ENCOUNTERS PARADOX

In the notebooks Coleridge indeed traces human mental development from "one sense." Referring to his infant son he says, "Hart[ley] seemed to learn to talk by touching his mother."[11] Elsewhere he locates the origin of mental life in one specific version of touch, the baby's nurture at the breast: "Babies touch *by taste* at first,— then about 5 months old they go from the Palate to the hand—& are fond of feeling what they . . . taste / Association of the Hand with the Taste—till the latter by itself recalls the former."[12] When we take note of these connections, the poem echoes loudly: "In the touch of this bosom there worketh a spell, / Which is lord of thy utterance, Christabel!" (ll. 267-68). The entry concerning speech is dated November 18, 1800; Coleridge had finished Part II of *Christabel* in October and wrote the letter to Poole the following March, about one week before he made the entry concerning taste. Although the spell is cast in Part I, written in 1798, we can see that these later psychological observations were on his mind at least by the time he completed Part II. In fact, there is evidence of some such connections as early as 1795.[13]

Several years after he completed what we now have of the poem, we find him still interested in the way in which ideas associated in the mind seemed to undergo a qualitative change, after the manner of elements combined chemically:

> Scratching & ever after in certain affections of the Skin, milder than those which provoke Scratching a restlessness for double Touch / Dalliance, & at its height, necessity of Fruition.—Fruition the intensest single Touch, &c &c &c; but I am bound to trace the Ministery [*sic*] of the Lowest to the Highest, of all things to Good.[14]

We can identify here an extension of the associations that begin orally, then supposedly develop into manual touching and further into speech.[15] Here in 1804 we see that Coleridge viewed sexuality as an intensification and complication of that sense of touch whose awakening he had described in 1800 as occurring at the breast. The development of sexuality is thus implicitly related to touch and therefore ultimately to what both the notebooks and the poem combine as the touch (and taste) of the breast, the same source as that of speech.

Unfortunately that which is reassuringly present can be lost. For Coleridge, the loss of the maternal touch causes fear, guilt, and finally death. When lost or withdrawn, the mother's influence seems actually destructive:

> Contact—the womb—the amnion liquor—warmth + touch / —air cold + touch + sensation & action of breathing—contact of the mother's knees + all those contacts of the Breast + taste & wet & sense of swallowing—Sense of diminished Contact explains the falling asleep— / this *is* Fear.

Again:

> To *fall* asleep—is not a real *event* in the body well represented by this phrase—is it in *excess,* when on first *dropping* asleep we *fall* down precipices, or *sink* down, all things *sinking* beneath us, or *drop down*.[16]

As one might expect from these notebook entries, the sleep that concludes Part I of **Christabel** is at first a "vision of fear" (l. 453). There the effect of losing the mother is portrayed not as passive suffering, however, but as active and intentional persecution by the Lady Geraldine, like the paranoid fantasies that Klein describes. Not only is the heroine's protective mother absent, but the wrong "mother" is there (l. 301). I suggest that Geraldine represents, among other things, Mother Nature, with her implacable demand that we leave our "real" mother, mature, and die. Much more thought must be given Geraldine, but at present we can speculate that the connection between touch and pain in the poem may well be the same one Coleridge records in the notebooks: the connection between love and loss. The pain that he portrays in **Christabel** is indeed the pain of loss; it culminates in that moment when Sir Leoline turns his back on "his own sweet maid" (l. 653). Indeed, loss and absence dominate the poem from the start. Christabel goes out at first to pray for her absent lover (ll. 25-30); her father commemorates every morning his wife's (her mother's) death (ll. 332-44).

Only a slight shift in viewpoint changes the terms of this problem from those of happiness vs. fear to those of innocence vs. guilt. The origins of such complex activities as sexual love and speech in the simple sensations of taste and touch lead Coleridge to ethical questions. Christabel's sleep with Geraldine is vicious and holy by turns. Geraldine tells Christabel that their night together will control the girl's speech (ll. 267-68), and the means of this control is guilt. The guilt results from Christabel's terrible visions (ll. 292-97), shows itself in her snakelike appearance and her hissing (ll. 589-612), and seems apparent (though we feel it is not real) in her final isolation (ll. 621-55).

In the notebooks, too, touch and its mental associations bring Coleridge to the question of moral choice. There he sees moral choice as emerging from the perpetual opposition between conscious will and sensuous inclination. He sometimes argues that without conscious interference physical impulses must inevitably cause evil. And conversely, at least once he seems to identify all virtue with the deliberate frustration of desire. On the other hand, Coleridge also observes instances in which what he terms "streamy association" or "Volition" accomplishes positive ends. But such exceptions make him uneasy, and we are left at last with his perception that automatic association is in itself amoral yet must answer to moral demands. In these speculations he can do no more than define that self-contradiction, but we can be grateful that he does not flinch from his difficult position. The constantly self-contradictory argument makes the notebook entries troublesome to follow, yet a careful look at them helps us to appreciate Coleridge's poetic achievement. In one entry dated December 26, 1803, he insists that the role of conscious will is to frustrate an impulse that is harmful or base:

> I resisted the Impulse—Why? because I could not endure my after Consciousness. Hence derive the immense Importance to Virtue of increasing and *enlivening* the Consciousness & press upon your own mind & as far as in you lies, on others, the connection between Consciousness & Conscience / the mutual Dependence of Virtue & the Understanding on each other.

Two days later he writes in the same vein, applying his idea yet more widely:

> I will at least make the attempt to explain to myself the Origin of moral Evil from the *streamy* Nature of Association, which Thinking = Reason, curbs & rudders / how this comes to be so difficult / Do not the bad Passions in Dreams throw light & shew of proof upon this Hypothesis?—Explain those bad Passions: & I shall gain Light, I am sure—A Clue! A Clue!

But next he confronts an example that threatens his hoped-for conclusion: "Take in the blessedness of Innocent Children, the blessedness of sweet Sleep, &c &c &c: are these or are they not contradictions to the evil from *streamy* association?" Then the longing for a coherent philosophy leads him close to misanthropy as he adds, "I hope not."[17]

Hoping the worst of human nature is not Coleridge's ruling passion, and in this same month he uses a water metaphor to describe beneficent sleep:

> O then as I first sink on the pillow, as if Sleep had indeed a material *realm,* as if when I sank on my pillow, I was entering that region & realized Faery Land of Sleep—O then what visions have I had, what dreams— the Bark, the Sea . . . all the shapes & sounds & adventures made up of the Stuff of Sleep & Dreams, & yet my Reason at the Rudder / . . . & I sink down the waters, thro' Seas & Seas—yet warm, yet a Spirit.[18]

Kathleen Coburn points out disguised puns on the word "breast" occurring elsewhere in this entry.[19] A preoccupation with the breast in connection with sleep, one that whimsically or otherwise Coleridge disguised, takes us back to Christabel's night with Geraldine. And the connection thus noted between the breast and "Reason" refers us to that source of all mental action in the "one sense" of taste.

In the notebooks, therefore, we see two purposes that nullify each other. We have the poet's "Hope of making out a radical distinction between . . . Volition & Free Will or Arbitrement, & the detection of the Sophistry of the Necessitarians / as having arisen from confounding the two." At the same time (and in the same entry) we see the opposite intention "to trace the Ministery . . . of all things to Good."[20] If free will differs from common association in a "radical" way, however—that is, at its very root—then the lowest does not minister to the highest. The question is how mental association can produce both moral vision and nightmare:

> What is the height, & ideal, of mere association?— Delirium.—But how far is this state produced by Pain & Denaturalization? And what are these?—In short, as far as I can see anything in this Total Mist, Vice is imperfect yet existing Volition, giving diseased Currents of association, because it yields on all sides & *yet* is—So think of Madness.[21]

When Coleridge translates this problem into artistic expression, poetic language and form (by their very nature, he later believed) resolve this dilemma. The contradiction he observes in human nature becomes the stuff of tragedy, that condition in which impulses good in themselves unfold naturally yet lead inevitably to disaster. The first impulse he considers in ***Christabel*** is that of dependence on the breast, that is, on the mother. This initial dependency proves to be the psychological origin of poetry and myth. As Coleridge develops his symbol of the lost paradise, the breast becomes a metaphor for the entire nourishing environment, some loss of which occurs at each stage of individual growth,

with a resultant increase in one's sense of vulnerability and isolation and therefore (however irrationally) of guilt. The breast symbol and its related suggestions in the poem therefore require a yet more careful look.

THE WOUNDED BREAST: THE TERRORS IN "SPLITTING"

Geraldine's curse specifies, as we have seen, the relation between breast and speech:

> "In the touch of this bosom there worketh a spell,
> Which is lord of thy utterance, Christabel!
> Thou knowest to-night, and wilt know to-morrow,
> This mark of my shame, this seal of my sorrow;
>   But vainly thou warrest,
>   For this is alone in
>   Thy power to declare,
>   That in the dim forest
>   Thou heard'st a low moaning,
> And found'st a bright lady, surpassingly fair;
> And didst bring her home with thee in love and in charity,
> To shield her and shelter her from the damp air."

> [ll. 267-78]

From her first appearance the poem portrays Geraldine as motherly. She appears behind "the huge, broad-breasted, old oak tree" (l. 42), and other references to motherhood occur here as in the prayer "Mary mother, save me now!" (l. 69). As they sleep, Coleridge compares the women to "a mother with her child" (l. 301). We resist the identification that he suggests because Geraldine perverts the touch of reassurance into one that creates horror and guilt. She is an evil, substitute mother—a wicked stepmother. The horrible visions that follow proceed from neither Geraldine nor Christabel alone, but from a particular, painful aspect of the mother-child relationship, the aspect of inevitable separation.

At the same time, however, an equally dismaying difficulty is perceived in the opposite impulse toward identification. In Part II the curse makes Christabel resemble Geraldine, as a child resembles its mother. But what aspect does the girl assume? Not that of the beautiful lady or of the protective mother, but of the hissing, dully malevolent snake (ll. 457-59, 583-612). Geraldine's serpentine qualities are obvious (ll. 583-87). Yet there are other ways in which to curse besides making one's victim resemble oneself. Perhaps the resemblance tells us of some latent and disturbing identification between the heroine and this aspect of the mother, which the curse merely completes and reveals. Coleridge seems to have used the spell not to create something new and antithetical to its victim's nature, but to make evident and perhaps distort or exaggerate what is already there.

The night's visions result in a new understanding on Christabel's part, sexual in nature but also recalling, at least insofar as the poem reflects Coleridge's mind, "all those contacts of the Breast + taste & wet & sense of swallowing." We are shown a state of mind in which feelings are not distinct. Genital sexuality is by no means the exclusive issue here; it is scarcely distinguished as sexuality, not because Coleridge shrank from the truth but because he evokes in this scene a mental state that reaches from adulthood back to the time in which sensations have not been clearly differentiated. The latent sexuality is mingled with equally strong impulses: toward plain animal nurture in one direction and toward that more distinctively human activity of speech in the other. In the poem these connections work against the heroine in a way that corresponds to the moral doubts that Coleridge expressed in the notebooks.

Psychoanalytic theory helps us to understand this pattern of ambivalence: of mixed love and fear, of simultaneous victimization and guilt. The night with Geraldine obviously suggests oedipal identification, which we must consider later. But the notebook entries on touch as the origin of speech lead us to Klein's research in preoedipal fantasy. She held that, whether resolved positively or negatively, those moments of frustration first create fantasies of persecution by an agent of evil, who unpredictably and terrifyingly replaces the superficially identical agent of good. The mother—more specifically, the concept of "breast"—is split into contrasting opposites. From this "splitting" into "good" breast and "bad" breast Klein derives her term for this early stage, calling it the "paranoid position."

These concepts may help explain the sharp dichotomy between good and evil found in melodrama and fairy tale, including within the latter category *Christabel*. Each of us has a wicked stepmother; she is that mother who denies us some pleasure; archaically, Klein maintained, she is the breast we could not perpetually possess. As Bruno Bettelheim remarks, "The typical fairy-tale splitting of the mother into a good (usually dead) mother and an evil stepmother serves the child well. . . . The fantasy of the wicked stepmother not only preserves the good mother intact, it also prevents having to feel guilty about one's angry thoughts and wishes about her."[22] This splitting into "good mother" and "bad mother" is an extension of what Klein defined as the "paranoid-schizoid position" in which the infant fantasies a "good" available breast and a "bad" or otherwise unsatisfying one. The child's first worries "go back beyond the beginnings of his understanding of speech." Klein observed that in response to inevitable dissatisfaction, infants, lacking intellectual concepts in which to formulate questions, lacking words in which to express them, and unable to understand the words of others, generate "an extraordinary amount of hate." The infant then at least partially turns this hatred against itself, in the fantasy of a persecuting breast.[23]

Here again is that "contact—the womb—amnion liquor—warmth + touch . . . all those contacts of the Breast + taste & wet & sense of swallowing," the loss of which, even in sleep, is to Coleridge "falling" and "Fear." Christabel's need and love for her mother focus, as Klein also discovered, on the breast. The breast and the woman who provides it indeed feed our mental as well as physical life. They may become hateful because we desire them yet cannot always and wholly possess them; we can fear the mother because we need her so much. In her analysis of children Klein found that the infant fantasies devouring its mother, emptying her so as to keep her forever. Geraldine's mutilated bosom ("and half her side" [l. 252]) therefore suggest the infant's cannibalistic fantasy as well as a sexual wound; to the latter the lady's abduction before we meet her (recalled in ll. 81-99) corresponds.

Like the splitting into "good" breast and "bad" breast and the start of symbol formation which that splitting entails, the poem's sexual—or to be more precise, genital—significance concerns life's requirement that one become independent and create an identity of one's own, that one relinquish the parental touch and recreate it symbolically elsewhere. But with that separation comes pain, anger, and finally death. Coleridge's metaphor for this predicament is Christabel's adolescence. She is old enough to leave her father; in fact, she is betrothed. Therefore it is while she prays for her beloved that she meets Mother Nature, the ambiguous Lady Geraldine, who seems to represent birth and growth, maturity and death.

When one relinquishes dependency in adolescence one paradoxically "touches" one's parents even more intimately than before: one assumes their identity as potentially a parent oneself and as a mortal being. Where the old intimacy brought reassurance, this later identification brings pain. Small wonder, then, that the heroine abhors what she sees in Geraldine: the wound demonstrating the body's vulnerability and therefore bringing that mingled awareness of life and death which maturity entails (ll. 250 and following). Besides reflecting the infant's fantasy, in which the mutilated breast horrifies, Christabel's "vision of fear" thus seems to include both intimations of genital sexuality and a premonition of the ultimate separation, that of death.

Manic Evasion vs. Mythic Resolution

As in Klein's theory, then, death real or fantasied may well be the source of the poem's horror. Death is indeed the event on which Coleridge focuses his study of guilt. Here, in what Klein defined as the "depressive position," the breast's taste and touch have to do with moral choice. In Klein's view, the infant's fantasies of "good breast" and "bad breast" gradually yield to a perception of the mother herself, a person by whom the baby can be both satisfied and pained. This realization comes when the child relinquishes the conviction that either itself or anything outside itself can provide constant and total pleasure. With that disappointment comes sorrow, hence Klein's term "depressive." There also arises guilt, from the impression of having destroyed the good with the bad in those earlier dreams (which seemed to the baby real acts) of aggression against the breast. Finally comes the desire to repair that damage, whence springs the impulse to preserve and satisfy the mother and also to recreate the mother symbolically in the rest of the world. "The acceptance of psychic reality involves . . . the lessening of splitting. . . . It means the acceptance of the idea of separateness—the differentiation of one's own self from one's parents, with all the conflicts that it implies. It also involves, as part of reparation, allowing one's objects to be free, to love and restore one another without depending on oneself."[24]

Besides the certainty of death, which accompanies this independence, there comes another realization, equally dismaying. By maturing, one actually replaces one's parents and apparently consigns them to irrelevance, symbolically also, then, to death. D. W. Winnicott, who has developed Klein's theories, states the problem as follows: "If, in the fantasy of early growth, there is contained *death,* then at adolescence there is contained *murder.* . . . Growing up means taking the parent's place. *It really does.* In the unconscious fantasy, growing up is inherently an aggressive act. And the child is now no longer child-size." This fantasy, he continues, may be inverted to provoke persecution, much as Christabel may be said to assist, however unconsciously, in her own rejection.[25]

Coleridge focuses our attention on death through yet another fantasy—not Christabel's this time, but her father's. Christabel tells us that her mother "died the hour that I was born" (l. 197). Some measure of guilt is implied by that statement. We feel it even though, rationally considered, Christabel is no more guilty than any other mother's child. That is, however, precisely the point: rationality has no exclusive province in the mind, any more than it has in external circumstance. In the mind, fantasy and fear impel us toward neurosis as well as toward balance, toward guilt as well as toward creative reconstruction. And as Klein describes, at times the two paths are the same.

Sir Leoline is the victim of neurosis, fixing his kingdom upon the fact—even the moment—of his wife's death. Part II of the poem begins:

> Each matin bell, the Baron saith,
> Knells us back to a world of death.
> These words Sir Leoline first said,
> When he rose and found his lady dead:
> These words Sir Leoline will say
> Many a morn to his dying day!
>
> And hence the custom and law began
> That still at dawn the sacristan,

> Who duly pulls the heavy bell,
> Five and forty beads must tell
> Between each stroke.
>
> [ll. 332-42]

With the perception of radical ambivalence characteristic of this poem, Coleridge uses the identification between mother and daughter to condense into one moment events usually separated by a lifetime, and thus to posit nature's paradox: that the joy in a new life implies, because it must someday confront, the sorrow of death. By his decree the Baron then attempts to create a world in which death is the only reality. Yet to do so requires the banishment of birth and growth. In such a world no one fully lives, but no one grieves because there is no joy to lose. This is very like the unproductive "manic evasion" of death and grief which Klein described. In its poverty the Baron's artificial kingdom is enviably if perversely under control. It is a civilization whose discontents are accepted, even worshiped, in which life and living women are out of place. Here mourning is really what Freud elsewhere described as melancholia. In Klein's terminology, it is the persistence of splitting and the identification of culture literally with the harsh, depriving alternative to satisfaction, the absence of woman and of that pleasure of which she is both source and symbol.

Klein held that this archaic splitting, though never wholly given up, does not dominate the healthy personality. As we have seen, she believed that in order even to enter the oedipal stage, one must see the parents as persons separate from oneself, capable of actions good, bad, and indifferent to oneself, yet also trusted and indeed loved. When she thus claimed that guilt for the fantasied destruction of the mother precedes and actually mitigates the aggression of the Oedipus complex, she was repudiated by Freud. Defended to some extent by Ernest Jones, she upheld the principles by which she had challenged psychoanalytic orthodoxy, and thereby prepared the way for such later theorists as Winnicott to claim that civilization is not wholly sadistic, but mediates between the archaic fantasies of absolute good and absolute evil. The symbolic re-creation of the mother becomes a means of union with her, accepted sorrowfully for what it is—and for what she is—loved but impermanent, intimate with us but free from our absolute control.[26]

The blending of good and evil is presented as confusion in *Christabel.* To understand it we do best to heed what may be the poem's one authoritative voice, that of Bracy the Bard. Bracy mocks the Baron's morbid religiosity, as does another strange company. "Three sinful sextons' ghosts" send back their own knell to meet the sacristan's tune, and they are often followed by "a merry peal" from the "devil" himself. Furthermore, hearing the devil's laughter, Geraldine "rises lightly from the bed" (ll. 345-63).

Bracy has had his own vision of fear in a dream of

> That gentle bird, whom thou dost love,
> And call'st by thy own daughter's name—
> Sir Leoline! I saw the same
> Fluttering, and uttering fearful moan.
> . . . .
> I stooped, methought, the dove to take
> When lo! I saw a bright green snake
> Coiled around its wings and neck.
> Green as the herbs on which it couched,
> Close by the dove's its head it crouched;
> And with the dove it heaves and stirs,
> Swelling its neck as she swelled hers!

[ll. 532-54]

"Christabel with Geraldine!" one wants to say, and the poem indeed involves Christabel intimately with the witch, as the dove is involved with the snake. Yet although at first glance Christabel's identity seems restricted to the dove, that attribution is made by her father, the Baron, who may not have interpretive authority. It may be that, more precisely, the dove and serpent together form one image for the mixed qualities of guilt and innocence in the suffering and contagion that afflict both women. If so, we can understand the exact form of the witch's curse, which takes effect a few lines after Bracy reports his dream (ll. 583-606). Here we learn that Christabel "passively did imitate" Geraldine's serpent-like qualities (l. 605), that is, the horrifying or "fallen" aspect of nature; both this event and Bracy's dream thus recall and interpret Christabel's sleep with Geraldine.

Two conflicting interpretations of Bracy's dream point up this implication of the one woman with the other. Bracy himself plans to cure the evil by oral magic, "with music strong and saintly song" (l. 561). The Baron, however (like any ordinary person, perhaps), thinks Bracy is quixotic. Sir Leoline uses only common practical sense: "With arms more strong than harp or song, / Thy sire and I will crush the snake!" he assures Geraldine (ll. 570-71). His interpretation of the dream is univocal and straightforward. But I believe that Coleridge here rejects the terms of chivalric romance, in which good defeats evil when the knight beheads the dragon. He works with the knowledge that physical force cannot eradicate evil from the world because evil never really appears in a melodramatic distillation. It may be illuminating to assume that the fallible Baron, whose rejection of Christabel later we perceive as a mistake, reads Bracy's dream mistakenly, too. He cannot, after all, "crush the snake" without also killing the dove. Only "song"—that is, art—can comprehend the problem as a paradox, and in so doing constructively contain its conflict.

It seems that Bracy's dream, like the poem itself, resumes Coleridge's inquiry at the point where it is left in "Total Mist" in the notebooks. If the dream presents one ambiguous symbol and not two simple opponents, then the dove and serpent finally represent the tangle of impulses in human minds and hearts. Univocal, abstract language misrepresents this confusion for the sake of logical order, and we must always effect a compromise between the confusion encountered in life and the logical constructs by which we try to manipulate the world. On the other hand, iconic, equivocal language in dreams, poetry, and myth faithfully represents human ambivalence and paradox, but therefore requires logical interpretation through the media of analysis and criticism. As both poet and literary theorist Coleridge came to understand this relationship—indeed, it was he who explained it to us. When the poem is read with these ideas in mind, *Christabel* implicitly emphasizes the inadequacy of abstract language and connects an overconfidence in logic (the Baron's clear-cut dualism) with the failure to perceive the fact that identifying real people with absolutes of good and evil is a projection of archaic splitting.

Like Bracy's account of his dream and like the words described in the poem's Conclusion, the dialogue between the tolling bell and its mocking echo is an example of expression whose meaning is not obvious or straightforward. In this manner the poem dramatically presents the confusion between good and evil which we have traced in the notebooks.

This blending illustrates one step by which the mind attunes itself to reality. It is what Geraldine requires of Christabel, even to the extent of alienating the girl from her father and from her illusion of immortality. Through the deliberate confusion of good with evil Coleridge prepares to consider the nature of art, using the ambiguous figure of Geraldine to save the Baron from his paralyzing resignation. The wounded lady, evidently tolerated and perhaps approved by heavenly powers (ll. 226-32), shows us that we need not be paralyzed, only, like her, badly scarred, or like "Clubfoot" (Oedipus), crippled.

Yet one must resist the opinion that whatever is, is right. In the poem, the concept of corruption contains both its moral and its physical meanings. Helpless victim though she may be, Geraldine perpetuates misery, imparts (perhaps unwillingly) the curse. As Mother Nature she is fallen, deadly, in league with the Devil, even while she bears her sad disfigurement. In secular terms she is both the victim of death (since nature is what dies) and its cause. Even if we admit that Christabel, being natural, is corruptible by herself, Geraldine precipitates and epitomizes that condition. She is everyone's tragic flaw, as Christabel is our image of innocence (and at last, beyond the scope of our present study, of redemption).

Christabel resists identification with the lady. "This woman send away!" she cries out (l. 617). By speaking against "this woman" (which is really "this womanhood"), she tries to preserve her father's kingdom as she has known it. Ironically, just at this time her father breaks his own law, takes Geraldine to himself, and rejects his daughter, who has now offended against two laws that are mutually exclusive, contradictory, and hence the cause of inevitable guilt. One is that of her father, who would erect a civilization resistant to time, growth, and change. Within the perspective of the Baron's fears all nature, Christabel included, is guilty because it leads to death. Since death is indeed implicit in growth and change, even in birth itself, the Baron is half right. But the poem does not approve his answer. Nature's own law opposes his arrangements, requiring Christabel to mature and eventually to die. Sharing her father's view, Christabel protests against nature and against "this woman" whom she has come to resemble, through whom she participates in nature's fallen state. To refuse natural growth, however, is precisely her father's error, and so, with cruel irony, Coleridge has the Baron change his mind. As Sir Leoline departs with Geraldine, he refuses to accept the implications of his own regime. He leaves Christabel to bear the hopelessly contradictory imperatives of nature and civilization, of maturing and yet of resisting the fate of all natural beings. At the point at which Christabel stands, ready to assume maturity and so to marry, she is damned if she does and damned if she does not.

Unable to possess the perfect mother and with her eternal joy and life, Christabel emerges into her own "world of death." One might say, with other readers, that she must also fail morally.[27] In our present context her moral corruption would then function as both a symbol of and a justification for her eventual death. Her father's paralyzing melancholy rightly yields to life; why not also her innocence? In the manner we have considered, it does: she cannot escape natural aging and death, yet she tries to stop that progression, or perhaps at least to block it from consciousness, to render it unspeakable, "a sight to dream of, not to tell" (l. 253). If language here represents civilized form, then Christabel's realization of death's inevitability eludes, in the dilemma in which the poem represents it, logical formulation. Yet civilization insists on overcoming the formless, the silent, on verbalizing that which nevertheless surpasses complete conceptualization.

If we apply here only the terms and methods of rational argument, the deadlock of paradox is the only possible result. We are indeed with Coleridge in "total mist," unable to resolve the contradiction between unconscious drives and conscious choice, between guilt and innocence, between natural flux and civilized form. Each logically negates the other. An alternative approach is needed, and it seems that Coleridge finds it in the moral neutrality of art.

As psychoanalysis, with its commitment both to scientific fact and to healing, looks on moral tempests and is never shaken, so also art, in this case the genre of tragedy, contemplates with equanimity what the poem portrays. Both disciplines find their model in Sophocles, and both take us beyond the realization that Christabel's guilt, however real it may be, is also irrational. Since her conscious will remains innocent and therefore, morally, so does she, it seems useful to distinguish between innocence and immunity: in relation to consciousness and moral choice, her innocence remains; what yields is her unawareness of the human dilemma and her wholly fictional immunity to anxiety.[28] Both her insouciance and her father's simplistic solution of the contradictions in human life must give way to a more complex realization. In Bracy's projected song, that realization introduces the alternative of forgiveness, much as growth into a new phase of unconscious fantasy enables the act that Klein terms "reparation."

At the start of the oedipal phase, Klein maintained, fallen as we are, separate, vulnerable to death, we begin our restorative work, remaking reality into the image of what we have lost, aware now, however, that the world cannot conform to a merely private version of perfection. Here the Oedipus myth, Genesis, and *Paradise Lost,* all seem traceable to the same psychological roots. Tasting the forbidden fruit (so like the breast in appearance and in function) brings the knowledge of good lost and evil got, but also of good to be restored—on the symbolic, therefore communal or cultural level now and, Klein would argue, through the work of the human imagination.

CIVILIZATION AND ITS CONTENTS: AMBIVALENCE AND THE LANGUAGE OF LOVE

Coleridge's use of iconic language to reconcile the conflict that he saw between sensuous stimulation and moral choice leads us to consider further the function of art in this pattern of guilt and reparation. Authorship repaired, for Coleridge, much of the painful conflict within himself. As he saw it, "affection and bodily feeling" direct that treacherous "streamy association," as the creative process shapes an otherwise chaotic mental flux into moral and intelligent structures.[29] This shaping, not any arbitrary or even wholly conscious power, is what he calls "Will . . . strictly synonimous [sic] with the individualizing Principle, the 'I' of every rational Being." His recollections center around physical pleasure or pain and around affection: joy in union and sorrow in loss. The artifact then produced results from a power whose exertion is both the effect and the cause of psychic healing, much as physical exercise both tests a set of muscles and improves their performance in the future.[30]

In poetry, therefore, Coleridge mastered the dilemma that he recorded in the notebooks. He did so perhaps inadvertently, anticipating in practice the theory that he developed later. Psychoanalytic theory also maintains that the evil he saw in the mind, the dangerous impulses and even madness, indeed exist inextricably with good. In *Christabel* this observation becomes more than a disturbing aspect of associative thought; it provides the irrational dilemma behind a rather startling analogy. Starting with the personal sense of love and loss, Coleridge leads us to consider universal guilt and reparation. Nor are consciousness, free will, and "arbitrement" negated in the poem, but they become much less important than they are in the notebooks because the poetic vision reveals the truth that such terms as "sense" and "matter," "will" and "spirit" could not make clear: that good and evil spring from a level that includes but goes beyond consciousness and logical opposites; that being good requires, as it does for the Ancient Mariner, that one bless life, unaware.

In this case only the poetic symbol could express Coleridge's complex perception of good and evil. As we see in the notebooks, without that symbol he was left either to condemn human nature, or to accept the shallow materialism that he abhorred, or to struggle incoherently with both these contradictory positions. The solution was the one that Klein and Winnicott seek to integrate with psychoanalytic theory: the sublimation of instinctual conflict into symbolic action, whereby literal expression that would be merely guilty and isolating (like murder or incest) finds its archetypal analogue. In this way individual pain opens out into sympathy and compassion. Instead of murdering one's father or mother, one fears and pities the sins of Adam and Cain, or the crime of Oedipus, or the horrified fascination of Christabel.

In telling his myth of the Fall, therefore, Coleridge may be said to have enacted the reparation whose psychic sources *Christabel* mysteriously presents. He analyzed the creative process while he practiced it. His poem stands as evidence of his individual effort toward psychic recovery, a recovery gained not by evading but by describing and recreating our tragic situation. We are left with further questions, especially about the possible links or parallels between the reparative state of mind and Coleridge's later ideas of justification or redemption. We would be mistaken if, while admiring his understanding of psychology, we were to lose sight of the puzzling relationship in the poem among Christabel, Geraldine, and "all . . . who live in the upper sky" (l. 227). Meanwhile, the way in which *Christabel* connects the psychological dynamics of love and loss with a radical sense of guilt lends additional credibility to Klein's views on symbol formation, including that which is involved in the production of language and literature. As Coleridge reflects on linguistic ambiguity at the poem's close, Klein's theory helps us to understand why he does so. Both the process by which the poem is made and the experience we have in reading it show

that, provided it accepts ambivalence and moral ambiguity, culture can nourish and, perhaps only approximately, heal. This puts one in mind of Bracy's song. When freed from the manic denial of the mother (and of all women, since they become the mother's symbolic equivalent), when women are perceived not as agents of male satisfaction or of its opposite but as the center of their own tragedy (exiles from the Garden like everyone else), then civilization is not deadly but redemptive. In creating Christabel to represent his own tragic situation, Coleridge inadvertently reveals this fact.

Nevertheless, the comparatively barbaric impulse to simplify life into fantasies of absolute good and evil never dies, and in its persistence, the poem suggests, the image of woman, so long as she is mother, is inextricably involved. Women must therefore come to terms not only with their own vulnerability as separate, mortal beings, but also with the anger of those, male and female, who cannot outgrow their infantile rage or cannot deal with their "depressive" guilt. One task of civilization, however, is to relieve this double jeopardy, directly and especially indirectly, through the symbolic reconstruction of community within the shared immortality that a cultural heritage provides. Coleridge's poem, as both an achieved work of art and a portrayal of the condition it seeks to rectify, is an insightful contribution to the communal effort at reparation.

Notes

1. Humphry House, *Coleridge* (London: Rupert Hart-Davis, 1953), 126, and *The Unpublished Letters of Samuel Taylor Coleridge,* ed. Earl Leslie Griggs, 2 vols. (London: Constable, 1932), II, 247.

2. See *The Notebooks of Samuel Taylor Coleridge,* ed. Kathleen Coburn, 3 vols. to date (New York: Pantheon, 1957-), item 2670 (September 15, 1805), and Coburn, *Experience into Thought* (Toronto: University of Toronto Press, 1979), 4.

3. *Collected Letters of Samuel Taylor Coleridge,* ed. Earl Leslie Griggs, 6 vols. (Oxford: Clarendon, 1956-71), III, 70; see also 92. This work is cited below as *Collected Letters.* Coleridge protested his unhappy marriage (see *Collected Letters,* III, 60-66). His view of love can be described as platonic in, for example, the Shakespeare lectures (*Coleridge on Shakespeare,* ed. R. A. Foakes [Washington, D.C.: Folger, 1978], lectures 7 and 8, pp. 75-97). For a discussion of this aspect of Coleridge's thought, see Anthony John Harding, *Coleridge and the Idea of Love* ([London]: Cambridge University Press, 1975).

4. *The Complete Poetical Works,* ed. Ernest Hartley Coleridge, 2 vols. (Oxford: Clarendon, 1912), I, 390-91, ll. 27-32, 50-end. This poem was originally written in a letter to Robert Southey, Sep-

tember 11, 1803. See *Collected Letters,* II, 982-84. For the remark about the dreams, see *Notebooks,* item 2398 (January 11, 1805). Critics from Roy K. Basler in 1948 to Barbara A. Schapiro in 1983 have discussed the ambivalence in *Christabel.* All these psychoanalytic readings, however, use the poem as an index to the poet's personality; although Basler does so much less than the others, he relates the suggestions of sexuality in the poem only to Coleridge's concern about his moral reputation. I find it interesting to relate *Christabel* to his psychological speculations, as they foreshadow and impinge upon his aesthetic theory. These earlier readings also view the ambivalence in the poem as abnormal, while I consider it appropriate to and permanent within the human situation as Coleridge, Freud, and others saw it. Furthermore, I believe that Coleridge shows ambivalence as the necessary condition for artistic creation, and it is here that Klein's theory is relevant. A partial list of psychoanalytic interpretations includes Basler, *Sex, Symbolism, and Psychology in Literature* ([1948] rpt. New York: Octagon Books, 1967); Arthur Wormhoudt, *The Demon Lover* (New York: Exposition Press, 1949); Edward Bostetter, *The Romantic Ventriloquists* (Seattle: University of Washington Press, 1963); Gerald E. Enscoe, *Eros and the Romantics* (The Hague: Mouton, 1967); Geoffrey Yarlott, *Coleridge and the Abyssinian Maid* ([London]: Methuen, 1967); Norman Fruman, *Coleridge, the Damaged Archangel* (New York: G. Braziller, 1971); and Schapiro, *The Romantic Mother* (Baltimore: Johns Hopkins University Press, 1983). Jonas Spatz argues that the ambivalence which Coleridge's portrayal suggests can be wholly overcome by a mature adjustment, and that the author assumed such an outcome. See "The Mystery of Eros: Sexual Initiation in Coleridge's 'Christabel,'" *PMLA,* 90 (1975), 107-16. One sensitive and well-balanced essay is "Coleridge's Anxiety," by Thomas McFarland, in *Coleridge's Variety,* ed. John Beer (Pittsburgh: University of Pittsburgh Press, 1975), 134-65.

5. Sandor Ferenczi, "Stages in the Development of the Sense of Reality," *Psychoanalytic Review,* 1 (1913-14), 223-25; Klein, "The Importance of Symbol-Formation in the Development of the Ego," in *Love, Guilt, and Reparation and Other Works,* vol. 1 of *The Writings of Melanie Klein,* 4 vols., ed. R. E. Money-Kyrle, International Psycho-analytical Library (London: Hogarth Press and Institute of Psycho-analysis, 1975), I, 219-32; quotations here from 232 and 220. See also in the same volume "Early Analysis," 100-105. For the application of Klein's theory to aesthetics, see her "Infantile Anxiety-Situations Reflected in a Work

of Art and in the Creative Impulse," *Writings,* I, 210-18, and Hanna Segal, "A Psycho-analytical Approach to Aesthetics," *International Journal of Psycho-analysis,* 33 (1952), 196-207. Segal's essay is reprinted in Klein et al., *New Directions in Psycho-analysis* (London: Tavistock, 1955), along with Adrian Stokes's "Form in Art." Stokes's later work is also significant. Simon Stuart's *New Phoenix Wings: Reparation in Literature* (London: Routledge, 1979) applies Klein's theory to Romantic poetry, especially to that of Blake and Wordsworth.

6. Klein, "Early Analysis," 105, and "Symbol-Formation," 221. Of interest is the history of Dick in "Symbol-Formation," 221-32. The concept of reparation also involves a repairing of the mother, whom, in the rage of desire and anxiety, the infant has imagined destroying. This reconstruction is the primary motive Klein ascribes to mature symbolization.

7. *Collected Letters,* II, 706-7 (Coleridge's emphasis).

8. See Edward E. Bostetter, "Christabel: The Vision of Fear," *Philological Quarterly,* 36 (1957), 186 n. 7.

9. For the poem's prepublication history, see *Poetical Works,* I, 213-14, and Arthur Nethercot, *The Road to Tryermaine* (Chicago: University of Chicago Press, 1939; rpt. Westport, Conn.: Greenwood, 1978), 3-21. The poem we have was written from 1798 to 1800. Coleridge planned to add three more sections and wrote some additional passages, which were never published. The first two parts circulated in manuscript until 1816. Even after their publication in that year, Coleridge hoped to compose more.

10. Quotations from *Christabel* are taken from *Poetical Works,* I, 213-36. Line numbers are cited in the text.

11. *Notebooks,* item 838.

12. *Notebooks,* item 924 (March 24, 1801). Parentheses denote Coleridge's dating.

13. See *Notebooks,* item 21, which Coburn tentatively dates 1795 and which connects the pillow with both sorrow and a soothing and buoyant love. These associations, which seem irrelevant at this point in the argument, nevertheless resemble others that relate to the poem (see below). Hence it would seem that on some level of consciousness, even before he wrote Part I of *Christabel,* Coleridge made some of the mental associations I describe.

14. *Notebooks,* item 827 [January 9, 1804]. Square brackets denote editor's dating.

15. On the relation of "double touch" to infant psychology, sublimation, and *Christabel,* see John Beer, *Coleridge's Poetic Intelligence* (London: Macmillan, 1977), 86-89.

16. *Notebooks,* items 1414 [July 16-19, 1803] and 1078 (May 10, 1803); Coleridge's emphasis.

17. *Notebooks,* items 1763 and 1770 (December 26, 28, 29, 1803); Coleridge's emphasis.

18. *Notebooks,* item 1718 [December 6-13, 1803]. See also item 21 [1795?].

19. *Notebooks,* note to item 1718. See Coburn's references here to psychoanalytic studies.

20. *Notebooks,* item 1827.

21. *Notebooks,* item 1770.

22. Bruno Bettelheim, *The Uses of Enchantment* (New York: Knopf, 1976), 69.

23. Klein, "Early Stages of the Oedipus Conflict," *Writings,* I, 186-98; quotation from 188.

24. Hanna Segal, *Introduction to the Work of Melanie Klein,* enl. ed. (New York: Basic Books, 1974), 102. See also Klein, "A Contribution to the Psychogenesis of Manic-Depressive States," *Writings,* I, 262-89.

25. D. W. Winnicott, *Playing and Reality* (New York: Basic Books, 1971), 144, 148 (Winnicott's emphasis). Beyond the scope of this paper, but so closely related to it that it should be studied at greater length, is Coleridge's later theological consideration of guilt in the origin of individual will. The terms of the argument are too abstruse to define here, but the following quotation suggests additional interesting comparisons between Coleridge's theological speculation and the issues relevant to *Christabel*: "What could follow but a world of contradictions, when the first self-constituting act is in its essence a contradiction [of God's will]?" ("Opus Maximum," Huntington MS, 39-43; quoted in J. Robert Barth, S.J., *Coleridge and Christian Doctrine* [Cambridge: Harvard University Press, 1969], 112).

26. See Klein, "Mourning and Its Relation to Manic-Depressive States," *Writings,* I, 344-69; and Freud, "Mourning and Melancholia," in *Standard Edition,* XIV, 243-58, whose implications Klein developed. The relevance of Freud's *Civilization and Its Discontents* is, I hope, apparent.

27. See Enscoe, *Eros and the Romantics*; Yarlott, *Coleridge and the Abyssinian Maid.*

28. This distinction permits us to avoid two critical difficulties. On the one hand we can accept the poem's presentation of sexuality as tragically flawed. In that case we need not adopt what seems to me a naive view, equating sexual activity wholly with freedom and joy, and we thus avoid the sentimentality I find in Enscoe and Yarlott, and even in the view of mature love described by Spatz. Nor need we allow the view that at first seems the logically necessary opposite: that Christabel is in some way actually corrupted (see Harding, *Coleridge and the Idea of Love,* 74, although earlier [72] he argues that she is not. See also Carl Woodring, "Christabel of Cumberland," *Review of English Literature* 7 [1966], 46-51). John Beer distinguishes carefully between her innocence and her role as victim: "She is to accept [evil], subsume it, and finally transfigure it. The demonic must nevertheless enter her so deeply that she takes on, temporarily, its actual appearance to unenlightened eyes" (*Coleridge the Visionary* [London: Macmillan, 1959; rpt. New York: Collier, 1962], 202). Of course I would argue that "the demonic" is more than appearance, and that it is not all externally caused. But Christabel's moral innocence remains.

29. Quoted in House, *Coleridge,* 148.

30. House, *Coleridge,* 155-56.

Charles J. Rzepka (essay date winter 1986)

SOURCE: Rzepka, Charles J. "Christabel's 'Wandering Mother' and the Discourse of the Self: A Lacanian Reading of Repressed Narration." *Romanticism Past and Present* 10, no. 1 (winter 1986): 17-43.

[*In the following essay, Rzepka examines representations of identity and desire in "Christabel," analyzing the poem within the framework of Jacques Lacan's theories of language and otherness.*]

"THE OTHER" AND OTHERS

If we think of Christabel [in Coleridge's ***Christabel***] at all, it is likely to be as the young woman who cannot tell what has happened to her. Twice confronted with the horror that she sees in the person of Geraldine, her seducer, she can only react "with forced unconscious sympathy," inarticulate. Here is the second such "vision of fear" [453]:[1]

One moment—and the sight was fled!
But Christabel in dizzy trance
Stumbling on the unsteady ground
Shuddered aloud, with a hissing sound;

The maid, alas! her thoughts are gone,
She nothing sees—no sight but one!

The maid, devoid of guile and sin,
I know not how, in fearful wise,
So deeply had she drunken in
That look, those shrunken serpent eyes,
That all her features were resigned
To this sole image in her mind:
And passively did imitate
That look of dull and treacherous hate!
And thus she stood, in dizzy trance,
Still picturing that look askance
With forced unconscious sympathy
Full before her father's view—
As far as such a look could be
In eyes so innocent and blue!

And when the trance was o'er, the maid
Pause awhile, and inly prayed:
Then falling at the Baron's feet,
'By my mother's soul do I entreat
That thou this woman send away!'
She said: and more she could not say:
For what she knew she could not tell,
O'er mastered by the mighty spell.

(588-620)

Such was the effect of the power exerted by Geraldine the night before, when she took Christabel in her arms and muttered, "In the touch of this bosom there worketh a spell / Which is lord of thy utterance, Christabel!" (267-68). Denied speech, Christabel the next morning enacts something she cannot articulate, something so horrifying, apparently, that she cannot put it into words. Critics are generally agreed that that "something" is sexual desire.[2] Christabel is afraid to grow up. The horror, of course, arises from Christabel's inchoate understanding that this desire is hers, that the "sole image" of desire—Geraldine's sinister "look"—is indeed all "in her mind." As Sandor Ferenczi, one of Freud's early disciples, observed of the hysteric, "When consciousness refuses to accept the positive unconscious desire, then we get . . . antipathy of various degrees up to loathing" (55).

And yet, however intensely desire may be denied, even consciously loathed, it finds expression. As Jacques Lacan points out, "the first object of desire is to be recognized by the 'other'" (31). Lacan is but one of many contemporary theorists of mind and identity to have placed primary emphasis on the role of "the Other" in the formation both of one's conscious sense of identity and one's unconscious mind.[3] The Other is that imagined presence, often embodied in real persons, "through whom and for whom the subject poses *his question,*" which is always the question of the Self (Lacan 67). The Self, for Lacan, is a social construct, and the Other is that spectral eye before which, alone or in company, consciously or unconsciously, we create such a construct, that voice through which we would tell our "story."

Among theorists on the role of the Other in the formation of identity, Lacan and his followers are notable for the stress they place on the essential importance of language in this process. Extrapolating from Freudian theory, Lacan believes that what differentiates the unconscious from conscious posing of the question of identity is the ability of the subject to *articulate* desire *as if for another.* Language, insofar as it transforms mere images—including the specular image of the embodied self—into symbols susceptible of conscious manipulation, characterization, or justification, puts the subject into possession of his or her Self as a symbolic object, an image that is named and characterized and that, therefore, stands for an individual person. But because language is a public and not a private system of signification, a form of discourse already determined in its categories of meaning by a society that exists prior to the subject, it also alienates the subject from the articulated Self he or she comes to possess. In the words of the Lacanian Anika Lemaire, "By mediating himself in his discourse, the subject in effect destroys the immediate relation of self to self, and constructs himself in language . . . as he wishes to see himself, as he wishes to be seen, and thereby alienates himself in language" (64). What cannot be mediated by language is repressed. Thus Freud: "A presentation which is not put into words remains thereafter in the Unconscious in a state of repression" (202).

The acquisition of language, then, splits the subject into a conscious Self, which is the construct of a language that compromises the full expression of desire, and the unconscious, in which unacknowledged desires must seek expression obliquely, by exploiting the infinite associative resources of ordinary speech, everyday gestures, common bodily functions, and trains of thought—for instance, in slips of the tongue, tics, compulsions, psychosomatic illnesses, and dreams. In this way, the desire which goes unarticulated, and thus remains unconscious, seeks nonetheless to be "recognized" by the Other as part of the Self.

It is through the use of language, in the Lacanians' view, that the subject can rise from the level of imaginary experience—in which consciousness does not distinguish between its own images and what it means by them, "cannot keep its distance from its own internal vision" (Lemaire 60)—to symbolic experience—in which the subject understands the images that present themselves to his mind as informed by his own desires. The desire which seeks, in Geraldine, its proper audience, and therein the proper response to the "question" of its identity, is Christabel's after all, not Geraldine's. But since Christabel cannot mediate her "vision of fear" by means of language, which would force her to adopt a perspective "outside" the mind in which it inheres, she cannot consciously recognize its *being* "in her mind" and, ultimately, question what she means by it. As a result, she succumbs to the power of the image without knowing why. As in a mirror, she *becomes* the "sole image" she beholds in Geraldine: "consciousness collapses into its double without keeping its distance from it" (Lemaire 81), unable to see itself as separate and independent, unable to articulate the "question" it has posed in the images that haunt it.

The desire which is unacceptable and inarticulable appears as a symptom—a compulsion, an error in diction, a hallucination—"a Language," says Lacan, "from which the Word must be liberated" (32). But that Word can only be "liberated" when one comes to understand the "discourse" that desire seeks to elicit in the Other, that specific recognition and acceptance which the language of the symptom anticipates. Indeed, the "unconscious *is* the discourse of the other," a "transindividual" discourse "which is not at the disposition of the subject to reestablish [in] the continuity of his conscious discourse" (Lacan 27, 20). In Paul Ricoeur's words, "It is only for someone other that I even possess an unconscious" (106-07).

In conscious reflection, the Other is that internalized presence whose "outside," discursive point of view I adopt so as to see—and judge and evaluate and comment upon—myself objectively, as another would. Repression results when the Other becomes completely split off, silenced and separated from consciousness, and is embodied entirely in a specific "other" who is perceived and responded to on the Imaginary level. To the extent that the "discourse of the other," the response anticipated and sought from the Other, cannot be articulated and thus owned by the subject in an interiorized, "conscious discourse" at the symbolic level, desire evades consciousness by seeking a tacit recognition inaccessible to symbolic representation and, thus, to conscious reflection.

For Christabel, the Other becomes another in Geraldine, to whom she poses, unconsciously, through her actions, the "question" of her sexual identity. As secret interlocutor, Geraldine possesses the "discursive" power to confirm, by her embrace and her "serpent eyes," the reality of Christabel's desire, a desire that Christabel must act out silently and passively because she cannot consciously accept it in herself. Geraldine's embrace and Christabel's later response to her "look," however, are less homoerotic in their significance than is often proposed by critics who base their interpretation on the ambiguous suggestions of lesbianism in the seduction scene. A more important clue to Geraldine's power over Christabel's sexual identity lies in the narrative's subtle insistence on Geraldine's maternalism,[4] which has been used to support traditional Freudian readings of Christabel's "vision of fear" as an expression of Oedipal jealousy over her father's love.

Geraldine's motherly features assume new significance, however, in the light of standard theories that trace the origins of self-consciousness to the infant's first identification with the parent as Other.[5] At every important stage of our development, we test our maturing sense of ourselves against our parent's sense of us, recapitulating our earliest adoption or "introjection"[6] of his or her presence as the very mirror of self-consciousness. The parent is, then, the prototypical interiorized Other. But Christabel's mother is dead: "She died the hour that I was born" (197), she tells Geraldine. Furthermore, she died in childbirth, a victim of desire. If we accept this death as the cause of Christabel's denial of her own adult desire (and much in the poem suggests we should), then Geraldine's ability to transform Christabel's perceptions and behavior in a sexually sinister way begins to make sense. Geraldine represents a surrogate mother, sexually mature and attractive, "through whom and for whom" Christabel can pose the question of her new womanhood without having to acknowledge it consciously and, thus, confront the fate it apparently entails.

The real mother is "wandering" (205), a ghost haunting the castle and its environs. Her very restlessness suggests Christabel's inability fully to "take her in" as the mirror of adult self-consciousness. She is the "guardian spirit" (212) of the girl's innocence only because her sad example prevents the conscious acceptance of desire. Accordingly, Christabel remains oblivious to the mother's spiritual proximity throughout Part I, as she leads Geraldine into the castle, up to her room, and finally to her bed. Often invoked and adverted to, the mother herself remains silent and invisible, unacknowledged even when Geraldine apparently struggles with her for mastery over the girl, and wins (204-13). Christabel can only assume her new identity in the presence of Geraldine, her new "mother," and only in a kind of dream or trance that prevents her from telling who this "lofty lady" has replaced, and why.

All that *can* be told in **Christabel** appears in the narrative itself, which speaks for and in the tone of voice (though not in the person) of Christabel as *naif,* blurring the description of her "vision of fear" at strategic moments and formally recapitulating the twists and turns of her denial of sexual curiosity. Unsophisticated, even child-like at times, the third-person narrative reads like a species of ventriloquism or metempsychosis. In Part I, especially, where the point of view is exclusively Christabel's, the disingenuousness and literalness of style are at times almost infantile. The effect is uncanny, as though the speaker were merely an instrument by which Christabel would represent herself and her actions from without, telling her "story" through the eyes of an adult who assumes she is innocent.

The narrator, in fact, speaks like that interiorized Other of self-consciousness to which Christabel would appeal for justice and self-justification. This is not to say he is the voice of Christabel's conscious self in the process of reflection, for such a voice would have to speak in the first person. Rather, his is the outside, discursive, third-person point of view which Christabel would adopt on her own actions and the events happening to her *were she to tell her story.* Forgiving, understanding, credulous, the narrator maintains the picture of Christabel which the girl would consciously affirm in the eyes of the adult world: she is still an asexual being, a "child," "so fair, so innocent, so mild." Or so the narrator affirms in an apostrophe to Christabel's father, the Baron Sir Leoline, admonishing him for his angry rejection of Christabel's plea to send Geraldine away:

> Why is thy cheek so wan and wild,
> Sir Leoline? Thy only child
> Lies at thy feet, thy joy, thy pride,
> So fair, so innocent, so mild!

>   (621-24)

The narrator is concerned here, as he is throughout the poem, with maintaining Christabel's passivity and innocence. To do so he must, like Christabel herself, consistently overlook the symbolic resonances of the images that obsess him, or look away from such images altogether.

Those resonances of obsession and denial are accessible in the first place only through the mediation of a symbolic structure like language, and thus (since the narrator will not take responsibility for them) only to the reader. If the narrator is the Other of self-conscious reflection, that articulate presence to which all of Christabel's actions and perceptions are directed, then the reader is the Other of the unconscious, that silent witness to whom, with a different intention, they are simultaneously referred. It is the reader who, in the process of critical reflection on the linguistically mediated image, enacts the raising of consciousness from the level of the Imaginary—in which the mind attends only to the procession of images conveyed by the poem—to that of the Symbolic—in which it can reflect on what these images mean in the context of the story as a whole. Focusing on the narrative ambiguities of the poem as expressing, in the words of the Other which Christabel's behavior anticipates, her failure to acknowledge the figure of the mother as the source of both paralyzing dread and self-transforming power, we can clarify the connection between the girl's emergent self and Geraldine's "occult relation to Christabel's mother" (Fogle 132), as well as the bizarre changes Christabel undergoes in the presence of Geraldine during her "vision of fear." The issue throughout the poem is fundamentally narrative: what the narrator can and cannot tell reflects the extent to which Christabel herself can "tell" who she is.

SEEING AND SAYING, KNOWLEDGE AND ACKNOWLEDGMENT

As Richard Harter Fogle has noted, the verse of ***Christabel*** is "exact almost to grotesqueness" (140). The unembarrassed repetitions, the transparent, simple diction, the innocent assurances of the narration attend so narrowly to what is happening as to inhibit reflection. We tend to lose ourselves in what we see, thus all but losing the inclination, if not the ability, to question it. The poetry performs a "kind of hypnotism," writes Fogle. "The poet acts as Ancient Mariner to the reader's Wedding Guest" (138).

That is, we see, but not with waking eyes. We see like the beguiled heroine herself in the aftermath of Geraldine's embrace,

> With open eyes (ah woe is me!)
> Asleep, and dreaming fearfully,
> Fearfully dreaming, yet, I wis,
> Dreaming that alone, which is.

>   (292-95)

Dreaming with "open eyes" suggests that the truth, "that alone, which is," cannot be faced and accepted in waking life. To dream awake is, momentarily, to become hysterical. In Lacanian terms, it is to remain at the level of the Image, to lack that distance from an experience which would allow one to recognize its psychological significance: "the imaginary lived experience does not allow a clear distinction between the image and its signification" (Lemaire 176).

The narrative itself at this point in the story refuses to tell us what Christabel sees with "open eyes": what Geraldine's embrace has revealed to her cannot be articulated, just as Geraldine predicted a moment before when she cast her spell. Thus, what has passed this night will remain a waking mystery not only to Christabel, but also to the reader. The narrator hides from us what Christabel will, in memory, hide from herself. A more vivid example of narrative paralysis appears in that passage which invites us to look at Geraldine's nude torso as she prepares to lie down beside Christabel:

> Beneath the lamp the lady bowed,
> And slowly rolled her eyes around:
> Then drawing in her breath aloud,
> Like one that shuddered, she unbound
> The cincture from beneath her breast:
> Her silken robe, and inner vest,
> Dropt to her feet, and full in view,
> Behold! her bosom and half her side—
> A sight to dream of, not to tell!
> O shield her! shield sweet Christabel!

>   (245-54)

In the act of revealing—"Behold!"—the narrator refuses to "tell" us what we are presumed to be seeing. He turns us aside at the crucial moment from that which is "full in view." Our eyes are open, but we cannot see. The point is not only that Geraldine's bosom and side are, we assume, obscene or hideous, but that nothing seen *can* enter consciousness unless it can also be *told,* admitted.

At the critical moment the narrator is unable to "admit" the truth in either of two important and related senses: because what has happened must not be "admitted" into consciousness, it is never "admitted" or acknowledged in that discourse of the Other which is always appropriated by self-consciousness. Thus, the story of Christabel is punctuated by strategic omissions and evasions, crippled by the amnesia and aphasia that, as Abse (8) observes, typify the trance-like state of dissociative hysteria.

That true knowledge anticipates acknowledgment, true seeing requires saying, is suggested by the way Coleridge plays with the word "tell." At her first meeting with Geraldine, under the oak in the "midnight wood" (29), Christabel hears her moan "as near as near can be": "But what it is, she cannot tell" (39-40), that is, discern. Geraldine says she has been kidnapped by five knights and left beneath the oak adding that her abductors "choked [her] cries with force and fright" (83). That detail is not lost on the highly suggestible girl, who will later find herself unable to object to her own curiously passive-aggressive encounter with Geraldine. More importantly, Geraldine's inability to cry out is linked, by the word "tell," to her present inability to see or discriminate, to understand what happened next. "Whither they went I cannot tell" (99): neither know, nor can say.

> For I have lain entranced I wis
> Since one, the tallest of the five,
> Took me from the palfrey's back,
> A weary woman, scarce alive.
>
> (92-95)

Geraldine provides Christabel with a model of denial. Following her own seduction, Christabel too will lie with "open eyes . . . asleep" (292-93) as in a "trance" (312), and her later loss of memory and speech seem as mercifully self-imposed a form of repression as Geraldine's own.

Later, when we read that Christabel beholds "a sight to dream of, not to *tell,*" the word is colored by Geraldine's protestations of ignorance and the description of Christabel's initial inability to see the woman clearly. Two senses of the word—as an act of perception and as an act of speech—here merge. This is a sight *we* are not allowed to see clearly because it is not "told." Our very

blindness turns on the narrator's failure of speech, which reflects Christabel's act of denial. The next day, the girl will not only be unable to speak of what is wrong with her: she will, as at her first meeting with Geraldine, be unable to see clearly, to "tell," the source of her uneasiness.

Although Geraldine, the previous night, had assured Christabel that she would "know to-morrow, / This mark of my shame, this seal of my sorrow" (269-70), her spell keeps the girl from "telling," discerning clearly, what she knows. Thus, the next morning, Christabel's anxieties lack a definite object until her first "vision of fear," and even after recoiling in horror, she is at a loss for words. "All will yet be well," she replies to her father's expression of concern at her behavior. "I ween," adds the narrator, "she had no power to *tell* / Aught else: so mighty was the spell" (472-74; italics mine). And as we have seen following her second "dizzy trance" at the sight of Geraldine's "serpent eyes," once Christabel has entreated the Baron to send the woman away, she can say—and see—no more: "For what she knew she could not *tell.*"

For Christabel to "tell" the truth about Geraldine, she would have to acknowledge—to admit in the words and thus to see through the eye of the Other—an entire field of possible choices as a sexual being. She would thereby assume the burden of choosing, of taking responsibility for her becoming the woman she would be. If she is responsible, literally "able to respond," say, to the Baron's question, "What ails then my beloved child?" (470), then she is capable of "answering" for her actions, desires, choices. Christabel, quite clearly, is incapable of answering, just as the narrator whose discourse consistently ratifies Christabel's innocence is incapable of "telling" the truth.

Instead, the untold truth is expressed obliquely. It appears in what consciousness insists on ignoring, in what discourse pointedly refuses to say, or "admits" only in a disguised manner, symbolically or by means of distortions in perception and speech. Here, discourse appears idle, innocent with respect to the symbolic significance of those events by which it is obsessed, events which "bespeak" an unacknowledged dread despite, or perhaps because of, the narrator's frequent failures to speak.

Repetition and question—begging are, like silence, failures of speech. As Emslie and Edwards point out, such devices also mark, in **Christabel,** a calculated attempt to make a naive impression on the reader, as though to ratify a certain portrayal of Christabel. For example, the rhetorical question with which the narrator begins to describe the night in the opening stanzas of Part I—"Is the night chilly and dark? / The night is chilly, but not dark" (14-15)—are "deliberately gauche" (57). The language is almost aggressively innocuous and the narrator is to be understood as reflecting the movements of Christabel's child-like mind.

But repetition can protest too much. Consider the following lines, which describe Christabel leading Geraldine into the courtyard of the castle:

> So free from danger, free from fear,
> They crossed the court: right glad they were.
> And Christabel devoutly cried
> To the lady by her side,
> Praise we the Virgin all divine
> Who hath rescued thee from thy distress!
> Alas, alas! said Geraldine,
> I cannot speak for weariness.
> So free from danger, free from fear,
> They crossed the court: right glad they were.
>
> (135-44)

These repeated assurances do not reassure us. They make us suspect not only that something is wrong, but that the speaker understands, and will not or cannot admit, that something is wrong. This is not language "free from fear," but language burdened with an unacknowledged fear.

What danger threatens innocence? And why must that danger not be acknowledged in the discourse of the Other who speaks for Christabel? Consider again the innocuous lines, "Is the night chilly and dark?" The question is not only rhetorical, and thus unnecessary (the speaker answers it himself), but it is also a cliché of Gothic romance,[7] in which the night is always "chilly and dark." Nonetheless, the question elicits a substantive reply: "The night is chilly but *not* dark." By correcting the cliché, the narrator implies that the question was not pointless after all, even while he ridicules it by self-mimicry. In the act of reassuring himself, the speaker pretends not to care. Why, then, ask the question? Why stress the unremarkable nature of what is marked?

In *Christabel,* writes Fogle, "one has some ominous hint of a hidden death that lies at the root of things" (144). Christabel leaves the protective walls of the family to pray for "her lover" (30) in the world of nature, and of "natural," instinctive desires.[8] But it is, in the Baron's words, "a world of death" (333) now that Christabel's mother is dead. Not insignificantly, the world of death awaits a belated spring. Its vital development has only been arrested, not ended. "'Tis a month before the month of May, / And the Spring comes slowly up this way" (21-22). Christabel's sexual blossoming, like its corresponding season, must also be understood to have been delayed by the fear engendered by her mother's death.

If the night may be taken to represent a region of forbidden self-knowledge, then it follows that death is clearly what has made "chilly and dark," i.e., forbid-ding, all previous nights. It is death that threatens a bold and too-curious innocence. But Christabel's future as a woman lies beyond the safe walls of the familial self, the self as child. The mind seeking reassurance for its unacknowledged fears must hide from itself its need for reassurance, or Christabel will never venture beyond the limits of her child-self. "Is the night chilly and dark?"—Is this the world of death? The cliché question masks an anxious expectancy, hope and fear. "The night is chilly," like death, "but not dark." Here is light, and enlightenment. Outside the fortress of maidenhood, beyond the "gate that was ironed within and without" (127), Christabel finds enough "moonlight cold" (146) to see by and something—or someone—to see: Geraldine,

> a damsel bright,
> Drest in a silken robe of white
> That shadowy in the moonlight shone,
>
> (58-60)

a "lady of a far countree" (225).

If we have been prepared for the appearance of anyone, however, it is another "lady of a far countree" who is also dressed in "robe of white": her shroud.[9] The ghostly presence of Christabel's mother has been hinted at as early as the second stanza, but the narrator, who perceives things as Christabel wishes to, refuses to acknowledge that presence, dismissing it even as he adverts to signs of it:

> Sir Leoline, the Baron rich,
> Hath a toothless mastiff bitch;
> From her kennel beneath the rock
> She maketh answer to the clock,
> Four for the quarters, and twelve for the hour;
> Ever and aye, by shine and shower,
> Sixteen short howls, not over loud;
> Some say, she sees my lady's shroud.
>
> (6-13)

"Some say" implies that the belief here called to mind is superstitious gossip. Why, then, bring it to mind? Precisely to dismiss it and, thereby, call attention to the dismissal. "Some say," but unless the narrator "admits" the mother's presence, we will not be able to "tell" for certain she is there. Later, when Christabel helps Geraldine across the castle threshold, we read:

> The mastiff old did not awake,
> Yet she an angry moan did make!
> And what can ail the mastiff bitch?
> Never till now she uttered yell
> Beneath the eye of Christabel.
> Perhaps it is the owlet's scritch:
> For what can ail the mastiff bitch?
>
> (147-53)

The repetition, the lame attempt at explanation, again, suggest less naiveté or innocence than denial.[10] The narrator, like his heroine, pointedly avoids coming to any conclusion about the events he observes. We know what, typically, "ails" the bitch: the mother's presence. But here it is Geraldine's presence that has triggered the mastiff's moan, an "angry moan," as though a sinister substitution has taken place. Two "mothers" are present in Part I, but only one is taken in. The other is left "wandering" (205).

The tale of Christabel, like its heroine, is caught up in the failure of speech, in uncalled-for reassurances, begged questions, silence. The girl's innocence is not so much a matter of simple ignorance as of not admitting—both in the sense of not accepting and of not acknowledging in that narrative of the internalized Other which implicitly ratifies her conscious self-image—the mother's ghostly presence in her life. It is not, after all, *eros* that Christabel dreads, but *thanatos,* death in the manner of her mother. It is the pressure of that dread, and not mere sexual squeamishness, which blinds Christabel at the moment the mother's sexually vital surrogate reveals herself: "Behold! her bosom and half her side— / A sight to dream of, not to tell!" (252-53).

We can gain some idea of what has here been repressed—literally, written out of the narrative—by consulting the three manuscript versions of **Christabel** that have survived, where these crucial lines read, "Behold! her bosom and half her side, / Are lean and old and foul of hue."[11] In other words, Geraldine appears corpse-like. Originally, what Christabel beheld was an image of morbidity and death, as confirmed in her first "vision of fear" the next day: "Again she saw that bosom old, / Again she saw that bosom cold" (467-68). Christabel's horror of degeneration and death finds expression in her fearful glimpse of Geraldine's maternal "bosom," symbol of that state which both frightens and fascinates her.

Despite strategic silences, then, the truth appears obliquely, in the maternal associations of those items that are repressed in the "telling" of the story: the presence of Christabel's dead mother and Geraldine's disfigured bosom and side. Sometimes the truth can appear in a "slip of the tongue," a momentary syntactic lapse. Consider the description of Geraldine as she first appears to Christabel the morning after their night together:

> her looks, her air
> Such gentle thankfulness declare,
> That (so it seemed) her girded vests
> Grew tight beneath her heaving breasts.
>
> (377-80)

Nearly all critical speculation on what happened the night before makes use of this passage, concentrating on the two lines describing Geraldine's "heaving breasts." Basler's response is typical. Taking Geraldine to be the projection of Christabel's repressed eroticism, he writes, "In a specific detail which Coleridge almost italicizes, as it were, [Geraldine's] figure has become more distinctly feminine. Her breasts seem to swell and '. . . her girded vests / Grew tight beneath her heaving breasts'" (40).[12]

Generations of readers have noticed the same "italics." And yet the passage which conveys this image of Geraldine's "distinctly feminine" figure is garbled syntactically in a significant manner. Let us add some italics of our own: "That (so it seemed) her girded *vests* / Grew tight *beneath* her heaving *breasts*." "Heaving" does suggest that Geraldine's bosom is full, swelling. But something else is swelling here as well, something the more significant for being so easily overlooked: Geraldine's abdomen, the area of her body "beneath" her breasts, has drawn the "girded vests" covering it "tight," or "so it seemed" to Christabel. We miss the meaning, quite naturally, by a syntactical misreading, transposing the end-line positions of "girded vests" and "heaving breasts."

In short, Geraldine, the image of Christabel as she unconsciously wishes to see herself, seems to be with child. "Sure *I* have sinn'd!" responds Christabel in unconscious self-projection. "Now heaven be praised if all be well!" (381-82). Christabel perceives something shameful and threatening in Geraldine's buxom sexual vitality, and the hidden cause of her dread appears in the confused syntax of the passage, for the way the narrator "tells" what Christabel sees subconsciously charges the image of Geraldine with the dread inspired by Christabel's mother's death in child-birth. Despite what the lines say, we do not read them right. Like Christabel, we are led to perceive Geraldine's "heaving breasts"—sexually vital and maternally nurturing—only by an act of denial, only by ignoring what the narrator in fact refers to: childbearing, the phase of womanhood intervening between sexual vitality and maternal nurturing.

"Sure I have sinn'd!" Geraldine. when casting her spell the night before, says that Christabel will "know tomorrow, / This mark of my shame, this seal of my sorrow" (269-70): here is the "mark" of the *mother's* "shame," the "seal" of the *mother's* "sorrow," her death warrant. But the words "mark" and "seal," though both denoting a sign, have different connotations, as demonstrated the next day: Christabel can recognize or "mark" the "shame" that accompanies her fear, but cannot recognize the "sorrow" that inspires it. The sorrow, the mother's death, remains "sealed." It is, however, on some level "known." The shameful after all can only be "marked" *as* shameful by being looked away from. Our inability to look at it is what "marks" it as shameful.

Thus, the "mark" of shame which turns Christabel away from the recognition of desire conveniently "seals" away from consciousness the "sorrow" that gives rise to her fear. Similarly, the "marks" on the page that constitute the narrative of *Christabel* "seal" from our view the true source of dread: for Christabel to "admit" or "tell" her desire in a straightforward way would require her to embrace, as a sexually aware being, her mother's fate. Desire must find expression in a dissociated manner, in a waking dream where the dream-self can enact desire inarticulately, anticipating self-recognition in a form of discourse for which, since all is understood, nothing need be told.

MOTHERS AND FATHERS

It is Christabel's actions that "speak" for her dream-self, not only in the confrontations of Part II, but throughout the events of Part I. "What makes her in the wood so late, / A furlong from the castle gate?" (25-26), asks the narrator, answering lamely, "She in the midnight wood will pray / For the weal of her lover that's far away" (29-30). The narrator's answer is insufficient to explain why this prayer must take place in the midnight wood at all, and we wonder what—or who—Christabel expects to find out there. It is Christabel, after all, who has made the encounter with Geraldine possible, she who has "raised up" (373) at the foot the "huge, *broad-breasted,* old oak tree" (42; italics mine) this "damsel bright," "richly clad," "beautiful exceedingly" (58, 67, 68), embodying all that the mother's world of death denies. "Raised up" suggests a conjuration, hinting at Christabel's responsibility for her fate: she comforts the "weary woman," takes her in, revives her, and asks her to share her bed (122).

Christabel's complicity in her own seduction, in the face of numerous indications of Geraldine's sinister aims, has long excited speculation.[13] But in the same way that Geraldine's spell, which prevents Christabel from telling what has happened to her, must be understood as self-imposed, a tactic resorted to in an ongoing psychomachia between her waking and dreaming selves, so Christabel's naiveté and passivity must be taken as signs of her unacknowledged intentions to transform herself. These intentions become more apparent when she offers Geraldine her mother's "cordial wine" (191), a "wild-flower wine" (220), and Geraldine's appropriation of the missing mother's role formally begins. Her first sip transforms Geraldine from a helpless, listless damsel into a proud and defiant figure:

> But soon with altered voice, said she—
> 'Off, wandering mother! Peak and pine!
> I have power to bid thee flee.'
> Alas! what ails poor Geraldine?
> Why stares she with unsettled eye?
> Can she the bodiless dead espy?
> And why with hollow voice cries she,
> 'Off, woman, off! this hour is mine—
> Though thou her guardian spirit be,
> Off, woman, off! 'tis given to me.'
>
> (204-13)

Though Christabel will not "take in" her real mother, the wanderer cannot easily be shaken off. Geraldine, who was up to now a "weary woman, scarce alive," "a weary weight," a "weary lady," who could not "speak for weariness" (95, 131, 190, 142), here withstands the mother's final challenge and drives *her* away to grow weak and weary, "to peak and pine." Christabel's confusion is once more reflected in disingenuous questions—"What ails poor Geraldine?"

> Then Christabel knelt by the lady's side,
> And raised to heaven her eyes so blue—
> Alas! said she, this ghastly ride—
> Dear Lady! it hath wildered you!
> The lady wiped her moist cold brow,
> And faintly said, ''tis over now!'
>
> (214-19)

Though puzzled, Christabel does not question Geraldine. Instead, she jumps to a safe conclusion, focusing on an efficient *cause* of Geraldine's behavior in order to blunt her awareness of its *symbolic* significance, in her own mind, as a response to the wild-flower wine Christabel herself has administered. In Lacanian terms, she remains at the imaginary level in her dealings with Geraldine, unaware of the symbolic intentionality informing her own actions. That symbolic level of meaning is accessible only in the context of her "story," as mediated by language, i.e., in the extended narrative itself and, thus, only for us, the readers. It is we who complete the circle of meaning initiated by Christabel's "discourse of the Other," we who raise it from the level of the imaginary to that of the symbolic. We are the Other to whom the unconscious structures of this anticipated discourse of self-consciousness are directed.[14]

Another drink, and the assimilation of the mother's role is complete.

> Again the wild-flower wine she drank!
> Her fair large eyes 'gan glitter bright,
> And from the floor whereon she sank,
> The lofty lady stood upright:
> She was most beautiful to see,
> Like a lady of a far countree.
>
> (220-25)

Following the ambiguous seduction scene, the narrator will call our attention to "the worker of these harms, / That holds the maiden in her arms": she "seems to slumber, still and mild, / As a mother with her child" (298-301). Twenty-five lines later Christabel smiles in her sleep "as infants at a sudden light" (318). "No doubt," the narrator suggests earnestly,

> she hath a vision sweet.
> What if her guardian spirit 'twere?
> What if she know her mother near?
>
> (326-28)

The last remark is, of course, compromised by Geraldine's presence, her embrace. The mother's wild-flower wine, symbolic of all the dangerously "wild," natural desires that have been distilled out of the mother's "bodiless" image, has transformed the "weary lady" into another mother, and thereby bestowed on her the power, so graphically expressed in Geraldine's newly glittering eyes and lofty stature, to transform the Baron's daughter into a woman like her. In Part II, Christabel will find herself compelled to behave in a manner which she unconsciously expects Geraldine, her "new" mother, will understand. Geraldine's covert resemblances to the dead mother, however, will make her image repulsive to the girl's waking mind.

Christabel's act of maternal substitution, her subsequent submission to Geraldine's mesmeric "serpent eyes," and her simultaneous revulsion at the "sole image" which she "passively did imitate" resemble what is clinically known as "transference"—in particular, that which characterizes hysteria and hypnotic states such as those which Christabel assumes in the presence of Geraldine.[15] In analysis, for instance, the hysterical subject attributes responsibility for all that happens to him or her to the analyst, the person apparently in charge.[16] Furthermore, the authority attributed to the analyst is "discursive" or interpretive in nature and clearly parental in character.[17]

In Lacanian terms, transference can be understood as a "putting of the question" to that parental Other whose tacit "discourse" the subject's behavior and speech unconsciously anticipate or refer to in order to be recognized. Like Geraldine, these are figures who cannot be interiorized or integrated by consciousness, presences whose points of view cannot be consciously adopted, identified with, and thus articulated by the subject, who thus relates to them on the imaginary rather than symbolic level. That Geraldine's mesmeric power to transform Christabel into a lamia like herself is "transferred" by Christabel's own unconscious mind is suggested by the fact that long before the narrative draws our attention to Geraldine's "shrunken serpent eyes" in the second vision of fear, Christabel has begun to *act out* the role of serpent: the first time that the "vision fell / Upon the soul of Christabel" (451-52), she "drew in her breath with a hissing sound" (459). Christabel's fascination with the abomination grows out of her own repressed personality, which insists on holding up to consciousness an image of the desire she fears and hates, now safely transferred to another. As a result, she can dissimulate her own responsibility for desire even as she acts in consonance with it: not she, but Geraldine is making her behave in a manner which consciously repulses her.

The Baron, by contrast, is that presence which brings Christabel "to" her waking self, that presence "through whom and for whom" she poses the question of her conscious identity as her father's "daughter mild" (471). When, in Part II, Christabel experiences her first "vision of fear" (453), as she "shrunk and shuddered" (454) and "drew in her breath with a hissing sound" (459) at the sight of Geraldine, it is the Baron's eye which composes her. When "the Knight turned wildly round," he "nothing saw, but his own sweet maid / with eyes upraised, as one that prayed" (460-62). The *consciously* anticipated "discourse of the other"—i.e., the Baron's interpretation of Christabel's behavior—here calls forth a different self-representation. Two different "parents" hold up to Christabel different mirrors in which to conceive herself. She becomes the person, takes on the identity, which she assumes the Other perceives in her.

But in fact, as Coleridge makes clear, the Baron's power to transform Christabel back into his innocent daughter is not his: it is a power appropriated, like Geraldine's, from the dead mother. For although, as a source of recognition, the mother is remote and wandering, her asexual, saintly image is made present for Christabel daily in the mournful litany of the Baron, the girl's only living source of self-esteem and acceptance.

> Each matin bell, the Baron saith,
> Knells us back to a world of death.
> These words sir Leoline first said,
> When he rose and found his lady dead:
> These words Sir Leoline will say
> Many a morn to his dying day!
>
>   (332-37)

The rhymes here—"saith"/"death," "said"/"dead," "say"/"dying day"—reinforce the associations made throughout the poem between speech and the recognition of the repressed. Sir Leoline's melancholy reflections maintain an image of the mother as a martyr to her sex, inadvertently reminding Christabel of the "world of death" to which she too must inevitably be knelled with the passing of time. If the mother's spiritual homelessness can be taken to symbolize her daughter's failure to internalize the mother's real image as Other, then the authority associated with that image would seem to have been delegated to the Baron, for the mother's last and thus self-definitive wish was that Christabel "might prove her dear lord's joy and pride" (631), might remain, in other words, the little girl her husband wants her to be. Significantly, when Christabel begs Sir Leoline to send Geraldine away, she invokes her dead "mother's soul" (616).

In order to understand fully the maternal basis of the Baron's authority in light of the Lacanian model of linguistic repression, we must take account of Lacan's version of the oedipal complex. For Lacan, the significance of the oedipal stage has only partly to do with the notions of latent sexuality conventionally focused upon by orthodox Freudians. The oedipal is, above all, the intrusion of the symbolic, of language itself, into the dyadic, wordless, and thus unselfconscious Imaginary relationship of the child with its mother, thus forcing the child to name itself and others and to see itself as a social object. The Father, in the traditional scenario centered on a male child, is the primary agent of this intrusion, the representative of a cultural structure of symbolization that is alien to the subject.

It is indeed appropriate, from a Lacanian standpoint, that Christabel be unable in the presence of her father to "tell," and thus put into the realm of the symbolic that the father represents, what "ails her." But Sir Leoline's associations with the dead mother also allow us to see how the Lacanian version of the oedipal might apply to female experience. For as Lemaire points out, the Lacanian father is merely the delegate of a symbolic system that transcends and antedates his authority: If "relations between men will be mediated by discourse or, to be more precise, by the concepts it engenders," then "in the domain of social symbolism, the third term which mediates the living will be the Ancestor, the Dead, God, the Sacred Cause, the Institution, Ideology, etc." (60). For Christabel, this mediating term is the dead mother—*she* is the ancestor who, as a "third term," must be assimilated by Christabel's waking mind if the girl is to see herself in the role which God, through his sacred institution—matrimony—has sanctioned for her as a woman.

The mother who can serve as such a "third term," however, is never fully interiorized, as we have seen. Christabel has never managed to integrate the mother's image as a sexual being with the mother's image as an adult, a parent. It is by means of the former image, a "third term" unassimilated by Christabel's mind, that Geraldine exerts her spell, and it is by means of the latter image, the assimilated "third term," that Sir Leoline is attributed the parental authority to keep Christabel a child. In trying to make sense of Geraldine's maternal resemblances, critics applying the traditional Oedipal theory to *Christabel* draw the main line of conflict between Christabel and Geraldine for the love of Sir Leoline (at the end of Part II, after the Baron rejects Christabel's plea, he leaves the room with Geraldine on his arm).[18] A Lacanian reading, while not directly contradicting such an interpretation, would seek the final meaning of Geraldine's maternalism in the opposition between Geraldine and Sir Leoline as figures of, ultimately, a *maternal* authority, figures reflecting a struggle in Christabel to resolve her own sense of identity.

The opposition between Geraldine and the Baron as wielders of maternal authority is implied by Coleridge at a number of points, the most significant being the one at which Christabel escorts Geraldine into Langdale Castle, her father's domain, and finally into her bedroom. Christabel's carrying Geraldine across the threshold (which the weary woman cannot cross under her own power) symbolically enacts that introjection of the sexual mother which Christabel cannot achieve psychologically as long as her barricaded psyche, like the castle itself,[19] belongs to her father and the image of the asexual mother he represents. Although her own symbolic intention is not recognized by Christabel's conscious self, it determines what she sees and how she reacts to it, as reported and responded to, again, by the voice of the narrator. Significantly, Geraldine must be kept out of Sir Leoline's sight:

> They passed the hall, that echoes still,
> Pass as lightly as you will!
> The brands were flat, the brands were dying,
> Amid their own white ashes lying;
> But when the lady passed, there came
> A tongue of light, a fit of flame;
> And Christabel saw the lady's eye,
> And nothing else saw she thereby,
> Save the boss of the shield of Sir Leoline tall,
> Which hung in a murky old niche in the wall.
> O softly tread, said Christabel,
> My father seldom sleepeth well.
>
> (154-65)

The feeling of stealth associated with entering the castle is unmistakable:

> Jealous of the listening air
> They steal their way from stair to stair;
> Now in glimmer, now in gloom,
> And now they pass the Baron's room,
> As still as death, with stifled breath!
>
> (167-71)

The castle, the very air, seems haunted by the presence of Christabel's slumbering father, and as Fogle observes, "The boss of the shield is another eye, a salient evidence that the castle is somehow awake and watchful" (146). In this tense moment Christabel feels herself caught in the glare of two opposing presences, made uncomfortably conscious of her father's, in fact, *because* Geraldine's presence causes the dying brands in the hallway—symbolic of repressed desire (Enscoe 45)—to flare up and gleam in the boss of the shield. As desire flares, so does conscience—strictly speaking, self-consciousness: the awareness, which Christabel here feels she must elude, of herself as the Baron sees her and as her ghostly mother, presumably, wished her to be. The Baron's eye, which represents Christabel's waking self-consciousness, threatens to destroy her unreflective absorption in a fantasized scenario of self-transformation.

Sir Leoline's shield symbolizes that very weapon by which the narrator would have Christabel "shielded" from the truth, against too intimate a knowledge of her own sexual identity. Self-consciousness flares in "a *tongue* of flame": once more Coleridge links seeing with saying, knowing with acknowledging. To the extent that the eye of conscience calls Christabel to acknowledge herself as her father's daughter, it will "shield" the truth that cannot be told. That Christabel's breath should be "stifled" when she confronts the gleaming boss is, thus, singularly apt: her inability to breathe reflects her inability to "admit"—both to her waking self and to her father—what she would now become, foreshadowing her failure in Part II to "tell" what she knows in his presence. The phrase "as still as death" once again links her paralysis to the dread associated with her mother's death.

Finally, the "maternal" derivation of the authority exerted by the paternal eye of self-consciousness is suggested by the fact that the "boss" of the shield is located at its midpoint, its "breast."[20] The power of Geraldine's spell over Christabel's utterance is exerted by the "touch" of her breast: the spell, Geraldine tells Christabel, "is lord of thy utterance" (268). Here the word "lord" reinforces the idea that Geraldine's new authority represents a direct challenge to Sir Leoline's. The challenge is underscored when, the next morning, greeting Christabel, the Baron presses "his gentle daughter to his breast" (398).[21] Christabel must serve two "lords," each of whom represents a different source of "maternal" self-validation. She is caught in a crossfire of anticipated parental expectations, conflicting "discourses" of the Other.

Summary and Postscript: The Power to Declare

Christabel's struggle to integrate her sexual and social identities can be understood as a severe crisis of recognition with respect to the Other, as represented in two conflicting images of the same-sex parent she never fully managed to internalize: that part of herself which Christabel can accept and about which she can speak seeks recognition from her father, the dead mother's familial and societal delegate; that part of herself—her sexual desire—which Christabel cannot accept and about which she cannot speak seeks tacit recognition from Geraldine, the dead mother's sexual surrogate. At the root of Christabel's sexual repression—and of its accompanying silence—lies the fear of death in the manner of her mother.

The ultimate value of such an analysis of repression in Coleridge's heroine is that it helps us to understand the appositeness of his ingenuous narrative style. The heroine's conflict of identity is expressed formally in the discrepancies between the symbolic significance of her actions, words, and perceptions and the naiveté that narrative "discourse of the Other" which represents them from without. The narrative defines and defends Christabel's waking self-image while denying or ignoring the symbolic level of meaning to which all images,

once mediated by language, advert. This is a level of meaning made accessible to the reader precisely by the obtrusiveness of narrative denial. Thus does desire insist on being recognized.

There is not space here for discussing adequately the relationship between Christabel's aphasia and amnesia; her dreams, desires, fears, and inhibitions; and the creative processes of the poet who conceived her. I think such a discussion would have to begin with Kathleen Coburn's observation that "the lost or orphan child and the dying or absent mother come too frequently into the poetry to be insignificant images" (#1991n.). We know that, probably as a result of his father's early death and his mother's *de facto* abandonment of him after his departure for Christ's Hospital, Coleridge considered himself, even at the age of thirty-seven and all during the years his mother was still alive, "a deserted orphan," "an orphan Brother" (***Letters*** [***Collected Letters***] III, 103, 105). Given these tendencies, and the recurrence of the orphaned child, usually female, in Coleridge's poetry, the close identification of the narrator with Christabel's point of view throughout most of the poem suggest that in his heroine Coleridge was personifying salient aspects of his own personality. Who then was he, as a poet, seeking—and in the person of Christabel recoiling from—when he created Geraldine?

The love-hate relationship of Christabel to Geraldine reflects Coleridge's own problematic relationship to his mother. Geraldine resembles sexually inimical, maternal figures in Coleridge's notebooks and other writings, figures which began to haunt his dreams more and more frequently during the writing of ***Christabel,*** and which critics like Bostetter, Yarlott (40-49), Beres (106-08), and Fruman have linked to the poet's subconscious feelings of guilt, shame, unworthiness, and even latent homoeroticism, all connected in some way with his mother's apparent abandonment of him from boyhood on. In his dreams and waking nightmares at this time, and for many years to follow, this mother, hated and feared, encouraged the most hideous expression of the sexual self in scenes of humiliation and pursuit.

But in ***Christabel*** the Mother is not only the ultimate arbiter of sexual identity: she is also, figuratively, the ultimate arbiter of a "poetic" identity closely associated with the sexual self—an identity expressed in speech. In terms of Coleridge's own poetic "aphasia" in failing to complete the poem—indeed, in giving up the serious pursuit of poetry altogether—Geraldine is the Muse turned mute, the "mother tongue" paralyzed. If it was a failure caused, as many have suggested, by his realization that the chthonic source of creative inspiration and imaginative power within him was becoming, in its sexually lurid suggestiveness, a threat to his conscious self-image—perhaps even to his sanity—then here lies the link between the mother-obsessed and mother-terrified heroine of Coleridge's gothic fragment and his own poetic desires and expectations. Geraldine, the predatory mother and muse, ruled that underworld, nurtured and tormented the dream-self that inhabited there, and finally enjoined silence. Coleridge's abandonment of his poetic profession, like Christabel's verbal paralysis, was a failure to "tell" "the desire which is there to be recognized and the object to whom this desire is addressed" (Lacan 33).

Notes

1. All citations from the poetry are from Ernest Hartley Coleridge's standard edition and are noted by line number in the text.

2. Basler (25-51) was the first to point out that the sinister theme of sexual perversion and repression that insinuates itself throughout the poem can be traced to Christabel's inability to accept her own sexual maturity, "her passionate though thwarted love for her absent 'betrothed knight'" (29). See also Wormhoudt (17-50), Spatz, Proffitt, and Beres. More broadly psychological approaches include Bostetter, Luther, Enscoe (25-60), and Emslie and Edwards, the last of which approaches Christabel's fall from sexual innocence from a Blakean perspective.

3. For all its currency, the term *Other* has a long history in existential and phenomenological thought going back to Hegel, who first affirmed, in *The Phenomenology of Mind,* that "self-consciousness exists in itself and for itself, in that, and by the fact that it exists for another self-consciousness; that is to say, it *is* only by being acknowledged or 'recognized'" (229). In the words of Lemaire, "It is in the other that the subject first lives and registers himself" (177), and in the words of the French phenomenologist, Maurice Merleau-Ponty, "The ego cannot emerge . . . without doubling itself *as an ego in the eyes of the other*" (153). Paul Ricoeur goes so far as to assert, "My existence for my self depends utterly on this self-constitution in the opinion of others. My Self—is I dare say so—is received from the opinion of others, who consecrate it" (112).

4. See, for instance, Spatz (112-13) and Fogle (142).

5. See, for instance, Klaus and Kennel: "The original mother-infant bond is the formative relationship in the course of which the child develops a sense of himself" (2). For a phenomenological treatment, see Merleau-Ponty (149-55).

6. I follow Erikson (215-18), who sees the process of adolescent and adult identity formation as repeating, with respect to authority figures outside the family, the earliest introjection of and identification with the parents. For Erikson, the attainment of a strong unitary sense of identity is a gradual process of integrating self-representations in public roles that receive recognition from family, friends, and at last the wider society. "The body, the personality, the role to which [one] is attached for life . . . are the various selves which make up our composite Self. There are constant and often shock-like transitions between these selves" (218). Christabel undergoes just such "shock-like transitions" during her confrontations with Geraldine.

7. Dramin notes that "Part I parodies conventional paraphernalia of gothic fiction: the gothic heroine, vignettes containing howling hounds and tolling clocks, crude devices arousing suspense and mystery, lurid sensationalism, and the gothic villain."

8. See Enscoe (42-44), to whom I am indebted for this reading.

9. Piper notes the same connection, and Magnuson (99) observes that Christabel, like the Hermit who confronts the Ancient Mariner, fears that the person she sees has come from the dead.

10. Emslie and Edwards: "Here, too, the effect is pointed by repetition. Coleridge is deliberately risking the flatness of naiveté for the sake of a special effect" (60).

11. See [Ernest Hartley] Coleridge's standard edition (40).

12. See also Nethercot (56), Luther (61), Radley (71), and Beyer (168).

13. See, for instance, Basler (32) and Luther (52). Spatz (112) notes that "despite the sinister overtones of Geraldine's invasion of the household, Christabel seems eager to consummate their relationship."

14. Lemaire points out, "It is characteristic of unconscious structures to include voices other than that of the first person; the unconscious discourse could, for example, take place in the alienated form of the second or third person" (136).

15. In addition to transference, Abse cites "restriction of consciousness, heightened suggestibility, alteration of memory function, and dissociative phenomena" (40-41) as salient characteristics of both hysteria and hypnosis. Christabel displays all of these symptoms at one point or another in the poem. Abse also notes that the hysteric "has difficulty in attaining actuality as a grown-up human being" (107) and that hysteria "provides an example of the onset of neurosis due to failure of adaptation as the result of conflict between individual needs and social opportunities and requirements" (9). Both these descriptions quite clearly apply to Christabel's situation.

16. So Ferenczi: "The consciousness that the physician is responsible for everything that happens (in his own room) favours the emergence of daydreams, first unconscious, later becoming conscious" (37).

17. Ferenczi concludes that the analyst, in order to succeed, must arouse in the subject "the same feelings of love or fear, the same conviction of infallibility, as those with which his parents inspired him as a child" (60).

18. For both Spatz and Proffitt, for instance, Geraldine's identification with and replacement of the mother are to be interpreted according to traditional Oedipal categories: The source of Christabel's "vision of fear" is her sense of being displaced in her father's affections by Geraldine. Wormhoudt observes "that Geraldine is unconsciously meant to represent Christabel's mother" (19), but does not relate the connection to the question of Christabel's identity.

19. Siegel (173) takes the castle to be symbolic of the human mind, in line with "the long tradition symbolizing the soul as a besieged castle."

20. Noted by Wormhoudt (25). One is reminded of Dr. John Polidori's anecdote, in the "Extract of a Letter to the Editor" which he prefixed to his horror tale, *The Vampyre,* describing *Christabel*'s effect on Shelley when the poet first heard it recited by Byron: "His wild imagination having pictured to him the bosom of one of the ladies with eyes (which was reported of a lady in the neighborhood where he lived) he was obliged to leave the room in order to destroy the impression" (260).

21. From an Eriksonian perspective, the emphasis on the breast would appear to be a symbolic recapitulation of the earliest stage of infant identity-formation in the working out of Christabel's adolescent identity-crisis. The touch of Geraldine's bosom holds Christabel spell-bound in the presence of her father because, as a symbol of maternal nurturance, it represents the mother's formative influence over her child's as yet inchoate sense of self—in this case, a self that is seeking mature erotic expression.

Works Cited

Abse, D. Wilfred. *Hysteria and Related Disorders: an Approach to Psychological Medicine.* Bristol: Wright, 1966.

Basler, Roy P. *Sex, Symbolism, and Psychology in Literature.* New Brunswick: Rutgers UP, 1948.

Beres, David. "A Dream, a Vision, and a Poem." *International Journal of Psycho-analysis* 32: 106-108.

Beyer, Werner W. *The Enchanted Forest.* Oxford: Blackwood, 1963.

Bostetter, Edward E. "*Christabel*: The Vision of Fear." *Philological Quarterly* 36 (1957): 183-94.

Coburn, Kathleen, ed. *The Notebooks of Samuel Taylor Coleridge.* 3 Vols. New York: Pantheon, 1961.

Coleridge, Samuel Taylor. *Poetical Works.* Ed. Ernest Hartley Coleridge. 1912. Oxford: Oxford UP, 1967.

———. *Collected Letters.* Ed. Earl Leslie Griggs. 5 Vols. Oxford: Clarendon, 1959-71.

Dramin, Edward I. "'Amid the Jagged Shadows': Parody, Moral Realism, and Metaphysical Statement in Coleridge's *Christabel.*" Diss. Columbia, 1972.

Enscoe, Gerald. *Eros and the Romantics: Sexual Love as a Theme in Coleridge, Shelley, and Keats.* The Hague: Mouton, 1967.

Emslie, Macdonald, and Paul Edwards. "The Limitations of Langdale: A Reading of Christabel." *Essays in Criticism* 20 (1970): 57-70.

Erikson, Erik. *Identity, Youth and Crisis.* New York: Norton, 1968.

Ferenczi, Sandor. *Sex in Psycho-analysis.* 1909; rpt. New York: Dover, 1956.

Fogle, Richard Harter. *The Idea of Coleridge's Criticism.* Berkeley: U California P, 1962.

Freud, Sigmund. "The Unconscious." *Standard Edition.* Trans. James Strachey. London: Hogarth Press, 1962. Vol. 14.

Fruman, Norman. *Coleridge: The Damaged Archangel.* New York: Braziller, 1971.

Hegel, Georg Wilhelm Friedrich. *The Phenomenology of Mind.* Trans. J. B. Baillie. 1910. New York: Harper, 1967.

Klaus, Marshall H. and John H. Kennel. *Maternal-Infant Bonding.* St. Louis: Mosby, 1976.

Lacan, Jacques. *The Language of the Self: The Function of Language in Psychoanalysis.* Trans. Anthony Wilden. Baltimore: Johns Hopkins UP, 1968.

Lemaire, Anika. *Jacques Lacan.* Trans. David Macey. London: Routledge, 1977.

Luther, Susan M. *Christabel as Dream Reverie.* Salzburg: Institut fur Englische Sprache, 1976.

Magnuson, Paul. *Coleridge's Nightmare Poetry.* Charlottesville: UP of Virginia, 1974.

Merleau-Ponty, Maurice. "The Child's Relations with Others." *The Primacy of Perception.* Ed. James M. Edie. Evanston: Northwestern UP, 1964.

Nethercot, Arthur H. *The Road to Tryermaine.* 1939. New York: Russell, 1962.

Piper, H. W. "The Disunity of *Christabel* and the Fall of Nature." *Essays in Criticism* 28 (1978): 216-227.

Polidori, John. "The Vampyre, A Tale." *Three Gothic Novels.* Ed. E. F. Bleiler. New York: Dover, 1966.

Proffitt, Edward. "'Christabel' and Oedipal Conflict." *Research Studies* 46 (1978): 248-51.

Radley, Virginia C. *Samuel Taylor Coleridge.* New York: Twayne, 1966.

Ricoeur, Paul. *The Conflict of Interpretations.* Ed. Don Ihde. Evanston: Northwestern UP, 1974.

Siegel, Robert H. "The Serpent and the Dove: *Christabel* and the Problem of Evil." *Imagination and the Spirit: Essays in Literature and the Christian Faith presented to Clyde S. Kilby.* Ed. Charles A. Huttar. Grand Rapids: Eerdmans, 1971.

Spatz, Jonas P. "The Mystery of Eros: Sexual Initiation in Coleridge's 'Christabel.'" *PMLA* 90 (1975): 107-116.

Wormhoudt, Arthur. *The Demon Lover: A Psychoanalytic Approach to Literature.* 1949. Freeport, N.Y.: Books for Libraries, 1968.

Yarlott, Geoffrey. *Coleridge and the Abyssinian Maid.* London: Methuen, 1967.

Andrew M. Cooper (essay date 1988)

SOURCE: Cooper, Andrew M. "Who's Afraid of the Mastiff Bitch? Gothic Parody and Original Sin in 'Christabel.'" In *Critical Essays on Samuel Taylor Coleridge,* edited by Leonard Orr, pp. 81-107. New York: G. K. Hall & Co., 1994.

[*In the following excerpt, originally published in 1988, Cooper examines "Christabel"'s comic elements. Cooper regards Coleridge's use of gothic motifs as a deliberate form of parody, one intended to expose the sensationalism and absurdity of the genre.*]

> In the establishment of principles and fundamental doctrines, I must of necessity require the attention of my reader to become my fellow-labourer. The primary facts essential to the intelligibility of my principles I can prove to others only so far as I can prevail on them to retire into themselves and make their own minds the objects of their stedfast attention.
>
> —*Coleridge,* **The Friend,** *Essay iii*

"The mastiff's howl is touched with a deathly horror," says G. Wilson Knight, speaking for many others who have found *Christabel* a genuinely chilling piece of gothic supernaturalism.[1]

'Tis the middle of night by the castle clock,
And the owls have awakened the crowing cock;
Tu-whit!—Tu-whoo!
And hark, again! the crowing cock,
How drowsily it crew.
Sir Leoline, the Baron rich,
Hath a toothless mastiff bitch;
From her kennel beneath the rock
She maketh answer to the clock,
Four for the quarters, and twelve for the hour;
Ever and aye, by shine and shower,
Sixteen short howls, not over loud;
Some say, she sees my lady's shroud.[2]

If we do a double take, however, the jocular reactions of contemporary reviewers seem closer to the truth. As William Hazlitt put it, "Is she a sort of Cerberus to fright away the critics? But—gentlemen, she is toothless."[3] Indeed, there is comedy in the spectacle of so grotesquely dilapidated a watchdog ("the picturesque old lady," commented another reviewer);[4] in the weltering fricatives with which she is introduced in line 7, a tongue-twister itself tending to induce momentary toothlessness; in the distinctly uneerie cacophony she generates together with hooting owls, crowing cock, and tolling clock; in the narrator's somewhat disoriented identification of the bird song, suggesting his affinity with Wordsworth's Idiot Boy who likewise asserts, topsy-turvy, "The cocks did crow, to-whoo, to-whoo";[5] in the metronomic regularity of the dog's howling, heard all day every day and hence not a spooky special effect of this particular midnight; in the tedious precision with which the howls are computed, recalling the obtuse arithmetic of Wordsworth's narrator in "We Are Seven"; and in the contrasting vague portentousness with which the obligatory rumored ghost is abruptly brought forward in the last line. Coleridge's opening set piece accumulates in a short space so much paraphernalia of horror that the effect is less ominous than bathetic.

I

Unless, of course, we approach the dog full of the expectations gratified by popular gothic subliterature. "If the poem seems awkward," the reader tells himself, "surely this only reflects my own distance from the conventions of the genre." As Romantic gothic was deliberately archaic from its inception, moreover, contemporaries would have rationalized in the same way we do today. And yet Coleridge implies in four highly critical reviews of gothic fiction—one written in 1794, the others about the time of *Christabel,* Part I, in 1797 and 1798—that a too-willing suspension of disbelief is delusion, even hypocrisy. If his pathetic relic of a watchdog looks less fearfully symmetrical than Blake's Tyger (which in some versions also looks distinctly tame and toothless), that is only Coleridge's characteristically unintimidating way of dramatizing the same irony: our horror at the beast is sheer self-deception, its monstrosity just a projection of our own alienated energies. Coleridge aims to elicit the same realization as Jane Austen does at the end of *Northanger Abbey,* another gothic parody with almost the same twenty-year interval between commencement and publication (1798-1817 versus 1797-1816 for *Christabel*): "Nothing could shortly be clearer, than that it had been all a voluntary, self-created delusion, each trifling circumstance receiving importance from an imagination resolved on alarm, and every thing forced to bend to one purpose by a mind which . . . had been craving to be frightened."[6]

The reviewers for the most part admitted straight out that *Christabel* fails laughably if judged as ordinary gothic. By constantly provoking doubts about the plausibility of his narrative, Coleridge satirizes the number and artificiality of the conventions required by such literature. When the two ladies enter Christabel's chamber (190-225), for example, Geraldine's discomfort ensues so rapidly after talk of Christabel's guardian mother-spirit, the episode seems perfunctory. She acts as though she is fending off a persistent bee, thereby unluckily emphasizing the crassly tangible nature of the spirit: "Off, wandering mother! . . . Off, woman, off! . . . Though thou her guardian spirit be, / Off, woman, off!"[7] Since Geraldine twice declares the identity of her assailant, the narrator's puzzlement does not seem perspicacious: "what ails poor Geraldine? / Why stares she with unsettled eye? / Can she the bodiless dead espy?" The comedy increases when next Christabel intervenes with more wildflower wine: "Alas! said she, this ghastly ride— / Dear lady! It hath wildered you!" Christabel's charitable euphemism for what must appear a rather violent attack of insanity; her failure to put two and two together by connecting the attack with mention of her guardian mother just seconds before, or else the crude stylization whereby Geraldine's cries are supposed to be stage whispers unheard by Christabel; finally, Geraldine's double shot of the home-brewed wildflower medication to such "speedy" and "excellent effect," as the *Edinburgh* reviewer quipped, that her eyes begin to "glitter bright" and she arises from the floor invigorated[8]—all evince the humorous creakings of stage machinery.

Such lapses are attributable not to the author, however, but to his narrator. Humphrey House observes that the landscape of Part I is skewed inasmuch as all its details seem to be "behaving oddly and ominously," but he interprets this as Coleridge's attempt to "heighten the mystery by suggestions of slight distortions in ordinary behavior, . . . as if proportion is thrown out and normal vision perplexed."[9] Yet such oddness suggests not only danger, but that something funny is going on in both senses of the word. Although the narrator's perplexed vision does intimate that supernatural matters are afoot, it also reveals his utterly mundane difficulty in discerning the dramatic action at all. Dim-witted,

nagging, sanctimonious, and overwrought, Coleridge's old duffer recalls the comically limited narrators of Wordsworth's "The Idiot Boy," "The Thorn," and "We Are Seven." He appears only partly in command of his story, so that his frequent querulous interpolations tend to break rather than heighten the suspense. Chiefly it is his frantic losing struggle to gratify the audience's sensational expectations—what the preface to *Lyrical Ballads* calls the "degrading thirst after outrageous stimulation" and "craving for extraordinary incident" (W [*Selected Poems and Prefaces by William Wordsworth*], p. 449)—that produces the comedy.[10] The stock exaggeration in an outburst like "Hush, beating heart of Christabel!" (53) could have passed if muttered by the lady to herself; spoken by the narrator, however, the suspense is (in House's phrase) thrown out of proportion, for the reader thus infers a telltale heart no less audible than Geraldine's moaning out loud. The narrator's clumsy identification with his heroine is reemphasized when she next confronts Geraldine: "Mary mother, save me now! / (Said Christabel,) And who art thou?" (69-70). The embarrassed parentheses are necessary, of course, to distinguish Christabel's exclamation from the narrator's previous "Jesu, Maria, shield her well!" (54), likewise addressed to the mother of God.

Ultimately, the poem's proliferation of rhetoric so plainly devised for effect threatens to undermine the narrator altogether, blurring his distance from the dramatic action and exposing him as just another gothic gimmick no more credible than the rest. His gullibility is further suggested in lines like: "It moaned as near, as near can be" (39)—how near is *that*? "Is the night chilly and dark? / The night is chilly, but not dark" (14-15)— since this distinction remains, as House puts it, "perplexed," either the question must be superfluous or the answer banal. "'Tis a month before the month of May" (21)—a pretentious circumlocution which, as the *British Review* pointed out, merely arouses "the strong suspicion . . . that it could not be, after all, any other than that month which a plain man would call April" (CH [*Coleridge: The Critical Heritage*], p. 225), specifically, April Fool's Day. Coleridge's criticism of Ann Radcliffe applies above all to his own narrator: "Curiosity is raised oftener than it is gratified; or rather, it is raised so high that no adequate gratification can be given it."[11] At the same time, the many rhetorical questions and exclamations underscore his abhorrence of the gothic writer's implicit condescension in pretending horror at tales that really amount to mere bedtime stories for a childishly credulous audience. Through the same "tedious protraction of events" and "redundancy of description" as Coleridge denounces in Ann Radcliffe and the same "flat, flabby, unimaginative Bombast" as he condemns in Monk Lewis,[12] *Christabel*'s heavy-handed narrator serves to hasten a "satiety" which, the author trusted, "will soon banish what good sense should have prevented; and . . . the public will learn . . . with how little expense of thought or imagination this species of composition is manufactured" (Greever, pp. 186, 191).

As a "hireling in the Critical Review," Coleridge himself became sated soon enough. His letter to Thomas Bowles of March 16, 1797, complains, "I am almost weary of the Terrible. . . . I have been lately reviewing The Monk, the Italian, Hubert de Sevrac, & &c & &c—in all of which dungeons, and old castles, & solitary Houses by the Sea Side, & Caverns, & Woods, & extraordinary characters, & all the tribe of Horror & Mystery, have crowded on me—even to surfeiting" (*CL* [*Collected Letters of Coleridge*] 1:225). Only if we regard the supernaturalism of *Christabel,* Part I, as parody is the contradiction averted of Coleridge undertaking a major gothic narrative within months of declaring himself "surfeited" with such writing. Only thus is he saved from the shameless double standard imputed to him by any straight reading of the poem, which he commenced so shortly after proclaiming in print that "a romance is incapable of exemplifying a moral truth. . . . Tales of enchantment and witchcraft can never be *useful,*" although they can be "*pernicious*" (Greever, pp. 192, 195). Even the philosophical plagiarisms of the *Biographia Literaria* assert ideas Coleridge shared and respected, and in large measure had already expressed in his own writing—as indeed he protested with guilty prolepsis in the *Biographia* itself.[13] Yet this would hardly be the case were *Christabel* intended to gratify his audience's detestable appetite for "the trite and the extravagant . . . the Scylla and Charybdis of writers who deal in fiction" (Greever, p. 169).

Recognizing that the "patent inconsistency" imputed of Coleridge's position puts an unusual burden of proof on the traditional reading of *Christabel,* Arthur Nethercot hedged. The poem was written, he argued fifty years ago, as a romance not of the supernatural but the "preternatural": events highly improbable but not, like the gothic fiction Coleridge abhorred, "contrary to nature" and so incapable of serving a moral purpose.[14] When Nethercot wrote, Donald Tuttle had just revealed numerous parallels between *Christabel* and works of gothic romance, including M. G. Lewis's *The Monk,* and had concluded the poem was another such work.[15] But useful as Nethercot's distinction is for the wholly serious Part II, it fails to explain Part I's additional resemblances to passages of *The Monk* whose leering salacity, far from being typical of 1790's gothic, represents Lewis's special contribution and which Coleridge evidently imitates for a specific purpose. Compare Geraldine's disrobing and the Peeping Tom hypocrisy of the poem's narrator with the monk Ambrosio's prurient discovery that Matilda is not a fellow novitiate after all:

> Then drawing in her breath aloud,
> Like one that shuddered, she unbound
> The cincture from beneath her breast:

> Her silken robe, and inner vest,
> Dropt to her feet, and full in view,
> Behold! her bosom and half her side—
> A sight to dream of, not to tell!

[247-53]

"She had torn open her habit, and her bosom was half-exposed . . . and, oh! that was such a breast! The moonbeams darting full upon it enabled the monk to observe its dazzling whiteness: his eye dwelt with insatiable avidity upon the beauteous orb: a sensation till then unknown filled his heart with a mixture of anxiety and delight."[16] The titillation of these episodes indeed does not run "contrary to nature." Yet contrary to Nethercot, Coleridge's February 1797 review excoriates *The Monk* for its "libidinous minuteness": "shameless harlotry . . . and trembling innocence . . . are seized . . . as vehicles of the most voluptuous images," making the book "a *mormo* [bugbear] for children, a poison for youth, and a provocative for the debauchee" (Greever, p. 195). One concludes that the implicit lesbianism of the poem's bedchamber scene deliberately burlesques the lubricious and implausible gender confusion at the heart of Lewis's tale. When Hazlitt spread the wicked rumor that Geraldine was really a man in disguise and Christabel's seduction therefore boringly routine, he was closer to divining Coleridge's satire than he suspected.[17] In short, we must stand Tuttle's argument on its head: *Christabel* does not passively reflect the influence of popular gothic subliterature; it reacts against that influence and the corruptions Coleridge saw therein. Less strenuously, his portrayal of the narrator reveals a tongue-in-cheek, essentially campy appreciation of the banality and melodrama of a literary fad insufficiently aware of its cultural determinants to be considered serious art.

Why then has Coleridge's humor eluded so many sensitive and intelligent readers, including Byron, Shelley, and Walter Scott? I can only guess, of course, but one reason must be the tendency to compensate for the poem's fragmentary status by interpreting Part I in terms of the less conventionally gothic and utterly unfunny Part II. Perhaps another is that the immediate satire was passé by the time it was published in 1816, almost twenty years after the height of the gothic craze. One suspects the poem's reputation as a chiller resulted from the downplaying or omission of comic details during its prolonged underground existence through recitations themselves seemingly in the oral tradition of authentic balladry. Shelley's notorious panic at the bedchamber scene—"Shelley suddenly shrieking and putting his hands to his head, ran out of the room with a candle," Polidori reported[18]—came from hearing Byron recite a few verses from memory when at "twelve o-clock" the company "really began to talk ghostly": circumstances not exactly conducive to critical discernment (this was the meeting in which "The Vampyre" and *Frankenstein* originated). At any rate, parody of a genre that is itself based on another genre—as eighteenth-century gothic romance is based on certain preconceptions, however ahistorical or self-serving, about the manners and mores of medieval romance—possesses a confusing double artificiality whose calculated distortions are naturally liable to be confounded, by an audience already expecting artificiality, with the distortions present unwittingly in the object of parody. In fact, the gross carnage of Lewis and Maturin clearly involves an element of self-parody from the outset, an exuberant and unpretentious nihilism that is perhaps their chief appeal. When *Tales of Terror,* Lewis's collection of gothic ballads published in 1799, led by popular demand to *Tales of Wonder* a year later, the companion volume supplied not only more thrills but several satires directed at its presumed audience of young females.[19] Somewhat similarly, William Empson notes that **The Rime of the Ancient Mariner** originally included a stanza expressing "the formula, '*fun* with corpse horror'"; and Leslie Brisman has recently elaborated Empson's proposal that the Mariner's experience is not, as he himself trusts, a type of Christ's redemption but "at best only a parody of it."[20] Not that the Mariner is a humorous figure, but his simplemindedness does yield a dramatic irony not unlike the black comedy of **Christabel**'s narrator.

Finally, if everyone was misreading **Christabel,** why didn't Coleridge set them straight? Mainly, I think, because he considered the imitative accuracy of Part I to reflect on his own integrity as an artist. As he later argued about, significantly, satires on "pretensions to the supernatural": "Whatever must be misrepresented in order to be ridiculed, is in fact not ridiculed; but the thing substituted for it. It is a satire on something else, coupled with a lie on the part of the satirist, who knowing, or having the means of knowing the truth, chose to call one thing by the name of another."[21] Thus an honest satire is self-evident, and either hits or misses. To explain the joke—a tedious task whose reward is not spontaneous shared amusement but only imposed intellectual understanding: my task in this essay—looks suspiciously like "calling one thing by the name of another." Since Coleridge believed the popularity of gothic to be a function of supply and demand, ultimately his satire aims not to deride "the multitude of the manufacturers" (Greever, p. 191) but to open the eyes of consumers whose self-ignorance is what makes the stuff marketable in the first place. And, of course, the whole thrust of Coleridgean philosophy is that consciousness-raising is not much helped by rational demonstration, tending as it does to answer "delving & difficulty" with "a set of parrot words, quite satisfied, clear as a pikestaff, . . . a stupid piece of mock-knowledge."[22]

II

The poem's parody turns serious when we consider that Christabel's relation to Geraldine parallels that of the stereotypical gothic reader to the seductive gothic villain-hero. The most jaded horror addicts were generally represented as well-bred young ladies like Jane Austen's Miss Andrews, "one of the sweetest creatures in the world, . . . an angel" who guarantees a book list of which the heroine Catherine anxiously inquires, "but are they all horrid, are you sure they are all horrid?" (pp. 34-35).[23] On the other hand, Geraldine's basilisk-eye, superb demeanor, and divided will, together with her momentary fits of compunction, manipulativeness based on uncanny insight into human nature, and apparent subordination to forces still more powerful than herself—all evoke such figures as Radcliffe's Schedoni, Lewis's Wandering Jew, or Joanna Baillie's de Monfort. Typical of these demons is their ambiguous identity, part human, part monster. Similarly, although critics have called Geraldine a vampire, witch, lamia, ghoul, metempsychosed spirit, and werewolf, nobody denies the equivocal nature of the evidence. Indeed, the real question is why we *prefer* that Geraldine be unequivocally supernatural, why (to munch an old critical chestnut) the evil in her seems more "interesting" than the good.

Coleridge's examination of this problem centers on Christabel's exaggerated notion of her own innocence. She scans the signature of Geraldine's wretchedness—"This mark of my shame, this seal of my sorrow"—but refuses to "declare" the human truth she thus "knows" "with open eyes" (270-92). For there is nothing necessarily supernatural about the spell with which Geraldine binds Christabel to silence. As Arthur Lovejoy points out, Coleridge's persistent concern was "that of vindicating philosophically man's moral freedom and accountability, and consequently the reality of genuinely moral evil—evil for which the individual is absolutely and alone responsible."[24] In his review of 1797, Coleridge accordingly objects that the victims of supernatural demons are made to beg the crucial question: why has this person been selected to encounter sin? "Human prudence can oppose no sufficient shield to the power and cunning of supernatural beings," Coleridge points out; therefore "let [the romance-writer] work *physical* wonders only, and we will be content to *dream* with him for a while; but the first *moral* miracle which he attempts, he disgusts and awakens us" (Greever, pp. 192, 194). Thus Geraldine no more commands Christabel's moral nature than one would expect in real life. It is hard to see how E. E. Bostetter's interpretation of "the helpless paralyzed good, invaded and violated without cause or warning" by an evil "imposed from without" constitutes anything but a mugging, much less "a nightmare vision of evil triumphant."[25] The critic's righteous assumption that Christabel's innocence should supply immunity from all earthly constraints reflects the same overidentification with the heroine as he proceeds to condemn in the poet. After all, her physical vulnerability does not necessarily entail moral capitulation.

Christabel's precursor, the Lady in Milton's *Comus,* is similarly liable to deception through her charity and, like Christabel, becomes paralyzed as a result, but upon discovering Comus's falsity she resolutely refuses to have anything more to do with him. She thus explicitly repudiates any personal guilt: "Thou canst not touch the freedom of the mind / With all thy charms, although this corporal rind / Thou hast immanacl'd."[26] In the same way, physical evil, no matter how supernatural its source, cannot touch Christabel's soul unless she consents to it, so forging manacles of the mind. Wrote Coleridge in a letter of March 10, 1795, "Almost all the physical Evil in the World depends on the existence of moral Evil" (*CL* 1:154)—not vice versa, as Bostetter's reading would suggest.[27] One could object that Coleridge here leaves room for the rare supernatural exception that proves the rule; but that the will was indeed susceptible to "forced unconscious sympathy" (409) with evil he reiterated throughout his life. "I believe most steadfastly in original sin," he wrote with ingratiating sternness to his older brother George, the reverend, exactly three years later, the probable date of Part I, "that from our mothers' womb our understandings are darkened; and even where our understandings are in the Light, that our organization is depraved, & our volitions imperfect" (*CL* 1:396).

So Christabel's innocence is not somehow exempt from human frailty. Yet she desperately desires to be perfect, and paradoxically this desperation corrupts her. Here lies the core dramatic irony that saves her character from the oversimplification alleged by Hazlitt and many others since. What makes Geraldine's spell insidious is that, in part at least, it is *not* supernatural but merely a lie or threat which Christabel embraces in order to keep believing in her own infallibility. The spell's power is psychological, based on Christabel's awareness that only forcible restraint can justify silence about her otherwise pardonable error in admitting evil into the castle (the poet thus analyzes his own growing self-enslavement to the spell of opium, a *"free-agency-annihilating* Poison" [*CL* 3:489] which he nevertheless chooses freely in the first place).[28] Hence Coleridge's well-known account of his poetic contributions to *Lyrical Ballads.* "The incidents and agents were to be, in part at least, supernatural; and the excellence aimed at was to consist in the interesting of the affections by the dramatic truth of such emotions, as would naturally accompany such situations, supposing them real. And real in this sense they *have* been to every human being who, from whatever source of delusion, has at any time believed himself under supernatural agency."[29] Thus Geraldine, who is not evil incarnate, only provides the opportunity for sinning; Christabel is free to stand or fall. But Christabel's fugitive and cloistered virtue is oblivious of the fine Miltonic distinction between feeling tempted and actually succumbing. She ignores her initial deception by Geraldine, thereby conniving at it.

As Bostetter aptly observes, Coleridge was much bemused at the way inadvertent sinful thoughts for which one bears no moral responsibility—his own nightmares being a major case in point—can elicit nonetheless an irrational sense of guilt and shame. This reaction would suggest that the thoughts are unconsciously perceived as deserved punishment for some previous unknown sin for which one does in fact bear responsibility. Coleridge attempts to explain the phenomenon through psychological association, as we'll see: sinful thoughts being in the final analysis products of the Fall, the mind associates them with that universal crime and the more appropriate guilt and shame which *it* elicits. Such identification with the aggressor forms the link connecting Christabel's latent sinfulness with Geraldine's actual evil. When Christabel awakens crying "'Sure I have sinn'd!'" (381), her moral innocence remains intact; still in bed, she hasn't yet had occasion to withhold confessing the evil to her father downstairs. What her shocked little outburst therefore expresses is simply an awareness of her ordinary human fallibility, an awareness provoked by the sudden recollection, upon coming fully awake, of her mistaken assumptions about Geraldine's beauty and innocence the night before. But with her black-and-white morality, Christabel misinterprets her dismay. She assumes herself guilty of actually choosing sin in some hidden way and hence prays that God "Might wash away her sins *unknown*" (390; italics mine). Unwilling to incur the heavy guilt which she deludedly believes she has incurred through a moment's inattention, the girl thus rejects all responsibility whatsoever for Geraldine's presence in the castle. Trapped by her self-deception, she refuses to warn others of the evil which in reality she encountered only by accident. In sum, Christabel as the poem opens is perfect in all respects but one: she lacks the knowledge that she is not perfect. Put less paradoxically, she is ignorant of the one imperfection she cannot help, her *potential* for sin, a potential intrinsic to earthly life. And yet so pervasive are the corruptions of earthly life, Coleridge shows, this one imperfection ineluctably becomes a tragic flaw.

For Geraldine, like Milton's tempter, sees right through her victim. She tells the girl exactly what she wants to hear. To have caused the death of one's mother in childbirth, as Christabel says has befallen her, would seem *prima facie* ample grounds for supposing oneself inherently iniquitous. Recognizing that Christabel takes the opposite view—she optimistically believes the mother has become her guardian spirit—and that someone convinced that her every move is divinely protected might well consider herself invulnerable, Geraldine smooths the way toward the spell with mesmerizing flattery:

> All they who live in the upper sky,
> Do love you, holy Christabel!
> And you love them, and for their sake
> And for the good that me befell,

Even I in my degree will try,
Fair maiden, to requite you well.

[227-32]

Christabel is here lulled into regarding herself as the special friend of all the angels, the focus of heavenly concern. At which point the seducer gets down to business: "But now unrobe . . ." (233). Similarly, one suspects an ulterior motive behind Geraldine's histrionic account of her arrival at the oak tree in lines 79-103. Notes Nethercot:

> The traditional nature of such an episode is conclusively, though unconsciously, proved by Tuttle . . . when he cites passages from *The Mysteries of Udolpho*, *The Romance of the Forest*, and *Hubert de Sevrac*, all of which Coleridge had been reading and all of which concern the abduction of a young girl by a band (of between three and five in number) who are invariably described as either "villains" or "ruffians" (the latter being Coleridge's term in some manuscripts), who bind her to a horse and who, in the last case at least, deposit her at the foot of a tree.
>
> [p. 162*n*]

Most likely Geraldine has been lurking by the tree some time, appraising her victim; like original sin, she is always already there. She moans, allows herself to be discovered, and tosses off a melodramatic tale like those she surmises the girl has been reading, placing her in the desired (although pathetically inappropriate) role of rescuer. Hence Christabel's prompt compliance with Geraldine's request:

> Stretch forth thy hand (thus ended she),
> And help a wretched maid to flee.
>
> Then Christabel stretched forth her hand.
>
> [102-04]

The suspect nature of her eagerness is further emphasized by the echo of Eve's temptation by Satan in *Paradise Lost*:

> Goddess humane, reach then, and freely taste.
> He ended . . .
> . . . .
>   . . . her rash hand in evil hour
> Forth reaching to the Fruit, she pluck'd she eat.
>
> [IX:733-81][30]

So not only does Geraldine seem, in Hazlitt's words, "to act without power—Christabel to yield without resistance" (*CH*, p. 207); as critics have noticed, Coleridge further implies the girl is a willing victim. Her warning as they enter the castle, "But we will move as if in stealth" (120; "stealth," with its whiff of corruption, recurs twice in describing Christabel's movements); her "prudent precaution," as the *Anti-Jacobin* reviewer sneered (*CH*, p. 218), of taking the castle key, and her calculation in removing her slippers as they glide past the sleeping Baron; above all, the "hyperbole of courtesy," as Carl Woodring calls it,[31] whereby she offers to take the stranger to bed—all arouse our mistrust. Since Christabel's playacting ("as if in stealth") plainly conceals a real fear of discovery, one wonders if her charity isn't a cloak for sin.

Finally, of course, one wonders why she left her shrine-like chamber in the first place and made her prayers in the wood, sin's traditional playground outside the Christian pale. The narrator's trite rhetorical questions only cloud this enigma. Why does Christabel go to the tree? To pray for her lover. But why to that tree, the very spot where danger lurks? Perhaps, as "mistletoe" (34) implies, it is a lovers' rendezvous. But then why does she "steal" there, as though acting illicitly? So as not to disturb the sleeping Baron. But why must she make these prayers at all? And at this point the answer defies analysis: "She had dreams" (27). Whether they were nightmares or not, Christabel's baffling misfortune evidently reflects original sin, "the evil which has its ground or origin in the agent, and not in the compulsion of circumstances. . . . It is a mystery, that is, a fact, which we see, but cannot explain" (*AR* [*Aids to Reflection*], pp. 245-46). Undeterred as usual, Coleridge does go on to explain the impossibility of an explanation: since "no natural thing or act" is known otherwise than as, in Hume's terms, "a mere link in a chain of effects," it follows "the moment we assume an origin in nature, a true beginning, an actual first—that moment we . . . are compelled to assume a supernatural power" (*AR*, p. 263). Thus the supernatural power of Geraldine's spell is a function of Christabel's desire to avoid facing the evil that originates in herself. Elsewhere Coleridge asserts that "the sensations which [objects appearing in dreams] seem to produce, are in truth the causes and occasions of the images. . . . The fact really is, as to apparitions, that the terror precedes the image instead of the contrary" (*LR* [*Literary Remains*] 1:202-03). Perhaps then it is Christabel's doubting anxiety toward her proper lover "far away" that leads her to his demonic surrogate.[32]

Once having awakened sin, the girl overestimates her ability to withstand it:

> They crossed the moat, and Christabel
> Took the key that fitted well;
> A little door she opened straight,
> All in the middle of the gate;
> The gate that was ironed within and without,
> Where an army in battle array had marched out.
>
> [123-28]

Since "strait is the gate," it appears she anticipates a similarly deft entry into heaven. Seemingly an afterthought, the last two lines reveal that Christabel's is a hard, violent world. If the fortress is secure, the reason is its vigilance, not its invulnerability:[33] "So free from danger, free from fear, / They crossed the moat, right glad they were" (135-36). The inanity of the gladness, emphasized by the pseudoarchaic jocundity of the last phrase and the sloganlike repetition of the couplet ten lines later (the ridiculousness of which did not escape the *Edinburgh* reviewer [*CH,* pp. 228-29]), exposes Christabel's naive belief in her complete security (of course, Geraldine's gladness reflects even more damningly on her hostess). "The doctrine of Election," Coleridge's *Aids to Reflection* reminds us, "in relation to the believer is a hope, which . . . will become a lively and an assured hope, but which cannot in this life pass into knowledge, much less certainty of foreknowledge" (*AR,* p. 169). By contrast, Christabel "knows, in joys and woes, / That saints will aid if men will call: / For the blue sky bends over all!" (329-31). Such faith appears commendable, but in this imperfect world the sky is overcast (16-17) and Christabel, bound to silence, cannot call. . . .

III

Part II shows Christabel living down a lie, hating it all the while she compounds it, thereby becoming the horror she beholds. Coleridge himself was about to live down the plagiarisms of the *Biographia Literaria,* published a year after the poem finally appeared; but of course his concern with neurotic vice was long-standing. Involving as it does subversion of the will, he finds habitual immorality, although in any single act less reprehensible than a crime, to be nevertheless "more hopeless and therefore of deeper Evil than any single Crime, however great" (*CL* 4:553). Christabel's continued silence is worse than the Ancient Mariner's criminal but merely momentary loss of control because it entails making herself over in the image of evil. As Laurence Lockridge remarks, Coleridge "comes to identify the origin and nature of evil with something more basic and frightening than fallibility, and yet, like fallibility, near at hand."[34] Speech, or the affirmation of moral identity sustained and tempered by a coherent community of relationships, would give consciousness back its waking dominance, anxiously incomplete but at least hopeful and meliorable, over the isolate unconscious will, as, for example, the Mariner's retelling of his tale helps to do. Christabel's muteness, on the other hand, involves not only acquiescence in her seduction but a despondent hardening of conscience at the further seduction of her father, in which she thus becomes Geraldine's accomplice.

Like daughter, like father: as with Christabel, Geraldine manipulates the Baron's eagerness to believe himself the rescuing hero of a gothic romance.[35] Her stagy behavior first provokes him to a blustering show of chivalry ill suited to one so "agéd" (431-46) and then to infatuation masked—from himself although not from the ladies—by high-minded concern for his former friend Lord Roland. Plainly, when Geraldine "meets" and "prolongs" his gratuitous second embrace, the spell that ostensibly lies "in the touch of this bosom" (267) is not operating in any *super*natural fashion. Finally the Baron, like Christabel, is led to choose evil: piqued, he rejects his daughter in favor of the beautiful stranger, thereby repeating the rashness of her own earlier rescue effort. Not that he hasn't good cause to doubt Christabel. Her stammering entreaty, "this woman send away!" (617), says the right thing but not necessarily for the right reason. Through procrastination, Christabel's stand upon conscience has become tainted by the complexities of other people's wills, so that the Baron's charge of jealousy seems likely enough.[36]

That actions can ramify in this fallen manner creates an uncertainty principle precluding foresight into their full consequences. Says Jeremy Taylor, the seventeenth-century divine quoted throughout *Aids to Reflection,* "then is it that every man dashes against another, and one relation requires what another denies; and when one speaks another will contradict him; and that which is well spoken is sometimes innocently mistaken" (*AR,* p. 245). In the same way, Christabel's charitable aid of Geraldine hurts herself and perhaps also the Baron; the Baron's chivalrous aid of Geraldine hurts Christabel and perhaps also himself; and Christabel's attempted filial aid of the Baron would perhaps deprive him of rejuvenating affections long overdue—affections for Lord Roland as well as for Geraldine—and so only perpetuate his death-in-life endured since his wife's demise (332-44). For these reasons Coleridge rejected Paley's necessitarianism as shallowly behaviorist: it "draws away the attention from the *will,* that is, from the inward motives and impulses which constitute the essence of *morality,* to the outward act,"[37] so divorcing the agent from his acts and, by extension, from any reassuringly concrete involvement with reality.

Christabel's self-alienation in Part II likewise discloses, on one hand, a delusive acceptance of responsibility for any and all misfortunes resulting from her initial act of charity, no matter how unpredictable, as though they reflected a necessarily evil motive, and on the other hand, a disavowal of all responsibility, even for conniving at the spell. Whether or not it is a demonic possession, her horrified hissing gasp at the Baron's courtship of Geraldine attests a divided self. Partly it shows Christabel's startled recognition of her own fallibility based on recollection of her experience the previous night, and partly it recalls the prudish voyeurism of the Part I narrator ("a sight to dream of, *not to tell*"), thus implying overreaction to the sight of ordinary lechery (454-59). Having gained awareness of sexuality through the sight of Geraldine's naked body, Christabel is now evidently reading sexual meaning into Geraldine's embrace of the

Baron. The abruptness of the metamorphosis suggests a schizophrenic antinomianism much like that of James Hogg's Justified Sinner:[38] when the Baron twice turns at the sound, he "nothing saw, but his own sweet maid / With eyes upraised, as one that prayed" (461-62). If Christabel here can "imitate" Geraldine's snake eyes with "all her features" (602-05) while outwardly acting the saint, then plainly a snake must be how she pictures herself. The reader, on the contrary, sees such envy as only too human. At the same time, Geraldine is by her own admission a very sinful woman, so she may really look reptilian; in which case the doting Baron, as fascinated by Geraldine's eyes as Christabel is, but rather inclined to see them as "large bright eyes divine," is an unreliable judge of either woman's face. What this baffling, wordless exchange of glances demonstrates is the impossibility of deducing who saw what first. Geraldine's snaky iridescence making her all things to all people evidently comprises the mystery of original sin, which originates in the agent but becomes activated by the ambiguities of human relationships.[39]

The Baron's diagnosis of jealousy is therefore only partly correct. Christabel's reactions evince what Coleridge, in a long notebook entry of 1803 describing Wordsworth's "*up*, askance, pig look" and his own ensuing "little ugly Touchlets of Pain & little Shrinkings Back at the Heart"—an episode that duplicates Geraldine's "look askance" and Christabel's "shrinking" at "the touch and pain"—deems "a vice of personal Uncharitableness, not Envy" although very like it (*N* [*The Notebooks of Samuel Taylor Coleridge*] I, entry 1606).[40] Envy Coleridge considers merely a secondary effect of "the instinct of all fine minds to *totalize*—to make a *perfectly congruous whole* of every character—& a pain at the being obliged to admit incongruities." Specifically, the pain results from disruption of one's "representative" or "phantom image" of the other based on the coalescence of accustomed impressions.[41] Confronting the inadequacy of that image produces a sense of "Self-degradation," leading to invidious comparison of oneself with the other such as Coleridge finds so pitiable in St. Teresa.

Christabel's "forced unconscious sympathy" with Geraldine's spiteful glance attests a repetition compulsion of which the spell is merely a neurotic symbol. In order to master it, the girl repeats her traumatic confrontation of evil, an experience the more painful, and hence the more inescapably repetitive, for being so alien to her self-image. Doomed to a similar vicious circle, the Ancient Mariner at least obtains temporary relief by attempting to *tell* his experience. Coleridge's analysis of the incident with Wordsworth shows him "deeplier than ever . . . the necessity of understanding the whole complex mixed character of our Friend." Similarly, Geraldine and the Baron—even Bard Bracy, whose subservience to his patron violates his poetic vow to purify

Langdale Wood—are all what Jane Austen likewise calls "mixed characters" containing "a general though unequal mixture of good and bad." Apparently Christabel has yet to realize, as the heroine of *Northanger Abbey* finally sees, that indeed "in Mrs Radcliff's works, and . . . the works of all her imitators, . . . such as were not as spotless as an angel, might have the dispositions of a fiend. . . . But in England it was not so" (p. 177). From Part I to Part II Christabel's view of Geraldine plunges between these simple extremes, and with the same paralyzing abstraction of good and bad from the complexities of real human relationships as Austen and Coleridge both condemn in the School of Sensibility.

Accordingly, the increasing fortitude of Coleridge's Christian faith leads him, beginning in late 1801, to a critique of his earlier associationism, a moral critique rooted in the staunch Miltonic premise that "good and evil we know in the field of this world grow up together almost inseparably. . . . And perhaps this is that doom which Adam fell into of knowing good and evil, that is to say, of knowing good by evil" (Hughes, p. 728). The perfectibilist Hartley believed the process of association to spiritualize the "sensible Pleasures and Pains" into "intellectual" ones, thus tending to "reduce the State of those who have eaten of the Tree of Knowledge of Good and Evil, back again to a paradisiacal one."[42] But Coleridge, who dedicated a youthful poem to Hartley's thesis, no longer envisions such a utopia. At the source of association he locates mankind's depraved will—that is, our animal apprehension of pain and pleasure as simple stimuli able indeed to be quantified and equated in behaviorist fashion, but for that reason all the more liable to be sadomasochistically confounded together to the detriment of the more complexly organized personality. A notebook jotting from this period offers a preview of *Christabel*'s tailpiece: "Laughter of Parents & Grandames at little children's motions, is Laughter in its original state—a little convulsive motion to get rid of a pleasure rising into pain" (*N* I, entry 1533).[43] Hence arises "the Origin of moral Evil from the *streamy* Nature of Association" (*N* I, entry 1770): although association supplies the basis for sympathetic identification with others, its "height, & ideal" is "Delirium," continuous self-enclosed reverie hostile to the higher-order moral distinctions that define the self's relation to the outer world. So whereas the youthful Coleridge developed his philosophy of organic unity in reaction to the soullessness of Newtonian mechanism, he later sees the enemy to be "this anti monadic feeling" itself, the selfish desire to unify, or "totalize," associations actually discrete and incompatible: "That deep intuition of *oneness*—is it not at the bottom of many of our faults as well as Virtues / the dislike that a bad man should have any virtues, a good man any faults / & yet something noble and incentive in this" (*N* 1, entry 2471).

The Conclusion to Part II explicitly confronts this paradox. "A very metaphysical account of Fathers calling their children rogues, rascals, & little varlets" (*CL* 2:729), the poet and recent father described it in the letter to Southey in which it first appeared. The passage doesn't only recapitulate the peculiar violence with which the Baron rebukes his beloved daughter, as commentators tend to point out.[44] By exposing the corruptness of our interest in gothic horror, it further offers a psychoreligious gloss on the parody of Part I, so bringing the poem full circle. "A little child," writes Coleridge,

> Makes such a vision to the sight
> As fills a father's eyes with light;
> And pleasures flow in so thick and fast
> Upon his heart, that he at last
> Must needs express his love's excess
> With words of unmeant bitterness.
> Perhaps 'tis pretty to force together
> Thoughts so all unlike each other;
> To mutter and mock a broken charm,
> To dally with wrong that does no harm.
> Perhaps 'tis tender too and pretty
> At each wild word to feel within
> A sweet recoil of love and pity.
> And what, if in a world of sin
> (O sorrow and shame should this be true!)
> Such giddiness of heart and brain
> Comes seldom save from rage and pain,
> So talks as it's most used to do.

[660-77]

The father tenderly abusing his own child images the reader's relation to his own purest feelings as embodied by Christabel. To feel "a sweet recoil . . . at each wild word" refers in this sense to the sadistic relish with which we peruse Christabel's seduction. The recoil involves "giddiness" because her innocence seems truly excessive; it disrupts our necessary familiarity with imperfections typical of "this world of sin," thrusting us back into the "streaminess" of associations not yet comfortably organized into a "representative image" of the other person.[45] For Coleridge, then, the great "sorrow and shame" of man's fallen estate is his inability to love deeply without selfish ambivalence. "To mutter and mock a broken charm" is to profess and imitate beliefs that are belied by one's conduct.[46] Similarly, Christabel's guardian mother, her superstitious charm against Geraldine's evil eye, is ineffectual so long as she hypocritically embraces the spell (this affords a perfectly naturalistic view of the mother, whose assault on Geraldine seems in any case to be an expression of the latter's remorse). Yet the reader, too, is guilty of "dallying with wrong." The speciousness of Geraldine's spell represents the falseness of gothic subliterature, of which Coleridge remarks that "the reader, when he is got to the end of the work, looks about in vain for the spell which had bound him so strongly to it" (Greever, pp. 169-70). Thus the Conclusion to Part II insists we rec-

ognize that the evils, which at the beginning of the poem we assumed to exist "out there" in the safely impersonal form of monsters, are in fact trivial compared to our own fascination with them. In a reversal of accustomed causality, it isn't so much the monsters that elicit our fascination; rather, our prior fascination with sin itself produces the monsters in order to enjoy the mixed pain and pleasure of a catharsis. "Words of unmeant bitterness" therefore characterize gothic authors unaware that their supernaturalism, seemingly so inventive and exotic, is only specious embellishment of an all-too-common sinfulness that simply "talks as it's most used to do," making the authors its mouthpiece.

In sum, the Conclusion reveals a forcing together of unlike thoughts on two levels. At the narrative level, such forcing occurs in Christabel's not-quite-innocuous visit to the midnight woods, in the Baron's somewhat lecherous chivalry, and in Geraldine's calculated but reluctant deceptions. At the thematic level, it occurs in the mind of the reader: since the idea of innocence (Christabel) inevitably tempts the idea of its corruption (Geraldine), the reader is led to face squarely the "mixed," fallen nature of his own mind. As Coleridge declares again and again in the notebooks, "Extremes meet."

Notes

1. G. Wilson Knight, *The Starlit Dome* (London: Oxford Univ. Press, 1941), p. 83.

2. *Poetical Works of Coleridge*, ed. Ernest Hartley Coleridge (London: Oxford Univ. Press, 1973), pp. 215-16. All quotations of Coleridge's poetry are from this edition. For the ensuing account of the mastiff bitch, I am heavily indebted to Edward Dramin, "'Amid the Jagged Shadows': Parody, Moral Realism, and Metaphysical Statements in Coleridge's *Christabel*" (Ph.D. Diss., Columbia Univ. 1972), a condensed version of which appeared as "'Amid the Jagged Shadows': *Christabel* and the Gothic Tradition," *Wordsworth Circle* 13 (1982):221.

3. *Examiner,* June 2, 1816, pp. 348-49. Rpt. in *Coleridge: The Critical Heritage,* ed. J. R. de J. Jackson (New York: Barnes & Noble, 1970), p. 206; henceforth cited as *CH.*

4. William Roberts, *British Review,* viii, August 1816, 64-81; in *CH,* p. 225.

5. *Selected Poems and Prefaces by William Wordsworth,* ed. Jack Stillinger (Boston: Houghton Mifflin Co., 1965), p. 69; henceforth cited as *W.*

6. Jane Austen, *Northanger Abbey and Persuasion,* ed. John Davie (London: Oxford Univ. Press, 1971), p. 177.

7. Elsewhere Coleridge observes that "pretensions to the supernatural . . . one and all have this for

their essential character, that the Spirit is made the immediate object of sense or sensation." This "absurdity" is "more or less offensive to the taste" (*Aids to Reflection,* 2nd ed., 1840 [1825; Port Washington, N.Y.: Kennikat, 1971], p. 113).

8. Thomas Moore, *Edinburgh Review,* xxvii, September 1816, 58-67; in *CH,* pp. 229-30.

9. Humphrey House, *Coleridge: The Clark Lectures, 1951-52* (London: Hart Davis, 1953), p. 124.

10. Cf. Mary Jacobus's description of Wordsworth's "The Idiot Boy" as a "burlesque of the supernatural ballad" in which "the reader is teased for wanting to be thrilled or scared" (*Tradition and Experiment in Wordsworth's "Lyrical Ballads"* (1798) [Oxford: Clarendon, 1976], pp. 251-52). Further, Carl Woodring notes that Wordsworth's "first stanza, beginning ''Tis eight o'clock,—a clear March night,' resembles the first stanza of *Christabel.* Of the same date, each evokes by onomatopoeia the shout of an owl. Both poems, throughout, employ such devices of medieval ballads and romances as the rhetorical question" (*Wordsworth* [Cambridge: Harvard Univ. Press, 1968], p. 29). In the comic Part I, at least, *Christabel* is Coleridge's "Idiot Boy." Indeed, Coleridge's exuberant recitals of his poem while hiking the Harz Mountains in 1799 sound gleefully tongue-in-cheek; as the impervious Dr. Carlyon recalled, "At the conclusion of . . . the first stanza . . . he would perhaps comment at full length upon such a line as—'Tu-whit!—Tu-whoo!' that we might not fall into the mistake of supposing originality to be its sole merit[!!!]" (Clement Carlyon, *Early Years and Late Reflections* [London: 1836], p. 134). Coleridge's reported reaction to *Blackwood's* 1819 takeoff is revealing: "I laughed heartily . . . [but] it is in appearance, and in appearance only, a good imitation; I do not doubt but that it gave more pleasure, and to a greater number, than a continuation by myself in the spirit of the two first cantos" (*The Table Talk and Omniana of Samuel Taylor Coleridge,* ed. T. Ashe [London: George Bell, 1884], p. 314). The insinuation is evidently that the *Blackwood's* parody appears successful for precisely the reason that it is in reality a failure—namely, its ignorance that *Christabel* is *already* a parody.

11. *Critical Review,* August 1794, ii, 361-72; rpt. in Garland Greever, *A Wiltshire Parson and His Friends* (London: Constable, 1926), p. 169. Greever includes Coleridge's other reviews from the *Critical Review* of February 1797, 194-200; June 1798, 166-69; and August 1798, 442.

12. *Critical Review,* June 1798; and letter to Wordsworth of January 23, 1798, in *Collected Letters of Coleridge,* ed. E. L. Griggs, 4 vols. (Oxford: Oxford Univ. Press, 1956-71), 1:378; henceforth cited as *CL.*

13. See Thomas MacFarland, *Coleridge and the Pantheist Tradition* (Oxford: Oxford Univ. Press, 1956), pp. 1-52.

14. Arthur H. Nethercot, *The Road to Tryermaine* (New York: Russell, 1939), pp. 189, 198-201. Influential as it has been, Nethercot's argument directly contradicts the opening premise of Coleridge's review of *The Monk:* "The horrible and the preternatural . . . can never be required except by the torpor of an unawakened, or the languor of an exhausted, appetite" (Greever, p. 191).

15. Donald R. Tuttle, "*Christabel* Sources in Percy's *Reliques* and Gothic Romance," *PMLA* 53 (1938):445.

16. Matthew G. Lewis, *The Monk* (1794; New York: Grove, 1952), pp. 98-100.

17. Coleridge's speculations on this rumor appear in *CL,* 4:917-18.

18. *The Diary of William Polidori,* ed. W. Rossetti (1911), entry for June 18, 1816; cited in Richard Holmes, *Shelley: The Pursuit* (London: Chaucer Press, 1974), pp. 328-29.

19. Consider, for example, Lewis's note at the end of "The Cloud-King," a tale where the heroine over-tasks the seemingly omnipotent Cloud-King and his demons by first commanding him to restore her lover, "the truest of lovers," and then commanding him to show her yet "a truer" one:

> Lest my readers should mistake the drift of the foregoing tale, and suppose its moral to rest upon the danger in which Romilda was involved by her insolence and presumption, I think it necessary to explain, that my object in writing this story was to show young ladies that it might possibly, now and then, be of use to understand a little grammar; and it must be clear to every one, that my heroine would infallibly have been devoured by the demons, if she had not luckily understood the difference between the comparative and superlative degrees.
>
> (*Tales of Terror and Wonder,* intro. Henry Morley [London: Routledge & Sons, 1887], p. 167)

Furthermore, in Lewis's "Introductory Dialogue" to *Tales of Terror,* the Friend urges objections to the Author's excesses in exactly the same moralistic terms as Coleridge uses in his reviews:

> These active pandars to perverted taste
> Shall mar their purpose by too anxious haste.
> . . . .

> The vicious taste, with such a rich supply
> Quite surfeited, "will sicken, and so die."

For a valuable account of the phenomenal but short-lived success of William Bürger's "Lenore," its various English translations, and the sense of parody to which the poem soon gave rise, see Mary Jacobus, *Tradition and Experiment,* pp. 215-24.

20. William Empson, Introduction to *Coleridge's Verse: A Selection,* ed. Empson and David Pirie (New York: Schocken, 1972), p. 62; Leslie Brisman, "Coleridge and the Supernatural," *Studies in Romanticism* 21 (1982):159.

21. *Aids to Reflection,* 2nd ed., 1840 (1825; Port Washington, N.Y.: Kennikat, 1971), p. 113; henceforth cited as *AR.*

22. *The Notebooks of Samuel Taylor Coleridge,* ed. Kathleen Coburn, 3 vols. (New York: Pantheon, 1957), 2, entry 2509; henceforth cited as *N.*

23. Arguing that the hostile reactions of contemporary reviewers disclose their fear of being rendered passive and "feminized" by the poem's ability "to hold the reader as if it were his *own* dream or fantasy," Karen Swann demonstrates that despite their attempts to reduce the poem to "a derided genre (the Gothic) and gender (the feminine), . . . it is the poem which contains its critics, whose two responses to it—a spellbound accession to play and a petrified and petrifying refusal of exchange—are figured in the text" ("Literary Gentlemen and Lovely Ladies: The Debate on the Character of *Christabel,"* *ELH* 52 (1985):406-07).

24. Arthur Lovejoy, "Coleridge and Kant's Two Worlds," in *Essays in the History of Ideas* (Baltimore: Johns Hopkins Univ. Press, 1948), pp. 254-55.

25. Edward E. Bostetter, *The Romantic Ventriloquists* (Seattle: Univ. of Washington Press, 1963), pp. 8, 118, 123.

26. *John Milton: Complete Poems and Major Prose,* ed. Merritt Y. Hughes (New York: Odyssey, 1957), p. 105. Martin Bidney's "*Christabel* as Dark Double of *Comus,"* *Studies in Philology* 83 (1986):182, points out numerous comparisons between the two poems, concluding that "strong verbal echoes and parallels of imagery show that Coleridge wishes not only to emphasize elements of metaphysical dualism in Milton's poem, but to augment or intensify them whenever possible. . . . In *Christabel,* metaphysical pessimism prevails" (p. 195). I concur with Bidney's observation but reject his assessment of it. Coleridge indeed emphasizes a dualistic, even "Gnostic"

separation of good and evil—at least in Part I of *Christabel*—but only in order to demonstrate our need to interpret such metaphysical absolutes in moral and psychological terms. Metaphysical pessimism prevails only if one takes the poem's surface of irrational gothic supernaturalism as a literal portrayal of the moral conditions of earthly life.

27. Cf. *The Friend,* ed. Barbara E. Rooke, 2 vols. (1818; Princeton: Princeton Univ. Press, 1969), 1:103: "it be a truth, attested alike by common feeling and common sense, that the greater part of human misery depends directly on human vices and the remainder indirectly."

28. Cf. *N* 1, entry 1717: "My will & I seem perfect Synonimes—whatever does not apply to the first, I refuse to the latter / —Any thing strictly of outward Force I refuse to acknowledge, as done *by* me / it is done *with* me." Thus Coleridge notes of the alchemists: "The supposed exercise of magical power always involved some moral guilt, directly or indirectly" (*Literary Remains,* ed. Henry Nelson Coleridge, 4 vols. [1836; New York: AMS Press, 1967], 1:209; henceforth cited as *LR.* Coleridge's observations of his opium despondency closely describe Christabel, who like him is "in a moral *marasmus* from negatives—from misdemeanours of Omission, and from Weakness & moral cowardice of moral Pain" (*CL* 3:48). Empson's Introduction to *Coleridge's Verse* likewise considers the spell cast by the dead sailors upon the Ancient Mariner to be a function of "neurotic guilt." Cf. also Coleridge's letter of March 12, 1811: "Moral obligation is to me so very strong a Stimulant, that in 9 cases out of ten it acts as a Narcotic. The Blow that should rouse, *stuns* me" (*CL* 3:307).

29. *Biographia Literaria,* ed. James Engell and W. Jackson Bate, 2 vols. (1817; Princeton, Princeton Univ. Press, 1983), 2:6.

30. For an examination of the poem's many parallels with *Paradise Lost,* see my unpublished article, "From Stereotypes to Truth: Christabel as Ironic Miltonic Eve."

31. Carl Woodring, "Christabel of Cumberland," *Review of English Studies* 7 (1966): 43.

32. Compare the opening lines of William Bürger's celebrated "Lenore" (first translated by William Taylor in March 1796; this is Matthew Lewis's rendering in *Tales of Terror and Wonder,* p. 273):

> At break of day, with frightful dreams
>   Lenora struggled sore:
> "My William, art thou slaine," said she,
>   "Or dost thou love no more?"

33. A similar glimpse of nature red in tooth and claw comes toward the end of *The Rime of the Ancient Mariner*: the ghost ship's sails remind the Hermit of dead leaves in winter, when "the owlet whoops to the wolf below, / That eats the she-wolf's young" (536-37; the rough-hewn syntax even suggests cannibalism). Like the passage from *Christabel,* this one works to undercut the simplistic piety of the Mariner's closing moral of love for all things great and small.

34. Laurence S. Lockridge, *Coleridge the Moralist* (Ithaca: Cornell Univ. Press, 1977), p. 53. Cf. Coleridge's letter to Josiah Wedgwood of January 5, 1798, written at the climax of his struggle whether or not to accept a Unitarian ministry: "If a man considered himself as acting in opposition to his principles *then only* when he gave his example or support to actions and institutions, the existence of which produces *unmingled* evil, he might perhaps with a safe conscience perpetrate any crime. . . . If on the other hand a man should make it *his principle* to abstain from all modes of conduct, the general practice of which was not permanently useful, or at least absolutely harmless, he must live, an isolated Being: his furniture, his servants, his very cloathes are intimately connected with Vice and Misery."

Starting from the assertion that "the nature of absolute evil is the insidious and inevitable corruption of good *into* evil, a corruption that is successful precisely in proportion to the real purity of the good," Walter H. Evert makes much the same argument about the Beatrice of Shelley's *Cenci* as I am making about Christabel. See his "Coadjutors of Oppression: A Romantic and Modern Theory of Evil," in *Romantic and Modern: Revaluations of Literary Tradition,* ed. George Bornstein (Pittsburgh: Univ. of Pittsburgh Press, 1977), p. 29. The Count's prediction that "what [Beatrice] most abhors / Shall have a fascination to entrap / Her loathing will" (IV, i, 85-87), distinctly echoes Christabel's "forced unconscious sympathy" with Geraldine.

35. Similarly, Edward Duffy sees parody in Sir Leoline's bombastic self-importance, which he calls "a literary caricature . . . [of] a specific kind of inadequate vision," namely gothic romance ("The Cunning Spontaneities of Romanticism," *Wordsworth Circle* 3 [1972]:237-40).

36. "There is one criterion by which we may always distinguish benevolence from mere sensibility— Benevolence impels to action, and is accompanied by self-denial" ([Coleridge in *The*] *Watchman,* [ed. Lewis Patton; Princeton: Princeton Univ. Press, 1970,] 140).

37. *The Friend,* ed. Barbara E. Rooke, 2 vols. (1818; Princeton: Princeton Univ. Press. 1969), 1:314.

38. James Hogg, *The Private Memoirs and Confessions of a Justified Sinner* (1824; New York: Norton, 1970).

39. Cf. Coleridge's frighteningly casual observation of Wordsworth during the Highlands tour of summer 1803: "My words & actions imaged on his mind, distorted & snaky as the Boatman's Oar reflected in the Lake" (*N* 1, entry 1473).

40. In reporting his visionary dream, Bracy stresses that the Christabel-dove appeared "Among the green herbs in the forest alone. / . . . / For nothing near it could I see, / Save the grass and green herbs underneath the old tree" (536-40); and hence in the dream Christabel is the one "uttering fearful moan"—not Geraldine, as the poem's opening scene leads one to believe. Bracy thus implies that the "bright green snake" coiled about Christabel, "Swelling its neck as she swelled hers" (549-54), is her own green envy and pride.

41. For further discussion of Coleridge's concept of the "phantom image," see Lockridge, pp. 154-56.

42. David Hartley, *Observations on Man: His Frame, His Duty, and His Expectations* (1749; Gainesville, Fla.: Scholar's Facsimiles and Reprints, 1966), pp. 82-83.

43. Compare *N* 1, entries 1185 and 1392.

44. See, e.g., Constance Hunting, "Another Look at 'The Conclusion to Part II' of *Christabel*," *English Language Notes* 12 (1975):171.

45. Compare Adam Smith's Humean discussion of the disutile aspects of "wonder" arising from a person's failure to "fill up the gap" or "interval" felt to exist between two events or objects not customarily connected together: "a person of the soundest judgment, who had grown up to maturity, and whose imagination had acquired those habits, and that mold, which the constitution of things in this world necessarily impress upon it . . . would soon feel the same confusion and giddiness begin to come upon him, which would at last end . . . in lunacy and distraction" ("The History of Astronomy," in *Essays on Philosophical Subjects,* ed. W. P. D. Wightman [1790; Indianapolis: Oxford Univ. Press, 1980], pp. 41-44).

The Ancient Mariner's shooting of the albatross can likewise be seen as a reaction against its disturbingly unworldly perfection. Cf. Stanley Cavell: "It seems to me that the focus of the search for motive should be on the statement in the poem that 'the bird . . . loved the man / Who shot him with his bow.' Then the idea may be that the killing is to be understood as the denial of some claim upon him. . . . He may only have wanted at once to silence the bird's claim upon him and to establish a connection with it closer, as it were, than his caring for it: a connection beyond the force of his human responsibilities" ("In Quest of the Ordinary: Texts of Recovery," in *Romanticism and Contemporary Criticism,* ed. Morris Eaves and Michael Fischer [Ithaca: Cornell Univ. Press, 1986], pp. 193, 197).

46. Cf. [Coleridge,] "Fears in Solitude":

> Oh! blasphemous! the Book of Life is made
> A superstitious instrument, on which
> We gabble o'er the oaths we mean to break;
>
> . . . .
>
> All, all make up one scheme of perjury,
> That faith doth reel; the very name of God
> Sounds like a juggler's charm.
>
> [70-80]

Andrea Henderson (essay date winter 1990)

SOURCE: Henderson, Andrea. "Revolution, Response, and 'Christabel.'" *ELH* 57, no. 4 (winter 1990): 881-900.

[*In the following essay, Henderson analyzes "Christabel" within the context of Coleridge's complex attitudes toward the French Revolution. According to Henderson, the poem's gothic imagery and erotic undertones represent a sublimation of Coleridge's more serious political concerns during the period of the work's composition.*]

> Amidst images of war and woe, amidst scenes of carnage and horror of devastation and dismay, it may afford the mind a temporary relief to wander to the magic haunts of the Muses, to bowers and fountains which the despoiling powers of war have never visited, and where the lover pours forth his complaint, or receives the recompense of his constancy. The whole of the subsequent Love Chant is in a warm and impassioned strain.
>
> —note accompanying **"Lewti"** in the *Morning Post,* 1798[1]

> A heavier objection may be adduced against the author, that in these times of fear and expectation, when novelties explode around us in all directions, he should presume to offer the public a silly tale of old-fashioned love: and five years ago, I own I should have allowed and felt the force of this objection. But alas! explosion has succeeded explosion so rapidly, that novelty itself ceases to appear new; and it is possible that now, even a simple story, wholly uninspired with politics or personality, may find some attention amid the hubbub of revolutions, as to those who have remained a long time by the falls of Niagara, the lowest whispering becomes distinctly audible.
>
> —from Coleridge's **"Introduction to the Tale of the Dark Ladie,"** 1799[2]

Readers of **"Christabel"** may well wonder why, during the years Coleridge was composing poems like **"France: An Ode,"** and **"Fire, Famine, and Slaughter,"** he began and returned again and again to what appears to be a gothic fantasy. But one may also wonder whether, as the first epigraph suggests, a poet's own passionate response to "scenes of carnage" may not be channeled into the presentation of erotic passion. As Coleridge's "Introduction" implies, it was impossible for him, in 1799, given his early interest in "the hubbub of revolutions," to write a poem that *was* "uninspired by politics or personality"; the very decision not to treat the political explicitly was itself politically meaningful, and to the modern reader the crashing sound of Niagara behind Coleridge's poetry may be more audible than it would have been to contemporaries. It is my contention that **"Christabel"** can be read as an extended, troubled (and in certain ways masked), meditation on modes of response to "exploding novelties"—extended because the question of response was complicated by Coleridge's own engagement with the French Revolution, and troubled because the matter had a direct bearing on the inspiration for and subject matter of poetry.

I

We can begin by examining the context within which the various types of response the poem explores are set. To do this requires that we take the social landscape of the poem seriously, and not simply as gothic machinery, mere intertextual pointers. The hermetic and disintegrating world of Leoline, a rich baron whose name suggests a kingly genealogy while his title ranks him among the lowest classes of the nobility, is forcefully figured in his "ironed" castle (127). As Geraldine and Christabel make their way through this silent castle in part one, all of its various characteristics suggest isolation and decay. Leoline is "weak in health" (118), the mastiff bitch is old and toothless (7, 145), the brands are dying and lying in their own white ashes (156-57), and Leoline's shield is hung in a "murky old niche" (163).

Our sight of the baron in action in part two only confirms our sense that he is part of a rapidly collapsing order. His chivalric response to Geraldine's supposed wrong sounds sadly antiquated; his "noble heart" (432) becomes enraged, and he swears to "proclaim it far and wide, / With trump and solemn heraldry, / That they, who thus had wronged the dame, / Were base as spotted infamy!" (434-37)—an empty gesture. The problem is not just that Leoline is wrong about Geraldine and therefore misled in his efforts to help her; in the world of this poem, which seems to contain only four people, it is difficult to imagine the public to whom this proclamation could be made, much less made meaningful. And the old baron's intention to take on five young men in his "tourney court" (441) seems not only hubristic, given his age and ill-health, but also inappropriate as a response to a crime committed not by knights but "warriors" (81) (in alternate versions "ruffians"). In retrospect, and as critics have long recognized, the leaf hanging "on the topmost twig" of the oak tree, the "last of its clan" (49), dancing madly, seems a pointed figuration of Leoline's line.

The poem opens with an equivocal movement out of this limited and disintegrating world: Christabel's walk—apparently the first such movement through the ironed gate since "an army in battle array had marched out" (128). Ostensibly Christabel goes out merely to pray, but the narrator hints from the outset that this is an anti-familial gesture: "The lovely lady, Christabel / Whom her father loves so well, / What makes her in the wood so late, / A furlong from the castle gate?" (23-26). It almost sounds as if Leoline's love for Christabel should have been sufficient to keep her inside, and in fact, the various incestuous impulses that will be played out on and through Geraldine (Christabel-Geraldine as mother, Leoline-Geraldine as wife, Leoline-Geraldine as daughter) suggest a family tendency toward aristocratic endogamy.

Christabel discovers in Geraldine de Vaux the epitome of disruptive foreignness; although Geraldine's first claim for herself is that her sire too "is of a noble line" (79), we soon learn that she has come not to augment but to shatter this household. The "army in battle array" has done no good; destruction in the form of Geraldine has entered by the back door, and has done so successfully precisely because she was able to trick her victims into identifying with her. Geraldine is possessed of a kind of revolutionary energy, one all the more threatening because it inspires confidence and sympathy. Her apparent purity, through its very excessiveness, proves to be a sign of radical impurity, rather in the way that the pure and rational ideals of the Revolution, carried further and further, finally led to the destructive and irrational rigor of the Terror. Even according to Geraldine's own story, she is carried to the castle by *warriors* whom she, oddly enough, leads ("they rode furiously behind" [86]). This woman resembling "a lady of a far countrée" (225), has, according to some commentators, characteristics of a vampire—she survives on the blood of others.[3]

The point here is not to draw an allegorical equivalence between Geraldine and the French Revolution but to lay a groundwork for understanding the implications of her relations to the other characters in the text. The problem that those characters face is that in the world of **"Christabel"** the only alternative to stifling tradition is terrifying indeterminacy. Of course, the contention that Geraldine can be understood as the embodiment of social disruptiveness—incomprehensible novelty—encoded as sexual and moral indeterminacy, immediately raises the question of why such a mystification

should be necessary, and how one can reasonably argue the existence of a connection which is, after all, more or less absent from the poem as we have it. These questions can only be answered cumulatively over the course of this paper, through the gradual unearthing of a social context which can finally help to bind together the poem, to ground this notoriously ungrounded text.

At this point it may be useful to suggest the fitness of a domestic setting as a field within which to work out broader social concerns. In *The Fall of Robespierre,* written a few years before **"Christabel"** was begun, the two principal victims of Revolutionary strife are family ties and free speech (significantly, Geraldine attacks these as well). And there, as in **"Christabel,"** the disruption of families not only provides a vivid picture of discord as registered on a personal or private level, but also suggests the threat of an uncontrolled intermingling of persons and bloodlines:

> O this new freedom! at how dear a price
> We've bought the seeming good! The peaceful virtues
> And every blandishment of private life,
> The father's cares, the mother's fond endearment,
> All sacrificed to liberty's wild riot.

(*LR* [*The Literary Remains of Samuel Taylor Coleridge*], 1:10-11)

That the loss of the fond endearments of private life should be so lamented in a fictional world where heads are falling every moment need not be taken simply as a sign of Coleridge's relative insulation from the events the poem treats—the perceived threat to the family reflects the dangers the middle class's "own" revolution presented to itself. Liberty, equality, and fraternity may make upward mobility possible for the middle class, but it also opens up that class to insurgence from below, a disruption which here takes the form of an attack not just on family lines (a more properly aristocratic concern), but on that peculiarly middle-class social unit, the affective nuclear family. The domestic may thus reasonably become the locus of the revolutionary's fears about revolution.

At the same time, however, the domestic realm may appear to afford refuge from political conflict. Insofar as it does, its use as poetic subject matter may provide welcome relief from overtly political concerns. Coleridge does assume that private and public life are usually opposed; as he says of Burke: "It might have been expected, that domestic calamity would have softened his heart, and by occupying it with private and lonely feelings, have precluded the throb and tempest of political fanaticism."[4]

II

In **"Christabel,"** what is ultimately more important than social upheaval per se (Geraldine) is that "throb and tempest" that marks involvement in it, and the way one stations oneself with respect to it (Christabel, Bracy, Leoline). All of the three latter characters have distinct ways of positioning themselves in relation to others, so that they become, for the reader, object-lessons in response.

We can begin, as the poem does, with Christabel's response to Geraldine. Of the three castle inhabitants, Christabel is the most susceptible to Geraldine's machinations, and, as several commentators have suggested, she seems almost complicit in her own undoing. The reasons offered for her leaving the castle seem insufficient, and she would appear at the very least to be aware at some level that something is amiss even before Geraldine displays "the seal of [her] sorrow" (270): "But through her brain of weal and woe / So many thoughts moved to and fro, / That vain it were her lids to close" (239-41). While many have taken unspoken motives for Christabel's midnight stroll as necessarily morally tainting, in the context of the poem's strictly social landscape Christabel's escape from the castle, so far as it really is an escape, would appear to be a healthy exogamous move. Christabel is open enough to identify willingly with the stranger, and draws her into her own world.

The results are, of course, equivocal. Christabel loses her innocent simplicity (or at least an innocence at the level of consciousness), and appears in some way to have fallen: the star that has set, though generally taken as a reference to her mother, could also refer to her, and the "wood and fell" (310) which end the same verse paragraph invite a punning reading. At the same time, the experience infantilizes Christabel; she is held like a child, she smiles like an infant. This is not simply a *felix culpa*—this is a fall which is somehow restorative.[5]

One can approach the positive, restorative aspect of the experience in a backward fashion by way of a later comment by Coleridge on the subject of childhood:

> To the idea of life victory or strife is necessary. . . . So it is in beauty. The sight of what is subordinated and conquered heightens the strength and pleasure. . . . And with a view to this, remark the seeming identity of body and mind in infants, and thence the loveliness of the former; the commencing separation in boyhood, and the struggle of equilibrium in youth; thence onward the body is first simply indifferent; then demanding the translucency of the mind not to be worse than indifferent; and finally all that presents the body as body becoming almost of an excremental nature.
>
> **(LR, 1:230)**

The concept of fruitful strife is here undermined rather than concretized through the example of the mind-body relation; the subordination of the body generates disgust, not beauty. As Karen Swann deduces from a line in a letter to Humphrey Davy in 1800, "'disgust' is not

the mind's critical pronouncement on a body (although it may masquerade as such), but a symptom of the subject's mourning or revulsion for the lost, mutual pleasures of mind and body."[6] Christabel's triumph lies precisely in the fact that she achieves what the Coleridge of this later lecture could no longer imagine; lying in bed, smiling like an infant and weeping, with the "blood so free" (324) tingling in her feet, Christabel represents a sort of ideal: she is characterized by an integration and plenitude characteristic of infancy but, in this case, achieved through strife. Her encounter, although disillusioning and distressing, has literally rejuvenated her. The outcome of part one suggests at least the possibility that sympathetic response can open one up to valuable experience.

But if part one is ambiguous about the value of Christabel's experience and therefore of her initial openness, when Coleridge resumes work on the poem in 1800 much of the ambiguity vanishes. It is not surprising that commentators who treat Christabel's experience as a necessary step towards maturity glean most of their evidence from part one. H. W. Piper is one of the few recent critics to discuss the differences between the two parts of the poem, differences which he relates to a shift in Coleridge's attitude toward nature. For him, the major distinction is that part one is "full of ambiguities," whereas part two is "comparatively unambiguous" and makes use of a relatively straightforward imagery.[7] Piper is right, I think, in judging that the difficulties and paradoxes raised in part one are not only not solved but are in fact not confronted in part two. In part two, the turbulent mixture of sensations that Christabel experiences at the end of the first part is schematized as two distinct, and distinctly unappealing, modes of knowledge. This knowledge comes only in flashes, and then only in the form of passive rapture, or grace ("in its stead that vision blest . . . Had put a rapture in her breast, / And on her lips and o'er her eyes / Spread smiles like light!" [464-69]), or passive imitation of Geraldine, or evil ("all her features were resigned / To this sole image in her mind: / And passively did imitate / That look of dull and treacherous hate!" [603-606]). The exclamation marks that close both descriptions are further signs of their excessive, overdetermined quality. This knowledge hardly qualifies as knowledge at all, and appears instead to be an effacement of Christabel's identity.

Why does Coleridge shift from a model wherein sympathy leads to experience which generates a state of chaotic abundance of sensation, to one wherein sympathy leads, not to development, but to passivity and self-erasure? The answer, I believe, can be grounded in the adjustments in response patterns which the course of the Revolution seemed to require. Peter Kitson traces the step by step shift in Coleridge's stand on the Revolution during the years 1792 through 1798.[8] He points to 1798 as a pivotal year, a year when Coleridge finally gave up any hope of social improvement through political action and made collective guilt a frequent poetic theme. This change of heart is perhaps best exemplified by the publication of **"France: an Ode"** under the title of **"The Recantation: an Ode."** Coleridge's mounting resistance to sensibility can best be understood in the context of his own desire to become less immediately responsive to Revolutionary enthusiasm.

Although aware of the "dangers" of sensibility as early as 1796, initially his objections to it are measured. In writing a brief epistolary autobiography for Thomas Poole in 1797 he claims that before age eight he "was a *character*—sensibility, imagination . . . were even then prominent & manifest."[9] In 1796 he defines benevolence as "*Natural sympathy* made permanent by an *acquired conviction,* that the interests of each and of all are one and the same"—sensibility with republican reason superadded (**ET** [**Essays on His Own Times**], 1: 139: my emphasis). At this point, Coleridge's principal objection to conventional sensibility is that in practice it often amounts to little more than hypocritical self-staging and precludes a more substantial involvement with real human suffering: "the fine lady's nerves are not shattered by the shrieks! She sips a beverage sweetened with human blood, even while she is weeping over the refined sorrows of Werter or of Clementina" (**ET,** 1: 151). Benevolence, Coleridge argues, is fundamentally different from sensibility in that it leads to socially meaningful action.

By 1825 his objections have shifted and deepened. In a piece devoted to the topic, he begins dispassionately enough, defining sensibility as "a constitutional quickness of sympathy," but going on to associate it with "shapeless feelings" and passivity.[10] Over the course of the essay, one senses a mounting anxiety as Coleridge recurs several times to the threat of seduction which for him inheres in sensibility: it becomes the "instrument[s] of seduction," and can lead a man to "attempt to seduce" his friend's wife or daughter (**AR** [**Aids to Reflection**], 32). It would appear then that sensibility, whether in men or women, poses a threat primarily to women—but this is not quite the case. The real threat here surfaces in the confusion of genders in the argument: the distinctions between men and women may break down, leaving the *men* in danger of being seduced. Finally, the introduction of the sentimental meaning of the word "Love" into scientific inquiry is figured as the presentation of the muse of science "*rouged* like an Harlot, and with the harlot's wanton leer" (**AR,** 33). Sensibility is no longer a problem by virtue of being a willed and self-serving inaction; it is now threatening primarily because it leaves one vulnerable to "seduction." Although Coleridge had long associated seduction with what he considered excessively radical principles, by this time his discussion of it has taken on a

surplus emotional charge. The dangers of sensibility now appear particularly acute to him because, as he says, his is "an over-stimulated age" (**AR,** 31). As his contemporary Josiah Conder notes in his review of **"Christabel,"** the power of Geraldine's spell to "so [work] on the sympathy, as to make its victim passively conform itself to the impression" is as "terrible [an] engine of supernatural malice" as one can conceive, but "the spells of vicious example in real life [are] almost a counterpart to this fiction."[11] A concern that people won't be politically active enough is replaced by a concern that they will not be able to maintain a necessary and general aloofness.

One can map out Coleridge's growing resistance to sensibility across the two parts of **"Christabel"**; Christabel's sensibility is at least of ambiguous value in part one, whereas in part two it is obvious that it has rendered her pathetically passive. This shift away from sensibility includes a shift away from qualities which were associated with both sensibility and republican feeling: childlike or youthful exuberance and infectious emotional intensity. In 1796 Coleridge wishes that France could settle into a state of peace, imagining that "the *juvenile ardour* of a *nascent* republic would carry her on, by a rapid progression, in a splendid career of various improvement" (**ET,** 1: 167: my emphasis). He praises General Pichegru for his ability to make a successful army out of "undisciplined boys": "he found no one principle of an army upon which to act, except *enthusiasm* in the cause in which they were engaged; he seized upon this great *passion* and made it equal to all the rest; discipline, science, *maturity,* fell before it" (**ET,** 1: 172: my emphasis). He could write of Burke that his admiration for him was increased rather than diminished by the fact that he "secured the aids of sympathy to his cause by the warmth of his own emotions," adding that those who find this characteristic a fault in Burke "disgrace the cause of freedom" (**ET,** 1: 108).

In 1796 Coleridge wrote to Benjamin Flower that he would be "unworthy the name of Man if I did not feel my Head and Heart awefully interested in the final Event" of the Revolution.[12] By 1799, however, all is changed, and it is imperative that one resist the temptation to sympathize with the French: "Alas, poor human nature! Or rather, indeed, alas, poor Gallic nature!" "the French are always children, and it is an infirmity of benevolence to wish, or dread aught concerning them" (**ET,** 1: 184). This refusal of identification and the shift in the connotation of youth signal a closing down of sympathy around 1800 which, as we shall see later, causes a broad range of problems for Coleridge. He will have learned to disengage and will find himself, at least temporarily, without any of the pleasures or powers that come of engagement.

III

The shift in the representation of Christabel's response is paralleled by another shift, this one from the example of one saint to another. In his notebooks Coleridge quotes lines 43-64 of Crashaw's "Hymn to St. Teresa" and says that "these verses were ever present to my mind whilst writing the second part of *Christabel*; if, indeed, by some subtle process of the mind they did not suggest the first thought of the whole poem."[13] The lines focus on the fact that Teresa must leave her home and native land to find martyrdom; it requires considerable imagination to connect this with the events of **"Christabel,"** part two. Several commentators have used the remark to support a reading of Christabel's experience as a vicarious expiation of some sin—the best way to make sense of the remark as it stands.[14] On one level, then, Coleridge was through this comment moralizing **"Christabel"** in retrospect, encouraging a more profound and doctrinal mystification of an already mystified piece, and hoping to bring even part one under a spiritual cloak. (Interestingly, a manuscript version of 1824 includes moralizing marginalia.)[15] But the reference to Saint Teresa makes more sense in light of her difference from another saint whose experiences truly do resemble Christabel's (particularly Christabel's experiences in part one): Coleridge's own St. Joan from **"Destiny of Nations,"** a poem written two years before part one of **"Christabel."**[16] Joan undergoes an experience strikingly similar to Christabel's:

Ah! suffering to the height of what was suffered,
Stung with *too keen a sympathy,* the Maid
Brooded with moving lips, mute, startful, dark!
And now her flushed tumultuous features shot
Such *strange vivacity,* as fires the eye
Of Misery fancy-crazed! and now once more
Naked, and void, and fixed, and all within
The unquiet silence of confuséd thought
And *shapeless feelings.* For *a mighty hand
Was strong upon her,* till in the heat of soul
To the high hill-top tracing back her steps.
Unconscious of the driving element,
Yea, *swallowed up in the ominous dream, she sate
Ghastly as broad-eyed Slumber*! a dim anguish
Breathed from her look! and still with pant and sob,
Inly she toiled to flee, and still subdued,
Felt an inevitable Presence near.

Thus she toiled in *troublous ecstasy,*
And a voice uttered forth unearthly tones,
"Maid beloved of Heaven!"[17]

Like Christabel, Joan has a supernatural encounter which is facilitated by her sensibility and results in a chaotic amplification of her passions. This general resemblance throws the differences between the two into relief. Joan, like Christabel, is led by "inexplicable sympathies" (187) to venture outside, but she encounters not a mysterious lady but a homeless and miserable family destroyed by war. It is Joan's responsiveness to

the family's tale, her "suffering to the height of what was suffered," that precipitates her supernatural vision, and it is in response to this vision that she determines to fight in the war. Joan's story has political meaning, and her fantastic experience leads to determinate action. Christabel's almost seems to be the same story, but so mythologized and abstracted that it hardly releases determinate meanings at all:

Yea, she doth smile, and she doth weep,
Like a youthful *hermitess,*
Beauteous in a wilderness,
Who, praying always, prays in sleep.
And, if she move unquietly,
Perchance, 'tis but the blood so free
Comes back and tingles in her feet.
No doubt, she hath a vision sweet.
What if *her guardian spirit* 'twere,
What if she knew her mother near?
But this she knows, in joys and woes,
That saints will aid if men will call:
For the blue sky bends over all!

(319-31, my emphasis)

Although, as we saw earlier, Christabel's encounter can be read for its social significance, the poem tends to overwhelm its social implications with moral and sexual ones. And even those implications are formally destabilized through the excessive use of conditionals and questions. The sing-song and sentimental quality of the third to the last line particularly unsettles our sense of the tone of the passage and strengthens our suspicion that faith in saints is ridiculous. Fittingly, in the abstract space within which the poem operates, Christabel herself seems to be suspended in a kind of half-consciousness; we certainly don't expect her to go off and lead a war.

Coleridge's swerve from a politicized and active Joan to a somnolent Christabel who operates in a hypothetical space is repeated in the further swerve to the Christabel of part two and finally to St. Teresa. Teresa, like Joan, felt a passionate enthusiasm to leave home in order to fight for a worthy cause. Teresa's enthusiasm, however, though beautifully sincere, was *childish*; as Crashaw argues, God did not intend for her devotion to lead to an early death among the Moors. She is brought home by concerned family members, and later in life founds an order of nuns. More important, she devotes herself to the refinement of her inner life, a process traced in the pages of her autobiography. Whether or not her own feelings would have been consonant with his, her life could serve as a demonstration of Coleridge's own disaffected convictions: "those feelings and that grand *ideal* of Freedom which the mind attains by its contemplation of its individual nature, and of the sublime surrounding objects . . . do not belong to men, as a society, nor can possibly be either gratified or realised, under any form of human government; but belong to the individual man, so far as he is pure. . . ."[18] One finds freedom not through social activity but private contemplation.[19] The connection drawn between **"Christabel"** and the "Hymn to St. Teresa" can then be taken as a (self) diversionary tactic. With Teresa rather than Joan serving as patron saint of the piece, what similarities there are between **"Christabel"** and **"Destiny of Nations"** are more thoroughly effaced, and a life of exemplary political involvement is displaced by a life of exemplary spirituality.[20]

IV

If Christabel's sensibility becomes by part two the sign of a dangerously passive sympathy, the first alternative model for response we are offered is Bard Bracy, who is himself immediately presented with a difficulty similar to the one created by Christabel's overactive sensibility. The baron's control of the production and meaning of the toll of the matin bell makes that toll a sign of the impression produced by established authority: "not a soul can choose but hear / From Bratha Head to Wyndermere" (343-4). Bracy's response to this imposition is in several respects unlike Christabel's response to the impression Geraldine makes. First, rather than simply passively "hear" the knell, he appropriates Leoline's position to command it: "Saith Bracy the bard, So let it knell! / And let the drowsy sacristan / Still count as slowly as he can!" (345-47). By accepting Leoline's power actively, Bracy gains a kind of derivative power for himself. He then proceeds to generate a power of his own by focussing on the gaps between the tolls: "There is no lack of such, I ween, / As well fill up the space between" (348-49). He goes on to construct an imaginative scene on the framework of the tolls, a scene not only of his own making, but one which forms a sort of contrapuntal response to the original sounds:

> With ropes of rock and bells of air
> Three sinful sextons' ghosts are pent,
> Who all *give back,* one after t'other,
> The death-note to their living brother . . .
>
> (352-55, my emphasis)

Initially, then, it would appear that Bracy, by literally working within the established power structure, is able to gain a critical purchase on it. Bracy's would seem to be an intermediate form of response, a simultaneous identification and distancing, which is at once marked by and productive of his mediating imaginative scenes, dreams, and so forth. Unfortunately, the double sense of lines 354-55 hints proleptically at Bracy's shortcoming: that the imaginatively animated echoes give the death-note to their living brother could indicate that they sound its death-note, that is, that they kill it; but, insofar as the note was declared a death-note to begin with, they are after all merely hollow reduplications of Leoline's power.

Bracy's bind is demonstrated more concretely in his next appearance, where Leoline appropriately commands him to act as mediator, to tell Roland that "Sir Leoline greets thee thus through me" (504). Bracy offers instead another form of mediation, which he hopes will convince Leoline to allow him to take independent action. His account of his dream is itself a thoroughly mediated representation of Christabel's novel situation, but it does not accomplish the task of bridging the gap between either Christabel and Leoline or himself and Leoline. Bracy's claim that he can purify the woods with "music strong and saintly song" (561) exaggerates the practical effect of his poetic power—he will not even be given an opportunity to go to the forest, which isn't where the "serpent" is anyway. Leoline prevails, and Bracy is sent off to act as a transparent, passive mediator: "'Why, Bracy! dost thou loiter here? / I bade thee hence!' The bard obeyed" (651-52). Leoline walks off with Geraldine and part two ends. Bracy is too completely co-opted to serve anyone effectively, even Leoline. His relation to those around him finally seems, not sympathetic while still critical, but insufficiently intimate while still circumscribed.

Of course, the reception of Bracy's vision also reflects on Leoline, who practices a third mode of response. If Bracy's failing lies in the fact that he tends to become little more than a passive mediator, Leoline's is that he habitually uses mediators. He uses both Geraldine and Bracy to mediate his relationship to Roland, and his romantic/fatherly interest in Geraldine looks like a deflection of an incestuous interest in his daughter and a lingering desire for his dead wife. This deflection is not unreasonably thought by the baron to provoke in Christabel "more than woman's jealousy" (646).

But Leoline's indirection is just one aspect of his tendency to maximize the distance between himself and other people or objects. Frequently the creation of this distance either requires a "misreading" on his part of the object at hand, or it produces such a misreading. This distanced and often antithetical response is examined most directly in the coda, but we see hints of it from the opening of part two: "Each matin bell, the Baron saith, / Knells us back to a world of death" (332-33)—the baron reads the announcement of a beginning as a reminder of endings. Leoline's first response to Geraldine, too, is symptomatic: "Sir Leoline, a moment's space, / Stood gazing on the damsel's face: / And the youthful Lord of Tryermaine / Came back upon his heart again" (427-30). The baron, unlike his daughter, waits a moment, temporally constructing a distance between himself and Geraldine. It would seem that he has what Coleridge called "manly benevolence," a considered and willed, rather than instinctive, kindness. As Swann notes, "separation is something of a habit with the Baron," who divides and opposes "potential 'sames' or potentially intermingling parts of 'the same,'"[21] a habit which Swann associates with paternal law struggling against feminine instability. This separation, unfortunately, both isolates the baron, and, rather than protecting him, opens him to more danger; he is no less a victim of Geraldine than his passive, unthinking daughter, and his effort to recover a lost noble friend leads him to relinquish his only child, who was to carry his blood and wealth into the future. Manly benevolence is no more useful a form of response than is sensibility.

The coda treats the problem of antithetical response in a purer and yet more cryptic form, and it poses a confrontation between the two extremes which Christabel and Leoline represent. The little child and father with which it opens have been associated both with Christabel and Leoline, and with Coleridge and his son Hartley, and both of these connections seem convincing and useful.[22] The dissimilarities between the pair of the coda and the other two, however, cease to be a critical problem if we take the relation between the characters and not the characters themselves as the central issue. The child, in its psychic self-sufficiency and plenitude ("Singing, dancing to itself . . . always finds, and never seeks" [657-59]), threatens its father in a two-pronged manner: first, simply by being a vision of abundance (arousing desire), and second, by impressing itself too directly and immediately upon its father (rendering him passive). "[P]leasures flow in so thick and fast / Upon his heart, that he at last / Must needs express his love's excess / With words of unmeant bitterness" (662-65). What we have here, then, is a final representation of antithetical response, but in this case, defenses are specifically being erected against the childish, full, and passive state of which Christabel herself is the prime representative in this poem. That is, it is as if the coda locates the true danger not in alien disruptiveness (Geraldine), but in the tendency to yield to that disruptiveness (Christabel); the real threat to Leoline is Christabel.[23]

The coda, then, is a final effort to exorcise Christabel, in all her shapeless sensibility, but the problem remains that no truly workable mode of response has been found. Leoline's antithetical responses are ridiculous and often worse than useless, and the coda itself cannot imagine a way out:

> Perhaps 'tis pretty to force together
> Thoughts so all unlike each other;
> To mutter and mock a broken charm,
> To dally with wrong that does no harm.
> Perhaps 'tis tender too and pretty
> At each wild word to feel within
> A sweet recoil of love and pity.
> And what, if in a world of sin
> (O sorrow and shame should this be true!)
> Such giddiness of heart and brain
> Comes seldom save from rage and pain,
> So talks as it's most used to do.

(666-677)

This passage mockingly uses sentimental language to describe antithetical response ("'tis tender too and pretty," "sweet recoil"). The speaker's wild words not only alienate him from his listener but also create in him a self-division, a sweet recoil from his own language. The "giddiness" which characterizes this separation marks a liberation from others which is both thrilling and dizzying (in Leoline's case, it is accompanied by a sense of power and a painful confusion). This giddiness is presented as being at once a response to loss and pain and a reduplication of it. The phrase "rage and pain," here the cause of "giddiness," is itself an echo from the description of the baron's response to Christabel's plea. That is, pain both spurs antithetical response and characterizes it. As Swann notes with reference to the death of the baron's wife, the "Baron's response to a traumatic event is to commemorate it," to recall it compulsively.[24] If Christabel's manner of response is naive, the baron's is jaded.

But perhaps the most troubling feature of antithetical response is its inflexibly conservative character. In talking "as it's most used to do," giddiness of heart leads not only to unkind words but also to the same ones. The baron's responses throughout the poem are not only inappropriate but also outdated, as we saw earlier. If Christabel's openness leads to too much change, the Baron's considered benevolence goes hand in hand with an unwillingness to change which, ironically, leaves him unable to resist change effectively. **"Christabel"** can offer no model for a successful engagement with novelty. It is entirely fitting that the poem never clarifies the mystery of Geraldine or shows her overcome. The text is helpless before her.

V

The poem's inability to present a productive response to novelty within the world it creates is reproduced at the textual level as a problem of reception. Contemporary reviewers are divided in their response to the poem just as the inhabitants of the castle are to Geraldine. Though perhaps in the minority, some reviewers did respond to the piece "sympathetically," finding in Christabel a pure and lovely heroine "all innocence, mildness, and grace" and in Geraldine a majestic but vicious Duessa (*RB* [*Romantic Bards and British Reviewers*], 141). Such reviewers tend to say little of Leoline or Bracy and find something charming and even sublime in the tale's indeterminacies: "it appeared to be one of those dream-like productions whose charm partly consisted in the undefined obscurity of the conclusion"; "the reader . . . must be prepared to allow for . . . the glorious and unbounded range which the belief in those mysteries permits" (*RB*, 140). It is precisely this kind of response that encapsulates for a reviewer like Hazlitt the threat of the poem: "the effect of the general story is dim, obscure, and visionary. It is more like a dream than a reality. The mind, in reading it, is spell-bound. The sorceress seems to act without power—*Christabel* to yield without resistance. The faculties are thrown into a state of metaphysical suspense and theoretical imbecility" (*RB*, 146). Hazlitt, in refusing to give in to a passive, Christabelian reception, responds, instead, like Leoline—antithetically. The temptation to lose oneself in the poem necessitates a powerfully negative response to it. The poem acts much like a figure/ground image: one can respond to it sympathetically or antithetically, but not both at once. Its generic instability and fragmentary form (the essence of the new, even in its "finished" form it is in the process of becoming) make it impossible for the reader to find a comfortable intermediate perspective from which to judge it; the text is as deformed and unstable as Geraldine herself.

Coleridge's own relation to the poem was similarly polarized. As Swann notes, he described the composition of part two as characterized by "labor-pangs," and compared the poem's publication to a miscarriage, saying it "fell almost dead-born from the press."[25] This painful and "feminine" engagement with the poem is later replaced with the controlled, masculine disengagement of Coleridge's chivalric relation to the poem-as-lady jokingly described in a letter to his wife.[26] The distinctness of male and female roles here parallels and acts as a metaphor for the distinctness of sympathetic and distanced modes of response. A productive androgyny does not seem to be attainable; one can do nothing but vacillate between extremes.

The bind presented in the world and fabric of the poem helps to account for Coleridge's lack of desire or capacity to complete it. As he was to say in a letter in 1800, "The delay in Copy has been owing in part to me, as the writer of **Christabel**—Every line has been produced by me with labor-pangs. I abandon Poetry altogether—."[27] The paralyzing conflicts which **"Christabel"** registers but cannot resolve can be traced to causes more specific than a growing sense that nature is fallen or a mysteriously increasing incapacity to confront "the ambiguities of the unconscious and its visionary exploration."[28] The need to gain a critical distance from early radical engagements requires the shutdown of sensibility (including sympathy, ardor, childlike enthusiasm), but in 1800 a distanced form of response seems heartless and foolishly conservative. Nor can the intermediate figure of Bracy provide consolation. Edward Dramin has not been alone in suggesting a connection between Bracy's failure and Coleridge's own "suspended animation" with regard to poetry in 1800.[29] Bracy's practice is specifically reminiscent of Coleridge's in some respects; his concern to fill "the space between" tolls is much

like the speaker's procedure in **"Frost at Midnight,"** a poem which almost seems to be generated out of the speaker's desire to fill up the silences between the owlet's cries. But Bracy is hemmed in rather than liberated by that aural framework; he never becomes anything more than a pawn in the hands of power. And Bracy's dream presents a practical problem in such mediated and mythic terms that it encourages a "Half-listening" (565) reception, a failure of sorts which **"Christabel,"** as a kind of dream vision, replicates. The profound inconclusiveness of **"Christabel"** indicates more than just a problem with that particular poem; a satisfying and workable way of responding to novelty was for Coleridge an essential part of poetic production. As Michael Holstein points out, Geraldine has much in common with the "intruders" of Coleridge's meditative poetry, such as the "stranger" of **"Frost at Midnight"**[30]—but Geraldine does not stimulate a productive response.

The danger of the decision Coleridge tries to justify in the second epigraph, the decision to write a poem "wholly uninspired with politics or personality," is that it might simply end up being "wholly uninspired." **"Christabel"** has simultaneously too much connection to politics and personality and too little connection to them; the piece has a high emotional charge but can propose no way to ground it. That Coleridge wrote less poetry over the next several years and focused more closely on his strictly theological and philosophical interests may indicate that the only way he could escape suspension was by retreating from this mode and subject of inquiry. When he finally published **"Christabel"** in 1816, he remarked in his introduction to it that if he had published it in 1800 "the impression of its originality would have been much greater"; but after all, around 1800 "exploding novelties" were to be avoided, not sought.

Notes

1. *Coleridge: Poetical Works*. ed. Ernest Hartley Coleridge (New York: Oxford Univ. Press, 1912), 253. All references to "Christabel" will be from this edition, 213-236.

2. *The Literary Remains of Samuel Taylor Coleridge*. ed. Henry Nelson Coleridge, 4 vols. (New York: AMS Press, 1967), 1:51 (hereafter cited as *LR*).

3. See, for example, Arthur H. Nethercot, *The Road to Tryermaine* (1939; rpt. New York: Russell & Russell, 1962); James Twitchell, *The Living Dead: A Study of the Vampire in Romantic Literature* (Durham: Duke Univ. Press, 1981), 40-51; and Edward Strickland, "Metamorphoses of the Muse in Romantic Poesis: *Christabel,*" *ELH* 44 (1977): 641-658. Insofar as Geraldine's behavior can be taken as vampiric, it is the appropriately horrify-

ing counterpart to the castle inhabitants' incestuous tendencies. Their desire to keep themselves "all in the family" is ironically paralleled by Geraldine's cannibalistic relation to them. But whereas they "feed on" each other in an effort to distinguish themselves from others, Geraldine's feeding on them marks them as indistinguishable from beasts—hers is the ultimate act of levelling.

4. S. T. Coleridge, *Essays on His Own Times,* ed. Sara Coleridge, 3 vols., (New York: AMS Press, 1971), 1:109 (hereafter cited as *ET*). In this case, of course, Coleridge is arguing against a kind of conservative "fanaticism," but these early, more radical writings already display a kind of preparatory defensive conservatism on Coleridge's part.

5. The dark underside of this, it should be noted, is the speechless, helpless character of infants; one could read Christabel's experience as having been so horrible as to have forced her to withdraw from it and to *regress to* rather than *recover* a childish state.

6. Karen Swann, "Literary Gentlemen and Lovely Ladies: The Debate on the Character of Christabel," *ELH* 52 (1985): 408.

7. H. W. Piper, "The Disunity of *Christabel* and the Fall of Nature," *Essays in Criticism* 28 (1978): 216.

8. Peter Kitson, "Coleridge, the French Revolution, and 'The Ancient Mariner': Collective Guilt and Individual Salvation," *The Yearbook of English Studies* 19 (1989): 197-207.

9. *Collected Letters of Samuel Taylor Coleridge,* ed. Earl Leslie Griggs, 6 vols., (Oxford: Clarendon Press, 1956-71), 1:348.

10. S. T. Coleridge, *Aids to Reflection,* ed. James Marsh (Burlington: Chauncey Goodrich, 1829), 31 (hereafter cited as *AR*).

11. John Hayden, ed., *Romantic Bards and British Reviewers: A Selected Edition of the Contemporary Reviews of the Works of Wordsworth, Coleridge, Byron, Keats, and Shelley* (Lincoln: Univ. of Nebraska Press, 1971), 143 (hereafter cited as *RB*).

12. Griggs (note 9), 1:266.

13. *The Table Talk and Omniana of Samuel Taylor Coleridge,* ed. H. N. Coleridge (London: Oxford Univ. Press, 1917), 441.

14. For a discussion of Christabel as a martyr, see, for example, Arthur Nethercot, *The Road to Tryermaine* (note 3), and Marjorie Levinson, "The True Fragment: 'Christabel,'" in *The Romantic Fragment Poem* (Chapel Hill: Univ. of North Carolina Press, 1986), 82.

15. See Barbara Rooke, "An Annotated Copy of Coleridge's 'Christabel,'" *Studia Germanica* 15 (1974): 179-92.

16. Piper (note 7) also notes the similarity but suggests that the differences simply reflect Coleridge's growth as a poet (221-22).

17. Coleridge (note 1), 139-40, lines 253-78, my emphasis.

18. Coleridge (note 1), 244 (from Coleridge's "Argument" to "France: An ode").

19. Coleridge's wish to make use of Teresa as a model is betrayed in his notes on her autobiography. He first describes her mystical experiences as "*deliquia*" caused in part by the fact that she had a "frame of exquisite sensibility by nature, rendered more so by a burning fever, which no doubt had some effect upon her brain." Later, however, he asserts that her raptures were the result of the perfect application of her reason: she felt the pleasure of "the effects . . . of the moral force after conquest, the state of the whole being after the victorious struggle, in which the will has preserved its perfect obedience to the pure or practical reason, or conscience." This shift from a picture of helpless madness to ideal Kantian citizen is a remarkable effort to salvage Teresa. We see here a lingering attraction to the passionate receptiveness of sensibility, an attraction which in this case is managed by rewriting sensibility as precisely what it is not: a reasoned act of will. (See *LR* 4:68-70).

20. Interestingly, Crashaw's "Hymn" is immediately followed in the original volume by "An Apologie for the Foregoing Hymn . . . As Having been writt when the Author was yet among the Protestants." The striking juxtaposition of poem and socially-grounded retraction suggests a further motivation for the already overdetermined reference to Crashaw's hymn.

21. Karen Swann, "'Christabel': The Wandering Mother and the Enigma of Form," *Studies in Romanticism* 23 (1984): 547, 548.

22. See Constance Hunting, "Another Look at 'The Conclusion to Part II' of *Christabel*," *English Language Notes* 12 (1975): 172.

23. It is worth noting that the coda also distances the poem from the reader, lines 664-670 reading almost like a commentary on the poem proper, the poem being the incarnation of the "juxtaposition of unlike thoughts" (at once comic and tragic, sentimental and brutal) and a "muttered and mocked charm" (sentimental and a parody of the sentimental, gothic and a parody of the gothic), which, after all, being only a poem, "does no

harm." Thus, the coda manages to be a serious treatment of the issues at stake in the poem while encouraging the reader not to take the poem seriously. The most direct treatment of the troubling question of response is necessarily the most mystified treatment.

24. Swann (note 21), 547.

25. Swann (note 6), 402.

26. Recounted in Swann (note 6), 397. Swann provocatively links the rather unusual relation of Coleridge (and his contemporaries) to the poem to "problematically invested literary relations" among various writers, readers, and texts.

27. Griggs (note 9), 1:623.

28. Strickland (note 3), 653.

29. Edward Dramin, "'Amid the Jagged Shadows': *Christabel* and the Gothic Tradition," *The Wordsworth Circle* 13 (1982): 225.

30. Michael Holstein, "Coleridge's *Christabel* as Psychodrama: Five Perspectives on the Intruder," *The Wordsworth Circle* 7 (1976): 120.

Dennis M. Welch (essay date 1992)

SOURCE: Welch, Dennis M. "Coleridge's 'Christabel': A/version of a Family Romance." *Women's Studies* 21, no. 2 (1992): 163-84.

[*In the following essay, Welch explores the symbolic import of the father-daughter relationship in "Christabel."*]

> The thin gray cloud is spread on high,
> It covers but not hides the sky.

I

As a great poem of concealment and mystery, *Christabel* raises many questions that continue to tease us. Why, for instance, does the young Christabel endanger herself by going out into a forest late at night to pray for her betrothed instead of praying in her chamber? What precisely is the relevance of Geraldine's experience with five warriors in the dark wood to Christabel's experience? Why does Christabel dread awakening her father Sir Leoline on the night she prays for her betrothed? What are the implications concerning Christabel of Leoline's obsession with his deceased wife? Why is Geraldine associated not only with the figure of motherhood but also with the "boss" on the Baron's shield? Why is Christabel's "look of dull and treacherous hate" said to be "Full before her father's view" (lines 606, 610). What are we to make of Coleridge's statement

that several verses about martyrdom in Richard Crashaw's "Hymn to . . . Sainte Teresa" were "ever present to my mind whilst writing the second part" of the ballad? Considering his claim of having the whole plan of the ballad in mind, why didn't Coleridge complete *Christabel*?

Although this poem is "entirely domestic," as one early reviewer suggested (Matthew 435-36), many of its critics see in Christabel and her relationship with Geraldine a neurotic struggle to cope with sexual maturation. To Roy Basler, for example, Geraldine represents "sexual necessity" that draws the repressed Christabel toward irrational behaviour (25-51). To Charles Tomlinson, Geraldine represents the "fatal woman" of the Gothic tale, an agent symbolizing guilt and neurosis in Christabel (105, 107). Susan Luther asserts that the protagonist projects her guilty feelings of sexuality onto the ghost Geraldine in a subconscious wish to grow up by a "self-imposed martyrdom" (50-86). Jonas Spatz avers likewise that Christabel struggles neurotically "to come to terms with her sexuality, . . . to progress from adolescence to womanhood" (111).

Observing that "By Part II of the poem Sir Leoline increasingly dominates the reader's attention," Wendy Flory argues that *the preservation of the bond between himself and Christabel somehow is the secret of Sir Leoline's continuing well being*" (7, 11). From traces of classical tragedy in the poem, Margorie Levinson says that Leoline's well-being is in danger because his "House . . . labors beneath a curse. . . ." Levinson conjectures that the curse involves a "triangle" among the Baron, his wife, and Lord Roland (Geraldine's father)—a triangle wherein Leoline suspected his wife of infidelity and thus rejected her and Lord Roland's child, Christabel (87). Accepting the idea of a curse on Sir Leoline's household yet unconvinced of the triangle that Levinson conjectures, this essay shows that "Leoline is [indeed] weak in health" (118)—not from any severing of the bond between himself and his daughter but precisely as a result of that "bond." His house labors under a curse—not involving spousal infidelity and rejection but instead incest. Although several scholars see in Christabel a dark unfulfilled desire for her father (e.g., Spatz 113; Proffitt 249), their relationship is not a matter of guilty desire or neurotic fantasy on her part. It is a *fait accompli*—wrought by none other than the Baron himself. As the narrator says naively, this "father loves [Christabel] so well" (24).

The theme of incest appears elsewhere in Coleridge's work. In **"The Three Graves"** the sexual desires of the widowed mother-in-law involve incestuous overtones and lead her to curse her own daughter. In *Osorio* incestuous implications are complicated by the fact that Maria is not only a sister in all but name but also a psychic twin of Albert—born on the same day and nursed in the same cradle. Regarding the crime of incest as well as other crimes explored by Coleridge, Norman Fruman asserts that they are usually "unmotivated" and "inexplicable" (353). In *Christabel,* however, Sir Leoline has definite motives for placing inordinate demands on his daughter. His wife, whose death he commemorates daily, passed away while bearing Christabel. In one form or another the theme of maternal absence appears almost universally in the incest "romance." As Judith Herman points out, "In the archetypal incest stories (e.g., the story of Lot and several variants of Cinderella), the mother's absence is literal and final" (44). The Baron's bitter resentment, obsessive need, and angry temperament combine to derange him so that he not only blames his daughter for his loss but also seeks in her a surrogate companion. "And to be wroth with one we love / Doth work like madness in the brain" (412-13).

Although Geraldine may seem irrelevant to the relationship between Christabel and her father, she is a psychological projection that represents the heroine's experience in at least four ways: as a victim, a would-be mother and female companion, and a lover. As a victim Geraldine has experienced sexual abuse just as Christabel has. Consequently, the heroine identifies with and gives succor to Geraldine. With a similarly maternal side to her nature, Geraldine in turn nurtures Christabel and plays the protective role of the mother that she longs for but never had. In the partly lesbian relationship between Geraldine and Christabel is the expression of their mutual fear of male abuse and their need for female companionship. With a distinctly masculine side also, Geraldine functions as Christabel's lover—image of her betrothed knight and the father that "loves [her] so well." In essence, Geraldine aside from her positive aspects is the abused as well as the abuser, standing for the anger and guilt of both. She represents Christabel's situation as one who has been forced to undertake the roles of daughter (child) *and* mother/lover (wife). According to Herman, a daughter's fulfillment of "her father's sexual demands may evolve almost as an extension of her role as 'little mother' in the family" that lacks a genuine maternal figure (45). Having been brought up in a male-dominated household, Christabel seeks bitterly to fulfill her various roles and feels guilty in doing so. Her martyrdom is anything but self-imposed.

Because Coleridge's relationship with his daughter Sara was—so far as we know—healthy (albeit brief),[1] this essay does not attempt to link the relationships in *Christabel* to his own family life. Instead, the following pages present a comprehensive analysis of this mysterious ballad, disclosing the concealed *reality* of incest *within it. Christabel* does not deal merely with the sick fantasies of a neurotic young woman. Nevertheless, since psychoanalysis was directed away from the reality of sexual abuse and its generation of neurosis (a con-

nection for which Freud found evidence and hence formulated his early theory of seduction) toward disturbed fantasy life (a major focus of his Oedipal theory), *Christabel* has come to be interpreted as a poem about the latter rather than the former. Such interpretation not only neglects the ballad's real significance but also fails to grasp a likely reason why Coleridge abandoned it as a fragment. After carefully examining the poem, this essay argues by way of analogy to Freud's abandonment of his seduction theory that the father-daughter relationship in *Christabel* was the "extremely subtle and difficult" matter that made the poet abandon his ballad—never to finish it properly. And yet his proposed continuations of *Christabel*—the so-called Gillman and Derwent endings—can be reconciled with its theme of incest.

II

As her name implies, CHRIST/ABEL is doubly a victim. And even before she appears in the ballad, the origins of her victimization are obliquely indicated through the yapping of Sir Leoline's "mastiff bitch," which (like himself) is overly sensitive to the midnight hour (6-13)—for that is the hour at which the Baron's wife died and at which her death is commemorated each day (197, 332-42). That Christabel yearns in part to escape the daily reminder of her father's obsessive love and grief is suggested by the extremity of her actions—an extremity observed by James Gillman: ". . . in these lawless times, for such were the middle ages, the young lady who ventured unattended beyond . . . the castle [after dark], would have endangered her reputation" (285). According to Lynda Boose, "Father-daughter stories are full of literal houses, castles, or gardens in which fathers . . . lock up their daughters . . . to prevent some rival male from stealing them" (33). Thus, instead of praying in the confines of her chapel or chamber for her betrothed, the defenseless and forlorn Christabel escapes into a dark wood at midnight to offer her prayers—"resigned to bliss or bale" (288). Clearly, her venture is associated not only with her beloved but also with paternal "affection":

> The lovely lady, Christabel,
> Whom her father loves so well,
> What makes her in the wood so late,
> A furlong from the castle gate?
>
> (23-26)

She seeks to escape, however briefly, the Baron's household because it fails to provide the security and privacy in which to offer her prayers for a competing male.

Though temporarily absent from Langdale Hall, Christabel cannot escape herself and so amid her "sighs" she meets her alter-ego Geraldine, who "moaned as near, as near can be" (32, 39). That each of these figures has been sexually abused can hardly be doubted from Geraldine's gravely repetitious "Me, even me" (implying the heroine as well as herself) and from her story about her presence in the dark wood—a story that is clearly about a rape:

> Five warriors seized me yestermorn,
> Me, even me, a maid forlorn:
> They choked my cries with force and fright,
> And tied me on a palfrey white.
>
> (81-84)

According to Spatz, Christabel recognizes in Geraldine's story "a maiden threatened by sexual violence" and hence imagines "herself, as a prospective bride, to be in the same position" (112). But the situations here are quite different. Christabel is betrothed to a knight whom she loves whereas Geraldine was seized by warriors whom she did not even know. The more likely connection between Christabel and Geraldine is *the fact*—not the threat—of sexual abuse. Admittedly, the poem is oblique about the matter. But such obliqueness is not surprising from Coleridge, especially considering the value he placed on it concerning women: ". . . a virtuous woman . . . is ever on the alert to discountenance & suppress the very embryos of Thoughts not strictly justifiable" (*Letters* [*Collected Letters of Samuel Taylor Coleridge*] 4: 905).

Having "crossed the shade of night" (88), Geraldine is so shocked by the rape that she represses it as well as the identities of her assailants and the duration of their attack:

> I have no thought what men they be;
> Nor do I know how long it is
> (For I have lain entranced I wis)
> Since one, the tallest of the five,
> . . . .
> . . . placed me underneath this oak;
> He swore they would return with haste;
> Whither they went I cannot tell—
> I thought I heard, some minutes past,
> Sounds as of a castle bell.
>
> (90-101)

Despite her shock and repression (the latter resembling Christabel's main defense mechanism), Geraldine knows exactly what has happened to herself—"(For I have lain entranced I wis)"—her word "entranced" being a pun that discloses the irreversible loss of innocence.

Although Geraldine does not know who her assailants are, it is suggested that they came from a nearby castle, quite probably Sir Leoline's—thus implying further that here is a household where women live in danger. Indeed, soon after Geraldine asserts that "Five warriors seized" her "yestermorn" (81), we learn that just recently "an army in battle array had marched out" the Baron's gate (128). Granted, this evidence is only circumstantial; but the following details reinforce it: (1) Geraldine's assailants abandoned her within earshot of a "castle bell" (101) that rang about the same time as Leoline's; (2) they promised to "return with haste" (98), implying that they did not have far to go; and (3) just as they are associated with the "palfrey white" to which they tied Geraldine (84), so the "numerous array" of the Baron's mission of intended reconciliation to Lord Roland is "White with their panting palfreys' foam" (510). No wonder Christabel's alter ego wishes so much "to flee" these environs (103).

Sympathetic to Geraldine's story, Christabel stretches "forth her hand" and offers assistance (104). But, since her plight and Geraldine's are so similar, why does the protagonist take her counterpart to Langdale Hall? The most obvious reason is that she has no alternative. Nor is her offer of assistance a case of misery seeking company. Instead, she seeks the empowerment of womanhood, her womanhood. She hopes that her alter-ego "may . . . command / The service of Sir Leoline" and his "stout chivalry" to "guide and guard" her "safe and free" (106-10). Moreover, Geraldine's situation gives Christabel an opportunity to work through the absence of her mother by being helpful and maternal to someone with the same qualities.

While entering the castle Christabel stresses exceeding quiet, for "Sir Leoline . . . weak in health . . . may not well awakened be" (118-19). The Baron's ill-health is never clearly defined, but concerning it two matters are certain: it either causes or results from restless sleep (this "father seldom sleepeth well"), and Christabel truly fears disturbing this man—fears even to the extent of walking the cold corridors of his castle barefooted in order not to rouse him:

> Sweet Christabel her feet doth bare,
> And jealous of the listening air
> They steal their way from stair to stair,
> Now in glimmer, and now in gloom,
> And now they pass the Baron's room,
> As still as death, with stifled breath!
>
> (166-71)[2]

Often attributed to the machinations of a witch or lamia, Geraldine's fainting and recovery at the threshold of the castle have been interpreted as signs of the difficulty and the evil of such creatures gaining access to a decent Christian household. But, as the text more likely suggests, the fainting points to Geraldine's weariness, which results from her ordeal with the five warriors. Having been made a "weary woman" (95), she is now a "weary weight" (131). And although Christabel thanks the Virgin Mary for helping to deliver them from their distress in the forest, Geraldine knows the real situation and hence "cannot speak for weariness" (139-42). As very specific instances of projection, Geraldine's fainting and sudden recovery reflect the following concerns of the heroine: her revulsion at being reminded of her mock marriage with Sir Leoline (a reminder piqued by the act of crossing the threshold without her betrothed), and at the same time her desire to find a substitute for herself in that marriage (hence Geraldine's quick recovery and readiness to meet the Baron).

When she looks directly into Geraldine's eyes for the first time, Christabel begins to enter a spell that condenses the most terrible aspects of her experience. Thus, when "Christabel saw the lady's eye / . . . nothing else saw she thereby, / Save the boss of the shield of Sir Leoline tall" (160-62). The emphatic association ("nothing else") between Geraldine's "eye" and Leoline's "boss" suggests that an aspect of Geraldine involves Christabel's father, in particular, his symbol of male power and authority—i.e., the boss, which is not only a metallic inset but also an emblematic protuberance on his shield (the shield being a substitute for his body). According to the *OED* [*Oxford English Dictionary*], a "boss" is a "round prominence in hammered or carved work . . . a metal stud." In addition, it can refer to a "protuberance or swelling on the body of an animal." The military and sexual implications here hark back to the five warriors, who raped Geraldine.

Upon her arrival in Christabel's chamber, Geraldine's actions include welcoming and then suddenly banishing the spirit of the protagonist's mother (203-06). Though at first puzzling, this behavior reflects Christabel's confused state of mind concerning her mother—longing for her protection, resenting her absence, and yet wanting at the same time to mature properly without maternal help. Left defenseless from birth at Langdale Hall, Christabel quite naturally associates Geraldine's sudden reversal of behavior with confusion and distress resulting from the rape: "Alas said she, this ghastly ride— / Dear lady! it hath wildered you!" (216-17). And Geraldine's response—"'tis over now!'"—implies her (as well as Christabel's) wish to put such abuse permanently into the past.

Because this wish is futile, they attempt to relive their trauma in a manner that seeks comfort—a manner that is both lesbian and maternal (262-63, 299-301). Little wonder is it that the Christian Christabel is so confused when she disrobes herself and watches Geraldine pray for her: ". . . through her brain of weal and woe / So many thoughts moved to and fro" (239-40). Little wonder is it, likewise, that Geraldine (of "noble line") hesitates to reveal her violated form to Christabel. (What is eventually revealed suggests the horror of not only past but possibly future violation. According to James Twitchell, a long-standing biological conjecture about sexual abuse was that it increased the possibility of

physical and even genetic deformity [*Forbidden Partners* 244].) In lines 255-261 Geraldine hesitates also to "couch" with Christabel. In manuscripts and the first edition of the ballad, these lines consisted of only a couplet: "She took two paces and a stride, / And lay down by the maiden's side" (p. 224). Expanded to emphasize Geraldine's hesitation, this passage has been interpreted to mean that she is not wholly evil (Fruman 358) and that she deserves "increased compassion" (Flory 6). Hence, though "defied" and made reprobate (*defy* means also to curse or reprobate), Geraldine seeks at the risk of incurring Christabel's revulsion to provide the kind of companionship denied her since birth: she "holds the maiden in her arms, / . . . As a mother with her child" (299-301).

Although Geraldine appears to befriend Christabel, we must ask why she inflicts upon the protagonist a spell that involves rationalization and half-truth:

> 'In the touch of this bosom there worketh a spell,
> Which is lord of thy utterance, Christabel!
> Thou knowest to-night, and wilt know to-morrow,
> This mark of my shame, this seal of my sorrow;
> But vainly thou warrest,
> For this is alone in
> Thy power to declare,
> That in the dim forest
> Thou heard'st a low moaning,
> And found'st a bright lady, surpassingly fair;
> And didst bring her home with thee in love and in charity,
> To shield her and shelter her from the damp air.'

(267-78)

Like her own en-*trance*ment under male domination, Geraldine's bespelling of Christabel becomes "lord" over (i.e., silences) explicit utterance. Geraldine enacts the roles of not only surrogate mother and female companion but also father, lord, and lover—seeking to conceal especially the latter set of relationships with her. This interpretation gains support from William Hazlitt's "Report that Geraldine was a man in disguise" (Coleridge, **Letters** 4: 918) and that there is "something disgusting at the bottom" of Coleridge's subject (Hazlitt 349)—something perhaps far worse in the mannish qualities of Geraldine than the suggestion of normal (albeit clandestine) heterosexuality with Christabel.

By the "Conclusion" of Part I, the heroine seems "resigned" (288), as the speaker says. Though open, her eyes dream "that alone, which is— / O sorrow and shame!" (296-97). Appearing like Christabel to have fallen under the spell of concealment inflicted by Geraldine, the speaker cannot utter exactly what this "sorrow" and "shame" refer to. But surely they are the physical mark of Geraldine's shame and the psychological seal of her sorrow (270), in which Christabel shares. Thus, after the night with Geraldine and the re-enactment of the primal sexual offense against this hero-ine, she awakens with a sense of wrong (381) although she cannot say what exactly the wrong is (390; see 385-86). Geraldine's bespellment of her fixes her attention on the surface details of her story (i.e., her kindliness to Geraldine), but it is not uncommon for the sexual abuse of children to result in their deep bewilderment—the sense that something is terribly wrong yet the inability to articulate what it is or who is responsible and why (Herman 30; Finkelhor *et al.* 180-84, 190, 192).

III

If Part I of this poem presents some of the effects of Christabel's circumstances, Part II presents their cause. Furthermore, if Part I focuses on the heroine and her alter-ego, Part II focuses on her father and the same alter-ego. From the outset Sir Leoline's apparent feel-ings of loss about his wife pervade this section:

> Each matin bell, the Baron saith,
> Knells us back to a world of death.
> These words Sir Leoline first said,
> When he rose and found his lady dead:
> These words Sir Leoline will say
> Many a morn to his dying day!
>
> (332-37)

And according to his "law," this knelling must continue daily from midnight till "dawn" (338-42). But the mock-ing way in which the narrator describes the knelling ("There is no lack of such, I ween") implies something inappropriate about this sign of Leoline's sorrow. Inap-propriateness of tone and detail continues with the nar-rator's observations that this solemn tolling is echoed throughout the Baron's land by "Three sinful sextons' ghosts" (353) and even by the devil himself, who "mocks the doleful tale / With a merry peal from Borodale" (358-59). The sources of these echoes sug-gest that something is amiss with the Baron's love. In-deed, the fact that he learned of his lady's death *after* he "rose"—presumably—from his bed indicates a hus-band without much regard for his wife as she suffered the pangs of childbirth. That his love and sorrow for his spouse may not be wholly sincere is suggested most immediately by his embrace of Geraldine upon first seeing her. The embrace is rather sudden, warm, and in-appropriate for a man in mourning (not to mention ill health).

Similarly, the way that he greets Christabel seems inap-propriate:

> The Baron rose, and while he prest
> His gentle daughter to his breast,
> With cheerful wonder in his eyes
> The Lady Geraldine espies,
> And gave such welcome to the same,
> As might beseem so bright a dame!
>
> (397-402)

Since Leoline was so sick and grumpy that Christabel dreaded awakening him the preceding night, what are we to make of his vigor and seeming kindliness only a few hours later? Either her fears did in fact involve his grouchiness or they involved something else—some-thing perhaps resembling "The vision of fear, the touch and pain" (453) that she experiences while watching the Baron embrace her alter-ego. If his greeting of Christa-bel herself appears too intimate, then so is "such wel-come" for Geraldine. Accordingly, the words "As might beseem so bright a dame" include a double entendre that makes his embrace even more suspect, for the root of "beseem" implies not only suitability or decorous-ness (as in "seemly") but also the idea of appearance and perhaps the idea of degradation (as in "seamy"). Leoline has more than a little in common with the "spot-ted infamy" (437) of the warriors who seized Geral-dine. This interpretation gains further support from the double-meaning of "espies," which suggests that the Baron lies "in wait for" as well as "looks intently at" (*OED*) this bright dame.

Although the story of Geraldine's plight and the men-tion of her father give Sir Leoline the opportunity to re-vive his comradery with Lord Roland, this does not ap-pear to be his primary concern. Instead, his oath and challenge against those who laid hands on Geraldine sound more like public posturings, for it is the "'beautiful'" and "'lovely'" Geraldine (503, 507) who at present interests him.[3] Recognizing this fact and re-pulsed at their embrace, Christabel sinks more deeply into her "vision of fear":

> She shrunk and shuddered, and saw again—
> . . . .
> Again she saw that bosom old,
> Again she felt that bosom cold. . . .
>
> (454, 457-58)

Nearly every Coleridgean believes that these lines refer to Christabel's experience with Geraldine the preceding night. Although that experience was in some ways frightening, nothing in the published version of the bal-lad suggests that Geraldine's bosom is either old or cold. Granted, in earlier manuscripts of *Christabel* the following verse appeared after the famous line "Be-hold! her bosom and half her side—" (252): "Are lean and old and foul of hue" ([*Coleridge: Poetical Works*] p. 224). But the fact that Coleridge deleted these words leaves open the possibility that the "old" and "cold" bo-som in Christabel's vision is as much her father's as Geraldine's. Moreover, the threefold repetition of "again" points to redundant experiences, mixing past traumas with the present one. Shuddering at the re-minder of sexual impropriety, Christabel hisses and is immediately hushed by her father and by Geraldine's repressive spell.

Soon an ominous dream (narrated by Leoline's bard) of a dove encircled by a snake shows us not only how much the Baron now disregards his daughter and pursues Geraldine but also how hidden the truth of male assault is in his domain. Although Bard Bracy clearly identifies the dove with Christabel (531-33), the Baron, who presumably would want to protect his daughter, completely misinterprets the dream and identifies the dove with Geraldine (509), toward whom he turns— "His eyes made up of wonder and love" (567). His misinterpretation reveals that he does not admit to the reality of male abuse. As Bracy's words indicate, that reality is well disguised in this manor: "'I wonder'd what might ail the bird; / For nothing near it could I see'" (538-39). Not until he stooped down and looked closely did he see "'a bright green snake / Coiled around its wings and neck'" (549-50)—a snake whose color makes it almost indistinguishable from its environment (551). Ultimately, whether this snake symbolizes Geraldine, whose eyes resemble a "serpent's" (585), or Sir Leoline makes little difference, for the midnight liaison with Geraldine reminds Christabel partly of her relationship with the Baron.

With bravado Leoline announces that he and Lord Roland will "'crush the snake'" (571) of Bracy's dream. The Baron's declaration to eliminate the snake makes psychological sense. Because the dream comes too close to the reality of his behavior and because he loathes himself for that behavior and wishes to perform some compensatory act, he seeks to displace this symbol of his dishonor. But, when he kisses Geraldine while promising to crush the snake, we see the displacement instead of Christabel and her mother in a kind of marriage rehearsal—complete with blushing "bride" and her wedding train:

> He kissed her forehead as he spake,
> And Geraldine in maiden wise
> Casting down her large bright eyes,
> With blushing cheek and courtesy fine
> She turned her from Sir Leoline;
> Softly gathering up her train,
> That o'er her right arm fell again;
> And folded her arms across her chest,
> And couched her head upon her breast,
> And looked askance at Christabel. . . .
>
> (572-81)

That displacement is the subject of this passage is suggested also in line 576, where Coleridge—instead of using the pronoun "herself" (meaning Geraldine)—used "her," thereby implying Christabel as well.[4] Geraldine looks askance at Christabel "with somewhat of malice, and more of dread" (586) precisely because the situation she is entering with Sir Leoline resembles the heroine's. The latter's angry hissing at Geraldine's snaky look (591) shows not only how similar these figures are but also how confused and upset Christabel is about being displaced. While deeply hoping to be free from her father's "love," she partly fears losing it.[5] Hence, she impulsively entreats Leoline to send Geraldine "'away'" (617).

The Baron's anger (621) in response to Christabel's entreaty stems not so much from her lack of hospitality as from her accusatory "look of . . . hate" (606) and *her* reminder of his wife's death ("'By my mother's soul do I entreat . . .'"). Though unaware of exactly what is going on between the Baron and his daughter, the narrator comes very close to critical insight: Leoline's

> . . . cheeks they quivered, his eyes were wild,
> Dishonoured thus in his old age;
> Dishonoured by his only child,
> And all his hospitality
> To the wronged daughter of his friend
> By more than woman's jealousy. . . .
>
> (641-46)

Although the narrator appears to blame Leoline's "pain and rage" on Christabel's dishonoring of his hospitality, the word "Dishonoured" is often a sexually charged term and there is little doubt it does involve him (even "in his old age"). Furthermore, in the verse "Dishonoured by his only child" the preposition "by" can mean "with" as well as "through." The Baron's dishonor includes "all" his hospitality, meaning presumably his entire household—its knights and warriors. This dishonor has surely been communicated "To the *wronged* daughter of his friend" (italics added). The narrator's phrase "By more than woman's jealousy" almost establishes intuitively Leoline's disgrace, for if it stems from more than Christabel's jealousy (the apparent source of her inhospitable actions) then what could that disgrace be other than sexual dishonor brought on by the Baron himself?

In spite of Coleridge's assertion that he "always had the whole plan [of *Christabel*] entire from beginning to end in . . . mind" (*Table Talk* [*The "Table Talk" and "Omniana" of Samuel Taylor Coleridge*] 241), he never completed the poem except for the addition of a brief coda to Part II—a "Conclusion" that originally appeared in his letter to Robert Southey on May 6, 1801. Of this letter's verses, which vary only slightly from their published version in the ballad, Coleridge said that they express "A very metaphysical account of Fathers calling their children . . . little varlets—&c—" (*Letters* 2: 729). Whether or not he originally intended the verses to Southey for *Christabel,* the fact is that with its first publication (1816) Coleridge thought they provided an adequate close to the poem and thereafter he never changed his mind about the matter. Scholars, however, generally consider the "Conclusion" to Part II more makeshift than suitable. Nevertheless, it is relevant, for it articulates the tragic paradox that in families "love's excess" is sometimes expressed with "unmeant bitter-ness" (664-65). This paradox Coleridge considered but found difficult to fathom. As he said laconically in **Table Talk,** ". . . in love there is a sort of antipathy, or op-posing passion" (112). That there are connections be-tween Christabel and the coda's "little child," for whom its father expresses "love's excess," is implied in the imagery of dance. Both Christabel and the child appear to be the only children in their respective families, for just as the child is described as a "limber elf, / Singing, dancing to itself" (i.e., alone, without siblings), so Christabel is associated with "The one red leaf, the last of its clan, / That dances as often as dance it can" (49-50).

Despite the tragic theme in and the connections be-tween the ballad and the coda, its paradox concerning the intimacy of love and hate appears rather facile. This is why the verses following the paradox are so self-reflexive:

> Perhaps 'tis pretty to force together
> Thoughts so all unlike each other;
> To mutter and mock a broken charm,
> To dally with wrong that does no harm.

(666-69)

If a paraphrase of this tonally self-deprecatory passage is permissible, the following might satisfy: It is quite clever to join, as this poem does, thoughts and feelings (like love and hate) which are so different. It is clever also to mimic charms and other deep psychic phenom-ena and to "dally with" evils that are merely fictional and therefore can do no harm. But, as subsequent verses indicate, the relationships between anger or "wild word[s]" and "love and pity" (671-72) are too sensitive and disturbing simply to "dally with." This is all the more so "if in a world of sin" (i.e., the non-fictive world) such confusion of heart and brain as the Baron's results "from rage and pain": "(O sorrow and shame should this be true!)" (673-76). Echoing Geraldine's words to Christabel in her chamber (270), the phrase "sorrow and shame" suggests a frightening connection between the fictive and non-fictive worlds—between the excess of love that leads to ire and abuse in Christa-bel's life, as the ballad particularizes, and the same in real life, as the coda generalizes.

IV

So dizzying is the confusion between heart and brain and between love and hate that this "giddiness" (675) is hard to silence: "So talks as it's most used to do" (677). And yet Coleridge did not finish **Christabel** according to his apparent plans. Nonetheless, his projected completions of the poem, as reported by his son Der-went and his early biographer James Gillman, can be reconciled with the theme of incestuous family romance.

While the so-called Gillman ending is predicated on the idea that Geraldine is an independent supernatural force of evil ("like the Weird Sisters in Macbeth"), she can be seen to reinforce "the anger" of a cruel father, which now exceeds his possessiveness such that he continues to abuse his daughter through the surrogacy of Geral-dine. In defiance of Christabel's entreaty, Leoline has retained Geraldine at Langdale Hall. And through this figure, whose gender is ambiguous also in the Gillman ending (she "changes her appearance to that of the ac-cepted though absent lover of Christabel" [301-02]), the Baron's behavior works its most insidious effect—namely, his victim's confusion of disgust and yearning for other men. The false lover's "courtship [is] most distressing to Christabel, who feels . . . great disgust for her once favoured knight." Though predictable her "coldness" to this suitor is "very painful to the Baron" because it reflects her deepest feelings toward him. Ac-cording to Gillman, Leoline "has no more conception" than Christabel does of Geraldine's "transformation" into the absent lover. But this obtuseness is just as likely his denial of responsibility for the fear and loathing in his child. With subordination largely expected of women in the medieval world,[6] Christabel finally "yields to her father's entreaties, and consents to approach the altar with this hated suitor" (302).

As every Coleridgean knows, the Gillman conclusion is eventually a happy one: the "real lover" suddenly re-turns and "the rightful marriage takes place, after which follows [sic] a reconciliation and explanation between the father and daughter" (302). While this ending seems as implausible as a fairy tale's, it does assert the reality of the incest taboo and especially its social effects. Whereas according to Freud the taboo divides sexually the young from the old and from each other, according to Talcott Parsons it ultimately unites them into a greater cohesive social framework. The taboo pushes the child to form new relationships beyond the nuclear family, thereby establishing new families and stabilizing spe-cific orders of authority within them (Parsons 101-05). Herein lie not only the significance of "the rightful mar-riage" between Christabel and her true lover but also the sub-text of the "explanation" between her and Sir Leoline. The bestowal of Christabel on her betrothed reconciles with the Baron's previous behavior and rein-forces his explanation, for as Lynda Boose observes: "The bestowal design places the daughter's departure from the father's house and her sexual union with an-other male into a text defined [i.e., explained] by obedi-ence. . . . So long as the strategy operates, the loss of a daughter can be psychologically mitigated, and defeat by a rival male constructed into public rituals that rede-fine this transfer as the father's magnanimous gift" (32). Leoline's bestowal changes Christabel from a posses-sion of his to an article in his transfer of male authority.

Derwent Coleridge, writing several years after the Gillman biography, disputed its account of Geraldine:

> The sufferings of Christabel were to have
> been represented as vicarious, endured for
> her 'lover far away'; and Geraldine [is]
> no . . . malignant being of any kind,
> but a spirit, executing her appointed task
> with the best good will, as she herself says:—
> All they, who live in the upper sky,
> Do love you, holy Christabel, &c. (ll. 227-32)
> In this form this is, of course, accommodated
> to a 'fond superstition,' in keeping with the
> general terms of the piece; but that the holy
> and the innocent do often suffer for the
> faults of those they love, and are thus made
> the instruments to bring them back to the
> ways of peace, is a matter of fact. . . .
>
>   (xlii)

While disagreeing with Gillman's suggestion that Geraldine is "evil," Derwent Coleridge did agree with the biographer's shorter account of the poem's continuation, namely, that "The story of the Christabel is partly founded on the notion, that the virtuous of this world save the wicked. . . . Christabel suffers and prays for 'The weal of her lover that is far away,' exposed to various temptations . . ." (Gillman 283). But just how temptations constitute wickedness or faults of any kind is unclear. And how the true lover's distant actions relate to Geraldine and the particular events of Parts I and II is equally unclear. To reconcile Derwent's views and Gillman's shorter account with the ballad's "romance," the distinction between the heroine's devotion and her suffering must be acknowledged: she prays for the "weal of her lover"; but she suffers directly at the hands of her father and vicariously through perhaps an ultimately benevolent Geraldine. Christabel may be said to be in harm's way *for* her beloved but *not because* of him, for if the Baron's jealousy weighs heavily in Derwent's all too sketchy version then this father may make his daughter suffer additionally for having a sexual interest beyond his domain.

In spite of all her circumstances, however, Christabel remains "innocent" and "holy." Even though she and her alter-ego experience moments of profound horror, it is in such moments that theologians such as Rudolf Otto locate the sense of awe that can lead to spiritual understanding. In *The Idea of the Holy* Otto suggests that from the shiver of "daemonic dread" visionary and mystical experience (the *mysterium tremendum*) arise (12-19). Thus, Christabel's circumstances reconcile with Coleridge's assertion that several verses about martyrdom in Crashaw's "Hymn to . . . Sainte Teresa" were ever on his mind "whilst writing the second part" of the ballad—"if, indeed, by some subtle process of the mind they did not suggest the first thought of the whole poem" (*Table Talk* 322). Undoubtedly, the closest similarity between Christabel and Teresa involves the act of ravishment: Christabel's physical and psychological ravishment and Teresa's spiritual embrace by God—her "fair Spouse." In radically different ways, Christabel and Teresa are "love's victime[s]" (Crashaw, lines 65, 75). But, as Derwent Coleridge implied, Christabel might have become a new Teresa. The language in Crashaw's hymn is so striking that Derwent may well have been thinking of it when he referred to Christabel as an instrument of peace:

> So rare,
> So spirituall, pure, and fair
> Must be th'immortall instrument
> Upon whose choice point shall be sent
> A life so lov'd. . . .
>
>   (87-91)

V

Despite the assertion that he envisioned *Christabel* in its entirety and despite the urging from his friends to finish it, Coleridge offered essentially one excuse for not doing so: "I could not carry on with equal success the execution of the idea, an extremely subtle and difficult one" (*Table Talk* 241). While most critics attribute this excuse to a failure of poetic powers, I suggest that there was more to it than that. His topic proved to offend his moral sensibility too much; and the idea that love and hate, desire and ire, could mingle so intimately and harmfully within a family was too terrible to fathom. In the words of Derwent Coleridge, his father "would not, could not, have produced anything . . . which did not satisfy his own taste and judgment,— which perhaps may be taken as one reason why he produced nothing" further of the poem (xlii). Its thoughts and feelings, "so all unlike each other," were ultimately too repugnant and incomprehensible for him to "force together" and bring to closure.

Nevertheless, it seems odd that this great poet of desire and dream-life could not finish *Christabel*. But incest, especially between fathers and daughters, is so abhorrent and the taboo against it so profound that studies of sexual *fantasies* indicate it is usually repressed even in them (Goleman 19). Indeed, as Jeffrey Masson points out in *The Assault on Truth: Freud's Suppression of the Seduction Theory*, the subject is so sensitive that before 1895-96 when Freud recognized that incest lurked in the background of his female patients,[7] the psychoanalysts who had heard their stories dismissed them as mere fantasies. After he proposed his seduction theory, arguing that "sexual abuses" are the foundation of neuroses (3: 199, 203, 206-07, 214), fellow psychoanalysts greeted his ideas with silence, ridicule, and outright rejection (Masson xxii-xxiii, 134-38). For various reasons, ranging from peer pressure to moral respectability, incredulousness, and other factors—all of which Masson sums up as "a failure of courage" (xxi), Freud aban-

doned his seduction theory in favour of the more socially acceptable view (his Oedipal theory) that neuroses
result not from the *fact* of sexual abuse but from the patient's own disturbed fantasy life.[8] For similar reasons,
which can be summed up also as a failure of courage,
Coleridge abandoned *Christabel.*

Though encouraged by friends to finish the poem, he
must have felt more *dis*couraged by the reviews that accused it of being obscene. Such reviews included not
only Hazlitt's in *The Examiner* (2 June 1816) but also a
review by (probably) Thomas Moore in the *Edinburgh
Review* (Sept. 1816), which suggested that Geraldine
seduces Christabel (63). In the anonymous pamphlet
*Hypocrisy Unveiled and Calumny Detected: In a Re-
view in Blackwood's Magazine,* the author (probably
James Grahame) called *Christabel* "the most obscene
poem in the English language" and compared it—interestingly—to Byron's *Parisina,* which deals also with a
form of incest (50). The reviews and the pamphlet agitated Coleridge (*Letters* 4: 918, 919) and appear to
have prompted him to tell DeQuincey on 8 August 1821
that, had it not been for Hartley's financial needs,
Christabel would never have been published (*Letters* 5:
162). In a letter to William Blackwood, whose magazine published one of the several vulgar and sometimes
obscene parodies of the ballad (*Blackwood's Edinburgh
Magazine,* June 1819), the poet took notice of the
parody, tacitly admitting grounds for it so long as no
questions of personal turpitude were raised (*Letters* 4:
944). I refer to this letter and the above not to imply
turpitude on Coleridge's part but to show his concern
(like Freud's) with public opinion and moral and professional respectability.

In addition, I proffer that the psychological readings of
Christabel which focus on the protagonist's fantasy life
and neglect or deemphasize Sir Leoline's behavior have
wittingly or unwittingly adhered to the ideology of psychoanalysis since Freud's suppression of the seduction
hypothesis.[9] According to Masson, ". . . once Freud
had decided that . . . parents had not done anything to
their children in reality, then . . . 'aggressive impulses'
[from the children] replaced seduction in his theories"
(113). Taking the form of repressed illicit desires and
disturbing projections, such impulses and the analysis
of them have been central to much psychological criticism of *Christabel.* Furthermore, this criticism perpetuates related aspects of Freud's "mainstream," post-
seduction-theory, views. Among these views, as Masson
paraphrases, ". . . early childhood traumas turn out to
be fantasies which are conjured up as a defense against
fully experiencing the events of adolescence. . . . The
'neurotic' adolescent does not want to acknowledge her
own sexual desires . . ." (122). How often have words
to this effect been said of Christabel!

In the histories of science and letters, it may appear insignificant that Freud suppressed his seduction hypoth-

esis and that *Christabel* has been interpreted repeatedly
from a perspective valorizing fantasy over experience,
but such matters are not trivial. Years after abandoning
(or, rather, transforming beyond recognition) the seduction theory, Freud wrote in his *Introductory Lectures on
Psycho-Analysis* (1916-17) that "if in the case of girls
who produce such an event [seduction] in the story of
their childhood their father figures fairly regularly as
the seducer, *there can be no doubt . . . of the imaginary nature of the accusation . . .*" (16: 370; italics
added). But to tell a young woman who has suffered the
trauma of incest that her memories are not anchored in
reality is to do even further violence to her. In the case
of Coleridge's ballad, to see Christabel's problems as a
matter primarily of disturbed fantasy (without any real
connection to her father) is both to beg the question—
how did her fantasy life become disturbed in the first
place?—and to sidestep the ballad's true topic and its
social import.

Although Freud's evasion of the reality of father-
daughter incest enabled him to develop a socially acceptable theory, there have undoubtedly been generations of deleterious effects by the psychoanalysis of
people with real events to narrate but who have been
treated as if nothing factual lay beneath their narratives.
As Boose argues, Freud's post-seduction Oedipal theories have been "used by the psychoanalytic institution
. . . to suppress the daughter's story and avoid acknowledging the father's guilt" (40-41). Just as in the
lives of Christabel and many of Freud's female patients
and no doubt many of his successors' patients, so in the
life of Claudia Draper in the recent motion picture *Nuts*:
a grim reality lurks beneath terrible female suffering.
And yet the prison psychiatrist in the film could not see
beneath the many signs in his patient's experience to
the fact of sexual abuse by her father. Even when she
painfully divulged in court this fact, the psychiatrist
could not accept it, for if in the case of girls who produce such stories their fathers figure regularly as the se-
ducers "there can be no doubt . . . of the imaginary nature of the accusation[s]." Thus, the psychiatrist unable
to reject father Freud's Oedipal theories still considered
Claudia "nuts," just as many critics consider Christabel
a victim of self-induced neurosis.

While understandable, Coleridge's unwillingness or inability to complete *Christabel* was more than a poetic
failure. R. D. Laing has written about the concept of
"potentration" or the way evasion of a subject reinvests
it with power. And in *Dangerous Secrets* Michael Weissberg has argued that silence renders morally and socially reprehensible acts such as child abuse and incest
with powers that are almost destined to fracture the self
as well as family order. Tragically, these are the very
circumstances in which we find Christabel at the end of
Part II—wronged, scorned, and then rejected by her father—her identity and her household in disarray. Such

circumstances are all too common in households where father-daughter incest occurs. "The displaced, unacknowledged fault [of the father] will perform its work of separation across generations, separation from others and from oneself" (Balmary 170). Furthermore, it does not appear that Christabel's circumstances would have improved in the next part of the ballad. As Coleridge wrote in a Notebook entry of 1823-24, when he was feeling particularly well on his birthday, "Were I free to do so I feel as if I could compose the third part of Christabel, or the song of her desolation" (qtd. in Coburn 127).[10]

Notes

1. Brief, for the poet "lived with his youngest child only . . . a period measurable in months" (Mudge 2; see also 19).

2. As experts in the research and treatment of incest victims have shown, fear is the most common reaction among such victims, especially when the victimizer is the father or a father-figure (Gagnon 184; Herman 28; Gelinas 315-17; and Finkelhor *et al.* 149, 192).

3. According to the narrator, these are the Baron's descriptors of Lady Geraldine.

4. The poet could just as easily have used "herself" since his meter is based (he asserted) on the number of accents per line, not the number of syllables ([*Poetical Works*] p. 215).

5. The paradoxical phenomenon of the incest victim wanting reprieve from yet fearing abandonment by the victimizer is not unusual, as clinicians and researchers have discovered (Sloane and Karpinski 669; Kaufman, Peck, and Tagiuri 271; Lustig *et al.* 35).

6. That such subordination was more the norm than the exception in the Middle Ages is argued by F. and J. Gies (27), Bornstein (12, 46-75), and Bullough, Shelton, and Slavin (129).

7. See, for example, the following letters by Freud in *The Origins of Psycho-analysis*: letter 29 (8 Oct. 1895), 30 (15 Oct. 1895), and 52 (6 Dec. 1896).

8. As Freud said later in his career, "In the period in which the main interest was directed to discovering infantile sexual traumas, almost all my women patients told me that they had been seduced by their father. I was driven to recognize in the end that these reports were untrue and so came to understand that hysterical symptoms are derived from phantasies and not from real occurrences. It was only later that I was able to recognize in this phantasy of being seduced by the father the expression of the typical Oedipus complex in women" (22: 120). See Balmary 114. Although David Willbern asserts that Freud did not completely reject his seduction hypothesis, he acknowledges that late in the evolution of Freud's thought "the father has become displaced as the agent responsible for childhood seduction . . ." (80). According to Jane Gallop, after repudiating it Freud did speak of "actual seduction"—but with the difference that he now deflected guilt from the father to the nurse, the mother, and (by way of fantasy life) the child herself (144-45). Like Masson, several commentators have argued that Freud turned away from his seduction theory because he was unable to come to terms with what he discovered: namely, the crucial role played in neurosis by the abuse of paternal power. These commentators and their perspectives include Luce Irigaray (from feminist theory), Alice Miller as well as Judith Herman and Lisa Hirschman (from clinical evidence), Florence Rush (from historical evidence), and Maria Balmary (from a psychoanalytic reading of the "text" of Freud's life and work).

9. Besides such critics as Basler, Tomlinson, Luther, Spatz, and Proffitt, who have been cited earlier, several others have slighted or ignored Christabel's experience, emphasizing instead her "neurotic" fantasies and desire (often in conjunction with Coleridge's) for the mother though sometimes also the father: Wormhoudt (19-29), Beres (97-116), Angus (663), Ware (345-50), Twitchell ("'Desire with Loathing'" 39-43), Fruman (405-07), and Schapiro (123-24).

10. My thanks go to Max Schulz and David Radcliffe for making helpful suggestions on earlier drafts of this paper and to Vara Neverow-Turk and Jane Lilienfeld for allowing me to present a shorter version of it at the 1989 MLA Convention.

Works Cited

Angus, Douglas. "The Theme of Love and Guilt in Coleridge's Three Major Poems." *Journal of English and Germanic Philology* 59 (1960): 655-68.

Balmary, Marie. *Psychoanalyzing Psychoanalysis: Freud and the Hidden Fault of the Father.* Trans. Ned Lukacher. Baltimore: Johns Hopkins UP, 1982.

Basler, Roy P. *Sex, Symbolism, and Psychology in Literature.* 1948. New York: Octagon, 1967.

Beres, David. "A Dream, a Vision, and a Poem." *International Journal of Psychoanalysis* 32 (1951): 97-116.

Boose, Lynda E., and Betty S. Flowers, eds. *Daughters and Fathers.* Baltimore: Johns Hopkins UP, 1989.

Boose, Lynda E. "The Father's House and the Daughter in It: The Structures of Western Culture's Daughter-

Father Relationship." *Daughters and Fathers.* Ed. L. E. Boose and B. S. Flowers. 19-74.

Bornstein, Diane. *The Lady in the Tower: Medieval Courtesy Literature for Women.* Hamden, Conn.: Archon, 1983.

Bullough, Vern L., Brenda Shelton, and Sarah Slavin. *The Subordinated Sex: A History of Attitudes Toward Women.* Athens: U of Georgia P, 1988.

Coburn, Kathleen, ed. *Inquiring Spirit: A New Presentation of Coleridge from His Published and Unpublished Prose Writings.* Rev. ed. Toronto: U of Toronto P, 1979.

Coleridge, Derwent, ed. *The Poems of Samuel Taylor Coleridge.* London, 1870.

Coleridge, Samuel Taylor. *Coleridge: Poetical Works.* Ed. Ernest Hartley Coleridge. London: Oxford UP, 1969.

————. *The "Table Talk" and "Omniana" of Samuel Taylor Coleridge.* Ed. T. Ashe. London: G. Bell, 1909.

————. *Collected Letters of Samuel Taylor Coleridge.* Ed. Earl Leslie Griggs. 6 vols. Oxford: Clarendon, 1956-71.

Crashaw, Richard. *The Complete Poetry of Richard Crashaw.* Ed. George W. Williams. New York: New York UP, 1972.

Finkelhor, David, *et al. A Sourcebook on Child Sexual Abuse.* Beverly Hills: Sage, 1986.

Flory, Wendy S. "Fathers and Daughters: Coleridge and 'Christabel'." *Women & Literature* 3 (1975): 5-15.

Freud, Sigmund. *The Standard Edition of the Complete Psychological Works of Sigmund Freud.* Gen. ed. and trans. James Strachey, with Anna Freud *et al.* 24 vols. London: Hogarth and the Institute of Psycho-analysis, 1953-74.

————. *The Origins of Psycho-Analysis: Letters to Wilhelm Fliess, Drafts and Notes: 1887-1902.* Ed. M. Bonaparte, A. Freud, and E. Kris. Trans. E. Mosbacher and J. Strachey. New York: Basic Books, 1954.

Fruman, Norman. *Coleridge, The Damaged Archangel.* New York: Braziller, 1971.

Gagnon, John. "Female Child Victims of Sex Offenses." *Social Problems* 13 (1965): 176-92.

Gallop, Jane. *The Daughter's Seduction: Feminism and Psychoanalysis.* Ithaca: Cornell UP, 1982.

Gelinas, Denise J. "The Persisting Negative Effects of Incest." *Psychiatry* 46 (1983): 312-32.

Gies, Frances, and Joseph Gies. *Women in the Middle Ages.* New York: Crowell, 1978.

Gillman, James. *The Life of Samuel Taylor Coleridge.* London: William Pickering, 1838.

Goleman, Daniel. "Sexual Fantasies: What Are Their Hidden Meanings?" *New York Times* 28 Feb. 1984: 19.

[Grahame, James.] *Hypocrisy Unveiled and Calumny Detected: In a Review in Blackwood's Magazine.* 4th ed. Edinburgh: F. Pillans, 1818.

Hazlitt, William. Rev. of *Christabel; Kubla Khan, a Vision; The Pains of Sleep,* by S. T. Coleridge. *The Examiner* 2 June 1816: 348-49.

Herman, Judith L., with Lisa Hirschman. *Father-Daughter Incest.* Cambridge: Harvard UP, 1981.

Irigaray, Luce. *The Sex Which Is Not One.* Trans. Catherine Porter and Carolyn Burke. Ithaca, N.Y.: Cornell UP, 1985.

Kaufman, Irwin, Alice L. Peck, and Consuelo K. Tagiuri. "The Family Constellation and Overt Incestuous Relations Between Father and Daughter." *American Journal of Orthopsychiatry* 24 (1954): 266-79.

Levinson, Marjorie. *The Romantic Fragment Poem: A Critique of a Form.* Chapel Hill: U of North Carolina P, 1986.

Lustig, Noel, *et al.* "Incest: A Family Group Survival Pattern." *Archives of General Psychiatry* 14 (1966): 31-40.

Luther, Susan M. Christabel *as Dream-Reverie.* Salzburg: Institut für Englische Sprache und Literatur Universität Salzburg, 1976.

Masson, Jeffery M. *The Assault on Truth: Freud's Suppression of the Seduction Theory.* New York: Farrar, 1984.

Matthew, George F. Rev. of *Christabel; Kubla Khan, a Vision; The Pains of Sleep,* by S. T. Coleridge. *European Magazine* 70 (Nov. 1816): 434-37.

Miller, Alice. *Thou Shalt Not Be Aware: Society's Betrayal of the Child.* Trans. Hildegarde Hannum and Hunter Hannum. New York: Farrar, 1984.

[Moore, Thomas.] Rev. of *Christabel. Kubla Khan, a Vision. The Pains of Sleep,* by S. T. Coleridge. *Edinburgh Review* 27 (Sept. 1816): 58-67.

Mudge, Bradford K. *Sara Coleridge, A Victorian Daughter: Her Life and Essays.* New Haven: Yale UP, 1989.

Otto, Rudolf. *The Idea of the Holy.* Trans. John W. Harvey. New York: Oxford UP, 1958.

Parsons, Talcott. "The Incest Taboo in Relation to Social Structure and the Socialization of the Child." *British Journal of Sociology* 5 (1954): 101-05.

Proffitt, Edward. "'Christabel' and Oedipal Conflict." *Research Studies* 46 (1978): 248-51.

Rush, Florence. *The Best-Kept Secret: Sexual Abuse of Children.* Englewood-Cliffs, N.J.: Prentice, 1980.

Schapiro, Barbara. "'Christabel': The Problem of Ambivalent Love." *Literature and Psychology* 30 (1980): 119-32.

Sloane, Paul, and Eva Karpinski. "Effects of Incest on the Participants." *American Journal of Orthopsychiatry* 12 (1942): 666-73.

Spatz, Jonas. "The Mystery of Eros: Sexual Initiation in Coleridge's 'Christabel'." *PMLA* 90 (1975): 107-16.

Tomlinson, Charles. "Coleridge: *Christabel.*" *Interpretations: Essays on Twelve English Poems.* Ed. John Wain. London: Routledge and Kegan Paul, 1955. 86-112.

Twitchell, James B. "'Desire with Loathing Strangely Mixed': The Dream of Christabel." *Psychoanalytic Review* 61 (1974): 33-44.

———. *Forbidden Partners: The Incest Taboo in Modern Culture.* New York: Columbia UP, 1987.

Ware, J. Garth. "Coleridge's Great Poems Reflecting the Mother Image." *American Imago* 18 (1961): 331-52.

Weissberg, Michael P. *Dangerous Secrets: Mal-Adaptive Responses to Stress.* New York: Norton, 1983.

Willbern, David. "*Filia Oedipi*: Father and Daughter in Freudian Theory." *Daughters and Fathers.* Ed. L. E. Boose and B. S. Flowers. 75-96.

Wormhoudt, Arthur. *The Demon Lover: A Psychoanalytic Approach to Literature.* New York: Exposition, 1949.

Avery F. Gaskins (essay date summer 1993)

SOURCE: Gaskins, Avery F. "Dramatic Form, 'Double Voice,' and 'Carnivalization' in 'Christabel.'" *European Romantic Review* 4, no. 1 (summer 1993): 1-12.

[*In the following essay, Gaskins examines "Christabel"'s complicated dramatic action within the context of Mikhail Bakhtin's theories of literature and language. In Gaskins's view, Coleridge's poem exhibits many of the qualities that Bakhtin considered exclusively novelistic.*]

M. M. Bakhtin contends in *The Dialogic Imagination* that both what he calls "double voice" and "heteroglossia" are the exclusive properties of a novel, and he targets the poem especially as being "single voiced" and "monologic." Double voice has to do with speech, either that of the narrator or characters, which expresses multiple intentions, and heteroglossia is the juxtaposition of the "languages" of various social classes and professions and allowing each to compete for attention and supremacy. Bakhtin believes that the poet's preoccupation with a unified construction militates against achieving either of these as he states in the following passage:

> The poet is a poet insofar as he accepts the idea of a unitary and singular language and a unitary, monologically sealed-off utterance. These ideas are immanent in the poetic genres with which he works. In a condition of actual contradiction, these are what determine the means of orientation open to the poet. The poet must assume a complete single-personed hegemony over his own language; he must assume equal responsibility for each of its aspects and subordinate them to his own, and only his own, intentions. Each word must express the poet's *meaning* directly and without mediation . . . [emphasis Bakhtin's].
>
> (296-97)

However, in recent years, critics have begun to find that even the most lyrical forms of poetry share the characteristics that Bakhtin wishes to claim are the exclusive property of the novel.[1] David H. Richter, in particular, indicates that the flaw in Bakhtin's overstating the antithetical qualities of the novel and the poem lies in his disagreements with the Russian Formalists as he says:

> Bakhtin was driven to valorize prose and prose fiction, and consequently to devalue those aspects of poetry which could not be made consonant with prose. Poetry as such was identified entirely with its tropological use of language. But that meant ignoring or shelving, for the sake of the polemic, those many elements which poetry shared with prose—including an astoundingly diverse architectonics of meaning.
>
> (26-27)

"Christabel" is an especially interesting example of a poem which exhibits these characteristics of double voice, heteroglossia, and carnivalization because of the unusual dramatic form in which it is cast.

In the fall of 1797, Coleridge finished a verse drama *Osorio* as he was also continuing work on his share of *Lyrical Ballads* (Bate 40). Among a number of poems in varying stages of completion upon which Coleridge worked at this time was **"Christabel."** Constructing a dramatic text for *Osorio* had left him with the habit of developing action through dialogue, especially questions and answers, a habit which he carried over into the writing of Part I of **"Christabel."** The result is a kind of hybrid text which is not drama, but has some of the feel of drama.[2] For example, after using just thirteen lines setting the scene, some unidentified narrator begins a series of dialogues with a second unidentified narrator in the form of questions and answers:

Is the night chilly and dark?
The night is chilly, but not dark.
The thin gray cloud is spread on high,
It covers but not hides the sky.
The moon is behind, and at the full;
And yet she looks both small and dull.
The night is chill, the cloud is gray:
'Tis a month before the month of May,
And spring comes slowly up this way.[3]

(14-22)

Exchanges such as this dominate Part I up to The Conclusion and are used by the author in the ways he might have used a single, omniscient narrator: to add further detail to the setting, to advance the action, to establish motives for the actions of characters, and to call special attention to important moments.[4]

It may occur to some persons that these exchanges may not be dialogues at all and that the questions posed are merely rhetorical devices utilized by a single narrator. To such a suggestion, I would have a number of answers. First, the narrator would have to establish a presence or persona as Byron does for himself in *Don Juan* before using rhetorical questions for effect. In the thirteen lines leading up to the first exchange, no such persona has been established. Second, since there is already firmly set up in the opening lines a pattern of narration which is assertive, there was little economy for the narrator to have broken in with a question to himself or the reader. Rather than letting line 15 "The night is chilly, but not dark" serve as an answer, if the narrator had moved to it directly, the story could have been narrated just as effectively. There must have been another reason for introducing the question at that point, and I feel it was to establish a questioner. Third, although a question such as "Is the night chilly and dark?" may seem rhetorical since the questioner could have had the answer merely by observing, there are many others which seem to be genuine requests for information that the questioner does not have. For example, the questioner has to be told why Christabel is outside the castle by herself and at night (25-6) and in the bedroom scene requests an interpretation of Geraldine's aside and to whom it is addressed (209-13).

Part II of **"Christabel"** was not begun until 1800, according to Coleridge's own headnote (***Poetical Works*** [***Complete Poetical Works***] 213). The time delay created some distance between Coleridge and his inclination to develop the plot through dialogue, and hence, this part is not so dominated by dialogic narration. However, Part II does contain one major break at the point where Geraldine claims to be the daughter of Sir Roland of Tryermaine. Sir Leoline's emotional response to this news is puzzling to one of the narrators who asks about it. The second narrator replies with a nineteen-line explanation which outlines the former friendship between the two men and their subsequent disaffection which Sir Leoline has come to regret (405-26).

If, then, one follows the leads offered by the text, it is possible to visualize one principal narrator and a questioner, or perhaps two narrators who alternate in narrating the story. Either way, these two function very much like a chorus would do in drama. They introduce the action and setting, intrude upon the action with questions and commentary, and sum up the action and its significance in The Conclusion. Such a quasi-dramatic form allows for narrators with a language and intentions all their own, and for characters whose quoted speeches express their own intentions, languages, and ideologies separate from those of the author.

Bakhtin argues that the metrical structure of a poem militates against heteroglossia. He says it creates a "unitary language" which eliminates the possibility of dialogues between languages as he defines the term (298). However, I would answer that even though **"Christabel"** has a metrical structure, it is a rather loose one as Coleridge explains in his headnote (***Poetical Works*** 215), and even though there is an attempt to approximate medieval speech, the poem leaves plenty of room for individual languages among the many speakers, as I shall demonstrate in the following examples.

The narrators speak the language of pious gossips. Their role in the story is to be feckless observers, often horrified or morally outraged at what they are observing, but without the power to intercede. In a number of places when they sense that Christabel is being morally or physically threatened, they are reduced to a ritualistic prayer, "Jesu, Maria, shield her well!"[5] In The Conclusion to Part I, as they reflect on the moral implications of what has transpired in Christabel's bedroom, they become indignant and do a great deal of clucking about. After establishing in the opening that "It was a lovely sight to see / The lady Christabel, when she / Was praying at the old oak tree" (279-81), they lament the fallen condition of Christabel:

O sorrow and shame! Can this be she,
The lady, who knelt at the old oak tree?
And lo! the worker of these harms,
That holds the maiden in her arms
Seems to slumber still and mild,
As a mother with her child.
A star hath set, a star hath risen,
O Geraldine! since arms of thine
Have been the lovely lady's prison.

(296-304)

They understand their own lack of power to correct the situation and must rely on the hope that Christabel herself will turn to prayer and bring about her own salvation: "And this she knows, in joys and woes, / The saints will aid if men will call: / For the blue sky bends over all!" (329-31)

In the early action of Part I, Geraldine and Christabel speak an almost indistinguishable language. Their discourse is that of well-bred daughters of northern aristo-cratic background. In revealing her supposed abduction, Geraldine says:

> My sire is of a noble line,
> And my name is Geraldine:
> Five warriors seized me yestermorn,
> Me, even me, a maid forlorn:
>
> (79-82)

After Geraldine has finished her story, Christabel re-plies in similar language:

> O well, bright dame! may you command
> The service of Sir Leoline;
> And gladly our stout chivalry
> Will he send forth and friends withal
> To guide and guard you safe and free
> Home to your noble father's hall.
>
> (106-11)

However, in Christabel's bedroom, Geraldine begins using the language of power, the power of the hi-erophant. Her first act is to establish her authority as an agent of spiritual powers:

> All they who live in the upper sky,
> Do love you, holy Christabel!
> And you love them, and for their sake
> And for the good which me befel,
> Even I in my degree will try,
> Fair maiden, to requite you well.
>
> (226-32)

This is the language of the holy messenger (or possibly unholy messenger, depending on whether or not one wishes to read lines 231-32 ironically) who speaks con-fidently knowing that her authority and inspiration come from beyond herself. As such, the language has appro-priate biblical overtones.

After having established her authority, Geraldine binds Christabel to secrecy with a magic spell whose chanting rhyme is true to the form one finds in the spells in fairy tales:

> In the touch of this bosom there worketh a spell,
> Which is lord of thy utterance, Christabel!
> Thou knowest tonight, and wilt know to-morrow,
> This mark of my shame, this seal of my sorrow;

and she goes on to specify just what Christabel may and may not reveal about Geraldine's identity.

Sir Leoline speaks the language of a different kind of power, that of social and political power. As one of the principal Barons in the north of England, he is accus-tomed to issuing commands and having them obeyed. He is aware of the formalities required of him when he makes public declarations, and as a military leader, he

prefers to settle problems with the use of force. A good case in point is his reaction to Geraldine's story that she has been abducted and mistreated by a group of men. The narrators paraphrase his speech in the early part of his reaction, but the phrasing gives a hint of its formal aspects, "He would proclaim it far and wide / With trump and solemn heraldry, / That they who thus had wronged the dame, / Were base as spotted infamy" (434-37). In the rest of the passage, the Baron speaks for himself:

> And if they dare deny the same,
> My herald shall proclaim a week,
> And let the recreant traitors seek
> My tourney court—that there and then
> I may dislodge their reptile souls
> From the bodies and forms of men!
>
> (438-43)

After giving Bard Bracy instructions to ride to Geraldi-ne's father and inform him of his daughter's safety, Sir Leoline becomes angry with the bard when he discov-ers he has not left as quickly as the Baron would have liked:

> He rolled his eye with stern regard
> Upon the gentle minstrel bard,
> And said in tones abrupt, austere—
> 'Why, Bracy! dost thou loiter here?
> I bade thee hence!' The bard obeyed;
>
> (648-52)

Bard Bracy acts, to some extent, as a foil to Sir Leo-line. He is described as "the gentle minstrel bard" (649), and his meekness stands out in contrast to the bold as-surance of his lord. Readers accustomed to the authori-tative figure of Gray's *Bard* would find him unusually submissive. Even though his dream of the snake and dove confirms that he has the vatic power associated with Bardic lore, he does not put forth the information concerning the dream and its evil implications with as-surance or authority. He speaks "with faltering voice" (521), and rather than asserting that he must delay the mission on which he has been sent, makes his request in servile language:

> Thy words, thou sire of Christabel
> Are sweeter than my harp can tell;
> Yet might I gain a boon of thee,
> So strange a dream hath come to me,
> That I had vowed with music loud
> To clear yon wood from thing unblest,
> Warned by a vision in my rest!
>
> (523-30)

He is so ineffective in conveying the serious nature of his vision that the Baron "Half-listening heard him with a smile"[6] (565).

These examples, it seems to me, demonstrate that there is anything but a "unitary language" taking place in this poem. Multiple languages and ideologies compete with each other for attention and supremacy.

However, Bakhtin goes beyond nothing the multiplicity of languages to be found in the novel. He often comments on their parodic tone, as he does when he analyzes the descriptions of Merdle in *Little Dorritt* and points out that the putative approval of Merdle's set of values is undercut by the ironic tone of the description (303-04). He says that parodic passages by characters or narrators have the ability to achieve what he calls "carnivalization," that is to say the undermining of the authority of an established custom, institution, or figure of power which opens it up to closer examination and questioning. His discussions work best in terms of comic or satiric novels, but Michael A. Bernstein has demonstrated the technique can be found in serious drama as well, as for example the exchanges between King Lear and the Fool (107).

That **"Christabel"** may have parodic qualities has not escaped the notice of critics. Both Edward Duffy and Edward Dramin have suggested that **"Christabel"** may be a parody which has as its target the Gothic Novel. Duffy finds the parody in the characterizations (237-39), and Dramin feels the entire work parodies the major conventions of the genre (232-33).

However, as has already been stated, "carnivalization" uses parody, but goes beyond it in the sociological and ideological implications it creates, and in **"Christabel,"** I can find parodic overtones here and there that work toward Bakhtinian "carnivalization." The objects in these cases are Sir Leoline and the class he represents.[7] Since the manuscript of **"Christabel"** is a fragment lacking a conclusion, the action leading up to where the narrative stops has the potential of developing into a genuine domestic tragedy concerning an aristocratic family, or a parodic treatment thereof,[8] and parodic language, where it is found in the poem, creates the effect of carnivalization.

Without imputing any conscious intent on Coleridge's part, I should like to suggest that the carnivalization of the De Vaux household may be a by-product of Coleridge's radical political activities from 1795 to 1798. The Pantiscocracy scheme had been an attempt to escape the class structure of England and set up a more democratic society in America. Since 1795, he had been making a number of public and private statements attacking privileged classes and urging governmental reform. During this period, Coleridge exchanged letters with the radical, John Thelwell, who had been tried for treason for supporting the French Revolution and advocating the overthrow of aristocratic power in government. His admiration for Thelwell was so great that in July of 1797, just as he was beginning to write **"Christabel,"** he invited Thelwell to come visit him in

Nether Stowey with the idea that he might settle there permanently and the two men might exchange ideas more frequently and easily (Roe 234-40). In October of 1797, he wrote to Francis Wrangham, "Kings, Wolves, Tygers, Generals, Ministers, and Hyaenas, I renounce them all" (Woodring 71). However, it may be preferable, in the best spirit of Bahktinian discourse study, to allow the text to speak for itself.

The major undercutting of Sir Leoline's authority is done by the narrators during an aside to the reader in Part II. After seeing that her father believes the story Geraldine has told him concerning her background, Christabel, in panic, urgently asks her father to send Geraldine away, but because she is under Geraldine's spell, she is unable to give a reason for her request. The narrators emphasize Sir Leoline's reaction to this request and stress how he should have reacted as opposed to how he does react:

> Why is thy cheek so wan and wild,
> Sir Leoline? Thy only child
> Lies at thy feet, thy joy, thy pride,
> So fair, so innocent, so mild;
> The same for whom thy lady died!
> O by the pangs of her dear mother
> Think thou no evil of thy child!
> For her, and thee, and for no other,
> She prayed the moment ere she died;
> Prayed that the babe for whom she died,
> Might prove her dear lord's joy and pride!
>   That prayer her deadly pangs beguiled,
>   Sir Leoline!
> And wouldst thou wrong thy only child,
>   Her child and thine?
> Within the Baron's heart and brain
> If thoughts, like these, had any share,
> They only swelled his rage and pain
>
>   (621-38)

These narrators had demonstrated earlier that they are not of the Baron's social class in their use of diction, "Sir Leoline, the Baron rich / Hath a toothless mastiff bitch" (6-7). In fact, the reviewers of 1817, assuming that Coleridge was the narrator scolded him for his lack of decorum in using a vulgar term such as "bitch" in a serious poem.[9] The very emphasis on the Baron's "richness" indicates that the narrators are from a lower social class since persons of his own class would not have thought it worth noting. Their values as expressed in describing Sir Leoline's anger are centered around the kind of sentimental view of family bonding that Coleridge and Wordsworth had intended to glorify as one of the virtues of commoners in *Lyrical Ballads.*

On the other hand, Sir Leoline's anger is occasioned by an opposing set of aristocratic values. He cares less about his obligations as a father than his obligations as a host:

> His cheeks they quivered, his eyes were wild,
> Dishonoured thus in his old age;

Dishonoured by his only child,
And all his hospitality
To the wronged daughter of his friend
By more than woman's jealousy
Brought thus to a disgraceful end—

(641-47)

Both these passages concerning Sir Leoline are ostensibly merely descriptive, but they are expressed in such melodramatic language as to suggest parody or caricature.

Yet, none of this is parody in the service of broad comedy, satire, or burlesque. Rather, the parodic overtones leave in question the authority of any figures who might oppose Geraldine, and thus, she is left at this point in the narrative, as the only empowered character. The narrators are clearly present during the events of the story as their use of present tense attests, but they appear to be there in spirit only since they do not interact with any of the characters. As has been stated earlier, they are powerless to intercede in any way and are left only the ability to moralize. Bard Bracy's inborn timidity and dependence on the good will of Sir Leoline cancel out any chance that the Bard will be able to find the source of his fears and take action. Sir Leoline, who normally would be the most powerful figure in the group, neutralizes himself in his fascination with Geraldine and in his obligation to aristocratic hospitality. Since Christabel is the potential victim in the narrative, she is not carnivalized, but she too, has lost any power to resist Geraldine, either because of a sense of guilt or as a result of magic. Her reactions to Geraldine's serpentine qualities hint strongly that Geraldine will use her empowerment to harm Christabel, and possibly Sir Leoline. The interplay of carnivalization with a sense of threat creates a tension that the Conclusion to Part II does not relieve.

Richard Holmes has best summed up the effect of **"Christabel"** as follows: "The sense of passionate emotions and explosive energies, locked and spellbound, frozen, dumb, struggling for release but always contained, becomes the ultimate character of the poem" (288). Alternations of carnivalization and dread play a large part in bringing about this result.

Notes

1. Bialostosky's Bakhtinian study of Wordsworth's poetry and Richter's recent article on dialogism in poetry, especially his cluster footnote (14n), indicate that despite Bakhtin's protestations to the contrary, his theories may be applied to a wide variety of poetic forms as well as to the novel.

2. "The Ancient Mariner" ["The Rime of the Ancient Mariner"] whose composition was contemporaneous with that of "Christabel" has an intrusion of

lines which look very much like the script of a play. These also advance the action through dialogue. See the opening five stanzas of Part VI of that poem.

3. All quotations from "Christabel" are taken from *Complete Poetical Works* (1.213-35).

4. For more on the multiple narrators and their functions, see Gaskins, 10-12.

5. At first, I thought these narrators might be the ghosts of the sinful sextons mentioned in line 365, but Molly Lefebure, who besides being a noted Coleridgean is also noted for her expertise in the folklore of the Lake District, assures me that Coleridge would have found no legend to support what the narrative says of them. Langdale Pike, Witch's Lair, and Dungeon-Ghyll do not have churches where the sextons could have served, St. Oswald's in Grasmere being the nearest. The sextons appear to have been made up out of whole cloth with no other purpose than to furnish atmosphere.

6. Janowitz (68-73) discusses Gray's role in the mystification of the Bard with the political intention of glorifying pre-Norman, "native" cultures and the personal intention of urging contemporary poets to reassume the power of their medieval precursors. It is interesting to see Coleridge demystifying a medieval bard while creating a mystified, "ideal" poet in his own theory. See *Biographia [Biographia Literaria]* 2.15-18.

7. Woodring notes that in "Christabel" the poet was able to use the word "noble" without an immediate expression of disgust, but he also cites a number of poems during the period from 1797-1801 in which the rhetoric remains heated and the position radical (165-85). My point is that Coleridge need not have been aware of the effects he was achieving which were the unconscious results of feelings he normally expressed overtly. At any rate, the text creates the effects regardless of the intent.

8. It is true that Coleridge talked to his physician, Dr. Gillman, of a plan to finish "Christabel" which furnished a happy ending by having Geraldine revealed as a supernatural being who then vanishes (McElderry 447). However this is one of many different versions he suggested to people, and it is impossible to know what he might actually have done if he had decided to do the writing.

9. See Jackson's summary of the reviews of "Christabel" (199-289). Of course, the term "bitch" would have been in the everyday vocabulary of all classes of people living in rural England at this time, appropriate for casual conversation, but un-

derstood to be at a low level of diction and not appropriate for serious literature unless for comic effect.

Works Cited

Bakhtin, M. M. "Discourse in the Novel." *The Dialogic Imagination.* Ed. Michael Holquist. Trans. Caryl Emerson and Michael Holquist. Austin: U of Texas P, 1981. 257-422.

Bate, Walter Jackson. *Coleridge.* New York: Macmillan, 1968.

Bialostosky, Don H. *Making Tales.* Chicago: U of Chicago P, 1984.

Bernstein, Michael A. "When the Carnival Turns Bitter: Preliminary Reflections Upon the Abject Hero." *Bakhtin. Reflections and Dialogues on His Work.* Ed. Gary Saul Morson. Chicago: U of Chicago P, 1986. 99-122.

Coleridge, Samuel Taylor. *Complete Poetical Works.* Ed. E. H. Coleridge. 2 vols. Oxford: Clarendon P, 1912.

————. *Biographia Literaria.* Eds. James Engell and W. Jackson Bate. Princeton, N.J.: Princeton UP, 1984.

Dramin, Edward. "Amid Jagged Shadows: *Christabel* and the Gothic Tradition." *The Wordsworth Circle* 3 (1972): 221-32.

Duffy, Edward. "The Cunning Spontaneities of Romanticism." *The Wordsworth Circle* 8 (1982): 232-40.

Gaskins, Avery F. "Catechistic Lines in 'Christabel'." *Bulletin of the West Virginia Association of College English Teachers* ns. 12 (Fall, 1990): 8-16.

Holmes, Richard. *Coleridge: Early Visions.* New York: Viking Penguin, 1990.

Jackson, J. R. de J. *Coleridge: The Critical Heritage.* New York: Barnes and Noble, 1970.

Janowitz, Anne. *England's Ruins: Poetic Purpose and the National Landscape.* Oxford: Blackwell, 1990.

McElderry, Jr. B. R. "Coleridge's Plan for Completing *Christabel*." *Studies in Philology* 33 (1936): 437-55.

Richter, David H. "Dialogism and Poetry," *Studies in the Literary Imagination* 23 (Spring, 1990): 9-28.

Roe, Nicholas. *Wordsworth and Coleridge. The Radical Years.* Oxford: Clarendon P, 1988.

Woodring, Carl. *Politics in the Poetry of Coleridge.* Madison: U of Wisconsin P, 1961.

Claire B. May (essay date autumn 1997)

SOURCE: May, Claire B. "'Christabel' and Abjection: Coleridge's Narrative in Process/on Trial." *Studies in English Literature, 1500-1900* 37, no. 4 (autumn 1997): 699-721.

[*In the following essay, May discusses Coleridge's narrative technique in "Christabel." In May's interpretation, "Christabel" represents a failure of narrative because the narrator finds the situation and events of the poem too disturbing to relate in a conventional or coherent manner. In this sense, the poem continually and deliberately undermines its own meaning.*]

In spite of Samuel Taylor Coleridge's claims that he always had in mind the completed narrative of **"Christabel,"** he never finished the story. Yet "incomplete" as it is, the poem has been a source of fascination—and an enigma—to its readers for almost two hundred years. For while they have been intrigued, drawn to read the poem again and again, a certain unintelligibility remains, problems and ambiguities that challenge their abilities to understand the poem itself and, perhaps, even to understand their responses to it. **"Christabel"** resists all attempts to impose determinate meaning. It remains unsettled and unsettling.

Many of the problems that most confound readers' expectations derive from the assumptions with which they are accustomed to make sense of a narrative. An obvious problem is the fragmentary nature of the poem and the seemingly unrelated conclusion to part 2, frustrating the desire for closure. Perhaps the most puzzling question, however, and the one giving rise to most critical debate, is the identity and significance of the central character, Geraldine, and the nature of her relationship with Christabel. While earlier readings emphasize in these two characters a bipolarity of good and evil,[1] many later readings of the poem prefer a psychosexual interpretation of their relationship, with Geraldine representing repressed desire, Christabel's unassimilated, possibly homoerotic, sexuality.[2] Kathleen M. Wheeler, emphasizing language, finds both moral and psychological interpretations unsatisfactory: Geraldine "is a force neither of evil nor desire, but of disruption, or . . . the meaningless at the heart of all language and meaning."[3] She points to the poem's unreliable narrative voice and "the difficulty of narration or communication of meaning and, more basically, the difficulty even of describing in factual terms what is happening, much less assigning value or meaning or interpretation to descriptions."[4]

The failure of **"Christabel"** as narrative, especially the inability of the narrative voice to describe clearly what happens, has not been fully addressed by previous studies and will be my focus here. This essay will first point out typical problems with the narrative that appear early in the poem and then show how Julia Kristeva's theories of poetic language and abjection may explain these textual aporias and others that appear throughout the text. I will then argue that the narrator becomes increasingly disturbed by the contents of his own discourse. Where his story becomes most distressing, his narrative becomes less coherent. Finally, overwhelmed by his story, he abandons any attempt to bring it to closure.

The place to begin is to identify the assumptions about the narrative genre that readers bring to the text but that **"Christabel"** fails to fulfill, thus providing obstacles to reading and interpretation. These assumptions may be described as three overlapping symbolic constructs: (1) Stable oppositions (good/evil, life/death) that underlie the structure of the narrative and that are resolved either through privileging one of the categories or through combining the two into a higher unity. Such movements toward narrative harmony reflect a teleological paradigm and are in (dis)harmony with it in some way.[5] (2) Narrative time as linear and purposive. The structure of the narrative (beginning, middle, end) as well as syntax and verb tenses are based on this assumption of progressive, uninterrupted time. (3) Stable, univalent language capable of transmitting without slippage the meaning intended by a narrating subject.[6]

"Christabel" fails to adhere to these assumptions, thus disrupting reading and interpretation. Oppositions are conflated; time is neither clearly sequential nor measurable; and signification is often ambiguous. These instabilities suggest a narrator who lacks mastery of the constructs that would make coherent narration possible.

The opening stanzas present a number of problems typical of the text. The poem begins with uncertainty about time: "'Tis the middle of night by the castle clock."[7] This sounds clear enough, but ensuing lines raise questions. "[T]he owls have awakened the crowing cock" (line 2): is it then midnight or dawn? The tense shifts in the first stanza throw the sequence of events into further uncertainty, including the chronology of the cock's crowing relative to the narrator's awareness of the sound, a shift from present to past: "*hark, again!* the crowing cock, / How drowsily it *crew*" (lines 4-5; emphasis added). In spite of this temporal confusion, the echolalia in the third line evokes a nocturnal atmosphere: "Tu—whit!——Tu—whoo!" (line 3). In these sounds are heard the call of the owl, creature of night—and harbinger of death.

Syntactic ambiguity in the second stanza adds to confusion about time:

> Sir Leoline, the Baron rich,
> Hath a toothless mastiff bitch;
> From her kennel beneath the rock
> She maketh answer to the clock
> Four for the quarters, and twelve for the hour;
> Ever and aye, by shine and shower,
> Sixteen short howls, not over loud;
> Some say, she sees my lady's shroud.
>
> (lines 6-13)

What is the sense of the "sixteen short howls," and how are they an "answer to the clock"? Can this number be reconciled with the twelve called for by the "middle of night" (line 1)? Are these sixteen howls a response to a clock the dog hears now, or are they her usual response to the clock "[e]ver and aye" (line 11)? The syntax and punctuation render these questions undecidable and reinforce the ambiguity about time introduced in stanza one. Or is there some other temporality in question here, one to which the bitch may be attuned, but different from the time measured by the clock?

The second stanza introduces other ambiguous identities as well, including the reference to the "toothless mastiff bitch" (line 7).[8] The overdetermination of this old, female guard dog resonates with ominous references to the feminine and the maternal. "Bitch" suggests the maternal tainted with sensuality, even obscenity.[9] And this mastiff, who should be protective, is "toothless," presumably weakened, except that "toothless" may also suggest a hag or witch. Moreover, this dog's kennel is "beneath the rock" (line 8), a more likely abode for some other kind of animal, a creature of the dark, hidden, like a snake. The hissing of alliterative sibilants in the last three lines of this stanza strengthens the suspicion that a snake may be present, out of sight, but beginning to announce its presence through sound.

The sibilants intensify in the final line of the stanza: "Some say, she sees my lady's shroud" (line 13), an allusion that compounds the vague sense of unease that has been accumulating and that now has a hint of defilement and decay—a shroud. The narrator speaks here of another female figure, not bodily present, because "my lady" is dead, yet the specter of her shroud suggests something sinister. The narrator's relation to "my lady" is also puzzling. While "my lady" or "milady" is a conventional medieval courtesy title, the "my" in relation to the narrative voice also suggests that the narrator may be identifying with, or appropriating, the narrative he is relating.[10] Is this dead lady who yet threatens somehow *his* lady? Possibly she is the lady of the manor, a presence the narrator might find disorienting, and thus disruptive of his attempts to tell the story. The reference to "my lady's shroud" appears just after the temporal confusion introduced by the sixteen howls. Could the difficulties encountered so far in understanding this narrative—ambiguous identities, conflated oppositions, and confusion about time—result from the narrator's disturbance by the unsettling story he is relating, especially his response to the female or maternal figured as sinister?

Random tense shifts continue in the following stanzas, indeed throughout the poem, revealing the narrator's persistent inability to represent time through the grammatical conventions of language. The narrator says, for instance, that while "The night is chill" (line 20), Christabel "stole along, she nothing spoke" (line 31), and then "in silence prayeth she" (line 36), a shift from present to past and back to present. The entry of Christabel into the narrative raises still other ambiguities, including cause and effect and the character of Christabel. Why is this denizen of the castle, this "lovely lady . . . / Whom her father loves so well" (lines 23-4), alone in the woods at midnight? The narrator asks this very question, and then provides an answer that only raises more questions: "she in the midnight wood will pray / For the weal of her lover that's far away" (lines 29-30). And pray she does, "beneath the huge oak tree" covered in "moss and rarest mistletoe" (line 35, 34): a strangely pagan, Druidic setting for a maiden's prayers in the heart of medieval Christendom, and one fraught with such danger that the narrator utters a plea in her behalf: "Jesu, Maria, shield her well!" (line 54). This blending of Christian and pagan suggests uncertainty about Christabel's character and her status as a representative of Christian values—an equation we might expect, given her name.

Puzzling as well is this danger about which the narrator expresses such concern. The first mention of the danger occurs in proximity to the oak tree under which Christabel prays, a threat referred to as an "[i]t" that "moaned" (line 39). While neither Christabel, the narrator, nor the poem's readers can tell with certainty what "it" is, or why it moaned, to the narrator it "seems to be" located on "the other side" (line 41) of the protective, "broad-breasted" oak tree (line 42), now figured as maternal. This hint that the mother's "other" side is the source of a moaning raises further questions. Who is moaning? And does this moan result from pleasure, pain, fear, or some other primal emotion? Christabel seems disturbed by these mysteries, her heart beating so loudly that the narrator himself becomes alarmed: "Hush, beating heart of Christabel!" (line 53).

Curious as well as frightened, Christabel steals to the other side of the tree and sees there an apparition that might be the answer to her questions, were it not yet another figure of ambiguous identity: "a damsel bright" (line 58), "richly clad" (line 67)—yet "frightful" (line 66), with "blue-veined feet unsandal'd" (line 63). These bared feet are a jarring detail, a reminder of the custom of burying the dead without shoes. Could this damsel be a specter like "my lady"? Equally provocative is the narrator's description of this damsel as "Beautiful exceedingly!" (line 68). The phrase might signify that the damsel is desirable, beautiful to an unusual degree, but it also suggests excess, more than is natural or proper. Following the mastiff bitch and "my lady's shroud," this damsel is yet another example of the female figured as uncanny—alluring, disturbing, a threat perceived by both the narrator, who has invoked Christian protection, and Christabel herself: "Mary mother, save me now!" (line 69).

Who (or what) then is this stranger, and how did she come to be where she is? Christabel herself asks these questions and then hears Geraldine's explanation that she is an innocent maiden abducted by warriors and left in the forest. The conventionality of this account may prepare for a certain moral ambivalence about Geraldine in later details. She will not be able to cross the castle threshold, which has presumably been blessed, nor join Christabel in praise of "the Virgin all divine" (line 139). Many readers have been convinced by these and similar passages that Geraldine is unequivocally evil, but textual evidence later in the poem will leave this conclusion open to question.

Another puzzling element in Geraldine's story adds to the confusion about narrative time. Geraldine says that her adventure began when the warriors seized her "yestermorn" (line 81); warriors and Geraldine then "rode furiously" (line 86) until they "crossed the shade of night" (line 88): crossing night (a measure of time) as movement through space. And how much time—spatially or sequentially—since the beginning of Geraldine's flight and her subsequent abandonment by the warriors? Even for Geraldine the measure of this episode is indeterminate: "Nor do I know how long it is" (line 91). At this point readers' expectations of stable, linear time are thoroughly unsettled. In addition to the opening stanza, which confuses midnight and dawn, and the shifting verb tenses as ambiguous reconstructions of time, time has now become unmeasurable and discontinuous, and time and space are conflated.

These sample passages from the first part of **"Christabel"** suggest the disruptions that create interpretative problems throughout the text: shifting signifiers and porous bipolar categories, destabilization of linear time, and a narrator who is unable to tell a story that readers can understand. The narrator's difficulties in telling this story are critical, since it is only through the narrative voice that readers have access to the narrative. Disruptions in the text, such as those just examined, reflect his inability to speak a narrative that coheres. Rather than maintaining control of his story, he is apparently determined by it, disturbed by the signifiers he introduces. He becomes absorbed into the narrative, overwhelmed, and finally silenced by it. The narrative, then, narrates the narrator: the text becomes an account of his attempts to narrate, and of the disruptions in the text that render the narrative act impossible.

The psychologies of selfhood current in Coleridge's day are inadequate to explain these aporias in **"Christabel."** The *Biographia Literaria* describes a transparent, monadic *cogito* possessed of the shaping powers of the will, a self accessible to itself. The narrator of **"Christabel,"** however, illustrates neither the Aristotelian associationism affirmed by Coleridge nor the mechanical associationism of David Hartley. Indeed, if consciousness were accessible to itself, as the *Biographia* argues, **"Christabel"** would be both narratable and completable.[11] Given the aporias in the text, however, some other model of consciousness (and of what lies beyond the ken of consciousness) is needed, a theory that describes a subject constituted by discourse, rather than autonomously in control of thought and discourse through the transcendental powers of the imagination.

To understand the instabilities in **"Christabel"** and the way in which they both determine and reflect the instability of the narrative voice, it will be helpful to consider Julia Kristeva's concepts of "poetic language."[12] Unlike the stable symbolic signification we expect to find in a narrative, poetic language assumes an interplay of two modalities of the signifying process, the semiotic with the symbolic, in a dialectic that constitutes both the text and the speaking/writing subject.[13] Text and subject then become not fixed, determinant identities, but "in process/on trial" (*en proces*), through language.[14]

As Kristeva explains in *Revolution in Poetic Language,* the symbolic modality of signification reflects the paternal order. It assumes a patriarchal hierarchy, fixed laws of grammar and syntax, univalent signification, the law. The expectations for the narrative which readers bring to the poem are dimensions of that symbolic order, including the assumptions that time is linear and that oppositions remain stable. Readers of narrative also assume a unitary voice, a stable identity capable of relating a coherent story. In psychoanalytic terms, this is a subject who has rejected the primal bond of the mother/child dyad in order to establish an ego and acquire language, an ego that has, in other words, completed the Oedipal stage and found its place as a functioning identity within the symbolic (paternal) order.[15]

Yet the drives that were repressed in order for the ego to acquire the father's language remain a threat both to the ego, the speaking subject, and to the symbolic within which it functions. Within language itself, including the language of a text, this threat may appear as disruptions of symbolic signification. These disruptions are signs of semiotic eruption, of repressed drives that attack fixed meanings and representation, thereby destabilizing social and linguistic order, and destabilizing the speaking subject as a unitary ego. Within the language of a text, semiotic disturbance may be recognized by polyvalent signs and symbols, connotation rather than denotation, and disrupted conventions of grammar and syntax. Traces of the semiotic appear at fault lines of the narrative where surges of presignifying affect register in language: as sound, the "musicalization of signifiers"[16]— rhythm, alliteration, echolalia; and as intonation—grief, fear, horror—and sometimes, fleetingly, by "joy, within, through, and across the Word."[17]

The textual instabilities identified so far in **"Christabel"** can now be described as indications of semiotic disruption. Random tense shifts and the confusing syntax of the second stanza raise questions about the stability of linear time; the "musicalization of signifiers" evokes the mysterious, the primal—including the echolalia of the owl's call, which resonates with the nocturnal and with death; and the alliteration of sibilants, which hints at the (unseen) presence of a snake. The opening also introduces a number of polyvalent signifiers, especially ambiguous female figures: the mastiff bitch, protective and obscene; "my lady," dead and yet present in the specter of her shroud; the old oak tree, with its "other side"; and especially Geraldine, with her frightening, excessive beauty. Two of these uncanny female figures, the mastiff bitch and the oak tree, have already been identified as provisionally maternal; "my lady" and Geraldine would be at least potentially maternal because they are female. Evocative of both the known and the unknown, the desirable and the repulsive, the appearance of these ambiguous female/maternal figures in the narrative disrupts the symbolic signification attempted by the narrative voice—not surprising, perhaps, given the repression of the maternal influence required for a subject to function within the symbolic order.

Yet elusive memories of the pre-Oedipal state before the mother/child dyad was ruptured must haunt every ego, including this narrator: shadowy recollections of joy from the bond with the good mother, the warmth of the mother's nourishing breast, and, at the same time, misgivings that this loving maternal warmth might be lost, the breast withheld. Union with the mother haunts the narrator as a bond he has rejected, a loss he never ceases to mourn—a loss that, nevertheless, "laid the foundations of [his] own being" as he became an individuated ego,[18] a speaking subject.

This loss, this abyss that ceaselessly threatens the narrator's integrity as a subject, Kristeva calls the abject: an excluded, "radically separate, loathsome" nonobject that haunts and harries the narrative voice (*PH* [*Powers of Horror*], p. 2). Living with this loss Kristeva terms living with abjection, a "weight of meaninglessness . . . [o]n the edge of non-existence and hallucination," a meaninglessness about which the narrator cannot speak (*PH*, p. 2). It is "other" and hence feminine to the masculine symbolic order, which seeks safety through its control, though never with complete success. Traces of abjection appear in discourse as semiotic disruption, registering in a text as figures, as sound, as style.

The most compelling instances of this disruption in **"Christabel"** are the poem's ominous figures—the uncanny, the hidden, the nocturnal, the unclean and the taboo, and especially the feminine, alluring and horrible, tainted with death and desire. Yet the poem also contains figures of abjection gendered as masculine, providing evidence that theories of abjection should not be limited by essentialist categories, which are themselves reifying, symbolic constructs.[19]

The question now is how the uncanny, the loathsome and alluring, erupts into the text as semiotic disturbance and affects the narrator's ability to narrate.[20] A further reading of the text will show that where these intrusions are most intense, the act of narration becomes most problematical, especially the passages in the text where Geraldine's presence is strongest, where she evokes in the narrator's affective response both horror and desire.

Part 1 of the narrative continues with evidences of semiotic intrusion similar to those just examined, intensifying as the narrator's ambivalent responses to Geraldine, his desire and fear, become stronger. The first hint of the central interaction between the two female characters occurs after Christabel has carried Geraldine across the threshold and is leading her through the castle to the room they will share. Christabel speaks here to Geraldine:

> All our household are at rest,
> The hall is silent as the cell;
> Sir Leoline is weak in health,
> And may not well awakened be,
> But we will move as if in stealth,
> And I beseech your courtesy,
> This night, to share your couch with me.
>
> (lines 116-22)

Several linguistic features of this passage suggest that semiotic intrusions may be disrupting the utterance. Sounds create an eerie effect, beginning with the repetition of *l* sounds in the first few lines, like the tolling of a bell to mark some significant event, a death perhaps. As the passage progresses the liquids give way to sibilants, stirring memories of the hissing heard earlier and hinting again at the (still unseen) presence of a snake.

Also puzzling is the unconventional syntax in this passage, the accumulation of coordinate clauses that have little relationship of meaning or sequence. The final clause, with its provocative suggestion of intimacy between the two women, also contains a confusing pronoun reference. Christabel beseeches Geraldine "to share *your* couch with me" (line 122; emphasis added), yet the couch belongs to Christabel. This possible infraction of grammatical convention appears as the foreshadowing of an episode that evokes both desire and fear, as the narrator anticipates the time when Geraldine and Christabel will lie together in the mysterious scene that is central to the story. The many linguistic anomalies in this passage suggest that the narrator has become agitated, ill at ease, as his consciousness of their impending intimacy grows.

This apprehensive mood intensifies in the final scene of part 1, which takes place in Christabel's room. Allusions to the ghost of Christabel's mother strengthen the mood of the uncanny; at the same time they suggest the ambiguity of the maternal, since this spirit seems also to offer the protection of a "good" mother. Geraldine seeks to ward off the mother's spirit, and yet, paradoxically, finds her cordial of wild flowers restorative. The feminine appears in this scene, then, as abject, both threatening and nurturing, fearful and desirable. In fact, desire for the feminine reaches the pitch of the erotic in the descriptions of both Christabel and Geraldine as they prepare for bed: Christabel, who undresses, then "[lies] down in her loveliness" and watches as Geraldine gradually removes her own clothing in preparation for joining her in bed (line 238).

But who experiences this desire, this eroticism in an atmosphere charged with dread? Perhaps Geraldine and Christabel, but most assuredly the narrator. So overwhelmed is he by the powerful drives that emerge in this scene that his control of the narrative becomes even more tenuous. The narrator never reveals what occurs between Geraldine and Christabel, whether lesbian eroticism, the kiss of a vampire, or maternal nurturing—but he does say that Geraldine slumbers "As a mother with her child" (line 301), thus aligning her with the maternal, however frightening and desirable. And this intimacy between the two women, whatever its nature, powerfully affects the narrator, who interrupts the narrative with laments that signify the strength of his own response—his grief, fear, and shame: "ah woe is me! / . . . / O sorrow and shame!" (lines 292-6).

The narrator not only fails to tell what happens between these two characters; he also seems uncertain about the most appropriate adjective for describing Christabel's appearance: "Her face, oh call it fair not pale" (line 289). More than a simple choice of words is at stake here, because "pale" connotes sickness and death, and the narrator's indecision suggests that he cannot represent the meaning of Christabel. The possibility that she might be contaminated with sickness and death also raises the possibility that Christabel is yet another feminine figure for abjection.

This scene is in fact permeated with traces of the abject, which receive their strongest representation in the ambiguous character of Geraldine. From her first appearance in the poem she has been associated with classic signs of the abject: the uncanny, death, and perhaps evil. And now the narrator reveals, in the lines that describe her disrobing, that she is physically marked with a sign of deformity and decay, the horror of her side and bosom, which she calls "[t]his mark of my shame, this seal of my sorrow" (line 270). This mark is so horrible that once again the narrator is unable to describe her appearance: Geraldine's unnamable bosom is "A sight to dream of, not to tell!" (line 253). Later the narrator will say that it is a "bosom old / . . . [a] bosom cold" (lines 457-8), often the mark of a witch, but even this mark of abjection remains ambiguous. Another reference to a marked side occurs in a subsequent passage, this time "the wounds in Jesu's side" (line 433). Taken together, these two references blur the distinction between damned and martyred, diabolical and divine, suggesting yet again the ambiguity of the abject as both abhorred and adored, and calling into question any gendered notions of abjection, which is neither masculine nor feminine, but indeterminate.

Semiotic traces indicating the presence of abjection often appear in the discourse of subjects for whom the symbolic is weak, and it is in connection with the subject's ability to speak meaningfully that Geraldine's defiled bosom is most ominous. This monstrous deformity, and the spell of which it is the emblem, is, in fact, the key to utterance within the narrative, both Christabel's and the narrator's flawed efforts to tell the story. At the beginning of their encounter in Christabel's bedroom, when Christabel sees Geraldine disrobed, Geraldine speaks these words: "'In the touch of this bosom there worketh a spell, / Which is lord of thy utterance, Christabel!'" (lines 267-8). Geraldine then tells Christabel that because of this spell she will be able to tell only a limited version of what had occurred between the two of them—a prediction that is borne out the next day when Christabel is unable to tell her father of her fearful recollections.

To understand the effects of this spell requires more thought about the "touch of this bosom." The image suggests the bond between mother and child in the pre-Oedipal stage: source of both primal joy and primal fear (should the breast be withheld). Of course Geraldine's bosom is deformed, a perversion of the nourishing breast of the good mother. In this sense, its touch becomes a contamination, an infection of Christabel with Geraldine's defilement. Such a contamination might then produce in Christabel the dis-ease that is the threat of abjection, a condition whose symptom is a rupture of the symbolic, a wound within language. This infectious touch, this spell, will be "lord of . . . utterance." A spell may be an enchantment or words with occult powers. "To spell" can also mean "to signify."[21] If a spell were a modality of signification, however, it would be semiotic rather than symbolic; enchantment would partake of the hidden, the uncanny, the disruptive: abjection. This spell, this infection, would then control utterance, would be "lord" of utterance, the source of its power, "a brutish suffering . . . sublime and devastated" (*PH*, p. 2). That this spell is gendered masculine may be surprising, since the spell has its origin in a feminine figure. Yet like "the wounds in Jesu's side" (line 433), this spell also suggests that figures of abjection should not be limited by essentialist notions of gender.

It is not only Christabel's powers of utterance that are limited, but those of the narrator as well. In fact,

Christabel is a correlative of the narrator in that her mastery of language, her ability to function within the symbolic order, is subverted by intercourse with the abject, the contamination of abjection. The narrator's ability to narrate the story has become undermined as Geraldine has come to dominate the narrative. He seems by the end of part 1 to be overwhelmed by the story he is relating, an utterance that has taken on a life of its own, independent of the speaking subject. The utterance, the narration, seems now to be determining the narrator's response, and interest has shifted from the narrative itself to the narrative voice, as the narrative narrates the narrator.

After the heightened emotion evoked by the exchange between Geraldine and Christabel there follows for both Christabel and the narrator a kind of post-coital repose, even, for Christabel, the suggestion that the encounter had not been a source of horror after all:

> And see! The lady Christabel
> Gathers herself from out her trance;
> Her limbs relax, her countenance
> Grows sad and soft; the smooth thin lids
> Close o'er her eyes; and tears she sheds—
> Large tears that leave the lashes bright!
> And oft the while she seems to smile
> As infants at a sudden light!
>
> (lines 311-8)

A smile "[a]s infants at a sudden light"—like that of infants in the loving embrace of a good mother. Later in the poem the narrator refers to this mood as a "rapture" (line 467). Do these lines provide a glimpse of the maternal as source of primal jouissance?

The last verse paragraph of the conclusion to part 1 ends with the narrator, like Christabel, more at peace, less caught up in the passion of the encounter with Geraldine, that carrier of disruption. The narrator is now able to make some gesture toward regaining control of the narrative, though only a gesture, because the repose he seems to have experienced, even with its elusive joy, will prove to be only an interlude in his distress. In an attempt to regain control over his narrative, to render its meaning determinate, he ventures an explanation of Christabel's perplexing response to her experience with Geraldine: "No doubt, she hath a vision sweet" (line 326). Of course interpretation can at best create only an illusion of fixed meaning, of mastery over what is finally indeterminate.

The narrator reinforces his illusion of mastery by reciting a platitude that invokes supernatural intervention:

> But this she knows, in joys and woes,
> That saints will aid if men will call:
> For the blue sky bends over all!
>
> (lines 329-31)

Saints may "aid if *men* will call," but Christabel is not a man, so she remains unprotected from Geraldine's power; and "the *blue* sky" may indeed "[bend] over all," but blue is not the color of the night sky, when Geraldine has worked her spell. This reassurance is thus also based on illusion. The narrator's repose, his attempted resumption of control over his narrative, is at best only a temporary respite from his distress.

Perhaps as a result of this illusion of mastery, part 2 opens with a voice more confident of the symbolic constructs that would make narrative possible. The narrator reports that Sir Leoline has ordered the matin bell to be tolled in a measured, precise way, to allow time for the prayers called for by "Five and forty beads" (line 341). The decree thus imposes "custom and law" (line 338) on the patriarchal demesne, as a shoring up of symbolic strength against the "world of death" (line 333), Sir Leoline's only life since the morning "[w]hen he rose and found his lady dead" (line 335). But Bard Bracy realizes that the interval between the peals opens a fissure, a space within this measure of time:

> Saith Bracy the bard, So let it knell!
> And let the drowsy sacristan
> Still count as slowly as he can!
> There is no lack of such, I ween,
> As well fill up the space between.

> (lines 345-9)

Bracy and the narrator then tell of the "such" that will "well . . . up" to fill these spaces: ghosts, the devil, mocking laughter, and—Geraldine. In spite of the confident tone with which part 2 began, signs of semiotic disturbance appear once again: conflation of life/death and time/space and intrusion of the uncanny and the horrific, rendering objects and meaning indeterminate, and narration problematical.

The notion of a rupture in symbolic order is also significant in the account of the youthful friendship between Sir Leoline and Lord Roland of Tryermaine, whom Geraldine claims is her father. This strong male friendship—each had been "his heart's best brother" (line 417)—had been broken by "whispering tongues" that "poison[ed] truth" (line 409). A whisper: secretive, almost a hiss, and "work[ing] like a madness in the brain" (line 413). Because of these whispers, these two fathers now stand apart, their "truth" overthrown, their solidarity broken, "[l]ike cliffs which had been rent asunder" (line 422). Again the ordered unity of the symbolic is broken by eruptions from the semiotic, here a whispering tongue, snakelike.

The narrative then continues to demonstrate just this pattern of disrupted signification, the symbolic destabilized as the semiotic breaks into the narrator's story. Increasingly the narrator is overwhelmed by Geraldine as

threat, to the point where once again he loses control over the narrative, becomes in a sense determined by it. Sir Leoline's prolonged embrace of Geraldine, for instance, is so disturbing to both Christabel and the narrator that they can only react with horror, but not with language that explains their response. Christabel shudders at the embrace. She remembers with apparent abhorrence the intimacy she had shared with Geraldine the previous night, but "she ha[s] no power to tell" her father what ails her (line 473). The narrator, also moved by this recollection and by the embrace between Geraldine and Sir Leoline that he is now relating, interrupts the narrative with a cry of distress: "Ah, woe is me!" (line 455). Both Christabel and the narrator are so distraught, in fact, that they emit animal sounds, the hiss of a snake: Christabel "[draws] in her breath with a hissing sound" (line 459) and the lines of the text itself, the speech of the narrator, echo with the repetition of sibilants. But fear and distress are not the only responses to the recollection of Geraldine's embrace of Christabel; the narrator recalls that in the repose following their intimacy, Christabel had experienced a "vision blest" (line 464) that "[h]ad put a rapture in her breast" (line 467). He seems aware that experience with Geraldine, that figure of the abject maternal, holds out the possibility of joy as well as pain.

Such a possibility is also suggested by Bard Bracy's dream, though not in Bracy's interpretation of the dream's images. Bracy relates to Sir Leoline this dream in which he finds in the forest a snake and dove:

> I stooped, methought, the dove to take,
> When lo! I saw a bright green snake
> Coiled around its wings and neck.
> Green as the herbs on which it couched,
> Close by the dove's its head it crouched;
> And with the dove it heaves and stirs,
> Swelling its neck as she swelled hers!

> (lines 548-54)

As these lines make clear, the dream imagery associates the snake with the healing power of greenery and herbs, fertility and health. The relationship between the snake and dove is symbiotic—"swelling its neck as she swelled hers"—not predatory, with an innocent dove the victim of the snake's violation. As Bard Bracy interprets the dream, however, the snake becomes "unholy" (line 563), a threat which the bard hopes to remove by walking through the forest with his "saintly song" (line 561).

Bracy interprets the snake and dove as a dualism of evil over good, constructed as a hierarchy which he hopes to reverse. But like all the dualisms in this text, this one is problematical. Ambiguity of metaphor and referent becomes apparent in the conflicting interpretations of the dream by Bracy and Sir Leoline. For Bracy, the dove is Christabel:

that dove,
That gentle bird, whom thou dost love,
And call'st by thy own daughter's name—

(lines 531-3)

In Sir Leoline's interpretation the metaphor refers to Geraldine, "'Lord Roland's beauteous dove'" (line 569).

This confusion about metaphors and referents destabilizes the identities of Christabel and Geraldine and reflects the narrator's ambiguous significations of these characters. Conflicting signs about Geraldine's ontology have already been noted, as well as uncertainty arising from Christabel's associations with the sacred, especially her prayer beneath the Druidic oak tree. Now Christabel's identity becomes even more problematical. For the most part, the narrator has portrayed Christabel as a pure and innocent maiden; he tells us that she is "devoid of guile and sin" (line 599), an innocence presumably violated by Geraldine in the episode in Christabel's bedroom when the two lie together. Now he tells how, under the influence of Geraldine's powerful gaze, "that look askance" (line 608), Christabel herself appears as a snake by virtue of mimesis:

So deeply had she drunken in
That look, those shrunken serpent eyes,
That all her features were resigned
To this sole image in her mind:
And passively did imitate
That look of dull and treacherous hate!

(lines 601-6)

Christabel, like Geraldine, has become a snake, and the narrator, as Bracy had done in his dream interpretation, now posits this figure as evil, an embodiment of treachery and hatred.

As part 2 of the poem draws to a close, Geraldine's ascendancy, her control of events and characters, has become almost absolute. She has displaced Christabel as the object of Sir Leoline's affections, who "turning from his own sweet maid, / . . . / [Leads] forth the lady Geraldine!" (lines 653-5). Bard Bracy has been sent away: "'Why, Bracy! dost thou loiter here? / I bade thee hence!'" (lines 651-2). Moreover, Geraldine has become so powerful that the narrator's attempts to control his characters, their actions, and signification itself have become impossible. He, like Christabel, is finally silenced by the strength of Geraldine's curse: "For what she knew she could not tell, / O'er-mastered by the mighty spell" (lines 619-20). Near the end of part 2, the narrator in fact enters his own narrative, though with no more success at influencing the outcome of events than when he maintained a position external to it. Almost as a character himself he addresses Sir Leoline: "O by the pangs of her dear mother / Think thou no evil of thy child!" (lines 626-7). But even this entreaty to a character who seems to have become autonomous is of no avail:

If thoughts, like these, had any share,
They only swelled his rage and pain,
And did but work confusion there.

(lines 637-9)

Soon, when Sir Leoline "[leads] forth the lady Geraldine," the narrative comes to an end, the narrator abandoning all attempts to tell the remainder of the story. There remain only the conclusion to part 2 and the measure of self-reflection for the narrator that that conclusion allows.

The conclusion ignores the events of the preceding narrative, reflecting instead on the difficulties of telling such a story. In lines that refer to the inadequacy of language, the narrator describes the inability of a speaking subject, a "father," to speak the love he feels for his little child, "his love's excess" (line 665), except through "words of unmeant bitterness" (line 665). The lines that reflect on this faulty signification show a similar disruption in the speech of the narrator, who describes the cruel words spoken to the beloved child as "tender" and "pretty" (line 670). The narrator also refers to the collapsing of binary categories, the inability to differentiate experiences of "love and pity" from those of "rage and pain" (lines 672, 676), an indeterminacy inherent, he speculates, in this "world of sin" (line 673).

Speaking from outside the narrative, the narrator thus reflects on the instability of the symbolic constructs on which narrative is based. Univalent language capable of transmitting the meaning intended by a unitary ego, fixed bipolar categories around which to structure a narrative or to make sense of a life—the narrator has found these symbolic constructs to be unstable and narration thus to be flawed. And yet the symbolic is only one modality of signification. Semiotic eruptions are inextricable from the signification of any speaking subject. Traces of the semiotic appear even in this conclusion, its presence revealed by the rhythm of the lines and the music of the signifiers, resonances of the semiotic disruptions that occurred in the narrative itself:

And what, if in a world of sin
(O sorrow and shame should this be true!)
Such giddiness of heart and brain
Comes seldom save from rage and pain,
So talks as it's most used to do.

(lines 673-7)

Alliteration of *s* sounds recalls the snake; the long *u* sounds recall the echolalia of the opening lines ("Tu—whit!——Tu—whoo!") (line 3). The semiotic continues to pulse in these sounds, evoking a lamentation from the narrator: "O sorrow and shame." In this lament echo the words Geraldine used to describe her side and bosom: "This mark of my shame, this seal of my sorrow" (line 270). The narrator speaks an awareness of abjection as a condition of life when he alludes to a "world of sin."[22] Does his lament then suggest as well an awareness of the abjection inherent in his own condition as a speaking subject? This world of sin, this life of abjection with its ruptures, its wounds, its abyss—such is the inevitable condition for any speaking being.

In *Powers of Horror* Kristeva points to a possibility of reconciling ourselves to the abjection that is intrinsic to life, if we can acknowledge our "particularity as *mortal and speaking.* 'There is an abject' is henceforth stated as, 'I am abject, that is, mortal and speaking'" (p. 88). The key to any act of narrating, then, is to acknowledge that abjection lies within ourselves as speaking subjects as "we recognize ourselves as always already altered by the symbolic—by language. Provided we hear in language—and not in the other, nor in the other sex . . . the wound, the basic incompleteness that conditions the indefinite quest of signifying concatenations. That amounts to joying in the truth of self-division" (pp. 88-9). "*Nor in the other sex*": while the abject is figured predominantly in **"Christabel"** as feminine, the marked sides of both Jesu and Geraldine and the spell that is "lord of . . . utterance" show that the abject is indeterminate (line 268), beyond any attempts to control it through essentialized constructs of gender.

This reading of **"Christabel"** suggests that the presence of abjection within the speaking subject, especially as manifest through disruptions of symbolic signification, may be a way to understand many narrative anomalies, especially instabilities of the symbolic constructs with which readers normally make sense of narrative. Where **"Christabel"** suspends closure and withholds determinate meaning, other Coleridge poems are likewise haunted with traces of abjection. The Ancient Mariner [*Rime of the Ancient Mariner*], journeying toward individuation, is arrested by sailors' corpses, slimy sea snakes, and the loathsome "[n]ight-mare Life-in-Death."[23] Anne Williams reads the Mariner's story as one of universal experience, "inevitable in the attainment of selfhood and subjectivity," emphasizing that "*The Rime*'s great power—and readers' urge to interpret the text—lies in the poem's discovery of intense, primitive anxieties fundamental to the self."[24] The Mariner as *speaking subject* figures abjection. His image and his story horrify the hermit, the Pilot's boy, the wedding guest, and the poetic voice, who attributes to the Mariner the poem's puerile moral: "He prayeth best, who loveth best / All things both great and small."[25] This moral fails to translate the Mariner's experience, as Coleridge acknowledged. It is an abstract and pietistic attempt to summarize and thus contain the uncontainable horror of abjection.

As **The Rime** tells of universal abjection in the journey toward self and language, **"Kubla Khan"** witnesses to the abject in the formation of the poetic voice. The fig-

ures in the poem evoke both fear and desire—the "woman wailing for her demon lover," the "sunny pleasure-dome with caves of ice," the Abyssinian maid and her abysmal song, and especially the poet, whose threat invokes ritual incantation and dance: "Beware! Beware!"[26] Yet all who hear him express ambivalence toward his vision and his song. The monstrous forbidden becomes the center as his hearers "[w]eave" in dance "a circle round him thrice."[27] Their fascination with the poet's song, like the ambivalent narrative of **"Christabel,"** reveals the power of poetry to speak their condition as fragile beings, forever desiring and dreading the memory of that savage, holy, and enchanted place, the mother's world. Coleridge's figures of abjection, like the narrator of **"Christabel,"** reveal no reified self, no unitary ego, but a subject speaking, a subject in process/on trial, unfinished, but open to joy.[28]

Notes

1. See, for example, Edward E. Bostetter, "Coleridge," in *The Romantic Ventriloquists: Wordsworth, Coleridge, Keats, Shelley, Byron* (Seattle: Univ. of Washington Press, 1963), pp. 82-135 (originally published in altered form as "*Christabel*: The Vision of Fear," *PQ* [*Philological Quarterly*] 36, 2 [April 1957]: 183-94); H. W. Piper, "The Disunity of *Christabel* and the Fall of Nature," *EIC* [*Essays in Criticism*] 28, 3 (July 1978): 216-27; Stuart Peterfreund, "The Way of Immanence, Coleridge, and the Problem of Evil," *ELH* 55, 1 (Spring 1988): 125-58; Susan M. Luther, "*Christabel* as Dream-Reverie," *Romantic Reassessment,* Salzburg Studies in English Literature 61 (Salzburg: Univ. of Salzburg, 1976); Macdonald Emslie and Paul Edwards, "The Limitations of Langdale: A Reading of *Christabel*," *EIC* [*Essays in Criticism*] 20, 1 (January 1970): 57-70; and Edwards and Emslie, "'Thoughts so all unlike each other': The Paradoxical in *Christabel*," *ES* [*English Studies*] 52, 3 (June 1971): 236-46.

2. Psychosexual readings include Jonas Spatz, "The Mystery of Eros: Sexual Initiation in Coleridge's 'Christabel,'" *PMLA* 90, 1 (January 1975): 107-16; Edward Proffitt, "'Christabel' and the Oedipal Conflict," *RS* [*Research Studies*] 46, 4 (December 1978): 248-51; Jane A. Nelson, "Entelechy and Structure in 'Christabel,'" *SIR* [*Studies in Romanticism*] 19, 3 (Fall 1980): 375-93; Barbara A. Schapiro, *The Romantic Mother: Narcissistic Patterns in Romantic Poetry* (Baltimore: Johns Hopkins Univ. Press, 1983); Karen Swann, "'Christabel': The Wandering Mother and the Enigma of Form," *SIR* [*Studies in Romanticism*] 23, 4 (Winter 1984): 533-53; Margery Durham, "The Mother Tongue: *Christabel* and the Language of Love," in *The (M)other Tongue: Essays in Feminist Psychoanalytic Interpretation,* ed. Shirley Nelson Garner,

Claire Kahane, and Madelon Sprengnether (Ithaca: Cornell Univ. Press, 1985), pp. 169-93; Charles Rzepka, "Christabel's 'Wandering Mother' and the Discourse of the Self: A Lacanian Reading of Repressed Narration," *Romanticism Past and Present* 10, 1 (Winter 1986): 17-43; Dennis M. Welch, "Coleridge's *Christabel*: A/version of a Family Romance," *WS* [*Women's Studies*] 21, 2 (Spring 1992): 163-84; Lore Metzger, "Modifications of Genre: A Feminist Critique of 'Christabel' and 'Die Braut von Korinth,'" *SECC* [*Studies in Eighteenth-Century Culture*] 22 (1992): 3-19; Douglas B. Wilson, "Coleridge and the Endangered Self," *WC* [*Wordsworth Circle*] 26, 1 (Winter 1995): 18-23. On Coleridge's relationship with his own mother, see, for example, Schapiro, Durham, Rzepka, and Wilson.

3. Kathleen M. Wheeler, "Disruption and Displacement in Coleridge's 'Christabel,'" *WC* [*Wordsworth Circle*] 20, 2 (Spring 1989): 85-90, 88.

4. Wheeler, "Disruption," p. 90.

5. In *Romanticism, Pragmatism, and Deconstruction* (Oxford: Blackwell, 1993), Wheeler notes that Coleridge described dualisms as relative, rather than absolute (pp. 152-4). See also Thomas McFarland, "A Complex Dialogue: Coleridge's Doctrine of Polarity and Its European Contexts," in *Reading Coleridge: Approaches and Applications,* ed. Walter B. Crawford (Ithaca: Cornell Univ. Press, 1979), pp. 56-115.

6. Rzepka's Lacanian reading discusses problems of narrativity and narrative voice: the narrator speaks "for and in the tone of voice (though not in the person) of Christabel . . . *were she to tell her story* . . . What the narrator can and cannot tell reflects the extent to which Christabel herself can 'tell' who she is" (pp. 21-3). Swann, identifying multiple narrators, believes "'Christabel' both dramatizes and provokes hysteria" (p. 535); the narrators, as hysterics, are unable to render meaning clear. See also Avery F. Gaskins, in "Dramatic Form, 'Double Voice,' and 'Carnivalization' in 'Christabel,'" *ERR* [*European Romantic Review*] 4, 1 (Summer 1993): 1-12. Andrew M. Cooper describes the problematic narrator as "[d]imwitted, nagging, sanctimonious, and overwrought" ("Who's Afraid of the Mastiff Bitch? Gothic Parody and the Original Sin in *Christabel*," 1988; rprt. in *Critical Essays on Samuel Taylor Coleridge* [New York: G. K. Hall, 1994], pp. 81-107, 83). Susan Eilenberg discusses the indeterminacy of time, syntax, and verb tenses in relation to narrative disturbance in "'Michael,' 'Christabel,' and the Poetry of Possession," *Criticism* 30, 2 (Spring 1988): 205-24; Geraldine's "evil" lies primarily "in her powers of displacement, which reveal her to be essentially linguistic in nature" (p. 219).

7. Samuel Taylor Coleridge, *Christabel,* in *Poems,* vol. 1 of *The Complete Poetical Works of Samuel Taylor Coleridge,* ed. Ernest Hartley Coleridge (1912; rprt. Oxford: Clarendon Press, 1957), pp. 213-36, line 1. All subsequent references to *Christabel* are to this edition and are cited parenthetically within the text.

8. See Jane Chambers, "Leoline's Mastiff Bitch: Functions of a Minor Figure in *Christabel*," *ELN* [*English Language Notes*] 22, 1 (September 1984): 38-43.

9. The *OED* [*Oxford English Dictionary*] defines *bitch* as "a lewd or sensual woman" as early as the Chester Play from the 1400s (2d edn., s. v. "bitch").

10. The narrator is assumed to be male because of his erotic response to the scene in Christabel's chamber. In truth, the narrative function cannot be decisively gendered, but that is the subject of another study.

11. For Coleridge's theory of the self in relation to associationism, see his *Biographia Literaria, or Biographical Sketches of My Literary Life and Opinions,* ed. James Engell and W[alter] Jackson Bate, vol. 7 of *The Collected Works of Samuel Taylor Coleridge,* ed. Kathleen Coburn (Princeton: Princeton Univ. Press, 1983), chaps. 5-8 and 12, pp. 89-115 and 232-94.

12. Julia Kristeva, *Revolution in Poetic Language,* trans. Margaret Waller (New York: Columbia Univ. Press, 1984).

13. In *Revolution in Poetic Language,* Kristeva defines *semiotic* and *symbolic*:

> We understand the term "semiotic" in its Greek sense . . . distinctive mark, trace, index, precursory sign, proof, engraved or written sign, imprint, trace, figuration . . . This modality is the one Freudian psychoanalysis points to in postulating not only the *facilitation* and the structuring *disposition* of drives, but also the so-called *primary processes* which displace and condense both energies and their inscription. Discrete quantities of energy move through the body of the subject who is not yet constituted as such and, in the course of his development, they are arranged according to the various constraints imposed upon this body—always already involved in a semiotic process—by family and social structures. In this way the drives, which

are "energy" charges as well as "psychical" marks, articulate what we call a *chora*: a nonexpressive totality formed by the drives and their stasis in a motility that is as full of movement as it is regulated.

(p. 25)

We shall distinguish the semiotic (drives and their articulation) from the realm of signification [the symbolic], which is always that of a proposition or judgment, in other words, a realm of *positions*. This positionality . . . is structured as a break in the signifying process, establishing the *identification* of the subject and its object as preconditions of propositionality. We shall call this break, which produces the positing of signification, a *thetic* phase.

(p. 43)

Kristeva quotes these passages herself in *Black Sun: Depression and Melancholia*, trans. Leon S. Roudiez (New York: Columbia Univ. Press, 1989), pp. 264-5. The definitions exclude mention of gender, a shift which may reflect Kristeva's efforts to distance herself from some feminists' use of the terms *semiotic* and *symbolic*, even though the terms are clearly gendered in *Revolution in Poetic Language* (published in French in 1974). *Black Sun* (published in French in 1987) attests to her continued valuing of the concepts of poetic language, even as she shifts her focus toward psychoanalysis. Issues of gender in relation to abjection, individuation, and language acquisition remain unresolved for many critics of psychoanalytic theory, like Luce Irigaray; see, for example, "The Poverty of Psychoanalysis," *The Irigaray Reader,* ed. Margaret Whitford (Oxford: Blackwell, 1991), pp. 79-104.

14. Kristeva, *Revolution in Poetic Language*, p. 63.

15. "Any narrative already assumes that there is an identity stabilized by a completed Oedipus and that . . . it can concatenate its adventures through failures and conquests of the 'objects' of desire" (Kristeva, *Black Sun*, p. 161).

16. Kristeva, *Black Sun*, p. 101.

17. Kristeva, *Desire in Language: A Semiotic Approach to Literature and Art,* trans. Roudiez (New York: Columbia Univ. Press, 1980), p. 158.

18. Kristeva, *Powers of Horror: An Essay on Abjection,* trans. Roudiez (New York: Columbia Univ. Press, 1982), p. 5; subsequent references to this source will occur parenthetically in the text designated as *PH*. Kristeva's theories of abjection develop the work of Mary Douglas and other anthropologists who have studied defilement in relation to cultural structures. To this work Kristeva has added theories taken from the structural anthropology of Claude Levi-Strauss and Freudian and Lacanian psychoanalysis to derive "a deep psycho-symbolic economy: the general, logical determination that underlies anthropological variants . . . and evinces a specific economy of the speaking subject, no matter what its historical manifestations may be" (*PH,* p. 68).

Elizabeth Grosz has explored Kristeva's understanding of corporeality and abjection as constitutive of the subject, but finds Kristeva's theories inadequate to an understanding of the sexual specificity of the body in relation to discourse. See Grosz, "The Body of Signification," in *Abjection, Melancholia, and Love: The Work of Julia Kristeva,* ed. John Fletcher and Andrew Benjamin (London: Routledge, 1990), pp. 86-103, 86.

In another study that considers "Christabel" in relation to Kristeva's theories, Wilson explains the "blurring of the boundaries between Christabel and Geraldine" in terms of abjection (p. 21). Durham, following Melanie Klein, notes the ambiguous affects associated with the mother in the pre-Oedipal stage, especially in relation to the child's acquisition of language.

19. Feminists such as Judith Butler and Grosz, in accusing Kristeva of essentialism, run the risk themselves of reifying the symbolic and semiotic. In contrast, Roudiez, Toril Moi, and Fletcher underscore the productive possibilities of Kristeva's theory, its mobile and provisional articulation of what lies at the ever-disintegrating border of language. See Roudiez, introduction to *Revolution in Poetic Language*, pp. 1-10; Moi, introduction to *The Kristeva Reader,* ed. Moi (New York: Columbia Univ. Press, 1986), pp. 1-22; Fletcher, introduction to *Abjection, Melancholia, and Love,* pp. 1-7.

20. Anne Williams, *Art of Darkness: A Poetics of Gothic* (Chicago: Univ. of Chicago Press, 1995), discusses the Gothic genre, including issues of narrativity, in light of Kristeva's theories of poetic language and abjection. Her Kristevan study of *The Rime of the Ancient Mariner,* which appeared originally as "An I for an Eye: Spectral Persecution in *The Rime of the Ancient Mariner*" in *PMLA* 108, 5 (October 1993): 1114-27, appears in a somewhat revised form in *Art of Darkness*.

21. *OED,* 2d edn., s.v. "spell." *Webster's Third New International Dictionary* defines "to spell" as "to signify." Williams, in a helpful discussion of the etymology and multiple meanings of *spell*, notes that one group of meanings "embodies the very

idea of a Symbolic Law . . . [in] notions of order, clarity, and correctness"; the word simultaneously has darker meanings, "hint[ing] at the uncanny power that lies at or below the roots of language" (*Art of Darkness*, pp. 179, 180).

22. Kristeva identifies the concept of sin as a figuration of abjection (*PH*, p. 118).

23. Coleridge, *The Rime of the Ancient Mariner*, in *Poetical Works*, pp. 186-209, line 193.

24. Williams, "An I for an Eye," pp. 1118, 1125.

25. Coleridge, *Rime*, lines 614-5.

26. Coleridge, "Kubla Khan," in *Poetical Works*, pp. 295-8, lines 16, 36, and 49.

27. Coleridge, "Kubla Khan," line 51.

28. I wish to thank Anne Mellor for helpful suggestions on an earlier version of this essay.

Christian La Cassagnère (essay date spring 2001)

SOURCE: La Cassagnère, Christian. "The Strangeness of 'Christabel.'" *Wordsworth Circle* 32, no. 2 (spring 2001): 84-8.

[*In the following essay, La Cassagnère discusses "Christabel"'s enigmatic qualities through an in-depth analysis of the characters of Geraldine and Christabel. According to La Cassagnère, the success of the poem lies in its ability to convey the essential inarticulateness of human desire.*]

Of Coleridge's "Mystery Poems," *Christabel* is the one that most deserves the title. For reading *Christabel* is to be confronted with two mysteries. There is, first, the inherent mystery of its significance, a significance that centres upon an opaque focus, the fascinating figure of the "lady strange," Geraldine, that eludes us like an anamorphosis: she fantastically changes with our travelling gaze, she reverses her significance depending on our reading position, to such a point that she could be viewed by readers close to Coleridge in his lifetime as impersonating "the power of evil"—to quote James Gillman's biography of 1838 [*The Life of Samuel Taylor Coleridge*] (183)—but as well as "a spirit executing her appointed task with the best good will," in the eyes of Derwent, the poet's son, according to a comment he made some fifteen years after the publication of Gillman's book.

This mystery is nested, so to speak, within a further mystery which is that of the production of the text. For the history of its genesis offers all the material for a mystery story—such a story as Henry James, I imagine,

might have written. Briefly, Coleridge wrote the first Part of *Christabel* at Nether Stowey, in February, 1798 (in the *annus mirabilis*, soon after the two other "Mystery Poems", *Kubla Khan* and *The Rime of the Ancient Mariner*); and it was not until more than two years later that he took up the poem, at the end of August, 1800, settled in Keswick, once again near the Wordsworths in Grasmere. As the writing of the second Part progressed, in September and October, Coleridge would walk to Grasmere and read his text to William and Dorothy, who were fascinated, it seems, judging by the evidence of Dorothy's *Journals* (57): "October 4th, 1800, Saturday.[. . .] Exceedingly delighted with the second part of *Christabel.*" Then, next entry: "October 5th, Sunday Morning. Coleridge read a 2nd time *Christabel*; we had increasing pleasure." Strangely enough, however, Coleridge never wrote anything beyond this second Part (with the exception of the brief "Conclusion to Part II" in the following year), although the poem was originally planned—so Coleridge kept on saying—as a composition in five Parts.

His failure to complete *Christabel* looks like a real enigma. Of course, it would be quite understandable that in 1800, Coleridge should have temporarily given up working on the poem because of his disappointment on learning that *Christabel,* which was intended as the concluding poem in the second edition of the *Lyrical Ballads,* was eventually rejected by Wordsworth who found it too "discordant"—as he wrote in a letter to his publisher (*Collected Letters of STC* [*Samuel Taylor Coleridge*], I, 643, n. 2)—with the rest of the volume and set about writing **"Michael"** which finally took the place of the vanishing *Christabel.* But, throughout the remaining thirty-four years of his life, Coleridge never added a word to the poem, even when, in 1816, he finally decided to publish it together with *Kubla Khan* and **"The Pains of Sleep."** He still presented it as unfinished, adding that he would be "able to embody in verse the three parts yet to come in the course of the present year" (*Poetical Works* [*Poetical Works of Samuel Taylor Coleridge*], 213). We are thus left, I should say, with a ghost-text, hovering as it does between presence and absence, between existence and virtuality: a textual ghost that haunted some of Coleridge's contemporaries, mesmerized such persons as Sir Walter Scott and Lord Byron during the sixteen years before publication when it was recited or circulated in manuscript form.

The end of the story—if such story has an end—is that in the two collected editions of his *Poetical Works,* 1828 and 1829, Coleridge retained the allusion to "the three parts yet to come," but omitted it in the last revised edition, a few months before his death, in 1834. Now—and this is the last question I would like to raise—was this just a renouncement? Or might it not have been the subliminal recognition at long last that

Christabel, as a poem, namely not as a story or as a thriller, but as a verbal construct, was indeed complete: that it projected a self-sufficient myth and that the text as it was—as it is—brought its creator, as well as the creative reader whom it implied, the revelation or the deep effect they were seeking? And in this case, of course, the two mysteries I have pointed out would be one: the supposedly unfinished poem would resolve into that of its intimate significance. Such is the reading I would like to suggest by concentrating primarily on what might be called the overture of *Christabel,* the nocturne on which the poem opens, because it contains, I think, the major keys to the myth that organizes the text.

On first looking into *Christabel,* the 19th century reader presumably expected to get the thrill of "supernatural terror" found in Gothic romances and verse equivalents (and indeed, incidentally, an anonymous poet, who had been able to have access to the unpublished manuscript, did better than Coleridge since he published a "Gothic Tale," as he called it, entitled **"Christobell"**, which offered at last the complete story.) But the reader's expectancy would have been frustrated; for, if Coleridge does introduce most of the main Gothic stock elements—the medieval period setting, the castle, the witching time of midnight and even a reference to the ghost world in the early mention of "my lady's shroud" (13)—he brings them into play derisively, to make them inoperative: the castle will never be described in its most thrilling aspects, there will be no Radcliffean flight through subterranean passages and the conjectural lady's ghost will remain out of use behind the arras. Making light of those referents of Gothic fiction, Coleridge builds up the eeriness of his world by playing purely on the signifier, thus creating an infinitely more searching "fantastic": a fantastic which the text generates in two ways, and this from the breathtaking opening stanza:

> 'Tis the middle of night by the castle clock,
> And the owls have awakened the crowing cock;
> Tu—whit!—Tu—whoo!
> And hark, again! the crowing cock,
> How drowsily it crew.

> (1-5)

What is breath-taking in this stanza—in the familiar though strangely distorted ballad design,—is the rupture that occurs in the discourse at the place of what should be the third line, since instead of the expected six syllabled line (or trimeter), a sheer sequence of sounds, "Tu—whit!—Tu—whoo!" makes itself heard. In the heart of the stanzaic pattern the speech flow is thus broken through by something—call it a cry or a pulsation—that comes straight from the Real, in the full sense of the term, that is the Real as radically distinct from the symbolic order, particularly, the order of language, which represents, without being, the Real. For

the four sounds that irrupt in the place of the third line are not linguistic signs (that would belong to the code of the English language and would be, as such, characterized by what linguistics calls, after Saussure, the arbitrary nature of the sign); neither do they belong, rhythmically, to the specific metrical code of the poem, since the metre, as Coleridge makes it clear in his preface, is defined as an accentual verse whose number of syllables "may vary" but only "from seven to twelve" (**Poetical Works** 215). The signifying chain is thus ruptured in its centre, and in the slit something tries to speak, although from beyond the world of words. Something, unspeakable and yet ready to speak, demands to be realized. This is the first *textual* occurrence of *Christabel*: an emblematic occurrence indeed, in that it plays out immediately, in a nutshell, the drama of emergence and of discovery which is to be the poem's drama.

At the same time the stanza as a whole brings into play a special strategy. Excluding the extraordinary, it focuses on such natural objects as could be seen in the English countryside on a quiet winter night, and, particularly on such trivial occurrences as are likely to be part of the heroine's everyday experience; but it transforms them in an "unrealization," to use Coleridge's term. In a letter of 1819, Coleridge illuminates an essential feature of his poetics: "From my very childhood I have been accustomed to abstract and as it were unrealize whatever of more than common interest my eyes dwelt on; and then by a sort of transfusion and transmission of my consciousness to identify myself with the object" (**Collected Letters** *IV,* 974-75). "Unrealize" is the master word: it means that the object the gaze dwells upon is "abstracted" in the literal sense, that is mentally detached from the context in which it is actually involved or with which it is usually associated, because that context prevents the subject from really seeing the object in its whatness. (In other words, as Coleridge had explained a few years earlier in **Biographia Literaria** [II, 6], the context and the mental routine that goes with it spread "a film of familiarity" on the object that blinds us to its spell.) In unrealization the object is thus removed from its ground and either insulated, suspended on no ground at all, or displaced onto a foreign ground and thus set in a thoroughly unusual association so that, in either case, it tends to turn into something strange—a process in which Coleridge, remarkably, initiates, one century ahead of surrealism, an essential feature of the surrealist aesthetics: that of the displaced object in painting and, in literature, the surrealist metaphor as it will be theorized by André Breton's *Manifeste du Surréalisme* in 1924, namely as an encounter of disparates within the image. This process is constantly at work in the overture of *Christabel*; it generates the specific nature of its fantastic: what was supposed to be well-known turns out unknown; the familiar turns into the alien; and, conversely, the alien turns into the familiar, the unknown into the intimate.

In the first two stanzas the description is exclusively devoted to sound, without any reference to sight: each sound—the chiming of the clock, the owl's cry, the cock's crow, the bitch's "short howls"—is thus suspended in a vacuum of invisibility and insulated with silence. And if two sounds are related, it is to form a disturbing association in which each unrealizes the other, as when the owl's midnight cry meets the cock's morning crow in an unthinkable coexistence—which, incidentally, may remind us of the surrealist metaphor on which Wordsworth's "Idiot Boy" culminates. Familiar sounds thus glide into strangeness. Then the third stanza carries on the process while transferring it onto the visual field (and on a conceptual plane as well) through the binary pattern of question and answer, which is actually a couple of two juxtaposed utterances: "Is the night chilly and dark? / The night is chilly, but not dark" (14-15). The first statement posits a normal association of two descriptive terms which the mind readily accepts as likely and rational (a winter night both cold and dark). Then the second statement dismisses one of the two terms ("not dark": the negation being here the unrealizing operator), so that the adopted term ("chilly") is unexpectedly deprived of its context. What seems to be a mere description in the traditional dialogic ballad style is indeed a potent rhetoric of unrealization, all the more so as it goes on working along the same lines throughout the stanza: each couplet establishes a pair of closely related items ("covering" and "hiding," "full moon" and "large moon"), then dissociates it, so that the remaining items ("covering" without "hiding," "full moon" without "large moon") build up an eerie landscape, a no man's land where the familiar and the unfamiliar merge disturbingly into each other.

In stanzas 4 and 5 that solitary night world, already strange in itself, now serves as a ground to a refined human figure, "The lovely lady Christabel," of stanza 4 abruptly superimposed on the description of stanza 3. This is Coleridge's presurrealist technique of the displaced figure: against a background where a human presence could not be expected, Christabel's appearance, in the instant when it occurs, takes on the value of an apparition. But that is not all, for in the following sequence (stanzas 6 to 8) the same type of occurrence, with exactly the same kind of effect, is repeated with the appearance of the stranger (that will turn out to be Geraldine) and here is a major clue to the myth. Just as Christabel appeared to us against the nocturnal background, as an unexpected presence, in the same way the stranger appears to Christabel (who is from now on the narrative focus at work in the story) as a disturbingly unexpected presence, a duplication which is stressed, moreover, by the narrator's choric discourse (which is

as well, incidentally, a self-description of unrealization): just as before "The lovely lady Christabel, [. . .] What makes her in the wood so late?" (23-25), now, as if in an echo, "I guess, 'twas frightful there to see / A lady so richly clad as she, / Beautiful exceedingly" (66-68). Geraldine, the eerie visitor, thus makes her entrance in the poetic space—that of poetic communication and poetic effect—like a *double* of Christabel.

Underlying Geraldine is indeed, so it seems to me, the mythological figure of the double as it has been investigated in the 20th century by psychoanalytic research, by Otto Rank who in an essay entitled "Der Doppelgänger" (published in 1914 in the third issue of *Imago* and later exploited by Sigmund Freud) offered a systematic study of "the double," pointing out its various modalities and manifestations in myth, folklore and works of imagination as being chiefly the echo, the portrait that comes alive, the shadow and the image in the mirror. Such modalities loom indeed behind the opening narrative of **Christabel** and they become perceptible if one visualizes this opening (and what it communicates) in spatial terms, either as a stage with personae or as a picture with figures. Geraldine enters the stage immediately after Christabel (in poetic time), projecting the same sort of unexpected silhouette: so like a shadow cast from Christabel.

From a pictorial point of view—in the surrealist painting I am suggesting as a correlative to the poem—Geraldine functions like Christabel's reflection, for the two figures stand to each other in spatial symmetry on either side of a virtual middle screen (the screen of the mirror) which is materialized, in the structure of the Coleridgean picture, by the tree trunk which is in the position of a central axis dividing the pictorial space in two: Christabel is seen, on one side, "beneath the huge oak tree" (35); and the "It" (the inaugural signifier is well worth noticing) manifests its presence "On the other side [. . .] Of the huge, broad-breasted, old oak tree" (41-42): on the other side of the mirror. And when Christabel makes up her mind to go and see, to find out about the nature of the "It," she has to glide "to the other side of the oak" (56): you will discover the nature of the Thing, of the Other, only by crossing the screen, by walking across the mirror into that other space, ever so close and yet foreign, where your double is living. Again, to note further converging textual effects, "The lovely lady" (first half of line 38 describing Christabel) reflects itself in "a damsel bright" (second half of line 58 describing Geraldine), its chiastic mirror image. A duplication moreover that makes itself heard in the rhythmical perception of the text: for brought together, the two phrases, "The lovely lady"/"a damsel bright", make up one complete tetrameter (the poem's metrical norm), which suggests that, distant as they may be in the space of the text, they are indeed two split off fragments of one and the same exploded unit.

The psychoanalytical theory I am referring to (Freud XVII, 233-45) has interpreted the figure of the double as objectifying aspects of the subject that are unknown to his consciousness and foreign to the ego, either because they are primitive modes of thought which have been overlaid by new, rational modes in the process of cultural development or because they are tendencies, drives or desires that have been repressed because they are at odds with the subject's ethical or social standards. They thus go on living a life of their own in the unconscious, still striving for expression.

The double in this view is not a copy of the ego, but rather what the ego is not, the stranger within: my double is what I have disowned or negated in myself and thus turned into a stranger that may meet me, sometime, somewhere, in a strange encounter. When such encounter takes place, it generates that special kind of anxiety which Freud has explored in a seminal essay (XVII, 217-56) and defined as "the Uncanny"—the standard English translation of the German "Unheimliche." Because it leaves out the metaphoric dimension of the German, this translation may not be satisfactory, especially applied to the literary field. We might prefer, as an equivalent, "the Unhomelike" (what does not seem to belong to one's home), a term that would restore the imaginary dimension of the Freudian concept. The experience of the Uncanny occurs when a psychic, intimate reality—a desire or the representative of a desire—which has been repressed and is not granted any symbolization, particularly any representation in language, returns, apparently in the outside world (where it has been projected) and confronts the subject as something alien. "This uncanny," Freud says, "is in reality nothing new or alien, but something which is familiar and old established in the mind, and which has become alienated from it through the process of repression." It is "something that ought to have remained secret and hidden but has come to light" (241).

The figure of Geraldine, as created by the poetic text, is exactly that alien within. Thoroughly mysterious, unknown to Christabel as "The lady strange" (71), she is yet, somehow, intimate, as suggested when she first manifests herself as "It": "It moaned as near as near can be" (39). What is "as near as near can be" if not inside, within the subject's own self? Geraldine does not exactly "appear" (at once, like a supernatural ghost that would come from the beyond): she follows in the wake of those small occurrences (the chiming of the clock, the cock's crow, and so on) which, in the ambiguous light of unrealization, are both familiar and strange and build up that quality of "the Unhomelike Homelike" which the figure of Geraldine capitalizes as the final term of the series, thus materializing as "the Homelike Unhomelike".

Above all, the utterance which introduces her visual discovery by Christabel, "What sees she there?" (57), is a singular line made of four monosyllables which thereby reproduces the sound sequence that was in the position of line 3 (Tu—whit! Tu—whoo!). The linguistic utterance of line 57 thus harbours the rhythmic structure of the pulsation which in the slit of the opening stanza manifested the irruption of the Real: as if the Real, first heard in the pulsation of the four beats, was now captured from beyond the limits of language and forced into the linguistic body of the poem at a point, then, where the unspeakable Real enters the text and makes the text pregnant with itself.

Here therefore—in the rhythmic isotopy which conflates the two lines and which the ear perceives as it comes to line 57—the poem exhibits its own genesis and its deeper economy: it describes itself as the expansion of an instant (say the few seconds taken by the sound heard in the slit of the third line), an instant brief like the pulsation of an artery but in which something of the Real flickers, "vacillates," to take up the word through which Jacques Lacan qualifies the characteristic way in which the unconscious manifests itself in the subject: "The unconscious," Lacan observes in *The Seminar,* "is always manifested as that which vacillates within a split in the subject from which there emerges a discovery [. . .] where the subject comes upon himself in some unexpected place" (Lacan 29, my translation). Coleridge's poem is the miraculous expansion and the poetic articulation of such "vacillation." And the meeting with the "lady strange" on the forest margin is the "discovery" Lacan speaks about, a discovery in which the subject, Christabel, "comes upon herself in some unexpected place": the secret place of her desire. Geraldine is thus desire in Christabel, the reality of unconscious desire which she meets in an uncanny moment. The poem explores this uncanny meeting, staging it in a mythical drama.

Christabel's grapple with that inner reality of hers thus constitutes the poem's drama: a drama played out in two acts which correspond to the two Parts of the poem as it is. The action of Part I, which is essentially a development of the overture, is the emergence of "what ought to have remained hidden," in other words the return of the repressed and the way in which it infiltrates the space of the ego. The text stages the (literally) haunting character and potency of that return in the irresistible trajectory of the upsurging Shade which fed, so to speak, with Christabel's life blood, steals into the castle (an image of the world of culture with its laws) and transgresses the bars of repression in a series of violations dramatized by the crossing of frontiers: the moat, the castle gate, the staircase, the threshold of Christabel's chamber, the ultimate metaphor of the ego.

In Part II, once the stranger has been established as an inmate of the castle—once "the Unhomelike" has turned back into "the Homelike"—, the drama becomes a specular confrontation between the subject and the Other: the operative mirror, which was already virtual in the opening scene and is now the basic structuring scheme of the text, being by no means the narcissistic mirror (that in which the subject finds the image of himself or herself as he or she thinks it to be), but the uncanny mirror which sends back Christabel an image she did not expect. That image flickers in the intensest moments of Part II, in the uncanny epiphanies where the secret reptilian identity of the Other shows forth, while the reptilian, although experienced as monstrous, keeps on being reflected, in the specular scheme, between the Other and the subject, the subject and the Other: the serpent first shows, most spectacularly, as a visual image in Geraldine's face (as perceived by Christabel) in a sort of fade-in:

> A snake's small eye blinks dull and shy:
> And the lady's eyes they shrunk in her head,
> Each shrunk up to a serpent's eye
>
> (583-585)

This is the serpent as "unhomelike". But first it had flickered as an auditive image when Christabel "drew in her breath with a hissing sound" (459): the serpent thus originates within before it is reflected outward onto Geraldine. And the monstrous will keep on travelling, back and forth, until the last.

Christabel is thus caught up in the spell of a nightmarish mirror, a spell from which she proves unable to break free because she is only, so to speak, half visionary: though she can meet the Other in her raid into the forest and see into the Other's secret reptilian identity, she falls short of recognizing that reptilian as her own, persisting as she does to repudiate it as monstrous, and therefore, unlike the Ancient Mariner, excluding all possibility of coming to terms with it.

We may be here touching upon the true ethics of Coleridge's poem, an ethics to which the traditional notions of "good" and "evil" are irrelevant. For Geraldine is neither good nor evil: she is the lawless Real, more precisely that Real which is internal to the subject but from which the subject's consciousness has become estranged, keeping him or her paralysed, locked up in neurotic conflict. Ethics, in such perspective, is a task of recognition and integration: such process as has been beautifully formulated in a terse statement of Freud I would like to introduce finally, because it seems to me illuminating to the myth of **Christabel**: *"Wo es war, soll Ich werden,"* "Where id was, there ego shall be" (XXII, 80) or, better (in a literal rendering of Freud's utterance), "Where It was, there I shall be," which means that in the field of the Real ("It"), that is to say of inner reality, the subject ("I") should feel at home. In other words, I should recognize the otherness of my desire, whatever it may be, as my own: where It (Geraldine) was, in the

night forest, I (Christabel) should come at last. Christabel is thus called to an appointment with the Real: a Real that offers itself to her grasp in a crucial but privileged moment of being.

But Christabel misses the encounter, being too weak to integrate that reality and, thereby, unable to mediate it in terms of language—which would be the only way to humanize it: to master it or to transform it through sublimation. This incapacity appears in the myth, in terms of witchcraft, in the guise of the "spell" (of the "ligature," in the technical term of witchcraft) that ties up Christabel's tongue and prevents her from "telling" anything concerning the nature of the "lady strange" who thus remains monstrous because she is not symbolized by Christabel's speech and has thus no existence in the world of language. Ironically then, Christabel believes that Geraldine's monstrousness is "lord of [her] utterance" (268), in other words causes her incapacity to speak, whereas it is indeed her incapacity to speak which generates, or at least maintains, Geraldine's monstrousness. For not only does Christabel deny her desire all access to language, but she uses language as a means to obliterate it when she finally calls on her father— here the symbolic Father whose function is to articulate the law—"That thou this woman send away" (617). In this speech act Christabel behaves indeed—surprising as the parallel may seem at first sight—very much like Urizen whose strategy is to speak the wilderness and its energy out of existence. Like Blake's fierce god striving "in battles dire / In unseen conflictions with shapes / Bred from his forsaken wilderness" (*The Book of Urizen,* Pl. 20, 49-51), "The lovely lady Christabel" uses language as a means of repression and of self-alienation. She widens the gap between the symbolic and the Real, she confirms the estrangement of speech from desire.

The story told by **Christabel** is of a missed encounter, and its myth that of a failing self-integration—which may throw light after all on the "true ending" and thereby on the problematic status of the poem. Left out unspoken and unspeakable in the field of an impossible Real, left unresolved in the fantastic play of her metamorphoses between beauty and horror, Geraldine will keep on pressing on the edges of the forest and haunting Christabel's nights: for dismissing a ghost without understanding it, is condemning oneself to live in anxiety and in the expectancy of its returns. The outcome of the **Christabel** myth is thus the ghost's interminable recurrence, the endlessness of a haunting in a poem, therefore, that has no real closure because the myth it projects finds no solution, so that the supposedly "unfinished" text has its proper significance as an interminable haunting. And in the uncanny experience, we, readers, are made to participate as we expect—and imaginatively create—the ghost-Parts of this extraordinary poem that keeps haunting us.

For **Christabel,** while it represents in the persona of the heroine a psychical failure, is as a text a poetic triumph in the representation of that failure and of the dim struggle that precedes it. **Christabel** is probably the masterpiece of Coleridge's exploration of what he was to call, in **Biographia Literaria** (II, 121), "the twilight realms of consciousness," the borderline between "I" and "It," between, as post-Freudian readers the ego and the id, namely the space of the Uncanny where the subject may meet, at times, his own secret desire. Coleridge's poetic triumph is in the inscription of that uncanny space and in its power to involve the reader in it, to put him, in the reading experience, in a position to encounter his own unrecognized desire.

And in this sense the poem is also, implicitly, a statement on the essence of poetic communication and a beautiful lesson on poetic reading: a lesson whose point is obliquely made through a special irony generated by the projection of the poet within the poem in the person of "Bracy the bard" (424). The bard, as he tells his (so called) vision of the "bright green snake" stifling the gentle dove in the night forest, in a fairly long passage of Part II (526-563), actually repeats the scenario of the overture, while degrading its magical language, its subtle atmosphere of strangeness and its incantatory rhythms into the stock-phrases of a fairly conventional rhetoric, and, thus, while turning the fascinating ambiguity of the stranger into the plain horror of the serpent, clearly and crudely presented as an allegory of evil.

In this allegorizing and moralizing self-parody, Coleridge's text is no doubt ironically projecting a counter-image of itself (this is what I am not, it says) and thereby, as well, a counter-model of the reader. This moralizing reader is represented (in the person and the speech of Bracy) in order to be excluded and to leave room for another kind of reader: a creative reader who cannot be represented since he is at work, as co-creator, in the process of reading. Such reader will fully respond to the monstrous beauty of the stranger in which he is invited to recognize—and enjoy—the dangerous beauty of his own desire.

Works Cited

Coleridge, Samuel Taylor, *The Poetical Works . . .* [*The Poetical Works of Samuel Taylor Coleridge*], ed. Ernest Hartley Coleridge (1912).

———, *Biographia Literaria,* ed. J. Shawcross, 2 vols. (1907).

———, *Collected Letters . . .* [*Collected Letters of Samuel Taylor Coleridge*], ed. Earl Leslie Griggs, 6 vols. (1956-1971).

Freud, Sigmund, *The Standard Edition of the Complete Psychological Works . . .* [*The Standard Edition of the Complete Psychological Works of Sigmund Freud*], trans. James Stratchey, 24 vols. (1964).

Gillman, James, *The Life of Samuel Taylor Coleridge* (1838).

Lacan, Jacques, *Le Séminaire, Livre XI: les quatre concepts fondamentaux de la psychanalyse* (1973).

Wordsworth, Dorothy, *Journals of . . .* [*Journals of Dorothy Wordsworth*], ed. Helen Darbishire (1958).

Anya Taylor (essay date autumn 2002)

SOURCE: Taylor, Anya. "Coleridge's 'Christabel' and the Phantom Soul." *Studies in English Literature, 1500-1900* 42, no. 4 (autumn 2002): 707-30.

[*In the following essay, Taylor examines Coleridge's depictions of feminine identity in "Christabel."*]

"Christabel" is Samuel Taylor Coleridge's longest poem, his least revised, the most satisfying to himself as its preface indicates, and his most troubling to readers. It is a poem that can drive readers "mad" or make them feel "stupid."[1] From its opening—"Tu-whit!—tu-whoo!"—its lulling, almost lobotomized repetitions—"Is the night chilly and dark? / The night is chilly but not dark"[2]—its shifting narrative voices, and its metrical hesitations and forward rushes, it lures listeners into its twilight.[3] Coleridge's opening section does to listeners what Geraldine does to Christabel: leaves them anxious and ungrounded. Critic after critic has tossed interpretations into the poem's "Dark fluxion, all unfixable by thought."[4] Each interpretation seems to work as well as the next, even if the interpretations are contradictory. Some see the heroine Christabel initiated into love; some see her as a more or less innocent Eve falling into the snares of a demon from preternatural realms or from Satan;[5] some see the poem as having no meaning besides the complex contradictions of language and voice,[6] as a Blakean examination of divided states of body and soul,[7] as a dream or many dreams with condensed or displaced images,[8] even as a meditation on Jean-Jacques Rousseau.[9] William Hazlitt called the poem "Obscene"; Tom Moore thought its gaps showed incompetence.[10] How do we cope with this tumult of uncertainty?

As one more reader transfixed like "a three year's child"[11] by the rhythms of this disturbing poem, I wish to see Coleridge's deliberate (and perhaps even gleeful) construction of mystery in **"Christabel"** in the context of his wider philosophical and psychological investigations. The poem can be seen as a thought-experiment, enacting ideas that he elaborates in other poems and in prose writings. To set **"Christabel"** in the context of these ideas is not to thin out its maddening density, but to reduce its isolation.[12] As a thought-experiment, a germ of future thought, **"Christabel"** participates in Coleridge's continuing work on the development of the human person, on how selves are made and lost. The poem narrates incidents in the emotional life of a young woman; it shows her acting and being acted upon; its segments—written at different times—circle backwards to address questions that had been left unanswered. The poem, part of Coleridge's lifelong meditation on the vulnerabilities of will and agency, is in many ways a female version of **"The Rime of the Ancient Mariner."**

Some of Coleridge's concerns emerging early and taking different emphases throughout his life provide an encircling context to help explain the purposes of **"Christabel."**

1) The first element of the context that bears on **"Christabel"** is Coleridge's belief in the necessity of preserving a distinction between persons and things at a time when human beings were increasingly tabulated as numbers, averages, and groups. Coleridge argued against the use of a vocabulary that would reduce persons to things to be used, means to an end. Fully aware that persons are not always coherent to others or to themselves, that persons fragment and lose control, and that persons allow themselves to be used as things as their dependencies require, Coleridge advocates in different ways at different times the sacred distinction between persons and things;[13] the necessity of not using others as things;[14] or not letting oneself be used by abdicating the will.[15]

2) A second context for gaining perspective on **"Christabel"** is Coleridge's interest in the interplay of souls and bodies, spirits and selves, in metamorphoses that merge substances. Such a flow of identities is familiar to contemporary American filmgoers who have watched the fusion of bodies and souls in Steve Martin and Lily Tomlin's "All of Me," but in Coleridge's day this interplay also had mesmerizing possibilities; ghosts, revenants, and diabolic possession were common superstitions, the topics of early anthropological research, and frequent invaders of dreams. Coleridge's plan to publish **"Christabel"** with an essay on the "Praeternatural" may have aimed to justify his use of such spiritualistic traditions to render human emotions.[16] For Coleridge such porous perimeters can be intimate, as when he writes his young friend Thomas Allsop "'we will exchange souls'";[17] at other instances they are frightening, as when he describes "the absence of a Self . . . the want or torpor of Will" that is the "mortal Sickness" of his son Hartley (**CL** [*Collected Letters of Samuel Taylor Coleridge*] 5:232). In his late *Opus Maximum* he finds the word for a soul that evaporates for want of a connection with others: this is "the phantom soul" of my title.[18]

3) Related to the two previous contexts is the biographical reality that one of the most influential and brilliant men of the romantic age saw himself as weak and empty and that he proliferated images for his own absence of personhood. One of the most famous appears in a letter to Robert Southey from 1803, wherein he confesses, "A sense of weakness—a haunting sense, that I was an herbaceous Plant, as large as a large Tree, with a Trunk of the same Girth, & Branches as large & shadowing—but with *pith within* the Trunk, not heart of Wood / —that I had *power* not *strength*—an involuntary Imposter—that I had no real Genius, no real Depth / — / This on my honor is as fair a statement of my habitual Haunting, as I could give before the Tribunal of Heaven / How it arose in me, I have but lately discovered / —Still it works within me / but only as a Disease, the cause & meaning of which I know" (**CL** 2:959). Watching himself experience this inner absence, he plays with botanical metaphors to amuse Southey with the spectacle of his insignificance.[19]

4) These fluctuations of power and weakness Coleridge often formulates in terms of gender. In **"To W. Wordsworth (1807),"** Coleridge calls William Wordsworth "Strong in thyself, and powerful to give strength" (p. 392, line 109), and describes himself as "passive" (p. 392, line 102) and "absorb'd" (p. 392, line 118). Marlon B. Ross shows that Coleridge, abased before Wordsworth's masculinity, "assumes a 'feminine' position in order to attain a distinctively 'masculine triumph.'"[20] a needy self-abasement that Donald H. Reiman explores as a continuation of Coleridge's adoring and resentful relation to his older brothers.[21] In a positive sense, Coleridge aspires to the androgyny that he finds in Shakespeare rather than to the masculine single-mindedness of Wordsworth, though Diane Long Hoeveler sees the androgyny in **"Christabel"** as a negative force.[22] In part because of his sense of himself as yielding, Coleridge is engrossed in the lives and feelings of his many women friends, who by nature or nurture must learn to yield; these affinities come to the surface in **"Christabel."**

5) Coleridge's search for "the cause and meaning" of feelings of emptiness takes him deep into child psychology. Why do some children develop a strong identity and others wither and collapse at the slightest trauma? While notes from 1796 already suggest a project on infants and infancy,[23] his fullest analysis of infant selfhood comes late in the 1820s, when he dictates to Joseph Henry Green his great final statement the *Opus Maximum.* In fragment 2 of the *Opus Maximum,* he examines mother and child bonding and argues that the nursing child who gazes at its mother's face does not gaze at a mirror but at an Other, whom the child learns to love and subsequently to leave.[24] A crisis of some kind occurs to startle the child into a separate identity: "The child now learns its own alterity, and sooner or later, as if some sudden crisis had taken

place in its nature, it forgets hence forward to speak of itself by imitation, that is, by the name which it had caught from without. It becomes a person; it is and speaks of itself as 'I,' and from that moment it has acquired what in the following stages it may quarrel with, what it may loosen and deform, but can never eradicate,—a sense of an alterity in itself, which no eye can see, neither his own nor others" (*OM* [*Opus Maximum*], p. 132).[25] If this bonding or the crisis that disconnects it does not occur, the child grows into a thing grasping after a world of things that will always recede. He or she becomes the "Mad Narcissus" (*OM*, p. 104) of Coleridge's age and of our own. The "Mad Narcissus" is the active side of "The Phantom Soul." Coleridge's scrutiny of early infant learning is revolutionary, 120 years in advance of John Bowlby and D. W. Winnicott. His interest in the formation of infant identity may inform the thought-experiment of the poem "Christabel" with its insistence on the girl's motherlessness, need, and vulnerability.

6) A last element of the context for "Christabel" is also related to the previous ones: it is Coleridge's lament that the yearnings that impel men and women cannot be satisfied. They lead to a chasm that he calls "self-insufficingness."[26] The hunger for love cannot be adequately returned in this world and so provokes imaginings of unearthly love. Yearning, craving, hunger, and need come increasingly to explain both loneliness and the aspiration to spiritual life; this "want" spreads through "Christabel" and many later poems.[27] In his 1826 essay "On the Passions," Coleridge specifically relates this hunger to puberty; he plans to quote from *King John*, from the Greek tragedians, from Dante, Chaucer, Shakespeare, and Ben Jonson to "prove Grief to be a Hunger of the Soul."[28]

These ideas and many others, modified or recharged over time, converge on "Christabel," and take specific form in a "character" who is imagined as growing and ceasing to grow. Coleridge's principles surround the poem; the poem embodies the principles, and at the same time suggests their limitations. The poem and the principles that it embodies are rooted in Coleridge's affinity with women.[29]

II

These surrounding preoccupations will cast a "peculiar tint of yellow green" ("Dejection: An Ode," p. 351, line 29) on the poem upon which we are gazing. If we see "Christabel" as one specific experiment furthering Coleridge's work in distinguishing between persons and things, in showing how the souls or spirits of one person pass in and out of another person in the form of dream-like phantoms, in understanding selves as fluctuating between strength and weakness and male and female, in exploring infant psychology for its formative

moments of developing identity, and in yearning for an ever-receding completion, we will be hard put to find the joy and sexual rapture that many critics have seen in the poem. We will see it instead as a companion piece to "The Rime of the Ancient Mariner." Where "The Rime" encapsulates one form of Coleridge's obsession with will, action, guilt, penance, perpetual torment, and the glimmer of blessing, "Christabel" hides at its center a different sort of pain. The poem in all three of its segments spins inward to an intricate knot of need, yearning, self-obliteration, and merging. It struggles with nonbeing and emptiness, the "horrible solitude" and "self-inquietude" of the notebooks (*CN* [*The Notebooks of Samuel Taylor Coleridge*] 1, entry 257), the reaching outward of the letters, the analysis of human development in the *Opus Maximum*. It catches in rhythms a deep and mournful emotion that "must pine" in words, struggling to escape (*CN* 2, entry 2998). Coleridge places this almost incommunicable emotion in the hidden life of a young woman.

Readers who find joy and exhilaration in sexual initiation concentrate on part 1, lines 230-64. They see a young woman on the verge of puberty venturing forth, defying her father, his walls, his guards, his rules, and his morbidity, acting on her own, inviting a young and unknown woman hospitably to her castle chamber, and making all the moves that will accomplish her own suddenly upsurging sexual desires. I think that we would all agree that these are the occurrences in the first part of the poem from lines 23-225. Susan Luther calls Christabel's "martyrdom" "the psychological 'death' which she must undergo in order to experience the 'life' of mature adult emotional functioning." Jonas Spatz emphasizes the importance of the "sexual maturation" as the basis of love and a happy marriage. H. W. Piper finds "enlightenment and joy as well as suffering"; John Beer also affirms a positive fulfillment in sexual initiation.[30] Camille Paglia exults in the "erection" of female power in the poem as a whole and throughout Coleridge's libidinous work.[31] These interpretations focus on the moment of entry, the initiation, the "liminality" of the narrative.[32]

It is certainly true that Christabel assertively wills her own adventure up to line 230. She leaves the castle at midnight of her own will. She is not prevented by guards or nurses from leaving the walls and going alone into a deep forest. She is left alone to do as she wishes; no one notices her absence or cares for her, despite the tag "whom her father loves so well" (line 24). She may or may not have a fiancé for whom she prays. The mysterious glittering female Geraldine, who moans and arises from the other side of the oak, may be a projection from a dream, an aspect of Christabel's personality, a witch, a young victim of gang rape, a specter of nature and fertility. Christabel actively courts Geraldine and invites, leads, and even carries her over the threshold as if she were her bride, saving her from the taboos that guard the entrances to the castle, determined to hold onto this one potential companion. Christabel moves in stealth, urging Geraldine to secrecy, and evades the mastiff bitch, the warning flames, and her father's closed door. She intoxicates her guest with wine made by her dead mother, softening her up for whatever purposes she intends. This is the opening, the crossing of the threshold and return over the threshold. It seems to promise release.

But the effects of this initiation undercut any hope of joy. The silencing and transformation in lines 265-78 of part 1; in the conclusion to part 1; in part 2, lines 381-92, 451-74, 589-635; and in the conclusion to part 2 constitute the Ovidian and Dantean metamorphoses of the poem. Like Ovid's tale of Philomela and Dante's description in canto 25 of the *Inferno* of the thieves absorbing each other's substance and being,[33] these sections show one person being absorbed and obliterated by another and then made to bear the imprint of the inner life of the other. The sexuality of the event is peripheral; it is one image for many kinds of intersubjective exchange and transformation. What occurs is a loss of self, from which there is no escape because there remains no one inside to cry out "from the inmost" (*CN* 2, entry 3353).

Coleridge is deliberate in presenting what he later calls "an extremely subtle and difficult" idea.[34] Once inside her bedroom, the girl's adventurous will seems to shrivel, whereas the visitor's will swells to overpower it. Geraldine struggles with the dead mother's hovering spirit for control of the body or soul of Christabel. Shifting her voice into a hollow reverberant supernatural vehicle, Geraldine intones:

> "Off, woman, off! this hour is mine—
> Though thou her guardian spirit be,
> Off, woman, off! 'tis given to me."
>
> (lines 211-3)

Geraldine, a ventriloquist or improvisatrice, assumes numerous voices, sighing in sweet weakness, speaking to spirits, summoning powers, vibrating magical force. Her different voices multiply while Christabel's go mute. Geraldine swells up and Christabel becomes the shell that two women—the bodiless mother and the excessively embodied love-object—try to enter. This exchange of power occurs by the means of commands; through the sight of flesh, variously described as old, withered, reptilian; through physical touch; through the spoken incantation; through an unspoken but implied sexual act; through lying beside each other asleep or just before sleep. Jack Stillinger shows that the variants in this otherwise quite stable text work to smudge these shocking details.[35]

While the aftermath of this exchange of power has sometimes been read positively, as a successful recap-

turing of the lost mother, the recuperation of neglected infancy, or a bland peace following initiation into mature sexuality, in my view the descriptions point to a sinister overtaking: the resigned obedience ("So let it be!" [line 235]) as she strips down to "her loveliness" (line 238); the agitated features that give no hint of the "many thoughts mov[ing] to and fro" (line 240) within her mind; the silent watching of the woman dropping her dress to the floor, revealing a bosom so horrific as to be beyond words; the silence as her naked body is pressed close to Geraldine's naked body, pressing her side (is it scaly, withered, prematurely old?) against her own side; the stillness as the spell is uttered and takes effect word by word (lines 267-8). One of the narrative voices closely watches the girl in the aftermath of this invasion. In stops and starts, hesitations and retractions, the narrator imagines what feelings may be stirring within the girl's head:

> With open eyes (ah woe is me!)
> Asleep, and dreaming fearfully,
> Fearfully dreaming, yet, I wis,
> Dreaming that alone, which is—
> O sorrow and shame! Can this be she,
> The lady, who knelt at the old oak tree?
>
> (lines 292-7)

Though we might see the fearfully dreaming girl as resting in satiety after finding the lost mother whom she had yearned for, we might also see this dreaming body ("ah woe is me! . . . O sorrow and shame!") as an altered being—"Can this be she"?—and in my negative reading, a broken being. For Christabel appears dazed like a prisoner stumbling from a torture chamber. So powerful is this moment of bewildered emergence that Percy Bysshe Shelley may have modeled on it his depiction of Beatrice Cenci, after the night when her father does or does not rape her, stumbling, speaking haltingly, shifting from topic to topic without her customary rhetorical elegance:

> *Beatrice Cenci.* No, I am dead! These putrefying limbs
> Shut round and sepulchre the panting soul
> Which would burst forth into the wandering air![36]

It was Geraldine's side, after all, that caused Shelley "to . . . run shrieking from the room because he 'suddenly thought of a woman he had heard of who had eyes instead of nipples, which, taking hold of his mind, horrified him.'"[37] The aftermath of ambiguous sexual initiation in **"Christabel"** may have suggested to Shelley a way to imply the breaking of a vital womanly spirit without stating it.[38]

With the silencing of Christabel's will, power surges inside Geraldine; the narrator by reflection adopts a more decisive voice:

> And lo! the worker of these harms,
> That holds the maiden in her arms,

Seems to slumber still and mild,
As a mother with her child.

A star hath set, a star hath risen,
O Geraldine! since arms of thine
Have been the lovely lady's prison.
O Geraldine! one hour was thine—
Thou'st had thy will!

(lines 298-306)

The narrator records that Geraldine is released, fulfilled, and rampant in will: "Thou'st had thy will!" echoes the phrase "The Marinere hath his will" from the **"Rime,"** when the mariner's will overpowers the wedding guest's will and reduces him to a "three year's child" (**"The Rime of the Ancient Mariner [1798],"** lines 19-20).

For Christabel, the child forced to listen to the spell and feel the sexual body, there seems to be no one left inside. The naked body, the blinking eyes, the vague smile, the leaking tears, the unquiet movements, and the baffled acquiescence suggest the draining out of selfhood from the empty shell:

And see! the lady Christabel
Gathers herself from out her trance;
Her limbs relax, her countenance
Grows sad and soft; the smooth thin lids
Close o'er her eyes; and tears she sheds—
Large tears that leave the lashes bright!
And oft the while she seems to smile
As infants at a sudden light!

(lines 311-8)

These behaviors suggest that the girl's will has been obliterated. The narrator tries to reassure us—"No doubt, she hath a vision sweet" (line 326)—and projects upon her blankness the faith "That saints will aid if men will call: / For the blue sky bends over all!" (lines 330-1). For some readers this hope for benevolence reassures, but for others it seems as ironic as **"The Rime"**'s "He prayeth best who loveth best / All things both great and small" (lines 647-8) or "Tintern Abbey"'s "Nature never did betray / The heart that loved her" (lines 122-3). The sky will still be blue whether the child suffers or not. Suspended in our judgments, we watch a girl lose inward drive and personal integrity, her boundaries broached and blurred. Only Bard Bracy will notice or care.

In May 1798, Coleridge's poem initially ended here as the girl awakens, but the meaning of what he had composed haunted him through the next fourteen months, some of which time he spent in Germany and some on a farm in Sockburn near Durham falling in love with a woman who was not his wife. During this interlude he mused on how his poem was to unfurl. He feared it would disgust people (*CL* 1:545), and yet he struggled to complete it, finally drinking so much wine, as he

writes Josiah Wedgwood, that his "verse making faculties returned" (*CL* 1:643). The happy result of this bibulous evening at a neighboring clergyman's house is part 2 of **"Christabel."**

Part 2 may be read as answering the questions roused by part 1: What is the cause of this child's neediness, susceptibility, and collapse? Why had she no will to resist, or, if she wanted and sought the seduction, to thrive in its release? Why does she cease to be an active agent or person? Once again **"Christabel"** pursues questions about agency that are asked hypothetically in **"The Rime of the Ancient Mariner"** in a different way: did the Mariner act with full intentional agency when he suddenly shot the albatross or did this "manly" act come from some unconscious impulse of perverse and unwilled cruelty? So, too, one asks if his repeated telling of his tale is willed or compulsive, and, if compulsive, from where the compulsion comes. In the case of Christabel, she can no longer speak of her present condition or her past desire, and her personal agency is more compromised than his.

In part 2 Coleridge shifts into a different voice, more assured that an evil had indeed occurred in the last section of part 1. He explains the causes of the girl's neediness by moving back a generation to imagine the formative family patterns. Christabel's mother died in childbirth. The infant has no known nurse or female relative to substitute for the mother.[39] Christabel's father began mourning his wife at the moment of Christabel's birth with lugubrious rituals of long, slow bells tolling obsessively day in and day out. He sequestered himself in his rooms, his halls were silent, his retinue only occasionally summoned. We could suppose that he hardly knew his child. Beneath this fixated mourning for his wife was an even more intense reason for his unavailability to his child: persistent mourning for a broken friendship, passionate in its absorption, with a male friend. Here, too, the feelings were dammed up by this taboo.[40] In part 2 of the poem we see Sir Leoline's feverish excitement about using Geraldine to reawaken his friendship with Sir Roland, her putative father, his determination to hunt down Geraldine's tormentors and "dislodge their reptile souls / From the bodies and forms of men" (lines 442-3; a reminder of the interfusion of souls and bodies that has just occurred in his daughter's bedroom and will recur in a few lines), and his rage at his own daughter for her appearance, her strange facial twitches, her garbled speech, her unseemly hisses, her embarrassing lack of graciousness to his new young friend, who represents his conduit to past happiness. We see him quickly abandon his daughter in her mute anguish, and take up her seducer and silencer as both his new daughter and his new lady. As an old man, Coleridge claims that Sir Leoline's feelings are paternal and not sexual (*TT* [*Table Talk*] 1, 494 n. 7), though he may be forgetting the phrases his earlier wild self included in the poem:

> And now the tears were on his face,
> And fondly in his arms he took
> Fair Geraldine, who met the embrace,
> Prolonging it with joyous look.

> (lines 447-50)

Sir Leoline's rage, his inappropriate sexual attraction to his daughter's "companion," his fierce rejection of his motherless daughter, point to his own self-absorption.

For Christabel's part this final abandonment erases her. Numerous details suggest the loss of personal identity within:

> She shrunk and shuddered, and saw again—
> (Ah, woe is me! Was it for thee,
> Thou gentle maid! such sights to see?)

> (lines 454-6)

So blank is she that in an instant her being takes the imprint of Geraldine's shrunken snake eyes (lines 583-7):

> But Christabel in dizzy trance
> Stumbling on the unsteady ground
> Shuddering aloud, with a hissing sound.

> (lines 589-91)

She exchanges faces and voices with her dominator:

> The maid, alas! her thoughts are gone,
> She nothing sees—no sight but one!
> The maid, devoid of guile and sin,
> I know not how, in fearful wise,
> So deeply had she drunken in
> That look, those shrunken serpent eyes,
> That all her features were resigned
> To this sole image in her mind:
> And passively did imitate
> That look of dull and treacherous hate!

> (lines 597-606)

Out of her vacancy of person and in defiance of Geraldine's spell, she summons a plea, in full suppliant's posture, gripping her father's knees—"'By my mother's soul do I entreat / That thou this woman send away!'" (lines 616-7). But this spark of will quickly subsides. Her changed look, taking over Geraldine's inner nature, her staggering walk, her inability to speak, explain herself, or protest, and her dazed and blank appearance attest to a childhood of terror.[41] Her father's anger is intense enough to be admonished by the narrator (lines 634-5).

In addition to his cold, narcissistic rage, Sir Leoline tyrannizes his court and creates in it a universe of death, censoring and silencing others. He censors the bard whose dream inspires him to help Christabel, forbidding him to travel around the countryside singing the symbolic tale that will tell the truth. This is the third and most outward layer of silencing in the poem, and one that makes Christabel a political prisoner as well as a "prisoner of childhood" (to cite Alice Miller's study of the needy offspring of narcissists[42]). For Christabel there is no exit from her hollowed-out core; either there is no one inside (consistent with children lacking nurture from birth and adopting false selves to cover this gap) or her enforced silence suffocates her. A motherless daughter with a grieving and distant father and no mentioned nurse surely sets up an experiment for any psychologist: what can happen to a girl with so little support and tenderness? Coleridge's thought-experiment catches his subject at the moment of sudden sexual quest. Her impulse misfires, and she is absorbed by the (M)other she has lured to her bed.

In the midsection of the poem, then, a transfer of power seems to occur; one young woman absorbs another, eradicates her will and her speech, deprives her of the imaginary protective spirit of her mother and the fragile loyalty of her father, and fills her with the underside of her own vicious features. A negative reading of this passage—that Christabel is not purring with sexual well-being or infantile reunion with the lost mother but is emptied out by a more wide-ranging invasion of her inward fountain of agency—is reinforced by the parallels between this central section of the poem and **"The Three Graves,"** written in the early spring of 1798 during the writing of the first part of **"Christabel."** **"The Three Graves,"** a 537-line poem in quatrains that fizzles out in mockery, explores some of the same ground as **"Christabel"**: women's passions and jealousies, the overpowering of a younger woman by an older one, and the incapacitation of one young woman by force of magic and will. Coleridge believes that the merits of **"The Three Graves,"** "if any, are exclusively psychological." Summarizing the plot in his preface to the poem, he says that "[the mother] practiced every art, both of endearment and of calumny, to transfer [the] affections [of her future son-in-law] from her daughter to herself." When he rejected her, she "fell on her knees, and in a loud voice that approached to a scream, she prayed for a curse both on him and on her own child" (p. 153). The phrases, "Away, Away!" (line 76) and "a deadly leer of hate" (line 81), and reactions to the spell such as silence, paralysis, and the inability to weep, link the mother's breaking of the daughter's will in **"The Three Graves"** with Geraldine's similar power over Christabel. As early as 1796 in **"The Destiny of Nations"** Coleridge uses some of the phrases describing blankness and self-loss for Joan of Arc (pp. 111-25, 118-9, lines 253-77), but these phrases apply to Joan of Arc's sorrow at seeing a family in desperate poverty. **"The Three Graves"** is the experimental ground for the disturbing elements in **"Christabel"**: the overpowering of another through passionate magical language and through the skin-penetrating vibrations of prohibited desires.[43] **"The Three Graves"** applies to women's passions Coleridge's study of Obeah witchcraft and Otaheitan Indian rites,[44] and his frequent re-readings in Greek of the powerful outcries of Electra and Antigone. **"Christabel"** climaxes these earlier representations of female passions and in turn prepares for later poems on jealousy and rage, such as **"Alice du Clos"** and **"Not at Home,"** that explore the smothering weight of unbearable emotion, the "dark fluxion" of Coleridge's death bed poem **"Self-Knowledge"** ("all unfixable by thought, / A phantom dim of past and future wrought" [pp. 489-90, 490, lines 7-8]).

Four years after the completion of part 2 (1804), Coleridge was still brooding about the meaning of his poem. In yet another new voice he added a coda to suggest by an elusive analogy that parental neglect and rage are not phenomena limited to the middle ages, but continue into the early nineteenth century, even among ostensibly well-meaning parents. The father of the coda speaks too much rather than too little, and this child, too, is left speechless, but at a younger age. The father's wounding words come from some inexplicable tangle of his own thwarted emotions, crashing in on his child in the midst of the child's whirling delight. A modern Sir Leoline, this father of the coda can blight a child's growth even in an enlightened time when children's psyches were known to be impressionable. In regard to the observation of child development, Coleridge was himself one of the most enlightened, and yet in this coda he obliquely confessed uncontrollable rage at his first-born son.[45]

The disturbing power of **"Christabel"** may come in part from its layers of grief. This grief works on many levels: the motherless daughter desperate for any touch of kindness; the widower secluded in mourning and coldly, furiously unavailable to his child, mourning in addition a severed intimacy with a male friend, a severance that has long choked him with frustration. Coleridge puts this *"wanting, the craving* of Grief," this "wasting and marasmus of Grief" (*SW&F* [*Shorter Works and Fragments*] 2, 1451) in the character of a girl who reaches puberty without having bonded with a parent or parent substitute; he expands it into a past generation in part 2 and applies it in the coda to a domestic personal situation in the present. The poem circles around obsessively unresolved loss that forces either inert or seething passivity. While **"The Rime of the Ancient Mariner"** also circles obsessively around a site of pain and guilt, **"Christabel"** focuses on what we now realize are difficult transitions in the personal development of young women, where what is done *to* them often feels like their own fault,[46] where they retreat from personhood into paralysis.[47] No wonder Algernon Charles Swinburne calls Coleridge's verse

"womanly rather than effeminate" (quoted in Beer, *Poems,* p. 505). **"Christabel"** explores a moral dimension that draws on Coleridge's horror of using other persons as things. Geraldine uses Christabel as a means to approach her father, if any such inner motivation can be ascribed to her; Sir Leoline uses Geraldine to recapture his past life and discards his daughter as now useless. Both violate Coleridge's fundamental principle: "Reverence the Individuality of your Friend" (*SW&F* 2:1335-7, 1335), or, less elegantly as in *The Friend,* "the reverence which [each person] owes to the presence of Humanity in the person of his Neighbour" (*CW,* 4.2:44).

III

In defending **"Christabel"** from the "rude breezes of disapprobation" stirred up by the 1816 volume, George Felton Mathew asks: "And shall it be considered unlawful for Coleridge to pay his addresses to more than one muse? or for the children of his imagination to be not only sons, but daughters?"[48] Mathew implies that the womanliness of the poem might make a difference in the appreciation of it. If seen as a study of abandonment and neglect in a girl child, and her susceptibility to being used by a dominant person, the poem might meet wider approval. Although Coleridge is one of the six male poets of the romantic era who have long monopolized the canon, he had many women friends, especially pairs of sisters, such as the Evanses, the Frickers, the Hutchinsons, the Brents, and the Gillmans; he encouraged women writers such as Mary Robinson, included sonnets by Charlotte Smith in a 1796 consolatory volume, admired Mary Wollstonecraft and Jane Austen, watched the too somber play of baby Mary Godwin, and late in life advised his younger friends about the necessity in marriage of not using the partner as a thing for one's own gratification. Instead of asking why Coleridge did not finish **"Christabel,"** we should ask how he knows as much as he does about the silencing of young women, anticipating what psychologists have discovered only since 1980 about girls' desires and repressions as they approach puberty, which Coleridge called "a distinct revolutionary Epoch in the human mind & body" (*CN* 1, entry 1637), when "sexual instincts begin to disquiet" the fourteen- or fifteen-year-old child. Just how unusual his discoveries are can be measured by the reactions of his manly critics, Hazlitt and Moore, who mock the poem's freakishness and titter nervously that Geraldine is a man in disguise. Rather, **"Christabel"** joins *Jane Eyre, Wuthering Heights,* and *Blithedale Romance* as studies of violent passions in women, the absorption of women's identities, and the potential collapse of their independent agency. All these girls are motherless, and Christabel's isolation is essential to Coleridge's experiment.

His knowledge may derive in part from his mother's degrading treatment of his sister Nancy, the only girl in the family of ten boys, five years older than Samuel.

New information about her fate emerges in James Engell's *The Early Family Letters*. Writing from India, the oldest brother John, helpless because of his distance from home, protests against their mother's sending Nancy off at age fourteen to sell ribbons. When Nancy was sent to work in Exeter, Coleridge was nine, away at Christ's Hospital, a ward of the institution. When Nancy died of consumption in 1791, Coleridge himself, as part of his mother's agreement with the school directors that he not come home for vacation, had not been brought home for ten years. There was no family mourning; each surviving brother locked away his grief in himself. Coleridge's sense of injustice for women may have been spurred by this banishment of his sister to a solitary and loveless exile and death.[49] His 1790-91 sonnet **"On Receiving an Account that His Only Sister's Death Was Inevitable"** (p. 11) expresses his sorrow. His sympathies for women were not just familial: while writing **"Christabel"** Coleridge was deeply concerned about the suicide of Dr. Joshua Toulmin's daughter, who, "in a melancholy derangement suffered herself to be swallowed up by the tide on the sea-coast between Sidmouth & Bere" (*CL* 1:407). Dorothy Wordsworth, too, may have fueled Coleridge's indignation at the uses made of young women. An orphan, Dorothy allowed herself to be absorbed into William's life, serving numerous functions for him. As she and Coleridge walked out in the moonlit nights, her emotions, what Meena Alexander describes as her "longing for the supportive love that she was robbed of," and her "terrible void of maternal loss,"[50] touched an answering pain in her companion Coleridge. Motherless at birth in 1797, Mary Godwin playing sadly in the house of the grieving William Godwin may also have stung Coleridge, who called the house and mingled children "catacombish" (*CL* 1:553). In her study of the ways that girls allow themselves to be turned into objects, Jessica Benjamin describes this self-loss in a formulation that could apply to Christabel: "When the self is felt to be buried or in chaos, powerless or destructive, penetration and mastery by the powerful one serves to ward off and express self-dissolution, to overcome abandonment."[51]

Where Wordsworth—in poems about mad mothers, lost daughters, and abandoned wives—watched women suffer,[52] Coleridge felt this crushing of the girl child from within as if it were his own. **"Christabel"** is the poem that recognizes this female pain, even as its author feels a correspondent vulnerability and emptiness as a man. Coleridge's own sense of stability teetered on the edge when Wordsworth without explanation rejected **"Christabel"** for volume two of the *Lyrical Ballads* of 1800. Life imitated Art as Wordsworth played Geraldine to Coleridge's Christabel. Coleridge, ecstatically completing his poem, strode over Helvellyn to place the beautiful object at Wordsworth's feet.[53] Dorothy Wordsworth's journal records his arrival on 29 August 1800, in "the still clear moonshine in the garden," the late

night reading of the poem, and the "pleasure" it gave on a later reading 5 October. The entries of 6 and 7 October are as cryptic as any of the difficult gaps in **"Christabel"**: "*Monday* [*6th*]. A rainy day. Coleridge intending to go but did not get off. We walked after dinner to Rydale. After tea read The Pedlar. Determined not to print **Christabel** with the LB. Tuesday [*7th*]. Coleridge went off at 11 o'clock."[54] The gaps between events, the absences, and silent departures mirror the suffocation of feeling within the poem itself.[55] The day after Coleridge left, Wordsworth began quickly transposing themes in **"Christabel"** into the poem **"Michael,"** to fill the gap at the end of the volume left by the withdrawal of **"Christabel."** Susan Eilenberg perceives how **"Michael"** shifts motifs in **"Christabel"** into a different register. She notes, for instance, that in both poems "the rival child displaces the true child from his secure place in the family, and the true child, abandoned, takes on the characteristics of the rival."[56] Wordsworth materializes the themes of **"Christabel"** in **"Michael,"** from spiritual possession into possession of property, from desire to inheritance, and in doing so enacts the very possession that the poems exchange, as the later poem appropriates and transforms the identity of the earlier poem.[57] In letters to friends, Coleridge tries to make light of Wordsworth's domination, so reminiscent of Geraldine's: he says that his "poem grew so long & in Wordsworth's opinion so impressive, that he rejected it from his volume as disproportionate both in size & merit, & as discordant in it's [sic] character" (*CL* 1:643); deep within, he felt that his career as a poet was over.

Despite Coleridge's seeming passivity to and collusion with Wordsworth's silencing of his poem (he helped copy **"Michael"** to send to press), Coleridge persisted in thinking about **"Christabel"** and in planning to expand it. He did not give up on it and changed very few lines.[58] Coleridge wrote Thomas Poole that he planned to publish it by itself, with "two Essays annexed to it, on the Praeternatural—and on Meter" (*CL* 1:707, 16 March 1801). By the time George Gordon, Lord Byron urged John Murray to publish it with **"Kubla Khan"** and **"Pains of Sleep"** in a twenty-three page volume of 1816, Coleridge is almost arrogant in defiance of critics, in marked contrast to the apologetic headnotes and anxious additions to **"The Rime of the Ancient Mariner"** and to **"Kubla Khan."** This poem, whatever people might think, especially after hearing Sir Walter Scott's metrically derivative "Lay of the Last Minstrel," came forth as a fountain, not as a leak in other men's tanks. And where the Ancient Mariner becomes an image of his own life as a wanderer and guilty talker, **"Christabel"** is an artwork apart, depicting the mysterious life of the Other. Standing in as the bewildered narrator, changing his voices, asking silly questions, gaping at human writhing and entrapment from different angles, wondering at the external evidence for the inward loss of force, he tries to enter the female world, to understand "someone the structure of whose experience is radically different from one's own."[59]

This essay centers the disturbing narrative **"Christabel"** in the context of Coleridge's works in other genres about the "forfeiture of Free-agency" (*CL* 5:252, to Thomas Allsop on 8 October 1822, concerning his son Hartley's disintegration). Christabel is a child brought up in gloomy vacancy who did not make the transition from *it* to *I* and thus did not learn to say *Thou*. She is a phantom soul. She demonstrates proleptically the formulation that Coleridge finds in his **Opus Maximum**: "A will that does not contain the power of opposing itself to another will is no will at all" (**OM**, p. 172). As Coleridge thinks about this vulnerability later in his life he finds it in people who are not technically motherless or parentless, but who in wealthy homes have been raised with things that reflect them, not loving faces and voices to connect with. To him there seem to be more and more phantom souls in the increasingly mechanistic world. **"Christabel"** is one of his first forays into the causes of this modern malaise.[60] The poem enunciates the silence of adolescent women, the passivity, punishment, paralysis, sense of guilt; it stands in counterpoint to its companion piece **"The Rime of the Ancient Mariner"** with its manly bloodthirstiness, guilty action, and loquacity. It demonstrates Coleridge's immersion in the depths of the sufferings of women, and his use of their life patterns to illustrate the violation of his ethical principles.

Notes

1. Karen Swann describes the reader's puzzlement: "'Christabel' contrives to have these alternatives redound on the reader, who continually feels mad or just stupid, unable to 'tell' how to characterize the verse at any given point" ("'Christabel': The Wandering Mother and the Enigma of Form," *SIR* [*Studies in Romanticism*] 23, 4 [Winter 1984]: 533-53, 545).

2. Samuel Taylor Coleridge, "Christabel," in *Poems*, ed. John Beer (London: Dent, 1993), pp. 260-78, 260, lines 3, 14-5. All further references to Coleridge's poetry will be to this edition and will be cited parenthetically in the text and in the endnotes.

3. In his preface, Coleridge insists on the originality of his poem and adds "that the metre of Christabel is not, properly speaking, irregular, though it may seem so from its being founded on a new principle: namely, that of counting in each line the accents, not the syllables. Though the latter may vary from seven to twelve, yet in each line the accents will be found to be only four. Nevertheless, this occasional variation in number of syllables is

not introduced wantonly, or for the mere ends of convenience, but in correspondence with some transition in the nature of the imagery or passion" (*The Complete Poetical Works of Samuel Taylor Coleridge,* ed. Ernest Hartley Coleridge [London: Oxford Univ. Press, 1912], p. 215). Marjorie Levinson suggests that the meter derives from Coleridge's close study of Greek meters, which he practices in his notebooks and marginalia (*The Romantic Fragment Poem: A Critique of a Form* [Chapel Hill: Univ. of North Carolina Press, 1986], pp. 77-96).

4. The poem "Self-Knowledge" from his last year recapitulates his lifelong questions: can one make oneself, what is one's own, can one know more than the "Dark fluxion, all unfixable by thought, / A phantom dim of past and future wrought / Vain sister of the worm" (pp. 489-90, 490, lines 7-9)?

5. Stuart Peterfreund discovers that Geraldine is "an anagram of *Dire Angel*" ("The Way of Immanence, Coleridge, and the Problem of Evil," *ELH* 55, 1 [Spring 1988]: 125-58, 143). Laurence Lockridge calls her bluntly "positive inexplicable evil" (*Coleridge the Moralist* [Ithaca: Cornell Univ. Press, 1977], p. 75).

6. Kathleen M. Wheeler, "Coleridge and Modern Critical Theory," in *Coleridge's Theory of Imagination Today,* ed. Christine Galant (New York: AMS Press, 1989), pp. 83-102, 90-2; Wheeler argues that Coleridge deconstructs meaning by "saturating the narrative voice with Henry Jamesian-type ambiguities, avowals, disavowals, questionings, uncertainties" (p. 90), by overlayering naïve and sophisticated narrative voices, by leaving open certain elements of the plot, by weaving stories inside stories, and by giving conflicting interpretations of the bard's dream (pp. 90-2).

7. Anthony John Harding, "Mythopoesis: The Unity of Christabel," in *Coleridge's Imagination: Essays in Memory of Peter Laver,* ed. Richard Gravil, Lucy Newlyn, and Nicholas Roe (Cambridge: Cambridge Univ. Press, 1985), pp. 207-17. But in "The Passions" in *Shorter Works and Fragments,* ed. H. J. Jackson and J. R. de J. Jackson (hereafter *SW&F*), vol. 11 of *The Collected Works of Samuel Taylor Coleridge,* ed. Kathleen Coburn (Princeton: Princeton Univ. Press, and London: Routledge and Kegan Paul, 1971-, hereafter *CW*), Coleridge argues that separating body and soul is "mischievous" (*SW&F*, bk. 2, p. 1421).

8. Swann sees all of the figures floating in and out of "the malady of hysteria, the womb whose vaporish fantasies were thought to block the hysteric's speech" ("'Christabel' and the Enigma of Form," *SIR* [*Studies in Romanticism*] 23, 4 [Winter 1984]:

533-53, 548). Swann's discovery of hysteria has important applications to Christabel's silence. But Claire Kahane defines hysteria as the repressed rage from having to reject the maternal body; since Christabel had never known her mother, she had nothing to reject and no bond to break (*Passions of the Voice: Hysteria, Narrative, and the Figure of the Speaking Woman, 1850-1915* [Baltimore: Johns Hopkins Univ. Press, 1995]).

9. Chris Rubinstein, "Rousseau and Coleridge: Another Look at Christabel," *Coleridge Bulletin* (Winter 1992): 9-14.

10. Coleridge's transitions, as H. J. Jackson has marvelously clarified, are "invisible, occurring in the blank spaces between sentences or stanzas. They conform to Coleridge's general preference for energy over matter in physical models of the universe and for mystery over evidence in the area of religious faith," a fine conceptualization of the "intangible powers," the subtle interconnections of thought, that characterize Coleridge's "method" ("Coleridge's Lessons in Transition: The 'Logic' of the 'Wildest Odes,'" in *Lessons of Romanticism: A Critical Companion,* ed. Thomas Pfau and Robert F. Gleckner (Durham: Duke Univ. Press, 1998), pp. 213-24, 220).

11. Coleridge, "The Rime of the Ancient Mariner (1798)," pp. 215-54, 216, line 19.

12. Tilottama Rajan suggests that "meaning" that is hidden in one work may be "made explicit somewhere else in the canon." The reader, adding his "supplement," "break[s] the hermeneutic circle at the level of the oeuvre, projecting into the individual text a set of meanings that it does not have in isolation, and perhaps even reversing the reading that emerges when the text is made its own context" (*The Supplement of Reading: Figures of Understanding in Romantic Theory and Practice* [Ithaca: Cornell Univ. Press, 1990], p. 26). In applying to "Christabel" themes and ideas that appear in Coleridge's own earlier and later writings I hope to bring to the surface meanings hidden in this one poem that are apparent elsewhere.

13. As in the 1811 essay "The Catholic Petition," in *Essays on His Times in "The Morning Post" and "The Courier,"* ed. David V. Erdman, *CW* vol. 3, bk. 3, p. 235; and in *Biographia Literaria,* ed. James Engell and W. Jackson Bate, *CW* vol. 7, bk. 1, p. 205.

14. As in his 1795 lecture on the slave trade, in *Lectures 1795 On Politics and Religion,* ed. Lewis Patton and Peter Mann, *CW* vol. 1, pp. 242-3; in *Lay Sermons,* ed. R. J. White, *CW* vol. 6, pp. 207, 218-20; and in *Constitution of Church and State,* ed. John Colmer, *CW* vol. 10, pp. 15-6.

15. As in *The Friend,* ed. Barbara E. Rooke, *CW* vol. 4, bk. 2, pp. 44, 71, 125. Other references to persons and things can be found in Anya Taylor, *Coleridge's Defense of the Human* (Columbus: Ohio State Univ. Press, 1986); Coleridge, *On Humanity,* ed. Taylor, vol. 2 of *Coleridge's Writings,* ed. Beer (London: Macmillan, 1994); and Taylor, "Coleridge on Persons in Dialogue," *MLQ* [*Modern Language Quarterly*] 50, 4 (December 1989): 357-74, and "Coleridge on Persons and Things," *ERR* [*European Romantic Review*] 1, 2 (Winter 1991): 163-80.

16. Beer explains that "the word 'preternatural' seems with him to carry a certain pejorative force, from which the word 'supernatural' is exempt, and it is not unlikely that he intended, when he wrote his poems, to distinguish between literature which simply made use of supernatural 'machinery' for the sake of sensationalism, and that which was concerned with the possible significance of extra-sensory phenomena as a revelation of the metaphysical" (*Coleridge the Visionary* [New York: Collier, 1962], p. 150).

17. *Collected Letters of Samuel Taylor Coleridge* (hereafter *CL*), ed. Earl Leslie Griggs (Oxford: Clarendon Press, 1971), 5:164.

18. Coleridge, *Opus Maximum,* ed. Thomas McFarland, with Nicholas Halmi, *CW* vol. 15, pp. 124-5, hereafter *OM.*

19. Later in life he continues to believe that his weakness is "a readiness to believe others my superiors and to surrender my own judgment to their's" (*CL* 5:231).

20. Marlon B. Ross writes, for instance, that "As the 'active' agent asserts its power by permeating the 'passive' medium, it also gives itself to that medium and becomes possessed by it" and "What Wordsworth joins, Coleridge subtly tears asunder" (*The Contours of Masculine Desire: Romanticism and the Rise of Women's Poetry* [New York: Oxford Univ. Press, 1989], pp. 93-108, 95, 101).

21. Donald H. Reiman, "Coleridge and the Art of Equivocation," *SIR* [*Studies in Romanticism*] 25, 3 (Fall 1986): 325-50.

22. Diane Long Hoeveler, *Romantic Androgyny: The Women Within* (University Park: Pennsylvania State Univ. Press, 1979), pp. 176-88. She finds that the poem "reveals a fear and hatred of women" and "his conscious and unconscious opinion of them as perverse, sexually voracious, predatory, and duplicitous" (p. 176). By contrast, Tim Fulford interprets Coleridge's androgyny as an impulse toward inclusiveness (*Romanticism and Masculinity: Gender, Politics, and Poetics in the*

Writings of Burke, Coleridge, Cobbett, Wordsworth, DeQuincey, and Hazlitt [Houndmills: Macmillan, 1999]).

23. *The Notebooks of Samuel Taylor Coleridge,* ed. Coburn (New York: Pantheon Books, 1957-61), vol. 1, entry 330; hereafter *CN.*

24. Madelon Sprengnether, *The Spectral Mother: Freud, Feminism, and Psychoanalysis* (Ithaca: Cornell Univ. Press, 1990) illuminates the power of the mother. Countering Sigmund Freud's attention to the father and the phallus, she turns to the biologism of the mother's body: "No longer an exile from the process of signification, the body of the (m)other may actually provide a new, and material, ground for understanding the play of language and desire" (p. 10). Sprengnether writes, "Whereas object relations theory stresses maternal presence (and plenitude) through the concept of mother-infant fusion, Jacques Lacan downplays the role of the biological mother to the point where she barely seems to exist in a corporeal sense" (p. 183). The recognition that the mother is a real body with a face and a breast, a being whose absence would be a deprivation, fulfills Coleridge's insights, and shows his connection to John Bowlby, D. W. Winnicott, and other Object Relations psychologists.

25. Here again Sprengnether helps to explain Coleridge's work on the loss of the mother and the crisis that forces identity. She writes, "the loss that precipitates the organization of a self is always implicitly the loss of a mother . . . The mother's body becomes that which is longed for yet cannot be appropriated, a representative of both home and not home, and hence, in Freud's terms, the site of the uncanny" ([ibid.] p. 9).

26. I discuss Coleridge's use of this term in "Romantic *Improvvisatori:* Coleridge, L. E. L., and the Difficulties of Loving," *PQ* [*Philological Quarterly*] 79, 4 (Fall 2000): 501-22.

27. David L. Clark writes of Schelling in a way that can be applied to Coleridge's "Christabel": "Primal craving is an important part of a more extensive rhetoric of affective states and borderline conditions (including melancholy)—in other words, a body language of 'flesh and blood'" ("Heidegger's Craving: Being-on-Schelling," *Diacritics* 27, 3 [Fall 1999]: 8-33, 17).

28. Coleridge, "On the Passions," in *SW&F* bk. 2, pp. 1438, 1451.

29. His capacity for friendship with women is in dispute. H. J. Jackson, "Coleridge's Women, or Girls, Girls, Girls Are Made to Love," *SIR* [*Studies in Romanticism*] 32, 4 (Winter 1993): 577-600, argues that he takes a dim view of female intelligence, while Reggie Watters, "Coleridge, Female Friendship, and 'Lines Written at Shurton Bars,'" *Coleridge Bulletin* (Spring 2000): 1-15, believes that he welcomes companionate love. Coleridge's observations of women are also noted in Taylor, "Coleridge, Wollstonecraft, and the Rights of Women," in *Coleridge's Visionary Languages: Essays in Honour of J. B. Beer,* ed. Fulford and Morton Paley (Cambridge: D. S. Brewer, 1993), pp. 83-98, and in Taylor, "Romantic *Improvvisatori.*"

30. Susan Luther, *Christabel as Dream-Reverie* (Romantic Reassessment: Salzburg Studies in English Literature 61. Salzburg: Institut für Englische Sprache und Literatur, Universität Salzburg, 1976), p. 11; Jonas Spatz, "The Mystery of Eros: Sexual Initiation in Coleridge's 'Christabel,'" *PMLA* 90, 1 (January 1975): 107-16, 109; H. W. Piper, "Nature and the Gothic in *Christabel,*" in *The Singing of Mount Abora: Coleridge's Use of Biblical Imagery and Natural Symbolism in Poetry and Philosophy* (Rutherford N.J.: Fairleigh Dickinson Univ. Press, 1987), pp. 74-84, 78; Coleridge, *Poems,* ed. Beer, pp. 256-9.

31. Camille Paglia, *Sexual Personae: Art and Decadence from Nefertiti to Emily Dickinson* (New Haven: Yale Univ. Press, 1990), pp. 331-46.

32. To borrow a term from Mark M. Hennelly Jr., "'As Well Fill Up the Space Between': A Liminal Reading of *Christabel,*" *SIR* [*Studies in Romanticism*] 38, 2 (Summer 1999): 203-22, a witty application of Victor Turner's anthropological work on initiations.

33. *Marginalia* 2, 131, notes that Coleridge borrowed Henry Boyd's translation of the *Inferno* from the Bristol Library in late June 1796. Soon after, he noted a project for a "Poem in one Book in the manner of Dante on the excursion of Thor" (*CN* 1, entry 170). Ralph Pite, *The Circle of Our Vision: Dante's Presence in English Romantic Poetry* (Oxford: Clarendon Press, 1994), mentions Coleridge's use of Henry Boyd's translation in 1796 (p. 69), but finds Dantean images only in the late poems such as "Ne Plus Ultra" and "Limbo" (p. 70 n. 5). I believe that "Christabel" shows the influence of the 1796 reading of Dante. See Eric C. Brown, "Boyd's Dante, Coleridge's *Ancient Mariner,* and the Pattern of Infernal Influence," *SEL* [*Studies in English Literature, 1500-1900*] 38, 4 (Autumn 1998): 647-67.

34. Coleridge, *Table Talk,* ed. Carl Woodring, *CW* vol. 2, p. 245 (hereafter *TT*).

35. Jack Stillinger writes, "While the numerous substantive differences among the texts have their lo-

cal effects and exemplify Coleridge's rhetorical skills as reviser, none of the rewritten passages alters the plot (such as it is), the characters, or the themes of the fragment. The most interesting revisions occur not in the verse but in a series of *Mariner*-like explanatory glosses that Coleridge added in the margins of one of the annotated *1816*s at Princeton" (*Coleridge and Textual Instability: The Multiple Versions of the Major Poems* [New York: Oxford Univ. Press, 1994], p. 80). For the smudging of the details about Geraldine's breast or side, see Stillinger, p. 88. In *Revision and Romantic Authorship* (Clarendon: Oxford Univ. Press, 1996), Zachary Leader argues against Stillinger that Coleridge's revisions are efforts to achieve perfection rather than signs that the text is unstable and the meaning uncertain (p. 142).

36. Percy Bysshe Shelley, *The Cenci,* III. 1.26-8, in *Shelley's Poetry and Prose: Authoritative Texts and Criticism,* ed. Reiman and Sharon B. Powers (New York: Norton, 1977), p. 262.

37. Quoted in Stillinger, p. 89.

38. Both Coleridge and Shelley may also draw from Dante's Vanni Fucci as he stumbles blinking and stupefied from his solitary prison (*Inferno*, canto 24, lines 112-8).

39. My understanding of the yearning and loneliness of daughters who lose their mothers comes from Hope Edelman, *Motherless Daughters: The Legacy of Loss* (Reading Mass.: Addison-Wesley Publishing Company, 1994). But even Edelman has no chapter on girls who never know their mothers. Coppelia Kahn explores the effect of the absent mother on the hysteria of King Lear himself, but not on the daughters left in his erratic care ("The Absent Mother in *King Lear,*" *New Casebooks: King Lear,* ed. Kiernan Ryan [New York: Macmillan, 1993], pp. 92-113).

40. After arguing into the night with Robert Southey about incest and other taboos, Coleridge in November 1803 writes in his notebook that the so-called "crime against Nature" is in many countries "a bagatelle, a fashionable Levity" (*CN* 1, entry 1637).

41. In *Coleridge's Poetic Intelligence* (New York: Macmillan, 1977), Beer writes that "if the acting self has lost contact with its own organic centre, it will be at the mercy of the energies that have invaded it, able only to mirror back a reflection of their form" (p. 233).

42. Alice Miller, *The Drama of the Gifted Child* (originally published as *Prisoners of Childhood*), trans. Ruth Ward (New York: Basic Books, 1981).

43. I have described these spells and incantations, and their relation to passions, in "Coleridge and the Potent Voice," in *Magic and English Romanticism* (Athens: Univ. of Georgia Press, 1979), pp. 99-133.

44. In Samuel Hearne, *A Journey to the Northern Ocean* (1795); Coleridge's copy is from Dublin, 1796, noted in *CN* 1, entry 1637 (November 1803).

45. I discuss the father and son interchange in chap. 5, "In the Cave of the Gnome: Hartley Coleridge," of *Bacchus in Romantic England: Writers and Drink, 1780-1830* (Basingstoke: Macmillan, 1999), pp. 126-56.

46. Lyn Mikel Brown and Carol Gilligan, *Meeting at the Crossroads: Women's Psychology and Girls' Development* (Cambridge Mass.: Harvard Univ. Press, 1992), pp. 28-73, describe the self-silencing fear of conflict, and corrosive suffering of girls at the onset of puberty.

47. Karen Horney tries to readjust the study of woman's development from a woman's point of view in "The Flight from Womanhood: The Masculinity-Complex in Women as Viewed by Men and Women" (1926), "Inhibited Femininity: Psychoanalytical Contribution to the Problem of Frigidity" (1926-7), "The Denial of the Vagina: A Contribution to the Problem of the Genital Anxieties Specific to Women" (1933), in *Feminine Psychology,* ed. Harold Kelman (New York: Norton, 1967). Coleridge in "Christabel" seems to be struggling with some such realization that male and female developments are not identical.

48. George Felton Mathew, in *European Magazine* 1816, in *Coleridge, The Critical Heritage,* ed. J. R. de J. Jackson (London: Routledge, 1970), p. 241.

49. *Coleridge: The Early Family Letters,* ed. James Engell (Oxford: Clarendon Press, 1994), pp. 52-5, 95-6.

50. Meena Alexander, *Women in Romanticism: Mary Wollstonecraft, Dorothy Wordsworth, and Mary Shelley* (Basingstoke: Macmillan, 1989), pp. 86 and 87.

51. Jessica Benjamin, *Like Subjects, Love Objects: Essays on Recognition and Sexual Difference* (New Haven: Yale Univ. Press, 1995), p. 150.

52. This includes the motherless heroine of "Ruth," a poem Coleridge wished that he had written. Judith W. Page, *Wordsworth and the Cultivation of Women* (Berkeley: Univ. of California Press,

1994), reveals a wealth of information on Wordsworth's women friends and helpers.

53. Coleridge's notebooks for this hike record detailed vistas but do not mention the treasure tucked in his pocket.

54. *Journals of Dorothy Wordsworth: The Alfoxden Journal 1798, The Grasmere Journals 1800-1803,* ed. Mary Moorman (London: Oxford Univ. Press, 1971), p. 43.

55. Richard Holmes, *Early Visions* (London: Hodder and Stoughton, 1989), pp. 281-6; Holmes, *Coleridge: Darker Reflections, 1804-1834* (London: HarperCollins, 1998), p. 458. Might Wordsworth's complete silence about "Christabel" after its 1816 publication hint at a resentment at some reference to his own absorption of his sister?

56. Susan Eilenberg, *Strange Power of Speech: Wordsworth, Coleridge, and Literary Possession* (New York: Oxford Univ. Press, 1992), pp. 87-107, 99.

57. With some ironies Coleridge calls this interloper poem "mild" and "unimposing" but "full of beauties to those short-necked men who have their hearts sufficiently near their heads—the relative distance of which (according to Citizen Tourdes, the French Translator of Spallanzani [a work on circulation]) determines the sagacity or stupidity of all Bipeds & Quadrupeds" (*CL* 1:649).

58. Stillinger, *Coleridge and Textual Instability,* pp. 79-91 and 189-215.

59. Rajan [see note 12], p. 114, writing about Coleridge's effort to understand Charles Lamb's experience in "This Lime-Tree Bower My Prison."

60. This malaise is probed by Julia Kristeva, *Powers of Horror: An Essay on Abjection,* trans. Leon S. Roudiez (New York: Columbia Univ. Press, 1982), pp. 1-89, as a turmoil.

FURTHER READING

Criticism

Berkoben, Lawrence D. "*Christabel*: A Variety of Evil Experience." *Modern Language Quarterly* 25 (December 1964): 400-11.

Examines Coleridge's use of an "echo motif," a poetic device that contributes to "Christabel"'s ambiguity.

Bostetter, Edward E. "*Christabel*: The Vision of Fear." *Philological Quarterly* 36, no. 4 (October 1957): 183-94.

Interprets "Christabel" within the context of Coleridge's letters, notebooks, and other poems, arguing that the relationship between good and evil in the poem is based on Coleridge's personal experience.

Byron, George Gordon. "To Samuel Taylor Coleridge." In *"Wedlock's the devil": Byron's Letters and Journals.* Vol. 4, edited by Leslie A. Marchand, pp. 318-19. Cambridge: Belknap Press of Harvard University Press, 1975.

Written on October 18, 1815; offers high praise for Coleridge's "Christabel," describing it as "the wildest & finest" poem of its kind.

Dramin, Edward. "'Amid the Jagged Shadows': *Christabel* and the Gothic Tradition." *Wordsworth Circle* 13, no. 4 (fall 1982): 221-28.

Examines Coleridge's exploration of moral issues in "Christabel."

Grossberg, Benjamin Scott. "Making Christabel: Sexual Transgression and Its Implications in Coleridge's 'Christabel.'" *Journal of Homosexuality* 41, no. 2 (2001): 145-65.

Analyzes questions of lesbianism, sexual transgression, and gender identity in "Christabel."

Hennelly, Mark M., Jr. "'As Well Fill Up the Space Between': A Liminal Reading of *Christabel*." *Studies in Romanticism* 38, no. 2 (summer 1999): 203-22.

Discusses states of marginality or "in-betweenness" in "Christabel" as they relate to the poem's fascination with crossing thresholds or rites of passage.

Holstein, Michael. "Coleridge's *Christabel* as Psychodrama: Five Perspectives on the Intruder." *Wordsworth Circle* 7 (1976): 119-28.

Examines the symbolic significance of the figure of Geraldine.

Knight, G. Wilson. "Coleridge's Divine Comedy." In *The Starlit Dome: Studies in the Poetry of Vision,* pp. 83-178. London: Oxford University Press, 1941.

Argues that "Christabel," "The Rime of the Ancient Mariner," and "Kubla Khan" represent Coleridge's own divine comedy, symbolizing hell, purgatory, and paradise, respectively.

Levinson, Marjorie. "The True Fragment: 'Christabel.'" In *The Romantic Fragment Poem,* pp. 77-96. Chapel Hill: University of North Carolina Press, 1986.

Examines "Christabel"'s unique formal qualities.

Liggins, Elizabeth M. "Folklore and the Supernatural in 'Christabel.'" *Folklore* 88 (1977): 91-104.

Discusses the interplay of natural and supernatural imagery in "Christabel."

Luther, Susan M. *Christabel as Dream-Reverie.* Salzburg: Institut für Englische Sprache und Literatur, 1976, 113 p.

Presents a psychological reading of "Christabel."

Magnuson, Paul. "A Ghost by Day Time." In *Coleridge's Nightmare Poetry,* pp. 94-106. Charlottesville: University Press of Virginia, 1974.

Argues that as Geraldine is transferred from Christabel's dream into the reality of daylight, the poem becomes a waking nightmare.

McElderry, B. R., Jr. "Coleridge's Plan for Completing *Christabel.*" *Studies in Philology* 33 (July 1936): 437-55.

Takes issue with critics who dismiss "Christabel" as too fantastical to be taken seriously, arguing that Coleridge's plan for completing the poem was both sound and credible.

Metzger, Lore. "Modifications of Genre: A Feminist Critique of 'Christabel' and 'Die Braut von Korinth.'" In *Borderwork: Feminist Engagements with Comparative Literature,* pp. 81-99. Ithaca, N.Y.: Cornell University Press, 1994.

Analyzes Johann Wolfgang von Goethe's "Die Braut von Korinth" and Coleridge's "Christabel" as poems that transgressed normative eighteenth-century definitions of genre and gender roles.

Nethercot, Arthur Hobart. *The Road to Tryermaine: A Study of the History, Background, and Purposes of Coleridge's "Christabel."* Chicago: University of Chicago Press, 1939, 230 p.

Discusses the influence of mythology on "Christabel"'s imagery and major themes.

O'Donnell, Brennan. "The 'Invention' of a Meter: 'Christabel' Meter as Fact and Fiction." *Journal of English and Germanic Philology* 100, no. 4 (fall 2001): 511-36.

Suggests that ambiguity in "Christabel" is heightened by the poet's archaic use of syllable, stress, and verse paragraphing.

Paglia, Camille. "'Christabel.'" In *Samuel Taylor Coleridge,* edited by Harold Bloom, pp. 217-29. New York: Chelsea House Publishers, 1986.

Provides a thorough analysis of the poem's sexual undertones. Praising "Christabel" for its "lurid pagan pictorialism," Paglia asserts that the poem represents the triumph of art over the moral constraints of Judeo-Christian civilization.

Piper, H. W. "The Disunity of *Christabel* and the Fall of Nature." *Essays in Criticism* 28 (1978): 216-27.

Analyzes the disunity between parts one and two of "Christabel," arguing that the disparity between the two reflects the evolution of Coleridge's poetics ideas and methods between 1798 and 1802.

Proffitt, Edward. "'Christabel' and the Oedipal Conflict." *Research Studies* 46 (1978): 248-51.

Discusses the psychological forces that motivate "Christabel"'s central characters.

Russett, Margaret. "Meter, Identity, Voice: Untranslating *Christabel.*" *Studies in English Literature, 1500-1900* 43, no. 4 (fall 2003): 773-97.

Examines issues of plagiarism and copyright law as they relate to "Christabel."

Schapiro, Barbara. "'Christabel': The Problem of Ambivalent Love." *Literature and Psychology* 30, nos. 3-4 (1980): 119-32.

Analyzes the relationship between Christabel and her dead mother.

Schwartz, Lewis M. "A New Review of Coleridge's *Christabel.*" *Studies in Romanticism* 9, no. 2 (spring 1970): 114-24.

Examines contemporary responses to "Christabel," arguing that one favorable review of the poem, published anonymously in the *London Times* in May 1816 was actually authored by Charles Lamb.

Spatz, Jonas. "The Mystery of Eros: Sexual Initiation in Coleridge's 'Christabel.'" *PMLA* 90, no. 1 (winter 1975): 107-16.

Reads "Christabel" as the culmination of Coleridge's poetic exploration of his ideas about sex, love, and marriage.

Strickland, Edward. "Metamorphoses of the Muse in Romantic Poesis: 'Christabel.'" *ELH* 44, no. 4 (winter 1977): 641-58.

Examines Geraldine as the embodiment of an ambivalent Muse—as Coleridge saw it, a figure capable of "demonic possession" and, at the same time, of "celestial exaltation" of the imagination.

Swann, Karen. "Literary Gentlemen and Lovely Ladies: The Debate on the Character of *Christabel.*" *ELH* 52, no. 2 (summer 1985): 397-418.

Through an evaluation of contemporary reactions to the poem, discusses the act of reading "Christabel" as a form of "feminine erotic experience."

Twitchell, James B. "The Female Vampire." In *The Living Dead: A Study of the Vampire in Romantic Literature,* pp. 39-73. Durham, N.C.: Duke University Press, 1981.

Includes an analysis of Coleridge's exploration of vampire motifs in "Christabel," while examining the sexual imagery used to depict the relationship between Geraldine and Christabel.

Wheeler, Kathleen M. "Coleridge and Modern Critical Theory." In *Coleridge's Theory of Imagination Today,* edited by Christine Gallant, pp. 83-102. New York: AMS Press, 1989.

Includes a discussion of "Christabel"'s ambiguous imagery.

Additional coverage of Coleridge's life and career is contained in the following sources published by Thomson Gale: *Authors and Artists for Young Adults,* **Vol. 66;** *Beacham's Guide to Literature for Young Adults,* **Vol. 4;** *British Writers,* **Vol. 4;** *British Writers Retrospective Supplement,* **Vol. 2;** *Concise Dictionary of British Literary Biography, 1789-1832; Dictionary of Literary Biography,* **Vols. 93, 107;** *DISCovering Authors; DISCovering Authors 3.0; DISCovering Authors: British Edition; DISCovering Authors: Canadian Edition; DISCovering Authors Modules: Most-studied Authors* **and** *Poets; Exploring Poetry; Literary Movements for Students,* **Vol. 1;** *Literature and Its Times Supplement,* **Vol. 1:1;** *Literature Resource Center; Nineteenth-Century Literature Criticism,* **Vols. 9, 54, 99, 111;** *Poetry Criticism,* **Vols. 11, 39, 67;** *Poetry for Students,* **Vols. 4, 5;** *Poets: American and British; Reference Guide to English Literature,* **Ed. 2;** *Twayne's English Authors; World Literature and Its Times,* **Vol. 3;** *World Literature Criticism;* **and** *World Poets.*

Johnson Jones Hooper
1815-1862

American short story writer and journalist.

INTRODUCTION

Hooper was among the earliest and most popular of the early nineteenth-century Southwestern humorists. Along with A. B. Longstreet and James Glover Baldwin, Hooper helped establish an American literary tradition that was rooted in life on the frontier, and his work captures the spirit of rugged individuality, as well as the unique vernacular, that characterized his era. He remains best known as the creator of Simon Suggs, an unscrupulous, flamboyant confidence man whose larger-than-life personality struck a chord with an American reading public hungry for outlandish depictions of frontier society. In addition to his acclaim as an author, Hooper also enjoyed prestige as an editor during his lifetime, and over the course of his journalism career he served in that position on a number of prominent Alabama newspapers. He also achieved renown late in his life for his involvement in Southern Whig political causes, and he became a vocal proponent of secession in the years leading up to the Civil War. Hooper devoted his final years to publishing vitriolic editorials on behalf of slavery and states' rights. Before his untimely death in 1862, he played an active role in the fledgling Confederate government. While Hooper has received relatively little attention from modern readers and scholars, he exerted a wide influence during his lifetime, particularly on writers like Mark Twain and Herman Melville, whose own depictions of confidence men owe a debt to Simon Suggs.

BIOGRAPHICAL INFORMATION

Hooper was born in Wilmington, North Carolina, on June 9, 1815, the youngest of six children. He was descended from prominent southern merchants and politicians—his great-uncle, William Hooper, was a signer of the Declaration of Independence and represented North Carolina in the Continental Congress—and throughout his early childhood he enjoyed the advantages of belonging to a prosperous and respected family. Hooper's father, Archibald Hooper, was an accomplished newspaperman and lawyer who served as editor of the *Cape-Fear Recorder* in the late 1820s and early 1830s; his mother, Charlotte DeBerniere, a cultivated and well-read woman from Charleston, South Carolina, played a prominent role in her children's intellectual upbringing. Hooper received his early education in the Wilmington public schools, and he intended to follow his older brothers to college. Financial difficulties eventually forced Hooper to abandon his formal education, however, and in his early adolescence he took a job as a printer's devil at his father's newspaper. Although forced to leave school, Hooper still read widely throughout his teenage years, and at the age of fifteen, he published his first piece of writing, a satirical poem titled "Anthony Milan's Launch," in the *Cape-Fear Recorder.*

When he was twenty, Hooper moved to La Fayette, Alabama, where his older brother George had recently established a law practice. For the next two years Hooper studied law at his brother's office, earning admittance to the Alabama bar in 1838. A year later Hooper was named Notary Public of Tallapoosa County, and in 1840 he became the county census taker. After completing his census duties, Hooper went to work at his brother's law firm, where he remained for two years. In 1842 he left the legal profession to join the staff of the *East Alabamian,* a weekly newspaper dedicated to promoting Whig political views. In December 1842 Hooper married Mary Mildred Brantley, the daughter of a prominent farmer and Whig politician. The couple would have three children.

Soon after launching his career as a newspaper editor, Hooper began to write his first humorous sketches. His debut effort, "Taking the Census in Alabama," appeared in the *East Alabamian* in 1843. Inspired by Hooper's census-taking experiences among the backwoods settlers and Creek Indians of rural Alabama, the story evokes the primitive social life and coarse humor of the South and is counted as one of the earliest satirical depictions of frontier life in American literature. Shortly after its publication, "Taking the Census in Alabama" attracted the attention of prominent New York newspaper editor William T. Porter, who republished the piece in his popular sporting magazine, *Spirit of the Times.* In 1844 Hooper published the first of his Simon Suggs stories in the *East Alabamian;* the piece was later reprinted by Porter in the *Spirit.* Porter proved instrumental in introducing Hooper to a national audience, republishing several of his sketches over the next two years and even including one of the stories, "How Simon Suggs Raised Jack," in his acclaimed 1845 anthology, *The Big Bear of Arkansas, and Other Sketches.*

In 1845 Hooper left his position with the *East Alabamian* to become the editor of the *Wetumpka Whig,* and a year later he moved to Montgomery to join the staff of the *Alabama Journal,* the state's leading Whig political journal. In 1846 Hooper published his first book, *Some Adventures of Captain Simon Suggs,* which he dedicated to Porter. The work made Hooper one of the nation's leading humorists.

Over the course of the next decade, Hooper published more than fifty stories and sketches in Porter's magazine; as his popularity grew, his identity as an author became inextricably linked with that of his fictional alter ego, Simon Suggs. Hooper soon began to feel ambivalent about his fame as a humorist, however, largely because of his growing involvement with politics. In 1849 Hooper returned to La Fayette, worked for several months as a lawyer, and ran unsuccessfully for a seat in the Alabama House of Representatives. He published a second book, *A Ride with Old Kit Kuncker,* that same year. In 1850 he became part owner and editor of the *Chambers Tribune.* During this time he began to publish new sketches in the *New Orleans Delta* and launched a successful campaign to become solicitor of the Ninth Judicial Circuit of Alabama, a position he held until 1853. In 1853 Hooper published a series of essays on the subject of hunting in the *Tribune* that would later form the core of his collection *Dog and Gun* (1856).

As the decade progressed and the threat of Civil War loomed over the nation, Hooper became more dedicated to secessionist politics, and his writings from the last years of his life reflect his staunchly pro-slavery views. Increasingly disillusioned with the official Whig platform, Hooper began to seek out alternatives to the mainstream political parties. He returned to Montgomery in 1854 to found the *Montgomery Mail,* an independent political newspaper. In January of the following year, Hooper became associated with the newly formed Know-Nothing party, which was dedicated to wiping out corruption in politics. After Democratic candidate James Buchanan won the 1856 presidential election, Hooper renounced his ties to all official political parties, offering his support only to candidates who wholeheartedly espoused states' rights. Hooper chronicled his experiences during the campaign in the satirical pamphlet *Read and Circulate* (1855).

Throughout the remainder of his life, Hooper continued to work as an editor at several Alabama newspapers, while devoting a great deal of his energy to the cause of states' rights. He played an active role in the presidential election of 1860, publishing a series of scathing editorials, as well as a poem entitled "The South," in the *Montgomery Mail.* His outspoken support of Southern rights earned him an appointment as secretary of the Provisional Confederate Congress in February 1861.

In July of that year, he moved with his family to Richmond, Virginia, the new capital of the Confederacy, where he continued to work on behalf of the Confederate Congress. Shortly after moving to Richmond, however, Hooper was overcome by illness, and he died of tuberculosis on June 7, 1862.

MAJOR WORKS

Hooper is remembered today as the author of *Some Adventures of Captain Simon Suggs.* The book is composed of twelve interrelated stories featuring the character of Simon Suggs, as well as two additional tales, "Taking the Census" and "Daddy Biggs' Scrape at Cockerell's Bend." In one sense, the book is a work of political parody: it is loosely modeled after the popular "campaign biographies" of contemporary public figures like Andrew Jackson, Martin van Buren, Henry Clay, and James Knox Polk. For the most part, however, the book is a character study of Hooper's hero and alter-ego, Simon Suggs. Based in part on a man named Bird H. Young, a notorious gambler and practical joker with whom Hooper had become acquainted in Alabama, Suggs is the prototypical American confidence man. Abiding by his famous motto, "It is good to be shifty in a new country," Suggs continually enters into social situations with an eye toward monetary gain, always hoping to profit at the expense of others. The opening chapter of the book finds the seventeen-year-old Suggs shirking his chores in order to gamble with one of his father's slaves. When Suggs's father, a Baptist preacher, discovers them with a deck of cards, punishment seems inevitable. Suggs, however, outwits his father by preying on the preacher's own greed and vanity, and by the end of the scene, he has swindled his father out of money and a horse. This pattern of deceit recurs again and again throughout the book, as Suggs travels the South in search of new scams. In the sketch "The Captain Attends a Camp-Meeting," Suggs dupes a revival meeting out of its collection money; in "Simon Becomes Captain," Hooper's protagonist poses as a military hero of the Creek Indian wars. Other notable stories from the collection include "Simon Fights 'the Tiger' and Gets Whipped—but Comes out not Much the 'Worse for Wear,'" in which Suggs impersonates a prosperous hog farmer in order to run up a large tab at a gambling house; "Simon Speculates Again," in which he defrauds a group of unscrupulous land speculators; and "The Captain Is Arraigned before a 'Jury of His Country,'" a satire of frontier justice.

Although Hooper's modern reputation rests almost exclusively on his first book, his other works have ellicited critical notice as well. *A Ride with Old Kit Kuncker,* a collection of twenty humorous pieces, includes two additional Simon Suggs sketches as well as Hooper's famous satire of frontier life, "A Night at the Ugly Man's." The brief sketch "Capt. Stick and Toney," which contains a depiction of the relationship between a plantation owner and one of his slaves, is noteworthy in that it embodies many of the stereotypical attitudes toward African Americans prevalent in the antebellum South, particularly in Hooper's rendition of slave manners of speech. Hooper republished the stories from *A Ride with Old Kit Kuncker*, along with an additional four sketches, in the 1851 collection *The Widow Rugby's Husband*.

CRITICAL RECEPTION

Hooper enjoyed widespread popularity during his lifetime, both among the reading public and among literary reviewers. His *Some Adventures of Captain Simon Suggs* went through eleven editions in the decade following its initial publication, and his stories and sketches were widely serialized in nationwide newspapers and journals. After the Civil War, however, Hooper and his eponymous protagonist fell into obscurity. It was only in the 1920s and 1930s that Hooper's writings experienced a revival of interest, when scholars like Jeanette Tandy, Walter Blair, and Franklin Meine evaluated Hooper's work in their pioneering studies of early American humor. In *Mark Twain and Southwestern Humor*, published in 1959, Kenneth Lynn examined the character of Simon Suggs within the context of the "confidence man" tradition in nineteenth-century American literature, a subject discussed at greater length by William Lenz in his 1985 study *Fast Talk & Flush Times: The Confidence Man as a Literary Convention*. Although only a handful of essays devoted to Hooper's life and career have been published since the late 1980s, a few important critical studies have emerged, notably Johanna Shields's 1990 essay "A Sadder Simon Suggs: Freedom and Slavery in the Humor of Johnson Hooper," which includes an exhaustive bibliography of writings on Hooper. Over the years some important biographies of Hooper have appeared, the most famous and influential of which is Stanley W. Hoole's *Alias Simon Suggs: The Life and Times of Johnson Jones Hooper*, which appeared in 1952.

PRINCIPAL WORKS

Some Adventures of Captain Simon Suggs, Late of the Tallapoosa Volunteers; Together with "Taking the Census," and Other Alabama Sketches (short stories) 1846

A Ride with Old Kit Kuncker, and Other Sketches, and Scenes of Alabama (short stories) 1849; enlarged as *The Widow Rugby's Husband, A Night at the Ugly Man's, and Other Tales of Alabama*, 1851

Read and Circulate: Proceedings of the Democratic and Anti-Know-Nothing Party in Caucus; or the Guillotine at Work, at the Capital, during the Session of 1855-'56 (journalism) 1855

Dog and Gun; A Few Loose Chapters on Shooting, Among Which Will Be Found Some Anecdotes and Incidents (sketches) 1856

*These collections contain stories or sketches that were originally published in periodicals.

CRITICISM

Henry Watterson (essay date 1883)

SOURCE: Watterson, Henry. "Simon Suggs." In *Oddities in Southern Life and Character*, pp. 39-91. Boston: Houghton, Mifflin and Company, 1883.

[*In the following excerpt, Watterson discusses the character of Simon Suggs, asserting that he is one of the most vital and original personalities in antebellum Southern literature.*]

Mr. Hooper was a most genial and entertaining person, and the central figure of a brilliant coterie of writers and speakers. Of these, S. S. Prentiss and George D. Prentice were the most conspicuous; and they always regarded him and spoke of him as their peer. He was not, in public life, so aggressive as they, and therefore he failed to leave so deep a personal impress upon his time. But he had both sense and wit, and was very effective in the party campaigns of the period.

His *History of the Life and Adventures of Captain Simon Suggs, of the Tallapoosa Volunteers*, may be, and indeed it is, but a charcoal sketch. Yet, in its way, it is a masterpiece. No one who is at all familiar with the provincial life of the South can fail to recognize the "points" of this sharp and vulgar, sunny and venal swash-buckler. As serio-comic as Sellers, as grotesque as Shingle, he possesses an originality all his own, and never for a moment rises above or falls below it. He is a gambler by nature, by habit, by preference, by occupation. Without a virtue in the world, except his good humor and his self-possession, there is something in his vices, his indolence, his swagger, his rogueries, which, in spite of the worthlessness of the man and the dishonesty of his practices, detains and amuses us. He is a representative character, the Sam Slick of the South; only, I should say, the Sam Slick of Judge Haliburton is not nearly so true to nature, so graphic, or so picturesque.

It has often been stated that Simon was taken from a real personage by the name of Bird, and the story goes that this individual did on a certain occasion call Mr. Hooper to account for making too free with his lineaments and practices. It may be so; but the likelihood is that the author in this instance followed the example of other writers of fiction, and drew his hero from many scraps and odd ends of individual character to be encountered at the time in the county towns and upon the rural highways of the South. At all events, Simon has survived the ephemeral creations of contemporary humor, and is as fresh and lively to-day as he was five and thirty years ago.

Carl Holliday (essay date 1906)

SOURCE: Holliday, Carl. "The Period of Expansion (1810-1850)." In *A History of Southern Literature*, pp. 117-239. New York: Neale Publishing Co., 1906.

[*In the following excerpt, Holliday examines the comic aspects of Hooper's writings. While Holliday concedes that much of the humor in Hooper's work is dated, he argues that the stories still have enduring literary value, primarily in their depictions of frontier society and culture during the antebellum era.*]

The last of these sketch writers here to be discussed, but by no means the last that might be discussed, is Johnson Hooper (1815-1863). He was born in North Carolina, but, while still a child, removed to Alabama, and there, as editor, lawyer, and statesman, performed notable services for the State and for the entire South. He was secretary of the provisional Confederate Congress, and during the Civil War held various important positions under the new government. The first work that called the attention of the public to Hooper as a writer, was his *Adventures of Captain Simon Suggs* (1845), a racy piece of literature, describing a gambling sharp of the Southwest during its first boom days. Six years later he followed this successful venture with his *Widow Rugby's Husband and Other Tales of Alabama*; but this was not a work of the same merit, and it very deservedly failed to gain the same wide popularity.

Here again we find the humorist dealing with the "poor whites," not Georgia Crackers this time, it is true, but Alabamians of the same type. Again, too, we find the same conflict between ignorant conservatism and progress. The ridiculous suspicions and, at the same time, the extreme credulity of these rustics of the back counties afford many a humorous situation. But beneath all the fun, as we read of the stern, gloomy ideas of God and religion, the inborn rascality found even among such well-meaning people, and the struggle between goodness and greed, we discover, perhaps unintention-

ally on the author's part, an element of pathos. The purpose of the book, however, is that of fun-making, and in that particular it is a decided success. For instance, the census officer comes to an old widow's house to secure the required information, and the suspicious lady threatens to "sick" the dogs on them.

> "Last week Bill Stonecker's two-year-old steer jumped my yard fence, and Bull and Pomp tuk him by the throat and they killed him afore my boys could break 'im loose to save the world."
>
> "Yes, ma'am," said we meekly; "Bull and Pomp seem to be very fine dogs."
>
> At length . . . we remarked that . . . we would just set down the age, sex, and complexion of each member of her family.
>
> "No sich a thing—you'll do no sich a thing," said she, . . . "I've got five in family, and they are all a plaguy sight whiter than you, and whether they are he or she is none of your consarns."

Thus the rant goes on, and the old woman finally offers, indeed begs for, the opportunity to kill the marshal, several government officers and at length President Van Buren himself. "'A pretty fellow to be eating his vittles out'n gold spoons that poor people's taxed for, and raisin' an army to get him made king of Ameriky.'" In time the census men give up their effort, but when safely on their horses, they decided to give her a parting compliment.

> "Do you want to get married?"
>
> "Here, Bull," shouted the widow, "sick him, Pomp . . . Si-c-k, Pomp—sick, sick, si-c-k him, Bull—suboy, suboy, suboy."

Humor has improved greatly since those times, and to-day it cannot be doubted that America's most original, and perhaps best, contributions to the world's literature have been along this line. Possessing a familiarity with the more subtle and refined efforts of the later wit, we may find the sketches that made our fathers laugh, rather common and even unentertaining, but placing ourselves, in imagination, among the same surroundings, and, remembering that many of the characters and scenes described were familiar to every Southerner, we can understand, perhaps, the wide popularity of these pioneers in American humor.

Jennette Tandy (essay date 1925)

SOURCE: Tandy, Jennette. "The Development of Southern Humor." In *Crackerbox Philosophers in American Humor and Satire*, pp. 65-102. New York: Columbia University Press, 1925.

[*In the following excerpt, Tandy provides a general reading of Hooper's* Some Adventures of Captain Simon Suggs. *Comparing Simon Suggs to other comic lit-*

erary characters of the period, Tandy concludes that, while Hooper's character is certainly original, he is in many ways too crass and profane to enjoy lasting widespread appeal.]

It will be seen that the conventions of Southern humor in the forties held for accurate observation and fresh material rather than technique. Piquancy was rather to be desired than form. A long step forward was taken when Johnson J. Hooper[1] centered his representation of the semi-civilized age of speculation in a single character, Simon Suggs.

The *Adventures of Captain Simon Suggs* is a campaign biography. In a year or two the captain may be running for office, so it is well to get his name before the public. His history must be revealed.

> It is an absolute, political necessity. His enemies *will* know enough to attack; his friends *must* know enough to defend.—Thus Jackson, Van Buren, Clay, and Polk have each a biography published while they live.[2]

The narrative of Simon's life begins with his preparations for migrating from Georgia to Alabama. When Simon was a boy of sixteen, his father, an old "hardshell" Baptist preacher, caught Simon and the negro boy Bill in a fence corner playing seven-up. The boys see him coming just in time to switch to a game of mumblepeg. But the old man picks up a dropped card and marches them off to the mulberry tree for chastisement. Bill gets a terrific "wallopin." When Simon's turn comes he tells his father that it is no use to whip him. He intends to play cards as long as he lives, and some day to make his living by it.

> Old Mr. Suggs groaned, as he was wont to do in the pulpit, at this display of Simon's viciousness.
>
> "Simon," said he, "you're a poor, ignunt creetur. You don't know nutin' and you've never b'en nowhars. If I was to turn you off, you'd starve in a week—."
>
> "I wish you'd try me," said Simon, "and jist see. I'd win more money in a week than you can make in a year. There ain't nobody round here kin make seed corn off o' me at cards. I'm rale smart."[3]

Half by boasting, half by cleverly laid baits to curiosity, Simon entices his father into a game. As for a bet on the cards—"Me bet!" thundered old Mr. Suggs.

> I didn't go to say *that* daddy; that warn't what I meant adzactly. I went to say that ef you'd let me off from this here maulin' you owe me, and *give me* "Bunch" ef I cut Jack, I'd *give you* all this here silver, ef I didn't— that's all. To be sure I alers knowed *you* wouldn't bet.[4]

The bet is laid on these terms. Simon palms the cards, cuts the Jack, escapes a licking and wins Bunch, the pony. Early the next morning he slips down, puts a thimbleful of gunpowder into his mother's pipe, and rides away.

After twenty mysteriously unexplained years he turns up, "snugly settled on public land on the Tallapoosa River, in the midst of that highly respectable town of Indians known as the Oakfuskees." He is pursuing a varied career as speculator and gambler, following his favorite aphorism, "IT IS GOOD TO BE SHIFTY IN A NEW COUNTRY."[5] He is now a soft-spoken, foul-mouthed, skinny gentleman, with an ever-present sneer on his face and an all-too-ready tear in his eye.

Many are his schemes and plentiful the silver he rakes in. He gets one hundred and seventy dollars and a good horse for not filing on a piece of land which he does not want, twenty dollars more from a politician who mistakes him for a venal member of the state legislature, and again several hundred by impersonating a wealthy Kentucky hog buyer. Simon does not rush into deceit. "What's a man without his inteegerty?"[6] But if mistakes come he knows how to make the most of them. If the ring of speculators who are trying to buy the land of the Big Widow, his squaw friend, assume that Simon has his saddlebags crammed full of coins, they must pay for their misapprehension. He will let them know the pouches contain only rocks and old iron—after he has pocketed their five hundred dollars.

Simon won his captaincy at the Creek War. When the alarm was sounded the little town on the Tallapoosa was in a panic. "Will any of the breethring lend me a horse?" asked the Reverend Snufflenosy, wildly, as he bounded out of the pulpit.[7] Furniture, bedding, and tom-cats were piled on wagons and hauled to the nearest crossroads store. Simon was on hand. His eloquence saved the day.

The village was in a quandary.

> "We shall be skelped," cried the Widow Haycock, "and our truck all burnt up and destr'yed! What shall we do?"
>
> "That's the question," remarked Simon, as he stooped to draw a glass of whiskey from a barrel of that article—the only thing on sale in the "store"—"that's the question. Now as for you women-folks"—here Suggs dropped a lump of brown sugar in his whiskey, and began to stir it with his finger, looking intently in the tumbler, the while—"as for our women-folks, it's plain enough what *you've* got to do"—here Simon tasted the liquor and added a little more sugar—"plain-*enough*! You've only got to look to the Lord and hold your jaws; for that's all you *kin* do! But what's the 'sponsible *men*"—taking his finger out of the tumbler, and drawing it through his mouth—"of this crowd to do? The inemy will be down upon us right away, and before morning"—Simon drank half the whiskey—"blood will flow like"—the Captain was bothered for a simile, and looked around the room for one, but finding none, continued—"like all the world"—an idea suggested itself—"and the Tallapussey river! It'll pour out," he continued, as his fancy got rightly to work, "like a

great guljin ocean!—d—d if it don't." And then Simon swallowed the rest of the whiskey, threw the tumbler down, and looked around to observe the effect of this brilliant exordium.

The effect was tremendous! . . .[8]

"My apinion," continued Simon, as he stooped to draw another tumbler of whiskey; "my apinion, folks, is this here. We ought to form a company right away, and make some man capting that ain't afeard to fight—mind what I say, now—*that-aint-afeard-to-fight!*—some, sober, stiddy feller"—here he sipped a little from the tumbler . . . "and more'n all, a man that's acquainted with the country and the ways of the Injuns!" Having thus spoken, Suggs drank off the rest of the whiskey, threw himself into a military attitude, and awaited a reply.

"Suggs is the man," shouted twenty voices.[9]

And so Suggs is made "capting of the Tallapoosy Volluntares," otherwise known as the "Forty Thieves." The band does noble service during the Creek War, for it succeeds in frightening an old woman half to death, and in running off at least thirty Indian ponies. On the conclusion of the uprising "Capting" Suggs retires with a proud title and a military record. Suggs next gets "convarted" at a camp-meeting. He also gets the collection-box.

A year or two afterwards the piety has worn off. He is arraigned before a jury for playing poker. Simon would have received a heavy sentence, but a note is handed in to the courtroom which causes him to weep bitterly. His two boys are dying. The judge is impressed by his grief.

> "I'll plead guilty," sobs Simon. "The boys will be dead afore I could get home anyhow! Let 'em send me to jail whar there won't be anybody to laugh at my misery."[10]

Of course the judge gives an order for his release. An hour later the prosecuting attorney finds him standing in front of a tavern in great glee, relating some laughable anecdote. Why is he not on the way home?

> "You see," quoth Simon, "it was this here way adzactly—that note I got in the court-house, was one Dr. Jourdan sent me last summer, when the boys *was* sick, and I was on a spree over to Sockapatoy—only I didn't know it was the same. It must 'a drapped outen my pocket here, somehow, and some of these cussed town boys picked it up, tore off the date at the bottom, and sent it to me up thar—which, my feelins was never hurt as bad before."[11]

The picaresque biography closes with an appeal to the public:

> Men of Tallapoosa, we have done! Suggs is before you!

> We have endeavored to give the prominent events of his life with accuracy and impartiality. If you deem that he has "done the state some service," remember that he

seeks the Sheriffalty of your county. He waxes old. He needs an office, the emoluments of which shall be sufficient to enable him to relax his intellectual exertions. His military services, his numerous family, and his long residence among you, his gray hairs—all plead for him! Remember him at the polls.[12]

The political satire in Simon Suggs is slight, but effective. It is the more interesting because of the dearth of Southern political satires. Thomas Cooper's *Memoirs of a Nullifier*,[13] Kennedy's *Quodlibet*,[14] and John Beauchamp Jones's *Adventures of Colonel Gracchus Vanderbomb*[15] are all that can be counted. In the last two the aspersions are too cautious to be convincing. The brief observations on current politics in Hooper's **Simon Suggs** [**Adventures of Captain Simon Suggs**], Thompson's *Major Jones's Travels,* and Bagby's *Letters of Mozis Addums* are only passing criticisms. Satire on Southern affairs assumed no importance until The Cause was lost.

The contrast between Simon Suggs and Jack Downing and Sam Slick illustrates the difference between the popular conceptions of the comic Southerner and the comic Yankee. The interest in Simon is founded upon his actions, not his point of view. He is far more vulgar than his Yankee prototypes. His "cuteness" is frequently not the invention of a scheme, but the turning to account of an unforeseen circumstance. He is, if it may be said, an individualist who has no interest in public affairs except as they may affect his own pocketbook. The advantage is on Hooper's side, however, when one considers the local color and historical background. The Creek Indian camps, the protracted meeting, the border faro den, are new material. Simon's adventures are not the stereotyped Yankee tricks. He has no wooden nutmegs to sell. But neither has he the wit of Sam Slick. His humor is too often mere profanity.

Notes

1. Johnson Joseph Hooper (1815-1863), was born in North Carolina, and went in his youth to Alabama, where he was first lawyer, then editor. Simon Suggs appeared first in Hooper's paper, the *East Alabamian,* Lafayette, Ala. Selections were reprinted in the *Spirit of the Times.* Hooper edited a number of newspapers, the most important of which was the *Montgomery Mail,* to which he gave a national reputation. At his death he was secretary to the Senate of the Southern Confederacy.

2. *Some Adventures of Captain Simon Suggs* [(1845)], p. 8.

3. *Some Adventures of Captain Simon Suggs,* p. 21.

4. *Ibid.,* pp. 24, 25.

5. *Ibid.,* p. 12.

6. *Ibid.,* p. 41.

7. *Ibid.,* p. 84.

8. *Ibid.,* p. 86.

9. *Ibid.,* p. 88.

10. *Ibid.,* p. 138.

11. *Ibid.,* p. 140.

12. *Ibid.,* p. 148.

13. Cooper, Thomas, *Memoirs of a Nullifier,* 1832.

14. Kennedy, J. P., *Quodlibet,* 1840.

15. Jones, J. B., *Adventures of Colonel Gracchus Vanderbomb,* 1852.

Walter Blair (essay date 1937)

SOURCE: Blair, Walter. "Humor of the Old Southwest (1830-1867)." In *Native American Humor (1800-1900),* pp. 62-101. New York: American Book Company, 1937.

[*In the following excerpt, Blair discusses Hooper's writings within the context of the frontier storytelling tradition.*]

That the oral humor of the Crockett tales, the Fink tales, the *Spirit of the Times,* and kindred publications affected the writings of many Southwestern humorists seems reasonably sure. . . .

Consider Hooper's book, **Widow Rugby's Husband,**[1] for example. Almost every tale in it might well be preceded by the quotation which prefaces **"The Res Gestae of a Poor Joke"** (pp. 142-145)—"We tell the tale as 'twas told to us." A series of little yarns told by a guide are reported in **"Dick McCoy's Sketches of His Neighbors"** (pp. 35-40); **"A Night at the Ugly Man's"** (pp. 41-51) is a tall tale told by a host, full, as Mr. De Voto has pointed out, of oral lore, some of it particularly linked with Crockett;[2] four stories are pretty clearly derived from yarn-spinning sessions on the law circuit;[3] **"A Ride with Old Kit Kuncker"** (pp. 86-96) is a reported oral yarn; **"The Evasive Soap Man"** (pp. 109-111) is made up chiefly of the spiel of a peddler, and **"Captain McSpadden"** (pp. 112-120) is a tall tale recounted by an Irishman. Less specifically acknowledged sources in oral tales are discoverable in three of the other sketches in the volume.

It is at least possible, furthermore, that without the example of the Crockett tales, the Fink stories, and the yarns in the *Spirit,* Hooper never would have written his masterpiece, *Adventures of Simon Suggs* (1845). This is a notable American contribution to the literature

of roguery as defined by Frank W. Chandler.[4] Hooper's book is an admirable account of a crafty rascal, Simon Suggs, who gorgeously lived up to his motto, "It is good to be shifty in a new country," by cheating or hoodwinking as many of his Alabama neighbors as possible. A series of chapters are given unity because they all reveal hawk-nosed, watery-eyed Simon Suggs brilliantly duping people. They are given variety because the backgrounds and the characters change as the hero— "as clear cut a figure as is to be found in the whole field of American humor"[5]—moves around the frontier, cheating his father at cards, collecting money on false pretenses from an over-anxious claim-filer, passing himself off as a rich uncle in Augusta, cozening the godly folk at a camp meeting by simulating repentance. They are humorous because they ludicrously display a series of comic upsets of poetic justice shrewdly arranged by a downright rascal who, in Hooper's words, "lives as merrily and comfortably as possible at the expense of others" by taking advantage of the frailties of human nature.

Three forces, conceivably, may be back of this book: the influence of European picaresque fiction, the influence of life on the frontier, and the influence, direct or indirect, of oral literature. How much Hooper knew of the literature of Europe which detailed the adventures of rogues it is impossible to say, and it is likewise impossible to presume that, even if he knew this literature, he would have been any quicker to imitate it than most of his countrymen were.[6] But it is possible to perceive that with nothing except a knowledge of life on the frontier and acquaintance with Southwestern humor, Hooper could have learned how to draw Simon Suggs.

For in the United States the frontier was to a large degree responsible for such a character as Hooper's shifty hero. As Miss Hazard has suggested, "To find the American picaro we must follow the American pioneer; the frontier is the natural habitat of the adventurer. The qualities fostered by the frontier were the qualities indispensable to the picaro: nomadism, insensibility to danger, shrewdness, nonchalance, gaiety."[7] As Watterson said of Suggs, "His adventures as a patriot and a gambler, a moralizer and cheat, could not have progressed in New England, and would have come to a premature end anywhere on the continent of Europe."[8] And in the oral literature of the frontier—literature which idolized Mike Fink for swigging a gallon of whisky without showing effects, for flaunting justice at the St. Louis court house, for stealing from his employer, for maltreating his spouse, and for cheating a gullible farmer, restraints which limited the stuff of other American fiction had disappeared.[9] Professor Boynton discerningly calls attention to the change:

> In all the accounts of the real figures of the frontier in South and Southwest the point is in one respect utterly different from that of the older North and East. The

conscious literature was consciously edifying; it was not only polite but also moral. The Saxon insistence on ethical motivation was seldom relaxed at any section of the Atlantic seaboard. But the unconscious, or un-literary, literature of the backwoodsman, plainsman, riverman, was frankly unethical, amoral. The prevailing practice is summed up in Simon Suggs's favorite saw, "It is good to be shifty in a new country" . . . Crockett boasted of his shiftiness as proudly as of his shooting prowess. Ovid Bolus is presented . . . with great gusto . . . as a natural liar. . . . If it is pertinent to refer to these tales as savoring of folk literature, it is pertinent to suggest that guile prevails in all of it, and that Reynard the Fox and Brer Rabbit move on the same plane as Simon Suggs. On the open, fluid frontier the ethics implicit in these stories is the ethics of success . . .[10]

The most notable precedent for Hooper's volume is the literature, oral and printed, about Fink and—to some extent—Crockett. Their tales, too, are told in loosely linked yarns, since oral narrative fosters episodes and anecdotes rather than thoroughly integrated plots. Their histories reveal wandering heroes who, like Suggs, despise book larnin', who know that mother wit is the best asset of a man in a new territory, and who consistently display their common sense in their dealings with others. And the book about Simon, like the first book about Crockett, is a campaign biography.

Notes

1. First published as *A Ride with Old Kit Kuncker* (Tuscaloosa, 1849), but generally known by the title given above, published in Philadelphia in 1851, since no copy of the first edition has been discovered.

2. [Bernard] De Voto, [*Mark Twain's America* (Boston, 1932)], pp. 93-94. Crockett makes much of his ugliness, alleging that he can bring a coon from a tree by grinning at it. Hooper's hero is so ugly that flies avoid lighting on his face even when he is a baby, so ugly that his wife has to practice before she can manage to kiss him, so ugly that a whole crowd of men who have been told to give their knives to any man uglier than they are shower knives upon him.

3. "The Bailiff that 'Stuck to His Oath'" (pp. 64-70), "Jim Bell's Revenge" (pp. 71-79), "Mrs. Johnson's Post Office Case" (pp. 80-82), and "A Fair Offender" (pp. 83-86).

4. *The Literature of Roguery* (Boston, 1907), I, 2-6.

5. C. Alphonso Smith, "Johnson Jones Hooper," *Library of Southern Literature* (New Orleans, 1909), VI, 2491.

6. Teague, in *Modern Chivalry* [H. H. Brackenridge, New York: American Book Co., 1937], is hardly worthy of the tradition. Birdofredum Sawin came

later. The best American predecessor of Simon is discoverable in Henry Junius Nott's *Novelettes of a Traveller* (1834) wherein the South Carolina author displayed the farcical adventures of Thomas Singularity. Singularity, as Professor Wauchope pointed out, is "a sharper 'deadbeat' and unscrupulous rascal—a lineal descendant of the earlier picaresque romances."—*The Writers of South Carolina* (Columbia, S. C., 1910), p. 59. But Nott's book is pretty generalized, pretty pallid, and rather dull.

7. Lucy L. Hazard, "The American Picaresque," *The Trans-Mississippi West* (Boulder, 1930), p. 198.

8. "The South in Light and Shade," in *The Compromises of Life* (New York, 1903), p. 78. Simon receives high praise from Watterson: "He is to the humor of the South what Sam Weller is to the humor of England, and Sancho Panza is to the humor of Spain . . . he stands out of the canvas whereon an obscure local Rubens has depicted him as lifelike and vivid as Gil Blas of Santillane."

9. [Walter] Blair and [Franklin J.] Meine, [*Mike Fink, King of Mississippi Keelboatmen* (New York, 1933)], p. x.

10. [Percy H. Boynton, *Literature and American Life* (Boston, 1936)], pp. 614-615.

Kenneth S. Lynn (essay date 1959)

SOURCE: Lynn, Kenneth S. "The Confidence Man, the Soldier, and the Mighty Hunter." In *Mark Twain and Southwestern Humor,* pp. 73-99. Boston: Little, Brown and Company, 1959.

[In the following excerpt, Lynn analyzes the character of Simon Suggs. Lynn argues that Suggs represents the consummate "confidence man," a literary type just beginning to emerge in the American literature of the period.]

The Confidence Man

His first appearance in Porter's magazine was as a loafer and pickpocket, hanging around nameless and dusty race tracks all across the Southwest. When he showed up again, he was a fixer, knowledgeable in the ways of tampering with horseflesh: the saddle burr, the cut rein, and various pills and sirups were now as familiar to him as the palm of his hand. On the rare occasions when he was caught out on a bet, he knew how to vanish into thin air. Sometimes, too, he was a trader in horses; on other occasions, a card-sharp, full of sly tricks. Along with his marked decks and extra aces he brought to the card table an air of amazed innocence: the mask of the greenhorn was the perfect disguise for the professional cheater. Soon he had other disguises as well. A born actor and boldly self-assured, he swaggered through a dazzling variety of parts, becoming by turns a doctor, lawyer, banker, long-lost relative. His favorite stage for acting his roles was the deck of a Mississippi steamboat. Another of his frequent haunts was the camp meeting revival, where he either played the ranting preacher or the sweaty sinner who "got religion"—whichever masquerade led most directly to the collection plate. From ignorant revivalists he moved on to bankers. Great gentlemen accustomed to deriving a handsome return from speculations in land or dealings in commercial paper found themselves outsmarted by his unscrupulous tactics. Avaricious, cruel, and utterly ruthless, always operating on the edge of the law, he moved through the land like a flight of seven-year locusts, leaving empty wallets behind him.

In his supreme incarnation he was known as Simon Suggs, the character created by Johnson J. Hooper. The editor of a struggling Whig newspaper in Chambers County, Alabama, Hooper was unknown as a humorist outside of Alabama until Porter reprinted one of his stories with the prefatory note, "This Hooper is a clever man, and we must enlist him among the correspondents of the *Spirit of the Times*." From that initial recognition, Hooper went on to become one of the magazine's most popular writers. When, in the mid-'40s, Hooper brought out a collection of Suggs's adventures in book form, he dedicated the volume to Porter, to whom he owed so much.

Some Adventures of Captain Simon Suggs (1845) is cast in the form of a campaign biography. Hooper's Confidence Man is running for office, we are informed by the Self-controlled Gentleman who is the narrator of the story, and the book is purportedly an *apologia pro vita sua*. In a tone of carefully extravagant admiration, the Gentleman introduces us to his candidate. He describes Suggs's gruesome face in minute and enthusiastic detail, mentioning in particular his four-inch mouth, on which "an ever-present sneer—not all malice, however—draws down the corners," and his "long and skinny, but muscular, neck." The Self-controlled Gentleman appears slightly embarrassed that the sample of Suggs's autograph which he wishes to describe to the voters was "only produced unblotted and in orthographical correctness, after three several efforts, 'from a rest,' on the counter of Bill Griffin's confectionary," but this momentary uneasiness is more than made up for by his apparent appreciation of the Suggsian wit: "His whole ethical system lies snugly in his favourite aphorism—'IT IS GOOD TO BE SHIFTY IN A NEW COUNTRY.'" Nature, the narrator says in fond summation, made Suggs "ready to cope with his kind, from his infancy, in all the arts by which men '*get along*' in the world; if she made him, in

respect to his moral conformation, a beast of prey, she did not refine the cruelty by denying him the fangs and the claws." Murderously ironic as these quotations are, they by no means get to the heart of Hooper's destructive humor. To appreciate the introductory "frame" to the full, one has to understand why Hooper chose to model his book on a political campaign biography.

It is by means of campaign biographies, the Self-controlled Gentleman explains, that "all the country has in its mind's eye, an image of a little gentleman with a round, oily face—sleek, bald pate, delicate whiskers, and foxy smile. . . . [called] Martin Van Buren; and future generations of naughty children who will persist in sitting up when they should be a-bed, will be frightened to their cribs by the lithograph of 'Major General Andrew Jackson,' which their mammas will declare to be a faithful representation of the Evil One—an atrocious slander, by the bye, on the potent, and comparatively well-favoured, prince of the infernal world." The comparison of the Devil's physiognomy to Jackson's prompts a second glance at the Gentleman's description of Suggs's diabolic appearance, and sure enough, in the hang of the nose, the slit of the mouth, and the hardness of the eyes we see who it is that Hooper's caricature resembles. Later references in the course of Suggs's adventures to Amos Kendall of Jackson's Kitchen Cabinet, and to the honorary degree that Harvard awarded Old Hickory, serve to keep Suggs's prototype lively in the mind: "Would that thy pen, O! Kendall, were ours! Then would thy hero and ours—the nation's Jackson and the country's Suggs—go down to posterity, equal in fame and honors, as in deeds! . . . Would that, like Caesar, he could write himself! Then, indeed, should Harvard yield him honors, and his country—justice!" In thus linking his Confidence Man with the idol of the Democracy, Hooper invited his audience to read political and cultural meanings of the broadest significance into the despicable life and times of Simon Suggs.

The son of a pious, austere, and "very avaricious" Baptist preacher, Simon has grown up in a home that has never been sanctified, to say the least, by the Whig harmonies. Watching his father administer a vicious lashing to a Negro boy, Simon says to himself, "'Drot it! what do boys have daddies for, anyhow? 'Tain't for nuthin' but jist to beat 'em and work 'em.—There's some use in mammies—I kin poke my finger right in the old 'oman's eye, and keep it thar, and if I say, it ain't thar, she'll say so, too." Deciding that his parents are of no use to him, Simon wins his father's horse from him by cheating at cards, and as he rides off in search of adventure he laughs aloud at the thought that he has secretly stuffed his mother's pipe with gunpowder instead of tobacco, and that soon she will be lighting it. The comedy in this opening sequence is in many ways reminiscent of [A. B.] Longstreet's work of the previous decade. Frame, point of view, and narrative style establish an aristocratic standard against which the antics of this Jacksonian boor are measured and evaluated. The differences between Hooper and Longstreet, between the Southwestern humor of the '40s and of the '30s, are as striking, however, as the similarities. Ransy Sniffle, to begin with, had been a solitary sadist in a fundamentally decent community; his victims, Stallions and Durham, had been upright and admirable men. The people whom Simon Suggs triumphs over, commencing with his parents, are a gross and greedy lot. Following the adventures of Simon Suggs, one is oppressed by the sense of moving through a darkening world, populated by dehumanized grotesques. Sensual and superstitious, gray with fear and green with envy, the people who are taken in by Hooper's Confidence Man are as morally degraded as he is. The perspective in which we view Simon Suggs is altered considerably as a result. The alteration is particularly evident in Simon Suggs's best-known adventure, the one which Mark Twain would draw upon for an episode in *Huckleberry Finn*: **"Simon Suggs Attends a Camp-Meeting."**

Camp meetings were one of the prime targets of the Southwestern humorists throughout the antebellum period. As Longstreet's remark about the Christian religion at the end of "The Fight" implied, the Whigs looked to the churches for allies in their battle against the Democracy. The Episcopalian minister and Whig propagandist, Calvin Colton, spoke for his class when he said that "Christian morality and piety, in connexion with the intelligence of the common people, are the last hope of the American Republic, and the only adequate means of bridling and holding in salutary check that rampant freedom, which is so characteristic of the American people." The one trouble with this pious hope was that by 1839, the year in which Colton voiced it, even the most myopic conservative, even Calvin Colton, must have realized that "the last hope of the American Republic" could no longer be counted on as a bulwark against rampant freedom. For in the voluntaristic denominations, at least, the techniques of revivalism were serving the cause of Jacksonism. Inviting all sinners to forget about doctrinal and ministerial guidance and save themselves by their own initiative, the revivalists bolstered the notion that "converted men by choice create the church"—an idea which, as Sidney E. Mead has seen, was "paralleled in the political realm by the notion that the people create the government." The religious emotion generated in the camp meetings was the political emotion of Jacksonian rallies in another form. Testifying to the Whigs' awareness of this fact was the amount of ammunition expended by the Southwestern humorists on demagogic preachers and their hallelujah-shouting congregations. When Simon Suggs rides into the camp meeting at Sandy Creek he enters an atmosphere that conservative Christians regarded with a mixture of contempt and extreme disquietude:

The excitement was intense. Men and women rolled about on the ground, or lay sobbing or shouting in promiscuous heaps. More than all, the negroes sang and screamed and prayed. Several, under the influence of what is technically called "the jerks," were plunging and pitching about with convulsive energy. The great object of all seemed to be, to see who could make the greatest noise. . . . "Bless my poor old soul!" screamed the preacher in the pulpit; . . . "Keep the thing warm!" roared a sensual seeming man, of stout mould and florid countenance, who was exhorting among a bevy of young women, upon whom he was lavishing caresses. "Keep the thing warm, breethring!— come to the Lord, honey!" he added, as he vigorously hugged one of the damsels he sought to save.

In this luridly lit scene of mendacity and sexuality, Simon Suggs is no longer a Clown in the sense that Ransy Sniffle had been: a puppet to be held at arm's length and laughed at. Hooper's Confidence Man is, rather, a comic hero, who—to a degree at least—enlists our sympathies on his side. Although he is a supreme hypocrite, we paradoxically admire his honesty, for unlike anyone else at the camp meeting, Simon Suggs admits his shiftiness; thus his cynical masquerade as a sinner who gets saved wins our surreptitious approval, while the censorship that would ordinarily prevent us from laughing along with him as he extracts a "handsome sum" from the congregation is lifted by the knowledge that the money would otherwise have lined the pockets of that fake religioso, the Reverend Bela Bugg. In a world of Buggs, we prefer Suggs.

The degradation of the society in which he moves is by no means the only factor responsible for the shift in comic perspective toward Simon Suggs. To compare Longstreet's book with Hooper's is to see that the clumps of vernacular dialogue judiciously planted by Longstreet in the early 1830s have grown rank and wild in the course of a decade. Once we are past Hooper's marvelously executed introduction, the gentlemanly style is kept up much less consistently than in Longstreet's sketches. For long periods, only the vernacular voices of the Confidence Man and the other Clowns can be heard. One effect of Hooper's increased use of the vernacular is to lend his scenes of Southwestern life a vitality unequaled by any humorist of the '30s. The sensory vividness of popular speech quickens his comedy with a ferocious energy; if the appearance and gestures of the poor whites are still described in the Gentleman's bland style, the extended use of quoted dialogue charges their characterizations with new life. The most important effect, however, is to blur the moral outlines of the comedy. As we listen to Hooper's characters "speak out of their own nature," the temperate voice of the Self-controlled Gentleman fades and we drift loose from the familiar assurances of the Whig universe into a featureless world of nightmarish sounds. Amidst the ecstatic screams of God-drunk revivalists, the shrieks of frontier settlers, their teeth chattering with fear at the prospect of an Indian attack, and the howls of pain of mothers, fathers, and slaves, it is no longer possible to pass a moral judgment when we hear the lying, cunning voice of the Confidence Man, because the very existence of a moral tradition in this world seems problematic. The triumph of the vernacular over the gentlemanly style is by no means definitive in *Simon Suggs* [*Some Adventures of Captain Simon Suggs*]. When the Confidence Man and his victims are finished talking, the Self-controlled Gentleman is heard once again, as disdainfully unruffled and impeccably refined as ever. Nevertheless, the total effect of the book's nervous alternation between two drastically different modes of expression is to obscure the comedy's didactic intent and to cause the reader's judgment of the central character to waver. Is Simon Suggs's motto, "IT IS GOOD TO BE SHIFTY IN A NEW COUNTRY," a despicable ethic, or the only one that makes survival possible? A. B. Longstreet would never have left such a question hanging fire.

As with language, so with point of view: there are times in Hooper's book when we leave the Gentleman's vantage point and enter the warped and vengeful mind of Simon Suggs. If the Gentleman quickly leads us out again and re-establishes his own distantly superior point of view, the momentary transposition is as shocking as though a puppeteer were temporarily to relinquish the direction of his show to Punch or Judy. For when we view men and events through the glittering eye of the Confidence Man, we are *in his world*, where no moral reference points exist; seen through the glass of the Suggsian consciousness, humanity has not the slightest dignity, while such terms as harmony, unity, stability—all the Whig shibboleths—are exposed as empty mockeries. The Gentleman, in Hooper's book, is no longer the supreme master, no longer quite so firmly in control of things. Our awareness of his presence is less vivid than previously, and so is our sense that the stories he tells have taken place in the past. In a footnote inserted in the **"Camp-Meeting"** story, Hooper attempted to assure his readers that "the scenes described in this story are not *now* to be witnessed," but the very fact that he felt constrained to add the footnote suggests his own awareness of the moral obscurities of his humor. When William Dean Howells deplored pre-Civil War Southwestern humor as being on the side of slavery, drunkenness and irreligion, he was almost certainly thinking of Hooper as a prime example, for no more famous character was ever produced by the tradition than Simon Suggs. Yet if slavery was defended by Hooper, drunkenness and irreligion were about as far from his temperate Whig precepts as possible. That a perceptive reader like Howells could have been so wide of the mark is eloquent testimony to Hooper's ambivalence. Wavering between two points of view as well as between two lin-

guistic modes, Hooper's humor is above all a nervous humor, brilliantly funny at times, but with no secure base anywhere.

The nervousness of *Simon Suggs* is the quality which beyond any other makes the book such an interesting documentation of the state of mind of conservative Southerners in a crucial decade in American history. For the vacillations of Hooper's book track the wide swings between optimism and pessimism to which the Southern Whigs were subject in the 1840s. Nothing in life seemed certain to them. If the Whigs won two out of three Presidential elections during the decade, both their candidates, being infirm generals, sickened and died in office. Their success in blunting the more radical reforms proposed in the constitutional conventions of the 1830s was scant solace in a decade which produced a new wave of populist agitation, including a scheme—pressed with particular fervor in Hooper's Alabama—for basing representation on white population alone, whereby the political strength of the slave-populated plantation counties would be severely reduced. And if slavery and cotton were bringing in bigger profits than ever, the world-wide outcry against the "peculiar institution" mounted ever higher in the '40s. Conservatives in the '30s had had their ups and downs, but the peaks had never been so sharp, nor the valleys so deep, and it is this psychological unsureness which *Simon Suggs* reflects. As his remarks about Andrew Jackson in his introduction indicated, Hooper desired with a fervor equal to Longstreet's to make his humor the instrument of political enlightenment. Like Longstreet, therefore, he turned to the serenely didactic Addison for his literary model. The complacent optimism of the *Spectator* manner was also admirably suited to express the sense of power and confidence that represented one strain of the Southern Whig mind in the '40s. But the Hooper who shared the well-nigh apocalyptic judgment of the *American Whig Review* in the mid-'40s that Jacksonism had brought America to the brink of "degradation and ruin"—and whose own editorials voiced the guilt, the indignation and the fear of the planters at the increasing fury of the slavery controversy—could not give vent to his feelings in the round tones of Joseph Addison. When Hooper confronted the Jacksonian saturnalia of the camp meeting, he was, consequently, a man divided against himself. In one guise, Hooper at Sandy Creek was the Self-controlled Gentleman, pointing with mild ridicule at violent excesses; in another, he was the Confidence Man, making war on a rotten world. In a decade of confusion, doubt, and growing uneasiness, halfway between the wide-open '30s and the dark and hate-filled '50s, Hooper's Jekyll-and-Hyde humor perfectly caught the ambivalent mood of Southern Whiggery.

Robert Hopkins (essay date fall 1963)

SOURCE: Hopkins, Robert. "Simon Suggs: A Burlesque Campaign Biography." *American Quarterly* 15, no. 3 (fall 1963): 459-63.

[*In the following essay, Hopkins discusses the satirical aspects of Hooper's* Some Adventures of Captain Simon Suggs, *examining the ways in which the work is modeled after, and at the same time parodies, the campaign biography of Andrew Jackson.*]

While it is generally recognized that Johnson Hooper's *Some Adventures of Simon Suggs* (1845) is written in the form of a campaign biography, no critic has yet recognized that the work is a *burlesque* of campaign biographies. This elementary distinction, however, is of some importance; for as in most great works of satire, the structure of *Simon Suggs* becomes itself a functional part of the humor. If one reads the story merely in terms of the Confidence-Man theme, there is a lengthy section (Chapters 7-9) that seems digressive and overly extended. This section becomes functional only when it is recognized as a direct burlesque of political biographies of Andrew Jackson. Hooper's title, *Some Adventures of Captain Simon Suggs Late of the Tallapoosa Volunteers,* parodies the title of John Henry Eaton's biography, *Memoirs of Andrew Jackson, Late Major-General and Commander In Chief of The Southern Division of The Army of The United States* (Boston, 1828). If Hooper's title would not have shown the alert reader of 1845 that burlesque was intended, the introductory chapter would surely have succeeded in doing so when the biographer defends his writing about a subject who is still alive by citing precedents:

> Thus Jackson, Van Buren, Clay and Polk have each a biography published while they live. Nay, the thing has been carried further; and in the first of each "Life" there is found what is termed a "counterfeit presentment" of the subject of the pages which follow. And so, not only are the moral and intellectual endowments of the candidate heralded to the world of voters; but an attempt is made to create an idea of his *physique.*[1]

Several paragraphs later, after comparing the lithograph of "Major General Andrew Jackson" to the "comparatively well-favoured, prince of the infernal world" (p. 9), the biographer describes Captain Suggs' physiognomy in such terms as to be an obvious caricature of Jackson.[2]

Kenneth Lynn has shown that the verbal description of Suggs and Darley's illustrations of Suggs are caricatures of Jackson, but he does not seem to see that the work is structurally burlesque.[3] Chapters 7, 8 and 9 deal with Suggs' escapades as the leader of the Tallapoosa Volunteers who band together in 1836 to protect themselves against a supposed Creek Indian uprising. Suggs

has himself elected the leader of the band, proclaims a state of martial law, conducts a farcical drumhead court-martial of a woman (who is sentenced to death but then released after paying Simon a fine), confiscates supplies from the surrounding area, and finally steals a large sum of money being wagered by two friendly Indian villages on an intratribal ballgame. The opening paragraph of Chapter 7 is such an important key to an understanding of the burlesque which follows, that it is necessary to quote it in full:

> By reference to memoranda, contemporaneously taken, of incidents to be recorded in the memoirs of Captain Suggs, we find that we have reached the most important period in the history of our hero—his assumption of a military command. And we beg the reader to believe, that we approach this portion of our subject with a profound regret at our own incapacity for its proper illumination. Would that thy pen, O! Kendall, were ours! Then would thy hero—and ours—the nation's Jackson and the country's Suggs—go down to far posterity, equal in fame and honors, as in deeds! But so the immortal gods have not decreed! Not to Suggs was Amos given! Aye, jealous of his mighty feats, the thundering Jove denied an historian worthy of his puissance! Would that, like Caesar, he could write himself! Then, indeed, should Harvard yield him honors, and his country—justice!

(p. 82)

Lynn mentions that the allusion is "to Amos Kendall of Jackson's Kitchen Cabinet"[4] and adds that Suggs' "ruthless use of the Creek War crisis as an excuse for looting his neighbor's possessions was understood by Whig readers to be a commentary on the Democrat's manipulation of the Texas question as a means of winning power."[5] In more immediate terms, however, the military episodes burlesque Jackson's military campaigns against the Creek Indians and ridicule mock-heroically Suggs' ludicrous attempts to emulate Jackson's exploits. Hooper's allusion is to Kendall primarily as a *writer,* not a cabinet member; in 1843-44 Kendall had published serially seven numbers of a biography of Jackson he never finished but which was published as a single volume in 1844 by Harper and Brothers.[6] The last seven chapters of Kendall's biography (Chapters 12-18) concern Jackson's military campaign against the Creek Indians in 1813-14. It is more than mere coincidence that much of this campaign was fought along the Tallapoosa River and that Suggs' campaign is fought in the same area. In reading the biographies of Jackson written before 1845 one is struck by the accounts of threatened and actual mutinies among the volunteers of Jackson's army, and in fact one private, John Wood, was court-martialed and executed.[7] The Battle of New Orleans is never reached, however, in Kendall's biography; and in connection with Suggs' drumhead court-martial of Mrs. Haycock a reader in 1845 would have recalled Jackson's proclamation of martial law at New Orleans, his arrest of Judge Hall who was escorted out of town, and his subsequent payment of a thousand-dollar fine after martial law had been suspended and civil law restored. In 1842 this episode was brought back into the lime-light when Senator L. F. Linn introduced a bill proposing that the federal government pay back the fine with interest to Jackson. In the ensuing national debate both inside and outside Congress the issue of martial law versus civil law was thoroughly explored, and it was not until 1844 that Jackson's fine was refunded by vote of Congress.[8]

Chapters 7, 8 and 9 in *Simon Suggs* can best be explained as a telescoped burlesque of Jackson's military campaign against the Creek Indians in 1813-14 (Kendall's biography) and Jackson's use of martial law in New Orleans in 1815 (Eaton's biography and others). Support for this interpretation is provided by Hooper's envelope pattern of allusions, first to Kendall as a writer at the beginning of Chapter 7 and last to Jackson's fine in the opening paragraph of Chapter 10:

> Captain Suggs found himself as poor at the conclusion of the Creek war, as he had been at its commencement. Although no "arbitrary," "despotic," "corrupt," and "unprincipled" judge had fined him a thousand dollars for his proclamation of martial law at Fort Suggs, or the enforcement of its rules in the case of Mrs. Haycock; yet somehow—the thing is alike inexplicable to him and to us—the money which he had contrived, by various shifts to obtain, melted away and was gone for ever.
>
> (p. 118)

The unity of this section would of course be destroyed if only one or two chapters are read out of context. It should also be pointed out that the burlesque need not be aimed so much at Jackson—by 1845 he was a legendary hero to the general public—as at the Confidence Man as demagogue using the Jacksonian myth as a smokescreen in order to achieve his own ulterior ends.

If then *Simon Suggs* is read not only as a picaresque narrative but also as a burlesque of campaign biography, certain restrictions will be imposed on its mode of expression. In his study of Southwestern humor Lynn distinguishes between the idiom of the Self-controlled Gentleman and the idiom of the Clown or Jacksonian Boor (the Self-controlled Gentleman is usually the narrator who in a dignified, somewhat verbose idiom satirizes or mocks the Clown whose idiom is vernacular). He implies that *Simon Suggs* is artistically defective in that the vernacular style is not allowed to triumph over the gentlemanly style.[9] If Hooper is to be consistent, however, in his burlesque of campaign biography he must retain the mode of expression of the genre as well. The strategy of campaign biography is to give the appearance of impartiality and seeming objectivity while in reality trying to convince the reader of the virtues of the candidate. Campaign biography is usually written in the gentlemanly idiom.

Simon Suggs burlesques this strategy by ironically inverting it: the gentleman-biographer's impartial rhetoric borders not on the edge of praise, but on the edge of sarcasm throughout the work, and at no time is there any doubt that Suggs is a comic butt of satire. The sudden return to the gentlemanly style to which Lynn is undoubtedly referring occurs in the last chapter. The reader is presented with a first person point of view of Suggs by the gentleman-biographer's introduction into the text of a signed letter from Suggs. Simon indicts himself so successfully and comically that the biographer in the last paragraph of the book can launch into a biased campaign oration that is easily understood as irony:

> Men of Tallapoosa, we have done! Suggs is before you! We have endeavoured to give the prominent events of his life with accuracy and impartiality. If you deem that he has "done the state some service," remember that he seeks the Sheriffalty of your county. He waxes old. He needs an office, the emoluments of which shall be sufficient to enable him to relax his intellectual exertions. His military services; his numerous family; his long residence among you; his gray hairs—all plead for him! Remember him at the polls!
>
> (pp. 147-48)

Such a shift back from the vernacular idiom of Suggs to the gentlemanly idiom of the biographer, made more abrupt because it is the last paragraph in the work, is not an artistic flaw if we recognize that *Simon Suggs* is burlesque. The return to the style of the campaign biography and the dropping of the pose of impartiality in order to make an impassioned plea to the voter burlesque the similar conclusions in American campaign biographies of the day. It is a conclusion that has been prepared for by the very genre in which *Simon Suggs* is written.

Notes

1. *Some Adventures of Captain Simon Suggs Late of The Tallapoosa Volunteers Together With "Taking the Census," And Other Alabama Sketches* (Philadelphia, 1847), pp. 8-9. All quotations in the text will refer by page numbers to this edition. See Walter Blair, *Horse Sense in American Humor* (New York, 1962), p. 103.

2. Many campaign biographies tended to be anticlimactic as a result of presenting the physical characteristics at the end. Hooper avoids this by giving a physical description of Suggs at the beginning.

3. *Mark Twain and Southwestern Humor* (Boston, 1959).

4. Lynn, p. 79.

5. Lynn, p. 87.

6. *Life of Andrew Jackson, Private, Military, and Civil* (New York, 1843-44).

7. Kendall, pp. 273-74.

8. See Robert S. Rankin, *When Civil Law Fails: Martial Law and Its Legal Basis in the United States* (Durham, N.C., 1939), pp. 3-25.

9. Lynn, p. 83.

Manly Wade Wellman (essay date 1969)

SOURCE: Wellman, Manly Wade. Introduction to *Adventures of Captain Simon Suggs, Late of the Tallapoosa Volunteers,* by Johnson Jones Hooper, pp. ix-xxiv. Chapel Hill: University of North Carolina Press, 1969.

[*In the following excerpt, Wellman analyzes the character of Simon Suggs. Describing Suggs as a "ribald colossus," Wellman asserts that he is wholly original, with no clear predecessor in English literature.*]

In December of 1844, a new and classic figure stalked out of the brush into American picaresque literature. Gaunt, disheveled Captain Simon Suggs, creature of the lively mind of Johnson Jones Hooper, always profiting but never thriving by shameless roguery, spoke for a whole gallery of frontier rascals when he drawled, "It's good to be shifty in a new country." Even those modern Southern humorists who never heard of Simon Suggs are strongly influenced by him. . . .

There is very little of Chateaubriand's noble savage or of Cooper's heroic woods-ranger in Captain Suggs. Not Sganarelle, Falstaff, or Tyll Eulenspiegel is more vividly characterized for complex deceit and utter lack of principle. Suggs would rather climb the tallest tree to plunder a trusting stranger than stand on the ground to earn an honest dollar. He is dishonest at cards to a degree remarkable even in Alabama's flush times. Though shambling and slovenly, he is able to impersonate an influential member of the State Legislature, a wealthy Kentucky drover, a prosperous slave-buyer.

Throughout all his exploits, he manifests a pungent bucolic repartee. "There ain't nobody round here kin make seed corn off o' me at cards," he boasts, with a confidence not fully justified. Of education: ". . . book-larnin' spiles a man if he's got mother-wit, and ef he ain't got that, it don't do him no good. . . ." Of trading: "Ef a feller don't make every aidge cut, he's in the background directly." But he never whines or goes mealy-mouthed save once, when he is on trial for gambling; and he may be forgiven for using every weapon at hand to talk himself out of a backwoods jail.

This genius for blackleg success and advancement appears at an early age. As a supremely delinquent teenager, Simon persuades his father to cut a stacked deck

for a pony, then rides away into decades of adventure which are mysteriously and perhaps significantly unchronicled. He turns up in Alabama in the 1830's, about the time of Hooper's own arrival. By now he is a middle-aged trickster and coney-catcher, going from strength to strength in his profitable deceptions. His high moment of glory is election to a militia captaincy by a huddle of neighbors who are terrified of an Indian raid that never takes place. Thus possessed of the military title so prized in that time and place, Suggs campaigns against the savages. Prudently he never fights them, but he robs them magnificently.

These various adventures appeared in the *East Alabamian* and the *Spirit* as separate stories, but through them runs a perceptible narrative continuity. In book form [*Some Adventures of Captain Simon Suggs, Late of the Tallapoosa Volunteers*], they fell into place as twelve chapters of a true novel. Hooper finished the saga with his hero offering for the post of sheriff of Tallapoosa County. There is something intriguing about Suggs's request that the author omit "that story bout the muscadine vine on the river . . . the old woman would be shure to hear bout it, and then the yeath *would* shake!"

Lively action in a half-wild setting makes the adventures move excitingly. And the character of Captain Simon Suggs, at once engaging and despicable, bestrides his world like a ribald colossus. . . .

Simon Suggs lived on.

For a while he lived in something like obscurity. ***Dog and Gun*** went into a fifth edition in 1863, a year after Hooper's death, and into a sixth and last in 1871. After the Civil War ended, the later decades of the nineteenth century saw new writers of folk humor becoming prolific and popular.

George W. Cable wrote in the accents of his Louisiana Creoles. Joel Chandler Harris took full and rich advantage of the plantation Negro's individual speech and legendry. A host of writers—dime-novelists, journalists, popular favorites of sleek publishing houses—exploited the picturesque cowboys, trappers, and bandits of the new Far West. The greatest of all the new folk humorists, and their lasting exemplar, was Samuel L. Clemens, called Mark Twain.

But newspapers reprinted stories about Suggs. In 1881, Peterson of Philadelphia brought him out in his twelfth edition, complete with the Darley illustrations. Two years after that, Henry Watterson included more than fifty pages of Simon Suggs, whose adventures he called a "masterpiece." In Mark Twain's *Library of Humor,* which appeared in 1888, appeared a Suggs adventure. Other anthologies have offered Suggs to new generations of readers. In 1928, the thirteenth edition of the book, with several other stories by Hooper, appeared in Americus, Georgia. There are also the Suggs influences and imitations, the captain's more or less legitimate children.

An early and highly distinguished Suggs enthusiast was William Makepeace Thackeray, who is said to have called Hooper "the most promising writer of his day" and to have praised *Simon Suggs* highly. It is not at all unlikely that something of Suggs went into Thackeray's seedy former captains with inglorious military records; his base-born, impudent claimants of bogus titles; his card sharps; and confidence men. More strongly discernible is the Suggs influence upon Clemens. Bernard de Voto's *Mark Twain's America* says outright that the twentieth chapter of *Huckleberry Finn,* in which the consummately unprincipled King fleeces an Arkansas camp meeting, is "all but identical" with Suggs's earlier plundering of a revival congregation [**"Simon Suggs Attends a Camp-Meeting"**]. This may be too flat a statement. Yet, to one who has companioned with the late captain of the Tallapoosa Volunteers, the King, with his white-whiskered plausibility, shabby finery, and masterful hoodwinking, looks and speaks and behaves exactly like an older Suggs, banished perhaps by an Alabama grown mistrustful to new and unsuspecting fields of endeavor along the Mississippi.

And William Faulkner's Snopeses are near cousins of Simon. The Suggs methods, gone country club, are employed by George Randolph Chester's Get-Rich-Quick Wallingford. Several Damon Runyan characters bring those same methods to the sidewalks of New York. *The Ballad of the Flim-Flam Man,* best-seller of the 1960's by Hooper's fellow North Carolinian Guy Owen, celebrates a modern Suggs.

The vigorous, racy, shameless strain is in no immediate danger of dying out.

Walter Blair and Hamlin Hill (essay date 1978)

SOURCE: Blair, Walter, and Hamlin Hill. "The Profile of a Prude." In *America's Humor: From Poor Richard to Doonesbury,* pp. 187-93. New York: Oxford University Press, 1978.

[*In the following excerpt, Blair and Hill discuss the relationship between the narrator and the main character in Hooper's* Some Adventures of Captain Simon Suggs.]

If [A. B.] Longstreet was equivocal about his gentry, making them sometimes ridiculous with their inflated language and highfalutin airs, Johnson J. Hooper created an anonymous narrator for *Simon Suggs's Adventures* [*Some Adventures of Captain Simon Suggs*] whose rhetoric was as purple as Hall's and Baldwin's and whose ridiculousness was even more dramatic. Hooper intended to burlesque campaign biographies, so he chose for his subject a rascal (one whose likeness to Old Hickory was unmistakable) and for his narrator a man who could work up to fever pitch over that rascal's skulduggery. "Would that thy pen, O! Kendall, were ours!" "Had not Romulus his Rome? Did not the pugnacious son of Philip call his Egyptian military settlement Alexandria? . . . Who then shall carp, when we say that Captain Simon Suggs bestowed *his* name upon the spot strengthened by his wisdom, and protected by his valour!"

Such rhapsodic carrying on inflates Simon's activities to heroic and monumental proportions; as it turns out, Simon is running only for sheriff of Tallapoosa County, Alabama. The narrator is able to ignore Simon's illegal and immoral intentions and to convert Simon's schemes and plots into valorous engagements. In short, although Hooper may have intended to ridicule Jackson, he also makes fun of the mock-heroic response to Simon that the narrator expresses. Blind to the true con-man attributes of Simon's biography, bombastic in his elegant praise, and ridiculous in his admiration of Suggs, the narrator is himself a fool—the character in the book whom Simon cons most successfully of all.

William E. Lenz (essay date 1985)

SOURCE: Lenz, William E. "The Emergence of the Confidence-Man Convention." In *Fast Talk & Flush Times: The Confidence Man as a Literary Convention,* pp. 57-96. Columbia: University of Missouri Press, 1985.

[*In the following excerpt, Lenz discusses the origins of the character of Simon Suggs. Describing* Some Adventures of Captain Simon Suggs *as a type of "literary masquerade," Lenz asserts that Suggs represents a new literary convention, one that embodies the spirit of the American frontier.*]

Hooper's first literary effort, **"Taking the Census in Alabama. By a Chicken Man of 1840,"** appeared in the La Fayette *East Alabamian* in 1843. This humorous reminiscence of misadventures in Tallapoosa was immediately applauded by William T. Porter, editor of the influential New York weekly *Spirit of the Times: A Chronicle of the Turf, Agriculture, Field Sports, Literature and the Stage.* Introducing **"Taking the Census,"** which the *Spirit* printed in September 1843, Porter outlined for his sixteen thousand subscribers Hooper's literary ancestry: "This Hooper is a clever man, and we must enlist him among the correspondents of the 'Spirit of the Times.' His sketch reminds us forcibly of the late Judge Longstreet's 'Georgia Scenes,' and the 'Adventures of Thomas Singularity,' by the late Prof. Nott, of S.C."[1] As Porter implies, **"Taking the Census"** is a linear descendant of traditional humorous sketches, an informal description of southwestern oddities: the low dialect is a characteristic element of 1830s frontier humor; the punctilious narrator, whose carefully chosen words contrast comically with those of the backwoodsmen, is likewise a conventional device. Hooper's comic perspective itself—based on such structural oppositions as those between the country and the city, the community and the stranger, and rebellion and authority—is a well-worn technique, and his deflation of both narrator and vernacular characters echoes Longstreet's methods in "Georgia Theatrics" and "The Horse-Swap."

The main structure of **"Taking the Census"** consists of humorous confrontations between the "chicken-man" and assorted residents of the Tallapoosa backcountry. In each of these, the narrator's repeated attempts to acquire information are frustrated—by mean dogs, fearful women, and artful circumlocution. A secondary structure emerges, however, which indicates a reorganization of conventional meanings and techniques.

Sol Todd, at first glance a conventional prankster like Longstreet's Ned Brace, lures the unsuspecting census-taker into the bottomless "Buck Hole" of the Tallapoosa River. Unlike Ned Brace, who frustrates Jacques Sancric's attempts at understanding ("The Character of a Native Georgian"), Sol intends more than the chicken-man's amusing embarrassment, for the ducking, we are told, is "but the fulfillment of a threat" ([Hooper] 155). The census man represents more than Ned Brace's archetypal foreigner; he is the visible agent of Van Buren, who would personally, the population of Tallapoosa believed, after taking the census levy "a tremendous tax" upon every Alabamian—every man, woman, child, and chicken. To make the chicken-man take a swim in the Buck Hole is therefore to strike out at the personal representative of the federal government. Sol's prank, as opposed to any of Ned's, is motivated by more than a rough sense of fun—it is a political statement. Seen in this light, each encounter in **"Taking the Census,"** although subordinate to a unifying comic structure, is informed by the rough individualism or rebelliousness characteristic of the frontier. Sol Todd and the other vernacular characters are not traditional pranksters playing traditional pranks.

Neither are they playing out the traditional action of the "biter bit." Hooper's **"Taking the Census,"** although containing the ducking of Sol Todd—the prankster pranked—directs attention beyond itself toward a symbolic interpretation of the *duello,* one that suggests new external forces impinging upon the frontier. The 1840 United States Census embodies the intrusion of national

political issues into the Southwest and gives particular literary form to the constitutional question of states' rights. The resistance of the vernacular characters to this form of federal regulation not only recalls the nullification crisis but also prefigures the impending Civil War. **"Taking the Census"** implies no political resolution to the debate, though as a loyal States' Rights Whig Hooper sees to it that the chicken-man's single victory is pyrrhic; rather, the sketch links opposed points of view. In this manner Hooper avoids judging the political issue, insisting instead on the "valueless action" of comedy.[2] Hooper focuses on the narrator's frustration, insulating the reader from the pressures of external problems. By withholding a final resolving action between the narrator and the vernacular characters, he allows the reader to try out each position, to evaluate each without commitment, and, at the tale's end, to retreat to a humorous vision of the whole.

"Taking the Census" reveals the method by which an author like Hooper could condition his audience to accept disturbing new perceptions; he utilizes familiar forms and techniques in order that his readers will be pleased rather than confused by deviations from the expected. The narrator's humorous observations and misadventures form the sketch's conventional main structure, one familiar to contemporary readers of *Georgia Scenes,* and one for which they share a conventional response: laughter. The implications of the confrontations between narrator and characters occupy a secondary position, held in check by equivalent pressures: the narrator, ducked in the Buck Hole by Sol Todd, immediately engineers Sol's own ducking—a balance is maintained.

From **"Taking the Census"** it is but a short imaginative step to Captain Simon Suggs.[3] The census-taker is, to Hooper's Whig Alabamians, no better than a shifty swindler, the Sixth U.S. Census no more nor less than a cleverly contrived game of theft. Simon Suggs, the "shifty man," is a chicken-man unrestrained by federal forms, a confidence man who at his leisure conducts his own personal census of the American frontier.

Some Adventures of Captain Simon Suggs (1845) borrows its form from nineteenth-century political biographies of prominent men like Andrew Jackson.[4] Written to present potential political candidates to the voters, campaign biographies normally contained information on the office seeker's youth, his mature exploits of honor, his portrait accompanied by a physical description, and a statement of his intentions when elected. Hooper provides Simon Suggs with all of these elements, yet each is informed—or malformed—by the comic perspective of frontier humor. "His whole ethical system," writes Hooper, "lies snugly in his favourite aphorism—'IT IS GOOD TO BE SHIFTY IN A NEW COUNTRY'— which means that it is right and proper that one should live as merrily and as comfortably as possible at the expense of others; and of the practicability of this in particular instances, the Captain's whole life has been a long series of the most convincing illustrations."[5] A portrait by Felix O. Darley complements a thorough anatomical analysis: the serpentine "lids without lashes," "An ever-present sneer—not all malice, however," and other "facial beauties" (11). "His autograph,—which was only produced unblotted and in orthographical correctness, after three efforts, 'from a rest,' on the counter of Bill Griffin's confectionary—we have presented with a view to humor the whim of those who fancy they can read character in a signature." Pointing out the discrepancy between appearance and reality—and between a conventional form and its humorous imitation—Hooper states plainly that "all such, we suspect, would pronounce the Captain *rugged, stubborn, and austere* in his disposition; whereas in fact, he is *smooth, even-tempered, and facile*" (10). To complete this parody, the author regrets the lapse of twenty years in Suggs's biography, and offers only one example from his formative years. It is, however, telling.

In his seventeenth year, Simon is caught playing "seven up" by his father, the Reverend Jedidiah Suggs. Hooper renders the hard-shell Baptist preacher, like Simon's Negro friend Bill, with conventionally exaggerated characteristics, attitudes, and language.

> "Soho! youngsters!—*you* in the fence corner, and the *crap* in the grass; what saith the Scriptur', Simon? 'Go to the ant, thou sluggard,' and so forth and so on."
>
> (15)

Jedidiah resembles Fielding's Thwackum, a familiar figure of pompous authority the reader is expected to resent. This conventional response Hooper insures by underscoring Jedidiah's unbending nature, an even mixture of self-righteous piety and greed. The reader sympathizes with Simon and desires the humorous deflation of his humorless dad, who appears to take more than spiritual enjoyment in disciplining the boys with canes. Escape, triumph, and laughter are Simon's goals: escape from punishment, triumph over his environment, and laughter to confirm his success. Simon is symbolically the champion of the individual, the reader's conventional hero of freedom, a truant not entirely unlike a frontier Tom Jones.

Facing a bout of discipline for playing cards with Bill, Simon boldly proclaims that the punishment will do no good, as he intends to make his living by gambling. Caught red-handed, the boy's brashness not only postpones his beating but redirects Jedidiah's thoughts: Simon's impassioned defense of his card-playing abilities astounds his father and arouses his righteous indignation and pity.

> "Simon! Simon! You poor unlettered fool. Don't you know that all card-players, and chicken-fighters, and

horse-racers go to hell? You crack-brained creetur you. And don't you know that them that plays cards always loses their money."
>
> (21)

Jedidiah's pulpit logic is no match for Simon's simple question: "Who wins it all then, daddy?" The reader appreciates Jedidiah's embarrassment and savors his fumbling efforts to assert his authority.

> "Shet your mouth, you imperdent, slack-jawed dog. Your daddy's a-tryin' to give you some good advice, and you a-pickin' up his words that way. I knowed a young man once, when I lived in Ogletharp, as went down to Augusty and sold a hundred dollars worth of cotton for his daddy, and some o' them gambollers got him to drinkin', and the *very first* night he was with 'em they got every cent of his money."
>
> (21-22)

Jedidiah's advice falls upon ears that are anything but deaf: "I'm as smart as any of 'em, and Bob Smith says them Augusty fellers can't make rent off o' me" (22). Simon's timely invocation of Bob Smith as a higher authority than his father on the perils of city life wounds Jedidiah's pride and arouses his contempt—for Bob Smith.

> "*Bob Smith* says, does he? And who's *Bob Smith*? Much does *Bob Smith* know about Augusty! he's *been thar*, I reckon! Slipped off yerly some mornin', when nobody warn't noticin', and got back afore night! It's *only* a hundred and fifty mile. Oh, yes, *Bob Smith* knows *all* about it! *I* a'n't never been to Augusty—I couldn't find the road thar, I reckon—ha! ha. *Bob-Smith*! The eternal stink! If he was only to see one o' them fine gentlemen in Augusty, with his fine broad-cloth, and bell-crown hat, and shoe-boots a-shinin' like silver, he'd take to the woods and kill himself a-runnin'. Bob Smith! that's whar all your devilment comes from, Simon."
>
> (23)

By a kind of logical sleight-of-hand, Simon confuses his father and severs the link connecting cause (caught gambling) and effect (immediate punishment).

Realizing his advantage, Simon insists that Bob Smith, his gambling tutor, assures him that he cannot be cheated by professional sharpers. "Bob Smith's as good as any body else, I judge; and a heap smarter than some. He showed me how to cut Jack . . . and that's more nor some people can do, if they *have* been to Augusty" (23). Simple Jedidiah, unwilling to admit his ignorance and to doubt his perceptions, agrees to witness Simon's attempt to cut jack: "If Bob Smith kin do it . . . I kin too. I don't know it by that name; but if it's book knowledge or plain sense, and Bob kin do it, it's reasonable to s'pose that old Jed'diah Suggs won't be bothered *bad*" (23-24). It is the very reasonableness of Simon's explanation that snares Jedidiah.

"Well, now the idee is, if you'll take the pack and mix 'em all up together, I'll take off a passel from the top, and the bottom one of them I take off will be one of the Jacks."

"Me to mix 'em fust?" said old Jed'diah.

"Yes."

"And you not to see but the back of the top one, when you go to 'cut,' as you call it?"

"Jist so, daddy."

"And the backs all jist as like as kin be?" said the senior Suggs, examining the cards.

"More alike nor cow-peas," said Simon.

"It can't be done, Simon," observed the old man, with great solemnity.

"Bob Smith kin do it, and so kin I."

"It's agin nater, Simon; thar a'n't a man in Augusty, nor on top of the yeath that kin do it!"

(24)

Simon has won his father's confidence, although Jedidiah knows "that them that plays cards always loses their money." It is this very distrust of others coupled with an intense faith in himself that makes the senior Suggs such a willing victim of the junior's "transaction." For Simon, acutely aware of the labyrinthine, contradictory impulses of human nature, appeals to the hard-shell preacher's egotistical confidence ("I *know* he can't do it, so there's no resk"), his sense of spiritual office ("I'll jist let him give me all his money, and that'll put all his wild sportin' notions out of his head"), his plastic morality ("It sartinly *can't* be nothin' but *givin'*, no way it kin be twisted"), and his greed ("Old Mr. Suggs ascertained the exact amount of the silver . . . he weighed the pouch of silver in his hand"). Jedidiah, whose instincts and emotions are now fully aroused, eagerly responds to a suggestion of the devil and removes all the "*picter*" cards from Simon's deck. Confidently awaiting the outcome of Simon's cut, Jedidiah is the quintessential victim, the dishonest man who is sure he is about to outsmart the confidence man. But by "a suspicious working of the wrist of the hand on the cards," Simon defeats his father's expectations, denies the validity of his perceptions, calls into question his powers of reasoning, and presents the jack of hearts for inspection. Astonished—and unwilling to admit his own dishonest manipulations—Jedidiah gives Simon the horse Bunch, a reprise from correction, and agrees with his son's ironic explanation of events.

"Daddy coun't help it, it was *predestinated*—'whom he hath, he will,' you know;" and the rascal pulled down the under lid of his left eye at his brother. Then addressing his father, he asked, "Warn't it, daddy?"

"To be sure—to be sure—all fixed aforehand," was old Mr. Suggs' reply.

"Didn't I tell you so, Ben?" said Simon—"*I* knowed it was all fixed aforehand."

(29)

The reader laughs with Simon, for he too understands that fate was fixed. He shares in the triumph of adolescence over sententious authority and delights in the exposure of the preacher's true qualities: avarice, egotism, and an ill-founded self-confidence. Had Jedidiah been a truly honest man, Simon could not have induced him under any circumstances to postpone his "correction" and take part in his "transaction"; Jedidiah reaps exactly as he sows. Hooper's use of the conventional frame technique further enlists the reader's sympathy, as the amused voice of the narrator assures him that this biography of Captain Simon Suggs chronicles the exploits of a humorous fellow worthy of note and that his behavior is completely under rational—narrative—control. It is also difficult to resist a boyish confidence man who wins an impractical horse and his freedom: Simon acts out a common fantasy of adolescent triumph. The confidence man is the youthful new country.

Simon's victory, however, is not without qualification. It is perhaps the result of the needs of frontier authors to reassert their superiority over low characters, or of these authors' awareness that shifty characters symbolize historical threats not completely dismissed by humor, that the confidence man is almost never entirely successful and admirable. His winnings are small, like the unmanageable horse Bunch, and his resolve to "git these here green feller's money" has social implications that are less than amusing. The reader is related, regardless of whether he acknowledges his kinship explicitly, to the confidence man's victim; in the broadest sense, he shares with every man the fate of the "green feller." By anticipating with pleasure Simon's hoodwinking of Jedidiah, the reader recognizes his own predicament and admits his own vulnerability. The same experience that teaches him to expect Jedidiah's victimization also teaches the reader that he too is susceptible to victimization. Although the reader overtly laughs with Simon, the entire episode acts as a kind of multiply refracting mirror in which the reader sees himself as both confidence man and foolish gull. The effect diminishes the confidence man's appeal and reinforces the reader's identification with the narrative voice.

When Simon appears to be the dispenser of poetic justice—Simon surely gives Jedidiah his just reward—his moral posture is vitiated by more than a streak of inhumanity: the malicious glee with which he "very wickedly" drives the mumble-peg deeper into the ground, knowing full well the inevitable consequence for his friend Bill, is bettered by the pipe he fills with gunpowder and leaves for his mother as a reminder of his affection. These are not the poetics of the confidence man, for they require neither confidence nor art—they are the dirty tricks of an irresponsible prankster. Twice Simon deliberately exposes Bill to painful beatings, and Simon's "involuntary sympathy" does little to enhance his appeal; his clear theft of his friend's pennies confirms the fact that the Negro is literally his whipping boy. Simon's often vile behavior clearly separates him from the normative frame-narrator (and author) and shows that the confidence man's ethical system is ultimately self-reflexive rather than social.

The distinction between artistic confidence tricks and blatant dirty tricks is crucial, revealing much more than a historical difference in standards of humor. The confidence man's occasional physical pranks resemble those of Longstreet's Ned Brace; they remind the reader of Simon's ancestry by their conventional form and provide the reader with a conventional model for response. They also invite comparison with confidence art, which implies an inchoate new standard. The confidence man becomes a literary convention precisely at the point that we can distinguish his aesthetic moneymaking schemes from the exploding gimmicks of the traditional prankster. As Hooper notes of Simon Suggs, it is the captain's ingenuity and wit which enable him "to detect the *soft spots* in his fellow . . . to assimilate himself to whatever company he may fall in with," and "which entitle him to the epithet '*Shifty*'" (12, 13). Further, the narrator insists that he will not be guilty of the cheap stunts to which Simon resorts; he can be trusted implicitly—the reader need not fear a similar betrayal of his confidence. As the confidence man triumphs over his victim, so too does the frame narrator triumph over his charismatic character, thereby assuring his audience that the harsh, chaotic world of Simon Suggs is carefully circumscribed. The confidence man's art appears subservient to the narrator's: stuffing his mother's pipe with gunpowder demonstrates Simon's tendency to forgo the rhetorical tools of his profession and seriously qualifies his success. These acts of rough sport signify that although the confidence man is decidedly the master of his frontier world, it is the frame narrator's rhetorical mastery that ultimately shapes and contains it.

Simon's youthful escapade provides a paradigm of expectations and response, its conventional and innovative elements fused through Hooper's overarching perspective of frontier humor. The momentary uneasiness the reader experiences when he recognizes himself in Jedidiah, Bill, Mrs. Suggs, or Simon himself is a defining characteristic of the American confidence man. Like the figure of the fool in Elizabethan drama, the confidence man makes the audience—the reader, not his victim—laugh, but it is laughter always tinged with anxiety: he who laughs at the fool's antics also laughs at himself, for the fool symbolically mirrors the folly to which every man is prone. The tension felt by the audience, common to both confidence man and fool, receives structural reinforcement by their peripheral social sta-

tus: both function as outsiders, outlaws who simultaneously represent the contradictory human impulses toward society and anarchy. Whether in an English court or the American Southwest, these figures inhabit a symbolic frontier where opposed pressures intersect and intermingle. Thus the fool, lording over his bauble, forms an ambiguous doppelgänger of the king ruling his court, and the confidence man, who abuses frontiersmen, functions as an analogue of those Americans who exploit the frontier.[6] Thus the confidence man embodies and recapitulates the continuous struggle between order and chaos in nineteenth-century America. A child of the frontier, the confidence man embodies its ambiguities; ruled by these ambiguities, he is also defined by the frontier and bound to it. Temporally and spatially, the confidence man symbolizes in a conventional literary form the flush times in the new country.

It is therefore altogether appropriate that Simon Suggs's first mature "operation" is speculation in frontier lands. Hooper carefully initiates the reader in the mysteries of flush times economics, detailing Simon's methods of speculation "without a dollar":

> We admit that there is a seeming incongruity in the idea but have those in whose minds speculation and capital are inseparably connected, ever heard of a process by which lands were sold, deeds executed, and all that sort of thing completely arranged, and all without once troubling the owner of the soil for an opinion even, in regard to the matter? Yet such occurrences were frequent some years since, in this country, and they illustrated *one* mode of speculation requiring little, if any, cash capital. But there were other modes of speculating without money or credit; and Captain Simon Suggs became as familiar with every one of them, as with the way to his own corncrib. As for those branches of the business requiring actual pecuniary outlay, he regarded them as only fit to be pursued by purse-proud clod-heads. Any fool, he reasoned, could speculate if he had money. But to buy, to sell, to make profits, without a cent in one's pocket—this required judgment, discretion, ingenuity—in short, genius!
>
> (35)

Simon's genius, undeniably, lies in "that tact, which enables man to detect the *soft spots* in his fellow, and to assimilate himself to whatever company he may fall in with" (12). The confidence man is proud of his ability, a national virtue, to make something out of nothing. Overhearing two speculators discuss a valuable piece of property, Simon, though unable to learn its exact location, formulates an inspired plan to profit from his greatest resource, human nature, and from the confident appearance of knowledge. The shifty man overtakes the speculator, Mr. Jones, and, knowing that one of any fellow's softest spots is his suspicion of others, insinuates that he, Simon Suggs, is also heading to Montgomery to lay claim to Mr. Jones's land. Jones, whose horse has been worn to the bone, allows his fear that Simon is his competition to cloud his reason, and within minutes reveals the coordinates of the property to the confidence man. Certain that Simon—whose horse is fresh—will be able to enter the claim first, Jones, whose blind greed is obvious, agrees to pay Simon $150 not to make the entry, furthermore "convincing" Simon to swap his own fine but tired horse plus $20 for the worthless but well-rested Ball. Using only his genius, Simon makes the speculator pay the price of his profession, for without Jones's desire to make a fast killing and the suspicion that attends such dishonest dealings, the shifty man would have remained the penniless owner of Ball; the victim's own fear and avarice give Simon the opportunity to speculate on him. The confidence man merely confirms (and profits by) Jones's apprehension that the world is filled with men as dishonest as himself.

Simon concludes the episode with a parodic paean to honesty.

> "Now some fellers, after makin' sich a little decent rise would milk the cow dry, by pushin' on to Doublejoy's, startin' a runner the nigh way to Montgomery, by the Augusty ferry, and enterin' that land in somebody else's name before Jones gits thar! But honesty's the best policy. Honesty's the bright spot in *any* man's character!—Fair play's a jewel, but honesty beats it all to pieces! Ah yes, *honesty,* HONESTY'S the stake that Simon Suggs will ALLERS tie to! What's a man without his inteegerty?"
>
> (40-41)

The confidence man's mock praise is humorous, for the reader knows that what really stops Simon is that the effort required to register the claim would be tiresome. He is honest only to his nature, which dictates "that one should live as merrily and comfortably as possible at the expense of others" (12). And his insistence on the truth of a traditional aphorism—"honesty's the best policy"—reminds the reader of Suggs's credo: "IT IS GOOD TO BE SHIFTY IN A NEW COUNTRY."

Simon's adventure with Mr. Jones, ending with a parody of conventional wisdom, appropriately introduces the sentimental address with which Hooper's fourth chapter commences.

> READER! didst ever encounter the Tiger?—not the bounding creature of the woods, with deadly fang and mutilating claw, that preys upon blood and muscle—but the stealthier and more ferocious animal which ranges amid "the busy haunts of men"—which feeds upon coin and banknotes—whose spots, more attractive than those of its namesake of the forest, dazzle and lure, like the brilliantly varying hues of the charmer snake, the more intensely and irresistibly, the longer they are looked upon—the thing, in short, of pasteboard and ivory, mother-of-pearl and mahogany—The FARO BANK!
>
> (42)

Hooper's rhetoric explores new possibilities for the artificial style of much sentimental fiction: the real and fictional worlds intersect, like the animal and mechanical images Hooper employs, and a new synthesis results. It also provides for his audience an immediately recognizable structure of understanding. The conventional address, humorously inflated, forms a familiar literary signpost for the reader and signals to him by its very nature as a set piece that not all traditional values will be inverted or burlesqued in *Simon Suggs* [*Some Adventures of Captain Simon Suggs*]. In addition, Hooper qualifies Simon's activities by devoting much of chapters 4 and 5 to his weakness: the Faro Bank. That Simon has a weakness proves that he is only human, not the Devil Incarnate, and that he is susceptible to other confidence men of greater quickness and skill. The reader reimagines with Hooper the character of Simon Suggs, recalling the truth of Jedidiah's biblical wisdom once so easily dismissed: "Them that plays cards always loses their money" (21). Jedidiah, it seems, may have been right, for "The Tiger" repeatedly makes a poor fool out of Simon.

Hooper's introductory digression, itself a conventional literary device, enforces the reevaluation by the sharp contrast between Simon's obsession and the narrator's normative rhetoric. The narrator's verbal "actions" may be imaginative and energetic, but they will never veer out of control. As in chapter 5, the descriptive digression is reassuring because of its substantiality; the physical details—the "mother-of-pearl and mahogany" Faro Bank, the "huge-lettered advertising cards" of Tuskaloosa—confirm the reader's knowledge of the historical frontier. They also acquaint the green fellow with the operations of gamblers and sharps. And finally, Hooper begins to flesh out the character of one particular confidence man; the shifty man is defined as an individual, a personality not to be confused with other types. Unlike Longstreet's Yellow Blossom or Ned Brace, Simon Suggs is the protagonist of fourteen stories. And as this confidence man becomes a more round character, there appears a trace of involuntary sympathy in Hooper's language; Simon's flaw, his "delusion," is lamentable, a consequence of his fuller personality. In this, Hooper reveals a new aspect of frontier humor, compassion for the confidence man, which will be fully developed by Harris, Melville, and Twain. The discovery of Simon's depth, his complexity of character, is Hooper's own, and implies an ambivalence toward the confidence man and an uncertainty of his identity as a mere comic device. Appropriately, Simon's next two exploits involve masquerade.

Simon Suggs is of course itself a form of literary masquerade, the "campaign biography" of an American who is the antiface of the Leatherstocking ideal, the ironic counterfeit or mirror image of Cooper's hero. More particularly, Hooper's fiction exemplifies what

Henry Nash Smith terms "the nineteenth-century fondness for disguises."[7] Simon Suggs puts on and takes off identities with less effort than that required to change hats: at one moment he becomes the representative from Tallapoosa, only to be transformed in the next into the heroic hog-driver General Witherspoon. These disguises, provided by acts of mistaken identity, suggest a traditional pattern of complication; in *Simon Suggs,* however, the conventional revelations of sentimental and romantic fiction Hooper shares only with the reader. Simon's victims do not learn his identity (or their folly) until he has made good his escape. The humor of each episode depends on concealment rather than on revelation. Finally, the comedy of errors the confidence man perpetuates ends neither in tragedy—as in James Nelson Barker's "Superstition" (1825)—nor in marriage—as in James Fenimore Cooper's *Pioneers* (1823)—but in an ironic ritual of good-fellowship. Having been mistaken for the representative from Tallapoosa by a man desirous of becoming—by the representative's influence—a bank director, Simon good-naturedly accepts a bribe, and with "his new friend travelled the remainder of the way to Tuskaloosa, in excellent companionship, as it was reasonable they should. They told their tales, sang their songs, and drank their liquor like a jovial pair as they were—the candidate paying all scores wherever they halted" (51). And after playing the part of General Witherspoon to the tune of two thousand dollars, Simon entertains the gentlemen of Tuskaloosa with an oyster supper (on the general's credit) and a farewell toast.

> "Gentle*men,*" said he "I'm devilish glad to see you all, and much obleeged to you, besides. You are the finest people I ever was amongst, and treat me a d—d sight better than they do at home"—which was a fact! "Hows'ever, I'm a poor hand to speak, but here's wishing of luck to you all"—and then wickedly seeming to blunder in his little speech—"and if I forget you, I'll be d—d if you'll ever forget me!"
>
> (66-67)

The reader, privy to the real import of Simon's speech, agrees with a smile that they will never forget "General Witherspoon," nor will they soon forget the ease with which they were manipulated. For Simon has only "to assimilate himself" to their expectations, parody their fantasies of the general's liberality, and allow his victims to deceive themselves.

As the legislator from Tallapoosa and as General Witherspoon, Simon acts in "a sublime moral spectacle" with unpleasant social ramifications. Chapter 4 demonstrates that "there are many reasons why gentlemen of distinction should at times desire to travel without being known" (49). The confidence man, of course, does not wish to be unmasked; this is the joke Simon shares with the reader. A dishonest legislator, as well, desires the protection of secrecy; this joke is on the reader. The suspicion that all representatives can be bought impinges upon our amusement, and Hooper's distrust of figures of authority manifests itself both in the confidence man's ability to assume the identity of a legislator or general and in the congruence between the practical methods of officials and con men. Hooper underlines the immorality of heroes and statesmen by noting that "General Witherspoon" is accepted in the Tuskaloosa gambling hall by gentlemen, "a large proportion members of the legislature" (55). The unamusing implication is that these crooked fools are actually Representative Men, not the worst America has to offer, like Captain Simon Suggs, but the best, those to whom the reader has entrusted his faith and his future.

That Hooper employs a central character whose business is dishonesty itself, that Simon Suggs never meets an honest man, and that the reader finds such characters entertaining all suggest a critical impulse to the confidence man's adventures. The new country, which in the 1830s had seemed to offer infinite opportunity, wealth, and security, by 1845 often appeared to have become—again, in the imagination—settlements plagued by necessity, poverty, and uncertainty. The cycle of boom-and-bust, culminating for many pioneers in financial ruin following the Panic of 1837, created anxiety in the Southwest that often appeared as suspicion of those in power who seemed to profit in proportion to the pioneers' loss. The confidence man, who returns to the 1830s in fiction to expose, profit from, and triumph over the speculators, expresses the common fantasy of the disillusioned who, as Timothy Flint noted, watched helplessly as their bubble of confidence burst. Simon Suggs is no frontier guardian angel; he, too, is helplessly tossed about, and though he may float high on the calm surface one day, on the next he must struggle not to go under.

Simon's dealings with Indians, a people who lost everything in the flush times, begin with the conventional *ubi sunt* theme, yet it is modified to accommodate contradictory impulses.

> In those days, an occasion of the sort drew together white man and Indian from all quarters of the "nation"—the one to cheat, the other to be cheated. The agent appointed by the Government to "certify" the sales of Indian lands was always in attendance; so that the scene was generally one of active traffic. The industrious speculator, with his assistant, the wily interpreter, kept unceasingly at work in the business of fraud; and by every species and art of persuasion, sought—and, sooner or later, succeeded—in drawing the untutored children of the forest into their nets. . . .
>
> And where are these speculators NOW?—those lords of the soil!—the men of dollars—the fortune-makers who bought with hundreds what was worth thousands!—they to whom every revolution of the sun brought a reduplication of their wealth! Where are they?
>
> (69)

By lamenting the passing of the flush times of rampant speculation Hooper fulfills a comic purpose, for it is amusing to mourn for confidence men and thieves. Yet his sobering answer to "Where are they, and what are they, now?" defeats the humorous expectations of the reader.

> They have been smitten by the hand of retributive justice! The curse of their victims has fastened upon them, and nine out of ten are houseless, outcast, bankrupt! In the flitting of ten years, the larger portion have lost money, lands, character, every thing! And the few who still retain somewhat of their once lordly possessions, mark its steady, unaccountable diminution, and strive vainly to avert their irresistible fate—an old age of shame and beggary. They are cursed, all of them—blighted, root and trunk and limb! The Creek is avenged!

(69-70)

The narrator attempts to have it both ways, affirming first with one set of values a comedic golden age, and then praising with a very different set of values that age's destruction. Hooper suspends the reader between two visions of the 1830s, one a comic pastoral in which the confidence man is king, and the other an antipastoral of retribution and wrath. The reader's confusion may be the result of Hooper's ambivalence toward the flush times and the confidence man, for the pastoral and antipastoral illuminate each other by contrast, mutually exclusive images evoking separate responses. The apparently humorous scene of speculation is by narrative fiat transformed into a court of ultimate justice, the comic perspective so comfortable to the reader becoming suddenly reflective and bitter. The reader may accept that the Indians have been wronged, that confidence men deserve their comeuppance, and that Hooper's sympathy and condemnation are equally genuine; but what, then, is the proper response to Hooper's Simon Suggs, who shamelessly speculates in Indian lands? Hooper appears to intend his literary devices to communicate contradictory attitudes: the Indians lost their ancestral lands to speculators who exploited their innocence; those speculators, though corrupt, were clever men, and one cannot help but admire their skill; the passing of both "races" should be mourned, for the wide-open frontier that gave them life is forever gone; and although some speculators hastened the death of the frontier through their monomaniacal pursuit of lucre, there was at least one, Simon Suggs, who was in harmony with the flush times and who loved the art, laughter, and personal triumph as much as a stack of golden double-eagles. . . .

Simon Suggs is, in fact, a literary convention that embodies and shapes perceptions of the American frontier, a device, like the term *confidence man*, created in the 1840s to express and control anxieties of boom and bust.

Hooper introduces Simon Suggs by means of conventional literary devices: the episodic structure, the form of a campaign biography, the narrative frame, the contrast between cultured narrator and dialect-spouting "low" characters, and the condescending narrative tone are all easily recognized elements of frontier humor. They structure the reader's response to Simon Suggs, trading upon the reader's familiarity with the works of Nott, Longstreet, Thompson, and others. Within the accepted context of frontier humor, Hooper creates a protagonist who redefines the frontier in terms appropriate to the 1840s, clarifying much of the uncertainty of intention present, for example, in Longstreet's "Georgia Theatrics." Hooper uses conventions from the 1830s to establish continuity: the frontier prankster, Ned Brace, reemerges as the frontier confidence man, taking its form from a synthesis of earlier models—Capt. John Farrago, Davy Crockett, Thomas Singularity, the Yellow Blossom, and Major Jones all join Ned Brace in contributing features to Capt. Simon Suggs. This multiplicity confirms the absence of a conventional figure and action before Hooper's hero, one that he might have merely rechristened and duplicated. A legion of tricksters, biters, shape-shifters, and rogues also crowds the works of Hooper's contemporaries: S. G. Goodrich's dishonest peddler, Philip B. January's rollicking dragoon, Poe's artful diddlers, Sol Smith's tricky steamboatmen, James Hall's wild backwoodsmen, and William Gilmore Simms's reformed gambler testify to the popularity of shifty sharpers, again demonstrating in their diversity the lack of a conventional literary form.[8] If the captain is in fact the conventional confidence man, there should appear following *Simon Suggs* a certain conformity to Hooper's model.

The example of Simon Suggs is visible first of all in the American public's appetite for editions of the captain's adventures. Obviously aware of Hooper's widespread popularity, the editors of the *New Orleans Picayune,* the *Boston Yankee Blade,* the *Cincinnati Great West,* and the *Baltimore Republican and Daily Argus* (to name a few) frequently reprinted Suggs's tales without a sign of embarrassment. The reading public was not alone in its admiration for Hooper; in addition to Griswold and Watterson, William E. Burton included four Suggs tales in his *Cyclopaedia of Wit and Humor* (1858), while James Wood Davidson, in *The Living Writers of the South* (1869), ranked *Simon Suggs* above Longstreet's *Georgia Scenes* because it was more "uniformly humorous." Of even more importance than critics are the fiction writers who applauded *Simon Suggs.* A minimal list would include Thomas A. Burke, John S. Robb, Sol Smith, Joseph M. Field, T. B. Thorpe, Stephen C. Massett, and William T. Porter, who reputedly held up publication of *The Big Bear of Arkansas, and Other Sketches* (1845) in order to include **"How Simon Suggs 'Raised Jack.'"** Porter also directs us to a clear example of Hooper's influence within *The Big Bear.* In his introduction to "The Way 'Lige' Shaddock 'Scared Up A Jack,'" he leaves no doubt as to its origin: "The following sketch was suggested to the writer—a capital Mississippi correspondent to the 'Spirit of the Times'—by Hooper's story (previously given in this volume) of **'How Simon Suggs raised Jack.'**"[9] A riverboat sharper bets Lige Shaddock fifty dollars that he can "turn a Jack" at one try, and, when challenged by Shaddock to perform, tosses the entire deck of cards face up on the table. The shifty descendant of Simon Suggs, however, observes, "If there is a Jack in THAT pack, I'll be d——d!" (177). In both title and action, "The Way 'Lige' Shaddock 'Scared Up A Jack'" pays tribute to Hooper's sketch; though he reverses the roles of Simon and Jedidiah, the author retains not only the structure of the snap but also a physical eccentricity of Simon's: "Lige has a way of dropping one corner of his eye and mouth at the same time—I don't know how he does it—it's a way he's got—but whenever you see it, there is *something out*" (176).

Old Tuttle, who appears in Porter's *A Quarter Race in Kentucky and Other Sketches* (1847), also bears Hooper's mark.

> Look at the picture of "Simon Suggs," and you'll see Old T. physically; in the *trial* scene you find him intellectually, and in the camp-meeting scene, morally. Were it not that Old T. never "samples" too much when on business, and fights the "*hoss* b'hoys" instead of the "Tiger," I should say they were one and the same person.[10]

Even the casual reader must note the resemblance at "Buckeye's" insistence. Old Tuttle's sleight-of-horse, as well, seems a variation on the confidence man's formula for fleecing Bela Bugg at the camp meeting, the Creeks at the ball game, and the slave-trading "Wetumpky Tradin Kumpiny": he wins his victim's confidence, allows him to think himself the smarter man, and then reaps the reward of his deception. Old Tuttle has learned more from Suggs than just how to wink at the reader.

Polly Peablossom's Wedding (1851), a humorous collection dedicated to "Johnson J. Hooper, Esq., of Lafayette, Alabama, (author of *Adventures of Simon Suggs*,) as a token of respect,"[11] contains several confidence games suggesting a close reading of the captain's exploits. Thomas A. Burke's "A Losing Game of Poker" imitates Suggs's method of turning the tables to turn a profit. Bennett, a gambler, enlists Cole to set up Andy Smith for a stacked deck by pretending to beat Bennett at cards. After winning over one thousand dollars from Bennett, Cole leaves as agreed; he is replaced by the eager Smith, who feels certain that Bennett is a loser. Bennett stacks the deck and cleans out Smith, yet wins only five hundred dollars from his not-so-stupid pigeon. The next day Bennett asks Cole, his decoy, for "a settlement."

"A settlement! what do you mean? I am not aware that there is anything to settle between you and me."

"Come, come, old hoss, none of your jokes. About that money you won last night; you know well enough what I mean."

"Well, didn't I win it fairly?"

"Why, yes, the playing was fair enough on your part, but you know the cards were stocked, so as to give you the hand you held," said the gambler, who began to feel slightly alarmed at Cole's manner.

"And who stocked them, pray? If you chose to deal me a better hand than you kept yourself, without my asking you to do so, it certainly wasn't my fault."

"I know that," said Bennett, really alarmed at the prospect of losing his money; "Still, it was understood that we were only playing for fun, and I hope you will refund that seventeen hundred, and take half my winnings from Smith."

"I understood the thing, Bennett, in no such way, and shall keep what I won from you, and you are perfectly welcome to *the whole* of what you took from Mr. Smith. Good morning, sir."

(48)

Cole springs the "Wetumpky Tradin Kumpiny" reversal quite as neatly as Simon Suggs.

"'Doing' a Sheriff" echoes Hooper's **"Muscadine Story,"** and "War's Yure Hoss?" and "The Thimble Game" recount games of chance not unlike the "soft snap" Simon gets from Jedidiah: in each a confidence man lures the sure but green sucker into an unwise trust in his perceptions. T. W. Lane's "The Thimble Game," moreover, contains a description of "Augusty" that parallels Hooper's in chapter 2 of *Simon Suggs* nearly word for word.

> Augusta was looked upon as Paris and London are now viewed by us. The man who had *never* been there, was a cipher in the community—nothing killed an opinion more surely, nothing stopped the mouth of "argyment" sooner, than the sneering taunt, "Pshaw! you ha'n't been to *Augusty*." The atmosphere of this favoured place was supposed to impart knowledge and wisdom to all who breathed it, and the veriest ass was a Solon and an umpire, if he could discourse fluently of the different localities, and various wonders, of *Augusty*.
>
> (*Polly Peablossom*, 28-29)

Finally, John S. Robb's confidence man in "'Doing' a Landlord" (in *Streaks of Squatter Life*, 1847) practices the manipulation of appearances Simon put to use in his Indian speculations with the "Big Widow"; the captain's saddlebags and Tom's trunk are both bulging with rocks rather than bullion.

Simon Suggs clearly formed the confidence man exemplum for Hooper's contemporaries. Recognizable in physical appearance, in speech, and in shifty style,

Suggs provided a model that proved eminently imitable, variable, and—in a literary, canonical sense—honorable. Once delineated, the narrative and thematic poetics of the confidence man are reimagined and the convention's structural devices are retooled to express new perceptions by succeeding generations of American writers. Baldwin, Harris, Warren, and Melville all demonstrate in their fictions the confidence they had in Hooper's example.

Notes

1. *Spirit of the Times* 13 (9 September 1843): 326. For more information on the relationship between Hooper and Porter, see Norris W. Yates, *William T. Porter and the "Spirit of the Times,"* chapter 2; and W. Stanley Hoole, *Alias Simon Suggs: The Life and Times of Johnson Jones Hooper.*

2. The phrase *valueless action* of comedy I have borrowed from a very different context in Elder Olson, *The Theory of Comedy,* p. 36.

3. Hooper's second sketch for the *East Alabamian,* "Our Hunt Last Week," Porter borrowed in 1843 for the *Spirit of the Times.* Like "Taking the Census," this humorous piece was well received; the *Spirit* even reprinted excerpts from it, retitled "The Biters Bit," in July 1844. Editors of such geographically diverse publications as the *Nashville Daily Gazette,* the *New Orleans Picayune,* and the *Boston Yankee Clipper* reprinted Hooper's sketches from the *Spirit,* and Hooper suddenly found himself with a national reputation.

4. See Robert Hopkins, "Simon Suggs: A Burlesque Campaign Biography" Hopkins argues that Hooper directly parodies specific biographies of Andrew Jackson, deriding Old Hickory's military and political achievements.

5. Johnson Jones Hooper, *Some Adventures of Captain Simon Suggs, Late of the Tallapoosy Volunteers,* p. 12. All future references to Hooper's work, unless otherwise indicated, will be from the first edition and will be cited parenthetically in the text.

6. See William Willeford, *The Fool and His Scepter: A Study in Clowns and Jesters and Their Audience,* for an excellent discussion of the fool's role.

7. Henry Nash Smith, *Virgin Land,* pp. 92-94.

8. These examples, typical of frontier humor, are chosen more or less at random: S. G. Goodrich ("Peter Parley"), "The Peddler" (1841); Philip B. January ("The Man in the Swamp"), "A Rollicking Dragoon Officer" (1843); Poe, "Diddling Considered as One of the Exact Sciences" (1843); Sol Smith, "A Bully Boat and a Brag Captain" (1845);

James Hall, "Peter Featherton" (1845); and William Gilmore Simms, "The Last Wager, or The Gamester of the Mississippi" (1845). For a wider contemporary sampling, see Griswold, *Prose Writers* (1857); William E. Burton, *Cyclopaedia of Wit and Humor* (1858); and James Wood Davidson, *The Living Writers of the South* (1869).

9. William T. Porter, ed., *The Big Bear of Arkansas and Other Sketches,* p. 175. All references to tales appearing in *The Big Bear* will be to this edition and will be cited parenthetically in the text.

10. "Old Tuttle's Last Quarter Race," by "Buckeye," in William T. Porter, ed., *A Quarter Race in Kentucky and Other Sketches,* p. 118. All references to tales appearing in *A Quarter Race* will be to this edition and will be cited parenthetically in the text.

11. Thomas A. Burke, *Polly Peablossom's Wedding and Other Tales,* p. 5. Burke also included Hooper's "Shifting the Responsibility" in this volume (143-45). The tales referred to are Burke's own "A Losing Game of Poker" (44-48) and "'Doing' A Sheriff" (98-101); "War's Yure Hoss?" by "a Missourian" (41-43); and Lane's "The Thimble Game" (28-40).

Bibliography

Barker, James Nelson. "Superstition." *Representative American Plays: From 1767 to the Present.* Ed. Arthur Hobson Quinn. New York: Appleton-Century-Crofts, 1953.

Burke, Thomas A. *Polly Peablossom's Wedding and Other Tales.* Philadelphia: T. B. Peterson and Brothers, 1851.

Burton, William E., ed. *Cyclopaedia of Wit and Humor; Containing Choice and Characteristic Selections from the Writings of the Most Eminent Humorists of America, Ireland, Scotland, and England.* 2 vols. New York: D. Appleton and Co., 1858, 1866.

Cooper, James Fenimore. *The Prairie: A Tale.* In *The Works of James Fenimore Cooper* ("Mohawk Edition"). 32 vols. New York & London: G. P. Putnam's Sons/The Knickerbocker Press, 1912.

Davidson, James Wood. *The Living Writers of the South.* New York: Carleton, 1869.

Griswold, Rufus W. *The Prose Writers of America.* 4th ed. rev. Philadelphia: Parry & McMillan, 1857.

Hoole, W. Stanley. *Alias Simon Suggs: The Life and Times of Johnson Jones Hooper.* University: University of Alabama Press, 1952.

Hooper, Johnson Jones. *Some Adventures of Captain Simon Suggs, Late of the Tallapoosy Volunteers; Together* with "Taking the Census," and Other Alabama Sketches. By a Country Editor. With a Portrait from Life, and Other Illustrations, by Darley. Philadelphia: Carey & Hart, 1845, 1846, 1848.

———. *Some Adventures of Capt. Simon Suggs.* Upper Saddle River, N.J.: Literature House/Gregg Press, 1970.

Hopkins, Robert. "Simon Suggs: A Burlesque Campaign Biography." *American Quarterly* 15 (1963): 459-63.

Longstreet, Augustus Baldwin. *Georgia Scenes, Characters, Incidents, &c., in the First Half Century of the Republic.* Augusta, Georgia: Printed at the S. R. Sentinel Office, 1835.

Nott, Henry Junius. *Novellettes of a Traveller; or, Odds and Ends from the Knapsack of Thomas Singularity, Journeyman Printer.* 2 vols. New York: Harper & Brothers, 1834.

Olson, Elder. *The Theory of Comedy.* Bloomington: Indiana University Press, 1968, 1975.

Porter, William T., ed. *The Big Bear of Arkansas and Other Sketches.* Philadelphia: T. B. Peterson, 1845.

———. *A Quarter Race in Kentucky and Other Sketches.* Philadelphia: Carey and Hart, 1847.

Robb, John S. *Streaks of Squatter Life, and Far-West Scenes.* Ed. John Francis McDermott. Gainesville, Fla.: Scholars' Facsimiles and Reprints, 1962.

Smith, Henry Nash. *Virgin Land: The American West as Symbol and Myth.* Cambridge: Harvard University Press, 1950. Rpt. 1970.

Thompson, William Tappan. *Major Jones' Scenes in Georgia.* Philadelphia: T. B. Peterson and Brothers, 1858.

Willeford, William. *The Fool and His Scepter: A Study in Clowns and Jesters and Their Audience.* Evanston, Ill.: Northwestern University Press, 1969.

Yates, Norris W. *William T. Porter and the "Spirit of the Times."* Baton Rouge: Louisiana State University Press, 1957.

Joseph H. Harkey (essay date 1986)

SOURCE: Harkey, Joseph H. "*Some Adventures of Captain Simon Suggs*: The Legacy of Johnson Jones Hooper." In *No Fairer Land: Studies in Southern Literature Before 1900,* edited by J. Lasley Dameron and James W. Mathews, pp. 200-10. Troy, N.Y.: Whitston Publishing Company, 1986.

[*In the following essay, Harkey examines the character of Simon Suggs. Harkey asserts that, while Suggs shares a number of similarities with Don Quixote, Tom Jones,* and other heroes of picaresque literature, he is also unique to the fiction of the Southwest and embodies the freedom, and precariousness, of life on the American frontier.]

In December of 1844, when Johnson Jones Hooper published in the LaFayette *East Alabamian* the first of his tales about Captain Simon Suggs, Hooper already had established himself as a humorist with a piece titled **"Taking the Census,"** which William T. Porter had reprinted in his *Spirit of the Times.* It was Suggs, however, who was to win Hooper immediate popularity as well as a permanent place in American literature. A month after the first Suggs tale had appeared in the *East Alabamian,* Porter began serializing it in the *Spirit,* and within a year Porter had arranged for a collection of Suggs' tales to be published by Carey and Hart of Philadelphia.[1] A dozen editions of the Suggs saga appeared during the nineteenth century, and individual selections were reprinted in dozens if not hundreds of anthologies, magazines, and newspapers in the United States and abroad.[2]

Of all the rascals that populated Southwestern humor, Suggs is not only one of the most memorable, but also one of the few of real literary interest. The Captain, his feet planted firmly in the hill country of Tallapoosa County, Alabama, occupies a clear position in the history of American fiction. As I show in this study, his *Adventures* [*Some Adventures of Captain Simon Suggs*] are a throwback to the picaresque literature of earlier centuries as well as a harbinger of the American local color movement, and the satire of the tales has not lost its edge in over a hundred and thirty years.

When one considers the time of Hooper's tales—in the 1840's when the short story was just beginning to receive its modern shape—the achievement is all the more impressive. In a literary sense, Hooper was as much a pioneer as any of his frontier neighbors who were carving farms and towns out of Indian lands.

There were models available to picaresque writers of the 1840's: the fiction of DeFoe, Fielding, and Smollett; translations of older European works, like *Gil Blas, Lazarillo de Tormes,* and *Don Quixote*; the oral tale, rich in local color and the humor of violence; and, for Hooper, *Georgia Scenes* and the Davy Crockett yarns. But models can not completely explain the accomplishment of *Some Adventures of Captain Simon Suggs, Late of the Tallapoosa Volunteers,* the first collection of Southwestern tales to feature a single, central character.[3]

One must temper his praise of Hooper's book, of course. It is hardly a novel, as some call it, and arbitrary chapter breaks often detract from a particular tale's "feel" of the modern short story, as does the narrator's typical

Southwestern insistence on framing each incident with urbane, ironic musings on the Captain. Despite such demerits the episodes are more than anecdotes, each having a beginning, middle, and end and satisfying expectations raised in the reader. All are rendered dramatically, and after the first tale, when Hooper offers exposition on the Captain and his character, the narrator generally does not intrude on the story, but is content to remain within the frame, aside from ironic references to "our hero." As Jay B. Hubbell has noted, Hooper allows the reader to draw the moral,[4] although he does on occasion interrupt a story to make moral comments on activities not involving Suggs, such as Hooper's denunciation of the land speculators who bled the Creeks.

One of the chief merits of the book is its realistic style. Granted that realistic elements had been found in English prose fiction at least since Malory—and traditionally satirists have relied on an exaggerated realism, there is still something quite modern about Hooper's realism. In addition to a verisimilitude of detail based upon close observation, Hooper's tales deal with representative rather than exceptional characters and actions, and the narrator usually reports Suggs' adventures objectively, as noted.[5] Above all, Hooper's reluctance to moralize—even when Suggs' volunteers to murder the Indian Cocher-Emartee—gives the tales a startlingly realistic quality.

If Hooper's realism is not pure, his tales nevertheless attain an "apparent fidelity, through style, to details of objects, manners, and speech," to cite Charles C. Walcutt's criterion for realism.[6] Admittedly, most realists were more affected by the social implications of the life they described than Hooper, whose ironic comments suggest a detached attitude toward Suggs' tricks. Yet the view of the life of the narrator in *Adventures* is anything but dispassionate, for he reveals a feeling of powerless outrage when he recounts the fate of the Creeks. But his satire, which suggests that the dull in this world are likely to be taken advantage of by the sharp, was meant to be funny—and is[7]—and each tale was aimed at an audience that enjoyed a good laugh and was hardly concerned about the world view of the author.

More striking than its realism is the collection's affinity with Spanish picaresque fiction of the sixteenth and seventeenth centuries. While scholars cannot agree on what constitutes a picaresque novel (whether, for example, it has a moral purpose, the pícaro is a villain, or satire is a necessary element of the genre[8]), there is extant a body of fiction dating from *Lazarillo de Tormes* (1554) that draws upon a common group of characteristics traditionally considered picaresque. Suggs has been linked to this tradition by many scholars, including Walter Blair, who in 1937 said that Suggs was a "notable contribution to the literature of roguery," while acknowledging that there is no way to determine whether Hooper had read Spanish picaresque novels or would have imitated them if he had.[9] There are some significant differences between *Adventures* and classic picaresque fiction.

Spanish pícaros usually sprang from disreputable families and were corrupted by contact with the world after being cast out at early ages to make their own ways in life. Pícaros celebrated in literature are those whose wits were sharp and morals flexible enough to enable them to survive, as in *Lazarillo*. But Suggs did not come from a disreputable family. His father, a hard-shell Baptist preacher, owned a farm and at least one slave, Bill—property enough to make him locally respectable.[10] Simon, always knavish and an accomplished gambler and swindler as a young boy, left home riding Bunch, the pony he won from his father by palming a card. In the Spanish picaresque, the protagonist rose by serving one master after another, and the novel develops his entire life. But Suggs never served a master, being nominally a yeoman farmer, and after one glimpse of him as a youth the reader loses sight of Simon until twenty years later. Then in middle age he surfaces in Tallapoosa County, a poor section of middle Alabama,[11] where he is a property owner and land speculator. He is not the "lowest of trash," as he has been called, though a Spanish pícaro might well have been, nor is he "socially inadequate," one scholar's characterization of a picaro.[12] To the contrary, he is a man of great social presence, though coarse of speech, and is comfortable in any company. Finally, love and marriage were portrayed as "deception and fraud" in Spanish picaresque fiction; but in *Adventures,* marriage is typically comic-American—Suggs fears his wife—and aside from a bland episode involving Betsy Cockerell and the hugging at the camp meeting, sex plays no role at all in the book.[13]

These differences notwithstanding, *Adventures* still has many of the features of Spanish picaresque fiction. It is realistic and is a "road" novel—Suggs never stays any place longer than six weeks, although he does operate from a base, his farm. The book is highly episodic, Suggs' *modus operandi* and his character offering the work's only unity.[14] The setting is contemporary—Alabama of the 1830's—and actual place names are used throughout. Irony is used frequently by Suggs himself: "'I ginnally makes my mark, so that I'm hard to forget,' said the Captain *truthfully*." The "old pícaro reborn as a frontier confidence man,"[15] Suggs is a rouge's rogue and prides himself on his ability to outcheat any other man in a "fair" contest. From the outset he consciously uses his wits to gain advantage. His amoral attitude coupled with a devotion to Providence not unlike that of Lazarillo—and his ability to be vicious when the need arises—make him very much a *pícaro* in the Spanish, as opposed to English, manner, except for perhaps the rogues of Greene and Smollett.

Despite the Captain's popularity in his own day and for half a century afterwards, reviews of his character have been less than complimentary. He has been called the "prince of rascals,"[16] adept at "brilliantly duping people";[17] a "character of hypocrisy and craft" of the "uttermost sharpness" who would "rather succeed by foul than fair means";[18] and an "old scoundrel" who as a "middle-aged trickster and coney-catcher" is "at once engaging and despicable."[19] His engaging qualities should not be minimized, for had Hooper created a mere Billy Fishback, Suggs would not have enjoyed the popularity he has. He is not just a quick-witted card sharp whose misdemeanors are less significant than his essential decency, like television's Maverick. For, as Arlin Turner has said, Suggs is "not simply a scamp operating outside all moral codes, but also a character of such uncouth speech and action, and such blythe unconcern through it all as to seem a deliberate challenge to current tastes";[20] and the Captain thus has a great deal to overcome with wit, style, and judicious choice of victims in order to seem engaging.

As a "shirt-tail" boy he already had "contrived to contract all the coarse vices incident" to a newly-settled region like middle Georgia and Alabama. As a man, Suggs, whose motto is "It's good to be shifty in a new country," illustrates completely the conception of a pícaro as defined in the 1726 edition of an authoritative Spanish dictionary: he is "low, deceitful, dishonest, and shameless."[21] An "incorrigible, irreclaimable devil" as a boy who stole his father's horses and mother's roosters for racing and cock-fighting, he displays in middle age his baseness by eavesdropping, lying, stealing, and cowardice. The one time he is challenged to fight he protests that he is "not a fightin' man." He demonstrates his baseness by making the Widow Haycock grovel for mercy at her court martial at "Fort Suggs" and by swindling the defenseless Indian Big Widow out of several hundred dollars with his sweet tongue and "sweet water."

His dishonesty and deceitfulness are implicit in his lowness; in addition to being a liar and a swindler, he is a thief and an imposter. He steals horses, a saddle, and a pouch of silver representing bets at an Indian game of ball-play (modern lacrosse). He bilks the congregation of a camp meeting; he lies about the dangers of Indian raids in order to gain his captaincy and daily levies of supplies; he allows himself to be mistaken for a legislator in order to swindle a political aspirant and impersonates General Witherspoon, an eccentric hog drover, in an attempt to make a "rise" at faro; and he pretends to be a friend of the family of the Widow Rugby in order to blackmail her new husband.

His "blythe unconcern" about all of this trickery is never tainted by remorse. In an apparent attempt to seduce Betsy Cockerell, he shamelessly tells her that his wife is dying and implies that Betsy will be his new wife. He even employs an outdated note informing himself that his "boys is a-dying" to persuade a judge to dismiss an indictment against him. (Later, as he is "gleefully" relating his trick to some friends, his lawyer approaches; Suggs assumes an irate air, accusing "the boys" of having played a trick *on him* with the note.) Shameless Simon even applies to the government for reimbursement for a pony he abandoned in order to steal a better horse during his "military career."

Of these characteristics, the one Hooper emphasized least in Suggs is viciousness. Readers who encounter Suggs only in the camp meeting and "Fort Suggs" episodes might doubt that he was capable of real viciousness, thinking of him as a rather mean version of that shifty contemporary confidence man, Professor Harold Hill, the Music Man. Evidently Hooper originally conceived of Suggs as basically vicious for in his early exposition he calls him a "beast of prey," not without "fangs and claws." Yet actual viciousness reveals itself in Suggs only three times. He swindles Big Widow, although he does not take all of her money as some of his counterparts would have done. In the muscadine tale, he leaves the sheriff dangling over the water of the river, clinging from a high vine, although the sheriff cannot swim. (The sheriff thinks Suggs is playing a practical joke on him, but the Captain tells him that "thar's just the smallest grain of a joke in this here, that you ever seed. It's the coldest sort of airnest.") Suggs shows his viciousness in all its ugliness, however, in ordering the death of Cocher-Emartee. After stealing the purse at the lacrosse game, the Captain and his volunteers cross the river to safety. When Cocher-Emartee, urging his warriors on, plunges into the river to pursue Suggs, the Captain orders his men to "blaze away." After the smoke of the volley clears, there is no Indian to be seen in the water, only a pony.

The murder of Cocher-Emartee, bringing to mind the shooting of Buck Grangerford in *The Adventures of Huckleberry Finn,* is the low point of Suggs' career. Given Hooper's attitude toward the "untutored children of the forest" whose fate at the hands of land speculators he protested in an earlier chapter of the book, it is difficult to imagine his involving Suggs in such a cold-blooded murder. Hooper may have presented a realistic incident from the times or intended it as another parallel between Suggs and Andrew Jackson, who were "equal in fame and honors." But the action is out of character for Suggs, whose only other act of violence is to kick the pestering Carolina "clay-eater" on one occasion.

While Captain Suggs is not a good man, ordinarily he is an affable, engaging confidence man whose victims are fools eager to be swindled. Among them, only Big Widow is pitiable. The self-righteousness of Suggs' father and his father's pride and avarice make him a gull one enjoys seeing cheated. The husband of the Widow Rugby is a fortune hunter himself; the political aspirant, a greedy hypocrite, is eager to bribe Suggs; and his victims at the camp meeting are guilty of hypocrisy and affectation, contributing money out of pride of purse. While the Captain himself is satirized in the book, most of the satire is directed at his victims, who are so gullible that Providence apparently placed them in Alabama for the sole purpose of supplying Suggs with money.

In his dealings with gulls, Suggs displays a consummate skill of which he is quite proud, knowing that he is not likely to be "throwed by ordinary men" and that he will not be easily forgotten. He is as vain about his achievements as was Davy Crockett of reselling a "useful coonskin" a number of times to get rum for his constituents during an election campaign; and like the Yankee merchant whom Davy cheated, Suggs believes that the sharper individual has a natural right to take advantage of his victim.[22] If language fails to charm Suggs' gulls, he readily supplies tears. He will strike the pose of a heroic Tallapoosa "Old Hickory" if need be, or grovel if that is more effective. An inveterate card player, he enjoys running a bluff in a swindle, as when he uses a saddlebag full of stones to persuade other speculators he has the money to buy Big Widow's property. He is masterful at appearing magnanimous, "giving" General Witherspoon's nephew ten hogs and setting up the house—on the general's credit. Because of his keen understanding of human nature and his "nose for the soft spot," his swindles are always successful.

The Captain's philosophy is of a piece with his behavior. His private musings reveal an implicit belief that man is by nature a predator: "Ef a feller don't make every aidge cut, he's in the background directly. It's tile and strive, and tussle every way, to make and honest livin." The word "honest" may be taken ironically, or as evidence of hypocrisy, but Suggs seems to use the word as seriously as Alan Sillitoe's long-distance runner, who holds that the outlaw's "honesty" differs from that of the "inlaws." To Suggs, in part, it means recognizing the fact that everyone cheats and lives accordingly: "Honesty's a bright watch-out, a hand o' cards in your fingers and one in your lap, with a little grain of help from Providence, will always fetch a man through!" But something keeps him from "milk[ing] the cow dry," for he never bleeds his victims, being content with the spoils of the moment. In this regard, "Fair play's a jewel, but honesty beats it all to pieces!" Hooper may have simply satirized Suggs' hypocrisy, but since Hooper does not comment on these passages himself, we have only Suggs' words to judge, and Suggs seems unaware of any hypocrisy on his part. "Honesty and Providence will never fail to fetch a man out!" Suggs

says, repeating one of his favorite themes. While it makes him appear ignorant at best when he imagines that Providence provides gulls for his benefit, he had learned his morals from life, and life on the frontier in the 1830's and 1840's taught him that the strong devour the weak, as was the case with the mistreatment of the Creeks and other Indians.[23]

J. DeLancy Ferguson insisted that Hooper "self-consciously patroniz[ed]" Suggs and the other backwoods characters he dealt with,[24] and certainly Hooper is at pains to distinguish his voice, in the frame, from that of Suggs. If Hooper's attitude toward Suggs reflected little fondness, it is difficult to imagine why he elaborated Suggs' character as he did. For the Captain is not merely droll but truly engaging; and although he seems like the very roughest of diamonds, he is a gem. Part of his charm lies in the richness of his language. He speaks of making "as much noise as a panter and a pack of hounds" and tells a man he would "see him as deep in h-ll as a pigeon could fly in a fortnight." Of his own patriotism, he says that "Simon Suggs will allers be found sticking thar, like a tick onder a cow's belly" and says of a swamp that "it'll mire butterflies." He has a nice sense of irony, also, confessing at the camp meeting that he came there to swindle the people when, in fact, he still intends to do so.

Occasionally Suggs discloses recognizably human feelings. As a boy leaving home, he is saddened to part from his mother, brother, and friends—although when he remembers he had filled her pipe with gunpowder his amusement banishes his sadness. Like most comic American husbands, he fears his wife, who will make the "yeath shake" if she learns of his peccadilloes. And at one point he mourns the fact that the family larder is almost empty and he has little money. "*Somebody* must suffer," he concludes and is determined that it will not be his family.

Ironically, his most engaging trait is his own "soft spot," a passion for faro, at which he always loses. In the course of the book he gets over two thousand dollars, but at the end he has less than twenty, for every time he makes a "rise," he battles the "tiger" with the loot and loses. While impersonating General Witherspoon, he wins fifteen hundred dollars at faro, but then loses it and his stake.

Suggs also has the appeal of the anchorless bachelor, and despite his concern for his family, he never stays at home. Rather he enjoys freedom from the responsibilities of work and the freedom to ignore laws, like a layabout Daniel Boone or Natty Bumppo. Few symbols are more compelling to American men during strenuous times than a symbol of freedom, and Hooper and his readers, especially the male ones, must have envied the Captain and his relatively free existence.

Not everyone appreciates a character like the Captain. The plantation owners William Gilmore Simms wrote for did not care for him, and some contemporary critics find him downright repellent.[25] Hooper, however, discovered the popularity of the Captain when he tried to wash his hands of him. Other men were much more interested in Simon Suggs than in Johnson Jones Hooper, political candidate. Such was the danger of creating a character capable of taking on a life of his own. His creation of Captain Simon Suggs in a narrative recapturing the flavor of the original picaresque novel was to become Hooper's legacy to American literature.

Notes

1. W. Stanley Hoole, *Alias Simon Suggs: The Life and Times of Johnson Jones Hooper* (University, Ala.: University of Alabama Press, 1952), pp. 51-59.

2. See Manly Wade Wellman's "Introduction," pp. xxv-xxvi, in *Adventures of Captain Simon Suggs, Late of the Tallapoosa Volunteers,* Southern Literary Classics (Chapel Hill: University of North Carolina Press, 1969). All quotations are from this edition.

3. Hoole, pp. 57, 204*n.* Two editions totaling 8,000 volumes were published in 1845.

4. Jay B. Hubbell, *The South in American Literature, 1607-1900* (Durham, N.C.: Duke University Press, 1954), p. 674.

5. George J. Becker, "Realism: An Essay in Definition," *Modern Language Quarterly,* 10 (June 1949), 184-97, sees objectivity, representative characters and actions, and verisimilitude of detail as the main characters of realism.

6. *American Literary Naturalism, A Divided Stream* (Minneapolis, Minn.: University of Minnesota Press, 1956), p. 23.

7. Carl Holliday, *A History of Southern Literature* (New York: Neale Publishing Co., 1906), p. 167, writes that the purpose of the Simon Suggs book was "fun making, and in that particular it is a decided success."

8. For recent views of what a pícaro is, for instance, see Alexander A. Parker, *Literature and the Delinquent: The Picaresque Novel in Spain and Europe* (Edinburgh: Edinburgh University Press, 1967), p. 4, who says a pícaro is "a 'delinquent'" who offends "against moral and social laws" but is not "vicious" but "dishonourable and anti-social in a less violent way"; and Robert Alter, *Rogue's Progress: Studies in the Picaresque Novel* (Cambridge, Mass.: Harvard University Press, 1965), p. 12, who sees the pícaro as one having a "natural inclination toward roguery" but who "is not by nature a scoundrel." The problems presented by labels like "picaresque" and "pícaro" are discussed by Percy G. Adams, "The Anti-Hero in Eighteenth-Century Fiction," *Studies in the Literary Imagination,* 9 (1967), 29-53.

9. Walter Blair, *Native American Humor (1800-1900)* (New York: American Book Co., 1937), p. 87.

10. Merrill MacGuire Skaggs, *The Folk of Southern Fiction* (Athens, Ga.: University of Georgia Press, 1972), p. 38, affirms that owning even one slave gave one respectability in his community.

11. Tallapoosa had poor market outlets and land not well-suited to cotton; the number of farms was greater and their value much smaller in Tallapoosa than in nearby cotton counties, according to William L. Barney, *The Secessionist Impulse, Alabama and Mississippi in 1860* (Princeton, N.J.: Princeton University Press, 1974), pp. 140-41.

12. Christine J. Whitbourne, ed., *Knaves and Swindlers: Essays on the Picaresque Novel in Europe* (London: Oxford University Press, 1974), p. 16.

13. Unless one interprets symbolically Suggs' rusted sword or the imaginary one he described to Betsy Cockerell.

14. Parker, pp. v-vi, says that structure should not be a consideration in any definition of the picaresque, but it has been commonplace to use structure in defining the form.

15. James M. Cox, "Humor in the Old Southwest," in Louis D. Rubin, Jr., ed., *The Comic Imagination in American Literature* (New Brunswick, N.J.: Rutgers University Press, 1973), p. 107.

16. Hubbell, p. 674.

17. Blair, p. 86.

18. William Jerdan, quoted in Hoole, p. 175.

19. Rubin, p. 9; Wellman, p. xvi.

20. Arlin Turner, "Seeds of Literary Revolt in the Humor of the Old Southwest," *Louisiana Historical Quarterly,* 39 (1956), 149.

21. *Dictionary of the Spanish Academy* (1726), quoted in Parker, p. 4.

22. Crockett did not write "A Useful Coonskin" himself, but he probably supplied notes for it, according to Hennig Cohen and William B. Dillingham, eds. *Humor of the Old Southwest* (Boston: Houghton Mifflin, 1964), p. 16.

23. Martin E. Marty, *Righteous Empire: The Protestant Experience in America* (New York: Dial Press,

1970), pp. 14-15. Marty notes, p. 14, that a school-book "published in 1793 argues that 'nature has formed the different degrees of genius, and the characters of nations, which are seldom known to change.'" He adds that schoolchildren were taught that it is only natural that when an inferior and a superior nation meet, the inferior one is likely to yield.

24. Ferguson, "The Roots of American Humor," *American Scholar,* 4 (1935), 49.

25. Shields McIlwaine, *The Southern Poor-White, From Lubberland to Tobacco Road* (Norman: University of Oklahoma Press, 1939), pp. 48-49, calls Suggs "unheroic," "prideless," and a "simon pure rogue"; Skaggs, p. 33, says that Suggs is a "rogue by any standards" and a "villain"; and Sylvia Jenkins Cook, *From Tobacco Road to Route 66: The Southern Poor White in Fiction* [(Chapel Hill: University of North Carolina Press, 1976)], p. 6, says that Suggs "has all the immorality and pious hypocrisy of the comic poor white."

Johanna Nicol Shields (essay date 1990)

SOURCE: Shields, Johanna Nicol. "A Sadder Simon Suggs: Freedom and Slavery in the Humor of Johnson Hooper." In *The Humor of the Old South,* edited by M. Thomas Inge and Edward J. Piacentino, pp. 130-53. Lexington: University Press of Kentucky, 2001.

[*In the following excerpt, originally published in 1990, Shields examines Hooper's writings within the context of the contentious social climate of the antebellum South. Shields argues that in spite of his virulent racism and contempt for human weakness, Hooper was essentially a political idealist. According to Shields, Hooper envisioned a future in which the frontier would be transformed into a just society rooted in strong moral values rather than in power or greed.*]

> "Well, mother-wit kin beat book-larnin, at any game! . . . Human natur' and the human family is my books, and I've never seed many but what I could hold my own with."
>
> Captain Simon Suggs

The variety of human experience in the Old South stands much more fully before us now than it did only decades ago. Today, however, while historians clearly perceive the complex relationships between white freedom and black slavery, they do not fully understand the alien mentality behind them. How could intelligent men and women have expected to perpetuate both slavery and freedom in a progressive world? Historians' efforts to answer this troubling question can be aided by a fresh look at old evidence: the abundant comic record left by popular southern humorists such as Johnson Hooper.[1] Humor had special use to people with deep potential conflicts among their values. Humor flows directly from the tension between what is and what ought to be—sometimes from conflicts so severe that they are tragic, as the twin faces of drama imply. But laughter has unique power to make all but the worst problems tolerable, if only by easing tensions or postponing resolutions. Johnson Hooper's famous comic saga, *Some Adventures of Captain Simon Suggs,* reflects the hopeful spirit of its Whig author in the early 1840s, when the stories were written, but it also reveals a strong undercurrent of anxiety. Thus Hooper's popular art demonstrates the instrumental relationship linking humor with freedom and slavery in southern society. His art provoked laughter that had tragic repercussions.

Hooper treated a southern problem while satirizing American social values. As a good Whig, he believed that the individual freedom that dissolved archaic forms of order would finally stimulate social progress but only when men worked together in a new spirit of cooperation.[2] In Suggs's ludicrous adventures, Hooper shows the crude results of unrestrained liberty on Alabama's frontier. With one eye on the future, he lampooned white men's ceaseless competition and savagely ridiculed the impact of their freedom on slaves. Ultimately, his jokes made slavery seem natural, even necessary, in an American jungle where "mother-wit" was a sine qua non for survival.

Simon Suggs was a predatory opportunist, a grotesque and bestial version of an American self-made man, but if his naturalistic traits derived from any explicit social theory, Hooper's humor hid it well. Hooper's understanding of the world drew instinctively from his experience as well as from formal ideas. "'Book larning spiles a man ef he's got mother-wit, and ef he aint got that, it don't do him no good,'" quipped Suggs, and the blue-blooded Hooper's career demonstrated the point. He claimed an ancient literary lineage that ran from Juvenal through Cervantes, Swift, and Addison to America. He read England's gentlemanly reviews, which reported intellectual life abroad. And he also knew the folk mythology that provided comic relief in the cabins and taverns of a dangerous frontier. But a newspaper editor's "mother-wit," a canny sense of ear and eye that captured the common tongue in a readable form, enabled Hooper to market his humor. First circulated in his Whig newspaper, the Suggs stories went through roughly a dozen antebellum printings issued mainly from northern presses. In a serious mood, Hooper used his newspaper's press to publish a proslavery tract in 1846 and agitated for southern nationalism in the late 1850s, but his humor betrayed no polemical intent. Instead, he buried his ideas so deeply in new images of "human natur' and the human family" that when readers laughed at Suggs's reckless freedom they may well have ignored how their amusement condoned slavery.[3]

Historians will not fail to see the ugly side of Hooper's humor, yet understanding why others laughed is important since it links slavery and freedom in an unfamiliar way. Historians like James Oakes and George M. Fredrickson have insisted that popular proslavery ideology used race rather than paternalism to justify a herrenvolk society. By making slaves outsiders in a liberal state, their status as property was guaranteed. These arguments, however, relegate paternalistic values to a minor, geographically restricted role, as if migrants left their ingrained habits behind when they moved westward from the coastal South. Such a view slights the force of memory, operating in the minds and upon the "manners"—to use the Jeffersonian word of the many people who were raised with the ethos by which patricians had long justified their moral right to dominate others.[4] In Hooper's humor, paternalistic standards covertly impugned the morality of a herrenvolk ethic. The spirit of freedom animated Suggs's world, creating a moral anarchy that naturally bred slavery, but such unstable freedom held no promise of equality since race quite imperfectly separated those people with "mother-wit" from those without it. For all of their brutish qualities, Hooper's black slaves are humans, while his free whites can be kin to animals—and witless, too.

At the same time, however, Suggs's inegalitarian society presented no case for planter dominance over plain folk. Eugene Genovese and Elizabeth Fox-Genovese have forcefully argued that slaveholders, "in but not of the capitalist world," were driven by the logic of paternalism to accept slavery in the abstract, implicitly renouncing the absolute value of freedom. Unquestionably, paternalistic values provided a coherent way to attribute morality to exploitative relationships. That many planters embraced an ideology enshrining themselves as Christian guardians for their benighted African wards is both logically consistent and historically demonstrable. It is much more difficult, however, to demonstrate that a paternalistic ideology pervaded southern white society. The notion that planters should rightfully be fatherly stewards for other free men sat poorly with many nonplanters—and Johnson Hooper thought it nonsense.[5]

Instead, Hooper made Suggs demonstrate again and again the comic futility of traditional conceptions of paternalism, hinting at a new moral order in which good men must earn the right to organize a progressive society. But Hooper's satire only hinted at moral standards he made explicit elsewhere, and therein lay its special suitability for joining freedom and slavery in popular thought. The apparent moral anarchy in Suggs's world stems from the literary model Hooper employed. In the underlying structure of satire, the targets of derisive laughter—Hooper's predators and their victims—stand judged by those who might be their opposites. Without the hopeful implicit standard, predators would not be funny. For thousands of amused readers, the pleasure of laughter affirmed hope without defining aspirations. . . .

Suggs is the common man writ large: dirty and disreputable but master of his world. More fundamentally, he is human nature in the raw. Hooper—later nicknamed "the Ugly Man"—resembled Suggs, whose physiognomy and spindly body are described in language that reveals the kinship.[6] Suggs, too, has just emerged from a "somewhat extended juvenility" and a long period of wandering without "authentic trace" of his whereabouts. Like Hooper, he is incurably fond of drinking and gambling. Suggs lives by his wits, making something out of nothing, needing no capital to "get along." He has something better: an infallible knowledge of human nature. He is "a sort of he-Pallas, ready to cope with his kind, from his infancy. . . ." If nature made Suggs a "beast of prey, she did not refine the cruelty by denying him the fangs and the claws." Simon Suggs is man as animal, his residence the jungle, not an abstract state of nature. Not only does no wrathful God intervene to punish Suggs for bestial behavior, but time and again the environment rewards it.[7]

Suggs's depraved world is too funny to be confused with Hell. In reflection of Hooper's dual allegiances—to the society which shaped his character and to that which promised his redemption—his genius made the freedom of Suggs's natural habitat both as frightening and as attractive as unbounded opportunity. Suggs roamed a frontier waiting for development, a jungle ready to be tamed, amusing because his wit was equal to the task. Although it bears some hints of a nightmare republic corrupted by unrestrained avarice, Hooper's vision was not retrogressive.[8] Order in the new society would have to take unfamiliar forms, tapping forces compatible with those unleashed by freedom. The license of satiric form did not require Hooper to explain precisely how the spirit of freedom might be retained as civilization advanced or exactly what moral glue would hold society together. A positivist by instinct, Hooper offered reality as he saw it. Decrying false visions defined by tradition or convention, he empowered Suggs, the scholar of human nature, to destroy them, suggesting the potentialities of freedom by what was left in ruins.[9]

The landscape of Suggs's world is littered with the victims of his destructive power, its creative strength purging the jungle of more venal predators. In story after story, Suggs defeats his fellow confidence men, who pose as false stewards while manipulating conventional standards to promote themselves. Suggs and Johns symbolize the great deception of Jacksonian politics, but

Suggs also triumphs over land speculators robbing the Indians, members of the legislature and profligate "men of fortune" outwitting each other in card games, lawyers and judges bilking the people at large, and preachers extorting money from their congregations.[10] Suggs can victimize these would-be nabobs because they are too busy exploiting others' "soft spots" to see ruin approaching. No moral superiority separates these beasts from their intended prey; their status in society rests only upon pretense. By any standards of moral responsibility, they deserve the laughter their foibles provoke.

Simon Suggs also exploits ignorant, gullible, and seemingly harmless poor whites, but only at first glance are most of them innocents.[11] The frontiersmen elevate Suggs to their captaincy for an Indian war he has conjured wholly from rumor, through feeding their prejudice and fear. These commoners are sorted out by wit, however, and significantly, it is their lowliest representative, a din-eating, "spindlelegged young man" called Yellow Legs, who sees right through Suggs's charade. He is too young and powerless to depose the captain, so Yellow Legs proclaims the truth to his fellows over Suggs's dire threats. Like knowledge unfettered, he bounces in and out of the plot, challenging Suggs with "a gesture expressive of the highest contempt."[12] When the dirt-eater's elders fail to act upon the truth he reveals, they become victims of the faulty order they have created. Hooper's satire has a kind of primitive moral truth: given freedom, men must be responsible for their own "soft spots."

But the nihilism inherent in Hooper's naturalism is more brutally revealed by the exploitation of those who do not seem to deserve their fate at all: slaves, whose weaknesses come directly from nature, in Hooper's view. They are perpetual victims, captives of their inferiority. Relative innocents, however deficient in wit, they are exploited by Suggs and by his other victims as well. Cruel laughter about slaves was important to the meaning of both the first and last stories in Simon Suggs's biography, and brief but grim jokes about slaves mark the center of Hooper's most effective piece of satire, **"The Captain Attends a Camp-Meeting."** Hooper cannily shifted his narrative from American white freedom to southern Negro slavery, confident that racism would allow his readers to share his amusement at slavery's ugly features, some of which could not be changed, even in a tamer world. The laughter of white people demeaned the black slaves, assuaging unease and fixing their place as victims with natural finality, as the same freedom that empowered whites forever entailed blacks to slavery.[13]

Black slavery first defines white freedom in the opening escapade of Simon Suggs, when he acquired the liberty that created his adult character. The story of Simon's escape from his parents drew power from Hooper's conviction that external restraints upon the anarchic impulses of human nature were useless. Simon's father, Jedediah Suggs, is a hard-shell Baptist preacher, avaricious and something of a hypocrite, but he believes himself duty-bound to save his son from gambling. While trying to do so, he is tricked by the precocious sharpster into a card game that costs Jedediah a horse and all control over young Simon. Jedediah's greed and his moral tyranny warrant his loss, but Simon's mother's self-deception seems quite minor: she merely entertains a sentimental view of her son. As the boy puts it: "'There's some use in mammies—I kin poke my finger right in the old 'omen's eye, and keep it thar, and if I say it aim thar, she'll say so too.'" Still, Suggs takes a parting shot at her, loading her favorite pipe with gunpowder. He rides away from home on his father's horse, laughing at the picture of the pipe exploding in his mother's face. False piety and sentiment were no match for Suggs's wit and his powerful thirst for freedom.[14]

Jedediah Suggs is no more a loving patriarch to his slave Bill than he is to his son. The slave cannot escape, however, and his punishment is essential to Simon's getaway. When Jedediah first catches his son and young Bill playing cards in a field, he declares that they both deserve a beating. Bill, already being beaten at poker, goes first, and as Simon watches in horrified expectation, "Bill was swung up a-tiptoe to a limb, and the whipping commenced, Simon's eye followed every movement of his father's arm; and as each blow descended upon the bare shoulders of his sable friend, his own body writhed and 'wriggled' in involuntary sympathy."[15] The shifty white boy vicariously felt the slave child's pain, but it gave him extra time to invent the card trick that wins his freedom. Simon triumphantly escapes both a beating and his confining home; Bill can avoid neither. The story begins with the two young men as playmates. It ends with their futures in sharp contrast.

The multiple meanings of this complicated parable touch upon the most basic human relations, conveying Hooper's sense that in free society the dissolution of familial order might be pervasive. The story bears witness to the rising influence of the cash nexus, and it heralds the arrival of a new era of oedipal tensions aggravated by the lure of recurring flush times. The competitive frontier seduced eastern sons to western freedom, to the irresistible promise of a future gained by wit, not given by family. Hooper assailed with equal enthusiasm the futile authority of patriarchy and the more manipulative order of sentimental families like his own. Both gave way before the appetite for self-determination. So if, like proslavery intellectuals, Hooper compared the moral obligations within families to the responsibilities of power over dependent slaves, he found that new and deeply felt tensions made the family an unusable model for slavery.[16] The loose ties of affection might "refine the cruelty" of nature, preventing fathers from whipping sons or slaves, but they would be inadequate to restrain slaves. With the same brutal frankness that would lead him later to defend burning alive a slave accused of murder as a wrong justifiably committed by respectable people, Hooper affirmed what he thought had to be.[17]

Jedediah Suggs points toward other predatory stewards whom Hooper, through Simon, punishes for creating social order false to nature's own. This moral is outrageously invoked in **"The Captain Attends a Camp-Meeting,"** a stunning satire of enthusiastic religion. In a scene dominated by nearly pornographic imagery, Simon steals the meeting's offering from impious preachers by posing as a "saved" sinner. The hedonism unveiled by Hooper's coarse humor lies in human nature, but its eruption at the meeting is the work of greedy preachers, whose bad faith exposes whites to petty theft and blacks to worse. The opening scene describes the emotional turmoil the preachers stir up among white and black people, who mix "promiscuously," though the "negroes sang and screamed and prayed" more wildly than the whites: "'Gl-o-ree!' yelled a huge, greasy negro woman, as in a fit of the jerks, she threw herself convulsively from her feet,"—falling all over a tiny white man in her ecstasy. In the middle of this biracial uproar, Suggs captivates the excited crowd with his theatrically sexual account of being born again. His "load o' sin" that had been "'a-mashin down on my back'" lifts as soon as Suggs relates his vision of the threatening jaws of a dreadful alligator: "'I jist pitched in a big rock which choked him to death, and that minit I felt the weight slide off, and I had the best feelins—sorter like you'll have from good sperrits—any body ever had!'" Throughout Suggs's spellbinding "discourse" the ministers, recognizing no difference between his theatrics and the conduct of other converts, maintain a steady flow of exhortations about the "'spe-rience" and its spiritual meaning, their commentary demonstrating the tools with which Suggs will soon defraud them all.[18]

But Hooper more ominously punctuates Suggs's performance with the exclamations of a hysterical old white woman dressed in black silk. Three times Mrs. Dobbs shrieks at her slave Sukey to fetch Mr. Dobbs so he can hear Simon "talk sweet":

> "Whar's John Dobbs? You Sukey!" screaming at a ne-gro woman on the other side of the square—"ef you don't hunt up your mass John in a minute, and have him here to listen to his [Suggs's] 'sperience, I'll tuck you up when I get home and give you a hundred and fifty lashes, madam!—see if I don't!" "Blessed Lord!"—referring again to the Captain's relation, "aint it a *precious* 'scource!"[19]

Aroused by Simon and the preachers, the frustrated old woman threatens her slave with a violence that underscores the mistress's animal qualities. Mrs. Dobbs's

threats appear as a dark counterpoint to her supposed religious enthusiasm. Yet like the murky "krick swamp" that adjoins the camp ground and provides shelter for Suggs's eventual escape, her shrill exclamations warn of the natural wildness never far removed from human experience. . . .

Although Hooper probably had a darker view of human nature than most members of his Whiggish audience, he too hoped that a free society's cultivation of human wit would engender progress. He hoped—one cannot say believed—that honorable, honest men with self-knowledge would have enough self-restraint to check their predatory instincts, to curb might with right. So even after northern antislavery politics had destroyed his nationalism, Hooper remained a Whiggish advocate of education and public improvement and an avid promoter of state aid for economic development. Moreover, he wanted slavery's cruelties, like those of other human relationships, to be meliorated, to make all "institushuns" consistent with a social order he later described as a "true, permanent, and homogeneous condition, in which a steady, well-regulated public sentiment is a powerful influence to direct and correct in every department of life."[20] He saw black slavery as a necessary cost of civilized freedom in a biracial society, but it was not to be confused with the goal of progress. During the long process, in order to sustain the effort, how much better to laugh than cry at every inevitable failure?

Johnson Hooper was not, then, an atavistic remnant of bygone patriarchy, nor was he an apologist for a tyrannical ruling class in the making. He belonged in a sense to a southern elite that never emerged. On the one hand, he drew his ideas from the larger currents of the Anglo-American world, as Mills Thornton has suggested for other Alabama fire-eaters of a decade later.[21] In his zeal for progress, his pragmatic naturalism, and his deep-seated racism, Hooper foreshadowed the laissez-faire ideology of the latter half of the nineteenth century. Yet he would have attacked the greed of industrial robber barons as strongly as he did the reigning planters of Alabama's senatorial aristocracy or, as Suggs did, the predatory false stewards of frontier Alabama. In 1845, in his thirtieth year, he at least hoped that strong southern whites would also be good men, democratically responsible to their peers and protective of their black charges. But then he also hoped that his own strengths would come to outweigh his youthful weaknesses. As it turned out, he was tragically wrong about both.[22]

At the spontaneous level from which humor springs, most of what was funny in *Some Adventures of Simon Suggs* stemmed from Johnson Hooper's fond toleration of his own shortcomings. It was the toleration of a young man, still expecting to succeed, writing for a new world, waiting to be civilized. Hooper's resistance to self-control—his reluctance to pay all of the psychological costs of becoming civilized, if you will—is reflected in the energies of Suggs's unbounded world. For all of his bestial nature, Simon Suggs was funny because civilized readers could take comfort in their expectation that his kind would be tamed with the frontier itself. Suggs is thus an emblem of the creative and destructive possibilities inherent in the American freedom that sustains his life, as air does fire. His energies, his wit, and his predatory instinct for human weaknesses required self-control but not elimination. Like Hooper himself, his readers could laugh at the excesses of their ambitions without ceasing to aspire.[23]

It seems worthwhile to underscore what may already be obvious: in the 1840s, Hooper had many national readers who, if they attended at all to the place of slaves in his stories, seem to have found it proper.[24] Hooper's slave characters were not really actors in his comedy. They were acted upon, forced into social passivity by the aggressiveness of the whites around them. Hooper hoped that this combination of human power—white wit and black brute force—would build a great society. That view was not explicit in Suggs, but the writer's hopes provided the contrast that made his stories funny rather than sad. Ironically, Hooper's covert standards contributed to Suggs's popularity across classes and regions, fitting the aspirations of men with quite differing notions of society but similar instincts for order and freedom. Some found his coarse humor vulgar; others perhaps despised his racial slurs; but in the decade before *Uncle Tom's Cabin* laid bare the connections between competitive freedom and slavery, Hooper found many amused readers.[25] His success compels modern readers to contemplate nineteenth-century white Americans so entranced by what they wanted to become that they could laugh at the slaves who might become hapless victims of white freedom. It also suggests that we reflect upon the popular foundations for their amusement: weaknesses in human nature that bound slavery with freedom and pervasive racial prejudice that cut across geographical lines. The world of Simon Suggs is sometimes vulgar, always coarse, but it is still alive with an energy that was not to be restrained. Hooper's images reflect the force of a southern mind fixed on the future, its outlines all the more ominous for their national appeal.

Notes

1. The best modern edition of Hooper's first and most famous book is *Adventures of Captain Simon Suggs, Late of the Tallapoosa Volunteers*, intro. by Manly Wade Wellman (Chapel Hill, N.C., 1969); all subsequent page references to Hooper, *Adventures of Captain Simon Suggs*, are to this edition, and the quoted headnote is from pages 49-50. The first edition was published in 1845 by Carey and Hart of Philadelphia. While recent historians have neglected southern white humor, there is a steadily growing body of criticism by literary scholars of the humorous tradition. For historians' purposes, the criticism is marred by insensitivity to social context and by a lumping together of humorists whose views of society are substantially different. Still, much of it is invaluable for placing Hooper in the proper literary context. Particularly helpful in this attempt to chart unfamiliar literary territory are four collections of essays: Louis D. Rubin Jr., ed., *The Comic Imagination in American Literature* (New Brunswick, N.J., 1973); M. Thomas Inge, ed., *The Frontier Humorists: Critical Views* (Hamden, Conn., 1975); William Bedford Clark and W. Craig Turner, *Critical Essays on American Humor* (Boston, 1984); and Ronald Paulson, ed., *Satire: Modern Essays in Criticism* (Englewood Cliffs, N.J., 1971). Edward A. Bloom and Lillian D. Bloom, in *Satire's Persuasive Voice* (Ithaca, N.Y., 1979), emphasize the reformist nature of satiric literature, but in Chapter I, entitled "Intention," cogently warn against "dogmatic" interpretations. See also Charles E. Davis and Martha B. Hudson, comps., "Humor of the Old Southwest: A Checklist of Criticism," *Mississippi Quarterly*, XXVII (Spring 1974), 179-99. Historical studies that specifically treat the subject of humor about blacks in the antebellum period include Jean H. Baker, *Affairs of Party: The Political Culture of Northern Democrats in the Mid-Nineteenth Century* (Ithaca, N.Y., 1983); and Joseph Boskin, *Sambo: The Rise and Demise of an American Jester* (New York, 1986). Research for this essay was undertaken with the support of grants from the National Endowment for the Humanities Program for Travel-to-Collections and the University of Alabama in Huntsville. The author wishes to thank Thomas B. Alexander, Ann Boucher, Vicki Johnson, Larry Kohl, Michael O'Brien, Stephen Waring, Carolyn White, John White, and Bertram Wyatt-Brown for their helpful comments and suggestions.

2. The standard biography of Hooper is W. Stanley Hoole, *Alias Simon Suggs: The Life and Times of Johnson Jones Hooper* (University, Ala., 1952), which is outdated in some respects, including its interpretation of Hooper's Whiggish views. A newer critical study by Paul Somers Jr., *Johnson J. Hooper* (Boston, 1984), treats Hooper's partisan ideas more effectively, though it repeats some of Hoole's errors.

3. Quoted passages from *Adventures of Captain Simon Suggs*, 49 (second quotation), 50 (first quotation). Among the growing number of studies about the market's influence upon nineteenth-century writers most useful for understanding

Hooper are Shelley Fisher Fishkin, *From Fact to Fiction: Journalism and Imaginative Writing in America* (Baltimore, 1985); Michael T. Gilmore, *American Romanticism and the Marketplace* (Chicago, 1985); and David S. Reynolds, *Beneath the American Renaissance: The Subversive Imagination in the Age of Emerson and Melville* (New York, 1988). John McCardell has briefly related Hooper's work to larger themes in southern culture in *The Idea of a Southern Nation: Southern Nationalists and Southern Nationalism, 1830-1860* (New York, 1979), 160-61. Essential to understanding the role Hooper played in the secession crisis is J. Mills Thornton III, *Politics and Power in a Slave Society: Alabama, 1800-1860* (Baton Rouge, 1978). The proslavery tract is Matthew Estes, *A Defence of Negro Slavery, as it Exists in the United States* (Montgomery, Ala., 1846).

4. The most cogent interpretations emphasizing the liberal character of southern society are those of George M. Fredrickson in *The Black Image in the White Mind: The Debate on Afro-American Character and Destiny, 1817-1914* (New York and other cities, 1971), and *The Arrogance of Race: Historical Perspectives on Slavery, Racism, and Social Inequality* (Middletown, Conn., 1988); and James Oakes in *The Ruling Race: A History of American Slaveholders* (New York, 1982), and *Slavery and Freedom: An Interpretation of the Old South* (New York, 1990). The "outsiders" usage is prominent in *Slavery and Freedom,* while *The Ruling Race* stresses coastal paternalism. That emphasis is also reflected in some scholarship in social and political history. See, for example, Michael P. Johnson, *Toward a Patriarchal Republic: The Secession of Georgia* (Baton Rouge, 1977); Orville Vernon Burton, *In My Father's House are Many Mansions: Family and Community in Edgefield, South Carolina* (Chapel Hill, N.C., 1985); and William H. Pease and Jane H. Pease, *The Web of Progress: Private Values and Public Styles in Boston and Charleston, 1828-1843* (New York, 1985). Lawrence Shore's *Southern Capitalists: The Ideological Leadership of an Elite, 1832-1885* (Chapel Hill, N.C., 1986), which stresses continuity between Old South and New South, treats with considerable sensitivity the flexibility of southern ideologues in addressing tensions between the values of liberal capitalism and aristocratic paternalism, especially as those were revealed in theories of labor; see especially Chap. 2, "Nonslaveholders in Slaveholders' Capitalist World." Among literary critics, Louis D. Rubin Jr. insists upon the similarities between North and South as part of an emerging industrial capitalist world, but his observation that the South produced no satiric "self-scrutinizing critique" is puzzling;

see the opening chapter to *The Edge of the Swamp: A Study in the Literature and Society of the Old South* (Baton Rouge, 1989), 46 (quotation).

5. Much of the recent scholarship emphasizing paternalism has been stimulated by Genovese's influential work *The World the Slaveholders Made: Two Essays in Interpretation* (New York, 1969). A more comprehensive treatment is Elizabeth Fox-Genovese and Eugene D. Genovese, *Fruits of Merchant Capital: Slavery and Bourgeois Property in the Rise and Expansion of Capitalism* (New York, 1983), 16 (quoted passage). Also important have been a series of books by Drew Gilpin Faust, *The Sacred Circle: The Dilemma of the Intellectual in the Old South, 1840-1860* (Baltimore, 1977); *The Ideology of Slavery: Proslavery Thought in the Antebellum South. 1830-1860* (Baton Rouge, 1981); and *James Henry Hammond and the Old South: A Design for Mastery* (Baton Rouge, 1982). For related interpretations in literary criticism, see the influential work of Lewis P. Simpson, especially *The Man of Letters in New England and the South: Essays on the History of the Literary Vocation in America* (Baton Rouge, 1973); his brief study, *The Dispossessed Garden: Pastoral and History in Southern Literature* (Athens, Ga., 1975); and his recent prizewinning *Mind and the American Civil War: A Meditation on Lost Causes* (Baton Rouge, 1989); and Elizabeth Fox-Genovese and Eugene D. Genovese, "The Cultural History of Southern Slave Society: Reflections on the Work of Lewis P. Simpson," in J. Gerald Kennedy and Daniel Mark Fogel, eds., *American Letters and the Historical Consciousness: Essays in Honor of Lewis P. Simpson* (Baton Rouge, 1987). Other recent works stressing patriarchal themes are Kenneth S. Greenberg, *Masters and Statesmen: The Political Culture of American Slavery* (Baltimore, 1985); and Larry E. Tise, *Proslavery: A History of the Defense of Slavery in America, 1701-1840* (Athens, Ga., 1987). The difficulty of explaining how slaveholders' views were accepted by nonslaveholders is discussed in Fox-Genovese and Genovese, "Yeoman Farmers in a Slaveholders' Democracy," in *Fruits of Merchant Capital,* 249-64. Also relevant are the summary comments of Greenburg in *Masters and Statesmen,* 102-3.

6. In Hoole's account, Suggs is patterned after Bird H. Young, a notorious resident of Tallapoosa County, who was a likely source for many of Suggs's characteristics; *Alias Simon Suggs,* 51-60; see also Somers, *Johnson J. Hooper,* 26-28, a more balanced evaluation. Suggs is described at length by Johns in Hooper, *Adventures of Captain Simon Suggs,* 6-7. Hooper's appearance was a standing joke in journalistic circles in Alabama, as his bi-

ographers have noted. The picture of him in the Alabama Department of Archives and History makes the resemblance to Suggs evident. One Alabamian who called himself "Captain Cuttle" in a series of articles about writers commented with typical insight: "Jonce Hooper is indeed a lucky man. Nature in marring his 'face divine,' conceived that she was clipping his wings and precluding his rise to fame, but she was grieviously [*sic*] at fault in her calculation, as his homeliness has contributed fully as much to his success as his mental resources and efforts. He is always on the look out for eccentricities of manner, thought, and expression, and when once detected, he transfers them to his canvass, and gives a portrait which would provoke a hearty laugh from the bedridden." See the *Livingston Sumter Democrat,* July 3, 1852; "Captain Cuttle" was not identified, but he seems to have been a resident of Livingston, Alabama, where the articles were published. Bertram Wyatt-Brown has pointed to the emphasis placed upon proper appearance in *Southern Honor,* noting (like "Captain Cuttle") that physical shortcomings could stimulate compensatory ambitions, (pp. 48-49).

7. Mrs. Suggs reflects on Suggs's "juvenality" on page 153; Suggs's wandering is described on page 28; and his character on pages 8-9; all in Hooper, *Adventures of Captain Simon Suggs.* Elliott Gorn in "'Gouge and Bite, Pull Hair and Scratch': The Social Significance of Fighting in the Southern Back Country," *American Historical Review,* XC (February 1985), 18-43, demonstrated how the frontier folklore of individualism "buttressed the emergent ideology of equality" (p. 30) at the same time it affirmed the older ethos of honor. Interestingly, Hooper himself wrote a "gouging" story, but in it the genteel frame is dominant, perhaps because the piece was written for New England's humorous magazine *The Yankee Blade.* The story was reprinted with the notation that it was "from *The Yankee Blade*" in the *Montgomery* [*Alabama*] *Journal,* July 9, 1850. See also David E. Sloane's introduction to Sloane, ed., *The Literary Humor of the Urban Northeast, 1830-1890* (Baton Rouge, 1983); reference to *The Yankee Blade* as one of a number of New England publications is on page 315.

8. The political manipulation of republican themes is satirized by Hooper in *Adventures of Captain Simon Suggs.* A corrupt office seeker comments, for example, on one of Suggs's deceptions: "Yes, sir, it was a sublime moral spectacle, worthy of a comparison with any recorded specimens of Roman or Spartan magnanimity, sir. How nobly did it vindicate the purity of the representative character, sir!" (p. 43).

9. As David Reynolds notes in *Beneath the American Renaissance,* "Suggs is the first figure in American literature who fully manipulates Conventional values—piety, discretion, honesty, entrepreneurial shrewdness—for purely selfish ends. The Conventional becomes fully relativized in the world of subversive humor" (p. 454).

10. See, for example, chapters entitled "Simon Speculates," "Simon Starts Forth to Fight the 'Tiger' [faro], and Falls in with a Candidate whom he 'Does' to a Cracklin',," and "Simon Fights 'the Tiger' and Gets Whipped—but Comes out Not Much the 'Worse for Wear',," all in Hooper, *Adventures of Captain Simon Suggs.*

11. These stories, in which Suggs manipulates poor whites, are parodies of Andrew Jackson's supporters' exploitation of his 1814 victory at Horseshoe Bend (in Tallapoosa County, thus Suggs's company of Tallapoosa Volunteers) and of the hysteria that seized Alabama during the Creek War of 1836. The three stories relating to the phony war and how Simon earned his rank are "Simon Becomes Captain," "Captain Suggs and Lieutenant Snipes 'Court-Martial' Mrs. Haycock," and "The 'Tallapoosy Volluntares' Meet the Enemy"; all in Hooper, *Adventures of Captain Simon Suggs.* Johnson's location during the Creek episode is questionable, but George wrote about the local uproar in reassuringly funny letters to Caroline Mallet before their marriage; see his letters of February 21 and 28, May 11 and 22, 1836, in CMH Papers [Caroline Mallet Hooper Papers in the Southern Historical Collection (University of North Carolina at Chapel Hill)].

12. Yellow Legs is another disguise for the author, as is indicated by his appearance and wit and by Suggs's comments that he earned his stained legs as "the mark of the huckleberry ponds . . . what the water come to when he was a-gatherin 'em in his raisin' in Northkurliny"; Hooper, *Adventures of Captain Simon Suggs,* 84. The young man is described by Johns as "spindle-legged" (p. 82) and by Suggs as "dirt eatin'" (p. 84). He flees contemptuously (quoted passage) on page 100 and "contumaciously" on page 103; he suggests that he is only a child and Suggs is a coward for mistreating him on page 83. In one sense, because he is like Hooper, the youth cannot be taken as lowborn, despite appearances to the contrary. But as in the case of Suggs, what matters is not the circumstance of Yellow Legs's birth but the presence of his wit. The character appears on pages 82-84, 88-89, 100, and 102-3. There are comments relevant to Hooper's portrayal of frontier commoners in Dickson Bruce Jr., *Violence and Culture in the Antebellum South* (Austin, Tex., 1979), 224-32, al-

though Bruce's emphasis on the distance established between the humorists and their frontier subjects and his insistence on their affinities for social control seem more relevant for Augustus Baldwin Longstreet, whom he discusses at some length, than for Hooper, whom he treats only incidentally. I would make the same criticism of Richard Gray's application of contemporary literary theory to the humorists, in which he asserts (p. 74) that they achieved a comfortable distance from their subjects by encoding the "rough beast" in an inherited populist vocabulary rather than seeing them freshly; see his *Writing the South: Ideas of an American Region* (Cambridge, Eng. 1986), 62-74.

13. The use of white racial humor as a device to demean blacks is a major theme in Boskin's *Sambo,* which also explores the national popularity of the derogatory stereotype. Thornton discusses the symbiotic relationship between white freedom and black slavery in *Politics and Power,* xviii; their psychological interdependence is also stressed in Orlando Patterson, *Slavery and Social Death: A Comparative Study* (Cambridge, Mass., 1982), especially sharply in his concluding remarks, 340-42. Also relevant is Bertram Wyatt-Brown. "The Mark of Obedience: Male Slave Psychology in the Old South," *American Historical Review,* XCIII (February 1988), 1228-52. Although Suggs himself is for Hooper the "shameless trickster" (as Wyatt-Brown described that role on p. 1242) and slaves are shamed, there are intriguing hints of affinities between white and black tricksters.

14. Suggs's departure from home runs across the first three chapters in Hooper, *Adventures of Captain Simon Suggs*: "Introduction—Simon Plays the 'Snatch' Game," "Simon Gets a 'Soft Snap' Out of his Daddy," and "Simon Speculates." The father's description is on page 9. "Daddies," who exist "jist to beat 'em [boys] and work 'em," are compared to the "use in mammies," who are more inclined to spoil their sons, on page 16. By way of comparison, see Johnson's father's letter to D. B. [John de Berniere Hooper, Johnson's brother] about his "anxieties . . . in respect to Johnson. He is at a critical period of life, and your mother's fondness has countenanced too much his scribbling propensity," A. M. [Archibald Maclaine Hooper, Johnson's father] to D. B., July 1, 1835, JDBH Papers [John de Berniere Hooper Papers in the Southern Historical Collection (University of North Carolina at Chapel Hill)], written after the time Johnson fled Charleston for Alabama. Hooper's crude humor here bears comparison with that of George Washington Harris in the Sut Lovingood stories; see the analysis of Sut's social significance in [Larzer] Ziff, *Literary Democracy*[:

The Declaration of Cultural Independence in America (New York, 1981)], 185-94. Dickson Bruce describes Suggs's leave-taking as a "virtual paradigm for a life spent skirting violence and convention for profit"; *Violence and Culture,* 230.

15. Hooper, *Adventures of Captain Simon Suggs,* 16.

16. Relevant analyses of the changing relationships between white southern parents and children are Jane Turner Censer, *North Carolina Planters and Their Children*[, 1800-1860 (Baton Rouge, 1984)]; and Ann Williams Boucher, "Wealthy Planter Families in Nineteenth-Century Alabama" (Ph.D. dissertation, University of Connecticut, 1978). See also Bertram Wyatt-Brown's observations about oedipal and other tensions in family life associated with changes in southern society in "Fathers, Mothers, and Progeny" (*Southern Honor*[: *Ethics and Behavior in the Old South* (New York, 1982)], Chap. 5); and those of Steven M. Stowe in *Intimacy and Power in the Old South: Ritual in the Lives of the Planters* (Baltimore, 1987), which emphasize especially the celebration of hierarchy by planters and the social tensions fostered by sex and gender differences that were emphasized in the planter ethos. The tensions of authority and gender in Hooper's family warrant more attention than they have been given in previous biographies or can be given here.

17. Comments about the burning of the slave at nearby Mt. Meigs (*Montgomery Weekly Mail,* August 31, 1859) made by Hooper when fear had gripped him tightly, should be compared with his earlier and somewhat less immoderate views in the *Montgomery Weekly Mail,* May 31, 1855. When Nature made Suggs bestial, "she did not refine the cruelty by denying him the fangs and the claws," and in his case, neither the tyranny of his father nor the affectionate tolerance of his mother had any meliorative influence; quoted passage in Hooper, *Adventures of Captain Simon Suggs,* 9.

18. Suggs refers to the salvation of sinners as "saving" on page 116. The description of the "promiscuous" audiences and the preachers' sexual motives and methods begins on page 112 and concludes with the black woman's falling upon the little white man on page 114; quoted passages on pages 112 and 114. Suggs's graphic account of his supposed salvation appears on pages 118 through 121; quoted passages on pages 119 and 121. Suggs commonly refers to the falsities by which he entraps his victims as "discourses" (see, for example, p. 72), but the minister Bela Bugg calls the salvation story a "discorse" (p. 123); and Mrs. Dobbs, a key observer, calls the narrative of Suggs's "'sperience" a "'scource" (p. 119); all quotations and page numbers from Hooper, *Ad-*

ventures of Captain Simon Suggs. The camp meeting episode was imitated by Twain in *Adventures of Huckleberry Finn* (New York, 1884), an imitation Bernard DeVoto finds inferior to the original; see his *Mark Twain's America* (Boston, 1932), 253. See Hooper, *Adventures of Captain Simon Suggs,* 111-26.

19. The whipping threat appears first on pages 118-19 (where "'scource" may suggest scourge) and is repeated by implication on page 120 ("I'll settle wi' you!"). Mrs. Dobbs's excitement interrupts the narrative from pages 118 to 121. Quoted passages and page numbers from Hooper, *Adventures of Captain Simon Suggs.* For relevant comments on sexuality in George Washington Harris's humor, see Ziff, *Literary Democracy,* 186-88; in "subversive" literature, see Reynolds, *Beneath the American Renaissance,* 211-24; in the humor of the "reverend rake," *ibid.,* 476; and in frontier humor, *ibid.,* 454-57.

20. *Montgomery Weekly Mail,* August 31, 1854; compare with the sentiments of Daniel Webster discussed in [Lawrence Frederick] Kohl, *Politics of Individualism*[*: Parties and the American Character in the Jacksonian Era* (New York, 1989)], 85.

21. Thornton, *Politics and Power,* 337. For a discussion of the implications of Thornton's study for southern intellectual history, see Michael O'Brien, "Modernization and the Nineteenth-Century South," in *Rethinking the South: Essays in Intellectual History* (Baltimore, 1988), 115-18.

22. Hooper's later difficulties were barely mentioned by Hoole in *Alias Simon Suggs,* but they are referred to in family letters, which suggest quite serious financial problems at the very least. See, for example, Charlotte Hooper to D. B., March 22, 1851, in which she mentions Johnson's "set back 4 years ago [that] cost him dearly," a line followed by a cut passage, a phenomenon that appears more than once in the family papers when negative references to Johnson were apparently the subject. Johnson's own letters refer to poverty, ill health, and hard work. See, for example, his letters to D. B., August 15 [?], 1855, and December 25, 1861; all in JDBH Papers. In the latter, a highly charged commentary on Alabama's secession and the family's personal trials, Johnson wrote his older brother: "When I think of your labors, however, and of your uncomplaining endurance, I feel ashamed both of my weakness and egotism. With more delicate health and harder work, you have fought the world even longer than I and without whining." See also a very funny letter in which Hooper acknowledges his gambling and drinking; letter written to his business associate E. Sanford Sayre in the winter of 1846 [?] in

the Sayre file, Thomas Hill Watts Papers (Alabama Department of Archives and History). The Sayre file also contains evidence relating to the financial problems of the *Montgomery [Alabama] Journal* between 1846 and 1848, when Hooper was its co-owner.

23. Both Hauck and Slotkin have commented in their literary studies on the extent to which laughter at the humor of the confidence men legitimized the exploitative tendencies in American society; see [Richard Boyd] Hauck, *Cheerful Nihilism*[*: Confidence and "The Absurd" in American Humorous Fiction* (Bloomington, Ind., 1971)], 71; and [Richard] Slotkin, *Regeneration through Violence*[*: The Mythology of the American Frontier, 1600-1860* (Middletown, Conn., 1973)], 416-17.

24. Given what little is known about book marketing and purchasers in the 1840s, this assessment rests on inference, but most recent scholars have treated Hooper's audience as national. Ronald J. Zboray, "The Transportation Revolution and Antebellum Book Distribution Reconsidered," *American Quarterly,* XXXVIII (Spring 1986), 53, 71, argues persuasively that most scholarly evaluations of the relationship between market tastes and book sales have failed to allow for the influence of regional differences in transportation upon marketing. Even with accurate figures for the total sales of Hooper's books, which surely numbered in the thousands, it would be impossible to say where they sold. See Hoole, *Alias Simon Suggs,* 58-59, 203-5, 207, 212-13, for figures on the printings of Carey and Hart, Hooper's publisher in Philadelphia.

25. The influence of Harriet Beecher Stowe's book has recently been evaluated by Thomas F. Gossett. *"Uncle Tom's Cabin" and American Culture* (Dallas, 1985); and Moira Davison Reynolds, *"Uncle Tom's Cabin" and Mid-Nineteenth Century United States: Pen and Conscience* (Jefferson, N.C., and London, 1985). The similarities between Stowe's slave character Sam and Hooper's Simon Suggs are sufficiently strong to suggest that Stowe knew Hooper's racist humor; see especially [Harriet Beecher] Stowe, *Uncle Tom's Cabin* [(Boston, 1852; rev. ed., New York, 1965)], 75-79; and Hooper, *Adventures of Captain Simon Suggs,* 76, 103.

Sheila Ruzycki O'Brien (essay date fall 1994)

SOURCE: O'Brien, Sheila Ruzycki. "Writing with a Forked Pen: Racial Dynamics and Johnson Jones Hooper's Twin Tale of Swindling Indians." *American Studies* 35, no. 2 (fall 1994): 95-113.

[*In the following excerpt, O'Brien explores the relationship between humor and race in Hooper's Simon Suggs stories. In O'Brien's view, Hooper's satire was primarily directed at human foolishness in general, rather than at a specific racial or social identity.*]

In Southwest humor those who lose out were born fools—or rather they were *created* damned fools and were fulfilling their destiny. And, although victims in Southwest humor could be drawn from any class and color, those who were non-white—African Americans and, most prominently, Native Americans—were especially vulnerable, likely because their non-fiction counterparts possessed land worth coveting.[1] Beneath a veneer of humor, these writers promoted a survival-of-the-fittest world to legitimate the accompanying practices of racial antagonism and swindling; their stories repeatedly portray these practices as being in accord with "Providence" and "natur." . . .

One of the most prominent Southwest humorists was Johnson Jones Hooper, whose Simon Suggs stories won enormous popularity in the mid-nineteenth century. The individual stories were widely reprinted, and *Adventures of Captain Simon Suggs* went through eleven editions between 1845 and 1856.[2] This collection, particularly his story of white men swindling Native Americans, **"Simon Speculates Again,"** provides insights into how Southwest humor's ostensibly regional preoccupation with justifying cutthroat business deals represents and responds to the larger social, political and economic concerns shaping U.S. society. Based on a foundation of a proto-Social Darwinism that pervaded Southwest humor, the story vindicated those lying to, sexually abusing, and cheating Native Americans; it also gave guidance to those predators who needed to develop sentimental "cover stories" that maintained a genteel facade, and it both placated and diverted those not in tune with a survival-of-the-fittest approach.

In Suggs, Johnson Jones Hooper created Southwest humor's greatest predator hero. Unlike George Washington Harris's Sut Lovingood, who toys with people by setting animal nature and human nature on collision courses, Simon focuses on human prey for personal gain. The animal elements in the Suggs' stories are chiefly metaphorical rather than physical. Simon is a con man whose wiles and honed selfishness keep him responsive to the offerings of "Providence." Although he is clearly no gentleman, he is also no fool. While readers would feel sufficiently detached from Simon to enjoy his victories without feeling in cahoots with him, his intelligence and cunning were clearly meant to be appealing. Hooper's Simon Suggs evaluates ethical principles in practical terms, and to him traditional ethics are invalid. "Goodness" does not mean abiding by a firm, traditional moral code. He perceives goodness as foolish and thus amoral; utility shapes his morality, and thus, in *Adventures of Captain Simon Suggs,* the narrator records Suggs' "favorite aphorism" as "IT IS

GOOD TO BE SHIFTY IN A NEW COUNTRY."[3] The word "shifty" functions on many levels here. Not only did it imply trickiness, but adaptability and industry as well. Simon Suggs' putative campaign biographer informs the reader that this shiftiness was a means of survival bestowed by reasonable Mother Nature, who also supplied him with a predator's instincts and natural weapons:

> He possesses, in an eminent degree, that tact which enables man to detect the *soft spots* in his fellow, and to assimilate himself to whatever company he may fall in with. . . . In short, nature gave the Captain the precise intellectual outfit most to be desired by a man of his propensities. She sent him into the world a sort of he-Pallas, ready to cope with his kind, from his infancy, in all the arts by which men "get along" in the world; if she made him, in respect to his moral conformation, a beast of prey, she did not refine the cruelty by denying him the fangs and the claws.
>
> (9)

Hooper added validity and status to Mother Nature's design of Simon by alluding to Greek mythology in the form of Pallas Athene, the goddess of might and wisdom who sprang fully armed from the head of Zeus. Simon was likewise armed. Like some other protagonists in Southwest humor (Sut Lovingood with his long legs that enabled his escapes and Davy Crockett with his grin—useful in hunts of both the backwoods and Congressional sort), Hooper's con man possessed a dominant physical feature that facilitates survival: appropriately, Hooper made his protagonist's "great feature" his huge mouth, the mouth of a predator. . . .

Johnson Jones Hooper framed *Adventures of Captain Simon Suggs* with tales in which black people remained subordinate. In **"Introduction—Simon Plays the 'Snatch' Game"** as well as in the following chapter, **"Simon Gets a 'Soft Snap' out of his Daddy,"** young Simon manipulates his father into venting his ire on the black boy Bill instead of on himself. Unlike Simon, Bill is not clever enough to avoid being kicked and beaten. Early in the final chapter, **"Conclusion—Autographic Letter from Suggs,"** Simon writes to his biographer "Johns" (who happened to be "The edditur of the eest Allybammyun" and to be publishing Suggs stories where Hooper did[4]); he claims to be particularly surprised with the likeness of Bill that appeared in the *Spirit* [*Spirit of the Times*], since Bill had been dead twenty years and "thar he is, in the picter, with more giniwine nigger in him and you'll find nowadaze owin to the breed bein so devilishly mixed" (134-5). Simon goes on to tell the tale of his conning a con man in the slave trade. Despite "the breed bein so devilishly mixed," black people remain merely trade goods to Simon here; like Bill they are maneuverable pawns.

All of the people whom Simon cons were fools, and Hooper's Indians fit this pattern. They were governed by appetite but lacked awareness, and Hooper's narratives were unsympathetic to them. James M. Cox has noted that "Hooper has to distort and demean his lower-class world so that it can receive Suggs's raids without offence to a civilized audience."[5] While I disagree with Cox that Hooper's world was always "lower-class," Suggs's victims were definitely demeaned, and Hooper thus made acceptable their further degradation by the predator Suggs.

The Creek War provided background for much of *Adventures of Captain Simon Suggs,* but the Creeks, like the African Americans in the collection, were far from threatening. In the text, the war merely provides Simon with the psychological weapon of fear—which facilitates some scams. In **"The 'Tallapoosy Vollantares' Meet the Enemy,"** it allows Simon to get away with murdering an Indian chief (lacking in cunning) in order to keep stolen goods. In **"Simon Speculates Again,"** as in all Suggs's tales and much of Southwest humor, lack of cunning determined who was valid prey. In this tale of swindling Indians, Hooper employed a complex narrative structure to convey his survival-of-the-fittest message. The story is comprised of a prologue and two mirror tales about cheating Indians. Both the prologue and the first, or "cover," story offer a perforated veneer of sympathy for the oppressed Indians, then the Suggs tale that mirrors the cover story clearly undercuts the already shaky fellow-feeling expressed. The narrative elements work together, the body of the tale supporting the theft of Indian lands while the cover story provides a sense of decorum.

The narrative begins with the upper-class narrator (Simon Suggs's "biographer") discussing "the Indian Council at Dudley's store, in Tallapoosa county, in September of the year 1835," which later forms the basis of the Suggs section of the narrative (65). Notably, the time frame for the tale occurs after many Creeks were fed up with the government's defaulting on the Treaty of 1832, an agreement which limited Creek territory while promising the natives protection from intruders. By 1835, largely at the mercy of poachers and other sorts of thieves, and literally fearing for their lives, moving west seemed the only option for many Indians. In 1836, after what may have been an uprising masterminded by speculators rather than the Creeks, the Indians were ordered to sell and move.[6] Hooper's tale, however, does not focus on Indian Removal itself. (Whigs were generally against Western expansion, preferring to concentrate economic power in the East.) The story details instead how speculators succeeded.

After setting the scene, the narrator continues with a surprisingly serious prologue about how the Creek tribe has been avenged for being mistreated, since of those who cheated them, "the larger portion have lost money, lands, character, everything!" (66). Hooper, however, sets up his opening statement to be undermined, since it

indicates that at least some portion of such cons have been successful. In addition, knowing that Simon is a speculator, the readers also know from stories preceding **"Simon Speculates Again,"** as well as from the Suggs section of this tale itself, that *his* sporadic poverty is not caused by the "hand of retributive justice" proffered by the prologue (65), but rather by his losses at Faro, a game in which survival of the fittest is moot since the player's opponent is a machine—called "the Tiger"—which has no "reason," only "springs and the like" (169). There can be no "fair fight" with the Faro bank, and Simon knows that his tangles with it are "runnin' agin Providence" (169). Simon does give his talents sufficient exercise among humans—where "Providence" works—to keep him from being totally mauled. Chances are, Hooper's readers also knew some speculators who had not lost "everything." The substance of the prologue is further undermined by the ironic assumption that speculators had "character" to lose.

The elevated style of both the prologue and the opening cover story seems incompatible with Suggs's "biographer's" standard, tongue-in-cheek approach, but the narrator accelerates his subversion of his high-toned style and sentiment. The prologue soon shifts into the sad story of Litka, a pretty Indian girl "with a Grecian face," and her chieftain father, who are duped by a speculator named Eggleston. The narrator ironically portrays Litka's father as a wise man, "one of the few who would not be contaminated by intercourse with the whites" (66), yet he foolishly gets suckered, not just by any white man, but by a man he knew to be a land shark. In fact, the narrator takes jabs at the chief even before he's swindled, calling him not only "Sky Chief" (perhaps a pun on his impending landlessness or his foolishness or both), but also "Sudo Micco," meaning "Pseudo Ape." ("Micco," a common name among the Creeks, is also figurative for "debauchee" in Italian.) Once he falls for the speculator, the narrator openly calls the chief a "simple-minded Indian" (67).

The chief's daughter's being "contaminated by intercourse" with the speculator at "the green corn dance" echoes the chief's own greenness (66) and clearly indicates Litka's own. She falls for Eggleston's "sweet tale" merely because "he was a very handsome young man" (67). In addition to being handsome, Eggleston, employed as a "striker," definitely knows where to strike. He tells Litka what she and her father want to hear, that they would be set above the rest of the tribe and could stay in their own ancestral home while the rest of the Creeks would be forced to Arkansas. Instead of being set above their tribe, however, the two foolish people are swindled, cast aside, and, despite Litka's pregnancy, forced to flee to Arkansas "in one of the 'public' wagons, among the '*poor*' of [the] tribe" (68).

Hooper's subversion of his rhapsody on the Indians' sad fate continues in the Suggs section of the story, an earthy parallel to the Indian tale. The language also reverts from the generally elevated tone of the prologue and the first tale to Hooper's standard style. The Suggs section gives details about those Indians cheated by the speculators, in particular the Deer people and the Alligator people. Both clans are depicted as foolish, bloodthirsty braggarts. While waiting to sell their land to speculators, they fight amongst themselves, hurling some accusations against each other that better suit their future "business" partners: the Deer people claim that the Alligator people "have two tongues" (68), and the Alligator people call the Deer "thieving" (69). The narrator emphasizes that the list of wrongs that the Creek have perpetrated exceeds the list of wrongs committed against them. The woman who parallels the Grecian-faced Indian maiden of the cover story is "Big Widow," who knows that other speculators would give her more money than Simon, but she fears losing Simon's gifts of "tobacco and *sweet water*"(70). While "sweet water" can mean "perfume" or "sweet grapes," underlining the words implies a pun or double entendre; since widows have a reputation in Southwest humor for sexual activity, as does Simon himself, I assume that "*sweet water*" connotes a sexual "gift." As such, it also parallels Eggleston's "sweet tale." Thus both Indian women give up land for sex—a warning to the male reader to beware of any "feminine weakness" in themselves and avoid placing their sexual desire over shrewdness, particularly since both women are abandoned. Litka heads west and the reader sees no more of "Big Widow."

The parallels between both tales are strong, and Indians get swindled in each, but the sad, sentimental tale is sufficiently subverted so that it loses its force. The success of Simon's con game itself counters the prologue and the cover story, since it occurs after the narrator's claim that the Creek have been avenged. In addition, the Indians are no better than the other fools Simon swindles, and they thus come across as deserving to be swindled. In fact, the focus of Simon's swindling activity is not conning the Indians, but rather other con artists. (The one illustration of **"Simon Speculates Again"** emphasizes this.) The Indian men's foolishness and the women's combined foolishness and sexual proclivity for shrewd white men are givens in both tales, factors which would bolster the egos of the tales' readership— and act as an advertisement for speculation. Simon's challenge is to outwit the other speculators, getting them to compete with each other for his partnership in buying "Big Widow's" land, a partnership that results in Suggs netting a substantial profit without his putting any money down—a business deal which would have been considered enviable by many of Hooper's ambitious readers.

While Hooper undermined the sentimentality of the cover story, that semi-sentimentalized section of the narrative does convey important information to Hooper's readers: the value of a "cover story." A sentimental, moralistic line to cover over dirty business (in this case, swindling Indians) is a technique still employed by Simon Suggs's relations rampant in the world today—as it was used by William Cullen Bryant in 1837. And Hooper's technique worked. Annie Mae Hollingsworth, in her 1931 newspaper article "Johnson Jones Hooper, Alabama's Mark Twain, Champion of the Creeks" in the *Montgomery Advertiser,* only noted the narrator's defense of the Creeks in this tale, not his subversion of this defense.[7] W. Stanley Hoole also claimed that Hooper "lamented the ill-treatment these naive people received at the hands of land-sharks, speculators and traders." However, although Hoole did not note the irony in Hooper's tale, he was in accord with its intent. Without acknowledging the bigotry of Hooper's view, Hoole said that Suggs's author was "[q]uick to see the Indians' . . . stupidity and general undesirability as citizens in a white man's country."[8]

Joanna Shields has contended that in Hooper's Suggs tales, Simon's adventures were those of a con man in "an American jungle where 'mother wit' was a *sine qua non* for survival" (["A Sadder Simon Suggs: Freedom and Slavery in the Humor of Johnson Hooper," *The Journal of Southern History,* 56 (1991),] 642), that slaves were "perpetual victims . . . deficient of wit" (655-6), and that Hooper's "jokes made slavery seem natural, even necessary" (642). Yet Shields, too, has partially accepted Hooper's "cover story." She has depicted Hooper's racism and pro-slavery stance as modified by his fictional "lampoon[ing of] white men's ceaseless competition" (642) as well as his mockery of blind hypocrisy, including that of slaveholders. She has noted that Hooper punished "predatory stewards" via Suggs, and has claimed that the writer "would have attacked the greed of industrial robber barons as strongly as . . . Suggs did the predatory false stewards of frontier Alabama" (662-3), including in this group the land sharks who swindled Indians in **"Simon Speculates Again."** While I am in accord with Shields's view of Hooper's racism, her claims for Hooper's modifications are tenuous. Simon swindled the "predatory false stewards" not for moral reasons, but because they are both foolish and in possession of loot. Greed was never mocked in Hooper's Suggs tales, only stupidity. . . .

In analyzing **"Simon Speculates Again,"** it is important to note that Simon did not provide the "cover story" dripping with high-sounding phrases, but rather the elite narrator, whom many readers conflated with Hooper himself. Through comments made by Porter in *Spirit of the Times* and by Hooper himself in *Adventures,* most readers knew Hooper to be an active Whig, and so the narrator's duplicity can be seen as a political lesson in how a gentleman could use fine-sounding, generous phrases and undercut their meaning.[9]

Simon himself does not dabble in recriminations and sentimentality, but like a gentleman, he credits God with his achievements, placing his success in Indian swindling, as well as in his other con games, firmly at the feet of "Providence." Throughout *Adventures of Captain Simon Suggs,* he claims that a man who does not believe in Providence is an unsuccessful man, and so Simon proclaims himself in harmony with the Protestant ethic. Not to take advantage of the opportunities that cross his path would be "'sputin' with providence" (159), turning aside supernatural gifts, and going against nature. Simon claims that he is continually gaining insight into scripture, particularly such Bible stories as "the manna in the wilderness, and ravens feedin' Elishy" (180). He believes that his honesty (the using of his natural gifts) and Providence combined will make him a survivor: "Jist give me that for a hand, and I'll 'stand' agin all creation!" (180).

The narrator of the Suggs tales does not condemn Simon for his behavior, nor does he overtly applaud it. He claims to be just "Captain Suggs's biographer" (28), and yet, within the tales, Suggs's victims are depicted as worse than Suggs himself. They were not only selfish, but stupid. The Suggs stories are clearly educational, and the education was meant for Hooper's audience of businessmen. Reading Simon's adventures is rather like attending a conference of salesmen and learning their gimmicks: it could make one wary and streetwise—or perhaps junglewise. In the opening of Hooper's story, **"Daddy Biggs Scrape at Cockerell's Bend,"** the narrator articulates a lesson in survival as he watches a mother duck with her brood:

> Take care! ye little downy rascals!—especially you, little fellow, with half an egg-shell stuck to your back!—true, there are not many or large trout in the Tallapoosa: but there are *some*; and occasionally one is found of mouth sufficient to engorge a young duck!—and almost always in a cool quiet shade just like—hist! snap!—there you go, precisely as I told you!
>
> (142)

The narrator's use of five, second-person personal pronouns in this passage draws the readers into the text, leading them to identify with the inexperienced rascal duck "with half an eggshell" still stuck to him—a novice in need of guidance. While neither white nor red fools learn and change in Hooper's tales, this passage implies that the white fools who were reading the tales had that capability. If Mother Nature endowed them with the proper tools, they only needed to recognize their true natures and act accordingly.

Hooper did not take a pro-Suggs stance publicly, but the humorist was wiser than the little rascal duck. Once Hooper became politically ambitious in Whig politics, he did not like being associated with Suggs,[10] the asso-

ciation being possibly disadvantageous, since Suggs operated without the mantle of decorum requisite of most politicians. But despite some distancing created by satiric elements in the Suggs tales, such as Suggs's lower-class speech and semi-literacy, I agree with Shields that Hooper possessed a sympathy for—even an empathy with—Simon Suggs.[11] Hooper's Whig Party, despite its pretense of being a party of the common man, was really governed by wealthy Americans, an elite which wanted to maintain (and expand) its position and which had no superficial similarities to Suggs: the similarities run deeper. Kenneth Lynn has claimed that the purpose of many Southwest humorists was "to convert the entire community to the temperate values of Whiggery";[12] however, though the veneer of these values may be temperate, the means of maintaining them were not. Whigs refined political trickery, as evidenced not only by their manipulation of Davy Crockett into a counter to Jackson, who would please foolish voters and romanticize swindling, but also by their log-cabin-and-apple-cider campaign of 1840, the first rip-roaring propaganda campaign in American history. While many verbally protested Indian Removal, actions to protect legal Indian claims were too often weak or non-existent—perhaps because they expected Indians to conveniently become extinct. Their slogan "Tippecanoe and Tyler, too" praised William Henry Harrison's role as an Indian conqueror. (He won the Battle of Tippecanoe in 1811.) During the campaign, however, both Harrison and his campaign biographers publicly softened his reputation in respect to Indians, providing a more gentlemanly demeanor.[13] Although Whigs were not generally exponents of Manifest Destiny,[14] they were men looking for ways to justifiably enhance their holdings, and Southwest humor provided justification. The Whig literary texts thus appropriate the potentially subversive power of folktales, folkheroes, and "low" anti-establishment comedy. The tales of such men as Hooper and Baldwin made *in*temperate values, among Whig and Democrat alike, more palatable, and even desirable, for if a wise man refused to strive for dominance, not only might he fail to survive and prosper, he also would have been betraying his God-given nature.

Notes

1. While the Whig Party was divided about Indian Removal, most Whigs opposed it; the Whigs preferred keeping the U.S. population concentrated in the east for economic reasons. See Daniel Walker Howe, *The Political Culture of the American Whigs* (Chicago, 1979). Johnson Jones Hooper's twin tales of swindling Indians is set after Indian Removal is a foregone conclusion, when a killing can be made in real estate.

2. The first edition was titled *Some Adventures of Captain Simon Suggs.* The word "Some" was later dropped.

3. Johnson Jones Hooper, "Introduction—Simon Plays the 'Snatch' Game," in *Adventures of Captain Simon Suggs* (Chapel Hill, 1969), 8. Further references will be included in the text and cited by page number.

4. These clear parallels between the narrator and Hooper counter the claim made by Walter Blair and Hamlin Hill that the narrator is "anonymous." Blair and Hill, *America's Humor: From Poor Richard to Doonesbury* (Oxford, 1978), 191.

5. Cox, "Humor" ["Humor of the Old Southwest," in *The Comic Imagination in American Literature* (New Brunswick, 1973)], 107.

6. [Michael D.] Green, *Indian Removal* [*The Politics of Indian Removal: Creek Government and Society in Crisis* (Lincoln, Nebraska, 1982)], 174-186.

7. Anne Mae Hollingsworth, "Johnson Jones Hooper, Alabama's Mark Twain, Champion of the Creeks," *Montgomery Advertiser,* 23 March 1931, 3.

8. Hoole, *Alias Simon Suggs,* [*Alias Simon Suggs, the Life and Times of Johnson Jones Hooper* (University, Ala., 1952)], 18.

9. Hoole quotes numerous comments by Porter in the *Spirit* that state Hooper's identity and affiliation with Whig newspapers in *Alias Simon Suggs.*

10. Hoole, *Alias Simon Suggs,* 102-03.

11. Shields claims that Hooper is both the narrator and Simon Suggs in "A Sadder Simon Suggs," 653.

12. Kenneth Lynn, as found in Wade Hall, *The Smiling Phoenix* (Gainesville, Fla., 1965), 2.

13. See [Daniel Walker] Howe, *Political Culture* [*Political Culture of the American Whigs* (Chicago, 1979)], 42.

14. Frederick Merk, *Manifest Destiny and Mission in American History: A Reinterpretation* (New York, 1963), 35, 39-40.

Adam L. Tate (essay date 2005)

SOURCE: Tate, Adam L. "The Whig Social Thought of Baldwin and Hooper." In *Conservatism and Southern Intellectuals, 1789-1861: Liberty, Tradition, and the Good Society,* pp. 307-54. Columbia: University of Missouri Press, 2005.

[*In the following excerpt, Tate examines the tension between representations of social order and individual freedom in Hooper's writings. Tate also evaluates Hooper's political writings from the latter phase of his career, arguing that the fervor of his pro-slavery views stemmed from his staunch desire to see the South liberated from economic and cultural dependence on the North.*]

HOOPER'S SOCIAL VISION

Hooper's Suggs stories revealed his social vision, which mirrored Baldwin's in many respects. Hooper, like Baldwin and other Whigs, doubted that the traditional order or liberalism could contain freedom. Hooper's portrait of traditional society was the opposite of Edmund Burke's. Whereas Burke saw virtue in traditional orders of society, Simon Suggs constantly exposes scions of the traditional order—religious leaders, legislators, and military leaders—as hypocrites who take advantage of those willing to trust in the efficacy of traditional order. The fact that Suggs escapes his scams largely unscathed or unpunished reveals Hooper's doubts about traditional conservatism's answers to the problems of modern freedom.[1]

Some Adventures of Captain Simon Suggs begins as a satire of the traditional order. The first two chapters, **"Simon Plays the 'Snatch Game'"** and **"Simon Gets a 'Soft Snap' Out of His Daddy,"** tell about Suggs's move to the frontier from his home in eastern Georgia. Hooper introduced Suggs as "a miracle of shrewdness" who possessed "that tact which enables man to detect the *soft spots* in his fellow, and to assimilate himself to whatever company he may fall in with." The story starts with seventeen-year-old Suggs playing cards with a black boy named Bill. Suggs's father, Jedediah, "an old 'hard shell' Baptist preacher," exemplifies a traditional source of authority. Hooper noted that Jedediah Suggs, "though very pious and remarkably austere, was very avaricious." He "reared his boys . . . according to the strictest requisitions of the moral law." Simon, however, adopted bad habits, like playing cards, whenever Jedediah was absent. Hooper portrayed the traditional order neither as nostalgic nor utopian. Rather, hypocrisy and corruption had tainted traditional forms of authority, a point Simon Suggs revealed.[2]

As Jedediah Suggs, armed with hickory switches, approaches the two boys, Simon grabs the pot over Bill's protests and pockets the cards. Jedediah begins to whip Bill for his laziness and then notices the Jack of Diamonds, which Simon had been sitting upon in an effort to cheat Bill. Jedediah realizes that the two boys had been playing cards and decides that both need a beating. The first chapter ends with traditional authority reestablished. Jedediah, though maligned by Hooper for his greed, has yet to display any weaknesses. He prepares to use coercion in order to preserve the traditional values of hard work, responsibility, and morality.

The second chapter opens with Simon trying to devise an escape while watching his father mercilessly beat Bill. Simon contemplates striking his father, but realizes that his brother Ben, who was plowing the adjoining field, would help Jedediah, leaving Simon outnumbered. Jedediah finishes with Bill and approaches Simon. Simon remonstrates with his father, telling him that a whipping would not deter him from his plan to make his living by playing cards. Jedediah replies that "all card-players, and chicken-fighters, and horse-racers go to hell," but the fear of eternal damnation does not change Simon's mind. Simon tells his father that a local man, Bob Smith, had seen Simon play cards, taught him a few tricks, and praised his deftness. Jedediah, who thinks himself better and more knowledgeable than Smith, agrees to play a card game with Simon to demonstrate his own superiority and to reveal Simon's ineptness. The game between father and son reveals the challenge of modernity to traditional society.

Simon gets Jedediah to place a bet on the game by appealing to his greed. If Simon cuts the Jack from the deck, his father would refrain from beating him and give him an Indian pony, Bunch. If Simon fails, he will give his father a sack of silver coins, which Jedediah greedily eyes in hopes of paying off his land. Simon gives the deck to his father to cut. Jedediah tries to cheat by moving some of the cards, but Simon, looking over his father's shoulder, catches the move and by sleight of hand cuts a Jack anyway. His father is devastated. Simon then uses religious rhetoric to humiliate his father by saying that his victory was "predestinated." Jedediah, not realizing Simon's sarcasm, agrees, "To be sure—to be sure—all fixed aforehand." Simon obtains Bunch and is "in high spirits . . . at the idea of unrestrained license in the future." As he rides off to the frontier, Suggs "roared with delight" at his last trick he had played on his mother—before he left he filled her pipe with gunpowder. The anarchic Suggs has vanquished through trickery and violence the corrupt traditional order represented by his parents.[3]

Suggs's success against traditional society formed part of Hooper's subversive message. William Lenz points out that while the reader cheers for Suggs in his trickery against his self-righteous, hypocritical father, Suggs's last trick on his mother turns the reader against him.[4] Suggs is not Hooper's hero, but only his tool to make social points. Suggs, by attacking his parents, reveals his lack of *pietas*. Hooper did not necessarily think that the destruction of the traditional order was always beneficial, but he believed that it fell under the weight of its own corruption. Suggs's victory and escape showed the inability of coercion and religion to order modern freedom. In the face of modern freedom, traditional society was incompetent. In fact, once the traditional order entertained modern ideas of freedom, it began to fall. That Hooper first attacked the traditional society in the eastern state of Georgia is significant, for the rest of the book deals with the frontier, which lacks even the rudiments of traditional society. In the first

few chapters, Hooper portrayed the West much as John Randolph did, as an escape from established communities. Suggs's escape to the West put traditional forms of keeping order in jeopardy, for in the face of coercion one could always flee. For Hooper, as for Baldwin, the frontier represented both the home of modern freedom and the destruction of traditional society.

Even religion was unable to keep order. Until the last two years of his life, Hooper was not a religious man, and, therefore, religion played little positive role in his social vision. In chapter 10 of *Some Adventures of Captain Simon Suggs,* Hooper subjected evangelicalism to withering satire. The theme of the chapter is that religion is the haven of hypocrites and often a thin veil covering human depravity. No virtuous religious figure appears in the Suggs tales, and Suggs's confidence games fit into the program of evangelical Protestantism as Hooper saw it. Whereas Hooper valued religion that was politically useful in shaping character, he had little love for Christianity for most of his life.[5]

The themes of greed, ignorance, and sexual perversion figure prominently in **"The Captain Attends a Camp Meeting."** The chapter begins with Suggs's family hungry and virtually penniless, a striking contrast to the wealth present at the camp meeting. Suggs decides to attend the nearby revival to find a way to alleviate his poverty. When he arrives at the revival tents, the scene is complete chaos. Hooper wrote: "The excitement was intense. Men and women rolled about on the ground, or lay sobbing or shouting in promiscuous heaps. More than all, the Negroes sang and screamed and prayed. Several, under the influence of what is technically called 'the jerks,' were plunging and pitching about with convulsive energy." For a Whig who praised self-restraint, such a scene was hellacious and dangerous. Social order had disappeared, replaced by heaps of men and women mixed with blacks. In the story it is Suggs who actually brings order to the meeting through his confidence scheme, a reversal of the usual nature of the stories in which Suggs introduces chaos into a controlled environment. Suggs "viewed the whole affair as a grand deception—a sort of 'opposition line' running against his own, and looked on with a sort of professional jealousy," Hooper stated. The preachers were confidence men who preyed on trusting victims for money or sexual pleasure. Suggs wonders why "these here preachers never hugs up the old, ugly women." He supplies an answer, saying, "I judge ef I was a preacher, I should save the purtiest souls fust, myself!" The greed of the preachers and the great number of wealthy people at the revival enable Suggs to implement a moneymaking scheme.[6]

Suggs plays a confidence game with the preacher, Rev. Bela Bugg. Gaining the trust of the congregation first, Suggs fakes an emotional religious experience and then tells the crowd that he has been converted. He gives credit for his change of heart to Rev. Bugg. He informs the crowd that originally he had come to the revival to steal money, but that God had changed his heart. He then joins the frenzy of religious enthusiasm until late in the night. The next morning Suggs declares his desire to build a church so that he can begin serving the Lord immediately and takes up a collection, using guilt and shame to persuade the wealthy to contribute. Rev. Bugg greedily eyes the collection and offers to "hold" it for Suggs until a church building could be obtained. Suggs, in a pious tone, explains that he must "pray over" the collection first in the nearby swamp (where his horse is tied). As Suggs leaves with the collection, he quips, "Ef them fellers aint done to a cracklin . . . I'll never bet on two pair agin!" He continues, "Live and let live is a good old motter, and it's my sentiments adzactly!" In other words, Rev. Bugg and the evangelicals could not complain about Suggs's thievery when they practiced the same thing under the guise of religion.[7]

After refuting both liberalism and traditional conservatism through the Suggs stories, Hooper tried to find a way to preserve order in modern society without abandoning freedom or adopting the arbitrary and hypocritical authority of the traditional world. The potential for freedom to devolve into chaos made Hooper's task difficult. Hooper's social vision highlighted the importance of social institutions in forming moral character. Hooper realized that the anonymity of modern society, caused by extensive social mobility, made it harder for traditional means of coercion to maintain social order. Simon Suggs often succeeded in swindling others by imitating respectable citizens such as legislators. Hooper thought that because frontier society was so fluid, personal accountability was lacking. Strong social institutions could solidify society and thus keep order by forming character in individuals. Hooper, like other Whigs, did not advocate the reestablishment of traditional society; he instead desired to tame the anarchic tendencies of modern freedom by teaching self-restraint and individual responsibility. Hooper advocated voluntary institutions that respected individualism and renounced the principles of coercion.

Like other Whigs and southern conservatives, Hooper resisted the egalitarian ethos of nineteenth-century America but did not desire to return to a traditional aristocratic order. He fully supported an individualistic society, which by its nature could not be egalitarian. He believed that people should possess the freedom to choose their own destinies (within certain social limits, of course) despite the fact that such an arrangement would result in inequality. Hooper idealized a meritocracy combined with strong social institutions to guide human behavior toward productive ends. Simon Suggs, in a perverted sense, represents meritocracy, one social

goal of Jeffersonian republicanism. "Well, mother-wit kin beat book-larnin, at any game," Suggs exclaimed. He continued, "As old Jed'diah used to say, book-larning spiles a man ef he's got mother-wit, and ef he aint got that, it don't do him no good."[8] "Mother-wit," innate talent and common sense, would separate superior and inferior persons in an individualistic society. The attractiveness for Hooper of both Suggs and the frontier was that despite the chaos each embodied, meritocracy seemed possible. Even the rascal Suggs could outwit better-educated and richer men. Extreme individualism and the inequality it produced both captivated and frightened Hooper.

Hooper's first major literary exploit, **"Taking the Census in Alabama,"** displayed the importance of wit in an individualistic society. As an assistant census marshal in 1840, Hooper, assigned to Tallapoosa County, had been ordered to count all the people and chickens in the county. He commented, "The popular impression, that a tremendous tax would soon follow the minute investigation of the private affairs of the people, caused the census-taker to be viewed in no better light than that of a tax-gatherer; and the consequence was, that the information sought by him was either withheld entirely, or given with great reluctance." Referring to part of his task, Tallapoosa residents called Hooper "the chicken man." The contrast between the gentlemanly narrator (Hooper) and the largely ignorant people created humorous situations.[9]

Hooper portrayed himself as the intellectual superior of the people of Tallapoosa. The common people accuse Hooper and President Martin Van Buren of all sorts of conspiracies. One old woman promised Hooper that she would kill Van Buren if he ever set foot on her property. She said, "A pretty fellow to be eating his vittils out'n gold spoons that poor people's taxed for, and raisin' an army to get him made King of Ameriky—the oudacious, nasty, stinking old scamp!" The woman refused to give Hooper the information he needed and even sicced her dogs on him after he made an insulting gesture toward her. Hooper also meets Kit Kuncker, a strong Democrat, whose parting line is always, "God bless the old Ginnul, and damn all nullifiers!" Kuncker's dog is even named "Andy" after General Jackson. Hooper encounters Mrs. Naron, who named her young son Thomas Jefferson. The toddler, when Hooper met him, did not wear any pants or diaper and soon urinated on the floor. Hooper relates that Mrs. Naron called to her son but he "did not heed the invitation, but continued to dabble and splash in a little pool of water, which had somehow got there, as proud, apparently, of his *sans-culottism,* as ever his illustrious namesake could have been of his." After making his dig at Jefferson, Hooper watches as Mrs. Naron whips her son, marveling at the crudity of the citizens of Tallapoosa.[10]

Hooper's aristocratic tone in the story was not meant to keep the lower classes in their places; Hooper appreciated frontier society. Wit, not Hooper's refinement, separates the citizens of Tallapoosa and all people in free societies. The people of Tallapoosa were equal in their ignorance and flawed natures, but some citizens rose above the others. While trying to cross the Tallapoosa River on horseback, Hooper meets Sol Todd, who tricks him into crossing over a deep hole, which results in a soaking for both Hooper and his horse on a "sharp September morning." Sol's wit had beaten Hooper's refinement. Thinking that turnabout is fair play, Hooper fabricates a story that he had dropped twenty-five dollars in specie in the middle of the deep hole while crossing. He convinces Sol to dive for the imaginary purse, promising to split the money with him. As Sol dives for the purse, Hooper announces that he has to leave for the next town but that Sol should bring him the purse if he should find it. Sol, greedy for the money, continues to dive in the icy water, "his blue lips" quivering. Hooper comments with pride, "The 'river ager' made Sol shake worse . . . that fall." Hooper's wit, not his refinement or learning, won him satisfaction. Hooper presents the frontier as an equalizer that marked sharply the differences between those who possessed the wit and self-restraint necessary to succeed in the modern order and those who could not cope with modern freedom.[11]

Hooper disdained traditional and artificial aristocracies with almost as much vehemence as did John Taylor of Caroline. In a November 1855 editorial, Hooper denounced the "Cow Heel Aristocracy," those of "low origin and contemptible pretensions" who based their pretentiousness on their new wealth. He declared: "In a republican country, there should be no aristocrats—no class to be rated superior to another, by the law, or by custom . . . But if we are to have an aristocracy *at all,* let it be an aristocracy of birth and blood—let it not be the base counterfeit of a contemptible original." The Cow Heel aristocracy forgot that wit, not wealth, was the great divider in modern society. But Hooper did not like traditional aristocracies either. He condemned the idea that virtue was a birthright or could be obtained by wealth.[12] Through the example of Simon Suggs, he showed that an aristocracy of wealth harmed society by denying freedom.

"Simon Starts Forth to Fight the 'Tiger'" begins with Suggs in a coach en route to Tuscaloosa ready to gamble at cards, his "Achilles' heel." The other passenger "was a gentleman who was about to visit the seat of government, with the intention of making himself a bank director, as speedily as possible." The aspiring banker mistakes Suggs for a legislator, an assumption Suggs does not discourage, and begins lobbying for Suggs's vote. He flatters Suggs, calling him a "man of high moral principles, refined feelings, pure patriotism."

Suggs claims that he forgot to bring the money necessary for the stage fare, and the gentleman offers Suggs a loan. Whereas Suggs speaks in a rough dialect in the story, the banker's speech is refined and aristocratic, making his flattery and greed transparent. The man gives Suggs an additional twenty dollars, an obvious bribe, and asks Suggs not to tell anyone about the "gift." The gentleman begs Suggs to vote him a bank charter, to which Suggs readily agrees. For the rest of the trip, the gentleman and Suggs drank, ate, and "sang their songs" with the gentleman "paying all scores wherever they halted."[13]

The banker represents the aristocracy of wealth seeking political power through corruption. He pays lip service to the wisdom of the common man while trying to establish himself as an aristocrat. Hooper did not repeat Old Republican invectives against banking in the story, but he hinted that the merger of political power with wealth originated in personal corruption. The gentleman is the antithesis of republicanism: selfish, greedy, and a corrupter of the legislature. Suggs is the hero in the story, preserving freedom through trickery and deceit, or as he would have it, through "mother-wit." The anonymity of frontier society plays to Suggs's advantage as the gentleman mistakes him for a man of importance. Clearly Suggs is superior in wit to the greedy gentleman and better exemplifies the individualistic ethic. The fact that Suggs preserves freedom through trickery reveals further the subversive aspect of the humor and Hooper's ambiguity about modern freedom. By having wit triumph in such circumstances, Hooper intimated that modern freedom always threatened to become moral anarchy.

Despite his disgust for an artificial aristocracy, Hooper believed that a natural hierarchy of talent existed among men. Traditional aristocracies had little room for merit, and thus Hooper rejected a return to a Burkean society. Hooper thought that men could retain the polite customs that elevated life and distinguished the talented from the average. Randolph of Roanoke had made a similar point in decrying the vulgarization of American life as a betrayal of virtue. Hooper commented on the customs of the South's gentlemanly pastime, hunting. In *Dog & Gun,* which he published in 1856, he advised southern gentlemen on the correct attitudes, practices, and equipment needed to maintain the genteel sport of hunting.

Hooper contrasted utility and gentility in order to support the need for gentlemanly society. He calls the "shooting of game birds" the "gentleman's amusement." Then, speaking of the quail, he writes, "Let all true sportsmen call him aright—leaving it to the pot-hunter who shoots the bevy as it huddles on the ground, or murders the whistling cock on the fence or stump, and the clown who nets or traps what he cannot fairly kill, to apply to him a name for which there is no owner on this continent." The pot-hunter kills only for utility and thus contributes to the decline of mannerly conduct. Worse, the pot-hunter vulgarizes the name of the bird, leading to a loss of propriety in speech. Hooper appealed to talent, sport, and custom to defend hunting as a sort of cultural ritual or tradition that had value beyond its usefulness or necessity in gaining food. He decried the cheap guns used by the pot-hunters as well. He disdained the method of catching quail in large nets, a technique practiced "quite extensively in this region." Usually "pot-hunting vagabonds" engaged in such a practice, but some gentlemen had been known to do it too. Hooper noted, "I do not mean that all who indulge in the villainous practice are worthless characters—though a majority of them are—but that the thing itself is so vile an outrage upon all sportsmanship, humanity, and magnanimity, that no man who *knows better* ought to countenance his best neighbor if he will not discontinue it."[14]

Such rhetoric seems silly and pedantic. The idea that one would passionately believe in the necessity and cultural importance of certain hunting tactics seems preposterous. *Dog & Gun,* however, reveals much about Hooper's social vision. For Hooper the culture of hunting was a circumscribed frontier in which talent could prevail. Freed from the demands of the cash nexus and the pretensions of the Cow Heel aristocracy, gentlemen competed for one prize, honor. The hunting culture contained certain rules, customs, and traditions that to Hooper elevated one from the crass utilitarianism of American life. The preservation of the hunting tradition without regard to utility seemed to Hooper important for maintaining some sense of meritocracy and hierarchy in society. Also, because hunting was voluntary, it did not carry the negative or coercive aspects of traditional society. *Dog & Gun* fit, oddly enough, into Hooper's Whig social vision.[15]

Throughout the Suggs stories Hooper discussed the collapse of traditional society and the ambiguity of modern freedom. Hooper recognized the necessity of both individual self-restraint and strong, but voluntary, institutions to check the excesses of modernity. Hooper expressed the sense of nostalgia that many Whigs felt toward traditional society. Though he had no desire to return to traditional society, he did acknowledge that it often represented good principles. The fact that Hooper selected hunting as a cultural reserve of gentility on the frontier shows just how deeply modernity had been established in Alabama in the 1850s. *Dog & Gun* represented Hooper's retreat into a space where he could celebrate his conservative social views without being penalized politically for his skepticism about American egalitarianism. Unlike Randolph, who defended the Western intellectual and social tradition, Hooper showed no enthusiasm for social or religious tradition. Hooper's love of gentility and honor reveal that some southern conservatives in the 1850s still cared about tradition, although the traditions they defended were not always the political and religious traditions of Western society. . . .

Issues of race and slavery absorbed a good deal of Hooper's energies in the 1850s. He was an inveterate racist. In his editorials he mentioned frequently the inferiority of blacks. In a February 1860 editorial, Hooper commented upon the election of the new Speaker of the House of Representatives in Washington. The new speaker, he charged, "is one of those who believe the African to be the equal of the Anglo-Saxon." The "unrelenting North forced him down the throats of the humble imbecile South."[16] Hooper's fear of racial equality drove some of his political defenses of the South too. In November 1860 he remarked, "Those who have these advantages [money and northern connections], may afford to be Union shriekers; but we, being poor at home and friendless in the North, must, (if Alabama submits to being held in the present Union,) stay here, and submit to all the horrors of an equality of the white and black races." Hooper believed that Lincoln would free the slaves and force racial equality on the South. He continued: "In the struggle for maintaining the ascendancy of our race in the South—our home—we see no chance for victory but in withdrawing from the Union. To remain in the Union is to lose all that white men hold dear in Government."[17] For Hooper, secession was more than a constitutional question. It was also a matter of maintaining white supremacy.

Hooper drew demeaning portraits of blacks in his fiction. He portrayed them as stupid and dull. He neither romanticized the master-slave relationship nor depicted the stock character of the loyal slave. One of his overtly racist humorous pieces, **"Captain Stick and Toney,"** appeared in *A Ride With Old Kit Kuncker* in 1849. The brief sketch concerned Captain Stick, "a remarkably precise old gentleman," who was "a conscientiously just man." The captain kept an account book of the daily conduct of his slaves. For each misdeed, the slave received a certain number of lashes, while for good deeds, the slave obtained credits. Captain Stick enjoyed whipping his slaves and settled their accounts every Saturday. After giving his slave Toney the "just" number of lashes, the Captain was not satisfied and wanted to whip him more. Toney, however, successfully convinced the captain to credit his "account" for some of the good deeds he had done that week about which the captain had forgotten. When Stick realized that Toney might escape next week's whipping because of his credits, he decided to "charge" Toney for the "cost" incurred in providing for him. The captain exclaimed, "[W]here's my costs—you incorrigible, abominable scoundrel? You want to swindle me do you, out of my costs, you black, deceitful rascal." Toney protested for naught, and the captain whipped him harshly.[18] The humor in the story is dark. The slave is completely helpless in the face of the unjust violence done against him. The cruelty of the story would hardly strike modern readers as funny, but it does reflect Hooper's racism.

The issue of slavery composed a major portion of Hooper's politics in the 1850s. He devoted time to promoting his Whig economic views, especially in state-aid railroad projects, but on the national scene he judged the protection of slavery to be the most important issue. He called slavery the South's "most important institution" and made it clear that any move against slavery by the federal government would provoke secession by the slave states.[19] He vigorously defended the constitutional right to own slaves and to take them into the territories. As a partisan editor, Hooper used slavery as a political weapon.

Hooper faced what historian William Cooper has termed the "politics of slavery." Hooper described the political tactic at length in an 1854 editorial. He began, "The newspapers of the Southern Whig party labor strenuously to prove that the Democratic party of the free States is very thoroughly demoralized by abolitionism and that even where the party shout is heard, in the North and West, for 'Nebraska and the Administration,' it is accompanied by the declaration that the measure and its promoters are the truest friends of *free soil.*" Once tarred with the brush of antislavery, the Democratic papers responded in kind and accused the Whigs of harboring abolitionist sentiment in their party. "Each establishes the correctness of its own partisans," Hooper noted, "by showing the unsoundness of its opponents." He thought such an argument fallacious. Hooper called for all southern politicians to realize that no party in the North "dares assume to yield to the plainest constitutional rights of the South." He acknowledged that the southern Whigs had been unfairly charged with antislavery sentiments but insisted that the southern Whigs had forgotten about reestablishing their fractured national party structure. Instead they should focus on electing "men of undoubted ability, nerve, and Southern feeling" so that the South could present a united front against antislavery agitation in the U.S. House of Representatives. Hooper called the politics of slavery a "party drill" and charged that it took away from the defense of the true interest of the South, slavery.[20]

Despite condemning the politics of slavery as divisive and harmful to southern interests, Hooper used the tactic in his editorials. As a Know-Nothing editor, he accused Alabama Democrats of endangering the safety both of American republicanism and of slavery. On August 3, 1857, state election day in Alabama, Hooper attacked anyone who planned to vote for a Democrat. Pointing out that President James Buchanan would not protect southern rights, he called Democrats party hacks and betrayers of southern rights. He wrote: "*This day* settles the question in Alabama. The man whose vote is given to those who stand by the Administration repudiates our rights in the Territories and consents to the 'restriction of slavery.' If a majority of the State so vote, Alabama can never again be called a Southern Rights State. If you would take 'high ground,' *ever,* take it now!" The Democrats swept the elections, leaving Hooper to comment that "the people . . . throw themselves willingly and with utmost confidence upon the tender mercies of the Freesoilers for all time to come."[21] Hooper's willingness to play the politics of slavery, even after having denounced it, reveals that he regarded slavery as both the fundamental issue in national politics and the basis of southern social interests.

Some historians have argued that fears of slave revolts gave impetus to the secessionist impulse, but Hooper seldom expressed fears of slave revolts in the context of his call for the protection of slavery. In 1859 and 1860, however, he did express a few fears of revolt as he began to press more urgently for secession. In November 1859, he reported that northern visitors and immigrants might try to "slip about among the plantations, endeavoring to corrupt the slaves." Anyone attempting such a thing should be hanged, insisted Hooper. In April 1860 he warned his readers that another Harper's Ferry raid could happen at any time because of anti-slavery and abolitionist rhetoric. His most extended comments on slave unrest appeared in a Christmas letter to his brother John DeBerniere Hooper in 1860. Hooper noted that the election returns in Alabama on the vote deciding to hold a secession convention were in, and the state would secede. "On all sides we have insurrectionary plots," he continued, "instigated by the North—thousands of dollars' worth of negro property destroyed by hanging—strychnine fixed for our food—and a general notion infused into the servile race, that Lincoln is to free them." Hooper described several hangings of slaves near Montgomery and a hanging of twenty-one men, mostly blacks, in Autauga County (next to Montgomery). Supposedly, the authorities found "Brown's pikes" in the possession of some slaves and poison in the possession of a miller. Someone confessed to the plot, and the conspirators were rounded up and killed. A few days later, on December 28, Hooper insisted that the state legislature ban all free blacks from Alabama and prevent all Yankees from migrating to the state, presumably to prevent any future uprisings.[22]

Hooper's fear of northern fanaticism drove him toward extreme sectionalism. As a Whig with a modern conservative social vision, he abhorred social radicalism. He thought that northerners interfered too much in southern affairs and called for independence from the North. With a libertarian attitude, he asked: "What right have the Northern people to meddle with the affairs and rights of the Southern states? Have the Southern people ever, in any manner, shape or form, meddled with the affairs of the Northern people?" Hooper attributed Yankees' social activism to their impiety: "Now if the Northern people—born such—would only agree to submit to the decrees of the Almighty, we might get along. But the genuine Free Soil Yankee believes Omnipotence to be a mere bungler and always wishes to improve his work."[23] Hooper shared his distrust of social activism with other southern conservatives who feared the interference of government in society. Northern reformers, according to Hooper, attempted to use the state as a means to re-make southern society. Therefore, as the Republican Party came closer to attaining the presidency, Hooper's fears of northern radicalism grew, causing him to embrace secession.

Hooper hated abolitionism the most, of course. In 1854 he reprinted comments made about abolitionists in a Virginia paper: "The Moslem zealots who think that they promote the Kingdom of God in this world by warring against the Bible and Christianity, do not exceed in fanaticism and criminality the men who are now at the North actively engaged in warring against the Constitution and the Laws." Abolitionists, by denouncing the Constitution and appealing to a higher law, frightened Hooper because they violated his Whig love of order. Abolitionists, in Hooper's mind, were anarchists who had to be stopped, by violence if necessary. He warned his readers, "The Masses of abolition are moving forward to attack us." The North would not help the South, and thus the South had to defend itself from ruin by meeting "the foe" with "firmness," "union," and "preparation." By 1860, a scared Hooper remarked: "We believe that abolitionists are by nature, or the operation of their principles, made liars, thieves and cowardly murderers. We believe that they have the supremacy in this government and will retain it and apply their principles." Hooper's fear of abolitionism was far from unique. He shared his hatred of social radicalism with both northern and southern conservatives.[24] Nevertheless, his hatred of abolitionism caused him to view other parts of northern society with suspicion.

Hooper portrayed northern society as driven by hatred, and he longed for retribution for the wrongs perpetrated upon the South. He believed that northerners taught their children from birth to hate the southern people. Such hatred drove northerners to applaud the efforts of John Brown to arm the slaves of Virginia and cause a rebellion. In December 1859, Hooper reprinted a story from a Philadelphia newspaper that lamented the economic hardship in the North caused by the South's 1859 boycott of northern businesses. The story told of the difficulties faced by the poor urban workers. Hooper commented: "It rejoices our soul to hear of this early justice. Every howl of the North West wind will bring sweet dreams to us, for we shall know that it is pinching the thin-clad limbs of some at least of those who

would place the knife at our throats, if they could." He regarded the situation as vengeance for northern support of the Harper's Ferry raid. He insisted: "'Workmen discharged,' eh! And 'particularly trying at this period of the year'—is it? It was not 'particularly trying,' was it, to send thousands of broad blades to Virginia, to put into the hands of our loyal slaves, for the purposes of rebellion and massacre! Oh, no!"[25] Hooper had faith in neither the northern people nor their politicians to protect the constitutional rights of the South. He made wild assertions that northerners wanted only to see southerners killed. His loss of faith in the North reflected his loss of trust in the benefits of the United States of America. The Whig ideal of a common social vision and a united effort for a common national good had passed.

Hooper also depicted the North as a place of hypocrisy and sexual depravity. In 1856 he printed a story about sexual immorality in a school for girls in Boston. He commented that "the saints of that city are not altogether free from those carnal weaknesses which their romances are inclined to saddle almost exclusively on slaveholders." Hooper relished the sexual depravity of hypocrites. It was "very apparent that 'the Flesh and the Devil' 'hold their own' among the descendants of the Mayflower Pilgrims, quite as fully as among the warmer regions of the South." He concluded: "That is a nice little kettle of fish, for pious, puritanic, nigger-loving, psalm singing Boston! It would be difficult to parallel such detestable pollution in the lowest sinks of rotten and rotting London." In another editorial he described a meeting of a Free Love Society in New York City that was frequented by intellectuals. He tied sexual license to social radicalism. "Can we wonder, that in a society where such elements as these exist, abolition vagaries should be produced! A society which submits to the existence of such an association, even on the most limited scale, in its midst, must be depraved to its inmost core." By painting northern society as inherently depraved, Hooper assured southerners of their own righteousness. He portrayed the radicalism of the North as culturally pervasive, much as the chaos on the frontier in the Suggs stories affected southern culture for a time. Social radicalism challenged the conservative principles and society of the South. "We can only look for destructive principles and action, social and political, where such infinite and ineffable impurity has found a 'local habitation and a name,'" commented Hooper on New York City.[26] Images of the North as Sodom and Gomorrah could hasten southerners' desires to separate from the radical and "evil" North.

Hooper drew on southern proslavery social rhetoric, although he did not offer a systematic defense of slavery. He held with other southern nationalists that the slave society of the South was superior to northern society. In a November 1857 editorial, Hooper reported that there had been a mob in New York City threatening the mayor and promising to loot the city unless they received relief from the food shortages plaguing the North. Hooper gleefully commented, "There's free society, for you." He believed that northern capitalist society would implode due to the tensions caused by its labor system, a common view among southern conservatives in the 1850s. Hooper seemed to have retreated from his earlier Whig defense of a free society and individualism. His corresponding Whig appreciation of meritocracy and inequality, however, could buttress his proslavery convictions because the superior wealth of the South was linked to slavery. In November 1860, shortly before the presidential election, Hooper encouraged Alabamians to stand firm on principle. He said that if secession occurred it would take place "with the wealth of a great nation in our depots and in those of the other Seceding States." He continued: "There will be no war and, after a few weeks, no distress. Our cotton bales are the bond which obligates the armies and navies of Europe to defend us." The wealth of the South formed "the subsistence" of the North. He predicted that without southern cotton both the North and European nations would suffer hardship. "We have only to be true to our own sense of right, to obtain Security and Prosperity," he exclaimed. Southern superiority, based on its cotton economy and slave society, would triumph.[27]

Hooper deeply loathed the North, particularly abolitionists and anyone who denied the South her constitutional rights. On Christmas Day 1860, he wrote a letter to his brother about the upcoming secession convention in Alabama. Hardly in keeping with the Christmas spirit, he launched into a bitter diatribe against northern radicals. He began: "You seem to think me bitter, perhaps too bitter, toward the fanatical portion of the North. . . . I *am* bitter towards them and I often regret that I cannot in some way help to destroy them." Blurring the distinction between radicals and New Englanders in general by using the Puritan myth, he asserted: "I hate them instinctively—I hate the race and the blood from which they spring—from Oliver Cromwell down to Ward Beecher, I regard them as one of God's punishments for a sinful world." Almost at a frenzy, Hooper wrote: "I hate them more than I do any thing in this world, or than I can hate any thing in that which is to come; and I cannot repress my joy, when I hear that they are starving and freezing and rotting around the factories of New England." He ended the thought with a final wish for violence: "They pursue me and mine; if I could, I would visit them with fire, pestilence, famine and the sword." Secession would rid Alabama of "the accursed tyranny of these demons." In Hooper's hatred of the North as a corrupt, radical, aggressive power, he revealed that he viewed the possible war in the future to be one of purification. By separating from the demonic North, a pure southern nation could preserve order, slavery, and constitutional liberty.[28]

Hooper's sectionalism and southern nationalism were largely negative in character, but they also reflected his Whig principles. He feared the chaos abolition would bring and the disrespect to the rule of law that a higher law approach to the Constitution brought. He hoped for an economically progressive, Whiggish southern nation that preserved the antiparty purity of republicanism.[29] He yearned for the realization of economic opportunity and individualism with the opening of the West to slaveholders. Although he possessed a positive vision of the future southern nation, he did not articulate it clearly or frequently. Instead, his fear of government interference with slavery and of northern radicalism drove his burgeoning southern nationalism in the late 1850s. Hooper believed that the primary goal of his southern nationalism was to protect and secure slavery in the South. . . .

Hooper passionately tried to build southern unity in order to form a national community. He realized that he faced a difficult task. In an 1858 editorial, Hooper noted that the *Mail* was "a most dedicated Southern Rights American paper." He continued, "Those who manage it have been in minorities during all of their political lives; they therefore are not likely to shrink from opposing majorities." Hooper promised that he would remain "steadfast to the end."[30] His admission that southern rights was a minority position indicated to him that he must create a consensus. He stressed unity on principles to do so. Hooper noted that the Constitution obviously protected the right to own slaves. Likewise, the right to bring slaves into the territories was a logical extension of the constitutional right to own slaves. These principles, Hooper insisted, were easy for all to grasp and defend. He did not appeal primarily to interest because he thought that all principled men could defend the Constitution regardless of whether or not they owned slaves. He did, however, warn southerners that if they did not stand up to the abolitionists and defend the Constitution, abolition of slavery would occur with devastating results. In Hooper's logic, unity on constitutional principles gave southerners a common interest in defeating abolitionism.

Hooper used various methods to attain southern unity. Rhetoric was extremely important. He used the term the "South," referring to the slave states, to suggest a degree of unity that went beyond mere geography. He also used the terms "Southern people" and "our people" to suggest a regional or southern national identity. He tried to reinforce the idea of a unified South in his newspaper. He reprinted stories from other southern newspapers, especially those in Virginia, Georgia, and South Carolina, to show Alabama readers of the *Mail* that all southerners faced problems such as abolitionism, the prohibition of slavery in the territories, and northern aggressiveness. By informing his Alabama readership of events of which they otherwise would have been ignorant, Hooper essentially tied the political reactions of

Alabamians to occurrences and opinions in other southern states. He used a similar tactic when reporting on different northern cities. He painted each of them as radical in order to portray a unified enemy, the "North." It was hoped such tactics could create a national community of southerners united around opposition to the North and constitutional principles.

Hooper stressed that all southerners faced a common plight of economic and cultural dependence on the North. In 1855 he declared that the South's "dependence on the North is most degrading." In 1858 he declared, "Today instead of reaping alike with the North the benefits and advantages resulting from the Union, the South stands forth—and has stood forth for years past—the recipient of injurious, insulting oppression." The North, he charged, had used its superiority in numbers to wear down the South and prevent her from prospering economically. Hooper linked his advocacy of a progressive Whig economy for the South to his southern nationalism. He wrote, "We shall strive to aid in stimulating the South to Industrial Independence, as the best preparation for political Independence." He also supported efforts at cultural independence. In an April 1860 editorial, Hooper praised the formation of the University of the South in Sewanee, Tennessee, as a means to celebrate southern culture's superiority. He noted that southerners discovered in such a scheme how to "fire every Southern heart with enthusiasm and patriotic pride."[31]

In the mid-1850s, Hooper began insisting that southerners unite in order to fight the northern threat to southern rights. In an 1855 editorial he warned southerners that northern Congressmen in the House of Representatives were incited to attack slavery "by frantic, howling constituencies at home." The South had to stand firm and united in national politics, rejecting party loyalty. The South could not back down. Hooper charged that if the South retreated from the fight, "Cuban vassalage would be too mild a doom for her degenerate sons."[32] By portraying the political fight as a litmus test for republicanism, Hooper hoped to unite southerners from both parties to defend their common constitutional rights.

Hooper readily admitted that disunity existed among southerners but hoped, through reason, to convince the southern people to unite. As the presidential election of 1860 approached, however, Hooper became much more frightened by the lack of a southern national community. In April 1860 he chastised southerners for being too tolerant of free soilers expressing their opinions in public. Hysterically, Hooper declared that all free soilers were abolitionists and that southerners must not allow any verbal dissent on slavery in social discourse. On November 6, 1860, fearing that a Lincoln victory was imminent, Hooper expressed hope that southerners would forget their party differences of the past and

unite. He wrote: "Shall not our people unite, then, under such circumstances? The political differences of the past—supposing Lincoln elected—ought to be buried among Southern men. We mean, of course, all true hearted men of the South, who only desire the welfare of their country and section. *After this day,* there is no cause for dispute among us. We can be, if we choose, one people; and we ought to be, and must be." Hooper opined that unity and loyalty were inextricably linked. Loyal southerners professed unity and abandoned parties. He implied that only disloyal southerners would disagree. "Let Southern Union be the word," he concluded. In a November 8 editorial, he hinted that one source of possible disloyalty in the South could be wealthy southerners who possessed the means to leave the South instead of fighting. His argument was an old republican one against luxury in republics. Some republicans had claimed that luxury would dissolve public virtue so much that the rich would refuse to fight for any good other than the protection of their wealth. After Alabama seceded in January 1861, Hooper proclaimed: "[A]ll hail! To the glorious, free and independent Flag of the Sovereign Republic of Alabama! Forever may it wave in honor over a happy, chivalrous, united people."[33] After secession Hooper reported as fact that the people of Alabama were united and desired independence. The imagined political community would be completed upon the formation of the Confederate States of America.[34]

Hooper used the image of the South as the *patria* in order to unite southerners to oppose northern aggression. In April 1860 he wrote a poem expressing the theme of southern unity:

> Men of the South! Your homes,
> Where peace and plenty smiled,
> Have been assailed by thieving bands,
> And by their tread defiled.
> The canting traitors of the North
> With lying tongues declaim,
> And spit at you their slime and froth,
> Their venom and their flame.[35]

Hooper's image of the South seems classical in inspiration. The virtuous southerners, like the ancient Romans, were to defend their homes, the foundations of society, against the aggressive, deceitful "thieving bands" of the North, the equivalent of the ancient barbarian tribes. Hooper shifted the focus away from slavery, his constant theme, to the defense of the home and civilization, a task all honorable men would gladly perform. His image was a conservative one—a united people fighting in self-defense for the very existence of society and civilization. It matched well the images of traditional society used by John Randolph. By focusing on the image of a virtuous protagonist against an utterly evil foe, Hooper revealed the urgency and desperation of his southern nationalism. All of civilization, he thought, hung in the balance.

Notes

1. Lynn, *Mark Twain and Southwestern Humor,* 52-64. Anderson, "Scholarship in Southwestern Humor—Past and Present," 70-77. See Bradford, review of *With the Bark On: Popular Humor of the Old South,* edited by John Q. Anderson, 377-81.

2. Hooper, *Adventures of Captain Simon Suggs,* 12-14.

3. Ibid., 28-30.

4. Lenz, *Fast Talk and Flush Times,* 72-73.

5. Hooper's irreligious attitudes were represented in his secular social views and his Freemasonry. Hooper thought that religion could have a positive influence on politics. If religion served the state, then it could be supported. *Montgomery* (Alabama) *Daily Mail,* July 26, 1855, "The surest mode of keeping this country republican, is to keep it Protestant."

6. Hooper, *Adventures of Captain Simon Suggs,* 119-23.

7. Ibid., 132-33. Suggs describes his conversion with crude sexual innuendo that the crowd does not understand. See Shields, "A Sadder Simon Suggs," 658-60. John Randolph also disliked evangelicalism. See also Robert M. Calhoon, *Evangelicals and Conservatives in the Early South, 1740-1861.*

8. Hooper, *Adventures of Captain Simon Suggs,* 53-54.

9. Ibid., 149.

10. Ibid., 152-53, 188, 169.

11. Ibid., 155-57.

12. *Montgomery* (Alabama) *Daily Mail,* November 27, 1855. For the Juvenal reference see Gilbert Highet, *Juvenal the Satirist: A Study,* 113-16. John Taylor made similar points about wealth and freedom.

13. Hooper, *Adventures of Captain Simon Suggs,* 44-50.

14. Johnson Jones Hooper, *Dog & Gun: A Few Loose Chapters on Shooting, Among Which Will Be Found Some Anecdotes and Incidents,* 9, 15, 60.

15. Greenberg, *Honor and Slavery.* Philip D. Beidler, introduction to Johnson Jones Hooper, *Dog & Gun,* vii-xxiii. Hooper also celebrated traditions such as the theater and literature. He was fond of Shakespeare in particular. See *Montgomery* (Alabama) *Daily Mail,* January 8, 1857, and December 16, 1858.

16. *Montgomery* (Alabama) *Daily Mail,* February 3, 1860. See Shields, "A Sadder Simon Suggs" and Introduction to Johnson Jones Hooper, *Adventures of Captain Simon Suggs,* xix, xliv-xlvii, for Hooper's racism.

17. *Montgomery* (Alabama) *Mail,* November 8, 1860.

18. Johnson Jones Hooper, *A Ride with Old Kit Kuncker, and Other Sketches, and Scenes of Alabama,* 58-60. It should be noted that the story differs greatly from Baldwin's story in *Flush Times* in which the Yankee schoolteacher leaves town after being told fictitious stories about cruelties perpetrated upon slaves. In Hooper's tale, the cruelty is real. In Baldwin's story, the horrors are concocted.

19. *Montgomery* (Alabama) *Mail,* August 12, 1857.

20. *Montgomery* (Alabama) *Daily Mail,* November 24, 1854.

21. Ibid., August 3 and 12, 1857.

22. Ibid., November 24, 1859. *Montgomery* (Alabama) *Weekly Mail,* December 28, 1860. Johnson Jones Hooper to John DeBerniere Hooper, December 25, 1860, reprinted in Edgar E. Thompson, "The Literary Career of Johnson Jones Hooper," 96-97.

23. *Montgomery* (Alabama) *Weekly Mail,* May 4, 1860. *Montgomery* (Alabama) *Daily Mail,* January 31, 1861.

24. *Montgomery* (Alabama) *Daily Mail,* November 17, 1854, May 25, 1855, and January 16, 1860. Part of the Alabama American Party's platform in 1855 contained a denunciation of a higher-law approach to the Constitution. Number five of the platform read: "Protection to all persons 'in the inestimable privilege of worshipping God in the manner most agreeable to their own consciences': opposition to the election to office of any man who recognizes the right of any religious denomination to power, or the authority of any 'higher law' than the Constitution of the United States." *Montgomery* (Alabama) *Daily Mail,* June 13, 1855.

25. *Montgomery* (Alabama) *Weekly Mail,* May 4, 1860. *Montgomery* (Alabama) *Daily Mail,* December 22, 1859.

26. *Montgomery* (Alabama) *Daily Mail,* November 26, 1856, and October 22, 1855. Somers, *Johnson J. Hooper,* 117-18.

27. *Montgomery* (Alabama) *Daily Mail,* November 12, 1857, and November 6, 1860. See Genovese, *The World the Slaveholders Made* for a discussion of slaveholding ideology and northern capitalism.

28. Johnson Jones Hooper to John DeBerniere Hooper, December 25, 1860, reprinted in Edgar E. Thomp-

son, "The Literary Career of Johnson Jones Hooper," 96-97. For southern views of the Civil War as an agent of purification see Genovese, *A Consuming Fire.* Some northern intellectuals had a similar view of the purifying nature of the war. See George Frederickson, *The Inner Civil War: Northern Intellectuals and the Crisis of the Union.*

29. Potter and Fehrenbacher, *The Impending Crisis,* 469-84. Hooper's southern nationalism reflects Potter's charge that southern nationalism was primarily negative in character. Shields, introduction to Johnson Jones Hooper, *Adventures of Captain Simon Suggs,* li.

30. *Montgomery* (Alabama) *Mail,* April 28, 1858, reprinted in Kelley, "The Life and Writing of Johnson Jones Hooper," 161.

31. *Montgomery* (Alabama) *Daily Mail,* May 9, 1855, and August 3, 1858. *Montgomery* (Alabama) *Mail,* January 2, 1860, reprinted in Kelley, "The Life and Writing of Johnson Jones Hooper," 162. *Montgomery* (Alabama) *Weekly Mail,* April 13, 1860.

32. *Montgomery* (Alabama) *Daily Mail,* April 16, 1855.

33. *Montgomery* (Alabama) *Weekly Mail,* April 27, 1860, and January 18, 1861. *Montgomery* (Alabama) *Daily Mail,* November 6, 1860.

34. The subject of secession in Alabama has produced many works. For book-length treatments see Clarence Phillips Denman, *The Secession Movement in Alabama.* Dorman, *Party Politics in Alabama from 1850-1860.* William L. Barney, *The Secessionist Impulse: Alabama and Mississippi in 1860.* Thornton, *Politics and Power in a Slave Society.* Two historiographical essays, though dated, offer good insights on conceptualizing the secession movement: William J. Donnelly, "Conspiracy or Popular Movement: The Historiography of Southern Support for Secession," 70-84. Ralph A. Wooster, "The Secession of the Lower South: An Examination of Changing Interpretations," 117-27. Ralph A. Wooster, "An Analysis of the Membership of Secession Conventions in the Lower South," 360-68. William H. Brantley, Jr., "Alabama Secedes," 165-85. Hugh C. Bailey, "Disloyalty in Early Confederate Alabama," 522-28. Hugh C. Bailey, "Disaffection in the Alabama Hill Country, 1861," 183-93. Thomas B. Alexander, "Persistent Whiggery in Alabama and the Lower South, 1860-1867" [Tuscaloosa, Ala.: Alabama Historical Association, 1959], 35-52. For a refutation of Bailey's thesis that the state was profoundly divided over secession, see Durward Long, "Unanimity and Disloyalty in Secessionist Alabama," 257-73. See also Marshal J. Rachleff, "Racial Fear and Political Factionalism: A Study of the Secession Movement in Alabama, 1819-1861." William J. Cooper, Jr., "The Politics of Slavery Affirmed: The South and the Secession Crisis," in Fraser and Moore, eds., *The Southern Enigma: Essays on Race, Class, and Folk Culture,* 199-215.

35. *Montgomery* (Alabama) *Weekly Mail,* April 20, 1860.

Works Cited

Books

Baldwin, Joseph Glover. *The Flush Times of Alabama and Mississippi.* New York: Appleton, 1853. Reprt., Baton Rouge: Louisiana State University Press, 1987.

Barney, William L. *The Secessionist Impulse: Alabama and Mississippi in 1860.* Princeton, N.J.: Princeton University Press, 1974.

Calhoon, Robert M. *Evangelicals and Conservatives in the Early South, 1740-1861.* Columbia: University of South Carolina Press, 1988.

Denman, Clarence Phillips. *The Secession Movement in Alabama.* Montgomery: Alabama State Department of Archives and History, 1933.

Dorman, Lewy. *Party Politics in Alabama from 1850 through 1860.* Tuscaloosa: University of Alabama Press, 1995; originally published Wetumpka, Ala.: Wetumpka Printing Company, 1935.

Fraser, Walter J., Jr., and Winfred B. Moore, Jr., eds. *The Southern Enigma: Essays on Race, Class, and Folk Culture.* Westport, Conn.: Greenwood Press, 1983.

Frederickson, George. *The Inner Civil War: Northern Intellectuals and the Crisis of the Union.* Urbana: University of Illinois Press, 1965.

Genovese, Eugene. *The World the Slaveholders Made: Two Essays in Interpretation.* New York: Pantheon Books, 1969.

———. *A Consuming Fire: The Fall of the Confederacy in the Mind of the White Christian South.* Athens: University of Georgia Press, 1998.

Greenberg, Kenneth S. *Honor and Slavery: Lies, Duels, Noses, Masks, Dressing as a Woman, Gifts, Strangers, Humanitarianism, Death, Slave Rebellions, the Proslavery Argument, Baseball, Hunting, and Gambling in the Old South.* Princeton, N.J.: Princeton University Press, 1996.

Highet, Gilbert. *Juvenal the Satirist: A Study.* Oxford: Clarendon Press, 1954.

Hooper, Johnson Jones. *A Ride with Old Kit Kuncker, and Other Sketches, and Scenes of Alabama.* Tuscaloosa, Ala.: M. D. J. Slade, 1849.

————. *Adventures of Captain Simon Suggs, Late of the Tallapoosa Volunteers; Together with "Taking the Census" and Other Alabama Sketches.* Philadelphia: T. B. Peterson and Brothers, 1858. Reprt., Tuscaloosa: University of Alabama Press, 1993.

————. *Dog & Gun: A Few Loose Chapters on Shooting, Among Which Will Be Found Some Anecdotes and Incidents.* New York: Orange Judd, 1856. Reprt., Tuscaloosa: University of Alabama Press, 1992.

Kelley, Marion. "The Life and Writing of Johnson Jones Hooper." Master's thesis, Alabama Polytechnic Institute, 1934.

Lenz, William. *Fast Talk and Flush Times: The Confidence Man as a Literary Convention.* Columbia: University of Missouri Press, 1985.

Lynn, Kenneth. *Mark Twain and Southwestern Humor.* Boston: Little, Brown, 1959.

Potter, David M., and Don E. Fehrenbacher. *The Impending Crisis, 1848-1861.* New York: Harper and Row, 1976.

Rachleff, Marshal J. "Racial Fear and Political Factionalism: A Study of the Secession Movement in Alabama, 1819-1861." Ph.D. diss., University of Massachusetts, 1974.

Randolph, John. *Letters of John Randolph to a Young Relative: Embracing a Series of Years, from Early Youth, to Mature Manhood.* Edited by Theodore Dudley. Philadelphia: Carey, Lea and Blanchard, 1834.

Somers, Paul, Jr. *Johnson J. Hooper.* Boston: Twayne Publishers, 1984.

Thompson, Edgar E. "The Literary Career of Johnson Jones Hooper: A Bibliographical Study of Primary and Secondary Material (With a Collection of Hooper's Letters)." Master's thesis, Mississippi State University, 1971.

Thornton, J. Mills, III. *Politics and Power in a Slave Society: Alabama, 1800-1860.* Baton Rouge: Louisiana State University Press, 1978.

ARTICLES

Bailey, Hugh C. "Disloyalty in Early Confederate Alabama." *Journal of Southern History* 23, no. 4 (November 1957): 522-28.

————. "Disaffection in the Alabama Hill Country, 1861." *Civil War History* 4, no. 2 (June 1958): 183-93.

Bradford, M. E. Review of *With the Bark On: Popular Humor of the Old South,* edited by John Q. Anderson. *Louisiana Studies* 6, no. 4 (1967): 377-81.

Brantley, William H., Jr. "Alabama Secedes." *Alabama Review* 7 (July 1954): 165-85.

Donnelly, William J. "Conspiracy or Popular Movement: The Historiography of Southern Support for Secession." *North Carolina Historical Review* 42, no. 1 (January 1965): 70-84.

Long, Durward. "Unanimity and Disloyalty in Secessionist Alabama." *Civil War History* 11 (1965): 257-73.

Shields, Johanna Nicol. "A Sadder Simon Suggs: Slavery and Freedom in the Humor of Johnson Hooper." *Journal of Southern History* 56, no. 4 (November 1990): 641-64.

Wooster, Ralph A. "An Analysis of the Membership of Secession Conventions in the Lower South." *Journal of Southern History* 24, no. 3 (August 1958): 360-68.

————. "The Secession of the Lower South: An Examination of Changing Interpretations." *Civil War History* 7, no. 2 (June 1961): 117-27.

FURTHER READING

Biography

Hoole, Stanley W. *Alias Simon Suggs: The Life and Times of Johnson Jones Hooper.* Tuscaloosa: University of Alabama Press, 1952, 283 p.

Provides a thorough account of Hooper's formative years, his career as a humorist and newspaper editor, and his later involvement with secessionist politics.

Criticism

Garrett, William. *Reminiscences of Public Men in Alabama.* Atlanta: Plantation Publishing Co., 1872, 809 p.

Includes a scathing critique of Hooper, accusing him of immorality in both his literary works and his personal life.

Rachal, John. "Language and Comic Motifs in Johnson Jones Hooper's *Simon Suggs.*" *Alabama Historical Quarterly* 38, no. 2 (summer 1976): 93-100.

Argues that the humor of Simon Suggs lies principally in his unique speaking mannerisms.

Reynolds, David S. "The Carnivalization of American Language." In *Beneath the American Renaissance: The Subversive Imagination in the Age of Emerson and Melville,* pp. 441-83. New York: Alfred A. Knopf, 1988.

Explores the "shiftiness" of Simon Suggs.

Somers, Paul, Jr. *Johnson J. Hooper.* Boston: Twayne Publishers, 1984, 168 p.

Offers a comprehensive evaluation of Hooper's writings, while also examining his work as a newspaper editor and his political activities in the years leading up to the Civil War.

Treadway, James L. "Johnson Jones Hooper and the American Picaresque." *Thalia* 6, no. 2 (fall 1983): 33-42.
Examines the character of Simon Suggs within the context of frontier society.

Watterson, Henry. *The Compromises of Life.* New York: Duffield & Company, 1906, 511 p.
Includes a brief evaluation of the character of Simon Suggs, reprinting many of his most memorable scenes.

West, Harry C. "Simon Suggs and His Similes." *North Carolina Folklore* 16 (May 1968): 53-7.

Examines Hooper's use of folk sayings, proverbs, and frontier vernacular in his Simon Suggs stories.

Williams, Benjamin Buford. *A Literary History of Alabama: The Nineteenth Century.* Rutherford, N.J.: Fairleigh Dickinson University Press, 1979, 258 p.

Includes an appraisal of Hooper's emergence as one of the foremost humorists of his day, arguing that his stories represented a new form of frontier humor, one dependent more on wit and dialogue than on depictions of physical violence.

Additional coverage of Hooper's life and career is contained in the following sources published by Thomson Gale: *Dictionary of Literary Biography,* **Vols. 3, 11, 248;** *Literature Resource Center*; **and** *Reference Guide to American Literature,* **Ed. 4.**

Christoph Martin Wieland
1733-1813

German novelist, playwright, poet, essayist, translator, short story writer, and librettist.

The following entry presents an overview of Wieland's life and works. For additional information on his career, see *NCLC,* Volume 17.

INTRODUCTION

Wieland is widely regarded as one of the most influential figures in eighteenth-century German literature. A versatile and prolific author, Wieland published more than seventy original works over the course of his fifty-year career. In addition, he produced the first significant translations of Shakespeare's plays into German and founded the journal *Der teutsche Merkur,* a literary journal that served as a forum for the most vital literary debates of the age. Wieland's most accomplished writings embody the wit and eloquence of the Rococo style while also anticipating the literary innovations of the Romantic era, both in Germany and throughout Europe. Regarded as one of the most elegant prose stylists of his period, Wieland was also a profound thinker, and his novel *Geschichte des Agathon* (1766-67; *The History of Agathon*) is considered the first work of psychological realism in the German language. An exploration of the tension between the forces of rationalism and sentimentality underlies Wieland's body of work, and his efforts to reconcile these two aspects of human nature, which drew to a large extent from the ideals of classical antiquity, dominate most of his mature writings. With the rise of German nationalism in the nineteenth century, Wieland's cosmopolitan sensibility and irreverent wit fell out of fashion among the nation's cultural elite, and his works fell into obscurity for several decades. In recent years, however, scholars have begun to reexamine his role in the development of modern German literature, and a number of modern commentators have argued that Wieland's significance, both as a great Enlightenment thinker and as a vital influence on the development of a new literary style, rivaled that of Johann Wolfgang von Goethe.

BIOGRAPHICAL INFORMATION

Wieland was born on September 5, 1733, in the Swabian village of Oberholzheim. His father, Thomas Adam Wieland, was a Lutheran minister, and his mother, Regina Catherina Kick, came from a military family. Wieland demonstrated extraordinary intellectual abilities as a young child, reading voraciously and writing verse by the age of three. In his youth Wieland also developed a reputation as an independent, often intractable spirit, and his earliest writings included satirical sketches of his instructors. He received his early education first from private tutors and later at the public schools in the nearby city of Biberach before enrolling in Klosterbergen, a boarding school outside the northern city of Magdeburg. Although his academic prowess impressed his teachers, his irreverent attitude led to constant clashes with school administrators, and he stayed only two years. Upon leaving Magdeburg he lived with Johann Wilhelm Baumer, a professor at the University of Erfurt and a family friend, under whose tutelage he prepared for his university studies. On a visit home in the spring of 1750, Wieland met Marie Sophie Gutermann, a distant cousin, to whom he became engaged. That fall Wieland left Biberach to study jurisprudence at the University of Tübingen, but the law held little interest for him, and he devoted almost all of his energies to corresponding with Sophie and composing verse. During his brief time in Tübingen, he completed several volumes of poetry, which he published anonymously. Upon abandoning his formal studies Wieland traveled to Zurich, where he settled for the next eight years. His decision not to return to Biberach effectively terminated his engagement with Sophie, a rupture that haunted Wieland for many years. Sophie still played a critical role in helping Wieland launch his literary career, however, and they remained close friends until her death in 1807.

For the next six years, Wieland worked as a tutor in Zurich, while continuing to write poetry and prose at a prodigious rate. His publications from these years included one of his most acclaimed early works, the play *Lady Johanna Gray* (1758). Wieland's writings from this period, which were characterized primarily by a pious, moral tone that proved popular among readers of the time, soon became famous throughout the German states, and in 1759 he received an invitation to become a private tutor to several wealthy families in Bern. In Bern Wieland met Julie von Bondeli, the city's most prominent woman intellectual, with whom he quickly became engaged. Under Julie's influence, Wieland's literary style began to exhibit a more cosmopolitan outlook, a change most readily apparent in the dialogue *Araspes und Panthea* (1760; *Araspes and Panthea*).

During this time Wieland also began his translations of the plays of William Shakespeare, published in the eight-volume *Shakespeares Theatralische Werke* (1762-66). Wieland's translation of the 1611 play *The Tempest, Der Sturm oder der erstaunliche Schiffbruch,* premiered in his hometown of Biberach in 1761, and was the first staging of a Shakespeare play in Germany.

Unfortunately, Wieland's headstrong personality caused him to clash with the wealthy burghers of Bern, and in 1760 he broke off his engagement to Julie and returned to Biberach. His emotional distress was exacerbated by the fact that his beloved Sophie had married another man during his long absence and was living in Biberach. In the midst of this turmoil, Wieland never hesitated in his commitment to his writing, and in fact the complications that beset Wieland's personal life during this period inspired one of his best known novels, *Der Sieg der Natur über die Schwärmerei, oder, die Abenteuer des Don Sylvio von Rosalva* (1764; *Reason Triumphant over Fancy, Exemplified in the Singular Adventures of Don Sylvio de Rosalva*). At around this time Wieland became acquainted with Count Stadion, a prominent aristocrat with ties to the most elevated writers and thinkers of the age, among them Voltaire. Wieland thrived in Stadion's prestigious salon, and his writings from this period reflect a changing sensibility as he began to address his work to the tastes of the upper classes. His most popular work from these years, *Comische Erzählungen* (1765), embodied the cosmopolitanism that would characterize Wieland's best-known work, marking a final break from the pious tone that had pervaded many of his earliest writings.

Throughout this period Wieland also worked steadily on the novel that would bring him fame. First published in 1766-67, *The History of Agathon* is the author's first truly mature work and captures the process of his literary coming-of-age while living in Biberach. Indeed, Wieland regarded the work as the most honest expression of himself, both as an artist and an individual, and he revised the work several times over the next three decades. Shortly after the publication of *The History of Agathon,* Wieland married Anna Dorothea von Hillenbrand, the daughter of a prosperous Augsburg businessman. They would have fourteen children together. The occasion marked a turning point in Wieland's life and career, but while his marriage and family brought him the stability and respectability he needed, he never achieved real happiness with Anna Dorothea, and he remained devoted to Sophie.

In 1769, frustrated by the stifling social and cultural atmosphere of Biberach, Wieland accepted an invitation to become a philosophy professor at the University of Erfurt. In Erfurt Wieland finally found a place where his intellectual and artistic abilities were fully appreciated, and he quickly became one of the most popular instructors on the faculty. Over the next half decade Wieland's reputation as a scholar spread, and he received offers to teach at some of the most prestigious universities in Central Europe. During his time in Erfurt, Wieland wrote the novels *Sokrates Mainomenos* (1771; *Socrates Out of His Senses*) and *Der goldene Spiegel* (1772). In spite of his popularity among his students, however, Wieland eventually found himself at odds with the other faculty members at Erfurt, most of whom were religious conservatives, and he once again began to seek a means of escape. In 1772, shortly after failing to obtain a professorship in Vienna, Wieland received a position as private tutor to Prince Karl August of Saxe-Weimar. In Weimar Wieland launched *Der teutsche Merkur,* the first significant literary journal in the German language. The journal sparked controversy soon after its founding, however, with the publication in 1773 of Wieland's two-part essay, "Briefe an einen Freund über das deutsche Singspiel *Alceste,*" in which he discussed the adaptation of classical ideals to modern culture. The essay provoked anger in the younger generation of writers, who took offense at what they perceived as Wieland's arrogant dismissal of the works of antiquity, and inspired Johann Wolfgang von Goethe to compose a short satirical play that appeared in 1774, *Götter, Helden und Wieland,* in which he suggested that Wieland had become decadent and irrelevant. Indeed, these years saw the emergence of a considerable backlash against Wieland, as young poets decried his cosmopolitanism and irreverence, organizing demonstrations against him and burning his books. Wieland met these outcries with equanimity, and his critical writings from this period, which included reviews of Goethe's work, are characterized by restraint and fairness.

After completing his duties as Karl August's tutor, Wieland remained in Weimar, where he helped form the nucleus of a thriving literary culture. He published an early version of one of his most accomplished novels, *Die Abderiten* (*The Republic of Fools*), in several issues of the *Merkur* in 1774. In 1775 Goethe visited Weimar, and he and Wieland became close friends. Wieland's influence over Goethe's development as an author is unmistakable; the younger poet renounced his early "Sturm und Drang" writings in order to cultivate a more classical attitude toward art. The presence of both Wieland and Goethe in Weimar also lent a new prestige to the city, and in the later years of the eighteenth century, it gained a reputation as the unofficial cultural capital of the German states. The arrival of prominent theologian Johann Gottfried Herder in 1776 heightened Weimar's fame, and Herder became a frequent contributor to *Der teutsche Merkur.* In 1780 Wieland completed *Oberon,* an epic poem inspired by his studies of the Middle Ages. After its publication Wieland stopped writing original works for several years, devoting much of the 1780s to translating the classical writers Horace, Lucian, and others into German. Throughout this time he continued to publish his work in and edit the *Merkur,* while also publishing the works of younger writers, among them Friedrich Schiller. In 1787, at the suggestion of a young Leipzig bookseller named Georg Joachim Göschen, Wieland arranged to publish his collected works. For the next decade and a half he worked diligently on revising his writings for republication, completing the thirty-sixth volume in 1802. Three more volumes, comprising his later writings, appeared in 1811.

Wieland remained in Weimar until 1797, when he purchased a small farm outside the village of Oßmannstedt. The maintenance of the estate proved too difficult for Wieland's meager finances, however, and in 1803, shortly after the death of his wife, he returned to Weimar. Near the end of his life, fearing that the early-nineteenth-century rise of nationalist and militarist forces posed a threat to Enlightenment ideals, Wieland embarked on a translation of the letters of Cicero, in hopes that the Roman orator's reflections on the end of the Republic would resonate with European audiences. He completed five volumes of the letters before his death on January 21, 1813. A sixth volume, prepared by Friedrich David Gräter, appeared posthumously in 1818.

MAJOR WORKS

The sheer breadth of Wieland's literary oeuvre, produced over the course of several decades, continues to astound modern scholars. Although his writings comprise more than a hundred individual works in a range of genres, he is remembered today primarily for a handful of works that define his unique style and sensibility while also embodying the underlying spirit of German literature in the latter half of the eighteenth century. Among his most significant early writings is the play *Lady Johanna Gray,* a dramatization of the life of England's tragic "nine-day queen." Many commentators credit the play with providing a model of the literary heroine, found later in the works of Friedrich Schiller and Goethe. Wieland's 1764 novel, *Reason Triumphant over Fancy, Exemplified in the Singular Adventures of Don Sylvio de Rosalva,* which was modeled loosely after Miguel de Cervantes's 1605-15 novel *Don Quixote,* explores the psychological divide between intellectual and emotional aspects of the human condition, a theme that would emerge again and again in Wieland's mature work. Regarded by many scholars to be the first modern novel written in German, *Reason Triumphant over Fancy, Exemplified in the Singular Adventures of Don Sylvio de Rosalva* is also noteworthy for its candid portrayals of human sexuality; indeed, in this novel Wieland introduced the word *erotisch* into the German lexicon. *The History of Agathon,* the story of a young man's intellectual coming-of-age, made Wieland the most important German writer of his era and is widely considered a foundational work in the German *Bildungsroman* tradition. Wieland's epic poem *Musarion* (1768), further examines the struggle between the opposing forces of rationalism and idealism. Set in ancient Greece, the work tells the story of Musarion, a wise hetaera (a highly cultured courtesan) who teaches a young hedonist the virtues of moderation. The work became a best seller and inspired many of Goethe's own writings on antiquity. Wieland's *The Republic of Fools* presents a scathing satire of numerous prominent literary and political figures of the age and in many ways represents the author's personal vengeance against the provincial attitudes that thwarted him in Biberach and Erfurt. The epic poem *Oberon,* inspired in part by Shakespeare's *A Midsummer Night's Dream,* which debuted circa 1595-96, is regarded by many to be an important early work in the Romantic tradition; it influenced John Keats, Percy Bysshe Shelley, and Samuel Taylor Coleridge, among others.

In addition to producing some of the most influential writings of eighteenth-century Germany, Wieland also played a crucial role in bringing the works of William Shakespeare to the German stage, and his translations of Shakespeare's body of work were regarded as the best in the German language for nearly a century. Wieland also enjoyed renown as an editor during his lifetime, and his journal *Der teutsche Merkur* played a central role in the development of modern German literature in the late eighteenth century.

CRITICAL RECEPTION

At the height of his career, Wieland enjoyed a prestige unmatched among eighteenth-century German authors. Although his irreverent wit and his disdain for accepted moral and cultural values alienated many of his contemporaries, his works achieved popularity with a wide audience while exerting a profound influence on the writings of Johann Wolfgang von Goethe, Friedrich Schiller, Heinrich von Kleist, and numerous others. By the early nineteenth century, however, as nationalist ideologies began to spread throughout the German-speaking states, Wieland's worldly outlook provoked scorn in younger generations of writers, and by the end of his life, his reputation as Germany's most important literary figure had been taken over by Goethe.

In the early twentieth century, scholars began to re-evaluate Wieland's significance, and a body of critical works devoted to his writings began to emerge. Scholars like F. W. Meisnest and George Leuca address Wieland's role in bringing Shakespeare's plays to a wider European audience, while Werner Beyer discusses his impact on the English Romantic poets. Derek Van

Abbé argues that, in spite of the charges of depravity leveled at him by his contemporaries, Wieland was in fact a deeply moral writer. Van Abbé further asserts that Wieland's cosmopolitanism embodies the essence of Enlightenment thought. More recently, scholars like Ellis Shookman and Claire Baldwin examine Wieland's role in the emergence of the German *Bildungsroman* tradition. Important book-length studies of Wieland's life and career include Van Abbé's *Christoph Martin Wieland (1733-1813): A Literary Biography,* which appeared in 1961, Lieselotte E. Kurth-Voigt's 1974 *Perspectives and Points of View: The Early Works of Wieland and their Background,* and John A. McCarthy's 1979 *Christoph Martin Wieland.*

PRINCIPAL WORKS

Lobgesang auf die Liebe [anonymous] (poetry) 1751

Anti-Ovid; oder, die Kunst zu lieben [anonymous] (poetry) 1752

Die Natur der Dinge [anonymous] (poetry) 1752

Zwölf moralische Briefe in Versen [anonymous] (poetry) 1752

Der geprüfte Abraham [anonymous; *The Trial of Abraham*] (poetry) 1753

Lady Johanna Gray (play) 1758

Araspes und Panthea [*Araspes and Panthea; or, The Effects of Love*] (prose) 1760

Clementina von Poretta (play) 1760

Der Sturm oder der erstaunliche Schiffbruch [translator; from William Shakespeare's play *The Tempest*] (play) 1761

*Shakespeares Theatralische Werke: Aus dem Englischen übersezt. 8 vols. [translator; from Shakespeare's plays] (plays) 1762-66

Der Sieg der Natur über die Schwärmerei; oder, die Abenteuer des Don Sylvio von Rosalva [anonymous; *Reason Triumphant over Fancy, Exemplified in the Singular Adventures of Don Sylvio de Rosalva*] (novel) 1764

Geschichte des Agathon. 2 vols. [anonymous; *The History of Agathon*] (novel) 1766-67; revised and enlarged as *Agathon,* 1773; revised and enlarged as *Geschichte des Agathon,* 1794

Comische Erzählungen [anonymous] (poetry) 1765; revised edition, 1768

Idris: Ein heroisch-comisches Gedicht [anonymous] (poetry) 1768

Musarion; oder, die Philosophie der Grazien [anonymous] (poetry) 1768; revised edition, 1769

Beiträge zur Geheimen Geschichte des menschlichen Verstandes und Herzens. 2 vols. [anonymous] (essays and short stories) 1770

Die Grazien [anonymous; *The Graces: A Classical Allegory, Interspersed with Poetry, and Illustrated with Explanatory Notes: Together with a Poetical Fragment Entitled Psyche among the Graces*] (poetry) 1770

Der neue Amadis. 2 vols. [anonymous] (poetry) 1771

Sokrates Mainomenos; oder, Die Dialogen des Diogenes von Sinope [anonymous; *Socrates Out of His Senses, or Dialogues of Diogenes of Sinope*] (novel) 1771

Der goldene Spiegel; oder, die Könige von Scheschian [anonymous] (novel) 1772

Alceste [anonymous] (libretto) 1773

"*Briefe an einen Freund über das deutsche Singspiel Alceste*" (essay) 1773; published in journal *Der teutsche Merkur*

Die Abderiten, eine sehr wahrscheinliche Geschichte [*The Republic of Fools: Being the History of the State and People of Abdera in Thrace*] (novel) 1774; published in journal *Der teutsche Merkur*; revised as *Geschichte der Abderiten,* 1781

Geschichte des Philosophen Danischmende (novel) 1775; published in journal *Der teutsche Merkur*

Oberon [anonymous] (poetry) 1780

Rosemunde (libretto) 1780

Briefe, aus dem Lateinischen übersetzt und mit historischen Einleitungen und auch nöthigen Erläuterungen versehen. 2 vols. [translator; from the works of Horace] (prose) 1782

Kleinere prosaische Schriften. 2 vols. (prose) 1785-86

Klelia und Sinibald; oder Die Bevölkerung von Lampeduse (poetry) 1785; published in journal *Der teutsche Merkur*

Satyren, aus dem Lateinischen übersetzt und mit Einleitungen und erläuternden Anmerkungen versehen. 2 vols. [translator; from the works of Horace] (prose) 1786

Sämmtliche Werke, aus dem Griechischen übersetzt und mit Anmerkungen und Erläuterungen versehen. 6 vols. [translator; from the works of Lucian] (prose) 1788-89

Die Geheime Geschichte des Philosophen Peregrinus Proteus. 2 vols. [*Private History of Peregrinus Proteus, the Philosopher*] (novel) 1791

Sämmtliche Werke. 39 vols. (poetry, prose, novels, plays, novellas, and essays) 1794-1811

Agathodämon (novel) 1799

Aristipp und einige seiner Zeitgenossen. 4 vols. (novella) 1800-01

Taschenbuch für 1804: Menander und Glycerion (novella) 1803

Krates und Hipparchia: Ein Seitenstück zu Menander und Glycerion von C. M. Wieland. [*Crates and Hipparchia*] (novella) 1804

Euthanasia: Drey Gespräche über das Leben nach dem Tode (prose) 1805

Sämmtliche Briefe, übersetzt und erläutert. 4 vols. [translator; from the letters of Cicero] (letters) 1808-12

Ausgewählte Briefe von C. M. Wieland an verschiedene Freunde in den Jahren 1751. bis 1810. geschrieben und nach der Zeitfolge geordnet. 4 vols. (letters) 1815-16

Auswahl denkwürdiger Briefe von C. M. Wieland. 2 vols. (letters) 1815

Sämmtliche Werke. 53 vols. (poetry, prose, novels, plays, novellas, and essays) 1818-28

Sämmtliche Werke. 36 vols. (poetry, prose, novels, plays, novellas, and essays) 1853-58

Wielands Werke. 40 vols. (poetry, prose, novels, plays, novellas, and essays) 1879

Wielands Werke. 4 vols. (poetry, prose, novels, and novellas) 1900

†*Wielands Gesammelte Schriften* (poetry, prose, novels, plays, novellas, and essays) 1909-

Wielands Briefwechsel. 5 vols. (letters) 1963-83

*Comprises the following plays: *Sommernachtstraum*; *König Lear*; *Wie es euch gefällt*; *Mass für Mass*; *Der Sturm*; *Der Kaufmann von Venedig*; *Timon von Athen*; *König Johann*; *Julius Cäsar*; *Antonio und Cleopatra*; *Komödie der Irrungen*; *Richard II*; *Heinrich IV, 1 und 2*; *Viel Lermen um Nichts*; *Macbeth*; *Die zween edlen Veroneser*; *Romeo und Julia*; *Othello*; *Was Ihr wollt*; *Hamlet*; and *Das Wintermärchen*.

†Not yet complete.

CRITICISM

F. W. Meisnest (essay date January 1914)

SOURCE: Meisnest, F. W. "Wieland's Translation of Shakespeare." *Modern Language Review* 9, no. 1 (January 1914): 12-40.

[*In the following excerpt, Meisnest discusses the diverse influences behind Wieland's translations of William Shakespeare's plays, while also examining the impact of these translations on German literary culture in the late eighteenth century.*]

Just when and through what means Wieland first became interested in Shakespeare cannot be definitely decided. Possibly the appreciative remarks on Shakespeare and the potentialities of English tragedy in Béat de Muralt's *Lettres sur les Anglais* (Berne, 1712; Zürich, 1725; Cologne, 1726) may have directed his attention to the English poet[1]. Other possible sources were Voltaire's works, of which Wieland confessed himself a constant reader and admirer[2]; and even Gottsched, who was to him in his youth a 'magnus Apollo[3],' may have been instrumental in interesting him in Shakespeare. The English periodicals, the *Tatler*, *Spectator*, and *Guardian*, were familiar to Wieland in his school-days; while the Leipzig journal, *Neue Erweiterungen der Erkenntniss und des Vergnügens* (1753), contained a

translation of Rowe's *Life of Shakespeare*. Lastly, Nicolai's *Briefe über die itzigen Zustände der schönen Wissenschaften* (1754) and Young's *Essay on Original Composition* (1759; translated, 1760), with their important references to Shakespeare, were no doubt known to him.

The immediate suggestion for translating Shakespeare was probably derived from various sources. Gervinus believed that if it had not been for Lessing's recommendation of a translation of Shakespeare's masterpieces (*Litteraturbriefe*, No. XVII), Wieland would not have undertaken the task[4]. The fact is that Wieland cared little for Lessing's opinions at this time. When Mendelssohn subjected Wieland's tragedy **Clementina von Porretta** (1760) to a severe criticism (*Litteraturbriefe*, Nos. CXXIII, CXXIV), Wieland remarked: 'der Missachtung meiner Clementina von Lessing und Compagnie achte ich nicht mehr als des Summens der Sommermücken oder des Quäckens der Laubfrösche[5].' Far more significant to Wieland must have been the urgent demand for a translation of English stage-plays, especially those of Shakespeare, contained in a review of *Neue Probestücke der englischen Schaubühne* (3 vols., Basel, 1758) in the *Bibliothek der schönen Wissenschaften* (VI, 1760, pp. 60-74). The work reviewed contains Shakespeare's *Romeo and Juliet* in iambic blank verse, besides dramas by Young, Addison, Dryden, Otway, Congreve and Rowe, all translated from the original 'von einem Liebhaber des guten Geschmacks.' The reviewer directs translators to Shakespeare as follows:

> Wir haben schon mehr als einmal gewünscht, dass sich ein guter Uebersetzer an die englische Schaubühne wagen, und seine Landsleute hauptsächlich mit den vortrefflichen alten Stücken des Shakespeare, Beaumont und Fletcher, Otway, und andern bekannt machen möchte. Es würde vielleicht für die deutsche Schaubühne weit vortheilhafter gewesen seyn, wenn sie jenen nachgeahmt hätte, als dass sie sich die französische Galanterie hinreissen lassen, und uns mit einer Menge höchst elender, obgleich höchstregelmässiger Stücke bereichert hat. . . . Wir empfehlen hauptsächlich dem Uebersetzer die Shakespeareischen Stücke: sie sind die schönsten, aber auch die schwersten, aber um deste eher zu übersetzen, wenn man nützlich seyn will[6].

No doubt the immediate and most direct call for translating Shakespeare came to Wieland from his friend W. D. Sulzer, who upon returning a volume of Wieland's copy of Shakespeare (Jan. 14, 1759), expressed the hope that some skilful genius would translate and analyse Shakespeare's plays in the manner of Brumoy's *Théâtre des Grecs* (see below, [Purpose and Conception]).

Furthermore the decade 1760-70 was characterised by an awakening of interest in English literature. Gottsched and his followers had lost their prestige, and the younger writers looked to England for their literary standards. In 1760 the Shakespeare cult, inaugurated by the forerunners of the 'Storm and Stress' movement—Lessing, Nicolai, Mendelssohn, Weisse and Meinhard—was well established. The French had their translation of Shakespeare by La Place, although it was very imperfect and incomplete. Besides the three scenes of Richard III (I, ii; IV, iv, 1-195; V, iii, 108-206, Globe ed.), which appeared in *Neue Erweiterungen der Erkenntniss und des Vergnügens* (Leipzig, 1755), only two dramas had been translated into German: *Julius Caesar* by von Borck (1741) and *Romeo and Juliet*. The time was auspicious for a complete German Shakespeare.

Soon after Wieland came to Biberach (1760) as 'Ratsherr' and 'Kanzleidirektor,' he was appointed director of the local theatrical society (Jan. 7, 1761), which had existed since 1686, and was composed of artisans and tradesmen of the town[7].

The successful presentation of his **Lady Johanna Gray** on the stage at Winterthur, Switzerland, on July 20, 1758, by the famous Ackermann company was heralded throughout the land, and much was expected of him. To meet this expectation he translated and arranged the *Tempest* for the stage. The performance in September, 1761, was received with great applause, and Wieland was encouraged to continue his work. He translated twenty-two dramas, published by Orell, Gessner and Co., Zürich, between 1762 and 1766, in eight volumes[8].

WIELAND'S SOURCES.

In order to realize fully the immensity of the task, we must consider that Wieland undertook the work without a Shakespeare library. There are no indications in his translation or writings which show that he used even the meagre critical works on Shakespeare in existence at that time, as: Theobald's *Shakespeare Restored* (1726), Samuel Johnson's *Miscellaneous Observations on the Tragedy of Macbeth* (1745), Upton's *Critical Observations on Shakespeare* (1746), Edward's *The Canons of Criticism and Glossary, being a Supplement to Warburton's Edition of Shakespeare* (1748), Grey's *Critical, Historical and Explanatory Notes on Shakespeare* (2 vols., 1755). According to all past investigations his working library consisted of three works: Warburton's edition of *Shakespeare's Works* (8 vols., Dublin, 1747), Boyer's *French-English and English-French Dictionary* (2 vols., Lyons, 1756), and a dictionary of Shakespearean Words and Phrases, which his friend La Roche recommended to him as indispensable, but whose author's name Wieland had forgotten[9]. . . .

PURPOSE AND CONCEPTION.

In order to do full justice to Wieland's translation it is necessary to take into consideration the attitude of contemporary critics and scholars towards such an undertaking. Custom had practically made it a fixed principle that the great foreign classics be made available by means of partial translations and synopses. This is what Brumoy in his *Théâtre des Grecs* (1730) and La Place in *Le Théâtre Anglois* (1746) had done. Thus Homer had been treated in Pope's translation (1715), and Milton's *Paradise Lost* in Bodmer's version (1732). Meinhard's *Versuche über den Charakter und die Werke der besten italienischen Dichter* (1763-4) followed the same plan. Sulzer had suggested this method in his letter of Jan. 14, 1759:

> Wenn doch ein geschickter Kopf die Arbeit übernehmen wollte, diese Schauspiele im Deutschen so zu analysiren, wie Père Brumoy mit dem griechischen Theater gethan hat. Soweit ich gekommen bin, ist kein Drama, das man ganz übersetzen dürfte. Man würde nur den Plan derselben durchgehen, die Scenen oder Stellen aber, welche wirkliche Schönheit besitzen, auszeichnen und alles auf eine kritische Manier verrichten[10].

Weisse in the *Bibliothek der schönen Wissenschaften* (IX, 261, 1763) in the review of Wieland's first volume insisted on Brumoy's plan:

> Wir glaubten also, dass wenn ja mit dem Shakespear in unsrer Sprache etwas vorzunehmen wäre, dass man den Weg des Brumoy mit dem griechischen Theater einschlagen sollte, und einen Auszug von Scene zu Scene liefern, um die Oekonomie des Stücks, und die Situationen, die Shakespear oft so glücklich herbey zu führen weiss, nicht zu verlieren, die schönsten und besten Stellen und Scenen aber ganz zu übersetzen.

In 1788 the same periodical, reviewing Eschenburg's *Über W. Shakespeare,* still insisted upon its former judgment:

> Wie sehr wäre es also nicht zu wünschen gewesen, Hr. Wieland hätte gleich damals den Weg eingeschlagen, auf den jene Rec. hinzeigte. Er war ganz der Mann dazu, ihn würdig zu betreten. . . . Wir wiederholen den Wunsch, dass man den Deutschen nur eine Auswahl der schönsten Scenen Shakespears und von den übrigen einen blossen Auszug und keine wörtliche Uebersetzung geliefert haben möchte, die sowohl dem Publikum, als dem Dichter selbst, der sich nun aus derselben, und gleichsam als unsern Zeitgenossen beurtheilen lassen muss, mehr geschadet als genutzt hat.

Even Lessing in his 17th *Litteraturbrief* (1759) recommended a translation of Shakespeare with the proviso: 'mit einigen bescheidenen Veränderungen.' With Garrick omitting the grave-diggers' scene in *Hamlet* on the Drury Lane stage in London, and playing Shakespeare's plays in an abridged and expurgated edition; with critics like Weisse, Nicolai and Gerstenberg publicly proclaiming the impossibility and undesirability of systematically translating Shakespeare, all the more credit is due to Wieland for boldly attempting the difficult task with a purpose far in advance of his time:

Es kann eine sehr gute Ursache haben, warum der Ue-
bersezer eines Originals, welches bey vielen grossen
Schönheiten eben so grosse Mängel hat, und überhaupt
in Absicht des Ausdruks roh, und incorrect ist, für gut
findet, es so zu übersezen, wie es ist. Shakespear ist an
tausend Orten in seiner eignen Sprache hart, steif,
schwülstig, schielend; so ist er auch in der Ueberse-
zung, denn man wollte ihn den Deutschen so bekannt
machen, wie er ist. Pope hat den Homer in Absicht des
Ausdruks verschönert, und wie die Kenner, selbst in
England sagen, oft zu viel verschönert. Das konnte bey
einem Homer angehen, dessen Simplicität sich schwer-
lich in irgend einer Sprache, welche nicht die eigentli-
chen Vorzüge der griechischen hat, ohne Nachtheil des
Originals copieren lässt. Bey unserm Engländer hat es
eine ganz andere Bewandtniss. Sobald man ihn ver-
schönern wollte, würde er aufhören, Shakespear zu
seyn.

Thus Wieland defended his translation in the last volume (III, p. 566), against the severe criticisms of Weisse,
Nicolai and Gerstenberg. Again in *Teutscher Merkur*
(III, pp. 187, 1773), referring to the proposed new edition of his translation he says:

Der Verbesserer wird nur zu manche Stellen, wo der
Sinn des Originals verfehlt oder nicht gut genug ausgedrückt worden, und überhaupt vieles zu polieren und
zu ergänzen finden. Aber möchte er sich vor der Ver-
schönerungssucht hüten, unter welcher Shakespears
Genie mehr leiden würde, als unter meiner vielleicht
allzu gewissenhaften Treue! Mein Vorsatz . . . war,
meinen Autor mit allen seinen Fehlern zu übersetzen;
und dies um so mehr, weil mir däuchte, dass sehr oft
seine Fehler selbst eine Art von Schönheiten sind.

That Wieland speaks of the faults of Shakespeare in
connection with his beauties is not surprising and is no
disparagement of his conception of the great dramatist.
In the preface of every Shakespeare edition of that time
we find his 'faults' enumerated and extensively discussed. Even Samuel Johnson who perhaps expressed
the most advanced view on Shakespeare in the eighteenth century, said in his *Preface* (1765): 'Shakespeare
with his excellencies has likewise faults, and faults sufficient to obscure and overwhelm any other merit. I
shall shew them in the proportion in which they appear
to me, without envious malignity or superstitious
veneration,' whereupon he proceeds to discuss not less
than twelve defects. Critics universally attributed these
faults, following the dictum of Alexander Pope in his
Preface (1725), to the perverted taste of the populace
for whom Shakespeare wrote. Wieland had a more rational explanation (*Merkur* [*Teutscher Merkur*], III, p.
184, 1773):

Die wahre Quelle dieser Mängel liegt nicht, (wie man
zu sagen gewohnt ist), in der Ansteckung des falschen
Geschmacks seiner Zeit,—denn ein Geist wie der
seinige lässt sich nicht so leicht anstecken—noch in
einer unedlen Gefälligkeit gegen denselben—denn wie
frey und stark sagt er nicht im Sommernachts-Traum

und im Hamlet den Dichtern, den Schauspielern und
dem Publico die Wahrheit?—sie liegt in der Grösse
und in dem Umfang seines Geistes. Sein Genius um-
fasst, gleich dem Genius der Natur, mit gleich scharfem
Blick Sonnen und Sonnenstäubchen, den Elephanten
und die Milbe, den Engel und den Wurm; er schildert
mit gleich meisterhaftem Pinsel den Menschen und den
Caliban, den Mann und das Weib, den Helden und den
Schurken, den Weisen und den Narren, die grosse und
die schwache, die reizende und die hässliche Seite der
menschlichen Natur, eine Kleopatra und ein Auster-
weib, den König Lear und Tom Bedlam, eine Miranda
und eine Lady Macbeth, einen Hamlet, und einen
Todtengräber. Seine Schauspiele sind, gleich dem grossen Schauspiele der Natur, voller anscheinenden Unor-
dnung;—Paradiese, Wildnisse, Auen, Sümpfe, bezauberte Thäler, Sandwüsten, fruchtbare Alpen, starrende
Gletcher; Cedern und Erdschwämme, Rosen und Dis-
telköpfe, Fasanen und Fledermäuse, Menschen und
Vieh, Seraphim und Ottergezüchte, Grosses und
Kleines, Warmes und Kaltes, Trocknes und Nasses,
Schönes und Ungestaltes, Weisheit und Thorheit, Tugend und Laster,—alles seltsam durcheinander gewor-
fen—und gleichwohl, aus dem rechten Standpuncte betrachtet, alles zusammen genommen, ein grosses,
herrliches unverbesserliches Ganzes!

How infinitely superior is this view of Shakespeare to
that of Voltaire, which is nowhere more tersely described than in Wieland's own words (*Merkur*, III, p.
184, 1773):

Es ist leicht, dem Sophisten Voltaire, (welcher von dem
Dichter Voltaire wohl zu unterscheiden ist), der weder
Englisch genug weiss, um ihn zu verstehen, noch, wenn
er Englisch genug könnte, den unverdorbnen Geschmack hat, der dazu gehört, seinen ganzen Werth zu
empfinden—es ist leicht, sage ich, diesem Voltaire und
seines gleichen nachzulallen: Shakespear ist un-
regelmässig; seine Stücke sind ungeheure Zwitter von
Tragödie und Possenspiel, wahre Tragi- Komi- Lyrico-
Pastoral-Farçen ohne Plan, ohne Verbindung der
Scenen, ohne Einheiten; ein geschmackloser Mischm-
asch von Erhabnen und Niedrigen, von Pathetischen
und Lächerlichen, von ächtem und falschem Witz, von
Laune und Unsinn, von Gedanken die eines Weisen,
und von Possen, die eines Pickelherings würdig sind;
von Gemählden, die einem Homer Ehre brächten, und
von Karrikaturen, deren sich ein Scarron schämen
würde. . . .

RECEPTION AND INFLUENCE.

Wieland's translation not only awakened a new interest
in Shakespeare in Germany, but also renewed that bitter
warfare begun by Gottsched in 1741 upon the appearance of Caspar von Borck's translation of *Julius Caesar*. The opposition now was no longer directed against
the poet, but against the translation, especially against
the plan of entire translations of the dramas. The most
violent attacks were made by the *Bibliothek der schönen
Wissenschaften* (IX, 257-70, 1763)[11], the *Allgemeine
deutsche Bibliothek*[12], Gerstenberg in his *Briefe über
Merkwürdigkeiten der Litteratur*, Nos. 14-18, 1766, and

Herder in his *Erste Sammlung der Fragmente, 4. kritisches Wäldchen* [1767], and private letters (*Lebensbild* [1846], vol. III). On the other hand the translation was defended with somewhat less enthusiasm and occasionally with reservations, by the *Neue Zeitungen von gelehrten Sachen,* Leipzig, 1763, Nos. 3, 58, 81; 1764, Nos. 58, 97; *Göttingische Anzeigen von gelehrten Sachen,* 1764, Nos. 26, 96, 156; 1766, No. 7; by Uz, Klotz, K. A. Schmid, Lessing, Goethe and Schiller[13].

Dr Stadler's excellent discussion of the reception of Wieland's Shakespeare may be supplemented by the following references. Severe judgment is pronounced upon Wieland's work by the reviewer of Meinhard's translation of Henry Home's *Elements of Criticism* in the *Allgemeine deutsche Bibliothek* (1766, vol. II, 1, p. 36):

> Wie gut diese Uebersetzung sey, kann der Augenschein gleich frappant lehren, wenn man nur ein paar Stellen aus dem Shakespear nach dieser Uebersetzung gegen die steife, geschmacklose Uebersetzung hält, die jetzt in der Schweiz erscheint, und wodurch dieser grosse englische Dichter mehr entstellt als in unsre Sprache herüber getragen worden.

The signature 'B' to this review corresponds to 'Westfeld,' in Parthey's *Mitarbeiter an der Allgemeinen deutschen Bibliothek.*

In a superficial review (signed 'Dtsch') of C. H. Schmidt's *Theorie der Poesie* in Klotz's *Deutsche Bibliothek der schönen Wissenschaften* (Halle, 1768, vol. I, p. 3) Wieland's translation receives favourable mention:

> Eben so ist es Ihnen, mein Herr S., mit Wielanden gegangen. Ist es nicht wahr, jetzt würden Sie ihr Urtheil von seinem Shakspear gerne zurücknehmen, nachdem Sie Lessings Dramaturgie gelesen haben? Schon lange zuvor habe ich geglaubt, dass Wielands Uebersetzung so schlecht nicht ist, als es den Kunstrichtern gefallen hat, sie abzumahlen. Diese Herren wollten uns, wenn es Ihnen geglückt hätte, die besten Schriften aus den Händen kritisiren, die nicht aus ihrer Litteraturschule herstammten. Sie, Herr Schmidt, und Herr Fll. und wie sie weiter heissen, mögen einmal eine Uebersetzung von Shakspear liefern, die die Wielandsche übertrifft. Sie soll uns, willkommen seyn: allein bis dahin bitte ich Sie, erlauben Sie uns andern, die Wielandsche Arbeit nicht schlecht zu nennen.

The estimate of Wieland's Shakespeare in Jördens' *Lexikon deutscher Dichter und Prosaisten* (Leipzig, 1810, vol. V, p. 404)—the standard work of reference of that time—may be regarded as expressing the sober and final judgment of the eighteenth century:

> Durch diese Uebersetzung (ein schweres Unternehmen, da die Bahn zu brechen war) hat sich Wieland um den theatralischen Geschmack in Deutschland grosse Verdienste erworben. Seine Verdeutschung und Lessings Anpreisungen zogen die Aufmerksamkeit auf den Englischen Dichter; man las, man studirte, und bekam allmählig andere und bessere Begriffe von Menschendarstellung in theatralischen und andern Werken.

Wieland's translation and the interest and criticism which it engendered brought about two significant results: first, the introduction of Shakespeare upon the German stage and secondly, a demonstration of the fact that a translation of Shakespeare was not only possible but desirable.

After the first successful performance of the *Tempest* on the stage at Biberach (1761) in Wieland's version this small Swabian town became the centre of a Shakespearian cult. The *Tempest* was the greatest favourite on this stage and the most frequently repeated. *Macbeth* (1771-2), *Hamlet* (1773-4), including the gravediggers' scene which even Garrick had expunged, *Romeo and Juliet* (1774-5) were each performed four times, and *Othello* (1774), *As You Like It* (1775), and *The Two Gentlemen of Verona* (1782) each three times in the years indicated—and all in Wieland's version. At least two members of the Biberach dramatic society of which Wieland was director (1761-9), Karl Fr. Abt and his wife, became leading members of various theatrical companies and carried the news of the Shakespeare performances at Biberach to the principal cities of northern and central Germany. With Madame Schröder they established the first German theatrical company at The Hague (1774) and in 1780 the first at Bremen, of which Abt was the director. Of Frau Abt in the role of *Hamlet* at Gotha (May 10, 1779) it is said: 'Madame Abt hat die Rolle des Hamlet göttlich gespielt[14].'

In 1773 *Hamlet* was performed at Vienna in Heufeld's version based on Wieland's translation, and three years later after Friedrich Ludwig Schröder had seen *Hamlet* on the stage at Prague, he hastened home and within a few days completed his version of the play, which was given Sept. 20, 1776, in the Hamburg theatre.

In making a complete and faithful translation of the great masterpieces his chief aim and purpose, Wieland was in advance of most of the best scholars and critics of his time, such as Weisse, Nicolai, Herder and Gerstenberg, who either opposed all translations of Shakespeare, or at most favoured the translation of selected passages with synopses of the remainder. His high ideal was best realised in *Midsummer Night's Dream,* where the metre, style and spirit of the original were so successfully reproduced that Eschenburg accepted the entire translation without averaging more than two or three changes, mostly formal, to a page. The rabble-scenes and the Pyramus and Thisbe play were exceptionally well done. Schlegel adopted the former with few changes and the latter without any. But often Wieland failed to accomplish his high aims, as is most evident in the *Tempest* and *Romeo and Juliet.* Shakespeare's subtle phraseology, his puns and quibbles often caused Wieland to despair. His much condemned 'footnotes' indicate that his attitude towards Shakespeare underwent temporary changes during the progress of the work, yet his general conception remained firm. Contemporary critics misjudged and greatly undervalued his work. He possessed a great part of the genius of a translator, but he lacked the patience and perseverance necessary for such a gigantic piece of work.

Notes

1. Cf. Otto von Greyerz, *B. L. von Muralt,* Berne, 1888; M. Koch in *Englische Studien,* XXIV [1897], p. 317; also Böttiger, *Litterarische Zustände und Zeitgenossen,* Leipzig, 1838, I, p. 174.

2. Cf. Wieland, *Ein Wort über Voltaire besonders als Historiker* (1773); (*Werke,* ed. Göschen, 1839-40, XXXVI, p. 174).

3. Letter to Bodmer, March 6, 1752 (*Ausgewählte Briefe,* [1815], I, p. 46).

4. *Geschichte der deutschen Dichtung,* 5th ed. [1871-74], IV, p. 422, a view which is concurred in by Dr Merscheberger (*Shakespeare-Jahrbuch,* XXV [1890], p. 209).

5. E. Schmidt, *Richardson, Rousseau und Goethe,* [Jena, 1875,] p. 48.

6. In January 1759 Nicolai surrendered the editorship of the *Bibliothek* to Ch. F. Weisse. But this review with its significant reference to Shakespeare is not in accord with the views of either of these editors. Both violently opposed entire translations of Shakespeare, as is evident from their reviews of Wieland's translation in the *Allg.* [*Allgemeine*] *deutsche Bibliothek* (I, 1, 1765, p. 300) and *Bibliothek der schönen Wissenschaften* (IX, 1763, p. 259). It seems probable that Joh. Nic. Meinhard was the author of the above review, which is quite in accord with his views and attitude (cf. *Denkmal des Herrn Joh. Nik. Meinhard von Friedr. Just Riedel, Sämmtlichte Schriften,* Wien, 1787, vol. V, pp. 97-158).

7. Dr L. F. Ofterdinger, *Geschichte des Theaters in Biberach* (*Württembergische Vierteljahreshefte,* VI, 1883, pp. 36-45), gives the most complete account.

8. Vol. I: Pope's *Preface, Mids., Lear*; II: *A.Y.L., Meas., Temp.*; III: *Merch., Tim., John*; IV: *Caes., Ant., Err.*; V: *Rich. 2, 1 Hen. IV, 2 Hen. IV*; VI: *Much Ado., Macb., Two Gent.*; VII: *Rom., Oth., Tw. N.*; VIII: *Haml., Wint.,* Rowe's *Life of Shak.* (abridged). Various editions or reprints of at least some of the volumes appeared. Of the four copies of Wieland's translation which I have seen, two contain the 'Account of the Life of Shakespeare'

in vol. I, following Pope's 'Preface,' instead of in vol. VIII. In one of the copies vol. I bears the date 1764 instead of 1762. The translation is now easily accessible in the splendid new edition of Wieland's *Übersetzungen,* Herausg. von Ernst Stadler, 3 Bde. Berlin, Weidmann, 1909-11.

9. Seuffert, *Prolegomena zu einer Wieland-Ausgabe,* Berlin, 1905, III 6; Böttiger, *Litterarische Zustände* [*und Zeitgenossen* (1838)], vol. I, p. 196; Stadler, *Quellen und Forsch.,* CVII [(Strasburg, 1910)], pp. 21-2. Brief glossaries were appended to the editions of Rowe (1714), Hanmer (1744) and Hugh Blair (1753); but I could find no work corresponding to that recommended by La Roche.

10. *Briefe von Sulzer,* Geilfuss, 1866, p. 8.

11. Eschenburg, *Über W. Shakespeare,* p. 506, attributed this review to Meinhard. According to Weisse's biographer (*Bibl. der schönen Wiss.* LXX, 203, 1804) Weisse was the author: 'Unter seinen eigenen Recensionen ist wohl die bedeutendste die von Wielands Uebersetzung des Shakespear.' This is probably Jördens' (*Lexikon* [*Lexikon deutscher Dichter und Prosaisten* (Leipzig, 1810) vol.] V, 404) authority for Weisse's authorship.

12. I, 1, 300, 1765, by Nicolai; XI, 1, 51-9, 1770, small part by Nicolai. In a letter to Wieland, Feb. 6, 1770, Nicolai reveals the authorship: 'Ich übersende Ew. H. das erste Stück des XI. B. der A. D. B[ibliothek]; die darin enthaltene Anzeige Ihres Deutschen Shakespears und Ihres Idris sind zwar nicht von mir. . . . der Anzeige des Shakespears habe ich die Erklärung S. 51, 52 und 54 selbst eingewebt. Ich gestehe es Ew. H., dass ich der Verf. der Anzeige der ersten Theile Ihres Shakespears in des. 1. Bds. 1. Stücke bin. Es ist mir sehr unangenehm, dass ich durch die darin gebrauchten nicht genug abgemessene Ausdrücke, Ihnen wahrhaftig wider meine Absicht Gelegenheit zum Missvergnügen gegeben habe. Durch die gedachte öffentliche Erklärung (i.e., pp. 51, 52, 54) suche ich meine wahre Meinung in ein näheres Licht zu setzen, und wenn Ew. H. auch nicht völlig damit zufrieden sein sollten, so kann sie wenigstens zur Bezeugung meiner aufrichtigen Hochachtung gegen Ihre Verdienste, dienen, die auch bey einer nicht völligen Übereinstimmung der Meinungen beständig bleiben wird.' Otto Sievers, *Akademische Blätter,* 1884, p. 268.

13. Cf. Stadler, *Q.-F.* [*Quellen und Forsch.*] CVII [(1910)], pp. 75-94.

14. Ofterdinger, *Geschichte des Theaters in Biberach, Württembergische Vierteljahreshefte,* VI (1883), pp. 113-126.

Kenneth C. Hayens (essay date November 1929)

SOURCE: Hayens, Kenneth C. "Heine and Wieland." *Modern Language Notes* 44, no. 7 (November 1929): 451-54.

[*In the following essay, Hayens explores some of the similarities between Wieland and the poet Heinrich Heine, paying particular attention to the qualities of wit and intelligence in their writings.*]

It is surprising that the literary historian can entirely ignore the possible influence of Wieland on Heine. Max J. Wolff in the last full biography of Heine makes absolutely no reference to the possibility of any such influence.[1] Possibly the literary historian has been too conscious of Heine's technical excellence to connect him with a predecessor of Wieland's technical deficiencies. Also, it appears likely that the emphasis laid on the connection between Byron and Heine has obscured an equally existent connection between Wieland and Heine. It is the object of this paper to suggest that there are sufficient grounds to warrant an investigation of the whole subject.

If the customary value be placed upon literary parallels, surely it cannot be denied that *Atta Troll,* Kaput III, owes something to **Oberon**? Here are Wieland's opening lines:

Noch einmal sattelt mir den Hippogryphen, ihr Musen
Zum Ritt ins alte, romantische Land!
Wie lieblich um meinen entfesselten Busen
Der holde Wahnsinn spielt! Wer schlang das magische
　Band
Um meine Stirn? Wer treibt von meinen Augen den
　Nebel,
Der auf der Vorwelt Wundern liegt?

And this is Heine:

Traum der Sommernacht! Phantastisch
Zwecklos ist mein Lied. Ja, zwecklos
Wie die Liebe, wie das Leben,
Wie der Schöpfer samt der Schöpfung!

Nur der eignen Lust gehorchend,
Galoppierend oder fliegend,
Tummelt sich im Fabelreiche
Mein geliebter Pegasus.

. . . .

Jede Blindheit weicht! Mein Blick
Dringt bis in die tiefste Steinkluft,
In die Höhle Atta Trolls—
Ich verstehe seine Reden!

Both poets are attracted and re-attracted by tales of magic and by the magic of the old tales, but their use of the magical can be understood only from a sophisticated standpoint. Both present a mingling of the romantic and the sceptic, picturing wonders to their own and their readers' delight, but with their tongues in their cheeks. Can this similarity of attitude and approach to the subject matter be quite fortuitous? Is there not sufficient in it to make one feel that Heine had not merely read and enjoyed Wieland's verse romances, but had learnt from them also? Perhaps admirers of Heine have been so engaged in laying stress on his development of suppleness, lightness and pointedness in the German language, that they have overlooked the work done by Wieland at his best exactly in this direction. Perhaps the orthodox view that Wieland had no literary descendants of note makes this oversight more intelligible. Yet among the tales in verse which lead up to **Oberon** there is one, **"Das Sommermärchen,"** the tone of which must have made a real appeal to Heine. If, again, Heine talks in the *Vorrede* to *Atta Troll* of "die Parodie eines freiligrathschen Gedichtes," Wieland's treatment of the tales of chivalry is certainly not respectful.

The reader finds in **"Das Sommermärchen"** something characteristic of Heine, the use of foreign words, often in rime, to mark the banter and irony in which both poets delight. The anthologies eschew Wieland. Were it not so, something of what appears to many as a revelation in Heine might achieve a truer perspective. A few examples are adduced.

l. 288 ff.　　Er war im Fliehn,
　　　　　　　Da kamen grosse Haufen
　　　　　　　Von Löwen gegen ihn
　　　　　　　Mit offnem Schlund gelaufen.
　　　　　　　Der arme Herr
　　　　　　　Testiert *mentaliter.*

l. 488 ff.　　Doch, übern Themsefluss
　　　　　　　Auf einem Draht
　　　　　　　Zu traben,
　　　　　　　Und das—*pardonnez-moi,*
　　　　　　　Um einen Kuss,
　　　　　　　Das sollte sich
　　　　　　　Der grosse Mithridat,
　　　　　　　Ma foi,
　　　　　　　Verbeten haben
　　　　　　　So gut als ich.

l. 1033 ff.　Dem Ritter rät nach solcher Motion
　　　　　　　Sein leerer Magen,
　　　　　　　Die Invitation
　　　　　　　Nicht auszuschlagen.

Not only **Oberon,** not only **"Das Sommermärchen"** could give Heine examples of the conscious imitation of medieval naïveté which, too, he could appreciate. This conscious imitation is itself, and very intelligibly, responsible for some of the charges of offending against good taste, which have been brought against both poets. Both enjoy introducing into their work scraps of information culled from many fields, a characteristic itself suggestive of that mental activity and quickness they cannot be denied. Both lack power to sustain a satiric approach.

One might well doubt if Heine read much of *Aristipp* [*Aristipp and einige seiner Zeitgenossen*], not to say of *Agathon*; but it can hardly be mere fancy to find in his writings something of the spirit of *Die Abderiten.*[2] Certainly Heine writes disparagingly of Wieland, ostensibly putting him in the same category as Iffland and August Lafontaine. "Wieland war der damalige grosse Dichter, mit dem es etwa nur Herr Odendichter Ramler zu Berlin in der Poesie aufnehmen konnte. Abgöttisch wurde Wieland verehrt, mehr als jemals Goethe."[3] No student of Heine, however, will believe that this necessarily reveals his true attitude. Much rather one might recall the fact, which other views of him have forced definitely into the background, that Wieland, in common with Heine, liked to consider himself a social and political critic and herald. The mocking tone is largely due to the lack of any ultimate personal conviction. If Wieland has genuine roots in a comfortable hedonism, Heine can lay claim at times to a greater honesty of opinion, for it comes from a greater depth of feeling. Neither on the one side, nor on the other, however, is there anything to prevent the conclusion that both writers are more characterised by wit, than by moral principle, or yet moral indignation. This recognition of an affinity in the spirit can be held to emphasise the call for an examination of the literary relationship.

Notes

1. Max J. Wolff, *Heinrich Heine,* 1922.

2. Cf. the sarcastic reference to "die abderitische Partei in Deutschland," *Vorrede zur Vorrede, Französische Zustände* [(1832)].

3. *Die Romantische Schule, Erstes Buch* [(1836)].

George Leuca (essay date November 1955)

SOURCE: Leuca, George. "Wieland and the Introduction of Shakespeare into Germany." *German Quarterly* 28, no. 4 (November 1955): 247-55.

[*In the following essay, Leuca discusses Wieland's role in bringing Shakespeare to the German stage.*]

The history of Shakespeare on the German stage begins only a few years after the appearance of his plays in the theaters of England, but his name was not mentioned in Germany in connection with these actual stage productions until 1761. In that year "Das evangelische Komö-

dienwesen" of Biberach in Suabia presented *Der erstaunliche Schiffbruch oder die verzauberte Insel (The Tempest)* in a translation by Senator Christoph Martin Wieland (1733-1813).[1] Not only was this the first attempt to present Shakespeare in Germany, "unter seinem Namen und ohne grobe Entstellung,"[2] it was the first such effort in all continental Europe.[3] Any Shakespeare plays presented up to that time had been "adapted" beyond recognition and the only pre-Wieland translations worth mentioning are Kaspar Wilhelm von Borck's version of *Julius Caesar,* in unwieldy German Alexandrines (1741), and the anonymous blank-verse translation (1758) of *Romeo and Juliet* by a citizen of Basel, finally identified as one Simon Grynaeus. In one respect these represented opposite extremes: Borck furnished too much rhyme, and Grynaeus none at all.[4]

To be sure, there had been the impossible but very popular travesties of Weisse, such as his *Richard III* (1759), which now serve only to show how relatively fine the other two translations were. But Gottsched's reaction to Borck's *Julius Caesar,* as could be expected, was one of violent opposition. To the mortal enemy of the "Haupt-und-Staatsaktion" this represented a revival of anarchy in the dramatic arts,[5] and in a sense Gottsched was right, in view of the effect of Shakespeare on the "Kraftgenies" of the Storm and Stress period. Ironically enough, two of the persons most influential in introducing Shakespeare to the Germans, Johann Elias Schlegel, a protégé of Gottsched, and Frau Gottsched herself, with her translations of the *Spectator,* were carrying on this activity under Gottsched's very nose, and Schlegel's "Vergleichung Shakespear's und Andreas Gryphs" appeared in Gottsched's *Beiträge zur critischen Historie der deutschen Sprache* in 1742.

Two years earlier Bodmer had deplored the lack of appreciation of good literature in Germany, comparing this to the times when there was no one to explain the beauties of Milton to the English, even though they had someone named "Saspar" who must have provided them with an opportunity to improve their tastes. This indicates how little Bodmer knew of Shakespeare in 1740, but by the time Wieland came to Switzerland (1752) Bodmer had learned considerably more. Young Wieland was urged to read Shakespeare in the original, and he began to study him as a model for his own plays. The result was *Johanna Gray* (1758), written in blank verse and performed with great success in Winterthur, Zürich and Basel by the famed Ackermann troupe. Its success, and that of an even worse play, *Clementina von Porretta* (1760), had made Wieland such a celebrity that he was entrusted with the directorship of the local theater company soon after he arrived at Biberach in 1761.

So it was that Wieland was privileged to introduce Shakespeare to the continent as a great playwright ought to be introduced, i.e., on the stage. The unheard-of success of *The Tempest* and of other Shakespeare adaptations in Biberach surely gave Wieland the final encouragement to undertake the translations of Shakespeare's complete dramatic works. He could not have realized the magnitude of this task, at least not until he had completed the eighth and last of the ten volumes he had planned. "Ich schaudere selbst, wenn ich zurücksehe und daran denke, dass ich den Shakespeare zu übersetzen gewagt habe," he wrote to his publisher in 1766. "Wenige können sich die Mühe, die Anstrengung, die oft zur Verweiflung und zu manchem Fluch treibende Schwierigkeit dieser Art vorstellen. Genug, diese herculische Arbeit ist nun gethan, und bey allen Göttinnen des Parnasses, ich würde sie gewiss nicht anfangen, wenn sie erst gethan werden sollte."[6]

The faults of Wieland's translations (1762-1766) are too obvious, and have been pointed out too often, to require detailed re-exposition here. He translated verse into prose, he omitted most of the songs, he aped Warburton in his comments on too many passages, he made ridiculous, sometimes hilarious blunders in translation, and he did not finish the work. But he did present the world with the first worth-while translation of Shakespeare on a large scale, and he translated twenty-two of the best plays, one of them, *Midsummer Night's Dream,* brilliantly and in appropriate verse.

La Place's anonymous work of 1746, *Le Théâtre Anglois,* followed the custom of the times: great foreign classics should be made available in partial translations and synopses. Meinhard's *Versuche über den Character der besten italienischen Dichter* (1763-4) followed the same pattern, and Dr. Dodd's *Beauties of Shakespeare, Properly Selected from Each Play* (1752) was long a favorite in Germany. In the light of this firmly established precedent and of the Shakespeare that was being staged in England, Wieland's work was truly revolutionary. It must be remembered that what we now consider a "complete" Shakespeare play was rarely if ever seen in eighteenth-century England. Throughout the whole of that century, and even until 1823, *King Lear,* for example, had a happy ending on the stage. Neither Coleridge nor Lamb nor Hazlitt ever saw this play acted as written by Shakespeare.[7]

Modern translators of Shakespeare have many more critical aids available than did Wieland, but even in the thirty years between Wieland's and Schlegel's translations much of importance was accomplished for Shakespeare studies, not the least of which was Johnson's great edition. There is evidence, however, that Wieland, too, had considerably more to work with than is generally supposed. In an excellent essay, "Wieland's Translation of Shakespeare,"[8] F. W. Meisnest offers plausible arguments indicating that Wieland, using Graf Stadion's library at Warthausen Castle near Biberach, was not restricted to Boyer's *Dictionnaire Royal Francois et An-*

glois and to a "Wörterbuch Shakespearescher Wörter und Phrasen" borrowed from Sophie la Roche's husband. In addition to Ludwig's *English, German and French Dictionary* (3rd ed., 1765), and *Deutsch-Englisches Lexikon,* he must have used Samuel Johnson's *Dictionary of the English Language,* published in 1755 and well known throughout Germany. And it is fairly certain that Wieland did not rely solely on the Warburton edition of 1747, but that Theobald's and even Hamner's editions were consulted, since Wieland does not always accept Warburton without question. But if he had, it would be understandable, since Warburton had advertised his edition as follows: "The Genuine text (collated with all the former editions and then converted and amended) is here settled: Being restored from the blunders of the first editors, and the interpretations of the two Last; with a Comment and Notes, Critical and Explanatory, by Mr. Pope and Mr. Warburton."

In re-examining Wieland's translation it should be recognized, in spite of Gundolf's left-handed compliments,[9] that Wieland is one of the greatest translators in all German literature, and that whatever his reason for translating almost all the plays into prose, it was not his distaste for verse. Wieland was above all a "leidenschaftlicher Verskünstler,"[10] and this facet of his genius shone brightly in the songs he chose to translate. Some of them Schlegel found so nearly perfect that he incorporated them into his own translation with little change or, as in the case of Bottom's song in *Midsummer Night's Dream* (I, iv), with no change at all:

> Der Felsen Schoss
> Und toller Stoss
> Zerbricht das Schloss
> Der Kerkertür
> Und Febbus [Schlegel: Phöbus, Phibbus] Karr'n
> Kommt angefahr'n
> Und macht erstarr'n
> Des stolzen Schicksals Zier!

In his interesting study, "Probleme des Musikalischen in der Sprache,"[11] Ronald Peacock has selected the Schlegel version of "Full fathom five" (*The Tempest,* I, ii) as an example, yet he might also have chosen Wieland's rendition, which has captured remarkably well the spirit of the English original. For the sake of comparison, the following quotations include a new translation by Richard Flatter:[12]

SCHLEGEL:

> Fünf Faden tief liegt Vater Dein,
> Sein Gebein wird zu Korallen,
> Perlen sind die Augen sein.
> Nichts an ihm, das soll verfallen,
> Das nicht wandelt Meeres-Hut
> In ein reich und seltenes Gut.

Nymphen läuten stündlich ihm,
Da horch! Ihr Glöcklein—Bim! bim! bim!

FLATTER:

Dein Vater, der liegt auf dem Meeresgrund,
So friedlich als ob er schliefe.
Die spielenden Wogen wiegen den Fund,
Verwandeln ihn sacht in der Tiefe.
Nichts ist verloren, nichts wird vergehn,
Mag alles auch zerfallen:
Aus den Augen werden Perlen entstehn,
Aus den Knochen werden Korallen.
Und die Meerfraun läuten die Glocken dazu,
sie läuten, läuten, läuten zur Ruh:
Ding—dong, ding, dong, dong—
Ding-dong-dong—

WIELAND:

Fünf Faden tief dein Vater liegt
Sein Gebein ward zu Korallen,
Zu Perlen seine Augenballen,
Und vom Moder unbesiegt,
Wandelt durch der Nymphen Macht
Sich jeder Teil von ihm und glänzt in fremder
  Pracht.
Die Nymphen lassen ihm zu Ehren
Von Stund zu Stund die Totenglocke hören.
Horch auf, ich höre sie, ding-dang, ding-dang.

An even better example of Wieland's skill is Ariel's song (*The Tempest,* V, i):

SCHLEGEL:

Wo die Bien, saug ich mich ein,
Bette mich in Maiglöcklein,
Lausche da, wenn Eulen schrein,
Fliege mit der Schwalben Reihn
Lustig hinterm Sommer drein,
Lustiglich, lustiglich leb' ich nun gleich,
Unter den Blüten, die hängen am Zweig.

FLATTER:

Wo das Bienlein, saug auch ich;
In ein Primlein bett ich mich;
Schreit ein Käuzlein, duck ich mich;
Auf ein Schwälblein schwing ich mich.
Flieg dem Lenz nach lustiglich.
Lustiglich, lustiglich leb ich nun bald,
Unter den Blüten im Feld und im Wald.

WIELAND:

Wo die Biene saugt, saug' ich;
Im Schoss der Primel lagr ich mich;
Dort schlaf ich, wenn die Eule schreit;
Ich flieg in steter Munterkeit,
Fern von des Winters Ungemach
Dem angenehmen Sommer nach;
Wie fröhlich wird künftig mein Aufenthalt sein,
Unter den Blüten im duftenden Hain!

It is quite apparent that even ultra-modern German translators cannot resist the temptation to make Shakespeare less "crude," less "natural," and thus "on the bat's back" becomes "auf ein Schwälblein" even in 1954!

That the so-called A. W. Schlegel-Ludwig Tieck translations were by no means the last word, is all too obvious when one considers the number of translations and "alterations" that have appeared since. Flatter, the latest of the Shakespeare translators, objects in particular to the "Verniedlichung Shakespeares," the attempt to prettify Shakespeare and his language. "Er [Schlegel] geht dahin gelegentlich so weit, dass er Shakespeare schulmeistert: er lässt ihn sagen, nicht was er schrieb, sondern was er, Shakespeare, nach Schlege's Meinung hätte schreiben sollen . . . überall finden wir die Tendenz, Shakespeares Sprache auf ein feineres, ein höheres Niveau zu heben."[13]

One of the more important voices raised in protest against the Schlegel translation was that of Friedrich Hebbel, who had to resort to a rewriting, an "Einrichten," as he called it, of the "unspeakable" Schlegel version of *Julius Caesar* for a performance at the Burgtheater in Vienna. "Unter Einrichten verstehe ich nichts weiter als ein simples Umschreiben der durchaus nicht sprechbaren Schlegelschen Uebersetzung."[14]

Whatever his shortcomings, "unspeakability" is one charge that cannot be brought against Wieland's language, and Hermann Hesse finds that even for modern readers Wieland's German "hat etwas musterhaft Klares und Gebändigtes."[15] If one of the chief attributes of good translation is its ability to recreate the atmosphere of the original, then Wieland was anything but a failure. If Shakespeare was "ganz Natur" to the Germans, why should not the most "natural" of German poets translate him? Long after Schlegel's work had appeared, Goethe remarked: "Es ist ein unvergleichliches Naturell was in ihm [Wieland] vorherrscht. Alles Fluss, alles Geist, alles Geschmack. Eben diese hohe Natürlichkeit ist der Grund, warum ich den Shakespeare, wenn ich mich wahrhaft ergötzen will, jedesmal in der Wielandschen Übersetzung lese."[16]

Wieland's efforts in behalf of Shakespeare had at least three significant results: (1) the introduction of Shakespeare upon the German (and continental) stage, (2) a demonstration of the fact that a faithful translation was not only possible but desirable, and (3) an enrichment of the German language. But with renewed interest in Shakespeare there came a renewal of the bitter warfare begun by Gottsched over Borck's *Julius Caesar.* Now, however, the opposition was no longer directed against the English poet, but against Wieland, the German translator. The leaders in this fight were Gerstenberg (*Briefe über Merkwürdigkeiten der Literatur,* Nos. 14-18, 1766),[17] and Herder (*Erste Sammlung der Fragmente, 4.*

Kritisches Wäldchen[, 1767]). These attacks, especially Gerstenberg's, were so devastating and the prestige of Gerstenberg was so great that the embittered Wieland felt it necessary to append a defense of the translation to the last volume of his *Shakespeare* [*Shakespeares Theatralische Werke*] (1766). Yet at this very time, when the rising tide of criticism threatened to engulf Wieland together with his translation, it remained for Lessing, the one authority of the day whose literary sense and critical judgment were least impeachable, and who had taken Wieland severely to task on other occasions, to vindicate Wieland and to praise his work with vigor and intelligence.[18]

Nevertheless, the young "Sturm-und-Drang" enthusiasts decided that Shakespeare was infallible and well-nigh untranslatable, and that if he could be translated, Wieland was the last person in the world to undertake the task. Yet it was Wieland's translation they read so avidly, and it was Wieland's prose they copied for their "Bürgerliche Trauerspiele." "Nun erschien Wielands Uebersetzung," Goethe tells us in *Dichtung und Wahrheit.* "Sie ward verschlungen, Freunden und Bekannten mitgeteilt und empfohlen . . . Shakespeare, prosaisch übersetzt, konnte als eine allgemeinverständliche und jedem Leser gemässe Lektüre sich schnell verbreiten und grosse Wirkung hervorbringen. Ich ehre den Rhythmus wie den Reim, wodurch Poesie erst zur Poesie wird, aber das eigentlich tief und gründlich Wirksame, das wahrhaftig Ausbildende und Fordernde ist dasjenige, was vom Dichter übrig bleibt, wenn er in Prosa übersetzt wird."[19]

Wieland's work is perhaps best described as an "Eindeutschung" or a "Verdeutschung" of Shakespeare. Sengle prefers "Uebertragung," but all these terms have a significant "Germanizing" connotation, a making-available of Shakespeare in a form that can be called faithful, yet one that was most acceptable to eighteenth-century Germany. The importance of this work for German literature must be re-emphasized. Through it Shakespeare became "naturalized" in Germany as he was nowhere else in the world.

Wieland's personal appreciation of Shakespeare, though perhaps limited, never wavered throughout his long life. None of his great contemporaries, no, not even Lessing,[20] was so consistent in his devotion. Goethe's Strassburg enthusiasm for Shakespeare had cooled considerably by the time he wrote "Shakespeare und kein Ende," and the mature Schiller, gravitating ever closer to classic French drama, was quite willing to forget the "Shakespearomanie" of his early plays. Even Herder had to admit sadly that the remoteness of his age from Shakespeare's time made Garrick's adaptations necessary.[21] Perhaps Goethe's last words were "mehr Licht," but Wieland ended with "Sein oder nicht sein, das ist die Frage."[22]

Notes

1. "Senator" was the high-sounding title of a relatively minor post in Wieland's home town of Biberach-on-the-Riss. Wieland was actually born in Oberholzheim, which however was included in the territory of the "Freie Reichsstadt" Biberach.

2. Ernst Stadler, *Wielands Shakespeare* (Strassburg, 1910: Quellen und Forschungen, 107) p. 12.

3. Paul van Tieghem, "La Découverte de Shakespeare sur le continent," *Le Préromantisme* (*Etudes d'histoire littéraire européene* [Paris, 1947] III, 232).

4. Grynaeus' translation was based on Garrick's adaptation for the stage. It appeared in a three-volume work, *Neue Probestücke der englischen Schaubühne* (Basel, 1758).

5. *Beiträge zur critischen Historie der deutschen Sprache,* VII (1741), 516.

6. *Archiv für Literaturgeschichte,* VII (1876), 505.

7. David Nichol Smith, *Shakespeare in the 18th Century* (Oxford, 1928) p. 24.

8. *MLR* [*Modern Language Review*], IX (1914), 21ff.

9. Friedrich Gundolf, *Shakespeare und der deutsche Geist* (Godesberg, 1947), p. 145ff.

10. Friedrich Sengle, *Wieland* (Stuttgart, 1949), p. 162.

11. *Weltliteratur, Festgabe für Fritz Strich zum 70. Geburtstag* (Bern, 1952).

12. *Shakespeare,* neu übersetzt von Richard Flatter (Wien, 1954) III, 412.

13. Ibid., I (1952), 24.

14. Letter to Felix Bamberg, Vienna, August 22, 1848. Friederich Hebbel, *Sämtliche Werke,* Werner, ed. (Berlin, 1906) *Briefe* IV, 132.

15. *Festschrift zum 200. Geburtstag des Dichters Christoph Martin Wieland,* hsrg. von dor Stadtgemeinde (*Biberach/Riss,* 1933), p. 116.

16. *Goethes Gespräche,* Biedermann, ed. (Leipzig, 1909-11), II, 166.

17. Also the *Rezensionen in der Hamburgischen Neuen Zeitung* (1767-71). Reprinted in *Deutsche Litteraturdenkmale des 18. und 19. Jahrhunderts,* nos. 29-30 [1888-90] and 128 [1904].

18. *Hamburgische Dramaturgie* [(1767-69)], No. 15.

19. *Weimarer Ausgabe* [(1907)], XXVIII, 73.

20. One cannot help agreeing with Pascal that "Lessing never enters into a full discussion of Shakes-

peare, and in his own theory of drama ignores him almost completely. His appreciation of Shakespeare was never incorporated into his outlook, and remained in a separate compartment of his brain." R. Pascal, *Shakespeare in Germany* (Cambridge, 1937), p. 6.

21. Ibid., p. 15.

22. Werner Deetjen, "Rede bei der 69. Hauptversammlung der Deutschen Shakespeare Gesellschaft zu Weimar," *Shakespeare Jahrbuch* LXIX (1933), 2.

John Fitzell (essay date January 1957)

SOURCE: Fitzell, John. "The Island Episode in Wieland's *Oberon.*" *German Quarterly* 30, no. 1 (January 1957): 6-14.

[*In the following essay, Fitzell evaluates Romantic elements in Wieland's* Oberon. *In Fitzell's view, Wieland's treatment of such themes as death, nature, and spirituality prefigured many of the central concerns of German Romanticism.*]

While it is true that the aesthetic discovery of nature as an all-pervading dynamic force may be attributed to writers of Storm and Stress, German Romanticists explored most profoundly and poetically the concept of death-longing (*Todessehnsucht*). It remained for them to equate that experience with a basic urge of the soul for reunion with nature (*Naturfrömmigkeit*).[1] In significant respects, Wieland is a forerunner of Romanticism, and his verse romance, **Oberon,**[2] is surely one of the most romantic of his works. The island episode (containing the events subsequent to the shipwreck of Hüon and Rezia) reveals to what specific degree this is so. The substance of the episode also lends a poetic depth to the poem not popularly associated with it. Most important, however, is the fact that Wieland's treatment of the hermit Don Alfonso represents a very early, searching exposition of death-longing and spiritualization in nature.[3] The purpose of this essay is to provide an interpretation of Don Alfonso's relationship to nature and so show that the episode is a striking expression of a theme subsequently central in German Romanticism.

Like Eichendorff's Don Diego (*Eine Meerfahrt*), Alfonso is a former Spanish knight who finds his earthly paradise on a remote tropical island and, for him, as for Novalis' Hohenzollern (*Heinrich von Ofterdingen*), the death of his wife and sons has, in part, motivated his hermithood. (The circumstances of shipwreck are similar to those in Chamisso's *Salas y Gomez,* the hero of which, however, is not properly a hermit.) Alfonso, like most subsequent romantic solitaries, is an aged man and, as such, personifies intimacy with nature; he is at a

stage preparatory to his impending union with it in death. Several lines referring to his shipwreck also suggest the sea as a source of eternal life surrounding his adopted world, the island (VIII, 16): "Bevor er aus den Wogen / Der Welt geborgen ward . . ." This suggestion is comparable to the visions of gleaming, endless waters symbolizing eternity in Kerner's *Die Heimatlosen,* for in the latter work Serpentin has such visions, while in Sililie's "Märchen" Goldener departs across such an infinite sea. The conception of the sea as an isolating medium and the island motif (insulate and isolate are variations of a common stem) also connect the hermit theme to that of the island-paradise in the "Robinsonaden." (There is some internal evidence that Wieland's picture was influenced by Robinson Crusoe—e.g., the "two-faced" island with one barren and one verdant portion.)

Alfonso thus has a background which might be termed traditional for the literary hermit-figure. Trevrizent in *Parzival,* Simplicissimus, Balduin in Droste-Hülshoff's *Walter,* Don Diego in Eichendorff's novella, Hohenzollern in Novalis' novel, and Paul in Uhland's *König Eginhard* all seek solitude after a life of rich and varied activity, usually knightly, courtly or military. Like many literary hermits, Wieland's has come to consider vain the empty splendor of worldly ways. He has been reared in royal service and has competed with countless others for glory and recognition (VIII, 16), "Dem schimmernden Gespenst, das ewige Opfer heischet / Und, gleich dem Stein der Narren, die Hoffnung ewig täuschet." Having evaluated this life as illusory and barren of all deeper validity, Alfonso regards the shipwreck as a bizarre stroke of fortune that has released him from the burdens of courtly existence and allows him, his wife and his best friend to pass their remaining years in isolation (VIII, 17). The event is for him providential, much as are the losses by fire for Balduin in Annette's *Walter.*

The successive deaths of his wife, three sons and friend, however, have turned his thoughts toward the grave, and the world itself seems to him a tomb. To escape the silent reminder of his sorrow, he has fled with a servant to the rocky isle which becomes the scene of his final hermithood.

Once every tie with the world is broken and the deaths of his loved ones have reoriented his entire being, Don Alfonso's senses are opened and made receptive to the elements of nature. Through them his spirit achieves awareness of its eternal relationship with all about him; a profound contentment comes over him and he finds a new life (VIII, 22):

> Die Nüchternheit, die Stille,
> Die reine freie Luft durchläuterten sein Blut,
> Entwölkten seinen Sinn, belebten seinen Mut.

> Er spürte nun, dass aus der ewigen Fülle
> Des Lebens Balsam auch für seine Wunden quille.

Nature is conceived (not only in the personification of its forces in the fairy rulers Titania and Oberon) as the positive medium through which the divine spirit reaches out to soothe and heal the soul of man.

Thus Alfonso's abode, shut off from the rest of the island by bleak cliffs and dense forest, suggests the pulsating heart of nature itself. Its eternal characteristics are indicated further by the green earth and rich foliage, which, even in autumn, are protected from the blighting northwind; it is another world, an enchanting fairyland where figs and oranges still bloom, although their season is past (VIII, 12). The remoteness of this "Elysium" from the outer world also implies a nearness to the spirit of nature, for Titania, its elfin queen and genius, had created the secluded paradise as a refuge for herself until she might be reconciled with Oberon (VIII, 65-66). The marvelous glade, then, assumes a supernatural, ethereal quality through her presence. It breathes a vital healing power and becomes for the hermit the medium of his metaphysical affinity with eternal life. Don Alfonso's intimate relationship with nature is the basis of his rapport with the spiritual beyond and, accordingly, his hermitage symbolizes the final stage and attenuation of his physical life.

As we have already inferred, the death of those closest to him had made him acutely sensitive to the world of the spirit; through its intermediary realm, nature, it effects its healing power. Nature is here the very revelation of the transcendental. Left utterly alone after the decease of his loyal servant, Don Alfonso's essential spiritualization (*Vergeistigung*) approaches an accomplished state through his heightened receptivity to the impulses about him; through nature he reaches toward his loved ones beyond (VIII, 26):

> Doch desto fester kehrte
> Sein stiller Geist nun ganz nach jener Welt sich hin,
> Der, was er einst geliebt, itzt alles angehörte,
> Der auch er selbst schon mehr als dieser angehörte.

Yet, as in the instance of Werdo Senne in Brentano's *Godwi*, the specific longing for the dead is transformed into a suprarational, harmonious intimacy with the ethereal-natural realm of his environment, and the process of this transformation is a recreation of the world from within (VIII, 27):

> Ihm wird, als fühl 'er dann die dünne Scheidwand
>   fallen,
> Die ihn noch kaum von seinen Lieben trennt;
> Sein Innres schliesst sich auf, die heil'ge Flamme
>   brennt
> Aus seiner Brust empor; sein Geist, im reinen Lichte
> Der unsichtbaren Welt, sieht himmlische Gesichte.

At night (to Wieland, as to the Romanticists, a realm of "Unendlichkeit" and other-worldliness), "Wenn vor dem äussern Sinn / Wie in ihr erstes Nichts die Körper sich verlieren," (VIII, 26), Don Alfonso feels a phantom touch upon his cheek and, in half-slumber, he is aware of the echoes of angelic voices from the grove outside his hut. Yet this consciousness of most intimate communion with the universal forces does not leave him during daylight hours of activity, for the experience has awakened in his innermost being completely and forever the purest of all senses (VIII, 29). This sense the poet refuses to name, preferring, as he says, to remain silent on the edge of the abyss. Undoubtedly "der reinste aller Sinne" is essentially "Todessehnsucht," equated here, as in *Hyperion, Heinrich von Ofterdingen* and Kerner's *Die Heimatlosen,* with the emotion of concord of the entire being with all elements. This conception is related, also, to the "Fühlbarkeit" of Werther.[4] It represents for Wieland the Unutterable, because it is a conscious insight into the Absolute beyond the thin "dividing wall" (VIII, 27). The partition between this life and the next has fallen before the hermit's inner eye, since his intimate communion with nature in solitude has granted him a means of penetrating it (VIII, 29): "So fliesst zuletzt unmerklich Erd' und Himmel / In seinem Geist in Eins" (cf. also note 3).

This sense of suprarational recognition gained through such a communion distinguishes the hermit from other men. Although he is a secular solitary, Don Alfonso is endowed with a natural-spiritual power. He becomes a kind of priest of nature. Indeed, suggestions of his identification with the pervading spirit are apparent from Amanda's (Rezia's) initial impression of him. She falls upon her knees before him as before the genius of the sacred, seemingly enchanted glade in which he dwells (VIII, 13). To both Amanda and Hüon, whom Alfonso receives into his hermitage, he often appears to be a protective genius (*Schutzgeist*), perhaps Oberon himself doing penance for their guilt in the guise of a hermit (VIII, 33).

In the capacity of confessor, Don Alfonso urges Hüon to disclose the source of his misery, offering to atone for him and to open to him the gates of redemption (VIII, 6). This theme is similar, of course, to the vicarious atonement of Trevrizent in *Parzival*. In the same capacity, he hears the tale of Hüon's adventures and of the guilt which Amanda and her knight had incurred through breach of trust with Oberon, nature's royal elf (VIII, 35-37). Since the lovers had offended Oberon and, through him, as it were, his realm, abstinence and the purifying effect of the simple, hardy life in nature combine as fitting penance, strengthening them for the ordeal of faith and loyalty which they are to endure at the court of Almansor in Tunis (X-XII). As the dedicated spokesman of nature, the hermit becomes, quite literally, the interpreter of that element through which the "Weltseele" works in the soul of man. He performs, in this respect, what might be called an educational function for the protagonists of the epic at a crucial stage of their development, like Trevrizent for Parzival, Hohenzollern for Heinrich von Ofterdingen and, to an extent, Don Diego for Antonio in Eichendorff's *Eine Meerfahrt.*

We have referred to implications of the hermit's identification with the genius of the secluded paradise and have indicated the essentially symbolic and spiritual character of his dwelling place, a quality derived specifically from the presence of Titania (cf. VIII, 66); we have also traced the development of his spiritualization through increased receptivity to the impulses about him. While the suggestions of his identification with the spirit pervading his abode cannot, of course, be taken at surface value, since Titania, the personification of this spirit, dwells there too, they do point directly toward his ultimate, utter identification with it in death.

The angelic voices which Alfonso had heard during the night (VIII, 27) were those of Titania and her attendant Sylphs (VIII, 66), and it was the elfin queen herself whose passing seemed a phantom brushing on his cheek. This fanciful connection of the hermit's sensitivity to the impulses from nature lends a definite, almost tangible, quality to the implication of his pending reunion with its essential spirit. A further word with respect to a possible symbolic connotation for Titania's grotto may add weight indirectly to our conception of her as the genius of the natural spirit and of the death of Alfonso as marking his complete reunification with it.

The entrance of Titania's grotto is impassable; it is as if an invisible gate barred all who would from entering. Hüon and Alfonso, tempted by its iridescent beauty in the morning sun, had often wished to go in, but they had felt an unusual resistance—"ein wunderbares Grauen" (VIII, 71). The invisible obstacle at the entrance to Titania's cave may well be considered the ultimate equivalent of the thin "Scheidwand" (VIII, 27) which had fallen before the inner eye of Alfonso's soul in his new-found intimacy with the universal (nature) spirit. The curious sense of horror felt at the brink of this portal is like that expressed by the poet when he refuses to name the "purest of all senses" (VIII, 29). It is the involuntary awe of confrontation with an aspect of the Absolute which one cannot comprehend in terms of this life (an emotion similar to, though less violent than, that which turns Faust's face from the Earth Spirit). Only Amanda is able to pass through the magic portal, for she is to give birth to her child within the sacred precinct of the grotto (VIII, 75), the heart of nature from which life emerges and into which, in death, it is finally taken.

Don Alfonso's life has its "diesseitig" aspects, however, for it is he who instructs Hüon in the cultivation of the garden and in the construction of shelter and hearth for Amanda (VIII, 40-41):

> "Nichts unterhält so gut," versichert ihn der Greis,
> "Die Sinne mit der Pflicht in Frieden,
> Als fleissig sie durch Arbeit zu ermüden;
> Nichts bringt sie leichter aus dem Gleis
> Als müss'ge Träumerei."

Through the activity recommended by the recluse, Hüon finds a means of maintaining his oath of abstinence. For Alfonso, as for Novalis' hermit in *Ofterdingen* and Eichendorff's in *Eine Meerfahrt,* hermithood is a way of life not for the young, to whom isolation is highly unnatural and in whose veins the strength for deeds yet unaccomplished still pulses. Although worldly existence has no further significance for Alfonso, he sympathizes with the young people, reading the unfulfilled hopes in their souls and in the tears which they vainly attempt to conceal (IX, 27):

> Tadelt nicht die unfreiwilligen Triebe
> Und frischt sie nur, so lang' als ihren Lauf
> Das Schicksal hemmt, zu stillem Hoffen auf.

Yet, the hermit's entire being is, as we have seen, directed toward its final absorption into the cosmos; his earthly life has become a dream and his mind dwells upon the flight of his soul into the essence of existence (IX, 29):

> Es war, als wehe schon
> Ein Hauch von Himmelsluft zu ihm herüber
> Und trag' ihn sanft empor, indem er sprach.

The more sensitive feminine intuition of Amanda is somehow aware that the pious man's final stage of withdrawal from life is at hand (IX, 29). "'Mir,' fuhr er fort, 'mir reichen sie die Hände / Vom Ufer jenseits schon, mein Lauf ist bald zu Ende'," and upon the threshold of his spiritualization he foretells the hardships which await the young couple. Joys and pleasures alternate through life; pleasures are a strengthening for subsequent pains. Worldly vicissitude and bliss become dreams, and nothing accompanies the soul to its goal (IX, 31):

> Nichts als der gute Schatz, den ihr in euer Herz
> Gesammelt, Wahrheit, Lieb' und innerlicher Frieden,
> Und die Erinnerung, dass weder Lust noch Schmerz
> Euch je vom treuen Hang an eure Pflicht geschieden.

At the close of the evening on which the hermit expresses the sum of his life experience, he embraces Hüon and Amanda in a last farewell and enters his hut with tear-filled eyes. In the past his soul at rest had heard ethereal voices from the enchanted grove, but on this night Titania, in fearful anticipation of Amanda's future peril, flies forth from her grotto, taking with her the baby for safe-keeping (IX, 32). In this very night, too, Alfonso's sublimation is completed; he is discovered dead on the following morning. The departure of Titania coincides with the hermit's death; his soul has passed through the sacred portal and has become united with the universal spirit of nature. Alfonso's "Naturvergeistigung" is conveyed not only by Titania's flight from the garden paradise, simultaneous with the hermit's decease, but also by the fact that the "Elysium" surrounding the hermitage has been transformed (IX, 44): the plants and garden have withered, the forest is blighted, and the entire glade becomes as bleak as the rest of the island. The departure of the genius, with which the hermit's soul in death is identified, robs the hermitage of its aspect of eternal life.

Don Alfonso's island hermithood thus represents the most remote station of life, one attained only after a wealth of experience and suffering and in advanced age, when the innermost being has been directed toward a sphere beyond the incapacities of the worldly self; hermithood is that phase in which the final stages of the spiritualization through nature take place and in which the soul is ultimately reunited and identified with nature's pervading spirit. Nature becomes the realm through which the individual attains to the cosmic harmony. Don Alfonso's relationship to nature accordingly provides a preview of the conceptions of "Todessehnsucht" and "Naturfrömmigkeit" in German Romanticism, and Wieland's recluse is a forerunner of the solitaries embodying that romantic "Naturfrömmigkeit" which takes the place of more traditionally orthodox Christian conceptions of the cosmos (cf. also Korff, *Geist der Goethezeit*, [1923-57,] IV, 372-374).

Not as a suggested substantiation of the findings here, but rather as a peculiarly applicable illustration of them, we may cite a thought of Schelling, perhaps the most representative of romantic philosophers. His dictum very nearly defines our interpretation of Don Alfonso's spiritualization and reunification with the spirit of nature. In his *Ideen zu einer Philosophie der Natur*[5] he says of the Absolute, which is embodied in nature: "da nun sein Wesen ein Produzieren ist und es die Form nur aus sich selbst nehmen kann, es selbst aber reine Identität ist, so muss auch die Form *diese Identität,* und also Wesen und Form in ihm *eines und dieselbe,* nämlich die gleiche reine Absolutheit sein." Wieland's recluse attains at last precisely that absolute identity of spirit in us and nature outside us of which Schelling speaks.

This episode, then, from a poem otherwise frequently designated a lighthearted fairy-tale epic, comprises a sensitive and incisive poetic document in the development of a major theme in the literature of the Age of Goethe and Romanticism.

Notes

1. Wackenroder's mad recluse in *Ein wunderbares morgenländisches Märchen,* Hyperion in Hölderlin's novel, Werdo Senne in Brentano's *Godwi,* the "Waldvater" in Justinus Kerner's *Die Heimatlosen,* Balduin in Droste-Hülshoff's *Walter,* and Don Diego in Eichendorff's *Eine Meerfahrt,* as well as, to an extent, Hohenzollern in Novalis' *Heinrich von Ofterdingen,* are all figures which embody variously the stages of spiritualization in nature—as, of course, do the anchorites in the closing scene of Goethe's *Faust.* All these literary characters are solitaries; for not a few poets, particularly those belonging properly to German Romanticism, incorporated their deepest interpretations of man's relationship to nature into the figure of the hermit.

2. Christoph Martin Wieland, *Oberon,* ed. Rheinhold Kohler (Leipzig, 1868). All references to the poem are from this edition by canto and strophe number.

3. Cf. also J. C. Blankennagel, "The Island Scene in Wieland's 'Oberon'," *PMLA,* XLI (1926), 161-166. Professor Blankennagel sees the episode as an almost "separate entity," standing in contrast with the substance and tone of the rest of the epic. He devotes only a modest portion of his essay to Alfonso, however. He speaks of the "mystic merging of heaven and earth in the soul of man" (p. 161) and refers to Alfonso's death (p. 166) with a paraphrase of lines from VIII, 29, which touches upon the subject of this essay, but in no real sense does the present article duplicate his study.

4. The noun "Fühlbarkeit" occurs in *Werther* (Jubiläums-Ausgabe, XVI, 86 and 392); it is "defined" in the letters "Am 4.Mai" (end) and "am 10.Mai" (XVI. 5-6).

5. Friedrich Wilhelm Joseph Schelling, *Werke, Auswahl in drei Bänden,* ed. Otto Weiss (Leipzig, 1907), I 158-159.

Israel S. Stamm (essay date February 1958)

SOURCE: Stamm, Israel S. "Wieland and Sceptical Rationalism." *Germanic Review* 33, no. 1 (February 1958): 15-29.

[*In the following excerpt, Stamm examines Wieland's attitude toward Enlightenment thought through an analysis of his later prose writings.*]

The more one reads in the eighteenth century, the more cautious one becomes in speaking of it simply as an age of reason. The century was not predominantly Rationalistic, if Rationalism is the philosophy that finds a true representation of reality in *a priori* conceptual thought.[1] It is true that Germany, under the influence of Leibniz and Wolff, was to a large extent still Rationalistic in this sense until the *Sturm und Drang* and Kant in their different ways undermined the dogmatic Rationalistic claims; but if we look at the Enlightenment of Western Europe as a whole, we find it definitely anti-Rationalistic.[2] It is instructive to notice that even Descartes, generally considered a great liberator, was in the eighteenth century criticized for his Rationalistic tendencies: "Descartes, et Bacon lui-même, malgré toutes les obligations que leur a la philosophie, lui auraient peut-être été encore plus utiles, s'ils eussent été plus physiciens de pratique et moins de théorie; mais le plaisir oisif de la méditation et de la conjecture même entraîne les grands esprits."[3]

It was a sensational empiricism, related largely to the Lockean psychology, that the century favored. There was a revulsion against *a priori* excogitations, against involved metaphysical analyses, against dogmatic creeds, against theological disputes, against the great mass of verbiage and prejudice and authority that obscured the face of the world and that the spirits of the Enlightenment wanted reformed and reduced to a simple, clear, direct sense of life. In this desire for simplicity and clarity the age was inspired considerably, it would seem, by the wonderfully convincing order of the new Newtonian picture. The same article "Expérimental" of the *Encyclopedia* [*The Encyclopédie of Diderot and D'Alembert*] that criticized Descartes wrote of Newton: "Newton parut et montra le premier ce que ses prédécesseurs n'avaient fait qu'entrevoir, l'art d'introduire la géométrie dans la physique et de former, en réunissant l'expérience au calcul, une science exacte, profonde, lumineuse et nouvelle" (pp. 73-74). The urge of the century was to reduce the human problem to comparable order and clarity. The urge was to see life afresh by the senses and the accurate mind (the equivalents of Newton's *expérience* and *calcul*) without the obfuscating mass of outworn ideas that misled human energy and kept it from coming to grips with the problems of man and society. It was the urge to clear directness that Voltaire expressed in his formulation: "La raison consiste à voir toujours les choses comme elles sont."[4] . . .

The simplists had their easy illusions, the Rationalists their *a priori* conviction. But the sceptics, who while they talked of reason could not mean by it an easy obedience to orderly ideas (the illusion of the simplist) or handsome metaphysical structure (the construction of the Rationalist), but in effect a reduction of illusion, tradition, metaphysics to a sense-and-science picture— these sceptics had reduced themselves to a simplicity and negativity inadequate to the complex requirements of man's nature. Voltaire, we have said, contradicted his

Lockean and Newtonian age and himself because as an alert, acute human being he came up against the fact of human complexity, perversity, misery, and against the persistent failure of man to solve his problems in any practical, worldly way. The Newtonian picture, the Lockean psychology, the simple Deistic belief of the time could not hold in their organization the complexity of the human soul. It would seem that the organizations best capable of dealing with the total human problem are the mythic ones such as religion and poetry. These do not solve man's problem, but resolve it into enduring forms of being that communicate to man his wanted harmony. But the eighteenth century typically had little sense for such mythic form.

II

The eighteenth century is not, then, entirely an age of light. One might more accurately designate its tone as *chiaroscuro,* mingling the brighter hope of reason and science with some darker recognition of man's failure in the rationality and order that were offered him. In reading a man like Voltaire, one may think of reason as a bright, steady star, but distant from man's actual life and only faintly illuminating it.

In such a context we shall set the mature Wieland, viewing him in the Enlightenment, but in its twilight character of scepticism. We shall chiefly cite discursive writing of his maturity less known than his more artistic work but useful, it is hoped, in sketching his general intellectual character.[5]

It is not difficult to set off Wieland's scepticism against the more positive rationalisms of his age: the formal conceptual Rationalism of men like Wolff, Mendelssohn, and sometimes Lessing; and the less formal, more practical rationalism that believed in the power of science and education to construct a new man, since at last an enlightened society would write on the fresh Lockean minds of its children only accurate and orderly ideas to match the order of the Newtonian world.[6]

Wieland's stand with the majority of the eighteenth century against formal Rationalism is quite explicit. He goes along with the common depreciation of *a priori* systems that seemed to the practical Enlightenment so wordy and so useless; and his anti-Rationalism stands out the more clearly for his location in Germany, where Rationalism persisted with much more force than in England or France.[7] In his **Abderiten** he uses the figure of the spider to designate and denigrate the Rationalist, in the person of the priest Stilbon: "Gleich einer unermüdeten Spinne saß er im Mittelpunkt seiner Gedanken- und Wortgewebe, ewig beschäftigt, den kleinen Vorrat von Begriffen . . . in so klare und dünne Fäden auszuspinnen, daß er alle die unzählbaren leeren Zellen seines Gehirns über und über damit austapezieren konnte"

(Klee [*Wielands Werke,* ed. Gotthold Klee], IV, 439). In *Diogenes* [*Sokrates Mainomenos; oder, Die Dialogen des Diogenes von Sinope*] Wieland burlesques the Rationalistic technique at some length. To counter a word-spinning Pythagorean transcendentalist, Diogenes, in the guise of a Chaldaean sage, holds forth on the weighty problem of the Man in the Moon. He plays with the conventional Rationalistic terminology of the possible and the actual. Confronted with the circular difficulty that to be actual the Man in the Moon must be possible, and to be possible must be actual, he resorts to an incisive solution: that the Man in the Moon is simply there: else how could he be the Man in the Moon? Etc., etc. (XIX, 93ff.).

So much to illustrate Wieland's patent rejection of Rationalism. But if he does not hold the faith in Pure Reason, neither does he believe in the Lockean man, in whom the age put so much of its hope. It is a crucial point about the eighteenth century that significant sceptical reasoners opposed to its hopeful Lockeanism[8] a view of human nature more traditional, more realistic, and more pessimistic. The mention of Voltaire's *Candide* or Johnson's *Rasselas* should be enough to indicate again the shadows that fell across the century in the bright sun of its Enlightenment.

In Germany it was Wieland who, with more distinction than any one else, represented the sceptical view of man against the claims of the age of progress. In Wieland's cultivated mind the old theme of human inadequacy rang sad but clear. We must always remind ourselves of the great influence—even still in the eighteenth century—of the realistic classical tradition on men whose education rested on Latin and Greek. When Wieland, against the common eighteenth-century hope, wants to document his doubt of the rational power of man to order himself and his destiny, it is natural for him to cite a concise classical formulation of his view. He lets Ovid's Medea speak for him:

> Video meliora proboque,
> Deteriora sequor.

> (XXX, 40)

Man sees the better and does the worse: this, Wieland goes on to say, will be true as long as man is man.

Whether Ovid's Medea speaks the truth or not, i.e., whether life dominates man's reason, or whether man's reason can dominate life—this division of opinion is a basic one in human history. In the eighteenth century the formal Rationalists and the more practical Lockeans are together, though in different ways, on the confident side. Against them stand the more realistic and sceptical spirits with their eye on the long actual record of man's failure and folly. When Wieland looks at this record, he finds that man is just about rational enough to recog-

nize his own irrationality: "Sie [i.e., die Menschen] haben just Vernunft genug, es immer hinterdrein zu merken, wenn sie was recht Albernes gethan haben, und so werden sie endlich durch lauter Thorheiten klug, wiewohl meistens erst, wenn es ihnen nichts mehr helfen kann" (Jupiter in *Göttergespräche,* Klee, II, 375).

It is clear that such a view of man will not support much of the faith in reason and progress that we commonly associate with the eighteenth century. Indeed, there is in the sceptical mind of the century a sense of human failure so intrinsic to man as to constitute a primal flaw in him comparable to the original sin of Christianity. If the Christian in relation to the perfection and beauty of God can speak of man's original sin, the disappointed rationalist of the eighteenth century in relation to his ideal of order may speak of *original folly*: "Zwar schmeicheln [die Menschen] sich immer, die letzte Albernheit, zu deren Erkenntnis sie kommen, werde auch die letzte sein, die sie begehen; Hoffnung besserer Zeiten ist ihre ewige Schimäre, von welcher sie immer betrogen werden, um sich immer wieder von ihr betrügen zu lassen, weil sie nie zu der Einsicht kommen, daß nicht die Zeit, sondern ihre angeborne unheilbare Thorheit die Ursache ist, warum es nie besser mit ihnen wird" (*Göttergespräche,* Klee, II, 384).

A passage of this kind, with its conviction of an intrinsic human defect, might even suggest a temperamental affinity of the sceptical rationalist and the Christian. There is an approach of the two in their sense of human weakness, but there is usually enough of the eighteenth century in the sceptic to assure his not being a Christian. In Wieland, for example, there is the characteristic eighteenth-century view of established religion as superstition and of priests as swindlers seeking their own profit. In the *Göttergespräche* Apollo speaks of Christian "Menschenfischerei" and of poor fish stupid enough to let themselves be taken (Klee, II, 383). And Jupiter charges the Christian priests with establishing a superstition worse than that it superseded:

> In diesem Augenblicke legen sie den Grund zu einem Aberglauben, der niemand als ihnen selbst nützlich sein . . . wird . . . Wenn man von dem Aberglauben, der die Welt bisher bethörte, das Ärgste gesagt hat, was sich mit Wahrheit von ihm sagen läßt, so wird man doch dereinst gestehen müssen, daß er weit menschlicher, unschuldiger und wohlthätiger war als der neue, den man an seine Stelle setzt. Unsere Priester waren unendlichemal harmlosere Leute als diejenigen, denen sie jetzt weichen müssen . . .

> (Klee, II, 385-386)

Then, too, in keeping with its *calculating* character, the eighteenth century often regarded established religion as something deliberately designed for social purposes. Long ago, we read in Wieland, the legislators of society recognized in the common fear of the gods the strongest means of keeping the lower classes in social order (Cf. **"Über den freien Gebrauch der Vernunft in Glaubenssachen,"** XXX, 20-21). This use of religion Wieland carries down to his own time. To undermine the public faith in God, is, he says, "ein öffentlicher Angriff auf die Grundverfassung des Staats, wovon die Religion einen wesentlichen Theil ausmacht, und auf die öffentliche Ruhe und Sicherheit, deren Stütze sie ist" (ibid., p. 81.). This functional view of religion contains, of course, much practical truth; but in the eighteenth century it was one-sided, it represented a bare utilitarianism without a complementary acknowledgment of religion as religion—that is, as mythic representation of man's most serious consciousness of his life and his death. The Enlightenment granted, for example, that Christ was a great moral teacher; but it had little use for the profound myth of man's fall and redemption. The time had sense for the obvious moralities of social life, but very little for the mystery of man's story. It was, after all, largely a prosaic, utilitarian age, deliberate, calculating, two-dimensional; it liked to shear off the dimension of depth and to work on the surface of life. Its God, when it had one, was an Engineer to account for Newtonian order or a Moral Accountant to make men behave. It had little sense for the high drama of God and man on the stage of the world. It was a limited, practical century, and its practical use of religion was in keeping with its character. When we encounter the practical conservatism of the eighteenth century, as in its use of established religion, we must distinguish it from the vivid and imaginative conservatism that came in with Burke and the Romantics. The newer conservatism was motivated not by calculation but by an empathetic sense of continuity in past and present; above all it contained the element of love, generally absent from the relation of the eighteenth century to the past.

The utilitarian view of Christianity dominated, we believe, Wieland's *Agathodämon,* though this work is by some considered to have a special quality of depth.[9] There is in *Agathodämon* a strong sense of human need and even some feeling for religious immediacy as against the usual calculation of the century. In his laudatory account of Christ (we remember that the age distinguished between Christ and Christianity) Agathodämon describes this immediacy in Christ's faith: "Was er Glauben nennt, ist eine aufs innige Gefühl gegründete Gesinnung des Gemüths, mit einer geistigen sinnlichen Vorstellung verbunden, welche eher Anschauung als räsonnirter Begriff zu nennen ist; mit Einem Worte, nicht Begreifen, sondern Ergreifen dessen, was nicht begriffen werden kann noch soll" (XVIII, 288). But while *Agathodämon* includes this deepening (the work dates from the later 1790's, when the eighteenth century was on the way out in more than a chronological sense), it explicitly contains an instrumental view of religion neither deep nor complimentary: religion as a crutch to hold up a man in his weakness, but then, if at all possible, to be cast aside: "Der Schwache und Lahme bedarf einer Stütze oder Krücke,—und welcher Mensch ist in keinem Zeitpunkt seines ganzen Lebens schwach? In diesem Fall ist es gut eine Krücke zu haben, an der man gehen kann; gleichwohl ist es unläugbar besser, ohne Krücke gehen zu können" (XVIII, 345). Not indeed a complimentary view of religion—yet a common one of it as sense but not substance.

There are also parts of *Agathodämon* that do not get beyond the obviousness of explaining away miracles, including the resurrection of Christ. The crucified one, we are told, was only seemingly dead when taken from the cross and buried; his tomb was burst open by an earthquake; he could then emerge and walk again among men (cf. XVIII, 291ff).

We have dwelt here somewhat on *Agathodämon* to indicate that even in his high maturity Wieland was kept from any essential relation to Christianity by various eighteenth-century calculations.

There is further a large spiritual difference between Christianity and rationalism in general that is relevant to our discussion. The Christian system holds an inclusive view of man: it includes his sin as well as his faith. ("If we say that we have no sin, we deceive ourselves, and the truth is not in us" [I John. i. 8]). The Christian as Christian participates with his whole nature in his fellow-man and through his Savior in God. Christianity is a community; but rationalism in its idea tends, we believe, to be exclusive. Rationalism is a counsel of perfection; there is not much room in it for folly, as there *is* room in Christianity for sin. This is why rationalism is essentially less human than Christianity and contains the danger of detachment.

When we speak of rationalistic aloofness, we may think of the stern Stoic *sapiens* looking down on the many *stulti*; but in the case of a sceptical, and therefore less rigorous, rationalist like Wieland it is rather an urbane Horatian detachment that may separate the man of reason from the foolish world. We hear Jupiter say to Juno in the *Göttergespräche*: "*Nil admirari,* liebe Frau!—Wie kannst du erwarten, daß einer, der dem Lauf der Welt schon so manches Jahrtausend aus einem so hohen Standpunkte zusieht, sich durch etwas, das bei diesen Lilliputern da unten vorgehen kann, aus der Fassung bringen lasse?" (Klee, II, 432). And as if to focus on our distinction of rationalistic detachment and Christian involvement, Jupiter declares in another part of the *Göttergespräche* that he will do for man what he can do without losing his equanimity; but "Zu schwärmen und mich für Undankbare und Narren kreuzigen zu lassen, das ist Jupiters Sache nicht. . . ." (Klee, II, 396). This realistic and practical reserve opposes the very "crux" of Christian devotion and sacrifice.[10]

Yet readers of Wieland know that for all the aloofness that is clear enough in him, he is also an understanding human being. The formal Rationalist may be rigoristic in his perfect ideas; the practical rationalist may in his urgency to reason and progress be dictatorial;[11] but the sceptical rationalist, who does not believe in absolutes and immutable essences nor in the power of man to behave rationally with any persistence, may, if he does not sour, be sadly indulgent of his fellow-men and tolerant of their weakness. After all, what wisdom can one expect of folly? Knowingly Jupiter asks, after remarking the helplessness even of the gods against the immutable way of the world: "Was können wir von den Sterblichen fordern, wenn Götter selbst nicht weiser sind?" (***Göttergespräche,*** Klee, II, 447). Even the much sharper Voltaire, as we all know, addressed men to mutual tolerance in bearing their common weaknesses: "Qu'est-ce que la tolérance? C'est l'apanage de l'humanité. Nous sommes tous pétris de faiblesses et d'erreurs; pardonnons-nous réciproquement nos sottises, c'est la première loi de la nature" (*Dict. Phil.* [*Dictionnaire philosophique*], III, 230, article "Tolérance"). The tone of Wieland's indulgent feeling for his fellow-men is indicated by such a remark as the following in the mouth of his Danischmend: "Wir sind. . . . am Ende nur arme schwache Menschlein" (IX, 21). This same Danischmend contradicts the detachment noted before in the ***Göttergespräche***: "Ich hasse die bloße Vorstellung von einem gleichgültigen Zuschauer des menschlichen Lebens" (IX, 46).

Sceptical reason, seeing the radical folly of man, seems capable of both cooling and warming the heart. The folly repels, but its victims may move compassion.[12] So we find Wieland in his sophisticated scepticism so often amused by the antics of men (***Abderiten***) and smiling at them from a superior distance; yet into this ironic superiority understanding and compassion weave their way. It is this same superior Wieland who through his Danischmend even defends those enthusiasts—so different from his sceptical self and generally so uncongenial to the deliberate eighteenth-century mind—who rush in to do good and in their idealistic zeal do harm as well as good: "Ich berufe mich auf die Geschichte . . . , wenn ich behaupte: daß das menschliche Geschlecht dieser Art von Enthusiasten Alles, was von Vernunft, Tugend und Freiheit noch auf dem Erdboden übrig ist, zu danken hat. Dieß Alles ist sehr wenig, wirst du sagen. Aber, so wenig es seyn mag, für uns ist es unendlich viel; denn diess Wenige macht, daß wir Menschen und keine Orang-Utangs oder noch was Aergeres sind" (IX, 73). It is the latter part of this declaration that draws our special attention for its special human quality. We see here how little Wieland's sceptical temperament really demanded of man, how grateful he was even for small achievements of humanity. It proves, we believe, a generous soul to recognize the achievement of being even modestly human in a world so massively hard and in-

different. A man must have been solidly decent who so esteemed small human accomplishment—much more solidly than those of his contemporaries who valued man for some perfection that they expected of him.

We should appreciate Wieland's human understanding. The position of the eighteenth-century sceptic was not easy. He was deprived of the mental faiths that sustained others around him: the verbal-intellectual confidence of the Rationalists and the practical confidence of the Lockeans. In his reduced position he had cast off much of the old, both good and bad, without finding much new substance to replace it. He could not go along with the progressive illusions of his time. We have noted above that sceptics like Voltaire and Wieland maintained a traditional classical realism about human nature in a time largely given to abstract illusion. For all their sense of reason they knew only too well the actual irrationality and perversity of man. It is such truthfulness that makes *Candide* so much more human than *L'an 2440*. There was this truthful knowledge of man in Wieland, and in the absence of an assistant faith this knowledge seems to have weighed on him as a problem. When a man knows so much that he knows little and believes even less, what position can he maintain? We find such a problematical condition in Wieland's essay **"Was ist Wahrheit?"**:

> Kinder sind leichtgläubig aus Unwissenheit dessen, was möglich oder unmöglich ist; Alte sind es, weil sie so oft unglaubliche Dinge sich haben zutragen sehen, daß ihnen nichts mehr unglaublich scheint. Jene glauben Alles, weil sie das Mißtrauen noch nicht kennen; bei diesen ist Mißtrauen eine der bittern Früchte des Lebens und macht sie eben so geneigt, an Allem zu zweifeln, als die Erfahrenheit auf der andern Seite, Alles für möglich zu halten.
>
> (XXIX, 142)

How far this knowing wariness is from the youthful hope of the century! In this sceptical world almost anything can happen; the order and regularity of rationalistic expectation are gone; and we encounter here a world so fluid and so complicated as to be beyond human arrangement:

> Und wenn . . . der weise Mann in einer so langen Lehrzeit auch noch gelernt hätte, daß eben diese Unermeßlichkeit und Unbegreiflichkeit, die für uns Erdebewohner eine Eigenschaft der ganzen Natur ist, sich auch in jedem einzelnen Stäubchen befindet; daß in jedem einzelnen Punkte der Natur Strahlen aus allen übrigen zusammenlaufen, und wie unbegreiflich alle diese Strahlen, Beziehungen, Aus- und Einflüsse aller Dinge auf jedes und jeden Dinges auf alle einander durchschneiden und durchkreuzen; wie unmöglich es also ist, nur eine einzige Erscheinung, eine einzige Bewegung oder Wirkung eines einzigen Theilchens der Natur recht zu erkennen, ohne zugleich die ganze Natur eben so zu durchschauen, wie der, in dem sie lebt und webt und ist: beim Himmel! ich denke, das müßte

den weisen Mann bescheiden gemacht haben, und es
sollte mich nicht wundern, wenn er alle seine Urtheile
und Meinungen in einem Tone vorbrächte, den ein
Mann wie Elihu, der Sohn Barachiel von Bus, des Geschlechts Ram, [Job xxxii. 2ff.] mit allem Unwillen
eines ehrlichen überzeugten Dogmatikers für baren
Skepticismus halten müßte.

(XXIX, 148)

We may here recall the Leibnizian picture of the
monads, each reflecting all the others; but in the Leibnizian system each distinct monad was fixed in a universal harmony, and the emphasis was on the power of
reason to see ever more clearly the beauty of the universal order. In Wieland's picture the harmony of the
monads is displaced—so far as human knowledge is
concerned—by a rushing tangle of all the parts of the
world; and the overpowered onlooker can only resign
himself to a careful scepticism. If the blank pages at the
close of Voltaire's *Micromégas* are a sceptical counterpoint to the fresh white pages of the Lockean psychology, then the infinitely complicated flux in Wieland's
description is likewise a twilight contrast to the bright
and beautiful order of the Leibnizian image.

With Wieland's picture of total interfluence we approach
the problem of Romanticism, for in Romanticism the
mechanical, discrete world of the eighteenth century is
displaced by a world-organism with one life flowing
continuously through all its parts. While Wieland's in-
terfluent world does not have the positive vitalistic quality given to nature by Romanticism, it is interesting that
even with his limited sense of fluidity he seems to approach the Romantics in a feeling for the power of music, the flowing art, at the expense of the word, which
is the proper medium of eighteenth-century rationalism.
In Wackenroder-Tieck's *Phantasien über die Kunst* we
read of "die zaghaften und zweifelnden Vernünftler, die
jedes der. . . . Tonstücke in Worten erklärt verlangen. . . . Streben sie die reichere Sprache nach der
ärmern abzumessen. . . . ?" (*Deut. Lit.* [*Deutsche Literatur*] *in Entwicklungsreihen, Reihe Romantik* [1930-
50], III, 115). In Wieland's *Agathodämon* the narrator,
on hearing beautiful three-part singing, speaks for pure
music without verbal interference:

Ich bedarf bei einer Musik, wie die heutige, keiner
Worte, die mir ihren Sinn erst erklären und sie gleichsam in meine Sprache übersetzen müßten; ich bedarf
nicht nur der Worte nicht dazu, sondern sie stören mich
sogar im reinen Genuß derselben, indem sie den reinen
Flug meiner durch sie leichter beflügelten Seele hem-
men, . . . und von dem, was mir die Musen in ihrer
eigenen geistigen Sprache unmittelbar mittheilen, durch
Vergleichung der Worte mit dem, was sie ausdrücken
sollen, abziehen.

(XVIII, 274-275)

Yet musicality is for Wieland by no means a surrender
to the mysterious flow of Nature and of the soul as it
sometimes is for the Romantics (cf. *Phantasien über*

die Kunst, 115-116). It is for him rather the purest representation of the ideal of harmony that he wants in the
world, the "Symphonie des Weltalls" (XVIII, 274).
Against the great flowing sea of mystery, so dear to the
Romantics, Wieland maintains his eighteenth-century
form: that is, he does not permit himself an immersion,
but keeps himself dry on the shore of scepticism and
common sense. Romanticism is mystery, largeness, inclusiveness, range, mixture, with the leaven of the infinite in it; but Wieland, for all his awareness of mystery
and large complexity, asserts deliberately his eighteenth-
century restriction to a limited and therefore more
sharply defined human form. His *Euthanasia* (1805) is
especially instructive on this matter. In these dialogues
Wieland argues against the likelihood of personal survival after death: this would, he says in his practical
way, require the survival of the individual physical apparatus. Those who simply must have the assurance of
personal continuance may indulge whatever illusions
they require. But, he continues, "wenn. . . . die Rede
von dem ist, was wir vernünftiger Weise als wahr oder
wenigstens als das Wahrscheinlichste anzunehmen
genöthigt sind, so sehe ich wenig Grund für die Hoffnung, nach meinem Tode dieselbe Person zu bleiben,
die ich im Leben war, und folglich die Verhältnisse und
Verbindungen, die einst das Glück meines Lebens aus-
machten, auch im künftigen fortzusetzen. Das Weiseste
dürfte also wohl seyn, uns in das gemeinschaftliche
Loos aller Sterblichen zu ergeben und etwa die Gründe
aufzusuchen, die uns über diesen Verlust trösten können" (XXX, 207). The end of the long dialogue approaches with a frank and smiling acceptance of our ignorance in certain deep matters; and the tone of the
passage is enlarged for us by an echo of Wieland's
mock excogitations on the Man in the Moon: "Wir thun
also wohl am besten. . . . , wenn wir uns unsere Un-
wissenheit in dämonischen Dingen aufrichtig gestehen
und uns darüber in dem Gedanken beruhigen, dass etwas, was wir unmöglich wissen können, uns vernünftiger Weise eben so wenig kümmern sollte, als was der
Mann im Mond (wenn einer ist, und wenn er was zu
essen braucht und hat) heute zu Mittag gegessen habe"
(XXX, 243). But how, it is asked, can we have peace of
mind when we know we must die and yet do not know
what lies beyond? Wieland has his sensible recommendation: The human answer to death is life! "Ich wenigstens kenne dazu kein anderes Mittel, als das Geheim-
niss des alten Sokrates, das Bewußtseyn eines
wohlgeführten Lebens" (XXX, 244). The soul that in
this life does its best, when its hour comes "senkt sich,
wie ein Kind in den Busen der Mutter, mit voller Zuver-
sicht in den Schoß des Unendlichen und schlummert
dann unvermerkt aus einem Leben hinaus, worin sie nie
wieder erwachen wird. Dieß . . . ist, nach meiner Ue-
berzeugung, im reinsten Sinne des Wortes, was meine
alten Griechen Euthanasia nannten, die schönste und
beste Art zu sterben. . . ." (XXX, 244). Again, since

he knows man's need, Wieland makes the point that we may, in our weaker moments, indulge whatever illusion our comfort requires, but—"von Allem, was guten Menschen gewiß ist, das Gewißeste bleibt doch immer, daß sie sich nicht betrügen können, wenn sie in ruhiger Ergebung und gleichsam mit geschlossenen Augen bis zum letzten Athemzug das Beste hoffen" (XXX, 245). The speaker's partner, bringing the dialogue to its close, responds: "Mein Herz sagt mir, daß du Recht hast, . . . und dabei soll es für immer bleiben" (XXX, 245).

This dialogue is cited at some length as a pronouncement of Wieland's eighteenth-century character in a high time of German Romanticism. Here the dimension of depth is deliberately cut off and man restricts himself to his human world. There are philosophies deeper than this, more intense, and probably more satisfying to our full human nature. But there is no reason why we should not appreciate, too, the more restricted and sceptical form of the eighteenth century. It is one of the possible modes of adjustment to a world infinitely beyond our smallness, for it may be a special tribute to Mystery and the Infinite not to plunge into them but to withdraw before them in sceptical respect. Indeed a position on the surface of life maintained against the deep below may build dialectical strength of character (Nietzsche: "oberflächlich aus Tiefe"). It is true that Wieland's sense of the deep was not strong or rich enough to give dramatic, let alone mythic, quality to his expression. Yet in his urbane way he knew well enough what was in the world around and beneath man, so that his superficiality, like that of the Rococo in general, may suggest a special quality of significance. Or does any one believe that Wieland found life in any way so light and gracious as it appears in his *Oberon*? We are so used to a literature of depth (as in Kierkegaard and Dostoevski) that we may have lost some valuable sense for the subtle depth of superficiality. If a writer like Wieland at least reminds us of such considerations, he may do us some good.

Notes

1. Cf. *Eislers Handwörterbuch der Philosophie, 2. Auflage* (Berlin, 1922), p. 520, article "Rationalismus": "Nur das reine, begriffliche Denken, nicht die sinnliche Erfahrung erfaßt die Realität, das Wesen der Dinge."

2. Cf. Ernst Cassirer, *Die Philosophie der Aufklärung* (Tübingen, 1932), p. 7. After discussing the *a priori* deductive Rationalism of the seventeenth century, Cassirer remarks: "Das achtzehnte Jahrhundert hat auf *diese* Art und auf *diese* Form der Deduktion, der systematischen Ableitung und Begründung verzichtet."

3. *The Encyclopédie of Diderot and D'Alembert, Selected Articles,* ed. Lough (Cambridge, 1954), ar-

ticle "Expérimental," p. 73. Note in the same volume the inference of Cartesian Rationalism in the article "Ecole (Philosophie de 1')": "Ce grand homme [i.e., Descartes] nous a détrompés de la philosophie de l'école (et peut-être même, sans le vouloir, de la sienne . . .)" (pp. 40-41).

4. *Dictionnaire philosophique, Éditions de Cluny* (Paris, 1930), II, 89, article "Enthousiasme."

5. Textual references will be to *Wielands Werke,* 4 vols., ed. Klee, *Bibliographisches Institut* (Leipzig, 1900), and to C. M. Wieland's *Sämmtliche Werke,* 36 vols. (Leipzig, 1853-58). The first will be cited as Klee; the second merely by volume and page.

6. Cf. J. B. Bury, *The Idea of Progress* (London, 1920), p. 165, where the optimism of the Encyclopedists is based on their theory of "the indefinite malleability of human nature by education and institutions. This had been . . . assumed by the Abbé de Saint-Pierre. It pervaded the speculation of the age, and was formally deduced from the sensational psychology of Locke and Condillac . . ."

7. Cf. Hans M. Wolff, *Die Weltanschauung der deutschen Aufklärung* (Bern, 1949), p. 112: "Dieser feste Glaube an den Erkenntniswert der Begriffe bildet von Wolff bis zu Mendelssohn die Grundlage des Denkens der deutschen Aufklärung."

8. It will have been noticed that the terms "Lockean" and "Lockeanism" are used in this paper in a general representative way for the view of man as unspoiled subject ready to be decisively molded by education and institutions.

9. Cf. Fritz Martini, "C. M. Wieland und das 18. Jahrhundert," in *Festschrift Paul Kluckhohn und Hermann Schneider* (Tübingen, 1948), pp. 243-265; and Friedrich Sengle, *Wieland* (Stuttgart, 1949), p. 479.

10. Cf. St. Augustine's Christian opposition to "apathy" in *The City of God,* Book XIV, Ch. ix. The opposition is summed up in the sentence: "When there shall be no sin in a man, then there shall be this apathy."

11. See, for example, Mercier, *L'an 2440* (London, 1772), ch. xxi, on the treatment of atheists who refuse, against the obvious truth, to believe in the God of natural religion.

12. Cf. Wieland's favorite Lucian in *Demonax*: "Though he assailed sins, he forgave sinners, thinking that one should pattern after doctors, who heal sicknesses but feel no anger at the sick." *Lucian* (Loeb Classical Library [1967-1979]), I, 147.

Derek Van Abbé (essay date 1962)

SOURCE: Van Abbé, Derek. "Unfair to Wieland?" *Publications of the English Goethe Society: Papers Read Before the Society, 1961-62* n.s. 32 (1962): 1-23.

[*In the following essay, Van Abbé reflects on Wieland's literary reputation, both during his lifetime and in the modern age. Van Abbé asserts that, in spite of his reputation for immorality among many contemporary critics, Wieland was in essence a profoundly ethical writer.*]

When I was being taught German Literature for the first time, I was given the apodictic statement that the German Classical period reposed on the four corner-stones of Klopstock, Wieland, Lessing and Herder. This was, of course, at school and I know that a great deal of material has to be handed down *ex cathedra* to schoolchildren merely in order to fill in the background against which they study their set texts. In the universities I am sure that study of the Classical period is carried out in a much more thorough fashion. Yet there are many unspoken assumptions even there in our teaching. We pass by many facts and many people in the way in which we pass the pub on the corner. What I mean is this: you pass the pub every day and you know it's there. But if an investigating detective were to ask you to describe it, all you would probably be able to say would be "Well, it's like a pub".

Now when we consider these four great corner-stones of the German Classical period, I have a nasty suspicion that most of us do treat Wieland rather as we treat the pub on the corner. I myself was not aware of any difference until I came, almost by accident, to study him more deeply a few years ago. In 1954 I visited Europe on leave from an Australian university and one of my ports of call was the German Academy of Sciences in Berlin. Here I had a good deal to do with Hans-Werner Seiffert, who also happens to be the present editor of the still unfinished definitive Wieland edition. Now *Die Abderiten* has long been a favourite of mine quite independently of its author's being a corner-stone. And Seiffert talked to me so enthusiastically about Wieland that I began to study Sengle's admirable biography and even to read some of his actual writings.

The result was that—for the first time—Wieland began to become a very real person for me. Then, realising that I was failing completely to pass on my enthusiasm to friends and colleagues—largely because of the absence of any great interest in Wieland in English Germanistics—I vowed to fill the gap with a biography, necessarily less learned than Sengle's, but written, I hope, in the flush of a convert's enthusiasm.

Now if I look up my school notebooks—the same ones in which there stands the "four corner-stones"—I find a number of what might gently be termed cliché phrases

about Wieland. I was told that he had great facility of expression and cultivated French grace, and a few more phrases which will now, I am sure, be calling forth echoes in your own minds. And all this is, as they say in Australia, fair enough, as far as it goes. But when you encounter judgments of this kind in the histories, you seldom encounter anything else—and the chances are that even these faint praises will be offset by at least some unfair judgment on this writer who was actually, all by himself, not so much one of the corner-stones as a great deal of the very foundation of a whole period of German literature.[1]

Wieland himself was to blame for some of the distortion in what might be called his 'public image'. From the literary point of view—and this is the standpoint from which in the past very many of our judgments have been made—he *is* a difficult poet to adjudge in the classroom prize-awarding competition we conduct in our lectures. He does not display obvious signs of having either that deep philosophical meaning many of us cherish, or a striking personal style which we can analyse with Leavite *Akribie*. He was not, that is, an original poet. He was, in fact, perfectly happy to use the devices of his age. He used them, of course, with superb mastery, but this, in a field like aesthetics, is not a virtue lecturers reward. The professional literary pundits, in fact, tend to behave like the Swiss who, since they live in a mountainous country, only regard the Eiger and the Matterhorn as real peaks, oblivious of the fact that even the Uetliberg is really quite remarkable!

As against this lack of a personal literary style, our modern democratic age tends to dislike Wieland's aristocratic airs and graces. We are all so down-to-earth these days that one of the most serious accusations that can be made against a writer is the charge of aristocratic dallying. Lack of seriousness is an accusation calculated to destroy a reputation almost as quickly as the stigma of immorality.

And indeed another reason why nasty legends have wreathed themselves round Wieland's name is the fact that he does often leave an impression of having displayed what we would call an aristocratic fondness for ambiguities on the moral side. I shall return to this point; to my mind the perpetuating of this particular accusation throws grave doubts on our own emergence from the narrow-mindedness of our nineteenth-century ancestors.

A third reason for the comparative disgrace into which Wieland has fallen is the charge that he was not an original writer, that, in fact, he adhered much too closely to French models. Nowadays I think we outside Germany do have some inkling of the permanent state of inferiority complex which has made Germans so sensitive to this particular failing in any of their writers. We

Anglo-Saxons are very conscious of the ease with which Germans entwine themselves in the obscurities of their own thought and their own language. And I feel that they have always been helped by close contact with the greater stylistic clarity of the French who, whatever we may think of them as a nation, *have* a remarkable literary tradition. It seems to me quite symptomatic that some of the most Frenchified Germans have written some of the clearest books in German. At random I would name Wieland, Heine, C. F. Meyer and Heinrich Mann. This is a point to which I also intend to return.

Finally I would like to finish this preamble by saying something positive. As opposed to those, especially amongst his contemporaries, who thought and think of Wieland as being wicked, it seems to me that he is a highly moral writer. I would give him this name, not merely because it sounds nice and paradoxical, but because this was what he wanted to be. He wanted to be moral, however, not in the sense of being professionally *erbaulich* like a parson; he wished, like a good publicist of the *Aufklärung,* to reach lots of people and influence their thinking. And in this, as you will see, he was more successful than any of his contemporaries, more successful, at least in his own day, than even Goethe and Schiller. He may not have had as much that was of lasting value to impart; but he had a very well-developed sense of the writer as *praeceptor Germaniae* and, flying in the face of the modern hero-worship of the inspired individual, I would say that this sense of communal responsibility is a worthwhile thing for a writer to have.

Wieland was born in 1733 in Biberach, a small *Reichsstadt* in Swabia. Being brought up in Biberach was as important for him as being educated in Frankfurt was for Goethe. He was, in his own eyes, the citizen of no mean city. We tend to think of Germany as having had a rising middle class that never got into the stage of being a risen one. Yet in the big cities of the Middle Ages and in the Imperial towns right up to the twentieth century, we can find all the symptoms which seem to us important for the successful *bürgerlich* culture of England and France. Never to the same extent, of course; but it is not uninteresting, for example, to compare near-contemporaries like Hans Sachs and Shakespeare as near-contemporaries and, making sensitive historical comparisons, the result is not as bad for the Germans as we tend to believe.

Biberach was a substantial city, centre of the surrounding region, and the Wieland family were more important in the local hierarchy than the Goethes were in Frankfurt. There were *Bürgermeister* in Wieland's ancestry, and *Senioren* of the local Reformed church. In fact, the family had a hereditary position, you might say, high up amongst the pastorate: one of their distant relations was Abraham Francke and there were close connections to the University of Halle. Moreover,

Wieland was to return later to Biberach as *Kanzleidirektor* and *Senator,* a position which, in such a municipal republic, however small, was tantamount to being Minister of the Interior. This is a point to bear in mind in relation to the later development of Wieland as political commentator.

Despite the family tradition young Wieland went to Erfurt and Tübingen and he studied Law not Theology. The *Aufklärung* and the Age of Rococo had him in its grip from the start: the family atmosphere was *aufgeklärt,* his father having started a secular course before he reverted to type, whilst it was the headmaster of the secularised abbey to which he was sent for schooling who introduced him to the Encyclopédistes and that other great influence on his early days, *Don Quixote.* A few years younger than Klopstock, he too was writing pietistic verse at the time the *Messias* appeared. His subject was just as Baroque as Klopstock's and indeed it probably came to him as directly as Milton's inspiration did, straight from the Italian, from Torquato Tasso, in fact.

We are no longer astonished at the strength of the religious element in German eighteenth-century thought. Time was when the word *Aufklärung* summoned up solely thoughts of Rationalism and the Leibniz tradition. From the time of Herbert Schöffler[2] we have, however, accustomed ourselves to seeing the links, especially the personal links, between the pastorate and the rationalists. Not for nothing does a French Germanist of my acquaintance call the *Aufklärung* "une symphonie pastorale". You have real pastors, like Herder and Gleim, Bodmer and Lavater, and you have sons of pastors, like Lessing and Wieland, and you have pastors *manqués,* like Schiller. What was common to them all was not so much their enlightenment as their desire to preach.[3] Above all, their desire to give comfort: far from them our modern despair and disbelief. They were certainly not orthodox Lutherans or Calvinists. But they had a belief and, whatever it was, they wished to share it.

Side by side with religious effusions young Wieland also carried out more conventional poetic exercises. In Tübingen he came into contact with the English, of the type of Prior, Thomson and Young. What he wrote was imitative enough; it is, however, interesting to see how he took the precaution of finding a genuine girlfriend to whom to address his springtime lyrics. This young lady was to become one of the most celebrated 'femmes savantes' of the century. She was Sophie von Gutermann, daughter of a wealthy physician in the still elegant Imperial city of Augsburg and, though she gave up the provincial law-student in favour of the adopted son of the mighty Graf Stadion, she remained Wieland's friend, despite literary differences of opinion, all his life. She became the writer of a celebrated sentimental novel, the mother of the beautiful Maximiliane and the grandmother of Clemens and Bettina von Brentano.

What Wieland wrote in Tübingen served at least to make his name known and soon he received an invitation to Zürich from one of the literary popes of the day, Professor Bodmer. Klopstock had shocked the professor's Calvinist household; he now hoped the young prodigy from just over the border would prove more amenable. In a sense he was not proved wrong. Wieland was a shrewed Swabian businessman as well as a poet and he was always willing to suit his tune to whichever Maecenas was paying. Too much, in this case, for his own good. The sophisticated Berlin critics, Nicolai and Lessing, saw that a steely-bright stylist like Wieland was out of place writing in Bodmer's 'seraphic' vein and the bad marks they gave him unfortunately stuck. In some quarters they have never been erased. This was one source of his bad reputation. Yet it applies strictly to a very early period in his development when he did have his way to make in a very difficult field.

There is one by-product of this Swiss period which is often overlooked. The really important field on which Wieland conquered here was, oddly enough, not one of those for which he is normally known. In Zürich Wieland attained wide acclaim as a dramatist.[4] For in the mid-eighteenth century there were only two fields in which a writer wanted to shine in the eyes of the real *cognoscenti*: the poetic (lyric or epic) and the dramatic. Today we acclaim Wieland because he adapted to German taste the novel. But in his youth this was regarded as a low-brow art-form.[5] What he succeeded in doing first was to conquer the two worlds in which it was mandatory to shine, Poetry and the Drama.

By modern standards his two dramas are poor 'comédies larmoyantes'. One was an adaptation of a sentimental Jacobean drama on Lady Jane Gray, the other a tearful episode taken from a Richardson novel. But the historical drama (especially if compared with the original) is remarkably concentrated. It was written, moreover, in iambics and was so successful that there is a strong suspicion that it was **Lady Johanna Gray** rather than *Nathan der Weise*, unpublished and little known at this time, that revived Goethe's and Schiller's interest in verse drama. For one thing Wieland was very close to both poets at the crucial time when they turned back to verse. **Lady Johanna,** moreover, could well have inspired a good deal of *Maria Stuart*, possibly for the worse.[6]

Wieland wrote his historical play for the Ackermann troupe when the Seven Years' War forced that company to take refuge in Switzerland. The play's success may well have owed something to the fact that it was a kind of martyr-play, even if in Rococo rather than Baroque dress. A Protestant princess under Catholic persecution was well calculated to appeal to the *Züricher.* This idea also underlies Wieland's second drama, **Clementina von Porretta,** which hinges entirely on the difficulties of a Protestant obstructed from marrying his Catholic love. It is a peculiar play; it may even strike you as inconsequential. But it was very popular in its day and when the Ackermanns returned to the *Reich* they opened their post-war season precisely with **Clementina.**

Wieland's reputation as a dramatist continued to haunt him, though he wrote no more major dramas. But it should not be forgotten that as soon as he was settled back in the comparative leisure of Biberach public life, he immediately began to translate Shakespeare, another undertaking which was a contemporary success—indeed Goethe confessed to preferring it to the more accurate versions later produced by Eschenburg and the Romantics. Translating Shakespeare was no surprising development in the 'seraphic' author of sentimental dramas: Wieland started with *Midsummer Night's Dream* and *The Tempest,* the fairy-plays. The great tragedies also appealed to him as romances more than as dramas, and he definitely flagged when it came to translating the histories.[7] Wieland, you see, was essentially a Rococo poet; in his enthusiasm for Shakespeare you can indeed see how the Renaissance imagination leads over directly into the fairy-tale imaginings of the Romantics. This is a little-regarded aspect of the *Aufklärung*: small wonder that critics play down this Wieland achievement.

Wieland did make one more serious attempt on the theatre. As a gesture to his ducal patrons at Weimar, who also thought of him as the successful dramatist, he was forced to write something soon after his translation to that Court. So he wrote the Singspiel **Alceste,** a play which is also important, though not for reasons which are easy to make capital out of when rapidly sketching a classroom Classical background. It fits neatly into Gluck's Classical reform of the opera and it appears to have been the final factor deciding Goethe to foresake what he had thought of as the realism of *Götz* and *Egmont*—the outcome of Herder's patriotic and organic philosophy—in favour of a return to the Renaissance stage-traditions displayed in *Iphigenie* and *Tasso.*

It was after Wieland's initial dramatic triumphs that Biberach bid for the return of the native son who had made his name abroad. This return was not as triumphal as he could have wished. He was involved in a ridiculous local political squabble which resulted in his being without pay for the first four years. And he had emotional complications as well.

But near Biberach was the castle where lived the retired Graf Stadion, formerly chief political official of the influential Elector of Mainz, Chancellor of the Empire; and in Schloss Warthausen Wieland experienced his last co-ordinated group of 'influences'. They came to him from contact with the Rococo miniature Court of Stadion, and through free access to an immense library covering the whole of the French literature of the modern period. Sophie von La Roche, his former fiancée, was already there and smoothed his way into this charmed circle. It is curious to note that Wieland remained friendly with Stadion despite the fact that, as a Biberach official, he was engaged in a running legal fight with him of a kind which was usual amongst feudal neighbours. I mention this fact since such anomalies gave him matter for later writings, especially for the political satire, *Die Abderiten.*

The Rococo note now introduced into Wieland's writing arose out of the necessity to show his aristocratic patrons that German served as well as French for literary ends. The German aristocracy could not believe this; as a conscientiously German poet Wieland could not ignore the challenge to his craft. This was the background to all his major works of the period, including, possibly, the Shakespeare translations: both the *Dream* and the *Tempest,* after all, show Shakespeare genuflecting hard in the direction of Elizabeth's Court.[8] But the main original works of this time were the *Komische Erzählungen* and the comic novel *Don Sylvio de Rosalva.*

The *Erzählungen* are the chief reason why Wieland has been called immoral. And indeed they are not nice-minded. The best that can be said of them is that Prior's poems which inspired many of them are much lewder. The well-known love-stories of Classical legend were used throughout the Rococo as a pretext for elegant depiction of near-pornography, whether in the form of poetic tales such as these, or in the form of boudoir-frescoes in pastel shades by Fragonard and Boucher. Wieland thought he carried it off well and *liked* to compare himself with these painters. Need *we* pass by with averted gaze? Have we not become schizophrenic in our approach to the Rococo? We brush aside the *Erzählungen* and even *Oberon*; but we rush to Rococo and Charles II exhibitions and make pious pilgrimages to Versailles, Schwetzingen and Würzburg. Occasionally we may even be heard to murmur: "How graceful. Isn't our modern world boorish by comparison?"

Frankly, the *Erzählungen* are excellent of their kind. Especially when you think that Wieland had no real *German* models for such airy trifles. Since the days of Peter Locher, no one in Germany had really succeeded in doing more with amusement love-poetry than gambolling like an elephant. The whole of contemporary German literature up to that time was, indeed, antipathetic to the internationally-minded German aristocracy, of whom Stadion was a very good specimen. How could such a gentleman appreciate *Simplicissimus*? Even the novels of the Freiherr von Ziegler or Duke Anton Ul-

rich could scarcely be praised for elegance of expression. The language had changed so much, moreover, that the would-be delicacies of the members of the *Fruchtbringende Gesellschaft* were no longer considered contemporary. As so frequently happened in earlier German letters, the backwardness of the national *literary* tradition made men of considerable culture express themselves in a German which seems more suitable for a peasant.

This was most noticeable during the Reformation, in the German writings of the Humanists (even more so in the writing of a self-trained humanist like Niclaus Manuel, who painted in the strict Renaissance manner but wrote an even cruder German than Hans Sachs);[9] it was still evident in the work of Nicodemus Frischlin, the most polished Classical scholar of his day, but a writer of the crudest German; it was still to be felt in the works of bilingual poets like Opitz, Fleming and Gryphius. The standard of literary German was doubtless rising by Wieland's day. But even Klopstock's language is still academic and pastoral. It was Wieland who made, as a jump, the final leap from the fair and the marketplace into the boudoir and the salon.

There remains the charge of smirking indecency, which I have no desire to extenuate. These tales were intended for a narrow audience which regarded itself as standing above bourgeois morality. Indeed the members of all the upper classes in those days *were* above it. Did Wieland, a member, not have in Biberach an illegitimate child by a Catholic girl whom he sincerely loved but who was forbidden *by her parents* to marry him? They preferred (what was obviously not the stigma of) illegitimacy to a mixed marriage. After which it is not surprising to find Sophie fixing up a suitable *mariage de convenance* for her ex-fiancé, a marriage which, incidentally, was thoroughly satisfying and happy for the poet throughout the remainder of his long life. There are, paradoxically, few more model bourgeois households in German Literature than the home of the allegedly immoral Wieland. Do not, however, confuse Wieland's two moralities with the normal run of Rococo 'carpe diem' or 'Küssen und Trinken' type of verse, as practised by solid citizens like Hagedorn and Gessner. Wieland's indecency was *intended* as indecency. His patrons were not jolly Hamburg or Zürich brokers; they were the morally libertine aristocrats of Warthausen and other courts and there is something to be said for a way of life which did not confine innuendo to the billiard-room but treated of it in serious literary vein.

Wieland never let this reading-public out of his sight. Considering the strength of German royalty up to 1918, there would seem to have been little reason why he should. His life was determined by patronage, to a degree which is true neither of Lessing nor Goethe. From

Biberach he was translated by the Archbishop of Mainz, no less, to the Chair of Political Philosophy at His Eminence's Erfurt University. From thence he was invited to become tutor to the two sons of the Dowager Duchess of Weimar. At one time there was even a chance that he might have been invited to Vienna by Josef II.[10]

This may explain immoral overtones *throughout* his work. **Don Sylvio [Don Sylvio de Rosalva]** contains all kinds of vague hints of indecency—its plot tells the story of a young man brought up to believe in the world of the *Märchen* and awakened gradually to reality by a mondaine countess (it was *intended* as an amatory *Don Quixote*). **Musarion,** written a little later than the **Erzählungen,** the most delicate of them all (and the most original), is fairly direct in its lack of bourgeois morality.[11] **Agathon,** Wieland's most popular novel, has passages of outrageous sensuality: one of its main characters is an hetæra of accomplished profligacy. And the novels of Wieland's old age all continued the practice of spicing the philosophy and politics with naughty amusement. It is nasty to us, maybe, but Wieland, for his part, and his patrons would have disapproved of the bluntness of *Fiesta* and *Room at the Top.*

There is one historiographic feature of great importance in our disapproval of the 'immoral' Wieland. Germanistics in the early nineteenth century was closely associated with the political pioneers of Democracy in Germany. The first Germanists came from the ranks of late Romantics and 'Young Germans': there were the Grimm Brothers and Gervinus and the other members of the 'Göttinger Sieben'. Then there were fierce democrats like Hermann Hettner and Rudolf Haym, Ludwig Feuerbach (the friend and teacher of Marx and Keller), Robert Prutz the '48er, Julian Schmidt (Freytag's friend), and David Friedrich Strauss. These worthy liberals and socialists of the *Katheder* thought Aristocracy an evil in itself. Goethe was more than slightly suspect to them for precisely this reason; Schiller's so-called 'revolutionary pathos' was much more to their liking.[12] Hence the relative estimation of the two throughout the nineteenth century.

Now revolutionaries are known to be somewhat deficient in a sense of humour. These German democratic publicists were helpless when faced with irony, as their attitude to Heine displays. We see it too in their failure to appreciate Jean Paul and Raabe. These last only began their rise in esteem with the growth of the art for art's sake movement in criticism. The post-1945 Wieland renaissance is largely the result of work done by German Germanists who are most unlike their nineteenth-century teachers: Martini, Kayser, Sengle, men of the world as well as pedagogues. Perhaps only their generation, battered unmercifully by utter catastrophe, could dare to take up again the attitude of superior amusement which was the basic attitude of the European aristocracy throughout an eighteenth century that they felt was their graveyard. It has been said that Beaumarchais and Mozart never let one forget the flash of the guillotine in the background: Wieland too, for all his surface roseate sensuality, was perhaps the only major writer of the century to understand precisely the scope and meaning of the French Revolution.

One reason for this was the depth of his Classical scholarship.[13] We talk of the Classical period in German Literature, gaily muddling various meanings of the term 'Classical'[14] And one thing which was not frightfully widespread in the German eighteenth century was *good* Classical scholarship. There was plenty of Classical teaching: one of the reasons for the longevity of the genuine tradition in European literature up to the nineteenth century was the fact that the reading public, especially the aristocrats and the upper-middle-class civil servants, were all educated in the Classics. Gone, of course, were the days when the *vir dicendi peritus* had to be a man able to make speeches and draw up treaties and contracts in Latin. But they were not *far* gone, as we know from the jargon of the German universities.

The educated classes shared a common background of Classical reading and Classical mythology. One has only to think of the wealth of Classical allusion that spills over into Dr. Schiller's ballads, to see what was taken for granted in the eighteenth century. As this education became watered down, not least through the necessity to spread it widely amongst ever-dropping social classes, Classical mythology became as much *Märchen* as the Land of Camelot. This is one reason why Wieland gained such a wide and enduring public for his **Oberon,** which made a synthesis of all these elements, its basic plot being the medieval legend-become-*Märchen* of Huon of Bordeaux. The newer reading public already saw the picturesqueness of the Rococo world (Herder and the Romantics developed precisely this cult of the picturesque) and Wieland was perfectly willing to oblige them by creating what one might call a literary 'Gothick ruin'.

Wieland moved throughout the world of Classical mythology with perfect ease precisely because he was a master of Classical scholarship. We know from our personal acquaintance with British secondary education that Classical teaching *fails* to impress a large proportion of its victims! The princely patrons of the eighteenth century knew the old Classical tales but largely as tales, somewhat as the children who hear such stories on the BBC Schools Programme do today. Even the writers were not deeply versed in the Classics. The normal range of Classical allusion is restricted: it was only a lifetime of purposeful reading and friendship with scholars like the Humboldts and F. A. Wolf that provided Goethe with the wealth of scholarship that he was able to display in *Faust II.*

But Wieland had a passion for scholarship, not only Latin but also Greek. In his old age he followed up his translations from Shakespeare and fashionable French authors with admirable German versions of Horace, Aristophanes, Lucian and Cicero.[15] One of the more important influences on his novel-writing was the Hellenistic novelist Heliodorus, whom he imitated in matter as well as manner. This is significant, since Heliodorus was a true epigone, a writer in the period of Classical decay. It is a mark of Wieland's political acumen that he *preferred* plots taken from the fourth century A.D. to the grand themes from the fourth century B.C. Syracuse under Dionysius the Tyrant was an appropriate dress for political moralising directed to the age of 'benevolent despotism'; this is as appropriate a piece of political symbolism as the French Revolutionaries' preference for the period of Roman Republicanism. And indeed Wieland's political consciousness was heightened by his close acquaintance with Classical history.

To us Wieland's actual training in the Classics may seem dilettante. It was not so by eighteenth-century standards. And his literary and political training were expert compared with his training in philosophy, as we would see it. Yet the poet and his century saw nothing strange about his holding such a Chair. The Archbishop chose him deliberately, doubtless at Stadion's prompting, because he wanted to bring new life into a constipated university. And the difficulties Wieland found in Erfurt were shared by a number of his younger colleagues, one of whom, the aesthetician Riedel, was to rise from Erfurt to some eminence in Josephine Vienna. Wieland's university career was made thorny, in fact, not because of lack of scholarship but through his own attempts at innovation, reinforced by common-room envy of success in public life. Indeed he was saved from a public trial on the accusation of corrupting students only by his acceptance of an offer to go to Weimar. As an example of significant continuity we may note that one of the students whom he might have been accused of corrupting at Erfurt was Wilhelm Heinse.

Life in Weimar did not put a stop to Wieland's scholastic interests. He proved a shocking tutor and the Duchess had hastily to engage a real one (this was the worthy Knebel). But Wieland continued to pursue Classical studies, many of his odd undertakings becoming the occasion for articles in his *Teutscher Merkur*. It is interesting too to note that when he finally lost interest in the journal and passed it over for a decade to one of Weimar's high-school professors, he founded yet another 'little magazine', the *Attisches Museum*, into which, as Goethe did with *Kunst und Alterthum*, he poured his scholastic writings, such as, for example, the Cicero translations.

I must now say something about Wieland's journalism, for this, as his contemporaries appreciated, was one of his main claims to be considered a foundation-platform for the Classical Period. An American student of Wieland's influence on British Romantic writers has said that Wieland "was read as eagerly by his rivals as by that growing reading-public which, more than any other, he attracted at home and abroad to German letters".[16] G. P. Gooch adds that Wieland's "cool and observant mind" made his readers look to him for guidance not only in literature and taste but in practical problems of life and politics: "the only political head among the classical writers of Germany . . . unlike Goethe and Schiller, he worked steadily at the formation of opinion".[17] In Goethe's memorial to Wieland, we read: "Die Wirkungen Wielands auf das Publikum waren ununterbrochen und dauernd. Er hat sein Zeitalter sich zugebildet, dem Geschmack seiner Zeitgenossen sowie ihrem Urteil eine entschiedene Richtung gegeben".[18] Finally, in the 1825 conversations with Eckermann, he summarised his influence thus: "Wielanden verdankt das ganze obere Deutschland seinen Stil. Es hat viel von ihm gelernt, und die Fähigkeit, sich gehörig auszudrücken, ist nicht das geringste." John Quincy Adams, finally, is quoted as saying of his stay in Germany round 1800: "Wieland was there, I think, decidedly the most popular of the German poets".

The most deliberate way in which Wieland influenced public opinion was through the editing and publishing of his periodical, *Der Teutsche Merkur*, from 1773 to 1799 (the journal continued, with only sporadic contributions from its ex-editor, until 1810). The first thing to note about the *Merkur* is that it was not just one more 'little magazine'. The eighteenth-century writer considered it almost a point of honour to run his own journal. Thus we have Gottsched's *Vernünftige Tadlerinnen* and its Zürich rival. Lessing made repeated excursions into journalism, especially in collaboration with his Berlin friend Friedrich Nicolai. Goethe and Schiller were constantly founding Classically titled magazines. The tradition continued over the turn of the century: the early Romantics had their *Athenäum*, Kleist his *Phöbus* and *Berliner Abendblätter*.[19]

But what is less appreciated is that most of these were horrifyingly short-lived. Most lasted little more than a few years: some of the most famous never got beyond three issues. Wieland's *Merkur*, however, lasted 30 years and more. The first issue was so popular that it had to be reprinted. And it never looked back: its finances have been investigated and we find that, even when circulation, round 1800, was down to a thousand, Professor Böttiger still found it profitable to keep it going for another decade.

This was not good luck. Wieland realised that earlier journals had been too narrow. With the *Standesdünkel* of the German academic, earlier editors had scared off the reading-public now growing amongst the educated middle classes. It is paradoxical that Wieland, the friend and protégé of aristocrats, should work consciously for the new classes. Is this not a sign of his intelligence? Like his admirer Heine, he was able to live in two worlds at once. He enjoyed life amongst the privileged; but he saw that this world was dying and a new one being born. Heine only made fun of the situation (in the columns of the—even newer—daily press). Wieland set himself to train the new masters, and much more high-mindedly than London's press-lords of the 1880's! As Goethe wrote in his *Annalen*: "das südliche Deutschland, besonders Wien . . . sind ihm ihre poetische und prosaische Kultur schuldig."

I would compare what Wieland did in the *Merkur* with the work of those later nineteenth-century Oxford and Cambridge academics to whom we are so deeply indebted for the WEA and our modern adult education. Indeed, though I personally consider Wieland great both as poet and novelist, I am more *impressed* with the sustained effort that went into the thirty years' life of the *Merkur,* even if it is difficult to pass this respect on to students in the course of lectures on the Classical Period.

For this success was one uphill battle. At the very time the journal was launched, in the early 1770's, Wieland's fame was at a surprisingly low ebb. He had nourished the idea of editing a magazine, possibly right from the time when he did Bodmer's 'ghosting' for him in Zürich. But neither there, nor in Biberach and Erfurt, had he the leisure. Only his sinecure in Weimar allowed him the opportunity to launch this new scheme. The post was poorly enough paid too to inspire him to this attempt, in order to increase the income necessitated by his large and constantly growing family.

But the 1770's was a bad time for him to have started. The Strassburg *Stürmer und Dränger* chose Wieland as the target for virulent attacks on what they considered the Frenchification of German Literature, mud that has stuck. But the *Merkur* survived. In the '80's Wieland rallied a remarkable team of writers to his mast-head, even, on occasion, Goethe. Then came a catastrophe. Sengle has shown how deliberately Wieland was chosen by the first Romantics, at a time when they felt that, as 'angry young men', they needed one specific victim to be angry about. But he carried on. What was more depressing was the official disapproval of the political comment with which he accompanied the French Revolution and, especially, the Coalition Wars: the German princes being on the opposing side could hardly stomach his criticism of their actions. It was, in fact, his growing gloom about the state of the political world which, it seems, finally decided him to give up his editorial chair in 1799.

The format of the *Merkur* was something like that of the *Reader's Digest* (as were most journals of the time) and about the same thickness, from 80 to 100 pages.

Wieland wrote a great deal of this himself, publishing many of his works in instalments (monthly, at times quarterly) in its columns, notably **Oberon.** But he had some faithful contributors, especially J. H. Merck, who wrote lively book-reviews at a time when high-brow books were also front-page news. This kind of opportunistic approach to adult education seems to me entirely legitimate. Later Wieland was to give wide popularisation to Kant's philosophy too. Here he employed his son-in-law, Professor Reinhold of Jena, who had already made a name for himself as an interpreter of modern philosophy to large popular audiences in his university lectures.

A journal aimed at what Wieland himself called "mässige Geister" could not, however, do much of this. There were many features of the kind which fill up our 'quality' Sunday papers—travel letters and articles on popular science. Even these Wieland could write himself: like Heine he was excellent at marrying middlebrow cultural chatter with sharp political comment. It was the acuity of his **Göttergespräche** which called down on him official reproof for too advanced and unpleasant political criticism.[20]

I have not dealt with many sides of Wieland's work. I have barely mentioned the filigree **Oberon,** scarcely the subtle *Agathon,*[21] the first psychological Bildungsroman, and not at all really my own favourite amongst the many novels, **Die Abderiten,** as wickedly pointed a comment on provincial politics today as at the end of the eighteenth century. What I wished to do was to plead the unfairness of our calm acceptance of an unread Wieland as merely having made a minute and entirely history-book contribution to the Classical Period.

I should like to conclude by saying once again that to me Wieland is a real moralist who also succeeds in being a good imaginative writer. *Agathon* seems to me no harder to read today than *Pamela* and a good deal wiser and more elegantly written, **Musarion, Oberon** and some of the Novelle-type poems just as worth constant re-reading as Herrick and Pope. In an age where there is so much in literature calculated merely to darken counsel and spread gloom and Angst, Wieland seems to me a valuable rock to which to cling. And if people will persist in periodic revivals, then let us revive Wieland. It will certainly be most unusual exercise for our risible nerves.

Notes

1. The purpose of this address was to deal with the general position of Wieland in the Classical hierarchy. It was not a summary of my book, which deals with the biography and works in much more detail, under the title *C. M. Wieland. A literary biography.* London, 1961.

2. E.g. in *Die Reformation. Einführung in eine Geistesgeschichte der deutschen Neuzeit.* Frankfurt, 1936.

3. This is a facet of German letters which seems to attract foreigners rather than Germans. Thus Robert Minder has meditated on it in *Das Bild des Pfarrhauses in der deutschen Literatur,* published by the Akademie der Wissenschaften in Mainz, 1960, and his remarks gave rise to an interesting comment, 'Le presbytère protestant dans la littérature allemande', by H. Plard, *EG [Etudes Germaniques]*, XVI (1961), 136.

4. I have studied this in much greater detail in my book. Amongst the sparse material, see especially E. Stilgebauer, 'Wieland als Dramatiker', *Zeitschrift für vergleichende Literaturgeschichte,* N.F., X (1897).

5. See the perceptive remarks by the late Wolfgang Kayser in 'Die Anfänge des modernen Romans im 18. Jh.', *DVLG [Deutsche Vierteljahrsschrift für Literaturwissenschaft und Geistesgeschichte]*, XXVIII (1954), 417-446.

6. My book prints some extracts from *Lady Johanna* which suggest influences.

7. Many important questions touching Wieland's attitude to Shakespeare were studied in Ernst Stadler's one lasting contribution to German studies, *Wielands Shakespeare.* Strassburg, 1910 (*Quellen und Forschungen,* 107). It may be of interest to list here the plays Wieland actually translated. They appeared in eight volumes: I—*Sommernachtstraum, König Lear*—appeared August 1762. II—*Wie es euch gefällt, Mass für Mass, Der Sturm*—finished by October 1762. III—*Der Kaufmann von Venedig, Timon von Athen, König Johann*—finished by autumn 1763. IV—*Julius Cäsar, Antonio und Cleopatra, Komödie der Irrungen*—printed by autumn 1763. V—*Richard II, Heinrich IV,* 1 und 2—finished by June 1763. VI—*Viel Lermen um Nichts, Macbeth, Die zween edlen Veroneser*—finished in mid-1764. VII—*Romeo und Julia, Othello, Was Ihr wollt*—finished by January 1765. VIII—*Hamlet, Das Wintermärchen*—finished by April 1766.

8. As Stadler says: "Wie später die Romantiker nimmt ihn Shakespeares Zauberwelt gefangen" (p. 97). He quotes Addison in the *Spectator,* Nos. 279 and 419, and notes that it was Wieland who introduced the word 'Elfen' from English into German.

9. See my *Renaissance Drama in Germany and Switzerland.* Melbourne and Cambridge, 1961.

10. There is direct flattery of Josef II in *Der goldene Spiegel,* 1772 ed., Book II, pp. 133 ff. Cf. also J.

Scheidl, 'Persönliche Verhältnisse und Beziehung zu den antiken Quellen in *Agathon*', *Studien zur vergleichenden Literaturgeschichte,* IV (1905/6), 389.

11. R. I. Asmus, 'Die Quellen von *Musarion*', *Euph.* [*Euphorion*], V (1898), 267-290.

12. See, on this too much neglected field: H. Kindermann, *Das Goethebild des 20 Jahrhunderts.* Wien, 1953; W. Leppmann, *The German Image of Goethe.* Oxford, 1961; and, above all, Thomas Mann's stimulating thoughts in his Goethe-essay in *Leiden und Grösse der Meister.* Berlin, 1935, and in his *Versuch über Schiller.* Berlin und Frankfurt, 1955. F. Martini makes some comment on this, both in his new *Deutsche Literatur im bürgerlichen Realismus.* Stuttgart, 1962, and in his excellent report on recent research, 'Deutsche Literatur in der Zeit des bürgerlichen Realismus', *DVLG,* XXXIV (1960), 581-666. The only other people to display interest in the actual motives of the nineteenth-century Germanists are the E. German Marxist scholars, as, for example, W. Harich in his introduction to Haym's *Herder.*

13. Some shrewd reflections (and one of the most interesting studies of Wieland *in petto*) in L. Edelstein, 'Wielands *Abderiten* und der deutsche Humanismus', *U. of Cal. Publs. in Mod. Phil.,* XXVI, no. 5 (1950), 441-72.

14. See the excellent article by K. H. Halbach, 'Zu Begriff und Wesen der Klassik' in *Festschrift für P. Kluckhohn und H. Schneider.* Tübingen, 1948, which also contains an illuminating article by Martini on Wieland. The loose talk about 'Classicism' impelled me to preface my Wieland biography with a chapter devoted to clarification of definitions on this subject. One could wish for more critical discussion of this.

15. E. G. Steinberger, *Lucians Einfluss auf Wieland.* Diss., Göttingen, 1902.

16. W. W. Beyer, *Keats and the Demon King.* New York, 1947. This is a study of Keats' use of the faery world and includes interesting notes on Wieland; the English quotations which follow all come from this source.

17. On Wieland as political commentator, see O. Vogt, *Der goldene Spiegel und Wielands politische Ansichten.* Berlin, 1904 (*Forschungen zur neueren Literaturgeschichte,* XXVII). This is a very concise and helpful study.

18. Herder called *Der goldene Spiegel* "ein politisches und Regierungskolloquium für grosse Herren" (quoted by Vogt, *op. cit.,* p. 6).

19. On the question of 'little magazines' see O. Lehmann, *Die moralischen Wochenschriften als päda-*

gogische Reformschriften. Leipzig, 1893. See also in this connection H. Böhnke, *Wielands publizistische Tätigkeit.* Progr., Oldenburg, 1883.

20. I have gone more deeply into the question of Wieland's political views in my biography.

21. On *Agathon* two useful monographs are C. Wildstake, *Wielands Agathon nud der französische Reise- und Bildungsroman.* Diss., Münster, 1933; and B. Schlagenhaft, *Wielands Agathon als Spiegelung seiner Zeit.* Erlangen, 1935.

W. E. Yuill (essay date 1965)

SOURCE: Yuill, W. E. "Abderitis and Abderitism: Some Reflections on a Novel by Wieland." In *Essays in German Literature—I*, edited by Frederick Norman, pp. 72-91. London: University of London, Institute of Germanic Studies, 1965.

[*In the following essay, Yuill offers an in-depth analysis of the major themes of Wieland's novel* Die Geschichte der Abderiten.]

One of the most striking things about the composition of *Die Geschichte der Abderiten* is the hiatus of four years between the publication of the first instalments comprising *Demokritus unter den Abderiten* and *Hippokrates in Abdera* and the continuation of the work with *Euripides unter den Abderiten.*[1] In an introduction to the resumed work the poet himself offers no very cogent explanation of the delay; there is probably a good deal of truth in the conjecture that he had simply lost interest and was prompted to take up his satire again only by certain experiences in Mannheim, where he had gone at the end of 1777 in order to witness the first performance of his *Rosemunde.*[2] Whatever the reasons for the hiatus may be, however, there are—perhaps not surprisingly—distinct differences in mood and pattern between the parts of the novel published in 1774 and the books published successively in 1778, 1779 and 1780. As far as the earlier part of the work is concerned, the description of its genesis which Wieland gives in a preface of 1776 may well be relevant:

> Es war ein schöner Herbstabend; ich war allein in einem Zimmer des obersten Stockwerks meiner Wohnung, und sah vor Langerweile zum Fenster hinaus; denn schon seit vielen Wochen hatte mich mein Genius gänzlich verlassen. Ich konnte weder denken noch lesen; alle meine Laune, alles Feuer meines Geistes schien erloschen; ich war dumm—aber ohne an den Seligkeiten der Dummheit Anteil zu haben, ohne einen Gran von dieser stolzen Zufriedenheit mit sich selbst, dieser unerschütterlichen Überzeugung, dass alles, was der Dummkopf träumt und sagt, witzig, weise und in Marmor gegraben zu werden würdig ist—einer Überzeugung, die den echten Sohn der Göttin Dumm-

> heit wie ein Muttermal kennbar und zum glücklichsten aller Menschen macht. Kurz, ich fühlte meinen Zustand; er lag schwer auf mir; ich schüttelte mich vergebens; und, wie gesagt, ich war dahin gebracht, dass ich zum Fenster hinaus in die Welt guckte, ohne zu wissen, was ich sah, und ohne dass in der Tat etwas Merkwürdiges zu sehen war. Auf einmal war mir, als ob ich eine Stimme hörte, die mir zurief: Setze dich und schreibe die *Geschichte der Abderiten*![3]

Jocular as it is, this circumstantial account, to which Wieland reverts both in his **'Auszug aus einem Schreiben an einen Freund in D . . .'** and in the **'Schlüssel zur Abderiten-Geschichte'**, is unlikely to be merely an example of the 'Autorkokotterie' attributed to the poet by incensed Philistines. It points, in fact, to the inspirational origin of something more than a 'personal and local satire', to the philosophical and 'ideal' nature of this attempt to represent an Abderite character conceived *in abstracto*. The opening episodes of *Die Abderiten* constitute an inspired illustration of certain ideas with which Wieland had been concerned for a number of years. These are ideas involved in the debate then being conducted in England, France and Germany on 'nature', 'man' and the evolution of society. Increasing knowledge of distant continents gave these discussions an anthropological rather than a theological character: in particular, the notion of an Arcadian condition gained new substance and topicality. One consequence of the debate was an interest in primitive communities and their art involving the kind of atavistic views that have sometimes been termed 'Kulturpessimismus'. Wieland's chief theoretical contribution to the discussion is represented by the essays of *Beiträge zur geheimen Geschichte des menschlichen Verstandes und Herzens.*[4] Compared with the practical statecraft of *Der goldne Spiegel,* these essays concern themselves more with actual varieties of rudimentary social organisation and the evolution of culture from its earliest stages. Wieland specifically joins issue with Rousseau and refutes the view of the savage as essentially unsociable. There can be no question for Wieland of man's return to a natural state, for man never ceases to be part of 'nature' in an extended sense; even in his cultured existence nature continues to manifest herself in him. A cultural instinct is part of man's nature:

> Wenn es die Natur ist, die im Feuer leuchtet, im Kristall sechseckig anschiesst, in der Pflanze vegitiert, im Wurme sich einspinnt, in der Biene Wachs und Honig in geometrisch gebaute Zellen sammelt, im Biber mit anscheinender Vorsicht des Zukünftigen Wohnungen von etlichen Stockwerken an Seen und Flüsse baut und in diesen sowohl als vielen andern Tierarten mit einer so zweckmässigen und abgezirkelten Geschicklichkeit wirkt, dass sie den Instinkt zu Kunst in ihnen zu erhöhen scheint: warum sollte es nicht auch die Natur sein, welche in Menschen nach bestimmten und gleichförmigen Gesetzen diese Entwicklung und Ausbildung seiner Fähigkeiten veranstaltet? Dergestalt, dass, sobald er unterlässt in Allem, was er unternimmt, auf ihren

Fingerzeig zu merken; sobald er aus unbehutsamem Vertrauen auf seine Vernunft sich von dem Plan entfernt, den sie ihm vorgezeichnet hat,—von diesem Augenblick an Irrtum und Verderbnis die Strafe ist, welche unmittelbar auf eine solche Abweichung folget.[5]

Departure from nature is not, then, departure from a state of innocence, but deviation from the path of natural evolution—a path which even in man is instinctive rather than rational. Wieland is confident that any people which deviates from this path will ultimately return, as it were, to the natural orbit:

> Das Beste ist, dass dieses Volk so gut als ein Komet, der sich einmal von seiner Sonne verlaufen hat (wofern ihm nicht unterwegs ein ausserordentliches Unglück zustösst), unfehlbar einmal wieder zu ihr zurückkommen wird.[6]

In spite of this rational confidence in the inevitability of progress, Wieland's imagination is still haunted by nostalgic visions of Arcadias in the past. Such visions persist beyond the supernatural 'moralische Unschuldswelten' of his seraphic period and they help to give his work its distinctive rococo colouring. There is hardly a major work in which some miniature Eden does not feature, and the poet's keenest indignation is reserved, as in **"Die Reise des Priesters Abulfauaris"** and *Die Geschichte des weisen Danischmend,* for those who shatter the idyll through cupidity or bigotry.

Wieland sees the process of human development, which he refers to in a striking prefiguration of Romantic imagery as "am Ende doch nur eine unmerklich fortrückende Spirallinie, die Alles ewig dem allgemeinen Mittelpunkt nähert",[7] as "der Kern oder der Zweck oder der Schlüssel von—oder zu allen meinen Werken". He resolves to foster the process "in Scherz und Ernst, in beweisender oder überredender Form".[8] The first two books of *Die Geschichte der Abderiten* might well be regarded as a humorous and illustrative sequel to the polemics of the *Beiträge*. A hint of this may be discovered, perhaps, in the *Vorbericht* to the edition of 1776, where the work is referred to as "einen, wiewohl geringen Beitrag zur Geschichte des menschlichen Verstandes und Herzens".[9] It is certainly true that these first two books of the novel embody ideas and images from the essays.

The Abderites of these books are an amalgam of traditional lore and personal experience. The primary aim is neither historical nor autobiographical: it is rather to illustrate a problem of cultural development that occupies the poet's mind. The Abderite way of life and thought represents a certain disorder, an aberration from the proper evolution of man in society, a psychopathic condition that might be called Abderitis. By an ironical paradox it is the Abderites who look upon Democritus as mad, but this is not an uncommon delusion of the mentally afflicted: "Darin liegt eben ihre Krankheit", says Democritus, "dass sie nicht fühlen, wo es ihnen fehlt".[10]

Abderitis is not characterised by brutishness or lack of intelligence: the Abderite lawyers, for instance, are renowned for their cunning. It consists rather in a discrepancy between the Abderites' actual sensibility and mode of thought, on the one hand, and their cultural potential, on the other. Abderitis is a condition of retarded development, or even of ingrowing instinct: its victims are marked by a naïveté that is out of keeping with their cultural environment. They cling stubbornly to the freedom of innocence, which, as the philosopher Tlantlaquakaptli in **"Koxkox und Kikequetzel"** points out, is neither more nor less than the innocence of early childhood:

> Wer erinnert sich nicht mit Vergnügen der schuldlosen Freuden seines kindischen Alters? Aber wer wollte darum ewig Kind sein? Die Menschen sind nicht dazu gemacht, Kinder zu bleiben . . .[11]

The Abderites, by refusing to accept the adult responsibilities of judgment, persist in an infantile condition. As Democritus tells them, "Eure Körper sind gewachsen, und Eure Seelen liegen noch in der Wiege".[12] And, like all children, they are self-willed:

> 'Ihr habt Euch einen falschen Begriff von Freiheit in den Kopf gesetzt, Eure Kinder von drei oder vier Jahren haben freilich den nämlichen Begriff davon; aber dies macht ihn nicht richtiger. Wir sind ein freies Volk, sagt Ihr; und nun glaubt Ihr, die Vernunft habe Euch nichts einzureden.'[13]

It is perhaps significant for German tradition, and certainly so for Wieland's humanism, that Abderitis is not a moral or specifically a political distemper but an aesthetic one. Abderite society is not so much corrupt as inert, tasteless and self-satisfied. Neither truly naive nor truly cultured, the Abderites dwell in a comfortably stagnant backwater, from which Democritus tries to drag them into the main stream of progress. Like true provincials the Abderites contrive to be both narrow-minded and undiscriminating in aesthetic matters. It is the aim of Democritus to instil in their minds a sense of the problematic and to make them develop a taste beyond the primitive or the purely traditional:

> 'Die Schwarzen an der Goldküste', sagte Demokrit, 'tanzen mit Entzücken zum Getöse eines armseligen Schaffells und etlicher Bleche, die sie gegen einander schlagen. Gebt ihnen noch ein paar Kuhschellen und eine Sackpfeife dazu, so glauben sie im Elysium zu sein. Wie viel Witz brauchte Eure Amme, um Euch, da Ihr noch Kinder waret, durch ihre Erzählungen zu rühren? Das albernste Märchen, in einem kläglichen Tone hergeleiert, war dazu gut genug. Folgt aber daraus, dass die Musik der Schwarzen vortrefflich, oder ein Ammenmärchen gleich ein herrliches Werk ist?'[14]

It is possible to detect here, perhaps, a gentle jibe at a contemporary cult of the primitive; the whole question of expertise and the refinement of taste was, however, apart from any topical reference, something which concerned Wieland throughout his life. It is after all a question which is central to the notion of classicism.

As a foil to the false naïveté of the Abderites the true innocence of the noble savage is embodied in "die gute, kunstlose, sanftherzige Gulleru". It is in her company that the despairing philosopher seeks comfort:

> . . . dein Herz ist rein und aufrichtig und fröhlich und fühlt mit der ganzen Natur. Du denkst nie Arges, sagst nie was Albernes, quälst weder andre noch dich selbst und tust nichts, was du nicht gestehen darfst. Deine Seele ist ohne Falsch, wie dein Gesicht ohne Schminke. Du kennst weder Neid noch Schadenfreude . . . Unbesorgt, ob du gefällst oder nicht gefällst, lebst du, in deine Unschuld eingehüllt, im Frieden mit dir selbst und der ganzen Natur . . .[15]

This 'effusion of the heart' as the author terms it, stands in contrast to the rational arguments which Democritus employs in his dealings with his fellow-citizens. It is, too, a characteristic expression of Wieland's nostalgia for the Arcadian condition and it indicates a certain tension between reason and imagination in the poet.

Although not actually congenital, Abderitis is endemic to the society that Wieland describes; it attacks its victims at an early age and, once established, can hardly be eradicated—even the refinements of an Athenian education simply turn an Abderite 'Bengel' into an Abderite 'Geck'. Apart from Democritus, who escaped the contagion by seclusion in his youth and extensive travel in early manhood, we only once encounter a native Abderite who has not contracted the disease—Nannion, "eine junge Abderitin von vierzehn Jahren", of whom it is said that "sie hatte eine sanfte Gesichtsbildung und Seele in den Augen". Democritus pities her:

> Schade für dich, dass du eine Abderitin bist! dacht' er. Was sollte dir in Abdera eine empfindsame Seele? Sie würde dich nur unglücklich machen. Doch es hat keine Gefahr! Was die Erziehung deiner Mutter und Grossmutter an dir unverdorben gelassen hat, werden die Söhnchen unsrer Archonten und Ratsherren zu Grunde richten. In weniger als vier Jahren wirst du eine Abderitin sein wie die andern.[16]

In his more sombre moments Democritus concludes that the Abderitic disease could be eradicated only by a 'tidy pestilence' which spared none but a handful of children old enough to dispense with parents or nurses.[17] This reflection is a distinct reminiscence of **"Koxkox und Kikequetzel"** and of the anthropological experiment suggested in the essay **"Über die von J. J. Rousseau vorgeschlagenen Versuche, den wahren Stand der Natur des Menschen zu entdecken."**[18]

One of the principal symptoms of Abderitis is a febrile condition of the imagination; it is this, above all, which leads the Abderites into positively foolish actions:

> . . . denn ihre Einbildung gewann einen so grossen Vorsprung über ihre Vernunft, dass es dieser niemals wieder möglich war, sie einzuholen. Es mangelte den Abderiten nie an Einfällen; aber selten passten ihre Einfälle auf die Gelegenheit, wo sie angebracht wurden, oder kamen erst, wenn die Gelegenheit vorbei war . . . Machten sie (welches sich ziemlich oft zutrug) irgend einen sehr dummen Streich, so kam es immer daher, weil sie es gar zu gut machen wollten . . .[19]

Although it is very active, the Abderitic imagination is of a particularly unsophisticated kind. It is, for instance, egocentric: the Abderites can visualise no canon of beauty other than their own—a black Venus is beyond their comprehension. Nor has their imagination any rational component: it is sensual and conative, conjuring up pictures of erotic delights or the pleasures of the table. It is perhaps significant that Abderites relapse readily into hallucinations of the Arcadian state which they are so reluctant to outgrow. The description of Ethiopia given by Democritus throws Lysandra into a voluptuous trance:

> . . . die schöne Juno sank mit dem Kopf auf ein Polster des Canapees zurück, schloss ihre grossen Augen halb und befand sich unvermerkt am blumigen Rand einer dieser schönen Quellen, von Rosen- und Citronenbäumen umschattet, aus deren Zweigen Wolken von ambrosischen Düften auf sie herabwallten. In einer sanften Betäubung von süssen Empfindungen begann sie eben einzuschlummern, als sie einen Jüngling, schön wie Bacchus und dringend wie Amor, zu ihren Füssen liegen sah. Sie richtete sich auf, ihn desto besser betrachten zu können, und sah ihn so schön, so zärtlich, dass die Worte, womit sie seine Verwegenheit bestrafen wollte, auf ihren Lippen erstarben.[20]

In this rococo vignette it is possible, perhaps, to detect an element of self-parody.

Even Abderite philosophers and moralists are afflicted by hypertrophy of the imagination: their cosmogonies are purely fantastic, and, what is of more consequence, their view of morality and happiness is determined by Arcadian visions. In his essay, **"Ob ungehemmte Ausbildung der menschlichen Gattung nachteilig sei?,"**[21] Wieland had deplored the enervating or frustrating effect on men of such visions or memories. Even Plato is not immune from the kind of idealised materialism represented by such legends or metaphors: his ideal condition is one of supreme physical well-being. In the novel Democritus denounces 'Schlaraffenland' as a goal of moral endeavour:

> . . . ein Land, wie Ihre Moralisten den ganzen Erdboden haben wollen, ist entweder ein Land, wo die Leute keinen Magen haben und keinen Unterleib, oder es muss schlechterdings das Land sein, das uns Telek-

lides schildert . . . Vollkommene Gleichheit, vollkommene Zufriedenheit mit dem Gegenwärtigen, immerwährende Eintracht—sind nur in dem Lande möglich, wo einem die Rebhühner gebraten in den Mund fliegen, oder (welches ungefähr ebenso viel sagen will) wo man keine Bedürfnisse hat . . . Gleichwohl ärgern sich Ihre Moralisten darüber, dass die Welt so ist, wie sie ist.[22]

The demands of idealistic moralists constitute part of the Abderitic false notion of freedom: they fail to take account of the fact that man is a part of nature and free only within her limits:

(Die Moralisten sollten) die Natur erst ein wenig kennen lernen, ehe sie sich einfallen lassen, es besser zu wissen als sie . . . und nicht verlangen, dass wir die Spitze eines Berges erreicht haben sollen, ehe wir hinaufgestiegen sind . . . so unsinnig sind neun Zehntel der Gesetzgeber, Projectmacher, Schulmeister und Weltverbesserer auf dem ganzen Erdenrund alle Tage![23]

The vehement denunciation of unrealistic moral standards—of *Schwärmerei*—is entirely characteristic of Wieland's mature common sense and humanism. It no doubt owes something of its vehemence to a memory of the youthful zeal which led him to describe the kind of moral Cloud-Cuckoo-Land that is to be found, for instance, in **"Gesicht von einer Welt unschuldiger Menschen."**[24]

It is by his acceptance of a natural order, by his interest in its detail and above all by his awareness that man forms part of this order that Wieland's Democritus differs essentially from his fellow-citizens. He is not a speculative philosopher but an empiricist, a 'Greek Bacon', with a characteristic interest in men and manners. To the Abderites he seems a necromancer, and this is the reputation that the historical figure often acquired in later ages. Wieland is concerned to discredit such legends: his Democritus is not a Faust, either in the traditional, or even in the Goethean mould. He believes, it is true, in the unremitting pursuit of knowledge, but he is also content to recognise limits set by nature: he is the ideal man of the Enlightenment, a Lessing rather than a Goethe. All the same, Democritus does embody a problem and he suffers an inner conflict that is at times desperate. His despair is not despair over the futility of reason or of human knowledge but despair of communicating his method of enquiry and the truths which he has discovered. Well-disposed as he is to his fellow-citizens, Democritus is frustrated in his efforts to enlighten them:

Allein, da man den Leuten nur insofern Gutes tun kann, als sie dessen fähig sind, so fand er sein Vermögen durch die unzähligen Hindernisse, die ihm die Abderiten entgegensetzten, in so enge Grenzen eingeschlossen, dass er Ursache zu haben glaubte, sich für eine der entbehrlichsten Personen in dieser kleinen Republik anzusehen. Was sie am nötigsten haben, dacht' er, und das Beste, was ich an ihnen tun könnte, wäre, sie ver-

nünftig zu machen. Aber die Abderiten sind freie Leute. Wenn sie nicht vernünftig sein wollen, wer kann sie nötigen.[25]

As tutor and administrator Wieland no doubt experienced this dilemma himself. And just as Wieland was often torn between his professional or journalistic duties and his poetic vocation, so Democritus is torn between his self-imposed obligations towards the Abderites and his duty to the order of cosmopolitans. In the end the frustrated philosopher retires to cultivate his garden, just as Wieland would retire to his 'Gartenhäuschen' outside Biberach or to his 'Osmantinum' near Weimar. Democritus becomes one of the hermit figures that feature so commonly in Wieland's tales. The final solution turns out to be after all the rather pessimistic ideal of an Arcadia for one:

Da er nun bei so bewandten Umständen wenig oder nichts für die Abderiten tun konnte, so hielt er sich für hinlänglich gerechtfertigt, wenn er wenigstens seine eigne Person in Sicherheit zu bringen suchte und einen so grossen Teil als immer möglich von derjenigen Zeit rettete, die er der Erfüllung seiner weltbürgerlichen Pflichten schuldig zu sein meinte.[26]

Democritus is in many ways a paragon, but, as an odd man out among these odd men in, he embodies doubts and frustrations felt by his creator. After all, he is in a minority of one. The Abderites may be fools, but in their own community they are the norm. They may be full of prejudice and superstition, but it is they, not the cosmopolitans, who are happy and self-satisfied. Abderitis is not a painful condition: on the contrary, its mark is euphoria, or *Hedypathie,* as Wieland calls it. It is little wonder that the doubts and misgivings of the poet, reflected in Democritus, make of the latter rather less than an urbane gentleman. When he returns from his travels, Democritus is "ein feiner, stattlicher Mann, höflich und abgeschliffen", but association with the Abderites soon drives him into an ironic defensive pose, and often into downright bad temper. There is bitter irony indeed in the way in which Wieland perverts the legend of the 'laughing philosopher': the man who uses laughter to provoke shameful incontinence on the part of the Abderite women is no Shaftesbury—nor, for that matter, is the poet who could invent such an episode.

Democritus is the organ of the author in the first two books of the novel. It is his voice which sustains the argument against a chorus of Abderites in the dialogue form that is so characteristic of Wieland. The philosopher represents, in effect, a standard by which the aberration of the Abderites is measured. When Wieland took up his 'curious history' again after an interval of four years he seems to have been prompted more by personal experience than by a general perplexity about the condition of man in society. Superficially at least the pattern of the earlier books—the wise man among fools—is preserved: ***Demokritus unter den Abderiten, Hippokrates in Abdera,*** now ***Euripides unter den Abderiten.*** The temper has changed, however. In the third book it is Euripides rather than Democritus who seems to speak with the author's voice, and Euripides is not the scold that Democritus so often is. He is amused rather than exasperated by his hosts:

> Euripides war in seinem Leben nie bei so guter Laune gewesen als bei diesem Abderitenschmause.[27]

Democritus fades from the work: he plays a minor part in the third book, and in Book 4 he features only in a brief epilogue, where he takes his leave with a comment that is positively benign:

> Diese Ähnlichkeit mit den Athenern muss man den Abderiten wenigstens eingestehen, dass sie recht treuherzig über ihre eignen Narrenstreiche lachen können. Sie werden zwar nicht weiser darum, aber es ist immer schon viel gewonnen, wenn ein Volk leiden kann, dass ehrliche Leute sich über seine Torheiten lustig machen, und mitlacht, anstatt wie die Affen tückisch darüber zu werden.[28]

From the third book onwards Wieland's novel is perceptibly more urbane; the poet is no longer diagnosing an Abderitic condition primarily by reference to another standard. He sets out instead to describe good-humouredly a pattern of behaviour that is so consistent as to have an ideal character. What he is describing now is not Abderitis but Abderitism. The change in conception and mood is particularly noticeable in the last two books, where, as the titles indicate, it is events and behaviour rather than the clash of outlooks that occupy the central place. In the later parts of the novel the Abderites are no longer just grotesque 'Zerrbilder'. They represent, rather, a kind of negative ideal. Possibly with an ironic reminiscence of his own earlier Platonism, Wieland seems to adopt here what might be described as aesthetic Manichaeism. Folly is seen not as a pathological condition, a deficiency, or a failure to reach a norm, but as a pattern of thought and action that gives the urbane 'cosmopolitan' aesthetic pleasure because of its coherence. In short, the Abderites are not simply fools—they are perfect fools:

> Die Dummheit hat ihr Sublimes so gut als der Verstand, und wer darin bis zum Absurden gehen kann, hat das Erhabene in dieser Art erreicht, welches für gescheite Leute immer eine Quelle von Vergnügen ist. Die Abderiten hatten das Glück, im Besitz dieser Vollkommenheit zu sein. Ihre Ungereimtheit machte einen Fremden anfangs wohl zuweilen ungeduldig; aber sobald man sah, dass sie so ganz aus *einem* Stücke war und (eben darum) so viel Zuversicht und Gutmütigkeit in sich hatte, so versöhnte man sich gleich wieder mit ihnen und belustigte sich oft besser an ihrer Albernheit als an andrer Leute Witz.[29]

The tone is clearly ironical. Wieland cannot regard stupidity as an ideal in the sense of something to be aimed at. This passage, amongst others, nevertheless indicates a significant change of attitude on the part of the author in that he now seems able to contemplate human folly with much greater equanimity. The more mellow temper cannot be the result of less intimate involvement in Abderite affairs; on the contrary, it was probably Wieland's experience with the Nationaltheater in Mannheim that prompted him to resume the work in 1778. It may well be precisely such first-hand experience that gives the third book greater coherence and verve than the alternately anecdotal and discursive opening chapters.

The later parts of the novel contain much evidence of sympathy with the Abderites. They are never again guilty of such dastardly behaviour as the plot by Thrasyllus to have his relative, Democritus, declared insane. In one respect at least the Abderites of Book 3 are the exact opposites of those in Book 1: whereas Democritus pitied Nannion for her sensitive soul, the Abderites of Book 3 are shown as responding in the liveliest manner to the *Andromeda* of Euripides. Their volatile sentiment is adduced, in fact, as evidence of their essential humanity:

> . . . und wem eine so grosse Empfindsamkeit an Abderiten befremdlich vorkommt, den ersuchen wir höflichst zu bedenken, dass sie bei aller ihrer Abderiteit am Ende doch Menschen waren wie andre; ja, in gewissem Sinne, nur desto mehr Menschen—je mehr sie Abderiten waren.[30]

In a long digression Wieland praises the naive response of the Abderites to art and deplores the unwelcome sophistication of so-called connoisseurs, remarking:

> . . . die grosse Disposition der Abderiten, sich von den Künsten der Einbildungskraft und der Nachahmung täuschen zu lassen, sei eben nicht das, was er [der Verfasser dieser Geschichte] am wenigsten an ihnen liebe.[31]

It is with a show of indignation that Wieland defends the Abderites against the scandalous account of their city given by Laurence Sterne in his *Sentimental Journey.*

Apart from evidences of greater urbanity and tolerance, the literary character of the novel appears to change from the third book onwards. A more coherent action and the elaboration of detailed character types—Agathyrsus, Strobylus, Pfriem, Salabanda, Stilbon, Korax—reinforce the impression of an autonomous pattern of behaviour. The irony is more delicate and there is not the impression of strenuous argumentation that marks the first two books. The poet has somehow emancipated himself from perplexity and exasperation by creating his 'ideal' of Abderite behaviour.

It is with the later books that the novel emerges most clearly as a product of 'wit' in the exact sense of that which "lies most in the assemblage of ideas and puts them together with quickness and variety, wherein can be found any resemblance or congruity, thereby to make up pleasant pictures and agreeable visions in the fancy"[32] or, in Adelung's definition of 'Witz', "das Vermögen der Seele, Ähnlichkeiten, und besonders verborgene Ähnlichkeiten, zu entdecken". In Wieland's poetical works, generally speaking, fantasy provides the fundamental impulse; wit is employed principally as an ornament. *Die Geschichte der Abderiten* is possibly the only one of his major works which is essentially witty in its conception. Here, wit is the soul of satire. It is wit that enables Wieland to perceive and represent with such finesse the affinities between life in a Greek city-state and life in the miniature republics of Germany, to link what he found in Aristophanes and Lucian with the pretensions and the spirit of emulation that he observed in German provincial life. It is wit that enables him to blend personal experience with legends and anecdotes from Classical sources. The Greek setting is not simply camouflage; it is itself involved in the satire, since it was one of the poet's aims to counter the modish admiration of the Greek 'ideal'. The negative ideal of Abderitism is an antidote to Winckelmania.[33] The ambition to foster a more discriminating view of Greek culture is borne out by certain of Wieland's essays, particularly **'Gedanken über die Ideale der Alten'** and **'Auch die Griechen hatten ihre Teniers und Ostaden'**, both published during 1777 in *Der Teutsche Merkur*.

It is in the fourth book, *Der Prozess um des Esels Schatten,* that the satire is most complex and the 'ideal' nature of the novel best epitomised. Here, above all, there is the essentially witty blend of traditional lore and personal experience, antiquity and topicality. But the tale of the donkey's shadow not only fuses these elements; it transcends them to form the most perfect account of Abderitism as a philosophy and a way of life. It has been frequently pointed out that *Der Prozess um des Esels Schatten* probably incorporates real personalities and incidents, but if it does, these are totally assimilated. Before we seek to isolate elements of personal experience we should perhaps heed what the poet says in the bogus 'key' to his work:

> . . . verständige Leute fühlten und erkannten den Geist, der in diesem Leibe webte, und liessen sich's nicht einfallen, scheiden zu wollen, was die Muse untrennbar zusammengefügt hatte . . .[34]

The great merit of the tale lies in its totally convincing account of the dynamic of communal behaviour. In the donkey's shadow—borrowed from something as rudimentary as a Greek idiom[35]—the author has lighted on a superb emblem of vain ideological dispute, and he makes characteristic use of it in puns. But shadowy as the pretext may be, the motives of the people involved are substantial enough. Individuals and groups are drawn into the vortex of the dispute by different but converging impulses and interests—the sycophants by hope of gain, Agathyrsus by sensuality and pride, Strobylus by envy, Salabanda by jealousy and spite, Pfriem by considerations of city politics, individual senators by an urge to conform or oppose, the mob by ignorance, venality and a general contentiousness. Once the process has begun, the original parties are almost forgotten and men are committed by their reason to a dialectic of unreason. The only escape is by the path of common sense, and nothing but the sovereign will and authority of Agathyrsus can force others to take this path and save them from themselves. The energy generated must be dissipated, however; there must be a scape-goat, and this is provided by the innocent donkey. Wieland's contemporaries may have been less disturbed by the animal's dreadful end than a modern reader is liable to be; they may even have joined in the 'inextinguishable laughter', but they can hardly have failed to recognise an ugly psychological truth in this violent scene, and some of them may even have remembered it when the French Revolution broke out just ten years later. Few German writers have shown such acute political insight as Wieland does in the apparently farcical incident of the donkey's shadow.

It is indeed only at first sight that the idea of a community being brought to the verge of civil war by such a dispute seems farcical or grotesque. When we reflect on the hair-raising, hair-splitting arguments that have been conducted from time to time on the highways to Berlin, then the tale of the donkey's shadow seems topical and plausible enough. It may appear improbable that the Abderites, in the fifth book, ignore the Korax report and allow themselves to be driven from their city by a plague of frogs; it seems less improbable if we substitute motor-cars for frogs. The fact is that Wieland's Abdera—especially as described in the later books of the novel—is everywhere and always—"und wir sind gewissermassen alle da zu Hause".[36] The Abderites are an immortal race, for Abderitism is an ideal—not a transcendental ideal of the Platonic kind, but an ideal deduced from the manifold of experience. It is true that in the later chapters of the novel a number of distinct figures emerge, but Agathyrsus, Strobylus, Salabanda, Pfriem and the others do not strike us as individuals— they are types carefully delineated. We have, for instance, little indication of their physical presence or gestures. At points we hear voices that are richly characteristic, but for the rest we are instructed as to their nature and motives by the narrator, who appeals explicitly to our own experience. These figures are 'ideals' belonging to what Wieland in his essay **"Über die Ideale der Alten"** calls the fourth category of artistic ideal—not the expression of some mystic inner vision, nor versions of an abstract canon, not even sublimated portraits of an individual, but composite empirical figures: "symmetrische Zusammensetzungen aus verschiedenen Modellen zu einem homogenen Ganzen zusammengeschmelzt".[37] This is surely the kind of ideal that is naturally adapted to narrative literature, an art that cannot make its impact direct upon the senses but depends for its response on the reader's imagination, and hence to a large extent on his experience. In striking this precise level of abstraction Wieland not only demonstrates his tact as a writer, but possibly also reveals an aspect of what is called classicism.

In the latter parts of the novel, and particularly in the superb fourth book, one has the impression that the scope of the satire is broadening, that it is no longer aimed simply at provincial *mores* but that we are indeed dealing with "eine idealisierte Composition der Albernheiten und Narrheiten des ganzen Menschengeschlechts". In the end it begins to seem that Abderitism is not even abnormal, that, as the poet says, "the more the Abderites are Abderites, the more they are men". That being so, their history is unlikely ever to lose its relevance for later generations—a fact that Wieland ironically hints at in parting words that are as benevolent as the parting words of Democritus himself:

> Und hiermit sei denn der Gipfel auf das Denkmal gesetzt, welches wir dieser einst so berühmten und nun schon so viele Jahrhunderte lang wieder vergessenen Republik zu errichten ohne Zweifel von einem für ihren Ruhm sorgenden Dämon angetrieben worden, nicht ohne Hoffnung, dass es, ungeachtet es aus so leichten Materialien, als die seltsamen Launen und jovialischen Narrheiten der Abderiten zusammengesetzt ist, so lange dauern werde, bis unsre Nation den glücklichen Zeitpunkt erreicht haben wird, wo diese Geschichte niemand mehr angehen, niemand mehr aufgeräumt machen wird; mit *einem* Worte, wo die Abderiten niemand mehr ähnlich sehen, und also ihre Begebenheiten ebenso unverständlich sein werden, als uns Geschichten aus einem anderen Planeten sein würden . . .[38]

Notes

1. The episodes which make up Books 1 and 2 of the completed novel were published in various issues of *Der Teutsche Merkur* during 1774 as Part I, along with a first chapter of a projected Part II. All of this, incomplete as it was, then appeared in book form in 1776 as *Die Abderiten, eine sehr wahrscheinliche Geschichte von Herrn Hofrath Wieland.* It was not until 1778 that the work was continued, again in *Der Teutsche Merkur,* with *Euripides unter den Abderiten* (Book 3 of the final form), the previous initial chapter of the projected Part II being scrapped. *Der Prozess um des Esels Schatten,* described as *Ein Anhang zur Geschichte der Abderiten,* appeared in the *Merkur* during 1779, and the work was brought to a rather hurried close in 1780 with *Die Frösche der Latona.* The complete novel was issued in two volumes by Weidmanns Erben und Reich, Leipzig, 1781.

2. For an account of this episode see B. Seuffert, *Wielands Abderiten,* Berlin 1878, p. 15 ff., and E.

Hermann: 'Wielands Abderiten und die Mannheimer Theaterverhältnisse', *Die Grenzboten,* xxxix (1880), 4, pp. 462-473.

3. *Gesammelte Schriften,* Berlin 1913 (Akademie-Ausgabe), Abt. I, Bd. 10, p. 3. Subsequent quotations are not from this (still incomplete) edition but from *Wielands Werke,* Berlin (Hempel), n.d., in 40 vols.

4. These comprise the following: 'Koxkox und Kikequetzel, eine mexicanische Geschichte'; 'Betrachtungen über J. J. Rousseaus ursprünglichen Zustand des Menschen'; 'Über die von J. J. Rousseau vorgeschlagenen Versuche, den wahren Stand der Natur des Menschen zu entdecken'; 'Über die Behauptung, dass ungehemmte Ausbildung der menschlichen Gattung nachteilig sei'; 'Reise des Priesters Abulfauaris ins innere Afrika'; 'Bekenntnisse des Abulfauaris'. These essays—not as yet under the titles given—were published anonymously in two parts, Leipzig 1770. When they were incorporated in the 'Ausgabe letzter Hand' Wieland added the essay, 'Über die vorgebliche Abnahme des menschlichen Geschlechts' from *Der Teutsche Merkur* (1777) to the first four of the above items and gave this collection the title of *Beiträge zur geheimen Geschichte der Menschheit.*

Apart from the literary cult of the noble savage as described by H. N. Fairchild in *The Noble Savage,* New York, 1928, there was in the 18th century a growing scientific or quasi-scientific interest in primitive men, societies and manners. Not only Rousseau and the French Encyclopédistes but writers like J. H. S. Formey, Charles Marie de la Condaminé, James Burnet (Lord Monboddo) and, of course, Herder concerned themselves with the origins of society and language. A characteristic theme is that of the 'wild boy' or, as in the case of the celebrated Marie Angélique Memmie le Blanc, the 'wild girl'. Speculation and enquiry were stimulated, too, and nourished by the numerous accounts of voyages and travels. Wieland shows a fair familiarity with these, referring to writers like the Dominican missionary Jean-Baptiste Labat, the explorers Jean Barbot and Amédée-François Frézier as well as Andrew Battel, Francis Moore of the Royal African Company and naval explorers like Commodore John Byron and Captain Samuel Wallis.

5. *Werke* (Hempel), xxxi, 36.

6. *Werke,* xxxi, 144.

7. *Werke,* xxxi, 171.

8. *Werke,* xxxi, 94.

9. *Werke,* vii, 9.

10. *Werke,* vii, 107.

11. *Werke,* xxxi, 64.

12. *Werke,* vii, 49.

13. Ibid.

14. *Werke,* vii, 46.

15. *Werke,* vii, 38.

16. *Werke,* vii, 76.

17. *Werke,* vii, 53.

18. Cf. *Werke,* xxxi, 97 ff.

19. *Werke,* vii, 14.

20. *Werke,* vii, 28.

21. *Werke,* xxxi, 127 ff.

22. *Werke,* vii, 60.

23. Ibid.

24. A fragment composed in 1755; cf. *Werke,* xxxix, 615 ff.

25. *Werke,* vii, 68.

26. Ibid.

27. *Werke,* vii, 151.

28. *Werke,* viii, 84.

29. *Werke,* vii, 150.

30. *Werke,* vii, 165 f.

31. *Werke,* vii, 166.

32. John Locke, *Essay concerning human understanding,* chap. 11, para. 2.

33. For a brief review of Wieland's changing attitude to Winckelmann, see W. H. Clark, 'Wieland and Winckelmann: Saul and the Prophets', *Modern Language Quarterly,* xvii (1956), pp. 1-16, and id., 'Wieland contra Winckelmann?', *Germanic Review,* xxxiv (1959), pp. 4-13.

34. *Werke,* viii, 141.

35. περὶ ὄνου σκιᾶς = 'about a donkey's shadow', used in the kind of contexts where English would speak of 'a storm in a tea-cup'. The phrase occurs, for instance, with reference to a law-suit in *The Wasps* of Aristophanes (l. 191).

36. *Werke,* xxxviii, 634.

37. *Werke,* xxxvii, 438.

38. *Werke,* viii, 137.

Charlotte Craig (essay date May 1968)

SOURCE: Craig, Charlotte. "From Folk Legend to Travesty: An Example of Wieland's Artistic Adaptations." *German Quarterly* 41, no. 3 (May 1968): 369-76.

[*In the following essay, Craig examines the influence of folk legends on Wieland's verse narratives. In Craig's*

reading, Wieland imbues his adaptations of popular fables with a distinctly Enlightenment sensibility.]

Christoph Martin Wieland's dependence upon models for his literary creations is a well-established fact. While he displayed notable affinity to themes from antiquity, to the Arthurian cycle, to French, to Oriental, and to other foreign sources which, by their nature, might be considered "legendary," he seemed to be indifferent to the stock of German *Sagen.* The folk legend was not Wieland's métier; his travesties, on the other hand, are styled with a degree of refinement which earned him the reputation of a prominent pioneer and one of the foremost exponents of the modern travesty in German literature. In view of Wieland's taste and his penchant for *Ausländerei,* it is amazing that he would make a naïve German folk legend of the Eisenach area the object of one of his travesties.

In his **"Der Mönch und die Nonne auf dem Mittelstein"** (1775),[1] Wieland's *Einkleidungskunst* achieves a triumph through the artistic metamorphosis of a crude folk legend to a charming poem which seems to deride, as it were, the banality of its model.

In the prose preface to **"Der Mönch und die Nonne auf dem Mittelstein: Ein Gedicht in drey Gesängen,"** Wieland acquaints the reader with the legendary nature, the setting, and the source of his poem. With slight sarcasm, he goes on record as defending the mutation which he has brought about and which, in his opinion, needs no justification. The following comment refers the reader to the source of the plot itself:

> Neben der berühmten Wartburg stund vorzeiten auf einem hohen Berg eine Burg, die (nach einigen Chronicken) schon in der Mitte des fünften Jahrhunderts von einem von Frankenstein erbaut, 700 Jahre drauf von der Herzogin Sophia von Brabant, während ihrer Händel mit dem Marggr. von Meissen, Heinrich dem Erlauchten, wieder aus den Ruinen gezogen worden, nun aber nur noch wenige Spuren ihres ehmaligen Daseyns aufzuweisen hat. Diese Burg hieß der Mittelstein, woraus der Nahme Mädelstein entstanden, den der Berg noch heutiges Tages in der Gegend führt. Auf diesem Mittelstein oder Mädelstein ragen zween ziemlich hohe Steine hervor, die von ferne, und in so fern die Einbildungskraft das Ihrige beyträgt, wie zwoo sich umarmende menschliche Figuren aussehen. Das gemeine Volk glaubte vorzeiten (und glaubt vielleicht noch) diese zween Steine seyen ein Mönch und eine Nonne gewesen, die aus wechselseitiger Liebe dem Kloster entsprungen und sich auf diesen Berg geflüchtet, daselbst aber zur Strafe ihres Verbrechens und andern ihres gleichen zum abscheulichen Exempel, in dem Augenblick, da sie sich umarmen und küssen wollen, in Stein verwandelt worden. Diese zu einer althergebrachten Sage gewordene Fabel konnte vielleicht zu nichts Bessern nutzen, als da sie die Entstehung des gegenwärtigen Gedichtes veranlaßt hat. Aus einem solchen Mährchen kann ein Dichter machen was er

will; er ist weder an Zeitrechnung, noch an Costume gebunden; die damit vorgenommene Veränderungen bedürfen also keiner Rechtfertigung. Von der Fabel selbst aber kann, wer Lust hat, in Limperts lebenden und schwebenden Eisenach das Mehrere lesen.

(***T.M.** [**Der teutsche Merkur**], III, 193-194)*

Gotthold Klee theorizes that the legend which has since become perpetuated in the region of Eisenach was not popularly known at the time Wieland fashioned his verse narrative. The poet, then, did not draw upon "living tradition."[2] Wieland's inaccurate bibliographical reference to the Limpert source, and a spelling or printing error in the alleged author's name—an error which persists through every existing Wieland edition—has long obscured the true identity of the work and its originator. Actually it was one Johann Limberg who included this legend among those collected in his volume entitled *Das im Jahr 1708. lebende und schwebende Eisenach* (1712).[3] Klee further reports that according to A. Oesterheld, onetime head librarian of the Eisenach library, the precursor to the Limberg source was *Das im Jahr 1708 lebende und schwebende Eisenach,* by Johann von Bergenelsen, a Swede, printed in Stralsund in 1709, most of the copies of which were sent to Eisenach and made available there at Wilhelmi's bookbindery.[4]

Johannes Limberg (exact dates unknown), is reported to have led an adventurous existence as a student, soldier, teacher, and cleric. Among Limberg's more notable publications are his *Denkwürdige Reisebeschreibungen durch Deutschland, Italien, Spanien, Portugal, England, und Schweiz* (1690).[5] Originally a Minorite Master of Novices, he converted to Protestantism in 1689—a circumstance which may account for his selection of the monastic topic and his slighting tone in the episode about to be examined.

Das im Jahr 1708. lebende und schwebende Eisenach is an anthology of multifarious local-color accounts rather than a systematic chronicle, incorporating descriptive as well as semi-statistical prose concerning the city of Eisenach and its environment. Following an elaborate dedication to Wilhelm-Henrich [sic], Hereditary Prince of Saxony, and Prince Carl August of Saxony, Limberg justifies his current opus through a reference to the learned English chancellor and historian, Verulamius, who in a treatise had encouraged the recording of noteworthy events not only at courts of nobles but also in less exalted strata. While Limberg's effort emulates the intention of his erudite example, his stylistic means are inadequate: The presentation suffers from limited vocabulary, faulty punctuation, indeed from lack of clarity or continuity. There is evidence of sententiousness, of objectionable taste—in short, crudity.

The account which served Wieland as a model is simply entitled *Der Mittelstein* (Limberg, pp. 273-278). The author frames his story with an *Ich*-experience:

while he is sight-seeing in the area, the castellan points out to him the Mittelstein, so called because of its medial location among five regions—Thuringia, Franconia, Buchen, Hesse, and the Eichsfeld. This elevation had formerly been the site of Herr von Franckenstein's castle, built in 455. Sufficiently intrigued by the legend surrounding the hill, the narrator undertakes to climb it. Having appraised the hilltop as a piece of real estate of doubtful value, he begins to relate the legend: "Von diesem Berge erzehlet man gar artige Sachen / wie nemlich einsmahls ein Münch eine Nonne lange Zeit caressirt / sie zu seinem Willen zu bringen / wirfft ihr in der Kirchen offters viel tausend blinde Küsse zu / (wie solches auch noch heutiges Tages Münch und Nonne im Gebrauch haben)" (Limberg, p. 275). Limberg treats it as a matter of common knowledge that questionable mores still persist in the monastic establishments of his time. Beyond that, he is grossly unkind in his portrayal of the young monk and nun who were punished for their "perfidy" through instant petrifaction. The narrative lacks subtlety of touch and development. The lascivious monk ". . . redet sie [die Nonne] mit gar süssen Worten an / kan sie aber zu seinen Willen nicht bringen sondern sagt / wenn ich das thue / mögen wir beyde wohl zu Steinen werden" (Limberg, p. 275). There is no indication of the time span involved in the unfortunate courtship. Crudely, it is a tangible object—a bottle of rare wine—that provides the stimulus for the nun to meet the monk on the mountain: ". . . da läst sie sich überreden / und gehen miteinander auf diesen Berg / und küssen einander so lange / daß die Mäuler an einander gewachsen . . ." (Limberg, p. 275). Limberg continues indulging in descriptive metaphor of doubtful taste, and goes out of his way to involve other members of the monastic community: the prior, who surprises the two in broad daylight; a lay brother who is dispatched to fetch the prior back; a fat monk; and a thin monk. In the tradition of primitive literature, Limberg's account favors readily observable basic traits—physical and moral—over more subtle characterization. The Limberg source expounds this aspect in such reference as ". . . ein dicker Noll-Bruder . . . / ist vielleicht der Koch . . ." or ". . . ein langer / schmaler / margerer [sic] Münch (ist vielleicht der Keller-Meister / dann die Keller in den Klöstern sind gemeiniglich tieff)" (Limberg, p. 277). The narrator awkwardly intermingles description of the scene and the action itself. He becomes so steeped in his censure of the institution which the monk and the nun represent that he fails to report the actual event of their punishment, the petrifaction. He simply ends his narrative (he calls it an amusing, if unlikely "Curiosität") with an invitation to any doubting reader to follow his, Limberg's, example—that is, to climb the hill and behold the scene himself.

1775, the year of publication of **"Der Mönch und die Nonne auf dem Mittelstein,"** marks the beginning of a new period in Wieland's verse narratives—a period which may be regarded as the starting point of his *humoristische Klassik* (ca. 1774-83).[6] We perceive a new objectivity and depth, qualities which bespeak his growing maturity and his conquest of the excesses of *Schwärmerei* and frivolity. Nevertheless, the spirit of *Empfindsamkeit* appears to have been lingering still at the court of Weimar, for in the same year, 1775, Wieland—by request of the Duchess Anna Amalia—wrote **"Seraphina,"** a sentimental cantata about a young nun's painful, hopeless love affair. Aside from certain plot elements, this product bears little resemblance to **"Der Mönch und die Nonne auf dem Mittelstein,"** which is unmistakably influenced by the *Sturm und Drang* in tone and atmosphere. Wieland was keenly aware of the growing penchant for *Volkstümlichkeit.* It is surely no coincidence that fairy and legendary themes (mostly foreign, it is true) constitute the plots of most of Wieland's verse narratives between 1774 and 1783. Yet Wieland, who never completely embraced any literary movement, was too much the enlightened skeptic and the poetic craftsman to feel at home in a genuine, undisciplined *Sturm und Drang* situation. It is, indeed, inconceivable that he would ever have produced true "folk" literature, because its naïveté was essentially incompatible with his subtlety and cosmopolitanism. Wieland's choice of the tale under consideration might be viewed as a concession to the *Sturm und Drang*—a gesture to meet the demands of the younger generation. He may also have been intrigued by the challenge of refashioning and embellishing an inferior literary product. We may observe a similar intention in certain aspects of *Das Wintermärchen* (1776), **"Vogelsang oder die drei Lehren"** (1778), and **"Pervonte oder die Wünsche"** (1779).

Wieland took monastic attitudes to task on other occasions.[7] His version of the legend is an articulate testimonial to his rejection of monasticism, of philistinism, and, in general, of hypocrisy; but his censure of an illicit relationship within a monastic community is secondary to his commiseration with the two unfortunate young people. As Sengle observes, "Es geht hier nicht um den Mönch und die Nonne als solche, sondern um das allgemein-menschliche Schicksal eines Liebespaares, dem . . . eine legitime Vereinigung verwehrt ist. Darum wurde wohl auch später der weniger mißverständliche Titel **'Sixt und Clärchen'** gewählt."[8]

Wieland's verse narrative begins with a *Prolog* humorously reflecting on the negligible value of the monastic vocation. The vow itself, which deprives a member of every mundane comfort and obligates him for life "bey wohlverschloßnen Thüren / Zu fasten und zu psalmodiren" (*T.M.* III, 195), elicits Wieland's awe as a "Wagstück" demanding profound conviction. It is this very quality which the hero and heroine of the narrative are

lacking. At the end of the prologue, Wieland hints at a forthcoming "lesson" and defends the inconspicuous genre of the fairy tale:

> Ergötzt es euch, so hat der Dichter halb erreicht,
> Was er dem Leser gerne gönnte;
> Denn, glaubet mir, kein Mährchen ist so seicht,
> Aus dem ein Mann nicht weiser werden könnte.
>
> (*T.M.,* III, 195)

In the opening lines of Canto I, diminutives give an ironical cast to the description of the sequestered pair's inexperienced youth:

> Ein frommes klösterliches Pärchen,
> Er, Bruder Sixt, Sie, Schwester Clärchen,
> Noch beyde jung und schön und zart
> Und fromm und gut nach teutscher Art.
>
> (*T.M.,* III, 196)

The poor unsuspecting souls fall prey to the ". . . süsse Gift der Liebe . . ." (*T.M.,* III, 197). As usual, Wieland does not preach or condemn. He merely warns of the consequences sure to ensue from an act branded as "sinful" by the moral codes of church and society alike. The poet makes his position clear when he speaks of Sixt's amorous ambition:

> In meinen Augen, daß ihrs wißt,
> Macht Sixten diese Schwachheit Ehre.
> Ein Mensch, der doch kein Engel ist,
> Kann traun! um kleinern Sold nicht minnen.
>
> (*T.M.,* III, 199)

Sixt and Clärchen experience all the nuances of passion: from the "dunkle nahmenlose Sehnen" to "stumpfen Schmerz" (*T.M.,* III, 197). Yet,

> Ihr Schmerz ist ein zu süsser Schmerz,
> Als daß man gleich an Heilung dächte.
>
> (*T.M.,* III, 200)

They reject the duty and comfort of confession for fear of ending their joys and their hopes—however faint—of ultimate union.

While Limberg makes no mention of the time element involved in the development of the relationship, Wieland heightens the dramatic impact of his version by taking this into account and tracing a slowly rising curve of action. The pair's mutual fixation secretly dominates every aspect of its monastic life and duty, including meditation. Three years of prayers and mortification fail to sublimate their passion.

In place of the bottle of wine in the Limberg source, Wieland employs the more refined device of the dream in Canto II of his poem. A thrice repeated dream vision arranged by a protective spirit serves not only as a promise of fulfillment, but also as an omen for guidance to which especially Clärchen clings. Her timid "Nie hätt' ich's aus mir selbst gewagt!" (***T.M.,*** IV, 12) reveals the degree of her dependence upon the supernatural phenomenon. Indeed, this welcome extraneous influence provides the impetus for her ultimate rendezvous with Sixt. This convenient shift of blame or responsibility may be open to question on moral grounds, but it cannot be denied that Wieland achieves artistic effect through this device without diminishing the genuinely human sentiment which pervades his work. Still plagued by misgivings—an impediment hardly considered in the earlier version—the two nevertheless yield to the omen. Wieland puts their escape at Easter time, thus compounding the gravity of the sacrilege for the purpose of impact.

In contrast to his source, Wieland concentrates solely on the two principal characters. When the two lovers meet at last, his version practices conscious discretion. Compared with the crudities of Limberg, Wieland's widely censured frivolity is the essence of aesthetic refinement.

Although Wieland parallels his source in retaining the motif of the lovers' petrifaction he is far from echoing Limberg's conclusion that they received their just deserts. Instead, he describes the bliss of their rendezvous in terms which suggest that they were practically transported to heaven:

> Ich seh, ich seh sie, Brust an Brust,
> Entseelt von grenzenloser Lust
> Die Augen starr gen Himmel heben;
> Er hat sich aufgethan, sie schweben
> In seinem Wonneglanz daher,
> Nichts sterblichs ist an ihnen mehr,
> Sie schweben auf ins ew'ge Leben.

(***T.M.,*** IV, 14)

Compared to this, Wieland's original concluding lines[9] speak only rather weakly of the punishment which follows illicit enjoyment:

> Glückselige, in euerm Wahn,
> (Wofern Empfindung Wahn zu nennen
> Erlaubt ist) labet euch daran,
> So lagn [sic] es Lieb und Schicksal gönnen!
> Es ist ein Traum, ein Augenblick!
> Ihr habt ihn wohl verdienen müssen,
> Und werdet für ein kurzes Glück
> Zu bald nur und zu lange büßen.

(***T.M.,*** IV, 15)

And Wieland later replaced them with a clear statement of his sympathetic attitude. Now it transpires that the lovers' souls indeed have gone to heaven, while their petrified bodies no longer signify punishment but stand as a touching reminder of the power of love:

> Versteinert bleibt ihr Leib zurück,
> Und zeigt, noch warm vom heil'gen Triebe,
> Des Wandrers sanft gerührtem Blick
> Dieß ew'ge Denkmal ihrer Liebe.[10]

Klee, whose inquiry is limited to the identification of Wieland's source and the intricacies surrounding the two versions of the conclusion, conceives of the mode of revision—its economy and effect—as a rare *tour de force*:[11] While the lovers' earthly felicity ends abruptly in death, their continued blissful companionship in the hereafter is virtually assured. Wieland displays his proverbial *Diesseitsfreudigkeit* by removing the threat of further atonement after death. In transforming a monument of shame into one that glorifies erotic love, Wieland successfully rounds out his travesty of the source material. Clearly, he is more concerned with aesthetic than with moral aspects, even though he retains a slight note of warning for those young lovers who disregard the potential dangers surrounding them. Wieland, the enlightened satirist, blends delicate irony and humorous skepticism with a diction which elevates the spirit and tone of the crude legend that served as his model.

Notes

1. The poem appeared originally with this title in *Der teutsche Merkur,* III (March 1775), 193-205 and IV (April 1775), 3-15, hereafter cited in the text as *T.M.* Later Wieland adopted the title "Sixt und Clärchen oder der Mönch und die Nonne auf dem Mädelstein" (a variant of "Mittelstein").

2. See "Wielands Gedicht 'Sixt und Klärchen,' sein ursprünglicher Plan und seine Quelle," *Zeitschrift für den deutschen Unterricht,* XIII, xi (1899), 728-730.

3. The title page of the work reads "Das im Jahr 1708. lebende und schwebende Eisenach / Welches Anno 1709. zum Erstenmahl gedruckt und zusammen getragen worden von Johann Limberg / der Zeit Waisen-Inspector, Anitzo wieder übersehen und mit einem Curiosen Appendice vermehret. Gedruckt im Jahr 1712. Eisenach / verlegt und zu bekommen bey Daniel Christian Wilhelmi / Buchbinder." This work is cited hereafter in the text as "Limberg."

4. "Wielands Gedicht 'Sixt und Klärchen,'" 730.

5. Wilhelm Kosch, *Deutsches Literatur-Lexikon,* 2nd ed. (Bern, 1949-58), II, 1536.

6. See Friedrich Sengle, *Wieland* (Stuttgart, 1949), pp. 344-345.

7. E.g., in his biting *Briefe über das Mönchswesen* (1771), which, to be sure, are credited chiefly to Georg Michael La Roche; in *Der goldene Spiegel* (1772); and in *Die Wasserkufe* (1795).

8. Sengle, p. 345.

9. These lines were evidently intended as a transition to an anticipated third canto.

10. *C. M. Wielands sämmtliche Werke,* ed. J. G. Gruber (Leipzig, 1824), xxi, 40.

11. "Wielands Gedicht 'Sixt und Klärchen,'" 729.

John A. McCarthy (essay date 1976)

SOURCE: McCarthy, John A. "Wieland as Essayist." *Lessing Yearbook* 8 (1976): 125-39.

[*In the following essay, McCarthy evaluates Wieland's career as an essayist. McCarthy asserts that Wieland introduced a number of significant innovations to the essay form.*]

The status of the essay in the 18th century has yet to be thoroughly determined. But the following picture has been sketched. For example, the Enlightenment is viewed as the cradle of the essay because it nurtured the urbanity, the intellectual agility, and the consciousness of stylistic technique which were prerequisite to the modern essay.[1] Lessing is generally seen as the "father of the essay," Möser, Hamann and Herder as early masters, Georg Forster as "the first sociable writer." Friedrich Schlegel is recognized as the first modern essayist, i. e., as a writer "who saw himself as an essayist and who reflected on the concept of the essay in modern fashion."[2] Although the precursors of the modern essay (the *Versuch, Aufsatz, Fragment, Entwurf*) made definite progress in gradually turning their attention from moral to aesthetic concerns (Cf. Rehder, p. 40), they are generally still closer to the *Traktat,* which is based on firm assumptions and which is more interested in communicating the results of cogitation than the process itself. Similarly, characteristics of the *Abhandlung* continue to adhere to the incipient essay forms: the *Abhandlung* is a scientific, impersonal monologue in unwavering pursuit of a specified goal. Thus Rohner contends: "Der deutsche Aufsatz riecht stehts ein wenig nach der blakenden Studierlampe."[3] There are of course the above mentioned authors, in whose hands the essay begins to free itself of pedantry.

One wonders why it is that Wieland is as often denied the attributes of an essayist as he is accorded them. In his book *Essay und Aufklärung,* Heinrich Küntzel cursorily speaks of Wieland not as an essayist, but as a consummator of classical German prose leading to the essay (Küntzel, p. 81). In his history of the essay Bruno Berger goes so far as to deny Wieland all claim to the title of essayist, stating that his contributions to the *Teutsche Merkur* bear no resemblance to the essay form.[4]

On the other hand Fritz Martini and Helmut Rehder do number Wieland among the authors of an authentic essay prose form in the 18th century,[5] and Rohner includes him in his anthology *Deutsche Essays* under the rubric "Essays avant la lettre." The phrase refers to the view that essays had existed in Germany before the term "essay" gained ascendancy.

It is curious that Georg Forster is definitely considered a genuine essayist (Küntzel, p. 79), while Wieland is not. I say curious because the two writers' styles are strikingly similar. Perhaps the lack of unanimity concerning Wieland's essayism is attributable to the 19th century bias against him which was transmitted by Friedrich and August Schlegel. At the time when Friedrich Schlegel lauded Georg Forster as a classical prose writer,[6] he also attacked Wieland. Consciousness of the essay as a legitimate poetic form emerged in the 19th century concurrently with the bias against Wieland; thus it would be understandable that Wieland be excluded from a 19th century consideration of the 18th century essay. The 19th century prejudice undoubtedly lingers on.

This study proposes to revise and focus the image of Wieland as essayist. On the one hand it will attempt to counter the denial of essayistic qualities in the writer; on the other it will endeavor to shift the emphasis from theory to practice. The lament is frequently heard in essay-research that too little attention is given to *explication de text,* that all energy has centered on the theory of the form.[7] Strides will now be taken to help alter the situation. I can best contribute to a revision of the author in the present spacial limitations by examining one of Wieland's better-known "*Merkur*-Aufsätze" in detail and, it is hoped, provide impulses for further study. An ancillary concern in the textual analysis will be to point out the extensive influence which the rhetorical tradition has exerted on the composition of the essay.

The article to be considered as a "Kostprobe"[8] of Wieland's essayistic writing is the short piece, **"Was ist Wahrheit?"**, in which Wieland raises the old question anew in succinct formulation. The article appeared in the April issue, 1778, of the *Teutsche Merkur,* subsumed under the general title, "Fragmente von Beiträgen zum Gebrauch derer, die sie brauchen können oder wollen." Later it was included under its own title in the first volume of his **Kleinere prosaischen Schriften** (1785) and in volume 24 of the **Sämmtliche Werke** (1794).[9] The general title under which **"Was ist Wahrheit?"** initially appeared is already a good omen for this undertaking, because the casual, even trifling attitude of the author reflected in it is a mark of "every truly great essayist."[10] Then too, the article is labeled a fragment, implying that no effort at comprehensiveness or finality is intended. This is also a mark of the true essay (cf. Rohner, pp. 23-24).

The article is divided into nineteen paragraphs of vary-ing length; none is very long, one (§ 14) is only one sentence long. From a purely optical point of view, therefore, the article does not intimidate or tax the pro-spective reader. The alternating length not only of para-graph but also of sentence structure creates optically and acoustically a sense of harmonious fluidity which invites the reader to continue. Wieland cites this quality of "wohlklingende Harmonie" as a rhetorical element.[11] "Das Lesbare" is an element of the modern essay as well.[12]

The main points of Wieland's position on the question of truth are formulated pithily in the short paragraphs. For example, § 3 presents his main thesis: truth is rela-tive (XXX, 181). This is in keeping with the directive for terseness which is necessary if the reader is to clearly comprehend the relationship of the parts to the whole; i. e., the subsumption of the *ideas partium* in the *idea totali.* Yet the writer must avoid extreme pithiness, for clarity would be ill-served by laconism (AA [*Wielands Werke,* Akademie Ausgabe], IV, 309). In analyzing the manner of his argument, we will want to pay close attention to the modes of persuasion, specifi-cally his appeals to our experience in the form of analo-gies, similes, metaphors, and the like. The accuracy, ap-propriateness, and the tact with which they are brought to bear will be of aesthetic interest.[13] The latter in rec-ognition of the fact that the essay appeals not to our in-tellect alone, but also to our emotions.[14]

Of the four categories of rhetoric—*inventio* (accumulation of evidence), *dispositio* (arrangement of evidence), *elocutio* (linguistic expression), and *executio* (oral delivery)—only *inventio* and *elocutio* are of im-portance for the composition of essays. Oral delivery is an obvious non-concern and the arrangement of evi-dence is less creative; it is mechanical, smacking of ra-tional ordering (AA, IV, 310). The internal structure of an essay is less the result of having thought a problem through than it is of actually thinking a problem out. Max Bense writes: "Essayistisch schreibt, wer . . . seinen Gegenstand während des Schreibens . . . fin-det."[15] Adorno contends: "Eigentlich denkt der Denk-ende gar nicht, sondern macht sich zum Schauplatz gei-stiger Erfahrung . . ." (Adorno, p. 81). Decisive for Lukacs is the essay as "der Prozeß des Richtens." (Lukacs, p. 53).

The categories of *inventio* and *elocutio* correspond to appeals to authority on the one hand and appeals to per-sonal experience on the other. The first presupposes an educated reader (cf. Rohner, p. 21), for it involves allu-sions to intellectual experiences. The influence of *in-ventio* on **"Was ist Wahrheit?"** is apparent. Wieland thrice refers to specific Biblical passages, once at the outset and twice at the conclusion. The first is to John XVIII.38, where Jesus announces that he has come into

the world "to bear witness to the truth." Pilate responds with the skeptical query: "what is truth?" The second Biblical reference is to Job XXXIIff., and alludes to Elihu's reaction to Job's righteous complaint to God. Elihu as a dogmatist misunderstood the tone of Job's lament, which resulted from true skepticism. The third reference, to Numbers XXII.28ff., is to the episode in-volving Balaam's talking ass, which served as God's mouthpiece. The incident is cited as evidence that God can express the truth through one of his creatures, even a dumb animal. Albeit such instances are rare. The reader is thus prepared and subsequently reminded of a relativistic concept of truth. Sandwiched in between these Biblical allusions are references to ancient and modern cultural history. It is expected that the reader is acquainted with Karneades, Pyrrho, Sextus, Francois de la Mothe le Vayer, Pierre Bayle, and David Hume. The reader is furthermore referred to the *Iliad*, the *Arabian Nights, Melusine, Orlando Furioso,* and *Don Quixote.* He is also presumed to know who the amphictyons and energumens were, and what the Areopagus and tripod represented. In short, the *Merkur*-article was obviously not intended for the common man.

Each of these allusions is an appeal to a reference point outside the author-reader relationship. It is sometimes a call to a judicial authority (Areopagus) or religious au-thority (tripod, Bible), sometimes an invocation of a mutual literary experience, and other times a reference to the wisdom of age (Nestor, cf. XXX, 190). The per-spective is constantly altered to illuminate the problem from dogmatic and skeptical angles in an approxima-tion of truth. In each case the appeal is to the reader's own experience, albeit intellectual experience.

Elocutio figures more prominently in this study of Wieland's essay; and it should because it has more to do with the poetic worth of this essay in particular and with the essay form in general. Like *inventio, elocutio* employs the literary principle which Bense calls "ars combinatoria" (Bense, p. 66). Unlike *inventio,* however, *elocutio* is more emotive, subjective, associative. Its al-lusions, metaphors, and rhythms aim at the responsive chords of the heart rather than play upon our critical perspicacity. Whereas the intellect still has the upper hand in the accumulation of evidence, poetic fantasy is allowed freer reign in the linguistic expression of ideas. **"Was ist Wahrheit?"**, as all essays, thus exists in a state of tension hovering between the poles of its her-maphroditic essence: reflexion and imagination. Gerke sums up this state in the following manner: "In diesem Spannungsfeld zwischen rationalem Mitteilungszweck und künstlerischer Gestaltungsabsicht gewinnt . . . der Essay seine Form."[16]

A major characteristic of this essay is the way in which it actively involves the reader. The opening sentence is highly effective in this respect: "Diese Frage ist dadurch, daß sie schon so mannichmal durch den Mund eines *Pilatus* ging, nichts desto schlechter geworden" (XXX, 181). It immediately catches the reader's attention by referring back to the title, **"Was ist Wahrheit?"** and immediately activates the reader's mind by forcing him to recollect the historical circumstances.[17] Wieland's remark that the question is not the worse for Pilate's use of it poses an additional task for the reader: what is *that* supposed to mean? Then too the reference is not just to the historical governor of Palestine, but to any person who posed or would pose the question in Pilate's skeptical manner (Wieland writes: "ein Pilatus!").

The second sentence of the paragraph continues the reader's active involvement by posing the rhetorical question: "Wessen Augen blinzen nicht, wenn er mit dieser Frage überrascht wird?" (XXX, 181). The reader is invited to imagine the enlightened man's response to the provocative query and his eager anticipation of a nimble discussion pursuant to it ("blinzen"). The sense of anticipation is subtly transferred to Wieland's own present inquiry. The third and final sentence of the initial paragraph makes this clear: "Schon tausend- und zehntausendmal entschieden, wird sie immer wieder als ein *Räthsel* aufgeworfen werden, und in zehntausendmal tausend Fällen ein *unauflösbares* bleiben" (XXX, 181). The rhythm and meaning of the formulation "zehntausendmal" etc. stress the elusive, enigmatic qualities of truth ("Räthsel, unauflösbares"). The sentence maintains the reader in a state of uncertainty as to the author's next move, but now he is interested enough to make it with him.

From the standpoint of content the opening paragraph (*exordium*) confronts the reader with the inscrutability of the problem. From the standpoint of style, a dialogic quality is evident. The reader is not going to be presented with *un fait accompli,* but rather with the author's reasoning process itself. The colloquy-like quality of the opening paragraph is representative of the entire essay. It is continued in the ensuing paragraphs through the use of the first person pronoun, pointed questions, and direct address. It is striking that the warm, personal note in the essay is not expressed until after the critical portion of Wieland's argument has been made in § 12 and 13. First the appeal is made to the head via rational categories of *confutatio* and *confirmatio* in which the pro and con of the main thesis are argued. Then follows the appeal to the heart.

Paragraph 15 is remarkable for its congeniality and style. It is quoted here in its entirety:

> Anstatt mit einander zu hadern, wo die Wahrheit sey? wer sie besitze? wer sie in ihrem schönsten Lichte gesehen? die meisten und deutlichsten Laute von ihr vernommen habe?—lasset uns in Frieden zusammen gehen, oder, wenn wir des Gehens genug haben, unter

den nächsten Baum uns hinsetzen, und einander offenherzig und unbefangen erzählen, was jeder von ihr gesehen und gehört hat, oder gesehen zu haben glaubt; und ja nicht böse darüber werden, wenn sichs von ungefähr entdeckt, daß wir falsch gesehen oder gehört, oder gar (wie es brünstigen Liebhabern, die ihr zu nahe kommen wollen, öfters begegnet) eine Wolke für die Göttin umarmt haben.

(XXX, 189)

The passage is in response to the preceding paragraph, the question: "Und was haben wir also zu thun?" Despite its length, the sentence does not seem long. The individual coda are clearly marked, the repetition of syntactical constructions creates a rhythmic regularity which enhances the clarity of expression. Even the parenthetical comment at the end does not obfuscate the basic lucidity of the passage. (The slight alteration in rhythm is quickly adjusted to). The stylistic features of the sentence can be taken as exemplary of other protracted sentences in the essay.

The passage contains the first first-person exhortative of the essay ("lasset uns") and that tends to draw author and reader closer together, especially since it follows closely upon the "wir" of the preceding paragraph ("Und was haben wir also zu thun?"). The author thereby conveys the impression that he is no better than his reader, that he does not consider himself teacher or preacher. More important is the topos of the congenial stroll to which Montaigne compared his own essayistic style.[18] Wieland invites the reader to go for a walk so that they can engage in frank, easy conversation and a friendly exchange of views. The cordiality of the notion is increased by Wieland's suggestion that they can always sit down in the shade of a tree if they should tire of walking. The amity of the situation also allows for greater honesty in the admission of folly, error, or misjudgment. Wieland's use of the *Spaziergangmotiv* is especially conducive to his argument.

The rapprochement between author and reader is continued in the ensuing paragraphs until it climaxes in an amusing twist in the final paragraph. Wieland alludes to the story of Balaam's talking ass as evidence that man is not always justified in rejecting those who proclaim their ideas to be dogmatic, for God can and does speak through his creatures. Thus an ass which serves as God's mouthpiece deserves respect, because it is not the animal which speaks, but God himself. By a subtle switch of stress Wieland next applies the analogy to man in a hypothetical case. The transfer involves some light irony. Man acquires not only the ass's inspiration but its other qualities as well. Wieland states: "Einem Menschen aber,—es sey denn er könne uns beweisen, daß er sich im Falle des besagten Esels befinde,—ziemt es, ungeachtet des aufgerichteten Angesichts und des Blicks gen Himmel der ihm gegeben ist, von Zeit zu

Zeit auf seine Füsse zu sehen und—*bescheiden zu seyn!*" (XXX, 191-192). Moreover, the burden of proof that he is like the ass falls upon the self-proclaimed prophet. Without discrediting the Biblical events, Wieland intensifies the unifying bond between himself and his reader through an ironic twist of images: man as ass, not just an ass. The irony is heightened even further by the concluding suggestion. The uplifted countenance is symbolic of the prophet (= ass) whom it nevertheless behooves to note from time to time that he is still earthbound. The reader smiles at the thought because he does not feel himself to be criticized.

A major aspect of the essay (and of the rhetorical category, *elocutio*) is the use of analogies, images, similes, and their appropriateness. **"Was ist Wahrheit?"** abounds in them. Wieland first introduces the thesis that innate feeling is of greater consequence than reason in the perception of truth in § 6. Although he follows the contention with examples and arguments to demonstrate the unassailability and inviolateness of innate feeling, it is not until § 11 that the reader encounters a salient analogy which impresses itself on his mind. Inner feeling is likened to a man's home which is surrounded by a fence. No one has the right to intrude into another's private sanctum and disrupt his innermost beliefs no matter how peculiar they might be: "Wer hat ein Recht in seines Nachbars Verzäunung einzudringen und den Frieden seiner Hausgötter zu stören? Mag doch seine *Melusine* einen Fischschwanz unter ihrem Rocke tragen; was geht das andre an?" (XXX, 187). The image of one penetrating the defenses of another without provocation is well chosen. Each can imagine the threat to his own private world, and reacts on an emotional rather than intellectual level. The hominess of the spirit generated comes across not only in the main image itself and the secondary one of the fish tail which must be concealed (= peculiarity of belief), but also in the choice of words. "Hausgötter" is a catchy, unique way of saying "one's private notions." The hominess adds of course to the sense of affinity between reader and author.

The first image is immediately followed by a second designed as a corollary to the first: the picture of Don Quixote charging through the countryside affronting strangers for the sake of his incomparable Dulcinea. It symbolizes the restriction Wieland placed on the inviolability of innermost convictions. As long as one's own beliefs are not constrained upon another, society should leave him alone (XXX, 187). However, if he crusades for his ideas, then society has the right to restrain him and attempt to set him right. Such knights-errant, Wieland suggests, are understandable to "kluge Leute," who see that aberrants bear their "Entschuldigung unter dem Hute" (XXX, 187). Naturally, the reader feels himself to be included by the author in the class of sagacious people. The phrase, "Entschuldigung unter dem Hute tragen," again continues the homey congeniality.

Both images contribute significantly to the reader's understanding, on the one hand, the inviolateness of notions kept to one's self and, on the other hand, the utter folly of trying to impose these private notions on anyone else. The final reference to the fate suffered by Don Quixote at the hands of hinny drivers and swindlers underscores the latter point (XXX, 188).

Two other analogies are worthy of note. Both concern the immeasurability of nature, each from a different perspective. One is a macrocosmic, the other a microcosmic view. Wieland returns to the topos of the wise man cited at the beginning of the essay to reaffirm man's relative ignorance in the face of the limitless possibilities and variations open to nature. The wise man, who is cited only as a prelude to the first of the images, has learned, "das man immer weniger von den Dingen *begreift,* je mehr man davon *weiss*" (XXX, 190).[19] Nature is more of an enigma to him than before. The recurrence of the phrase "zehnmal zehntausend" brings with it the implications of incalculability included in its first use in § 4. The wise man has learned that our tiny world ("Erdklümpchen"), which seems so immense to us, is actually of little account, when viewed from the sun's vantage point. The effect of that view point would be sobering since the earth would then appear as merely "a luminous point in the immense darkness of nature" (XXX, 190), and our planetary system itself would seem only another luminous point in the immensity of space. Through this analogy Wieland convincingly argues that each point of view is relative; that which strikes us as being undoubtedly important and true now, will strike us as much less so from a point further removed from the original one. The original point does not cease to exist; one learns to see it in its true relationship as part of the whole. The final words of the paragraph are "Nacht der Natur," a concept symbolizing man's feeble intellectual capacity. The final impression is effective.

The garden analogy in the next paragraph is the counterpart of the foregoing one. Instead of moving to a point even more distant from the earth, the new viewpoint is achieved by going ever deeper into the garden. The result is the recognition that each particle of dust ("Stäubchen") is a miniature planetary system. Each point of nature is a reservoir of all natural forces and influences and simultaneously the result of these influences, so that it is impossible to know a single phenomenon without learning something about the workings of nature *in toto*. Very Leibnizian in concept. The effect upon the observer is to make him aware of his littleness and of the relativity of so-called 'dogmatic' stances. Why, even Elihu himself would react here more like a skeptic than a sincere enthusiast (XXX, 191). Here, as previously, Wieland concludes his analogy-argument with an allusion to an accepted authority. Before it was to actual everyday experiences; here it is to Holy Writ.

The first allusion underscored the obviousness of the argument by its own commonplaceness. The second stresses the purblindness of dogmatic excess via reference to the canon of holy experience. Both allusions seem highly appropriate in context, effectively drawing out principal points of the author's argument.

The analogies of outward and inward infinity reintroduce the theme of "Kreis der Möglichkeiten" sounded at the beginning of the essay (XXX, 182). Herein is reflected a mark of the true essay which weighs the possibilities.[20] The concepts of myriad possibilities, the wisdom of age, the incomprehensibility of nature, and skepticism all reappear in the concluding paragraphs to round out the essay. After leading the reader on a tour through the problems associated with the perception of truth and the roles played by reason and emotion, Wieland deftly pulls the strings together into one tidy bundle at the end. His view is made more palatable through the use of the congenial irony discussed earlier. The essay concludes with the request, "*bescheiden zu seyn*" (XXX, 192).

It seems to me that Wieland succeeds in arguing his case concisely and succinctly by appealing alternately to the head and the heart, by inviting the reader himself to reason the difficulties through, by climaxing the main points of his contention with salient analogies and appropriate appeals to experience and accepted authorities. His essay would seem to fulfill the content criteria and the stylistic demands of the modern essay, which is concerned with truth or truthful representation. Bense states that the essay "is concerned not with a deductive proof of truth, but with . . . an essayistic pragmatic proof" (p. 60). For the 18th century essay, Rehder stressed the importance of the *search* for truth and the covalue of totality as the fulcrum both of the essay and of the search (p. 40). Adorno also speaks of the essay's need in the 20th century to relate the individual to the whole (cf. p. 85).

Many of the stylistic marks of the modern essay were formulated by Friedrich Schlegel at the end of the 18th century. So, for example, the dialogic quality of the essay, the reflection of the tentative thought processes themselves, or the hermaphroditic character of the essay. Schlegel writes: "Der Essay is so zu schreiben, wie wir denken, sprechen, für uns schreiben oder im Zusammenhang frei reden, Briefe schreiben—über einen sittlichen Gegenstand, aus reinem Interesse, nicht philosophisch und nicht poetisch." (Schlegel, XVIII, pt. 2, 206). He describes the essay further as "a reciprocal galvanism between author and reader" and also as "an inner galvanism in each individually" (Schlegel, XVIII, pt. 2, 221). Both these characteristics—the subjective, casual manner of expounding personal views and the dialectic interplay *within* author and reader as well as *between* author and reader—are apparent in Wieland's

"Was ist Wahrheit?" Moreover, the emphasis of Wieland's essay has been throughout on the framework of the whole to which the individual view and person must constantly be related. The intellectual thrust was the ongoing approximation of truth achieved through the stylistic devices of perspectivity, dialog, congeniality, and the intermingling of rhetoric and irony.

Schlegel called for this intermingling, suggesting that it begin rhetorically and conclude ironically (Schlegel, XVIII, pt. 2, 202). It is truly striking how Wieland's article completely fulfills this demand. It begins with a rhetorical question and ends with an ironic reference to Balaam's ass and Elihu's dogmatism. Not only is the indebtedness of the essay to the principle of *inventio* and *elocutio* clear, but the content of our essay is also distinctly organized according to the traditional subdivisions of *dispositio*:

exordium	—§ 1-2, introduction;
expositio	—§ 3, main thesis;
divisio	—§ 4-5, roles of the head and heart;
confirmatio	—§ 6-9: main thrust of argument, inadequacy of reason;
confutatio	—§10-11: concedes dangers of intuition alone despite its clear advantage;
	—§ 12-14: return to the main thesis of relativity, fulcrum of argument;
conclusio	—§ 15-19: exhortation to tolerance and diffidence; preponderance of metaphors and analogies.

Despite the strong influence of rhetoric on the composition of **"Was ist Wahrheit?"**, the essay is not merely rhetorical. For one thing the sophistry of the orator is subjugated to the "Wahrheitsgehalt" of the true essay. (Adorno, p. 91, cites this subordination as a sign of the modern essay). For another, Wieland the poet transcends the mere art of Wieland the orator. In his instructions on composition to his students Wieland notes that the difference between rhetorician and poet is one of intention. The rhetorician wants to instruct and persuade; the poet to entertain and move. Still the poet is dependent upon rhetorical techniques to achieve his aesthetic ends (AA IV, 335). It cannot be denied that Wieland was a teacher; by the same token it cannot be doubted that he was a genuine poet. The arrangement of evidence shows the orator at work in **"Was ist Wahrheit?"**. The selection of images and allusions and their appropriateness, the choice of diction, and the prose rhythm reveal the poet at work as well. What Bense said of the essay, would seem to fit Wieland's article: "Der Essay ist ein selbständiges Stück Realität in Prosa, aber interessiert an Poesie, die sich häufig in Pathos und Rhetorik verbirgt" (p. 59).

Wieland's proclivity to the essay form seems to have been unjustly questioned. To be sure, "the essay is the most difficult literary form to judge" (Bense, p. 66); yet when we compare the traits we have discovered here with a modern definition of the essay based on hundreds of examples, Wieland's article fares well. Ludwig Rohner, one of the most informed critics, defines the German essay as: ". . . ein kürzeres, geschlossenes, locker komponiertes Stück betrachtsamer Prosa, das in ästhetisch anspruchsvoller Form einen einzigen, inkommensurablen Gegenstand kritisch deutend umspielt, dabei am liebsten reihend, verknüpfend, anschauungsbildend verfährt, den fiktiven Partner im geistigen Gespräch virtuos unterhält und dessen Bildung, kombinatorisches Denken, Phantasie erlebnishaft einsetzt" (p. 22). These qualities of aesthetic concern, vividness of depiction, and discursive virtuosity in which the total man is involved are also widely noted features of Wieland's style in general. The "deutende Umspielung" of an incommensurable topic gave rise in particular to a sense of desultoriness in Wieland's writing which, according to Walter Benjamin,[21] was never quite understood, until Friedrich Beißner suggested that a latent earnestness lay below the shimmering surface.[22] Not surprisingly (after the foregoing), Adorno cites the reciprocity of desultoriness and earnestness also as a quality of essayistic style (cf. p. 87). This combination of apparent superficiality and latent earnestness is probably connected to the essay's desire to represent the universal through the flitting association of feelings and concepts. Friedrich Schlegel recognized this causal relationship when he wrote in 1799: "Nur in der *Universalität* liegt die Entschuldigung und Erklärung daß der Essay wesentlich Oberflächlichkeit—" (Schlegel, XVIII, pt. 2, 240).

Buffon once stated: "Le style est l'homme même."[23] The assertion is certainly true of Wieland, based on what we know of his life and work. Part of his style in the broadest sense was his penchant for innovation: he opened new possibilities for the novel, anticipated the enthusiastic reception of Shakespeare's realism, prepared the ground for the form and spirit of German classicism, and even nurtured the Romantic aesthetic ideal.[24] It is hoped that it has become apparent in the meantime that his use of the essay was also innovative in his age. He conceived of the essay mature in style and content in 1778 as it was to evolve in the later 19th century. His writings preceded Forster's by several years and Friedrich Schlegel's by twenty. Although Wieland apparently did not see himself as an essayist and although he did not theorize on the genre, it would not be inappropriate, I think, to see Wieland's essayistic style as a direct link between Montaigne, Bacon, and the classical German essay.

Notes

1. H. Küntzel, *Essay und Aufklärung* (München, 1969), 103. See also H. Rehder, "Die Anfänge des deutschen Essays," *DVjs* [*Deutsche Vierteljahrsschrift*] 40 (1966), 39. Hereafter these works will be cited in the text as "Küntzel" and "Rehder."

2. L. Rohner, "Versuch über den Essay," in *Deutsche Essays,* I (Neuwied und Berlin, 1968), 15. This sketch of the status of the essay in the 18th century is based on Rohner, 14-15; Rehder, 39-40; G. Haas, *Essay* (Stuttgart, 1969), 19-23; M. Bense, "Über den Essay und seine Prosa," in *Deutsche Essays,* I, 62; and F. Martini, "Essay," in *Reallexikon der deutschen Literatur,* I (1958), 409.

3. Rohner, "Versuch," 20. Hereafter cited in text as "Rohner."

4. B. Berger, *Der Essay: Form und Geschichte* (Bern, 1964), 201.

5. Martini, 409; Rehder, 37.

6. See Schlegel's "Georg Forster: Fragment einer Charakteristik der deutschen Klassiker" which appeared in 1797. Friedrich Schlegel, *Sämmtliche Werke,* ed. E. Behler (München, 1967), II, pt. 1, 81. Hereafter cited in text as "Schlegel."

7. See Haas, 22 f.; E.-O. Gerke, *Der Essay als Kunstform bei Hugo von Hofmannsthal* (Lübeck und Hamburg, 1970), 27 f.

8. H. Grimm, "Zur Geschichte des Begriffs Essay", in *Deutsche Essays,* I, 29.

9. *Sämmtliche Werke,* ed. J. G. Gruber (Leipzig, 1825), XXX, 181-192. Hereafter citations will appear in text with volume and page number.

10. G. Lukacs, "Über Wesen und Form des Essays", in *Deutsche Essays,* I, 42. Hereafter cited in text as "Lukacs."

11. C. M. Wieland, "Theorie und Geschichte der Red-Kunst und Dicht-Kunst, Anno 1757", *Wielands Werke,* IV, Akademie Ausgabe (Berlin, 1916), 312: "Unter dem *numerus oratoribus* versteht man eine gewisse wohlklingende Harmonie, wodurch dem Ohr geschmeichelt wird, und die aus dem geschickten Arrangement der Sätze und Perioden entspringt. Es ist ein Mittelding zwischen dem nachlässigen Klang der gemeinen Prosa und zwischen dem poetischen *Metro* oder der Versification." This edition cited hereafter in the text as AA. A fleeting glance at Wieland's "Theorie und Geschichte . . ." would suffice to demonstrate the influence of rhetoric on this essay.

12. Cf. Th. Adorno, "Der Essay als Form", in *Deutsche Essays,* I, 82. Hereafter cited in text as "Adorno." Cf. also Grimm, 31.

13. Cf. R. Scholes and C. H. Klaus, *Elements of the Essay* (New York, 1969), 8.

14. Berger, 27. Cf. also AA, IV, 307, 310.

15. Bense, 59. Hereafter cited in text as "Bense."

16. Gerke, 22.

17. See Wieland's definition of *exordium* and the specific content of *inventio* appropriate to it, AA, IV, 308.

18. Haas, 47, has the following to say about the topos: "Montaigne hat sein Vorgehen wiederholt mit einem Spaziergang verglichen . . . ., um die Gelöstheit und Freiheit der Denkbewegung zu bezeichnen. Die Formel 'promener mon jugement' (I, 50) betont das ohne Anstrengung gehandhabte, von jedem Systemzwang freie Verfahren; zugleich enthält sie auch ein ironisches Infragestellen alles endgültigen Urteilens." The relevancy of this topos to Wieland's use of it is incontestable. The question remains, however, whether Wieland consciously imitated Montaigne. A subject for further study beyond the scope of the current investigation. The "ironic questioning of all definitive judgements" is especially appropriate to Wieland's intellectual skepticism, which is transparent in this essay as well as elsewhere.

19. This passage offers us perhaps an important indication as to how best to assess the topos of wisdom and the wise man in Wieland's writings. See Müller, *Wielands späte Romane* (München, 1971), 83, note 5.

20. Cf. Haas, 25: "Der Essay umkreist eine mögliche, eine wahrscheinliche Wahrheit: dabei kann sich sein Stil ändern, nicht aber seine Denkhaltung und die grundsätzliche Art des Vorgehens."

21. W. Benjamin, "C. M. Wieland", *Schriften,* II (Frankfurt, 1955), 331.

22. Fr. Beißner, "Versuch einer Rehabilitation Wielands", *Welt und Wort* 19 (1964), 236.

23. Cited by O. Brückl, "Poesie des Stils bei Wieland", *Festschrift für H. Seidler* (Salzburg und München, 1966), 32. Cf. also Goethe's remark to Eckermann of April 14, 1824: "Im ganzen ist der Stil eines Schriftstellers ein treuer Abdruck seines Innern . . . ."

24. Several recent studies deal with these problems. For a revision of Wieland as dramatist see H. J. Meesen, "Wielands Briefe an einen jungen Dichter", *Monatshefte* 47 (1955), 193-208; and A. Pellegrini, *Wieland e La Classicità Tedesca* (Firenze, 1968). J. B. Gardiner and A. R. Schmitt, "C. M. Wieland: Theorie und Geschichte der Red-Kunst und Dicht-Kunst. Anno 1775. An Early Defense of Shakespeare," *Lessing Yearbook* V (1973), 219-241, reassess Wieland's stance toward Shakespeare, and his relationship to Romanticism is clarified by H. Müller-Solger, *Der Dichtertraum* (Göppingen, 1970), and K. Oettinger, *Phantasie und Erfahrung* (München, 1970). Underlying Wieland's penchant for innovation is his awareness of the importance of perspective in the presentation of one's views. Lieselotte Kurth-Voight's recent study, *Perspectives and Points of View* (Baltimore and London, 1974), provides valuable insights into the mode of narrative perspective and its role in Wieland's early works. The impact of point of view on the composition of "Was ist Wahrheit?" should be apparent.

Lieselotte Kurth-Voigt (essay date 1978)

SOURCE: Kurth-Voigt, Lieselotte. "Wieland and the French Revolution: The Writings of the First Year." In *Studies in Eighteenth-Century Culture.* Vol. 7, edited by Roseann Runte, pp. 79-103. Madison: University of Wisconsin Press, 1978.

[*In the following essay, Kurth-Voigt examines Wieland's attitude toward the French Revolution. Kurth-Voigt analyzes the distinctions between Wieland's essays, which provide a straightforward expression of the author's political views, and his fictional writings, in which his impressions of the events in France are voiced by a range of characters. In Kurth-Voigt's opinion, Wieland's fiction allowed him to examine the struggle from a variety of points of view; thus, it offers a more far-reaching commentary on the revolution and its aftermath.*]

Although the writings of Christoph Martin Wieland that treat, exclusively or incidentally, the French Revolution have received a fair share of scholarly attention ever since the first comprehensive study by Harald von Koskull appeared in 1901,[1] these works deserve still further analyses and interpretation. Close and detailed readings of the texts should prove particularly rewarding if significant factors of historical and literary contextuality are carefully considered, if the identities of the *personae* are meticulously analyzed, and if precise attention is given to the complex interrelation of these variants as they are uniquely combined in each of Wieland's relevant contributions. More specifically, every one of these pieces should be treated strictly in chronological order and in the context of the actual occurrences that are mirrored in the work. Furthermore, each work has to be viewed in its relation to contemporary publications, with which the author and his fictional figures were well acquainted; their critical reactions to crucial incidents and public documents always reach beyond the frame of a single work and must be understood as a participation in the continuing controversy of political reality. Most important, however, it is necessary to define the personalities of the fictional characters, their prejudices and idiosyncrasies, for Wieland created many of his figures with the distinct purpose of making them present subjective views on the controversial events of his time.[2]

Several of the relevant works are dialogues, and it is essential to remember Wieland's reasons for selecting a specific variant of this form for the treatment of political matters. From Cicero, Lucian, and, later, Shaftesbury he had learned that in contrast to Plato's biased characterizations, the creation of intelligent and well-informed interlocutors enables a writer to present various perspectives, each well-founded and seriously meant,[3] none necessarily revealing the author's personal stance. The resulting neutrality, so very carefully designed by Wieland, has often been violated by critics who interpret fictional statements as expressions of his own views, thus creating inconsistencies or contradictions which they then attack as evidence of his vacillation. Goethe, for one, knew better. Although he recognized the danger inherent in the artistic manipulation of opinions, he did not reject Wieland's intentions but defended them perceptively in one of his conversations with Falk: ". . . es war Wieland in allen Stücken weniger um einen festen Standpunkt als um eine geistreiche Debatte zu tun."[4] The undogmatic consideration of men and matters from different points of view was characteristic of Wieland,[5] and as he looks back upon his participation in the critical examination of historic events he admits these tendencies: "Meine natürliche Geneigtheit, Alles (Personen und Sachen) von allen Seiten und aus allen möglichen Gesichtspunkten anzusehen, und ein herzlicher Widerwille gegen das nur allzu gewöhnliche einseitige Urtheilen und Parteynehmen, ist ein wesentliches Stück meiner Individualität."[6]

In the analysis of his literary works it is necessary, of course, to distinguish carefully between the essays in which Wieland distinctly voices his own opinions and other writings in which mythological, historical, or invented figures express their personal convictions. Wieland, it will be remembered, was an acknowledged master of the art of characterization, and the literary figures he created were convincingly human, each unique in its make-up but at the same time frequently sharing the beliefs and antipathies of the groups they were meant to represent. Therefore, instead of seeing the individual spokesman as a mask for Wieland, it would be more enlightening to analyze each as an independent, self-determining personality with a well-defined part in the at times inharmonious chorus of voices that accompanied the events in France.

The first work directly concerned with the Revolution is the dialogue **"Eine Unterredung über die Rechtmässigkeit des Gebrauchs, den die Französische Nazion dermahlen von ihrer Aufklärung und Stärke macht.**

Geschrieben im August 1789."[7] The identities of its participants are immediately established by carefully chosen, meaningful names: Walther, "ruler of the host," acts as a supporter of the people in rebellion, and Adelstan, "from the camp of the nobility," defends the position of the king and his loyal followers. Walther begins the dialogue with a diatribe against journalists who, he claims, defame the French people, and in support of his accusation he quotes a paragraph from the *Cahiers de Lecture* which had recently published what he considers a "hideous portrait of the moral depravity" of the capital of France. Walther, however, is an unreliable explicator who falsifies the document he is using to make his point. The title of the article, "Le camp des Tartares au Palais-royal, à Paris," circumscribes the "portrait," and, underlining this first impression, the detailed description of the notorious section surrounding the Palais explicitly states that among the crowd of young fools and their companions one will seldom find a sensible man and rarely a respectable woman or a decent girl.[8] But Walther could not have used such a discriminating depiction; he needed a grossly biased, generalizing account so that he could discredit the critics and replace their "portrait" by a more favorable image of the nation which, he believes, has astonished the whole of Europe with its "patriotism, wisdom, bravery, and perseverance."

It is at this moment that Adelstan interrupts Walther in midsentence and completes the statement with a contrasting characterization. Europe, he maintains, is filled with horror and loathing precisely because the anonymous author of the article in the *Cahiers de Lecture* has accurately described "terrible" and "cannibalistic" scenes that can be observed everywhere in France and are symptomatic of the lawless disorder that has spread through the entire country. Exploiting Walther's distorting generalization and using it against him, Adelstan does not at all consider the unfavorable depiction an exaggeration, because the reality of the "outrageous arrogance of the National Assembly" and the "insane rage of the people" is actually still more sordid; in fact, it transcends the imagination of even the most severe critic.

Walther's reply to this indictment is an enthusiastic laudation of the French in which he expresses his compassion for a desperate people, a fierce contempt for the tyrants who enslave it, and an effusive admiration for the sound reason of the National Assembly, the manly spirit, enlightened minds, and the true nobility of its members. Adelstan is amused by the fervor of Walther's "recitation" and cautions him to remember that such excessive ardor coming from the heart may easily becloud the mind and impair the reason. Yet his own statements demonstrate that he is no less a *Schwärmer* than Walther as he defends the king and his cause with equal enthusiasm. And when he cites Mirabeau's famous address

of July 10, he too changes the text of the speech to illustrate his own contentions more effectively.[9]

This first exchange of views establishes the basic positions of the two dialogists, and these remain unaltered
throughout the conversation as they attempt to augment
their arguments and to justify their stances.[10] The tactics
they use to extol their ideals forcefully underscore their
argumentation. Both men are skillful advocates of their
causes and masters of the art of persuasion. They manipulate the language, carefully selecting a biased vocabulary, particularly when they discuss the contending
parties, and they are sensitively aware of their linguistic
subjectivity. For example, when Adelstan uses terms
like *Pöbel, Aufruhr,* and *Anmassung,* Walther corrects
him and suggests the use of less derisive terms, perhaps
Volk, Aufstand zu rechtmässiger Selbstverteidigung, and
Behauptung seiner Würde, which are of course equally
slanted, with their emphasis on "rightful," "self-
defense," and "dignity." The two men also use suggestive imagery and metaphors to reinforce their polemics.
Walther has a preference for the vocabulary of steady,
forward movement (*fester Gang, Schritt für Schritt*) and
natural processes, seeing for example the outcome of
the conflict as the rebirth of a monarchy that is at
present struggling with political death. Adelstan inter-
mittently uses the metaphors of the *theatrum mundi* and
interprets the events as a "play" (*Schauspiel*), refers to
the "place of action" (*Schauplatz*), mentions "scenes,"
and speaks of "appearances on the stage" (*Auftritte*).
Although these phrases characterize the Revolution as a
"drama," its merely "theatrical" aspects are later negated when he predicts that the princes of other nations
will most certainly not idly witness the events as if they
were nothing more than a stage tragedy
(*Schauspielertragödie*).

Like most of Wieland's figures, Walther and Adelstan
are well educated and at home with allusions to the
classics, which lend their views an air of authority and
establish meaningful perspectives in depth. When, for
example, they discuss some of the recent motions and
actions, but more important, the indecisiveness of the
National Assembly, Adelstan fears that soon it will be
too late for the new demagogues to turn from their abstract speculations to specific practical tasks, for the patient they wanted to "regenerate in Medea's magic
kettle" may well have died meanwhile. The allusion is
well chosen, because it carries appropriately political
overtones and plays on the idea of rebirth Walther had
previously introduced. Medea, legend relates, had cunningly convinced the daughters of Pelias that she knew
how to rejuvenate their aging father. She suggested that
they drug Pelias, cut him into small bits, and throw the
pieces into a kettle of boiling water. She then would utter the magic charm and Pelias would emerge, younger
and stronger. Trusting her promise, the women carry
out these instructions, only Medea never speaks the

magic words but disappears, and the king's daughters
realize with horror that they have murdered their father.
With his allusion to this event Adelstan establishes
rather unflattering parallels: the naïve and unsuspecting
among the French are duped into believing that there is
a kind of magic cure for the ills of the nation. Misled
by false promises, they share in sacrifices that seem
necessary to bring about the rebirth or rejuvenation of
their country, but they are betrayed and manoeuvered
into disaster. Walther, of course, rejects these implications and believes that neither a *deus ex machina* nor
Medea's magic kettle is needed to rescue a nation that
in spirit, courage, and sense of honor surpasses all others and possesses effective means to help itself. Through
further allusions Adelstan contrasts Louis XVI with Dionysius and Aristion, suggesting characteristic differences between the modern French king, the ancient tyrant of Syracuse, whom Wieland had portrayed in
Agathon, and the philosopher-king of Athens, whom he
had depicted in an article published August 1781 in the
Teutsche Merkur.

Walther's allusions establish equally important connections. His advice that a monarch should not object to a
necessary curtailment of his powers but should recognize the wisdom of Hesiod, who maintained that a half
is sometimes better than a whole, becomes even more
meaningful when it is seen in the context of Hesiod's
Works and Days. It immediately precedes the explanation that the dismal sorrows of mankind are the ines-
capable punishment of Zeus; man's misery is thus part
of a larger design and not unique to the French condition.[11] A more significant context is evoked when
Walther attempts to look at the conflict "aus dem
gewöhnlichen Gesichtspunkte der Politiker, . . . wo
Der Recht hat, für den sich der Erfolg, oder (wie Lukan
sagt) die Götter erklären" (312). The reference is to the
first book of the *Pharsalia,* and the reader familiar with
the work (as Wieland's contemporaries were) will perceive ominous overtones.[12] The text immediately surrounding the quotation (126-29) questions the right of
any party to involve another in a violent contest for superiority. Later lines indicate that the ancient rivals
were ill matched, one representing an aging power,
"tamed by declining years" (129), the other an ambitious, progressive, and easily challenged contestant who
cleared "the way before him by destruction" (150). Lucan further suggests in this section that the division of
power among "three masters"—a condition temporarily
paralleled in France—precipitated the decline of a great
nation and set the stage for a most horrible war, a "fierce
orgy of slaughter" and fratricide (9). Of course, Walther
would not have encouraged this kind of allusive speculation, for his position is severely jeopardized when the
context of the reference is made to bear upon his interpretation of events. But Wieland no doubt hoped that
the creative reader, his favorite reader, would accept the
challenge of the allusion, establish its broader contex-

tual meaning, and recognize the irony of reference by which the tenuousness of Walther's reasoning is exposed.

Adelstan and Walther are well informed on current publications and support their cases by citing relevant articles or by quoting distinguished orators who appeared before the National Assembly. They do not, however, use these documents with complete reliability, but adapt and supplement them, occasionally even falsifying the texts so that in their altered form they strengthen their arguments.

A characteristic example of their subjective exploitation of sources is provided by their use of the king's speech, delivered before the Estates-General on May 5, 1789.[13] Adelstan, a staunch advocate of Louis XVI, is fairly accurate when he combines the king's words with his own explanations as he attempts to prove that the deplorable state of the nation is not the sole responsibility of its present ruler. But ever so subtly he exonerates the king by interspersing a few phrases of his own into the indirect quotations from the speech. Whereas Louis had only mentioned "a costly, but honorable war" as part of the cause of the country's financial difficulties, Adelstan is more explicit as he speaks of the "American War" and reminds his opponent that this war "was enthusiastically supported by the entire nation." The king had merely mentioned the necessity for an increase in taxes, yet Adelstan does not allow Walther to forget that the burden of taxes had already been unbearable before Louis ascended the throne; and whereas Louis had only referred to the unequal distribution of taxes, Adelstan vindicates the king as he maintains that Louis was not at all responsible for this inequality in taxation but inherited it from his predecessors.

Walther is more overtly deceptive in his use of the address, as he supplements indirect quotations in such a fashion that all of it must be understood as the king's words. To be sure, he rephrases parts of the address correctly when he recalls that Louis had assembled the representatives to strengthen the nation and provide new sources for its monetary needs. But he clearly invents the continuation of this statement when he claims that the king had "admitted" the financial situation of France to be "a most miserable" one, never before encountered by this nation which under a wise government would have been destined to be "the very first in this world" but under his own rule is now "led to the brink of political destruction." Louis did not make these humble self-accusations, yet Walther needed this "confession" to build his case and did not hesitate to invent it.[14]

There are other moments of strong disagreement between the dialogists, and they clearly disclose the clashing views of these fictional yet plausibly real figures.

Again and again Adelstan is convincingly characterized as a traditionalist and an "ardent royalist," and Walther is credibly portrayed as an enthusiastic progressive who zealously supports the Revolution against the Ancient Regime.

Wieland's second contribution, the **"Kosmopolitische Addresse an die Französische Nazionalversammlung,"**[15] has equally fictional qualities.[16] Its speaker, Eleutherius Filoceltes, looks at the events in France as an "individual unimportant *Weltbürger,*" but he is identified as one who has, as his name indicates, a sincere affection for the French and who would be inclined to set free the enslaved.[17] The historical event that motivated the address was the crucial session of the National Assembly on the night of August 4, when inequalities were emotionally denounced and sweeping reforms, particularly the abolition of privileges in taxation, were initiated. Filoceltes assumes a moderate position between those of Walther and Adelstan as he examines recent decisions of the Assembly relating to the new constitution, the question of sovereignty, and the mounting national debt. Although he is less emotional and not as biased as his predecessors, he is as clever a disputant as they were. The address is well structured and carefully worded, and his case is convincingly argued, occasionally supported by appropriate references to published documents and by shrewdly chosen quotations.

His favorite device is the kind of rhetorical question that leads to a conditional supposition and finally implies exactly the answer he needs in order to make his point. The events of the night session and their aftermath have disenchanted Filoceltes, and he doubts that the French have chosen the proper methods to bring about the intended palingenesis of the monarchy. The first set of questions probes the right of the Assembly to overthrow the old constitution and establish a new one. He is critical of this action and hopes that the French will not claim to have based their decision on a "general, inalienable law of nature" that would apply to all nations and might thus encourage others to undertake similar steps whenever they have "the mood and inclination" (*Lust und Belieben*) to do so. Nor does he believe that dissatisfaction with imperfect conditions always justifies drastic measures. A change in constitution would then happen too frequently, for it is "fysisch und moralisch unmöglich . . . , dass eine Nazion im Ganzen und in allen ihren Theilen immer mit ihrem Zustande zufrieden sey" (319). He expects—and states this rather sarcastically—that the French will find "in den Archiven der grossen Göttin Natur . . . das Original eines Freybrietes" (320) establishing the exclusiveness of their right to select a new constitution whenever it would please their people—a unique privilege that should for the sake of peace and security not be granted to any other nation. Filoceltes does not deny the French the right to declare their opposition to monarchic and aristocratic despotism, but he questions their expectation that the type of "democratic despotism" they are about to establish will make the nation "happier, wealthier, and better." Until experience confirms the extent and duration of the national bliss of which the people in their intoxication with freedom sweetly dream, one should be permitted to doubt whether a realm that for centuries was one of the mightiest monarchies on earth can easily be transformed into a democracy.

To be sure, France still claims to be a monarchy, as was confirmed during the session of August 28, and although the Assembly declared Louis XVI the "restorer of French freedom," it also impaired his dignity by claiming sovereignty for the French people. All this has been done by those who call themselves "representatives of the people"; actually, Filoceltes believes, they are a small band of men who are at times as high-handed and demagogic as their opponents. Many of the reforms they introduced brought about "disorder, disadvantages, and abuses," and the most pressing problem, that of the heavy national debt, they not only neglected to solve but in fact seriously compounded. Why, Filoceltes asks, did they not simply reject financial responsibilities that are completely unrelated to the business of governing the nation and were caused by "excessive pomp, extravagance, and poor management at court"? How is it possible, he asks, that the representatives of the people who rejected so much of the past now "despotically" force them into a "scheme" that is clearly contrary to the principles of the new order?

In the final section of his address Filoceltes considers it necessary to identify and justify his position. He is neither a "Slave" nor a defender of the divine rights of kings, nor does he begrudge the French nation its newly found happiness and glory. He is, rather, as he had initially implied, the observer of a unique drama who in fairly objective conclusions sums up matters of which he approves and indicates actions he cannot possibly sanction. These latter aspects are often the subject of an unsparing satire that ridicules questionable decisions and dubious undertakings, occasionally with gentle irony—more often, however, with mocking sarcasm. The quarrel of the French over whether to call their new form of government "monarchic" reminds Filoceltes of Octavian who concealed the monarchical nature of his rule under the form of a republic, and he derisively asks: "Warum sollte die monarchische Form nicht eben so gut der neuen Demokratie in Frankreich zur Maske dienen können?" (323). Yet this is a minor matter; more serious disturbances seem to lie ahead, for the nation is apparently possessed by a strange kind of "freedom-fever" that is quite similar to the notorious *Abderitenfieber*,[18] an allusion obviously meant to imply that France is at the moment as much a republic of fools as Abdera was in ancient times. Continuing his

satire, Filoceltes facetiously analyzes a statement contained in the "Declaration of the Rights of Man" which states that every citizen may either "personally or through a representative" participate in the enactment of legislation for the nation. He finds the implication of this statement ludicrous, for on the basis of this provision every one of about five million Frenchmen could "als eben so viele Solone und Lykurge" (325) appear in person in Versailles, though of course not all of them will come; many are too poor to dress appropriately, and it would simply not be decent to stand before the august body in wooden shoes and torn pants.

In his compassionate defense of Louis XVI, Filoceltes also scorns the "sentimental *Fastnachtsspiel*" the French have staged in the king's "honor"; the performance sadly reminds him of the cruel game the soldiers played with Christ when they draped him in a torn robe, placed a crown of thorns on his head, abused him, and mockingly proclaimed him King of the Jews.

Despite its at times severe criticism, the address concludes in an open-ended fashion and Filoceltes' final *subjectio* is slightly optimistic:

> Wird die neue Ordnung, die aus diesem Chaos . . . entspringen wird, die unzähligen Wunden, welche der demokratische Kakodämon der freyheitstrunknen Nazion geschlagen hat, bald und gründlich genug heilen können, um als eine Vergütung so vielen Übels angesehen zu werden?

> Die Zeit allein kann auf diese Fragen die wahre Antwort geben.

(335)

The cautious attitude expressed in these lines is reminiscent of Adelstan's scepticism at the end of his dialogue with Walther. Yet despite some agreement, the views of these men on crucial matters are basically different, and although each of the three is depicted as having a distinctly individual personality, they also represent the ideals of larger segments of society and thus fulfill an important symbolic function.

Wieland's third contribution to the topic, **"Unparteyische Betrachtungen über die dermalige Staats-Revolution in Frankreich,"** adds further perspectives.[19] The essay appeared in 1790 in the *Teutsche Merkur,* is signed with the initial W., and contains the author's personal views. Wieland begins his reflections with a quotation from one of his earlier works, **"Eine Lustreise ins Elysium"** (1787), in which he had assigned a role to himself, the *Ich* conversing with Menippus and Xenophon, and had virtually predicted the inevitability of the Revolution.[20] The *Unparteilichkeit* indicated in the title must be understood in a specific sense. It does not mean that Wieland is strictly neutral, but it implies that he is an outside observer who does not belong to either one of the parties in conflict. Yet these factions are so unequal, so different in their ideals and in the means they employ to achieve their goals, that it is impossible for a conscientious witness to remain impartial. The presentation that precedes this admission shows that Wieland's own sympathies lie with the people, "ein Jahrhunderte lang misshandeltes Volk" (336), and their representatives in the National Assembly. Although he finds it natural that the outsiders' points of view from which the Revolution is observed continue to shift, often as a reflection of the Assembly's actions which change its course, he does not approve of undiscerning judgments which, for example, label the Assembly "unjust" and "tyrannical" or claim that it merely replaces the despotic aristocratic and monarchic system by a democratic despotism. Wieland thus sets himself apart from Filoceltes who had voiced exactly this kind of censure.[21] But he is not as uncritically enthusiastic in his support of the king's opponents as Walther was and cautiously identifies his position: "Ich bin weit entfernt, mich zum schwärmerischen Lobredner der französischen National-Versammlung aufzuwerfen, und alle ihre Handlungen, alle ihre Decrete und Einrichtungen, ohne Ausnahme und Einschränkung, für die bestmöglichsten zu halten . . ." (350). He is aware of the fallibility of these men and of the haste with which they have reached certain decisions; he is conscious of the mixed character of this political body and therefore distinguishes carefully between destructive insurgents and the "most noble and enlightened" faction of the Assembly that possesses his regard.

The events in France are receiving much praise as well as a large share of criticism, some of it unjustly slanted. These prejudicial opinions, Wieland believes, are tolerable if they are expressed in a private manner. But distortingly subjective views become indefensible when they are maintained by well-known writers and published in widely read journals, for they then unfairly influence a public that trusts the author's judgment and has perhaps no other means to inform itself more objectively. Characteristic examples of such biased depictions had appeared in the *StatsAnzeigen,* a politically influential periodical whose editor was the renowned historian August Ludwig Schlözer, and a large portion of Wieland's **"Betrachtungen"** [**"Unparteyische Betrachtungen über die dermalige Staats-Revolution in Frankreich"**] is a critical analysis of dubious views made public in this magazine. Although Schlözer had recently published a brief description of the disruption in France that was partly correct, he had supplemented it by a traveller's report which was unbelievably one-sided. As evidence of its irresponsible distortions Wieland reproduces a full page of the text and exposes the most blatant misrepresentations in extensive notes. These are often ironic, more frequently even sarcastic. When, for example, the traveller states that his searching inquiries about the reason and nature of the disrup-

tion in France were answered by "them"—"Und jedesmal antwortete man mir"—Wieland mockingly questions the precision of this identification: "Wer waren wohl diese wackern Leute, die dem ehrlichen (vermuthlich Teutschen) Frager eine so einhellige Antwort gaben?" (340). France, he believes, is too severely divided into many factions ever to have expressed agreement on all the topics the traveller claims to have discussed with its citizens.

The answers allegedly given seem equally ridiculous to Wieland. They attempt to place the blame for much of the disorder upon "a dozen most wicked villains," who follow in the footsteps of Cromwell, and fifty "second-rate villains" commanded by a man identified as M—, who manipulates the rabble of Paris as if they were marionettes. Wieland questions these insinuations; if the "villains" can be associated with Cromwell, at least they are "ganz respectable Bösewichter," although the English would rightfully resent any comparison of this nature. The puppeteer is obviously none other than Mirabeau, but Wieland ironically rejects this reading as erroneous: "Der Graf Mirabeau kann es wohl nicht seyn" (340), for he is by no means the kind of subordinate villain and inferior mind Schlözer's reporter makes him out to be. In this fashion Wieland's notes satirize other assertions of the speaker; they expose the prejudice of his report and caution the reader to doubt the reliability of similar vituperative articles in Schlözer's *StatsAnzeigen* and other contemporary periodicals with comparable tendencies.

Yet in his own documentation Wieland himself is not completely reliable. Like his fictional characters he also changes, albeit ever so slightly, the texts he uses. For instance, in one of his articles Schlözer quoted a French source that had stated: "Beim 'Schimmer der patriotischen Laternen in Paris,' lässt sich *noch* nicht eine Geschichte des dermaligen französischen Reichs Tags schreiben" (italics mine),[22] and he suggested to those who would like to contemplate the Revolution from a different point of view that they consider historical parallels that might reveal the better solutions earlier generations and other countries, particularly England, had found in the past. Although these thoughts are not alien to Wieland, he denies them an accurate representation. He only quotes the introductory sentence of the essay, thus treating it out of context; and by omitting the limiting particle *noch,* he converts the relative formulation into a dogmatic statement which he then rather unfairly analyzes as untenably doctrinaire.

The more broadly intended censure contained in Wieland's **"Betrachtungen"** is directed against those critics who draw their information from slanted sources, relying on the "ephemerischen Scarteken, womit der Parteygeist, zumal auf der missvergnügten Seite, Paris und die Provinzen überschwemmt" (355). Playing on words, Wieland does not consider such publications pure sources (*reine Quellen*), but dung puddles (*Mistpfützen*). The critic sincerely searching for the truth must consult other materials, public records, and official documents, and should rely on indisputable facts if he hopes to make a permanent contribution to the history of the Revolution.

To offset "one-sided" accounts Wieland will attempt to search more objectively for the truth, ". . . mit Beseitigung aller Vorurtheile, einseitiger Nachrichten, Anekdoten, angeblicher geheimer Aufschlüsse, and entweder wirklich passionierter oder absichtlich mit künstlicher Wärme geschriebener Declamationen" (342). The time for a conclusive judgment has not yet arrived; the outcome of the conflict is still uncertain; in fact, there is no doubt that the proponents of a counterrevolution are diligently at work. Wieland broadly indicates the direction toward which the nation should ideally be moving as he presents his characterization of the three factions involved in the struggle: the representatives of the people participating in the National Assembly, the aristocratic and court party, and the people themselves, who may profess loyalty to either of the groups but can be persuaded to alter their allegiance. Wieland's depiction of the two major parties is by no means as objective as one would have the right to expect on the basis of his promise to eliminate bias and prejudice. The comparison of the opponents is unfairly selective; the worst offenses of the "royal-aristocratic" party are contrasted with the achievements of the "most noble and enlightened part" of the National Assembly. The possible idealism of the royalists is lightly passed over, and the misdeeds of the people's party are understated or seen as regrettable exceptions. Language and images are shrewdly chosen and the *exempla* are cleverly designed to underline the contrast. Among those who are interested in a reactionary movement are the clergy and nobility, courtiers, parliamentarians, and financiers "mit dem ganzen ungeheuern Schweife, den dieser vielköpfige Drache nach sich schleppt" (344). They are constantly active with "unermüdeten, geheimen und zum Theil öffentlichen Machinationen" (344) trying to intimidate the true friends of freedom. They are politically clever enough to know, "dass man den Vögeln, die man locken will, liebliche Töne vorpfeifen muss" (347), and are patiently waiting for the moment at which they can spring the trap and lead the people back into slavery. If unchecked, this legion of evil spirits (*unsaubere Geister*) is bound to launch a civil war that will inflict intolerable misery on the French, cast the nation into anarchy, and cause its ruin and destruction.

Wieland is certain that in contrast to these "demons of doom," the noble members of the National Assembly will lead the French toward a better future. Guided by the benevolent genius of the nation, these patriotic men (he quotes Lafayette) "welche die Freyheit eben so

gesetzt und entschlossen gegen die Licenz als gegen den Despotismus vertheidigten" (350), who possess the energies and the will to effect the best possible results, will surely accomplish the demanding task of providing France with an equitable constitution and an orderly system of finances. In an *exemplum* that leaves no doubt about Wieland's strong sympathies, he compares the National Assembly with a true physician able to cure his patient, though perhaps slowly and painfully, who is drawn into a contest with a charlatan, symbolizing the court party, who provides spectacular but temporary relief and is handsomely paid but who has with his magic *arcanum* actually hastened the death of his patient. In the final section of his **"Unpartheyische Betrachtungen"** Wieland discusses a particular aspect of the projected constitution in greater detail. He would not sanction the granting of exceptional privileges to any one Estate, because this might again cause the enslavement of other classes, but he expects that each of the three Estates will assume an important role under the new system. It is his hope that the French will follow the English model and establish a sound balance of power by creating two houses in which the representatives of the people together with the clergy and nobility will share in the government of the nation.

The National Assembly, however, was to move in a different direction. An initial step was taken on February 13 when the privileges of the clergy were curtailed and monastic vows and orders were abolished. Wieland, who in earlier works had occasionally satirized the *Mönchswesen,* did not voice any criticism of the Assembly's action but wholeheartedly supported the decision in his article **"Die zwey wichtigsten Ereignisse des vorigen Monats,"** which was published in March 1790 in the *Teutsche Merkur*.[23] This is less an explanation of the edict than a defense of measures that must be taken to insure the efficacy of a new constitution. He admits that he cannot look at the consequences of the decree from the standpoint of those who suffer from the cancellation of privileges, but must see these matters in a larger perspective as an unavoidable move to "heal" the "ills and injuries of the nation."

Almost a third of the text is, by Wieland's own definition, an allegory poetically designed to persuade his readers of the justice of the edict. A perfect constitution is like a fine piece of architecture, he argues, and the process of its creation will delight an unbiased observer as much as if he were watching a skilled craftsman shape a work of art. The new constitution must be unencumbered by the rubble of the old "gothic monster" it is to replace; the ancient foundation must be razed. It is, of course, unavoidable that those who were securely and comfortably entrenched in the old structure—among them, according to a negatively selective listing by Wieland, mice and rats, spiders and sparrows—must be driven out when making room for the new building;

and it would be unfair to accuse the craftsmen who perform the work and by necessity disturb these creatures of "ill will, secret envy, or other maliciousness." The constitution should not be a patchwork of the old and the new. By using the image of *Flickwerk* Wieland can even refer to an authority the bishops and monks affected by this measure are bound to accept, for it was Christ himself who had advised that "no man putteth a piece of a new garment upon an old; if otherwise, then both the new maketh a rent, and the piece that was *taken* out of the new agreeth not with the old" (Luke 5:36). The nation must free itself from the burden of obsolete customs if it wants to establish "the most rational constitution"; and France is indeed fortunate to have made great progress in the enlightenment of its people, most of whom enthusiastically welcome the reform of antiquated traditions, an undertaking which Wieland at this moment approves without reservations.

The next of his works concerned with the events in France is the essay **"Zufällige Gedanken über die Abschaffung des Erbadels in Frankreich."**[24] It expresses a much more critical attitude toward a new decree, an edict which shattered his confident hope that the French would establish the best possible form of government modeled after the English example. The introduction of these "Incidental Thoughts" reveals his disappointment: "Die Französische Nazionalversammlung," he writes, "hätte meiner politischen Sagacität keinen schlimmern Streich spielen können, als durch das schreckliche Dekret vom neunzehnten Junius, wodurch sie den erblichen Adel in Frankreich auf immer abgeschafft . . . hat" (363).

The presentation of arguments in this essay is more complex than in previous pieces. Before Wieland reaffirms his earlier judgment he pursues his intellectual habit of having an important matter viewed from multiple vantage points. During the debate preceding the formal motion, a man who would not have been affected by the decree, Abbé Maury, a zealous supporter of the monarchy, eloquently defended the privileges of the nobility, while ironically, Matthieu de Montmorency, a nobleman who stood to lose much, spoke strongly in favor of the edict. Since Wieland does not know the exact content of Montmorency's statement, he attempts to discover the reasons for his decision by borrowing an appropriate method from Shaftesbury, who in his "Advice to an Author" had recommended the soliloquy as a useful process of "Self-dissection" and an effective device for the analysis of a personal dilemma in need of a sensible solution. "By virtue of this SOLILOQUY" the man who practices it "becomes two distinct *Persons*. He is Pupil and Preceptor. He teaches, and he learns."[25] Every man has "two distinct separate souls," one good, the other evil, an inner state which Xenophon's Araspes, who is quoted in the "Advice," had much earlier discovered.[26] Since, according to Shaftesbury, this is true, a soliloquy will enable a troubled man to look at a problem from opposing points of view in a dialogue with himself as the rational soul argues with the irrational in search of satisfactory solutions.

In Wieland's essay it is Matthieu de Montmorency who by design of the author "divides" himself into "two Parties" and argues both sides of the question of whether or not hereditary nobility should be abolished. Significantly, this debate is the kind of Socratic dialogue of which Wieland himself did not fully approve, for it depicts poorly matched opponents. One of the interlocutors is unrealistically inarticulate, naive, and emotional; the other is unusually eloquent and mature. One could maintain, of course, that these characteristics accurately reflect the nature of the two souls performing their "Duodrama." However, the rational side of Montmorency is not completely reasonable, but overemphasizes the negative side of tradition and is occasionally even deceptive. He ridicules, for example, his opponent's pride in noble heritage and illustrious family tradition, and when he argues that such pride is comparable to the conceit of a wooden stick that carries the wig of the famous Marshal of Luxemburg, he exaggerates absurdly; when he further identifies the origin of noble privileges as the usurpation of rights cunningly taken away from the people during a time when murder and robbery were favorite pastimes of the nobility, he clearly overstates his case. Yet the irrational being does not perceive the sophistry of such arguments and is at the end of the soliloquy easily persuaded to agree.

In contrast to Montmorency, other noblemen had voiced different views on the significance of hereditary titles, and the Count of Landenberg-Vagginbourg spoke for many when he stated that no decree and no power in the world could prevent them from living and dying as *Gentilshommes*. The introduction of this term spurs Wieland to offer an ironic "explication de mot" in which he exposes the meaninglessness of mere titles when contrasted to the true essence of nobility.

The final section of the work contains Wieland's personal thoughts as he considers the "ticklish matter of nobility" from a "cosmopolitan point of view." For thousands of years humanity has nourished its superstitions and prejudices, and among these is the belief that noble birth endows a child with physical and moral superiority. To be sure, this conclusion is commonly recognized as a false assumption, and it could not survive if man were a creature of pure reason. Yet since human beings always participate, at least to a modest degree, in irrationality, they are inclined to subscribe to traditional prejudices, particularly if the underlying phenomenon has the appearance of being empirically true. Although the assumption is false, it does have certain advantages. Pride in one's heritage, for example, often quickens a desire to be worthy of one's name, and the dignity of a young nobleman who is heir to the distinguished achievements of an illustrious family may well inspire in others affection and respect. Wieland believes that a nation will not gain anything by suddenly effacing all consciousness of noble heritage or by striking all memories of fame and glory. The liberation of France from the despotism of an intolerable aristocratic monarchy was a splendid advancement of humanity. To replace it by a limited monarchy that insures the rights of all people would be equally laudable. But to establish in its place "a monstrous, immensely complicated, clumsy, and insecure democracy" seems to Wieland an inglorious undertaking that will no doubt demand many more tragic sacrifices of the French.

These "Incidental Thoughts" were recorded on July 12, 1790;[27] this, then, is the moment at which Wieland becomes disenchanted with the developments in France, and it is a specific incident, the abolition of hereditary nobility, which initiates a gradual change in his attitude. Two days later the nation was to celebrate the first anniversary of the storming of the Bastille, and despite his disappointment Wieland treated the events of the day in another work, albeit of quite a different nature, in the dialogue of the Gods, **"Der vierzehnte Julius,"** which was published in September 1790 in the *Teutsche Merkur* and depicts the celebration on the Field of Mars as it is observed from humorously "superior" points of view.[28]

The first scene opens with a conversation between Jupiter Olympius and Louis IX. Jupiter begins the dialogue with a question and is so carried away by his enthusiasm for the achievements of the French that he rudely interrupts Louis' answer in mid-sentence to continue his laudation. He is overwhelmed with amazement: "Hat man jemahls von einem so schnellen Uebergang von Knechtschaft zu Freyheit, einem raschern Sprung von der schmählichsten Herabwürdigung der Menschheit zum lebendigsten Bewustseyn ihrer ganzen Würde und zur glänzendsten Entfaltung ihrer edelsten Kräfte, gehört?" (59). Jupiter's language—carefully chosen by Wieland to underline his *Schwärmerei*—, his excessive use of superlatives, and his overemphasis on the rapidity of changes as well as his unquestioning approval of all that has happened, indicates a bias that is modestly corrected by Louis, who fears that in their eagerness to change matters the French might well have taken "ein paar gefährliche Sätze zuviel" (60).

The selection of Louis, the ideal French king of the Middle Ages, as a judge of modern France is particularly appropriate, since he too had ruled the nation during difficult times, but with greater success. As a peer of Louis XVI he is uniquely qualified to evaluate his performance. As he recalls how centuries ago he had kept rebellious nobility and clergy under control, emancipated scholars, burghers, and peasants, and promoted

the welfare of the people, he suggests that Louis XVI might have avoided some of his problems by similar measures.

During the remainder of the scene the gods discuss the impending rains and hope that they may be averted so that Paris can hold its celebration in splendid weather. Jupiter Horkius is inordinately passionate in his praise of the French, and since it is usually easier to discover excessive ardor in others than in oneself, Jupiter Olympius is amused by the enthusiasm of Horkius and with a touch of satire, ironically reflecting back upon himself, praises the progress his "sub-delegate" has made in the study of rhetoric.

The course of the rains cannot be changed and gods and kings move onto a cloud above Paris where they continue their conversations. They are joined by Henry IV, perhaps the most popular of the French kings, who remembers the difficulties he had faced during his reign. He does not hesitate to give some of the credit for his success to the competent advisors he had chosen, among them d'Aubigné, the critical and outspoken member of his council, and the Duke of Sully, who had conducted the country's finances with exceptional skill. Thus Louis could have learned from Henry that a king must surround himself with frank, loyal, and resourceful counsellors, who are aware of the needs of the nation and introduce reforms before they are demanded. Jupiter, wishing to be fair, interjects a note of caution: In all these comparisons one must realize that Louis XVI is a man quite different from his predecessors and perhaps his unique personality is at least partly responsible for the misfortunes he is now suffering. Henry and Jupiter also exchange their views on political matters. Although Henry forcefully supports a "free constitution" and believes that sound attempts have already been made to establish one, he nevertheless fears that some serious and incorrigible mistakes have been committed because of hasty decisions and secret intrigues, that in fact the nation has by now gone too far in the wrong direction. Jupiter cannot deny these charges; yet he explains that previous excesses are responsible for present abuses, that the French went too far simply because they are human and thus imperfect. To live life properly is a difficult task and to govern a people is hardest of all. Even Jupiter admits that he has learned the best of what he knows from making mistakes.

A formidable duty the French still face is the enactment of an equitable and workable system of laws, a need Jupiter discusses with Numa Pompilius, the legendary lawgiver of ancient Rome, who would find it most troublesome if he had to devise legislation for a newly liberated people. Yet despite his misgivings he does suggest specific measures that would have prevented the embarrassing predicaments with which the French had to cope at the end of the century. His proposals for remedial legislation are so cleverly contrasted with things he would not do, but the French did, that concomitantly his advice is sarcastic criticism of their action; so much so in fact that Mercury is amused at the Satire Numa has, perhaps involuntarily, created.

The last to converse with Jupiter is Louis XIV, who recalls the power and honor of France during his own time, but not the unsettling crises toward the end of his reign that foreshadowed the decline of the nation. From his position of glory and dignity he can only despise the French for behaving like barbarians, and he is angry with Jupiter for his inactive observance of the degrading *Schauspiel,* which should not be viewed with compassionate understanding but should incite in other rulers the desire for revenge. He fears that the "demon of democracy" has conquered Olympus too, and that Jupiter, like Louis XVI, can do nothing but give in to everything his subjects demand.

The many and various opinions expressed in this dialogue are individually biased, but in its totality the work contains a fair balance of views, none of which, however, fully approves the actions of any of the contending parties. It is precisely this moderation and fairness that reflects Wieland's intentions, for all the dialogues of the Gods concerned with the Revolution are meant to convey "einen Geist von Mässigung und Billigkeit, der ihnen bei keiner Partei zur Empfehlung dient, aber desto gewisser auf den Beifall späterer Zeiten rechnet."[29]

These six works written during the first year of the Revolution establish formal patterns and literary techniques that foreshadow the artistic features of Wieland's later political contributions. In all of them different figures, usually characterized as intelligent and serious individuals who simultaneously serve as representatives of larger segments of society, are permitted to voice their opinions and to present a challenging variety of views, ranging from mutually supportive to clashingly contrasting positions, collectively reflecting the diversity of attitudes that existed in reality. Enthusiastic admirers of the Revolution, ardent royalists, and middle-of-the-road advocates; Frenchmen and foreigners; fictional figures and men of history or contemporary life—among them, of course, Wieland himself—judge the spectacular events of the time, some of them emotionally involved, others calmly observing. Taken together, these works are to be understood as a running commentary on intricate, complex, at times even irrational developments, and they should not be interpreted as evidence of Wieland's own vacillating attitude toward a single event, which the Revolution manifestly was *not.* The presentation of the many views contained in these writings affirms Wieland's vision of the ideal method to be applied in man's search for the truth.[30] It is the joining together of different perspectives that

supplement and correct single fields of vision which is more informative and reliable than the isolated subjective perception of each individual observer.

Notes

1. Harald von Koskull, *Wielands Aufsätze über die Französische Revolution* (Riga: W. F. Häcker, 1901). The following works are also importantly concerned with the topic: Klaus Bäppler, *Der philosophische Wieland* (Bern and Munich: Francke, 1974), pp. 86-115; Maurice Boucher, *La Révolution de 1789 vue par les écrivains allemands* (Paris: Marcel Didier, 1954), pp. 51-72; Jacques Droz, *L'Allemagne et la révolution française* (Paris: Presses Universitaires de France, 1949), pp. 320-31; Gonthier-Louis Fink, "Wieland und die Französische Revolution," in *Deutsche Literatur und Französische Revolution* (Göttingen: Vandenhoeck & Ruprecht, 1974), pp. 5-38; G. P. Gooch, *Germany and the French Revolution* (London: Longmans, Green and Co., 1920), pp. 142-60; Enrico Rambaldi, "La crisi dell'illuminismo moderato di C. M. Wieland, di fronte alla rivoluzione francese," *ACME* [*Annali della Facoltà di Lettere e Filosofia*], 19, No. 3 (Sept.-Dec. 1966), pp. 281-339; Friedrich Sengle, *Wieland* (Stuttgart: Metzler, 1949), pp. 440-53; Alfred Stern, "Wieland und die Französische Revolution," in *Reden, Vorträge und Abhandlungen* (Stuttgart and Berlin: Cotta, 1914), pp. 134-67; Alfred Stern, *Der Einfluss der Französischen Revolution auf das deutsche Geistesleben* (Stuttgart and Berlin: Cotta, 1928), pp. 108-19; Bernd Weyergraf, *Der skeptische Bürger, Wielands Schriften zur Französischen Revolution* (Stuttgart: Metzler, 1972); Hans Würzner, "Christoph Martin Wieland, Versuch einer politischen Deutung," Diss. Heidelberg 1957, pp. 95-120.

2. Although Wieland permits a variety of distinctly different and, in their individuality, masterfully characterized first-person speakers to voice their subjective prejudices, scholars have virtually disregarded the care with which he created these independent identities and have instead considered them as "masks" or "spokesmen" for Wieland. Indeed, some have stated explicitly that such fictional figures clearly reveal Wieland's own opinions (Koskull, p. 34) or are "relevante Hypostasierungen der Meinungsäusserung des Autors" (Bäppler, p. 106). It is almost customary to combine "Wieland" or "er"—the pronoun unmistakably referring to Wieland—with statements actually made by invented figures and to treat them as an expression of Wieland's personal views.

3. During a conversation with Goethe, Wieland expressed his preference for Lucian and Shaftesbury

over Plato, whose dialogues, he felt, often suffered from an unfair bias against the interlocutors whose views Plato did not share; see *Literarische Zustände und Zeitgenossen,* In *Schilderungen aus Karl Aug. Böttiger's handschriftlichem Nachlasse,* ed. K. W. Böttiger (Leipzig: F. A. Brockhaus, 1838), I, 239.

4. *Goethes Gespräche,* ed. Wolfgang Pfeiffer-Belli, (Zurich: Artemis, 1949), I, 670.

5. For a more extensive study of these aspects, see my monograph *Perspectives and Points of View: The Early Works of Wieland and Their Background* (Baltimore and London: Johns Hopkins Univ. Press, 1974); pp. 174-80 contain a brief treatment of his writings concerned with the French Revolution.

6. *Der Neue Teutsche Merkur,* 1 (1800), 256. It is in this connection (p. 253) that Wieland himself cautions his reader to consider carefully the identities of the speakers in his dialogues so that he will not arrive at the wrong conclusions.

7. *Wielands Gesammelte Werke,* ed. Deutsche Kommission der Preussischen Akademie der Wissenschaften. Erste Abteilung: *Werke,* XV (Berlin: Weidmannsche Buchhandlung, 1930), ed. Wilhelm Kurrelmeyer, pp. 295-315. Subsequent parenthetical references are to this edition. Further references will be identified as *Werke,* Akademieausgabe. The dialogue was first published in Wieland's periodical *Der Teutsche Merkur,* 3 (1789), 225-62.

8. *Cahiers de Lecture,* 2 (1789), 97.

9. Adelstan's reference (p. 297) is no doubt to Mirabeau's speech "On the Removal of the Troops Concentrated Round Paris," read to the king on the evening of July 10 by the Comte de Clermont-Tonnere, on behalf of the National Assembly. For the complete text of the address see *The Principal Speeches of the Statesmen and Orators of the French Revolution 1789-1795,* ed. Morse Stephens (Oxford: Clarendon Press, 1892), pp. 91-95.

10. Walther does not really "convince" Adelstan of his views, nor does the dialogue end with a victory of "liberalism," as Koskull (p. 6) believes.

11. Hesiod, *The Works and Days,* trans. Richmond Lattimore (Ann Arbor: Univ. of Michigan Press, 1959), p. 23.

12. Lucan, *The Civil War,* trans. J. D. Duff, The Loeb Classical Library (Cambridge, Mass.: Harvard Univ. Press, 1951), pp. 3-13; parenthetical references are to the lines of the text.

13. The German version of the speech, which Wieland used (see *Werke,* Akademieausgabe, XV, 86A),

was published in *Politisches Journal nebst Anzeige von gelehrten und andern Sachen,* 1 (1789), 605. The French text appeared in the *Gazette Nationale, ou Le Moniteur Universel,* No. 1. (1789), 1. Wieland was well acquainted with this paper and frequently used it as his source.

14. Neither the French original nor the German translation contains the statements Walther pretends to quote. In another connection Walther allegedly quotes from a "Mémoire" of the "Commission intermédiaire de Bretagne" (308) in support of his argument. Yet the published version of June 22, 1788, "Mémoire adressé au Roi par la Commission Intermédiaire" (Rennes: Nicolas-Paul Vatar, 1788), pp. 1-35, does not contain the statement Walther uses. For his edition of the *Werke* Kurrelmeyer was unable to locate the "Mémoire" (86A). One of its locations is the Archives d'Ille-et-Vilaine at Rennes; the *Directeur* of the Archives kindly made a copy of the document available to me.

15. *Werke,* Akademieausgabe, XV, 316-35. The work was first published in *Der Teutsche Merkur,* 4 (1789), 24-60.

16. The differences between the views of Filoceltes and those of Wieland himself as they are expressed in the "Unpartheyische Betrachtungen" (see pp. 86-90 of this article) clearly reveal that Filoceltes' address is by no means "Wieland's political confession of faith" (*Glaubensbekenntnis,* Koskull, p. 17), nor is the name Eleutherius Filoceltes a "*nom de plume*" (Bäppler, p. 92) or a pseudonym (Rambaldi, p. 291) for Wieland.

17. *Eleutherius,* "the Deliverer," is an epithet of Dionysius, or of Zeus, as a god who sets free a slave or an enslaved people; *Filoceltes,* or *Philoceltes,* is one who has a love or fondness for the ancient Gauls or Britons.

18. Wieland's novel *Die Abderiten* was published in 1774 in the *Teutsche Merkur* and appeared in 1776 in book form (Weimar: Carl Ludolf Hoffmann, 1776). An expanded version, *Geschichte der Abderiten,* was published in 1781 in Leipzig.

19. *Werke,* Akademieausgabe, XV, 336-62. See also *Merkur,* 2 (1790), 40-69.

20. *Werke,* Akademieausgabe, XV, 92. Although the dialogue has three participants—Wieland, who explicitly identifies himself as *Ich,* Menippus, and Xenophon—critics usually ignore this meaningful division of views. Weyergraf, for example, repeatedly claims to cite Wieland when he actually quotes Xenophon (pp. 8-10).

21. See note 16 of this article.

22. *StatsAnzeigen,* 14, No. 53 (January 1790), 101.

23. *Weilands Gesammelte Werke,* ed. Deutsche Akademie der Wissenschaften zu Berlin. Erste Abteilung: *Werke,* ed. William Clark, (Berlin: Akademieverlag, 1969), XXIII, 307-15. See also *Merkur,* 2 (1790), 315-28.

24. *Werke,* Akademieausgabe, XV, 363-80. See also *Merkur,* 2 (1790), 392-424.

25. Anthony Ashley Cooper, Earl of Shaftesbury, *Characteristicks of Men, Manners, Opinions, Times,* 4th ed. (n.p., 1727), I, 158.

26. Shaftesbury, *Characteristicks,* I, 184.

27. *Werke,* Akademieausgabe, XV, 380.

28. *Der Neue Teutsche Merkur,* 4 (1790), 58-96; subsequent parenthetical references are to this edition.

29. *Wielands Werke* (Berlin: Gustav Hempel, 1879), IX, 6.

30. "Wahrheit," *Der Teutsche Merkur,* 2 (1778), 9-17.

Charlotte C. Prather (essay date spring 1980)

SOURCE: Prather, Charlotte C. "C. M. Wieland's Narrators, Heroes and Readers." *Germanic Review* 55, no. 2 (spring 1980): 64-73.

[*In the following essay, Prather discusses the relationship between comedy and morality in Wieland's writings. According to Prather, Wieland's comic fiction arose out of his conviction that characterization and humor could have a more edifying effect on readers than righteous moralizing.*]

The goals of fiction and the tasks, responsibilities and privileges of the novelist were questions of considerable concern to the eighteenth century. Moralizing novels, Richardson's *Sir Charles Grandison* (1753) or Gellert's *Leben der schwedischen Gräfin von G.* (1747-48) for example, purport to instruct and edify by presenting figures of great moral stature and unflinching virtue. The object of these novels is clearly to provoke the reader to a more righteous way of life. Christoph Martin Wieland prefers the more humorous morality of his two great models, Henry Fielding and Miguel de Cervantes Saavedra.

Der Sieg der Natur über die Schwärmerei oder die Abenteuer des Don Sylvio von Rosalva (1763-64) reflects Wieland's admiration for and indebtedness to Don Quixote. The later Don's relation to the earlier one is frequently invoked in comic-satiric or at least ambivalent terms. After an analytic description of Don Sylvio's particular form of madness, the narrator concludes:

. . . so werden wir nicht unbegreiflich finden, dass er nur noch wenige Schritte zu machen hatte, um auf so abenteuerliche Sprünge zu geraten, als seit den Zeiten seines Landsmannes, des Ritters von Mancha, jemals in ein schwindlichtes Gehirn gekommen sein mögen . . .[1]

The saucy Laura responds with ironic praise to Pedrillo's account of his master's quest for an enchanted butterfly: "Hier ist ja noch mehr als Don Quischotte" (H. [*Werke* (Hanser edition)], 1, 133). Don Sylvio himself makes the comparison, but with resentment, when Pedrillo has mistaken an oak for a giant: "Ich glaube zum Henker, du willst einen Don Quischotte aus mir machen, und mich bereden, Windmühlen für Riesen anzusehen? (H., 1. 87).

Wieland's final judgment of the Andalusian knight is one of wonder, however. If Don Quixote is a fool, there is much virtue to be seen in his folly. Wieland writes in *Der teutsche Merkur*:

Don Quischotte war freilich ein Narr, was den Punkt der irrenden Ritterschaft anbetraf, aber seiner Narrheit ungeachtet, ein so edelmüthiger, frommer, und tugendhafter Mann, als irgend eine wahre Geschichte einen aufzuweisen hat.[2]

Wieland points out the potential power for good latent in the enthusiasm of such fools in *Der goldene Spiegel* (1772). King Tifan's desire to help all people is "eine Begierde, die in gewissem Sinn etwas Romanhaftes hat."[3] But in a footnote, Wieland defends the "romantic" spirit of his hero:

In der That fällt das Ungereimte in dem Verhältnis der Kräfte eines einzelnen Menschen, gegen die ungeheure Unternehmung allen Unbilden und Fehden in der Welt steuern zu wollen, einem jeden in die Augen. Und gleichwohl ist nichts wahrscheinlicher, als dass ein Dutzend Don Quischotten, die sich miteinander verständen, und anstatt auf die Feinde des Don Gaiferos und der schönen Melisandra, auf die Feinde des menschlichen Geschlechts mit eben dem Muthe, mit welchem der Held von Mancha seine schimärischen Gegner bekämpfte, (nur freylich mit einem gesundern Kopfe als der seinige war) los gingen,—die Gestalt unsrer sublunarischen Welt binnen einem Menschenalter mächtig ins Bessere verändern würden.

(P.A. [*Gesammelte Schriften* (Preussische Akademie der Wissenschaften edition)], 9, 221-222)

Of *Don Quixote* itself, Wieland writes: "Gleichwohl sind wenig Bücher in der Welt, welche ernsthafter gelesen und öfter wieder gelesen zu werden verdienten, als der Don Quischotte" (*Merkur* [*Der teutsche Merkur*], August 1773, p. 120). Don Quixote represents for Wieland the kind of ambiguity in a hero which he himself strives to present. His heroes suffer from differing degrees of quixotic follies but are, nonetheless, good. One must view them from more than a single point of view and conclude that they are neither models of virtue nor of vice. Their goodness of heart is burdened by errors and misconceptions as the result of an unfortunate education. Their ignorance may yet yield to enlightenment and mature judgment.

In contrast to his enthusiasm for *Don Quixote,* Wieland expresses little faith in the ability of humorless and moralizing novels to instruct and reform. In *Agathon [Die Geschichte des Agathon]* (1766-67), he belittles the novels of his predecessors, praiseworthy teachers of public morals, who produce supernatural characters, of whom parallels are to be found nowhere on earth:

> Daher finden wir die Liebesgeschichten, Ritterbücher und Romane, von den Zeiten des guten Bischofs Heliodorus bis zu den unsrigen, von Freunden, die einander alles, sogar die Förderungen ihrer stärksten Leidenschaften, und das angelegenste Interesse ihres Herzens aufopfern, von Rittern, welche immer bereit sind, der ersten Infantin, die ihnen begegnet, zu gefallen, sich mit allen Riesen und Ungeheurern der Welt herumzuhauen; und (biss Crébillon eine bequemere Mode unter unsre Nachbarn jenseits des Rheins aufgebracht hat) beynahe von lauter Liebhabern angefüllt, welche nichts angelegners haben, als in der Welt herumzuziehen, um die Nahmen ihrer Geliebten in die Bäume zu schneiden, ohne dass die reizendesten Versuchungen, denen sie von Zeit zu Zeit ausgesetzt sind, vermögend wären, ihre Treue nur einen Augenblick zu erschüttern.[4]

Such novels present a delightful and entertaining utopia, but hardly a moral example for the real world. Wieland contends that the heroes he here depicts are more seldom to be found in the realms of nature than winged lions and fishes with the bodies of women. They are "moralische Grotesken," who are all the more idolized, the farther removed they are from true human nature, which, he concludes, with all its faults and deficiencies, is nonetheless the best, most lovable, and complete form of being which we can ever truly know. Agathon, therefore, is able to instruct by means of his experiences and even through his mistakes (*Ag. [Die Geschichte des Agathon]*, p. 258). When describing the attitude of the Greeks towards love and friendship, which is presented as cool and reasonable, Wieland points out the extremes of the romances. The Greeks honored marriage and friendship, but knew little or nothing of the passion of love, raised by the French and the English to the level of a heroic virtue. Nor would the ancients have recognized the "whiney-comic" and adventurous brain-children of some modern writers, notably women, who depict in thick volumes a love which consists solely in silent gazing at the loved one, and is nourished by sighs and tears, and which, without any trace of hope, is nevertheless ever faithful (*Ag.*, p. 33).

In "Die Zweite Unterredung mit dem Pfarrer von ***" (1775), where Wieland discusses the morality of a true-to-life and sometimes attractive portrayal of vice,

he contrasts the relative merits of novels presenting imperfect but believable characters and those whose heroes are ideal models of virtue and wisdom. While not denying the usefulness of moralizing literature altogether, he nevertheless does not consider books in which "die Menschen geschildert werden, wie sie seyn sollten" to be generally beneficial (*Merkur,* September 1775, p. 252). After arguing that man can only be reformed to a certain degree of virtue and can never be made perfect, he concludes:

> Wenn dies ist, so ist auch kein Streit mehr unter uns, ob die Bücher, worinn die Menschen abgebildet werden, wie sie sind, oder jene, worinn man uns idealische Menschen, z.B. Clarissen, Grandisons, Henrietten, Byrons u. dergl. schildert, die nützlichern seyen?
>
> (September 1775, p. 268)

Wieland points out that, if it is a question of the relative usefulness of one kind of writing over the other, then that genre should be preferred which has an effect on the greatest number of readers: ". . . aus diesem Grunde dürfte wohl der Vorzug eines Tom Jones über einen Karl Grandison bald ausgemacht seyn" (September 1775, p. 268). Novels which present ideal or exotic places, times, and adventures are also assailed. Wieland prefers a presentation of characters within situations with which the reader (he refers here particularly to the young reader, who may be deeply influenced by the reading of novels) can associate his own life and circumstances:

> Sagen Sie mir, wär es nicht tausendmal besser, diese jungen Menschenkinder, anstatt sich immer in Zeiten, die nie gewesen sind, und zu Menschen, wie es nie keine gegeben hat, zu versetzen, lernten den Menschen kennen wie er ist, die Welt kennen wie sie ist, lernten begreifen wie dieser Zustand die nothwendige Würkung dieser Ursachen ist; lernten einsehen, wie sie selbst seyn müssen, um in die Zeit, in den Platz, in die Umstände, unter die Menschen zu passen, in und unter welche die Vorsicht sie gesetzt hat . . .
>
> (September 1775, pp. 265-266)

In *Don Sylvio [Der Sieg der Natur über die Schwärmerei oder die Abenteuer des Don Sylvio von Rosalva]* and *Agathon,* one encounters neither purely fantastic and frivolous nor purely edifying characters, but rather figures who are at times ridiculous, often virtuous, frequently misguided, consistently confused, searching, and involved in a continual process of learning and transformation. Such mixed characters must evoke a variety of responses from the reader, including salutary laughter. Wieland, moreover, defends the value of humor for its own sake in the preface to the *Comische Erzählungen* (1765), where he quotes Pliny:

> Es ist wahr, ich mache zuweilen Verse, und nicht sehr ernsthafte; ich mache Komödien, ich liebe alle Arten der Schauspiele; ich lese mit Vergnügen die Lyrischen

Dichter; ich lese die Satyren-Schreiber, selbst die aller-
freiesten, und brauche keinen Ausleger dazu; es gibt
Stunden, wo es mir angenehm ist zu lachen, zu scherzen
und zu kurzweilen; kurz, und um alle Arten der unschuldigen Ergötzungen in einem Wort zusammenz-
ufassen: Ich bin ein Mensch.

(H., 4, 74)

Humor justifies itself by virtue of its basic humanness.
But laughter is not solely an end in itself for Wieland.
He endows it with truly moral properties and contends
that the comic novel must of necessity also be instructive. In the preface to *Beyträge zur geheimen Geschichte des menschlichen Verstandes und Herzens*
(1770), he declares his objective in writing: "Meine
geringste Absicht ist, dass es euch amüsieren, meine
vornehmste, dass es euch besser machen möchte" (P.A.,
7, 315). Indeed, it is the first of these intentions which
makes the second possible.

A novel demanding comic and satiric presentation of
normal people and events for the purposes of entertainment and moral edification employs a personal and extremely opinionated fictive narrator, who implicates the
reader in the doings of the novel as well. This narrator
does not hesitate to exhort the reader to pay greater attention or even to reread particularly significant chapters (a technique undoubtedly learned from *Tristram
Shandy*).[5] In *Sokrates Maimonenos* (1769), the narrator
takes on a fatherly and benevolent tone and exhorts the
reader:

Ohne Ruhmredigkeit, das vorhergehende Capitel ist
eines von den lehrreichsten, die jemals geschrieben
worden sind, und ich rate euch wohlmeinend, es mehr
als einmal mit aller möglichen Aufmerksamkeit zu
überdenken.

(H., 2, 56)

At another point, the narrator makes his recommendations for more frivolous reasons:

Gönnet mir, dass ich mich der Empfindung überlasse,
die mich glücklich macht,—und überleset inzwischen
die drei vorhergehenden Nummern noch einmal—wenn
ihr wollt,—und so langsam oder flüchtig ihr wollt.

(H., 2, 32)

In *Beyträge zur geheimen Geschichte des menschlichen Verstandes und Herzens,* the narrator demands
active participation from his readership. Their minds
are necessary as well as his; he himself cannot accomplish the entire task of narration alone:

Aber erlaubet mir zu sagen, dass ich eine eben so gere-
chte Gegenförderung an euch zu machen habe. Wenn
ich euren Witz belustigen, und euer Herz unterhalten
soll, so kann ich mit der äussersten Billigkeit nicht
weniger von euch verlangen, als—dass ihr schon Witz
und Herz habet, eh ihr zu lesen anfangt; denn kein
Prometheus bin ich nicht.

(P.A., 7, 316)

Such an involvement of the reader or, indeed, such an
admission of vulnerability by the narrator could not
have been conceived in a novel where the impersonal
narrator related unquestionable facts about figures
whose deeds and statements were accurate registers of
their character.

The world as viewed in Wieland's novels is never totally accessible to the reader. Even if a given body of
facts comes within the narrator's perceptions, he may
arbitrarily choose to withhold some information. In
Don Sylvio, a small concern of the hero's aunt remains
a secret:

. . . allein die Vorsichtigkeit der Donna Mencia und
die Verschwiegenheit der Dame Beatrix hielten so gut
aus, dass die Sache ein Geheimnis blieb; und das wollen wir sie auch bleiben lassen . . .

(H., 1, 38)

At another point the reader is admitted into some classified information, but a call is made to his discretion—
Don Sylvio must not yet know. (H., 1, 135).

At times the narrator assumes a teasing attitude toward
the reader or even directs his irony towards himself. He
seems particularly sardonic towards his female readers
and feigns solicitude for their delicate sensibilities. In
Don Sylvio, for example, he expressed concern that certain coarse metaphors may be offensive—nevertheless,
he uses them for the sake of clarity! (H., 1, 139). In
"Koxkox und Kikequetzel" (1770), the narrator observes that the book may be becoming all too indecent
for delicate types, and advises them not to read the next
chapter. Clearly this technique will only persuade the
reader to go on reading. It creates a sense of expectation (which is then often disappointed) and, in general,
produces an atmosphere of witty familiarity, at times
bordering on the contemptuous, but always lively, between narrator and reader. Jürgen Jacobs sees the existence of irony within the understanding between narrator
and reader as making possible an element of distanced
playing.[6] The prodding to critical review and judgment
is produced by means of the humorous playing, which
is in itself also an object of the writing. The wit may
even attack the mode of narration itself. This is perhaps
the most self-conscious narrative technique. In *Don
Sylvio,* the narrator interrupts himself to ask the reader's pardon for relating trivialities. He does not understand how he could have let himself do this. (H., 1, 11).
Later he comments that he has somehow unwittingly
lapsed into verse. Before he even noticed, he might
have plagued the poor reader with a string of hexameters. He prescribes for himself a rest until his blood
can again flow in prose. (H., 1, 35). In another interruption, the narrator notes:

Unsere Leser befinden sich vermutlich durch die narko-
tische Kraft unsrer Erzählung in den nämlichen Um-

ständen, und damit sie, wenn sie Lust haben, unsern Schläfern Gesellschaft leisten können, so wollen wir hier eine kleine Pause machen.

(H., 1, 128)

Not only does the narrator stand back and view Don Sylvio and his friends with an objective and witty eye, but then he steps even farther back, rereads what he himself has just written; and that too evokes an objectively critical comment. Not even the narrator can be taken at his word.[7] Such passages also serve to summon the reader back to alertness as well. The disorienting, sudden inclusion of his own state of sleepiness or his possible dismay at having to read hexameters forces him to become aware of his own relationship to the process of the novel. He is not a simple observer who may amuse himself without any personal commitment. His moral judgment and intellect, as well as his literary taste, are in constant demand to consider the events and style of the narrative.

The narrator in Wieland's novels is not, however, a simple fictional character placed somewhere between the other fictional characters and the fictional reader, with whom Wieland would like the empirical reader to identify.[8] A further shield of distance exists between the narrator and his narrative: the fiction of the historical manuscript. Wieland consistently purports to be writing histories and not novels: *Die Geschichte des Agathon* (1767), *Die Geschichte der Abderiten* (1781), *Die Geschichte des weisen Danischmend* (1775). In *Don Sylvio,* the narrator assumes the position of translator from the Spanish; *Der goldene Spiegel* is supposed to be a translation from Scheschian. *Agathodämon* bears the sub-title: "Aus einer alten Handschrift." The narrator, Hegesias, communicates his experiences in a letter to a friend. Wieland deliberately underscores the use of this narrative technique by having Hegesias explain that he finds it better to write down his story than to merely tell it in person. (H., 2, 459). The old manuscript, in this case the letter, much of which is even further removed from its source by being a report of what Apollonius relates as his history, gives fictional testimony to the factuality of the tale. The manuscript has documentary status by virtue of its alleged preservation since antiquity. *Sokrates Maimonenos oder die Dialogen des Diogenes von Sinope* (1769) is also sub-titled "Aus einer alten Handschrift"—the editor-narrator claims to have found the manuscript in an abbey library. The narrator of *Die Abderiten* [*Die Geschichte der Abderiten*] quotes dubious sources to support his tale,

. . . deren historische Gewissheit durch das Zeugnis des von Justinus in einem Auszug gebrachten Geschichtschreibers Trojus Pompejus, Buch 15, Kapitel 2, ausser allem Zweifel gesetzt wird . . .

(H., 2, 443)

The narrator is quite conscious of his role as historian. He intends to represent both factions in the dispute regarding the expanding frog population, for instance, and notes that "Unparteilichkeit" is the first duty of the writer of history. (H., 2, 423).

Even the comic poems make use of the fictive manuscript device, which often provides Wieland with the opportunity to leave unsaid what can be all too well imagined by the reader in any event. In *Idris und Zenide* (1767), as Itifall is about to ambush a bathing nymph, the narrator interjects:

Hier, liebe Leute, zeigt sich eine kleine Lücke

Im Manuskript—"Warum denn eben hier?"—

Das weiss ich nicht, allein wer kann dafür?

(H., 4, 282)

The presence of a manuscript also allows for the possibility of its being incomplete. An omission of this sort would not have been allowed the traditional omniscient narrator.

The narrator of the story of Koxkox and Kikequetzel claims to be relating the tale, as well as the opinions, of the old Mexican philosopher, Thantlaquakapatli. Unfortunately for history and fortunately for the narrator, the manuscript has been lost. Unable to consult it, we must trust to his veracity and accuracy in the retelling. He can only assure us of Thantlaquakapatli's powers of observation, for example, in the detailed description of Koxkox's changing feelings upon first sight of Kikequetzel. (P.A., 7, 329). The editor, however, always stands as the last instance because of his right to select which of Thantlaquakapatli's discourses he will reproduce.

The editor-narrator of *Agathon* makes the claim for his tale that it too is based upon an old Greek manuscript. Surprisingly, however, he does not seem to expect the readers to believe him:

Der Herausgeber der gegenwärtigen Geschichte siehet so wenig Wahrscheinlichkeit, das Publikum überreden zu können, dass sie in der That aus einem alten Griechischen Manuskript gezogen sey; dass er am besten zu thun glaubt, über diesen Punct gar nichts zu sagen, und dem Leser zu überlassen, davon zu denken, was er will.

(*Ag.,* p. 1)

Clearly the claim to historical validity is not supported with great vigor, and yet it has been made and will be repeated often within the course of the novel. When a monologue of Agathon's is communicated, the narrator is at pains to satisfy the reader as to the authenticity of the information. He explains that the author of his manuscript bases most of his story upon a personal diary, kept by Agathon, a copy of which he has obtained through a mutual friend. He stresses how these facts protect him from the possible reproach that the historian may not indulge in poetry, that is writing of monologues. In a later chapter, the narrator refers to the author of the manuscript as having digressed:

> Soviel man sehen kann, ist dieses Capitel eines von den merkwürdigsten, und sonderbarsten in dem ganzen Werke. Aber unglücklicher Weise, befindet sich das Manuscript an diesem Ort halb von Ratten aufgegessen; und die andre Hälfte ist durch Feuchtigkeit so übel zugerichtet worden . . .

> (*Ag.*, p. 363)

Again Wieland introduces the motif of the lost (destroyed, illegible) manuscript, not for the purpose of conveying information—one does not learn the nature of the author's digression. Rather an atmosphere is created, the fiction of the manuscript is re-invoked, and the reader is temporarily diverted from the course of Agathon's adventures.

One interesting effect of maintaining the manuscript fiction is that the narrator may dissociate his own opinions from parts of his narrative and yet continue to relate the tale. There appear, in effect, two narrators: the Greek author and the eighteenth century one. When the manuscript author rejoices that Agathon has succeeded in leaving the court of Dionys with his virtue intact, the present narrator expresses doubt:

> Es würde allerdings et was seyn, das einem Wunder ganz nahe käme, wenn es sich würklich so verhielte; aber wir besorgen, dass er mehr gesagt habe, als er der Schärfe nach zu beweisen im Stande wäre.

> (*Ag.*, p. 364)

The result is a double perspective with neither point of view able to claim absolute authority, although the reader is compelled to align himself for the most part with the later narrator. The effect produced is similar to that which results when the narrator steps back to critically examine his own reporting. The reader is presented with a variety of attitudes and the absolute infallibility of a narrative voice exists nowhere.

Although Wieland has made a great effort to establish in most of his novels an elaborate narrative scheme with weighty historical verification, old manuscripts, letters, and the citing of ancient sources to confirm the story told, still he does not seem to want one to take the complex superstructure seriously. He calls his ancient authors to task through his modern narrator, who himself is often lacking information. At times, he even subjects the carefully built up system to tests other than documentation. In *Die Abderiten* (1781) another unfortunate manuscript failure deprives the reader of the speeches of the opposing lawyers in the trial over the donkey's shadow. The narrator, however, takes comfort,

aus den Papieren, aus welchen gegenwärtige Fragmente der Abderiten-geschichte genommen sind, wenigstens einen Auszug dieser Reden liefern zu können, dessen Echtheit um so unverdächtiger ist, da kein Leser der eine Nase hat, den Duft der Abderitheit, der daraus emporsteigt, verkennen wird. Ein innerliches Argument, das am Ende doch immer das beste zu sein scheint, das für das Werk irgendeines Sterblichen, er sei ein Ossian oder ein abderitischer Feigenredner, sich geben lässt.

> (H., 2, 368)

Suddenly historical authenticity must submit to the test of inner logic. That which is documented is not necessarily as historically accurate and, hence, to be believed as that which makes sense. Verisimilitude becomes a criterion for history.

Wieland claims to be writing histories, and yet makes no attempt to make his claim believable. On the contrary, he ensures that the reader does not take the matter seriously. The question remains: what does Wieland mean by "history"? Clearly he is not thinking of the recording of actual events which may be verified and documented. Facts and events antecedent to and independent of the human psyche to be the subject of his history (Agathon's, for instance) may be absolutely proven, but are, nonetheless, irrelevant. Wieland uses the term history (*Geschichte*) not to indicate that the events he relates happened *once*, but that they *might* happen at any time.[9] Probable and typical events, then, are for Wieland the substance of history. Wieland writes history as a means of establishing his book in opposition to that genre which he assures us he does not write—the novel.[10]

The narrator points out that he never had the intention of writing a novel, "wie sich vielleicht manche, ungeachtet des Titels und der Vorrede zu glauben in den Kopf gesetzt haben mögen . . ." (*Ag.*, p. 381), and adds that, in so far as he has any part in the story at all, it is indeed not a novel. Wieland describes, in the preface to *Agathon,* the kind of figures with which he wants to populate his work—true characters. The truth of such a work implies not that the persons and events are verifiable by documentation, but rather by common human experience:

> . . . dass alles mit dem Lauf der Welt übereinstimme, und dass die Charakter nicht willkürlich, und bloss nach der Phantasie, oder den Absichten des Verfassers gebildet, sondern aus dem unerschöpflichen Vorrath der Natur selbst hergenommen; in der Entwicklung derselben so wol die innere als die relative Möglichkeit, die Beschaffenheit des menschlichen Herzens, die Natur einer jeden Leidenschaft, mit allen den besondern Farben und Schattierungen, welche sie durch den Individual-Charakter und die Umstände einer jeden Person bekommen, auf genaueste beybehalten; daneben auch der eigene Charakter des Landes, des Orts, der Zeit, in welche die Geschichte gesezt wird, niemal aus

den Augen gesezt; und also alles so gedichtet sey, dass kein hinlänglicher Grund angegeben werden könne, warum es nicht eben so wie es erzählt wird, hätte geschehen können, oder noch einmal wirklich geschehen werde.

(Ag., p. 1)

Agathon, having unknowingly come to the home of Danae for shelter from a storm, is about to be brought into her presence. The narrator clarifies his hero's emotional state in terms of his historical existence and the fact that he is *not* a figure in a novel:

> Wäre hier die Rede von solchen fantasierten Charaktern, wie diejenige, welche aus dem Gehirn der Verfasserin der "geheimen Geschichte von Burgund" und der "Königin von Navarra" hervorgegangen sind, so würden wir uns kaum in einer kleineren Verlegenheit befinden, als Agathon selbst, da er mit pochendem Herzen und schweratmender Brust dem Sclaven folgte, der ihn ins Vorgemach einer Unbekannten führte, von der er fast mit gleicher Heftigkeit wünschte und fürchtete, dass es Danae seyn möchte. Allein da Agathon und Danae so gut historische Personen sind als Brutus, Portia, und hundert andre . . .

(Ag., p. 404)

For Wieland, that his characters rank among "hundert andre" is of greater significance than if they were in any way to dissociate themselves from the endless course of history by being different. Stephen R. Miller contends that the fiction of the historical source is a game which narrator plays with reader in order to destroy the traditional illusion of literal truth in the novel, which prevents the reader from recognizing the *general* validity of what is there represented.[11]

Wieland's characters are developed in great detail, spiritually, intellectually, and socially. Moreover, they are consistent. The inner logic of an individual figure's psyche is not usually violated by atypical decisions or actions. One would not claim, however, that the events of Wieland's novels follow a pattern of causality. They are often arranged in a totally arbitrary way, in order to manipulate the characters into a desired position. That the opportunity is presented to Agathon to become effective at the court of Syracus, at just the moment when he is hesitating on his decision to leave Danae, or that he happens upon the home of the long unseen Danae in the midst of a storm are highly artificial developments. His behavior in these situations, however, is quite natural and only what one would expect from him. As Guy Stern notes, Wieland is presenting a "practical and positive corrective" to the novels of his predecessors: "a dynamic hero . . . developed not by preconceived principles, but by inner and outer determinants."[12]

When Agathon, spurned by his native city Athens, makes a speech condemning republics, Wieland admonishes his readers to be neither too critical nor surprised by this seeming lack of loyalty:

> Hat die Empfindung des Unrechts, welches ihm selbst zu Athen zugefügt worden, etwas Galle in seine Kritik gemischt; so ersuchen wir unsre Leser (nicht dem Agathon zu lieb; denn was kan diesem durch ihre Meynung von ihm zu- oder abgeben?) sich an seinen Platz zu stellen, und sich alsdann zu fragen, wie werth ihnen ein Vaterland seyn würde, welches ihnen so mitgespielt hätte?

(Ag., p. 319)

Wieland indicates that Agathon is behaving in a totally expected manner, based upon his sensitivity and bitter experiences. Nor must the reader express discontent because the behavior of Agathon at this point does not seem to correspond to the selflessness expected of a "hero." Some readers may be displeased by his ingratitude and hatred toward his native country. Others may find his behavior since arriving at the court of Dionys to be artificially clever and calculating. But, the narrator insists:

> Wir haben uns schon mehrmalen erklärt, dass wir in diesem Werke die Pflichten eines Geschichtschreibers und nicht eines Apologisten übernommen haben . . .

(Ag., p. 318)

The psychological development of characters, as well as causality in their behavior and the typicality aimed at in their portrayal are aspects of Wieland's work which only much later were to become key characteristics of the German realistic novel.

Essential for the portrayal of psychologically believable characters is the aspect of development and education which determines their story. Characters behave in ways strongly dependent upon their environment, education (especially the reading of books) and personal experiences. This principle is derived from Wieland's belief that natural figures must be produced and not the superhuman models of virtue found in moral novels. He maintains in **Agathon** that it is impossible not to change in a world which is constantly undergoing change. "Andre Zeiten erfordern andre Sitten; andre Umstände andre Stimmungen und Wendungen unsers Verhaltens" *(Ag.,* p. 320). In the moralizing novels, however, one is presented with unchanging heroes, ever deserving of praise, who by their twentieth year have obtained the wisdom and virtue normally achieved by great men only in their sixtieth. In life, however, Wieland maintains, we find things to be otherwise *(Ag.,* p. 320). With the presupposition that heroes are not born heroes, Wieland presents, in **Don Sylvio** and **Agathon,** young men of an extremely callow, inexperienced, and at times foolish nature. It will be the development of their character in the course of their experiences which provides the "portrait of their innermost soul" and the material for the moral novel.

The developing portrait presented in Wieland's novels is actually a process with predictable—indeed inevitable—stages. The normal starting point for the hero is a state of naive illusion. He is alone. His first disillusionment and knowledge of life results from a romantic involvement, either love or infatuation. He enters into a private relationship with another person. He is then further enlightened by contact with the world at large and becomes conscious of his position and role in human society. Finally, he transcends the pettiness and folly of business and politics and attains the wise, detached, and humane status of the cosmopolitan. For Don Sylvio, the novel ends after the first step. He has been awakened by love, and is about to encounter the larger world. Agathon, after his initiation to the private world of Danae, passes through the trials and intrigues of public life. But only with the later philosopher heroes, Democritus, Apollonius (Agathodämon), and Danischmend, do we see cosmopolitanism realized. It is important to note, however, that even here Wieland is not concerned with a perfect and changeless character but still with a developing human with flaws and foibles.

At the outset of **Don Sylvio,** the hero has his early reading of fairy stories and knights' adventures to thank for his unbounded imagination and his exaggerated conception of the world, a fantasy realm to which Lieselotte Kurth refers as a "zweite Wirklichkeit."[13] His fatal mistake was in considering the fairy stories to be histories:

> Die Vermischung des Wunderbaren mit der Einfalt der Natur, welche der Charakter der meisten Spielwerke von dieser Gattung ist, wurde für ihn ein untrügliches Kennzeichen ihrer Wahrheit.
>
> (H., 1, 25)

We learn that the reading of poetry had a similar effect on Donna Felicia of Cardena, as the fairies on Don Sylvio (H., 1, 135). Agathon, having grown up at the temple in Delphi, places far more credence in spiritual beings and abstract qualities (virtues, for example) than in the persons and happenings, as well as the material goods of the physical world. Alfred Martens notes in particular of Wieland's heroes, that they are all brought up in social isolation, and stresses the "romanhafte Erziehung" which they receive.[14] They stand in a line from *Don Quixote* to Walter Scott's *Waverley,* and are led astray by the hours spent in the library, and might have been admonished: ". . . of making many books there is no end; and much study is a weariness of the flesh." (Ecclesiastes 12:12).

Gradually, through exposure to the world of commerce, love and its intrigues, and politics and its intrigues, Agathon loses contact with the spiritual realms, becomes aware of the presence of physical reality and susceptible to its pressures. The luxuries of the home of Hippias and the seductive charms of Cyane merely provoke revulsion from him in his naive freshness, accustomed only to the serene spirituality of Delphi. But through gradual contact, the world slowly binds Aga-

thon to itself. True, his eventual seduction by Danae comes about because of the great spiritual and artistic beauty which Agathon perceives in her. It is in exercising the physical rites of love that he begins to value them. Only through direct experience of the tangible goods of life, does he begin to desire them and with them to replace his former love for the ideals of which there were no earthly models. The presence of a physical being whom he loves subjugates his concern for the approbation of spiritual beings:

> Vor Begierde der Beherrscherin seines Herzens zu gefallen, vergass er, sich um den Beyfall unsichtbarer Zuschauer seines Lebens zu bekümmern; und der Zustand der entkörperten Seelen däuchte ihn nicht mehr so beneidenswürdig, seitdem er im Anschauen dieser irrdischen Göttin ein Vergnügen genoss, welches alle seine Einbildungen überstieg.
>
> (*Ag.,* p. 107)

It is important to note that the placing of value upon physical objects or persons provokes Agathon to re-evaluate his own physical existence. Where he formerly desired to join the ranks of the pure spirits, he now appreciates his own corporeality for the contact it gives him with the rest of the material world.

Not only does Agathon change in his beliefs and desires as a result of his love for Danae; his character and personality also begin to take on qualities associated with her nature and way of life. His earnest demeanor gradually yields to a certain cheerfulness. Moreover, his former critical judgments of many things yield to more favorable opinions. His standards of morality become freer and more pleasant, and the narrator concludes ironically,

> . . . seine ehmaligen guten Freunde, die etherischen Geister, wenn sie ja noch einigen Zutritt bey ihm hätten, müssten sich gefallen lassen, die Gestalt der schönen Danae anzunehmen, um vorgelassen zu werden.
>
> (*Ag.,* p. 107)

Nor is Agathon the only one of the enamored pair to undergo a transformation. Danae too is influenced by her attachment to him to become more retiring and philosophical and less extravagant. The change in the two is described as so great, that neither Alcibiades nor the priestess at Delphi would now recognize the former objects of their respective affections. The transformation would have provoked considerable surprise from the former associates of both:

> Dass dieser aus einem spekulativen Platoniker ein praktischer Aristipp geworden; dass er eine Philosophie, welche die reinste Glückseligkeit in Beschauung unsichtbarer Schönheiten setzt, gegen eine Philosophie, welche sie in angenehmen Empfindungen in ihren nächsten Quellen, in der Natur, in unsern Sinnen und in un-

sern Herzen sucht, vertauschte; dass er von den Göttern
und Halbgöttern, mit denen er vorher umgegangen war,
nur die Grazien und Liebesgötter beybehielt . . . Dass
diese Danae izt verächtliche Blike in die grosse Welt
zurükwarf, und nichts angenehmers fand als die ländli-
che Einfalt, nichts schöners als in Haynen herumzuir-
ren, Blumenkränze für ihren Schäfer zu winden, an
einer murmelnden Quelle in seinen Arm einzuschlüm-
mern . . .

(Ag., pp. 125-126)

Of course, the radical changes indicated here in the
character of Agathon represent a first step in his whole
education. He will retain his idealistic nature which
made his love for Danae possible, but will recover from
the seductive laziness of love-sickness. Education by
means of experience seems to be synonymous with disillusionment. The naive hero, after enthusiastically embracing a new aspect of life (in this case, Danae and a
leisurely life in the country), recognizes its inability to
completely satisfy him forever and is forced back into
the stream of changing experience. The cloying sweetness and indolence of Agathon's life in Smyrna eventually leave him discontented and guilty about the waste
of his energy. He then seeks recovery by means of intense political activity, devotion of his resources to the
public good. This project too is undertaken with a good
degree of enthusiasm. Its failure drives him again out of
the arena of public affairs and elicits the reaction of disillusionment. The observations which he makes in Athens and Smyrna about the character of the powerful
greatly diminish his belief in the inborn beauty and dignity of human nature (*Ag.*, p. 366). Each incident of
disillusionment strips the psyche of preconceived beliefs, unconfirmed by experience, and replaces these
with a more accurate estimate of human nature. Agathon is forced to give up ideals not based on worldly
experience, for his self-delusion has prompted him to
behave in imprudent ways. Typical of such delusion is
the arrogant assumption that he will be able to be effective at the court of Dionys, after Plato has failed. The
greatest disservice which Agathon suffers in that episode is through his own naive trust of calculating and
underhanded courtiers. Had he been more perceptive—
more disillusioned—he might have been able to deal
with them more effectively and not have become easy
prey to their plotting.

Eventually, Agathon is made to realize that blind virtuous idealism is as removed from reality and as vain an
objective as the utter sensuality depicted by the painters
and poets. His former self-defeating extremism is replaced by more moderate views, which take into account the inevitable imperfection of human nature and
the corporeal as well as spiritual necessities of human
beings. Agathon concludes that to urge the spirit of man
to superhuman heights of purity and strength may by as
disadvantageous as to completely immerse oneself in
sensuality,

weil es ein widersinniges und vergebliches Unterneh-
men scheine, sich besser machen zu wollen, als uns die
Natur haben will, oder auf Unkosten des halben Theils
unsers Wesens nach einer Art von Vollkommenheit zu
trachten, die mit der Anlage desselben in Widerspruch
steht; theils weil solche Menschen, wenn es ihnen auch
gelänge, sich selbst zu Halbgöttern und Intelligenzen
umzuschaffen, eben dadurch zu jeder gewöhnlichen
Bestimmung des geselligen Menschen desto untaugli-
cher werden.

(Ag., p. 252)

If Agathon had recognized these facts at the court of
Dionys, he would not have expected from himself, the
king, or the courtiers, a virtue that was not compatible
with their respective natures. It would not have been a
question here of compromising principles, but rather of
working effectively with the ever variable human nature
to achieve not perfection—the ideal government ruled
according to Platonic teachings—, but at least an improvement on the former tyranny and perhaps a stabili-
zation of the king's unpredictable whims or their direction into harmless channels. Agathon's maintenance of
his own idealistic stance withdraws him from the workings of the rest of society and thus eliminates his potential usefulness. Unfortunately—and this is the sad message conveyed by presenting the development of the
hero's inner life—Agathon can only learn these facts by
means of his failure at the court. Only experience, and
usually the experience of one's mistakes, provides the
wisdom to deal more usefully with such crises in the
future. Agathon's failure in Syracus illustrates Wieland's
conception of historical accuracy.[15] Perfectly virtuous
and wise heroes do not exist in real life. The very rare
ones only achieve such status in old age. Agathon is not
yet sufficiently astute to prevail over the intrigues of a
corrupt court. Moreover, if he were not permitted mistakes, there would be no possibility of psychological
development within the novel. He would stand still in a
moving world, a condition not only improbable, but
also grotesque (*Ag.*, p. 320).

The chief vice—one might better call it a foible—which
the educational process seeks to destroy is *Schwärmerei*. Hardly one of Wieland's heroes escapes without
having to deal with it at great length. The word itself is
difficult to define. Perhaps a good approximation would
be emotional extremism. Wieland takes care to distinguish it from simple enthusiasm which may be a very
desirable quality.[16] In November of 1775, he writes in
Der teutsche Merkur:

> Ich nenne Schwärmerey eine Erhitzung der Seele von
> Gegenständen die entweder gar nicht in der Natur sind,
> oder wenigstens das nicht sind, wofür die berauschte
> Seele sie ansieht.

(November 1775, p. 152)

One notes that an essential element of *Schwärmerei* is a
misconception of the nature of things, a false point of
view. The *Schwärmer* is excited by something which

exists, as he sees it, only in his imagination. Enthusiasm, on the other hand, is a commendable excitement over the good and the true in nature, as it really is. Wieland writes further: "Schwärmerey ist Krankheit der Seele, eigentliches Seelenfieber: Enthusiasmus ist ihr wahres Leben" (November 1775, p. 153). Wieland does not intend to foster a cold and calculating attitude towards life. He even writes in his review of *Werther*:

> Unzufriedenheit mit dem Schicksale ist eine der allgemeinen Leidenschaften und daher sympathisirt hier jeder, zumal da Werthers liebenswürdige Schwärmerey und wallendes Herz jeden anstecken müssen.
>
> *(Merkur,* December 1774, p. 242)

Wieland expresses here great affinity with the suffering Werther—he valued Goethe's novel very highly—and yet in his view for man's optimal life, such a self-destructive passion finds no place.

It is the task of education to lead the enthusiast to a serene and productive life. The enthusiasm must be moderated, but Wieland seems to love the enthusiast, the primary first role for all of his heroes. Indeed, in **Peregrinus Proteus** (1791), it is the final role of the hero as well. For all the logic in the arguments of Hippias, the reader sides unequivocally with the young Agathon. There is a grace and beauty typical of the enthusiasts, which the coarse Hippias may never attain. Schindler-Hürlimann's analysis of this seeming dilemma discloses a perceptive observation. She sees the close association between enthusiasm and art as the reason why a love proceeding from this combination (for example, Agathon's for Danae) is invariably superior to a purely sensual love according to the principles of Hippias. The love of the beautiful and harmonious is a potentially good form of enthusiasm.[17]

Don Sylvio is presented as imaginative, naive, guileless, and wholly gullible. Credibility is his predominant characteristic. He is described as tender, delicate, and sensitive.

> Junge Leute von dieser Art lieben überhaupt alle Vorstellungen, welche lebhafte Eindrücke auf ihr Herz machen, und Leidenschaften erwecken, die in einem leichten Schlummer liegend, bereit sind von dem kleinsten Geräusch aufzufahren.
>
> (H., 1, 21)

We learn further of his remarkable capacity to integrate the material world with the creations of his fantasy:

> Unvermerkter Weise verwebt sich die Einbildung mit dem Gefühl, das Wunderbare mit dem Natürlichen und das Falsche mit dem Wahren.
>
> (H., 1, 22)

Agathon, too, is presented as sensitive and impressionable, with an imagination willing to accept as truth quite fantastic theories. He entertains himself with contemplation of the spiritual world and describes his reflections thus:

> Dieses brachte mich hernach auf die Gedanken, wie glüklich der Zustand der Geister sey, die den groben thierischen Leib abgelegt haben, und im Anschauen des wesentlichen Schönen, des Unvergänglichen, Jahrtausende durchleben, die ihnen nicht länger scheinen als mir dieser Augenblick.
>
> *(Ag.,* p. 38)

Agathon's preoccupation with the ideally beautiful and the pure spirits is not very different from Don Sylvio's obsession with the society of fairies. Both fantasies are equally diverting from the material world and both are the result of a highly specialized and completely solitary early education. The only difference might be one of tone rather than of substance. That is, Don Sylvio's fantasies are funnier than Agathon's, perhaps because Don Sylvio is himself a more lightly sketched character than Agathon, or perhaps because fairies are a fantasy normally reserved to children, whereas the realms of pure spirit and ideal beauty are matters of serious concern for philosophy. Whatever the reason, Agathon's enthusiasm is a rather earnest matter, while Don Sylvio's provides constant amusement by its guilelessness.

Agathon's recovery from his first fantasy world yields to another form of idealism, his love of Danae, whom he imagines to be the most artistic and virtuous of women, as well as the most beautiful. He imagines that the fantastic strain in his character has now been eradicated, replaced with more accurate perceptions. And yet, we learn that he has never been such a blind enthusiast as in this very love, which he declares to her in glowing superlatives. The narrator corrects the declaration of love with appropriate irony:

> Mit einem Wort: Agathon hatte vielleicht in seinem Leben nie so sehr geschwärmt, als izt, da er sich in dem höchsten Grad der verliebten Bethörung einbildete, dass er alles das, was er der leichtgläubigen Danae vorsagte, eben so gewiss und unmittelbar sehe und fühle . . .
>
> *(Ag.,* p. 211)

Again the prosaic Hippias must listen to the rapturous outpourings of Agathon's sensitive heart:

> Er überliess sich hierauf der ganzen Schwärmerey seines Herzens, um dem Hippias eine Abschilderung zu machen, was er von dem ersten Anblick an bis auf diese Stunde für die schöne Danae empfunden; er beschrieb eine so wahre so delicate, so vollkommene Liebe, breitete sich mit einer so begeisterten Entzükung über die Vollkommenheiten seiner Freundin, über die Sympathie ihrer Seelen, und die fast vergötternde Wonne, welche er in ihrer Liebe geniesse aus, dass man entweder die Bosheit eines Hippias, oder die freundschaftliche Hartherzigkeit eines Mentors haben müsste, um fähig zu seyn, ihn einem so beglükenden Irrthum zu entreissen.
>
> *(Ag.,* p. 229)

In fact, Hippias does play the role of a mentor, albeit unintentionally. It is his cold irony and the revelation of the facts about Danae's past, which bring about Agathon's disillusionment and, as a result, his further development. Although, at first, Agathon retains his original conception of virtue and leaves Danae because he is disappointed in her supposed lack of morality, the process of disillusionment is eventually turned inward upon the hero himself. Because of the experience, he will now call into question those standards by which he judged Danae, and in the end reject them as illusions. He will not regret having left her, but he will recognize the falseness of the grounds for that desertion, as well as its harshness.

In later reflection over his love for Danae, Agathon realizes that, in the end, he was seduced as much by his own enthusiastic heart as by the artifices of the talented Danae:

> War nicht dieses zauberische Licht, welches seine Einbildungskraft gewöhnt war, über alles, was mit seinen Ideen übereinstimmte, auszubreiten; war nicht diese unvermerkte Unterschiebung des Idealen an die Stelle des Würklichen, die wahre Ursache, warum Danae einen so ausserordentlichen Eindruk auf sein Herz machte? War es nicht diese begeisterte Liebe zum Schönen, unter deren schimmernden Flügeln verborgen, die Leidenschaft mit sanftschleichenden Progressen sich endlich durch seine ganze Seele ausbreitete?
>
> (*Ag.*, p. 251)

Another manifestation of Agathon's enormous capacity for *Schwärmerei* is cured, but only as a result of the illuminating experience. Only after having been sated with the luxurious infatuation, and then hearing the tale told by Hippias, can Agathon recognize the extravagance of his behavior. Each experience throughout the novel produces a similar enlightenment, and since Agathon benefits from the lessons thus taught, the process of education is proven successful. It would be contrary to Wieland's expressed intentions to contend that Agathon assumes the role of the perfect hero at the end. He will undoubtedly encounter the disillusioning effect of experience again and again. For this reason, the original version of the novel (1766) in its fragment form, written when Wieland first embarked upon the writing of "true-to-life" narratives, is more interesting for this study than the philosophic ending of the final version (1794) which attempts to bring harmony and to resolve the conflicts of the hero, disillusioned with human nature but committed to public life. At the end of the first version, the narrator sums up his hero's progress:

> Nicht als ob es uns eben so leid sey, unsern Helden (den wir mit allen seinen Fehlern eben so sehr lieben, als ob er ein Sir Karl Grandison wäre) auf dem Wege zu sehen, von allen Arten der Schwärmerey von Grund aus geheilt zu werden—Denn so viel schönes und gutes sich immer zu ihrem Vortheil sagen lassen mag, so

> bleibt doch gewiss, dass es besser ist gesund seyn, und keine Entzükungen haben, als die Harmonie der Sphären hören, und an einem hizigen Fieber liegen.
>
> (*Ag.*, p. 374)

The novel, comically moral, a true-to-life narrative, the story of a hero of mixed character but with vast potential for development towards greatness, is the history of a life as it might be actually lived. It points toward an accuracy of vision and a pragmatism of action, which are the goals of the hero's education. Reasonable efficiency might be viewed as the product of the experiential education which Wieland's heroes undergo. Agathon does not arrive at any ultimate station towards which he has been striving, but he has sufficient education to continue his progress. The educational process has not been a matter of didactic tuition, but a game played by narrator, reader, hero, and the latter's fictive mentors, a game of changing perspectives and the flippant manipulation of conventions of historiography and fiction-writing.

Notes

1. Christoph Martin Wieland, *Werke,* ed. Fritz Martini and Hans Werner Seiffert (Munich: Hanser, 1964-68), 1, 23. This edition will be referred to in the text as H.

2. *Der Teutsche Merkur* (Weimar, 1773-1810), August 1773, p. 120.

3. *Gesammelte Schriften* (Berlin: Preussische Akademie der Wissenschaften, 1909-56), 9, 221-222. This edition will be referred to in the text as P.A.

4. *Geschichte des Agathon,* unveränderter Abdruck der Editio princeps, ed. Klaus Schaefer (Berlin, 1961), pp. 115-116 [This edition will be referred to in the text as *Ag.*].

5. For a detailed discussion of relations between Wieland's novels (*Don Sylvio* in particular) and *Tristram Shandy,* see Peter Michelsen, *Laurence Sterne und der deutsche Roman des 18. Jahrhunderts* (Göttingen, 1962), pp. 181-186. Wolfgang Iser points out that both Richardson and Sterne intended their readers to assume a role in the actual creation of the novel. Iser stresses the necessary changes in narrative form which are the result of such an implication of the reader in the story-telling. ". . . the formulated text must shade off, through allusions and suggestions, into a text that is unformulated, though nonetheless intended." *The Implied Reader* (Baltimore, 1974), p. 31.

6. Jürgen Jacobs, *Wielands Romane* (Bern, 1969), p. 28.

7. Lieselotte Kurth-Voigt states that Wieland's use of a varying perspective in the narrative structure is

not a wholly new phenomenon in German literature, nor was *Don Sylvio* Wieland's first work to
exploit this technique. "Wilhelm Ehrenfried Neugebauer—Der teutsche Don Quichotte: ein Beitrag
zur Geschichte des deutschen Romans im 18. Jahrhundert," *Jahrbuch der deutschen Schillergesellschaft,* XI (1965), 106-130, and *Perspectives and
Points of View: The Early Works of Wieland and
their Background* (Baltimore, 1974).

8. As Wolfgang Iser sees it, a division occurs within
the reader of the novel himself; a boundary is created, by the very process of reading, between the
reader, as he normally is and thinks, and the reader
involved in the action of the novel and thinking
the thoughts of its author. "The Reading Process:
A Phenomenological Approach," *New Literary
History,* 3 (Winter 1972), 298.

9. According to Guy Stern, historical accuracy means
for Wieland "strict adherence to the laws of probability." "Fielding, Wieland and Goethe: A Study
in the Development of the Novel" (Diss: Columbia, 1954), p. 99. Regina Schindler-Hürlimann
agrees that probability of plot is more important
to Wieland than whether what he presents has actually happened. *Wielands Menschenbild: Eine Interpretation des Agathon* (Zürich, 1963), pp. 24-
25.

10. Leo Braudy points to a simultaneous development
in both fiction and history writing which causes
the alliance of true "biographers" (a term which
Henry Fielding applied to himself) and objective
historians against the writers of romances and partisan histories. *Narrative Form in History and
Fiction* (Princeton, 1970), p. 93. Questions of historiography and the 18th century confusion as to
the task of the historian, biographer, and novelist
are also examined by Lieselotte Kurth in "Historiographie und historischer Roman: Kritik und
Theorie im 18. Jahrhundert," *Modern Language
Notes,* 79 (1964), 337-362.

11. *Die Figur des Erzählers in Wielands Romanen*
(Göppingen, 1970), p. 137.

12. Stern, p. 111.

13. Lieselotte Kurth-Voigt, *Die zweite Wirklichkeit:
Studien zum Roman des 18. Jahrhunderts* (Chapel
Hill, 1969), pp. 142-143.

14. *Untersuchung über Wielands Don Sylvio* (Halle,
1901), p. 56. John McCarthy also points out the
"hermit's way of life" common to Wieland's heroes. *Fantasy and Reality: An Epistemological
Approach to Wieland* (Bern, 1974), p. 29.

15. Lieselotte Kurth-Voigt refers to Agathon's imperfection as a "'comic flaw' of which . . . he is

never completely cured." *Perspectives and Points
of View,* p. 169. Agathon is hardly a comic figure.
It is his humane enthusiasm which preserves him
from the despair and tragedy into which his error
might otherwise lead him.

16. John McCarthy stresses Wieland's distinction between true and false enthusiasm: "Schwärmerei
generally denotes aberration from the norm, lack
of contact with reality, and loss of *gesunde Vernunft*. On the other hand, in Wieland's terminology . . . enthusiasm denotes the ability immediately to perceive the Beautiful, the True, and the
Good." *Fantasy and Reality,* p. 30. McCarthy further traces the development of the use of and distinction between the two terms in "Shaftesbury
and Wieland: The Question of Enthusiasm," *Studies in Eighteenth-Century Culture,* VI (1977), 85-
95.

17. Schindler-Hürlimann, p. 100.

Herbert Rowland (essay date April 1980)

SOURCE: Rowland, Herbert. "Wieland's 'Der
Vogelsang': *Prodesse* between Enlightenment and Idealism." *Modern Language Notes* 95, no. 3 (April 1980):
655-63.

[*In the following essay, Rowland explores the didactic
elements in Wieland's writings, focusing in particular
on his 1778 verse narrative "Der Vogelsang."*]

Whenever asked about the ultimate purpose of literature, Wieland responded in good enlightenment fashion
by emphasizing that literary art, in addition to providing pleasure, should instruct.[1] What he understood by
such instruction, however,—its specific nature and manner of realization in practice—underwent a profound
change which is reflected in the shift from overt didacticism in his early writings to implied didacticism in the
works beginning with ***Don Sylvio*** [***Die Abenteuer des
Don Sylvio von Rosalva***] (1764).[2] His later attitude
finds poetic expression in a short verse narrative called
"Der Vogelsang, oder die drei Lehren" (1778), which
is a recreation or adaptation of "Le lai de l'oiselet," an
anonymous early thirteenth century French *fabliau* first
published by Étienne Barbazan in 1756.[3] Especially in
comparison with its source, this work provides an opportunity to study Wieland's understanding of the didactic dimension of literature and to view one portion
of the interface between enlightenment and idealism.

The narrator sets the scene in Swabia some five hundred years in the past and then describes the opulent estate of a medieval parvenu called "der reiche Hans". On
this estate there is a paradisiacal grove formed by a

seven-fold circle of linden trees with branches inter-twined so as to create eternal twilight; in the center a rose hedge surrounds a marble fountain which bubbles forth clear, ice-cold refreshment. Twice a day a little bird endowed by fairies with magical powers appears at the fountain to sing. As long as it is present the beauty of the grove endures; as soon as it leaves, however, the foliage withers, the flowers die, and the fountain runs dry, leaving nothing but rock and sand behind. One day the Philistine Hans snares the bird in order to receive a handsome reward from the king. Finding its arguments of no avail, the bird buys its freedom by promising to tell Hans three things,

> Die nie ein Mann von Euerem Stamm
> Gewußt, von Sinn gar wundersam;
> Die sollen Euch groß Gut gewähren![4]

From the safety of a nearby branch the bird announces its *Lehren*: "Glaub nicht gleich Alles, was Du hörst!", (p. 108) "Weine nicht um etwas, das Du nicht gehabt!", (p. 109) and "Narr, was Du in den Händen hast, halt fest und laß' es nimmer fahren!" (p. 110) Hans, who expected another kind of "groß Gut", tears his clothing and hair in rage, claiming he has known these banalities all his life. However, the bird chides him for not living by them and then flies away, whereupon the grove becomes a wasteland.

The tale of the little bird can be read as an allegory of art and the artist and their place in life. The grove with its mystical seven circles of lindens and its clear fountain forever shaded from the sun represents the realm of art. The bird, which through its presence and song creates this enchanted world apart, stands for the artist. It can change the mood of its listeners at will with its melodies:

> Da war kein Schmerz noch Gram so groß,
> Der nicht in seinem Sang zerfloß;
> . . . .
> Und sang er Freud' im bunten Kranz,
> Gleich hob sich jeder Fuß zum Tanz;
> Und wenn er Ritterthaten sang,
> Ward einem stracks nach Kämpfen bang,
>
> (p. 103)

The artist, like the little bird, has the power to allay the troubles of life, to beautify existence, and to point the way to a more perfect world. Without him and his creation life is barren, like the wasteland remaining after the bird leaves the grove. The artist also has a refining and ennobling influence on his audience. With the knights and ladies of the court in mind the bird sings:

> . . . desto lieber
> War ich ihnen und mein Liederspiel,
> Und vor wonniglichem, pressendem Gefühl,
> Gingen manche klare Äuglein über,
> Und der liederwerthen Thaten wurden viel',

> Viel' gethan, und mancher Dank erstritten,
> Und sie lohnten deß der Lieb' und mir;
>
> (p. 106)

In this sense the artist can be said to instruct or to improve his audience. To fulfill his two-fold purpose of embellishing life and cultivating man the artist requires freedom; any stricture placed upon him from without threatens his art. The bird explains to Hans:

> Der Käfig ist mir stark zuwider.
> Ich liebe freien Himmel, ich,
> Drum, lieber Herr, seid nun so bieder
> Und schenkt mir meine Freiheit wieder!
> Denn, glaubt mir, da geht nichts davon,
> Im Bauer sing' ich keinen Ton.
>
> (p. 107)

In the crassly materialistic Hans one sees a representation of all those forces which would in some way circumscribe the province of art:

> Zwar singt er hübsch; allein, was schere
> Ich mich um seine Dudelei?
> Kommt doch zuletzt nichts 'raus dabei!
>
> (p. 105)

The art of the little bird is autonomous, obeying the law of its creator alone. Through its mere existence, however, it has the power to quicken one's experience of life and to heighten one's sensibilities.

In **"Der Vogelsang"** Wieland remains closer to his source than in any of his many other adaptations of French works; according to Albert Fuchs, to summarize one is to outline the other.[5] Despite the obvious similarities, however, often subtle differences exist between the two works. And these differences, which Fuchs sometimes criticizes or dismisses as insignificant, prove to be important in an attempt to understand Wieland's attitude toward didacticism in literature.

Fuchs mentions the digressions in **"Der Vogelsang"** as one of the features which distinguish it from the "Lai de l'oiselet," criticizing Wieland for a lack of conciseness.[6] Now, concision was admittedly not one of Wieland's virtues, nor, however, was it cultivated by him. The lack of it here simply bears testimony to a narrative posture different from that of the "Lai."

Close to the beginning of the work the narrator launches into a long, detailed description of Hans' estate, the beauty of the grounds and mansion, the richness of the furnishings, and the opulence of the cellars and larders. He even jests about his own garrulity: "Ich sage nichts von all dem feinen / Geräthe drin", (p. 101) and then proceeds to wander leisurely through the mansion enumerating all he sees. After an equally leisurely—and descriptive—stroll through the garden the narrator reflects:

Es geht doch, sagt mir, was Ihr wollt,
Nichts über Wald-und Gartenleben
Und schlürfen ein Dein trinkbar Gold,
O Morgensonn', und sorglos schweben
Daher im frischen Blumenduft
Und, mit dem sanften Weben
Der freien Luft,
Als wie aus tausend offnen Sinnen
Dich in sich ziehn, Natur, und ganz in Dir zerrinnen!

(p. 102)

Suddenly becoming aware of his self-indulgence, the narrator halts:

Wo war ich?—Gutes Volk, verzeiht!
Ich ließ Euch doch nicht lange warten?
Der Abweg ist zum Glück nicht weit;
Wir sind ja noch in Hansens Garten.

(p. 102)

In his description of the beautiful magical grove only a few lines later the narrator sinks into reverie once again and must catch himself and regain his reader's attention with a sharp "Nun merket auf!" (p. 103)

The narrator of **"Der Vogelsang"** is indeed more loquacious than his counterpart in the "Lai," especially at the outset. Wieland's work is some thirty lines longer than the old French *fabliau,* and fully half of these occur before the tale of the little bird and Hans ever begins. This fact is less important in itself, of course, than for the narrative stance to which it attests. By emerging from the impersonality of the third person in his praise of nature the narrator fictionalizes himself as a character within his own fictive world; the second person "Ihr" indicates the presence of a fictional reader, whom he also draws into the narrative act. The narrator becomes so absorbed by the sensual splendor of the estate he is forming that he is reluctant to end the description. He becomes so caught up in the *Naturstimmung* of his own making that he forgets momentarily what he set out to do, and both he and his reader would gladly linger in the enchanted grove. Together, they—and the real reader—consciously create and enjoy the aesthetic experience of this fictitious world, of which the bird, Hans, and their fortunes are only part. One concludes that this aesthetic experience itself, rather than the specific elements which form it, is the true *raison d'être* of the work. As Müller-Solger has said, "Daher ist es letzten Endes nicht von Belang, *was* erzählt wird . . . Ebenso ist es für den Erzähler erst in zweiter Linie von Bedeutung, *wie* diese Erzählung im Einzelnen verläuft. Wichtig ist allein, *daß* erzählt wird. . . ."[7] Strictly speaking, the allegory with its specific motifs of the bird and the parvenu is less important in itself than the aesthetic experience which it provides; it could be exchanged for another form and set of motifs, as long as the effect remained the same. Of course, the theme of the allegory—the embellishing and cultivating power of the artist and his art—is a mirror image of the ethos of the narrative technique; together, they give the work its unity. However, the form as such remains subordinate to the spirit in which it is used.[8] This is not true of the old French "Lai," where there is no self-conscious attempt to create an aesthetic experience on the order of **"Der Vogelsang."** The narrator of the "Lai" is, as might be expected, more conventional than his German counterpart.

Despite similarities, there is a basic difference in the specifically didactic content of the two works.[9] The "Lai" passes on a sort of wisdom not found in **"Der Vogelsang."** In one of his songs the *oiselet,* addressing himself to the *monde courtois,* recommends a union of religion and love, saying that they have the same goals and are thus of one accord. If the listener holds to the values of *courtoisie* he can both attain God and have the good life here on earth.[10] The theme of *courtoisie,* with its religious overtones, is central to the medieval work. Indeed, the three proverbs presented at the end, around which so much of the work revolves, are considered to be individual aspects of the greater complex.[11] In **"Der Vogelsang"** the bird sings in praise of eternal love and honor, but the connection between the two is not essential, and the religious dimension of the "Lai" is completely missing. The three *Lehren* stand at the end with no explicit or implicit relationship to the bird's song nor, even more important, to the theme of art and the artist.

More important for our purposes than the didactic content itself is the narrative attitude toward it. The narrator of the "Lai" makes a gesture of having direct access to truth and presents the tale of the *oiselet* and *vilain* as a kind of illustration, stating unequivocally that one can take a profitable example from it.[12] At the end of the work he summarizes the significance of the story: He who covets all loses all.[13] The bird's musical pronouncement on the identity of divine and earthly love and his three proverbs are made with the same gesture; indeed, the narrator and the *oiselet* are identical in the oracular nature of their statements. The relationship between the narrator and his narration here is similar to that of a fable. Thus, despite the imaginative, playful character of the "Lai," it seems reasonable to say that instruction of a direct kind is its main purpose. In Wieland's work, on the other hand, the narrator never strikes an omniscient pose, nor does he evaluate the events of the allegory; there is no identification of narrator and bird. Within the framework of the tale the little bird does wax didactic in presenting the *Lehren* and chastising Hans for not living according to the truths he professes to know. While valid enough in themselves, however, these proverbs and the imperative to realize one's insights have no relation to any attitude or body of wisdom presented as ideal and, as a result, give an impression of the random and dispensable. As part of a larger aesthetic whole, of an experience created primarily for its own sake, their purely didactic thrust is vitiated. The bird does not serve to impart some higher truth; it and its fantasy world are the truth of the work.

The appearance of a fictionalized personal narrator in **"Der Vogelsang"** signals a subjectification of the narrative process. This figure drops the pretense of possessing objective truth characteristic of his counterpart in the "Lai" or the personas of contemporary *Lehrgedichte*.[14] The truth of the work—the finery of the mansion, the beauty of the grounds, the bird's song with all that it means—is the truth, the vision, of one person alone, the creator, and resides within the boundaries of the work itself. The work is no longer a medium; it is the "Ding an sich". Implicit in this subjectification is an indirectness of statement. Allegory, while it occasionally comprised entire pieces and was frequently used for purposes of illustration in overtly didactic works, was frowned upon by enlighteners precisely because of its indirectness. It was felt that allegory insulted the intelligence of the reader, treated him as an "einfältiger Tropf", by emphasizing ornamentation rather than addressing itself to the logical structures of content and thereby the intellect of the reader.[15] In **"Der Vogelsang"** the allegory is still less strict than in works typical of the period. The little bird and Hans do not represent specific principles of morality or scientific knowledge; rather, they are suggestive of various aspects of art and the limitations imposed on it in life. The bird evokes the multifarious power of art to enrich existence and to enhance the individual's capacity to live; in Hans, on the other hand, one can see any inhibitive force, from the narrow moralist on down to the censor himself. The presence of a fictional narrator and reader serves as a prism through which the truth of the work is further refracted. By comparison, the instruction of **"Der Vogelsang"** appears indeed indirect.

The avowedly didactic poets of the enlightenment addressed themselves principally to the rational faculty of their readership and, when concerned with matters of character, usually turned to individual issues, in accordance with Gottsched's dictum.[16] In the aesthetic experience of **"Der Vogelsang,"** however, Wieland appeals to the senses at least as much as to the intellect; for him morality appears to involve the whole person. In a short essay entitled **"Über das Verhältnis des Angenehmen und Schönen zum Nützlichen"** (1775) Wieland, following in the footsteps of Shaftesbury, states than man possesses an innate sense of the pleasing and beautiful which distinguishes him from and lifts him above the other animals; indeed, he becomes more human the more he refines it.[17] This sense operates in all areas of life. On the one hand man improves the useful in the narrow sense of the word, i.e., those necessities which he has in common with the animals—food, shelter, and the like—, passing from the indispensable to the com-

fortable and ultimately on to the beautiful. On the other hand he cultivates his manners and intellect, which leads to advances in social living and to creativity in the arts and sciences. **"Der Vogelsang"** addresses precisely this sense in all its emotional-rational and aesthetic-pragmatic compass and in so doing, even in its artistic autonomy, influences the entire character of its listener. Ideally, virtuous action should follow as a natural consequence. In the final analysis morality, truth, and beauty are, for Wieland as for Shaftesbury, identical.[18] In his essay Wieland says that to approve only of the useful in the usual sense of the word, as commonly occurs, would be to deny the most human element of human nature—that sense for what goes beyond the essential. If one accepts as useful all that perfects man and his condition, however, then all discrepancies between the useful and beautiful vanish, and the two appear closely related. If we, in turn, view instruction in **"Der Vogelsang"** in terms of this broader concept of the useful, then the discrepancies between *prodesse* and *delectare* disappear as well, and they too would seem to be closely related.

In its obliqueness and its appeal to the total character the didactic mode of **"Der Vogelsang"** is identical to the classical-romantic position outlined fifteen years later by Schiller in his essay "Über das Pathetische":

> Aber was die Dichtkunst mittelbar ganz vortrefflich macht, würde ihr unmittelbar nur sehr schlecht gelingen. Die Dichtkunst führt bei dem Menschen nie ein besondres Geschäft aus, und man könnte kein ungeschickteres Werkzeug erwählen, um einen enzelnen Auftrag, ein Detail, gut besorgt zu sehen. Ihr Wirkungskreis ist das Total der menschlichen Natur, und bloß, insofern sie auf den Charakter einfließt, kann sie auf seine einzelnen Wirkungen Einfluß haben.[19]

In this respect **"Der Vogelsang"** represents a significant departure from attitudes and practices typical of the enlightenment. Wieland does not take the step to symbolism made by Goethe and Schiller.[20] Here, as in most of his other verse narratives, he relies on older sources for specific forms and motifs. Yet, he alters his sources in varying degrees to suit his own purposes, and the result is thus a work essentially distinct from the original. Historically speaking, Wieland's attitude toward didacticism in literature, as revealed in **"Der Vogelsang,"** lies somewhere along the continuum between enlightenment and idealism and represents either a transition or, more charitably and perhaps more accurately, another possibility.

Notes

1. Hermann Müller-Solger, *Der Dichtertraum: Studien zur Entwicklung der dichterischen Phantasie im Werk Christoph Martin Wielands,* Göppinger Arbeiten zur Germanistik, 24 (Göppingen: Kümmerle, 1970), p. 128.

2. Müller-Solger discusses aspects of this change in *Der Dichtertraum,* pp. 130-131, as does Regine Schindler-Hürlimann in *Wielands Menschenbild: Eine Interpretation des Agathon,* Zürcher Beiträge zur deutschen Literatur- und Geistesgeschichte, 21 (Zurich: Atlantis, 1963), pp. 21-23.

3. Gaston Paris, Introduction to "Le lai de l'oiselet," *Legendes du moyen âge* (1903; rpt., Amsterdam: Rodopi, 1970), p. 269.

4. "Der Vogelsang, oder die drei Lehren," *Wielands Werke,* ed. Heinrich Düntzer (Berlin: Hempel, 1879 ff.), XII, 108. Subsequent references to the work will be cited in the text as page numbers in parentheses.

5. Albert Fuchs, *Les apports français dans l'oeuvre de Wieland de 1772 à 1789,* Bibliothèque de la Revue de Littérature Comparée, 101 (Paris: Champion, 1934), p. 69.

6. ibid., pp. 72-73.

7. Müller-Solger, *Der Dichtertraum,* p. 243.

8. Cornelius Sommer says of Wieland's verse narratives as a whole, "Es ist also von vornherein auszuschließen, daß es der Zweck der Dichtung sei, das Inhaltliche durch eine schöne und überzeugende Gestaltung eingängiger zu machen; sondern die Dichtung soll *als Dichtung* wirken, als Erlebnis der Seelenkräfte." "Wielands Epen und Verserzählungen: Form und dichtungstheoretischer Hintergrund," Diss. Tübingen, 1966, pp. 22-23.

9. While the concept of art and the artist as discussed does not fall appropriately under the heading of "didactic content", this may be the proper point to comment on the problem in connection with the "Lai." I do not feel that the author of the "Lai" has actually thematicized an attitude toward art, as Fuchs suggests (*Les apports français,* p. 74). Paris is not aware of any such aspect of the work; he discusses the bird merely as a traditional symbol of the priest of the religion of love. More recently, Grente fails to make mention of the theme with regard to the "Lai": Cardinal Georges Grente, ed., *Dictionnaire des lettres françaises, Le Moyen Age* (Paris: Librairie Arthème Fayard, 1964), p. 449. The bird creates an enchanted orchard with its presence and song and destroys it upon leaving, just as in Wieland's work. However, it does so more to relay wisdom from a higher source than to create an autonomous aesthetic experience. A rather minor discrepancy between the two works may serve to show the difference in emphasis. On being released by Hans the bird

> .. schnurrt heraus aus seiner Höhle,
> So froh wie eine arme Seele,

> Die aus des Fegfeu'rs Flammennacht
> Ein frommer Klausner frei gemacht.
> Er hüpft und tanzt im Kreis umher,
> Als ob er neu geboren wär',

(p. 108)

Such a reaction to newly-won freedom, true to nature or not (Fuchs finds it somehow unnatural, p. 73), is quite appropriate, perhaps necessary, in terms of the theme of the artist's need for free expression. In the corresponding passage in the "Lai" the bird simply preens its ruffled feathers. Wieland recognized the potential in the old work and made use of it for his own purposes.

10. "Le lai de l'oiselet," *Fabliaux et contes des poètes françois des XII, XIII, XIV & XVes siécles. tirés des meilleurs auteurs,* ed. Étienne Barbazan (Paris: Vincent, 1756), I, 186-187.

> Et por verité vos recort,
> Diex & amors sont d'un acort,
> . . . .
> Et se vos à ce vos tenez,
> Deu & le siecle avoir poez.

11. In chastising the *vilain* for not living the truths he claims to know the *oiselet* makes the following generalization ("Le lai," p. 198):

> On dist que tex n'entent qui ot
> Que ces paroles de grans sens
> Qui n'et pas de sage porpens,
> Tex parole de cortoisie
> Qu'il ne la saroit faire mie,

12. "Exemples y pourroit-on prendre, / Dont on vaurroit miex en la fin,"

13. "Le lai," p. 199:

> Et bien sachiez toutes & tuit,
> Que li prodons dist en apert,
> Cils qui tout convoite tout pert.
> . . . .
> Il [the *vilain*] perdi par son convoitier
> Et son deduit & son vergier.

14. Leif Ludwig Albertsen discusses the posture of the didactic poet in *Das Lehrgedicht: eine Geschichte der antikisierenden Sachepik in der neueren deutschen Literatur mit einem unbekannten Gedicht Albrecht von Hallers* (Aarhus: Akademisk Boghandel, 1967), p. 38.

15. Christoph Siegrist, *Das Lehrgedicht der Aufklärung,* Germanistische Abhandlungen, 43 (Stuttgart: Metzler, 1974), p. 43.

16. Gottsched, *Versuch einer critischen Dichtkunst,* 4th ed. (1751; rpt., 5th ed. Darmstadt: Wissenschaftliche Buchgesellschaft, 1962), p. 611.

17. *Werke,* XXXII, 36 and 38.

18. Charles Elson, *Wieland and Shaftesbury,* Columbia University Germanic Studies, 16 (1913; rpt., New York: AMS Press, 1966), p. 60.

19. Friedrich Schiller, "Über das Pathetische," *Werke in drei Bänden,* ed. Herbert G. Göpfert (Munich: Hanser, 1966), II, 443.

20. Karl Heinz Kausch discusses the difference between Wieland's *Eigenart* and Schiller's *Symbolkunst* in "Die Kunst der Grazie: Ein Beitrag zum Verständnis Wielands," *Jahrbuch der deutschen Schillergesellschaft,* 2 (1958), pp. 36-42.

Richard G. Rogan (essay date May 1981)

SOURCE: Rogan, Richard G. "The Reader in Wieland's *Die Abenteuer des Don Sylvio von Rosalva.*" *German Studies Review* 4, no. 2 (May 1981): 177-93.

[*In the following essay, Rogan examines Wieland's use of the reader as a fictional character in* Die Abenteuer des Don Sylvio von Rosalva. *Rogan argues that the interaction between narrator and reader in the novel is primarily intended to serve as a means of educating the actual reader of Wieland's work.*]

A number of contemporary literary critics have begun to devote considerable attention to the concept of the reader and his role within a literary text. To be sure, the novel of eighteenth-century England itself, since it is clearly characterized by the actual appearance within the work of fictional reader figures who are frequently addressed by the narrator and who are themselves on occasion allowed to speak, has had consideration from such a methodological perspective. In such works as Henry Fielding's *Tom Jones* and *Joseph Andrews* or Laurence Sterne's *Tristram Shandy,* for example, the appearance of fictional readers is always apparent.[1] Such reader figures also appear with particular definition in the novel of eighteenth-century Germany,[2] and one of the first works in which their presence is especially clear is C. M. Wieland's *Die Abenteuer des Don Sylvio von Rosalva.*

In the recent past several critical studies have appeared that have treated various aspects of this Wieland novel. Jörg Schönert in his analysis of satire and its relationship to the German novel of the eighteenth century points out that *Don Sylvio* is in essence a narrated comedy whose most important aspect is not its satire but rather the actual process of narration through which an interchange between the narrator and the reader is facilitated.[3] Although he attaches importance to the reader with *Don Sylvio,* Schönert does not analyze the fic-

tional figures or their actual significance. In his consideration of irony in *Don Sylvio* Wolfgang Jahn indeed stresses how closely tied an understanding of this irony is to the real reader's awareness of literary allusion, but like Schönert he does not concern himself with the fictional reader figures within the novel.[4] Although Lieselotte Kurth-Voigt's treatment of narrative perspective in Wieland's early works includes a discussion of this novel which focuses upon the various narrative voices within, and their significance for, the work, she does not consider the matter of the reader.[5] John McCarthy's study *Fantasy and Reality* approaches *Don Sylvio* from the perspective of its philosophical and satirical aspects and is primarily concerned with the subject of truth and its apprehension in the novel.[6] Once again, however, although there is reference made to a reader, no thorough attention is given to this topic. Using Wolfgang Kayser's assessment of *Don Sylvio* as a starting point, Keith Leopold approaches the work from the aspect of its modernity and concludes that it is significant as "the first German third-person humorous novel on a high intellectual plane."[7] But, while clearly acknowledging that *Don Sylvio*'s importance lies primarily in its narrative technique, Leopold neglects to treat with any thoroughness a matter that is certainly a basic part of that technique, namely the reader figures and their significance.

To be sure, other critics have in their studies of Wieland shown somewhat more awareness of the reader. Gerd Matthecka in his dissertation on the theory of the novel held by Wieland and his predecessors amply demonstrates awareness of the narrator and his communication with the reader but makes no attempt to investigate the matter.[8] That the proximity of the narrator to the reader is significant for Wieland and has a pedagogical purpose is the concern of Jürgen Jacobs in his book *Wielands Romane,* but like Matthecka, Jacobs neglects to probe in detail the matter of the fictional readers and their significance for the real reader.[9] Steven R. Miller explores the topic of the narrator as a purveyor of truth through conversation and does not ignore the narrator's relationship to the reader, but in his study one again misses a truly detailed analysis of the fictional readers and their role in *Don Sylvio.*[10] In M. H. Würzner's article on *Agathon* the emphasis is upon a consideration of the reader and his significance, and even though his treatment is valid, Würzner by no means exhausts the subject.[11] The most recent discussion of the reader in Wieland involves *Don Sylvio* and *Agathon.* Christiane Seiler in her essay analyzes on the basis of very few textual examples from the two novels the relationship between the narrator and his reader. She neglects, however, to demonstrate awareness of the important distinction between the fictional and real reader.[12]

On the whole, therefore, Wieland scholarship has shown that it is aware of the existence of reader figures within the novels, but it has generally failed to distinguish between a real and fictional reader and has not, in all, treated the topic of the reader with the detailed attention it deserves. In this article I propose to look carefully at the fictional readers in *Don Sylvio* and to discuss their relationship to, and significance for, the real reader. It is hoped that in this way new awareness and understanding can be brought to a previously little treated aspect of a work whose role in the development of the German novel has been quite significant and, at the same time, that a model may be provided for future research in this area.

To be sure, any discussion of a reader must begin with a definition of terms and an answer to the question of "which reader," but first, however, one must realize the important distinction between author and narrator: whereas the actual author is the one having written the novel, the narrator is the fictive personality (or, in the case of *Don Sylvio*, fictive personalities[13]) within the framework of the novel who comments on the action and through whose eyes the action is, in general, interpreted. Wolfgang Kayser has said in this regard, ". . . der Erzähler ist eine gedichtete Person . . ."[14] and elsewhere, "Der Erzähler ist immer eine gedichtete, eine fiktive Gestalt, die in das Ganze der Dichtung hineingehört."[15] In an analogous way the real reader is that individual who holds the book in his hands and actually engages in the process of reading, while the fictional reader (or, again in the case of *Don Sylvio*, fictional readers) is that figure whose personality is in fact indicated within the narrative: his identity is either implicit or explicit within the text. Walker Gibson describes the distinction in these terms: "I am arguing, then, that there are two readers distinguishable in every literary experience. First, there is the 'real' individual upon whose crossed knees rests the open volume, and whose personality is as complex and ultimately inexpressible as any dead poet's. Second, there is the fictitious reader—I shall call him the 'mock reader' . . ."[16]

Don Sylvio involves not a single fictional reader but in fact various such individuals who are described in many ways but who themselves do not actually speak within the novel. One may therefore say that passive fictional readers are present whose existence is indicated through the narrator's description but who are never themselves allowed to speak. As might be expected, there are various ways in which these fictional readers are referred to in the novel. They are addressed simply as "Leser,"[17] "geneigter Leser,"[18] or "günstiger Leser" (p. 173, l. 25). In each such instance the desire of the narrator is to compliment these reader figures, to scold them mildly, to gain their attention, or simply to demonstrate trust and confidence in them. At other times the narrator's reference to the readers involves the word "unser," the use of which shows that the narrator considers his fictional readers to be close to him and feels responsible for their welfare.[19] In most instances "unsere Leser" are

simply expected to do, recognize, or observe something,[20] but at other times certain qualities are indicated about them: in one instance they are viewed as sleepy (p. 128, l. 23); at another time they are said not to be in love (p. 135, l. 3); another passage shows their eagerness to see the end of an episode (p. 262, l. 12). A certain playfulness on the part of the narrator towards these readers is quite apparent here, a playfulness which indeed characterizes the narrator/reader relationship in general. Three other words used in connection with the readers are "wert,"[21] "geliebt" (p. 192, l. 33), and "weise" (p. 202, ll. 20-21), each of which serves here not so much to characterize the readers as to show an attempt on the part of the narrator to gain intimacy and favor: the words stress the high regard in which the readers are held. Although these qualitative words are used in reference to the fictional readers, there are also quantitative adjectives applied to them, words like "die meisten Leser" (p. 346, l. 15) and "einige" (p. 370, l. 16). As is apparent from their meanings, these adjectives show that the narrator's perception of his readers involves groups, in the one instance a group due to whose possible lack of understanding the translator is said to have omitted certain speculations, in the other instance a group that is reproved for its "Trägheit." That the narrating figure amusingly conceives of his readers as less than perfect is again abundantly clear; that his wish is to improve them is equally clear.[22]

Although the word "Leser" in conjunction with various adjectives provides the most frequent reference to the fictional reader, it does not provide the only direct reference. On several occasions the word "Leserinnen" is employed with such adjectives as "unser" (p. 224, l. 24), "einige" (p. 370, l. 16), and "schön" (p. 34, l. 6). In these instances it is clear that the narrator wishes to involve the female segment of his imagined reading public, to compliment (or even scold) its members, and ultimately to gain their favor. There are other words used in the novel which also act as synonyms for "Leser." In the work's foreword the expression "dem hochansehnlichen Publiko" (p. 11, ll. 9-10) appears, which is indeed a very positive way to describe and flatter these readers but which, on the other hand, can also be understood as an ironic reference to them, a further demonstration of the playfulness characterizing the work. Somewhat later the term "solche Liebhaber" (p. 139, l. 26) is used of those readers who the narrator thinks would be interested in hearing more about the character Laura but who will be disappointed because the narrator is not about to discuss her any more. This thus refers to a specific portion of the fictional public. Much the same is true later when negative reference is made to certain readers. When speaking of a group of readers who expect no more than "eine eitle Belustigung" from this novel, the narrator calls them "junge leichtsinnige Schwindelköpfe" (p. 192, ll. 30-31). In the same section of the work "einige" (p. 192, l. 35) is used of readers who lack understanding and thus will be unable to see that the novel's purpose is more than simple entertainment. Once more the narrator is very frank in his realization of some imagined readers as less than perfect and demonstrates that he is more than willing to reprimand them for their inadequacies.

Although the existence of truly fictional readers is apparent, it remains to be seen how these readers involved in the fictional world are related to the real reader. In **Don Sylvio** an authorial narrative situation exists which involves constant direct comment from the narrating figures regarding both action and characters. This intrusion destroys epic illusion and makes it impossible for the real reader to become part of the illusion which the narrator describes: the direct entry of the narrating figure into the novel precludes constant empathy with the fictional characters. Steven R. Miller says, "Im Grunde wirkt das im Werk enthaltene Erzähler-Leser-Verhältnis wie eine Art Verfremdungseffekt, der den Leser davon zurückhält, sich in die Geschichte zu versenken und sich mit den Charakteren zu identifizieren."[23] Consequently, the real reader comes to identify not with the hero of this novel or with any of the characters included in the tale but rather with the fictional reader figures: the real reader thus plays the role of the fictional reader and in this way manages to take an active part in the novel. Kayser describes this process when he writes, "Der Leser ist etwas Gedichtetes, ist eine Rolle, in die wir hineinschlüpfen und bei der wir uns selber zusehen können."[24] Elsewhere he says, "Ebenso aber, wie der Erzähler nicht mit der biographisch faßbaren Gestalt des Dichters identisch ist, ist der biographisch faßbare und sich selbst bekannte Besitzer eines Romans identisch mit dem Leser, der im Roman angesprochen, getäuscht, befragt und auf mancherlei Weise einbezogen ist: auch dieser Leser ist ein fiktives Wesen, in das wir uns erst verwandeln."[25] More recently Walter Ong has made essentially the same point: "A reader has to play the role in which the author has cast him, which seldom coincides with his role in the rest of actual life."[26] This is then the situation that prevails in **Don Sylvio.**

Now that the relationship between the real reader and his fictional counterparts is clear, one may more easily understand the reason for it; it is, namely, an attempt to manipulate the real reader by means of the fictional readers. Such manipulation may be direct or indirect.

Direct manipulation involves an attempt to bring the real reader, through the fictional reader, to a certain attitude, opinion, or way of looking at something, and its initial appearance occurs in the introduction, ironically called "Nachbericht," where the reader is taken into especially great regard. In this introduction an effort is made to present the reader with an idea of the source for the work as well as to establish its "Wahrheit." However, also important in terms of the reader is the very

fact that the basic pattern of narrator/reader involvement with one another is established, a pattern which recurs constantly throughout the novel. After the real reader confronts the introduction and comes into close contact with the editorial figure through the figure of the fictional reader, he is well prepared for the almost constant contact with the editorial and author figures which occurs in the main body of the novel.

In **Don Sylvio** the fictional editor points out in the introduction that the reader must himself decide the validity of the work's origin; he says, "Ich muß es dem guten Willen der Leser überlassen, ob sie glauben wollen oder nicht daß dieses Buch den Don Ramiro von Z***, der einige Jahre Gesandtschafts-Secretarius bei einem bekannten Spanischen Minister an einem deutschen Hofe gewesen, zum Verfasser habe" (p. 9, ll. 4-8). However, the editor must admit that he never had the Spanish original in his hands. He has to rely on the translator as a witness who is so trustworthy "daß ich mir die Mühe nicht geben mag, an der Wahrheit seiner Erzählung zu zweifeln" (p. 9, ll. 17-18). Thus, by the editor's expressed confidence in the reliability of this source as well as by his stated interest in the reader, the latter is subtly manipulated into acceptance of the former's point of view. Yet, the fact will not escape the careful reader that the editor has really not given any proof whatsoever and the problem of historical origin is not being settled. The question is actually left undecided: "Ich lasse alles dieses an seinen Ort gestellt sein" (p. 9, l. 25).

Having thus commented on the work's origin, the editorial figure proceeds to a consideration of how the reader is expected to react to the novel. By showing laughter as his own reaction, he obviously demonstrates that this is a reasonable and desirable reaction: "Was ich gewiß sagen kann, ist, daß mich Don Sylvio von Rosalva so sehr belustiget als irgend ein Buch von dieser Art, und daß ich bei Durchlesung des Manuscripts so oft und so herzlich lachen mußte, daß meine Frau . . . mich fragte, was mir fehle . . ." (p. 9, ll. 26-32). Not only is this his own response but also that of his wife, whom he describes as "eine gute Art von einem Hausweibe" (p. 9, l. 35) and "kein gelehrtes Frauenzimmer" (p. 10, l. 1) but one who has "so viel Vernunft, daß sie weiß, wenn man lachen und wenn man weinen muß" (p. 10, ll. 1-2). By showing that he, an educated individual, and his wife, an uneducated one, both respond in the same manner, the editor demonstrates that laughter is a common response to the work and therefore conditions his readers to react in a similar manner.

Indeed his wife is not the only one who is amused by the novel; several other members of the household are as well. The normally serious "Schreiber" enters and thinks that his employer and his wife have gone insane, but after hearing the editor read some of the novel aloud, he too breaks into laughter. The maid, or the "Stuben-Mensch", is attracted by this laughter, hears the editor read part of the novel, and she also begins to laugh. The same happens to both the "Köchin" and the "Hausknecht." Eventually the chain reaction even reaches to people on the street who laugh along "ohne daß sie wußten warum?" (p. 10, l. 37). The editor finally stops reading aloud but not without first saying that this laughter could have spread throughout the whole town if he had not ceased. In a comment to "den geneigten Leser" he apologizes for having allowed his description to get somewhat out of hand and indicates that he is fully aware of the respectful stance which an editor has to take toward his audience in a preface. The only point he wanted to make is that he is convinced that ". . . Don Sylvio und sein getreuer Pedrillo nicht wenig beitragen werden, der Hypochondrie und dem Spleen Einhalt zu tun . . ." (p. 11, ll. 12-13), a process which laughter will expedite.

Although great emphasis is obviously put upon laughter, the editor does not overlook other possibilities of reader reaction. Again, in order to strengthen the reader's confidence in him and to lead the reader to appreciate the editor's integrity, he says, "Weil man aber doch aufrichtig sein, und das eine sagen muß wie das andre, so kann ich nicht bergen, daß ich einen gewissen Papefiguier kenne, der dieses Buch in einem ganz andern Lichte betrachtet . . ." (p. 11, ll. 19-22). This individual after having read the book "geriet in einen so heftigen Eifer über ein so gottloses und gefährliches Buch, daß ich Gewalt brauchen mußte um ihn zu verhindern, daß er es nicht auf der Stelle ins Camin warf" (p. 12, ll. 6-9). It is thus conceded that this is a possible reaction, but it is not one which the editor considers acceptable: he does, after all, portray this person as a negative individual, a Jansenist who is discontented with everything. Since the typical conception of the Jansenist was of one who was very serious and uncompromisingly obedient to rigid moral principles, it is understandable that the editor depicts him as unable to respond to the novel in the way that most others have responded.

In order to find out the extent to which this Jansenist's feelings about the book might be shared by others, the editor, in what appears to be a pursuit of fairness, speaks of "einem angesehen Geistlichen, welcher dermalen Dechant zu*** ist und bei jedermann den Namen eines der gelehrtesten und frömmsten Priestern in unsrer ganzen Revier hat" (p. 12, ll. 22-24), to whom he gave the book for criticism. Since this particular priest is obviously considered by the editor and others as a fine individual whose opinion is to be valued, the reader is manipulated into viewing his judgment with respect.[27] This priest too has an opinion about the novel; the editor says, ". . . er vermute sehr, daß der Verfasser kaum eine andere Absicht gehabt habe als sich und seinen

Lesern eine Kurzweil zu machen . . ." (p. 12, ll. 31-32). The priest also views the novel as "nützlich" (p. 12, l. 37) "mehr zur Belustigung als zum Unterricht geschrieben" (p. 12, l. 38, p. 13, l. 1), and as one "worin guter Humor und scherzende Satyre herrsche" (p. 13, ll. 1-2); in all, he regards the work in a positive light and says that the satire contained within it is definitely valuable. By thus combining the principles of pleasure and education to recommend the book, the priest clearly employs the "prodesse et delectare" principle of Enlightenment poetics.

After having discussed this priest's view, the editor says "Ich überlasse es nun den Lesern, was sie tun wollen, ob sie dabei lachen, lächeln, sauer sehen, schmälen oder weinen wollen" (p. 13, ll. 25-26). By ostensibly allowing the reader complete freedom, the editorial figure again manages to gain his reader's confidence by a demonstration of respect for and consideration of him. However, since he has already shown which reactions are preferable and more acceptable, he has managed to manipulate the real reader to his own point of view and has thus not allowed as much latitude of response as he pretends. This manipulation is, though, so playful that it completely lacks any sinister qualities that one might associate with the term.[28]

Such direct manipulation of the reader as occurs in the introduction to the novel is indeed no less obvious in the main body of the work. Those numerous instances already discussed where the fictional reader actually appears in the text all serve as further means of directly manipulating the real reader through his fictional counterparts. Through subtle manipulation, therefore, the real reader is brought to an attitude of respect for and trust in the narrating figure (be he the fictional editor or the supposed author); in all, the fictional editor and author become for the reader teachers who are not dogmatic but who nonetheless clearly, if subtly, demonstrate their own attitude and their wish for acceptance of this attitude.

Although the direct appearance for the fictional reader in the text is an important means of manipulating the real reader, it is not the only means. Rather, there are several indirect, but certainly no less important or effective, ways in which this individual is subtly taken in hand and led about. One of the most apparent such devices is the use of the first-person plural forms "wir" and "unser." Although these words upon occasion refer exclusively to the narrator,[29] at other times their use clearly involves the reader. The most obvious instance of reader inclusion involves a statement with "wir" or "unser" that is viewed as universally applicable. The fictional author says, for example, in reference to "Schwärmerei": "So wie es nämlich allen Egoisten zu Trotz, Dinge gibt, die würklich außer uns sind, so gibt es andre, die bloß in unserem Gehirn existieren."[30] Here it is not the author alone to whom the observation applies but rather the reader as well.

To be sure, one of the most frequent appearances of "unser" occurs in conjunction with "Held," "Geschichte," and other words referring to various characters or the narrative itself. The question is, of course, whether the reader is or is not included in these particular words, and, in general, the answer is an affirmative one. Indeed the real reader, through the close contact with the narrative and its narrating figures, comes into proximity with the characters, not necessarily because he is allowed to empathize and identify with them but rather because he is allowed, through the very conversational mood of the novel as well as through the figure of the fictional readers, to feel himself as a coparticipant in the production of the work:[31] when the narrator speaks therefore of "unser Held" or "unsere Geschichte," the reader is generally involved as one who, because of the narrating figures' attitude of concern for him, is allowed to feel a bond with these figures and the very process of narrating. He consequently assumes an ironic detachment and distance from the narrative and its characters as such.

A further such device which also serves indirectly to involve the reader in the work is the use of "man." Of course, it cannot be maintained that each time this particular word is employed it involves the reader;[32] but when the reader's involvement is sought, one goal that is attained is the bringing of narrator and reader into greater intimacy. This is the case, for instance, where the narrator says, ("denn man weiß, daß die Liebe in Träumen nicht alle die Gradationen beobachtet, die einem Schäfer an den Ufern des Lignon vorgeschrieben sind.)" (p. 29, ll. 8-10) or "Aber die Liebe ist, wie man weißt, so furchtsam, daß . . ." (p. 267, ll. 33-34). On such occasions "man" is used as a commonplace to call upon a general or universal experience which the narrator and the informed reader can share and which therefore brings them closer to one another. Thus, with "man weiß" it is not only shown that the narrator himself has learned from personal experience the import of the statement but also that the reader and the narrator, human beings that they are, should both have this experience in common.

A further device which affects the reader is the use of the phrase "die Wahrheit zu sagen." Although examples of it are not found in as great profusion as those of the other devices discussed, even in their limited number their effect is still important. For instance, when the narrator points out "Die Wahrheit zu sagen, er hatte sie jederzeit mehr gefürchtet als geliebt . . ." (p. 26, ll. 27-28), he not only provides the reader with important information but, further, demonstrates his desire for intimacy. A similar example is this: "Die Wahrheit zu sagen, so kam bei dem guten Pedrillo alles auf die Um-

stände des gegenwärtigen Augenblicks an" (p. 125, ll. 304). This statement not only reinforces the presence of the narrator in the work but also conveys reliability and authority with the goal of obtaining trust. In a subtle way, therefore, this phrase achieves essentially two goals: it serves first to reinforce the impression of the narrator's trustworthiness and sincerity vis-à-vis the reader through the very idea that the former is providing the latter with all that he knows about a particular matter; second, the phrase suggests that what is provided to the reader by the narrator is an intimate or secret bit of information, which again leads the reader to increase his trust and confidence in the narrator.

A variant of the "die Wahrheit zu sagen" statement is the "es ist wahr" type, which also has special significance for the reader but whose effect is somewhat different. In **Don Sylvio** one finds the following: "Es ist wohl wahr, die Torheit des Don Sylvio wird dadurch nicht kleiner; aber es ist auch zu seiner Entschuldigung genug, daß er wenigstens keine schlimmere Schlüsse macht als andere ehrliche Leute" (p. 32, ll. 1-5). The importance of this device is twofold: first, the narrator, after having described a number of situations in which human beings show stupidity and self-deception, concedes what is implicitly attributed to the reader, namely that Don Sylvio's self-deception does not become less significant simply because others in their own way have been equally lacking in awareness; secondly, though, (and well in keeping with the pattern established earlier in the novel's "Nachbericht") the narrating figure starting with "aber" presents an interpretation which is considered more valid and which he expects the reader to accept, namely that Don Sylvio's "Torheit" can at least partially be excused in that it is a phenomenon prevalent even among perfectly honest people (including, by implication, the reader himself): it is thus a universal malady (and therefore one which the reader himself may suffer from). Again manipulation of the real reader is apparent.

A variation of this device which is also observable in **Don Sylvio** is the "es ist leicht" statement. At one point in the novel the narrator says, for example, "Es ist leicht zu erachten daß man über die Ursache derselben allerlei Vermutungen anstellte . . ." (p. 38, ll. 26-27). The question arises of what effect such a statement is supposed to have upon the reader. The first important element is that the narrator suggests the simplicity involved in whatever observation he happens to make; consequently, it is expected that the real reader has made the observation already or will accept it very quickly since it is so obvious. The second item of importance is the playful implication that what the narrator observes is indeed so obvious that the reader who does not see it or does not accept it is lacking in perception. As a result, the real reader is again manipulated into viewing a certain situation in a particular way, namely the narrator's way; however, the method is again so subtle and playful that the reader, who may again be flattered to be taken into consideration at all, responds positively. Thus again unobtrusive persuasion is possible.

Although the real reader becomes involved in **Don Sylvio** in the several ways enumerated above, he also becomes involved in the work in another way: he is directly called upon to contribute to the text as judge or creator. In several instances the reader is asked to exercise his judgment and make a decision. At one point, for example, the narrator says, "Wir können also unsre Erklärung für mehr nicht geben als für eine bloße Vermutung und wenn die Liebhaber des Wunderbaren geneigter sein sollten, hierüber dem Don Sylvio selbst zu glauben, welcher unstreitig ein Augen-Zeuge und außer allem Verdacht eines vorsetzlichen Betrugs ist; so haben wir nicht das geringste dagegen einzuwenden" (p. 57, ll. 22-27). Explicitly the reader is given the opportunity to judge; this judgment, however, is not as free as one might expect, for the narrator with effectively playful irony presents that choice which he considers the correct one. The result is, of course, that the reader is once more led into a particular attitude: he may theoretically decide in any way he wishes; however, the correct decision has already been clearly indicated by the narrating figure.

Throughout **Don Sylvio** the problem of the discrepancy between the hero's "Schwärmerei" and the empirical reality of a particular situation is made clear to the real reader by means of the narrating figure's comments and digressions: the reader is continually aware of the fact that the hero is unable to differentiate between what is real and what is imagined and that he in fact constructs his own reality. For example, in Book I, Chapter 6, Don Sylvio encounters a frog which he saves from certain death; although he expects the animal to turn into a fairy and repay him for his kindness, this does not happen. The conclusion which he reaches is that the fairy is either not allowed to appear at this moment or else is waiting for a time when she may be of greater help. Don Sylvio does not interpret empirical reality as his reality: rather than coming to the reasonable conclusion that the frog is no more than a frog, he allows his "Einbildungskraft" to reach beyond all limits of "Vernunft." In order to make this abundantly clear to the reader, the narrator points it out explicitly:

> Vermutlich werden einige Leser sich wundern, wie es möglich sei, daß Don Sylvio albern genug habe sein können, um aus dem widrigen Ausgang dieses Abenteurs nicht den Schluß zu ziehen, der am natürlichsten daraus folgte, nämlich daß der Frosch keine Fee gewesen sei. Allein sie werden uns erlauben, ihnen zu sagen, daß sie die Macht der Vorurteile und vielleicht ihre eigene Erfahrung nicht genugsam in Erwägung ziehen. Nichts ist unter den Menschen gewöhnlicher als diese

Art von Trug-Schlüssen; das Vorurteil und die Leidenschaft macht keine andre.

> (p. 31, ll. 10-18)

Real reader involvement is sought here: not only does the narrator make clear by means of direct reference to the fictional readers ("einige Leser") what the reasonable, realistic conclusion should be but more importantly points out through his use of a commonplace in the last sentence ("unter den Menschen") that this situation is prevalent among human beings in general. Since the real reader is himself such a creature, the implication that he too may be guilty of similar unreasonable and undesirable actions is obvious.

In the next chapter the same type of situation exists. Don Sylvio encounters a beautiful butterfly, catches it, and then frees it after thinking that it may be a fairy or princess. As the creature flies away, the hero discovers a locket containing the picture of a beautiful woman and draws the conclusion that the fairy in butterfly form left it for him. To be sure, he considers the woman the most beautiful he has ever seen: ". . . je mehr er es betrachtete, desto mehr beredete er sich, daß es das Bildnis einer Göttin, oder doch zum wenigsten der Allerschönsten Sterblichen sei, die jemals gewesen, oder künftig sein werde" (p. 34, ll. 2-5). Although on the basis of the hero's already demonstrated tendency toward "schwärmerische" interpretations this conclusion might appear extreme, the narrator asserts the opposite; in a digression involving "unsre schönen Leserinnen" he explains that this was in fact the first time that Don Sylvio had seen a woman who could really be thought of as belonging "zum schönen Geschlecht;" his prior upbringing had been in such solitude that, aside from the unattractive females in the immediate household, he had never seen a beautiful woman: "Don Sylvio mußte also notwendig von der Schönheit dieser Schäferin außerordentlich gerührt werden, da sie unter den Figuren, an die er seine Augen hatte gewöhnen müssen, nicht anders ausgesehen hätte, als wie Latona unter den Einwohnern von Delos, als sie in Frösche verwandelt, ihr am Ufer entgegen quäkten" (p. 34, ll. 21-26).

Real reader involvement is here sought both through the word "Leserinnen" and through the presentation of what might be a possible reaction of these readers to Don Sylvio's actions; however, the reasonable conclusion of the "Leserinnen" is shown to be incorrect, and the reader must not only alter his assessment of things in this particular situation but also exercise his ability to reach a conclusion in future instances only after the necessary facts have been provided by the narrator. Playful irony is apparent here: the narrator had initially portrayed Don Sylvio as an unreasonable individual whose conclusions were founded upon excessive "Einbildungskraft;" obviously he desired that the reader accept this appraisal; in this instance, however, what seems to be the hero's "schwärmerisch" conclusion about the woman's beauty is quite correct, whereas the reasonable conclusion of the "Leserinnen" is not. That the readers must, therefore, rely upon the narrator's guidance for proper understanding in the novel is clear.

In general the narrator is, as we have seen, concerned with demonstrating Don Sylvio's inability to interpret reality without "Schwärmerei;" he explains the problem in these terms:

> Unvermerkter Weise verwebt sich die Einbildung mit dem Gefühl, das Wunderbare mit dem Natürlichen und das Falsche mit dem Wahren. Die Seele, welche nach einem blinden Instincte Schimären eben so regelmäßig bearbeitet als Wahrheiten, bauet sich nach und nach aus allem diesem ein Ganzes, und gewöhnt sich an, es für wahr zu halten, weil sie Licht und Zusammenhang darin findet, und weil ihre Phantasie mit den Schimären, die den größten Teil davon ausmachen, eben so bekannt ist als ihre Sinnen mit den würklichen Gegenständen, von denen sie ohne sonderliche Abwechslung immer umgeben sind.

> (p. 22, ll. 3-13)

The use of a generalized statement here demands the reader's involvement. Later in this section the narrator contrasts the poetic and the real worlds, showing that Don Sylvio exchanged "die poetische und bezauberte Welt in seinem Kopf an die Stelle der würklichen" (p. 22, ll. 24-25); in another section he makes essentially the same point: ". . . so werden wir . . . bei der Erzählung unsers jungen Ritters einen Unterschied machen müssen zwischen demjenigen was ihm würklich begegnet war, und zwischen dem, was seine Einbildungs-Kraft hinzugetan hatte" (p. 56, ll. 26-28). It is clear that the narrator's concern is the education of the reader to a more appropriate perception of reality: this instructive tone not only describes a scene but also explicitly indicates its significance in terms of "Wirklichkeit/Schwärmerei." Noteworthy too is that the destruction of illusion resulting in an awareness of what is real and what is illusory occurs for the reader continually from the novel's start while it occurs for the hero primarily during the recounting of the Biribinker tale. It is then that Don Sylvio is able to perceive empirical reality with reason rather than imaginative excess. Through the character of Don Sylvio, therefore, the real reader is himself educated to a perception of the difference between empirical and literary reality. (The final playful irony is, of course, that at the novel's end what was portrayed for the reader as the empirical reality of Don Sylvio is shown to be just as illusory as the reality that Don Sylvio has created for himself: when Donna Felicia identifies herself as the granddaughter of Gil Blas, the reader sees that the novel is itself a literary illusion. As Wolfgang Jahn says, "Das realitische Konzept der Fabel, die Antithese von Wirklichkeit und Einbildung, wird damit durchbrochen.

Entgegen aller Regel präsentiert Wieland seine Figuren als das, was sie, freilich uneingestandenermaßen, schon immer waren, als reine Ausgeburten eines die gesamte Romanschöpfung umgreifenden dichterischen Humors."[33]

In all, the varied means of reader involvement serve a specific purpose in this novel, namely the education of the real reader. Through such involvement the author is not only assured of the reader's correct understanding of the work but also of his development to reality and reason. Consequently, the author manipulates the reader into a realization of the general validity and reliability of the narrator's observations and internalizes them for him. Thus, just as Don Sylvio himself eventually learns to distinguish between reality and his own "Schwärmerei," so too does the real reader's own education reach this goal. In the end it is clear that the work's goal has been achieved, a goal described by the narrator as ". . . nicht etwan . . . eine eitle Belustigung, sondern das gemeine Beste, und die Beförderung der Gesundheit unsrer geliebten Leser an Leib und Gemüte . . ." (p. 192, ll. 29-34).

In contrast to "der Menge schlechter und mittelmäßiger moralischer Bücher" (p. 193, ll. 35-36) which the narrator views as worthless, he feels that those books are much more useful "in denen die Wahrheit mit Lachen gesagt, die der Dummheit, Schwärmerei und Schelmerei ihre betrügliche Masken abziehen, die Menschen mit ihren Leidenschaften und Torheiten, in ihrer wahren Gestalt und Proportion weder vergrößert noch verkleinert abschildern, und von ihren Handlungen diesen Firniß wegwischen, womit Stolz, Selbstbetrug oder geheime Absichten sie zu verfälschen pflegen; Bücher, die mit desto besserm Erfolg unterrichten und bessern, da sie bloß zu belustigen scheinen . . ." (p. 194, ll. 6-14). *Don Sylvio* is indeed such a book: its "Unterrichten" occurs through "Belustigen" and not through sentimental tears or moral preaching. Further, it is a work that may be categorized as an "Erziehungsroman" not simply because it portrays the education of its hero but, just as importantly, because it seeks to initiate an actual process of education within the real reader.

Notes

1. The matter of the reader in literature with, in some cases, particular emphasis upon eighteenth-century English literature is discussed in the following critical works: Wayne C. Booth, "The Self-conscious Narrator in Comic Fiction Before *Tristram Shandy*," *PMLA*, 67 (1952), 163-185; Gunter Grimm, ed., *Literatur und Leser* (Stuttgart: Reclam, 1975); Wolfgang Iser, *The Act of Reading* (Baltimore, London: Johns Hopkins University Press, 1978); Wolfgang Iser, *Der implizite Leser; Kommunkationsformen des Romans von Bunyan*

bis Beckett (München: Fink, 1972); Peter Michelsen, *Laurence Sterne und der deutsche Roman des 18. Jahrhunderts,* Palaestra, Nr. 232 (Göttingen, 1962); Manfred Naumann, ed., *Gesellschaft-Literatur-Lesen* (Berlin, Weimar: Aufbau, 1973); Walter J. Ong, S.J., "The Writer's Audience Is Always a Fiction," *PMLA,* 90 (1975), 9-21; John Preston, *The Created Self: The Reader's Role in Eighteenth-Century Fiction* (New York: Barnes & Noble, 1970); Dietrich Rolle, *Fielding und Sterne: Untersuchungen über die Funktion des Erzählers,* Neue Beiträge zur englischen Philologie (Münster, 1964); Erwin Wolff, "Der intendierte Leser," *Poetica,* 4/2 (April 1971), 141-166.

2. The reader in eighteenth-century German literature is treated with varying degrees of thoroughness in these works: Eva Becker, *Der deutsche Roman um 1780* (Stuttgart, 1964); Michael Hadley, *The German Novel in 1790,* European University Papers, Vol. 87 (Frankfurt, Bern: Lang, 1973); Wolfgang Kayser, "Die Anfänge des modernen Romans im 18. Jahrhundert," *DVjs* [*Deutsche Vierteljahrsschrifte*], 28 (1954), 417-446; Erich Kleinschmidt, "Fiktion und Identifikation: Zur Ästhetik der Leserrolle im deutschen Roman zwischen 1760 und 1780," *DVjs,* 53 (1979), 49-73; Victor Lange, "Erzählformen des Romans im 18. Jahrhundert," *Anglia,* 76 (1958), 129-144; M. von Poser, *Der abschwiefende Erzähler,* Respublica Literaria, Vol. 5 (Bad Homburg, 1969); William D. Wilson, "The Narrative Strategy of Wieland's *Don Sylvio von Rosalva,*" Diss. Cornell University 1978; Hans-Gerhard Winter, "Probleme des Dialogs und des Dialogromans in der deutschen Literatur des 18. Jahrhunderts," *Wirkendes Wort,* 20 (1970), 33-51.

3. Jörg Schönert, *Roman und Satire im 18. Jahrhundert,* Germanistische Abhandlungen, Bd. 27 (Stuttgart: J. B. Metzlersche Verlagsbuchhandlung, 1969).

4. Wolfgang Jahn, "Zu Wielands *Don Sylvio,*" *Wirkendes Wort,* 18 (1968), 320-328.

5. Lieselotte Kurth-Voigt, *Perspectives and Points of View: The Early Works of Wieland and Their Background* (Baltimore: Johns Hopkins University Press, 1974).

6. John McCarthy, *Fantasy and Reality: An Epistemological Approach to Wieland,* European University Papers, Vol. 97 (Frankfurt/M, Bern: Lang, 1974).

7. Keith Leopold, "Wieland's *Don Sylvio von Rosalva*: The First Modern German Novel?," *Festschrift for Ralph Farrell,* ed. Anthony Stephens et al., Australian and New Zealand Studies in German Language and Literature, Vol. 7 (Bern: Lang, 1977), p. 16.

8. Gerd Matthecka, "Die Romantheorie Wielands und seiner Vorläufer," Diss. Tübingen 1957.

9. Jürgen Jacobs, *Wielands Romane* (Bern: Francke, 1969).

10. Steven R. Miller, *Die Figur des Erzählers in Wielands Romanen,* Göppinger Arbeiten zur Germanistik, Nr. 19 (Göppingen: Kümmerle, 1970).

11. M. H. Würzner, "Die Figur des Lesers in Wielands 'Geschichte des Agathon'," *Dichter und Leser: Studien zur Literatur,* hrsg. v. Ferdinand van Ingen et al. (Groningen, 1972), pp. 151-155.

12. Christiane Seiler, "Die Rolle des Lesers in Wielands *Don Sylvio* und *Agathon,*" *Lessing Yearbook* IX (München: Max Hueber Verlag, 1977), pp. 152-165.

13. Lieselotte Kurth-Voigt, p. 118, refers to the "complex cast of narrators and spokesmen" found in *Don Sylvio.*

14. Wolfgang Kayser, "Wer erzählt den Roman?," in *Die Vortragsreise* (Bern, 1958), p. 91.

15. Kayser, "Anfänge," 429.

16. Walker Gibson, "Authors, Speakers, Readers, and Mock Readers," *College English,* 11 (1949-50), 265-266.

17. C. M. Wieland, *Der Sieg der Natur über die Schwärmerei oder Die Abenteuer des Don Sylvio von Rosalva,* Wielands Werke, Vol. I, ed. Fritz Martini and Hans Werner Seiffert (München: Carl Hanser Verlag, 1964), p. 9 (l. 1, 23); p. 104 (l. 3); p. 181 (l. 11); p. 348 (l. 2, 26, 33); p. 368 (l. 1). All subsequent references to the novel are cited according to page and line number of this edition.

18. *Don Sylvio,* p. 11 (l. 6); p. 191 (l. 22); p. 208 (l. 17); p. 269 (l. 30); p. 364 (l. 8); p. 370 (l. 3).

19. Steven R. Miller, p. 98, points out how such first-person forms demonstrate an attempt "die erhoffte Gemeinschaft zwischen Leser und Erzähler beim Beobachten, Bewerten, Vermuten usw. auch sprachlich anklingen zu lassen."

20. *Don Sylvio,* p. 45 (l. 12); p. 59 (l. 18); p. 62 (l. 27); p. 138 (l. 27); p. 141 (l. 6); p. 224 (l. 24); p. 268 (l. 21).

21. *Don Sylvio,* p. 349 (l. 23); p. 361 (ll. 7-8).

22. Jürgen Jacobs, p. 32, speaks of the "pädagogische Absichten" that characterize the narration in both *Don Sylvio* and *Abderiten.*

23. Steven Miller, p. 125.

24. Kayser, "Wer erzählt?," p. 88.

25. Kayser, "Anfänge," p. 430.

26. Ong, "Writer's Audience," p. 12.

27. In her book *Perspectives and Points of View,* p. 120, Kurth-Voigt also discusses this point.

28. Jürgen Jacobs, p. 29, says in this regard, ". . . die Manipulation des Lesers in verfängliche oder lächerliche Situationen ist nicht Vergewaltigung, sondern geschieht mit urbaner selbstironischer Zustimmung des Betroffenen."

29. *Don Sylvio,* p. 57 (l. 15, 22); p. 108 (ll. 10-11); p. 170 (l. 12); p. 191 (l. 4); p. 268 (ll. 23-26).

30. *Don Sylvio,* p. 55 (ll. 32-34). Other examples include: p. 22 (ll. 31-35); p. 23 (ll. 3-9); p. 269 (ll. 20-25).

31. Wolfgang Iser, "The Reading Process: A Phenomenological Approach," in *New Directions in Literary History,* ed. by Ralph Cohen (Baltimore: Johns Hopkins University Press, 1974), p. 130, points out, "The literary text activates our own faculties, enabling us to recreate the world it presents. The product of this creative activity is what we might call the virtual dimension of the text, which endows it with its reality. This virtual dimension is not the text itself, nor is it the imagination of the reader: it is the coming together of the text and imagination."

32. *Don Sylvio,* p. 105 (l. 38); p. 106 (ll. 1-3); p. 183 (l. 3).

33. Jahn, "Wieland's *Don Sylvio,*" p. 326

Heidi Glockhamer (essay date summer 1988)

SOURCE: Glockhamer, Heidi. "The Apprenticeship of a Hetaera: Gender and Socialization in Wieland's *Geschichte des Agathon.*" *German Quarterly* 61, no. 3 (summer 1988): 371-86.

[*In the following essay, Glockhamer presents a feminist reading of Wieland's* Geschichte des Agathon. *Glockhamer examines Danae's relationship with Agathon within the context of eighteenth-century social conventions, arguing that her decision to abandon her marriage in order to pursue an ascetic life reflects the essential inequality that confronted women during the period.*]

Christoph Martin Wieland's **Geschichte des Agathon** (1794) is usually read as a *Bildungsroman*—as the account of Agathon's development from a sensitive, naïve youth into a mature, productive man of the world. One of Agathon's principal challenges and areas of ignorance is sex. His prudishness stems largely from his having been raised by priests at Delphi. At one point, he is so immersed in mysticism and so enthralled by the possibility of a theophanic experience that he takes the croaking of frogs for a seraphic hymn and the sexual advances of a priest for Apollo's blessing. The only relationship he has is a platonic one with a young temple maiden appropriately named Psyche. But Agathon, as we are repeatedly told, has a body and face to rival those of Adonis, and if his attractiveness is lost on Psyche's love of his soul, it is more than appreciated by the priestess Pythia. Pythia tries almost everything—including threatening to murder the temple maiden Psyche—to get Agathon into her bed. Frightened and disgusted, Agathon runs away to Athens, where he is reunited with his father and enters politics, only to fall victim to the jealousy of powerful citizens. Framed for treason and forever banished from the republic, Agathon must run away again. This time he is captured by pirates who sell him to Hippias, a wealthy sophist residing in Smyrna.

Hippias treats Agathon more like a companion with odd notions than a servant. He is particularly intrigued and somewhat irritated by Agathon's lack of interest in sensual pleasure and attempts to convince Agathon of the absurdity of self-denial and sexual abstinence, first by having a series of discussions with him about human nature, and second by offering him one of the sexiest women in his household. Agathon admits that although he finds the woman in question sexually attractive, he would find more pleasure in the performance of a benevolent act. Not in the least convinced, Hippias decides that a stronger test is needed to prove to Agathon that his notions of virtue and celibacy are misguided.

The "test" is Danae, a wealthy hetaera. She not only succeeds in seducing Agathon, but to her surprise and much to Hippias' chagrin, she and Agathon fall in love. From the onset, their relationship has promise. In addition to compatibility of personality and intellect, they enjoy the type of sympathetic communion of souls Danae has longed for and Agathon values so highly. However, as the narrator informs us, love, sex, intimacy and female companionship are important but not the sole elements of a young man's *Bildung*. Agathon is destined to *do* something in the world, and when Hippias tells him that Danae is a hetaera, the affront to his pride is enough to make him leave her in Smyrna for the promise of a political career in Syracuse. The two lovers meet again in Tarent on the Italian mainland. Danae has retired. Agathon is no longer an impetuous idealist. In the household of Archytas, Tarent's Pythagorean sage and ruler, he finds Psyche, the long-lost love of his adolescence. She turns out to be his real sister. All obstacles that prevented Agathon from accepting Danae now removed, he proposes. Danae, however, declines the offer. For the time being she wishes to live in celibacy and friendship.

The failure of the text to end in Agathon's and Danae's marital bliss is a dissatisfactory conclusion for some readers, a disappointing one for others. One ready way of coming to terms with Danae's insistence on a platonic relationship is to read it against Archytas's philosophy. According to Archytas, who acts as spiritual teacher and personal advisor to both Danae and Agathon, the inclinations of our "animal half" cannot be allowed even moderate indulgence if happiness, harmony, justice and order are to be attained. Personal peace and universal morality come only through suppression of the senses.[1] Because Archytas's *Lebensweisheit* follows Danae's account of her life as a hetaera and functions to help Agathon accept Danae's choice of celibacy over marriage to him, some scholars, such as John McCarthy, interpret Danae's continence as validating Archytas's ascetic prescription for happiness.[2] Similar to this plot-oriented interpretation is the suggestion that Danae's continence and Archytas's philosophy be read against the background of the German intelligentsia's response to the French Revolution. Wieland, like many eighteenth-century German intellectuals, was distressed by events in France. The third and final edition of *Geschichte des Agathon,* which introduces Archytas, appeared in 1794—the same year that saw the death of Robespierre and the end of the Reign of Terror. Viewed within this time frame, Agathon's and Danae's celibacy actualizes Archytas's claim that the highest personal and social good resides in the subordination of the physical to the mind and the heart. Their celibacy and his ascetic philosophy function as correctives to social corruption and physical excess.[3] And finally, there is the option of the ironic ending. The fact that the lovers Agathon and Danae become spiritual brother and sister rather than a married couple functions as a tease, a foil to the reader's almost automatic expectations that lovers, so tested, true and well-suited, should be united in marriage at the end of their story.

Although these three interpretations are not invalid, I find them as dissatisfactory as I did the resolution of Agathon's and Danae's love affair when I first read *Geschichte des Agathon.* All three fail to take a thorough account of the explanation Danae and the narrator offer and consequently overlook a strong feminist current in the text. According to my reading, Wieland's *Geschichte des Agathon* lays bare the disparity in men's and women's socially prescribed experiential horizons. There can be no marriage because there exists no synchronicity in Agathon's (man's) and Danae's (woman's) development, no equality in their social participation and no actual reciprocity in their personal relationship.

My reading of the failure of Agathon's and Danae's romantic relationship and the asynchronicity of their re-

spective personal development takes its cue from the narrator and concentrates on Danae's *Geheime Geschichte.* Like Danae's life story, the discussion features two distinct identity formulations. I look first at Danae's identity as a hetaera and her similarity to the Juliette of Sade's *La nouvelle Justine.* The comparison may strike some as too radical. Its basis will become apparent, I hope, when I look at Jane Gallop's feminist reading of *Justine.* The second part of my discussion receives its direction from the narrator's identification of Danae as a "schöne Seele." I examine Danae's life as an ascetic, the inwardness of her development, its contrast to Agathon's *Bildung* and its similarities to the spiritual apprenticeship of a woman in another eighteenth-century *Bildungsroman,* the *schöne Seele* of Goethe's *Wilhelm Meisters Lehrjahre.*

Danae's narrative of how she came to be a hetaera contains many of the characters and situations which since the nineteenth century have been regarded as stock features of the prostitute's story, but what distinguishes her life from the tawdry victimization of the fictional streetwalker and courtesan is a quality of selflessness which is so transparent that it is archetypal. An excellent discussion of the notion of selflessness and the ideal whore occurs in Jane Gallop's analysis of Blanchot's reading of Sade's *La nouvelle Justine suivie l'histoire de Juliette.* Despite radically different attitudes toward sex, the sisters Justine and Juliette have in common integrity of self. Justine, for all the times she is sexually violated, remains virginal. "No event is sufficient to violate her integrity, her identity, her propriety."[4] By the same token, the whore Juliette, a willing participant and perpetrator of countless sexual and violent acts, never loses her integrity either. The reason lies in the fact that Juliette knows only her partners' desires:

> Juliette as woman (whore/slave) passes through her story with no particular tastes or perversions of her own, always open to the imprint of her friends' tastes. Juliette's peculiar devotion to her friends consists in being in perfect harmony with them, until she responds to the desire of another friend—going through a total metamorphosis. . . . It is not a betrayal of a friend, for the betrayed is no longer a friend. Juliette merely responds to the wishes of whomever she enters into conjuncture with. . . . The "reality" of the whore (woman) is inseparable from the "reveries" of men. Juliette attains to the apotheosis of perversion by having absolutely no desires of her own. She is absolutely inappropriable by being totally available and positively inconstant. Juliette's strength is her complete lack of resistance.[5]

To what extent is the ancient Greek hetaera, on which Danae's character is modeled, a *whore/slave* in the same sense Juliette is? Although the hetaera, whose name means companion, was well educated and trained in the arts, she provided more than a stimulating and decorative presence to men's social gatherings and intellectual discussions. According to Eva Cantarella, she was also "paid for a relationship (including sex) which was neither exclusive nor merely occasional."[6] If, then, the hetaera's "inappropriability" ensues from the inconstancy dictated by her professional persona, her "reality" is also inextricable from men's "reveries" of a compliant sexual partner and charming social companion. The hetaera avails not just her body to men for a price but her talents and mind as well. This is one sense in which Danae the hetaera resembles Juliette the companion, she who is utterly "responsive" and "available" to the other's desires. The other similarity goes beyond the specifics of Danae's professional persona. Sexual gratification is just part of the point of Gallop's use of the convertible terms *woman, whore* and *slave* to identify Juliette's nature. It is the *appropriability* of a woman's self to the other (a man) which appropriately defines a whore and, most important, spotlights in what respect woman and whore can be thought of as synonymous in Gallop's discussion of Sade's Juliette and in mine of Wieland's Danae. The openness of Juliette to the "imprint" of the other's tastes and wishes and her singular "devotion" to one friend until another comes along also characterize Danae's life. The substance of her fantasies, the way she directs her affections—even the names she calls herself by and the identities she assumes—are so literally determined by her current mistress, client or lover as to function allegorically. Like the whore-woman-slave Juliette epitomizes, Danae is "totally available," and it is significant that this availability to the other begins—as does her life story—in the last year of puberty or just when she is entering womanhood.[7]

Danae's given name is Myris. At age fourteen, after the death of her mother, Myris leaves her home in the country for Athens. Her foster mother Krobyle gets her work as a dancer in a club with the hope of eventually prostituting her. Feeling she is destined for something more noble and spiritual, Myris initially hates her employment. Within a short period, however, she responds to Krobyle's dreams of wealth. These borrowed fantasies of sumptuous chambers, beautiful clothes, servants and luxuries keep Myris in a state of "giddy ecstasy" or *Taumel*—a kind of sexual excitement that is further fired by the wanton appreciation of the club's clientele. The allegiance to Krobyle lasts until the painter Aglaophon hires Myris to pose for a portrait the famous Athenian Alcibiades has commissioned of Hebe.

During the sittings, the painter Aglaophon becomes as impassioned of the Myris in the portrait as he is of the real Myris. In fact, the narrator compares Aglaophon's confused desire to Pygmalion's and, as we might expect from Danae's openness to others' reveries, she is so enamored of her portrait that she runs the same danger Narcissus did with his reflection (Bk. 14, Ch. 2, 493). The difference between portrait and model is, on the other hand, all too clear to the painting's commissioner Alcibiades. Desiring to meet the model and suspecting that Aglaophon will use the same one again, Alcibiades orders a painting of the Argivan Danae and conceals himself in Aglaophon's studio during the first sitting. He is in luck, for Myris, desirous to be all the Danae that the painter and its commissioner imagine, has agreed to pose with no more covering than a loose drape. Alcibiades is so taken with her figure that he jumps out from his hiding place:

> "Du kannst deine Pinsel nur auswaschen, Freund Aglaophon," sagte er zu ihm; "deine Danae—würde zwar etwas sehr schönes, aber doch—keine Danae werden. Überlaß mir die Sorge, das reizende Modell erst dazu zu bilden! So bald es Zeit sein wird, will ich dich rufen lassen; dann sollst du malen! . . ."

> (Bk. 14, Ch. 2, 495)

After comforting Myris, who soon stops crying when she notices his attractive features and friendly demeanor, Alcibiades announces that he has decided to introduce her to Aspasia and that henceforward she shall cease to be called Myris. Her new name will be Danae. The scene ends with a shower of gold—of a kind, for Alcibiades takes Krobyle aside and presses money into her hand. He then kisses Danae and disappears.[8]

Danae admits to Agathon that had Alcibiades taken her somewhere private instead of to the hetaera Aspasia's house, she would have immediately yielded to him. However, like Sade's Juliette, "whose particular devotion to her friends consists in being in perfect harmony with them until she responds to the desires of another friend," as soon as Danae sees Aspasia she loses all desire to please Alcibiades. To her Aspasia represents the ideal of feminine perfection. Within a few moments after the two women meet, the desire to become an Aspasia emerges as the ruling passion in Danae's soul: "Der erste Augenblick, da ich *Aspasien* sah, schien mich zu einer andern Person umzuschaffen" (Bk. 14, Ch. 4, 502). Hence, when Alcibiades drops by that very evening on his way to another engagement, Danae notices that although she still savors his attractive body and face, his charms dull next to Aspasia's brightness.

Seeing in Danae the self of her youth, Aspasia willingly instructs her in the arts of a hetaera. One of the crucial attitudes she attempts to impress on Danae is that men do not allow women to reach their full potential. They have imprisoned women in a world of superfluous interests and tasks because they fear the power women would have if female sexuality became augmented by a developed intellect and spirit. Unfortunately, men's usurpation of women's right to growth has become permanent with time. The only recourse left to women is to see that men imprison them as little as possible. The first step in protecting themselves is to realize that men call women's sensuality, warmth, lively imaginations and capacity for deep, tender feelings the greatest female assets because these qualities make women vulnerable to male domination. Women should not attempt to eradicate these qualities, but they should never allow themselves to be taken in by men's appeal to these qualities, and most important, should never lose sight of the fact that men ultimately view women as the means by which they satisfy their lust and their vanity (Bk. 14, Ch. 6, 516-18).[9]

While Danae is a member of Aspasia's household, she becomes everything her mistress desires—prize student, close companion, happy participant in the sport Aspasia has with Alcibiades' attempts to satisfy his lust and vanity. After Aspasia dies, however, Danae undergoes another metamorphosis, brought on, as always, by her utter openness to whoever is her present companion. Just as easily as slipping out of one garment into another, Danae exchanges Aspasia's philosophy of feminist protectionism for self-abandoned love of Alcibiades. True to what Aspasia had told her, conquest and familiarity soon cool his passion. When the affair ends, Danae decides to leave Athens. While at sea, she is captured by pirates who deliver her to a slaver headed for Sardes. There she is purchased by Prince Cyrus and soon becomes his favorite. Cyrus likes to think that she is to him what Aspasia had been to Pericles. He calls Danae Aspasia—an identity which she willingly assumes, as well as that of a man, when she accompanies Cyrus into battle against his brother Artaxerxes. The battle is lost. Cyrus dies. Danae, no longer Aspasia, slave to Cyrus, becomes Danae again and establishes herself as a hetaera in Smyrna.

Danae does not receive a new name from her relationship with Agathon. The transformation she undergoes is, nonetheless, fundamental. Hippias warns her, as we recall, that Agathon values only virtue and sentiment. Danae thus arouses the first stirrings of sexual passion within him by singing about the merits of a love based on mutual sympathy and sensitivity over a love based on physical attraction. After they become lovers, appearing to share Agathon's tastes and outlook is no longer necessary. The narrator informs us that Danae, in executing Hippias' challenge, "war nur darüber unruhig, wie sie sich entschuldigen wollte, über der Bemühung den Charakter Agathons umzubilden, ihren eignen, oder doch einen guten Teil davon, verloren zu haben" (Bk. 6, Ch. 1, 166). She cuts off contact with all her former friends and clientele, abandons her customary pleasures and habits, and spends her time in groves with Agathon, making garlands and lying in his arms. Whereas in the past she ridiculed "empfindsame Liebe," she now thinks nothing of watching Agathon for hours while he sleeps or of being moved to tears by the song of a nightingale (Bk. 5, Ch. 9, 163).

It is important to note that it is not Danae but the narrator who relates the story of her love affair with Agathon. Significantly, the only difference between the narrator's account of her as a woman in love and her own description of herself as Aglaophon's model, Aspasia's student, Alcibiades' mistress or Cyrus's slave is that the narrator calls attention to her malleability of self. He does not, however, connect Danae's extreme openness to the other's desires and tastes to her identity as a hetaera. Instead, he introduces her individual metamorphosis from a worldly hetaera into a sentimental Chloe by attributing the same malleability to all women. According to the narrator, the best gift Nature has bestowed on women is the ability to please, but whereas this gift was chiefly determined to ensure the happiness of men, it endangers women in the bargain. In finding so much pleasure in pleasing men, women too easily lose themselves.[10] This identification of the hetaera's art with the natural inclination of any woman in love also evidences itself in the narrative agenda. The account of Danae's and Agathon's affair begins when Hippias asks Danae to seduce Agathon and ends when he tells Agathon that Danae has slept with the sons of the best families in Greece—himself included (Bk. 9, Ch. 3, 279). Danae's identity as hetaera thus frames her identity as a woman in love—a configuration which pinpoints the mutuality of the two identities. The hetaera, hired for sex and for participation in social gatherings and intellectual discussions, underscores woman's identity as supplemental—as defined by men to please and serve.

Logically, when Danae begins the process of discovering and developing her own identity, she adamantly refuses to involve herself sexually or romantically. The environments she chooses for the initiation and completion of this process are to a certain degree problematic. On the one hand, Danae would not be able to sell her property in Smyrna and purchase an isolated dwelling in Tarent had she not the income and independence of a hetaera. On the other hand, after she meets Agathon again, she leaves her hermitage for Archytas's household, where she becomes his doting daughter and novitiate—ever repentantly silent about her past. Danae's financial independence is in keeping with the text's ancient Greek setting. Her final attitude toward her past as well as Agathon's rejection of her because she was a hetaera and his later proposal to her after she has given up her profession are not.

The anachronism of Agathon's self-disgust at having loved a hetaera and Danae's discreet silence about her past identity has two functions. The first is to acquaint the implied woman reader, to whom the section containing the anachronism is primarily addressed, with sexual attitudes in Periclean Greece and thereby give her a lesson in the cultural relativism of sexual mores. The second and far more interesting function pertains to the status of the hetaera specifically. During the time

Agathon and Danae were to have lived, it was socially acceptable for a man to have relationships with three types of women—a wife, a concubine and a hetaera. A wife was intended to provide a suitable number of legitimate male offspring and thus ensure that the patrimony remained within the family. Concern over the family's inheritable property was such that families with no sons sought suitors for their daughters from those able to verify the closest blood connection. Sex comprised the function of the concubine, who was required by law to be faithful to her lover. Men did bring concubines to live in their family homes, but there existed strict legal distinctions regarding the status of a concubine's children and those of a wife. As mentioned earlier, the hetaera's role was both less and more than that of concubine and wife. In contrast to his relationship with a concubine, a man could expect sex as part of the relationship he paid the hetaera for, but he had no legal right to expect fidelity. Unlike the wife, the hetaera was well educated and not sequestered to one part of the family home and to exclusive contact with female slaves and family members.[11] Whereas a citizen's wife could not even shop in the market or attend a banquet, the hetaera, as Cantarella points out, was "intended 'professionally' to accompany men where wives and concubines could not go."[12] She "was a sort of remedy provided by a society of men which, having segregated its women, still considered that the company of some of them could enliven social activities, meetings among friends, and discussions which their wives, even if they had been allowed to take part, would not have been able to sustain."[13]

The narrator of *Geschichte des Agathon* provides a similar account of the differing status of citizen wives and daughters, concubines and hetaerae when he comments on Agathon's desertion of Danae. Although he does not specifically mention the production of legitimate male heirs as the intended role of citizen women, he does emphasize strictly enforced protection of their virtue (*Tugend*) along with the social acceptability of a man's having sex with a hetaera in so far as "die Pflichten seines Standes nicht darunter leiden mußten" (Bk. 9, Ch. 8, 309-10). Hence, the narrator makes it quite clear that the functional differentiation of women's roles in Greek society existed to serve male needs—one type of woman, "Mütter der Bürger," intended and protected for the transmission of his property and status and another type specified for his pleasure. After drawing this distinction, the narrator takes up the question of Agathon's outrage. We already know from a previous chapter that Agathon would have eventually left Danae for broader and challenging vistas in the political world of men. However, if Danae's profession is not the impetus for Agathon's departure, it is nonetheless enraging and the reason is not, as we might initially expect, that he transgressed the social code and tried to make a hetaera a citizen wife. His outrage—and herein lies the anach-

ronism—issues from a notion of virtue which is quite foreign to his Greek contemporaries, but very much that of Wieland's eighteenth-century readers (Bk. 9, Ch. 8, 310-13).

The anachronism of Agathon's singular conflict with virtue and sexual love pulls the novel's ancient Greek setting into the present of its readership, so that the two contexts stand in momentary juxtaposition, and what began as a lesson for the novel's female readership in historical difference now reveals a similarity between women's roles in ancient Greece and late eighteenth-century Germany. Who would be in a better position to perceive the parallel than the woman reader—even if she did not call the basis of male prescriptions for female identities into question. As Ruth Dawson rightly observes:

> [F]eminist consciousness—the awareness of women's oppression and the vigorous demand for change—first began to assume its modern aspect in the late eighteenth century. It came soon after the newest ideology of sexual character and separate spheres had gained acceptance, with its vision of women as supplementary to men. . . . Evolving during the period when the private and the public worlds were being increasingly separated, this ideology meant assigning women to the private and excluding them from the public, in effect eliminating them from the best opportunities for meaningful work and good pay, restricting them to housekeeping and jobs which could be carried out in the home.[14]

It is appropriate to remember here that women in Germany did not have the right of admission to universities until 1901. Admission of women to universities in the eighteenth century was infrequent and frowned upon. Despite the appearance of such aggressive feminist tracts as Gottlieb von Hippels *Über die bürgerliche Verbesserung der Weiber* and Mary Wollstonecraft's *Vindication of the Rights of Woman* (1792), Rousseau's *Émile ou de l'éducation* (1762) largely remained the canon on the sagacity of women's exclusively sexual and domestic function. A woman's subordinate role allowed her *Bildung* to include English, French, music and painting. Any other discipline was considered just too analytical for the female disposition, if not threatening to her new domestic bourgeois persona of beauty, charming passivity and housewife virtue.[15] According to Helga Madland, women's journals, which addressed "the 'vacuum' created by the early discontinuation of a young girl's limited education," lent further validation to the image of women as "passive and decorative objects."[16] Of the eighty-five which appeared during the eighteenth century, Gottsched's *Vernünftige Tadlerinnen,* Marianne Ehrmann's *Amaliens Erhohlungsstunden* and Sophie von La Roche's *Pomona* were the only journals to attempt a broadening of women's prescribed scope of interest and identification.[17]

As we know, Wieland expressed a concerted interest throughout his life in women's education, social roles and personal relationships. The best known discussion of his attitudes is probably **"Über weibliche Bildung,"** which appeared as the preface to the *Allgemeine Damenbibliothek* of 1785. There he decries, as he does in his fiction, the oppressive condition of slavery men have relegated women to, acknowledges women's intellectual equality, and argues strenuously for the improvement of their education. Wieland, however, was no Hippel, who advocated admittance of women to all professions but the military. In lieu of strong pragmatic suggestions, he sets no restrictions on the educational ambitions of women, for he is confident that temperament and domestic activity will ensure the proper direction. The direction Wieland likes best is that which inculcates wisdom, loveliness, and happiness, and what ultimately constitutes happiness for both women *and men* is marriage.[18]

If such was Wieland's stance, what are we to make of the fact that Danae finds happiness not in marriage to Agathon, but rather in celibate sisterhood? Far from Greece, off the Italian mainland in Tarent and in her new identity as Chariklea, conditions seem propitious for her to be with Agathon as she so ardently desired back on Smyrna. In fact, in Tarent she almost fits the ideal of the eighteenth-century German bourgeois woman described earlier. She is still lovely, educated in the arts, now discreet and virtuous, happy to take her place in the respectable, domestic environment of Archytas's household. The only attributes lacking are the attributes crucial to appropriability—passivity and sexual compliance. Ironically, Danae expressed these attributes when she was a hetaera. Now when Agathon wants to marry her, she is no longer imprisoned in the cycle of becoming what the other desires and insists on her right to sexual abstinence and self-development. The brunt of this asynchronicity falls most hard on Agathon, not just because Danae tells him that their meeting on Smyrna started this process, but also because of the bad timing of his own perceptional development (Bk. 15, Ch. 3, 542). When Danae was a hetaera, Agathon had appreciation only for a woman who was spiritually oriented. When he finally appreciates woman in her role as sexual partner, Danae opts for chastity and the development of her spiritual potential. Not coincidentally, and as Elizabeth Boa points out in her essay on sexual relationships in the *Geschichte des Agathon,* Agathon's role expectations coincide with two of the three roles described in eighteenth-century discussions about women and not integrated by the prescribed feminine bourgeois persona:

> The first two, mother and sexual partner, are based in biology. The third is religious in origin, woman as bearer of virtue within the family or as the chaste and equal partner of a platonic friendship. The main tensions arise between woman as purveyor of morality

and woman as sexual partner, especially in the works of Wieland's generation.[19]

Agathon's desertion of Danae when he learns she is a hetaera and his later disappointment when she answers his marriage proposal with the desire, for the time being, to be his platonic friend, enact the "tension" arising from narrowly defined, conflicting role prescriptions for women. The nature of the role prescriptions themselves is elucidated by Danae's socialization and personal development. We have already seen the self-effacement inherent to her role as sexual partner. Albeit in a different way, the same qualities attend her role as moral purveyor. This becomes especially apparent when we compare Danae's development with that of the *schöne Seele* in Goethe's *Wilhelm Meisters Lehrjahre.*

In an interesting essay tracing patterns of female development in Goethe's *Wilhelm Meisters Lehrjahre* (1796), Eliot's *The Mill on the Floss* (1860), Fontane's *Effi Briest* (1895) and Chopin's *The Awakening* (1899), Marianne Hirsch defines the fictional concept of male *Bildung* in the eighteenth and nineteenth centuries as signifying "progress, heterosexuality, social involvement, healthy disillusionment, 'normality,' and adulthood." Female *Bildung,* by contrast, focuses on "the purely subjective, psychological, emotional and spiritual" and is marked by frustration with strictly defined avenues for women's self-expression in society, "strong emotional and spiritual desires in childhood," attraction to "an invisible spiritual realm," self-denial, illness, alienation and death. In Hirsch's view, the "Bekenntnisse einer schönen Seele" in Goethe's *Wilhelm Meister* epitomizes the type of female development outlined above. The Beautiful Soul's cyclical inward experience inverts the linear outward progress of Wilhelm's *Bildung,* which literally and figuratively encases her own.[20]

The Beautiful Soul becomes seriously ill at age eight. She spends her convalescence learning about the Bible from her mother, nature from her father, and love and fairy stories from her aunt. Her passage from childhood into womanhood is a difficult one. The spiritual inclinations, emotional sensitivity and confident intellectuality she had been allowed to develop in childhood collide with the familial and social expectations of adult society. She falls in love but, eventually finding the role of fiancée and its indication of what married life holds too constrictive, she withdraws from all human society to a religious, introspective, bodiless sphere of self-actualization. In this fluid reality her soul becomes a mirror. All boundaries between "self and other, inner and outer, art and life" dissolve. Even the distinction between God and worshipper no longer obtains. God is her "unsichtbarer Freund," the locus for all her spiritual and emotional inclinations. Before her self-imposed isolation, her father had called her his "mißratner Sohn." Now her uncle considers her so detrimental to the family that he forbids any contact between her and her sister's children:

> The only form of communication she can establish is a posthumous one, through her writing. And here she is confined to play the role of other to Wilhelm's self: here, her voice is confined and contained, balanced in such a way as to make her experience no more than the example of one extreme of human development. By "killing" the emotional Mignon and the spiritual Beautiful Soul, by elevating the Amazon mother, Nathalie, as an ideal of femininity, Goethe protects society from the subversive extremes into which women are channeled. Pushed into absolute subjectivity, the exceptional woman is cut off from social intercourse; pushed into the role of posthumous confessor, her narrative remains virtually separate from the rest of the plot.[21]

Danae's confessions are not written, posthumous, or a separate narrative. What she tells Agathon that day in the garden is meant to explain why the two cannot resume their former footing as lovers. Hence, Danae's story of her life has an effect on what course Agathon's development will take. There are, on the other hand, sufficient parallels between Danae's and the Beautiful Soul's confessions to posit a sisterhood in individual development and, to some degree, textual function. Like the *schöne Seele* and Maggie Tulliver in *The Mill on the Floss*, Danae experiences in childhood an attraction to "an invisible spiritual realm" portrayed by Goethe and Eliot through "Edenic, paradisal, imagery."[22] In fact, the only aspect mentioned about those childhood years preceding Danae's arrival in Athens at age thirteen is her attraction to one of her mother's household gods. She tells Agathon that she was particularly drawn to a statuette of Venus adorned with representations of the Graces. She decorated it every morning with flowers and longed to see Venus and the Graces in their true form. One day as she heard a Theban minstral sing Pindar's ode to the Graces, it seemed to her as if "ein himmlischer Lichtstrahl" illumined her soul. She had a vision of the Graces and swore to make them her guides in all she undertook (Bk. 14, Ch. 2, 489-90).

The adult *schöne Seele* and Maggie Tulliver encounter constant roadblocks to the fulfillment of the intellectual and spiritual longings they formed in childhood. In Danae's case, the conflict between her childhood memory of the Graces and her occupations of tavern dancer and prostitute is not personally more painful, but certainly stylistically more blatant. During the time she works as a dancer, she attempts to block out Krobyle's pressuring her into prostitution and the lascivious looks from the club's clientele by withdrawing into an imaginary world where her true spiritual desires are given forms. As do the *schöne Seele* and Maggie, she "fühlte Fähigkeiten in sich, welche entwickelt zu werden strebten" (Bk. 14, Ch. 2, 492), but finds no rewarded,

productive environment in society. These capabilities and longings are destined, however, to remain latent for a long time. They become supplanted by the equally strong emotions Danae has for Alcibiades and Aspasia. It is not until she is an independently wealthy hetaera in Smyrna that thoughts about the Graces and a "higher" spiritual destiny resurface. She responds to the draw of the spiritual, inner world she created in childhood by, on the one hand, building a temple for the Graces and, on the other, filling her life with so much amusement and beauty as never to become bored or sad. Years later Danae confesses to the self-denial and the rationalization behind these two responses. She tells Agathon that she had deluded herself into believing that she had found the secret of combining "die *Weisheit* mit den *Grazien* und die *Grazien* mit der *Wollust* in eine schöne schwesterliche Gruppe" (Bk. 15, Ch. 3, 538).

Her fiancé Narcissus's hemorrhage, her own second serious hemorrhage, and a disappointing association with a Pietist society signal the Beautiful Soul's withdrawal from her family and community into a personalized relationship with God and self-absorbed, isolated existence. Danae's movement towards withdrawal also begins with a disappointing love affair, for it is his approach to women solely as objects of aesthetic and sexual pleasure that reactivates her longings for matters spiritual and motivates her first decision to become celibate. As we know when Danae talks about this with Hippias, the only soul she will come to know is not her own but Agathon's. The pain she experiences when he deserts her seals her renunciation of a social and personal identity determined by the desires of men.

Like that of the *schöne Seele,* Danae's self-actualization is religious in character—an untenable solution for George Eliot's Maggie Tulliver, who leaves Stephen and attempts to withdraw within the familiar environment of family and home. Danae's inward process toward self-knowledge bridges the developmental spheres of both the *schöne Seele* and Maggie. Her rejection of the nurturing roles of wife and mother and concentration on the spiritual longings she felt in childhood are accepted by Archytas's family. The moral, religious and idyllic character of Danae's new family is not crucial to the success of her development, as it is in Maggie's case. The atmosphere of Archytas's household is just incremental, for, as the narrator informs us, Danae had always been a "schöne Seele"—an identity outwardly signified by the name of Chariklea Danae adopts when she moves to Tarent. One should not think, the narrator remarks, that the nature of Danae's past should prevent her return to a life passionately dedicated to virtue:

> Aber warum sollte sie nicht von ihrem Irrwege zurück kommen können? . . . Die Grundzüge der Seele bleiben unveränderlich. Eine schöne Seele kann sich verirren, kann durch Blendwerke getäuscht werden;

aber sie kann nicht aufhören eine schöne Seele zu sein.
Laßt den magischen Nebel zerstreut werden, laßt sie
die Gottheit der *Tugend* kennen lernen! Dies ist der
Augenblick, wo sie *sich selbst* kennen lernt. . . .

(Bk. 13, Ch. 7, 483-84)

According to Hirsch, withdrawal from society and the
deaths of the *schöne Seele* and her nineteenth-century
sister protagonists Maggie Tulliver and Effi Briest constitute the only "viable response" to the "lack of
'harmony' between the outer and the inner life, the di-
chotomization that propels man outside and confines
woman inside."[23] Danae does not physically die, but her
identity as Danae, the prostitute and entertainer, selfless
and therefore perfect in her gratification of men's desires, does. Two indications of this social "death" are
her new name, Chariklea, and her severing of practically all ties with her past. Only the woman servant she
brings with her from Smyrna and Agathon know of her
former professional associations and tastes. A third and
most telling indication is the way Agathon eventually
views her. At the end of her *Confessions,* Danae tells
Agathon that she waits happily for the time when he
who now so ardently desires to be her lover can look at
her and see only a soul (Bk. 15, Ch. 3, 543). After Agathon sees that Danae is not to be dissuaded from her
new life of inwardness, he leaves Tarent for a lengthy
voyage. When he returns it is to actualize his life-long
goal as governor of a republic, Danae no longer exists
for him. As she wished, he sees only the beautiful soul
Chariklea and makes no distinction in his behavior between her and his sister Psyche (Bk. 16, Ch. 4, 578).

The novel ends here. Agathon has developed from a
naïve, judgmental and overly sensitive youth into a mature political leader able to use his knowledge of self
and the world for the public good. His *Bildung* has
been linear and progressive. It results in a position of
political power and social influence—an obvious sign
for men's outwardly-oriented existence and activity.
Danae, on the other hand, has undergone a circular development. From an innocent country girl of humble
origins and strong emotional and spiritual longings, she
develops into a worldly, financially independent hetaera
and then into an ascetic with an individuality of her
own making. This last stage is a return to origins. She
recoups her lost innocence through celibacy and love of
virtue. The spiritual potential she longed to develop
when she was a dancer in Athens finally finds expression. Like Agathon's, the end result of her *Bildung* involves knowledge of self and a philosophy based on
moral rigorism and benevolence. The orientation is,
however, exclusively inward. Danae dies to the world
and is reborn to herself as Chariklea—a kind of lay sister in the cloister-like atmosphere of Archytas's household.

Viewed from a twentieth-century intertextual perspective, Danae's life story is the cliché of the beautiful

courtesan finding grace and peace in religion. Within
the context of the late eighteenth century's interest in
education and socialization, on the other hand, the juxtaposition of the circularity of Danae's *Bildung* and the
linearity of Agathon's spotlights a profound inequality
in options of development. The significance of the divergence in these developmental patterns becomes radically clear when we remember that the story of Agathon's *Bildung* begins from a position of self-absorption,
ecstatic spirituality and celibacy. Within the value structure of Wieland's text in particular, and the German *Bildungsroman* in general, Agathon must move beyond
this position if he is to become a mature, happy and socially contributing individual. That Danae's development leads to a position which for the male protagonist
is regarded as personally confining and socially debili-
tating underscores and validates Aspasia's notion of
men's restriction of women's development. Aspasia, as
we recall, tells Danae that as men are afraid to let
women reach their full social and personal potential,
the only way a woman can avoid total subservience and
attain some degree of self-actualization is by not giving
herself emotionally. Interestingly, it is from a position
of asceticism and inwardness that Danae finally attains
the independence, integrity and knowledge of self that
Aspasia has in her position of hetaera. Combined as
moral purveyor and sexual partner, these positions
would constitute what Agathon desires in a wife. As
prescribed in eighteenth-century discussions on wom-
en's socialization, they testify to the restrictions set on
women's individual and social potential. Incorporated
by Wieland in the characters Danae and Aspasia, the
prescribed roles of moral purveyor and sexual partner
function as prisons, which through these women's refusal to devote themselves to men lead to a kind of liberation in self-development.

Notes

1. *Geschichte des Agathon,* in *Ausgewählte Werke in
   vier Bänden,* ed. Friedrich Beißner, Vol. II
   (München: Winkler Verlag, 1964), Bk. 16, Ch. 3,
   562-73. I am using the third version of *Agathon* to
   which Wieland added Hippias's visit to Agathon
   in jail at Dionysius's court in Syracuse and Archytas's *Lebensweisheit.* The second version introduced Danae's account of her life.

2. John McCarthy, *Fantasy and Reality: An Epistemological Approach to Wieland* (Bern: Herbert
   Lang, 1974), pp. 77, 83-98. McCarthy discusses
   all the reasons for Agathon's desertion of Danae,
   Archytas's philosophy and the question as to
   whether Wieland shared Archytas's philosophy.
   McCarthy's view that Archytas's asceticism "sums
   up the Weltanschauung that Agathon is gradually
   formulating for himself and places Danae
   (Chariklea) in the proper spiritual perspective for
   the hero" (p. 77) is similar to Wolfgang Paulsen's

metaphorical reading. The resolution of Danae's and Agathon's relationship "beruht auf dem Wissen, daß die Abenteuer der Sinne über alle Beglückungen hinaus zu bestehen sind, der wahre Friede mit sich selbst aber jenseits all der durch sie verursachten Fährnisse liegt. Deutlicher ausgedrückt: die Frau ist mit all den die Sinne berauschenden Erlebnismöglichkeiten zu erleben, am Ende aber auch zu überwinden und an den ihr gebührenden Platz zu verweisen. . . . Die Harmonie, von der Archytas spricht, ist nur möglich, wenn auch sie—als reiner Mensch und 'schöne Seele'—in sie mitaufgeht" (*Christoph Martin Wieland: Der Mensch und sein Werk in psychologischen Perspektiven* [Bern: Francke, 1975], p. 189).

3. See H. W. Reichert, "The Philosophy of Archytas in Wieland's *Agathon,*" *Germanic Review* 24 (1949), 8-17.

4. Jane Gallop, *Intersections: A Reading of Sade with Bataille, Blanchot, Klossowski* (Lincoln: Univ. of Nebraska Press, 1981), p. 57.

5. Gallop, pp. 57-59.

6. Eva Cantarella, *Pandora's Daughters: The Role and Status of Women in Greek and Roman Antiquity,* trans. Maureen B. Fant (Baltimore: John Hopkins Univ. Press, 1987), pp. 49-50.

7. Citizen daughters in Periclean Greece were married at ages fourteen or fifteen. Cantarella, p. 44.

8. Trivialized as it is, the scene does bear a sexual parallel to the story of the Argivan Danae. Arcrisius locks his daughter in a tower inaccessible to mortal man because he fears the prophesy that Danae's son would kill him. Like the Danae she is to model, Myris is imprisoned in a life she is beginning to find distasteful. Alcibiades releases her from the greedy would-be panderess Krobyle. And although he does not defloriate her until a good time later, his unforeseen appearance in the artist's studio does unleash the first sexual attraction she has ever had.

9. See Ruth P. Dawson, "'And this shield is called—self-reliance': Emerging Feminist Consciousness in the Late Eighteenth Century," in *German Women in the Eighteenth and Nineteenth Centuries: A Social and Literary History,* ed. Ruth-Ellen B. Joeres and Mary Jo Maynes (Bloomington: Indiana Univ. Press, 1986), pp. 157-74. Dawson examines the feminist texts of Theodor Gottlieb von Hippel, Marianne Ehrmann and Emilie Berlepsch. The passages she cites echo Aspasia's thoughts on the myth of female inferiority. For example, Hippel's *Über die bürgerliche Verbesserung der Weiber* (1792) and Berlepsch's *Einige zum Glueck der Ehe notwendige Eigenschaften und Grundsätze* (1791), a two-part essay published at Wieland's insistence in the *Teutscher Merkur,* both emphasize that men limit the sphere of women's activity because they fear what women might become and accomplish if given the opportunity. Berlepsch focuses the problem of female oppression on how men have educated women to please and to seek praise. Accordingly, women must learn to protect themselves by seeing through the image men have constructed and becoming self-reliant (165-67).

10. "Unser Augenmerk ist bloß auf euch gerichtet, ihr liebreizenden Geschöpfe, denen die Natur die schönste ihrer Gaben, *die Gabe zu gefallen,* geschenkt hat—ihr, welche sie bestimmt hat *uns glücklich zu machen,* aber, welche eine einzige kleine Unvorsichtigkeit bei Erfüllung dieser schönen Bestimmung so leicht in Gefahr setzen kann, durch die schätzbarste eurer Eigenschaften, durch das was *die Anlage zu jeder Tugend ist,* durch *die Zärtlichkeit eures Herzens,* selbst, unglücklich zu werden! . . . Möchten die Unsterblichen . . . über die eurige wachen! Möchten sie euch zu rechter Zeit warnen, euch einer Zärtlichkeit nicht zu vertrauen, welche, bezaubert von dem großmütigen Vergnügen den Gegenstand ihrer Zuneigung glücklich zu machen, so leicht *sich selbst* vergessen kann!" (Bk. 5, Ch. 8, 158-59).

11. Cantarella, pp. 38-51. See also Sarah B. Pomeroy, *Goddesses, Whores, Wives and Slaves. Women in Classical Antiquity* (New York: Schocken Books, 1975), pp. 87-91. Pomeroy lists the average marrying age of thirty for men, the severe penalties for adultery and the high population ratio of men to women as factors contributing to multiple sexual relationships for men.

12. Cantarella, p. 49.

13. Cantarella, pp. 49-50.

14. Dawson, p. 157. See also Silvia Bovenschen, *Die imaginierte Weiblichkeit. Exemplarische Untersuchungen zu kulturgeschichtlichen und literarischen Präsentationsformen des Weiblichen* (Frankfurt: Suhrkamp, 1979).

15. Helga Madland, "Three Late Eighteenth-Century Women's Journals: Their Role in Shaping Women's Lives" in *Women in German Yearbook* 4, ed. Marianne Burkhard and Jeanette Clausen (Lanham: Univ. Press of America, 1988), p. 168. See also Beverly Brown, "Philosophy and Sexual Difference. I Read the Metaphysic of Morals and the Categorical Imperative and It Doesn't Help Me a Bit. Maria von Herbert to Immanuel Kant, August 1791," *Oxford Literary Review,* 8, 1-2

(1986), 155-63, and Kant's chapter "Von dem Unterschiede des Erhabenen und Schönen in dem Gegenverhältnis beider Geschlechter" in *Beobachtung über das Gefühl des Schönen und Erhabenen.* See also Chapter Five in Rousseau's *Emile.*

16. Madland, p. 168.

17. Madland, p. 169.

18. See the chapters on feminism, education, love and marriage in Matthew G. Bach, *Wieland's Attitude toward Woman and Her Cultural and Social Relations* (New York: AMS Press, 1966), pp. 53-79. Hipparchia in *Krates und Hipparchia* (1804), Glycerion in *Menander and Glycerion* (1804), Lais in *Aristipp* (1801-02) and of course Aspasia in *Agathon* all expatiate on the wrongful subordination of women to men.

19. Elizabeth Boa, "Sex and Sensibility: Wieland's Portrayal of Relationships Between the Sexes in the *Comische Erzählung, Agathon,* and *Musarion,*" *Lessing Yearbook* XII (1980), 193. Also see Virginia Allen, *The Femme Fatale: Erotic Icon* (Troy: Whitson Publishing Co., 1983).

20. Marianne Hirsch, "Spiritual *Bildung*: The Beautiful Soul as Paradigm," in *The Voyage In: Fictions in Female Development,* ed. Elizabeth Abel, Marianne Hirsch and Elizabeth Langland (Univ. Press of New England, 1983), pp. 23-27.

21. Hirsch, p. 32.

22. Hirsch, p. 34.

23. Hirsch, pp. 28, 26.

James M. van der Laan (essay date spring 1995)

SOURCE: van der Laan, James M. "Christoph Martin Wieland and the German Making of Greece." *Germanic Review* 70, no. 2 (spring 1995): 51-6.

[*In the following essay, van der Laan offers an in-depth analysis of Wieland's* Die Geschichte der Abderiten. *According to van der Laan, Wieland's depiction of ancient Greek culture is primarily a satire of eighteenth-century German society.*]

With *Die Geschichte der Abderiten* (1774-1780), Christoph Martin Wieland created a masterpiece of narrative prose and satiric force. This multilayered work (in many ways representative of his literary production) remains both exceptional and distinctive.[1] His portrait of eighteenth-century German culture, especially his representation of Greece within that context, sets *Die Abderiten* apart, for his view of Greece and the Greek character differs radically from that held by most of his contemporaries. A critical response to the German making of Greece, Wieland's novel also inquires into the notion of "culture" and in doing so raises provocative questions about cultural identity, authority, and diversity.[2]

In *Die Abderiten,* Wieland has not so much reflected as refracted his culture through a prism of satire and parody. He has painted a satiric picture of eighteenth-century German culture imbedded in a satiric portrait of ancient Greek culture. As Thomas Starnes explains, Wieland "borrowed subject matter from mythology and ancient history, behind which he disguised irreverent commentary on the mores of his own day" (7). Although I am not specifically interested in *Die Abderiten* as an allegory, nor in any particular one-to-one correspondence between the events and characters portrayed, nor actual contemporary people and occurrences, a synopsis of the topics and issues, that is, of the various aspects of the eighteenth-century German cultural reality contained in Wieland's novel, proves instructive.[3]

Divided into five books, *Die Abderiten* illuminates a broad spectrum of cultural phenomena both in general and in particular. A veritable rogues' gallery of human folly, Wieland's novel exposes and criticizes the social, artistic, literary, political, religious, and intellectual life of his age. As Wieland indicates in his key to the novel, it portrays human life "in seinen mancherlei Ständen, Verhältnissen und Scenen" (447).

In book 1, *Demokritus unter den Abderiten,* Wieland introduces the reader to an uncivilized, superstitious, naive, gullible, lazy, foolish, hyperrational, closed-minded, ignorant, prejudiced, banausic folk—in many ways suggestive of his fellow Germans. Throughout the novel, Wieland lampoons a provincialism and anti-intellectualism evocative of his contemporary experience. The philosopher Democritus is clearly a prophet without honor in his own country, a misunderstood genius (not altogether unlike Wieland, who found himself at one point dismissed as both a heathen and a sensualist) whom his fellow Abderites consequently declare mentally ill.

The meeting in book 2 between Democritus and the preeminent physician Hippocrates (who has been brought to Abdera to "heal" the philosopher) affords Wieland an opportunity to unveil for the first time the *Order of Cosmopolites* to which both men belong. The *Kosmopolitenorden* suggests an alternative to the popular secret societies of the eighteenth century, but the cosmopolite expressly represents the Enlightenment's idea of the *vir bonum.* Christiane Bohnert also recognizes in that portrait of the cosmopolite a self-affirmation of the literary elite who read Wieland's *Teutscher Merkur* (553).

The events of book 3, *Euripides unter den Abderiten,* call to mind Wieland's experiences in Mannheim, where his opera **Rosemunde** had its premiere (Tronskaja 198). He takes the Abderites (and his contemporaries) to task for their inane aesthetic judgment (an indiscriminate philistine taste) and what amounts to an "I know what I like" criterion. "Schlecht oder gut," the narrator writes, "was sie amüsirte, war ihnen recht" (244). Wieland's interests extend far beyond the specifically personal, however. At this point in the narrative, he interpolates a survey of eighteenth-century dramatic theory. Although the story affirms Euripides' (read Lessing's) dramaturgy (Tronskaja 195), it disparages both Hyperbolus's (that is, *Sturm und Drang*) plays (Tronskaja 196) and the Thlapsodies (the petit-bourgeois domestic dramas of a Gemmingen, Iffland, or Kotzebue) (Tronskaja 197).

Material for the fourth book, **Der Prozeß um des Esels Schatten,** probably derives from several sources: from Wieland's experiences in Biberach, for instance, where he witnessed a heated controversy between Catholics and Protestants over the appointment of a clergyman (Tronskaja 204), from Klopstock's notion of a *Gelehrtenrepublik* (Bohm 656-58), as well as from a quarrel between two members of the illustrious French *Académie* (Perrault and Boileau) over a popular narrative form called "Peau-d'Ane" or "Donkey Skin" (Bohm 658-59). In the clash between asses and shadows, Wieland also depicts the friction between aristocracy and mob, between haves and have-nots, not to mention the ongoing power struggle between church and state.

* * *

Although the conflict depicted in book 5, **Die Frösche der Latona,** may correspond to specific circumstances in Erfurt (McCarthy, *Wieland,* 117) and the infamous Lessing-Goetze controversy (Rudolph 93), Wieland emphasizes more a general religious and political corruption. It is not an indictment of religion per se, as Maria Tronskaja believes (210), but of corrupted and politicized religion, as John McCarthy explains (*Wieland,* 115). Besides the religious dogmatism and fanaticism of his day, Wieland mirrors the collision of a spurious orthodoxy and a pseudoliberalism (Tronskaja 210-11). In the silly dispute over the biological history of frogs, moreover, Wilfried Rudolph discerns a parody of two competing scientific theories, one advanced by Nonnet, the other by Buffon (94). All in all, the novel is a picture of political legerdemain, religious intolerance, extreme contentiousness, outrageous legal and paralegal chicanery, and inveterate pettiness.

Scholars have typically concerned themselves with the novel as a document and critique of eighteenth-century German culture and thus have been reluctant to read it as a portrait and characterization of ancient Greece. At the same time, they have tended to neglect Wieland's caricature of ancient Greek culture as a satire and parody of another aspect of the German reality, namely, the German reverence for everything Greek and the preoccupation with Greece as cultural ideal.

Even though he recognizes an indictment of German Graecomania in **Die Abderiten,** Rudolph concentrates on its historicity. McCarthy similarly considers the novel "another corrective to Winckelmann's idealization of ancient Greece," yet does not discuss it in those terms (*Wieland,* 125). William Clark likewise identifies Wieland's skepticism toward the German cult of Greece in his insightful article about Wieland and Winckelmann but only in reference to Wieland's *Merkur* essay on the ideals of the Ancients and not in relation to **Die Abderiten.** Friedrich Sengle also notes that Wieland had no desire to glorify, let alone venerate, Greek art and poetry (191), but his comment nevertheless does not indicate that with **Die Abderiten** Wieland attempts to bring the Greeks from the heights of Mt. Olympus back down to earth. For Tronskaja, the Greek dress of **Die Abderiten** serves only to illuminate "die deutsche Wirklichkeit" (189). She perceives nothing more than "die Summe der Merkmale des deutschen Kleinbürgers" in Wieland's novel (199). What she and so many critics fail to address is that **Die Abderiten** at the same time depicts the sum of the attributes of the typical, ordinary citizen of ancient Greece. Lieselotte Kurth-Voigt, in contrast, acknowledges and incisively describes Wieland's critique of German Hellenism (174). Her book is devoted to Wieland's early works, however; she discusses **Die Abderiten** only in passing. To my knowledge, only Ludwig Edelstein deals expressly with **Die Abderiten** as a parody of both ancient Greek culture and the German cult of Greece. Even so, Wieland's humanism remains the real subject of Edelstein's study.

In consequence, I direct attention to an often overlooked aspect of German culture—the contrasting images of Greece—with which the novel deals: one developed and disseminated by Johann Joachim Winckelmann and his followers, the other portrayed by Christoph Martin Wieland in various works, but especially in **Die Abderiten.**

In her book *The Tyranny of Greece over Germany,* E. M. Butler attests to the impact of Greece on German culture in the eighteenth century. "The Germans," she writes, "have imitated the Greeks more slavishly; they have been obsessed by them more utterly, and they have assimilated them less than any other race. The extent of the Greek influence is incalculable throughout Europe; its intensity is at its highest in Germany" (6). She was interested in what the Greeks made of the Germans (7); however, I am interested in what the Germans made of the Greeks. The Germans in a sense "made" Greece in the same way England and France—as Edward Said argues—made the Orient. Indeed, the Germans of Wieland's time interpreted and represented ancient Greece, its people and its arts, in terms of their own particular interests, needs, and ideas and in effect gave rise to what Vico has called pseudomyths.

Wieland's novel challenges such myths, specifically the idealized, even hypostatized view of Greece engendered and propagated first by Winckelmann, then taken up to a greater or lesser extent by his German contemporaries, among them Lessing, Garve, Herder, Forster, Moritz, Schiller, Goethe, Hölderlin, and Wilhelm von Humboldt, to name only a few. It is precisely that Greece, actually a concept of Greece born of a preoccupation with and veneration of its art, and the cultural hegemony of Greece over Germany that Wieland contests.

With his "Gedanken über die Nachahmung der Griechischen Wercke in der Mahlerey und Bildhauer-Kunst" (1755), Winckelmann asserted an "absolute standard of beauty for his countrymen" (Butler 4-5) and inspired an unprecedented enthusiasm for everything Greek. In his opinion,

> Der gute Geschmack, welcher sich mehr und mehr durch die Welt ausbreitet, hat sich angefangen zuerst unter dem griechischen Himmel zu bilden. Alle Erfindungen fremder Völker kamen gleichsam nur als der erste Same nach Griechenland, und nahmen eine andere Natur und Gestalt an in dem Lande, welches Minerva, sagt man, vor allen Ländern, wegen der gemäßigten Jahreszeiten, die sie hier angetroffen, den Griechen zur Wohnung angewiesen, als ein Land welches kluge Köpfe hervorbringen würde.
>
> (29)

* * *

Winckelmann galvanized the eighteenth century with his definition of the Greek ideal and the now famous remark: "Das allgemeine vorzügliche Kennzeichen der Griechischen Meisterstücke ist endlich eine edle Einfalt, und eine stille Größe, sowohl in der Stellung als im Ausdruck" (43). According to Ludwig Uhlig, Winckelmann's stylistic ideal "ist als Ausdruck eines idealen Menschenbildes zu verstehen, dem auch über die künstlerische Darstellung hinaus vorbildliche Geltung zukommt" (22). In effect, Greece came to represent *the* standard of beauty, humanity, and culture.

Roughly twenty years later, Johann Caspar Lavater's *Physiognomische Fragmente* (1777) appeared with a characterization of the Ancients ("Ueber die Ideale der Alten, schöne Natur, Nachahmung"). Like Winckelmann, he believed in the identity of the ideal and the real. "Jedes Ideal," he wrote, "so hoch es über unsere Kunst, Imagination, Gefühl erhaben sein mag, ist doch nichts, als Zusammenschmelzung von gesehenen Wirklichkeiten" (215). Goethe's *Iphigenie* (1787), Schiller's "Götter Griechenlands" (1788-1800) and his "Über na-

ive und sentimentalische Dichtung" (1795), likewise Hölderlin's poems about Greece as well as *Hyperion* (1797-99) and the unfinished *Empedokles* (1797ff.), although published ten to twenty years after *Die Abderiten,* all reinforce the idealized conception of Greece. Schiller's poem, for example, celebrates ancient Greece as the "schöne Welt" and "holdes Blüthenalter der Natur" (1: 194). In his masterful essay on naive and sentimental poetry, Schiller again represents the ancient Greeks as the flower of humanity. He imagines the ancient Greek at one with himself and content in the realization of his humanity (20: 431). "Wie kommt es," he asks, "daß wir, die in allem, was Natur ist, von den Alten so unendlich weit übertroffen werden?" (20: 430). Ancient Greece stands apart as exemplary and consummate. "Sehr viel anders war es mit den alten Griechen," he writes, "Bey diesen artete die Kultur nicht so weit aus, daß die Natur darüber verlassen wurde" (20: 430-31).

Wilhelm von Humboldt's essay, "Über den Charakter der Griechen, die idealische und historische Ansicht desselben" (circa 1807), may best exemplify and sum up how Germans, in particular German Hellenists, envisioned the ancient Greeks. In his opinion, "wahrer und allgemeingeltender Vorzug" distinguishes classical antiquity from the present day (200). Greek character in fact provides "das Ideal alles Menschendaseins" (203). Humboldt does not refer to a few exceptional individuals but to all Greeks in general. According to him, the Greeks represent "als Nation das höchste Leben" (200). Once again, one hears echoes of Winckelmann: "Das Vorherrschende im griechischen Geist ist daher Freude an Gleichgewicht und Ebenmaß; auch das Edelste und Erhabenste nur da aufnehmen zu wollen, wo es mit einem Ganzen zusammenstimmt" (200). His comments might well serve as credo for German Hellenism.

That image of Greece as the *non plus ultra* and *the* criterion of culture enjoyed wide reception, acceptance, and authority. The Greece that Wieland portrays is radically different from the one envisioned and promulgated by the likes of Winckelmann, Lavater, Schiller, and Humboldt, however. Such poets and pundits hold up Greek notions of beauty and taste as models of a cultural ideal, but Wieland casts Greece in an altogether different light and so calls into question, indeed, lampoons the contemporary devotion to that ideal. He considers the uncritical perception of an all-embracing reverence for ancient Greece both unwarranted and undeserved. He takes his contemporaries to task for confusing the ideal with the real, art with nature, ancient Greek statuary with the actual appearance and character of the typical, ancient Greek man or woman. With his novel, he not only points out the fallacy of an idealized and idolized Greece, he also attempts to rectify an inaccurate and all too one-sided conception of Greece.

In response, he turns classical allusion against an illusion. His caricature of Greek society debunks and dispels the myth of Greece as *the* model and *the* standard of culture. Wieland's Greece is not the birthplace of civilization, culture, and the Classical ideal. His Greeks exhibit none of the ideal qualities so often attributed to them. There were indeed great individuals (such as Democritus in Abdera), but as a whole, the Greeks were not a particularly "vorzügliches Volk," nor were they especially "schöne Menschen." Wieland subverts the Winckelmannian version of Greece as contrasting image (as *other*) and casts ancient Greece instead as mirror. He does not present a picture of the highest humanity but of ordinary human beings, neither much better nor worse than any others. They are hardly models of harmony, balance, serenity, dignity, moderation, and restraint, in short, of "edle Einfalt und stille Größe." They are neither extraordinary nor heroic; rather they have all the faults and foibles of any other people. As Wieland portrays ancient Greece, it could never serve as the normative model for culture.

* * *

The implicit content of the novel receives explicit formulation in what might be considered a companion piece to **Die Abderiten,** his *Merkur* [*Teutscher Merkur*] essay on the ideals of the Ancients (**"Gedanken über die Ideale der Alten,"** 1777). Like the novel, the essay attacks "die überspannte Meinung von der höhern körperlichen und sittlichen Vollkommenheit der Griechen" (367) and "eine zu große, aus flüchtiger unvollständiger Kenntnis ihrer glänzenden Seite entsprungene Bewunderung" (368). Wieland recognizes the greatness of individual Greeks but also acknowledges and declares the limitations of Greek character:

> Daß die Griechen überhaupt ein wohlgebildetes Volk, und schöne Personen unter ihnen nichts seltnes gewesen, läßt sich allerdings beweisen, und es leugnen zu wollen wäre würklich unverschämt. Aber womit man den historischen Beweis führen wollte, daß sie zu des Phidias oder irgend einer andern Zeit schöner gewesen als die Perser, Tscherkassen, Georgier, oder als die Römer, Gallier, Germanen, Britten, Normannen, ja selbst als die heutigen Italiäner, Engländer, Franzosen, Teutschen u.s.w.—davon weiß ich zur Zeit nichts.
>
> (368-69)

In the *Merkur* essay, Wieland calls attention to a side of the Greeks others either fail to notice or ignore. "Die Griechen," he writes, "waren als sittliche Menschen betrachtet, ein noch sehr rohes und allen Excessen der wildesten Leidenschaften überlassenes Volk" (372). Wieland even characterizes the Athenians as "nicht weniger leichtsinnig, auffahrend, wankelmütig, ungerecht, undankbar, gewalttätig, und also wenigstens nicht besser gewesen als der Charakter irgend eines Pöbels in der Welt" (373), a comment completely in accord with

the picture of the Greeks Wieland's **Abderiten** affords. Indeed, both remarks describe the Greeks of his novel precisely. McCarthy is even of the opinion that the essay in question offers "die Summe der kunst- und kulturtheoretischen Ansichten Wielands, welche er seit Anfang der 1770er Jahre der unkritischen Nachahmungsschwärmerei der Zeit entgegenhielt" ("Klassisch lesen," 421). One could well make the same claim for the novel, in which Wieland emphasizes the common Greek, warts and all, not so much to lambast Greek art as to counteract an inflated, sanitized, idealized image of the ancient Greeks. As McCarthy explains in reference to the *Merkur* essay, "das umstrittene Verhältnis zwischen Subjekt und Objekt beziehungsweise zwischen Idealität und Realität bei der Rezeption des Kunstobjekts [steht für Wieland] im Mittelpunkt" ("Klassisch lesen," 421).

The novel as a whole satirizes the German veneration of ancient Greece as cultural ideal, but two episodes deserve and repay particular attention, for they specifically parody and undermine the normative authority of the Greek paragon. The first appears in book 1, where Democritus tells of his travels abroad and of Gulleru, the quintessence of feminine beauty—in Ethiopia! In every way, she falls short of the Greek ideal. All her features—the color of her skin, the texture of her hair, the line of her nose, the form of her lips, the shape of her eyes—depart from the Greek norm. According to Democritus, she embodies "das völlige Gegentheil des griechischen Ideals der Schönheit" (147). Nevertheless, she personifies beauty in Ethiopia, where in turn the Greek brow, complexion, hair, nose, and eyes would count for naught.

Here Wieland subtly renders one of Winckelmann's key premises moot: that the Greeks in all probability by far surpassed other peoples in physical beauty.[4] Likewise, he invalidates the requirement born of German Hellenism "that truly beautiful human beings must have Greek faces" (Clark 12). He denies the absolute and universal validity of Greek notions of beauty and instead asserts their cultural relativity. The Greek ideal might be suitable for the Greeks, not however for Ethiopians and by implication not necessarily for Germans either. Wieland in effect interrogates the notions of "civilization" and "barbarism" and exposes them as pseudomyths, saying, in other words, that one person's barbarism is another person's civilization and vice versa.

Wieland clearly criticizes the domination of one culture over another. In this regard, his eighteenth-century attack on normativity, as it were, anticipates the more recent controversy surrounding "diversity" and "multiculturalism."[5] **Die Abderiten** could hardly be said to advocate all that is now meant by those terms, but the novel promotes a pluralism indicative of things to come.

Indeed, "Einsicht in den historischen Relativismus aller Kulturepochen" (McCarthy, "Klassisch lesen," 418-19) distinguishes *Die Abderiten,* not to mention many of Wieland's other works. (For example, *Oberon* with its positive treatment of Islam comes to mind here.)

* * *

Book 3 provides a second representative passage. In this case, a bust of Euripides is at issue. The great playwright has come to Abdera on his way to another engagement only to find one of his plays in production. When he raises objections, Abdera's own dramaturge questions the visitor's identity, hence his right to criticize. To settle the matter, Euripides shall be compared to a sculptural representation of himself. Upon inspection, however, the bust looks nothing like the original, the great dramatist it supposedly depicts. It is, to put it bluntly, a joke. With great subtlety, Wieland both parodies and discredits Winckelmann's so highly respected reflections on Greek sculpture and in effect makes a mockery of the entire intellectual and cultural orientation to which those reflections gave rise.

Once again, the *Merkur* essay and McCarthy's commentary serve as a useful point of reference. Wieland expressed his opinions carefully, McCarthy writes, "ohne Anspruch auf normgebende Autorität, doch in der Hoffnung, einige wenige Leser zum Nachdenken über wichtige Kunstfragen anzuregen" ("Klassisch lesen," 424). With its almost indiscernible satiric allusion to Winckelmann, the passage discussed above gives evidence of the same strategy.

Butler asserts that "Heine and not Nietzsche gave the coup de grâce to Winckelmann's Greece [that is, the idealized and idolized image of ancient Greece]" (7), but she fails to note that Wieland had launched the attack earlier still. Already in such works as *Die Komischen Erzählungen, Musarion, Agathon, Die Dialogen des Diogenes,* and *Die Geschichte der Abderiten* (as well as a host of essays), Wieland had begun to counteract Winckelmann's image of Greece. Probably because of its deftness, subtlety, and congeniality, however, his assault (or more accurately, his corrective) went largely unnoticed.

Ironically, Wieland's novel may be a subtle act of self-parody. After all, he himself did much to generate and facilitate the cultural dominance of Greece over Germany, not least of all with the novel under consideration. According to Hans Henning, "in besonderer Weise haben wir Wieland die Verbreitung und Umsetzung der Antike im 18. Jahrhundert zu danken, wie es nicht nur aus den Briefen, sondern auch aus seinen Werken hervorgeht" (22). Many of his works are set in Greece, employ Greek characters, and are spiced with quotations from and allusions to classical antiquity. He also acted as translator and mediator of classical authors (Horace, Lucian, Euripides, Cicero, and Aristophanes) to the German reading public, not to mention published an *Attisches Museum* (Henning 21).

Even as he challenges and mocks it, Wieland may actually augment and bolster a German Hellenism. He himself borrows topoi, plots, and devices from classical antiquity. As Gerda von Bülow points out, Wieland found inspiration for his novel in Lucian's anecdote about Abdera, a story Wieland had previously translated (99). According to Tronskaja, Wieland owes his most important stylistic devices ("die Ironisierung und die satirisch-possenhafte Darstellung") to Lucian and the fictional prose epics of classical authors (191). Although he ridicules the blind imitation and admiration of Greek culture, he has nevertheless imitated Greek authors and literary forms with *Die Abderiten.* In Herrmann Funke's opinion, Wieland's literary production is "der Antike in einem solchen Maße verpflichtet, daß es ohne sie gar nicht denkbar wäre" (25).

As a result, Wieland's novel both withholds and resists solution. The text literally works against itself. It does afford a critique of the German preoccupation with Greece but nevertheless remains an adaptation of a Greek source, a work indebted to and harking back to classical antiquity, which consequently reinforces the place and authority of Greece in German culture. Wieland is in a sense product, proponent, and critic of the German Graecomania. But what else should one expect from the man some called the German Aristippus and whom Goethe labelled the German Lucian?

If the apparent contradiction finds any resolution, it is as a function of Wieland's complex ironic strategy. As Goethe knew so well, Wieland's talent manifested itself specifically in the tension between "Scherz und Ernst" (271). Similarly, Goethe recognized and prized the plasticity in Wieland's genius and the state of flux he thereby achieved in his works. *Die Abderiten* is one such work and for that very reason is also exemplary of the novel per se, which Milan Kundera defines as a world of ambiguity and relativity (14).

Wieland explains himself and his *modus scribendi* in a piece aptly enough entitled **"Meine Erklärung"**:

> Meine natürliche Geneigtheit, Alles (Personen und Sachen) von allen Seiten und aus allen möglichen Gesichtspunkten anzusehen, und ein herzlicher Widerwille gegen das mir allzu einseitige Urtheilen und Parteynehmen, ist ein wesentliches Stück meiner Individualität. Es ist mir geradezu unmöglich, eine Partey gleichsam zu heyrathen.
>
> (256)

Kurth-Voigt finds such perspectivity especially emblematic of Wieland's talent. In her opinion, "Wieland's presentation of multiple points of view and his introduction of supplementary or corrective perspectives continued to be distinctive characteristics of his later novels, indeed of virtually every one of his contributions to literature" (174). Likewise, James W. Marchand considers Wieland's "ability to see a problem from all sides and his inability to choose sides" one of his most characteristic traits as a writer (1). In *Die Abderiten,* however, it is not so much that Wieland was unable to choose sides as that he was able to have it both ways.

* * *

Wieland's *Abderiten* beautifully illustrates Kundera's description of the novel as "die einzige Kunstform, die immer imstande war, sich selbst zu ironisieren" (from a talk given at the Stockholm "Conference sur le Roman," as cited by Guy Stern [199]). It is precisely Wieland's virtuosic irony, his chameleonlike versatility, and his oscillation between two worlds "that makes him ambivalent and fascinating. Hence he can turn iconoclast and upholder of the Greek tradition in successive works or even in the same one"—as in *Die Abderiten.*[6]

Far from quaint and dated, Wieland's novel documents the foibles and flaws of any time and culture. Abderites, he reminds his audience, are alive and well, everywhere and in every age. One need only look at oneself and today's modern culture with its overly litigious citizens, its overabundance of lawyers, its television aesthetic, its gullible and duped populace, and its sophistical politicians. Abderites might even be discovered within the intellectual community, where pettiness, closedmindedness, and contentiousness are not altogether unheard of. After all: "Abdera," Wieland writes, "ist allenthalben und wir sind gewissermaßen alle da zu Hause" (**"Auszug"** [**"Auszug aus einem Schreiben an einen Freund D*** über die Abderiten"**] II: 743).

Certainly, *Die Abderiten* speaks to pivotal, muchdebated questions of modern time. In the deeper issues it addresses—image making, cultural authority and hegemony, multiculturalism and diversity—Wieland's novel proves unexpectedly and remarkably current.

Notes

1. John A. McCarthy points out, for example, that *Die Abderiten* renewed "the tradition of fool's literature so popular from the fifteenth to the seventeenth centuries" (*Wieland* 114). As the first serialized novel in German literature, it also paved the way for one of the most popular genres of the nineteenth century (114). According to Christiane Bohnert, Wieland's *Abderiten* broke ground for yet another genre, namely, the Enlightenment *Romansatire* (548). Fritz Martini likewise deems it "der erste umfassende gesellschaftskritische Roman in der deutschen Literatur des 18. Jahrhun-

derts," (the first comprehensive, socially critical novel in German literature of the eighteenth century"), as well as "die erste, künstlerisch durchgestaltete, literarische Dokumentation einer bürgerlichen Selbstkritik," ("the first aesthetically composed, literary documentation of a bourgeois selfcriticism") (77).

2. I use such "loaded" terms advisedly and somewhat reluctantly, given they are today's concepts and are associated with a specific, late twentiethcentury discourse on culture. Even so, such terms lend themselves *mutatis mutandis* to a discussion of Wieland's novel and to an illumination of its key themes.

3. Several scholars (notably Arnd Bohm, Christiane Bohnert, Fritz Martini, Wilfried Rudolph, and Maria Tronskaja) have identified many of the parallels to Wieland's own time and furnish more such detailed information.

4. According to Winckelmann, "ueberhaupt war alles, was von der Geburt bis zur Fülle des Wachsthums zur Bildung der Cörper, zur Bewahrung, zur Ausarbeitung und zur Zierde dieser Bildung durch Natur und Kunst eingeflößet und gelehret worden, zum Vortheil der schönen Natur der alten Griechen gewürckt und angewendet, und kan die vorzügliche Schönheit ihrer Cörper vor den unsrigen mit der grösten Wahrscheinlichkeit zu behaupten Anlaß geben" (33).

5. Articles in *The New York Times* and *The Chronicle of Higher Education*; books by Allan Bloom, E. D. Hirsch, and Dinesh D'Souza; recent essays in *Profession 92* (by Henry Louis Gates, Jr. and Edward J. Mullen), in *Profession 93* (by Gates and Sara Suleri), and in *Academic Questions* (by Lawrence Auster, Diane Ravitch, and Glenn M. Ricketts)—not to mention countless other publications—all attest to the ongoing concern with "civilization," "barbarism," "multiculturalism," and "cultural diversity," as well as to the concomitant divergence of opinion.

6. Here I must acknowledge a debt to Guy Stern, who has graciously given me permission to quote his insightful, albeit unpublished observations on Wieland's irony.

Works Cited

Auster, Lawrence. "America: Multiethnic, Not Multicultural." *Academic Questions* 4.4 (1991): 72-84.

———. "A Reply to Ravitch." *Academic Questions* 4.4 (1991): 88-90.

Bloom, Allan. *The Closing of the American Mind. How Higher Education Has Failed Democracy and Impoverished the Souls of Today's Students.* New York: Simon, 1987.

Bohm, Arnd. "Ancients and Moderns in Wieland's 'Prozeß um des Esels Schatten.'" *MLN* [*Modern Language Notes*] 103 (1988): 652-61.

Bohnert, Christiane. "Der Weg vom Wort zur Tat: Maßstab und Wirklichkeitsbezug der Satire 1774-1792." *German Quarterly* 60 (1987): 548-66.

Bülow, Gerda von. "Das historische Vorbild für Wielands Abdera." *Christoph Martin Wieland und die Antike: Eine Aufsatzsammlung.* Beiträge der Winckelmann-Gesellschaft, 14. Ed. Max Kunze. Stendal: Winckelmann-Gesellschaft, 1986. 95-99.

Butler, E. M. *The Tyranny of Greece over Germany.* New York: Macmillan; Cambridge: UP, 1935.

Clark, William H. "Wieland *contra* Winckelmann." *The Germanic Review* 34 (1959): 4-13.

D'Souza, Dinesh. *Illiberal Education. The Politics of Race and Sex on Campus.* New York: Free Press, 1991.

Funke, Herrmann. "Arno Schmidt: Wieland und die Antike." *Christoph Martin Wieland und die Antike.* 23-30.

Gates, Henry Louis, Jr. "Beyond the Culture Wars: Identities in Dialogue." *Profession 93.* New York: MLA, 1993. 6-11.

———. "Pluralism and Its Discontents." *Profession 92.* New York: MLA, 1992. 35-38.

Goethe, Johann Wolfgang von. *Aus meinem Leben Dichtung und Wahrheit. Autobiographische Schriften I.* Ed. Lieselotte Blumenthal and Erich Trunz. 10th ed. München: Verlag C. H. Beck, 1981. Vol. 9 of *Goethes Werke.* Hamburger Ausgabe. Ed. Erich Trunz. 14 vols. 1982.

Henning, Hans. "Wielands Verhältnis zur Antike, dargestellt nach seinen Briefen bis 1772." *Christoph Martin Wieland und die Antike.* 7-22.

Hirsch, E. D., Jr. *Cultural Literacy: What Every American Needs to Know.* Boston: Houghton Mifflin, 1987.

Humboldt, Wilhelm von. "Über den Charakter der Griechen, die idealische und historische Ansicht desselben." *Griechenland als Ideal: Winckelmann und seine Rezeption in Deutschland.* Ed. Ludwig Uhlig. Tübingen: Gunter Narr, 1988. 199-206.

Johne, Renate. "Wieland und der antike Roman." *Christoph Martin Wieland und die Antike.* 45-54.

Kundera, Milan. "The Depreciated Legacy of Cervantes." *The Art of the Novel.* Trans. Linda Asher. New York: Grove Press, 1988. 3-20.

Kunze, Max. "'In Deiner Mine diese stille Größe und Seelenruh' zu sehn!'—Winckelmann bei Wieland." *Christoph Martin Wieland und die Antike.* 65-75.

Kurth-Voigt, Lieselotte E. *Perspectives and Points of View: The Early Works of Wieland and their Background.* Baltimore and London: The Johns Hopkins UP, 1974.

Lavater, Johann Caspar. "Ueber die Ideale der Alten, schöne Natur, Nachahmung (Fragment, wie's eins sein kann)." *Ausgewählte Schriften.* Ed. Johann Kaspar Orelli. 3rd ed. Vol. 1. Zürich: Friedrich Schultheß, 1859. 4 vols. 212-21.

Marchand, James W. "Wieland's Style and Narratology." *Christoph Martin Wieland: Nordamerikanische Forschungsbeiträge zur 250. Wiederkehr seines Geburtstages 1983.* Ed. Hansjörg Schelle. Tübingen: Max Niemeyer Verlag, 1984. 1-32.

Martini, Fritz. "Wieland—*Geschichte der Abderiten.*" *Der deutsche Roman vom Barock bis zur Gegenwart.* Ed. Benno von Wiese. Vol. 1. Düsseldorf: Bagel, 1965. 64-94.

McCarthy, John A. *Christoph Martin Wieland.* Boston: Twayne, 1979.

———. "Klassisch lesen: Weimarer Klassik, Wirkungsästhetik und Wieland." *Jahrbuch der Deutschen Schiller-Gesellschaft* 36 (1992): 414-32.

Mullen, Edward J. "Foreign Language Departments and the New Multiculturalism." *Profession 92.* New York: MLA, 1992. 54-58.

Ravitch, Diane. "A Response to Auster." *Academic Questions* 4.4 (1991): 85-87.

Ricketts, Glenn M. "Multiculturalism Mobilizes." *Academic Questions* 3.3 (1990): 56-62.

Rudolph, Wilfried. "Einige Aspekte des Antike- und Zeitbezugs in Wielands Roman 'Geschichte der Abderiten'." *Christoph Martin Wieland und die Antike.* 89-94.

Said, Edward W. *Orientalism.* New York: Pantheon Books, 1978.

Schiller, Friedrich. "Die Götter Griechenlands." *Gedichte in der Reihenfolge ihres Erscheinens 1776-1799.* Ed. Julius Petersen and Friedrich Beißner. Weimar: Hermann Böhlaus Nachfolger, 1943. Vol. 1 of *Schillers Werke.* Nationalausgabe. Ed. Julius Petersen and Gerhard Fricke. 36 vols. to date. 1943. 190-95.

———. "Über naive und sentimentalische Dichtung." *Philosophische Schriften.* Ed. Helmut Koopman and Benno von Wiese. Weimar: Böhlau, 1962. Vol. 20, part 1 of *Schillers Werke.* 413-503.

Sengle, Friedrich. *Wieland.* Stuttgart: Metzler, 1949.

Starnes, Thomas C. *Musarion and Other Rococo Tales by Christoph Martin Wieland.* Trans. and Intro. T. Starnes. Studies in German Literature, Linguistics, and Culture 59. Columbia, S.C.: Camden House, 1991.

Stern, Guy. "Wieland als Herausgeber der *Sternheim.*" *Christoph Martin Wieland: Nordamerikanische Forschungsbeiträge 1983.* 195-208.

Suleri, Sara. "Multiculturalism and Its Discontents." *Profession 93.* New York: MLA, 1993. 16-17.

Tronskaja, Maria. *Die deutsche Prosasatire der Aufklärung.* Trans. Brigitta Schröder. Berlin: Rütten und Loening, 1969.

Uhlig, Ludwig, ed. *Griechenland als Ideal: Winckelmann und seine Rezeption in Deutschland.* Deutsche TextBibliothek 4. Ed. Gotthart Wunberg. Tübingen: Gunter Narr, 1988.

Wieland, Christoph Martin. "Auszug aus einem Schreiben an einen Freund D*** über die Abderiten." *Christoph Martin Wieland Werke.* Ed. Fritz Martini and Hans Werne Seiffert. Vol. 2. Ed. Fritz Martini and Reinhard Döhl. München: Hanser, 1966. 5 vols. 742-52.

———. "Gedanken über die Ideale der Alten." *Christoph Martin Wieland Werke.* Ed. Martini and Seiffert. Vol. 3. Ed. Martini and Döhl. München: Hanser, 1967. 359-411.

———. *Geschichte der Abderiten. Christoph Martin Wieland Werke.* Vol. 2. München: Hanser, 1966.

———. "Meine Erklärung." *Der Neue Teutsche Merkur* 1.4 (1800): 243-76.

Winckelmann, Johann Joachim. "Gedanken über die Nachahmung der Griechischen Wercke in der Mahlerey und Bildhauer-Kunst." *Kleine Schriften, Vorreden, Entwürfe.* Ed. Walther Rehm. Berlin: Walter de Gruyter, 1968. 27-59.

Simon Richter (essay date 1996)

SOURCE: Richter, Simon. "Wieland and the Homoerotics of Reading." In *Outing Goethe and His Age,* edited by Alice A. Kuzniar, pp. 47-60. Stanford, Calif.: Stanford University Press, 1996.

[*In the following essay, Richter examines depictions of the female breast in Wieland's writings. Richter argues that because the erotic elements in Wieland's work were directed almost exclusively toward male readers, Wieland's descriptions of sexuality are essentially homoerotic in nature. In this sense, according to Richter, Wieland's representations of the breast take on a decidedly phallic quality.*]

> Is not Wieland's poetry Wieland's person?
>
> —Caroline Schlegel-Schelling

Christoph Martin Wieland is about the last person one would expect to find implicated in a homoerotics of reading, even if, as Gleim once teasingly pointed out, it is "from his mouth that the German youth first heard of Greek love" (Derks 234). Gleim was referring to one of Wieland's scandalous *Comic Tales* (*Komische Erzählungen*) entitled **"Juno and Ganymede,"** a story that Wieland himself later expunged from his collected works. Wieland is generally known as the celebrator of heterosexual love, not in its spiritualized form, but in its mildly titillating sensuousness. Perhaps nothing figures Wieland's desire as precisely as the contour of the woman's breast. He never tires of inventing situations in which a woman's breast is exposed, and never fails to linger. These passages themselves become breasts in the text, gratuitous folds for the reader's delectation.[1] How could Wieland, of all people, be involved in a homoerotic network?

The reading that follows is itself like the breast. It will trace the line of a prodigious arc that connects Wieland and his (male) readers by means of the proffered breast. This particular homoerotics of reading might best be understood as an extreme instance of the triangle of homosocial desire (Sedgwick, *Between Men* 21-27) mapped onto a model of reader reception. What enhances and complicates the picture is that the mediating breast itself turns out to be phallic. Wieland is locked in a triple bind that is thoroughly gay, and of which he is the reluctant author.

I

It must have surprised the young Wilhelm Heinse when Wieland, his "wise high priest of the graces and Apollo" (Seiffert 5:210), so vociferously rejected the verses he had submitted to Wieland's literary journal, the *Merkur* [*Der teutsche Merkur*]. Heinse almost certainly believed that he was merely continuing in the tradition of Wieland's *Comic Tales* and **Musarion.** Wieland, however, was so upset that he refused to communicate directly with Heinse. As if to protect himself from contact, he required the mediation of his older friend Gleim to return the provocative poem. The explanation for his extreme reaction is disclosed in an accompanying letter (Seiffert 5:212-13). Heinse's "entire soul," he charges, is "a Priap." He calls Heinse "Mentula" and "mutoniato," characteristically resorting to Latin and Greek when it comes to naming the phallus.[2] He speaks of the "damned Tentigo that incessantly swells [Heinse's] soul." If Heinse's translation of Petronius's *Satyricon* amounted, in Wieland's opinion, to an assault on Ganymede, then these latest verses are nothing less than a rape of the graces. The sheer coherence of the formulations used to interpret Heinse's text and soul urges the hypothesis that Wieland is not merely indulging in a bit of scatological invective, but that he is vitally concerned to differentiate himself from Heinse, and to do so with reference to the male member. It is this difference and the process of differentiation that we will pursue in what follows.

Heinse's unfinished poem, announced to Wieland in an earlier letter as a "heroic poem," consists of 42 strophes: "a mere episode," writes Heinse, a song "that reveals only the slightest portion of the whole" (Seiffert 5:189). The poem begins with a bathing woman, Almina, and a hidden observer, Kleon. Precisely as in a Wieland text, Almina reveals one body part after another to the gaze of the voyeur:

> Now she began to undo her straps
> Mischievously her young bosom sprang forth.
> Now I saw her remove her dress,
> And seat herself on flowers in the moss.
> Already her thighs begin to spread,
> Here the foot and there the shoulder are exposed—
> My spirit burns! In my heart what tumult!—
> And now everything, and opened is heaven.
>
> Jetzt fing sie an die Bänder aufzuschleifen,
> Mutwillig sprang der junge Busen los.
> Jetzt sah ich sie das Kleid hinauf sich streifen,
> Und setzen sich auf Blumen in das Mooß.
> Schon fangen an die Schenkel auszuschweifen,
> Hier wird der Fuß und dort die Schulter bloß—
> Mir brennt mein Geist! im Herzen welch Getümmel!—
> Und alles nun, und aufgetan der Himmel.
>
> (Seiffert 5:191)

Kleon is not content with mere observation, and the scene of voyeurism becomes one of rape. Kleon plunges after Almina, but does not capture her until she has injured herself:

> . . . the thorns had scratched open
> Cheeks and bosom, and divine blood
> Flowed over snow to the shrine of love—
> This offering flowed to the honor of you graces.
>
> . . . die Dornen hatten Wange
> Und Busen aufgeritzt, und göttlich Blut
> Floß über Schnee zur Liebe Heiligthume—
> Dieß Opfer floß euch Grazien zum Ruhme.
>
> (Seiffert 5:194)

Three strophes were particularly upsetting to Wieland: "Read, dear Gleim, the 15th, 20th, 21st of these stanzas, and tell me whether I judge too harshly" (Seiffert 5:221). In the latter two, the recurring motif of blood implies the violence involved in the act of love.

XX

> She struggled still, and my souls wandered,
> Stimulated by this fight to fever pitch,
> They wandered full of rage, so that all nerves boiled,
> Already injured, stained with sweet blood—
> And finally, after a thousand strokes of thunder,
> Sweet rain broke forth in joyful storm.

XXI

> Kisses flare up like lightning around the lips—
> After every pause a stroke of thunder follows—
> The blood of mad love's penance sprays—

> The drunkenness of pleasure steals the day
> Causes hands, body, and feet
> Each one, to lie full of enraptured souls,
> Coursing with the nectar of sensation
> That Amor had poured into the flames.

XX

> Sie kämpfte noch, und meine Seelen irrten,
> Von diesem Kampf zum höchsten Sturm geschreckt,
> Voll Wut herum, daß alle Nerven girrten,
> Verwundet schon mit süßem Blut befleckt—
> Und endlich brach, nach hundert Donnerschlägen,
> Im Sturm hervor entzückend süßer Regen.

XXI

> Gleich Blitzen flammen um die Lippen Küße—
> Auf jede Stille folgt ein Donnerschlag—
> Es spritzt das Blut der tollen Liebesbüße—
> Die Trunkenheit von Wonne raubt den Tag
> Den Augen, macht, daß Hände, Leib und Füße—
> Ein jedes voll verzückter Seelen lag,
> Vom Nektar der Empfindungen durchfloßen,
> Die Amor in die Flammen uns gegoßen.
>
> (Seiffert 5:195)

The fifteenth strophe is distinguished by a single Petronic verse: "For this arrow is there the most beautiful target!" (*Zu diesem Pfeil ist dort das schönste Ziel!* Seiffert 5:193).

What connects the stanzas that disturbed Wieland, and what separates them from the rest, is that they point to distinct signs of the phallus. The phallus in the text does violence not only to Almina, but to the graces and the reader as well. Wieland instructs Gleim to teach Heinse "that the mysteries of nature and love must not be uncovered, and that one need not rape the graces in order to bring them an offering" (Seiffert 5:212). Silence should cover the male part in the writing of the text; as phallus, the male member is the mystery of nature and love. Wieland does not thereby deny the male part in the writing of the text; rather, he insinuates that the text originates from the phallus. As will become apparent in the course of this reading of Wieland, the phallus is, on the one hand, the hidden condition for the writing of the text and, on the other, the equally concealed object of (male) desire. Between these functions of the phallus the line of an arc extends that is nothing other than the breast and the female body, the rhetoric of male fantasy and of male poetry about women, a triangle of homosocial desire inscribed on the model of reception. Heinse's text violated this poetic logistics: Heinse does not offer the breast, he extends the uncovered phallus. Wieland understandably declined. Perhaps this is how Wieland is to be differentiated from Heinse: if Heinse's entire soul is a Priap, then Wieland's entire soul is a breast. It remains to examine the logic of this differentiation and its tenability.

II

The breast, it would seem, is one of the least deceptive signs of sexual differentiation. And yet the cultural meaning of the female breast in the eighteenth century was far from stable. Analysis of the multiple discourses of aesthetics, fashion, morality, and physiology shows that the more the breast was examined and theorized, the more it resembled the penis.

We will begin with aesthetic discourse in which the discussion of the reproductive body parts anticipates the concept of aesthetic autonomy. In his exhaustive catalog of body parts in the *History of the Art of Antiquity* (*Geschichte der Kunst des Alterthums*), Winckelmann writes: "The breast or bosom of female figures [in Greek statuary] is never excessively endowed, since beauty was placed in the moderate growth of the breasts" (*Geschichte* 183). In another place, he speaks of the breasts of the goddesses, which "are like those of young girls, and which have not yet received the fruit of love; I mean to say, the nipple is not visible on the breast" (*Geschichte* 156). By insisting on small breasts and missing nipples, Winckelmann denies the functionality and the sex-specific quality of the breast. In other words, he dismisses the maternal from aesthetic consideration. In a private letter, however, Winckelmann as much as admits that for him the female breast can and should be reduced to its functional aspect: "What beautiful thing does the woman have that we do not also have; for a beautiful breast is but of short duration, and Nature fashioned this part not for beauty, but for the rearing of children, and to this end it cannot remain beautiful" (Rehm 3:277). Beauty and functionality are mutually exclusive, as both Karl Philipp Moritz and Kant would insist some thirty years later.

While Winckelmann's aesthetics seems to be constructed within the visual gaze, Johann Gottfried Herder attempts to develop an aesthetics based on touch. In contrast to Winckelmann, Herder discovers beauty precisely in the functionality of the breast: "Nature gave woman not breast, but bosom, draped therefore the girdle of grace around her—since the springs of necessity and love should be presented here for the delicate suckling infant—and created, as is her maternal wont, sensuous pleasure of necessity" (8:52). It is not only a matter of sucking, but even more of touching—this is the *Urszene* of Herder's aesthetics: "When the drink of innocence is prepared and the immature babe clings to the sources of the first joys of mother- and childhood, and his little hand snuggles and taps and is sated . . ." (8:52). The beauty of the breast is in the touching.

Aesthetic and moral discourse intersect. In the aftermath of Rousseau's *Emile,* many voices protest the use of wet nurses. Women of both the noble and the bourgeois classes, according to the familiar polemic, would rather engage a wet nurse than nurse the child themselves. In the anonymous *Physical Treatise Concerning the Maternal Duty of Nursing and Its Influence on the Welfare of the State, According to the Prescription of Dr. Tissot and Other Famous Doctors,* the author asserts: "Just as soon as luxury, sensuous pleasure and prejudice won the upperhand among people, so the band of motherly love was finally torn without shame" (*Physische Abhandlung* [*Physical Treatise*] 10). City life is to be blamed for this unnatural practice, and particularly the vanity of women: "The tenderness of German women for their men is now too great to allow them to destroy the firmness and roundness of their bosom in the fulfillment of their maternal duty" (*Physische Abhandlung* 13). The fashion of the 1770s required the décolletage to be so low that "the slightest movement of the upper body was sufficient to expose the breast almost entirely" (Pomezny 112; cf. Hollander 203). The immoral use of wet nurses is combated by the detailed description of all sorts of repulsive conditions that putatively arise from the failure to nurse. The self-centered preservation of the beautiful breast is thus equated with masturbation.

For its part, the physiological discourse concentrates primarily on the nipple and its ability to become erect. In *Treatise Concerning the Inner Construction of the Female Breasts,* Alexander Kölpin writes: "In the middle of the brownish ring, there is the nipple (papilla), about whose spongy substance (substantia cavernosa) much fuss has been made, by means of which in the event of pleasurable sensations it attains an erect state, a certain hardness and stiffness, and becomes very sensitive" (15-16). In his *Primae lineae physiologiae,* Albrecht von Haller utters what appears to be self-evident: the blood collects in the nipple "& erectionem facere, ut in pene" (512). The erection of the nipple is irresistibly compared with that of the penis. Kölpin, it is true, is skeptical about the appropriateness of the comparison. In dissecting the breast, he had encountered no muscle that would have been capable of sealing the blood in the nipple. The pleasurable sensation should "merely be attributed to the nerves" (21).

Kölpin's sober analysis is powerless against the irresistible force of the analogy. The comparison is not limited to the erection, but rests on the deep-seated conviction that milk is essentially a diluted form of semen, and that the latter is a precious distillate of the blood, possessed in scarce supply by both sexes and expelled with orgasm—hence the constant diatribes against masturbation.[3] In 1719, Christoph Hellwig theorizes sexual intercourse as an inverse variant of nursing: "Just as the child draws the milk from his mother with the greatest desire, so the vagina draws into itself the semen that ejaculates from the male member during amorous skirmishes" (quoted in Meyer-Knees 52). Even the translator of Kölpin's Latin treatise cannot resist appending a long footnote to indicate his diverging opinion:

> It will certainly remain an undeniable experience that, in the case of young fertile women, the nipples, which are normally, in indifferent moments, entirely withdrawn and hidden in a navel-like hollow, will, when stimulated through pleasurable sensations and thoughts, soft rubbing with the tip of a finger, nipping of the lips, and the like, emerge in their true, nearly cylindrical form, standing erect and bursting, and, after some time, once the pleasant tickle has had its effect, disappear again.
>
> (16)

Even more important than every anatomical similarity is the question, assumed by the translator, as to whether the nipple, like the penis, can be stimulated by the imagination (i.e., "pleasurable thoughts"). Hermann Boerhaave stated early in the eighteenth century that "the muscles concerned in this action [male erection] are not to be reckoned among the class of vital or spontaneous muscles, since of themselves they do not act in the most healthy man; but they are rather in a class sui generis, being under the influence of the imagination. The will has no influence either to suppress, excite, or diminish their action" (quoted in *Tabes dorsalis* 14). Haller and the British physiologist Robert Whytt engaged in a hotly contested debate concerning the erection (Gilman, *Sexuality* 194-97). The penis, to use Haller's terms, is neither irritable nor sensitive, but somehow both. The penis is governed by the imagination, a dubious (and feminine) power, that mediates between body and soul in mysterious ways. The eighteenth century was inclined to accord this same unique status to the nipple.

Already in Herder a connection between the breast and the sense of touch had emerged. He could have found corroboration in seventeenth-century emblems of touch (Gilman, *Sexuality* 148-60). Typically they show a woman whose one hand is injured by a bird while the other fingers a tortoise's shell, thus displaying the passive and active aspects of touch, as well as the fact that touch is essentially a form of pain. The invariably naked bosom of the woman combines these opposing aspects in the erect nipples. The papilla becomes a physiological emblem of the sense of touch merely by virtue of its Latin name: the term "papillae" (nipples) also designates the vascular protuberances of the dermal layer of the skin which often contain the tactile corpuscles. One sees in the nipple what transpires microscopically in the finger—the papillae become erect. As Haller writes in the *tactus* chapter of his anatomy:

> The papillae of the fingertips on the inside of the hand, which are somewhat larger and arranged in regular, ring-shaped folds, can receive an impression of an ob-

ject in their nerve tissue and transmit it to the nerve fibers and the brain, when they erect themselves somewhat through a psychical effort—in the manner in which a shiver shows itself in female nipples [*papillae muliebres*]—and when they, under the pressure of gentle friction, are pressed against the tactile object.

> (241)

The papillae rise both when touched and in order to touch. Thus the discourses of the breast proceed—from aesthetics, by way of morality, fashion, and physiology—back to art. The undecidable oppositions are clustered around the related concepts of *Anmut* and *Reiz* (cf. Richter, "Ästhetischer und medizinischer Diskurs"), two German versions of the word "grace," and constitute what Wieland called the philosophy of the graces. The concept of grace in German anacreontic poetry was virtually coined on the female breast. But grace itself is riddled with the same ambiguities. Pomezny notes that

> *Anmut* belongs to those words that have undergone a notable change of meaning. *Anmut*—meaning desire, lust—became the quality of stimulating desire. The word occurs as masculine and feminine. The former has the exclusive meaning of *affectus*. Regarding the latter, Grimm states: "The feminine word also shows in the sixteenth and seventeenth centuries that masculine meaning of desire and lust."
>
> (15)

This is an all too familiar figure: the image of the attractive woman is inserted into the scene of rape, displacing all questions regarding the perpetrator and the violence of his act (cf. Heinse's poem). Either the sexual charms of the woman are blamed, or the "charming" image covers the violence of the rape. The older language use, by contrast, conceded that the woman—the feminine—could also be conceived of in terms of desire and lust, which by the eighteenth century was the exclusive resort of the masculine. In all of these discourses, and in the very language itself, the breast emerges as a highly unstable sign of difference, a final characteristic that it shares with the phallus—except for the fact that one speaks of the breast and reveals its forms.

III

The emblem of touch also occurs in Wieland's *History of Agathon (Geschichte des Agathon)*. Hippias, sophist and materialist philosopher, visits the bathing Danae, a hetaira, in the hope of persuading her to seduce Agathon. Asked what shape he would choose if he were Jupiter, Hippias replies:

> What shape could I choose that would be more pleasing to you and more amenable to my intention than this sparrow that so often has provoked justified envy in your lovers; encouraged by the most tender names, it flutters impertinently around your neck, or mischievously nips at the most beautiful bosom, and is rewarded with double the caresses it bestowed on you.
>
> (*Agathon* 121)

The bosom-touching bird, emblem of touch, mediates in the imagination between male desire and female body. *Agathon,* along with the *Comic Tales,* is one of Wieland's first works since his break with Breitinger and his turn to empirical psychology. This turn was reinforced by his friendship with Johann Georg Zimmermann, who had published a dissertation on *Reizbarkeit* (irritability) under Haller in Göttingen ten years earlier. Zimmermann is one of the many readers who watched with fascination as Wieland presided over the seduction of his hero as if it were a scientific experiment. The remaining interpretation will concentrate on the meaning of the breast in the seduction and the connection between text and body.

Hippias's sophistics, his theory of rhetoric, is based on what he has learned from the persuasive powers of the female body:

> He was so clever as to have discovered very early how important the favor of these charming creatures is, who in the more polished parts of the world possess the real power; who, with a single glance, or through a small shift of their scarf, are more persuasive than Demosthenes and Lysias with their long speeches; who, with a single tear, disarm the general of an army; and who, through the mere advantage they extract from their shape and a certain need in the stronger sex, raise themselves to become the unhindered rulers of those in whose hands the fates of entire peoples lie. Hippias had found this discovery to be so useful that he spared no effort in bringing its application to the highest degree of perfection.
>
> (*Agathon* 44-45)

The cliché-ridden stereotypes are, of course, annoying. What is crucial for the interpretation, however, is that according to Hippias, rhetoric achieves with words what women achieve with their bodies. This body-rhetoric consists in "a single glance," "the shifting of a scarf," or, as in *Musarion,* the exposing of the bosom (Wieland, *Musarion* 41); in other words, in "grace," beauty in motion. The woman who was a master of this rhetoric was Aspasia, the famous hetaira, wife of Pericles, and the frequent object of Wieland's fantasies.[4] She is alleged to have established a school of rhetoric and love in Athens. Wieland strives to recuperate her honor in several texts.[5] The Danae in *Agathon* is reputed to have been schooled by Aspasia. As Wieland says, "This group of women was to its sex what the sophists were to theirs" (*Agathon* 119)—one more indication of the equivalence of female grace and sophistic rhetoric.

Hippias attempts to persuade Agathon of the validity of his philosophy of pleasure by laying out its theoretical principles. The central concept is that of sensuous pleasure—for every pleasure can be reduced to the senses. Three maxims can be deduced from the concept of pleasure: "Satisfy your needs, delight all your senses, and spare yourself as much as possible from all painful sensations" (*Agathon* 77). Hippias speaks theoretically, not rhetorically, of the body and its senses. That is why he fails to convince Agathon. (To that extent, Hippias could be compared to Heinse: both expose the part of the phallus.) If Agathon is to be persuaded, then only through rhetoric—that is, through the female body. Hippias deploys Danae. She knows that she must conquer Agathon's imagination in order to seduce him (*Agathon* 131). What else does this mean—to speak with Haller—but that she must cause him an erection? The first encounter and the first mimic dance, in which Danae plays the part of Daphne entirely according to Agathon's desire, make a big impression on him. Yet his imagination transmutes the actual, corporeal Danae into "an ideal perfection" (*Agathon* 144), thus neutralizing her body-rhetoric.

The vision of this ideal image "set his spirit in such a pleasant and calm ecstasy that he, as if now all his wishes were satisfied, did not feel the least bit restless, nor suffered, on account of desires, inner ferment, the alteration of cold and fever" (*Agathon* 144). Agathon negates the signifier, the body, in order to loll in the signified, the spirit, as in an undeserved afterglow; thus Wieland skirts the erection. If Danae should ever succeed in seducing Agathon, she will have to draw his imagination back to her body; she will have to understand and use his imagination rhetorically.

> Agathon had to be manipulated into deceiving himself without being aware of it; and should he be made sensitive to subaltern stimuli, then it would have to be through the mediation of the imagination and in such a manner that the spiritual and material beauties were mixed in his eyes so that he would believe he saw in the latter nothing but the reflection of the former. Danae knew very well that intelligible beauty arouses no passion and that virtue itself (as Plato said), should it appear in visible form, would awaken ineffable love, but that this effect would be more attributable to the blinding whiteness and the charming contour of a beautiful bosom than to the innocence that it shimmered forth.
>
> (*Agathon* 145)

The bosom is not merely the image of what Danae hopes to achieve, the confusion of signifier and signified; it will be *her* bosom against which she will press Agathon's head, through which and for which she will master his imagination. The body, the sign, is more powerful than the spirit, its meaning—not innocence, but breast, blindingly white, with a charming contour. In *Musarion,* Wieland footnotes a passage regarding the "bursting contour" of the bosom: "Contour actually designates the representation of a corporeal form that we have acquired by means of feeling and touching" (41). Vision is blinded; touch takes over. The signified is dissolved in the signifier.

Danae's success confirms our reading. Agathon finds her in feigned sleep in a tiny hut. He observes her "for a long time in immobile ecstasy and with a tenderness, the sweetness of whose inner feeling surpasses all bodily pleasure until finally - - - - compelled by the power of almighty love, he can no longer constrain himself, kneels at her feet, takes one of her casually outstretched hands, and kisses it with an ardor few lovers would be capable of imagining" (*Agathon* 172-73). There is the erection, plainly indicated in the physiognomy of the text. One senses the movement in "finally"; one sees it in the four hyphens "- - - -,"[6] and measures it in "longer"—and yet there is a slippage: he kisses her hand passionately. Because of the previous analysis of the discourses of the breast, however, we realize that the hand substitutes for the breast; the word "papilla" alone guarantees it. Further confirmation comes when Danae wakes from her feigned sleep:

> O Callias [her name for Agathon] (she called with a tone of voice that resounded on all his heartstrings, while she wound her beautiful arms around him and pressed the happiest of all lovers into her bosom,)— what new being you give to me? Enjoy, o! enjoy, you most lovable among the mortals, enjoy the entire unlimited tenderness that you have poured into me.
>
> (*Agathon* 176)

Here is the pleasure of which Hippias spoke: "Enjoy, o! enjoy"—this is virtually a pictograph of the body she offers him. And Agathon does enjoy: the breast, at the breast. Wieland declines to sketch the scene further; he leaves "the paintbrush to a Correggio" (*Agathon* 176)— which in itself is ambiguous, since Correggio was commonly known as the painter of grace. The act of love for Wieland amounts to pleasure at the breast. What differentiates him from Heinse, it would seem, is that he describes the female seduction of a male, and not a rape. Wieland offers his reader the breast.

IV

There is no greater indication of the interaction between text and body than the reader's erection while reading. The seduction of Agathon by means of the rhetorical body/female rhetoric—that is, by means of the breast—is repeated on the body of the reader. The role of the phallus, in spite of its concealment, protrudes. Wieland is aware of this, though ambivalent. In a letter to his friend Zimmermann, he writes: "I'm glad that the *Comic Tales* appeal to you, but shall I tell you the truth? I was not glad to hear that they even caused such an older married man and such a wise man as yourself to have erections" (Seiffert 3:345). Wieland is in a triple bind. Confronted by Heinse, he conceals the phallus in the text. His text, in turn, cross-dresses the phallus as breast. The relation of the text to the reader is precisely analogous to that of Danae and Agathon. Wieland seduces the imagination; he offers his reader the breast. In the eighteenth-century discourses of the breast, however, it seems to be impossible to decisively differenti-

ate between the female breast and the male member: the apotheosis of the breast in Wieland is at the same time the disclosure of the breast as phallus. The phallic breast enables the seduction of the reader; if the seduction is successful, then there is nothing Wieland can do to prevent the reader, stimulated by this breast/text, from finally - - - - also having an erection. Everywhere he turns, Wieland encounters the erect phallus. While Zimmermann may seem to be admitting to masturbation, Wieland must deal with the realization that through *Agathon* and similar writings he has established a homoerotic network of readers in which he is implicated as chief seducer. The breast, where the seduction of Agathon is duplicated by the seduction of the reader, is an arc that connects the desire of every possible (male) reader with Wieland himself.

The key to understanding this eighteenth-century reading network is to be found in the numerous and popular antimasturbation treatises of the time. An analysis of the endless anecdotes that fill their pages indicates that masturbation is irrevocably linked with the imagination, the imagination with reading, and, most important, that masturbation is *not* by definition a solitary vice. Indeed, behavior that we would call homosexual or homoerotic at the very least is classified as onanism and spared any taint of sodomy. One of countless examples will suffice to display the analogy between Wieland's reading network and that of eighteenth-century group masturbation. In a book entitled *Regarding the Secret Sins*, Christian Gotthilf Salzmann writes:

> I know from the story of an older colleague that a young man, now a pastor, was seduced by a boy in school and practiced the vice. The entire school, primary and secondary, became infected. I know from experience that during lectures, while the professor held forth, this disgrace was practiced under the long cloaks worn by the students. Some of my acquaintances have admitted that they did the same thing in school. They had no cloaks, nor did they sit behind benches, but since there were few of them, they simply sat on chairs around a table. I know that two of them performed this service for each other at the deathbed of a fellow student.
>
> (Quoted in Villaume 54-55)

Wieland's effort to distinguish Heinse's poetics from his own by reference to the phallus fails in the final analysis. Not only can the distinction between penis and breast not be maintained insofar as both are phallic, but the moral implications of reading Wieland are even more dubious than those of reading Heinse. The repugnance and discomfort he showed in dealing with the rapacious desire of Heinse's verses may, according to eighteenth-century morality, be even more appropriate for the homoerotic community formed in the contact between Wieland and his readers, between text and body. This is one conclusion that cannot be skirted.

Notes

All translations from the German and Latin are by the author. The original version of this essay, with some differences of content, appeared first in German under the title "'Erektionen machen': Wieland und die Erotik der weiblichen Physiognomie," in *Geschichten der Physiognomik. Text-Bild-Wissen,* ed. Rüdiger Campe and Manfred Schneider (Freiburg: Rombach Verlag, in press).

1. The Greek word for bosom, *kolpos,* also means fold or pocket.

2. Cf. Wieland's refusal to translate *katapugon,* discussed by Derks 233.

3. With this conviction the eighteenth century duplicated a belief shared by many ancient and contemporary kinship-structured societies. See Gilbert H. Herdt's essay "Semen Transactions in Sambia Culture": "Sambia practice secret homosexual fellatio. . . . The symbolism of the first homosexual teachings in initiation is elaborate and rich; the meaning of fellatio is related to secret bamboo flutes, and ritual equations are made between flutes, penis, and mother's breast, and between semen and breast milk. Boys must drink semen to grow big and strong" (173).

4. Wieland had the habit of calling his girlfriends "Aspasia" and "Diotima"; see Sengle 75.

5. See, for example, *Ehrenrettung dreyer berühmter Frauen des Alterthums, der Aspasia, Julia und jungern Faustina.*

6. In Kleist's *Marquise von O*—these hyphens cover the space of the rape.

Works Cited

Derks, Paul. *Die Schande der heiligen Päderastie. Homosexualität und Öffentlichkeit in der deutschen Literatur, 1750-1850.* Berlin: Rosa Winkel, 1990.

Gilman, Sander L. *Sexuality: An Illustrated History.* New York: John Wiley, 1989.

Haller, Albrecht von. *Primae lineae physiologiae in usum praelectionum academicarum nunc quarto conscriptae emedatae et pluribus animadversionibus auctae ab Henrico Augusto Wrisberg.* Göttingen: Vandenhoeck, 1780.

Herder, Johann Gottfried. *Sämtliche Werke.* Ed. Bernhard Suphan. 33 vols. Berlin: Weimannsche Buchhandlung, 1877-1913.

Herdt, Gilbert H. "Semen Transactions in Sambia Culture." In *Ritualized Homosexuality in Melanesia,* ed. G. Herdt. Berkeley: University of California Press, 1984. 167-210.

Hollander, Anne. *Seeing Through Clothes.* New York: Avon Books, 1980.

Kleist, Heinrich von. *Sämtliche Werke und Briefe.* Ed. Helmut Sembdner. 2d ed. 2 vols. Munich: Hanser, 1961.

Kölpin, Alexander Bernhard. *Abhandlung von dem innern Bau der weiblichen Brüste.* Berlin, 1767.

Meyer-Knees, Anke. *Verführung und sexuelle Gewalt. Untersuchung zum medizinischen und juristischen Diskurs im 18. Jahrhundert.* Tübingen: Stauffenburg, 1992.

Physische Abhandlung von der mütterlichen Pflicht des Selbststillens und ihrem Einfluß auf das Wohl des Staates. Nach der Vorschrift des Herrn D. Tissot und anderer berühmten Aerzte. Augsburg: Eberhard Kletts Wittwe & Franck, 1788.

Pomezny, Franz. *Grazie und Grazien in der deutschen Dichtung des 18. Jahrhunderts.* Hamburg and Leipzig: Leopold Voss, 1900.

Rehm, Walther, ed. *Winckelmann Briefe.* 4 vols. Berlin: Walter de Gruyter, 1952-57.

Richter, Simon. "Ästhetischer und medizinischer Diskurs im 18. Jahrhundert: Herder und Haller über Reiz." *Lessing Yearbook* 27 (1993): 83-95.

Sedgwick, Eve Kosofsky. *Between Men: English Literature and Male Homosocial Desire.* New York: Columbia University Press, 1985.

Seiffert, Hans Werner, ed. *Wielands Briefwechsel.* 5 vols. Berlin: Akademie, 1983.

Sengle, Friedrich. *Wieland.* Stuttgart: Metzler, 1949.

Tabes dorsalis; or, The Cause of Consumption in Young Men and Women. London: M. Copper, W. Reeve & C. Sympson, 1752.

Villaume, Peter. *Ueber die Unzuchtsünden in der Jugend.* Wolfenbüttel: In der Schulbuchhandlung, 1787.

Wieland, Christoph Martin. *Geschichte des Agathon.* 1st ver. Stuttgart: Reclam, 1981.

———. *Musarion, oder die Philosophie der Grazien.* Stuttgart: Reclam, 1979.

Winckelmann, Johann Joachim. *Geschichte der Kunst des Alterthums.* Dresden: In der Waltherischen Hof-Buchhandlung, 1764.

Ellis Shookman (essay date 1997)

SOURCE: Shookman, Ellis. "*Geheime Geschichte des Philosophen Peregrinus Proteus* (1791)." In *Noble Lies, Slant Truths, Necessary Angels: Aspects of Fictionality in the Novels of Christoph Martin Wieland,* pp. 135-52. Chapel Hill: University of North Carolina Press, 1997.

[*In the following essay, Shookman discusses Wieland's explorations of the art of fiction in the novel* Die Geheime Geschichte des Philosophen Peregrinus Proteus.]

*Seine Phantasie glich einem neugierigen Wanderer,
der die einladenden baumbestandenen Nebenpfade
der geraden Hauptstraße vorzieht, seine
Geschichten umspannten in kühnem Wurf den
Erdkreis, und im Moment, da er sie erfand, warf er
das Netz seiner Imagination weiter aus, über die
Ränder der Welt hinaus.*

—Michael Kleeberg, *Proteus der Pilger* (1993)

The issues of imagination and ideals raised in Wieland's essays as well as in his early and middle novels remain important in his late ones—*Peregrinus Proteus* [*Die Geheime Geschichte des Philosophen Peregrinus Proteus*] (1791), *Agathodämon* (1799), and *Aristipp* [*Aristipp und einige seiner Zeitgenossen*] (1800-02)—but they are regarded there along with the concept of illusion, the *Täuschung* considered both in his **"Versuch über das deutsche Singspiel"** and in *Die Abderiten.* The late novels show how such illusion concerns not only aesthetic enjoyment like the Abderites', moreover, but also the epistemological and ontological problems posed in *Agathon* [*Geschichte des Agathon*] and *Don Sylvio* [*Die Abenteuer des Don Sylvio von Rosalva*]. Those problems pervade the plots as well as narration of all three, which explore how closely *il*lusion and *de*lusion are related in their characters' attempts to lead either spiritual lives inspired by early Christianity or the examined kind famously favored by Socrates. Wieland thereby draws parallels between life and fictional literature that demonstrate as well as help resolve ambiguities inherent in the illusion created by his own novels, not least in the idealistic, Kantian acceptance of fictionality apparent at the end of the third version of *Agathon.* The *Täuschung* thus studied in *Peregrinus Proteus,* which first appeared in *Der teutsche Merkur* in late 1788 and early 1789, is so severe as to be fatal, but it is explained, defended, and justified in ways that recall the sense and structure of Wieland's earlier novels. Here too both the marvelous found in literary fiction and the visual images conveyed by painting and sculpture reveal the power of a vivid imagination and high ideals. Wieland's title character succumbs to theatrical illusion even more completely than the Abderites, moreover, so much so that such illusion seems "romantic," a term with historical links to the genre of the *Roman.* Illusion also informs Peregrinus's belief in Gnostic Christianity and his conversion to Cynicism, both of which are related to Lavater's dubious science of physiognomy. Like Lavater's body language, Peregrinus learns, figurative language too can be extremely misleading, an insight that connects his story to its complex narration by Peregrinus himself, his interlocutor Lucian, Lucian's sources, and Wieland's narrator. *Peregrinus Proteus* thereby indicates how Wieland's late novels continue to probe the complex, larger realm of fictionality.

The novel is mostly a story told by Peregrinus to Lucian when they meet in Elysium sixteen centuries after their deaths. The historical Lucian died sometime after A.D. 180, and the historical Peregrinus set himself on fire at the Olympic games of A.D. 165, an act recorded in Lucian's "Passing of Peregrinus" (c. A.D. 169). Wieland translated this work as part of his *Lucians von Samosatas Sämmtliche Werke* (1788), and his novel begins with an excerpt from it, which shows Lucian doubting claims that Peregrinus was wise and divine, dismissing him instead as a vainglorious fool. Wieland then adds a dialogue between his fictional characters that is modeled on Lucian's *Dialogues of the Dead.*[1] That dialogue constitutes an autobiography of Peregrinus, an apology punctuated by Lucian's occasional comments. Peregrinus rejects slander reported in Lucian's treatise, but Lucian replies that he meant no harm and agrees to hear Peregrinus set the record straight. Peregrinus does so by recounting the main events of his life, which result from his erratic imagination and his pursuit of spiritual happiness. Such eudaemonism is so otherworldly that he fails to foresee how his attraction to young people in Parium as well as Athens can be construed as sexual, a mistake that he repeats when he travels to Smyrna and seeks the philosopher Apollonius of Tyana, whose supposed daughter Dioklea and her Roman mistress Mamilia Quintilla seduce him by posing as a priestess and the goddess she serves. Similar problems arise when Peregrinus is swindled out of his fortune by two mysterious men named Kerinthus and Hegesias, who preach Christianity to achieve secret political aims. Peregrinus's stint as a Cynic in Rome proves equally futile, for he is seduced there by its emperor's daughter Faustina, a lapse that demonstrates how badly he can still be deceived. Reflecting on these repeated *Täuschungen,* Peregrinus confesses his folly but consoles himself with having convinced Lucian that though he was an enthusiast, he was at least an honest one: *"Peregrinus Proteus* steht nun, als ein *Schwärmer,* wenn du willst, aber wenigstens als ein *ehrlicher* Schwärmer vor dir da" (28:219).

This admission of forthright *Schwärmerei* develops a theme found in Wieland's earlier novels, and its significance emerges from its similar connections to their settings, characters, plots, and narrative forms. Much like Don Sylvio, Peregrinus misinterprets sense impressions because he has a lively imagination, a poetic cast of mind that Mamilia Quintilla shares with him as surely as Donna Felicia does with Don Sylvio: "Ihre Fantasie hatte, wie die meinige, in früher Jugend einen gewissen dichterischen Schwung bekommen" (27:187). In retrospect, Peregrinus dismisses Dioklea's rituals as so much "*Feerey*" (27:138), but when she visits the prison where he is held for professing his Christian beliefs, she makes his cell seem like a "Zimmer eines Feenpalasts" (28:48). Indeed, Peregrinus and Lucian debate the right to deride *Schwärmerei,* invoking the same test of ridicule applied in *Don Sylvio.* With his poetic streak, Peregrinus also resembles Agathon. He too, moreover, recites poetry like a professional rhapsodist and meets an important mentor in Smyrna. His attempt to improve Roman morals recalls Agathon's similar effort in Syracuse, and a friend warns him that an idyllic Christian family he once met could not possibly live up to his ideals for long and that he would have to escape it by taking "einen Sprung aus dem Fenster" (28:128), the same kind of leap that the fictional Greek author of *Agathon* is said to take when his story fails to turn out well. Peregrinus similarly longs to get away from pagan "Kind[er] der Finsternis" (28:6) and to live among Christian "Kinder des Lichts" (28:7), who seem just as utopian as the "Kinder der Natur" posited in *Diogenes [Sokrates Mainomenos; oder Die Dialogen des Diogenes von Sinope]*, *Der goldne Spiegel,* and *Danischmend [Geschichte des Philosophen Danischmend]*. Finally, like Schach Gebal, Lucian takes increasing interest in the story that he hears, a willing and grateful listener curious about its details and convinced that it justifies Peregrinus. These many thematic and formal links to Wieland's earlier novels suggest that *Peregrinus Proteus* takes up business left unfinished there, returning to the multifarious problem of fictionality.

This suggestion is clearest in the case of illusion. Here such *Täuschung* goes beyond the purely aesthetic kind that the Abderites experience in the theater. It is so important that *täuschen* is the first word of the novel proper, which conveys Peregrinus's surprise at seeing Lucian again: "Täuschen mich meine Augen, oder ist es wirklich mein alter Gönner *Lucian von Samosata,* den ich nach so langer Zeit wiedersehe?" (27:29). This question is legitimate, since Peregrinus later recalls his irrational tendency, "immer auf eine oder andere Art zu schwärmen und getäuscht zu werden" (27:219). Actually, others deceived him less than he deceived himself, as Dioklea explains when describing his love for Mamilia Quintilla, whom he imagined to be a kind of Venus: "Sie täuscht dich! oder vielmehr du täuschest dich selbst mit einer Art von *fantasierter Liebe*" (27:159). Lucian too finds him highly prone to self-deception, a diagnosis that Peregrinus accepts with the help of hindsight: "Ach! was mich täuschte, war immer *in mir selbst!*" (28:54). Illusion is not as simple, however, as such skepticism implies. Peregrinus calls Lucian its foe, a "Feind aller Täuschungskünste" (28:98), but Lucian notes that even sworn "Gegner aller Täuschungen" (27:164) would envy Peregrinus's imagination. Apprised of his erotic fulfillment, Lucian goes so far as to find delusion worthwhile: "Täuschung oder nicht! welcher König . . . ja welcher Weise in der Welt hätte sich nicht um diesen Preis täuschen lassen wollen!" (27:239). When he hears how Peregrinus was tricked by sham evangelists, Lucian again values deception: "Armer— oder vielmehr *nicht* armer, reicher, an süßen Täuschungen reicher Peregrin!" (28:54). Dioklea explains the "ganze Kette von Täuschungen" (28, Inhalt: 7) that misled Peregrinus, moreover, and says that it is always better to know the truth, "auch dann, wenn sie uns der

schmeichelhaftesten Täuschungen beraubt" (28:77), but she describes nature itself as the source of fantasies that, guided by reason, are a boon to humanity: "Täuscht sie etwa nicht uns alle durch Fantasie und Leidenschaften? und sind, dieser Täuschung ungeachtet, Fantasie und Leidenschaften, von Vernunft geleitet, nicht unentbehrliche Springfedern des menschlichen Lebens?" (28:79). Although it causes him so much trouble, *Täuschung* thus rightly seems Peregrinus's reason for living.

Täuschung proves so important throughout Peregrinus's life because it determines the way he thinks. For him, it is not just an accidental state of mind, but an unavoidable part of perceiving truth. He notes the difficulty of telling truth from mere appearances when he calls his weakness for *Täuschung* unwitting and unintentional: "Ich bin getäuscht *worden,* und habe andere getäuscht; aber *jenes* immer unwissend, *dieses* immer ohne Vorsatz: ich gestehe beides offenherzig; aber am Ende ist es doch nur Gerechtigkeit, wenn ich sage, daß ich zu beiden fast immer durch *Anscheinungen* verleitet wurde, die so lebhaft auf mich wirkten daß ich sie für *Wahrheit* hielt" (28:100). Peregrinus's feelings are equally strong when he describes sensing sights and sounds during daydreams so vivid that "das, was wir . . . *erfahren,* es uns vielleicht durch unser ganzes Leben unmöglich macht, dem Gedanken Raum zu geben, daß es Täuschung gewesen seyn könnte" (27:127-28). Such powerful experiences seem less subjective when Peregrinus insists that something in nature really corresponds to Gnostic concepts, just as Juno corresponds to the cloud that the mythological king Ixion mistakes for her. Skeptics like Lucian knew that such mystical concepts are *Täuschungen,* he recalls, but dreamers like himself saw much more in them: "*Wir Ixionen . . .* glaubten in der Wolke *die Göttin,* deren Gestalt sie uns vorspiegelte, *selbst* zu umfassen, und fühlten uns selig, nicht nur, weil wir *nicht wußten,* daß wir getäuscht wurden, und also unser *Genuß* (so lange die Täuschung dauerte) *wirklich* war; sondern auch, weil die *Ähnlichkeit der Wolke mit der Göttin etwas wirkliches,* und also der *Gegenstand,* der uns in diese Entzückungen setzte, mehr als ein bloßes Hirngespenst war" (28:14). Peregrinus here resembles Agathon, who similarly perceives something ideal in Archytas. What is more, Dioklea persuades Peregrinus that his *Täuschung* by Kerinthus concerned only the apparent form of Christianity, not its actual truth—"daß diese Täuschung nicht in der Sache selbst, sondern bloß in den Formen, oder vielmehr in den *Hüllen* liege, worin die Wahrheit sich zeigen müsse" (28:81). Peregrinus proves so susceptible to *Täuschung,* then, not only because he thinks it true and trusts his own instincts but also because he believes that it neither diminishes his happiness nor discredits truth itself.

Peregrinus's *Täuschung* is thus an epistemological problem posed in terms like those spelled out in *Don Sylvio* and *Agathon* and more or less explicit in Wieland's subsequent novels as well. Research on *Peregrinus Proteus* has sometimes stressed its allusions to people, politics, and other fiction of Wieland's day, occasionally asking whether this *Roman* about illusion can be called "romantic." Peregrinus has been compared to Franz Anton Mesmer, Alexander Cagliostro, Lavater, and Rousseau—contemporaries whose psychic excesses Wieland exposed in his *Teutscher Merkur*.[2] Parallels with Lavater are drawn especially often (Wieland later confessed having intended them),[3] not least because Wieland's narrator claims to write "zu dem unschuldigen Zweck, *Menschenkunde und Menschenliebe zu befördern*" (27, Vorrede: 6), an echo of the title of Lavater's *Physiognomische Fragmente zur Beförderung der Menschenkenntniß und Menschenliebe*. Sengle thinks that Wieland softens harsh judgments passed on Lavater, but others find him critical or refer to the Swiss pastor when calling Peregrinus the butt of Wieland's satire.[4] Some prefer to see Peregrinus as politically relevant, tying his personal striving to the emancipation desired by bourgeois secret societies during the French Revolution.[5] The dim view of those societies taken in his tale has seemed a "quotation" of Schiller's "Der Geisterseher" (1787), one revealing how indirectly Wieland's novel represents reality, and his similarity to the hero of *Don Quixote*—Lucian, though not above criticism himself,[6] dubs him an "irrende[r] Ritter der cynischen Tugend" (28:153)—has seemed proof that his moral heroism is romantic (*romanhaft*) in a prosaic world.[7] The main phases of Peregrinus's life have even been likened to the major kinds of novels written in the Enlightenment.[8] It has also been noted that Wieland links the word "romantic" to literary imagination, not always negatively in *Peregrinus Proteus,* where references to Dionysian cults likewise help mark him as a forerunner of romanticism.[9] While the novel has struck some as pre-romantic in its sympathy for illusion and its dialogic form, however, others argue that Wieland was still ambivalent about Peregrinus's *Schwärmerei* and that romanticism only later regarded such fantasies as objectively real.[10] The extent to which this *Roman* is romantic thus seems debatable.

Closer consideration of Wieland's narration in *Peregrinus Proteus* has suggested how the illusion that he describes is related to the fact that the novel itself is fiction. Most scholars agree that the subjectivity apparent in the narrative frame, a conversation between characters whose knowledge is limited, makes it difficult to define or distinguish truth, though they differ in their readiness to accept the concomitant illusion in life as well as art. Matthecka compares Peregrinus's and Lucian's subjective views with the narrative voice of Wieland's earlier novels, taking the relativity of their respective judgments as a sign of Wieland's growing skepticism.[11] Jan-Dirk Müller writes that all the episodes in *Peregrinus Proteus* have to do with illusion

and disillusion, adding that subjectivity is not regarded primarily as a source of error in the novel but that the notion of *Täuschung* makes sense only if illusion is measured against the real. Like Lucian, moreover, readers can consciously enjoy the artful illusion created by Peregrinus's story.[12] McCarthy argues that the structure and style of the novel, which he regards as "a vindication of the sincere fantast," correspond to Peregrinus's epistemology. Imagination is implicitly necessary to the cognition of truth there, he explains, which shows how closely fantasy and reality are related.[13] Peregrinus's initial critique of Lucian's storytelling has also been said to indicate that Wieland's own narration is pure fiction, removing any illusion of adhering to historical fact.[14] Similarly, Michael Voges contrasts the *Täuschung* connected to secret societies in the novel—Hegesias and Kerinthus stand for such *Geheimbünde*—with the transparency of Wieland's narrative frame, the latter a literary fiction plainly revealed as such.[15] Voges thus examines the artificial character of Wieland's fiction together with the reality of Peregrinus's illusions, a reality that he thinks adds a new dimension to the novel.[16] Given the complexity of *Täuschung* noted above, further study of it along such narratological lines is needed.

Wieland mentions illusion together with literary fiction from the moment that Peregrinus starts to look back on his life. His *Schwärmerei*, like Don Sylvio's, is a product of his boyhood bookishness, which he recalls in terms of imagination and the marvelous, and which connects his quixotic career to Bodmer and Breitinger's semantics. He explains his belief in spirits by citing Plato's *Symposium,* where Diotima defines love as a daemon that appeared to him "durch eine sonderbare Art von Täuschung" (27:68). Such illusion reflects his earlier reading too. He was naturally receptive to sense impressions, he notes, and blessed with an extremely vivid imagination, talents tapped when his literary schooling began with Homer, who "unbeschreiblich auf meine Imaginazion wirkte; vornehmlich alles Wunderbare" (27:55). He eagerly devoured such fiction in his grandfather's library, which included all kinds of marvelous stories, legends of gods and heroes, ghost tales, "Milesian fables," and the like. This grandfather was a dreamer, but he read about the marvelous merely for amusement, while his grandson took it seriously: "Ihm war das Wunderbare nichts als eine Puppe, womit seine immer kindisch bleibende Seele spielte; bey mir wurde es der Gegenstand der ganzen Energie meines Wesens. Was bey ihm Träumerey und Mährchen war, füllte mein Gemüth mit schwellenden Ahndungen und helldunkeln Gefühlen großer Realitäten, deren schwärmerische Verfolgung meine Gedanken Tag und Nacht beschäftigte" (27:62-63). Lucian sums up the confusion caused by such keen reading when he implies that Peregrinus is like Don Quixote: "Dein Großvater las die Geschichte der Abenteurer zum Zeitvertreib, und *Du* machtest alle mögliche Anstalten selbst auf Abenteuer auszuziehen"

(27:63). Recounting a dangerous liaison with his cousin Kallippe, Peregrinus too speaks of acting like a fictional character, explaining that he never expected to be "der unglückliche Held dieses Mährchens" (27:71), the hero of a lascivious tale told by one of Lucian's sources. Lucian observes that experience should teach one to be more careful, but Peregrinus objects that what *has* happened is no guide to what *might,* distinguishing "was *meistens* geschieht" from "was *möglich* ist" (27:76).

In addition to thus tracing Peregrinus's *Täuschung* to a weakness for possible-worlds semantics induced by fictional literature, Wieland frequently associates it with the visual arts. As in his middle novels, such art connotes ideals, but the effect of painting is not strong enough for Peregrinus, who is aesthetically entranced by sculpture instead. In Smyrna, he asks to see a bust of Apollonius, an echo of the Abderites' encounter with Euripides, and this need for images of his ideals proves serious indeed. It derives from his belief that eudaemonism means seeing and enjoying increasing degrees of beauty, which he discovers thanks to Dioklea, whose scheme to seduce him defies common sense but strikes him as plausible: "Meine Einbildung war von früher Jugend an mit allen Arten des Wunderbaren vertraut, und was im gemeinen Laufe der Dinge wunderbar heißt, war, nach meiner Vorstellungsart, in dem höhern Kreise, zu welchem Dioklea gehörte, natürlich" (27:138). Such stress on the marvelous lends special weight to a painting instrumental in Peregrinus's seduction, "ein wunderschönes Gemählde" (27:138-39) of Venus and Adonis, which preoccupies him for hours since it seems to augur well for his meeting with Venus Urania, the goddess whose servant Dioklea pretends to be. The painted Venus falls short of his ideal, however, because she does not have the full effect that he expects to feel when he meets the goddess herself. Dioklea teaches him greater respect for such images, which she calls monuments of former theophanies, and Peregrinus soon mistakes a statue of Venus for the actual goddess, an example of the force of aesthetic illusion. "In der That war es doch wohl Täuschung" (27:151), he recalls, but Dioklea mentions that it might have been "bloße Täuschung" (27:155) only so that she can further manipulate him. As she later reveals, the sculpture was modeled on Mamilia Quintilla, whom Peregrinus therefore thinks a goddess when he meets her—another "abgezielte Täuschung" (27:217). Craving the marvelous, then, Peregrinus overreacts to aesthetic illusion induced by a piece of sculpture.

Wieland discusses illusion not only by citing such paintings and sculptures but also by referring to visual art metaphorically. Peregrinus's mental images are presented as *Bilder,* his seduction and conversion are cast in terms of chiaroscuro, and such terms are tied to the effect of verbal narration. He envisions Kallippe's *Bild* and searches for Apollonius, "dessen Bild keine Zeit aus meinem Gedächtniß auslöschen kann" (27:122). He returns from seeing Mamilia Quintilla's sculpture "mit einem neuen Bilde in meiner Seele" (27:152), moreover, and says of Kerinthus, "sein Bild folgte mir" (27:256). Mamilia Quintilla, Dioklea, and Kerinthus mislead Peregrinus by making such images seem *helldunkel.* The first appears "in einer helldunkeln Wolke" (27:162), the second puts her charms "in das vorteilhafteste *Licht* oder *Helldunkel*" (27:208), and the third keeps Peregrinus's reason cloaked "in dem gehörigen *Helldunkel*" (28:10). While *helldunkel* suggests Peregrinus's dim awareness of the world,[17] such terms borrowed from painting are related to verbal narration when Lucian notes that Peregrinus is unable to give him an idea of the true colors of invisible objects, an inability that Peregrinus finds frustrating: "Immer bleibt zwischen deiner Vorstellung, mein lieber Lucian, und dem was damahls in *meiner* Seele gegenwärtiges Gefühl und Anschauen war, der Unterschied, wie zwischen einem gemahlten Feuer und einem wirklichen" (27:339). Verbal and visual art are related yet again when Peregrinus talks about his idyllic Christian family. He fondly recalls its "Bild in meiner Seele" (28:103), praising the mother as an artist's model for the Virgin Mary: "Ein Mahler oder Bildner hätte, um die Mutter des Gottgesandten darzustellen, kein vollkommneres Modell finden können" (27:298). He himself, however, cannot paint a convincing verbal picture of the family for his friend Dionysius: "Ich bot also alle meine Mahlerkunst auf, ihm eine Abschilderung von [m]einer Familie . . . zu machen: aber ich trug meine Farben so dick auf, daß mein Gemählde gerade das Gegentheil dessen, was ich beabsichtigte, bey ihm wirken mußte" (28:118). Indeed, Dionysius says that such colorful rhetoric is a trick played by a wizard in Peregrinus's breast: "Die Farben, womit er dir die Seligkeit vormahlt, die im Schooße der vermeintlichen Engel . . . deiner warten soll, sind *Zauberfarben*; das Licht, worin du diese guten Menschen siehst, ist *Zauberlicht*" (28:127). Here too a kind of "painting" fails to tell the whole story.

Peregrinus succumbs to the *Täuschung* common to verbal and visual art most completely when it is presented as theatrical. Like the Abderites, he loses his head when he sees good acting, a momentary lapse that has lasting consequences. He does not attend an actual play, but Dioklea and Mamilia Quintilla put on erotic performances for him that literally leave nothing to be desired. Mamilia's villa is built for such dramatic purposes, a place "wo alles zu jedem Schauspiel, jeder Theaterveränderung, die zu ihrer Absicht nöthig seyn konnten, aufs sinnreichste eingerichtet und vorbereitet war" (27:188). The morning after she takes the place of her statue and first embraces him, Peregrinus accordingly finds himself "in einem großen Parterre" (27:191), a rococo garden where he gazes upon Mamilia Quintilla as she demonstratively bathes in the nude. She soon tires of this role, though, and they consummate their relationship, an act that delights but also disillusions Peregrinus, who finally understands the farcical part he has played, "der Held einer lächerlichen Posse" (27:202). He uses this same vocabulary when he tells Lucian "noch einige Scenen meines *Lebens-Mimus*" (27:210), and Dioklea drops her pretensions to priestliness as if they were a theatrical costume "mit der Gleichgültigkeit einer Schauspielerin, die ihre Theaterkleidung von sich wirft" (27:211), proof that Peregrinus had been no more than the plaything of a merry widow and an aging actress, "einer—alternden Griechischen Schauspielerin" (27:189). He failed to foresee this sobering "Entwicklung des Lustspiels" (27:189), and even later his shame is mixed with fond memories of such a pleasant illusion: "Ich schämte mich . . . eine Theatergöttin für Venus Urania genommen zu haben, und erinnerte mich doch mit Entzücken der Augenblicke, wo mich diese Täuschung zum glücklichsten aller Sterblichen machte" (27:223). Indeed, when Mamilia Quintilla stages a bacchanal, he is publicly caught in the act of having sex with her, a humiliating conclusion to "dieses ächte Satyrspiel" (27:244). As is clear from his choice of such words, Peregrinus takes theatrical illusion to even greater extremes than the Abderites, unable or unwilling to tell life from art.[18]

In the same erotic scenes that Peregrinus explains by likening them to theater, Wieland often uses the expression "romantic," connecting illusion to concepts of fantasy and the marvelous that confirm its literary import. For all her rational plotting to seduce Peregrinus, Mamilia Quintilla seems romantic in this sense. He himself describes her as a young widow who decides to enjoy her husband's fortune "nach einem eigenen romantischen, aber . . . nicht übel ausgedachten Plane" (27:186), a wealthy Roman lady, "deren Einbildung auf einen so romantischen Lebensgenuß gestimmt war" (27:188). Her desire to play the part of Venus Urania attests to her "Hang zu romantischen Einfällen" (27:232), moreover, a romantic inclination that lends Peregrinus what Dioklea calls "allen möglichen Reitz der Neuheit und des Wunderbaren" (27:212-13). Bodmer and Breitinger similarly linked the new and the marvelous in their aesthetics of literary fiction, which may well account for the poetic cast—the "dichterischen Schwung" (27:187)—of Mamilia Quintilla's imagination. To be sure, she leaves Peregrinus for a new object of her "launenvolle Fantasie" (27:226), letting Dioklea have him, like all her other men, "so bald ihr die Fantasie zu ihnen vergangen wäre" (27:232). She seduces Peregrinus so easily, however, that she is tempted to see in him more than a mortal, he recalls, and just as he thinks that she embodies an ideal of beauty, she wants to make her charms come close to a certain ideal perfection. Like Peregrinus, Mamilia Quintilla thus seems to have an imagination that is more than merely whimsical. She does not doubt the effect of putting him in a romantic spot where the marvelous serves her ends, of

the "bloße Versetzung in einen so romantischen, mit lauter schönen Gegenständen angefüllten Ort, verbunden mit dem Scheine des *Wunderbaren,* den alles von sich werfen sollte" (27:214-15). Peregrinus adds that this romantic landscape pales beside the sight of Mamilia bathing, which he calls "ein ganz anderes Schauspiel" (27:195). In this seductive setting, then, "romantic" connotes illusion closely tied to the marvelous and to poetic imagination.

Peregrinus's *Täuschung* also pervades his religion. His imagination and ideals predispose him to believe in miracles and the men who perform them, but such faith is shown to be ambiguous, often abused though apparently justified in the case of Jesus. Lucian notes that miracles attributed to the early Christians must have appealed to Peregrinus's imagination, and Peregrinus himself explains his attraction to their sect by citing his moral enthusiasm, which he says subjected him to new "Illusionen der Einbildung und des Herzens" (27:324) but also brought him closer to human perfection. These illusions result from his urge to forget old fantasies and to live according to his ideals of harmony and beauty, "ohne Furcht vor Täuschung und Reue" (27:324). Kerinthus exploits this aversion to illusion, telling Peregrinus that he has been deceived long enough: "Du bist lange genug getäuscht worden, Peregrin!" (27:260). Hegesias similarly dupes Peregrinus by calling his zeal to convert to Christianity a "Täuschung deines noch nicht ganz überwältigten Selbst" (27:329). A proselyte whose own fear of illusion is thus used to fool him, Peregrinus has not lost his sense of the marvelous. He calls Kerinthus a "Wunderbares Wesen" (27:260) and defends his own credulity by finding a weakness for illusion necessary to the success of such miracle workers: "Wie wollten die Wundermänner auch zurechte kommen, wenn es nicht solche gutwillige, jeder Täuschung immer selbst entgegen kommende Seelen in der Welt gäbe?" (27:277). Lucian is less generous, claiming that such figures either deliberately deceive their followers or unwittingly deceive themselves as well. As Kerinthus's agent, Peregrinus acts in the second way, respected by believers "deren größter Theil sich eben so treuherzig von mir täuschen ließ als ich selbst getäuscht war" (28:30). Jesus, however, seems to behave in the first. Dionysius describes Jesus as an enthusiast in the best sense of the word, one who did not deceive himself about the marvelous means that he used to achieve his moral end. Is Peregrinus therefore right, at the height of his *Schwärmerei,* to consider Jesus the ideal of humanity? Is Wieland arguing that morally motivated *Täuschung* can be condoned and called religion?

Maintaining religious illusions for the sake of humane ideals is an issue treated thoroughly in *Agathodämon.* *Peregrinus Proteus* simply raises it before Peregrinus succumbs to other *Täuschungen.* When he embraces Cynicism, he sees his prior illusions for what they are, but does so only as a prelude to worse ones yet to come. While he is in prison for spreading the Christian gospel, Dioklea appears and identifies herself as Kerinthus's sister, revealing the political motives behind her brother's religious order. She has already explained the elaborate pains taken to create the "beneidenswürdige Täuschungen" (28:68) that Peregrinus enjoyed while living with Mamilia Quintilla, and when she exposes Kerinthus's similar machinations, he exclaims, "*O so war auch dies alles Täuschung!*" (28:52). Worried that Dioklea too might be deceiving him, he soon runs away. Perhaps he is suspicious because she says that their reunion is "ganz natürlich zugegangen" (28:74), an echo of **Don Sylvio** that hardly encourages faith in facticity. In any case, he thus escapes "die Täuschung, die mir eine Wolke statt der Juno in die Arme gespielt hatte" (28:84), a modern Ixion no longer in love with a mirage. Peregrinus is nonetheless still idealistic, going off in search of the philosopher Agathobulus, whom Dionysius describes as a model Cynic, and doing all he can to live up to such an ideal. He falls short of it in Rome, however, thirty years older than when first seduced by Mamilia Quintilla but still sensual enough to make a fool of himself by desiring Faustina and thereby betraying his asceticism. Misanthropic because he has so often been deceived, Peregrinus is now sure that he always will be, and he becomes a bitter recluse. A few students seek him out, but only because they entertain "die täuschende Hoffnung, durch den Unterricht eines weisen Mannes selbst weise zu werden" (28:209), and his own best hope seems suicide, the only way out of a world that he regards as "dieses verhaßte Land der Täuschungen" (28:215). Although his religious illusions might be morally justified, then, and though he was satisfied while deceived by Mamilia Quintilla, *Täuschung* makes Peregrinus cynical to the point of self-destruction.

Peregrinus's flings with Christianity and Cynicism both show illusion at work on another level as well—that of physiognomy. If **Peregrinus Proteus** is critical of Lavater, it might also be expected to criticize his association of facial features with moral character. Faces are indeed important in the novel, where they sometimes correspond to morals but often seem misleading. Peregrinus recalls being blessed with "einer glücklichen Gestalt und Gesichtsbildung" (27:55), and he is struck by Dioklea's similarity to Apollonius, "es sey nun daß es Täuschung oder Wahrheit war" (27:131). Such traits speak truly when they draw him to his friend Dionysius: "Die Heiterkeit und anscheinende Ruhe, die sich in der Fysionomie dieses Dionysius ausdrückte, zog mich eben so stark zu ihm, als ihn ich weiß nicht was in der meinigen hinwieder anzuziehen und zu interessieren schien" (28:23). Peregrinus is saved by a Cyprian merchant, moreover, whom he once lent money "auf die bloße Bürgschaft seiner Fysionomie" (28:144), trusting the face of a man who proved true to his word: "Glücklicher Weise mußte es sich fügen, daß die Fy-

sionomie des Cypriers die Wahrheit gesagt hatte" (28:144). Peregrinus never suspects foul play from pretty Faustina, however, "unter deren so lieblich lächelnden Gesichtzügen ich keine Schalkheit ahndete" (28:176), and Hegesias is likewise more dangerous than he looks. Peregrinus remembers trusting him at first sight: "Es war etwas in der Fysionomie dieses Mannes, das mir Vertrauen einflößte" (27:291). Even after Hegesias starts to mislead him, Peregrinus cannot distrust a man, "der . . . ein so sprechendes Zeugniß seiner Redlichkeit in seinem Gesichte trug" (27:292). He even believes stories about Jesus' miracles solely "auf das Wort und die ehrliche Miene meines Freundes Hegesias" (27:326). He also says that his cynicism had "eine ziemlich *christianische Miene*" (28:133), and he never doubted his religious calling, which Kernithus once seemed to see written all over his face: "Hatte nicht der *Unbekannte das Zeichen meiner Erwählung* auf meiner Stirne gesehen?" (27:318-19). Peregrinus's faith in physiognomy thus seems part of his all-around *Täuschung*.

Parallels with Lavater lie less in Peregrinus's analysis of faces, however, than in his animosity toward language. Like Lavater, he pays attention to facial features because spoken and written words seem poor means of communication. He too desires a more transparent medium of human expression and divine significance, and his habit of feeling ineffably moved makes him receptive to music and dance as well as to Gnosticism. His sensations seem beyond words when he tries to tell Lucian how he felt at the foot of Mamilia Quintilla's statue: "Doch ich will nicht versuchen, unbeschreibliche Empfindungen, oder Täuschungen, wenn du willst, beschreiben zu wollen" (27:151). Similarly, he cannot say what it was like to see Mamilia Quintilla herself: "Du wirst mir gern glauben, daß mein Gefühl bey dieser Erscheinung—möchte sie nun Täuschung oder Wahrheit seyn—alle Beschreibung zu Schanden machen würde" (27:182). In both cases, ineffability is tied to illusion, as it is when Peregrinus has the feeling that he is experiencing a daemonic *unio mystica,* "ein Gefühl, unter welchem (wie viel Täuschung auch dabey seyn mag) alle menschliche Sprache einsinkt" (28:11). Such illusion seems avoided when Dioklea performs a pantomime for him, speaking to him "in einer allgemein verständlichen, unmittelbar zur Empfindung und Einbildungskraft redenden Sprache" (27:238), and he is similarly moved by both the antiphonal chant of a Christian congregation and the singing of his Christian family. The language that affects him most, though, is that of Gnosticism. Kerinthus speaks convincingly of supernatural powers, and he promises to tell him the secrets hidden in Gnostic images. As Peregrinus tells Lucian in turn, Gnostic theosophy expresses philosophical concepts in symbols, imbuing empty words with unknown beings and forces. He repeatedly translates such symbolic terms "aus der räthselhaften Bildersprache unsrer

Sekte in die gewöhnliche Menschensprache" (28:8), assuring Lucian that they made sense: "Alle diese pompösen Bilder waren keine Worte ohne Sinn" (28:9). Indeed, he sincerely believed that they were more than just illusions like the cloud that Ixion mistook for Juno. Peregrinus's problem with *Täuschung* thus includes such language too. Far from merely unable to describe religious experience,[19] that is, Wieland is interested in semiotic questions of language here.

Mindful of Lavater, one might say that Peregrinus takes Gnostic concepts and language at face value. He describes them both in terms of physiognomy, believing in them as strongly and taking them as literally as an overeager reader of fiction. Lucian notes the "mien" of Gnosticism when he scorns its philosophy, "die sich die Miene giebt, das *unergründliche Geheimniß der Natur* ausfündig gemacht zu haben" (28:13). Even more reminiscent of physiognomy are occurrences of the terms *Schatten, Schattenriß,* and *Schattenbild,* which all mean "silhouette" in Lavater's *Fragmente.* Kerinthus promises to initiate Peregrinus into "*Mysterien,* wovon jene zu *Eleusis* nur täuschende Schatten sind" (27:265), and Peregrinus recounts a sermon in which Kerinthus claimed that words to describe his eschatological vision failed him, though he exhausted the resources of language to trace "einen matten Schattenriß davon" (27:282). Verbal language here, like a silhouette, can give only a vague idea of what it represents. Lavater relied heavily on silhouettes, however, which could be drawn with the help of mechanical instruments and thus showed their sitters' profiles accurately. Peregrinus too places great faith in such *Schattenbilder* when he insists on the reality of objects that one can only imagine: "Immerhin mögen also die Bestrebungen der wärmsten Einbildungskraft, sich zum wirklichen Anschauen dieser unerreichbaren Gegenstände zu erheben, vergeblich seyn: so sind doch diese Gegenstände selbst wirklich; so besitzt doch die menschliche Seele das Vermögen sich eine Art von *Schattenbildern* von ihnen zu machen" (28:15). This plea for the existence of ideal objects, then, alludes not only to the shadows cast in Plato's famous cave but also to Lavater's silhouettes. Such objects are related to fiction as well when Dioklea tells Peregrinus that he took Gnosticism and its symbols too literally: "Die erhabnen Offenbarungen der unsichtbaren Welt, . . . die du . . . im *buchstäblichen Verstande* genommen hast, scheinen mir weder mehr noch weniger als die unschuldigste *Poesie*; entweder bildliche Einkleidungen großer Wahrheiten . . . oder Versinnlichung edler Zwecke" (28:78). Peregrinus thus fails to grasp the fictionality of concepts conveyed in figurative, "physiognomic" language.

If Peregrinus's *Täuschung* consists of such verbal, visual, theatrical, religious, philosophical, and physiognomic confusion so often and so closely tied to the issue of fictionality, how are readers to approach Wieland's novel itself? Should they suspend their disbelief but therefore risk repeating Peregrinus's mistakes, which start with avid reading? Should they avoid all *Täuschung* but thereby violate the aesthetic contract explained in **"Versuch über das deutsche Singspiel"** and exemplified in *Die Abderiten*? In other words, how are Peregrinus's fatal illusions related to the effect that Wieland thought his fiction should have? To answer such questions, one needs to regard the multiple levels of Wieland's narration, which show marked ambivalence toward its fictionality but also leave little doubt that Peregrinus's susceptibility to illusion is a weakness that readers of his story would do well to indulge, albeit with greater caution than he. That narration is the sum of tales told by Peregrinus, Lucian, a source cited in Lucian's "Passing of Peregrinus," and the narrator of *Peregrinus Proteus,* whose remarks are confined to a foreword added to the novel when it appeared as a book in 1791 and whose tone resembles the one that Wieland takes in two related works—**"Eine Lustreise ins Elysium"** (1787) and **"Ueber die Glaubwürdigkeit Lucians in seinen Nachrichten vom Peregrinus"** (1788). Each of these narrative voices expresses a different attitude toward imagination, the marvelous, and literary fiction, and only by considering their combination can one fully understand how Wieland treats the topic of fictionality here. Examined in this way, in fact, the concept of *Täuschung* connects its plot to problems of fictionality posed by its own narrative form. *Peregrinus Proteus* too might thus be called "metafiction."

The foreword to the novel shows both the narrator's sympathy with its hapless hero and a playful attitude toward imagination, the exact opposite of Peregrinus's *Schwärmerei.* The narrator rejects Lucian's "Passing of Peregrinus," but his irony about his own omniscience recalls Lucian's skepticism. In **"Ueber die Glaubwürdigkeit Lucians in seinen Nachrichten vom Peregrinus,"** moreover, Wieland defends Lucian against the charge of calumny. The narrator recalls Lucian's portrait of Peregrinus as a foolish, half-crazed charlatan, wondering whether Lucian was sufficiently impartial and doubting that Peregrinus could have been both a deceitful fraud and an enthusiastic fantast. This moral puzzle, he observes, remains insoluble for readers who want to be fair to a man no longer around to defend himself. His own respect for Peregrinus seems diminished, though, when he explains overhearing the two dead men in Elysium, a feat that he claims to perform by means of a dubious psychic ability, "einer kleinen Naturgabe . . . die ich (ohne Ruhm zu melden) mit dem berühmten Geisterseher *Swedenborg* gemein habe, und vermöge deren mein Geist zu gewissen Zeiten sich in die Gesellschaft verstorbener Menschen versetzen, und, nach Belieben, ihre Unterredungen mit einander ungesehen behorchen, oder auch wohl, wenn sie dazu geneigt sind, sich selbst in Gespräche mit ihnen einlassen kann" (27, Vorrede: 5-6). In this variant of

Wieland's usual *Quellenfiktion,* the narrator ridicules visionaries like Peregrinus. He also professes to use his own spiritualistic gift only for pleasant distraction, not to found a new religion or hasten the millennium, schemes that Peregrinus supports as a tool of Gnosticism. By contrast, the narrator regards Lucian as a good friend. Wieland too likes Lucian, whom he assumes meant to tell the truth about Peregrinus and whose story he thinks credible, if incomplete. Hardly "eine verläumderische Erdichtung," he argues, it plausibly explains Peregrinus's death, which is "ein *innerer* Beweis ihrer Wahrheit."[20] Lucian thus meets some of Wieland's own criteria for writing fiction true to life. Psychological likelihood and internal coherence, in fact, are primary characteristics of **Peregrinus Proteus** too.

Despite intending to clear Peregrinus's name, both Wieland and his narrator thus sound closer to Lucian when discussing products of literary imagination. The narrative case is not always so clear. In the introduction to **Peregrinus Proteus,** and in the novel proper as well, Lucian is shown to use imagination more earnestly than he allows, and Peregrinus seems anything but an advocate of the marvelous, talking of narrative truth and verisimilitude instead. The two regard imagination together with *Schwärmerei,* and Lucian recalls scorning the latter, while Peregrinus replies that their very presence in Elysium now proves him wrong. Lucian agrees but adds that only "das hitzige Fieber in einem hohen Grade" (27:31) could have made him imagine that they would ever meet there. This high fever recalls the Abderites' *Schauspielfieber,* likewise a symptom of vivid imagination. Peregrinus also says that Lucian's writings certainly show no lack of imagination, but Lucian explains that he used his imagination only in jest, "daß ich die Imaginazion nie anders als zum *Spielen* gebrauchte" (27:32). He also objects to people who use their own more seriously, prophets and dreamers whom he thinks dangerous fools. Lucian himself nonetheless significantly embellishes the main source cited in "The Passing of Peregrinus," an unnamed speaker who sharply criticizes its title character. Lucian explains that this speaker was not made up, "kein Geschöpf von meiner Erfindung" (27:44), but that his oracle unfavorable to Peregrinus was, being "eine Verschönerung von meiner eigenen Erfindung" (27:46). Peregrinus censures such inventive half-truths, a fault that he finds common to other writers too: "Man kann, denke ich, immer darauf rechnen, daß Schriftsteller, denen es mehr um Beyfall als um strenge Wahrheit zu tun ist, sich eben kein Gewissen daraus machen werden, der Komposizion zu Liebe manchen Eingriff in die Rechte der letztern zu thun" (27:46). Peregrinus promises to tell Lucian the truth, moreover, and he excuses the anonymous speaker's poetic embellishments: "Übrigens sind diese Verzierungen . . . zu gewöhnlich, als daß man dem Ungenannten ein großes Verbrechen daraus machen könnte, sie, vielleicht ohne historischen Grund, der

bloßen Wahrscheinlichkeit zu Ehren hinzu gedichtet zu haben" (27:92). Here it is Peregrinus who seems closer to Wieland's idea of credible literary fiction.

Not only do Lucian and Peregrinus show a complex attitude toward concocting fiction; Lucian's admission that Peregrinus was right to imagine places such as Elysium also makes the narrator's initial irony about traveling there ring hollow. Lucian is soon persuaded by Peregrinus's story, moreover, and the narrator never reappears. His significance seems clear from **"Eine Lustreise ins Elysium,"** however, where a similar narrator mocks his own gift for reaching Elysium but then also betrays sincere faith in at least some fiction. As in **Peregrinus Proteus,** this second narrator possesses a gift that enables his spirit to roam beyond his body. He explains this psychic talent not only by citing the mystic Emanuel Swedenborg but also by referring to *Arabian Nights* and to fairy tales, which he ironically claims are as credible as they are well-known. Lavater seems chided too when the narrator adds that this rare gift furthers "die . . . *allgemeine Menschenliebe*" (28:237) and when souls in Elysium have familiar physiognomies. The narrator's skeptical opinion of fiction changes, though, when he mentions Homer. He apologizes for writing a prologue that tries the patience of readers used to Homer's style of starting in medias res, he expects that finding the philosophers' stone and fountain of youth in Germany would unleash "eine ganze *Ilias* von Verwirrung und Unheil" (28:232), and he invokes "*Vater Homer*" (28:256) to prove his point that monarchy is the best form of government. In matters of literary form, metaphors, and politics, then, this narrator relies on Homer, the same poet who initially inspires Peregrinus. He also relies on Lucian. As Wieland's mouthpiece, he explains that he wanted to visit Elysium after translating Lucian's *Dialogues of the Dead,* and he does not know what to do there until he meets "den Lucianischen *Menippus*" (28:243). Such references to Lucian's writings also occur in **Peregrinus Proteus,** where Peregrinus tells Lucian that Dionysius recommended "das Ideal, das du in deinem *Cyniker* aufgestellt hast" (28:132) and that a certain Cejonius described Rome "mit den Worten deines *Nigrinus*" (28:158). In the foreword to the novel, moreover, Lucian himself is identified only as "*Lucian der Dialogenmacher*" (27, Vorrede: 8), a name that likewise stresses his own narration of literary fictions. Indirectly, the ironic narrator of **Peregrinus Proteus** thus shows sincere respect for characters, concepts, places, and authors associated with such fictions.

Knowing how to read **Peregrinus Proteus,** then, is not simply a matter of finding its narration more like Lucian's skepticism or Peregrinus's *Schwärmerei.* With his subtle comments on that narration itself, Wieland recommends an attitude toward fictionality more balanced than such extremes. In other words, one needs to know how the *Täuschung* recurring throughout Peregrinus's life also pertains to reading Wieland's literature. This narrative knowledge involves some unexpected twists and turns. Enthusiastic Peregrinus criticizes skeptical Lucian for writing about him in ways inconsistent with verisimilitude and truth, and the narrator of Wieland's novel feels sympathetic but dubious about Peregrinus, while the similar narrator of **"Eine Lustreise ins Elysium"** ends up relying on the same poet, Homer, whose stories set Peregrinus on the road to suicide. This ambivalence audible in Wieland's narrative voices makes sense when compared to his plot, which shows his hero repeatedly taking aesthetic illusion too far. First, the taste for the marvelous that Peregrinus acquires as an avid reader of fiction exaggerates the possible-worlds semantics connecting Wieland to some current theories of fictionality. Second, the erotic traps set by Dioklea and Mamilia Quintilla are sprung by Peregrinus's overreaction to painting and sculpture and reveal him to be a Pygmalion misled by his own mental images. Third, his seduction succeeds because he submits to theatrical illusion even more completely than the Abderites. Citing Wieland's allusions to physiognomy helps explain Peregrinus's similar submission to Gnosticism, given his interest in faces and his impatience with verbal language. He takes the abstract terms of Gnosticism literally, misconstruing figures of speech that are as suggestive but also as imprecise as Lavater's silhouettes. Peregrinus never knows that *Täuschung* can be temporarily induced by art without directly affecting life, despite all its seriousness. Readers shown the ambivalence toward fictionality apparent in Wieland's several narrative voices are better able to draw such distinctions and thus to see how aesthetic illusion is a state of mind appropriate to perceiving Wieland's novel itself. Thanks to such highly "self-conscious" suggestions about its own fictionality, which are often made with regard to other arts, **Peregrinus Proteus** certainly does seem a romantic *Roman*.

Notes

1. See Rutledge, *The Dialogue of the Dead*; see also Weinreich, *Der Trug des Nektanebos*, 87.

2. See Raab, "Studien zu Wielands Romane 'Peregrinus Proteus,'" 13-14, 30.

3. See Starnes, *Christoph Martin Wieland*, 2:256, 404, and 521.

4. See Sengle, *Wieland*, 482; Starnes, review of *Fantasy and Reality*, by John McCarthy, 280; Mickel, "Peregrinus Proteus oder die Nachtseite der Pädagogischen Revolution," 835; Schostack, "Wieland und Lavater," 116-29.

5. See Thorand, "Zwischen Ideal und Wirklichkeit," 91-93, and Höhle, "Die Auseinandersetzung mit der Großen Französischen Revolution," 7-9.

6. Braunsperger, *Aufklärung aus der Antike*, 241.

7. Voges, *Aufklärung und Geheimnis*, 420, 445.

8. See Mickel, "Peregrinus Proteus," 826.

9. See Immerwahr, "'Romantic' and Its Cognates," 56, 60; see also Kistler, "Dionysian Elements in Wieland," 83, 85-86.

10. See Sengle, *Wieland*, 472, 479-80; see also Viering, *Schwärmerische Erwartung*, 10, 289.

11. See Matthecka, "Die Romantheorie Wielands," 222, 227.

12. See Jan-Dirk Müller, *Wielands späte Romane*, 136, 33, 44, 182.

13. McCarthy, *Fantasy and Reality* [1974], 112, 154.

14. Strauss, "Wieland's Late Novel *Peregrinus Proteus*," 51-52.

15. Voges, *Aufklärung und Geheimnis*, 416.

16. Ibid., 436.

17. Viering, *Schwärmerische Erwartung*, 95, 96.

18. Cf. Sträßner, *Tanzmeister und Dichter*, 160.

19. See Schostack, "Wieland und Lavater," 123.

20. Wieland, "Ueber die Glaubwürdigkeit Lucians in seinen Nachrichten vom Peregrinus," 93, 107.

Bibliography

Braunsperger, Gerhard. *Aufklärung aus der Antike: Wielands Lukianrezeption in seinem Roman "Die geheime Geschichte des Philosophen Peregrinus Proteus."* Frankfurt am Main: Lang, 1993.

Höhle, Thomas. "Die Auseinandersetzung mit der Großen Französischen Revolution in den späten Romanen Christoph Martin Wielands." In Höhle, *Das Spätwerk Christoph Martin Wielands*, 5-19.

Immerwahr, Raymond. "'Romantic' and its Cognates in England, Germany, and France before 1790." In *"Romantic" and Its Cognates: The European History of a Word*, ed. Hans Eichner, 17-97. Toronto: University of Toronto Press, 1972.

Kistler, Mark O. "Dionysian Elements in Wieland." *Germanic Review* 35 (1960): 83-92.

Matthecka, Gerd. "Die Romantheorie Wielands und seiner Vorläufer." Diss., Tübingen, 1956.

Mickel, Karl. "Peregrinus Proteus oder die Nachtseite der pädagogischen Revolution." *Sinn und Form* 35 (1983): 814-35.

Müller, Jan-Dirk. *Wielands späte Romane: Untersuchungen zur Erzählweise und zur erzählten Wirklichkeit.* Munich: Fink, 1971.

Raab, Karl. "Studien zu Wielands Romane 'Peregrinus Proteus.'" *Prag-Altstadt, Staats-Gymnasium mit deutscher Unterrichtssprache, Jahresbericht* (1908-9), 3-32.

Rutledge, John. *The Dialogue of the Dead in Eighteenth-Century Germany.* Bern: Lang, 1974.

Schostack, Renate. "Wieland und Lavater: Beitrag zur Geschichte des ausgehenden 18. Jahrhunderts." Diss., Freiburg, 1964.

Sengle, Friedrich. *Wieland.* Stuttgart: Metzler, 1949.

Starnes, Thomas. Review of *Fantasy and Reality: An Epistemological Approach to Wieland,* by John McCarthy. *Lessing Yearbook* 8 (1976): 279-80.

———. *Christoph Martin Wieland: Leben und Werk.* 3 vols. Sigmaringen: Thorbecke, 1987.

Sträßner, Matthias. *Tanzmeister und Dichter: Literatur-Geschichte(n) im Umkreis von Jean Georges Noverre: Lessing, Wieland, Goethe, Schiller.* Berlin: Henschel, 1994.

Strauss, D. Pieter. "Wieland's Late Novel *Peregrinus Proteus.*" Diss., Cornell, 1972.

Thorand, Brigitte. "Zwischen Ideal und Wirklichkeit—Zum Problem des Schwärmertums im 'Peregrinus Proteus.'" In Höhle, *Das Spätwerk Christoph Martin Wielands,* 91-100.

Viering, Jürgen. *Schwärmerische Erwartung bei Wieland, im trivialen Geheimnisroman und bei Jean Paul.* Cologne: Böhlau, 1976.

Voges, Michael. *Aufklärung und Geheimnis: Untersuchungen zur Vermittlung von Literatur- und Sozialgeschichte am Beispiel der Aneignung des Geheimbundmaterials im Roman des späten 18. Jahrhunderts.* Tübingen: Niemeyer, 1987.

Weinreich, Otto. *Der Trug des Nektanebos.* Berlin: Teubner, 1911.

Wieland, Christoph Martin. "Ueber die Glaubwürdigkeit Lucians in seinen Nachrichten vom Peregrinus." In *Lucians von Samosata Sämmtliche Werke,* trans. Christoph Martin Wieland, 93-110. Leipzig: Weidmann, 1788.

———. *C. M. Wielands Sämmtliche Werke.* 45 volumes. Leipzig: Göschen, 1794-1811; Hamburg, 1984.

———. *Wielands gesammelte Schriften.* Ed. Bernhard Seuffert et al. 23 vols. to date. Berlin: Weidmann, 1909-54; Akademie-Verlag, 1954-.

———. *Christoph Martin Wieland: Werke.* Ed. Fritz Martini and Hans Werner Seiffert. 5 vols. Munich: Hanser: 1964-68.

Claire Baldwin (essay date 2002)

SOURCE: Baldwin, Claire. "Seductive Strategies and the Promise of Knowledge: Wieland's *Geschichte des Agathon.*" In *The Emergence of the Modern German Novel: Christoph Martin Wieland, Sophie von La Roche, and Maria Anna Sagar,* pp. 73-102. Rochester, N.Y.: Camden House, 2002.

[*In the following excerpt, Baldwin examines Wieland's novel* Geschichte des Agathon *within the context of the German bildungsroman tradition. Baldwin asserts that the work's self-reflective qualities make it an early example of metafiction.*]

Christoph Martin Wieland's novel **Geschichte des Agathon** became known, in literary history, as the most important precursor (if not the first example) of the German genre par excellence, the Bildungsroman. Its status as pivotal text was established by Friedrich von Blanckenburg's reading of the novel as the core of his influential novel theory, *Versuch über den Roman* (1774).[1] Such prominence obscures the fact that when **Agathon** first appeared in 1766-67, Wieland, like other authors, had to contend with debates on the viability of the novel as genre.

In **Agathon,** as in **Don Sylvio** [**Die Abenteuer des Don Sylvio von Rosalva**], Wieland addresses the contemporary discourse on the novel through metafictional commentary on the kind of narrative fiction he offers. As in his first published novel, Wieland develops this metafiction not only through his narrator's digressions, but also through elements of his novel's plot. Like **Don Sylvio,** **Agathon** focuses on aesthetic reception and aesthetic creation. And specifically, **Agathon,** too, takes up the central question of how best to narrate stories of identity. In the earlier novel, these issues were addressed overtly through the novel's characters, whose tales about their own experiences were modeled directly on the generic conventions of the stories they favored. In **Agathon,** the questions of aesthetic reception and creation are approached less schematically. Instead, the novel assesses various autobiographical and biographical stories by means of abstract rules of good narrative. In ways that reflect on his own practice in **Agathon,** Wieland explores how to portray the relationship between historical truth and moral precepts and how to balance entertainment and edification in the design of a story. Underlying these and other narrative quandaries are the recurrent questions of how to capture the readers' desires and how, simultaneously, to educate the novel's readers to appreciate the qualities of the new type of novel that **Agathon** represents.

Wieland held high expectations for the first work he claimed he was writing for the world: "Ich sehe den **Agathon** als ein Buch an das kaum anders als einen grossen Succeß in der Welt haben kan; es ist für alle Arten von Leuten, und das Solide ist darinn mit dem ergötzenden und interessanten durchgehends vergesellschaftet."[2] His endeavor to captivate his readers was not entirely successful, as is evident in **Agathon**'s controversial reception by contemporary reviewers.³ Many critics did recognize *Agathon* as, indeed, a new type of novel. The praise for the novel emphasizes its originality and distances it from other contemporary novels through terms like "wit," "strength," "classicism," and "intellect" that were associated with masculinity. Albrecht von Haller writes, "überhaupt ist Agathon der witzigste Roman, den die Deutschen aufweisen können."⁴ Gotthold Ephraim Lessing offers this famous parenthetical judgment: "Es ist der erste und einzige Roman für den denkenden Kopf, vom klassischen Geschmacke. Roman? Wir wollen ihm diesen Titel nur geben, vielleicht, daß es einige Leser mehr dadurch bekömmt."⁵ Johann Georg Meusel praises the narrative as "noble, masculine, strong."⁶ Yet some critics, even some who lauded aspects of *Agathon,* also charged the novel and its author with the kind of ethical improprieties that are often associated with the genre as a whole.⁷ Heinrich Wilhelm von Gerstenberg, who praises Wieland for his "nearly attic eloquence," chides him for his skepticism and eroticism;⁸ Christian Friedrich Daniel Schubart misses "a heart purified by the spirit of religion";⁹ the reviewer for the *Allgemeine deutsche Bibliothek* complains that there is an unethical emphasis on amorous affairs;¹⁰ in private, Lessing allegedly likewise attacked the immorality of *Agathon.*¹¹

The acclaim given *Agathon* as intellectually ambitious and therefore new and the critique of it as dangerously erotic both rely on a negative image of the novel form and on moral and aesthetic standards of judging novels that Wieland was attempting to overcome. Wieland complained that no reader had comprehended the novel: "Insonderheit wird der arme Agathon so abscheulich gelobt, und so dumm getadelt, daß man nicht weiß, ob man lachen, weinen oder nach dem spanischen Rohre greifen soll. . . . Das Lustigste ist, daß keiner, auch nicht ein einziger, die Absicht und den Zusammenhang des Ganzen ausfindig gemacht hat."¹² And he asserted in a letter to Johann Georg Zimmermann: "Die Art wie Agathon aufgenommen worden ist, hat mich radicaliter von dem Einfall geheilt, mir Verdienste um die Köpfe und Herzen meiner Zeitgenossen machen zu wollen."¹³ The critics found the narrative propriety of the philosophical novel marred by Wieland's thematic interest in love and his enticing depictions of sensual scenes, its wisdom diminished by a disregard for virtue. The amorous aspects of the novel were thus cast as aesthetic weaknesses that detracted from the novel's appeal for the "masculine" thinking mind, a concession to readers attracted to the novel form by a "feminine" desire for affairs of the heart that directly engaged the senses. But one of the foundational themes of the novel is that an appeal to the intellect depends on and proceeds through sensory impressions, and that the relationship between "wisdom" and "virtue" is complex. Wieland's novel champions both intellectual and sensual pleasures and persistently investigates the ways in which good art depends on their synthesis.

The Horatian citation Wieland offers his readers as the motto to *Agathon*—"Quid Virtus, et quid Sapientia possit / Utile proposuit nobis exemplar"—at first suggests a conventional understanding of his novel's purpose as morally instructive example. The life story of the hero Agathon, "the good," appears to be the vehicle through which to illustrate virtue and wisdom. Yet the traditional expectations raised by the motto are challenged in an adept fashion typical for Wieland: the authoritative gesture of the motto is transformed into an investigation of earnest questions accompanying the reader throughout the narrative. What, indeed, constitutes "wisdom" or "virtue?" What are their respective capabilities and limits? Such queries are raised with respect to Agathon's developmental journey, as he seeks wisdom and a virtuous lifestyle. The questions likewise refer to the way that Agathon's story itself is told. The narrator asks the readers to consider what makes a biographical narrative virtuous or wise and what makes it credible and compelling. The narrator leads the readers to ponder how an individual's story can best illuminate virtue and wisdom, and how it stands in relation to the exemplary function of literature lauded by Horace.¹⁴

Wieland addresses the theoretical concerns of aesthetic education and the status of art by making the tension between the two key terms of his motto a constant dilemma in Agathon's biography. The apparent incompatibility of virtue and wisdom occasions many of Agathon's trials. Furthermore, the novel stresses how hard it can be to differentiate between being guided toward wisdom and being led astray. In doing so, *Agathon* takes recourse to one of the most volatile terms in the debates on the novel as a cornerstone of its narrative scheme. It embraces seduction—the worst censure against the novel from the side of the moralists—as a figure through which to explore questions of narrative propriety. In order to expand the narrative possibilities of the novel, Wieland adopts the reproach of seductiveness as the description of his own efforts to arouse readers' desires and to captivate the audience, yet he does not accept the charge of immorality. Seduction functions in the novel to draw attention to matters of narrative style and strategy, to the relationships between reader and text, and to those between aesthetics and ethics. The nature of desire is at issue in the novel beginning with its opening scenes, which contrast images of the uncontrolled and threatening female passion of the Bacchic worshipers with images of the chaste, idealistic love of Psyche and Agathon. And plots of seduction structure much of Agathon's story, as he faces repeated challenges to his virtue and seeks to direct his own passions wisely. Seductive enchantment is often considered in relation to artistic enchantment in *Aga-*

thon; thus Wieland underscores ways in which the narrative charms its audience and probes the acceptable limits of this quintessential poetic power.

Wieland uses Homeric texts to represent the power of poetic enchantment in *Agathon,* and their authority provides him with one legitimation for styling his novel itself as seductive. The motto from Horace's epistles that introduces *Agathon* is a comment on the *Odyssey* and the parallels between the heroes of the ancient epic and Wieland's modern philosophical novel, drawn throughout the text, suggest a noble literary ancestry for *Agathon.* But Homeric texts also appear in the plot of the novel prominently in scenes of seduction, and the power of these narratives to captivate an audience is apostrophized repeatedly as magical. In addition to Greek epics, Wieland calls on another text to emphasize literature's potent sway over its readers, for Agathon, like Don Sylvio, is likened to Don Quixote. This parallel is first drawn in Book I and recurs near the end of the novel in the metafictional chapter identified as the apology of the Greek author, "Apologie des griechischen Autors" ([*Geschichte des Agathon*] XI, 1), in reference to both Agathon's appealing enthusiasm and the novel's task of reconciling virtue and wisdom. Wieland's direct reference to Cervantes's novel as a point of comparison for his story of Agathon makes one of the guiding themes of his metafiction more conspicuous, namely, the role of the arts and specifically of literature in shaping stories of identity. By placing his protagonist Agathon in relation to both Quixote and Ulysses and by evoking both the modern and the ancient narratives in the context of literature's capacity to enchant its audience, Wieland points to the generic innovation of *Agathon.* His seductive narrative of a male protagonist's development claims status as the legitimate heir to the exalted epic, but also self-consciously and unapologetically incorporates aspects of the more lowly novel tradition into its modern form.

Seductive Arts: Agathon's Aesthetic Education

Plots of seduction in *Agathon* are a vehicle for the novel's metafictional reflection on its own aesthetic qualities. Agathon is marked for seduction in various fashions by Theogiton, by Pythia, by Hippias, and by Danae, while Agathon's own aims to lead the sybaritic ruler Dionysius to a path of virtue prove similar to seductive efforts directed at him. Each ploy involves efforts to use the influence of art to manipulate the object of seduction and thus integrates into the novel's plot issues fundamental to the novel's metafictional commentary: aesthetic enchantment, the intent of the artist and the artistic performer, and the role of the audience in assessing and responding to aesthetic quality.

Hippias and the materialist philosophy he advocates present the first serious threat to Agathon's idealistic virtue, a threat of both physical and intellectual seduc-

tion. In an early theoretical text, Wieland describes the Sophists as "masters in the art of seduction."[15] In *Agathon,* he endows his fictional figure Hippias, the master Sophist, with this trait: "Er hatte alles, was die Art von Weisheit, die er ausübte, verführisch machen konnte."[16] Hippias believes that the similarities he perceives between himself and Agathon will allow him to make of his new slave a disciple who will further propagate his sophistic wisdom and fame. And indeed, the two characters share many traits. Like Hippias, Agathon is extraordinarily handsome and makes a strong, positive first impression on others. Like Hippias, Agathon is intellectually distinguished. He is a connoisseur of the arts and a lover of beauty and he too has powerful rhetorical skills. Each of the two men presumes to accurately assess the other based on his ability to "read" visages and souls.[17] Despite these affinities, Hippias errs in his assumptions that he can win over Agathon, for they disagree on what motivates human behavior and on what provides pleasure and happiness. The conflict between the two is initially drawn as a battle between the calculating, manipulative Sophist, who lives hedonistically at the cost of others and whose wisdom amounts to a system for achieving this goal, and the guileless Platonist given to introversion and reveries. Yet the apparently distinct moral contours of this contest between Hippias, the consummate seducer, and Agathon, the youthful champion of ideal virtue, soon become obscured. While Agathon, like Don Sylvio, perceives the world naively, Hippias is an intelligent and attractive immoralist—indeed, so attractive that Wieland was compelled to defend and refine his attitude toward his character in later editions of the novel. The celebrated wisdom of Hippias rests on psychological insight and a logic constructed on the principles of nature, reason, empiricism, and critical thought. Hippias's arguments echo many of the standard eighteenth-century theories of knowledge, while Agathon's enthusiasm and melancholy are typically deviant, a sign of an overactive or underemployed imagination: "romanhaft" is the epithet Hippias chooses for Agathon's behavior. Hippias believes that Agathon deceives himself as to the truly sensual source of his philosophical pleasures, which Agathon believes derive purely from his intellect and a disembodied moral sensibility. Hippias thus pursues an Enlightenment program of curing Agathon from his enthusiastic follies by demonstrating the logical errors in his ideological system.[18] The program of Hippias's seduction is to educate Agathon from idealistic excess to greater understanding of the laws of Nature.[19] In this fashion, the contest between the two characters becomes one between wisdom and virtue; the terms of the novel's Horatian motto are played off against each other disruptively rather than appearing in harmony.

Wieland complicates the assessment of the two characters Hippias and Agathon and the conception of the terms virtue and wisdom and hinders an easy judgment about the characters. While the Sophist's wisdom remains subject to moral criticism, the philosophical system he expounds at great length is superior to Agathon's in its realistic assessment of the world. And while Agathon's Platonic enthusiasm sustains his exemplary virtue and reveals his noble character, the narrator also presents it as a sign of immaturity and opens it to skeptical critique through the arguments of Hippias and the narrator's own gentle irony. As in *Don Sylvio,* Wieland sets up an apparent contest in his narrative between nature and enthusiasm, but instead mediates between the two poles, a convergence that his "philosophical novels" represent. As in *Don Sylvio,* the teachings of nature prove a problematic and insufficient weapon against enthusiasm, for nature provides the enthusiast with inspiration and justification. Agathon's imaginative visions, like those of Don Sylvio, also reveal aspects of the poetic fiction that tells his tale. If in *Don Sylvio* Wieland refused to condemn his protagonist's enthusiastic imagination, here he refuses to celebrate it without qualification. The novelistic enthusiasm and the ideal virtue of the hero reinforce each other and reflect the novel's fictionality, for only in a novel could such unwavering virtue be upheld. This in turn calls attention to the narrative's conceit of offering a solid, probable biography rather than a fanciful novelistic tale, while the ambivalence shown toward the protagonist's ideals simultaneously allows for narrative distance from the common conceptions of "the novelistic." The protagonist's youthful ideal of virtue is tempered through experience and he matures in his knowledge of himself and the ways of the world. The parallel metafictional commentary of the novel emphasizes that the narrative portrayal of Agathon's incredible virtue gains poetic validity not through the celebration of an ideal morality, but rather as realistic biography that reveals insights about human nature through astute psychological interpretation of its characters.

The unsuccessful efforts of Hippias to seduce Agathon to share his sensualist understanding of the world proceed through the allures of the young women in his household, through the art that adorns his home, and through his own persuasive rhetoric. Agathon's responses to these seductive measures reveal how the philosophical differences between him and Hippias lead to opposing positions on what constitutes or vitiates aesthetic power. For Hippias, aesthetic pleasure derives from the direct excitement of the senses and the task of art is to arouse and manipulate human passions. The artist or performer wields power over the passions of a malleable audience through psychological insight, founded on careful study of human nature. The more sensually overwhelming the art work, the better it achieves its aim and the better the artist can direct audience response to his or her own ends. For Agathon, the foundation of aesthetic pleasure is spiritual harmony. He claims that love of beauty is concurrently a love of

truth and a recognition of ideals, and that art should speak to the innermost soul. Art wields a sensual power over its audience which, however, derives from a spiritual response rather than merely sensual excitement. The moral judgment of an artwork centers not only on its aesthetic effect but also on the artist's intent, on whether the artist abuses the power which good art necessarily holds over its audience. For Agathon, not all seductive art is good art, but good art is always seductive and this seduction is justified by its principled beauty, while for Hippias, seductive art is always good.

Agathon delineates these differences in taste and aesthetic judgment as a conflict between art that is under the guidance of the muses and art defined by the wanton tones of the sirens. The first two paths to convert the idealist to sensualism—the attentions of the seductive Cyane and the impressions mediated through art—offend Agathon's moral sensibility and disturb his equanimity, for Hippias's art and the arts of Cyane indeed evince exquisite talent and achieve the desired effect of arousing Agathon's passions. However, Agathon anticipates Hippias's efforts at intellectual seduction with pleasure. As a talented speaker himself, Agathon can appreciate the skill involved in effective rhetoric. He thus approaches the demonstration of Hippias's renowned eloquence as artistic spectacle and is anxious to witness the performance, "weil er sich von der Beredsamkeit desselben diejenige Art von Ergötzung versprach, die uns ein geschickter Gaukler macht, der uns einen Augenblick sehen läßt, was wir nicht sehen, ohne es bei einem klugen Menschen so weit zu bringen, daß man in eben demselben Augenblick nur daran zweifeln sollte, daß man betrogen wird" (69).[20] The comparison of the rhetorician to the illusion artist describes the relationship between illusion and deception—the artist must tease both the senses and the intellect with the illusion of something not actually there. The pleasure in this appearance derives precisely from the knowledge of its illusory nature. Agathon reveals his increasing maturity and his growing understanding of art through these expectations. In Delphi he was easily fooled by the seductive plot of Theogiton, who donned the guise of Apollo, precisely because of his initial inability to distinguish between deception and illusion. Hippias's eloquence, Agathon imagines, is a tool of fabrication and fiction, which challenges the intellect, yet cannot deceive it outright. While sophistic rhetoric does aim to seduce and deceive the audience for political or personal gain, Agathon's notion of brilliant eloquence prizes linguistic dexterity and the capacity to create illusion. The effect of the Sophists' ideal rhetoric is to overwhelm the impressionable listeners to passivity.[21] That of Agathon's ideal is aesthetic pleasure, which actively engages the audience intellectually, spiritually, and sensually.

Agathon is confident that he will remain impervious to Hippias's eloquent assault on his idealistic virtue. Since his receptive stance allows him to withstand the seduction Hippias represents, he can indulge in the pleasures of Hippias's art, rather than avoiding them as he attempts to avoid the other seductive snares set out for him. This ability demonstrates progress in Agathon's aesthetic education in comparison to Delphi, but he is still unwilling to give the sensual pleasures of art the recognition they deserve. As Don Gabriel similarly discovered with his efforts to enlighten Don Sylvio, the appeal to reason, for all his eloquence, is ineffective in curing the enthusiast. Hippias therefore turns to the lovely Danae for help in bringing the stubborn youth to his senses. Through her artistic performances, Agathon learns that it is more difficult than he imagined to distinguish between the arts of the sirens and those of the muses. And through the portrayal of the love between Danae and Agathon, Wieland again represents a mediation between the poles of sensualism and idealism.

Agathon stages issues of aesthetic production and reception central to the self-reflection of its narrative through scenes of Danae's successful seduction of the protagonist.[22] Danae's plan to capture Agathon's heart and senses proceeds in a methodical and calculated fashion. The penultimate step in this strategy is the musical performance of the battle between the sirens and the muses that she stages at her country house. Here seduction and pure artistic appeal are set up through these familiar feminine archetypes as opposing qualities, yet Danae's designs rely on the close relation between the two. As Danae courts Agathon's desire through her performance, she casts him in the role of judge and calls upon him to render an aesthetic verdict on two counts. He is to be the audience for the work considered a musical masterpiece by connoisseurs. His good taste ought to concur and to confirm the artistic merit of the piece and the artistic talents of its performers. Agathon thus functions as distanced critic of the entire performance, but he also has a second, participatory role to play within it, for he is to be the adjudicator between the two parties that are, in the conceit of the piece, competing. In the scheme of the novel, Agathon's twofold judgment entails negotiating the aesthetic and ethical dilemmas debated in the eighteenth-century controversies on the genre of the novel and posited in *Agathon* as fundamental to the protagonist's conflict with Hippias. However, the division between the artistic appeal to sensual and sexual desires indulged by the Sophist and the artistic appeal to a more abstract aesthetic imagination championed by Agathon is profoundly challenged through Danae's performance. While the distinction between the two aesthetic ideologies proves less than clear, the subjective desirous attitude of the interpreter takes on great significance when assessing aesthetic achievement.

The contest between the two styles and philosophies of art represented by the figures of the muses and the si-

rens recalls the conflict between the ideological systems of Agathon and Hippias described in these same terms. Thus the choice required of Agathon for either the sirens or the muses is a further test of his own personal virtue: he ought (as upright hero) once again to reject the seduction instigated by Hippias. In addition, Agathon's verdict in the competition is implicitly a matter of aesthetic principle, a statement on the proper criteria for evaluating beauty and art, and a demonstration of how aesthetic judgments are formed. A predilection for one style or the other, however, is integrally linked with the ethical dimension of the choice Agathon faces. The performance enacts and literalizes the contest between Hippias and Agathon, incorporating and thus appropriating the aesthetic positions of each.

The role imposed upon Agathon as judge between two discrete and dissimilar styles proves to be falsely defined. Even a choice for the muse Danae as the winner of the competition is still paramount to succumbing to Hippias's system and would mean the triumph of the Sophist's philosophy represented by the sirens, since the entire performance of the battle is Danae's elaborate seductive ploy and the culmination of the conspiracy between her and Hippias to seduce, and convert, the young Platonist. Danae's strategy of seduction and the importance of her performance in this design are clearly outlined. She aims to inflame Agathon's imagination and his senses and to weaken his resistances while heightening his desire for her. Her skill in arousing and thwarting desire simultaneously is itself a highly developed art: "Die große Kunst war, unter der Masque der Freundschaft seine Begierden zu eben der Zeit zu reizen, da sie selbige durch eine unaffektierte Zurückhaltung abzuschrecken schien" (153).[23] The ultimate maneuver in her strategy of seduction repeats this duplicity. Under the mask of the muse she pursues the siren's aim of arousing Agathon's desires, enrapturing his senses, and winning his heart. As in the pantomime of Daphne and Apollo, the first such enactment designed to charm Agathon, Danae proves herself here to be both consummate artist and irresistible seductress. There, too, Agathon becomes ensnared by Danae's exquisite enactment of his ideal of virtue and, as shown in Kurt Wölfel's perspicacious interpretation of this pantomime in *Agathon,* Agathon's roles as critic and participant become profoundly entangled.[24]

Danae's talent on the lute and in song manifests itself through the magical powers of her music, the "Zauberkräfte der Kunst" (157), which efface even the visual impression of her initial pose:

> Man muß ohne Zweifel gestehen, daß das Gemälde, welches sich in diesem Augenblick unserm Helden darstellte, nicht sehr geschickt war, weder sein Herz noch seine Sinnen in Ruhe zu lassen; allein die Absicht der Danae war nur, ihn durch die Augen zu den Vergnügungen eines andern Sinnes vorzubereiten, und ihr Stolz

verlangte keinen geringern Triumph, als ein so rei-
zendes Gemälde durch die Zaubergewalt ihrer Stimme
und ihrer Saiten in seiner Seele auszulöschen.

(156)[25]

The "magical power of music" announced in the title of
the chapter (V, 7) already reminds the reader of the
magical power of literature, which the priestess Pythia
drew on to enhance *her* chances of seducing Agathon.
Pythia's attempt to adorn herself with the magically seductive power of Homer's poetry is likened to the way
Juno sought the magical belt of Venus to seduce and
ensnare Zeus. Danae appears dressed for her performance as muse in a pure white gown with a golden
belt, and is compared favorably with Juno. This again
recalls the Homeric passage Pythia asked Agathon to
read in her efforts to seduce him; it describes the shimmering veil "that glimmered pale like the sunlight" and
Aphrodite's magical belt adorning Juno, "the elaborate,
pattern-pierced / zone, and on it are figured all beguile-
ments, and loveliness / is figured upon it, and the passion of sex is there, and the whispered / endearment
that steals the heart away even from the thoughtful."[26]
Danae's performance thus suspends the sharp distinction between the muses and the sirens. Her art of seduction and her artistic talent mutually reinforce each other.
Similarly, the performance of the sirens is artistically
exquisite. The enacted battle of the sirens and muses reveals how thin the dividing line truly is between disreputable and acceptable art, between deceitful artistry
and artistic illusion.

Agathon's physical position as judge of the performance
under Danae's direction gives him the distance necessary for aesthetic appreciation. He is separated from the
singers by water, which both stages the mythical danger
of the sirens' song and offers a measure of protection
from the danger of their art. It also establishes an additional barrier between Agathon and the seductive muse
Danae. On hearing the "nearly irresistible seduction" in
the song of the siren performers, Agathon still has
enough presence of mind to reflect on Ulysses's wisdom in binding himself to the mast: "'Wenn die Si-
renen, bei denen der kluge Ulysses vorbeifahren mußte,
so gesungen haben,' (dachte Agathon) 'so hatte er wohl
Ursache, sich an Händen und Füßen an den Mastbaum
binden zu lassen'" (157).[27] He himself can barely avoid
succumbing to the lure of Danae's tones, as her performance as muse tempts him to flee his safe position.
Danae registers "wie sehr er außer sich selbst war, und
wie viel Mühe er hatte, um sich zu halten, aus seinem
Sitz sich in das Wasser herabzustürzen, zu ihr hinüber
zu schwimmen, und seine in Entzückung und Liebe zer-
schmolzene Seele zu ihren Füßen auszuhauchen" (158).[28]
This response is far from the exalted one Agathon normally associates with the muses. It does correspond to
the expectations Danae harbored before the performance
and to her plan to test the entire force of her charms on

him, which demands: "eine zärtliche Weichlichkeit
mußte sich vorher seiner ganzen Seele bemeistern, und
seine in Vergnügen schwimmende Sinnen mußten von
einer süßen Unruhe und wollüstigen Sehnsucht ein-
genommen werden" (153).[29] This is reminiscent of the
artistic style favored in Hippias's household, "Syrenen-
Gesänge . . . welche die Seele in ein bezaubertes Vergessen ihrer selbst versenkten, und, nachdem sie alle
ihre edlere Kräfte entwaffnet hatte, die erregte und wil-
lige Sinnlichkeit der ganzen Gewalt der von allen Seiten
eindringenden Wollust auslieferten" (55).[30] Danae as
muse is even more compelling than the sirens; her musical art is greater. Yet her song, which attests to the superior art of the muses, poses the sirens' threat of a wa-
tery death. While Agathon's status as competent critic
of the aesthetic performance is indeed threatened, it
may seem extreme to compare his position to that of
Ulysses. The performance is ostensibly a harmless artistic entertainment rather than an existential ethical dilemma. Nonetheless, in the novel's plot, Agathon is at
yet unable to control his own desires while still indulging them and cannot maintain the epic hero's distance
from danger. The seductive artistic performance does
lead to the modern hero's actual seduction and to the
loss of his independent, masculine self in his true love
for Danae.[31]

Danae's final performance fully transforms Agathon:
"Sein ganzes Wesen war Ohr, und seine ganze Seele
zerfloß in die Empfindungen, die in ihrem Gesange herr-
scheten" (158).[32] This seems to confirm the triumph of
Hippias's aesthetic sensibilities over Agathon's, for it
precisely captures the expectations he placed on Agathon as reader—as Homerist—in his household, and is
the measure of artistic quality for him: "Ein Jonisches
Ohr will nicht nur ergötzt, es will bezaubert sein . . .
kurz, die Art, wie gelesen wird, soll das Ohr an die
Stelle aller übrigen Sinne setzen" (51-52).[33] Agathon's
dilemma as judge and the substance of the battle staged
by Danae, then, recast the quandaries explored in and
for the novel ***Agathon*** itself, for it questions the nature
of aesthetic and ethical judgment and explores the psychological standpoint and engagement of the audience,
the reader. The consideration of Danae's intended influence on Agathon also occasions self-reflective gestures
of the novel more directly, namely by weighing Danae's skills as a storyteller and explicitly evaluating the
qualities and the quality of her narrative.

DANAE'S AUTOBIOGRAPHICAL TALE: A MODEL POETIC NARRATIVE

The narrator's extended deliberations on how best to interpret and judge Danae's autobiographical tale again
direct reader attention to the complexities of assessing
the aesthetic value that Agathon faced as participant-
critic of Danae's *Gesamtkunstwerk*. Generic definitions
and common criteria for measuring narrative worth

come under scrutiny in the commentaries on Danae's story. The narrator puts theoretical distinctions to the test of critical reflection, analyzing the concrete practice of constructing narrative to specific ends and pondering the symbiotic relationship between author and audience, still openly explored through figures of seduction, that both defines and is defined through a text. Subjective interests and desires influencing narrative production and reception are taken as significant aspects in the exchange between storyteller and listener, and these interests become part of the basis of judgment over Danae's tale for the narrator of *Agathon*. These specular reflections underscore for *Agathon*'s readers the interested, participatory role of the audience in establishing an interpretation of a narrative and insist that rendering a considered, self-aware aesthetic judgment is a serious and demanding task.

The self-interested story of Danae's life that she constructs for Agathon is prized in many respects as a model poetic narrative, and the qualities of Danae's autobiography that the narrator of *Agathon* commends are closely bound to her talents as seductress, as well as to her fine artistic sensibilities. The narrator denotes Danae's narrative principles as "the laws of beauty and decency," which shape her tale, he surmises, to the disadvantage of "the duties of precise historical faithfulness" (307). Danae's priority of aesthetics over factual truth corresponds to the effect she intends to produce in Agathon, for whom her narrative is specifically conceived. Her desire to please him and to appear in the best possible light so that his love for her is intensified leads her to embellish certain aspects of her tale while slighting others. The design of her narrative is thus also an extension of her seductive designs on Agathon, as its aim is to further secure his affections and desire. The means of realizing this goal, the technique of her narrative, is, furthermore, described in terms strikingly similar to those used to specify her art of seduction. Her narrative art consists primarily in achieving a tantalizing and favorable balance between revelation and concealment through the skillful and tactical control of language: "es gibt eine gewisse Kunst, dasjenige was einen widrigen Eindruck machen könnte, aus den Augen zu entfernen; es kömmt soviel auf die Wendung an; ein einziger kleiner Umstand gibt einer Begebenheit eine so verschiedene Gestalt von demjenigen, was sie ohne diesen kleinen Umstand gewesen wäre" (308).[34] Danae alters the shape of events with attention to minutiae and carefully chooses which details of her life to divulge. Where artistic skill cannot beautify an aspect of her tale, she hides it strategically with simple silence: "Allein was diejenigen Stellen betraf, an denen sie alle Kunst, die man auf ihre Verschönerung wenden möchte, für verloren hielt . . . über diese hatte sie klüglich beschlossen, sie mit gänzlichem Stillschweigen zu bedecken" (308-9).[35] Danae weighs the variables of her story matter and the taste of her intended listener when

shaping her narrative. The character of her audience influences the narrative design as both limitation and challenge; her artistic and amorous success in captivating her audience is contingent upon her ability to manipulate her listener's responses through well-considered linguistic disclosure and secrecy.

Despite the proximity of Danae's autobiographical tale to the realm of seduction in technique and intent, the narrator makes Danae no reproach. On the contrary, he even takes a stand in her defense, insisting that she neither deceives Agathon with fiction nor distorts her tale inappropriately through omission, for she tells him everything: "Sie sagte ihm alles" (308). Indeed, this narrative technique, with attention to aesthetic detail and the beautiful effect of the whole prized by good artists above all else, attests to Danae's artistic skill. Aesthetically pleasing narrative is contingent upon an encompassing design and upon a selective recounting of the story's material.

Danae's autobiographical narrative as told to Agathon is considered under the rubric of history, *Geschichte*. Her style and her decision to follow the aesthetic dictums of beauty and propriety is initially contrasted with the principle of historical faithfulness that the public generally demands from its authors. Yet instead of faulting Danae for the priorities she sets, the narrator questions the appropriateness of such clamor for rigid adherence to fact. Rather than striving for a definitive judgment about the truth of the story, the narrator focuses on the characters' psychological constitution and raises questions about their narratives from this perspective. The narrator draws on insights gleaned from the analysis of Danae's autobiography to venture suggestions on how to read other works, even those of authoritative authors like Xenophon and Montaigne. Her narrative is taken as an example to illuminate the general possibilities and perils of historical narrative. Absolute factual truth as the primary criteria of judgment, it is suggested, is quite misplaced. Autobiographies in particular must be read with consideration of the truths of human nature, for example the power of human vanity—such are the exigencies of even historical narration.

Modern historical narrative, in the theory of the time, was contrasted with the notion of the chronicle, in which every detail was listed with encyclopedic extravagance. The primary opposition was understood to lie between styles of presentation rather than between fact and fiction. The good narrator ought to order the crucial moments and events of the story at hand so as to reveal an inner and necessary causality, and ought further to adhere to rules of probability and to distinguish the narrative by a clarity and harmony achieved in large part through sparseness. (Pedrillo's ignorance of this rule was the fault which so exasperated Don

Sylvio, as Pedrillo's attempt to include all details of his experience only led to incoherence in his tale.) Only fundamental elements of the story, with selective elaboration and embellishments to enhance the vigor of the writing, should appear. Explicit explanations or excessive details bore and insult the readers. The task of the good narrator is to engage and satisfy both the imagination and the intellect of the creative and critical audience.

History was further contrasted with the fantastic falsehood of novels. Yet the terms *Roman* and *Geschichte* as generic classifications were unclear and fluctuating. Lieselotte Kurth traces these shifts in historical and literary criticism, and exposes how historians explicitly redefined their task over and against poetic histories.[36] The novel as immoral romance was derided, but the novel as fictional history of human emotions, including love, had the advantage of offering models of moral behavior. *Geschichte* communicated truths, whether factual or fictional, by corresponding to and reflecting what were taken to be universal natural laws. As stated programmatically in the foreword to *Geschichte des Agathon*:

> Die Wahrheit . . . bestehet darin, daß alles mit dem Lauf der Welt übereinstimme, daß die Charakter nicht willkürlich, und bloß nach der Phantasie, oder den Absichten des Verfassers gebildet, sondern aus dem unerschöpflichen Vorrat der Natur selbst hergenommen; . . . und also alles so gedichtet sei, daß kein hinlänglicher Grund angegeben werden könne, warum es nicht eben so wie es erzählt wird, hätte geschehen können, oder noch einmal wirklich geschehen werde. Diese Wahrheit allein kann Werke von dieser Art nützlich machen.

(11-12)[37]

To adhere to this truth, then, the author must portray credible human characters rather than exemplary moral heroes—must follow the example of Fielding rather than Richardson, authors taken to represent two poles in literary orientation.[38] No moral scheme, but only the varieties and peculiarities of human nature can truly capture the imagination and concern of readers and ultimately contribute to their moral betterment.

This interest in psychological complexity motivates biographical histories. The value and appeal of autobiographies lies likewise in readers' consideration of human nature. Thus Danae's narrative fulfills the demands placed on good history writing. She presents an aesthetically ordered, harmonious whole in an interesting, engaging fashion. Her ability to enchant the intended audience is a measure of her skill, and is in turn the primary criterion for judging her story. As long as the standards for reading are clear, the narrator concedes freedom of composition within this realm. Danae is exonerated from moral blame, for her tale follows the

rules of beauty and propriety.[39] Yet by describing her exemplary narrative ploys in terms similar to those of seductive strategies, the narrator pointedly revisits the issue of the nexus between ethics and aesthetics. Indeed, the consideration of Danae's narrative also reveals the extent to which aesthetic beauty and propriety is ethically suspect. Loveliness fosters Danae's seductive schemes, disarms the audience, and deviates from absolute factual truth. It can be quite deceptive. Specifically, aesthetic propriety can serve to mask ethical impropriety. Danae conceals the impropriety of her past as part of her strategy of propriety in narration. The refinement in her story leaves her audience room for misunderstanding and for a multiplicity of interpretations.

Hippias can, therefore, influence Agathon's reading of Danae's autobiography by revealing additional facts. The inclusion of this supplementary information does not, however, make Hippias's version of the story more true than Danae's account. The narrator again defends both Danae's virtue and the value of her narrative: "Danae erzählte ihre Geschichte mit der unschuldigen Absicht zu gefallen. Sie sah natürlicher Weise ihre Aufführung, ihre Schwachheiten, ihre Fehltritte selbst in einem mildern, und (lasset uns die Wahrheit sagen) in einem wahrern Licht als die Welt" (315).[40] Hippias's rendition of Danae's life is, like Danae's, a construct designed to affect Agathon in a specific manner, in this case to arouse his passions to Danae's disadvantage. Hippias skillfully spurs Agathon's jealousy and reignites his dormant love of an ideal virtue, figured in Psyche, in order to destroy his trust in Danae and to end their relationship. Under the sway of the adept Sophist, Agathon reinterprets Danae's story to confirm his new fears: "Er verglich ihre eigene Erzählung mit des Hippias seiner, und glaubte nun, da das Mißtrauen sich seines Geistes einmal bemächtiget hatte, hundert Spuren in der ersten wahrzunehmen, welche die Wahrheit des letztern bekräftigten" (319).[41] Agathon's divergent readings of the same story reveal the importance of the reader's particular approach to a narrative in constructing an interpretation, yet they also point to the storyteller's responsibility in this process. Allowing that too much discretion can invite readers to misconstrue the story, the narrator of *Agathon* reflects on the balance between narrative decorum and narrative clarity with respect to his own practice. He then uses this theoretical front to cover for his narrative practice, for he justifies transgression of social etiquette—namely explicit love scenes—as a means of counteracting the potential ambiguity of decorous presentation. Narrative virtue, the narrator muses, lies in correctly assessing the appropriate degree of candor required, in weighing the demands of artistry and ethics.

> Es ist ohne Zweifel wohl getan, wenn ein Schriftsteller, der sich einen wichtigern Zweck als die bloße Ergötzung seiner Leser vorgesetzt hat, bei gewissen Anläs-

sen, anstatt des zaumlosen Mutwillens vieler von den
neuern Franzosen, lieber die bescheidne Zurückhaltung
des jungfräulichen Virgils nachahmet, welcher . . .
sich begnügt uns zu sagen: "Daß Dido und der Held in
Eine Höhle kamen." Allein wenn diese Zurückhaltung
so weit ginge, daß die Dunkelheit, welche man über
einen schlüpfrigen Gegenstand ausbreitete, zu Mißver-
stand und Irrtum Anlaß geben könnte: So würde sie,
deucht uns, in eine falsche Scham ausarten; und in
solchen Fällen scheint uns ratsamer zu sein, den
Vorhang ein wenig wegzuziehen, als aus übertriebener
Bedenklichkeit Gefahr zu laufen, vielleicht die Unschuld selbst ungegründeten Vermutungen aus-
zusetzen.[42]

(165)

Narrative impropriety is justified as a means of revealing the virtue of the characters, for a modest silence is
open to misreading. The narrator provocatively adopts
the pose of apologizing for presenting the love scenes,
which are precisely those the reader (and especially,
Wieland teasingly claims, the female reader) most desires. Here the text, as if grudgingly, tells of novelistic
romance while posing as more serious educational history.

Yet the narrator also employs the opposite strategy as
part of his program to enchant readers, for, as he well
knows, marked silence directly invites interpretation.
By choosing at times to conceal pointedly, rather than
to disclose, Wieland's narrator aims to seduce the readers under the mask of propriety. The text plays with the
readers' anticipation and curiosity to arouse the imagination under the pretext of corralling it, and teases the
readers with silence after piquing their interest. After
introducing the central love scenes with protestations of
the need for historical precision, the text affects understanding for reader disinterest and leaves these scenes,
in the end, to the readers' fantasy: "Und hier, ohne den
Leser unnötiger Weise damit aufzuhalten, was sie ferner
sagte, und was er antwortete, überlassen wir den Pinsel
einem Correggio, und schleichen uns davon" (168).[43]
Correggio's sixteenth-century painting of Danae depicts
precisely the suspension between revelation and concealment and its concurrent suspense for the imagination that Wieland's narrative employs. As Danae re-
clines on a bed, she and Cupid, who faces her, each
hold a corner of the sheet partially covering her naked
body, while two cherubim sharpen their arrows in a corner. The moment between covering and uncovering
Danae is captured in the erotic image in which Cupid
catches and guides the golden rain, the guise Jupiter
adopts to mate with Danae. Wieland's reference to Correggio's painting evokes this visual image and thereby
enhances and emphasizes his own tantalizing narrative
tactics in *Agathon,* rather than diffusing them, as the
narrator innocently suggests.

The narrator's theoretical digressions on poetics lead
him to challenge the novel's readers to question the sincerity of Agathon's own autobiographical story as told

to Danae. The dilemma of how to evaluate its virtues
and those of the hero is thereby raised once more. If the
reader approaches Agathon's story with suspicion, as
Agathon did Danae's, his tale appears in another light.
The voice of such a skeptical reader is raised and it
provides the impetus for a reconsideration of Agathon's
narrative: "Und woher wissen wir auch, daß Agathon
selbst, mit aller seiner Offenherzigkeit, keinen Umstand
zurück gehalten habe, von dem er vielleicht, wie ein
guter Maler oder Dichter, vorausgesehen, daß er der
schönen Würkung des Ganzen hinderlich sein könnte.
Wer ist uns Bürge dafür, daß die verführische Priesterin
nicht mehr über ihn erhalten habe, als er eingestanden?"
(307).[44] Seduction is again the focus of this renewed investigation. The narrator recalls the situations in which
Agathon found himself the intended target of seduction
in Delphi and underscores the temptations that placed
him in jeopardy. The authority of the priestess, not to
mention her beauty, was bound to threaten any young
man's virtue, the narrator reasons. Moreover, Pythia in-
geniously heightened her chances of successful seduction by weaving the magical power of literature over
the soul—a force with indisputable impact on the enthusiast Agathon—into her schemes to fully overcome
his resistance. Given such consideration, the narrator
reflects, Agathon's story as he told it becomes increasingly incredible. If Agathon were truly able to withstand the combined charms of the priestess and Homer's seductive poetry expressly depicting seduction
scenes, then literature must not possess its acclaimed
power of enchantment. But the enchanting qualities of
Agathon's own narrative invalidate this hypothesis: the
skeptical fictive reader judges Agathon's story itself to
be so seductive in the mere retelling of the plots against
his virtue that it belies his reported stoicism. The figurative potency of Agathon's narrative would communicate the effects of Pythia's allures more truly than his
allegations.

The power which Agathon's narrative exerts over this
vocal fictive reader thus attests to his artistic skill as a
storyteller while marring his moral reputation. The narrator of **Agathon** is ostensibly concerned with weighing
the truth content of Agathon's story, yet in reconsider-
ing the scenes of Agathon's seductions, he piques the
novel reader's voyeuristic interest and curiosity. Although he approaches the investigation of the narrative
with the criterion of truth, he returns quickly to the examination of narrative enchantment and indirectly
praises exactly the quality in Agathon's autobiography
that initially arouses the suspicions of the moralist.

Seduction is portrayed throughout the novel, then, as
clever, artistic, and artful manipulation, effected by establishing and controlling the tension between revealing
and concealing the object of desire. Good narrative, the
text implies, functions similarly: it excites and maintains reader interest by manipulating the relationship

between revelation and concealment, and induces readers to continue reading in order to satisfy their desires for the pleasures of fiction. Like the art of seduction, narration fascinates by what is shown to be hidden. The narrative plays on the boundaries between silence and expression, and points to language as a medium of dissemblance as well as of disclosure. By explicitly leaving particularly intimate or erotic scenes to the imagination of the reader, provoking through prankish omission, the narrator can absolve himself of any blame. This ruse points to reading as deciphering, reassigning much of the responsibility for the moral quality of the work from the text to the reader's interpretive style. Yet Wieland also reconsiders the traditional notions of virtue. The virtue of the narrative lies precisely in its ability to seduce the reader. By exploring issues of aesthetic and ethical judgment, he subverts rigid categories of moral understanding and encourages the readers to approach the novel's complex questions of truth, wisdom, and virtue with greater sophistication.

Notes

1. [Jürgen] Jacobs, "Die Theorie und ihr Exempel[: Zur Deutung von Wielands Agathon in Blanckenburgs Versuch über den Roman]," [*Germanisch-Romanische Monatsschrift* 31, 1 (1981): 32-42,] exposes Blanckenburg's misreadings of *Agathon*.

2. Letter to Salomon Gessner, April 28, 1763. *Wielands Briefwechsel* 3: Nr. 161, 162.

   "I regard *Agathon* as a book that can hardly be anything but successful in the world; it is for every type of person, and what is solid is combined with what is pleasing and interesting throughout."

3. On the reception of the first edition, see Erich Gross, *C. M. Wielands Geschichte des Agathon: Entstehungsgeschichte* (1930; Nendeln/Liechtenstein: Kraus Reprint Limited, 1967), 159-79; Klaus Manger, "Kommentar," *Geschichte des Agathon,* ed. Klaus Manger (Frankfurt/Main: Deutscher Klassiker Verlag, 1986), 858-71; and Lieselotte E. Kurth-Voigt, "Wielands 'Geschichte des Agathon': Zur journalistischen Rezeption des Romans," *Wieland Studien* 1, ed. Wieland Archiv Biberach and Hans Radspieler (Sigmaringen: Jan Thorbecke, 1991), 9-24.

4. Albrecht von Haller, review of *Agathon, Göttingsche Anzeigen* 141, 23 (1767) 1127-28, cited here from Kurth-Voigt, "Wielands 'Geschichte des Agathon,'" 12.

   ". . . in general *Agathon* is the wittiest novel that the Germans have to show."

5. Gotthold Ephraim Lessing, *Hamburgische Dramaturgie* 69 (December 29, 1767), in *Werke,* ed. Herbert G. Göpfert (München: Hanser, 1970-79), 4:555.

   "It is the first and only novel for the thinking mind, in classical taste. Novel? We will go ahead and give it this title, perhaps it will receive a few more readers thereby."

6. Johann Georg Meusel, review of *Agathon, Deutsche Bibliothek der schönen Wissenschaften,* cited from Kurth-Voigt, "Wielands 'Geschichte des Agathon,'" 15.

7. The charges that Wieland lacked originality, which were to damage his reputation most severely, came from the Romantics at the turn of the century: their polemics against the authoritative Enlightenment author in Weimar colored Wieland reception even past the renewed critical interest in Wieland of the 1950s, which was instigated by Friedrich Sengle's important biography, *Wieland* (Stuttgart: Metzler, 1949). In the past fifty years, critics have ensconced *Agathon* as first important developmental novel or Bildungsroman. See, for example, Michael Beddow, *The Fiction of Humanity: Studies in the Bildungsroman from Wieland to Thomas Mann* (Cambridge: Cambridge UP, 1982); Jürgen Jacobs, *Wielands Romane* (Bern and München: Franke, 1969); Liisa Saariluoma, *Die Erzählstruktur des frühen deutschen Bildungsromans* (Helsinki: Suomalainen Tiedeakatemia, 1985); [Martin] Swales, *The German Bildungsroman* [*The German Bildungsroman from Wieland to Hesse* (Princeton: Princeton UP, 1978)].

8. Heinrich Wilhelm von Gerstenberg, *H. W. Gerstenbergs Rezensionen in der Hamburgischen Neuen Zeitung, 1767-1771,* ed. O. Fischer, Deutsche Literatur-Denkmale des 18. und 19. Jahrhunderts, 128, 3. Folge, Nr. 8. (Berlin: 1904), 47-48.

9. Christian Friedrich Daniel Schubart, letter to Christian Gottfried Böckh, June 6, 1766, cited from Manger, "Kommentar," 861.

10. Probably Issak Iselin. See Manger, "Kommentar," 863-64.

11. As Friedrich Heinrich Jacobi writes to Wieland, October 27, 1772, *Wielands Briefwechsel* [(1963-83)] 5: Nr. 19, 15.

12. Letter to Gessner, May 7, 1768, *Wielands Briefwechsel* 3: Nr. 522, 512.

    "In particular, poor Agathon is so terribly praised and so stupidly criticized that one doesn't know if one should laugh, cry, or reach for the Spanish cane. . . . The funny thing is, that nobody, not a single person, has figured out the intention and the unity of the whole."

13. Letter to Johann Georg Zimmermann, August 24, 1768, *Wielands Briefwechsel* 3: Nr. 555, 542.

"The kind of reception Agathon has received has radically cured me from the idea of wanting to be of service to the heads and hearts of my contemporaries."

14. W. Daniel Wilson discusses the differences between the first and third version of *Agathon* with respect to its motto and Horatian poetics in "'Prächt'ge Vase' or 'halber Topf'? A Horatian Verse in Wieland's Agathon," *Modern Language Notes* 95, 3-4 (1980): 664-69. The first version rejects an artificial reconciliation between the two terms as inappropriate for its status as the story of a soul, while the last version attempts to achieve a classical poetic harmony between them.

15. Wieland, *Theorie und Geschichte der Red-Kunst und Dichtkunst* (1757), in *Wielands Gesammelte Schriften,* ed. Deutsche Kommission der Königlich Preußischen Akademie der Wissenschaften (Berlin: 1909ff), I, 4, 330.

16. *Agathon,* cited from the text of the first edition of 1766-67, *Geschichte des Agathon,* ed. Klaus Manger (Frankfurt/Main: Deutscher Klassiker Verlag, 1986), 48. Further page references to this edition will be included in the text.

"He had everything that could make the type of wisdom he practiced seductive."

17. The widespread interest in physiognomy, most prominently represented by Johann Caspar Lavater's controversial *Physiognomische Fragmente* (1775-78), was one expression of eighteenth-century efforts to approach the realm of psychology with scientific claims and to channel and control knowledge of sentiment, "Empfindung," through rational categories. In *Agathon,* ten years older than Lavater's publications, Agathon's "natural ability to read in souls" provides him with a source of knowledge which compensates for his lack of worldly experience (II, 8, 69). On the personal relationship of Wieland and Lavater, as well as on their aesthetic controversies, see Renate Schostack, "Wieland und Lavater: Beitrag zur Geistesgeschichte des ausgehenden 18. Jahrhunderts" (Ph.D. diss., Freiburg, 1964), especially 4-52.

18. Horst Thomé traces the elements of "radical Enlightenment" in the discourse of Hippias in his article "Menschliche Natur und Allegorie sozialer Verhältnisse: Zur politischen Funktion philosophischer Konzeptionen in Wielands 'Geschichte des Agathon,'" *Jahrbuch der deutschen Schillergesellschaft* 22 (1978): 205-34, here 209. John A. McCarthy states that Agathon counters the intellectual arguments of Hippias by simply trusting his heart and his passions: *Fantasy and Reality:*

An Epistemological Approach to Wieland (Frankfurt/Main and Bern: Lang, 1974), 80.

19. The relation between seduction and knowledge, and the potential seducer lurking in the educator, is certainly familiar from such texts as Plato's *Symposion* or Rousseau's modern version of Abelard and Héloïse, "the most dangerous and most edifying novel in the world" (*Agathon,* 348).

20. . . . "because he imagined that Hippias's eloquence would provide the kind of enjoyment offered to us by a skilled magician, who makes us see for one moment something that we do not see, without taking it so far, for the clever person, that one would even doubt, in this very same moment, that one was being deceived."

21. The effect of rhetorical brilliance on listeners was described by the Sophists in analogy to magic and to narcotics; the issue of responsibility in the employment of this power over others surfaces in their earliest texts on rhetoric. See Renato Barilli, *Rhetoric,* trans. Giuliana Menozzi (Minneapolis: U of Minnesota P), 1989, 3-5.

22. Wieland mitigates the degree of outrage his positive seductress Danae might elicit with recourse to the customs and morals of his Greek setting, as Wulf Köpke notes in "Die emanzipierte Frau in der Goethezeit und ihre Darstellung in der Literatur," in *Die Frau als Heldin und Autorin: Neue kritische Ansätze zur deutschen Literatur.* ed. Wolfgang Paulsen (Bern and München: Franke, 1979), 96-110. Furthermore, the gender division of their roles account for the possibility of a positive seduction. It is not necessarily tragic for a young man to be seduced by an experienced woman, as would be the opposite case—see Ursula Fries, *Buhlerin und Zauberin: Eine Untersuchung zur deutschen Literatur des 18. Jahrhunderts* (München: Fink, 1970), 121-33. Dietlinde S. Bailet, *Die Frau als Verführte und als Verführerin in der deutschen und französischen Literatur des 18. Jahrhunderts* (Bern: Lang, 1981), argues that Danae's seduction of Agathon is, for him, "eine positive Etappe der Menschwerdung" (201). Yet, as discussed in Sven-Aage Jørgensen's article "Der unverheiratete Held," *Orbis Litterarum* 42, 3-4 (1987): 338-52, Wieland's novel is unable to overcome the crisis in the "codification of intimacy" (Luhmann) to arrive at a reconciliation of terms, for example in the form of marriage between Agathon and Danae. For a general discussion of Wieland's often liberal views on gender relations, see Elizabeth Boa, "Sex and Sensibility: Wieland's Portrayal of Relationships between the Sexes in the Comische Erzählungen, Agathon, and Musarion," *Lessing Yearbook* 12 (1980): 189-218.

23. "The great art was to arouse his desires under the mask of friendship, while simultaneously appearing to rebuff them through an unaffected reserve."

24. See Kurt Wölfel, "Daphnes Verwandlung: Zu einem Kapitel in Wielands 'Agathon,'" in *Christoph Martin Wieland,* ed. Hansjörg Schelle [(Darmstadt: Wissenschaftliche Buchgesellschaft, 1981)], 232-50.

25. "One must undoubtedly admit that the painting which presented itself to our hero in this moment was not well suited to leave either his heart or his senses tranquil; but Danae's intention was only to prepare him, through the eyes, for the pleasures of another sense, and her pride demanded no smaller triumph than to obliterate such an attractive image in his soul through the magical power of her voice and her strings."

26. Homer, *The Iliad,* translated and with an introduction by Richmond Lattimore, 1951 (Chicago: U of Chicago P, 1961), 14, v. 185 and 214-17, 299-300.

27. "'If the sirens, whom the clever Ulysses had to pass, sung this way,' (thought Agathon), 'then he truly had cause to have himself bound by his hands and feet to the mast.'"

28. . . . "how much he was beside himself and how much effort it cost him to hold himself back, not to throw himself out of his seat into the water and to swim over to her, and to expire, dissolved in delight and love, at her feet."

29. . . . "a tender softness had to first gain mastery over his entire soul and his senses, swimming in pleasure, had to be captured by a sweet uneasiness and a lustful longing."

30. . . . "siren-songs . . . which sank the soul into an enchanted forgetting of itself and, after it disarmed all its more noble powers, delivered the aroused and willing sensuality up to the entire force of lust which was entering from all sides."

31. In Dorothea von Mücke's trenchant study of the final version of *Agathon (Virtue and the Veil of Illusion[: Generic Innovation and the Pedagogical Project in Eighteenth-Century Literature* (Stanford: Stanford UP, 1991)], 229-73), she reads this challenge to Agathon's identity as a temporary loss of the "narcissistic integrity" on which the new paradigms of organizing male subjectivity in the late eighteenth-century are founded.

32. "His entire being was in his sense of hearing and his entire soul dissolved into the sentiments that dominated her song."

33. "An Ionic ear not only wants to be pleased, it wants to be enchanted . . . in short, the style of reading ought to put the ear in the place of all the other senses."

34. "There is a certain art of removing from sight whatever could make a negative impression; so much depends on the turn of phrase; a single small circumstance gives an event such a different appearance from the one it would have had without this small circumstance."

35. "But as regards those places where she considered as inadequate all the art that one could apply towards making them more beautiful . . . these she cleverly decided to conceal with complete silence."

36. Lieselotte E. Kurth, "Historiographie und historischer Roman: Kritik und Theorie im 18. Jahrhundert," *Modern Language Notes* 79, 3 (1964): 337-62.

37. "Truth . . . resides therein, that everything be commensurate with the way of the world, that characters are not arbitrary and simply generated from the fantasy or the intentions of the author, but are instead drawn from the inexhaustible sources of Nature herself; . . . and thus that everything is invented in such a way, that no sufficient reason can be given, why it could not have happened, or might not once happen, exactly as it was told. This truth alone can make works of this sort useful."

38. Wieland defends the label "history" for his work and positions himself in relation to Xenophon and Fielding in "Über das Historische in Agathon," 573. See Shookman's reading of the ambivalences in the concept of history for *Agathon* in *Noble Lies [Noble Lies, Slant Truths, Necessary Angels: Aspects of Fictionality in the Novels of Christoph Martin Wieland* (Chapel Hill and London: U of North Carolina P, 1997)], 52-58.

39. In "Unterredungen mit dem Pfarrer von ***" (1775), Wieland defends his artistic works and his person against charges of ethical transgressions. Danae's guidelines are expressly recalled as poetic ones: "Ich bin als Dichter bekannt. . . . Man würde sagen, daß ich (wie Danae) mehr die Gesetze des Schönen und Anständigen als der historischen Treue zum Augenmerke genommen" (*Wielands Gesammelte Schriften* [(1909ff)], I, 14, 30).

40. "Danae narrated her story with the innocent aim of pleasing. She naturally regarded her performance, her weaknesses, even her missteps in a milder and (let us tell the truth) in a truer light than did the world."

41. "He compared her own narrative with that of Hippias and now, once mistrust had taken over his

mind, he thought to perceive a hundred traces in the first which supported the truth of the second."

42. "It is undoubtedly good, when an author who has aimed to reach a more important goal than merely pleasing his readers, given certain situations, does not imitate the unbridled wantonness of many of the newer Frenchmen, but rather imitates the modest reservation of the innocent Virgil, who . . . finds it sufficient to tell us: 'that Dido and the hero came to a cave.' However if this reservation were carried so far that the obscurity with which one covers a delicate circumstance could give rise to misunderstanding and error: then, we think, it would be misplaced modesty and in such instances we think it advisable to lift the curtain a little bit, rather than to risk exposing innocence itself to unfounded suspicions because of exaggerated caution."

43. "And here, without unnecessarily detaining the reader with what she said further and what he answered, we will leave the brush to a Correggio and slip away."

44. "And how do we even know that Agathon himself, for all his candor, did not hold back any circumstance which he foresaw, like a good painter or poet, could hinder the beautiful effect of the whole. Who will vouch for the fact that the seductive priestess did not achieve more influence over him than he admitted?"

John P. Heins (essay date October 2003)

SOURCE: Heins, John P. "Quixotism and the Aesthetic Constitution of the Individual in Wieland's *Don Sylvio von Rosalva*." *Journal of English and Germanic Philology* 102, no. 4 (October 2003): 530-48.

[*In the following essay, Heins discusses the relationship between art and the individual in Wieland's novel* Don Sylvio von Rosalva.]

Cervantes's *Don Quixote* has often been referred to as the first modern work of literature, particularly because of the way in which it thematizes fictionality, or the relationship between representations and that which is represented.[1] Since its publication in 1605, this text has inspired a wide variety of appropriations and critical engagements that have played a central role in ongoing debates about literature's relationship to the empirical realm. Tracing these appropriations, particularly in the form of explicitly quixotic figures in literary works, can illustrate changing conceptions of the nature and function of literature, and of the arts more generally, in modern societies. In the eighteenth century in particular, the literary engagement with quixotism addresses the role of aesthetic illusion in the constitution of individuals as it satirically or humorously portrays the purported effects of reading imaginative literature.

The eighteenth century in Germany was particularly busy with the question of the proper function of art, going through substantial shifts from Gottsched's normative poetics in the early part of the century through the rise of *Wirkungsästhetik* to the varying conceptions of aesthetic autonomy at the end of the century.[2] Therefore it should not be surprising that this century was fascinated by the Quixote figure's relationship to the fictional realm, although the reception of *Don Quixote* in the following century, among the Romantics who were prone to see this text as "the most romantic book," has received considerably more attention over the last two centuries.[3] The reception of Cervantes's novel took various forms in the eighteenth century, one of the most prevalent being adaptations of its theme in contemporary settings. While Neugebauer's *Der Teutsche Don Quichotte* of 1753 and Musäus's *Der deutsche Grandison* of 1760-62 are of considerable historical interest, Wieland's *Der Sieg der Natur über die Schwärmerei, oder die Abenteuer des Don Sylvio von Rosalva* of 1764 (hereafter *Don Sylvio*) is generally acknowledged the most successful of the German quixotes of the eighteenth century and has attracted considerable literary-historical commentary.[4] The quality of Wieland's engagement with quixotism, in combination with the importance of quixotism in the development of European thought generally, suggests that this text merits further attention.[5] The present study seeks to discover what Wieland's quixotic novel ultimately implies about how individual consciousness is formed and conditioned by the reception of art works, that is, by a particularly intense form of sensual and intellectual experience. The focus on a young, developing mind here (unlike the case of *Don Quixote*) is particularly significant, since Wieland interrupted the writing of what became the first Bildungsroman, *Geschichte des Agathon,* to write this novel in 1763. Thus, the writing of *Don Sylvio* might be seen as an integral part of Wieland's historically innovative and influential narrative theorization of individual development in the *Agathon* project. Other commentators have reasonably suggested that Wieland wished to address in *Don Sylvio* the question of fictionality that was troubling him with *Agathon*; I wish to focus on the corollary issue of the *effects* of fictions and artistic illusions on the young, developing mind. Studying the approach of *Don Sylvio* to the problem of quixotism should yield insights into the German eighteenth century's understanding of subjective development in general.[6]

The novel *Don Sylvio,* in the form of a story about a quixotic or literal-minded reader, engages debates about mimesis and fictionality in the novel form, and through those debates, about representation in general. On the one hand, the first part of the title, ***Der Sieg der Natur über die Schwärmerei,*** claims that the novel will illustrate the cure of this quixotic reader of fairytales, a cure that will come about through the ostensible intervention of the empirical into Don Sylvio's text-derived psychic world. That is, "nature" triumphs over "enthusiasm" or "fancy" as Don Sylvio learns that fairytales are works of the imagination with no necessary correspondence to the real world. On the other hand, the text in the end exposes the fictionality of the so-called "nature" which ostensibly triumphs, through a series of references to the novel's own fictionality.[7] In Wieland's self-conscious narrative, nature exposes itself as an artifact of the literary text rather than the unproblematic and unquestionable ground of all existence and all cognition. In this way the novel undermines easy claims of verisimilitude in novels, and in so doing problematizes an important part of the argument which advocates of the novel in the German context made for the form's legitimacy.[8] The text illustrates Wieland's move away from the twin pillars of verisimilitude and moral efficacy, and toward the independent value of the imagination and the aesthetic.[9]

This novel's contribution to the debates about the novel as genre and about the particular nature of the art work's autonomy has been often noticed and variously interpreted. Less often commented upon are two aspects I would like to bring into focus here: the role of ideas specifically about the visual arts in the text, and the importance of the debate about representations to the text's notions of subject-formation, that is, about how individuals are constituted. On one level, the text works with a dichotomy of illusion and reality, of representation and original, and purports to destroy the former in the service of the latter, in the satirical tradition of *Don Quixote.*[10] Don Sylvio is indeed in one sense lost in representations; his cure does entail an aspect of destroying illusions and perceiving a reality, in the sense that he must appreciate originals over representations. Yet on another level there is no absolute separation between the original and the representation; he perceives the original through or by virtue of the representation. Wieland implicitly claims that representations or illusions, both visual and literary, are not mere cognitive tricks to be seen through and overcome, nor the sugar on the pill of moral teachings, nor exercises for the imagination or the soul; more than all this, they are indeed constitutive in the development of the individual psyche, and by extension in the building of what we might generally call intersubjective reality. For Wieland, representations are an integral part of the individual's perception of the world; they are elements which constitute the individual's world as much as the reality they represent does.[11] This constitutive function of representations amounts to Wieland's particular contribution to the discourse of quixotism.[12]

As I define it here, quixotism is the tendency of a literary character to read texts literally, to understand the world portrayed in literature to be literally true, and then to interpret the empirical world according to the terms and forms supplied by the particular category of literary fictions—in the case of Don Quixote, the category is medieval courtly romances; in the case of Don Sylvio, it is *Feenmärchen*—specifically, seventeenth-century literary fairytales. Hence quixotism is an effect of reading, characterized by a confusion of the artificial (or artistic) and the real, resulting in an inability to interact appropriately with the empirical world of objects.[13] The quixote's model texts present a world governed by high ideals, and hence the quixote is idealistic; satirical eighteenth-century German texts generally criticize this idealism as derived from unrealistic representations. The exception to this rule is Wieland, who as we will see prefigures the romantic reimagining of Don Quixote as an admirable idealist rather than the target of satirical critique. The quixote, then, interprets sensory input according to the worldview contained in his or her favorite class of texts. This process of interpretation is thus not strictly irrational or insane, but rather a rational, systematic process that is not shared by others, a process which evidences what Motooka calls "the irreducible diversity of mind" (p. 24). This state of mind is caused by an unlucky confluence of a particular predisposition (according to psychological character type, age, circumstance, marital status) and too much uninformed reading of low-quality literary texts.[14]

Wieland's particular characterization of the quixotic figure can lead us to a clearer understanding of the phenomenon. The young Don Sylvio, an avid reader of fairytales who lacks adequate instruction in their essential difference from reality, believes in the literal existence of fairies. He suffers from that peculiar ailment referred to in eighteenth-century German discourse as *Schwärmerei,* the inability to distinguish between objects of one's imagination and empirical reality.[15] The necessary precondition for this state of mind in Don Sylvio's case is an extremely impressionable sensibility: he is predisposed to this particular *Schwärmerei* because his soul is sensitive to stimulation by objects without regard to their real existence or lack thereof. In his reading, then, the represented world takes on the status of a real world, through the erasure of the printed text's mediation. The natural gifts which Don Sylvio possesses, "eine ungemeine Empfindlichkeit, und, was unmittelbar damit verbunden ist, eine starke Disposition zur Zärtlichkeit" occupy a semantic field which is soon to be dominated by the term *Empfindsamkeit,* and point in the first instance to a receptivity to physical sensation.[16] His tendency to be deceived by his reading, or his undiscerning receptivity to intellectual stimulation, stems in great part from the purity of his soul, that is, its relative lack of permanent obstructing impressions: "Die natürliche Lauterkeit seiner Seele war des Argwohns, ob er etwan betrogen werde, unfähig" (*DS* [*Don Sylvio*], p. 22).

The purity of his soul, though, is thus ironically also an emptiness. Don Sylvio is impressionable because his character is unsolid, or in a sense because he does not quite have a character. In Adelung's dictionary, *Charakter* has two basic meanings: a figure on paper or stone, as a sign or a letter; and figuratively, whatever mark distinguishes one thing from another of its type (I: 1323). The specification under the second definition includes the term *Gemüthsart,* which corresponds to "disposition" or "personality." These two definitions, roughly a sign and a personality, combine in the idea of an impression that creates or enhances a personality trait. Wieland's narrator writes of Don Sylvio in this regard: "Junge Leute von dieser Art lieben überhaupt alle Vorstellungen, welche lebhafte Eindrücke auf ihr Herz machen, und Leidenschaften erwecken, die, in einem leichten Schlummer liegend, bereit sind von dem kleinsten Geräusch aufzufahren" (*DS,* p. 21). In a commonplace in the critical discourse about sentimentalism, the sentimental individual is composed of a soft material upon which external impressions easily make their mark and establish (problematic) "character." The sentimental reader is a sort of blank sheet of paper upon which any type is easily received and stands out boldly. But in Wieland's version here, the easily accepted impressions awaken preexisting passions; in this ambiguity one can see the complexity of Wieland's thinking about the sentimental reader. The uniformity of Don Sylvio's life, the isolation and indolence of a noble, labor-free country existence facilitate his impressionability; fantasy fills the emptiness which "die beständige Einförmigkeit der Gegenstände, die sich den Sinnen darstellen, in der Seele zurück läßt" (*DS,* p. 22).

Developing out of these sense impressions are emotions and *Einbildungskraft,* or imagination, a term which is ambiguous in this period because it points to an aspect of forming or creativity on the one hand, but also to ungrounded imagining on the other—the power to create, but also the tendency to succumb to illusion.[17] Lest the reader focus too exclusively on the susceptibility to illusion as an illness (as was common in other eighteenth-century quixotes), Wieland consistently reminds us of the inherent reason in imagination:

> Die Seele, welche nach einem blinden Instincte Schimären eben so regelmäßig bearbeitet als Wahrheiten, bauet sich nach und nach aus allem diesem ein Ganzes, und gewöhnt sich an, es für wahr zu halten, weil sie Licht und Zusammenhang darin findet, und weil ihre Phantasie mit den Schimären, die den größten Teil davon ausmachen, eben so bekannt ist als ihre Sinnen mit den würklichen Gegenständen, von denen sie ohne sonderliche Abwechslung immer umgeben sind. . . . Seine Einbildung faßte also die schimärischen Wesen, die ihr die Poeten und Romanen-

> Dichter vorstellten, eben so auf, wie seine Sinnen die Eindrücke der natürlichen Dinge aufgefasset hatten. Je angenehmer ihm das Wunderbare und Übernatürliche war, desto leichter war er zu verführen, es würklich zu glauben.

> (*DS,* p. 22)

Here the information that his senses deliver about natural objects and the information his imagination delivers about chimaeras are processed in a parallel way, as long as they are pleasant information or impressions. Reason appears as a blind instinct for order, no matter whether the data are reported by imagination or the senses. The basic principle of the soul, its tendency to form coherent unities, does not differentiate between real and unreal objects, or between sensual and intellectual impressions. Since Don Sylvio's soul does indeed work in a regular manner, that is, since it succeeds in finding *Licht und Zusammenhang* in the objects it treats, the conclusions he comes to are only natural. The narrator here implies that Don Sylvio is perfectly healthy and merely needs criteria for differentiating objects according to their real existence. As we shall see below, those criteria are to be found not in an unquestioning or simple reference to a given world, but in a complicated intersubjective reality.

If it is natural for Don Sylvio's soul to operate in this manner, then nature must somehow share the blame for his illusions. Indeed, nature plays a double role with regard to Don Sylvio's way of knowing: on the one hand, the title suggests that nature will cure Don Sylvio ("Der Sieg der Natur über die Schwärmerei"), while on the other hand, the narrator points out that nature causes *Schwärmerei* in the first place: "Die Natur selbst, deren anhaltende Beobachtung das sicherste Mittel gegen die Ausschweifungen der Schwärmerei ist, scheint auf der andern Seite durch die unmittelbaren Eindrücke, so ihr majestätisches Schauspiel auf unsre Seele macht, die erste Quelle derselben zu sein" (*DS,* p. 22). In this formulation, all of us share with Don Sylvio an impressionable soul, at least when confronted by the spectacle of nature's majesty. Here Wieland's narrator denies the simple categorical division of *Natur* from *Schwärmerei* necessary for the triumph of the former over the latter. In doing so, of course, the narrator also conflates "nature" as physical laws governing the world, that is, nature as the object of scientific knowledge, with "nature" as the appearance of plants, animals, earth forms, and presumably celestial phenomena, that is, nature as the object of aesthetic perception. Wieland's ironic text implicitly pleads with those whom Lieselotte Kurth aptly calls the *Wahrscheinlichkeits-Fanatiker* of his time to define their "nature" before taking it as an unquestioned point of reference.[18]

In Don Sylvio's case, the representation of nature in the fairytales predisposes him to believe in them:

So oft er konnte, begab er sich in den Garten oder in den angrenzenden Wald, und nahm seine Märchen mit. Die Lebhaftigkeit, womit seine Einbildungskraft sich derselben bemächtigte, war außerordentlich, er las nicht, er sah, er hörte, er fühlte. Eine schönere und wundervolle Natur, als die er bisher gekannt hatte, schien sich vor ihm aufzutun, und die Vermischung des Wunderbaren mit der Einfalt der Natur, welche der Charakter der meisten Spielwerke von dieser Gattung ist, wurde für ihn ein untrügliches Kennzeichen ihrer Wahrheit.

(*DS*, p. 25)

He perceives an environment more beautiful and wonderful than the nature he knows, but still understandable as nature, and as therefore true. This cognitive operation erases the mediation of the printed word: because of the liveliness of his imagination, "er las nicht, er sah, er hörte, er fühlte." All sense of mediation disappears as the represented world, through the medium of reading, "immediately" imprints the soft, receptive soul in the same way as phenomena of the natural world would through simple visual perception. This blindness to mediation characterizes Don Sylvio as a reader: the reader interpolates himself or herself into the text and forgets the fundamental difference between fiction and reality. Don Sylvio's habit of erasing mediation and imagining himself into the text causes him in turn to misperceive the empirical world outside the texts. This faulty processing of empirical data leads to all of Don Sylvio's mistakes and misadventures throughout the novel, even as the ambiguous character of "imagination" suggests that his mind is fundamentally healthy and his reading is not entirely misreading.

Don Sylvio's adventures and misadventures can be quickly summarized. One day the young man finds a locket containing the image of a beautiful woman, and he becomes convinced that a certain butterfly is the same woman in enchanted form. Further prompted by his guardian aunt's plan to marry him off to an undesirable mate in order to facilitate an advantageous match for herself, Don Sylvio and his servant Pedrillo escape this domestic entrapment and set out to find the butterfly, that is, to find his "Princess" pictured in the locket. They wander the countryside having comic episodes in the mode of his model Don Quixote (that is, misinterpreting prosaic real-world occurrences, here as manifestations of the powers of fairies and wizards), eventually stumbling onto the palatial home of the young widow Donna Felicia, coincidentally the owner of the locket and the granddaughter of the woman pictured therein. She and Don Sylvio immediately fall in love. The cast of characters is rounded out when Donna Felicia's brother Eugenio and his friends Gabriel and Hyacinthe arrive. Don Sylvio had earlier assisted this party in fighting off an attack by a band of villains seeking to steal Hyacinthe, who is under the protection of Don Gabriel and of her suitor Don Eugenio, and who turns out to be Don Sylvio's long-lost sister. Don Sylvio must be cured of his *Schwärmerei* to enable the general pairing off, which will include the servant Pedrillo and Donna Felicia's chambermaid.

The very idea of the cure, though, is disturbed by the central irony of the story, the fact that the story itself is fundamentally improbable and unbelievable, a work of fiction rather than a realistic account. Most recent commentators agree that the text does not act as a simple satire of Don Sylvio, nor does "nature" triumph in some unequivocal way over "enthusiasm." Rather, Wieland uses these categories ironically, in the end to point out their proximity to each other rather than their absolute difference.[19] Certainly Don Sylvio's relationship to texts, and to artistic representations in general, changes as a result of his discovery that his fairytales are not strictly true, but that change cannot adequately be referred to as a cure from an illness, or a complete reform of his way of thinking. Wieland uses the complexity of the end of the novel to point out that—unlike many other eighteenth-century quixotes—Don Sylvio's mistakes are not entirely mistakes. The disenchantment of the protagonist leaves him not in a prosaic real world of struggle and disappointment, but in a world fully as enchanted as the one he has left behind. Thus, in ***Don Sylvio*** there are what we might call two separate levels of illusion: the one level of illusion is the world of fairies in whose real existence Don Sylvio passionately believes, while the other level of illusion is the actual events in the novel, wherein the young nobleman's pursuit of a butterfly leads him directly into the path of the woman he is destined to wed at the happy end. Wieland presents the destruction of the one level of enchantment in such a way as to call attention ironically to the enchanted nature of the other level. When we leave the world of fairies behind, we are still caught in a world of improbable happy coincidences, symmetries, and artistic satisfactions. We end up back in a novel—specifically, a novel that self-consciously exposes its indebtedness to the conventions of romance.[20] Don Sylvio is disabused of his belief in fairytales only that the reader may find him in a story whose structure is just as *märchenhaft*.[21]

Still, the other characters, of course unaware that they themselves are characters in an improbable fiction, insist that Don Sylvio should be cured of his belief in fairytales, although in the end the process of this ostensible cure suggests that fictions cannot be simply opposed to the real, but rather their status depends on intersubjective agreement. The other characters attempt to cure Don Sylvio by attacking his beliefs on two fronts: the combination of his love for Donna Felicia and a hermeneutic exercise regarding the story of Prince Biribinker, they imagine, should cure him. The Biribinker story is a particularly unrealistic fairytale which the character Don Gabriel concocts for this purpose, asking

Don Sylvio to judge its believability. The debate begins with Don Sylvio's defending the story's veracity:

> Mich deucht, (fuhr er fort) die wahre Quelle der irrigen Urteile, die man über alles dasjenige, was man wunderbare Begebenheiten heißt, zu fällen pflegt, entspringe aus der falschen Einbildung, als ob alles unmöglich sei, was sich nicht aus körperlichen und in die Sinne fallenden Ursachen erklären läßt; gleich als ob die Kräfte der Geister, von denen die körperlichen Dinge bloß tote und grobe Werkzeuge sind, nicht notwendiger Weise die mechanischen und geborgten Kräfte eben dieser Werkzeuge unendlich übersteigen müßten.
>
> (*DS,* p. 342)

Don Sylvio here moves the question onto the level of the mystery of life-energy or the principle of animation itself, arguing that before we have understood that principle fully, we cannot exclude manifestations of that unknown power that we simply do not understand. His suggestion is a version of a religious argument against a mechanistic universe.[22]

Having made this general theoretical point that stories which include the fantastic are not impossible, Don Sylvio goes on to conclude that there is nothing even necessarily improbable about the Biribinker story, with one crucial condition: that the teller of the tale is trustworthy. Don Gabriel then disillusions Don Sylvio by admitting that he made up the whole story. In the course of the discussion, Don Gabriel creates a new category for Don Sylvio which includes narratives, such as fairytales, containing events which are logically consistent with each other without therefore being believable as representations of the empirical world. The criterion for belonging to the strictest category of probability Don Gabriel spells out as accordance "mit dem ordentlichen Lauf der Natur, in so fern sie unter unsern Sinnen liegt, oder mit demjenigen hat, was der größte Teil des menschlichen Geschlechts alle Tage erfährt" (*DS,* p. 345). Here Don Gabriel emphasizes not the role of nature as an unproblematic absolute, but rather the orderly interpretation of subjective perceptions ("Natur, in so fern sie unter unsern Sinnen liegt") and the intersubjective ("was der größte Teil des menschlichen Geschlechts alle Tage erfährt") as correctives to purely subjective (however rational) interpretations of the world, or quixotism. Don Sylvio is provisionally convinced that fairies might not be real by Don Gabriel's rather sophisticated intersubjective argument, not by the other characters' simplistic references to the real.[23]

Still, at this point Don Sylvio does not admit that he was simply wrong about the fairies; the discussion (and with it the process of the "cure") is suspended for the time being, while the other curing force, Don Sylvio's love for Felicia, is allowed to take its course. As Don Eugenio has said, "die Natur und die Liebe werden das meiste tun; die Phantasie wird nach und nach der Empfindung Platz machen, und wenn nur diese einmal die Oberhand hat, so wird es leicht sein, ihm Vorurteile und irrige Begriffe zu benehmen, die keinen Fürsprecher mehr in seinem Herzen haben" (*DS,* pp. 219-20). When we seek to understand the nature and effect of Don Sylvio's love, we become embroiled in a complicated set of circumstances regarding the locket, circumstances which suggest a compelling parallel between the literary and the visual.

Since this text is so closely concerned with questions about the relationship between representations and the real, it is particularly significant that, at a moment when the discussion around textual representations remains inconclusive (the hermeneutic argument among the characters is suspended, not concluded), the narrative turns to visual representations, specifically to the portrait, an art form closely associated with verisimilitude, the natural, and the representation of character. The details emerge around a pair of portraits of the heroine and her grandmother. When confronted by these two paintings, the memory of the image in the locket, and the living Donna Felicia, Don Sylvio is put into a severe state of confusion about the identity of his beloved. These details suggest that Wieland sees not only literature, but the arts in general as overburdened by a narrow view of the task "imitation of nature"; he attempts ironically to expose as untenable a simplistic dichotomy between the natural and the artificial, the original and the representation.

The portrait, on one level the art form with the clearest and most obvious division and causal relationship between a model (the empirical person) and a representation (the painted portrait), raises the issue of "imitation of nature" in a particularly direct way. In eighteenth-century European portraiture, the perennial tension between beauty and similarity takes on a great urgency.[24] Even as the focus on the empirically perceptible increases, the era also wants to read the soul in the face, as the entry under *Portrait* in Sulzer's *Allgemeine Theorie der Schönen Künste* suggests: "wir sehen die Seele in dem Körper. Aus diesem Grunde können wir sagen, der Körper sey das Bild der Seele, oder die Seele selbst, sichtbar gemacht."[25] Sulzer here agrees in general principle with the physiognomics of Lavater, for whom the artistic representation of that face carries a heavy load of responsibility both to similarity and to beauty, the latter being the worldly and human expression of divine perfection. Lavater writes: "Wenn der Portraitmaler . . . durchdrungen wäre von Ehrfurcht gegen das beste Werk des besten Meisters . . . welch' eine wichtige, heilige Arbeit wäre ihm das Portraitmalen! Heilig wenigstens, wie der Text heiliger Schriften dem Uebersetzer sein sollte, sollte ihm ein lebendes Menschengesicht sein! wie sorgsam er, nicht zu verfälschen das Werk Gottes, wie ihrer so viele das Wort Gottes!"[26] Here again we see the tension, as we did in Adelung's definition of *Charakter,* between the particular or individual and the typological, between individual characteristics and general beauty. The aspect of abstract beauty has the important task of presenting in a sensually perceptible way an idea of divine perfection in order to fill the viewer with an appropriate awe for the Creator's works. On the other hand, the aspect of particular similarity has the role of guaranteeing that what we admire is not an abstraction, but a real human being, since only the real is credited with the power of most intensely affecting us. Since nothing in the divinely created universe is more important than a thinking and feeling soul, Sulzer continues, the human being in which that soul is visible is "der wichtigste aller sichtbaren Gegenstände," and not simply in its generality as beautiful object, but as "ein Wesen, in welchem Verstand, Neigungen, Gesinnungen, Leidenschaften, gute und schlimme Eigenschaften des Geistes und des Herzens auf eine ihm eigene und besondere Art gemischt sind" (p. 719), that is, in its particularity as that irreducible individual. "Dieses sehen wir sogar im Portrait meistentheils besser, als in der Natur selbst" (p. 719), and thus the portrait carries the very heavy burden of more truly representing its original, that is, the soul-identity of the person represented, than even the immediate physical impression of that person might.

Thus, when Don Sylvio is confused about who is represented in the portrait in the locket, that is, whose image he has fallen in love with, this confusion not only manifests his quixotism in another form, but also and more importantly points to this tension between abstract beauty and concrete similarity. First, we should try to understand Don Sylvio's confusion and the steps he goes through in achieving clarity. He has fallen in love with the woman pictured in the locket. When he meets Donna Felicia, he immediately falls in love with her but does not at first think she is the woman in the locket (which he has lost). In comic naiveté, he fears that this new love for Donna Felicia will make him untrue to the original woman, to whom he refers variously as his "Shepherdess" or "the Princess." This fear and confusion make him question the reality of his notions about the fairies and the butterfly. He seeks clarity by going through an exercise in Cartesian methodical doubt in order to ascertain what is beyond doubt. The image of his beloved shepherdess is the only thing, "was in seiner von Zweifeln gleichsam überschwemmten Seele noch empor ragte, und im allgemeinen Umsturz seiner Ideen unerschüttert blieb. Wenn auch alles andre Einbildung ist, rief er, so weiß ich doch gewiß, o! du namenlose Unbekannte, daß es keine Einbildung ist, daß ich dich liebe" (*DS,* p. 201). His belief in fairies he can rid himself of; that is, the way of knowing attached to his reading and to the world conjured up by books is subject to skeptical dismissal in this moment (he thinks), but the emotion attached to a visual representation remains beyond doubt. Don Sylvio does not assert that he is sure

that the image of the shepherdess corresponds to a real existing person, but only that he is sure of his love for her ("daß ich dich liebe"). His emotion is the empirical datum. This emotional fixation on the image provides the last hurdle he must overcome in his cure, but at the same time also remains necessary for the cure insofar as it "prepares him" to love the real existing Donna Felicia, who happens to resemble quite closely her grandmother pictured in the locket. Much is made of the power of his actual love to cure him of his belief in fairies, and this love is enabled and prefigured by his fixation on the image.

The transfer of emotion from the image of the grandmother to the real granddaughter Donna Felicia requires several steps which begin in a chapter entitled "Streit zwischen der Liebe zum Bilde und der Liebe zum Original." Slightly afraid of Donna Felicia's power, Don Sylvio, in his next self-disciplining mental game, tries to picture his Princess as being "noch reizender, liebenswürdiger und vollkommener" than Donna Felicia, "aber, es sei nun, daß die Einbildungs-Kraft nicht im Stande ist etwas vollkommeners hervor zu bringen als die Natur, oder daß ihm die Liebe hierin einen ihrer gewöhnlichen Streiche spielte: gewiß ist, das Bild der schönen Felicia stand jedesmal an der Stelle der Princessin, und alle seine Bestrebungen, sich dieselbe unter andern Zügen vorzustellen, waren vergeblich" (*DS,* p. 223). Thus nature triumphs over imagination, in the sense that his passion for Felicia overcomes his passion for an image. But here's the rub: Felicia wins not so much by cancelling the image as by merging with the image. The image of Donna Felicia now stands in the place defined by the Princess; he can only imagine the Princess in the features of Donna Felicia. In this way, the portrait in effect prefigures Donna Felicia, and his love will always be marked by its original object. Don Sylvio's logical conclusion, then, is that the image in the locket is a portrait of Donna Felicia, but she assures him that it is not: "Sie bemerkte die Verlegenheit, worein ihre Versicherung den guten Don Sylvio setzte, ob er gleich immer fort behauptete, daß er in diesem Bildnis, es möchte nun auch vorstellen sollen wen es wollte, niemand als sie selbst geliebt habe" (*DS,* pp. 359-60). Here Don Sylvio, in what from one point of view seems an embarrassed political move to avoid offending Donna Felicia in loving another, reinterprets the visual object as a pre-formation of Donna Felicia for him, claiming that he loved her "in" the portrait. It is as if the image conditions his soul for the subsequent encounter with a real love-object. For the portrait to have this function, however, requires that we de-emphasize its "similarity" aspect, that is, its correspondence to a real original.

In order fully to clarify the nature of the picture in the locket, Donna Felicia takes Don Sylvio to a cabinet containing two almost identical life-size portraits, one of herself and one of her grandmother, asking him to guess whom they represent. Don Sylvio guesses that one painting is a copy of the other; Donna Felicia sets him straight, pointing out that one is a painting of her grandmother, of which the image in the locket is a miniature copy.

> Dieses ist die Entwicklung des ganzen Knotens, und nun, setzte sie lächelnd hinzu, überlasse ich ihnen, da die Großmutter und die Enkelin gleich viel Recht an ihre Neigung hat, für welche von beiden sie sich erklären wollen. . . . Don Sylvio erzählte ihr jetzt sein ganzes Feen-Märchen, die Geschichte des Sommer-Vogels, und die Erscheinung der Fee Radiante; und er gestund desto williger, daß seine mit Feen-Wundern angefüllte Einbildungs-Kraft einen großen Anteil an diesem vermeinten Gesichte gehabt habe, da ihn Donna Felicia auf der andern Seite nicht ohne Vergnügen erlaubte die andere Hälfte dieses sonderbaren Phänomeni auf die Rechnung einer geheimen Divination oder Vorwissenschaft seiner Seele zu schreiben, der es ahnete, daß er in kurzem *das Urbild dieses geliebten Schattenbildes finden würde.*

(*DS*, pp. 360-361, my italics)

The confusing and fascinating part of this quotation is the expression "das Urbild dieses geliebten Schattenbildes"; if he means that he would find Donna Felicia, then the expression does not quite fit. In the most literal sense, the *Urbild* is the painting of the grandmother, since the *Schattenbild* is the miniature copy of it. Donna Felicia has just explained that the image in the locket is not of her at all, although in another sense she herself is a *Schattenbild* of her grandmother. In fact, Donna Felicia's father had the portrait made of his daughter in the same clothing and same position as the portrait of his mother precisely because of the uncanny resemblance of the two. When Don Sylvio confuses the two, then, he is not simply "wrong"; in fact, the organic continuity between the grandmother and the granddaughter means that the fact that he falls in love with both makes sense. In the quotation, though, we presume that what Donna Felicia will allow is that Don Sylvio's soul had a presentiment that he would find *her*, Donna Felicia. In this sense, we could call Donna Felicia the *Urbild* of the conceptual *Schattenbild*, the category "my Princess." Donna Felicia satisfies Don Sylvio's longing inspired by the image of her grandmother, insofar as she completely fills the preexisting category "my Princess" in such a way as to suggest that the category has been created as a copy of her. Such an explanation of this puzzling passage would suggest that because of the effects of aesthetic objects on the depths of an individual psyche, the empirical objects encountered later will always only be graspable through the preexisting categories created by those early illusions (whether innate or derived entirely from experience, whether archetypal or purely acquired).

Don Sylvio's cure does entail an aspect of destroying illusions and perceiving a reality, in the sense that he must appreciate originals over representations, the real existing Donna Felicia over the image of her grandmother or the resulting abstraction "my Princess," and the reality of the novel over the illusory fairytale. But subjectively for the individual there seems no absolute separation between the original and the representation. Rather, the only semi-cured and yet fully sane Don Sylvio perceives the original through the representation, that is, the portrait can never be dismissed, but rather will always inform his love for his Princess, Donna Felicia. So the cure involves a de-cathexis of the image (both the portrait and the fairytales), and yet the cathected image plays the role of a primary motivator. (The portrait taught him to love, and the fairytale belief led him on this successful search for his mate.)

Despite the opinions of his contemporary *Wahrscheinlichkeits-Fanatiker*, then, Wieland argues here against emphatic reference to "nature" as a pre-given point of orientation for the arts, an immediately present empirical realm to which the arts must refer and which the arts must imitate. It is not that the work of art and the empirical object of representation are completely indistinguishable; rather, in the inner workings of the psyche there is an intimate relationship between them, even if we must and do distinguish between them. Paintings, like novels or like fairytales, contain both truth and lies, are both products of imagination and representations of the world outside of them, exercise both healthy and dangerous influences on those who perceive them. To address the debate about the legitimacy of the novel form, in his focus on fictionality in this work Wieland explicitly calls attention to the much greater dependence of the novel on its forerunners than on the empirical realm it is said to mirror; he writes the novel back into the tradition of the romance, but not in order to fault it for that (as the novel form's detractors did), but rather as a preliminary step in establishing its rightful place among the arts.

If, as Georg Jäger argued convincingly, the genre of the novel rose to legitimacy in eighteenth-century Germany in the particular form of the moral-didactic sentimental novel, then it is significant that **Don Sylvio** refers not only to the problem of verisimilitude in general, but to the sentimental novel in particular. With regard to this literary form, Wieland's critique of the pretensions of verisimilitude complements his differing argument in favor of the novel's legitimacy. Wieland had earlier been a proponent of the sentimental epistolary novels of Samuel Richardson, texts which attempt to illustrate and impress on their readers a moral teaching through the sensual aesthetic form of a narrative. The German argument in favor of the sentimental novel as a legitimate form rested on the combination of moral efficacy and verisimilitude. Wieland's commitment to the project of moral sentimentalism is perhaps best illustrated by the fact that he had gone so far, in 1760, as to write a dramatized version of an episode from Richardson's third novel, *Sir Charles Grandison,* a drama called **Clementina von Poretta.** Subsequently, though, Wieland had taken to reading that other and very different giant of the eighteenth-century English novel, Henry Fielding, whose comic works *Joseph Andrews* and especially *Tom Jones,* both of which take *Don Quixote* as a reference point, play ironically with the conventions of the novel.[27] Fielding lightly ridicules the pretensions of novels to be "histories," emphasizing the ways in which the new form of the novel actually reinscribes the conventions of romance—improbable happy coincidences, symmetries, and artistic satisfactions—that create a consciously artificial, rather than verisimilar, world.[28] Wieland's novel exposes the artificial novelistic quality not only of Don Sylvio's story, but also of that of his sister Hyacinthe, and here the connection to sentimentalism appears in the form of references to its characteristic genre, the novel of virtue in distress.

In Hyacinthe's story, which she recounts for the company, she was kidnapped at age three and raised by a gypsy woman to be a courtesan. When she has come of age and the gypsy sells her to a Marquis, she refuses to comply with the money-making scheme, defending her virtue against the Marquis. Eventually Don Eugenio, believing in her innocence and virtue, saves her from her predicament. This clear case of "virtue rewarded" functions as a kind of Richardson episode in the novel: the heroine defends her virtue and is rewarded with the heart of an honest, rich nobleman. But after she finishes telling her story, Don Sylvio's response is quite revealing:

> Indessen konnte er doch nicht umhin, seine Verwunderung darüber zu bezeugen, daß in einer Geschichte, die ihm außerordentlich genug schien, die Feen nicht das geringste zu tun gehabt haben sollten, und er fragte sie ganz ernsthaft; woher es komme, daß sie über diesen Punct ein so genaues Stillschweigen beobachtet habe, da es doch ganz und gar nicht begreiflich sei, daß die Feen und Zauberer an den Begebenheiten einer so vollkommenen jungen Dame keinen Anteil gehabt haben sollten?

> (*DS,* p. 263)

On the one hand, Don Sylvio's literal belief in fairies prevents him from seeing "reality" accurately, that is, seeing that all of the actors in Hyacinthe's drama were human beings. On the other hand, his question ironically exposes Hyacinthe's story as improbable and unbelievable. Wieland suggests here that any story so artificially constructed to illustrate "virtue rewarded," like those of Richardson, might as well include fairies and wizards. Precisely the kind of novel which prides itself on what Ian Watt calls "formal realism" and probability is exposed as unbelievable and *romanhaft*; in this sense, the pretensions of the sentimental novel to verisimilitude are satirized. But again, if we take the lesson of Don Sylvio's story seriously, we must concede that here

too Wieland's intention is not simply to expose the novelistic as fiction, but also to suggest the positive value, perhaps the indispensability, of such fictions. In the happy outcome of Hyacinthe's story, as in that of Don Sylvio, we sense an unabashed, if complicated, celebration of artificial happy endings. Such an argument moves Wieland's version of quixotism close to the Romantics' conception, but with the difference that Wieland does not suggest the superiority of the artistic realm over the real, but rather suggests that the two will never be strictly separable. As Wieland in the end presents the semi-cured Don Sylvio as a model reader, he is suggesting that we have access to the empirical realm through representations; that our cognitive faculties are informed by representations; and that we must necessarily interpret the empirical in their terms.

This conception of the relationship between artistic representations and cognition should have major implications for Wieland's ideas about subject-formation, particularly since he was working at the time on **Geschichte des Agathon,** which comes down to us as the first major Bildungsroman. Friedrich Sengle argues that Wieland, as he was writing **Agathon,** was undergoing a kind of slow conversion which paralleled Agathon's own movement away from his enthusiastic Platonism.[29] Wieland as a young man had been extremely sentimental, involved in a kind of mystical spiritualism (his "seraphic period"); **Agathon,** then, was begun in this spirit and the spirit of Richardson, but completed in the spirit of Fielding. Wieland's interruption of **Agathon** to write the quixotic **Don Sylvio** then could be understood in biographical terms as the process whereby this conversion takes place. Sengle refers to the change as a "disenchantment," parallel to Don Sylvio's own. This last point illustrates the loophole in the argument: Don Sylvio's disenchantment, as we have seen, is only relative and partial, and in the text as a whole Wieland suggests that the wondrous world of fiction maintains its central role in the development of the individual; it is and should be constitutive, rather than merely reflective. A more convincing argument is offered by Wilson, who suggests that since in **Don Sylvio** the marvelous is not simply reduced to the verisimilar, and hence the treatment of the *Schwärmer-Figur* is fundamentally ambiguous, the novel form has reached a very high level of self-questioning which must have a complicating impact on the Bildungsroman (pp. 129-45). And indeed, if the corroborating evidence of the novel's complicated references to the visual arts holds, then Wieland may be suggesting something further: an epistemological necessity for seeing the empirical world through fictions, artistic representations, conventions, and artifice.

As the materialist mentor Hippias charges the young Agathon with *Schwärmerei* in **Geschichte des Agathon,** and Agathon's *Bildung* consists in part, ostensibly, with the cure of that *Schwärmerei,* it seems reasonable to seek there the traces of the ideas Wieland has worked out in **Don Sylvio** during his hiatus from **Agathon.** Without exploring here the complexity of Agathon's *Schwärmerei* (or even quixotism), we can venture the general point that the Platonic idealism and belief in virtue with which this character begins are never entirely defeated by Hippias's materialist corrective.[30] If the Bildungsroman as a form imagines building individuals for self-determination, then on the one hand Wieland's engagement with quixotism points out that it is necessary to provide some corrective to the quixotic generalization of individual experience. In modifying the satirical negation of the quixotic figure in **Don Sylvio,** though, Wieland suggests that the principle of intersubjective agreement would be a better corrective than a simplistic reference to what Hippias calls "die wahre Beschaffenheit der Dinge" (**Agathon** [in **Werke**], p. 424). This principle would acknowledge a wide compass for the role of artworks in the constitution of the individual, and consequently in the intersubjective constitution of the world.

Notes

1. For instance, Foucault writes, "*Don Quixote* is the first modern work of literature . . . because in it language breaks off its old kinship with things, and enters into the lonely sovereignty from which it will reappear, in its separated state, only as literature." Michel Foucault, *The Order of Things* (New York: Vintage, 1973), pp. 48-49.

2. For the best overview of these developments with regard to the novel form, see Dieter Kimpel, *Der Roman der Aufklärung (1670-1774),* 2nd ed. (Stuttgart: Metzler, 1977). See also Wilhelm Vosskamp, *Romantheorie in Deutschland. Von Martin Opitz bis Friedrich von Blanckenburg* (Stuttgart: Metzler, 1973) and Klaus Scherpe, *Gattungspoetik im 18. Jahrhundert. Historische Entwicklung von Gottsched bis Herder* (Stuttgart: Metzler, 1968).

3. A recent exception to this rule is Jürgen Jacobs, *Don Quijote in der Aufklärung* (Bielefeld: Aisthesis, 1992). On the Romantics' celebration of Don Quixote's idealism, his role as a sort of "God's fool" for the modern age, see Jacobs pp. 71-74; Werner Brüggemann, *Cervantes und die Figur des Don Quijote in Kunstanschauung und Dichtung der deutschen Romantik* (Münster: Aschendorff, 1958); and Theo In der Smitten on Tieck's translation in *Don Quixote (der "richtige" under der "falsche") und sieben deutsche Leser* (Bern: Lang, 1986), pp. 91-98.

4. Most helpful for me have been Ellis Shookman, *Noble Lies, Slant Truths, Necessary Angels: Aspects of Fictionality in the Novels of Christoph Martin Wieland* (Chapel Hill: Univ. of North Caro-

lina Press, 1997), pp. 1-45, and W. Daniel Wilson, *The Narrative Strategy of Wieland's Don Sylvio von Rosalva* (Bern: Lang, 1981). See also John A. McCarthy, *Christoph Martin Wieland* (Boston: Twayne, 1979), pp. 58-68; Jacobs, *Don Quijote,* pp. 38-50; and Lieselotte Kurth, *Die zweite Wirklichkeit. Studien zum Roman des achtzehnten Jahrhunderts* (Chapel Hill: Univ. of North Carolina Press, 1969), pp. 141-57.

5. For recent views of the importance of quixotism in eighteenth-century England, for instance, see Wendy Motooka, *The Age of Reasons: Quixotism, Sentimentalism and Political Economy in Eighteenth-Century Britain* (London: Routledge, 1998), and Ronald Paulson, *Don Quixote in England: The Aesthetics of Laughter* (Baltimore and London: Johns Hopkins Univ. Press, 1998).

6. For the importance of *Don Sylvio* for *Agathon,* see Wilson, *Narrative Strategy,* pp. 121-45, who argues that Wieland interrupted the writing of *Agathon* in order to explore the whole problem of narrative illusion.

7. For an account of the different *levels* on which the text provides these two insights, that is, an account of the differing implicit readers, see Wilson, *Narrative Strategy.*

8. See especially Dieter Kimpel, *Der Roman der Aufklärung,* and Georg Jäger, *Empfindsamkeit und Roman. Wortgeschichte, Theorie und Kritik im 18. und frühen 19. Jahrhundert* (Stuttgart: Kohlhammer, 1969). Kurth aptly characterizes this aspect of the text as "eine Parodie der unpoetischen Forderungen der Wahrscheinlichkeits-Fanatiker der Zeit" (p. 156).

9. Shookman argues that Wieland attempts to justify the novel form by reflecting on its fictionality within the novel (p. 2).

10. Despite writers like Wieland, the eighteenth century generally understood *Don Quixote* strictly as a satire. See Jacobs, *Don Quijote,* and In der Smitten, *Don Quixote.*

11. Shookman's reference to the neo-Kantian Hans Vaihinger's ideas about the necessary heuristic use of fictive constructs is suggestive in this regard (p. 11).

12. I wish to claim that a general "discourse of quixotism" is as central to German literary debates in the eighteenth century as Motooka and Paulson have recently and newly demonstrated it to be in England.

13. My definition here differs from several others in that it prioritizes misreading over the naive belief in ideals and the reader's tragi-comic sympathy

(Jacobs), the idealistic madness and the form of the quest (Paulson), and "idiosyncratic reason" (Motooka).

14. The problem of eighteenth-century quixotism is intimately linked with the emerging hierarchy of literary genres under a market system; critiques of misreading appear inextricable from critiques of bad literature, beginning with the contested "rise" of the novel form. In the German-language context, many sociological-literary studies of the late 1960s and early 1970s documented and analyzed this problem for our historical understanding; my purpose is to illustrate how satirical literary works created images of these threatening new kinds of reading. See especially Helmuth Kiesel and Paul Münch, *Gesellschaft und Literatur im 18. Jahrhundert. Voraussetzungen und Entstehung des literarischen Markts in Deutschland* (München: Beck, 1977).

15. Wieland defines *Schwärmerei* in *Der Teutsche Merkur* in 1775 as "eine Erhitzung der Seele von Gegenständen die entweder gar nicht in der Natur sind, oder wenigstens das nicht sind, wofür die berauschte Seele sie ansieht" (quoted from Jäger, *Empfindsamkeit und Roman*, p. 56). Originating as a label for religious fanaticism, the term becomes secularized as designating the tendency to believe in illusions, appearing prominently as a target of critique for the Enlightenment. The illusions may proceed, as Adelung explains, either from sense impressions or from the imagination unaided (Johann Christoph Adelung, *Grammatisch-kritisches Wörterbuch der hochdeutschen Mundart*, 2d ed. [Leipzig: 1793-1801], III, 1716-17. Subsequent citations will appear parenthetically in the text.) For the particular relationship between *Schwärmerei* and sentimentalism, see Jäger, *Empfindsamkeit und Form*, Wolfgang Doktor, *Die Kritik der Empfindsamkeit* (Frankfurt am Main: Lang, 1975), and Nikolaus Wegmann, *Diskurse der Empfindsamkeit. Zur Geschichte eines Gefühls in der Literatur des 18. Jahrhunderts*, (Stuttgart: Metzler, 1988).

16. Christoph Martin Wieland, *Werke*, Bd. 1 (München: Hanser, 1964), p. 21. Further references, identified as *DS*, appear in the text. For an account of the semantic development of the term *Empfindsamkeit*, see Gerhard Sauder, *Empfindsamkeit*, vol. 1 (Stuttgart: Metzler, 1974). The term in this particular meaning appears to have been born in the process of Bode's translating Laurence Sterne's *A Sentimental Journey* in 1769, and was subsequently applied to the literary movement of sentimentalism.

17. See Adelung, *Grammatisch-kritisches Wörterbuch*, I, 1689, and *Historisches Wörterbuch der Philoso-*

phie, ed. Joachim Ritter (Basel/Stuttgart: Schwabe, 1972), II, 346-58.

18. See n. 8 above.

19. See Kurth, pp. 141-57; McCarthy, *Wieland*, p. 64; Wilson, *Narrative Strategy*, pp. 19-66; Shookman, *Noble Lies*, pp. 27-45; and Jacobs, *Don Quijote*, pp. 44-50.

20. Wieland's novel in this way demonstrates its indebtedness to the novels of Henry Fielding, texts which embody a critique of his antagonist Samuel Richardson's claims of verisimilitude. In my view, the most useful explication of this English debate (which had a great impact on the German debate) for an understanding of the emergence of the novel out of the romance has been provided by Michael McKeon, *The Origins of the English Novel, 1600-1740* (Baltimore: Johns Hopkins Univ. Press, 1987), pp. 1-22. Where the English usage of "romance" and "novel" overstates the discontinuity between the two forms, the German use of the term "Roman" for both perhaps overstates the continuity.

21. Wilson writes: "Thus Sylvio may be seen as the hero of a fairytale, not only in his own imagination, but also in the fictive world of the novel" (p. 34).

22. Throughout the eighteenth century a variety of debates arose around the mechanistic implications of the emerging empirical sciences and Enlightenment philosophies. For perhaps the most pertinent example in eighteenth-century Germany, see Frederick Beiser's account of the "Pantheism Controversy" in *The Fate of Reason: German Philosophy from Kant to Fichte* (Cambridge: Harvard Univ. Press, 1987), pp. 44-126.

23. Jacobs formulates Wieland's ambivalent position on *Schwärmerei* particularly well: "Hinsichtlich der Schwärmerei räumt Wieland ein, daß ihr eine subjektive Wahrheit zukommt: Niemand kann dem jungen Sylvio die Erscheinung der Fee Radiante wegdemonstrieren. Aber der Glaube an solche Dinge bleibt dem Einwand ausgesetzt, daß er sich mit der Erfahrung anderer Menschen nicht in Einklang bringen läßt" (p. 47).

24. Werner Busch, *Das sentimentalische Bild. Die Krise der Kunst im 18. Jahrhundert* (München: Beck, 1993), p. 381.

25. Johann Georg Sulzer, *Allgemeine Theorie der Schönen Künste* (Hildesheim, 1994; reprint of neue vermehrte zweyte Auflage, Leipzig 1793), III, 719.

26. Johann Kaspar Lavater, *Ausgewählte Schriften*, ed. Johann Kaspar Orelli (Zürich, 1842), III, 177.

27. Wilson has argued convincingly that Wieland's debt to Laurence Sterne is greater, although certainly Wieland's novels themselves bear a closer resemblance to Fielding's. Wilson writes: "The crucial point is that Wieland's authoritarian narrator turns out to be unreliable, a *parody* of this type, and the intended reader is supplied with an alternative to blind submission; thus Wieland both understands and attempts to overcome the crisis of the novel laid bare by Sterne" (p. 135).

28. See Ian Watt, *The Rise of the Novel* (Berkeley: Univ. of California Press, 1957), and McKeon, *Origins,* on the Richardson/Fielding split.

29. Friedrich Sengle, *Wieland* (Stuttgart: Metzler, 1949), pp. 179-86.

30. See the discussion of *Agathon* in Dorothea von Mücke's *Virtue and the Veil of Illusion: Generic Innovation and the Pedagogical Project in Eighteenth-Century Literature* (Stanford: Stanford Univ. Press, 1991), pp. 229-73, especially pp. 240-44 and pp. 258-71.

Florian Gelzer (essay date January 2004)

SOURCE: Gelzer, Florian. "'Nenne doch, o Muse, den Sitz der kleinen Kolonie': Wieland's Portrayals of Nature Utopias in Verse and Prose." *Neophilologus* 88, no. 1 (January 2004): 1-18.

[*In the following essay, Gelzer examines Wieland's attitudes toward the ideas of Jean-Jacques Rousseau, paying particular attention to Wieland's poem* Oberon.]

I.

In one of his very early poems, Novalis praises the beauty of the "Plauischer Grund," a well-known region in his native Thuringia:

> O! Tal, so paradiesisch schön,
> Dich hat Natur mit Zauberreiz geschmücket,
> Durch dich wird mancher Wanderer beglücket,
> Und mancher frohe Musensohn entzücket
> Auf deinen unbegrenzten Höhn.
>
> Romantischer war Tempe nicht
> Und nicht das Tal, das Hüon einst erquickte,
> Als ihn sein Unstern zu Alfonsen schickte
> Und Hunger ihn und durstge Liebe drückte
> Durchwebt mit sanftem Rosenlicht. [. . .][1]

Not only the famous Tempe valley (where, at the foot of Mount Olympos, Apollon is said to have chased the nymph Daphne) serves as a simile to the paradisiac qualities of the landscape, but foremost that valley "das Hüon einst erquickte." The source of the allusion can

easily be detected. Novalis refers to Christoph Martin Wieland's adaptation of the story of Huon de Bordeaux, a tale from the court of Charlemagne, in his epic *Oberon* (1780). The context is the following: Oberon, the king of fairies, is at odds with his wife Titania. The two witnessed how the vivacious Rosette cheated on her husband, the blind and impotent old man Gangolf, with Walter, a stableman.[2] Oberon took sides with Gangolf and gave him back his eyesight, whereas Titania defended Rosette's deed. This was the cause of their discord, and Oberon swore no sooner to reconcile himself with his wife, than another human couple had expiated Rosette's misconduct by the example of their perfect love and steadfast fidelity.[3] Huon de Bordeaux, a Christian knight of Charlemagne, and Rezia (who is later baptised Amanda), the daughter of a caliph, are selected for this difficult test of steadfastness. Oberon despatches them with a strict injunction to remain chaste and a warning not to anticipate the sanctioning of their union by the Pope in Rome. However, while they are on a lonely journey across the sea, the lovers find the command impossible to keep. Immediately after they have given in to their passion, a storm arises, and the two lovers throw themselves into the waves. (In the bowdlerised "Schulausgaben" from the last century, this scene—as well as the whole story of Gangolf and Rosette—is taken out entirely!)[4] They strand on a deserted island, where, after initial privations, they live together with and are educated by an old and pious hermit, Alfonso. After the latter's death, Huon and Rezia, having internalised the hermit's counsels and his religiousness, are able to overcome the strongest temptations and trials.

It is this island episode, narrated in Cantos Seven and Eight of *Oberon,* which Novalis referred to as the embodiment of a paradisiac idyll. The epic reappears in other poems of the young Hardenberg, too, foremost in scenes of idyllic sentimental landscapes or occasions of conviviality. In the sonnet "Das süsseste Leben" (about 1789), for instance, the lines of the sestet run as following:

> [. . .] Süßer aber schleicht sie [die Liebe] sich davon,
> Wenn ich unter traurenden [!] Ruinen
> Efeugleich geschmiegt an Karolinen,
>
> Wehmutlächelnd les im *Oberon*
> Oder bei der milchgefüllten Schale
> Bürgers Lieder sing im engen Tale.[5]

Novalis' sentimental-anacreontic approbation of Wieland's epic stands in sharp contrast to another reference to *Oberon,* found in Heinrich Heine's fragmentary *Memoiren* (1853/54). Huon's heroic deeds—Charlemagne orders him to travel to Bagdad, behead the courtier sitting next to the caliph, kiss the princess as his bride, and demand from the caliph four molars and a handful of hair from his beard—,[6] are associated by

Heine with his own great-uncle ("halb Schwärmer, [. . .] halb Glücksritter"):

> Sein [des "Großoheims"] Charlatanismus, den wir nicht in Abrede stellen, war nicht von gemeiner Sorte—er war kein gewöhnlicher Charlatan, der den Bauern auf den Märkten die Zähne ausreißt, sondern er drang muthig in die Paläste der Großen, denen er den stärksten Backzahn ausriß, wie weiland Ritter Hüon von Bordeaux dem Sultan von Babylon that. Und welcher bedeutende Mensch ist nicht ein bischen Charlatan?[7]

Whereas Novalis associated *Oberon* with idyllic landscapes and anacreontic conviviality, Heine underlines the protagonist's smart "Charlatanerie," his likeable shrewdness. Novalis' and Heine's intertextual references are not only typical examples of the epic's literary impact, but also representative of the two main scholarly approaches to the epic. From the late 19th century on, positivistic studies have scrutinised the author's method of using and weaving together diverse motifs, especially his transformation of the norms of the classic chivalric epic. For instance, how the proud swashbuckling knight Huon from the *chanson de geste* turns into a likeable and clumsy, even somewhat foolish hero (whose "Charlatanerie" Heine had already alluded to).[8] On the other hand, numerous studies have been concerned with Wieland's idiosyncratic 'art of depiction', his fusion of medieval tales with the fabulous sphere of fairies and spirits, and with the epic's predominantly ironic undertone.[9] According to these studies, *Oberon* can be understood not only as a pivotal work of German Enlightenment and Classicism; it is also said to anticipate important features of Romanticism (as it had already served as a source of romantic motives for Novalis).

The scholarly work to *Oberon* as a whole—which is far from sparse—shows one peculiar characteristic: The epic has been unanimously praised as a masterly and formally perfect *tour de force*. Wieland's parodying method of depiction, however, has led to a considerable preponderance of studies of *formal* aspects. It seems that scholars tend to take the—seemingly whimsical—content of this epic not too seriously.[10] (It is telling that no less than six of the relevant articles to the subject are rather humorous contributions to *Festschriften*.) This becomes apparent even in the most important and comprehensive analyses: those of Friedrich Sengle, Fritz Martini and Wolfgang Preisendanz. Sengle talks of an "Ausgleich von Ironie und Ernst, von Leichtigkeit und Gewicht, von Märchenhaftigkeit und Menschlichkeit."[11] *Oberon* is said to contain all typical features of a product of "Spätheit," namely irony and parody (Hans Mayer). The epic thus appears as an impeccable, but rather harmless product of Wieland's 'art of depiction'. Fritz Martini summarises the general opinion as follows:

> Der Zauber dieses Epos in zwölf Gesängen liegt weniger in seinem ideellen und menschlichen [!] Gehalt als in der Souveränität des bewußten Formens, in der dichterischen Kunstleistung Wielands und nur dort, wo ein gewecktes, hellhöriges Formgefühl die Fähigkeit der reinen Aufnahme, zunächst unabhängig von allen stofflichen Reizen, schenkt, findet der '**Oberon**' das rechte Verstehen.[12]

It is exactly the "ideelle[r] Gehalt" of *Oberon* which will be examined here. There is a philosophical conception of society which underlies the burlesque and fairytale character of *Oberon* (and other verse-tales, too)[13] whose foundations—this is my main argument—can be found in Wieland's prose works of the 1770s. The concept of a 'Naturutopie' is interwoven with the plot of Huon de Bordeaux, which is related to Wieland's discussion of the writings of Jean-Jacques Rousseau.[14] It is epitomised in the island episode mentioned above, but it also influences the character of the epic as a whole. Yet how is it to be explained that Wieland, the antagonist of Rousseau, puts a scene of Rousseauian innocence in the centre of his epic?

II.

Huon's and Rezia's willingness to sacrifice themselves when their ship founders (Johann Heinrich Fuseli illustrated the scene impressively), their salvation on a deserted island, the depiction of the valley "das Hüon einst erquickte, / Als ihn sein Unstern zu Alfonsen schickte," the encounter between the castaways and the hermit—all these are classic motifs of the 'Robinsonade'.[15] Especially in the German examples of this genre inaugurated by Defoe's novel, the sojourn on a lonely island with an old hermit is *the* central element of the plot. There is no doubt that the island episode in *Oberon* has been heavily influenced by this tradition. The figure of Alfonso in particular bears some remarkable parallels with Don Cyrillo de Valaro, the first inhabitant of Felsenburg Island in Johann Gottfried Schnabel's tetralogy *Wunderliche Fata einiger Seefahrer* (1731-43).[16] Like Don Cyrillo, Alfonso is a former Spanish knight, "zum Fürstendienst erzogen," who had been "dem Blendwerk nachgerannt" (had been a gold prospector). And like the hermit in Schnabel's novel, after having been shipwrecked, he withdrew from the world in search of true contentment in a simple life in harmony with nature.[17] There are further elements which can be paralleled with the *Insel Felsenburg*: the shipwreck scene, the discovery of the idyllic valley,[18] Rezia-Amandas delivery of her child, Huonnet, as well as details such as Alfonso's features.[19]

Within the plot of *Oberon,* the castaway scene serves as a decisive changing point. Huon's sojourn on the island does not represent Baroque 'Weltflucht' (as in the *Continuatio* of Grimmelshausen's *Simplicissimus,* for instance), but the process of the hero's purification and repentance. To use the classic distinction suggested by Fritz Brüggemann: Alfonso's island is an 'asylum', not an'exile'.[20] Wieland stages the life of a small family living close to nature, a positive contrast to the over-refinements of civilisation and the flawed social'realities'. More than a merely incidental episode, the island scene can thus be read as the depiction of an ideal state of nature: an utopia. Alfonso's perfect moral values, which he gained after years full of privation, have become the basis of his critical views on the hollowness and corruption of the life'outside'[21] (Rousseau's famous image of man bound in the chains of civilisation—"L'homme est né libre, et partout il est dans les fers"—is clearly evoked):[22]

> Und als er [Alfonso] dergestalt des Lebens beste Zeit
> Im Rausch des Selbstbetrugs an Könige verpfändet,
> Und Gut und Blut, mit feur'ger Willigkeit
> Und unerkannter Treu', in ihrem Dienst verschwendet,
> Sah er ganz unverhofft, im schönsten Morgenroth
> Der Gunst, durch schnellen Fall sich frey von seinen
>   Ketten;
> Noch glücklich, aus der Schiffbruchsnoth
> Das Leben wenigstens auf einem Bret zu retten.[23]

Alfonso's isolated idyll is far from unique in Wieland's works. A whole number of his tales and novels which were completed during his time in Erfurt (1769-1772) comprise similar accounts of bucolic utopias. In the philosophical tale **"Koxkox and Kikequetzel"** (1769/70), for instance, the story of an idyllic love and family life develops on a deserted island.[24] The novel *Der goldne Spiegel, oder die Könige von Scheschian* (1772/1794)[25] contains even two interpolated bucolic "Naturutopien": the community of the "Children of Nature" and the account of the Colony of Dschengis. In the *Geschichte des Philosophen Danischmende* (1774/75),[26] an egalitarian utopian state is portrayed. Finally, in *Die Republik des Diogenes* (1769),[27] the necessary prerequisites of (the literary representation of) an utopian state are reflected on. What function do these isolated natural idylls have within the context of the respective works?[28]

"Koxkox und Kikequetzel" opens a collection of (originally six) tales and essays, the *Beiträge zur geheimen Geschichte der Menschheit* (1770). With these *Beiträge* Wieland responded overtly, but rather late, to the theses of Jean-Jacques Rousseau, especially to the *Discours* on the Sciences and Arts (1750) and on the Origin of Inegality (1755)[29]—both being essays on subjects proposed by the Academy of Dijon.[30] As it is generally known, Wieland contradicts the main thesis "unser[es] Freund[es] *Jean-Jacque*" formulated in the discourse on inegality, which is concerned with the relationship between *état naturel* and civic state: Rousseau's (Epicurean) perception of man as originally being a solitary and unsociable creature is contrasted with Wieland's own (Stoic) evolutionary concept.[31] Whereas Rousseau portrays the dissatisfaction and perpetual agitation of modern social man, who is condemned to servitude to preserve the institution of private property,

Wieland assumes that mankind is sociable by nature. In his essay **"Über das Verhältniss des Angenehmen und Schönen zum Nützlichen"** (1775), an important supplement to the argumentation of the *Beiträge,* he defines the characteristics of the "thierische Mensch" as well as of the innate "Trieb zur Schönheit," thereby emphasising the'naturalness'of beauty:

> Schönheit und Grazie sind zwar durch die Natur selbst mit dem Nützlichen *verwandt:* aber sie sind nicht darum begehrenswürdig weil sie nützlich sind, sondern weil es der Natur des Menschen gemäss ist, in ihrem Anschauen ein reines Vergnügen zu geniessen: ein Vergnügen das mit demjenigen, so uns das *Anschauen der Tugend* macht, völlig gleichartig, und eben so sehr ein *Bedürfnis vernünftiger Wesen* ist, als Nahrung, Kleidung und Wohnung Bedürfnisse des thierischen Menschen sind.
>
> Ich sage *des thierischen Menschen,* weil er sie mit allen andern oder doch mit den meisten *Thieren gemein* hat. Aber weder diese thierischen Bedürfnisse, noch die Fähigkeit und Bestrebung sie zu befriedigen, machen ihn zum *Menschen.* Indem er für sein Futter sorgt, sich ein Nest baut, sich zu einem Weibchen hält, seine Jungen ätzt, und sich mit einem andern herumbeisst der ihm sein Futter nehmen, oder sich in den Besitz seines Nestes setzen will,—in allen diesem handelt er, was das *Materielle* betrifft, als ein *Thier.* Bloss durch die *Art* und Weise, *wie* der Mensch—wofern er nicht durch zwingende äussre Ursachen zu einem viehischen Stande gebracht und darin erhalten wird—alle diese thierischen Dinge thut, unterscheidet und erhebt er sich über alle übrige Thierarten, und zeigt seine *Menschheit.*[32]

The "Fantom" of the unsociable, brutish *homme naturel* is thus rejected as a mental construct. Rousseau, Wieland writes in another *Beitrag,* should accept the simple fact that "die Menschen aller Wahrscheinlichkeit nach *von Anfang an in Gesellschaft lebten*—und von allen Seiten mit *natürlichen* Mitteln umgeben sind, die ihnen die Entwicklung ihrer Anlagen *erleichtern* helfen."[33] If we accept this original sociable drive of mankind, it is also legitimate to imagine the "ersten Menschen als in eine Familie vereinigt":

> Ist aber der Trieb der Geselligkeit dem Menschen so natürlich: so haben diejenigen, welche sich die *ersten Menschen* in eine *Familie vereinigt* vorstellen, den Vorwurf nicht verdient, Begriffe aus der *bürgerlichen* Gesellschaft in den Stand der Natur hinein getragen zu haben: so lösen sich alle die Schwierigkeiten von selbst auf, welche Rousseau in dem Übergang aus dem Stande der Natur in den gesellschaftlichen findet; so war es kein *Übergang* in einen *entgegengesetzten,* sondern ein bloßer *Fortgang* in dem *nehmlichen Stande* [. . .] .[34]

This general view—mankind is sociable by nature, and the development of civilisation is essential to its perfectibility—is held by Wieland in all his writings from the 1770s. It is depicted with biting irony in *Die Grazien* (1770), a prose narrative interspersed with verse. The beginning of the tale repeats the caricature of Rousseau's portrayal of man's natural state:

> Die Menschen, womit *Deukalion* und *Pyrrha* das alte *Gräcien* bevölkerten, waren anfänglich ein sehr rohes Völkchen; so, wie man es von Leuten erwarten mag, die aus Steinen Menschen geworden waren.
>
> > Sie irren, mit Fellen bedeckt, in dunkeln Eichenhainen,
> > Der Mann mit der Keule bewehrt, das Weib mit ihren Kleinen
> > Nach Affenweise behangen; und sank die Sonne, so blieb
> > Ein jedes liegen, wohin der Zufall es trieb. [. . .]
>
> Ich weiß nicht, *Danae,* wie geneigt Sie sich fühlen, es dem Verfasser der *Neuen Heloise* zu glauben, dass dieses der selige Stand sey, den uns die Natur zugedacht habe. Aber, wenn wir alle die Übel zusammen rechnen, wovon diese Kinder der rohen Natur keinen Begriff hatten, so ist es unmöglich, ihnen wenigstens eine Art von negativer Glückseligkeit abzusprechen.[35]

Only by the help of the Graces—that is, the Sciences and Arts—, mankind can be led into Rousseau's *juste milieu:*[36]

> Wer sollte denken, daß jene *Autochthonen,* (erschrecken Sie nicht vor dem gefährlichen Worte!) jene rohen *Kinder der Mutter Erde,* die wir, mit zottigen Fellen bedeckt, unter Eichen und Nußbäumen herum liegen sahen,—Geschöpfe, die in diesem Zustande den grossen Affen in Ostindien und Afrika nicht so gar ungleich sehen mochten,—und diese glücklichen Kinder des goldnen Alters, eben dieselben seyn sollten?
>
> Aber wie hätten sie auch etwas besseres sein können, eh sich die Grazien mit den Musen vereinten, um Geschöpfe, welche die Natur nur angefangen hatte, zu Menschen auszubilden; sie die Künste zu lehren, die das Leben *erleichtern, verschönern, veredeln,* ihren *Witz* zugleich mit ihrem *Gefühl* zu verfeinern, und tausend *neue Sinne* dem edlern Vergnügen in ihrem Busen zu eröffnen?[37]

It is this'middle state'in the development of mankind, which is equated with the harmonious state of nature in Wieland's later works. In his judgement about the relationship between natural state and civic state, however, he seems to vacillate between a rather optimistic estimation and the opposite, pessimistic opinion of Rousseau.[38] According to Wieland, man's rational forces, which enforce the development of culture, may also cause the development of egotistical drives—inertia, for instance—, which impede the realisation of harmonious circumstances. He thus does not disavow Rousseau's criticism of the depravation of civilisation, but solely contradicts his hypothesis of the origin of mankind.

III.

"Koxkox und Kikequetzel" can be read as a literary illustration of Wieland's *optimistic* position. In South America, the tail of a comet had come too near to the earth, so that large parts of Mexico have been flooded. The victims of this cataclysm "hatte[n] sich noch in den ersten Anfangsgründen des geselligen Standes befunden. Zufrieden mit den freywilligen Geschenken der Natur hatten sie noch wenig Gelegenheit gehabt, ihre Fähigkeiten zur *Kunst* zu entwickeln."[39] Koxkox and Kikequetzel, two survivors of the catastrophe, are the living proof that'Naturmenschen'can have "zärtliche Empfindungen," too. In contrast to their civilised counterparts, human and'brutish'love, that is, sympathy and sexual drives, have not yet drifted apart. The charming *conte philosophique* contains a revealing thought: For humans used to the amenities of social life, the involuntary isolation and the loneliness of the two castaways ("die gänzlich[e] Beraubung aller menschlichen Gesellschaft") must appear as a "unerträgliches Übel." Only "der Dichter, der Platonist, der schwärmerische Liebhaber [. . .] , kurz die *Penserosi* aller Gattungen [. . .] würden sichs, wenigstens eine Zeit lang, auf einer einsamen Insel gefallen lassen können."[40] Thus the portrayal of an ideal state of nature might well be suitable to provide evidence against the defectiveness of the cultural state, yet it contains a dangerous aspect, too: Both the literary characters and the reading public might misunderstand the utopias as an invitation to escapism and enthusiasm.

As I mentioned above, ***Der goldne Spiegel*** contains two utopias of a natural state. One tells the story of Prince Tifan, the last surviving legal heir to the throne of the kingdom Scheschian. Prince Tifan had been saved by his mentor Dschengis from the henchmen of the tyrannical sultan Isfandiar. In a remote valley—"von der Natur selbst zu einer Freystätte bestimmt für den Tugendhaften, der sein Glück in sich selbst findet"[41]—, Dschengis had founded a cultivating ground ("Pflanzstätte") of simple people living in egalitarian equality and in harmony with nature:

> Die Natur belohnte seinen [Dschengis'] Fleiss mit dem glücklichsten Erfolge. In wenigen Jahren verwandelte sich der grösste Theil dieser angenehmen Wildniss in Kornfelder, Gärten und Auen [. . .] . Die frohen Bewohner lebten im *Überflusse des Nothwendigen,* und in dieser glücklichen Armuth an entbehrlichen Dingen, welche für den Weisen oder für den Unwissenden Reichthum ist. [. . .]
>
> Alle Ungleichheit, welche nicht von der Natur selbst herrührt, war aus den Hütten dieser Glückseligen verbannt.[42]

In another part of the novel, the story of a wealthy and lecherous emir is told. Having escaped from an assault in the mountains, he is welcomed by the community of the "Kinder der Natur," in an area completely unknown to him. They are a crowd of herdsmen and farmers, who live in strict isolation and in idyllic harmony with nature, without the need of a "höheren Grades der Verfeinerung." Psammis, a sage, had given them a set of simple statutes[43] which prescribe "*Arbeit, Vergnügen und Ruhe, jedes in kleinem Masse, zu gleichen Theilen vermischet, und nach dem Winke der Natur abgewech-selt.*"[44] And again, these children of nature have settled in a lovely valley. There, the emir encounters the head of the community—an old sage.[45] The two utopias (and the whole story of the kingdom of Scheschian) are narrated by the court philosopher Doctor Danischmend, in order to entertain and educate Shah Gebal, a spoiled Indian sultan who leaves the governing of his country to the women around him. However, the didactic intent of the utopias—Shah Gebal should gain insight into his poor governance—has very little effect. The sultan is both the embodiment of *acedia* (which, as we have seen, hinders cultural development) and an astute critic of utopias. Whenever he is encouraged to alter his rule, he threatens to impose sanctions. The novel concludes in a pessimistic mode: The irksome moral philosopher Danischmend is put into jail.

In *Die Geschichte des Philosophen Danischmend,* the sequel to *Der goldne Spiegel,* the eponymous hero retires from public life after having left Shah Gebal's court. Together with a handful of kindred spirits, he moves into an inaccessible valley in the Himalayas, where they hope to lead a simple life in close touch with nature, without all the trappings of society.

> Unterdessen hatte Danischmend [. . .] in den Gebirgen, welche Kischmir von Tibet absondern, sich einen Wohnplatz ersehen, wo er, fern von Sultanen und Fakirn, nach seinem Geschmack und nach seinem Herzen glücklich zu leben hoffte. Es war ein langes, zwischen fruchtbaren Hügeln und waldigen Bergen sich hinziehendes Thal, *Jemal* genannt, von tausend Bächen und Quellen aus dem Gebirge bewässert, und von den glücklichsten Menschen bewohnt, die vielleicht damahls auf dem ganzen Erdboden anzutreffen waren.[46]

Danischmends starts a family and lives, for the time being, in a "Zustan[d] [. . .] , den er *häusliche Glückseligkeit* nannte."[47]

Starting with the *Beiträge,* Wieland's essays written in the 1770s can be regarded as a comprehensive and detailed response to Rousseau's perception of man's social and political environment. In the fictitious realm of the Erfurt novels, Wieland then goes through various possibilities of the literary representation of utopias, which mirror his ambivalent attitude towards the views of the "Citoyen de Genève." According to Wieland, it is only in society, by living together with his equals, that the individual can reach true contentment and balance. In sharp contrast to what Rousseau's early theories suggest, this goal can be reached with the help of social and aesthetical cultural achievements only. Despite all polemic against Rousseau, this model of the harmonious individual—who integrates sensuality and spirit, aesthetics and ethics—is nevertheless based to a large part precisely on his, Rousseau's, presentations of the problem: All the Erfurt prose works present idylls of domestic bliss, of small communities living in harmonious balance, whose portrayals have clearly been influenced by Rousseau. Moreover, the "Naturutopien" in Wieland's novels have a decidedly satirical character: The moral perfection of the utopias is contrasted with the depravity of 'reality'.

With the exception of **"Koxkox and Kikequetzel,"** Wieland does not, however, depict *primitive* original states. The utopias incorporated in his novels are, on the contrary, the result of cultural developments, which great pain has been expended over. In addition, their status is also described as a very difficult and unstable one. The "Naturutopien" in *Der goldne Spiegel* and its sequel serve as examples of an ideal; at the same time, their instability—or rather the impossibility of their realisation—is underlined in many ways. First, critical commentaries and satirical reflections constantly interrupt and undermine the illusionary power of the tales. A critical apparatus of fictitious translators and commentators thwarts the main narrative. Secondly, the fragility of the utopian undertakings is shown in the narratives themselves. Already in **"Koxkox und Kikequetzel,"** the initial feelings of innocence and harmony become degenerate, as soon as other people join the original family. In *Danischmend* as well, the idyll does not remain untouched for a long time: Due to the discord and devastating luxury of the inhabitants, Danischmend has to leave the valley, only to return—an ironical final twist!—as a delegate of Shah Gebal.

The depictions of isolated utopia scenes in Wieland's prose and verse productions thus contain a double argumentative structure. On the one hand—in the classic manner of utopian literature—, they visualise the lost innocence of the natural state of man. Here, in the "Naturkinderutopie" of *Der goldne Spiegel* for instance, Wieland comes surprisingly close to the positions of Rousseau. On the other hand, the natural state must *not* serve as an absolute ideal. Rather it has to be seen in critical perspective, in order to underline the necessity of cultural development. This is achieved by the inclusion of different opinions and critical views ("cum notis variorum").[48] According to these commentaries, rural idyllic life in happiness and harmony without restricting legislation is possible *only* in small populations and *only* in exceptional cases. It is more likely that a ruler—Tifan, for instance—can be made sagacious and laws can be made wise than that a nation could evolve and persevere in a state of nature. Confronted with 'intruders' from outside, the instability of such "Naturutopien" is clearly brought to light. It is no coincidence that Prince Tifan's ideal state in *Der goldne Spiegel* ends in decay, and that the wise philosopher Danischmend is sent away from the court because of his unpleasant warnings.

Wieland's ambivalent opinions concerning the natural state of man and its portrayal are epitomised in *Die Re-*

publik des Diogenes (1770). In this novel, the (utopian) narrative has been replaced by ironical reflections on the possibilities and structures of utopian thinking, and on the construction of utopias in general. Once more, "Hans Jakob Rousseau von Genf" is explicitly mentioned.[49] This time, the utopian island-colony, presented by the philosopher Diogenes, does not refer to a cultural state of mankind any more, but to an original state of nature—which, however, can be realised by magic only:

> Ich [Diogenes] will mir einbilden, ich wär' ein *weiser Zauberer,* der mit Hülfe einer *magischen Ruthe* alle seine Ideen realisieren könnte; und hätt' eine noch *unbewohnte Insel* vor mir liegen, welche gross und fruchtbar genug wäre, einige hundert tausend Männer, mit den dazu gehörigen Weibern und Kindern, auf jeden Mann höchstens zwey Weiber und sechs Kinder gerechnet, hinlänglich zu ernähren.
>
> Ich setze ferner voraus, dass diese Insel—Ja, das ist eben die Frage, *was* ich voraussetzen soll?—Ob, zum Exempel, meine künftigen Unterthanen noch *ungezeugt* und *ungeboren,*—oder zwar erwachsen aber noch *wild,*—oder ob sie wirklich schon so *policiert,* so *geschickt,* so *wohl erzogen* und *fromm* seyn sollen, als wir *Griechen* sind?
>
> Die Sache verdient Überlegung.[50]

In order to protect the islanders from negative influences from outside, Diogenes, again by a wave of his magic wand, causes the island republic to disappear: "Alle Mühe, die sich eure Seefahrer jemahls um ihre Entdeckung geben möchten, würde verloren seyn; sie würden sie in Ewigkeit nicht finden!"[51] Wieland's most ambitious 'Naturkinder-Projekt' thus turns out to be an utopia in the literal sense of the word: an unattainable and unrealistic ideal.

IV.

Back to *Oberon.* The episode of Huon's and Rezia's sojourn on Alfonso's island apparently has a lot in common with the bucolic idylls in Wieland's earlier writings. Like in **"Koxkox und Kikequetzel,"** the idyll is placed on an isolated island; as in Dschengis' colony in *Der goldne Spiegel,* the pair learns to know privation, and the healing impact of hard physical labour;[52] Alfonso's philosophy is largely identical with the one the sage Psammis had left to the colony of the Children of Nature.[53] And, like in that "Naturkinderutopie," it is the piety and wisdom of a venerable old man (of eighty years, too) who refines the characters of the two castaways. Moreover, the valley where Alfonso lives has striking resemblances to the one of the little colony of the philosopher Danischmend. Furthermore, the island episode has a function similar to the 'Naturutopien' in *Der goldne Spiegel.* Also in *Oberon,* the picture of an egalitarian isolated community living according to the laws of nature serves as a counterpart to the portrayal

of 'feudal' power, which is illustrated by the example of Charlemagne himself and of Sultan Almansor (and his wife Almansaris). Both are rulers whose actions and decisions are—similar to those of Shah Gebal in *Der goldne Spiegel*—determined by moods and arbitrariness, by irrational passions.[54] Alfonso's biography, and the island episode as a whole, add emphasis to the criticism of the feudal ruling system.

In contrast to the utopias in Wieland's *novels* however, the island scene in the *verse epic* entirely lacks any qualifying detachment. The ironic narrative mode and the unobtrusive comical tone, which are predominant before and after the episode, are entirely gone. The plea for marriage and family, the education according to the ideals of responsibility and fidelity, the goal of the balance between sensual and spiritual love—[55] all these values imparted on the protagonists are presented in a distinctively serious and grave tone, without being peppered by controversial opinions. The same counts for the descriptions of the heroes' everyday life:

> Indessen Hüon sich im Wald ermüdet, pflegt
> Der edle Greis, der mit noch festem Tritte
> Die schwere Last von achtzig Jahren trägt,
> Der Ruhe nicht; nur daß er von der Hütte
> Sich selten weit entfernt. Kein heitrer Tag entflieht,
> Der nicht in seinem lieben Garten
> Ihn dieß und das zu thun beschäftigt sieht.
> Amandens Sorge ist des kleinen Herds zu warten.[56]

The Alfonso episode thus underlines once more, plainly and unambiguously, the central message of the utopias in the earlier narratives. Only in a small circle—within the family—, "Unabhängigkeit, Zufriedenheit mit sich selbst, und reine[r] Lebensgenuß"[57] can be reached. And typically enough, like in *Danischmend,* the "Sultan- und Bonzenschaft" (Almansor) is set against this uncorrupted ideal.

Does this not contradict what has just been said above: that the sentimental idylls in valleys and on islands are usually put into perspective by disillusioning remarks, and that the reader is cautioned to accept other divergent opinions which question the incorporated narratives? Could it be that the island episode does not display an utopian tale at all, but (as some scholars have argued) a discreet resurrection of Wieland's former mysticism and Platonism?[58] Or even a prelude of romantic "Naturfrömmigkeit" *avant la lettre?*[59] True, the hermit's religiousness does not have much to do with Christianity, but rather resembles a mystic-platonic, or Spinozistic, "Schau des Göttlichen im Irdischen":

> [. . .] sein [Alfonsos] Geist, im reinen Lichte
> Der unsichtbaren Welt, sieht himmlische Gesichte.
> . . . .
> So fliesst unmercklich Erd' und Himmel
> In seinem Geist in Eins. Sein Innerstes erwacht.
> In dieser tiefen Ferne vom Getümmel

Der Leidenschaft, in dieser heil'gen Nacht
Die ihn umschliesst, erwacht der reinste aller Sinne—
Doch—wer versiegelt mir mit unsichtbarer Hand
Den kühnen Mund, dass nichts unnennbars ihm en-
trinne?
Verstummend bleib' ich stehn an dieses Abgrunds
Rande.[60]

The decisive difference between the island episode in *Oberon* and comparable scenes in earlier narratives—and the answer to the above questions—lies in Wieland's concept of genre, rather than the variations of the respective scenes. In Wieland's Erfurt production, the decision between verse or prose stands for a choice between two fundamentally different modes of depiction:[61] In the "Laboratoriumswirklichkeit" (Jan-Dirk Müller) of the Erfurt prose works, human actions and psychological processes are presented without any allusions to the supernatural and miraculous. An abstract form of representation predominates, and controversial voices are worked in, in order to avoid simple moralising and as a disillusionment of escapist reactions to the narrative. In the verse productions, on the other hand, the inclusion of the miraculous world of fairies and spirits removes the action from the world of experience right from the start. (Interestingly enough, Wieland had named no other than the horn and the cup of Oberon as prominent examples of the silly belief in supernatural things in his essay **"Über den Hang der Menschen an Magie und Geistererscheinungen zu glauben"**!)[62] A certain'alienation effect'is thus inherent in his concept of the verse-tale, and the inclusion of dissenting voices is superfluous, for the artificialness and the model character of the narrated world are part of the conventions of the genre. In this context, the sentimental utopia of *Der goldne Spiegel* reappears in *Oberon* (some of the maxims of Psammis included); this time it is told, however, in the form of an island episode, the classical module of a story of shipwreck and probation.

From this point of view, *Oberon* appears as a late response to the problem case Wieland had intensively discussed before: Against Rousseau, he had emphasised man's inherent sociability, his striving for harmony, his urge for creativity and improvement, and had illustrated this view in various poetic forms. For this purpose, he had used the model of the utopian'valley idyll', which largely corresponds to Rousseau's *juste milieu*, the hypothetical'middle state'in the development of mankind, to illustrate is ideal. This theoretical background has faded, however, and the island episode has been read by contemporary writers as well as by scholars merely as a conventional *locus amoenus*. The meaningful utopian realm of Alfonso has turned into a lovely "Tal, das Hüon einst erquickte," and the epic as a whole into a harmless and whimsical fairy-tale.

The thesis that Wieland's portrayals of nature utopias are based on his reception of Rousseau as well as strongly influenced by conventions of genre, shall be substantiated by another example. It has often been claimed, in the wake of Friedrich Sengle's verdict, that Wieland's epic *Klelia and Sinibald* (1782/83),[63] which was written three years after *Oberon,* marked a decisive conceptual and stylistic turning point in his verse production: the dismissal of a miraculous mode of depiction (as in *Oberon*) in favour of a greater amount of realism. And indeed, Wieland draws a clear dividing line between the two epics in the latter's very first lines:

Für dieses Mahl—doch ohne Präjudiz—
Soll keine Muse sich mit unserm Spiel bemühen,
Kein Hippogryf, behender als der Blitz,
Mit uns davon ins Land der Elfen fliehen:
Der Dichter mag mit seinem Bischen Witz
So gut er selber kann sich aus der Sache ziehen!
. . . .
Hier ist demnach von *Feen* und von *Zwergen,*
Von *Lilienstab* und *Horn* und *Becher* keine Spur[.][64]

This renunciation of the earlier epic, and of the miraculous in general, is, however, constantly undermined in the course of the epic.[65] Whereas the narrator claims in the opening lines to have written the poem without the support of a Muse, later on, he concedes that he might actually have been helped by a friendly genius. Moreover, the turns of fortune the heroes go through are attributed to supernatural powers: The story turns out to be motivated by the conflicting forces of St. Catherine and the evil spirit Asmodeus, respectively. All in all, *Klelia and Sinibald* appears to be anything but a refutation of *Oberon,* but rather a variation of the same motifs. This counts especially for the second half of the epic (the intricate plot of which cannot be retold here), which tells the love-story between Rosine and Sinibald, the separation of the lovers (shipwreck!) and their final reunion in slavery. The similarities between the two epics become so obvious, that the later has to be regarded as a conscious rewriting of the earlier one.

Moreover, Wieland-scholarship has failed to notice that *Klelia and Sinibald* contains . . . a nature utopia, too. It is displayed in the last Canto, and, as in *Oberon,* it is more earnest in its tone than the rest of the epic. There is one main difference however: Whereas the island idyll in *Oberon* depicts a transitory state—'asylum'—, *Klelia and Sinibald* provides an example of another classic module: the island idyll as'exile'. As far as the concept and the function of the nature utopia are concerned, *Oberon* follows the tradition of the'Robinsonade', *Klelia and Sinibald* the conventions of the'Felsenburgiade'. The protagonists—two pairs of lovers (Rosine and Sinibald, Klelia and Guido) as well as their maids (Klara and Laurette)—are, after a shipwreck, cast ashore on a lonesome island. It turns out to be inhabited solely by a hermit, the preacher Paul, and his nephew. After a fourfold marriage (not only the two pairs are married, but also the two maids to the islanders), the castaways decide to start a colony on the island:

Die Gäste haben zwar
Ihr reich beladnes Schiff verlohren:
Allein was giebt der Mensch nicht gern für Haut und
  Haar?
Aus solcher Noth so wunderbar
Erhalten, sehen sie sich nun wie neu geboren,
Und, gleich dem ersten Menschenpaar,
In diesem Paradies (für ihr Palerm verloren)
Zu Pflanzern einer neuen Schaar
Von Dienern Gottes auserkohren.[66]

Once again, Wieland revives all the motifs from the tradition of 'Robinsonaden'- and 'Felsenburg'-literature. The castaways are "gleich dem ersten Menschenpaar," they find a new "Paradise," they build up a "*neue[s] Eden.*"[67] But whereas Huon and Rezia in **Oberon** pursue their tasks after their sojourn on the island—eventually Huon regains his lands, is pardoned by Charlemagne and reintegrated into the chivalric society—, the castaways in **Klelia and Sinibald** decide to remain on the island and establish a little colony in true *Felsenburg*-style. In an ironic mode, Wieland turns to his—dubious—Muse: "Nenne doch, o Muse, / Den Sitz der kleinen Kolonie, / Die hier so glücklich war und selbst nicht wusste wie?"[68] Although the name of the island, Lampedusa, is given, the idyll is nevertheless portrayed as an utopian ideal—feasible on a more or less desert island, perhaps, but not in society.[69]

Notes

1. Novalis. *An den plauischen* [!] *Grund*, in *Schriften*. Eds. Paul Kluckhohn and Richard Samuel. Stuttgart: Kohlhammer, 1960, vol. 1, p. 490.

2. Wieland. *Oberon*, in *Sämmtliche Werke* [in the following: *SW*], vol. 22/23. Leipzig: Göschen, 1796. [Reprint, Hamburg: Greno, 1984, vol. VII], cant. VI, stanzas 35-107.—The story of Gangolf and Rosette is no other than *January and May,* the *Merchant's Tale* from Chaucer's *Canterbury Tales*.

3. *Oberon* VI, 101.

4. See Wieland. *Oberon*. Ed. Edmund von Sallwürk. Bielefeld, Leipzig: Velhagen & Klasing, 1912 (Velhagen & Klasings Sammlung dt. Schulausgaben. 120), pp. 72, 76 and 124.

5. In *Schriften*, p. 496.—See also *Burgunderwein*, p. 486.

6. *Oberon* I, 66f.

7. Heine, Heinrich. *Memoiren*, in *Historisch-kritische Gesamtausgabe der Werke*. Ed. Manfred Windfuhr. Hamburg: Hoffmann und Campe, 1982, vol. 15, pp. 59-100, here p. 72.

8. See: Düntzer, Heinrich. *Wielands 'Oberon'*. Jena: Hochhausen, s. a. [1855] (Erl. zu den dt. Klassikern. 2); Köhler, Reinhold. "Einleitung," in *Oberon*. Leipzig: Weidmann, 1868, pp. V-XXII; Koch,

Max. *Das Quellenverhältnis von Wielands'- Oberon'*. Marburg: Elwert, 1880; Fuchs, Albert. *Les apports français dans l'œuvre de Wieland de 1772 à 1789*. Paris: Champion, 1934 (Bibl. de la revue de litt. comp. 101), pp. 105-134; Teesing, H[ubert] P[aul] H[ans]. "Die Motivverschlingung in Wielands *Oberon*." *Neophilologus* 31 (1947): 193-201.

9. Sengle, Friedrich. "Von Wielands Epenfragmenten zum 'Oberon'. Ein Beitrag zu Problem und Geschichte des Kleinepos im 18. Jhdt.," *Festschrift P. Kluckhohn/H. Schneider*. Tübingen: Mohr, 1948, pp. 266-285 (again in *C. M. Wieland*. Ed. Hansjörg Schelle [Darmstadt: Wissenschaftliche Buchgesellschaft, 1981], pp. 44-66); Martini, Fritz. "C. M. Wielands 'Oberon'," *Vom Geist der Dichtung. Gedächtnisschrift für R. Petsch*. Hamburg: Hoffmann und Campe, 1949, pp. 206-233; Mayer, Hans. "Wielands 'Oberon'," *Zur dt. Klassik und Romantik*. Pfullingen: Neske, 1963, pp. 30-47, 359 (again in *Wieland*, ed. Schelle, pp. 189-204); Preisendanz, Wolfgang. "Die Kunst der Darstellung in Wielands 'Oberon'," *Formenwandel. Festschrift P. Böckmann*. Hamburg: Hoffmann und Campe, 1964, pp. 236-260 (again in *Wieland*, ed. Schelle, pp. 205-231); Friedrich, Cäcilia. "Zur Idee von Liebe und Ehe in Wielands 'Oberon'," Thomas Höhle, Ed. *Wieland-Kolloquium Halberstadt 1983*. Halle 1985, pp. 85-100; Yuill, William E. "A Poem far too little known. Wielands 'Oberon' Revisited." *Publ. of the Engl. Goethe Society* 54 (1984): 123-147; Jørgensen, Sven-Aage. "'Sing, komische Muse, in freier irrenden Tönen . . .'. Zur Museninvokation im 18. Jahrhundert," *Idee. Gestalt. Geschichte. Festschrift K. v. See*. Ed. G. W. Weber. Odense: Odense University Press, 1988, pp. 467-479; Jørgensen, Sven-Aage. "Nachwort," in *Oberon*. Ed. Jørgensen. Stuttgart: Reclam, 1990, pp. 328-357; Albertsen, Leif Ludwig. "Die Metrik in Wielands 'Oberon'," *Aufklärung als Problem und Aufgabe. Festschrift S.-A. Jørgensen*, K. Bohnen and P. Øhrgaard, Eds. München, Kopenhagen: Fink, 1994 (Text & Kontext. 33), pp. 89-98; Rowland, Herbert. "Autotextuality in Wieland: The Presence of *Oberon* in *Klelia und Sinibald*." *Goethe Yearbook* 7 (1994): 133-145.

10. The only dissenting opinion is expressed by Jan-Philipp Reemtsma in his (again humorous) essay: "Die Kunst aufzuhören oder: Warum Wieland nach 1784 keine Verse mehr geschrieben hat," in *Der Liebe Maskentanz*. Zürich: Haffmanns, 1999, pp. 277-303, p. 283: "Der 'Oberon' ist eine Rittergeschichte um Mut, Liebe und Keuschheit—und ganz unironisch."

11. Sengle, p. 281f.

12. Martini, p. 206f.

13. For an overview see: Müller, Joachim. "Wielands Versepen." *Jb. des Wiener Goethe-Vereins* 69 (1965): 5-47.

14. On the following see: Klein, Timotheus. *Wieland und Rousseau.* Berlin: Duncker, 1903; Baudach, Frank. *Planeten der Unschuld—Kinder der Natur. die Naturstandsutopie in der dt. und westeurop. Lit. des 17. und 18. Jhdts.* Tübingen: Niemeyer, 1993 (Hermaea. 66), chap. III.

15. See Fohrmann, Jürgen. *Abenteuer und Bürgertum. Zur Geschichte der dt. Robinsonaden im 18. Jhdt.* Stuttgart: Metzler, 1981.—On the island scene see: Blankenagel, John C. "The island scenes in Wieland's 'Oberon'." *PMLA* 41 (1926): 161-166; Fitzell, John. "The island episode in Wieland's 'Oberon'." *GQ* [*German Quarterly*] 30/1 (1957): 6-14.

16. Cf. the "Lebensbeschreibung des Don Cyrillo de Valaro," in Schnabel, Johann Gottfried. *Insel Felsenburg.* Eds. Günter Dammann and Marcus Czerwionka. Frankfurt a. M.: Zweitausendeins, 1997, vol. I, pp. 527-650.

17. *Oberon* VIII, 16-21.

18. Ibid., 10; Schnabel I, p. 123f.

19. Cf. the account of Albert Julius in: Schnabel, vol. 1, pp. 134-301; see also Düntzer, pp. 47-49.

20. Brüggemann, Fritz. *Utopie und Robinsonade. Untersuchungen zu Schnabels Insel Felsenburg (1731-1743).* Weimar: Duncker, 1914 (Forschungen zur neueren dt. Literaturgeschichte; Bd. 46), p. 36 and passim.

21. Oberon VIII, 40-48.

22. See J.-J. Rousseau. *Über Kunst und Wissenschaft,* in *Schriften zur Kulturkritik.* Ed. Kurt Weigand. Hamburg: Meiner, 1978 (Philos. Bibl.; Bd. 243), pp. 1-59, p. 6ff.: "Tandis que le gouvernement et les lois pourvoient à la sûreté et au bien-être des hommes assemblés, les sciences, les lettres, et les arts [. . .] étendent des guirlandes de fleurs sur les chaînes de fer dont ils sont chargés."

23. *Oberon* VIII, 17.

24. In *SW,* vol. 14 [V], pp. 3-118.

25. In *SW,* vol. 6/7 [II].—Cf. Fohrmann, Jürgen: "Utopie, Reflexion, Erzählung. Wielands *Goldner Spiegel,*" in Wilhelm Vosskamp, Ed. *Utopieforschung,* vol. 3. Stuttgart: Metzler, 1982, pp. 24-49.

26. In *SW,* vol. 8 [III].

27. Earlier title: *Socrates mainomenos oder Die Dialogen des Diogenes von Sinope.* In *SW,* vol. 13 [IV], pp. 159-201.

28. The best introduction into the subject still is the commentary as well as the "Nachwort" in Herbert Jaumann's edition of Wieland's political writings (*Der goldne Spiegel und andere politische Dichtungen* [München: Winkler, 1979], pp. 724-889.

29. See note 22 above and: Jean-Jacques Rousseau, *Diskurs über die Ungleichheit = Discours sur l'inégalité.* Ed. Heinrich Meier, 3rd edn. Paderborn e. a.: Schöningh, 1984 (UTB für Wissenschaft, 725).

30. Cf. Rousseau, *Sciences et Arts* [Über Kunst und Wissenschaft], p. 4: "Le rétablissement des sciences et des arts a-t-il contribué a épurer les mœurs?"; Rousseau, *Inégalité,* p. 64f.: "Quelle est l'origine de l'inégalité parmi les hommes, et si elle est autorisée par la Loy naturelle."

31. Wieland perpetuates a standard argumentation of German Rousseau-criticism of the time, which is based on an (intentional?) misreading of the *discours.* Rousseau indeed propagated the *retour à la nature,* but not to *primitivism,* as Wieland and many others insinuated.

32. In *SW,* Supplemente, vol. 6 [XIV], pp. 123-138, p. 127f.—Wieland alludes to Rousseau, *Inégalité,* p. 78ff.

33. *Betrachtungen über J. J. Rousseaus ursprünglichen Zustand des Menschen,* in *SW,* vol. 14 [V], pp. 119-175, p. 142.

34. Ibid., p. 147f.—Wieland here explicitly refers to Rousseau, *Inégalité,* p. 68ff.

35. In *SW,* vol. 10 [III], pp. 10-119, here pp. 10f.

36. Rousseau, *Inégalité,* p. 192: "[C]e période du développement des facultés humaines, tenant un juste milieu entre l'indolence de l'état primitif et la pétulante activité de nôtre amour propre, dut être l'époque la plus heureuse, et la plus durable."

37. Ibid., p. 15f.

38. Cf. the pessimistic tale "Reise des Priesters Abulfauaris ins innere Afrika" and the sequel "Bekenntnisse des Abulfauaris" (1770) (in *SW,* vol. 15 [V], pp. 1-28; 29-66.).

39. "Koxkox," p. 12f.

40. Ibid., p. 11f.

41. *Der goldne Spiegel* II, p. 108.

42. Ibid., p. 108f.

43. Ibid. I, pp. 103-114.

44. Ibid., p. 96.

45. Ibid., p. 82f.

46. *Danischmend,* p. 16.

47. Ibid., p. 19f.

48. *Danischmend,* subtitle.

49. *Republik des Diogenes,* p. 23.

50. Ibid., p. 161f.

51. Ibid., p. 201.

52. *Oberon* VIII, 40.

53. *Der goldne Spiegel* I, pp. 106-108.

54. See *Oberon* I, 52.

55. Cf. *Der goldne Spiegel,* pp. 111-114.

56. *Oberon* VIII, 45f.

57. *Danischmend,* p. 365.

58. Blankenagel, p. 166; Yuill, p. 143f.

59. Fitzell, p. 14: "This episode [. . .] comprises a sensitive and incisive poetic document of a major theme in the literature of the Age of Goethe and Romanticism [namely "Naturfrömmigkeit"]."

60. *Oberon* VIII, 27-29.—This is, with the exception of the proemium, the only instance in the whole epic, where the narrator, or rather the muse, rises her voice—only to turn silent. Alfonso's spiritualisation through nature and his near-death experiences put the narrative to an extreme, too. The quintessence of *Oberon* cannot be found in the hermit's cosmic visions, since the "reinste aller Sinne" he has reached remains unutterable. The mystical spiritualisation is attributed to him alone (and he explains it mainly as a consequence of his age); the 'message 'for Huon und Rezia on the other hand, the belief in the godliness of human nature and in its sublimity, is not imparted to the pair by vision or awakening, but experienced in the classic manner of the "Robinsonade": through regular physical work and a life full of privations.

61. See Martini, passim.

62. In *SW,* vol. 24 [VIII], pp. 71-92, here pp. 91f.

63. *Klelia und Sinibald oder Die Bevölkerung von Lampeduse* in *SW,* vol. 21 [VII], pp. 161-396.— The story is based on an Italian novel from the 16th cent., Giacopo Caviceo's *Il Peregrino,* extracts of which Wieland read in the *Mélanges tirés d'une grande bibliothèque* (Paris, 1780).—Cf. Köhler, Reinhold. "Zu Wielands Clelia und Sinibald." *Archiv für Litteraturgeschichte* 5 (1876): 78-83.

64. *Klelia und Sinibald* I, vv. 1-12. See *Oberon* I, 1.—In Canto Two it says: "*Der Dämon steckt in unsrer eignen Haut. / Du selber bist dein Teufel oder Engel: / Und Oberon sogar, mit seinem Lilienstängel / Und seinem Horn, (das sonst sehr wohl zu brauchen ist) / Hilft dir zu nichts, wenn du kein Hüon bist*" (vv. 189-196).

65. See Rowland, 136-139.

66. *Klelia und Sinibald* X, vv. 114-148.

67. Ibid., v. 178.

68. Ibid., vv. 202-204.

69. Why Lampedusa? Wieland took the idea apparently from Diderot's *Second Entretien sur Le Fils naturel* (1757). In a note to his epic *Der neue Amadis* (1768-71; in *SW* 4/5 [II]) he writes: "'Ich wurde verdrießlich, (lässt *Diderot* seinen Enthusiasten Dorval in den Dialogen hinter dem *Fils naturel* sagen) wenn ich in die Komödie ging, und den Nutzen, den man von dem Schauplatz ziehen könnte, mit der wenigen Aufmerksamkeit verglich, die man anwendet, gute Schauspieler zu bilden. O meine Freunde, rief ich dann aus, *wenn wir jemahls bis nach Lampeduse ziehen, um fern vom festen Lande, mitten in den Wogen des Meeres, ein kleines Völkchen von Glücklichen zu stiften,* so sollen die *Schauspieler* unsre Prediger seyn, u. s. w. [. . .]'" (p. 236). In the first version (1771) Wieland added: "Aber was sollte denn dieses kleine Volk von Glückseligen auf der kleinen Insel Lampeduse anders vorstellen können als eine Republik des Diogenes?"

FURTHER READING

Biography

Van Abbé, Derek Maurice. *Christoph Martin Wieland (1733-1813): A Literary Biography.* London: George G. Harrap, 1961, 191 p.

Provides one of the few full-length studies in English of the author's life and work.

Criticism

Beddow, Michael. *The Fiction of Humanity: Studies in the Bildungsroman from Wieland to Thomas Mann.* Cambridge: Cambridge University Press, 1982, 325 p.

Includes an analysis of Wieland's innovative approach to the novel form.

Beyer, Werner W. Introduction to *Keats and the Daemon King,* pp. 3-52. New York: Oxford University Press, 1947.

Examines Wieland's poem *Oberon* while analyzing its impact on the English Romantic poets.

Boa, Elizabeth. "Wieland's *Musarion* and the Rococo Verse Narrative." In *Periods in German Literature: Texts and Contexts.* Vol. 2, edited by James M. Ritchie, pp. 23-41. London: Oswald Wolff, 1969.

Argues that a critical analysis of Wieland's *Musarion* provides valuable insight into Rococo literary forms in general.

Clark, William H. "Wieland and Winckelmann: Saul and the Prophet." *Modern Language Quarterly* 17, no. 1 (March 1956): 1-16.

Discusses the impact of the influential art historian Johann Joachim Winckelmann's work on Wieland's philosophical views.

Craig, Charlotte. *Christoph Martin Wieland as Originator of the Modern Travesty in German Literature.* Chapel Hill: University of North Carolina Press, 1970, 146 p.

Examines Wieland's unique contributions to the tradition of parody in German literature.

Elson, Charles. *Wieland and Shaftesbury.* New York: Columbia University Press, 1913, 143 p.

Offers an analysis of the philosophical aspects of Wieland's work.

Kurth-Voigt, Lieselotte E. *Perspectives and Points of View: The Early Works of Wieland and their Background.* Baltimore: Johns Hopkins University Press, 1974, 189 p.

Discusses the rhetorical and philosophical elements in Wieland's early writings.

————. "Existence after Death: Changing Views in Wieland's Writings." *Lessing Yearbook* 17 (1985): 153-76.

Examines Wieland's evolving attitudes, throughout his body of work, toward questions of existence and mortality.

Larson, Kenneth E. "Wieland's Shakespeare: A Reappraisal." *Lessing Yearbook* 16 (1984): 229-49.

Offers an in-depth analysis of Wieland's translations of Shakespeare, maintaining that Wieland's versions of the plays still retain much of the rhythm and attention to language found in the originals.

McCarthy, John A. *Fantasy and Reality: An Epistemological Approach to Wieland.* Bern: Herbert Lang, 1974, 166 p.

Analyzes the emergence of Wieland's distinctive literary style within the context of his philosophical beliefs.

————. *Christoph Martin Wieland.* Boston: Twayne Publishers, 1979, 192 p.

Offers a detailed evaluation of Wieland's life, his writings, and his influence on modern German literature.

McNeely, James. "Historical Relativism in Wieland's Concept of the Ideal State." *Modern Language Quarterly* 22 (1961): 269-82.

Examines Wieland's ideas concerning government and the law, arguing that his fundamental pragmatism signifies a distinct break from Enlightenment notions of the perfectibility of man.

Menhennet, Alan. "The 'Romanticism' of a Rationalist: Wieland and the Aeronauts." *Lessing Yearbook* 13 (1981): 229-51.

Discusses the relationship between science and Romanticism in Wieland's work, paying particular attention to the author's writings on the subject of ballooning.

Rogan, Richard G. *The Reader in the Novels of C. M. Wieland.* Las Vegas: Peter Lang, 1981, 87 p.

Examines the relationship between narrator and reader in Wieland's major novels.

Shookman, Ellis. "Fictionality and the Bildungsroman: Wieland's *Agathon.*" *Michigan Germanic Studies* 13, no. 2 (fall 1987): 156-68.

Analyzes the narrative structure of Wieland's *Geschichte des Agathon* within the context of the German bildungsroman tradition.

Swales, Martin. "An Unreadable Novel? Some Observations on Wieland's *Agathon* and the *Bildungsroman* Tradition." *Publications of the English Goethe Society* 45 (1975): 101-30.

Discusses questions of genre as they relate to *Geschichte des Agathon.*

Timpe, Eugene F. "Wieland's *Singspiele* and the Rebirth of the German Opera." *Seminar* 13, no. 4 (November 1977): 203-14.

Examines the diverse influences behind Wieland's musical dramas.

How to Use This Index

CDALBS = *Concise Dictionary of American Literary Biography Supplement*
CDBLB = *Concise Dictionary of British Literary Biography*
CMW = *St. James Guide to Crime & Mystery Writers*
CN = *Contemporary Novelists*
CP = *Contemporary Poets*
CPW = *Contemporary Popular Writers*
CSW = *Contemporary Southern Writers*
CWD = *Contemporary Women Dramatists*
CWP = *Contemporary Women Poets*
CWRI = *St. James Guide to Children's Writers*
CWW = *Contemporary World Writers*
DA = *DISCovering Authors*
DA3 = *DISCovering Authors 3.0*
DAB = *DISCovering Authors: British Edition*
DAC = *DISCovering Authors: Canadian Edition*
DAM = *DISCovering Authors: Modules*
   DRAM: *Dramatists Module;* **MST:** *Most-studied Authors Module;*
   MULT: *Multicultural Authors Module;* **NOV:** *Novelists Module;*
   POET: *Poets Module;* **POP:** *Popular Fiction and Genre Authors Module*
DFS = *Drama for Students*
DLB = *Dictionary of Literary Biography*
DLBD = *Dictionary of Literary Biography Documentary Series*
DLBY = *Dictionary of Literary Biography Yearbook*
DNFS = *Literature of Developing Nations for Students*
EFS = *Epics for Students*
EXPN = *Exploring Novels*
EXPP = *Exploring Poetry*
EXPS = *Exploring Short Stories*
EW = *European Writers*
FANT = *St. James Guide to Fantasy Writers*
FW = *Feminist Writers*
GFL = *Guide to French Literature,* Beginnings to 1789, 1798 to the Present
GLL = *Gay and Lesbian Literature*
HGG = *St. James Guide to Horror, Ghost & Gothic Writers*
HW = *Hispanic Writers*
IDFW = *International Dictionary of Films and Filmmakers: Writers and Production Artists*
IDTP = *International Dictionary of Theatre: Playwrights*
LAIT = *Literature and Its Times*
LAW = *Latin American Writers*
JRDA = *Junior DISCovering Authors*
MAICYA = *Major Authors and Illustrators for Children and Young Adults*
MAICYAS = *Major Authors and Illustrators for Children and Young Adults Supplement*
MAWW = *Modern American Women Writers*
MJW = *Modern Japanese Writers*
MTCW = *Major 20th-Century Writers*
NCFS = *Nonfiction Classics for Students*
NFS = *Novels for Students*
PAB = *Poets: American and British*
PFS = *Poetry for Students*
RGAL = *Reference Guide to American Literature*
RGEL = *Reference Guide to English Literature*
RGSF = *Reference Guide to Short Fiction*
RGWL = *Reference Guide to World Literature*
RHW = *Twentieth-Century Romance and Historical Writers*
SAAS = *Something about the Author Autobiography Series*
SATA = *Something about the Author*
SFW = *St. James Guide to Science Fiction Writers*
SSFS = *Short Stories for Students*
TCWW = *Twentieth-Century Western Writers*
WLIT = *World Literature and Its Times*
WP = *World Poets*
YABC = *Yesterday's Authors of Books for Children*
YAW = *St. James Guide to Young Adult Writers*

Literary Criticism Series
Cumulative Author Index

20/1631
See Upward, Allen

A/C Cross
See Lawrence, T(homas) E(dward)

A. M.
See Megged, Aharon

Abasiyanik, Sait Faik 1906-1954
See Sait Faik
See also CA 123; 231

Abbey, Edward 1927-1989 .... **CLC 36, 59; TCLC 160**
See also AMWS 13; ANW; CA 45-48; 128; CANR 2, 41, 131; DA3; DLB 256, 275; LATS 1:2; MTCW 2; MTFW 2005; TCWW 1, 2

Abbott, Edwin A. 1838-1926 .... **TCLC 139**
See also DLB 178

Abbott, Lee K(ittredge) 1947- .... **CLC 48**
See also CA 124; CANR 51, 101; DLB 130

Abe, Kobo 1924-1993 ...... **CLC 8, 22, 53, 81; SSC 61; TCLC 131**
See also CA 65-68; 140; CANR 24, 60; DAM NOV; DFS 14; DLB 182; EWL 3; MJW; MTCW 1, 2; MTFW 2005; NFS 22; RGWL 3; SFW 4

Abe Kobo
See Abe, Kobo

Abelard, Peter c. 1079-c. 1142 ..... **CMLC 11, 77**
See also DLB 115, 208

Abell, Kjeld 1901-1961 .... **CLC 15**
See also CA 191; 111; DLB 214; EWL 3

Abercrombie, Lascelles 1881-1938 .... **TCLC 141**
See also CA 112; DLB 19; RGEL 2

Abish, Walter 1931- .... **CLC 22; SSC 44**
See also CA 101; CANR 37, 114, 153; CN 3, 4, 5, 6; DLB 130, 227; MAL 5; RGHL

Abrahams, Peter (Henry) 1919- .... **CLC 4**
See also AFW; BW 1; CA 57-60; CANR 26, 125; CDWLB 3; CN 1, 2, 3, 4, 5, 6; DLB 117, 225; EWL 3; MTCW 1, 2; RGEL 2; WLIT 2

Abrams, M(eyer) H(oward) 1912- ... **CLC 24**
See also CA 57-60; CANR 13, 33; DLB 67

Abse, Dannie 1923- .... **CLC 7, 29; PC 41**
See also CA 53-56; CAAS 1; CANR 4, 46, 74, 124; CBD; CN 1, 2, 3; CP 1, 2, 3, 4, 5, 6, 7; DAB; DAM POET; DLB 27, 245; MTCW 2

Abutsu 1222(?)-1283 .... **CMLC 46**
See Abutsu-ni

Abutsu-ni
See Abutsu
See also DLB 203

Achebe, Chinua 1930- .. **BLC 1; CLC 1, 3, 5, 7, 11, 26, 51, 75, 127, 152; WLC 1**
See also AAYA 15; AFW; BPFB 1; BRWC 2; BW 2, 3; CA 1-4R; CANR 6, 26, 47, 124; CDWLB 3; CLR 20; CN 1, 2, 3, 4, 5, 6, 7; CP 2, 3, 4, 5, 6, 7; CWRI 5; DA; DA3; DAB; DAC; DAM MST, MULT, NOV; DLB 117; DNFS 1; EWL 3; EXPN; EXPS; LAIT 2; LATS 1:2; MAICYA 1, 2; MTCW 1, 2; MTFW 2005; NFS 2; RGEL 2; RGSF 2; SATA 38, 40; SATA-Brief 38; SSFS 3, 13; TWA; WLIT 2; WWE 1

Acker, Kathy 1948-1997 .... **CLC 45, 111**
See also AMWS 12; CA 117; 122; 162; CANR 55; CN 5, 6; MAL 5

Ackroyd, Peter 1949- .... **CLC 34, 52, 140**
See also BRWS 6; CA 123; 127; CANR 51, 74, 99, 132; CN 4, 5, 6, 7; DLB 155, 231; HGG; INT CA-127; MTCW 2; MTFW 2005; RHW; SATA 153; SUFW 2

Acorn, Milton 1923-1986 .... **CLC 15**
See also CA 103; CCA 1; CP 1, 2, 3, 4; DAC; DLB 53; INT CA-103

Adam de la Halle c. 1250-c. 1285 .... **CMLC 80**

Adamov, Arthur 1908-1970 .... **CLC 4, 25**
See also CA 17-18; 25-28R; CAP 2; DAM DRAM; DLB 321; EWL 3; GFL 1789 to the Present; MTCW 1; RGWL 2, 3

Adams, Alice 1926-1999 .... **CLC 6, 13, 46; SSC 24**
See also CA 81-84; 179; CANR 26, 53, 75, 88, 136; CN 4, 5, 6; CSW; DLB 234; DLBY 1986; INT CANR-26; MTCW 1, 2; MTFW 2005; SSFS 14, 21

Adams, Andy 1859-1935 .... **TCLC 56**
See also TCWW 1, 2; YABC 1

Adams, (Henry) Brooks 1848-1927 .... **TCLC 80**
See also CA 123; DLB 47

Adams, Douglas 1952-2001 .... **CLC 27, 60**
See also AAYA 4, 33; BEST 89:3; BYA 14; CA 106; 197; CANR 34, 64, 124; CPW; DA3; DAM POP; DLB 261; DLBY 1983; JRDA; MTCW 2; MTFW 2005; NFS 7; SATA 116; SATA-Obit 128; SFW 4

Adams, Francis 1862-1893 .... **NCLC 33**

Adams, Henry (Brooks) 1838-1918 .... **TCLC 4, 52**
See also AMW; CA 104; 133; CANR 77; DA; DAB; DAC; DAM MST; DLB 12, 47, 189, 284; EWL 3; MAL 5; MTCW 2; NCFS 1; RGAL 4; TUS

Adams, John 1735-1826 .... **NCLC 106**
See also DLB 31, 183

Adams, John Quincy 1767-1848 .. **NCLC 175**
See also DLB 37

Adams, Mary
See Phelps, Elizabeth Stuart

Adams, Richard (George) 1920- ... **CLC 4, 5, 18**
See also AAYA 16; AITN 1, 2; BPFB 1; BYA 5; CA 49-52; CANR 3, 35, 128; CLR 20; CN 4, 5, 6, 7; DAM NOV; DLB 261; FANT; JRDA; LAIT 5; MAICYA 1, 2; MTCW 1, 2; NFS 11; SATA 7, 69; YAW

Adamson, Joy(-Friederike Victoria) 1910-1980 .... **CLC 17**
See also CA 69-72; 93-96; CANR 22; MTCW 1; SATA 11; SATA-Obit 22

Adcock, Fleur 1934- .... **CLC 41**
See also BRWS 12; CA 25-28R, 182; CAAE 182; CAAS 23; CANR 11, 34, 69, 101; CP 1, 2, 3, 4, 5, 6, 7; CWP; DLB 40; FW; WWE 1

Addams, Charles 1912-1988 .... **CLC 30**
See also CA 61-64; 126; CANR 12, 79

Addams, Charles Samuel
See Addams, Charles

Addams, (Laura) Jane 1860-1935 . **TCLC 76**
See also AMWS 1; CA 194; DLB 303; FW

Addison, Joseph 1672-1719 .... **LC 18**
See also BRW 3; CDBLB 1660-1789; DLB 101; RGEL 2; WLIT 3

Adler, Alfred (F.) 1870-1937 .... **TCLC 61**
See also CA 119; 159

Adler, C(arole) S(chwerdtfeger) 1932- .... **CLC 35**
See also AAYA 4, 41; CA 89-92; CANR 19, 40, 101; CLR 78; JRDA; MAICYA 1, 2; SAAS 15; SATA 26, 63, 102, 126; YAW

Adler, Renata 1938- .... **CLC 8, 31**
See also CA 49-52; CANR 95; CN 4, 5, 6; MTCW 1

Adorno, Theodor W(iesengrund) 1903-1969 .... **TCLC 111**
See also CA 89-92; 25-28R; CANR 89; DLB 242; EWL 3

Ady, Endre 1877-1919 .... **TCLC 11**
See also CA 107; CDWLB 4; DLB 215; EW 9; EWL 3

A.E. .... **TCLC 3, 10**
See Russell, George William
See also DLB 19

Aelfric c. 955-c. 1010 .... **CMLC 46**
See also DLB 146

Aeschines c. 390B.C.-c. 320B.C. .. **CMLC 47**
See also DLB 176

Aeschylus 525(?)B.C.-456(?)B.C. . **CMLC 11, 51; DC 8; WLCS**
See also AW 1; CDWLB 1; DA; DAB; DAC; DAM DRAM, MST; DFS 5, 10; DLB 176; LMFS 1; RGWL 2, 3; TWA; WLIT 8

Aesop 620(?)B.C.-560(?)B.C. .... **CMLC 24**
See also CLR 14; MAICYA 1, 2; SATA 64

Affable Hawk
See MacCarthy, Sir (Charles Otto) Desmond

Africa, Ben
See Bosman, Herman Charles

Afton, Effie
See Harper, Frances Ellen Watkins

Agapida, Fray Antonio
See Irving, Washington

Agee, James (Rufus) 1909-1955 .... **TCLC 1, 19, 180**
See also AAYA 44; AITN 1; AMW; CA 108; 148; CANR 131; CDALB 1941-1968; DAM NOV; DLB 2, 26, 152; DLBY 1989; EWL 3; LAIT 3; LATS 1:2; MAL 5; MTCW 2; MTFW 2005; NFS 22; RGAL 4; TUS

Aghill, Gordon
See Silverberg, Robert

Agnon, S(hmuel) Y(osef Halevi) 1888-1970 .... **CLC 4, 8, 14; SSC 30; TCLC 151**
See also CA 17-18; 25-28R; CANR 60, 102; CAP 2; DLB 329; EWL 3; MTCW 1, 2; RGHL; RGSF 2; RGWL 2, 3; WLIT 6

Agrippa von Nettesheim, Henry Cornelius 1486-1535 .... **LC 27**

Aguilera Malta, Demetrio 1909-1981 .... **HLCS 1**
See also CA 111; 124; CANR 87; DAM MULT, NOV; DLB 145; EWL 3; HW 1; RGWL 3

Agustini, Delmira 1886-1914 .... **HLCS 1**
See also CA 166; DLB 290; HW 1, 2; LAW

Aherne, Owen
See Cassill, R(onald) V(erlin)

Ai 1947- .... **CLC 4, 14, 69; PC 72**
See also CA 85-88; CAAS 13; CANR 70; CP 6, 7; DLB 120; PFS 16

Aickman, Robert (Fordyce) 1914-1981 .... **CLC 57**
See also CA 5-8R; CANR 3, 72, 100; DLB 261; HGG; SUFW 1, 2

Aidoo, (Christina) Ama Ata 1942- .... **BLCS; CLC 177**
See also AFW; BW 1; CA 101; CANR 62, 144; CD 5, 6; CDWLB 3; CN 6, 7; CWD; CWP; DLB 117; DNFS 1, 2; EWL 3; FW; WLIT 2

Aiken, Conrad (Potter) 1889-1973 .. **CLC 1, 3, 5, 10, 52; PC 26; SSC 9**
See also AMW; CA 5-8R; 45-48; CANR 4, 60; CDALB 1929-1941; CN 1; CP 1; DAM NOV, POET; DLB 9, 45, 102; EWL 3; EXPS; HGG; MAL 5; MTCW 1, 2; MTFW 2005; PFS 24; RGAL 4; RGSF 2; SATA 3, 30; SSFS 8; TUS

Aiken, Joan (Delano) 1924-2004 ..... **CLC 35**
See also AAYA 1, 25; CA 9-12R, 182; 223; CAAE 182; CANR 4, 23, 34, 64, 121; CLR 1, 19, 90; DLB 161; FANT; HGG; JRDA; MAICYA 1, 2; MTCW 1; RHW; SAAS 1; SATA 2, 30, 73; SATA-Essay 109; SATA-Obit 152; SUFW 2; WYA; YAW

Ainsworth, William Harrison 1805-1882 .... **NCLC 13**
See also DLB 21; HGG; RGEL 2; SATA 24; SUFW 1

Aitmatov, Chingiz (Torekulovich) 1928- .... **CLC 71**
See Aytmatov, Chingiz
See also CA 103; CANR 38; CWW 2; DLB 302; MTCW 1; RGSF 2; SATA 56

Akers, Floyd
See Baum, L(yman) Frank

Akhmadulina, Bella Akhatovna 1937- .... **CLC 53; PC 43**
See also CA 65-68; CWP; CWW 2; DAM POET; EWL 3

Akhmatova, Anna 1888-1966 ... **CLC 11, 25, 64, 126; PC 2, 55**
See also CA 19-20; 25-28R; CANR 35; CAP 1; DA3; DAM POET; DLB 295; EW 10; EWL 3; FL 1:5; MTCW 1, 2; PFS 18; RGWL 2, 3

Aksakov, Sergei Timofeyvich 1791-1859 .... **NCLC 2**
See also DLB 198

Aksenov, Vasilii (Pavlovich)
See Aksyonov, Vassily (Pavlovich)
See also CWW 2

Aksenov, Vassily
See Aksyonov, Vassily (Pavlovich)

Akst, Daniel 1956- .... **CLC 109**
See also CA 161; CANR 110

Aksyonov, Vassily (Pavlovich) 1932- .... **CLC 22, 37, 101**
See Aksenov, Vasilii (Pavlovich)
See also CA 53-56; CANR 12, 48, 77; DLB 302; EWL 3

Akutagawa Ryunosuke 1892-1927 .. **SSC 44; TCLC 16**
See also CA 117; 154; DLB 180; EWL 3; MJW; RGSF 2; RGWL 2, 3

Alabaster, William 1568-1640 .... **LC 90**
See also DLB 132; RGEL 2

Alain 1868-1951 .... **TCLC 41**
See also CA 163; EWL 3; GFL 1789 to the Present

Alain de Lille c. 1116-c. 1203   **CMLC 53**
See also DLB 208

Alain-Fournier .... **TCLC 6**
See Fournier, Henri-Alban
See also DLB 65; EWL 3; GFL 1789 to the Present; RGWL 2, 3

Al-Amin, Jamil Abdullah 1943- .... **BLC 1**
See also BW 1, 3; CA 112; 125; CANR 82; DAM MULT

Alanus de Insluis
See Alain de Lille

Alarcon, Pedro Antonio de 1833-1891 .... **NCLC 1; SSC 64**

Alas (y Urena), Leopoldo (Enrique Garcia) 1852-1901 .... **TCLC 29**
See also CA 113; 131; HW 1; RGSF 2

Albee, Edward (III) 1928- ... **CLC 1, 2, 3, 5, 9, 11, 13, 25, 53, 86, 113; DC 11; WLC 1**
See also AAYA 51; AITN 1; AMW; CA 5-8R; CABS 3; CAD; CANR 8, 54, 74, 124; CD 5, 6; CDALB 1941-1968; DA; DA3; DAB; DAC; DAM DRAM, MST; DFS 2, 3, 8, 10, 13, 14; DLB 7, 266; EWL 3; INT CANR-8; LAIT 4; LMFS 2; MAL 5; MTCW 1, 2; MTFW 2005; RGAL 4; TUS

Alberti (Merello), Rafael
See Alberti, Rafael
See also CWW 2

Alberti, Rafael 1902-1999 .... **CLC 7**
See Alberti (Merello), Rafael
See also CA 85-88; 185; CANR 81; DLB 108; EWL 3; HW 2; RGWL 2, 3

Albert the Great 1193(?)-1280 ..... **CMLC 16**
See also DLB 115

Alcaeus c. 620B.C.- .... **CMLC 65**
See also DLB 176

Alcala-Galiano, Juan Valera y
See Valera y Alcala-Galiano, Juan

Alcayaga, Lucila Godoy
See Godoy Alcayaga, Lucila

Alciato, Andrea 1492-1550 .... **LC 116**

Alcott, Amos Bronson 1799-1888 .. **NCLC 1, 167**
See also DLB 1, 223

Alcott, Louisa May 1832-1888 ...... **NCLC 6, 58, 83; SSC 27; WLC 1**
See also AAYA 20; AMWS 1; BPFB 1; BYA 2; CDALB 1865-1917; CLR 1, 38, 109; DA; DA3; DAB; DAC; DAM MST, NOV; DLB 1, 42, 79, 223, 239, 242; DLBD 14; FL 1:2; FW; JRDA; LAIT 2; MAICYA 1, 2; NFS 12; RGAL 4; SATA 100; TUS; WCH; WYA; YABC 1; YAW

Alcuin c. 730-804 .... **CMLC 69**
See also DLB 148

Aldanov, M. A.
See Aldanov, Mark (Alexandrovich)

Aldanov, Mark (Alexandrovich) 1886-1957 .... **TCLC 23**
See also CA 118; 181; DLB 317

Aldington, Richard 1892-1962 .... **CLC 49**
See also CA 85-88; CANR 45; DLB 20, 36, 100, 149; LMFS 2; RGEL 2

Aldiss, Brian W. 1925- . **CLC 5, 14, 40; SSC 36**
See also AAYA 42; CA 5-8R, 190; CAAE 190; CAAS 2; CANR 5, 28, 64, 121; CN 1, 2, 3, 4, 5, 6, 7; DAM NOV; DLB 14, 261, 271; MTCW 1, 2; MTFW 2005; SATA 34; SCFW 1, 2; SFW 4

Aldrich, Bess Streeter 1881-1954 .... **TCLC 125**
See also CLR 70; TCWW 2

Alegria, Claribel
See Alegria, Claribel
See also CWW 2; DLB 145, 283

Alegria, Claribel 1924- ... **CLC 75; HLCS 1; PC 26**
See Alegria, Claribel
See also CA 131; CAAS 15; CANR 66, 94, 134; DAM MULT; EWL 3; HW 1; MTCW 2; MTFW 2005; PFS 21

Alegria, Fernando 1918-2005 .... **CLC 57**
See also CA 9-12R; CANR 5, 32, 72; EWL 3; HW 1, 2

Aleichem, Sholom .... **SSC 33; TCLC 1, 35**
See Rabinovitch, Sholem
See also TWA

Aleixandre, Vicente 1898-1984 ...... **HLCS 1; TCLC 113**
See also CANR 81; DLB 108, 329; EWL 3; HW 2; MTCW 1, 2; RGWL 2, 3

Alekseev, Konstantin Sergeivich
See Stanislavsky, Constantin

Alekseyer, Konstantin Sergeyevich
See Stanislavsky, Constantin

Aleman, Mateo 1547-1615(?) .... **LC 81**

Alencar, Jose de 1829-1877 .... **NCLC 157**
See also DLB 307; LAW; WLIT 1

Alencon, Marguerite d'
See de Navarre, Marguerite

Alepoudelis, Odysseus
See Elytis, Odysseus
See also CWW 2

Aleshkovsky, Joseph 1929-
See Aleshkovsky, Yuz
See also CA 121; 128

Aleshkovsky, Yuz .... **CLC 44**
See Aleshkovsky, Joseph
See also DLB 317

Alexander, Lloyd (Chudley) 1924- .. **CLC 35**
See also AAYA 1, 27; BPFB 1; BYA 5, 6, 7, 9, 10, 11; CA 1-4R; CANR 1, 24, 38, 55, 113; CLR 1, 5, 48; CWRI 5; DLB 52; FANT; JRDA; MAICYA 1, 2; MAICYAS 1; MTCW 1; SAAS 19; SATA 3, 49, 81, 129, 135; SUFW; TUS; WYA; YAW

Alexander, Meena 1951- .... **CLC 121**
See also CA 115; CANR 38, 70, 146; CP 5, 6, 7; CWP; DLB 323; FW

Alexander, Samuel 1859-1938 .... **TCLC 77**

Alexeiev, Konstantin
See Stanislavsky, Constantin

Archer, Jeffrey Howard
See Archer, Jeffrey
Archer, Jules 1915- .... **CLC 12**
See also CA 9-12R; CANR 6, 69; SAAS 5;
SATA 4, 85
Archer, Lee
See Ellison, Harlan
Archilochus c. 7th cent. B.C.- ...... **CMLC 44**
See also DLB 176
Arden, John 1930- .... **CLC 6, 13, 15**
See also BRWS 2; CA 13-16R; CAAS 4;
CANR 31, 65, 67, 124; CBD; CD 5, 6;
DAM DRAM; DFS 9; DLB 13, 245;
EWL 3; MTCW 1
Arenas, Reinaldo 1943-1990 . **CLC 41; HLC 1**
See also CA 124; 128; 133; CANR 73, 106;
DAM MULT; DLB 145; EWL 3; GLL 2;
HW 1; LAW; LAWS 1; MTCW 2; MTFW
2005; RGSF 2; RGWL 3; WLIT 1
Arendt, Hannah 1906-1975 .... **CLC 66, 98**
See also CA 17-20R; 61-64; CANR 26, 60;
DLB 242; MTCW 1, 2
Aretino, Pietro 1492-1556 .... **LC 12**
See also RGWL 2, 3
Arghezi, Tudor .... **CLC 80**
See Theodorescu, Ion N.
See also CA 167; CDWLB 4; DLB 220;
EWL 3
Arguedas, Jose Maria 1911-1969 ... **CLC 10,
18; HLCS 1; TCLC 147**
See also CA 89-92; CANR 73; DLB 113;
EWL 3; HW 1; LAW; RGWL 2, 3; WLIT
1
Argueta, Manlio 1936- .... **CLC 31**
See also CA 131; CANR 73; CWW 2; DLB
145; EWL 3; HW 1; RGWL 3
Arias, Ron 1941- .... **HLC 1**
See also CA 131; CANR 81, 136; DAM
MULT; DLB 82; HW 1, 2; MTCW 2;
MTFW 2005
Ariosto, Lodovico
See Ariosto, Ludovico
See also WLIT 7
Ariosto, Ludovico 1474-1533 . **LC 6, 87; PC
42**
See Ariosto, Lodovico
See also EW 2; RGWL 2, 3
Aristides
See Epstein, Joseph
Aristophanes 450B.C.-385B.C. ...... **CMLC 4,
51; DC 2; WLCS**
See also AW 1; CDWLB 1; DA; DA3;
DAB; DAC; DAM DRAM, MST; DFS
10; DLB 176; LMFS 1; RGWL 2, 3;
TWA; WLIT 8
Aristotle 384B.C.-322B.C. .... **CMLC 31;
WLCS**
See also AW 1; CDWLB 1; DA; DA3;
DAB; DAC; DAM MST; DLB 176;
RGWL 2, 3; TWA; WLIT 8
Arlt, Roberto (Godofredo Christophersen)
1900-1942 .... **HLC 1; TCLC 29**
See also CA 123; 131; CANR 67; DAM
MULT; DLB 305; EWL 3; HW 1, 2;
IDTP; LAW
Armah, Ayi Kwei 1939- ...... **BLC 1; CLC 5,
33, 136**
See also AFW; BRWS 10; BW 1; CA 61-
64; CANR 21, 64; CDWLB 3; CN 1, 2,
3, 4, 5, 6, 7; DAM MULT, POET; DLB
117; EWL 3; MTCW 1; WLIT 2
Armatrading, Joan 1950- .... **CLC 17**
See also CA 114; 186
Armin, Robert 1568(?)-1615(?) .... **LC 120**
Armitage, Frank
See Carpenter, John (Howard)

Armstrong, Jeannette (C.) 1948- ...... **NNAL**
See also CA 149; CCA 1; CN 6, 7; DAC;
SATA 102
Arnette, Robert
See Silverberg, Robert
**Arnim, Achim von (Ludwig Joachim von
Arnim)** 1781-1831 . **NCLC 5, 159; SSC
29**
See also DLB 90
Arnim, Bettina von 1785-1859 .... **NCLC 38,
123**
See also DLB 90; RGWL 2, 3
Arnold, Matthew 1822-1888 .... **NCLC 6, 29,
89, 126; PC 5; WLC 1**
See also BRW 5; CDBLB 1832-1890; DA;
DAB; DAC; DAM MST, POET; DLB 32,
57; EXPP; PAB; PFS 2; TEA; WP
Arnold, Thomas 1795-1842 .... **NCLC 18**
See also DLB 55
Arnow, Harriette (Louisa) Simpson
1908-1986 .... **CLC 2, 7, 18**
See also BPFB 1; CA 9-12R; 118; CANR
14; CN 2, 3, 4; DLB 6; FW; MTCW 1, 2;
RHW; SATA 42; SATA-Obit 47
Arouet, Francois-Marie
See Voltaire
Arp, Hans
See Arp, Jean
Arp, Jean 1887-1966 ...... **CLC 5; TCLC 115**
See also CA 81-84; 25-28R; CANR 42, 77;
EW 10
Arrabal
See Arrabal, Fernando
Arrabal (Teran), Fernando
See Arrabal, Fernando
See also CWW 2
Arrabal, Fernando 1932- .. **CLC 2, 9, 18, 58**
See Arrabal (Teran), Fernando
See also CA 9-12R; CANR 15; DLB 321;
EWL 3; LMFS 2
Arreola, Juan Jose 1918-2001 ...... **CLC 147;
HLC 1; SSC 38**
See also CA 113; 131; 200; CANR 81;
CWW 2; DAM MULT; DLB 113; DNFS
2; EWL 3; HW 1, 2; LAW; RGSF 2
Arrian c. 89(?)-c. 155(?) .... **CMLC 43**
See also DLB 176
Arrick, Fran .... **CLC 30**
See Gaberman, Judie Angell
See also BYA 6
Arrley, Richmond
See Delany, Samuel R., Jr.
Artaud, Antonin (Marie Joseph) 1896-1948
.... **DC 14; TCLC 3, 36**
See also CA 104; 149; DA3; DAM DRAM;
DFS 22; DLB 258, 321; EW 11; EWL 3;
GFL 1789 to the Present; MTCW 2;
MTFW 2005; RGWL 2, 3
Arthur, Ruth M(abel) 1905-1979 .... **CLC 12**
See also CA 9-12R; 85-88; CANR 4; CWRI
5; SATA 7, 26
Artsybashev, Mikhail (Petrovich) 1878-1927
.... **TCLC 31**
See also CA 170; DLB 295
Arundel, Honor (Morfydd) 1919-1973
.... **CLC 17**
See also CA 21-22; 41-44R; CAP 2; CLR
35; CWRI 5; SATA 4; SATA-Obit 24
Arzner, Dorothy 1900-1979 .... **CLC 98**
Asch, Sholem 1880-1957 .... **TCLC 3**
See also CA 105; EWL 3; GLL 2; RGHL
Ascham, Roger 1516(?)-1568 .... **LC 101**
See also DLB 236
Ash, Shalom
See Asch, Sholem

Ashbery, John 1927- .. **CLC 2, 3, 4, 6, 9, 13,
15, 25, 41, 77, 125, 221; PC 26**
See Berry, Jonas
See also AMWS 3; CA 5-8R; CANR 9, 37,
66, 102, 132; CP 1, 2, 3, 4, 5, 6, 7; DA3;
DAM POET; DLB 5, 165; DLBY 1981;
EWL 3; INT CANR-9; MAL 5; MTCW
1, 2; MTFW 2005; PAB; PFS 11; RGAL
4; TCLE 1:1; WP
Ashdown, Clifford
See Freeman, R(ichard) Austin
Ashe, Gordon
See Creasey, John
Ashton-Warner, Sylvia (Constance)
1908-1984 .... **CLC 19**
See also CA 69-72; 112; CANR 29; CN 1,
2, 3; MTCW 1, 2
Asimov, Isaac 1920-1992 .... **CLC 1, 3, 9, 19,
26, 76, 92**
See also AAYA 13; BEST 90:2; BPFB 1;
BYA 4, 6, 7, 9; CA 1-4R; 137; CANR 2,
19, 36, 60, 125; CLR 12, 79; CMW 4;
CN 1, 2, 3, 4, 5; CPW; DA3; DAM POP;
DLB 8; DLBY 1992; INT CANR-19;
JRDA; LAIT 5; LMFS 2; MAICYA 1, 2;
MAL 5; MTCW 1, 2; MTFW 2005;
RGAL 4; SATA 1, 26, 74; SCFW 1, 2;
SFW 4; SSFS 17; TUS; YAW
Askew, Anne 1521(?)-1546 .... **LC 81**
See also DLB 136
Assis, Joaquim Maria Machado de
See Machado de Assis, Joaquim Maria
Astell, Mary 1666-1731 .... **LC 68**
See also DLB 252; FW
Astley, Thea (Beatrice May) 1925-2004
.... **CLC 41**
See also CA 65-68; 229; CANR 11, 43, 78;
CN 1, 2, 3, 4, 5, 6, 7; DLB 289; EWL 3
Astley, William 1855-1911
See Warung, Price
Aston, James
See White, T(erence) H(anbury)
Asturias, Miguel Angel 1899-1974 ... **CLC 3,
8, 13; HLC 1; TCLC 184**
See also CA 25-28; 49-52; CANR 32; CAP
2; CDWLB 3; DA3; DAM MULT, NOV;
DLB 113, 290, 329; EWL 3; HW 1; LAW;
LMFS 2; MTCW 1, 2; RGWL 2, 3; WLIT
1
Atares, Carlos Saura
See Saura (Atares), Carlos
Athanasius c. 295-c. 373 .... **CMLC 48**
Atheling, William
See Pound, Ezra (Weston Loomis)
Atheling, William, Jr.
See Blish, James (Benjamin)
Atherton, Gertrude (Franklin Horn)
1857-1948 .... **TCLC 2**
See also CA 104; 155; DLB 9, 78, 186;
HGG; RGAL 4; SUFW 1; TCWW 1, 2
Atherton, Lucius
See Masters, Edgar Lee
Atkins, Jack
See Harris, Mark
Atkinson, Kate 1951- .... **CLC 99**
See also CA 166; CANR 101, 153; DLB
267
Attaway, William (Alexander) 1911-1986
.... **BLC 1; CLC 92**
See also BW 2, 3; CA 143; CANR 82;
DAM MULT; DLB 76; MAL 5
Atticus
See Fleming, Ian; Wilson, (Thomas) Wood-
row
Atwood, Margaret 1939- ...... **CLC 2, 3, 4, 8,
13, 15, 25, 44, 84, 135; PC 8; SSC 2,
46; WLC 1**
See also AAYA 12, 47; AMWS 13; BEST
89:2; BPFB 1; CA 49-52; CANR 3, 24,
33, 59, 95, 133; CN 2, 3, 4, 5, 6, 7; CP 1,

Barrett, William (Christopher) 1913-1992
.... **CLC 27**
See also CA 13-16R; 139; CANR 11, 67;
INT CANR-11

Barrett Browning, Elizabeth 1806-1861
...... **NCLC 1, 16, 61, 66, 170; PC 6, 62;
WLC 1**
See also AAYA 63; BRW 4; CDBLB 1832-
1890; DA; DA3; DAB; DAC; DAM MST,
POET; DLB 32, 199; EXPP; FL 1:2; PAB;
PFS 2, 16, 23; TEA; WLIT 4; WP

Barrie, J(ames) M(atthew) 1860-1937
.... **TCLC 2, 164**
See also BRWS 3; BYA 4, 5; CA 104; 136;
CANR 77; CDBLB 1890-1914; CLR 16;
CWRI 5; DA3; DAB; DAM DRAM; DFS
7; DLB 10, 141, 156; EWL 3; FANT;
MAICYA 1, 2; MTCW 2; MTFW 2005;
SATA 100; SUFW; WCH; WLIT 4; YABC
1

Barrington, Michael
See Moorcock, Michael

Barrol, Grady
See Bograd, Larry

Barry, Mike
See Malzberg, Barry N(athaniel)

Barry, Philip 1896-1949 .... **TCLC 11**
See also CA 109; 199; DFS 9; DLB 7, 228;
MAL 5; RGAL 4

Bart, Andre Schwarz
See Schwarz-Bart, Andre

Barth, John (Simmons) 1930- .. **CLC 1, 2, 3,
5, 7, 9, 10, 14, 27, 51, 89, 214; SSC 10,
89**
See also AITN 1, 2; AMW; BPFB 1; CA
1-4R; CABS 1; CANR 5, 23, 49, 64, 113;
CN 1, 2, 3, 4, 5, 6, 7; DAM NOV; DLB
2, 227; EWL 3; FANT; MAL 5; MTCW
1; RGAL 4; RGSF 2; RHW; SSFS 6; TUS

Barthelme, Donald 1931-1989 . **CLC 1, 2, 3,
5, 6, 8, 13, 23, 46, 59, 115; SSC 2, 55**
See also AMWS 4; BPFB 1; CA 21-24R;
129; CANR 20, 58; CN 1, 2, 3, 4; DA3;
DAM NOV; DLB 2, 234; DLBY 1980,
1989; EWL 3; FANT; LMFS 2; MAL 5;
MTCW 1, 2; MTFW 2005; RGAL 4;
RGSF 2; SATA 7; SATA-Obit 62; SSFS
17

Barthelme, Frederick 1943- .... **CLC 36, 117**
See also AMWS 11; CA 114; 122; CANR
77; CN 4, 5, 6, 7; CSW; DLB 244; DLBY
1985; EWL 3; INT CA-122

Barthes, Roland (Gerard) 1915-1980
.... **CLC 24, 83; TCLC 135**
See also CA 130; 97-100; CANR 66; DLB
296; EW 13; EWL 3; GFL 1789 to the
Present; MTCW 1, 2; TWA

Bartram, William 1739-1823 ...... **NCLC 145**
See also ANW; DLB 37

Barzun, Jacques (Martin) 1907- .... **CLC 51,
145**
See also CA 61-64; CANR 22, 95

Bashevis, Isaac
See Singer, Isaac Bashevis

Bashkirtseff, Marie 1859-1884 ..... **NCLC 27**

Basho, Matsuo
See Matsuo Basho
See also RGWL 2, 3; WP

Basil of Caesaria c. 330-379 .... **CMLC 35**

Basket, Raney
See Edgerton, Clyde (Carlyle)

Bass, Kingsley B., Jr.
See Bullins, Ed

Bass, Rick 1958- .... **CLC 79, 143; SSC 60**
See also AMWS 16; ANW; CA 126; CANR
53, 93, 145; CSW; DLB 212, 275

Bassani, Giorgio 1916-2000 .... **CLC 9**
See also CA 65-68; 190; CANR 33; CWW
2; DLB 128, 177, 299; EWL 3; MTCW 1;
RGHL; RGWL 2, 3

Bastian, Ann .... **CLC 70**

Bastos, Augusto Roa
See Roa Bastos, Augusto

Bataille, Georges 1897-1962 .... **CLC 29;
TCLC 155**
See also CA 101; 89-92; EWL 3

Bates, H(erbert) E(rnest) 1905-1974
.... **CLC 46; SSC 10**
See also CA 93-96; 45-48; CANR 34; CN
1; DA3; DAB; DAM POP; DLB 162, 191;
EWL 3; EXPS; MTCW 1, 2; RGSF 2;
SSFS 7

Bauchart
See Camus, Albert

Baudelaire, Charles 1821-1867 ...... **NCLC 6,
29, 55, 155; PC 1; SSC 18; WLC 1**
See also DA; DA3; DAB; DAC; DAM
MST, POET; DLB 217; EW 7; GFL 1789
to the Present; LMFS 2; PFS 21; RGWL
2, 3; TWA

Baudouin, Marcel
See Peguy, Charles (Pierre)

Baudouin, Pierre
See Peguy, Charles (Pierre)

Baudrillard, Jean 1929- .... **CLC 60**
See also DLB 296

Baum, L(yman) Frank 1856-1919 . **TCLC 7,
132**
See also AAYA 46; BYA 16; CA 108; 133;
CLR 15, 107; CWRI 5; DLB 22; FANT;
JRDA; MAICYA 1, 2; MTCW 1, 2; NFS
13; RGAL 4; SATA 18, 100; WCH

Baum, Louis F.
See Baum, L(yman) Frank

Baumbach, Jonathan 1933- .... **CLC 6, 23**
See also CA 13-16R; CAAS 5; CANR 12,
66, 140; CN 3, 4, 5, 6, 7; DLBY 1980;
INT CANR-12; MTCW 1

Bausch, Richard (Carl) 1945- .... **CLC 51**
See also AMWS 7; CA 101; CAAS 14;
CANR 43, 61, 87; CN 7; CSW; DLB 130;
MAL 5

Baxter, Charles 1947- .... **CLC 45, 78**
See also CA 57-60; CANR 40, 64, 104, 133;
CPW; DAM POP; DLB 130; MAL 5;
MTCW 2; MTFW 2005; TCLE 1:1

Baxter, George Owen
See Faust, Frederick (Schiller)

Baxter, James K(eir) 1926-1972 ...... **CLC 14**
See also CA 77-80; CP 1; EWL 3

Baxter, John
See Hunt, E(verette) Howard, (Jr.)

Bayer, Sylvia
See Glassco, John

Bayle, Pierre 1647-1706 .... **LC 126**
See also DLB 268, 313; GFL Beginnings to
1789

Baynton, Barbara 1857-1929 .... **TCLC 57**
See also DLB 230; RGSF 2

Beagle, Peter S. 1939- .... **CLC 7, 104**
See also AAYA 47; BPFB 1; BYA 9, 10,
16; CA 9-12R; CANR 4, 51, 73, 110;
DA3; DLBY 1980; FANT; INT CANR-4;
MTCW 2; MTFW 2005; SATA 60, 130;
SUFW 1, 2; YAW

Beagle, Peter Soyer
See Beagle, Peter S.

Bean, Normal
See Burroughs, Edgar Rice

Beard, Charles A(ustin) 1874-1948
.... **TCLC 15**
See also CA 115; 189; DLB 17; SATA 18

Beardsley, Aubrey 1872-1898 .... **NCLC 6**

Beattie, Ann 1947- .... **CLC 8, 13, 18, 40, 63,
146; SSC 11**
See also AMWS 5; BEST 90:2; BPFB 1;
CA 81-84; CANR 53, 73, 128; CN 4, 5,
6, 7; CPW; DA3; DAM NOV, POP; DLB
218, 278; DLBY 1982; EWL 3; MAL 5;
MTCW 1, 2; MTFW 2005; RGAL 4;
RGSF 2; SSFS 9; TUS

Beattie, James 1735-1803 .... **NCLC 25**
See also DLB 109

Beauchamp, Kathleen Mansfield 1888-1923
See Mansfield, Katherine
See also CA 104; 134; DA; DA3; DAC;
DAM MST; MTCW 2; TEA

Beaumarchais, Pierre-Augustin Caron de
1732-1799 .... **DC 4; LC 61**
See also DAM DRAM; DFS 14, 16; DLB
313; EW 4; GFL Beginnings to 1789;
RGWL 2, 3

Beaumont, Francis 1584(?)-1616 . **DC 6; LC
33**
See also BRW 2; CDBLB Before 1660;
DLB 58; TEA

Beauvoir, Simone de 1908-1986 ... **CLC 1, 2,
4, 8, 14, 31, 44, 50, 71, 124; SSC 35;
WLC 1**
See also BPFB 1; CA 9-12R; 118; CANR
28, 61; DA; DA3; DAB; DAC; DAM
MST, NOV; DLB 72; DLBY 1986; EW
12; EWL 3; FL 1:5; FW; GFL 1789 to the
Present; LMFS 2; MTCW 1, 2; MTFW
2005; RGSF 2; RGWL 2, 3; TWA

**Beauvoir, Simone Lucie Ernestine Marie
Bertrand de**
See Beauvoir, Simone de

Becker, Carl (Lotus) 1873-1945 .... **TCLC 63**
See also CA 157; DLB 17

Becker, Jurek 1937-1997 .... **CLC 7, 19**
See also CA 85-88; 157; CANR 60, 117;
CWW 2; DLB 75, 299; EWL 3; RGHL

Becker, Walter 1950- .... **CLC 26**

Becket, Thomas a 1118(?)-1170 ... **CMLC 83**

Beckett, Samuel 1906-1989 .. **CLC 1, 2, 3, 4,
6, 9, 10, 11, 14, 18, 29, 57, 59, 83; DC
22; SSC 16, 74; TCLC 145; WLC 1**
See also BRWC 2; BRWR 1; BRWS 1; CA
5-8R; 130; CANR 33, 61; CBD; CDBLB
1945-1960; CN 1, 2, 3, 4; CP 1, 2, 3, 4;
DA; DA3; DAB; DAC; DAM DRAM,
MST, NOV; DFS 2, 7, 18; DLB 13, 15,
233, 319, 321, 329; DLBY 1990; EWL 3;
GFL 1789 to the Present; LATS 1:2;
LMFS 2; MTCW 1, 2; MTFW 2005;
RGSF 2; RGWL 2, 3; SSFS 15; TEA;
WLIT 4

Beckford, William 1760-1844 .... **NCLC 16**
See also BRW 3; DLB 39, 213; GL 2; HGG;
LMFS 1; SUFW

Beckham, Barry (Earl) 1944- .... **BLC 1**
See also BW 1; CA 29-32R; CANR 26, 62;
CN 1, 2, 3, 4, 5, 6; DAM MULT; DLB 33

Beckman, Gunnel 1910- .... **CLC 26**
See also CA 33-36R; CANR 15, 114; CLR
25; MAICYA 1, 2; SAAS 9; SATA 6

Becque, Henri 1837-1899 .. **DC 21; NCLC 3**
See also DLB 192; GFL 1789 to the Present

Becquer, Gustavo Adolfo 1836-1870
.... **HLCS 1; NCLC 106**
See also DAM MULT

Beddoes, Thomas Lovell 1803-1849 . **DC 15;
NCLC 3, 154**
See also BRWS 11; DLB 96

Bede c. 673-735 .... **CMLC 20**
See also DLB 146; TEA

Bedford, Denton R. 1907-(?) .... **NNAL**

Bedford, Donald F.
See Fearing, Kenneth (Flexner)

Beecher, Catharine Esther 1800-1878
.... **NCLC 30**
See also DLB 1, 243

Beecher, John 1904-1980 .... **CLC 6**
See also AITN 1; CA 5-8R; 105; CANR 8;
CP 1, 2, 3

Beer, Johann 1655-1700 .... **LC 5**
See also DLB 168

Beer, Patricia 1924- .... **CLC 58**
See also CA 61-64; 183; CANR 13, 46; CP
1, 2, 3, 4, 5, 6; CWP; DLB 40; FW

Beerbohm, Max
See Beerbohm, (Henry) Max(imilian)

Beerbohm, (Henry) Max(imilian) 1872-1956
.... **TCLC 1, 24**
See also BRWS 2; CA 104; 154; CANR 79;
DLB 34, 100; FANT; MTCW 2

Beer-Hofmann, Richard 1866-1945
.... **TCLC 60**
See also CA 160; DLB 81

Beg, Shemus
See Stephens, James

Begiebing, Robert J(ohn) 1946- ...... **CLC 70**
See also CA 122; CANR 40, 88

Begley, Louis 1933- .... **CLC 197**
See also CA 140; CANR 98; DLB 299;
RGHL; TCLE 1:1

Behan, Brendan (Francis) 1923-1964
.... **CLC 1, 8, 11, 15, 79**
See also BRWS 2; CA 73-76; CANR 33,
121; CBD; CDBLB 1945-1960; DAM
DRAM; DFS 7; DLB 13, 233; EWL 3;
MTCW 1, 2

Behn, Aphra 1640(?)-1689 . **DC 4; LC 1, 30,**
42; PC 13; WLC 1
See also BRWS 3; DA; DA3; DAB; DAC;
DAM DRAM, MST, NOV, POET; DFS
16; DLB 39, 80, 131; FW; TEA; WLIT 3

Behrman, S(amuel) N(athaniel) 1893-1973
.... **CLC 40**
See also CA 13-16; 45-48; CAD; CAP 1;
DLB 7, 44; IDFW 3; MAL 5; RGAL 4

Bekederemo, J. P. Clark
See Clark Bekederemo, J.P.
See also CD 6

Belasco, David 1853-1931 .... **TCLC 3**
See also CA 104; 168; DLB 7; MAL 5;
RGAL 4

Belcheva, Elisaveta Lyubomirova 1893-1991
.... **CLC 10**
See Bagryana, Elisaveta

Beldone, Phil "Cheech"
See Ellison, Harlan

Beleno
See Azuela, Mariano

Belinski, Vissarion Grigoryevich 1811-1848
.... **NCLC 5**
See also DLB 198

Belitt, Ben 1911- .... **CLC 22**
See also CA 13-16R; CAAS 4; CANR 7,
77; CP 1, 2, 3, 4, 5, 6; DLB 5

Belknap, Jeremy 1744-1798 .... **LC 115**
See also DLB 30, 37

Bell, Gertrude (Margaret Lowthian)
1868-1926 .... **TCLC 67**
See also CA 167; CANR 110; DLB 174

Bell, J. Freeman
See Zangwill, Israel

Bell, James Madison 1826-1902 .... **BLC 1;**
TCLC 43
See also BW 1; CA 122; 124; DAM MULT;
DLB 50

Bell, Madison Smartt 1957- ... **CLC 41, 102,**
223
See also AMWS 10; BPFB 1; CA 111; 183;
CAAE 183; CANR 28, 54, 73, 134; CN
5, 6, 7; CSW; DLB 218, 278; MTCW 2;
MTFW 2005

Bell, Marvin (Hartley) 1937- ...... **CLC 8, 31**
See also CA 21-24R; CAAS 14; CANR 59,
102; CP 1, 2, 3, 4, 5, 6, 7; DAM POET;
DLB 5; MAL 5; MTCW 1

Bell, W. L. D.
See Mencken, H(enry) L(ouis)

Bellamy, Atwood C.
See Mencken, H(enry) L(ouis)

Bellamy, Edward 1850-1898 .... **NCLC 4, 86,**
147
See also DLB 12; NFS 15; RGAL 4; SFW
4

Belli, Gioconda 1948- .... **HLCS 1**
See also CA 152; CANR 143; CWW 2;
DLB 290; EWL 3; RGWL 3

Bellin, Edward J.
See Kuttner, Henry

Bello, Andres 1781-1865 .... **NCLC 131**
See also LAW

Belloc, (Joseph) Hilaire (Pierre Sebastien
Rene Swanton) 1870-1953 .... **PC 24;**
TCLC 7, 18
See also CA 106; 152; CLR 102; CWRI 5;
DAM POET; DLB 19, 100, 141, 174;
EWL 3; MTCW 2; MTFW 2005; SATA
112; WCH; YABC 1

Belloc, Joseph Peter Rene Hilaire
See Belloc, (Joseph) Hilaire (Pierre Sebastien Rene Swanton)

Belloc, Joseph Pierre Hilaire
See Belloc, (Joseph) Hilaire (Pierre Sebastien Rene Swanton)

Belloc, M. A.
See Lowndes, Marie Adelaide (Belloc)

Belloc-Lowndes, Mrs.
See Lowndes, Marie Adelaide (Belloc)

Bellow, Saul 1915-2005 .... **CLC 1, 2, 3, 6, 8,**
10, 13, 15, 25, 33, 34, 63, 79, 190, 200;
SSC 14; WLC 1
See also AITN 2; AMW; AMWC 2; AMWR
2; BEST 89:3; BPFB 1; CA 5-8R; 238;
CABS 1; CANR 29, 53, 95, 132; CDALB
1941-1968; CN 1, 2, 3, 4, 5, 6, 7; DA;
DA3; DAB; DAC; DAM MST, NOV,
POP; DLB 2, 28, 299, 329; DLBD 3;
DLBY 1982; EWL 3; MAL 5; MTCW 1,
2; MTFW 2005; NFS 4, 14; RGAL 4;
RGHL; RGSF 2; SSFS 12, 22; TUS

Belser, Reimond Karel Maria de 1929-
See Ruyslinck, Ward
See also CA 152

Bely, Andrey .... **PC 11; TCLC 7**
See Bugayev, Boris Nikolayevich
See also DLB 295; EW 9; EWL 3

Belyi, Andrei
See Bugayev, Boris Nikolayevich
See also RGWL 2, 3

Bembo, Pietro 1470-1547 .... **LC 79**
See also RGWL 2, 3

Benary, Margot
See Benary-Isbert, Margot

Benary-Isbert, Margot 1889-1979 ... **CLC 12**
See also CA 5-8R; 89-92; CANR 4, 72;
CLR 12; MAICYA 1, 2; SATA 2; SATA-
Obit 21

Benavente (y Martinez), Jacinto 1866-1954
.... **DC 26; HLCS 1; TCLC 3**
See also CA 106; 131; CANR 81; DAM
DRAM, MULT; DLB 329; EWL 3; GLL
2; HW 1, 2; MTCW 1, 2

Benchley, Peter 1940-2006 .... **CLC 4, 8**
See also AAYA 14; AITN 2; BPFB 1; CA
17-20R; 248; CANR 12, 35, 66, 115;
CPW; DAM NOV, POP; HGG; MTCW 1,
2; MTFW 2005; SATA 3, 89, 164

Benchley, Peter Bradford
See Benchley, Peter

Benchley, Robert (Charles) 1889-1945
.... **TCLC 1, 55**
See also CA 105; 153; DLB 11; MAL 5;
RGAL 4

Benda, Julien 1867-1956 .... **TCLC 60**
See also CA 120; 154; GFL 1789 to the
Present

Benedict, Ruth 1887-1948 .... **TCLC 60**
See also CA 158; CANR 146; DLB 246

Benedict, Ruth Fulton
See Benedict, Ruth

Benedikt, Michael 1935- .... **CLC 4, 14**
See also CA 13-16R; CANR 7; CP 1, 2, 3,
4, 5, 6, 7; DLB 5

Benet, Juan 1927-1993 .... **CLC 28**
See also CA 143; EWL 3

Benet, Stephen Vincent 1898-1943 ... **PC 64;**
SSC 10, 86; TCLC 7
See also AMWS 11; CA 104; 152; DA3;
DAM POET; DLB 4, 48, 102, 249, 284;
DLBY 1997; EWL 3; HGG; MAL 5;
MTCW 2; MTFW 2005; RGAL 4; RGSF
2; SSFS 22; SUFW; WP; YABC 1

Benet, William Rose 1886-1950 .... **TCLC 28**
See also CA 118; 152; DAM POET; DLB
45; RGAL 4

Benford, Gregory (Albert) 1941- .... **CLC 52**
See also BPFB 1; CA 69-72; 175; CAAE
175; CAAS 27; CANR 12, 24, 49, 95,
134; CN 7; CSW; DLBY 1982; MTFW
2005; SCFW 2; SFW 4

Bengtsson, Frans (Gunnar) 1894-1954
.... **TCLC 48**
See also CA 170; EWL 3

Benjamin, David
See Slavitt, David R(ytman)

Benjamin, Lois
See Gould, Lois

Benjamin, Walter 1892-1940 .... **TCLC 39**
See also CA 164; DLB 242; EW 11; EWL
3

Ben Jelloun, Tahar 1944-
See Jelloun, Tahar ben
See also CA 135; CWW 2; EWL 3; RGWL
3; WLIT 2

Benn, Gottfried 1886-1956 . **PC 35; TCLC 3**
See also CA 106; 153; DLB 56; EWL 3;
RGWL 2, 3

Bennett, Alan 1934- .... **CLC 45, 77**
See also BRWS 8; CA 103; CANR 35, 55,
106, 157; CBD; CD 5, 6; DAB; DAM
MST; DLB 310; MTCW 1, 2; MTFW
2005

Bennett, (Enoch) Arnold 1867-1931
.... **TCLC 5, 20**
See also BRW 6; CA 106; 155; CDBLB
1890-1914; DLB 10, 34, 98, 135; EWL 3;
MTCW 2

Bennett, Elizabeth
See Mitchell, Margaret (Munnerlyn)

Bennett, George Harold 1930-
See Bennett, Hal
See also BW 1; CA 97-100; CANR 87

Bennett, Gwendolyn B. 1902-1981 ... **HR 1:2**
See also BW 1; CA 125; DLB 51; WP

Bennett, Hal .... **CLC 5**
See Bennett, George Harold
See also CAAS 13; DLB 33

Bennett, Jay 1912- .... **CLC 35**
See also AAYA 10; CA 69-72; CANR 11,
42, 79; JRDA; SAAS 4; SATA 41, 87;
SATA-Brief 27; WYA; YAW

Bennett, Louise 1919-2006 . **BLC 1; CLC 28**
See also BW 2, 3; CA 151; CDWLB 3; CP
1, 2, 3, 4, 5, 6, 7; DAM MULT; DLB 117;
EWL 3

Bennett-Coverley, Louise
See Bennett, Louise

Binchy, Maeve 1940- .... **CLC 153**
See also BEST 90:1; BPFB 1; CA 127; 134;
CANR 50, 96, 134; CN 5, 6, 7; CPW;
DA3; DAM POP; DLB 319; INT CA-134;
MTCW 2; MTFW 2005; RHW

Binyon, T(imothy) J(ohn) 1936-2004
.... **CLC 34**
See also CA 111; 232; CANR 28, 140

Bion 335B.C.-245B.C. .... **CMLC 39**

Bioy Casares, Adolfo 1914-1999 .. **CLC 4, 8,
13, 88; HLC 1; SSC 17**
See Casares, Adolfo Bioy; Miranda, Javier;
Sacastru, Martin
See also CA 29-32R; 177; CANR 19, 43,
66; CWW 2; DAM MULT; DLB 113;
EWL 3; HW 1, 2; LAW; MTCW 1, 2;
MTFW 2005

Birch, Allison .... **CLC 65**

Bird, Cordwainer
See Ellison, Harlan

Bird, Robert Montgomery 1806-1854
.... **NCLC 1**
See also DLB 202; RGAL 4

Birkerts, Sven 1951- .... **CLC 116**
See also CA 128; 133, 176; CAAE 176;
CAAS 29; CANR 151; INT CA-133

Birney, (Alfred) Earle 1904-1995 ..... **CLC 1,
4, 6, 11; PC 52**
See also CA 1-4R; CANR 5, 20; CN 1, 2,
3, 4; CP 1, 2, 3, 4, 5, 6; DAC; DAM MST;
POET; DLB 88; MTCW 1; PFS 8; RGEL
2

Biruni, al 973-1048(?) .... **CMLC 28**

Bishop, Elizabeth 1911-1979 .... **CLC 1, 4, 9,
13, 15, 32; PC 3, 34; TCLC 121**
See also AMWR 2; AMWS 1; CA 5-8R;
89-92; CABS 2; CANR 26, 61, 108;
CDALB 1968-1988; CP 1, 2, 3; DA;
DA3; DAC; DAM MST; DLB 5;
169; EWL 3; GLL 2; MAL 5; MBL;
MTCW 1, 2; PAB; PFS 6, 12; RGAL 4;
SATA-Obit 24; TUS; WP

Bishop, John 1935- .... **CLC 10**
See also CA 105

Bishop, John Peale 1892-1944 .... **TCLC 103**
See also CA 107; 155; DLB 4, 9, 45; MAL
5; RGAL 4

Bissett, Bill 1939- .... **CLC 18; PC 14**
See also CA 69-72; CAAS 19; CANR 15;
CCA 1; CP 1, 2, 3, 4, 5, 6, 7; DLB 53;
MTCW 1

Bissoondath, Neil (Devindra) 1955-
.... **CLC 120**
See also CA 136; CANR 123; CN 6, 7;
DAC

Bitov, Andrei (Georgievich) 1937- .. **CLC 57**
See also CA 142; DLB 302

Biyidi, Alexandre 1932-
See Beti, Mongo
See also BW 1, 3; CA 114; 124; CANR 81;
DA3; MTCW 1, 2

Bjarme, Brynjolf
See Ibsen, Henrik (Johan)

Bjoernson, Bjoernstjerne (Martinius)
1832-1910 .... **TCLC 7, 37**
See also CA 104

Black, Benjamin
See Banville, John

Black, Robert
See Holdstock, Robert P.

Blackburn, Paul 1926-1971 .... **CLC 9, 43**
See also BG 1:2; CA 81-84; 33-36R; CANR
34; CP 1; DLB 16; DLBY 1981

Black Elk 1863-1950 .... **NNAL; TCLC 33**
See also CA 144; DAM MULT; MTCW 2;
MTFW 2005; WP

Black Hawk 1767-1838 .... **NNAL**

Black Hobart
See Sanders, (James) Ed(ward)

Blacklin, Malcolm
See Chambers, Aidan

Blackmore, R(ichard) D(oddridge)
1825-1900 .... **TCLC 27**
See also CA 120; DLB 18; RGEL 2

Blackmur, R(ichard) P(almer) 1904-1965
.... **CLC 2, 24**
See also AMWS 2; CA 11-12; 25-28R;
CANR 71; CAP 1; DLB 63; EWL 3;
MAL 5

Black Tarantula
See Acker, Kathy

Blackwood, Algernon (Henry) 1869-1951
.... **TCLC 5**
See also CA 105; 150; DLB 153, 156, 178;
HGG; SUFW 1

Blackwood, Caroline (Maureen) 1931-1996
.... **CLC 6, 9, 100**
See also BRWS 9; CA 85-88; 151; CANR
32, 61, 65; CN 3, 4, 5, 6; DLB 14, 207;
HGG; MTCW 1

Blade, Alexander
See Hamilton, Edmond; Silverberg, Robert

Blaga, Lucian 1895-1961 .... **CLC 75**
See also CA 157; DLB 220; EWL 3

Blair, Eric (Arthur) 1903-1950 ... **TCLC 123**
See Orwell, George
See also CA 104; 132; DA; DA3; DAB;
DAC; DAM MST, NOV; MTCW 1, 2;
MTFW 2005; SATA 29

Blair, Hugh 1718-1800 .... **NCLC 75**

Blais, Marie-Claire 1939- ... **CLC 2, 4, 6, 13,
22**
See also CA 21-24R; CAAS 4; CANR 38,
75, 93; CWW 2; DAC; DAM MST; DLB
53; EWL 3; FW; MTCW 1, 2; MTFW
2005; TWA

Blaise, Clark 1940- .... **CLC 29**
See also AITN 2; CA 53-56, 231; CAAE
231; CAAS 3; CANR 5, 66, 106; CN 4,
5, 6, 7; DLB 53; RGSF 2

Blake, Fairley
See De Voto, Bernard (Augustine)

Blake, Nicholas
See Day Lewis, C(ecil)
See also DLB 77; MSW

Blake, Sterling
See Benford, Gregory (Albert)

Blake, William 1757-1827 ...... **NCLC 13, 37,
57, 127, 173; PC 12, 63; WLC 1**
See also AAYA 47; BRW 3; BRWR 1; CD-
BLB 1789-1832; CLR 52; DA; DA3;
DAB; DAC; DAM MST, POET; DLB 93,
163; EXPP; LATS 1; LMFS 1; MAI-
CYA 1, 2; PAB; PFS 2, 12, 24; SATA 30;
TEA; WCH; WLIT 3; WP

Blanchot, Maurice 1907-2003 .... **CLC 135**
See also CA 117; 144; 213; CANR 138;
DLB 72, 296; EWL 3

Blasco Ibanez, Vicente 1867-1928
.... **TCLC 12**
See Ibanez, Vicente Blasco
See also BPFB 1; CA 110; 131; CANR 81;
DA3; DAM NOV; EW 8; EWL 3; HW 1,
2; MTCW 1

Blatty, William Peter 1928- .... **CLC 2**
See also CA 5-8R; CANR 9, 124; DAM
POP; HGG

Bleeck, Oliver
See Thomas, Ross (Elmore)

Blessing, Lee (Knowlton) 1949- ...... **CLC 54**
See also CA 236; CAD; CD 5, 6; DFS 23

Blight, Rose
See Greer, Germaine

Blish, James (Benjamin) 1921-1975
.... **CLC 14**
See also BPFB 1; CA 1-4R; 57-60; CANR
3; CN 2; DLB 8; MTCW 1; SATA 66;
SCFW 1, 2; SFW 4

Bliss, Frederick
See Card, Orson Scott

Bliss, Reginald
See Wells, H(erbert) G(eorge)

Blixen, Karen (Christentze Dinesen)
1885-1962
See Dinesen, Isak
See also CA 25-28; CANR 22, 50; CAP 2;
DA3; DLB 214; LMFS 1; MTCW 1, 2;
SATA 44; SSFS 20

Bloch, Robert (Albert) 1917-1994 ... **CLC 33**
See also AAYA 29; CA 5-8R, 179; 146;
CAAE 179; CAAS 20; CANR 5, 78;
DA3; DLB 44; HGG; INT CANR-5;
MTCW 2; SATA 12; SATA-Obit 82; SFW
4; SUFW 1, 2

Blok, Alexander (Alexandrovich) 1880-1921
.... **PC 21; TCLC 5**
See also CA 104; 183; DLB 295; EW 9;
EWL 3; LMFS 2; RGWL 2, 3

Blom, Jan
See Breytenbach, Breyten

Bloom, Harold 1930- .... **CLC 24, 103, 221**
See also CA 13-16R; CANR 39, 75, 92,
133; DLB 67; EWL 3; MTCW 2; MTFW
2005; RGAL 4

Bloomfield, Aurelius
See Bourne, Randolph S(illiman)

Bloomfield, Robert 1766-1823 .... **NCLC 145**
See also DLB 93

Blount, Roy (Alton), Jr. 1941- .... **CLC 38**
See also CA 53-56; CANR 10, 28, 61, 125;
CSW; INT CANR-28; MTCW 1, 2;
MTFW 2005

Blowsnake, Sam 1875-(?) .... **NNAL**

Bloy, Leon 1846-1917 .... **TCLC 22**
See also CA 121; 183; DLB 123; GFL 1789
to the Present

Blue Cloud, Peter (Aroniawenrate) 1933-
.... **NNAL**
See also CA 117; CANR 40; DAM MULT

Bluggage, Oranthy
See Alcott, Louisa May

Blume, Judy (Sussman) 1938- .. **CLC 12, 30**
See also AAYA 3, 26; BYA 1, 8, 12; CA 29-
32R; CANR 13, 37, 66, 124; CLR 2, 15,
69; CPW; DA3; DAM NOV, POP; DLB
52; JRDA; MAICYA 1, 2; MAICYAS 1;
MTCW 1, 2; MTFW 2005; NFS 24;
SATA 2, 31, 79, 142; WYA; YAW

Blunden, Edmund (Charles) 1896-1974
.... **CLC 2, 56; PC 66**
See also BRW 6; BRWS 11; CA 17-18; 45-
48; CANR 54; CAP 2; CP 1, 2; DLB 20,
100, 155; MTCW 1; PAB

Bly, Robert (Elwood) 1926- ..... **CLC 1, 2, 5,
10, 15, 38, 128; PC 39**
See also AMWS 4; CA 5-8R; CANR 41,
73, 125; CP 1, 2, 3, 4, 5, 6, 7; DA3; DAM
POET; DLB 5; EWL 3; MAL 5; MTCW
1, 2; MTFW 2005; PFS 6, 17; RGAL 4

Boas, Franz 1858-1942 .... **TCLC 56**
See also CA 115; 181

Bobette
See Simenon, Georges (Jacques Christian)

Boccaccio, Giovanni 1313-1375 .. **CMLC 13,
57; SSC 10, 87**
See also EW 2; RGSF 2; RGWL 2, 3; TWA;
WLIT 7

Bochco, Steven 1943- .... **CLC 35**
See also AAYA 11, 71; CA 124; 138

Bode, Sigmund
See O'Doherty, Brian

Bodel, Jean 1167(?)-1210 .... **CMLC 28**

Bodenheim, Maxwell 1892-1954 ... **TCLC 44**
See also CA 110; 187; DLB 9, 45; MAL 5;
RGAL 4

Bodenheimer, Maxwell
See Bodenheim, Maxwell

Brown, Sterling Allen 1901-1989 ..... **BLC 1;**
CLC 1, 23, 59; HR 1:2; PC 55
  See also AFAW 1, 2; BW 1, 3; CA 85-88;
  127; CANR 26; CP 3, 4; DA3; DAM
  MULT, POET; DLB 48, 51, 63; MAL 5;
  MTCW 1, 2; MTFW 2005; RGAL 4; WP
Brown, Will
  See Ainsworth, William Harrison
Brown, William Hill 1765-1793 .... **LC 93**
  See also DLB 37
Brown, William Wells 1815-1884 ..... **BLC 1;**
DC 1; NCLC 2, 89
  See also DAM MULT; DLB 3, 50, 183,
  248; RGAL 4
Browne, (Clyde) Jackson 1948(?)- .. **CLC 21**
  See also CA 120
Browne, Sir Thomas 1605-1682 .... **LC 111**
  See also BRW 2; DLB 151
Browning, Robert 1812-1889 .... **NCLC 19,**
79; PC 2, 61; WLCS
  See also BRW 4; BRWC 2; BRWR 2; CD-
  BLB 1832-1890; CLR 97; DA; DA3;
  DAB; DAC; DAM MST, POET; DLB 32,
  163; EXPP; LATS 1:1; PAB; PFS 1, 15;
  RGEL 2; TEA; WLIT 4; WP; YABC 1
Browning, Tod 1882-1962 .... **CLC 16**
  See also CA 141; 117
Brownmiller, Susan 1935- .... **CLC 159**
  See also CA 103; CANR 35, 75, 137; DAM
  NOV; FW; MTCW 1, 2; MTFW 2005
Brownson, Orestes Augustus 1803-1876
  .... **NCLC 50**
  See also DLB 1, 59, 73, 243
Bruccoli, Matthew J(oseph) 1931- .. **CLC 34**
  See also CA 9-12R; CANR 7, 87; DLB 103
Bruce, Lenny .... **CLC 21**
  See Schneider, Leonard Alfred
Bruchac, Joseph 1942- .... **NNAL**
  See also AAYA 19; CA 33-36R; CANR 13,
  47, 75, 94, 137; CLR 46; CWRI 5; DAM
  MULT; JRDA; MAICYA 2; MAICYAS 1;
  MTCW 2; MTFW 2005; SATA 42, 89,
  131, 172
Bruin, John
  See Brutus, Dennis
Brulard, Henri
  See Stendhal
Brulls, Christian
  See Simenon, Georges (Jacques Christian)
Brunetto Latini c. 1220-1294 .... **CMLC 73**
Brunner, John (Kilian Houston) 1934-1995
  .... **CLC 8, 10**
  See also CA 1-4R; 149; CAAS 8; CANR 2,
  37; CPW; DAM POP; DLB 261; MTCW
  1, 2; SCFW 1, 2; SFW 4
Bruno, Giordano 1548-1600 .... **LC 27**
  See also RGWL 2, 3
Brutus, Dennis 1924- .. **BLC 1; CLC 43; PC**
24
  See also AFW; BW 2, 3; CA 49-52; CAAS
  14; CANR 2, 27, 42, 81; CDWLB 3; CP
  1, 2, 3, 4, 5, 6, 7; DAM MULT, POET;
  DLB 117, 225; EWL 3
Bryan, C(ourtlandt) D(ixon) B(arnes) 1936-
  .... **CLC 29**
  See also CA 73-76; CANR 13, 68; DLB
  185; INT CANR-13
Bryan, Michael
  See Moore, Brian
  See also CCA 1
Bryan, William Jennings 1860-1925
  .... **TCLC 99**
  See also DLB 303
Bryant, William Cullen 1794-1878
  .... **NCLC 6, 46; PC 20**
  See also AMWS 1; CDALB 1640-1865;
  DA; DAB; DAC; DAM MST, POET;
  DLB 3, 43, 59, 189, 250; EXPP; PAB;
  RGAL 4; TUS

Bryusov, Valery Yakovlevich 1873-1924
  .... **TCLC 10**
  See also CA 107; 155; EWL 3; SFW 4
Buchan, John 1875-1940 .... **TCLC 41**
  See also CA 108; 145; CMW 4; DAB;
  DAM POP; DLB 34, 70, 156; HGG;
  MSW; MTCW 2; RGEL 2; RHW; YABC
  2
Buchanan, George 1506-1582 .... **LC 4**
  See also DLB 132
Buchanan, Robert 1841-1901 ..... **TCLC 107**
  See also CA 179; DLB 18, 35
Buchheim, Lothar-Guenther 1918- ... **CLC 6**
  See also CA 85-88
Buchner, (Karl) Georg 1813-1837
  .... **NCLC 26, 146**
  See also CDWLB 2; DLB 133; EW 6;
  RGSF 2; RGWL 2, 3; TWA
Buchwald, Art 1925- .... **CLC 33**
  See also AITN 1; CA 5-8R; CANR 21, 67,
  107; MTCW 1, 2; SATA 10
Buchwald, Arthur
  See Buchwald, Art
Buck, Pearl S(ydenstricker) 1892-1973
  .... **CLC 7, 11, 18, 127**
  See also AAYA 42; AITN 1; AMWS 2;
  BPFB 1; CA 1-4R; 41-44R; CANR 1, 34;
  CDALBS; CN 1; DA; DA3; DAB; DAC;
  DAM MST, NOV; DLB 9, 102, 329; EWL
  3; LAIT 3; MAL 5; MTCW 1, 2; MTFW
  2005; RGAL 4; RHW; SATA 1, 25; TUS
Buckler, Ernest 1908-1984 .... **CLC 13**
  See also CA 11-12; 114; CAP 1; CCA 1;
  CN 1, 2, 3; DAC; DAM MST; DLB 68;
  SATA 47
Buckley, Christopher 1952- .... **CLC 165**
  See also CA 139; CANR 119
Buckley, Christopher Taylor
  See Buckley, Christopher
Buckley, Vincent (Thomas) 1925-1988
  .... **CLC 57**
  See also CA 101; CP 1, 2, 3, 4; DLB 289
Buckley, William F., Jr. 1925- .... **CLC 7, 18,**
37
  See also AITN 1; BPFB 1; CA 1-4R; CANR
  1, 24, 53, 93, 133; CMW 4; CPW; DA3;
  DAM POP; DLB 137; DLBY 1980; INT
  CANR-24; MTCW 1, 2; MTFW 2005;
  TUS
Buechner, Frederick 1926- ... **CLC 2, 4, 6, 9**
  See also AMWS 12; BPFB 1; CA 13-16R;
  CANR 11, 39, 64, 114, 138; CN 1, 2, 3,
  4, 5, 6, 7; DAM NOV; DLBY 1980; INT
  CANR-11; MAL 5; MTCW 1, 2; MTFW
  2005; TCLE 1:1
Buell, John (Edward) 1927- .... **CLC 10**
  See also CA 1-4R; CANR 71; DLB 53
Buero Vallejo, Antonio 1916-2000 . **CLC 15,**
46, 139, 226; DC 18
  See also CA 106; 189; CANR 24, 49, 75;
  CWW 2; DFS 11; EWL 3; HW 1; MTCW
  1, 2
Bufalino, Gesualdo 1920-1996 .... **CLC 74**
  See also CA 209; CWW 2; DLB 196
Bugayev, Boris Nikolayevich 1880-1934
  .... **PC 11; TCLC 7**
  See Bely, Andrey; Belyi, Andrei
  See also CA 104; 165; MTCW 2; MTFW
  2005
Bukowski, Charles 1920-1994 .. **CLC 2, 5, 9,**
41, 82, 108; PC 18; SSC 45
  See also CA 17-20R; 144; CANR 40, 62,
  105; CN 4, 5; CP 1, 2, 3, 4, 5; CPW; DA3;
  DAM NOV, POET; DLB 5, 130, 169;
  EWL 3; MAL 5; MTCW 1, 2; MTFW
  2005

Bulgakov, Mikhail 1891-1940 .... **SSC 18;**
TCLC 2, 16, 159
  See also BPFB 1; CA 105; 152; DAM
  DRAM, NOV; DLB 272; EWL 3; MTCW
  2; MTFW 2005; NFS 8; RGSF 2; RGWL
  2, 3; SFW 4; TWA
Bulgakov, Mikhail Afanasevich
  See Bulgakov, Mikhail
Bulgya, Alexander Alexandrovich 1901-1956
  .... **TCLC 53**
  See Fadeev, Aleksandr Aleksandrovich;
  Fadeev, Alexandr Alexandrovich; Fadeyev,
  Alexander
  See also CA 117; 181
Bullins, Ed 1935- . **BLC 1; CLC 1, 5, 7; DC**
6
  See also BW 2, 3; CA 49-52; CAAS 16;
  CAD; CANR 24, 46, 73, 134; CD 5, 6;
  DAM DRAM, MULT; DLB 7, 38, 249;
  EWL 3; MAL 5; MTCW 1, 2; MTFW
  2005; RGAL 4
Bulosan, Carlos 1911-1956 .... **AAL**
  See also CA 216; DLB 312; RGAL 4
Bulwer-Lytton, Edward (George Earle
  Lytton) 1803-1873 .... **NCLC 1, 45**
  See also DLB 21; RGEL 2; SFW 4; SUFW
  1; TEA
Bunin, Ivan
  See Bunin, Ivan Alexeyevich
Bunin, Ivan Alekseevich
  See Bunin, Ivan Alexeyevich
Bunin, Ivan Alexeyevich 1870-1953 . **SSC 5;**
TCLC 6
  See also CA 104; DLB 317, 329; EWL 3;
  RGSF 2; RGWL 2, 3; TWA
Bunting, Basil 1900-1985 ..... **CLC 10, 39, 47**
  See also BRWS 7; CA 53-56; 115; CANR
  7; CP 1, 2, 3, 4; DAM POET; DLB 20;
  EWL 3; RGEL 2
Bunuel, Luis 1900-1983 .. **CLC 16, 80; HLC**
1
  See also CA 101; 110; CANR 32, 77; DAM
  MULT; HW 1
Bunyan, John 1628-1688 . **LC 4, 69; WLC 1**
  See also BRW 2; BYA 5; CDBLB 1660-
  1789; DA; DAB; DAC; DAM MST; DLB
  39; RGEL 2; TEA; WCH; WLIT 3
Buravsky, Alexandr .... **CLC 59**
Burckhardt, Jacob (Christoph) 1818-1897
  .... **NCLC 49**
  See also EW 6
Burford, Eleanor
  See Hibbert, Eleanor Alice Burford
Burgess, Anthony . **CLC 1, 2, 4, 5, 8, 10, 13,**
15, 22, 40, 62, 81, 94
  See Wilson, John (Anthony) Burgess
  See also AAYA 25; AITN 1; BRWS 1; CD-
  BLB 1960 to Present; CN 1, 2, 3, 4, 5;
  DAB; DLB 14, 194, 261; DLBY 1998;
  EWL 3; RGEL 2; RHW; SFW 4; YAW
Burke, Edmund 1729(?)-1797 .... **LC 7, 36;**
WLC 1
  See also BRW 3; DA; DA3; DAB; DAC;
  DAM MST; DLB 104, 252; RGEL 2;
  TEA
Burke, Kenneth (Duva) 1897-1993 .. **CLC 2,**
24
  See also AMW; CA 5-8R; 143; CANR 39,
  74, 136; CN 1, 2; CP 1, 2, 3, 4, 5; DLB
  45, 63; EWL 3; MAL 5; MTCW 1, 2;
  MTFW 2005; RGAL 4
Burke, Leda
  See Garnett, David
Burke, Ralph
  See Silverberg, Robert
Burke, Thomas 1886-1945 .... **TCLC 63**
  See also CA 113; 155; CMW 4; DLB 197

Clark, Kenneth (Mackenzie) 1903-1983
.... **TCLC 147**
See also CA 93-96; 109; CANR 36; MTCW
1, 2; MTFW 2005
Clark, M. R.
See Clark, Mavis Thorpe
Clark, Mavis Thorpe 1909-1999 ..... **CLC 12**
See also CA 57-60; CANR 8, 37, 107; CLR
30; CWRI 5; MAICYA 1, 2; SAAS 5;
SATA 8, 74
Clark, Walter Van Tilburg 1909-1971
.... **CLC 28**
See also CA 9-12R; 33-36R; CANR 63,
113; CN 1; DLB 9, 206; LAIT 2; MAL 5;
RGAL 4; SATA 8; TCWW 1, 2
Clark Bekederemo, J.P. 1935- .... **BLC 1;
CLC 38; DC 5**
See Bekederemo, J. P. Clark; Clark, J. P.;
Clark, John Pepper
See also BW 1; CA 65-68; CANR 16, 72;
DAM DRAM, MULT; DFS 13; EWL 3;
MTCW 2; MTFW 2005
Clarke, Arthur C. 1917- ... **CLC 1, 4, 13, 18,
35, 136; SSC 3**
See also AAYA 4, 33; BPFB 1; BYA 13;
CA 1-4R; CANR 2, 28, 55, 74, 130; CLR
119; CN 1, 2, 3, 4, 5, 6, 7; CPW; DA3;
DAM POP; DLB 261; JRDA; LAIT 5;
MAICYA 1, 2; MTCW 1, 2; MTFW 2005;
SATA 13, 70, 115; SCFW 1, 2; SFW 4;
SSFS 4, 18; TCLE 1:1; YAW
Clarke, Austin 1896-1974 .... **CLC 6, 9**
See also CA 29-32; 49-52; CAP 2; CP 1, 2;
DAM POET; DLB 10, 20; EWL 3; RGEL
2
Clarke, Austin C. 1934- ...... **BLC 1; CLC 8,
53; SSC 45**
See also BW 1; CA 25-28R; CAAS 16;
CANR 14, 32, 68, 140; CN 1, 2, 3, 4, 5,
6, 7; DAC; DAM MULT; DLB 53, 125;
DNFS 2; MTCW 2; MTFW 2005; RGSF
2
Clarke, Gillian 1937- .... **CLC 61**
See also CA 106; CP 3, 4, 5, 6, 7; CWP;
DLB 40
Clarke, Marcus (Andrew Hislop) 1846-1881
.... **NCLC 19; SSC 94**
See also DLB 230; RGEL 2; RGSF 2
Clarke, Shirley 1925-1997 .... **CLC 16**
See also CA 189
Clash, The
See Headon, (Nicky) Topper; Jones, Mick;
Simonon, Paul; Strummer, Joe
Claudel, Paul (Louis Charles Marie)
1868-1955 .... **TCLC 2, 10**
See also CA 104; 165; DLB 192, 258, 321;
EW 8; EWL 3; GFL 1789 to the Present;
RGWL 2, 3; TWA
Claudian 370(?)-404(?) .... **CMLC 46**
See also RGWL 2, 3
Claudius, Matthias 1740-1815 ...... **NCLC 75**
See also DLB 97
Clavell, James 1925-1994 ...... **CLC 6, 25, 87**
See also BPFB 1; CA 25-28R; 146; CANR
26, 48; CN 5; CPW; DA3; DAM NOV,
POP; MTCW 1, 2; MTFW 2005; NFS 10;
RHW
Clayman, Gregory .... **CLC 65**
Cleaver, (Leroy) Eldridge 1935-1998
.... **BLC 1; CLC 30, 119**
See also BW 1, 3; CA 21-24R; 167; CANR
16, 75; DA3; DAM MULT; MTCW 2;
YAW
Cleese, John (Marwood) 1939- .... **CLC 21**
See Monty Python
See also CA 112; 116; CANR 35; MTCW 1
Cleishbotham, Jebediah
See Scott, Sir Walter
Cleland, John 1710-1789 .... **LC 2, 48**
See also DLB 39; RGEL 2

Clemens, Samuel Langhorne 1835-1910
See Twain, Mark
See also CA 104; 135; CDALB 1865-1917;
DA; DA3; DAB; DAC; DAM MST, NOV;
DLB 12, 23, 64, 74, 186, 189; JRDA;
LMFS 1; MAICYA 1, 2; NCFS 4; NFS
20; SATA 100; YABC 2
Clement of Alexandria 150(?)-215(?)
.... **CMLC 41**
Cleophil
See Congreve, William
Clerihew, E.
See Bentley, E(dmund) C(lerihew)
Clerk, N. W.
See Lewis, C.S.
Cleveland, John 1613-1658 .... **LC 106**
See also DLB 126; RGEL 2
Cliff, Jimmy .... **CLC 21**
See Chambers, James
See also CA 193
Cliff, Michelle 1946- .... **BLCS; CLC 120**
See also BW 2; CA 116; CANR 39, 72; CD-
WLB 3; DLB 157; FW; GLL 2
Clifford, Lady Anne 1590-1676 .... **LC 76**
See also DLB 151
Clifton, Lucille 1936- .. **BLC 1; CLC 19, 66,
162; PC 17**
See also AFAW 2; BW 2, 3; CA 49-52;
CANR 2, 24, 42, 76, 97, 138; CLR 5; CP
2, 3, 4, 5, 6, 7; CSW; CWP; CWRI 5;
DA3; DAM MULT, POET; DLB 5, 41;
EXPP; MAICYA 1, 2; MTCW 1, 2;
MTFW 2005; PFS 1, 14; SATA 20, 69,
128; WP
Clinton, Dirk
See Silverberg, Robert
Clough, Arthur Hugh 1819-1861
.... **NCLC 27, 163**
See also BRW 5; DLB 32; RGEL 2
Clutha, Janet Paterson Frame 1924-2004
See Frame, Janet
See also CA 1-4R; 224; CANR 2, 36, 76,
135; MTCW 1, 2; SATA 119
Clyne, Terence
See Blatty, William Peter
Cobalt, Martin
See Mayne, William (James Carter)
Cobb, Irvin S(hrewsbury) 1876-1944
.... **TCLC 77**
See also CA 175; DLB 11, 25, 86
Cobbett, William 1763-1835 .... **NCLC 49**
See also DLB 43, 107, 158; RGEL 2
Coburn, D(onald) L(ee) 1938- .... **CLC 10**
See also CA 89-92; DFS 23
Cocteau, Jean (Maurice Eugene Clement)
1889-1963 .... **CLC 1, 8, 15, 16, 43; DC
17; TCLC 119; WLC 2**
See also CA 25-28; CANR 40; CAP 2; DA;
DA3; DAB; DAC; DAM DRAM, MST,
NOV; DLB 65, 258, 321; EW 10; EWL
3; GFL 1789 to the Present; MTCW 1, 2;
RGWL 2, 3; TWA
Codrescu, Andrei 1946- .... **CLC 46, 121**
See also CA 33-36R; CAAS 19; CANR 13,
34, 53, 76, 125; CN 7; DA3; DAM POET;
MAL 5; MTCW 2; MTFW 2005
Coe, Max
See Bourne, Randolph S(illiman)
Coe, Tucker
See Westlake, Donald E.
Coen, Ethan 1958- .... **CLC 108**
See also AAYA 54; CA 126; CANR 85
Coen, Joel 1955- .... **CLC 108**
See also AAYA 54; CA 126; CANR 119
The Coen Brothers
See Coen, Ethan; Coen, Joel

Coetzee, J.M. 1940- ..... **CLC 23, 33, 66, 117,
161, 162**
See also AAYA 37; AFW; BRWS 6; CA 77-
80; CANR 41, 54, 74, 114, 133; CN 4, 5,
6, 7; DA3; DAM NOV; DLB 225, 326,
329; EWL 3; LMFS 2; MTCW 1, 2;
MTFW 2005; NFS 21; WLIT 2; WWE 1
Coetzee, John Maxwell
See Coetzee, J.M.
Coffey, Brian
See Koontz, Dean R.
Coffin, Robert P(eter) Tristram 1892-1955
.... **TCLC 95**
See also CA 123; 169; DLB 45
Cohan, George M. 1878-1942 .... **TCLC 60**
See also CA 157; DLB 249; RGAL 4
Cohan, George Michael
See Cohan, George M.
Cohen, Arthur A(llen) 1928-1986 .... **CLC 7,
31**
See also CA 1-4R; 120; CANR 1, 17, 42;
DLB 28; RGHL
Cohen, Leonard 1934- .... **CLC 3, 38**
See also CA 21-24R; CANR 14, 69; CN 1,
2, 3, 4, 5, 6; CP 1, 2, 3, 4, 5, 6, 7; DAC;
DAM MST; DLB 53; EWL 3; MTCW 1
Cohen, Leonard Norman
See Cohen, Leonard
Cohen, Matt(hew) 1942-1999 .... **CLC 19**
See also CA 61-64; 187; CAAS 18; CANR
40; CN 1, 2, 3, 4, 5, 6; DAC; DLB 53
Cohen-Solal, Annie 1948- .... **CLC 50**
See also CA 239
Colegate, Isabel 1931- .... **CLC 36**
See also CA 17-20R; CANR 8, 22, 74; CN
4, 5, 6, 7; DLB 14, 231; INT CANR-22;
MTCW 1
Coleman, Emmett
See Reed, Ishmael
Coleridge, Hartley 1796-1849 .... **NCLC 90**
See also DLB 96
Coleridge, M. E.
See Coleridge, Mary E(lizabeth)
Coleridge, Mary E(lizabeth) 1861-1907
.... **TCLC 73**
See also CA 116; 166; DLB 19, 98
Coleridge, Samuel Taylor 1772-1834
... **NCLC 9, 54, 99, 111, 177; PC 11, 39,
67; WLC 2**
See also CA 66; BRW 4; BRWR 2; BYA
4; CDBLB 1789-1832; DA; DA3; DAB;
DAC; DAM MST, POET; DLB 93, 107;
EXPP; LATS 1:1; LMFS 1; PAB; PFS 4,
5; RGEL 2; TEA; WLIT 3; WP
Coleridge, Sara 1802-1852 .... **NCLC 31**
See also DLB 199
Coles, Don 1928- .... **CLC 46**
See also CA 115; CANR 38; CP 5, 6, 7
Coles, Robert (Martin) 1929- .... **CLC 108**
See also CA 45-48; CANR 3, 32, 66, 70,
135; INT CANR-32; SATA 23
Colette, (Sidonie-Gabrielle) 1873-1954
.... **SSC 10, 93; TCLC 1, 5, 16**
See Willy, Colette
See also CA 104; 131; DA3; DAM NOV;
DLB 65; EW 9; EWL 3; GFL 1789 to the
Present; MTCW 1, 2; MTFW 2005;
RGWL 2, 3; TWA
Collett, (Jacobine) Camilla (Wergeland)
1813-1895 .... **NCLC 22**
Collier, Christopher 1930- .... **CLC 30**
See also AAYA 13; BYA 2; CA 33-36R;
CANR 13, 33, 102; JRDA; MAICYA 1,
2; SATA 16, 70; WYA; YAW 1
Collier, James Lincoln 1928- .... **CLC 30**
See also AAYA 13; BYA 2; CA 9-12R;
CANR 4, 33, 60, 102; CLR 3; DAM POP;
JRDA; MAICYA 1, 2; SAAS 21; SATA 8,
70, 166; WYA; YAW 1

Daly, Mary 1928- .... **CLC 173**
See also CA 25-28R; CANR 30, 62; FW;
GLL 1; MTCW 1

Daly, Maureen 1921-2006 .... **CLC 17**
See also AAYA 5, 58; BYA 6; CANR 37,
83, 108; CLR 96; JRDA; MAICYA 1, 2;
SAAS 1; SATA 2, 129; WYA; YAW

Damas, Leon-Gontran 1912-1978 ... **CLC 84**
See also BW 1; CA 125; 73-76; EWL 3

Dana, Richard Henry Sr. 1787-1879
.... **NCLC 53**

Daniel, Samuel 1562(?)-1619 .... **LC 24**
See also DLB 62; RGEL 2

Daniels, Brett
See Adler, Renata

Dannay, Frederic 1905-1982 .... **CLC 11**
See Queen, Ellery
See also CA 1-4R; 107; CANR 1, 39; CMW
4; DAM POP; DLB 137; MTCW 1

D'Annunzio, Gabriele 1863-1938 .. **TCLC 6,
40**
See also CA 104; 155; EW 8; EWL 3;
RGWL 2, 3; TWA; WLIT 7

Danois, N. le
See Gourmont, Remy(-Marie-Charles) de

Dante 1265-1321 ... **CMLC 3, 18, 39, 70; PC
21; WLCS**
See Alighieri, Dante
See also DA; DA3; DAB; DAC; DAM
MST, POET; EFS 1; EW 1; LAIT 1;
RGWL 2, 3; TWA; WP

d'Antibes, Germain
See Simenon, Georges (Jacques Christian)

Danticat, Edwidge 1969- . **CLC 94, 139, 228**
See also AAYA 29; CA 152, 192; CAAE
192; CANR 73, 129; CN 7; DNFS 1;
EXPS; LATS 1:2; MTCW 2; MTFW
2005; SSFS 1; YAW

Danvers, Dennis 1947- .... **CLC 70**

Danziger, Paula 1944-2004 .... **CLC 21**
See also AAYA 4, 36; BYA 6, 7, 14; CA
112; 115; 229; CANR 37, 132; CLR 20;
JRDA; MAICYA 1, 2; MTFW 2005;
SATA 36, 63, 102, 149; SATA-Brief 30;
SATA-Obit 155; WYA; YAW

Da Ponte, Lorenzo 1749-1838 ...... **NCLC 50**

d'Aragona, Tullia 1510(?)-1556 .... **LC 121**

Dario, Ruben 1867-1916 ..... **HLC 1; PC 15;
TCLC 4**
See also CA 131; CANR 81; DAM MULT;
DLB 290; EWL 3; HW 1, 2; LAW;
MTCW 1, 2; MTFW 2005; RGWL 2, 3

Darley, George 1795-1846 .... **NCLC 2**
See also DLB 96; RGEL 2

Darrow, Clarence (Seward) 1857-1938
.... **TCLC 81**
See also CA 164; DLB 303

Darwin, Charles 1809-1882 .... **NCLC 57**
See also BRWS 7; DLB 57, 166; LATS 1:1;
RGEL 2; TEA; WLIT 4

Darwin, Erasmus 1731-1802 .... **NCLC 106**
See also DLB 93; RGEL 2

Daryush, Elizabeth 1887-1977 .... **CLC 6, 19**
See also CA 49-52; CANR 3, 81; DLB 20

Das, Kamala 1934- .... **CLC 191; PC 43**
See also CA 101; CANR 27, 59; CP 1, 2, 3,
4, 5, 6, 7; CWP; DLB 323; FW

Dasgupta, Surendranath 1887-1952
.... **TCLC 81**
See also CA 157

**Dashwood, Edmee Elizabeth Monica de la
Pasture** 1890-1943
See Delafield, E. M.
See also CA 119; 154

da Silva, Antonio Jose 1705-1739
.... **NCLC 114**

Daudet, (Louis Marie) Alphonse 1840-1897
.... **NCLC 1**
See also DLB 123; GFL 1789 to the Present;
RGSF 2

Daudet, Alphonse Marie Leon 1867-1942
.... **SSC 94**
See also CA 217

d'Aulnoy, Marie-Catherine c. 1650-1705
.... **LC 100**

Daumal, Rene 1908-1944 .... **TCLC 14**
See also CA 114; 247; EWL 3

Davenant, William 1606-1668 .... **LC 13**
See also DLB 58, 126; RGEL 2

Davenport, Guy (Mattison, Jr.) 1927-2005
.... **CLC 6, 14, 38; SSC 16**
See also CA 33-36R; 235; CANR 23, 73;
CN 3, 4, 5, 6; CSW; DLB 130

David, Robert
See Nezval, Vitezslav

Davidson, Avram (James) 1923-1993
See Queen, Ellery
See also CA 101; 171; CANR 26; DLB 8;
FANT; SFW 4; SUFW 1, 2

Davidson, Donald (Grady) 1893-1968
.... **CLC 2, 13, 19**
See also CA 5-8R; 25-28R; CANR 4, 84;
DLB 45

Davidson, Hugh
See Hamilton, Edmond

Davidson, John 1857-1909 .... **TCLC 24**
See also CA 118; 217; DLB 19; RGEL 2

Davidson, Sara 1943- .... **CLC 9**
See also CA 81-84; CANR 44, 68; DLB
185

Davie, Donald (Alfred) 1922-1995 ... **CLC 5,
8, 10, 31; PC 29**
See also BRWS 6; CA 1-4R; 149; CAAS 3;
CANR 1, 44; CP 1, 2, 3, 4, 5, 6; DLB 27;
MTCW 1; RGEL 2

Davie, Elspeth 1918-1995 .... **SSC 52**
See also CA 120; 126; 150; CANR 141;
DLB 139

Davies, Ray(mond Douglas) 1944- .. **CLC 21**
See also CA 116; 146; CANR 92

Davies, Rhys 1901-1978 .... **CLC 23**
See also CA 9-12R; 81-84; CANR 4; CN 1,
2; DLB 139, 191

Davies, Robertson 1913-1995 . **CLC 2, 7, 13,
25, 42, 75, 91; WLC 2**
See Davies, William Robertson; March-
banks, Samuel
See also BEST 89:2; BPFB 1; CA 33-36R;
150; CANR 17, 42, 103; CN 1, 2, 3, 4, 5,
6; CPW; DA; DA3; DAB; DAC; DAM
MST, NOV, POP; DLB 68; EWL 3; HGG;
INT CANR-17; MTCW 1, 2; MTFW
2005; RGEL 2; TWA

Davies, Sir John 1569-1626 .... **LC 85**
See also DLB 172

Davies, Walter C.
See Kornbluth, C(yril) M.

Davies, William Henry 1871-1940 .. **TCLC 5**
See also BRWS 11; CA 104; 179; DLB 19,
174; EWL 3; RGEL 2

Da Vinci, Leonardo 1452-1519 ... **LC 12, 57,
60**
See also AAYA 40

Davis, Angela (Yvonne) 1944- .... **CLC 77**
See also BW 2, 3; CA 57-60; CANR 10,
81; CSW; DA3; DAM MULT; FW

Davis, B. Lynch
See Bioy Casares, Adolfo; Borges, Jorge
Luis

Davis, Frank Marshall 1905-1987 ..... **BLC 1**
See also BW 2, 3; CA 125; 123; CANR 42,
80; DAM MULT; DLB 51

Davis, Gordon
See Hunt, E(verette) Howard, (Jr.)

Davis, H(arold) L(enoir) 1896-1960
.... **CLC 49**
See also ANW; CA 178; 89-92; DLB 9,
206; SATA 114; TCWW 1, 2

Davis, Hart
See Poniatowska, Elena

Davis, Natalie Zemon 1928- .... **CLC 204**
See also CA 53-56; CANR 58, 100

Davis, Rebecca (Blaine) Harding 1831-1910
.... **SSC 38; TCLC 6**
See also AMWS 16; CA 104; 179; DLB 74,
239; FW; NFS 14; RGAL 4; TUS

Davis, Richard Harding 1864-1916
.... **TCLC 24**
See also CA 114; 179; DLB 12, 23, 78, 79,
189; DLBD 13; RGAL 4

Davison, Frank Dalby 1893-1970 ... **CLC 15**
See also CA 217; 116; DLB 260

Davison, Lawrence H.
See Lawrence, D(avid) H(erbert Richards)

Davison, Peter (Hubert) 1928-2004
.... **CLC 28**
See also CA 9-12R; 234; CAAS 4; CANR
3, 43, 84; CP 1, 2, 3, 4, 5, 6, 7; DLB 5

Davys, Mary 1674-1732 .... **LC 1, 46**
See also DLB 39

Dawson, (Guy) Fielding (Lewis) 1930-2002
.... **CLC 6**
See also CA 85-88; 202; CANR 108; DLB
130; DLBY 2002

Dawson, Peter
See Faust, Frederick (Schiller)
See also TCWW 1, 2

Day, Clarence (Shepard, Jr.) 1874-1935
.... **TCLC 25**
See also CA 108; 199; DLB 11

Day, John 1574(?)-1640(?) .... **LC 70**
See also DLB 62, 170; RGEL 2

Day, Thomas 1748-1789 .... **LC 1**
See also DLB 39; YABC 1

Day Lewis, C(ecil) 1904-1972 .... **CLC 1, 6,
10; PC 11**
See Blake, Nicholas; Lewis, C. Day
See also BRWS 3; CA 13-16; 33-36R;
CANR 34; CAP 1; CP 1; CWRI 5; DAM
POET; DLB 15, 20; EWL 3; MTCW 1, 2;
RGEL 2

Dazai Osamu .... **SSC 41; TCLC 11**
See Tsushima, Shuji
See also CA 164; DLB 182; EWL 3; MJW;
RGSF 2; RGWL 2, 3; TWA

de Andrade, Carlos Drummond
See Drummond de Andrade, Carlos

de Andrade, Mario 1892(?)-1945
See Andrade, Mario de
See also CA 178; HW 2

Deane, Norman
See Creasey, John

Deane, Seamus (Francis) 1940- ..... **CLC 122**
See also CA 118; CANR 42

de Beauvoir, Simone
See Beauvoir, Simone de

de Beer, P.
See Bosman, Herman Charles

De Botton, Alain 1969- .... **CLC 203**
See also CA 159; CANR 96

de Brissac, Malcolm
See Dickinson, Peter (Malcolm de Brissac)

de Campos, Alvaro
See Pessoa, Fernando (Antonio Nogueira)

de Chardin, Pierre Teilhard
See Teilhard de Chardin, (Marie Joseph)
Pierre

de Crenne, Helisenne c. 1510-c. 1560
.... **LC 113**

Dee, John 1527-1608 .... **LC 20**
See also DLB 136, 213

Deer, Sandra 1940- .... **CLC 45**
See also CA 186

Doctorow, E.L. 1931- ...... **CLC 6, 11, 15, 18, 37, 44, 65, 113, 214**
See also AAYA 22; AITN 2; AMWS 4; BEST 89:3; BPFB 1; CA 45-48; CANR 2, 33, 51, 76, 97, 133; CDALB 1968-1988; CN 3, 4, 5, 6, 7; CPW; DA3; DAM NOV, POP; DLB 2, 28, 173; DLBY 1980; EWL 3; LAIT 3; MAL 5; MTCW 1, 2; MTFW 2005; NFS 6; RGAL 4; RGHL; RHW; TCLE 1:1; TCWW 1, 2; TUS

Dodgson, Charles L(utwidge) 1832-1898
See Carroll, Lewis
See also CLR 2; DA; DA3; DAB; DAC; DAM MST, NOV, POET; MAICYA 1, 2; SATA 100; YABC 2

Dodsley, Robert 1703-1764 .... **LC 97**
See also DLB 95; RGEL 2

Dodson, Owen (Vincent) 1914-1983
.... **BLC 1; CLC 79**
See also BW 1; CA 65-68; 110; CANR 24; DAM MULT; DLB 76

Doeblin, Alfred 1878-1957 .... **TCLC 13**
See Doblin, Alfred
See also CA 110; 141; DLB 66

Doerr, Harriet 1910-2002 .... **CLC 34**
See also CA 117; 122; 213; CANR 47; INT CA-122; LATS 1:2

Domecq, H(onorio Bustos)
See Bioy Casares, Adolfo

Domecq, H(onorio) Bustos
See Bioy Casares, Adolfo; Borges, Jorge Luis

Domini, Rey
See Lorde, Audre
See also GLL 1

Dominique
See Proust, (Valentin-Louis-George-Eugene) Marcel

Don, A
See Stephen, Sir Leslie

Donaldson, Stephen R(eeder) 1947-
.... **CLC 46, 138**
See also AAYA 36; BPFB 1; CA 89-92; CANR 13, 55, 99; CPW; DAM POP; FANT; INT CANR-13; SATA 121; SFW 4; SUFW 1, 2

Donleavy, J(ames) P(atrick) 1926- ... **CLC 1, 4, 6, 10, 45**
See also AITN 2; BPFB 1; CA 9-12R; CANR 24, 49, 62, 80, 124; CBD; CD 5, 6; CN 1, 2, 3, 4, 5, 6, 7; DLB 6, 173; INT CANR-24; MAL 5; MTCW 1, 2; MTFW 2005; RGAL 4

Donnadieu, Marguerite
See Duras, Marguerite

Donne, John 1572-1631 .. **LC 10, 24, 91; PC 1, 43; WLC 2**
See also AAYA 67; BRW 1; BRWC 1; BRWR 2; CDBLB Before 1660; DA; DAB; DAC; DAM MST, POET; DLB 121, 151; EXPP; PAB; PFS 2, 11; RGEL 3; TEA; WLIT 3; WP

Donnell, David 1939(?)- .... **CLC 34**
See also CA 197

Donoghue, Denis 1928- .... **CLC 209**
See also CA 17-20R; CANR 16, 102

Donoghue, P. S.
See Hunt, E(verette) Howard, (Jr.)

Donoso (Yanez), Jose 1924-1996 .. **CLC 4, 8, 11, 32, 99; HLC 1; SSC 34; TCLC 133**
See also CA 81-84; 155; CANR 32, 73; CD-WLB 3; CWW 2; DAM MULT; DLB 113; EWL 3; HW 1, 2; LAW; LAWS 1; MTCW 1, 2; MTFW 2005; RGSF 2; WLIT 1

Donovan, John 1928-1992 .... **CLC 35**
See also AAYA 20; CA 97-100; 137; CLR 3; MAICYA 1, 2; SATA 72; SATA-Brief 29; YAW

Don Roberto
See Cunninghame Graham, Robert (Gallnigad) Bontine

Doolittle, Hilda 1886-1961 ...... **CLC 3, 8, 14, 31, 34, 73; PC 5; WLC 3**
See H. D.
See also AAYA 66; AMWS 1; CA 97-100; CANR 35, 131; DA; DAC; DAM MST, POET; DLB 4, 45; EWL 3; FW; GLL 1; LMFS 2; MAL 5; MBL; MTCW 1, 2; MTFW 2005; PFS 6; RGAL 4

Doppo, Kunikida .... **TCLC 99**
See Kunikida Doppo

Dorfman, Ariel 1942- .... **CLC 48, 77, 189; HLC 1**
See also CA 124; 130; CANR 67, 70, 135; CWW 2; DAM MULT; DFS 4; EWL 3; HW 1, 2; INT CA-130; WLIT 1

Dorn, Edward (Merton) 1929-1999
.... **CLC 10, 18**
See also CA 93-96; 187; CANR 42, 79; CP 1, 2, 3, 4, 5, 6, 7; DLB 5; INT CA-93-96; WP

Dor-Ner, Zvi .... **CLC 70**

Dorris, Michael 1945-1997 .... **CLC 109; NNAL**
See also AAYA 20; BEST 90:1; BYA 12; CA 102; 157; CANR 19, 46, 75; CLR 58; DA3; DAM MULT, NOV; DLB 175; LAIT 5; MTCW 2; MTFW 2005; NFS 3; RGAL 4; SATA 75; SATA-Obit 94; TCWW 2; YAW

Dorris, Michael A.
See Dorris, Michael

Dorsan, Luc
See Simenon, Georges (Jacques Christian)

Dorsange, Jean
See Simenon, Georges (Jacques Christian)

Dorset
See Sackville, Thomas

Dos Passos, John (Roderigo) 1896-1970
.. **CLC 1, 4, 8, 11, 15, 25, 34, 82; WLC 2**
See also AMW; BPFB 1; CA 1-4R; 29-32R; CANR 3; CDALB 1929-1941; DA; DA3; DAB; DAC; DAM MST, NOV; DLB 4, 9, 274, 316; DLBD 1, 15; DLBY 1996; EWL 3; MAL 5; MTCW 1, 2; MTFW 2005; NFS 14; RGAL 4; TUS

Dossage, Jean
See Simenon, Georges (Jacques Christian)

Dostoevsky, Fedor Mikhailovich 1821-1881
.. **NCLC 2, 7, 21, 33, 43, 119, 167; SSC 2, 33, 44; WLC 2**
See Dostoevsky, Fyodor
See also AAYA 40; DA; DA3; DAB; DAC; DAM MST, NOV; EW 7; EXPN; NFS 3, 8; RGSF 2; RGWL 2, 3; SSFS 8; TWA

Dostoevsky, Fyodor
See Dostoevsky, Fedor Mikhailovich
See also DLB 238; LATS 1:1; LMFS 1, 2

Doty, M. R.
See Doty, Mark (Alan)

Doty, Mark
See Doty, Mark (Alan)

Doty, Mark (Alan) 1953(?)- ... **CLC 176; PC 53**
See also AMWS 11; CA 161, 183; CAAE 183; CANR 110; CP 7

Doty, Mark A.
See Doty, Mark (Alan)

Doughty, Charles M(ontagu) 1843-1926
.... **TCLC 27**
See also CA 115; 178; DLB 19, 57, 174

Douglas, Ellen .... **CLC 73**
See Haxton, Josephine Ayres; Williamson, Ellen Douglas
See also CN 5, 6, 7; CSW; DLB 292

Douglas, Gavin 1475(?)-1522 .... **LC 20**
See also DLB 132; RGEL 2

Douglas, George
See Brown, George Douglas
See also RGEL 2

Douglas, Keith (Castellain) 1920-1944
.... **TCLC 40**
See also BRW 7; CA 160; DLB 27; EWL 3; PAB; RGEL 2

Douglas, Leonard
See Bradbury, Ray

Douglas, Michael
See Crichton, Michael

Douglas, (George) Norman 1868-1952
.... **TCLC 68**
See also BRW 6; CA 119; 157; DLB 34, 195; RGEL 2

Douglas, William
See Brown, George Douglas

Douglass, Frederick 1817(?)-1895 .... **BLC 1; NCLC 7, 55, 141; WLC 2**
See also AAYA 48; AFAW 1, 2; AMWC 1; AMWS 3; CDALB 1640-1865; DA; DA3; DAC; DAM MST, MULT; DLB 1, 43, 50, 79, 243; FW; LAIT 2; NCFS 2; RGAL 4; SATA 29

Dourado, (Waldomiro Freitas) Autran 1926-
.... **CLC 23, 60**
See also CA 25-28R; 179; CANR 34, 81; DLB 145, 307; HW 2

Dourado, Waldomiro Freitas Autran
See Dourado, (Waldomiro Freitas) Autran

Dove, Rita 1952- . **BLCS; CLC 50, 81; PC 6**
See Dove, Rita Frances
See also AAYA 46; AMWS 4; BW 2; CA 109; CAAS 19; CANR 27, 42, 68, 76, 97, 132; CDALBS; CP 5, 6, 7; CSW; CWP; DA3; DAM MULT, POET; DLB 120; EWL 3; EXPP; MAL 5; MTCW 2; MTFW 2005; PFS 1, 15; RGAL 4

Doveglion
See Villa, Jose Garcia

Dowell, Coleman 1925-1985 .... **CLC 60**
See also CA 25-28R; 117; CANR 10; DLB 130; GLL 2

Dowson, Ernest (Christopher) 1867-1900
.... **TCLC 4**
See also CA 105; 150; DLB 19, 135; RGEL 2

Doyle, A. Conan
See Doyle, Sir Arthur Conan

Doyle, Sir Arthur Conan 1859-1930
.... **SSC 12, 83, 95; TCLC 7; WLC 2**
See Conan Doyle, Arthur
See also AAYA 14; BRWS 2; CA 104; 122; CANR 131; CDBLB 1890-1914; CLR 106; CMW 4; DA; DA3; DAB; DAC; DAM MST, NOV; DLB 18, 70, 156, 178; EXPS; HGG; LAIT 1; MSW; MTCW 1, 2; MTFW 2005; RGEL 2; RGSF 2; RHW; SATA 24; SCFW 1, 2; SFW 4; SSFS 2; TEA; WCH; WLIT 4; WYA; YAW

Doyle, Conan
See Doyle, Sir Arthur Conan

Doyle, John
See Graves, Robert

Doyle, Roddy 1958- .... **CLC 81, 178**
See also AAYA 14; BRWS 5; CA 143; CANR 73, 128; CN 6, 7; DA3; DLB 194, 326; MTCW 2; MTFW 2005

Doyle, Sir A. Conan
See Doyle, Sir Arthur Conan

Dr. A
See Asimov, Isaac; Silverstein, Alvin; Silverstein, Virginia B(arbara Opshelor)

Drabble, Margaret 1939- ..... **CLC 2, 3, 5, 8, 10, 22, 53, 129**
See also BRWS 4; CA 13-16R; CANR 18, 35, 63, 112, 131; CDBLB 1960 to Present; CN 1, 2, 3, 4, 5, 6, 7; CPW; DA3; DAB; DAC; DAM MST, NOV, POP; DLB 14, 155, 231; EWL 3; FW; MTCW 1, 2; MTFW 2005; RGEL 2; SATA 48; TEA

Drakulic, Slavenka 1949- .... **CLC 173**
See also CA 144; CANR 92

Drakulic-Ilic, Slavenka
See Drakulic, Slavenka

Drapier, M. B.
See Swift, Jonathan

Drayham, James
See Mencken, H(enry) L(ouis)

Drayton, Michael 1563-1631 .... **LC 8**
See also DAM POET; DLB 121; RGEL 2

Dreadstone, Carl
See Campbell, (John) Ramsey

Dreiser, Theodore 1871-1945 .... **SSC 30; TCLC 10, 18, 35, 83; WLC 2**
See also AMW; AMWC 2; AMWR 2; BYA 15, 16; CA 106; 132; CDALB 1865-1917; DA; DA3; DAC; DAM MST, NOV; DLB 9, 12, 102, 137; DLBD 1; EWL 3; LAIT 2; LMFS 2; MAL 5; MTCW 1, 2; MTFW 2005; NFS 8, 17; RGAL 4; TUS

Dreiser, Theodore Herman Albert
See Dreiser, Theodore

Drexler, Rosalyn 1926- .... **CLC 2, 6**
See also CA 81-84; CAD; CANR 68, 124; CD 5, 6; CWD; MAL 5

Dreyer, Carl Theodor 1889-1968 .... **CLC 16**
See also CA 116

Drieu la Rochelle, Pierre 1893-1945
.... **TCLC 21**
See also CA 117; 250; DLB 72; EWL 3; GFL 1789 to the Present

Drieu la Rochelle, Pierre-Eugene 1893-1945
See Drieu la Rochelle, Pierre

Drinkwater, John 1882-1937 .... **TCLC 57**
See also CA 109; 149; DLB 10, 19, 149; RGEL 2

Drop Shot
See Cable, George Washington

Droste-Hulshoff, Annette Freiin von
1797-1848 .... **NCLC 3, 133**
See also CDWLB 2; DLB 133; RGSF 2; RGWL 2, 3

Drummond, Walter
See Silverberg, Robert

Drummond, William Henry 1854-1907
.... **TCLC 25**
See also CA 160; DLB 92

Drummond de Andrade, Carlos 1902-1987
.... **CLC 18; TCLC 139**
See Andrade, Carlos Drummond de
See also CA 132; 123; DLB 307; LAW

Drummond of Hawthornden, William
1585-1649 .... **LC 83**
See also DLB 121, 213; RGEL 2

Drury, Allen (Stuart) 1918-1998 ..... **CLC 37**
See also CA 57-60; 170; CANR 18, 52; CN 1, 2, 3, 4, 5, 6; INT CANR-18

Druse, Eleanor
See King, Stephen

Dryden, John 1631-1700 .... **DC 3; LC 3, 21, 115; PC 25; WLC 2**
See also BRW 2; CDBLB 1660-1789; DA; DAB; DAC; DAM DRAM, MST, POET; DLB 80, 101, 131; EXPP; IDTP; LMFS 1; RGEL 2; TEA; WLIT 3

du Bellay, Joachim 1524-1560 .... **LC 92**
See also DLB 327; GFL Beginnings to 1789; RGWL 2, 3

Duberman, Martin (Bauml) 1930- ... **CLC 8**
See also CA 1-4R; CAD; CANR 2, 63, 137; CD 5, 6

Dubie, Norman (Evans) 1945- .... **CLC 36**
See also CA 69-72; CANR 12, 115; CP 3, 4, 5, 6, 7; DLB 120; PFS 12

Du Bois, W(illiam) E(dward) B(urghardt)
1868-1963 .... **BLC 1; CLC 1, 2, 13, 64, 96; HR 1:2; TCLC 169; WLC 2**
See also AAYA 40; AFAW 1, 2; AMWC 1; AMWS 2; BW 1, 3; CA 85-88; CANR 34, 82, 132; CDALB 1865-1917; DA; DA3; DAC; DAM MST, MULT, NOV; DLB 47, 50, 91, 246, 284; EWL 3; EXPP; LAIT 2; LMFS 2; MAL 5; MTCW 1, 2; MTFW 2005; NCFS 1; PFS 13; RGAL 4; SATA 42

Dubus, Andre 1936-1999 .... **CLC 13, 36, 97; SSC 15**
See also AMWS 7; CA 21-24R; 177; CANR 17; CN 5, 6; CSW; DLB 130; INT CANR-17; RGAL 4; SSFS 10; TCLE 1:1

Duca Minimo
See D'Annunzio, Gabriele

Ducharme, Rejean 1941- .... **CLC 74**
See also CA 165; DLB 60

du Chatelet, Emilie 1706-1749 .... **LC 96**
See Chatelet, Gabrielle-Emilie Du

Duchen, Claire .... **CLC 65**

Duclos, Charles Pinot- 1704-1772 .... **LC 1**
See also GFL Beginnings to 1789

Dudek, Louis 1918-2001 .... **CLC 11, 19**
See also CA 45-48; 215; CAAS 14; CANR 1; CP 1, 2, 3, 4, 5, 6, 7; DLB 88

Duerrenmatt, Friedrich 1921-1990 .. **CLC 1, 4, 8, 11, 15, 43, 102**
See Durrenmatt, Friedrich
See also CA 17-20R; CANR 33; CMW 4; DAM DRAM; DLB 69, 124; MTCW 1, 2

Duffy, Bruce 1953(?)- .... **CLC 50**
See also CA 172

Duffy, Maureen (Patricia) 1933- ..... **CLC 37**
See also CA 25-28R; CANR 33, 68; CBD; CN 1, 2, 3, 4, 5, 6, 7; CP 5, 6, 7; CWD; CWP; DFS 15; DLB 14, 310; FW; MTCW 1

Du Fu
See Tu Fu
See also RGWL 2, 3

Dugan, Alan 1923-2003 .... **CLC 2, 6**
See also CA 81-84; 220; CANR 119; CP 1, 2, 3, 4, 5, 6, 7; DLB 5; MAL 5; PFS 10

du Gard, Roger Martin
See Martin du Gard, Roger

Duhamel, Georges 1884-1966 .... **CLC 8**
See also CA 81-84; 25-28R; CANR 35; DLB 65; EWL 3; GFL 1789 to the Present; MTCW 1

Dujardin, Edouard (Emile Louis) 1861-1949
.... **TCLC 13**
See also CA 109; DLB 123

Duke, Raoul
See Thompson, Hunter S.

Dulles, John Foster 1888-1959 ..... **TCLC 72**
See also CA 115; 149

Dumas, Alexandre (pere) 1802-1870
.... **NCLC 11, 71; WLC 2**
See also AAYA 22; BYA 3; DA; DA3; DAB; DAC; DAM MST, NOV; DLB 119, 192; EW 6; GFL 1789 to the Present; LAIT 1, 2; NFS 14, 19; RGWL 2, 3; SATA 18; TWA; WCH

Dumas, Alexandre (fils) 1824-1895 .... **DC 1; NCLC 9**
See also DLB 192; GFL 1789 to the Present; RGWL 2, 3

Dumas, Claudine
See Malzberg, Barry N(athaniel)

Dumas, Henry L. 1934-1968 .... **CLC 6, 62**
See also BW 1; CA 85-88; DLB 41; RGAL 4

du Maurier, Daphne 1907-1989 . **CLC 6, 11, 59; SSC 18**
See also AAYA 37; BPFB 1; BRWS 3; CA 5-8R; 128; CANR 6, 55; CMW 4; CN 1, 2, 3, 4; CPW; DA3; DAB; DAC; DAM MST, POP; DLB 191; GL 2; HGG; LAIT 3; MSW; MTCW 1, 2; NFS 12; RGEL 2; RGSF 2; RHW; SATA 27; SATA-Obit 60; SSFS 14, 16; TEA

Du Maurier, George 1834-1896 .... **NCLC 86**
See also DLB 153, 178; RGEL 2

Dunbar, Paul Laurence 1872-1906 .. **BLC 1; PC 5; SSC 8; TCLC 2, 12; WLC 2**
See also AFAW 1, 2; AMWS 2; BW 1, 3; CA 104; 124; CANR 79; CDALB 1865-1917; DA; DA3; DAC; DAM MST, MULT, POET; DLB 50, 54, 78; EXPP; MAL 5; RGAL 4; SATA 34

Dunbar, William 1460(?)-1520(?) ..... **LC 20; PC 67**
See also BRWS 8; DLB 132, 146; RGEL 2

Dunbar-Nelson, Alice .... **HR 1:2**
See Nelson, Alice Ruth Moore Dunbar

Duncan, Dora Angela
See Duncan, Isadora

Duncan, Isadora 1877(?)-1927 ...... **TCLC 68**
See also CA 118; 149

Duncan, Lois 1934- .... **CLC 26**
See also AAYA 4, 34; BYA 6, 8; CA 1-4R; CANR 2, 23, 36, 111; CLR 29; JRDA; MAICYA 1, 2; MAICYAS 1; MTFW 2005; SAAS 2; SATA 1, 36, 75, 133, 141; SATA-Essay 141; WYA; YAW

Duncan, Robert 1919-1988 .. **CLC 1, 2, 4, 7, 15, 41, 55; PC 2, 75**
See also BG 1:2; CA 9-12R; 124; CANR 28, 62; CP 1, 2, 3, 4; DAM POET; DLB 5, 16, 193; EWL 3; MAL 5; MTCW 1, 2; MTFW 2005; PFS 13; RGAL 4; WP

Duncan, Sara Jeannette 1861-1922
.... **TCLC 60**
See also CA 157; DLB 92

Dunlap, William 1766-1839 .... **NCLC 2**
See also DLB 30, 37, 59; RGAL 4

Dunn, Douglas (Eaglesham) 1942- .. **CLC 6, 40**
See also BRWS 10; CA 45-48; CANR 2, 33, 126; CP 1, 2, 3, 4, 5, 6, 7; DLB 40; MTCW 1

Dunn, Katherine 1945- .... **CLC 71**
See also CA 33-36R; CANR 72; HGG; MTCW 2; MTFW 2005

Dunn, Stephen 1939- .... **CLC 36, 206**
See also AMWS 11; CA 33-36R; CANR 12, 48, 53, 105; CP 3, 4, 5, 6, 7; DLB 105; PFS 21

Dunn, Stephen Elliott
See Dunn, Stephen

Dunne, Finley Peter 1867-1936 .... **TCLC 28**
See also CA 108; 178; DLB 11, 23; RGAL 4

Dunne, John Gregory 1932-2003 .... **CLC 28**
See also CA 25-28R; 222; CANR 14, 50; CN 5, 6, 7; DLBY 1980

Dunsany, Lord .... **TCLC 2, 59**
See Dunsany, Edward John Moreton Drax Plunkett
See also DLB 77, 153, 156, 255; FANT; IDTP; RGEL 2; SFW 4; SUFW 1

Dunsany, Edward John Moreton Drax Plunkett 1878-1957
See Dunsany, Lord
See also CA 104; 148; DLB 10; MTCW 2

Duns Scotus, John 1266(?)-1308 . **CMLC 59**
See also DLB 115

du Perry, Jean
See Simenon, Georges (Jacques Christian)

Farina, Richard 1936(?)-1966 .... **CLC 9**
See also CA 81-84; 25-28R

Farley, Walter (Lorimer) 1915-1989
.... **CLC 17**
See also AAYA 58; BYA 14; CA 17-20R;
CANR 8, 29, 84; DLB 22; JRDA; MAI-
CYA 1, 2; SATA 2, 43, 132; YAW

Farmer, Philip Jose 1918- .... **CLC 1, 19**
See also AAYA 28; BPFB 1; CA 1-4R;
CANR 4, 35, 111; DLB 8; MTCW 1;
SATA 93; SCFW 1, 2; SFW 4

Farquhar, George 1677-1707 .... **LC 21**
See also BRW 2; DAM DRAM; DLB 84;
RGEL 2

Farrell, J(ames) G(ordon) 1935-1979
.... **CLC 6**
See also CA 73-76; 89-92; CANR 36; CN
1, 2; DLB 14, 271, 326; MTCW 1; RGEL
2; RHW; WLIT 4

Farrell, James T(homas) 1904-1979
.... **CLC 1, 4, 8, 11, 66; SSC 28**
See also AMW; BPFB 1; CA 5-8R; 89-92;
CANR 9, 61; CN 1, 2; DLB 4, 9, 86;
DLBD 2; EWL 3; MAL 5; MTCW 1, 2;
MTFW 2005; RGAL 4

Farrell, Warren (Thomas) 1943- ..... **CLC 70**
See also CA 146; CANR 120

Farren, Richard J.
See Betjeman, John

Farren, Richard M.
See Betjeman, John

Fassbinder, Rainer Werner 1946-1982
.... **CLC 20**
See also CA 93-96; 106; CANR 31

Fast, Howard 1914-2003 ...... **CLC 23, 131**
See also AAYA 16; BPFB 1; CA 1-4R, 181;
214; CAAE 181; CAAS 18; CANR 1, 33,
54, 75, 98, 140; CMW 4; CN 1, 2, 3, 4, 5,
6, 7; CPW; DAM NOV; DLB 9; INT
CANR-33; LATS 1:1; MAL 5; MTCW 2;
MTFW 2005; RHW; SATA 7; SATA-
Essay 107; TCWW 1, 2; YAW

Faulcon, Robert
See Holdstock, Robert P.

Faulkner, William (Cuthbert) 1897-1962
..... **CLC 1, 3, 6, 8, 9, 11, 14, 18, 28, 52,
68; SSC 1, 35, 42, 92; TCLC 141;
WLC 2**
See also AAYA 7; AMW; AMWR 1; BPFB
1; BYA 5, 15; CA 81-84; CANR 33;
CDALB 1929-1941; DA; DA3; DAB;
DAC; DAM MST, NOV; DLB 9, 11, 44,
102, 316, 330; DLBD 2; DLBY 1986,
1997; EWL 3; EXPN; EXPS; GL 2; LAIT
2; LATS 1:1; LMFS 2; MAL 5; MTCW
1, 2; MTFW 2005; NFS 4, 8, 13, 24;
RGAL 4; RGSF 2; SSFS 2, 5, 6, 12; TUS

Fauset, Jessie Redmon 1882(?)-1961
.... **BLC 2; CLC 19, 54; HR 1:2**
See also AFAW 2; BW 1; CA 109; CANR
83; DAM MULT; DLB 51; FW; LMFS 2;
MAL 5; MBL

Faust, Frederick (Schiller) 1892-1944
.... **TCLC 49**
See Brand, Max; Dawson, Peter; Frederick,
John
See also CA 108; 152; CANR 143; DAM
POP; DLB 256; TUS

Faust, Irvin 1924- .... **CLC 8**
See also CA 33-36R; CANR 28, 67; CN 1,
2, 3, 4, 5, 6, 7; DLB 2, 28, 218, 278;
DLBY 1980

Fawkes, Guy
See Benchley, Robert (Charles)

Fearing, Kenneth (Flexner) 1902-1961
.... **CLC 51**
See also CA 93-96; CANR 59; CMW 4;
DLB 9; MAL 5; RGAL 4

Fecamps, Elise
See Creasey, John

Federman, Raymond 1928- .... **CLC 6, 47**
See also CA 17-20R, 208; CAAE 208;
CAAS 8; CANR 10, 43, 83, 108; CN 3,
4, 5, 6; DLBY 1980

Federspiel, J(uerg) F. 1931- .... **CLC 42**
See also CA 146

Feiffer, Jules (Ralph) 1929- ..... **CLC 2, 8, 64**
See also AAYA 3, 62; CA 17-20R; CAD;
CANR 30, 59, 129; CD 5, 6; DAM
DRAM; DLB 7, 44; INT CANR-30;
MTCW 1; SATA 8, 61, 111, 157

Feige, Hermann Albert Otto Maximilian
See Traven, B.

Feinberg, David B. 1956-1994 .... **CLC 59**
See also CA 135; 147

Feinstein, Elaine 1930- .... **CLC 36**
See also CA 69-72; CAAS 1; CANR 31,
68, 121; CN 3, 4, 5, 6, 7; CP 2, 3, 4, 5, 6,
7; CWP; DLB 14, 40; MTCW 1

Feke, Gilbert David .... **CLC 65**

Feldman, Irving (Mordecai) 1928- ... **CLC 7**
See also CA 1-4R; CANR 1; CP 1, 2, 3, 4,
5, 6, 7; DLB 169; TCLE 1:1

Felix-Tchicaya, Gerald
See Tchicaya, Gerald Felix

Fellini, Federico 1920-1993 .... **CLC 16, 85**
See also CA 65-68; 143; CANR 33

Felltham, Owen 1602(?)-1668 .... **LC 92**
See also DLB 126, 151

Felsen, Henry Gregor 1916-1995 .... **CLC 17**
See also CA 1-4R; 180; CANR 1; SAAS 2;
SATA 1

Felski, Rita .... **CLC 65**

Fenno, Jack
See Calisher, Hortense

Fenollosa, Ernest (Francisco) 1853-1908
.... **TCLC 91**

Fenton, James Martin 1949- ... **CLC 32, 209**
See also CA 102; CANR 108; CP 2, 3, 4, 5,
6, 7; DLB 40; PFS 11

Ferber, Edna 1887-1968 .... **CLC 18, 93**
See also AITN 1; CA 5-8R; 25-28R; CANR
68, 105; DLB 9, 28, 86, 266; MAL 5;
MTCW 1, 2; MTFW 2005; RGAL 4;
RHW; SATA 7; TCWW 1, 2

Ferdowsi, Abu'l Qasem 940-1020(?)
.... **CMLC 43**
See Firdawsi, Abu al-Qasim
See also RGWL 2, 3

Ferguson, Helen
See Kavan, Anna

Ferguson, Niall 1964- .... **CLC 134**
See also CA 190; CANR 154

Ferguson, Samuel 1810-1886 .... **NCLC 33**
See also DLB 32; RGEL 2

Fergusson, Robert 1750-1774 .... **LC 29**
See also DLB 109; RGEL 2

Ferling, Lawrence
See Ferlinghetti, Lawrence

Ferlinghetti, Lawrence 1919(?)- ... **CLC 2, 6,
10, 27, 111; PC 1**
See also BG 1:2; CA 5-8R; CAD; CANR 3,
41, 73, 125; CDALB 1941-1968; CP 1, 2,
3, 4, 5, 6, 7; DA3; DAM POET; DLB 5,
16; MAL 5; MTCW 1, 2; MTFW 2005;
RGAL 4; WP

Ferlinghetti, Lawrence Monsanto
See Ferlinghetti, Lawrence

Fern, Fanny
See Parton, Sara Payson Willis

Fernandez, Vicente Garcia Huidobro
See Huidobro Fernandez, Vicente Garcia

Fernandez-Armesto, Felipe .... **CLC 70**
See Fernandez-Armesto, Felipe Fermin
Ricardo
See also CANR 153

Fernandez-Armesto, Felipe Fermin Ricardo
1950-
See Fernandez-Armesto, Felipe
See also CA 142; CANR 93

Fernandez de Lizardi, Jose Joaquin
See Lizardi, Jose Joaquin Fernandez de

Ferre, Rosario 1938- .... **CLC 139; HLCS 1;
SSC 36**
See also CA 131; CANR 55, 81, 134; CWW
2; DLB 145; EWL 3; HW 1, 2; LAWS 1;
MTCW 2; MTFW 2005; WLIT 1

Ferrer, Gabriel (Francisco Victor) Miro
See Miro (Ferrer), Gabriel (Francisco
Victor)

Ferrier, Susan (Edmonstone) 1782-1854
.... **NCLC 8**
See also DLB 116; RGEL 2

Ferrigno, Robert 1948(?)- .... **CLC 65**
See also CA 140; CANR 125

Ferron, Jacques 1921-1985 .... **CLC 94**
See also CA 117; 129; CCA 1; DAC; DLB
60; EWL 3

Feuchtwanger, Lion 1884-1958 .... **TCLC 3**
See also CA 104; 187; DLB 66; EWL 3;
RGHL

Feuerbach, Ludwig 1804-1872 ... **NCLC 139**
See also DLB 133

Feuillet, Octave 1821-1890 .... **NCLC 45**
See also DLB 192

Feydeau, Georges (Leon Jules Marie)
1862-1921 .... **TCLC 22**
See also CA 113; 152; CANR 84; DAM
DRAM; DLB 192; EWL 3; GFL 1789 to
the Present; RGWL 2, 3

Fichte, Johann Gottlieb 1762-1814
.... **NCLC 62**
See also DLB 90

Ficino, Marsilio 1433-1499 .... **LC 12**
See also LMFS 1

Fiedeler, Hans
See Doeblin, Alfred

Fiedler, Leslie A(aron) 1917-2003 .... **CLC 4,
13, 24**
See also AMWS 13; CA 9-12R; 212; CANR
7, 63; CN 1, 2, 3, 4, 5, 6; DLB 28, 67;
EWL 3; MAL 5; MTCW 1, 2; RGAL 4;
TUS

Field, Andrew 1938- .... **CLC 44**
See also CA 97-100; CANR 25

Field, Eugene 1850-1895 .... **NCLC 3**
See also DLB 23, 42, 140; DLBD 13; MAI-
CYA 1, 2; RGAL 4; SATA 16

Field, Gans T.
See Wellman, Manly Wade

Field, Michael 1915-1971 .... **TCLC 43**
See also CA 29-32R

Fielding, Helen 1958- .... **CLC 146, 217**
See also AAYA 65; CA 172; CANR 127;
DLB 231; MTFW 2005

Fielding, Henry 1707-1754 ..... **LC 1, 46, 85;
WLC 2**
See also BRW 3; BRWR 1; CDBLB 1660-
1789; DA; DA3; DAB; DAC; DAM
DRAM, MST, NOV; DLB 39, 84, 101;
NFS 18; RGEL 2; TEA; WLIT 3

Fielding, Sarah 1710-1768 .... **LC 1, 44**
See also DLB 39; RGEL 2; TEA

Fields, W. C. 1880-1946 .... **TCLC 80**
See also DLB 44

Fierstein, Harvey (Forbes) 1954- .... **CLC 33**
See also CA 123; 129; CAD; CD 5, 6;
CPW; DA3; DAM DRAM, POP; DFS 6;
DLB 266; GLL; MAL 5

Figes, Eva 1932- .... **CLC 31**
See also CA 53-56; CANR 4, 44, 83; CN 2,
3, 4, 5, 6, 7; DLB 14, 271; FW; RGHL

Filippo, Eduardo de
See de Filippo, Eduardo

Forman, James D(ouglas) 1932- ..... **CLC 21**
See also AAYA 17; CA 9-12R; CANR 4, 19, 42; JRDA; MAICYA 1, 2; SATA 8, 70; YAW

Forman, Milos 1932- .... **CLC 164**
See also AAYA 63; CA 109

Fornes, Maria Irene 1930- .... **CLC 39, 61, 187; DC 10; HLCS 1**
See also CA 25-28R; CAD; CANR 28, 81; CD 5, 6; CWD; DLB 7; HW 1, 2; INT CANR-28; LLW; MAL 5; MTCW 1; RGAL 4

Forrest, Leon (Richard) 1937-1997
.... **BLCS; CLC 4**
See also AFAW 2; BW 2; CA 89-92; 162; CAAS 7; CANR 25, 52, 87; CN 4, 5, 6; DLB 33

Forster, E(dward) M(organ) 1879-1970
..... **CLC 1, 2, 3, 4, 9, 10, 13, 15, 22, 45, 77; SSC 27, 96; TCLC 125; WLC 2**
See also AAYA 2, 37; BRW 6; BRWR 2; BYA 12; CA 13-14; 25-28R; CANR 45; CAP 1; CDBLB 1914-1945; DA; DA3; DAB; DAC; DAM MST, NOV; DLB 34, 98, 162, 178, 195; DLBD 10; EWL 3; EXPN; LAIT 3; LMFS 1; MTCW 1, 2; MTFW 2005; NCFS 1; NFS 3, 10, 11; RGEL 2; RGSF 2; SATA 57; SUFW 1; TEA; WLIT 4

Forster, John 1812-1876 .... **NCLC 11**
See also DLB 144, 184

Forster, Margaret 1938- .... **CLC 149**
See also CA 133; CANR 62, 115; CN 4, 5, 6, 7; DLB 155, 271

Forsyth, Frederick 1938- .... **CLC 2, 5, 36**
See also BEST 89:4; CA 85-88; CANR 38, 62, 115, 137; CMW 4; CN 3, 4, 5, 6, 7; CPW; DAM NOV, POP; DLB 87; MTCW 1, 2; MTFW 2005

Forten, Charlotte L. 1837-1914 .... **BLC 2; TCLC 16**
See Grimke, Charlotte L(ottie) Forten
See also DLB 50, 239

Fortinbras
See Grieg, (Johan) Nordahl (Brun)

Foscolo, Ugo 1778-1827 .... **NCLC 8, 97**
See also EW 5; WLIT 7

Fosse, Bob 1927-1987
See Fosse, Robert L.
See also CA 110; 123

Fosse, Robert L. .... **CLC 20**
See Fosse, Bob

Foster, Hannah Webster 1758-1840
.... **NCLC 99**
See also DLB 37, 200; RGAL 4

Foster, Stephen Collins 1826-1864
.... **NCLC 26**
See also RGAL 4

Foucault, Michel 1926-1984 ..... **CLC 31, 34, 69**
See also CA 105; 113; CANR 34; DLB 242; EW 13; EWL 3; GFL 1789 to the Present; GLL 1; LMFS 2; MTCW 1, 2; TWA

Fouque, Friedrich (Heinrich Karl) de la Motte 1777-1843 .... **NCLC 2**
See also DLB 90; RGWL 2, 3; SUFW 1

Fourier, Charles 1772-1837 .... **NCLC 51**

Fournier, Henri-Alban 1886-1914
See Alain-Fournier
See also CA 104; 179

Fournier, Pierre 1916-1997 .... **CLC 11**
See Gascar, Pierre
See also CA 89-92; CANR 16, 40

Fowles, John 1926-2005 ... **CLC 1, 2, 3, 4, 6, 9, 10, 15, 33, 87; SSC 33**
See also BPFB 1; BRWS 1; CA 5-8R; 245; CANR 25, 71, 103; CDBLB 1960 to Present; CN 1, 2, 3, 4, 5, 6, 7; DA3; DAB; DAC; DAM MST; DLB 14, 139, 207;

EWL 3; HGG; MTCW 1, 2; MTFW 2005; NFS 21; RGEL 2; RHW; SATA 22; SATA-Obit 171; TEA; WLIT 4

Fowles, John Robert
See Fowles, John

Fox, Paula 1923- .... **CLC 2, 8, 121**
See also AAYA 3, 37; BYA 3, 8; CA 73-76; CANR 20, 36, 62, 105; CLR 1, 44, 96; DLB 52; JRDA; MAICYA 1, 2; MTCW 1; NFS 12; SATA 17, 60, 120, 167; WYA; YAW

Fox, William Price (Jr.) 1926- .... **CLC 22**
See also CA 17-20R; CAAS 19; CANR 11, 142; CSW; DLB 2; DLBY 1981

Foxe, John 1517(?)-1587 .... **LC 14**
See also DLB 132

Frame, Janet .. **CLC 2, 3, 6, 22, 66, 96; SSC 29**
See Clutha, Janet Paterson Frame
See also CN 1, 2, 3, 4, 5, 6, 7; CP 2, 3, 4; CWP; EWL 3; RGEL 2; RGSF 2; TWA

France, Anatole .... **TCLC 9**
See Thibault, Jacques Anatole Francois
See also DLB 123, 330; EWL 3; GFL 1789 to the Present; RGWL 2, 3; SUFW 1

Francis, Claude .... **CLC 50**
See also CA 192

Francis, Dick
See Francis, Richard Stanley
See also CN 2, 3, 4, 5, 6

Francis, Richard Stanley 1920- . **CLC 2, 22, 42, 102**
See Francis, Dick
See also AAYA 5, 21; BEST 89:3; BPFB 1; CA 5-8R; CANR 9, 42, 68, 100, 141; CD-BLB 1960 to Present; CMW 4; CN 7; DA3; DAM POP; DLB 87; INT CANR-9; MSW; MTCW 1, 2; MTFW 2005

Francis, Robert (Churchill) 1901-1987
.... **CLC 15; PC 34**
See also AMWS 9; CA 1-4R; 123; CANR 1; CP 1, 2, 3, 4; EXPP; PFS 12; TCLE 1:1

Francis, Lord Jeffrey
See Jeffrey, Francis
See also DLB 107

Frank, Anne(lies Marie) 1929-1945
.... **TCLC 17; WLC 2**
See also AAYA 12; BYA 1; CA 113; 133; CANR 68; CLR 101; DA; DA3; DAB; DAC; DAM MST; LAIT 4; MAICYA 2; MAICYAS 1; MTCW 1, 2; MTFW 2005; NCFS 2; RGHL; SATA 87; SATA-Brief 42; WYA; YAW

Frank, Bruno 1887-1945 .... **TCLC 81**
See also CA 189; DLB 118; EWL 3

Frank, Elizabeth 1945- .... **CLC 39**
See also CA 121; 126; CANR 78, 150; INT CA-126

Frankl, Viktor E(mil) 1905-1997 .... **CLC 93**
See also CA 65-68; 161; RGHL

Franklin, Benjamin
See Hasek, Jaroslav (Matej Frantisek)

Franklin, Benjamin 1706-1790 .... **LC 25; WLCS**
See also AMW; CDALB 1640-1865; DA; DA3; DAB; DAC; DAM MST; DLB 24, 43, 73, 183; LAIT 1; RGAL 4; TUS

Franklin, (Stella Maria Sarah) Miles (Lampe) 1879-1954 .... **TCLC 7**
See also CA 104; 164; DLB 230; FW; MTCW 2; RGEL 2; TWA

Franzen, Jonathan 1959- .... **CLC 202**
See also AAYA 65; CA 129; CANR 105

Fraser, Antonia 1932- .... **CLC 32, 107**
See also AAYA 57; CA 85-88; CANR 44, 65, 119; CMW; DLB 276; MTCW 1, 2; MTFW 2005; SATA-Brief 32

Fraser, George MacDonald 1925- ..... **CLC 7**
See also AAYA 48; CA 45-48, 180; CAAE 180; CANR 2, 48, 74; MTCW 2; RHW

Fraser, Sylvia 1935- .... **CLC 64**
See also CA 45-48; CANR 1, 16, 60; CCA 1

Frayn, Michael 1933- .... **CLC 3, 7, 31, 47, 176; DC 27**
See also AAYA 69; BRWC 2; BRWS 7; CA 5-8R; CANR 30, 69, 114, 133; CBD; CD 5, 6; CN 1, 2, 3, 4, 5, 6, 7; DAM DRAM, NOV; DFS 22; DLB 13, 14, 194, 245; FANT; MTCW 1, 2; MTFW 2005; SFW 4

Fraze, Candida (Merrill) 1945- .... **CLC 50**
See also CA 126

Frazer, Andrew
See Marlowe, Stephen

Frazer, J(ames) G(eorge) 1854-1941
.... **TCLC 32**
See also BRWS 3; CA 118; NCFS 5

Frazer, Robert Caine
See Creasey, John

Frazer, Sir James George
See Frazer, J(ames) G(eorge)

Frazier, Charles 1950- .... **CLC 109, 224**
See also AAYA 34; CA 161; CANR 126; CSW; DLB 292; MTFW 2005

Frazier, Ian 1951- .... **CLC 46**
See also CA 130; CANR 54, 93

Frederic, Harold 1856-1898 . **NCLC 10, 175**
See also AMW; DLB 12, 23; DLBD 13; MAL 5; NFS 22; RGAL 4

Frederick, John
See Faust, Frederick (Schiller)
See also TCWW 2

Frederick the Great 1712-1786 .... **LC 14**

Fredro, Aleksander 1793-1876 .... **NCLC 8**

Freeling, Nicolas 1927-2003 .... **CLC 38**
See also CA 49-52; 218; CAAS 12; CANR 1, 17, 50, 84; CMW 4; CN 1, 2, 3, 4, 5, 6; DLB 87

Freeman, Douglas Southall 1886-1953
.... **TCLC 11**
See also CA 109; 195; DLB 17; DLBD 17

Freeman, Judith 1946- .... **CLC 55**
See also CA 148; CANR 120; DLB 256

Freeman, Mary E(leanor) Wilkins 1852-1930
.... **SSC 1, 47; TCLC 9**
See also CA 106; 177; DLB 12, 78, 221; EXPS; FW; HGG; MBL; RGAL 4; RGSF 2; SSFS 4, 8; SUFW 1; TUS

Freeman, R(ichard) Austin 1862-1943
.... **TCLC 21**
See also CA 113; CANR 84; CMW 4; DLB 70

French, Albert 1943- .... **CLC 86**
See also BW 3; CA 167

French, Antonia
See Kureishi, Hanif

French, Marilyn 1929- .... **CLC 10, 18, 60, 177**
See also BPFB 1; CA 69-72; CANR 3, 31, 134; CN 5, 6, 7; CPW; DAM DRAM, NOV, POP; FL 1:5; FW; INT CANR-31; MTCW 1, 2; MTFW 2005

French, Paul
See Asimov, Isaac

Freneau, Philip Morin 1752-1832 . **NCLC 1, 111**
See also AMWS 2; DLB 37, 43; RGAL 4

Freud, Sigmund 1856-1939 .... **TCLC 52**
See also CA 115; 133; CANR 69; DLB 296; EW 8; EWL 3; LATS 1:1; MTCW 1, 2; MTFW 2005; NCFS 3; TWA

Freytag, Gustav 1816-1895 .... **NCLC 109**
See also DLB 129

Galt, John 1779-1839 .... **NCLC 1, 110**
See also DLB 99, 116, 159; RGEL 2; RGSF
2

Galvin, James 1951- .... **CLC 38**
See also CA 108; CANR 26

Gamboa, Federico 1864-1939 .... **TCLC 36**
See also CA 167; HW 2; LAW

Gandhi, M. K.
See Gandhi, Mohandas Karamchand

Gandhi, Mahatma
See Gandhi, Mohandas Karamchand

Gandhi, Mohandas Karamchand 1869-1948
.... **TCLC 59**
See also CA 121; 132; DA3; DAM MULT;
DLB 323; MTCW 1, 2

Gann, Ernest Kellogg 1910-1991 .... **CLC 23**
See also AITN 1; BPFB 2; CA 1-4R; 136;
CANR 1, 83; RHW

Gao Xingjian 1940- .... **CLC 167**
See Xingjian, Gao
See also MTFW 2005

Garber, Eric 1943(?)-
See Holleran, Andrew
See also CANR 89

Garcia, Cristina 1958- .... **CLC 76**
See also AMWS 11; CA 141; CANR 73,
130; CN 7; DLB 292; DNFS 1; EWL 3;
HW 2; LLW; MTFW 2005

Garcia Lorca, Federico 1898-1936 ..... **DC 2;**
HLC 2; PC 3; TCLC 1, 7, 49, 181;
WLC 2
See Lorca, Federico Garcia
See also AAYA 46; CA 104; 131; CANR
81; DA; DA3; DAB; DAC; DAM DRAM,
MST, MULT, POET; DFS 4, 10; DLB
108; EWL 3; HW 1, 2; LATS 1:2; MTCW
1, 2; MTFW 2005; TWA

Garcia Marquez, Gabriel 1928- .. **CLC 2, 3,**
8, 10, 15, 27, 47, 55, 68, 170; HLC 1;
SSC 8, 83; WLC 3
See also AAYA 3, 33; BEST 89:1, 90:4;
BPFB 2; BYA 12, 16; CA 33-36R; CANR
10, 28, 50, 75, 82, 128; CDWLB 3; CPW;
CWW 2; DA; DA3; DAB; DAC; DAM
MST, MULT, NOV, POP; DLB 113, 330;
DNFS 1, 2; EWL 3; EXPN; EXPS; HW
1, 2; LAIT 2; LATS 1:2; LAW; LAWS 1;
LMFS 2; MTCW 1, 2; MTFW 2005;
NCFS 3; NFS 1, 5, 10; RGSF 2; RGWL
2, 3; SSFS 1, 6, 16, 21; TWA; WLIT 1

Garcia Marquez, Gabriel Jose
See Garcia Marquez, Gabriel

Garcilaso de la Vega, El Inca 1539-1616
.... **HLCS 1; LC 127**
See also DLB 318; LAW

Gard, Janice
See Latham, Jean Lee

Gard, Roger Martin du
See Martin du Gard, Roger

Gardam, Jane (Mary) 1928- .... **CLC 43**
See also CA 49-52; CANR 2, 18, 33, 54,
106; CLR 12; DLB 14, 161, 231; MAI-
CYA 1; MTCW 1; SAAS 9; SATA 39,
76, 130; SATA-Brief 28; YAW

Gardner, Herb(ert George) 1934-2003
.... **CLC 44**
See also CA 149; 220; CAD; CANR 119;
CD 5, 6; DFS 18, 20

Gardner, John, Jr. 1933-1982 .. **CLC 2, 3, 5,**
7, 8, 10, 18, 28, 34; SSC 7
See also AAYA 45; AITN 1; AMWS 6;
BPFB 2; CA 65-68; 107; CANR 33, 73;
CDALBS; CN 2, 3; CPW; DA3; DAM
NOV, POP; DLB 2; DLBY 1982; EWL 3;
FANT; LATS 1:2; MAL 5; MTCW 1, 2;
MTFW 2005; NFS 3; RGAL 4; RGSF 2;
SATA 40; SATA-Obit 31; SSFS 8

Gardner, John (Edmund) 1926- ...... **CLC 30**
See also CA 103; CANR 15, 69, 127; CMW
4; CPW; DAM POP; MTCW 1

Gardner, Miriam
See Bradley, Marion Zimmer
See also GLL 1

Gardner, Noel
See Kuttner, Henry

Gardons, S. S.
See Snodgrass, W.D.

Garfield, Leon 1921-1996 .... **CLC 12**
See also AAYA 8, 69; BYA 1, 3; CA 17-
20R; 152; CANR 38, 41, 78; CLR 21;
DLB 161; JRDA; MAICYA 1, 2; MAIC-
YAS 1; SATA 1, 32, 76; SATA-Obit 90;
TEA; WYA; YAW

Garland, (Hannibal) Hamlin 1860-1940
.... **SSC 18; TCLC 3**
See also CA 104; DLB 12, 71, 78, 186;
MAL 5; RGAL 4; RGSF 1, 2; TCWW 1, 2

Garneau, (Hector de) Saint-Denys 1912-1943
.... **TCLC 13**
See also CA 111; DLB 88

Garner, Alan 1934- .... **CLC 17**
See also AAYA 18; BYA 3, 5; CA 73-76,
178; CAAE 178; CANR 15, 64, 134; CLR
20; CPW; DAB; DAM POP; DLB 161,
261; FANT; MAICYA 1, 2; MTCW 1, 2;
MTFW 2005; SATA 18, 69; SATA-Essay
108; SUFW 1, 2; YAW

Garner, Hugh 1913-1979 .... **CLC 13**
See Warwick, Jarvis
See also CA 69-72; CANR 31; CCA 1; CN
1, 2; DLB 68

Garnett, David 1892-1981 .... **CLC 3**
See also CA 5-8R; 103; CANR 17, 79; CN
1, 2; DLB 34; FANT; MTCW 2; RGEL 2;
SFW 4; SUFW 1

Garnier, Robert c. 1545-1590 .... **LC 119**
See also DLB 327; GFL Beginnings to 1789

Garrett, George (Palmer, Jr.) 1929-
.... **CLC 3, 11, 51; SSC 30**
See also AMWS 7; BPFB 2; CA 1-4R, 202;
CAAE 202; CAAS 5; CANR 1, 42, 67,
109; CN 1, 2, 3, 4, 5, 6, 7; CP 1, 2, 3, 4,
5, 6, 7; CSW; DLB 2, 5, 130, 152; DLBY
1983

Garrett, David 1717-1779 .... **LC 15**
See also DAM DRAM; DLB 84, 213;
RGEL 2

Garrigue, Jean 1914-1972 .... **CLC 2, 8**
See also CA 5-8R; 37-40R; CANR 20; CP
1; MAL 5

Garrison, Frederick
See Sinclair, Upton

Garrison, William Lloyd 1805-1879
.... **NCLC 149**
See also CDALB 1640-1865; DLB 1, 43,
235

Garro, Elena 1920(?)-1998 .... **HLCS 1;**
TCLC 153
See also CA 131; 169; CWW 2; DLB 145;
EWL 3; HW 1; LAWS 1; WLIT 1

Garth, Will
See Hamilton, Edmond; Kuttner, Henry

Garvey, Marcus (Moziah, Jr.) 1887-1940
.... **BLC 2; HR 1:2; TCLC 41**
See also BW 1; CA 120; 124; CANR 79;
DAM MULT

Gary, Romain .... **CLC 25**
See Kacew, Romain
See also DLB 83, 299; RGHL

Gascar, Pierre .... **CLC 11**
See Fournier, Pierre
See also EWL 3; RGHL

Gascoigne, George 1539-1577 .... **LC 108**
See also DLB 136; RGEL 2

Gascoyne, David (Emery) 1916-2001
.... **CLC 45**
See also CA 65-68; 200; CANR 10, 28, 54;
CP 1, 2, 3, 4, 5, 6, 7; DLB 20; MTCW 1;
RGEL 2

Gaskell, Elizabeth Cleghorn 1810-1865
.... **NCLC 5, 70, 97, 137; SSC 25**
See also BRW 5; CDBLB 1832-1890; DAB;
DAM MST; DLB 21, 144, 159; RGEL 2;
RGSF 2; TEA

Gass, William H. 1924- ...... **CLC 1, 2, 8, 11,**
15, 39, 132; SSC 12
See also AMWS 6; CA 17-20R; CANR 30,
71, 100; CN 1, 2, 3, 4, 5, 6, 7; DLB 2,
227; EWL 3; MAL 5; MTCW 1, 2;
MTFW 2005; RGAL 4

Gassendi, Pierre 1592-1655 .... **LC 54**
See also GFL Beginnings to 1789

Gasset, Jose Ortega y
See Ortega y Gasset, Jose

Gates, Henry Louis, Jr. 1950- . **BLCS; CLC**
65
See also BW 2, 3; CA 109; CANR 25, 53,
75, 125; CSW; DA3; DAM MULT; DLB
67; EWL 3; MAL 5; MTCW 2; MTFW
2005; RGAL 4

Gatos, Stephanie
See Katz, Steve

Gautier, Theophile 1811-1872 . **NCLC 1, 59;**
PC 18; SSC 20
See also DAM POET; DLB 119; EW 6;
GFL 1789 to the Present; RGWL 2, 3;
SUFW; TWA

Gay, John 1685-1732 .... **LC 49**
See also BRW 3; DAM DRAM; DLB 84,
95; RGEL 2; WLIT 3

Gay, Oliver
See Gogarty, Oliver St. John

Gay, Peter 1923- .... **CLC 158**
See also CA 13-16R; CANR 18, 41, 77,
147; INT CANR-18; RGHL

Gay, Peter Jack
See Gay, Peter

Gaye, Marvin (Pentz, Jr.) 1939-1984
.... **CLC 26**
See also CA 195; 112

Gebler, Carlo 1954- .... **CLC 39**
See also CA 119; 133; CANR 96; DLB 271

Gee, Maggie 1948- .... **CLC 57**
See also CA 130; CANR 125; CN 4, 5, 6,
7; DLB 207; MTFW 2005

Gee, Maurice 1931- .... **CLC 29**
See also AAYA 42; CA 97-100; CANR 67,
123; CLR 56; CN 2, 3, 4, 5, 6, 7; CWRI
5; EWL 3; MAICYA 2; RGSF 2; SATA
46, 101

Gee, Maurice Gough
See Gee, Maurice

Geiogamah, Hanay 1945- .... **NNAL**
See also CA 153; DAM MULT; DLB 175

Gelbart, Larry
See Gelbart, Larry (Simon)
See also CAD; CD 5, 6

Gelbart, Larry (Simon) 1928- ... **CLC 21, 61**
See Gelbart, Larry
See also CA 73-76; CANR 45, 94

Gelber, Jack 1932-2003 ..... **CLC 1, 6, 14, 79**
See also CA 1-4R; 216; CAD; CANR 2;
DLB 7, 228; MAL 5

Gellhorn, Martha (Ellis) 1908-1998
.... **CLC 14, 60**
See also CA 77-80; 164; CANR 44; CN 1,
2, 3, 4, 5, 6 7; DLBY 1982, 1998

Genet, Jean 1910-1986 . **CLC 1, 2, 5, 10, 14,**
44, 46; DC 25; TCLC 128
See also CA 13-16R; CANR 18; DA3;
DAM DRAM; DFS 10; DLB 72, 321;
DLBY 1986; EW 13; EWL 3; GFL 1789
to the Present; GLL 1; LMFS 2; MTCW
1, 2; MTFW 2005; RGWL 2, 3; TWA

Genlis, Stephanie-Felicite Ducrest 1746-1830
.... **NCLC 166**
See also DLB 313

Gladkov, Fyodor (Vasilyevich) 1883-1958
.... **TCLC 27**
See Gladkov, Fedor Vasil'evich
See also CA 170; EWL 3

Glancy, Diane 1941- .... **CLC 210; NNAL**
See also CA 136, 225; CAAE 225; CAAS 24; CANR 87; DLB 175

Glanville, Brian (Lester) 1931- .... **CLC 6**
See also CA 5-8R; CAAS 9; CANR 3, 70; CN 1, 2, 3, 4, 5, 6, 7; DLB 15, 139; SATA 42

Glasgow, Ellen (Anderson Gholson)
1873-1945 .... **SSC 34; TCLC 2, 7**
See also AMW; CA 104; 164; DLB 9, 12; MAL 5; MBL; MTCW 2; MTFW 2005; RGAL 4; RHW; SSFS 9; TUS

Glaspell, Susan 1882(?)-1948 ... **DC 10; SSC 41; TCLC 55, 175**
See also AMWS 3; CA 110; 154; DFS 8, 18; DLB 7, 9, 78, 228; MBL; RGAL 4; SSFS 3; TCWW 2; TUS; YABC 2

Glassco, John 1909-1981 .... **CLC 9**
See also CA 13-16R; 102; CANR 15; CN 1, 2; CP 1, 2, 3; DLB 68

Glasscock, Amnesia
See Steinbeck, John (Ernst)

Glasser, Ronald J. 1940(?)- .... **CLC 37**
See also CA 209

Glassman, Joyce
See Johnson, Joyce

Gleick, James (W.) 1954- .... **CLC 147**
See also CA 131; 137; CANR 97; INT CA-137

Glendinning, Victoria 1937- .... **CLC 50**
See also CA 120; 127; CANR 59, 89; DLB 155

Glissant, Edouard (Mathieu) 1928-
.... **CLC 10, 68**
See also CA 153; CANR 111; CWW 2; DAM MULT; EWL 3; RGWL 3

Gloag, Julian 1930- .... **CLC 40**
See also AITN 1; CA 65-68; CANR 10, 70; CN 1, 2, 3, 4, 5, 6

Glowacki, Aleksander
See Prus, Boleslaw

Gluck, Louise 1943- .... **CLC 7, 22, 44, 81, 160; PC 16**
See also AMWS 5; CA 33-36R; CANR 40, 69, 108, 133; CP 1, 2, 3, 4, 5, 6, 7; CWP; DA3; DAM POET; DLB 5; MAL 5; MTCW 2; MTFW 2005; PFS 5, 15; RGAL 4; TCLE 1:1

Glyn, Elinor 1864-1943 .... **TCLC 72**
See also DLB 153; RHW

Gobineau, Joseph-Arthur 1816-1882
.... **NCLC 17**
See also DLB 123; GFL 1789 to the Present

Godard, Jean-Luc 1930- .... **CLC 20**
See also CA 93-96

Godden, (Margaret) Rumer 1907-1998
.... **CLC 53**
See also AAYA 6; BPFB 2; BYA 2, 5; CA 5-8R; 172; CANR 4, 27, 36, 55, 80; CLR 20; CN 1, 2, 3, 4, 5, 6; CWRI 5; DLB 161; MAICYA 1, 2; RHW; SAAS 12; SATA 3, 36; SATA-Obit 109; TEA

Godoy Alcayaga, Lucila 1899-1957 . **HLC 2; PC 32; TCLC 2**
See Mistral, Gabriela
See also BW 2; CA 104; 131; CANR 81; DAM MULT; DNFS; HW 1, 2; MTCW 1, 2; MTFW 2005

Godwin, Gail 1937- .... **CLC 5, 8, 22, 31, 69, 125**
See also BPFB 2; CA 29-32R; CANR 15, 43, 69, 132; CN 3, 4, 5, 6, 7; CPW; CSW; DA3; DAM POP; DLB 6, 234; INT CANR-15; MAL 5; MTCW 1, 2; MTFW 2005

Godwin, Gail Kathleen
See Godwin, Gail

Godwin, William 1756-1836 . **NCLC 14, 130**
See also CDBLB 1789-1832; CMW 4; DLB 39, 104, 142, 158, 163, 262; GL 2; HGG; RGEL 2

Goebbels, Josef
See Goebbels, (Paul) Joseph

Goebbels, (Paul) Joseph 1897-1945
.... **TCLC 68**
See also CA 115; 148

Goebbels, Joseph Paul
See Goebbels, (Paul) Joseph

Goethe, Johann Wolfgang von 1749-1832
... **DC 20; NCLC 4, 22, 34, 90, 154; PC 5; SSC 38; WLC 3**
See also CDWLB 2; DA; DA3; DAB; DAC; DAM DRAM, MST, POET; DLB 94; EW 5; GL 2; LATS 1; LMFS 1:1; RGWL 2, 3; TWA

Gogarty, Oliver St. John 1878-1957
.... **TCLC 15**
See also CA 109; 150; DLB 15, 19; RGEL 2

Gogol, Nikolai (Vasilyevich) 1809-1852
..... **DC 1; NCLC 5, 15, 31, 162; SSC 4, 29, 52; WLC 3**
See also DA; DAB; DAC; DAM DRAM, MST; DFS 12; DLB 198; EW 6; EXPS; RGSF 2; RGWL 2, 3; SSFS 7; TWA

Goines, Donald 1937(?)-1974 .. **BLC 2; CLC 80**
See also AITN 1; BW 1, 3; CA 124; 114; CANR 82; CMW 4; DA3; DAM MULT, POP; DLB 33

Gold, Herbert 1924- .. **CLC 4, 7, 14, 42, 152**
See also CA 9-12R; CANR 17, 45, 125; CN 1, 2, 3, 4, 5, 6, 7; DLB 2; DLBY 1981; MAL 5

Goldbarth, Albert 1948- .... **CLC 5, 38**
See also AMWS 12; CA 53-56; CANR 6, 40; CP 3, 4, 5, 6, 7; DLB 120

Goldberg, Anatol 1910-1982 .... **CLC 34**
See also CA 131; 117

Goldemberg, Isaac 1945- .... **CLC 52**
See also CA 69-72; CAAS 12; CANR 11, 32; EWL 3; HW 1; WLIT 1

Golding, Arthur 1536-1606 .... **LC 101**
See also DLB 136

Golding, William 1911-1993 .... **CLC 1, 2, 3, 8, 10, 17, 27, 58, 81; WLC 3**
See also AAYA 5, 44; BPFB 2; BRWR 1; BRWS 1; BYA 2; CA 5-8R; 141; CANR 13, 33, 54; CD 5; CDBLB 1945-1960; CLR 94; CN 1, 2, 3, 4; DA; DA3; DAB; DAC; DAM MST, NOV; DLB 15, 100, 255, 326, 330; EWL 3; EXPN; HGG; LAIT 4; MTCW 1, 2; MTFW 2005; NFS 2; RGEL 2; RHW; SFW 4; TEA; WLIT 4; YAW

Goldman, Emma 1869-1940 .... **TCLC 13**
See also CA 110; 150; DLB 221; FW; RGAL 4; TUS

Goldman, Francisco 1954- .... **CLC 76**
See also CA 162

Goldman, William 1931- .... **CLC 1, 48**
See also BPFB 2; CA 9-12R; CANR 29, 69, 106; CN 1, 2, 3, 4, 5, 6, 7; DLB 44; FANT; IDFW 3, 4

Goldman, William W.
See Goldman, William

Goldmann, Lucien 1913-1970 .... **CLC 24**
See also CA 25-28; CAP 2

Goldoni, Carlo 1707-1793 .... **LC 4**
See also DAM DRAM; EW 4; RGWL 2, 3; WLIT 7

Goldsberry, Steven 1949- .... **CLC 34**
See also CA 131

Goldsmith, Oliver 1730-1774 ... **DC 8; LC 2, 48; WLC 3**
See also BRW 3; CDBLB 1660-1789; DA; DAB; DAC; DAM DRAM, MST, NOV, POET; DFS 1; DLB 39, 89, 104, 109, 142; IDTP; RGEL 2; SATA 26; TEA; WLIT 3

Goldsmith, Peter
See Priestley, J(ohn) B(oynton)

Gombrowicz, Witold 1904-1969 ... **CLC 4, 7, 11, 49**
See also CA 19-20; 25-28R; CANR 105; CAP 2; CDWLB 4; DAM DRAM; DLB 215; EW 12; EWL 3; RGWL 2, 3; TWA

Gomez de Avellaneda, Gertrudis 1814-1873
.... **NCLC 111**
See also LAW

Gomez de la Serna, Ramon 1888-1963
.... **CLC 9**
See also CA 153; 116; CANR 79; EWL 3; HW 1, 2

Goncharov, Ivan Alexandrovich 1812-1891
.... **NCLC 1, 63**
See also DLB 238; EW 6; RGWL 2, 3

Goncourt, Edmond (Louis Antoine Huot) de
1822-1896 .... **NCLC 7**
See also DLB 123; EW 7; GFL 1789 to the Present; RGWL 2, 3

Goncourt, Jules (Alfred Huot) de 1830-1870
.... **NCLC 7**
See also DLB 123; EW 7; GFL 1789 to the Present; RGWL 2, 3

Gongora (y Argote), Luis de 1561-1627
.... **LC 72**
See also RGWL 2, 3

Gontier, Fernande 19(?)- .... **CLC 50**

Gonzalez Martinez, Enrique
See Gonzalez Martinez, Enrique
See also DLB 290

Gonzalez Martinez, Enrique 1871-1952
.... **TCLC 72**
See Gonzalez Martinez, Enrique
See also CA 166; CANR 81; EWL 3; HW 1, 2

Goodison, Lorna 1947- .... **PC 36**
See also CA 142; CANR 88; CP 5, 6, 7; CWP; DLB 157; EWL 3

Goodman, Paul 1911-1972 .... **CLC 1, 2, 4, 7**
See also CA 19-20; 37-40R; CAD; CANR 34; CAP 2; CN 1; DLB 130, 246; MAL 5; MTCW 1; RGAL 4

GoodWeather, Harley
See King, Thomas

Googe, Barnabe 1540-1594 .... **LC 94**
See also DLB 132; RGEL 2

Gordimer, Nadine 1923- .... **CLC 3, 5, 7, 10, 18, 33, 51, 70, 123, 160, 161; SSC 17, 80; WLCS**
See also AAYA 39; AFW; BRWS 2; CA 5-8R; CANR 3, 28, 56, 88, 131; CN 1, 2, 3, 4, 5, 6, 7; DA; DA3; DAB; DAC; DAM MST, NOV; DLB 225, 326, 330; EWL 3; EXPS; INT CANR-28; LATS 1:2; MTCW 1, 2; MTFW 2005; NFS 4; RGEL 2; RGSF 2; SSFS 2, 14, 19; TWA; WLIT 2; YAW

Gordon, Adam Lindsay 1833-1870
.... **NCLC 21**
See also DLB 230

Gordon, Caroline 1895-1981 ...... **CLC 6, 13, 29, 83; SSC 15**
See also AMW; CA 11-12; 103; CANR 36; CAP 1; CN 1, 2; DLB 4, 9, 102; DLBD 17; DLBY 1981; EWL 3; MAL 5; MTCW 1, 2; MTFW 2005; RGAL 4; RGSF 2

Gordon, Charles William 1860-1937
See Connor, Ralph
See also CA 109

Green, Anna Katharine 1846-1935
.... **TCLC 63**
See also CA 112; 159; CMW 4; DLB 202, 221; MSW

Green, Brian
See Card, Orson Scott

Green, Hannah
See Greenberg, Joanne (Goldenberg)

Green, Hannah 1927(?)-1996 .... **CLC 3**
See also CA 73-76; CANR 59, 93; NFS 10

Green, Henry .... **CLC 2, 13, 97**
See Yorke, Henry Vincent
See also BRWS 2; CA 175; DLB 15; EWL 3; RGEL 2

Green, Julian .... **CLC 3, 11, 77**
See Green, Julien (Hartridge)
See also EWL 3; GFL 1789 to the Present; MTCW 2

Green, Julien (Hartridge) 1900-1998
See Green, Julian
See also CA 21-24R; 169; CANR 33, 87; CWW 2; DLB 4, 72; MTCW 1, 2; MTFW 2005

Green, Paul (Eliot) 1894-1981 .... **CLC 25**
See also AITN 1; CA 5-8R; 103; CAD; CANR 3; DAM DRAM; DLB 7, 9, 249; DLBY 1981; MAL 5; RGAL 4

Greenaway, Peter 1942- .... **CLC 159**
See also CA 127

Greenberg, Ivan 1908-1973
See Rahv, Philip
See also CA 85-88

Greenberg, Joanne (Goldenberg) 1932-
.... **CLC 7, 30**
See also AAYA 12, 67; CA 5-8R; CANR 14, 32, 69; CN 6, 7; NFS 23; SATA 25; YAW

Greenberg, Richard 1959(?)- .... **CLC 57**
See also CA 138; CAD; CD 5, 6

Greenblatt, Stephen J(ay) 1943- ..... **CLC 70**
See also CA 49-52; CANR 115

Greene, Bette 1934- .... **CLC 30**
See also AAYA 7, 69; BYA 3; CA 53-56; CANR 4, 146; CLR 2; CWRI 5; JRDA; LAIT 4; MAICYA 1, 2; NFS 10; SAAS 16; SATA 8, 102, 161; WYA; YAW

Greene, Gael .... **CLC 8**
See also CA 13-16R; CANR 10

Greene, Graham 1904-1991 . **CLC 1, 3, 6, 9, 14, 18, 27, 37, 70, 72, 125; SSC 29; WLC 3**
See also AAYA 61; AITN 2; BPFB 2; BRWR 2; BRWS 1; BYA 3; CA 13-16R; 133; CANR 35, 61, 131; CBD; CDBLB 1945-1960; CMW 4; CN 1, 2, 3, 4; DA; DA3; DAB; DAC; DAM MST, NOV; DLB 13, 15, 77, 100, 162, 201, 204; DLBY 1991; EWL 3; MSW; MTCW 1, 2; MTFW 2005; NFS 16; RGEL 2; SATA 20; SSFS 14; TEA; WLIT 4

Greene, Robert 1558-1592 .... **LC 41**
See also BRWS 8; DLB 62, 167; IDTP; RGEL 2; TEA

Greer, Germaine 1939- .... **CLC 131**
See also AITN 1; CA 81-84; CANR 33, 70, 115, 133; FW; MTCW 1, 2; MTFW 2005

Greer, Richard
See Silverberg, Robert

Gregor, Arthur 1923- .... **CLC 9**
See also CA 25-28R; CAAS 10; CANR 11; CP 1, 2, 3, 4, 5, 6, 7; SATA 36

Gregor, Lee
See Pohl, Frederik

Gregory, Lady Isabella Augusta (Persse)
1852-1932 .... **TCLC 1, 176**
See also BRW 6; CA 104; 184; DLB 10; IDTP; RGEL 2

Gregory, J. Dennis
See Williams, John A(lfred)

Gregory of Nazianzus, St. 329-389
.... **CMLC 82**

Grekova, I. .... **CLC 59**
See Ventsel, Elena Sergeevna
See also CWW 2

Grendon, Stephen
See Derleth, August (William)

Grenville, Kate 1950- .... **CLC 61**
See also CA 118; CANR 53, 93, 156; CN 7; DLB 325

Grenville, Pelham
See Wodehouse, P(elham) G(renville)

Greve, Felix Paul (Berthold Friedrich)
1879-1948
See Grove, Frederick Philip
See also CA 104; 141; 175; CANR 79; DAC; DAM MST

Greville, Fulke 1554-1628 .... **LC 79**
See also BRWS 11; DLB 62, 172; RGEL 2

Grey, Lady Jane 1537-1554 .... **LC 93**
See also DLB 132

Grey, Zane 1872-1939 .... **TCLC 6**
See also BPFB 2; CA 104; 132; DA3; DAM POP; DLB 9, 212; MTCW 1, 2; MTFW 2005; RGAL 4; TCWW 1, 2; TUS

Griboedov, Aleksandr Sergeevich
1795(?)-1829 .... **NCLC 129**
See also DLB 205; RGWL 2, 3

Grieg, (Johan) Nordahl (Brun) 1902-1943
.... **TCLC 10**
See also CA 107; 189; EWL 3

Grieve, C(hristopher) M(urray) 1892-1978
.... **CLC 11, 19**
See MacDiarmid, Hugh; Pteleon
See also CA 5-8R; 85-88; CANR 33, 107; DAM POET; MTCW 1; RGEL 2

Griffin, Gerald 1803-1840 .... **NCLC 7**
See also DLB 159; RGEL 2

Griffin, John Howard 1920-1980 .... **CLC 68**
See also AITN 1; CA 1-4R; 101; CANR 2

Griffin, Peter 1942- .... **CLC 39**
See also CA 136

Griffith, D(avid Lewelyn) W(ark)
1875(?)-1948 .... **TCLC 68**
See also CA 119; 150; CANR 80

Griffith, Lawrence
See Griffith, D(avid Lewelyn) W(ark)

Griffiths, Trevor 1935- .... **CLC 13, 52**
See also CA 97-100; CANR 45; CBD; CD 5, 6; DLB 13, 245

Griggs, Sutton (Elbert) 1872-1930
.... **TCLC 77**
See also CA 123; 186; DLB 50

Grigson, Geoffrey (Edward Harvey)
1905-1985 .... **CLC 7, 39**
See also CA 25-28R; 118; CANR 20, 33; CP 1, 2, 3, 4; DLB 27; MTCW 1, 2

Grile, Dod
See Bierce, Ambrose (Gwinett)

Grillparzer, Franz 1791-1872 .... **DC 14; NCLC 1, 102; SSC 37**
See also CDWLB 2; DLB 133; EW 5; RGWL 2, 3; TWA

Grimble, Reverend Charles James
See Eliot, T(homas) S(tearns)

Grimke, Angelina (Emily) Weld 1880-1958
.... **HR 1:2**
See Weld, Angelina (Emily) Grimke
See also BW 1; CA 124; DAM POET; DLB 50, 54

Grimke, Charlotte L(ottie) Forten
1837(?)-1914
See Forten, Charlotte L.
See also BW 1; CA 117; 124; DAM MULT, POET

Grimm, Jacob Ludwig Karl 1785-1863
.... **NCLC 3, 77; SSC 36**
See Grimm Brothers
See also CLR 112; DLB 90; MAICYA 1, 2; RGSF 2; RGWL 2, 3; SATA 22; WCH

Grimm, Wilhelm Karl 1786-1859 . **NCLC 3, 77; SSC 36**
See Grimm Brothers
See also CDWLB 2; CLR 112; DLB 90; MAICYA 1, 2; RGSF 2; RGWL 2, 3; SATA 22; WCH

Grimm and Grim
See Grimm, Jacob Ludwig Karl; Grimm, Wilhelm Karl

Grimm Brothers .... **SSC 88**
See Grimm, Jacob Ludwig Karl; Grimm, Wilhelm Karl
See also CLR 112

Grimmelshausen, Hans Jakob Christoffel von
See Grimmelshausen, Johann Jakob Christoffel von
See also RGWL 2, 3

Grimmelshausen, Johann Jakob Christoffel von 1621-1676 .... **LC 6**
See Grimmelshausen, Hans Jakob Christoffel von
See also CDWLB 2; DLB 168

Grindel, Eugene 1895-1952
See Eluard, Paul
See also CA 104; 193; LMFS 2

Grisham, John 1955- .... **CLC 84**
See also AAYA 14, 47; BPFB 2; CA 138; CANR 47, 69, 114, 133; CMW 4; CN 6, 7; CPW; CSW; DA3; DAM POP; MSW; MTCW 2; MTFW 2005

Grosseteste, Robert 1175(?)-1253
.... **CMLC 62**
See also DLB 115

Grossman, David 1954- .... **CLC 67, 231**
See also CA 138; CANR 114; CWW 2; DLB 299; EWL 3; RGHL; WLIT 6

Grossman, Vasilii Semenovich
See Grossman, Vasily (Semenovich)
See also DLB 272

Grossman, Vasily (Semenovich) 1905-1964
.... **CLC 41**
See Grossman, Vasilii Semenovich
See also CA 124; 130; MTCW 1; RGHL

Grove, Frederick Philip .... **TCLC 4**
See Greve, Felix Paul (Berthold Friedrich)
See also DLB 92; RGEL 2; TCWW 1, 2

Grubb
See Crumb, R.

Grumbach, Doris 1918- .... **CLC 13, 22, 64**
See also CA 5-8R; CAAS 2; CANR 9, 42, 70, 127; CN 6, 7; INT CANR-9; MTCW 2; MTFW 2005

Grundtvig, Nikolai Frederik Severin
1783-1872 .... **NCLC 1, 158**
See also DLB 300

Grunge
See Crumb, R.

Grunwald, Lisa 1959- .... **CLC 44**
See also CA 120; CANR 148

Gryphius, Andreas 1616-1664 .... **LC 89**
See also CDWLB 2; DLB 164; RGWL 2, 3

Guare, John 1938- ... **CLC 8, 14, 29, 67; DC 20**
See also CA 73-76; CAD; CANR 21, 69, 118; CD 5, 6; DAM DRAM; DFS 8, 13; DLB 7, 249; EWL 3; MAL 5; MTCW 1, 2; RGAL 4

Guarini, Battista 1537-1612 .... **LC 102**

Gubar, Susan (David) 1944- .... **CLC 145**
See also CA 108; CANR 45, 70, 139; FW; MTCW 1; RGAL 4

Harris, Christie (Lucy) Irwin 1907-2002
.... **CLC 12**
See also CA 5-8R; CANR 6, 83; CLR 47;
DLB 88; JRDA; MAICYA 1, 2; SAAS 10;
SATA 6, 74; SATA-Essay 116
Harris, Frank 1856-1931 .... **TCLC 24**
See also CA 109; 150; CANR 80; DLB 156,
197; RGEL 2
Harris, George Washington 1814-1869
.... **NCLC 23, 165**
See also DLB 3, 11, 248; RGAL 4
Harris, Joel Chandler 1848-1908 ... **SSC 19;
TCLC 2**
See also CA 104; 137; CANR 80; CLR 49;
DLB 11, 23, 42, 78, 91; LAIT 2; MAI-
CYA 1, 2; RGSF 2; SATA 100; WCH;
YABC 1
**Harris, John (Wyndham Parkes Lucas)
Beynon** 1903-1969
See Wyndham, John
See also CA 102; 89-92; CANR 84; SATA
118; SFW 4
Harris, MacDonald .... **CLC 9**
See Heiney, Donald (William)
Harris, Mark 1922- .... **CLC 19**
See also CA 5-8R; CAAS 3; CANR 2, 55,
83; CN 1, 2, 3, 4, 5, 6, 7; DLB 2; DLBY
1980
Harris, Norman .... **CLC 65**
Harris, (Theodore) Wilson 1921- ... **CLC 25,
159**
See also BRWS 5; BW 2, 3; CA 65-68;
CAAS 16; CANR 11, 27, 69, 114; CD-
WLB 3; CN 1, 2, 3, 4, 5, 6, 7; CP 1, 2, 3,
4, 5, 6; DLB 117; EWL 3; MTCW 1;
RGEL 2
Harrison, Barbara Grizzuti 1934-2002
.... **CLC 144**
See also CA 77-80; 205; CANR 15, 48; INT
CANR-15
Harrison, Elizabeth (Allen) Cavanna
1909-2001
See Cavanna, Betty
See also CA 9-12R; 200; CANR 6, 27, 85,
104, 121; MAICYA 2; SATA 142; YAW
Harrison, Harry (Max) 1925- .... **CLC 42**
See also CA 1-4R; CANR 5, 21, 84; DLB
8; SATA 4; SCFW 2; SFW 4
Harrison, James (Thomas) 1937- .... **CLC 6,
14, 33, 66, 143; SSC 19**
See Harrison, Jim
See also CA 13-16R; CANR 8, 51, 79, 142;
DLBY 1982; INT CANR-8
Harrison, Jim
See Harrison, James (Thomas)
See also AMWS 8; CN 5, 6; CP 1, 2, 3, 4,
5, 6, 7; RGAL 4; TCWW 2; TUS
Harrison, Kathryn 1961- .... **CLC 70, 151**
See also CA 144; CANR 68, 122
Harrison, Tony 1937- .... **CLC 43, 129**
See also BRWS 5; CA 65-68; CANR 44,
98; CBD; CD 5, 6; CP 2, 3, 4, 5, 6, 7;
DLB 40, 245; MTCW 1; RGEL 2
Harriss, Will(ard Irwin) 1922- .... **CLC 34**
See also CA 111
Hart, Ellis
See Ellison, Harlan
Hart, Josephine 1942(?)- .... **CLC 70**
See also CA 138; CANR 70, 149; CPW;
DAM POP
Hart, Moss 1904-1961 .... **CLC 66**
See also CA 109; 89-92; CANR 84; DAM
DRAM; DFS 1; DLB 7, 266; RGAL 4
Harte, (Francis) Bret(t) 1836(?)-1902
.... **SSC 8, 59; TCLC 1, 25; WLC 3**
See also AMWS 2; CA 104; 140; CANR
80; CDALB 1865-1917; DA; DA3; DAC;
DAM MST; DLB 12, 64, 74, 79, 186;
EXPS; LAIT 2; RGAL 4; RGSF 2; SATA
26; SSFS 3; TUS

Hartley, L(eslie) P(oles) 1895-1972 .. **CLC 2,
22**
See also BRWS 7; CA 45-48; 37-40R;
CANR 33; CN 1; DLB 15, 139; EWL 3;
HGG; MTCW 1, 2; MTFW 2005; RGEL
2; RGSF 2; SUFW 1
Hartman, Geoffrey H. 1929- .... **CLC 27**
See also CA 117; 125; CANR 79; DLB 67
Hartmann, Sadakichi 1869-1944 .. **TCLC 73**
See also CA 157; DLB 54
Hartmann von Aue c. 1170-c. 1210
.... **CMLC 15**
See also CDWLB 2; DLB 138; RGWL 2, 3
Hartog, Jan de
See de Hartog, Jan
Haruf, Kent 1943- .... **CLC 34**
See also AAYA 44; CA 149; CANR 91, 131
Harvey, Caroline
See Trollope, Joanna
Harvey, Gabriel 1550(?)-1631 .... **LC 88**
See also DLB 167, 213, 281
Harwood, Ronald 1934- .... **CLC 32**
See also CA 1-4R; CANR 4, 55, 150; CBD;
CD 5, 6; DAM DRAM, MST; DLB 13
Hasegawa Tatsunosuke
See Futabatei, Shimei
Hasek, Jaroslav (Matej Frantisek)
1883-1923 .... **SSC 69; TCLC 4**
See also CA 104; 129; CDWLB 4; DLB
215; EW 9; EWL 3; MTCW 1, 2; RGSF
2; RGWL 2, 3
Hass, Robert 1941- . **CLC 18, 39, 99; PC 16**
See also AMWS 6; CA 111; CANR 30, 50,
71; CP 3, 4, 5, 6, 7; DLB 105, 206; EWL
3; MAL 5; MTFW 2005; RGAL 4; SATA
94; TCLE 1:1
Hastings, Hudson
See Kuttner, Henry
Hastings, Selina .... **CLC 44**
Hathorne, John 1641-1717 .... **LC 38**
Hatteras, Amelia
See Mencken, H(enry) L(ouis)
Hatteras, Owen .... **TCLC 18**
See Mencken, H(enry) L(ouis); Nathan,
George Jean
Hauptmann, Gerhart (Johann Robert)
1862-1946 .... **SSC 37; TCLC 4**
See also CA 104; 153; CDWLB 2; DAM
DRAM; DLB 66, 118, 330; EW 8; EWL
3; RGSF 2; RGWL 2, 3; TWA
Havel, Vaclav 1936- .... **CLC 25, 58, 65, 123;
DC 6**
See also CA 104; CANR 36, 63, 124; CD-
WLB 4; CWW 2; DA3; DAM DRAM;
DFS 10; DLB 232; EWL 3; LMFS 2;
MTCW 1, 2; MTFW 2005; RGWL 3
Haviaras, Stratis .... **CLC 33**
See Chaviaras, Strates
Hawes, Stephen 1475(?)-1529(?) .... **LC 17**
See also DLB 132; RGEL 2
Hawkes, John 1925-1998 . **CLC 1, 2, 3, 4, 7,
9, 14, 15, 27, 49**
See also BPFB 2; CA 1-4R; 167; CANR 2,
47, 64; CN 1, 2, 3, 4, 5, 6; DLB 2, 7, 227;
DLBY 1980, 1998; EWL 3; MAL 5;
MTCW 1, 2; MTFW 2005; RGAL 4
Hawking, S. W.
See Hawking, Stephen W.
Hawking, Stephen W. 1942- .... **CLC 63, 105**
See also AAYA 13; BEST 89:1; CA 126;
129; CANR 48, 115; CPW; DA3; MTCW
2; MTFW 2005
Hawkins, Anthony Hope
See Hope, Anthony
Hawthorne, Julian 1846-1934 .... **TCLC 25**
See also CA 165; HGG

Hawthorne, Nathaniel 1804-1864 .. **NCLC 2,
10, 17, 23, 39, 79, 95, 158, 171; SSC 3,
29, 39, 89; WLC 3**
See also AAYA 18; AMW; AMWC 1;
AMWR 1; BPFB 2; BYA 3; CDALB
1640-1865; CLR 103; DA; DA3; DAB;
DAC; DAM MST, NOV; DLB 1, 74, 183,
223, 269; EXPN; EXPS; GL 2; HGG;
LAIT 1; NFS 1, 20; RGAL 4; RGSF 2;
SSFS 1, 7, 11, 15; SUFW 1; TUS; WCH;
YABC 2
Hawthorne, Sophia Peabody 1809-1871
.... **NCLC 150**
See also DLB 183, 239
Haxton, Josephine Ayres 1921-
See Douglas, Ellen
See also CA 115; CANR 41, 83
Hayaseca y Eizaguirre, Jorge
See Echegaray (y Eizaguirre), Jose (Maria
Waldo)
Hayashi, Fumiko 1904-1951 .... **TCLC 27**
See Hayashi Fumiko
See also CA 161
Hayashi Fumiko
See Hayashi, Fumiko
See also DLB 180; EWL 3
Haycraft, Anna 1932-2005
See Ellis, Alice Thomas
See also CA 122; 237; CANR 90, 141;
MTCW 2; MTFW 2005
Hayden, Robert E(arl) 1913-1980 ... **BLC 2;
CLC 5, 9, 14, 37; PC 6**
See also AFAW 1, 2; AMWS 2; BW 1, 3;
CA 69-72; 97-100; CABS 2; CANR 24,
75, 82; CDALB 1941-1968; CP 1, 2, 3;
DA; DAC; DAM MST, MULT, POET;
DLB 5, 76; EWL 3; EXPP; MAL 5;
MTCW 1, 2; PFS 1; RGAL 4; SATA 19;
SATA-Obit 26; WP
Haydon, Benjamin Robert 1786-1846
.... **NCLC 146**
See also DLB 110
Hayek, F(riedrich) A(ugust von) 1899-1992
.... **TCLC 109**
See also CA 93-96; 137; CANR 20; MTCW
1, 2
Hayford, J(oseph) E(phraim) Casely
See Casely-Hayford, J(oseph) E(phraim)
Hayman, Ronald 1932- .... **CLC 44**
See also CA 25-28R; CANR 18, 50, 88; CD
5, 6; DLB 155
Hayne, Paul Hamilton 1830-1886
.... **NCLC 94**
See also DLB 3, 64, 79, 248; RGAL 4
Hays, Mary 1760-1843 .... **NCLC 114**
See also DLB 142, 158; RGEL 2
Haywood, Eliza (Fowler) 1693(?)-1756
.... **LC 1, 44**
See also BRWS 12; DLB 39; RGEL 2
Hazlitt, William 1778-1830 ..... **NCLC 29, 82**
See also BRW 4; DLB 110, 158; RGEL 2;
TEA
Hazzard, Shirley 1931- .... **CLC 18, 218**
See also CA 9-12R; CANR 4, 70, 127; CN
1, 2, 3, 4, 5, 6, 7; DLB 289; DLBY 1982;
MTCW 1
Head, Bessie 1937-1986 ..... **BLC 2; CLC 25,
67; SSC 52**
See also AFW; BW 2, 3; CA 29-32R; 119;
CANR 25, 82; CDWLB 3; CN 1, 2, 3, 4;
DA3; DAM MULT; DLB 117, 225; EWL
3; EXPS; FL 1:6; FW; MTCW 1, 2;
MTFW 2005; RGSF 2; SSFS 5, 13; WLIT
2; WWE 1
Headon, (Nicky) Topper 1956(?)- ... **CLC 30**
Heaney, Seamus 1939- ...... **CLC 5, 7, 14, 25,
37, 74, 91, 171, 225; PC 18; WLCS**
See also AAYA 61; BRWR 1; BRWS 2; CA
85-88; CANR 25, 48, 75, 91, 128; CD-
BLB 1960 to Present; CP 1, 2, 3, 4, 5, 6,

7; DA3; DAB; DAM POET; DLB 40,
330; DLBY 1995; EWL 3; EXPP; MTCW
1, 2; MTFW 2005; PAB; PFS 2, 5, 8, 17;
RGEL 2; TEA; WLIT 4

Hearn, (Patricio) Lafcadio (Tessima Carlos)
1850-1904 .... **TCLC 9**
See also CA 105; 166; DLB 12, 78, 189;
HGG; MAL 5; RGAL 4

Hearne, Samuel 1745-1792 .... **LC 95**
See also DLB 99

Hearne, Vicki 1946-2001 .... **CLC 56**
See also CA 139; 201

Hearon, Shelby 1931- .... **CLC 63**
See also AITN 2; AMWS 8; CA 25-28R;
CANR 18, 48, 103, 146; CSW

Heat-Moon, William Least .... **CLC 29**
See Trogdon, William (Lewis)
See also AAYA 9

Hebbel, Friedrich 1813-1863 .... **DC 21;
NCLC 43**
See also CDWLB 2; DAM DRAM; DLB
129; EW 6; RGWL 2, 3

Hebert, Anne 1916-2000 .... **CLC 4, 13, 29**
See also CA 85-88; 187; CANR 69, 126;
CCA 1; CWP; CWW 2; DA3; DAC;
DAM MST, POET; DLB 68; EWL 3; GFL
1789 to the Present; MTCW 1, 2; MTFW
2005; PFS 20

Hecht, Anthony (Evan) 1923-2004 ... **CLC 8,
13, 19; PC 70**
See also AMWS 10; CA 9-12R; 232; CANR
6, 108; CP 1, 2, 3, 4, 5, 6, 7; DAM POET;
DLB 5, 169; EWL 3; PFS 6; WP

Hecht, Ben 1894-1964 ... **CLC 8; TCLC 101**
See also CA 85-88; DFS 9; DLB 7, 9, 25,
26, 28, 86; FANT; IDFW 3, 4; RGAL 4

Hedayat, Sadeq 1903-1951 .... **TCLC 21**
See also CA 120; EWL 3; RGSF 2

Hegel, Georg Wilhelm Friedrich 1770-1831
.... **NCLC 46, 151**
See also DLB 90; TWA

Heidegger, Martin 1889-1976 .... **CLC 24**
See also CA 81-84; 65-68; CANR 34; DLB
296; MTCW 1, 2; MTFW 2005

Heidenstam, (Carl Gustaf) Verner von
1859-1940 .... **TCLC 5**
See also CA 104; DLB 330

Heidi Louise
See Erdrich, Louise

Heifner, Jack 1946- .... **CLC 11**
See also CA 105; CANR 47

Heijermans, Herman 1864-1924 ... **TCLC 24**
See also CA 123; EWL 3

Heilbrun, Carolyn G(old) 1926-2003
.... **CLC 25, 173**
See Cross, Amanda
See also CA 45-48; 220; CANR 1, 28, 58,
94; FW

Hein, Christoph 1944- .... **CLC 154**
See also CA 158; CANR 108; CDWLB 2;
CWW 2; DLB 124

Heine, Heinrich 1797-1856 ...... **NCLC 4, 54,
147; PC 25**
See also CDWLB 2; DLB 90; EW 5; RGWL
2, 3; TWA

Heinemann, Larry 1944- .... **CLC 50**
See also CA 110; CAAS 21; CANR 31, 81,
156; DLBD 9; INT CANR-31

Heinemann, Larry Curtiss
See Heinemann, Larry

Heiney, Donald (William) 1921-1993
See Harris, MacDonald
See also CA 1-4R; 142; CANR 3, 58; FANT

Heinlein, Robert A. 1907-1988 ..... **CLC 1, 3,
8, 14, 26, 55; SSC 55**
See also AAYA 17; BPFB 2; BYA 4, 13;
CA 1-4R; 125; CANR 1, 20, 53; CLR 75;
CN 1, 2, 3, 4; CPW; DA3; DAM POP;
DLB 8; EXPS; JRDA; LAIT 5; LMFS 2;

MAICYA 1, 2; MTCW 1, 2; MTFW 2005;
RGAL 4; SATA 9, 69; SATA-Obit 56;
SCFW 1, 2; SFW 4; SSFS 7; YAW

Helforth, John
See Doolittle, Hilda

Heliodorus fl. 3rd cent. - .... **CMLC 52**
See also WLIT 8

Hellenhofferu, Vojtech Kapristian z
See Hasek, Jaroslav (Matej Frantisek)

Heller, Joseph 1923-1999 ..... **CLC 1, 3, 5, 8,
11, 36, 63; TCLC 131, 151; WLC 3**
See also AAYA 24; AITN 1; AMWS 4;
BPFB 2; BYA 1; CA 5-8R; 187; CABS 1;
CANR 8, 42, 66, 126; CN 1, 2, 3, 4, 5, 6;
CPW; DA; DA3; DAB; DAC; DAM MST,
NOV, POP; DLB 2, 28, 227; DLBY 1980,
2002; EWL 3; EXPN; INT CANR-8;
LAIT 4; MAL 5; MTCW 1, 2; MTFW
2005; NFS 1; RGAL 4; TUS; YAW

Hellman, Lillian 1906-1984 ...... **CLC 2, 4, 8,
14, 18, 34, 44, 52; DC 1; TCLC 119**
See also AAYA 47; AITN 1, 2; AMWS 1;
CA 13-16R; 112; CAD; CANR 33; CWD;
DA3; DAM DRAM; DFS 1, 3, 14; DLB
7, 228; DLBY 1984; EWL 3; FL 1:6; FW;
LAIT 3; MAL 5; MBL; MTCW 1, 2;
MTFW 2005; RGAL 4; TUS

Helprin, Mark 1947- .... **CLC 7, 10, 22, 32**
See also CA 81-84; CANR 47, 64, 124;
CDALBS; CN 7; CPW; DA3; DAM NOV,
POP; DLBY 1985; FANT; MAL 5;
MTCW 1, 2; MTFW 2005; SUFW 2

Helvetius, Claude-Adrien 1715-1771 . **LC 26**
See also DLB 313

Helyar, Jane Penelope Josephine 1933-
See Poole, Josephine
See also CA 21-24R; CANR 10, 26; CWRI
5; SATA 82, 138; SATA-Essay 138

Hemans, Felicia 1793-1835 ..... **NCLC 29, 71**
See also DLB 96; RGEL 2

Hemingway, Ernest (Miller) 1899-1961
... **CLC 1, 3, 6, 8, 10, 13, 19, 30, 34, 39,
41, 44, 50, 61, 80; SSC 1, 25, 36, 40,
63; TCLC 115; WLC 3**
See also AAYA 19; AMW; AMWC 1;
AMWR 1; BPFB 2; BYA 2, 3, 13, 15; CA
77-80; CANR 34; CDALB 1917-1929;
DA; DA3; DAB; DAC; DAM MST, NOV;
DLB 4, 9, 102, 210, 308, 316, 330; DLBD
1, 15, 16; DLBY 1981, 1987, 1996, 1998;
EWL 3; EXPN; EXPS; LAIT 3, 4; LATS
1:1; MAL 5; MTCW 1, 2; MTFW 2005;
NFS 1, 5, 6, 14; RGAL 4; RGSF 2; SSFS
17; TUS; WYA

Hempel, Amy 1951- .... **CLC 39**
See also CA 118; 137; CANR 70; DA3;
DLB 218; EXPS; MTCW 2; MTFW 2005;
SSFS 2

Henderson, F. C.
See Mencken, H(enry) L(ouis)

Henderson, Sylvia
See Ashton-Warner, Sylvia (Constance)

Henderson, Zenna (Chlarson) 1917-1983
.... **SSC 29**
See also CA 1-4R; 133; CANR 1, 84; DLB
8; SATA 5; SFW 4

Henkin, Joshua .... **CLC 119**
See also CA 161

Henley, Beth .... **CLC 23; DC 6, 14**
See Henley, Elizabeth Becker
See also AAYA 70; CABS 3; CAD; CD 5,
6; CSW; CWD; DFS 2, 21; DLBY 1986;
FW

Henley, Elizabeth Becker 1952-
See Henley, Beth
See also CA 107; CANR 32, 73, 140; DA3;
DAM DRAM, MST; MTCW 1, 2; MTFW
2005

Henley, William Ernest 1849-1903 . **TCLC 8**
See also CA 105; 234; DLB 19; RGEL 2

Hennissart, Martha 1929-
See Lathen, Emma
See also CA 85-88; CANR 64

Henry VIII 1491-1547 .... **LC 10**
See also DLB 132

Henry, O. . **SSC 5, 49; TCLC 1, 19; WLC 3**
See Porter, William Sydney
See also AAYA 41; AMWS 2; EXPS; MAL
5; RGAL 4; RGSF 2; SSFS 2, 18; TCWW
1, 2

Henry, Patrick 1736-1799 .... **LC 25**
See also LAIT 1

Henryson, Robert 1430(?)-1506(?) .... **LC 20,
110; PC 65**
See also BRWS 7; DLB 146; RGEL 2

Henschke, Alfred
See Klabund

Henson, Lance 1944- .... **NNAL**
See also CA 146; DLB 175

Hentoff, Nat(han Irving) 1925- .... **CLC 26**
See also AAYA 4, 42; BYA 6; CA 1-4R;
CAAS 6; CANR 5, 25, 77, 114; CLR 1,
52; INT CANR-25; JRDA; MAICYA 1,
2; SATA 42, 69, 133; SATA-Brief 27;
WYA; YAW

Heppenstall, (John) Rayner 1911-1981
.... **CLC 10**
See also CA 1-4R; 103; CANR 29; CN 1,
2; CP 1, 2, 3; EWL 3

Heraclitus c. 540B.C.-c. 450B.C. . **CMLC 22**
See also DLB 176

Herbert, Frank 1920-1986 . **CLC 12, 23, 35,
44, 85**
See also AAYA 21; BPFB 2; BYA 4, 14;
CA 53-56; 118; CANR 5, 43; CDALBS;
CPW; DAM POP; DLB 8; INT CANR-5;
LAIT 5; MTCW 1, 2; MTFW 2005; NFS
17; SATA 9, 37; SATA-Obit 47; SCFW 1,
2; SFW 4; YAW

Herbert, George 1593-1633 ...... **LC 24, 121;
PC 4**
See also BRW 2; BRWR 2; CDBLB Before
1660; DAB; DAM POET; DLB 126;
EXPP; RGEL 2; TEA; WP

Herbert, Zbigniew 1924-1998 .... **CLC 9, 43;
PC 50; TCLC 168**
See also CA 89-92; 169; CANR 36, 74; CD-
WLB 4; CWW 2; DAM POET; DLB 232;
EWL 3; MTCW 1; PFS 22

Herbst, Josephine (Frey) 1897-1969
.... **CLC 34**
See also CA 5-8R; 25-28R; DLB 9

Herder, Johann Gottfried von 1744-1803
.... **NCLC 8**
See also DLB 97; EW 4; TWA

Heredia, Jose Maria 1803-1839 ...... **HLCS 2**
See also LAW

Hergesheimer, Joseph 1880-1954 .. **TCLC 11**
See also CA 109; 194; DLB 102, 9; RGAL
4

Herlihy, James Leo 1927-1993 .... **CLC 6**
See also CA 1-4R; 143; CAD; CANR 2;
CN 1, 2, 3, 4, 5

Herman, William
See Bierce, Ambrose (Gwinett)

Hermogenes fl. c. 175- .... **CMLC 6**

Hernandez, Jose 1834-1886 .... **NCLC 17**
See also LAW; RGWL 2, 3; WLIT 1

Herodotus c. 484B.C.-c. 420B.C. . **CMLC 17**
See also AW 1; CDWLB 1; DLB 176;
RGWL 2, 3; TWA; WLIT 8

Herr, Michael 1940- .... **CLC 231**
See also CA 89-92; CANR 68, 142; MTCW
1

Herrick, Robert 1591-1674 ..... **LC 13; PC 9**
See also BRW 2; BRWC 2; DA; DAB;
DAC; DAM MST, POP; DLB 126; EXPP;
PFS 13; RGAL 4; RGEL 2; TEA; WP

Hobbs, Perry
See Blackmur, R(ichard) P(almer)
Hobson, Laura Z(ametkin) 1900-1986
.... **CLC 7, 25**
See also BPFB 2; CA 17-20R; 118; CANR 55; CN 1, 2, 3, 4; DLB 28; SATA 52
Hoccleve, Thomas c. 1368-c. 1437 ..... **LC 75**
See also DLB 146; RGEL 2
Hoch, Edward D(entinger) 1930-
See Queen, Ellery
See also CA 29-32R; CANR 11, 27, 51, 97; CMW 4; DLB 306; SFW 4
Hochhuth, Rolf 1931- .... **CLC 4, 11, 18**
See also CA 5-8R; CANR 33, 75, 136; CWW 2; DAM DRAM; DLB 124; EWL 3; MTCW 1, 2; MTFW 2005; RGHL
Hochman, Sandra 1936- .... **CLC 3, 8**
See also CA 5-8R; CP 1, 2, 3, 4, 5; DLB 5
Hochwaelder, Fritz 1911-1986 .... **CLC 36**
See Hochwalder, Fritz
See also CA 29-32R; 120; CANR 42; DAM DRAM; MTCW 1; RGWL 3
Hochwalder, Fritz
See Hochwaelder, Fritz
See also EWL 3; RGWL 2
Hocking, Mary (Eunice) 1921- .... **CLC 13**
See also CA 101; CANR 18, 40
Hodgins, Jack 1938- .... **CLC 23**
See also CA 93-96; CN 4, 5, 6, 7; DLB 60
Hodgson, William Hope 1877(?)-1918
.... **TCLC 13**
See also CA 111; 164; CMW 4; DLB 70, 153, 156, 178; HGG; MTCW 2; SFW 4; SUFW 1
Hoeg, Peter 1957- .... **CLC 95, 156**
See also CA 151; CANR 75; CMW 4; DA3; DLB 214; EWL 3; MTCW 2; MTFW 2005; NFS 17; RGWL 3; SSFS 18
Hoffman, Alice 1952- .... **CLC 51**
See also AAYA 37; AMWS 10; CA 77-80; CANR 34, 66, 100, 138; CN 4, 5, 6, 7; CPW; DAM NOV; DLB 292; MAL 5; MTCW 1, 2; MTFW 2005; TCLE 1:1
Hoffman, Daniel (Gerard) 1923- ...... **CLC 6, 13, 23**
See also CA 1-4R; CANR 4, 142; CP 1, 2, 3, 4, 5, 6, 7; DLB 5; TCLE 1:1
Hoffman, Eva 1945- .... **CLC 182**
See also AMWS 16; CA 132; CANR 146
Hoffman, Stanley 1944- .... **CLC 5**
See also CA 77-80
Hoffman, William 1925- .... **CLC 141**
See also CA 21-24R; CANR 9, 103; CSW; DLB 234; TCLE 1:1
Hoffman, William M.
See Hoffman, William M(oses)
See also CAD; CD 5, 6
Hoffman, William M(oses) 1939- .... **CLC 40**
See Hoffman, William M.
See also CA 57-60; CANR 11, 71
Hoffmann, E(rnst) T(heodor) A(madeus)
1776-1822 .... **NCLC 2; SSC 13, 92**
See also CDWLB 2; DLB 90; EW 5; GL 2; RGSF 2; RGWL 2, 3; SATA 27; SUFW 1; WCH
Hofmann, Gert 1931-1993 .... **CLC 54**
See also CA 128; CANR 145; EWL 3; RGHL
Hofmannsthal, Hugo von 1874-1929 . **DC 4; TCLC 11**
See also CA 106; 153; CDWLB 2; DAM DRAM; DFS 17; DLB 81, 118; EW 9; EWL 3; RGWL 2, 3
Hogan, Linda 1947- .... **CLC 73; NNAL; PC 35**
See also AMWS 4; ANW; BYA 12; CA 120, 226; CAAE 226; CANR 45, 73, 129; CWP; DAM MULT; DLB 175; SATA 132; TCWW 2

Hogarth, Charles
See Creasey, John
Hogarth, Emmett
See Polonsky, Abraham (Lincoln)
Hogarth, William 1697-1764 .... **LC 112**
See also AAYA 56
Hogg, James 1770-1835 .... **NCLC 4, 109**
See also BRWS 10; DLB 93, 116, 159; GL 2; HGG; RGEL 2; SUFW 1
Holbach, Paul-Henri Thiry 1723-1789
.... **LC 14**
See also DLB 313
Holberg, Ludvig 1684-1754 .... **LC 6**
See also DLB 300; RGWL 2, 3
Holcroft, Thomas 1745-1809 .... **NCLC 85**
See also DLB 39, 89, 158; RGEL 2
Holden, Ursula 1921- .... **CLC 18**
See also CA 101; CAAS 8; CANR 22
Holderlin, (Johann Christian) Friedrich
1770-1843 .... **NCLC 16; PC 4**
See also CDWLB 2; DLB 90; EW 5; RGWL 2, 3
Holdstock, Robert
See Holdstock, Robert P.
Holdstock, Robert P. 1948- .... **CLC 39**
See also CA 131; CANR 81; DLB 261; FANT; HGG; SFW 4; SUFW 2
Holinshed, Raphael fl. 1580- .... **LC 69**
See also DLB 167; RGEL 2
Holland, Isabelle (Christian) 1920-2002
.... **CLC 21**
See also AAYA 11, 64; CA 21-24R; 205; CAAE 181; CANR 10, 25, 47; CLR 57; CWRI 5; JRDA; LAIT 4; MAICYA 1, 2; SATA 8, 70; SATA-Essay 103; SATA-Obit 132; WYA
Holland, Marcus
See Caldwell, (Janet Miriam) Taylor (Holland)
Hollander, John 1929- .... **CLC 2, 5, 8, 14**
See also CA 1-4R; CANR 1, 52, 136; CP 1, 2, 3, 4, 5, 6, 7; DLB 5; MAL 5; SATA 13
Hollander, Paul
See Silverberg, Robert
Holleran, Andrew .... **CLC 38**
See Garber, Eric
See also CA 144; GLL 1
Holley, Marietta 1836(?)-1926 ...... **TCLC 99**
See also CA 118; DLB 11; FL 1:3
Hollinghurst, Alan 1954- .... **CLC 55, 91**
See also BRWS 10; CA 114; CN 5, 6, 7; DLB 207, 326; GLL 1
Hollis, Jim
See Summers, Hollis (Spurgeon, Jr.)
Holly, Buddy 1936-1959 .... **TCLC 65**
See also CA 213
Holmes, Gordon
See Shiel, M(atthew) P(hipps)
Holmes, John
See Souster, (Holmes) Raymond
Holmes, John Clellon 1926-1988 ..... **CLC 56**
See also BG 1:2; CA 9-12R; 125; CANR 4; CN 1, 2, 3, 4; DLB 16, 237
Holmes, Oliver Wendell, Jr. 1841-1935
.... **TCLC 77**
See also CA 114; 186
Holmes, Oliver Wendell 1809-1894
.... **NCLC 14, 81; PC 71**
See also AMWS 1; CDALB 1640-1865; DLB 1, 189, 235; EXPP; PFS 24; RGAL 4; SATA 34
Holmes, Raymond
See Souster, (Holmes) Raymond
Holt, Victoria
See Hibbert, Eleanor Alice Burford
See also BPFB 2

Holub, Miroslav 1923-1998 .... **CLC 4**
See also CA 21-24R; 169; CANR 10; CD-WLB 4; CWW 2; DLB 232; EWL 3; RGWL 3
Holz, Detlev
See Benjamin, Walter
Homer c. 8th cent. B.C.- ... **CMLC 1, 16, 61; PC 23; WLCS**
See also AW 1; CDWLB 1; DA; DA3; DAB; DAC; DAM MST, POET; DLB 176; EFS 1; LAIT 1; LMFS 1; RGWL 2, 3; TWA; WLIT 8; WP
Hongo, Garrett Kaoru 1951- .... **PC 23**
See also CA 133; CAAS 22; CP 5, 6, 7; DLB 120, 312; EWL 3; EXPP; RGAL 4
Honig, Edwin 1919- .... **CLC 33**
See also CA 5-8R; CAAS 8; CANR 4, 45, 144; CP 1, 2, 3, 4, 5, 6, 7; DLB 5
Hood, Hugh (John Blagdon) 1928-
.... **CLC 15, 28; SSC 42**
See also CA 49-52; CAAS 17; CANR 1, 33, 87; CN 1, 2, 3, 4, 5, 6, 7; DLB 53; RGSF 2
Hood, Thomas 1799-1845 .... **NCLC 16**
See also BRW 4; DLB 96; RGEL 2
Hooker, (Peter) Jeremy 1941- .... **CLC 43**
See also CA 77-80; CANR 22; CP 2, 3, 4, 5, 6, 7; DLB 40
Hooker, Richard 1554-1600 .... **LC 95**
See also BRW 1; DLB 132; RGEL 2
hooks, bell 1952(?)- .... **CLC 94**
See also BW 2; CA 143; CANR 87, 126; DLB 246; MTCW 2; MTFW 2005; SATA 115, 170
Hooper, Johnson Jones 1815-1862
.... **NCLC 177**
See also DLB 3, 11, 248; RGAL 4
Hope, A(lec) D(erwent) 1907-2000 ... **CLC 3, 51; PC 56**
See also BRWS 7; CA 21-24R; 188; CANR 33, 74; CP 1, 2, 3, 4, 5; DLB 289; EWL 3; MTCW 1, 2; MTFW 2005; PFS 8; RGEL 2
Hope, Anthony 1863-1933 .... **TCLC 83**
See also CA 157; DLB 153, 156; RGEL 2; RHW
Hope, Brian
See Creasey, John
Hope, Christopher (David Tully) 1944-
.... **CLC 52**
See also AFW; CA 106; CANR 47, 101; CN 4, 5, 6, 7; DLB 225; SATA 62
Hopkins, Gerard Manley 1844-1889
.... **NCLC 17; PC 15; WLC 3**
See also BRW 5; BRWR 2; CDBLB 1890-1914; DA; DA3; DAB; DAC; DAM MST, POET; DLB 35, 57; EXPP; PAB; RGEL 2; TEA; WP
Hopkins, John (Richard) 1931-1998 . **CLC 4**
See also CA 85-88; 169; CBD; CD 5, 6
Hopkins, Pauline Elizabeth 1859-1930
.... **BLC 2; TCLC 28**
See also AFAW 2; BW 2, 3; CA 141; CANR 82; DAM MULT; DLB 50
Hopkinson, Francis 1737-1791 .... **LC 25**
See also DLB 31; RGAL 4
Hopley-Woolrich, Cornell George 1903-1968
See Woolrich, Cornell
See also CA 13-14; CANR 58, 156; CAP 1; CMW 4; DLB 226; MTCW 2
Horace 65B.C.-8B.C. .... **CMLC 39; PC 46**
See also AW 2; CDWLB 1; DLB 211; RGWL 2, 3; WLIT 8
Horatio
See Proust, (Valentin-Louis-George-Eugene) Marcel

Jeake, Samuel, Jr.
See Aiken, Conrad (Potter)
Jean Paul 1763-1825 .... **NCLC 7**
Jefferies, (John) Richard 1848-1887
.... **NCLC 47**
See also DLB 98, 141; RGEL 2; SATA 16;
SFW 4
Jeffers, (John) Robinson 1887-1962
... **CLC 2, 3, 11, 15, 54; PC 17; WLC 3**
See also AMWS 2; CA 85-88; CANR 35;
CDALB 1917-1929; DA; DAC; DAM
MST, POET; DLB 45, 212; EWL 3; MAL
5; MTCW 1, 2; MTFW 2005; PAB; PFS
3, 4; RGAL 4
Jefferson, Janet
See Mencken, H(enry) L(ouis)
Jefferson, Thomas 1743-1826 .... **NCLC 11,
103**
See also AAYA 54; ANW; CDALB 1640-
1865; DA3; DLB 31, 183; LAIT 1; RGAL
4
Jeffrey, Francis 1773-1850 .... **NCLC 33**
See Francis, Lord Jeffrey
Jełakowitch, Ivan
See Heijermans, Herman
Jelinek, Elfriede 1946- .... **CLC 169**
See also AAYA 68; CA 154; DLB 85, 330;
FW
Jellicoe, (Patricia) Ann 1927- .... **CLC 27**
See also CA 85-88; CBD; CD 5, 6; CWD;
CWRI 5; DLB 13, 233; FW
Jelloun, Tahar ben 1944- .... **CLC 180**
See Ben Jelloun, Tahar
See also CA 162; CANR 100
Jemyma
See Holley, Marietta
Jen, Gish .... **AAL; CLC 70, 198**
See Jen, Lillian
See also AMWC 2; CN 7; DLB 312
Jen, Lillian 1955-
See Jen, Gish
See also CA 135; CANR 89, 130
Jenkins, (John) Robin 1912- .... **CLC 52**
See also CA 1-4R; CANR 1, 135; CN 1, 2,
3, 4, 5, 6, 7; DLB 14, 271
Jennings, Elizabeth (Joan) 1926-2001
.... **CLC 5, 14, 131**
See also BRWS 5; CA 61-64; 200; CAAS
5; CANR 8, 39, 66, 127; CP 1, 2, 3, 4, 5,
6, 7; CWP; DLB 27; EWL 3; MTCW 1;
SATA 66
Jennings, Waylon 1937-2002 .... **CLC 21**
Jensen, Johannes V(ilhelm) 1873-1950
.... **TCLC 41**
See also CA 170; DLB 214, 330; EWL 3;
RGWL 3
Jensen, Laura (Linnea) 1948- .... **CLC 37**
See also CA 103
Jerome, Saint 345-420 .... **CMLC 30**
See also RGWL 3
Jerome, Jerome K(lapka) 1859-1927
.... **TCLC 23**
See also CA 119; 177; DLB 10, 34, 135;
RGEL 2
Jerrold, Douglas William 1803-1857
.... **NCLC 2**
See also DLB 158, 159; RGEL 2
Jewett, (Theodora) Sarah Orne 1849-1909
.... **SSC 6, 44; TCLC 1, 22**
See also AMW; AMWC 2; AMWR 2; CA
108; 127; CANR 71; DLB 12, 74, 221;
EXPS; FL 1:3; FW; MAL 5; MBL; NFS
15; RGAL 4; RGSF 2; SATA 15; SSFS 4
Jewsbury, Geraldine (Endsor) 1812-1880
.... **NCLC 22**
See also DLB 21

Jhabvala, Ruth Prawer 1927- ...... **CLC 4, 8,
29, 94, 138; SSC 91**
See also BRWS 5; CA 1-4R; CANR 2, 29,
51, 74, 91, 128; CN 1, 2, 3, 4, 5, 6, 7;
DAB; DAM NOV; DLB 139, 194, 323,
326; EWL 3; IDFW 3, 4; INT CANR-29;
MTCW 1, 2; MTFW 2005; RGSF 2;
RGWL 2; RHW; TEA
Jibran, Kahlil
See Gibran, Kahlil
Jibran, Khalil
See Gibran, Kahlil
Jiles, Paulette 1943- .... **CLC 13, 58**
See also CA 101; CANR 70, 124; CP 5;
CWP
Jimenez (Mantecon), Juan Ramon
1881-1958 ...... **HLC 1; PC 7; TCLC 4,
183**
See also CA 104; 131; CANR 74; DAM
MULT, POET; DLB 134, 330; EW 9;
EWL 3; HW 1; MTCW 1, 2; MTFW
2005; RGWL 2, 3
Jimenez, Ramon
See Jimenez (Mantecon), Juan Ramon
Jimenez Mantecon, Juan
See Jimenez (Mantecon), Juan Ramon
Jin, Ba 1904-2005
See Pa Chin
See also CA 244; CWW 2; DLB 328
Jin, Xuefei
See Ha Jin
Jodelle, Etienne 1532-1573 .... **LC 119**
See also DLB 327; GFL Beginnings to 1789
Joel, Billy .... **CLC 26**
See Joel, William Martin
Joel, William Martin 1949-
See Joel, Billy
See also CA 108
John, Saint 10(?)-100 .... **CMLC 27, 63**
John of Salisbury c. 1115-1180 .... **CMLC 63**
John of the Cross, St. 1542-1591 .... **LC 18**
See also RGWL 2, 3
John Paul II, Pope 1920-2005 .... **CLC 128**
See also CA 106; 133; 238
Johnson, B(ryan) S(tanley William)
1933-1973 .... **CLC 6, 9**
See also CA 9-12R; 53-56; CANR 9; CN 1;
CP 1, 2; DLB 14, 40; EWL 3; RGEL 2
Johnson, Benjamin F., of Boone
See Riley, James Whitcomb
Johnson, Charles (Richard) 1948- ... **BLC 2;
CLC 7, 51, 65, 163**
See also AFAW 2; AMWS 6; BW 2, 3; CA
116; CAAS 18; CANR 42, 66, 82, 129;
CN 5, 6, 7; DAM MULT; DLB 33, 278;
MAL 5; MTCW 2; MTFW 2005; RGAL
4; SSFS 16
Johnson, Charles S(purgeon) 1893-1956
.... **HR 1:3**
See also BW 1, 3; CA 125; CANR 82; DLB
51, 91
Johnson, Denis 1949- ..... **CLC 52, 160; SSC
56**
See also CA 117; 121; CANR 71, 99; CN
4, 5, 6, 7; DLB 120
Johnson, Diane 1934- .... **CLC 5, 13, 48**
See also BPFB 2; CA 41-44R; CANR 17,
40, 62, 95, 155; CN 4, 5, 6, 7; DLBY
1980; INT CANR-17; MTCW 1
Johnson, E(mily) Pauline 1861-1913
.... **NNAL**
See also CA 150; CCA 1; DAC; DAM
MULT; DLB 92, 175; TCWW 2
Johnson, Eyvind (Olof Verner) 1900-1976
.... **CLC 14**
See also CA 73-76; 69-72; CANR 34, 101;
DLB 259, 330; EW 12; EWL 3

Johnson, Fenton 1888-1958 .... **BLC 2**
See also BW 1; CA 118; 124; DAM MULT;
DLB 45, 50
Johnson, Georgia Douglas (Camp)
1880-1966 .... **HR 1:3**
See also BW 1; CA 125; DLB 51, 249; WP
Johnson, Helene 1907-1995 .... **HR 1:3**
See also CA 181; DLB 51; WP
Johnson, J. R.
See James, C(yril) L(ionel) R(obert)
Johnson, James Weldon 1871-1938 . **BLC 2;
HR 1:3; PC 24; TCLC 3, 19, 175**
See also AFAW 1, 2; BW 1, 3; CA 104;
125; CANR 82; CDALB 1917-1929; CLR
32; DA3; DAM MULT, POET; DLB 51;
EWL 3; EXPP; LMFS 2; MAL 5; MTCW
1, 2; MTFW 2005; NFS 22; PFS 1; RGAL
4; SATA 31; TUS
Johnson, Joyce 1935- .... **CLC 58**
See also BG 1:3; CA 125; 129; CANR 102
Johnson, Judith (Emlyn) 1936- .. **CLC 7, 15**
See Sherwin, Judith Johnson
See also CA 25-28R; 153; CANR 34; CP 6,
7
Johnson, Lionel (Pigot) 1867-1902
.... **TCLC 19**
See also CA 117; 209; DLB 19; RGEL 2
Johnson, Marguerite Annie
See Angelou, Maya
Johnson, Mel
See Malzberg, Barry N(athaniel)
Johnson, Pamela Hansford 1912-1981
.... **CLC 1, 7, 27**
See also CA 1-4R; 104; CANR 2, 28; CN
1, 2, 3; DLB 15; MTCW 1, 2; MTFW
2005; RGEL 2
Johnson, Paul 1928- .... **CLC 147**
See also BEST 89:4; CA 17-20R; CANR
34, 62, 100, 155
Johnson, Paul Bede
See Johnson, Paul
Johnson, Robert .... **CLC 70**
Johnson, Robert 1911(?)-1938 ...... **TCLC 69**
See also BW 3; CA 174
Johnson, Samuel 1709-1784 .... **LC 15, 52,
128; WLC 3**
See also BRW 3; BRWR 1; CDBLB 1660-
1789; DA; DAB; DAC; DAM MST; DLB
39, 95, 104, 142, 213; LMFS 1; RGEL 2;
TEA
Johnson, Uwe 1934-1984 . **CLC 5, 10, 15, 40**
See also CA 1-4R; 112; CANR 1, 39; CD-
WLB 2; DLB 75; EWL 3; MTCW 1;
RGWL 2, 3
Johnston, Basil H. 1929- .... **NNAL**
See also CA 69-72; CANR 11, 28, 66;
DAC; DAM MULT; DLB 60
Johnston, George (Benson) 1913- ... **CLC 51**
See also CA 1-4R; CANR 5, 20; CP 1, 2, 3,
4, 5, 6, 7; DLB 88
Johnston, Jennifer (Prudence) 1930-
.... **CLC 7, 150, 228**
See also CA 85-88; CANR 92; CN 4, 5, 6,
7; DLB 14
Joinville, Jean de 1224(?)-1317 ... **CMLC 38**
Jolley, (Monica) Elizabeth 1923- ... **CLC 46;
SSC 19**
See also CA 127; CAAS 13; CANR 59; CN
4, 5, 6, 7; DLB 325; EWL 3; RGSF 2
Jones, Arthur Llewellyn 1863-1947
See Machen, Arthur
See also CA 104; 179; HGG
Jones, D(ouglas) G(ordon) 1929- .... **CLC 10**
See also CA 29-32R; CANR 13, 90; CP 1,
2, 3, 4, 5, 6, 7; DLB 53

Jones, David (Michael) 1895-1974 ... **CLC 2, 4, 7, 13, 42**
See also BRW 6; BRWS 7; CA 9-12R; 53-56; CANR 28; CDBLB 1945-1960; CP 1, 2; DLB 20, 100; EWL 3; MTCW 1; PAB; RGEL 2

Jones, David Robert 1947-
See Bowie, David
See also CA 103; CANR 104

Jones, Diana Wynne 1934- .... **CLC 26**
See also AAYA 12; BYA 6, 7, 9, 11, 13, 16; CA 49-52; CANR 4, 26, 56, 120; CLR 23, 120; DLB 161; FANT; JRDA; MAICYA 1, 2; MTFW 2005; SAAS 7; SATA 9, 70, 108, 160; SFW 4; SUFW 2; YAW

Jones, Edward P. 1950- .... **CLC 76, 223**
See also AAYA 71; BW 2, 3; CA 142; CANR 79, 134; CSW; MTFW 2005

Jones, Gayl 1949- ..... **BLC 2; CLC 6, 9, 131**
See also AFAW 1, 2; BW 2, 3; CA 77-80; CANR 27, 66, 122; CN 4, 5, 6, 7; CSW; DA3; DAM MULT; DLB 33, 278; MAL 5; MTCW 1, 2; MTFW 2005; RGAL 4

Jones, James 1921-1977 .... **CLC 1, 3, 10, 39**
See also AITN 1, 2; AMWS 11; BPFB 2; CA 1-4R; 69-72; CANR 6; CN 1, 2; DLB 2, 143; DLBD 17; DLBY 1998; EWL 3; MAL 5; MTCW 1; RGAL 4

Jones, John J.
See Lovecraft, H. P.

Jones, LeRoi .... **CLC 1, 2, 3, 5, 10, 14**
See Baraka, Amiri
See also CN 1, 2; CP 1, 2, 3; MTCW 2

Jones, Louis B. 1953- .... **CLC 65**
See also CA 141; CANR 73

Jones, Madison (Percy, Jr.) 1925- ..... **CLC 4**
See also CA 13-16R; CAAS 11; CANR 7, 54, 83; CN 1, 2, 3, 4, 5, 6, 7; CSW; DLB 152

Jones, Mervyn 1922- .... **CLC 10, 52**
See also CA 45-48; CAAS 5; CANR 1, 91; CN 1, 2, 3, 4, 5, 6, 7; MTCW 1

Jones, Mick 1956(?)- .... **CLC 30**

Jones, Nettie (Pearl) 1941- .... **CLC 34**
See also BW 2; CA 137; CAAS 20; CANR 88

Jones, Peter 1802-1856 .... **NNAL**

Jones, Preston 1936-1979 .... **CLC 10**
See also CA 73-76; 89-92; DLB 7

Jones, Robert F(rancis) 1934-2003 ... **CLC 7**
See also CA 49-52; CANR 2, 61, 118

Jones, Rod 1953- .... **CLC 50**
See also CA 128

Jones, Terence Graham Parry 1942-
.... **CLC 21**
See Jones, Terry; Monty Python
See also CA 112; 116; CANR 35, 93; INT CA-116; SATA 127

Jones, Terry
See Jones, Terence Graham Parry
See also SATA 67; SATA-Brief 51

Jones, Thom (Douglas) 1945(?)- .... **CLC 81; SSC 56**
See also CA 157; CANR 88; DLB 244; SSFS 23

Jong, Erica 1942- .... **CLC 4, 6, 8, 18, 83**
See also AITN 1; AMWS 5; BEST 90:2; BPFB 2; CA 73-76; CANR 26, 52, 75, 132; CN 3, 4, 5, 6, 7; CP 2, 3, 4, 5, 6, 7; CPW; DA3; DAM NOV, POP; DLB 2, 5, 28, 152; FW; INT CANR-26; MAL 5; MTCW 1, 2; MTFW 2005

Jonson, Ben(jamin) 1572(?)-1637 .... **DC 4; LC 6, 33, 110; PC 17; WLC 3**
See also BRW 1; BRWC 1; BRWR 1; CDBLB Before 1660; DA; DAB; DAC; DAM DRAM, MST, POET; DFS 4, 10; DLB 62, 121; LMFS 1; PFS 23; RGEL 2; TEA; WLIT 3

Jordan, June 1936-2002 . **BLCS; CLC 5, 11, 23, 114, 230; PC 38**
See also AAYA 2, 66; AFAW 1, 2; BW 2, 3; CA 33-36R; 206; CANR 25, 70, 114, 154; CLR 10; CP 3, 4, 5, 6, 7; CWP; DAM MULT, POET; DLB 38; GLL 2; LAIT 5; MAICYA 1, 2; MTCW 1; SATA 4, 136; YAW

Jordan, June Meyer
See Jordan, June

Jordan, Neil 1950- ....- **CLC 110**
See also CA 124; 130; CANR 54, 154; CN 4, 5, 6, 7; GLL 2; INT CA-130

Jordan, Neil Patrick
See Jordan, Neil

Jordan, Pat(rick M.) 1941- .... **CLC 37**
See also CA 33-36R; CANR 121

Jorgensen, Ivar
See Ellison, Harlan

Jorgenson, Ivar
See Silverberg, Robert

Joseph, George Ghevarughese .... **CLC 70**

Josephson, Mary
See O'Doherty, Brian

Josephus, Flavius c. 37-100 .... **CMLC 13**
See also AW 2; DLB 176; WLIT 8

Josiah Allen's Wife
See Holley, Marietta

Josipovici, Gabriel (David) 1940- .... **CLC 6, 43, 153**
See also CA 37-40R; 224; CAAE 224; CAAS 8; CANR 47, 84; CN 3, 4, 5, 6, 7; DLB 14, 319

Joubert, Joseph 1754-1824 .... **NCLC 9**

Jouve, Pierre Jean 1887-1976 .... **CLC 47**
See also CA 65-68; DLB 258; EWL 3

Jovine, Francesco 1902-1950 .... **TCLC 79**
See also DLB 264; EWL 3

Joyce, James (Augustine Aloysius) 1882-1941 ... **DC 16; PC 22; SSC 3, 26, 44, 64; TCLC 3, 8, 16, 35, 52, 159; WLC 3**
See also AAYA 42; BRW 7; BRWC 1; BRWR 1; BYA 11, 13; CA 104; 126; CDBLB 1914-1945; DA; DA3; DAB; DAC; DAM MST, NOV; DLB 10, 19, 36, 162, 247; EWL 3; EXPN; EXPS; LAIT 3; LMFS 1, 2; MTCW 1, 2; MTFW 2005; NFS 7; RGSF 2; SSFS 1, 19; TEA; WLIT 4

Jozsef, Attila 1905-1937 .... **TCLC 22**
See also CA 116; 230; CDWLB 4; DLB 215; EWL 3

Juana Ines de la Cruz, Sor 1651(?)-1695 .... **HLCS 1; LC 5; PC 24**
See also DLB 305; FW; LAW; RGWL 2, 3; WLIT 1

Juana Inez de La Cruz, Sor
See Juana Ines de la Cruz, Sor

Judd, Cyril
See Kornbluth, C(yril) M.; Pohl, Frederik

Juenger, Ernst 1895-1998 .... **CLC 125**
See Junger, Ernst
See also CA 101; 167; CANR 21, 47, 106; DLB 56

Julian of Norwich 1342(?)-1416(?) ..... **LC 6, 52**
See also BRWS 12; DLB 146; LMFS 1

Julius Caesar 100B.C.-44B.C.
See Caesar, Julius
See also CDWLB 1; DLB 211

Junger, Ernst
See Juenger, Ernst
See also CDWLB 2; EWL 3; RGWL 2, 3

Junger, Sebastian 1962- .... **CLC 109**
See also AAYA 28; CA 165; CANR 130; MTFW 2005

Juniper, Alex
See Hospital, Janette Turner

Junius
See Luxemburg, Rosa

Junzaburo, Nishiwaki
See Nishiwaki, Junzaburo
See also EWL 3

Just, Ward 1935- .... **CLC 4, 27**
See also CA 25-28R; CANR 32, 87; CN 6, 7; INT CANR-32

Just, Ward Swift
See Just, Ward

Justice, Donald (Rodney) 1925-2004
.... **CLC 6, 19, 102; PC 64**
See also AMWS 7; CA 5-8R; 230; CANR 26, 54, 74, 121, 122; CP 1, 2, 3, 4, 5, 6, 7; CSW; DAM POET; DLBY 1983; EWL 3; INT CANR-26; MAL 5; MTCW 2; PFS 14; TCLE 1:1

Juvenal c. 60-c. 130 .... **CMLC 8**
See also AW 2; CDWLB 1; DLB 211; RGWL 2, 3; WLIT 8

Juvenis
See Bourne, Randolph S(illiman)

K., Alice
See Knapp, Caroline

Kabakov, Sasha .... **CLC 59**

Kabir 1398(?)-1448(?) .... **LC 109; PC 56**
See also RGWL 2, 3

Kacew, Romain 1914-1980
See Gary, Romain
See also CA 108; 102

Kadare, Ismail 1936- .... **CLC 52, 190**
See also CA 161; EWL 3; RGWL 3

Kadohata, Cynthia (Lynn) 1956(?)-
.... **CLC 59, 122**
See also AAYA 71; CA 140; CANR 124; SATA 155

Kafka, Franz 1883-1924 . **SSC 5, 29, 35, 60; TCLC 2, 6, 13, 29, 47, 53, 112, 179; WLC 3**
See also AAYA 31; BPFB 2; CA 105; 126; CDWLB 2; DA; DA3; DAB; DAC; DAM MST, NOV; DLB 81; EW 9; EWL 3; EXPS; LATS 1:1; LMFS 2; MTCW 1, 2; MTFW 2005; NFS 7; RGSF 2; RGWL 2, 3; SFW 4; SSFS 3, 7, 12; TWA

Kahanovitsch, Pinkhes
See Der Nister

Kahn, Roger 1927- .... **CLC 30**
See also CA 25-28R; CANR 44, 69, 152; DLB 171; SATA 37

Kain, Saul
See Sassoon, Siegfried (Lorraine)

Kaiser, Georg 1878-1945 .... **TCLC 9**
See also CA 106; 190; CDWLB 2; DLB 124; EWL 3; LMFS 2; RGWL 2, 3

Kaledin, Sergei .... **CLC 59**

Kaletski, Alexander 1946- .... **CLC 39**
See also CA 118; 143

Kalidasa fl. c. 400-455 .... **CMLC 9; PC 22**
See also RGWL 2, 3

Kallman, Chester (Simon) 1921-1975
.... **CLC 2**
See also CA 45-48; 53-56; CANR 3; CP 1, 2

Kaminsky, Melvin .... **CLC 12, 217**
See Brooks, Mel
See also AAYA 13, 48; DLB 26

Kaminsky, Stuart M. 1934- .... **CLC 59**
See also CA 73-76; CANR 29, 53, 89; CMW 4

Kaminsky, Stuart Melvin
See Kaminsky, Stuart M.

Kamo no Chomei 1153(?)-1216 ... **CMLC 66**
See also DLB 203

Kamo no Nagaakira
See Kamo no Chomei

Kandinsky, Wassily 1866-1944 ..... **TCLC 92**
See also AAYA 64; CA 118; 155

1890-1914; CLR 39, 65; CWRI 5; DA; DA3; DAB; DAC; DAM MST, POET; DLB 19, 34, 141, 156, 330; EWL 3; EXPS; FANT; LAIT 3; LMFS 1; MAICYA 1, 2; MTCW 1, 2; MTFW 2005; NFS 21; PFS 22; RGEL 2; RGSF 2; SATA 100; SFW 4; SSFS 8, 21, 22; SUFW 1; TEA; WCH; WLIT 4; YABC 2

Kircher, Athanasius 1602-1680 .... **LC 121**
See also DLB 164

Kirk, Russell (Amos) 1918-1994 . **TCLC 119**
See also AITN 1; CA 1-4R; 145; CAAS 9; CANR 1, 20, 60; HGG; INT CANR-20; MTCW 1, 2

Kirkham, Dinah
See Card, Orson Scott

Kirkland, Caroline M. 1801-1864
.... **NCLC 85**
See also DLB 3, 73, 74, 250, 254; DLBD 13

Kirkup, James 1918- .... **CLC 1**
See also CA 1-4R; CAAS 4; CANR 2; CP 1, 2, 3, 4, 5, 6, 7; DLB 27; SATA 12

Kirkwood, James 1930(?)-1989 .... **CLC 9**
See also AITN 2; CA 1-4R; 128; CANR 6, 40; GLL 2

Kirsch, Sarah 1935- .... **CLC 176**
See also CA 178; CWW 2; DLB 75; EWL 3

Kirshner, Sidney
See Kingsley, Sidney

Kis, Danilo 1935-1989 .... **CLC 57**
See also CA 109; 118; 129; CANR 61; CD-WLB 4; DLB 181; EWL 3; MTCW 1; RGSF 2; RGWL 2, 3

Kissinger, Henry A(lfred) 1923- .... **CLC 137**
See also CA 1-4R; CANR 2, 33, 66, 109; MTCW 1

Kittel, Frederick August
See Wilson, August

Kivi, Aleksis 1834-1872 .... **NCLC 30**

Kizer, Carolyn 1925- .... **CLC 15, 39, 80; PC 66**
See also CA 65-68; CAAS 5; CANR 24, 70, 134; CP 1, 2, 3, 4, 5, 6, 7; CWP; DAM POET; DLB 5, 169; EWL 3; MAL 5; MTCW 2; MTFW 2005; PFS 18; TCLE 1:1

Klabund 1890-1928 .... **TCLC 44**
See also CA 162; DLB 66

Klappert, Peter 1942- .... **CLC 57**
See also CA 33-36R; CSW; DLB 5

Klein, A(braham) M(oses) 1909-1972
.... **CLC 19**
See also CA 101; 37-40R; CP 1; DAB; DAC; DAM MST; DLB 68; EWL 3; RGEL 2; RGHL

Klein, Joe
See Klein, Joseph

Klein, Joseph 1946- .... **CLC 154**
See also CA 85-88; CANR 55

Klein, Norma 1938-1989 .... **CLC 30**
See also AAYA 2, 35; BPFB 2; BYA 6, 7, 8; CA 41-44R; 128; CANR 15, 37; CLR 2, 19; INT CANR-15; JRDA; MAICYA 1, 2; SAAS 1; SATA 7, 57; WYA; YAW

Klein, T(heodore) E(ibon) D(onald) 1947-
.... **CLC 34**
See also CA 119; CANR 44, 75; HGG

Kleist, Heinrich von 1777-1811 ..... **NCLC 2, 37; SSC 37**
See also CDWLB 2; DAM DRAM; DLB 90; EW 5; RGSF 2; RGWL 2, 3

Klima, Ivan 1931- .... **CLC 56, 172**
See also CA 25-28R; CANR 17, 50, 91; CDWLB 4; CWW 2; DAM NOV; DLB 232; EWL 3; RGWL 3

Klimentev, Andrei Platonovich
See Klimentov, Andrei Platonovich

Klimentov, Andrei Platonovich 1899-1951
.... **SSC 42; TCLC 14**
See also Platonov, Andrei Platonovich; Platonov, Andrey Platonovich
See also CA 108; 232

Klinger, Friedrich Maximilian von
1752-1831 .... **NCLC 1**
See also DLB 94

Klingsor the Magician
See Hartmann, Sadakichi

Klopstock, Friedrich Gottlieb 1724-1803
.... **NCLC 11**
See also DLB 97; EW 4; RGWL 2, 3

Kluge, Alexander 1932- .... **SSC 61**
See also CA 81-84; DLB 75

Knapp, Caroline 1959-2002 .... **CLC 99**
See also CA 154; 207

Knebel, Fletcher 1911-1993 .... **CLC 14**
See also AITN 1; CA 1-4R; 140; CAAS 3; CANR 1, 36; CN 1, 2, 3, 4, 5; SATA 36; SATA-Obit 75

Knickerbocker, Diedrich
See Irving, Washington

Knight, Etheridge 1931-1991 .. **BLC 2; CLC 40; PC 14**
See also BW 1, 3; CA 21-24R; 133; CANR 23, 82; CP 1, 2, 3, 4, 5; DAM POET; DLB 41; MTCW 2; MTFW 2005; RGAL 4; TCLE 1:1

Knight, Sarah Kemble 1666-1727 .... **LC 7**
See also DLB 24, 200

Knister, Raymond 1899-1932 .... **TCLC 56**
See also CA 186; DLB 68; RGEL 2

Knowles, John 1926-2001 . **CLC 1, 4, 10, 26**
See also AAYA 10; AMWS 12; BPFB 2; BYA 3; CA 17-20R; 203; CANR 40, 74, 76, 132; CDALB 1968-1988; CLR 98; CN 1, 2, 3, 4, 5, 6, 7; DA; DAC; DAM MST, NOV; DLB 6; EXPN; MTCW 1, 2; MTFW 2005; NFS 2; RGAL 4; SATA 8, 89; SATA-Obit 134; YAW

Knox, Calvin M.
See Silverberg, Robert

Knox, John c. 1505-1572 .... **LC 37**
See also DLB 132

Knye, Cassandra
See Disch, Thomas M.

Koch, C(hristopher) J(ohn) 1932- .. **CLC 42**
See also CA 127; CANR 84; CN 3, 4, 5, 6, 7; DLB 289

Koch, Christopher
See Koch, C(hristopher) J(ohn)

Koch, Kenneth 1925-2002 .... **CLC 5, 8, 44**
See also AMWS 15; CA 1-4R; 207; CAD; CANR 6, 36, 57, 97, 131; CD 5, 6; CP 1, 2, 3, 4, 5, 6, 7; DAM POET; DLB 5; INT CANR-36; MAL 5; MTCW 2; MTFW 2005; PFS 20; SATA 65; WP

Kochanowski, Jan 1530-1584 .... **LC 10**
See also RGWL 2, 3

Kock, Charles Paul de 1794-1871
.... **NCLC 16**

Koda Rohan
See Koda Shigeyuki

Koda Rohan
See Koda Shigeyuki
See also DLB 180

Koda Shigeyuki 1867-1947 .... **TCLC 22**
See Koda Rohan
See also CA 121; 183

Koestler, Arthur 1905-1983 . **CLC 1, 3, 6, 8, 15, 33**
See also BRWS 1; CA 1-4R; 109; CANR 1, 33; CDBLB 1945-1960; CN 1, 2, 3; DLBY 1983; EWL 3; MTCW 1, 2; MTFW 2005; NFS 19; RGEL 2

Kogawa, Joy Nozomi 1935- ..... **CLC 78, 129**
See also AAYA 47; CA 101; CANR 19, 62, 126; CN 6, 7; CP 1; CWP; DAC; DAM MST, MULT; FW; MTCW 2; MTFW 2005; NFS 3; SATA 99

Kohout, Pavel 1928- .... **CLC 13**
See also CA 45-48; CANR 3

Koizumi, Yakumo
See Hearn, (Patricio) Lafcadio (Tessima Carlos)

Kolmar, Gertrud 1894-1943 .... **TCLC 40**
See also CA 167; EWL 3; RGHL

Komunyakaa, Yusef 1947- . **BLCS; CLC 86, 94, 207; PC 51**
See also AFAW 2; AMWS 13; CA 147; CANR 83; CP 6, 7; CSW; DLB 120; EWL 3; PFS 5, 20; RGAL 4

Konrad, George
See Konrad, Gyorgy

Konrad, Gyorgy 1933- .... **CLC 4, 10, 73**
See also CA 85-88; CANR 97; CDWLB 4; CWW 2; DLB 232; EWL 3

Konwicki, Tadeusz 1926- ...... **CLC 8, 28, 54, 117**
See also CA 101; CAAS 9; CANR 39, 59; CWW 2; DLB 232; EWL 3; IDFW 3; MTCW 1

Koontz, Dean R. 1945- .... **CLC 78, 206**
See also AAYA 9, 31; BEST 89:3, 90:2; CA 108; CANR 19, 36, 52, 95, 138; CMW 4; CPW; DA3; DAM NOV, POP; DLB 292; HGG; MTCW 1; MTFW 2005; SATA 92, 165; SFW 4; SUFW 2; YAW

Koontz, Dean Ray
See Koontz, Dean R.

Kopernik, Mikolaj
See Copernicus, Nicolaus

Kopit, Arthur (Lee) 1937- ..... **CLC 1, 18, 33**
See also AITN 1; CA 81-84; CABS 3; CAD; CD 5, 6; DAM DRAM; DFS 7, 14; DLB 7; MAL 5; MTCW 1; RGAL 4

Kopitar, Jernej (Bartholomaus) 1780-1844
.... **NCLC 117**

Kops, Bernard 1926- .... **CLC 4**
See also CA 5-8R; CANR 84; CBD; CN 1, 2, 3, 4, 5, 6, 7; CP 1, 2, 3, 4, 5, 6, 7; DLB 13; RGHL

Kornbluth, C(yril) M. 1923-1958 ... **TCLC 8**
See also CA 105; 160; DLB 8; SCFW 1, 2; SFW 4

Korolenko, V.G.
See Korolenko, Vladimir G.

Korolenko, Vladimir
See Korolenko, Vladimir G.

Korolenko, Vladimir G. 1853-1921
.... **TCLC 22**
See also CA 121; DLB 277

Korolenko, Vladimir Galaktionovich
See Korolenko, Vladimir G.

Korzybski, Alfred (Habdank Skarbek)
1879-1950 .... **TCLC 61**
See also CA 123; 160

Kosinski, Jerzy 1933-1991 ... **CLC 1, 2, 3, 6, 10, 15, 53, 70**
See also AMWS 7; BPFB 2; CA 17-20R; 134; CANR 9, 46; CN 1, 2, 3, 4; DA3; DAM NOV; DLB 2, 299; DLBY 1982; EWL 3; HGG; MAL 5; MTCW 1, 2; MTFW 2005; NFS 12; RGAL 4; RGHL; TUS

Kostelanetz, Richard (Cory) 1940- . **CLC 28**
See also CA 13-16R; CAAS 8; CANR 38, 77; CN 4, 5, 6; CP 2, 3, 4, 5, 6, 7

Kostrowitzki, Wilhelm Apollinaris de
1880-1918
See Apollinaire, Guillaume
See also CA 104

Kotlowitz, Robert 1924- .... **CLC 4**
See also CA 33-36R; CANR 36

Kotzebue, August (Friedrich Ferdinand) von 1761-1819 .... NCLC 25
See also DLB 94

Kotzwinkle, William 1938- .... CLC 5, 14, 35
See also BPFB 2; CA 45-48; CANR 3, 44, 84, 129; CLR 6; CN 7; DLB 173; FANT; MAICYA 1, 2; SATA 24, 70, 146; SFW 4; SUFW 2; YAW

Kowna, Stancy
See Szymborska, Wislawa

Kozol, Jonathan 1936- .... CLC 17
See also AAYA 46; CA 61-64; CANR 16, 45, 96; MTFW 2005

Kozoll, Michael 1940(?)- .... CLC 35

Kramer, Kathryn 19(?)- .... CLC 34

Kramer, Larry 1935- .... CLC 42; DC 8
See also CA 124; 126; CANR 60, 132; DAM POP; DLB 249; GLL 1

Krasicki, Ignacy 1735-1801 .... NCLC 8

Krasinski, Zygmunt 1812-1859 ...... NCLC 4
See also RGWL 2, 3

Kraus, Karl 1874-1936 .... TCLC 5
See also CA 104; 216; DLB 118; EWL 3

Kreve (Mickevicius), Vincas 1882-1954
.... TCLC 27
See also CA 170; DLB 220; EWL 3

Kristeva, Julia 1941- .... CLC 77, 140
See also CA 154; CANR 99; DLB 242; EWL 3; FW; LMFS 2

Kristofferson, Kris 1936- .... CLC 26
See also CA 104

Krizanc, John 1956- .... CLC 57
See also CA 187

Krleza, Miroslav 1893-1981 ...... CLC 8, 114
See also CA 97-100; 105; CANR 50; CD-WLB 4; DLB 147; EW 11; RGWL 2, 3

Kroetsch, Robert (Paul) 1927- ... CLC 5, 23, 57, 132
See also CA 17-20R; CANR 8, 38; CCA 1; CN 2, 3, 4, 5, 6, 7; CP 6, 7; DAC; DAM POET; DLB 53; MTCW 1

Kroetz, Franz
See Kroetz, Franz Xaver

Kroetz, Franz Xaver 1946- .... CLC 41
See also CA 130; CANR 142; CWW 2; EWL 3

Kroker, Arthur (W.) 1945- .... CLC 77
See also CA 161

Kroniuk, Lisa
See Berton, Pierre (Francis de Marigny)

Kropotkin, Peter (Aleksieevich) 1842-1921
.... TCLC 36
See Kropotkin, Petr Alekseevich
See also CA 119; 219

Kropotkin, Petr Alekseevich
See Kropotkin, Peter (Aleksieevich)
See also DLB 277

Krotkov, Yuri 1917-1981 .... CLC 19
See also CA 102

Krumb
See Crumb, R.

Krumgold, Joseph (Quincy) 1908-1980
.... CLC 12
See also BYA 1, 2; CA 9-12R; 101; CANR 7; MAICYA 1, 2; SATA 1, 48; SATA-Obit 23; YAW

Krumwitz
See Crumb, R.

Krutch, Joseph Wood 1893-1970 .... CLC 24
See also ANW; CA 1-4R; 25-28R; CANR 4; DLB 63, 206, 275

Krutzch, Gus
See Eliot, T(homas) S(tearns)

Krylov, Ivan Andreevich 1768(?)-1844
.... NCLC 1
See also DLB 150

Kubin, Alfred (Leopold Isidor) 1877-1959
.... TCLC 23
See also CA 112; 149; CANR 104; DLB 81

Kubrick, Stanley 1928-1999 .... CLC 16; TCLC 112
See also AAYA 30; CA 81-84; 177; CANR 33; DLB 26

Kumin, Maxine 1925- .. CLC 5, 13, 28, 164; PC 15
See also AITN 2; AMWS 4; ANW; CA 1-4R; CAAS 8; CANR 1, 21, 69, 115, 140; CP 2, 3, 4, 5, 6, 7; CWP; DA3; DAM POET; DLB 5; EWL 3; EXPP; MTCW 1, 2; MTFW 2005; PAB; PFS 18; SATA 12

Kundera, Milan 1929- ...... CLC 4, 9, 19, 32, 68, 115, 135; SSC 24
See also AAYA 2, 62; BPFB 2; CA 85-88; CANR 19, 52, 74, 144; CDWLB 4; CWW 2; DA3; DAM NOV; DLB 232; EW 13; EWL 3; MTCW 1, 2; MTFW 2005; NFS 18; RGSF 2; RGWL 3; SSFS 10

Kunene, Mazisi 1930-2006 .... CLC 85
See also BW 1, 3; CA 125; CANR 81; CP 1, 6, 7; DLB 117

Kunene, Mazisi Raymond
See Kunene, Mazisi

Kung, Hans .... CLC 130
See Kung, Hans

Kung, Hans 1928-
See Kung, Hans
See also CA 53-56; CANR 66, 134; MTCW 1, 2; MTFW 2005

Kunikida Doppo 1869(?)-1908
See Doppo, Kunikida
See also DLB 180; EWL 3

Kunitz, Stanley 1905-2006 .... CLC 6, 11, 14, 148; PC 19
See also AMWS 3; CA 41-44R; 250; CANR 26, 57, 98; CP 1, 2, 3, 4, 5, 6, 7; DA3; DLB 48; INT CANR-26; MAL 5; MTCW 1, 2; MTFW 2005; PFS 11; RGAL 4

Kunitz, Stanley Jasspon
See Kunitz, Stanley

Kunze, Reiner 1933- .... CLC 10
See also CA 93-96; CWW 2; DLB 75; EWL 3

Kuprin, Aleksander Ivanovich 1870-1938
.... TCLC 5
See Kuprin, Aleksandr Ivanovich; Kuprin, Alexandr Ivanovich
See also CA 104; 182

Kuprin, Aleksandr Ivanovich
See Kuprin, Aleksander Ivanovich
See also DLB 295

Kuprin, Alexandr Ivanovich
See Kuprin, Aleksander Ivanovich
See also EWL 3

Kureishi, Hanif 1954- . CLC 64, 135; DC 26
See also BRWS 11; CA 139; CANR 113; CBD; CD 5, 6; CN 6, 7; DLB 194, 245; GLL 2; IDFW 4; WLIT 4; WWE 1

Kurosawa, Akira 1910-1998 .... CLC 16, 119
See also AAYA 11, 64; CA 101; 170; CANR 46; DAM MULT

Kushner, Tony 1956- .. CLC 81, 203; DC 10
See also AAYA 61; AMWS 9; CA 144; CAD; CANR 74, 130; CD 5, 6; DA3; DAM DRAM; DFS 5; DLB 228; EWL 3; GLL 1; LAIT 5; MAL 5; MTCW 2; MTFW 2005; RGAL 4; RGHL; SATA 160

Kuttner, Henry 1915-1958 .... TCLC 10
See also CA 107; 157; DLB 8; FANT; SCFW 1, 2; SFW 4

Kutty, Madhavi
See Das, Kamala

Kuzma, Greg 1944- .... CLC 7
See also CA 33-36R; CANR 70

Kuzmin, Mikhail (Alekseevich) 1872(?)-1936
.... TCLC 40
See also CA 170; DLB 295; EWL 3

Kyd, Thomas 1558-1594 . DC 3; LC 22, 125
See also BRW 1; DAM DRAM; DFS 21; DLB 62; IDTP; LMFS 1; RGEL 2; TEA; WLIT 3

Kyprianos, Iossif
See Samarakis, Antonis

L. S.
See Stephen, Sir Leslie

Laȝamon
See Layamon
See also DLB 146

Labe, Louise 1521-1566 .... LC 120
See also DLB 327

La Bruyere, Jean de 1645-1696 .... LC 17
See also DLB 268; EW 3; GFL Beginnings to 1789

LaBute, Neil 1963- .... CLC 225
See also CA 240

Lacan, Jacques (Marie Emile) 1901-1981
.... CLC 75
See also CA 121; 104; DLB 296; EWL 3; TWA

Laclos, Pierre-Ambroise Francois 1741-1803
.... NCLC 4, 87
See also DLB 313; EW 4; GFL Beginnings to 1789; RGWL 2, 3

La Colere, Francois
See Aragon, Louis

Lacolere, Francois
See Aragon, Louis

La Deshabilleuse
See Simenon, Georges (Jacques Christian)

Lady Gregory
See Gregory, Lady Isabella Augusta (Persse)

Lady of Quality, A
See Bagnold, Enid

La Fayette, Marie-(Madelaine Pioche de la Vergne) 1634-1693 .... LC 2
See Lafayette, Marie-Madeleine
See also GFL Beginnings to 1789; RGWL 2, 3

Lafayette, Marie-Madeleine
See La Fayette, Marie-(Madelaine Pioche de la Vergne)
See also DLB 268

Lafayette, Rene
See Hubbard, L. Ron

La Flesche, Francis 1857(?)-1932 ..... NNAL
See also CA 144; CANR 83; DLB 175

La Fontaine, Jean de 1621-1695 .... LC 50
See also DLB 268; EW 3; GFL Beginnings to 1789; MAICYA 1, 2; RGWL 2, 3; SATA 18

LaForet, Carmen 1921-2004 .... CLC 219
See also CA 246; CWW 2; DLB 322; EWL 3

LaForet Diaz, Carmen
See LaForet, Carmen

Laforgue, Jules 1860-1887 ...... NCLC 5, 53; PC 14; SSC 20
See also DLB 217; EW 7; GFL 1789 to the Present; RGWL 2, 3

Lagerkvist, Paer (Fabian) 1891-1974
.... CLC 7, 10, 13, 54; TCLC 144
See Lagerkvist, Par
See also CA 85-88; 49-52; DA3; DAM DRAM, NOV; MTCW 1, 2; MTFW 2005; TWA

Lagerkvist, Par .... SSC 12
See Lagerkvist, Paer (Fabian)
See also DLB 259; EW 10; EWL 3; RGSF 2; RGWL 2, 3

Lagerloef, Selma (Ottiliana Lovisa)
.... **TCLC 4, 36**
See Lagerlof, Selma (Ottiliana Lovisa)
See also CA 108; MTCW 2

Lagerlof, Selma (Ottiliana Lovisa)
1858-1940
See Lagerloef, Selma (Ottiliana Lovisa)
See also CA 188; CLR 7; DLB 259; RGWL
2, 3; SATA 15; SSFS 18

La Guma, Alex 1925-1985 . **BLCS; CLC 19; TCLC 140**
See also AFW; BW 1, 3; CA 49-52; 118;
CANR 25, 81; CDWLB 3; CN 1, 2, 3;
CP 1; DAM NOV; DLB 117, 225; EWL
3; MTCW 1, 2; MTFW 2005; WLIT 2;
WWE 1

Lahiri, Jhumpa 1967- .... **SSC 96**
See also DLB 323

Laidlaw, A. K.
See Grieve, C(hristopher) M(urray)

Lainez, Manuel Mujica
See Mujica Lainez, Manuel
See also HW 1

Laing, R(onald) D(avid) 1927-1989
.... **CLC 95**
See also CA 107; 129; CANR 34; MTCW 1

Laishley, Alex
See Booth, Martin

Lamartine, Alphonse (Marie Louis Prat) de
1790-1869 .... **NCLC 11; PC 16**
See also DAM POET; DLB 217; GFL 1789
to the Present; RGWL 2, 3

Lamb, Charles 1775-1834 .... **NCLC 10, 113; WLC 3**
See also BRW 4; CDBLB 1789-1832; DA;
DAB; DAC; DAM MST; DLB 93, 107,
163; RGEL 2; SATA 17; TEA

Lamb, Lady Caroline 1785-1828 . **NCLC 38**
See also DLB 116

Lamb, Mary Ann 1764-1847 ...... **NCLC 125**
See also DLB 163; SATA 17

Lame Deer 1903(?)-1976 .... **NNAL**
See also CA 69-72

Lamming, George (William) 1927- . **BLC 2; CLC 2, 4, 66, 144**
See also BW 2, 3; CA 85-88; CANR 26,
76; CDWLB 3; CN 1, 2, 3, 4, 5, 6, 7; CP
1; DAM MULT; DLB 125; EWL 3;
MTCW 1, 2; MTFW 2005; NFS 15;
RGEL 2

L'Amour, Louis 1908-1988 .... **CLC 25, 55**
See also AAYA 16; AITN 2; BEST 89:2;
BPFB 2; CA 1-4R; 125; CANR 3, 25, 40;
CPW; DA3; DAM NOV, POP; DLB 206;
DLBY 1980; MTCW 1, 2; MTFW 2005;
RGAL 4; TCWW 1, 2

Lampedusa, Giuseppe (Tomasi) di
.... **TCLC 13**
See Tomasi di Lampedusa, Giuseppe
See also CA 164; EW 11; MTCW 2; MTFW
2005; RGWL 2, 3

Lampman, Archibald 1861-1899 .. **NCLC 25**
See also DLB 92; RGEL 2; TWA

Lancaster, Bruce 1896-1963 .... **CLC 36**
See also CA 9-10; CANR 70; CAP 1; SATA
9

Lanchester, John 1962- .... **CLC 99**
See also CA 194; DLB 267

Landau, Mark Alexandrovich
See Aldanov, Mark (Alexandrovich)

Landau-Aldanov, Mark Alexandrovich
See Aldanov, Mark (Alexandrovich)

Landis, Jerry
See Simon, Paul

Landis, John 1950- .... **CLC 26**
See also CA 112; 122; CANR 128

Landolfi, Tommaso 1908-1979 .. **CLC 11, 49**
See also CA 127; 117; DLB 177; EWL 3

Landon, Letitia Elizabeth 1802-1838
.... **NCLC 15**
See also DLB 96

Landor, Walter Savage 1775-1864
.... **NCLC 14**
See also BRW 4; DLB 93, 107; RGEL 2

Landwirth, Heinz 1927-
See Lind, Jakov
See also CA 9-12R; CANR 7

Lane, Patrick 1939- .... **CLC 25**
See also CA 97-100; CANR 54; CP 3, 4, 5,
6, 7; DAM POET; DLB 53; INT CA-97-
100

Lane, Rose Wilder 1887-1968 ..... **TCLC 177**
See also CA 102; CANR 63; SATA 29;
SATA-Brief 28; TCWW 2

Lang, Andrew 1844-1912 .... **TCLC 16**
See also CA 114; 137; CANR 85; CLR 101;
DLB 98, 141, 184; FANT; MAICYA 1, 2;
RGEL 2; SATA 16; WCH

Lang, Fritz 1890-1976 .... **CLC 20, 103**
See also AAYA 65; CA 77-80; 69-72;
CANR 30

Lange, John
See Crichton, Michael

Langer, Elinor 1939- .... **CLC 34**
See also CA 121

Langland, William 1332(?)-1400(?) .. **LC 19, 120**
See also BRW 1; DA; DAB; DAC; DAM
MST, POET; DLB 146; RGEL 2; TEA;
WLIT 3

Langstaff, Launcelot
See Irving, Washington

Lanier, Sidney 1842-1881 ...... **NCLC 6, 118; PC 50**
See also AMWS 1; DAM POET; DLB 64;
DLBD 13; EXPP; MAICYA 1; PFS 14;
RGAL 4; SATA 18

Lanyer, Aemilia 1569-1645 ... **LC 10, 30, 83; PC 60**
See also DLB 121

Lao Tzu c. 6th cent. B.C.-3rd cent. B.C.
.... **CMLC 7**

Lao-Tzu
See Lao Tzu

Lapine, James (Elliot) 1949- .... **CLC 39**
See also CA 123; 130; CANR 54, 128; INT
CA-130

Larbaud, Valery (Nicolas) 1881-1957
.... **TCLC 9**
See also CA 106; 152; EWL 3; GFL 1789
to the Present

Lardner, Ring
See Lardner, Ring(gold) W(ilmer)
See also BPFB 2; CDALB 1917-1929; DLB
11, 25, 86, 171; DLBD 16; MAL 5;
RGAL 4; RGSF 2

Lardner, Ring W., Jr.
See Lardner, Ring(gold) W(ilmer)

Lardner, Ring(gold) W(ilmer) 1885-1933
.... **SSC 32; TCLC 2, 14**
See Lardner, Ring
See also AMW; CA 104; 131; MTCW 1, 2;
MTFW 2005; TUS

Laredo, Betty
See Codrescu, Andrei

Larkin, Maia
See Wojciechowska, Maia (Teresa)

Larkin, Philip (Arthur) 1922-1985 .. **CLC 3, 5, 8, 9, 13, 18, 33, 39, 64; PC 21**
See also BRWS 1; CA 5-8R; 117; CANR
24, 62; CDBLB 1960 to Present; CP 1, 2,
3, 4; DA3; DAB; DAM MST, POET;
DLB 27; EWL 3; MTCW 1, 2; MTFW
2005; PFS 3, 4, 12; RGEL 2

La Roche, Sophie von 1730-1807
.... **NCLC 121**
See also DLB 94

La Rochefoucauld, Francois 1613-1680
.... **LC 108**

**Larra (y Sanchez de Castro), Mariano Jose
de** 1809-1837 .... **NCLC 17, 130**

Larsen, Eric 1941- .... **CLC 55**
See also CA 132

Larsen, Nella 1893(?)-1963 ..... **BLC 2; CLC 37; HR 1:3**
See also AFAW 1, 2; BW 1; CA 125; CANR
83; DAM MULT; DLB 51; FW; LATS
1:1; LMFS 2

Larson, Charles R(aymond) 1938- . **CLC 31**
See also CA 53-56; CANR 4, 121

Larson, Jonathan 1960-1996 .... **CLC 99**
See also AAYA 28; CA 156; DFS 23;
MTFW 2005

La Sale, Antoine de c. 1386-1460(?)
.... **LC 104**
See also DLB 208

Las Casas, Bartolome de 1474-1566
.... **HLCS; LC 31**
See Casas, Bartolome de las
See also DLB 318; LAW

Lasch, Christopher 1932-1994 ...... **CLC 102**
See also CA 73-76; 144; CANR 25, 118;
DLB 246; MTCW 1, 2; MTFW 2005

Lasker-Schueler, Else 1869-1945 .. **TCLC 57**
See Lasker-Schuler, Else
See also CA 183; DLB 66, 124

Lasker-Schuler, Else
See Lasker-Schueler, Else
See also EWL 3

Laski, Harold J(oseph) 1893-1950
.... **TCLC 79**
See also CA 188

Latham, Jean Lee 1902-1995 .... **CLC 12**
See also AITN 1; BYA 1; CA 5-8R; CANR
7, 84; CLR 50; MAICYA 1, 2; SATA 2,
68; YAW

Latham, Mavis
See Clark, Mavis Thorpe

Lathen, Emma .... **CLC 2**
See Hennissart, Martha; Latsis, Mary J(ane)
See also BPFB 2; CMW 4; DLB 306

Lathrop, Francis
See Leiber, Fritz (Reuter, Jr.)

Latsis, Mary J(ane) 1927-1997
See Lathen, Emma
See also CA 85-88; 162; CMW 4

Lattany, Kristin
See Lattany, Kristin (Elaine Eggleston)
Hunter

Lattany, Kristin (Elaine Eggleston) Hunter
1931- .... **CLC 35**
See Hunter, Kristin
See also AITN 1; BW 1; BYA 3; CA 13-
16R; CANR 13, 108; CLR 3; CN 7; DLB
33; INT CANR-13; MAICYA 1, 2; SAAS
10; SATA 12, 132; YAW

Lattimore, Richmond (Alexander) 1906-1984
.... **CLC 3**
See also CA 1-4R; 112; CANR 1; CP 1, 2,
3; MAL 5

Laughlin, James 1914-1997 .... **CLC 49**
See also CA 21-24R; 162; CAAS 22; CANR
9, 47; CP 1, 2, 3, 4, 5, 6; DLB 48; DLBY
1996, 1997

Laurence, Margaret 1926-1987 .... **CLC 3, 6, 13, 50, 62; SSC 7**
See also BYA 13; CA 5-8R; 121; CANR
33; CN 1, 2, 3, 4; DAC; DAM MST; DLB
53; EWL 3; FW; MTCW 1, 2; MTFW
2005; NFS 11; RGEL 2; RGSF 2; SATA-
Obit 50; TCWW 2

Laurent, Antoine 1952- .... **CLC 50**

Lauscher, Hermann
See Hesse, Hermann

Lautreamont 1846-1870 . **NCLC 12; SSC 14**
See Lautreamont, Isidore Lucien Ducasse
See also GFL 1789 to the Present; RGWL 2, 3

Lautreamont, Isidore Lucien Ducasse
See Lautreamont
See also DLB 217

Lavater, Johann Kaspar 1741-1801
.... **NCLC 142**
See also DLB 97

Laverty, Donald
See Blish, James (Benjamin)

Lavin, Mary 1912-1996 .... **CLC 4, 18, 99; SSC 4, 67**
See also CA 9-12R; 151; CANR 33; CN 1, 2, 3, 4, 5, 6; DLB 15, 319; FW; MTCW 1; RGEL 2; RGSF 2; SSFS 23

Lavond, Paul Dennis
See Kornbluth, C(yril) M.; Pohl, Frederik

Lawes, Henry 1596-1662 .... **LC 113**
See also DLB 126

Lawler, Ray
See Lawler, Raymond Evenor
See also DLB 289

Lawler, Raymond Evenor 1922- ..... **CLC 58**
See Lawler, Ray
See also CA 103; CD 5, 6; RGEL 2

Lawrence, D(avid) H(erbert Richards)
1885-1930 .... **PC 54; SSC 4, 19, 73; TCLC 2, 9, 16, 33, 48, 61, 93; WLC 3**
See Chambers, Jessie
See also BPFB 2; BRW 7; BRWR 2; CA 104; 121; CANR 131; CDBLB 1914-1945; DA; DA3; DAB; DAC; DAM MST, NOV, POET; DLB 10, 19, 36, 98, 162, 195; EWL 3; EXPP; EXPS; LAIT 2, 3; MTCW 1, 2; MTFW 2005; NFS 18; PFS 6; RGEL 2; RGSF 2; SSFS 2, 6; TEA; WLIT 4; WP

Lawrence, T(homas) E(dward) 1888-1935
.... **TCLC 18**
See Dale, Colin
See also BRWS 2; CA 115; 167; DLB 195

Lawrence of Arabia
See Lawrence, T(homas) E(dward)

Lawson, Henry (Archibald Hertzberg)
1867-1922 .... **SSC 18; TCLC 27**
See also CA 120; 181; DLB 230; RGEL 2; RGSF 2

Lawton, Dennis
See Faust, Frederick (Schiller)

Layamon fl. c. 1200- .... **CMLC 10**
See Laȝamon
See also DLB 146; RGEL 2

Laye, Camara 1928-1980 .... **BLC 2; CLC 4, 38**
See Camara Laye
See also AFW; BW 1; CA 85-88; 97-100; CANR 25; DAM MULT; MTCW 1, 2; WLIT 2

Layton, Irving 1912-2006 .... **CLC 2, 15, 164**
See also CA 1-4R; 247; CANR 2, 33, 43, 66, 129; CP 1, 2, 3, 4, 5, 6, 7; DAC; DAM MST, POET; DLB 88; EWL 3; MTCW 1, 2; PFS 12; RGEL 2

Layton, Irving Peter
See Layton, Irving

Lazarus, Emma 1849-1887 ..... **NCLC 8, 109**

Lazarus, Felix
See Cable, George Washington

Lazarus, Henry
See Slavitt, David R(ytman)

Lea, Joan
See Neufeld, John (Arthur)

Leacock, Stephen (Butler) 1869-1944
.... **SSC 39; TCLC 2**
See also CA 104; 141; CANR 80; DAC; DAM MST; DLB 92; EWL 3; MTCW 2; MTFW 2005; RGEL 2; RGSF 2

Lead, Jane Ward 1623-1704 .... **LC 72**
See also DLB 131

Leapor, Mary 1722-1746 .... **LC 80**
See also DLB 109

Lear, Edward 1812-1888 .... **NCLC 3; PC 65**
See also AAYA 48; BRW 5; CLR 1, 75; DLB 32, 163, 166; MAICYA 1, 2; RGEL 2; SATA 18, 100; WCH; WP

Lear, Norman (Milton) 1922- .... **CLC 12**
See also CA 73-76

Leautaud, Paul 1872-1956 .... **TCLC 83**
See also CA 203; DLB 65; GFL 1789 to the Present

Leavis, F(rank) R(aymond) 1895-1978
.... **CLC 24**
See also BRW 7; CA 21-24R; 77-80; CANR 44; DLB 242; EWL 3; MTCW 1, 2; RGEL 2

Leavitt, David 1961- .... **CLC 34**
See also CA 116; 122; CANR 50, 62, 101, 134; CPW; DA3; DAM POP; DLB 130; GLL 1; INT CA-122; MAL 5; MTCW 2; MTFW 2005

Leblanc, Maurice (Marie Emile) 1864-1941
.... **TCLC 49**
See also CA 110; CMW 4

Lebowitz, Fran(ces Ann) 1951(?)- .. **CLC 11, 36**
See also CA 81-84; CANR 14, 60, 70; INT CANR-14; MTCW 1

Lebrecht, Peter
See Tieck, (Johann) Ludwig

le Carre, John 1931- .... **CLC 9, 15**
See also AAYA 42; BEST 89:4; BPFB 2; BRWS 2; CA 5-8R; CANR 13, 33, 59, 107, 132; CDBLB 1960 to Present; CMW 4; CN 1, 2, 3, 4, 5, 6, 7; CPW; DA3; DAM POP; DLB 87; EWL 3; MSW; MTCW 1, 2; MTFW 2005; RGEL 2; TEA

Le Clezio, J. M.G. 1940- .... **CLC 31, 155**
See also CA 116; 128; CANR 147; CWW 2; DLB 83; EWL 3; GFL 1789 to the Present; RGSF 2

Le Clezio, Jean Marie Gustave
See Le Clezio, J. M.G.

Leconte de Lisle, Charles-Marie-Rene
1818-1894 .... **NCLC 29**
See also DLB 217; EW 6; GFL 1789 to the Present

Le Coq, Monsieur
See Simenon, Georges (Jacques Christian)

Leduc, Violette 1907-1972 .... **CLC 22**
See also CA 13-14; 33-36R; CANR 69; CAP 1; EWL 3; GFL 1789 to the Present; GLL 1

Ledwidge, Francis 1887(?)-1917 ... **TCLC 23**
See also CA 123; 203; DLB 20

Lee, Andrea 1953- .... **BLC 2; CLC 36**
See also BW 1, 3; CA 125; CANR 82; DAM MULT

Lee, Andrew
See Auchincloss, Louis

Lee, Chang-rae 1965- .... **CLC 91**
See also CA 148; CANR 89; CN 7; DLB 312; LATS 1:2

Lee, Don L. .... **CLC 2**
See Madhubuti, Haki R.
See also CP 2, 3, 4, 5

Lee, George W(ashington) 1894-1976
.... **BLC 2; CLC 52**
See also BW 1; CA 125; CANR 83; DAM MULT; DLB 51

Lee, Harper 1926- .. **CLC 12, 60, 194; WLC 4**
See also AAYA 13; AMWS 8; BPFB 2; BYA 3; CA 13-16R; CANR 51, 128; CDALB 1941-1968; CSW; DA; DA3;

DAB; DAC; DAM MST, NOV; DLB 6; EXPN; LAIT 3; MAL 5; MTCW 1, 2; MTFW 2005; NFS 2; SATA 11; WYA; YAW

Lee, Helen Elaine 1959(?)- .... **CLC 86**
See also CA 148

Lee, John .... **CLC 70**

Lee, Julian
See Latham, Jean Lee

Lee, Larry
See Lee, Lawrence

Lee, Laurie 1914-1997 .... **CLC 90**
See also CA 77-80; 158; CANR 33, 73; CP 1, 2, 3, 4, 5, 6; CPW; DAB; DAM POP; DLB 27; MTCW 1; RGEL 2

Lee, Lawrence 1941-1990 .... **CLC 34**
See also CA 131; CANR 43

Lee, Li-Young 1957- .... **CLC 164; PC 24**
See also AMWS 15; CA 153; CANR 118; CP 6, 7; DLB 165, 312; LMFS 2; PFS 11, 15, 17

Lee, Manfred B. 1905-1971 .... **CLC 11**
See Queen, Ellery
See also CA 1-4R; 29-32R; CANR 2, 150; CMW 4; DLB 137

Lee, Manfred Bennington
See Lee, Manfred B.

Lee, Nathaniel 1645(?)-1692 .... **LC 103**
See also DLB 80; RGEL 2

Lee, Shelton Jackson
See Lee, Spike
See also AAYA 4, 29

Lee, Spike 1957(?)- .... **BLCS; CLC 105**
See Lee, Shelton Jackson
See also BW 2, 3; CA 125; CANR 42; DAM MULT

Lee, Stan 1922- .... **CLC 17**
See also AAYA 5, 49; CA 108; 111; CANR 129; INT CA-111; MTFW 2005

Lee, Tanith 1947- .... **CLC 46**
See also AAYA 15; CA 37-40R; CANR 53, 102, 145; DLB 261; FANT; SATA 8, 88, 134; SFW 4; SUFW 1, 2; YAW

Lee, Vernon .... **SSC 33; TCLC 5**
See Paget, Violet
See also DLB 57, 153, 156, 174, 178; GLL 1; SUFW 1

Lee, William
See Burroughs, William S.
See also GLL 1

Lee, Willy
See Burroughs, William S.
See also GLL 1

Lee-Hamilton, Eugene (Jacob) 1845-1907
.... **TCLC 22**
See also CA 117; 234

Leet, Judith 1935- .... **CLC 11**
See also CA 187

Le Fanu, Joseph Sheridan 1814-1873
.... **NCLC 9, 58; SSC 14, 84**
See also CMW 4; DA3; DAM POP; DLB 21, 70, 159, 178; GL 3; HGG; RGEL 2; RGSF 2; SUFW 1

Leffland, Ella 1931- .... **CLC 19**
See also CA 29-32R; CANR 35, 78, 82; DLBY 1984; INT CANR-35; SATA 65; SSFS 24

Leger, Alexis
See Leger, (Marie-Rene Auguste) Alexis Saint-Leger

Leger, (Marie-Rene Auguste) Alexis Saint-Leger 1887-1975 . **CLC 4, 11, 46; PC 23**
See Perse, Saint-John; Saint-John Perse
See also CA 13-16R; 61-64; CANR 43; DAM POET; MTCW 1

Leger, Saintleger
See Leger, (Marie-Rene Auguste) Alexis Saint-Leger

Le Guin, Ursula K. 1929- .... **CLC 8, 13, 22, 45, 71, 136; SSC 12, 69**
See also AAYA 9, 27; AITN 1; BPFB 2; BYA 5, 8, 11, 14; CA 21-24R; CANR 9, 32, 52, 74, 132; CDALB 1968-1988; CLR 3, 28, 91; CN 2, 3, 4, 5, 6, 7; CPW; DA3; DAB; DAC; DAM MST, POP; DLB 8, 52, 256, 275; EXPS; FANT; FW; INT CANR-32; JRDA; LAIT 5; MAICYA 1, 2; MAL 5; MTCW 1, 2; MTFW 2005; NFS 6, 9; SATA 4, 52, 99, 149; SCFW 1, 2; SFW 4; SSFS 1, 2; SUFW 1, 2; WYA; YAW

Lehmann, Rosamond (Nina) 1901-1990
.... **CLC 5**
See also CA 77-80; 131; CANR 8, 73; CN 1, 2, 3, 4; DLB 15; MTCW 2; RGEL 2; RHW

Leiber, Fritz (Reuter, Jr.) 1910-1992
.... **CLC 25**
See also AAYA 65; BPFB 2; CA 45-48; 139; CANR 2, 40, 86; CN 2, 3, 4, 5; DLB 8; FANT; HGG; MTCW 1, 2; MTFW 2005; SATA 45; SATA-Obit 73; SCFW 1, 2; SFW 4; SUFW 1, 2

Leibniz, Gottfried Wilhelm von 1646-1716
.... **LC 35**
See also DLB 168

Leimbach, Martha 1963-
See Leimbach, Marti
See also CA 130

Leimbach, Marti .... **CLC 65**
See Leimbach, Martha

Leino, Eino .... **TCLC 24**
See Lonnbohm, Armas Eino Leopold
See also EWL 3

Leiris, Michel (Julien) 1901-1990 ... **CLC 61**
See also CA 119; 128; 132; EWL 3; GFL 1789 to the Present

Leithauser, Brad 1953- .... **CLC 27**
See also CA 107; CANR 27, 81; CP 5, 6, 7; DLB 120, 282

le Jars de Gournay, Marie
See de Gournay, Marie le Jars

Lelchuk, Alan 1938- .... **CLC 5**
See also CA 45-48; CAAS 20; CANR 1, 70, 152; CN 3, 4, 5, 6, 7

Lem, Stanislaw 1921-2006 .... **CLC 8, 15, 40, 149**
See also CA 105; 249; CAAS 1; CANR 32; CWW 2; MTCW 1; SCFW 1, 2; SFW 4

Lemann, Nancy (Elise) 1956- .... **CLC 39**
See also CA 118; 136; CANR 121

Lemonnier, (Antoine Louis) Camille
1844-1913 .... **TCLC 22**
See also CA 121

Lenau, Nikolaus 1802-1850 .... **NCLC 16**

L'Engle, Madeleine 1918- .... **CLC 12**
See also AAYA 28; AITN 2; BPFB 2; BYA 2, 4, 5, 7; CA 1-4R; CANR 3, 21, 39, 66, 107; CLR 1, 14, 57; CPW; CWRI 5; DA3; DAM POP; DLB 52; JRDA; MAICYA 1, 2; MTCW 1, 2; MTFW 2005; SAAS 15; SATA 1, 27, 75, 128; SFW 4; WYA; YAW

Lengyel, Jozsef 1896-1975 .... **CLC 7**
See also CA 85-88; 57-60; CANR 71; RGSF 2

Lenin 1870-1924
See Lenin, V. I.
See also CA 121; 168

Lenin, V. I. .... **TCLC 67**
See Lenin

Lennon, John (Ono) 1940-1980 ...... **CLC 12, 35**
See also CA 102; SATA 114

Lennox, Charlotte Ramsay 1729(?)-1804
.... **NCLC 23, 134**
See also DLB 39; RGEL 2

Lentricchia, Frank, Jr.
See Lentricchia, Frank

Lentricchia, Frank 1940- .... **CLC 34**
See also CA 25-28R; CANR 19, 106, 148; DLB 246

Lenz, Gunter .... **CLC 65**

Lenz, Jakob Michael Reinhold 1751-1792
.... **LC 100**
See also DLB 94; RGWL 2, 3

Lenz, Siegfried 1926- .... **CLC 27; SSC 33**
See also CA 89-92; CANR 80, 149; CWW 2; DLB 75; EWL 3; RGSF 2; RGWL 2, 3

Leon, David
See Jacob, (Cyprien-)Max

Leonard, Elmore 1925- ...... **CLC 28, 34, 71, 120, 222**
See also AAYA 22, 59; AITN 1; BEST 89:1, 90:4; BPFB 2; CA 81-84; CANR 12, 28, 53, 76, 96, 133; CMW 4; CN 5, 6, 7; CPW; DA3; DAM POP; DLB 173, 226; INT CANR-28; MSW; MTCW 1, 2; MTFW 2005; RGAL 4; SATA 163; TCWW 1, 2

Leonard, Hugh .... **CLC 19**
See Byrne, John Keyes
See also CBD; CD 5, 6; DFS 13; DLB 13

Leonov, Leonid (Maximovich) 1899-1994
.... **CLC 92**
See Leonov, Leonid Maksimovich
See also CA 129; CANR 76; DAM NOV; EWL 3; MTCW 1, 2; MTFW 2005

Leonov, Leonid Maksimovich
See Leonov, Leonid (Maximovich)
See also DLB 272

Leopardi, (Conte) Giacomo 1798-1837
.... **NCLC 22, 129; PC 37**
See also EW 5; RGWL 2, 3; WLIT 7; WP

Le Reveler
See Artaud, Antonin (Marie Joseph)

Lerman, Eleanor 1952- .... **CLC 9**
See also CA 85-88; CANR 69, 124

Lerman, Rhoda 1936- .... **CLC 56**
See also CA 49-52; CANR 70

Lermontov, Mikhail Iur'evich
See Lermontov, Mikhail Yuryevich
See also DLB 205

Lermontov, Mikhail Yuryevich 1814-1841
.... **NCLC 5, 47, 126; PC 18**
See Lermontov, Mikhail Iur'evich
See also EW 6; RGWL 2, 3; TWA

Leroux, Gaston 1868-1927 .... **TCLC 25**
See also CA 108; 136; CANR 69; CMW 4; MTFW 2005; NFS 20; SATA 65

Lesage, Alain-Rene 1668-1747 ... **LC 2, 28**
See also DLB 313; EW 3; GFL Beginnings to 1789; RGWL 2, 3

Leskov, N(ikolai) S(emenovich)
See Leskov, Nikolai (Semyonovich)

Leskov, Nikolai (Semyonovich) 1831-1895
.... **NCLC 25, 174; SSC 34, 96**
See Leskov, Nikolai Semenovich

Leskov, Nikolai Semenovich
See Leskov, Nikolai (Semyonovich)
See also DLB 238

Lesser, Milton
See Marlowe, Stephen

Lessing, Doris 1919- . **CLC 1, 2, 3, 6, 10, 15, 22, 40, 94, 170; SSC 6, 61; WLCS**
See also AAYA 57; AFW; BRWS 1; CA 9-12R; CAAS 14; CANR 33, 54, 76, 122; CBD; CD 5, 6; CDBLB 1960 to Present; CN 1, 2, 3, 4, 5, 6, 7; CWD; DA; DA3; DAB; DAC; DAM MST, NOV; DFS 20; DLB 15, 139; DLBY 1985; EWL 3; EXPS; FL 1:6; FW; LAIT 4; MTCW 1, 2; MTFW 2005; RGEL 2; RGSF 2; SFW 4; SSFS 1, 12, 20; TEA; WLIT 2, 4

Lessing, Gotthold Ephraim 1729-1781
.... **DC 26; LC 8, 124**
See also CDWLB 2; DLB 97; EW 4; RGWL 2, 3

Lester, Richard 1932- .... **CLC 20**

Levenson, Jay .... **CLC 70**

Lever, Charles (James) 1806-1872
.... **NCLC 23**
See also DLB 21; RGEL 2

Leverson, Ada Esther 1862(?)-1933(?)
.... **TCLC 18**
See Elaine
See also CA 117; 202; DLB 153; RGEL 2

Levertov, Denise 1923-1997 . **CLC 1, 2, 3, 5, 8, 15, 28, 66; PC 11**
See also AMWS 3; CA 1-4R; 178; 163; CAAE 178; CAAS 19; CANR 3, 29, 50, 108; CDALBS; CP 1, 2, 3, 4, 5, 6; CWP; DAM POET; DLB 5, 165; EWL 3; EXPP; FW; INT CANR-29; MAL 5; MTCW 1, 2; PAB; PFS 7, 17; RGAL 4; RGHL; TUS; WP

Levi, Carlo 1902-1975 .... **TCLC 125**
See also CA 65-68; 53-56; CANR 10; EWL 3; RGWL 2, 3

Levi, Jonathan .... **CLC 76**
See also CA 197

Levi, Peter (Chad Tigar) 1931-2000
.... **CLC 41**
See also CA 5-8R; 187; CANR 34, 80; CP 1, 2, 3, 4, 5, 6, 7; DLB 40

Levi, Primo 1919-1987 ..... **CLC 37, 50; SSC 12; TCLC 109**
See also CA 13-16R; 122; CANR 12, 33, 61, 70, 132; DLB 177, 299; EWL 3; MTCW 1, 2; MTFW 2005; RGHL; RGWL 2, 3; WLIT 7

Levin, Ira 1929- .... **CLC 3, 6**
See also CA 21-24R; CANR 17, 44, 74, 139; CMW 4; CN 1, 2, 3, 4, 5, 6, 7; CPW; DA3; DAM POP; HGG; MTCW 1, 2; MTFW 2005; SATA 66; SFW 4

Levin, Meyer 1905-1981 .... **CLC 7**
See also AITN 1; CA 9-12R; 104; CANR 15; CN 1, 2, 3; DAM POP; DLB 9, 28; DLBY 1981; MAL 5; RGHL; SATA 21; SATA-Obit 27

Levine, Albert Norman 1923-2005
See Levine, Norman
See also CN 7

Levine, Norman 1923-2005 .... **CLC 54**
See also CA 73-76; 240; CAAS 23; CANR 14, 70; CN 1, 2, 3, 4, 5, 6; CP 1; DLB 88

Levine, Norman Albert
See Levine, Norman

Levine, Philip 1928- . **CLC 2, 4, 5, 9, 14, 33, 118; PC 22**
See also AMWS 5; CA 9-12R; CANR 9, 37, 52, 116, 156; CP 1, 2, 3, 4, 5, 6, 7; DAM POET; DLB 5; EWL 3; MAL 5; PFS 8

Levinson, Deirdre 1931- .... **CLC 49**
See also CA 73-76; CANR 70

Levi-Strauss, Claude 1908- .... **CLC 38**
See also CA 1-4R; CANR 6, 32, 57; DLB 242; EWL 3; GFL 1789 to the Present; MTCW 1, 2; TWA

Levitin, Sonia (Wolff) 1934- .... **CLC 17**
See also AAYA 13, 48; CA 29-32R; CANR 14, 32, 79; CLR 53; JRDA; MAICYA 1, 2; SAAS 2; SATA 4, 68, 119, 131; SATA-Essay 131; YAW

Levon, O. U.
See Kesey, Ken

Levy, Amy 1861-1889 .... **NCLC 59**
See also DLB 156, 240

Lewes, George Henry 1817-1878 . **NCLC 25**
See also DLB 55, 144

Lobb, Ebenezer
　See Upward, Allen
Locke, Alain (Le Roy) 1886-1954
　.................... **BLCS; HR 1:3; TCLC 43**
　See also AMWS 14; BW 1, 3; CA 106; 124;
　　CANR 79; DLB 51; LMFS 2; MAL 5;
　　RGAL 4
Locke, John 1632-1704 .... **LC 7, 35**
　See also DLB 31, 101, 213, 252; RGEL 2;
　　WLIT 3
Locke-Elliott, Sumner
　See Elliott, Sumner Locke
Lockhart, John Gibson 1794-1854 . **NCLC 6**
　See also DLB 110, 116, 144
Lockridge, Ross (Franklin), Jr. 1914-1948
　.. **TCLC 111**
　See also CA 108; 145; CANR 79; DLB 143;
　　DLBY 1980; MAL 5; RGAL 4; RHW
Lockwood, Robert
　See Johnson, Robert
Lodge, David 1935- .... **CLC 36, 141**
　See also BEST 90:1; BRWS 4; CA 17-20R;
　　CANR 19, 53, 92, 139; CN 1, 2, 3, 4, 5,
　　6, 7; CPW; DAM POP; DLB 14, 194;
　　EWL 3; INT CANR-19; MTCW 1, 2;
　　MTFW 2005
Lodge, Thomas 1558-1625 .... **LC 41**
　See also DLB 172; RGEL 2
Loewinsohn, Ron(ald William) 1937-
　... **CLC 52**
　See also CA 25-28R; CANR 71; CP 1, 2, 3,
　　4
Logan, Jake
　See Smith, Martin Cruz
Logan, John (Burton) 1923-1987 ...... **CLC 5**
　See also CA 77-80; 124; CANR 45; CP 1,
　　2, 3, 4; DLB 5
Lo Kuan-chung 1330(?)-1400(?) .... **LC 12**
Lombard, Nap
　See Johnson, Pamela Hansford
Lombard, Peter 1100(?)-1160(?) .. **CMLC 72**
Lombino, Salvatore
　See Hunter, Evan
London, Jack 1876-1916 . **SSC 4, 49; TCLC**
　　9, 15, 39; WLC 4
　See London, John Griffith
　See also AAYA 13; AITN 2; AMW; BPFB
　　2; BYA 4, 13; CDALB 1865-1917; CLR
　　108; DLB 8, 12, 78, 212; EWL 3; EXPS;
　　LAIT 3; MAL 5; NFS 8; RGAL 4; RGSF
　　2; SATA 18; SFW 4; SSFS 7; TCWW 1,
　　2; TUS; WYA; YAW
London, John Griffith 1876-1916
　See London, Jack
　See also CA 110; 119; CANR 73; DA; DA3;
　　DAB; DAC; DAM MST, NOV; JRDA;
　　MAICYA 1, 2; MTCW 1, 2; MTFW 2005;
　　NFS 19
Long, Emmett
　See Leonard, Elmore
Longbaugh, Harry
　See Goldman, William
Longfellow, Henry Wadsworth 1807-1882
　. **NCLC 2, 45, 101, 103; PC 30; WLCS**
　See also AMW; AMWR 2; CDALB 1640-
　　1865; CLR 99; DA; DA3; DAB; DAC;
　　DAM MST, POET; DLB 1, 59, 235;
　　EXPP; PAB; PFS 2, 7, 17; RGAL 4;
　　SATA 19; TUS; WP
Longinus c. 1st cent. - .... **CMLC 27**
　See also AW 2; DLB 176
Longley, Michael 1939- .... **CLC 29**
　See also BRWS 8; CA 102; CP 1, 2, 3, 4, 5,
　　6, 7; DLB 40
Longstreet, Augustus Baldwin 1790-1870
　.. **NCLC 159**
　See also DLB 3, 11, 74, 248; RGAL 4
Longus fl. c. 2nd cent. - .... **CMLC 7**

Longway, A. Hugh
　See Lang, Andrew
Lonnbohm, Armas Eino Leopold 1878-1926
　See Leino, Eino
　See also CA 123
Lonnrot, Elias 1802-1884 .... **NCLC 53**
　See also EFS 1
Lonsdale, Roger ed. .... **CLC 65**
Lopate, Phillip 1943- .... **CLC 29**
　See also CA 97-100; CANR 88, 157; DLBY
　　1980; INT CA-97-100
Lopez, Barry (Holstun) 1945- .... **CLC 70**
　See also AAYA 9, 63; ANW; CA 65-68;
　　CANR 7, 23, 47, 68, 92; DLB 256, 275;
　　INT CANR-7, -23; MTCW 1; RGAL 4;
　　SATA 67
Lopez de Mendoza, Inigo
　See Santillana, Inigo Lopez de Mendoza,
　　Marques de
Lopez Portillo (y Pacheco), Jose 1920-2004
　.. **CLC 46**
　See also CA 129; 224; HW 1
Lopez y Fuentes, Gregorio 1897(?)-1966
　.. **CLC 32**
　See also CA 131; EWL 3; HW 1
Lorca, Federico Garcia
　See Garcia Lorca, Federico
　See also DFS 4; EW 11; PFS 20; RGWL 2,
　　3; WP
Lord, Audre
　See Lorde, Audre
　See also EWL 3
Lord, Bette Bao 1938- .... **AAL; CLC 23**
　See also BEST 90:3; BPFB 2; CA 107;
　　CANR 41, 79; INT CA-107; SATA 58
Lord Auch
　See Bataille, Georges
Lord Brooke
　See Greville, Fulke
Lord Byron
　See Byron, George Gordon (Noel)
Lorde, Audre 1934-1992 ... **BLC 2; CLC 18,**
　　71; PC 12; TCLC 173
　See Domini, Rey; Lord, Audre
　See also AFAW 1, 2; BW 1, 3; CA 25-28R;
　　142; CANR 16, 26, 46, 82; CP 2, 3, 4, 5;
　　DA3; DAM MULT, POET; DLB 41; FW;
　　MAL 5; MTCW 1, 2; MTFW 2005; PFS
　　16; RGAL 4
Lord Houghton
　See Milnes, Richard Monckton
Lord Jeffrey
　See Jeffrey, Francis
Loreaux, Nichol .... **CLC 65**
Lorenzini, Carlo 1826-1890
　See Collodi, Carlo
　See also MAICYA 1, 2; SATA 29, 100
Lorenzo, Heberto Padilla
　See Padilla (Lorenzo), Heberto
Loris
　See Hofmannsthal, Hugo von
Loti, Pierre .... **TCLC 11**
　See Viaud, (Louis Marie) Julien
　See also DLB 123; GFL 1789 to the Present
Lou, Henri
　See Andreas-Salome, Lou
Louie, David Wong 1954- .... **CLC 70**
　See also CA 139; CANR 120
Louis, Adrian C. .... **NNAL**
　See also CA 223
Louis, Father M.
　See Merton, Thomas (James)
Louise, Heidi
　See Erdrich, Louise

Lovecraft, H. P. 1890-1937 .... **SSC 3, 52;**
　　TCLC 4, 22
　See also AAYA 14; BPFB 2; CA 104; 133;
　　CANR 106; DA3; DAM POP; HGG;
　　MTCW 1, 2; MTFW 2005; RGAL 4;
　　SCFW 1, 2; SFW 4; SUFW
Lovecraft, Howard Phillips
　See Lovecraft, H. P.
Lovelace, Earl 1935- .... **CLC 51**
　See also BW 2; CA 77-80; CANR 41, 72,
　　114; CD 5, 6; CDWLB 3; CN 1, 2, 3, 4,
　　5, 6, 7; DLB 125; EWL 3; MTCW 1
Lovelace, Richard 1618-1657 ... **LC 24; PC**
　　69
　See also BRW 2; DLB 131; EXPP; PAB;
　　RGEL 2
Lowe, Pardee 1904- .... **AAL**
Lowell, Amy 1874-1925 .. **PC 13; TCLC 1, 8**
　See also AAYA 57; AMW; CA 104; 151;
　　DAM POET; DLB 54, 140; EWL 3;
　　EXPP; LMFS 2; MAL 5; MBL; MTCW
　　2; MTFW 2005; RGAL 4; TUS
Lowell, James Russell 1819-1891 .. **NCLC 2,**
　　90
　See also AMWS 1; CDALB 1640-1865;
　　DLB 1, 11, 64, 79, 189, 235; RGAL 4
Lowell, Robert (Traill Spence, Jr.)
　　1917-1977 ... **CLC 1, 2, 3, 4, 5, 8, 9, 11,**
　　15, 37, 124; PC 3; WLC 4
　See also AMW; AMWC 2; AMWR 2; CA
　　9-12R; 73-76; CABS 2; CAD; CANR 26,
　　60; CDALBS; CP 1, 2; DA; DA3; DAB;
　　DAC; DAM MST, NOV; DLB 5, 169;
　　EWL 3; MAL 5; MTCW 1, 2; MTFW
　　2005; PAB; PFS 6, 7; RGAL 4; WP
Lowenthal, Michael (Francis) 1969-
　... **CLC 119**
　See also CA 150; CANR 115
Lowndes, Marie Adelaide (Belloc) 1868-1947
　.. **TCLC 12**
　See also CA 107; CMW 4; DLB 70; RHW
Lowry, (Clarence) Malcolm 1909-1957
　.......................... **SSC 31; TCLC 6, 40**
　See also BPFB 2; BRWS 3; CA 105; 131;
　　CANR 62, 105; CDBLB 1945-1960; DLB
　　15; EWL 3; MTCW 1, 2; MTFW 2005;
　　RGEL 2
Lowry, Mina Gertrude 1882-1966
　See Loy, Mina
　See also CA 113
Lowry, Sam
　See Soderbergh, Steven
Loxsmith, John
　See Brunner, John (Kilian Houston)
Loy, Mina .... **CLC 28; PC 16**
　See Lowry, Mina Gertrude
　See also DAM POET; DLB 4, 54; PFS 20
Loyson-Bridet
　See Schwob, Marcel (Mayer Andre)
Lucan 39-65 .... **CMLC 33**
　See also AW 2; DLB 211; EFS 2; RGWL 2,
　　3
Lucas, Craig 1951- .... **CLC 64**
　See also CA 137; CAD; CANR 71, 109,
　　142; CD 5, 6; GLL 2; MTFW 2005
Lucas, E(dward) V(errall) 1868-1938
　.. **TCLC 73**
　See also CA 176; DLB 98, 149, 153; SATA
　　20
Lucas, George 1944- .... **CLC 16**
　See also AAYA 1, 23; CA 77-80; CANR
　　30; SATA 56
Lucas, Hans
　See Godard, Jean-Luc
Lucas, Victoria
　See Plath, Sylvia
Lucian c. 125-c. 180 .... **CMLC 32**
　See also AW 2; DLB 176; RGWL 2, 3

Maclean, Norman (Fitzroy) 1902-1990
.... **CLC 78; SSC 13**
See also AMWS 14; CA 102; 132; CANR
49; CPW; DAM POP; DLB 206; TCWW
2

MacLeish, Archibald 1892-1982 .. **CLC 3, 8,
14, 68; PC 47**
See also AMW; CA 9-12R; 106; CAD;
CANR 33, 63; CDALBS; CP 1, 2; DAM
POET; DFS 15; DLB 4, 7, 45; DLBY
1982; EWL 3; EXPP; MAL 5; MTCW 1,
2; MTFW 2005; PAB; PFS 5; RGAL 4;
TUS

MacLennan, (John) Hugh 1907-1990
.... **CLC 2, 14, 92**
See also CA 5-8R; 142; CANR 33; CN 1,
2, 3, 4; DAC; DAM MST; DLB 68; EWL
3; MTCW 1, 2; MTFW 2005; RGEL 2;
TWA

MacLeod, Alistair 1936- .... **CLC 56, 165;
SSC 90**
See also CA 123; CCA 1; DAC; DAM
MST; DLB 60; MTCW 2; MTFW 2005;
RGSF 2; TCLE 1:2

Macleod, Fiona
See Sharp, William
See also RGEL 2; SUFW

MacNeice, (Frederick) Louis 1907-1963
.... **CLC 1, 4, 10, 53; PC 61**
See also BRW 7; CA 85-88; CANR 61;
DAB; DAM POET; DLB 10, 20; EWL 3;
MTCW 1, 2; MTFW 2005; RGEL 2

MacNeill, Dand
See Fraser, George MacDonald

Macpherson, James 1736-1796 .... **LC 29**
See Ossian
See also BRWS 8; DLB 109; RGEL 2

Macpherson, (Jean) Jay 1931- .... **CLC 14**
See also CA 5-8R; CANR 90; CP 1, 2, 3, 4,
6, 7; CWP; DLB 53

Macrobius fl. 430- .... **CMLC 48**

MacShane, Frank 1927-1999 .... **CLC 39**
See also CA 9-12R; 186; CANR 3, 33; DLB
111

Macumber, Mari
See Sandoz, Mari(e Susette)

Madach, Imre 1823-1864 .... **NCLC 19**

Madden, (Jerry) David 1933- ..... **CLC 5, 15**
See also CA 1-4R; CAAS 3; CANR 4, 45;
CN 3, 4, 5, 6, 7; CSW; DLB 6; MTCW 1

Maddern, Al(an)
See Ellison, Harlan

Madhubuti, Haki R. 1942- . **BLC 2; CLC 6,
73; PC 5**
See Lee, Don L.
See also BW 2, 3; CA 73-76; CANR 24,
51, 73, 139; CP 6, 7; CSW; DAM MULT,
POET; DLB 5, 41; DLBD 8; EWL 3;
MAL 5; MTCW 2; MTFW 2005; RGAL
4

Madison, James 1751-1836 .... **NCLC 126**
See also DLB 37

Maepenn, Hugh
See Kuttner, Henry

Maepenn, K. H.
See Kuttner, Henry

Maeterlinck, Maurice 1862-1949 ... **TCLC 3**
See also CA 104; 136; CANR 80; DAM
DRAM; DLB 192; EW 8; EWL 3; GFL
1789 to the Present; LMFS 2; RGWL 2,
3; SATA 66; TWA

Maginn, William 1794-1842 .... **NCLC 8**
See also DLB 110, 159

Mahapatra, Jayanta 1928- .... **CLC 33**
See also CA 73-76; CAAS 9; CANR 15,
33, 66, 87; CP 4, 5, 6, 7; DAM MULT;
DLB 323

Mahfouz, Naguib 1911(?)-2006 .... **CLC 153;
SSC 66**
See Mahfuz, Najib
See also AAYA 49; BEST 89:2; CA 128;
CANR 55, 101; DA3; DAM NOV;
MTCW 1, 2; MTFW 2005; RGWL 2, 3;
SSFS 9

Mahfouz, Naguib Abdel Aziz Al-Sabilgi
See Mahfouz, Naguib

Mahfuz, Najib .... **CLC 52, 55**
See Mahfouz, Naguib
See also AFW; CWW 2; DLBY 1988; EWL
3; RGSF 2; WLIT 6

Mahon, Derek 1941- .... **CLC 27; PC 60**
See also BRWS 6; CA 113; 128; CANR 88;
CP 1, 2, 3, 4, 5, 6, 7; DLB 40; EWL 3

Maiakovskii, Vladimir
See Mayakovski, Vladimir (Vladimirovich)
See also IDTP; RGWL 2, 3

Mailer, Norman 1923- . **CLC 1, 2, 3, 4, 5, 8,
11, 14, 28, 39, 74, 111**
See also AAYA 31; AITN 2; AMW; AMWC
2; AMWR 2; BPFB 2; CA 9-12R; CABS
1; CANR 28, 74, 77, 130; CDALB 1968-
1988; CN 1, 2, 3, 4, 5, 6, 7; CPW; DA;
DA3; DAB; DAC; DAM MST, NOV,
POP; DLB 2, 16, 28, 185, 278; DLBD 3;
DLBY 1980, 1983; EWL 3; MAL 5;
MTCW 1, 2; MTFW 2005; NFS 10;
RGAL 4; TUS

Mailer, Norman Kingsley
See Mailer, Norman

Maillet, Antonine 1929- .... **CLC 54, 118**
See also CA 115; 120; CANR 46, 74, 77,
134; CCA 1; CWW 2; DAC; DLB 60;
INT CA-120; MTCW 2; MTFW 2005

Maimonides, Moses 1135-1204 .... **CMLC 76**
See also DLB 115

Mais, Roger 1905-1955 .... **TCLC 8**
See also BW 1, 3; CA 105; 124; CANR 82;
CDWLB 3; DLB 125; EWL 3; MTCW 1;
RGEL 2

Maistre, Joseph 1753-1821 .... **NCLC 37**
See also GFL 1789 to the Present

Maitland, Frederic William 1850-1906
.... **TCLC 65**

Maitland, Sara (Louise) 1950- .... **CLC 49**
See also BRWS 11; CA 69-72; CANR 13,
59; DLB 271; FW

Major, Clarence 1936- .. **BLC 2; CLC 3, 19,
48**
See also AFAW 2; BW 2, 3; CA 21-24R;
CAAS 6; CANR 13, 25, 53, 82; CN 3, 4,
5, 6, 7; CP 2, 3, 4, 5, 6, 7; CSW; DAM
MULT; DLB 33; EWL 3; MAL 5; MSW

Major, Kevin (Gerald) 1949- .... **CLC 26**
See also AAYA 16; CA 97-100; CANR 21,
38, 112; CLR 11; DAC; DLB 60; INT
CANR-21; JRDA; MAICYA 1, 2; MAIC-
YAS 1; SATA 32, 82, 134; WYA; YAW

Maki, James
See Ozu, Yasujiro

Makine, Andrei 1957- .... **CLC 198**
See also CA 176; CANR 103; MTFW 2005

Malabaila, Damiano
See Levi, Primo

Malamud, Bernard 1914-1986 . **CLC 1, 2, 3,
5, 8, 9, 11, 18, 27, 44, 78, 85; SSC 15;
TCLC 129, 184; WLC 4**
See also AAYA 16; AMWS 1; BPFB 2;
BYA 15; CA 5-8R; 118; CABS 1; CANR
28, 62, 114; CDALB 1941-1968; CN 1, 2,
3, 4; CPW; DA; DA3; DAB; DAC; DAM
MST, NOV, POP; DLB 2, 28, 152; DLBY
1980, 1986; EWL 3; EXPS; LAIT 4;
LATS 1:1; MAL 5; MTCW 1, 2; MTFW
2005; NFS 4, 9; RGAL 4; RGHL; RGSF
2; SSFS 8, 13, 16; TUS

Malan, Herman
See Bosman, Herman Charles; Bosman,
Herman Charles

Malaparte, Curzio 1898-1957 .... **TCLC 52**
See also DLB 264

Malcolm, Dan
See Silverberg, Robert

Malcolm, Janet 1934- .... **CLC 201**
See also CA 123; CANR 89; NCFS 1

Malcolm X .... **BLC 2; CLC 82, 117; WLCS**
See Little, Malcolm
See also LAIT 5; NCFS 3

Malebranche, Nicolas 1638-1715 ..... **LC 133**
See also GFL Beginnings to 1789

Malherbe, Francois de 1555-1628 .... **LC 5**
See also DLB 327; GFL Beginnings to 1789

Mallarme, Stephane 1842-1898 ..... **NCLC 4,
41; PC 4**
See also DAM POET; DLB 217; EW 7;
GFL 1789 to the Present; LMFS 2; RGWL
2, 3; TWA

Mallet-Joris, Francoise 1930- .... **CLC 11**
See also CA 65-68; CANR 17; CWW 2;
DLB 83; EWL 3; GFL 1789 to the Present

Malley, Ern
See McAuley, James Phillip

Mallon, Thomas 1951- .... **CLC 172**
See also CA 110; CANR 29, 57, 92

Mallowan, Agatha Christie
See Christie, Agatha (Mary Clarissa)

Maloff, Saul 1922- .... **CLC 5**
See also CA 33-36R

Malone, Louis
See MacNeice, (Frederick) Louis

Malone, Michael (Christopher) 1942-
.... **CLC 43**
See also CA 77-80; CANR 14, 32, 57, 114

Malory, Sir Thomas 1410(?)-1471(?)
.... **LC 11, 88; WLCS**
See also BRW 1; BRWR 2; CDBLB Before
1660; DA; DAB; DAC; DAM MST; DLB
146; EFS 2; RGEL 2; SATA 59; SATA-
Brief 33; TEA; WLIT 3

Malouf, David 1934- .... **CLC 28, 86**
See also BRWS 12; CA 124; CANR 50, 76;
CN 3, 4, 5, 6, 7; CP 1, 3, 4, 5, 6, 7; DLB
289; EWL 3; MTCW 2; MTFW 2005;
SSFS 24

Malraux, (Georges-)Andre 1901-1976
.... **CLC 1, 4, 9, 13, 15, 57**
See also BPFB 2; CA 21-22; 69-72; CANR
34, 58; CAP 2; DA3; DAM NOV; DLB
72; EW 12; EWL 3; GFL 1789 to the
Present; MTCW 1, 2; MTFW 2005;
RGWL 2, 3; TWA

Malthus, Thomas Robert 1766-1834
.... **NCLC 145**
See also DLB 107, 158; RGEL 2

Malzberg, Barry N(athaniel) 1939- .. **CLC 7**
See also CA 61-64; CAAS 4; CANR 16;
CMW 4; DLB 8; SFW 4

Mamet, David 1947- . **CLC 9, 15, 34, 46, 91,
166; DC 4, 24**
See also AAYA 3, 60; AMWS 14; CA 81-
84; CABS 3; CAD; CANR 15, 41, 67, 72,
129; CD 5, 6; DA3; DAM DRAM; DFS
2, 3, 6, 12, 15; DLB 7; EWL 3; IDFW 4;
MAL 5; MTCW 1, 2; MTFW 2005;
RGAL 4

Mamet, David Alan
See Mamet, David

Mamoulian, Rouben (Zachary) 1897-1987
.... **CLC 16**
See also CA 25-28R; 124; CANR 85

Mandelshtam, Osip
See Mandelstam, Osip (Emilievich)
See also EW 10; EWL 3; RGWL 2, 3

Marti, Jose
　　See Marti (y Perez), Jose (Julian)
　　See also DLB 290
Marti (y Perez), Jose (Julian) 1853-1895
　　................................ **HLC 2; NCLC 63**
　　See Marti, Jose
　　See also DAM MULT; HW 2; LAW; RGWL
　　2, 3; WLIT 1
Martial c. 40-c. 104 .... **CMLC 35; PC 10**
　　See also AW 2; CDWLB 1; DLB 211;
　　RGWL 2, 3
Martin, Ken
　　See Hubbard, L. Ron
Martin, Richard
　　See Creasey, John
Martin, Steve 1945- .... **CLC 30, 217**
　　See also AAYA 53; CA 97-100; CANR 30,
　　100, 140; DFS 19; MTCW 1; MTFW
　　2005
Martin, Valerie 1948- .... **CLC 89**
　　See also BEST 90:2; CA 85-88; CANR 49,
　　89
Martin, Violet Florence 1862-1915 . **SSC 56;
　　TCLC 51**
Martin, Webber
　　See Silverberg, Robert
Martindale, Patrick Victor
　　See White, Patrick (Victor Martindale)
Martin du Gard, Roger 1881-1958
　　................................... **TCLC 24**
　　See also CA 118; CANR 94; DLB 65; EWL
　　3; GFL 1789 to the Present; RGWL 2, 3
Martineau, Harriet 1802-1876 .... **NCLC 26,
　　137**
　　See also DLB 21, 55, 159, 163, 166, 190;
　　FW; RGEL 2; YABC 2
Martines, Julia
　　See O'Faolain, Julia
Martinez, Enrique Gonzalez
　　See Gonzalez Martinez, Enrique
Martinez, Jacinto Benavente y
　　See Benavente (y Martinez), Jacinto
Martinez de la Rosa, Francisco de Paula
　　1787-1862 .... **NCLC 102**
　　See also TWA
Martinez Ruiz, Jose 1873-1967
　　See Azorin; Ruiz, Jose Martinez
　　See also CA 93-96; HW 1
Martinez Sierra, Gregorio
　　See Martinez Sierra, Maria
Martinez Sierra, Gregorio 1881-1947
　　.. **TCLC 6**
　　See also CA 115; EWL 3
Martinez Sierra, Maria 1874-1974
　　.. **TCLC 6**
　　See also CA 250; 115; EWL 3
Martinsen, Martin
　　See Follett, Ken
Martinson, Harry (Edmund) 1904-1978
　　................................ **CLC 14**
　　See also CA 77-80; CANR 34, 130; DLB
　　259; EWL 3
Martyn, Edward 1859-1923 .... **TCLC 131**
　　See also CA 179; DLB 10; RGEL 2
Marut, Ret
　　See Traven, B.
Marut, Robert
　　See Traven, B.
Marvell, Andrew 1621-1678 ... **LC 4, 43; PC
　　10; WLC 4**
　　See also BRW 2; BRWR 2; CDBLB 1660-
　　1789; DA; DAB; DAC; DAM MST,
　　POET; DLB 131; EXPP; PFS 5; RGEL 2;
　　TEA; WP
Marx, Karl (Heinrich) 1818-1883
　　.. **NCLC 17, 114**
　　See also DLB 129; LATS 1:1; TWA

Masaoka, Shiki -1902 .... **TCLC 18**
　　See Masaoka, Tsunenori
　　See also RGWL 3
Masaoka, Tsunenori 1867-1902
　　See Masaoka, Shiki
　　See also CA 117; 191; TWA
Masefield, John (Edward) 1878-1967
　　................................ **CLC 11, 47**
　　See also CA 19-20; 25-28R; CANR 33;
　　CAP 2; CDBLB 1890-1914; DAM POET;
　　DLB 10, 19, 153, 160; EWL 3; EXPP;
　　FANT; MTCW 1, 2; PFS 5; RGEL 2;
　　SATA 19
Maso, Carole 1955(?)- .... **CLC 44**
　　See also CA 170; CANR 148; CN 7; GLL
　　2; RGAL 4
Mason, Bobbie Ann 1940- .. **CLC 28, 43, 82,
　　154; SSC 4**
　　See also AAYA 5, 42; AMWS 8; BPFB 2;
　　CA 53-56; CANR 11, 31, 58, 83, 125;
　　CDALBS; CN 5, 6, 7; CSW; DA3; DLB
　　173; DLBY 1987; EWL 3; EXPS; INT
　　CANR-31; MAL 5; MTCW 1, 2; MTFW
　　2005; NFS 4; RGAL 4; RGSF 2; SSFS 3,
　　8, 20; TCLE 1:2; YAW
Mason, Ernst
　　See Pohl, Frederik
Mason, Hunni B.
　　See Sternheim, (William Adolf) Carl
Mason, Lee W.
　　See Malzberg, Barry N(athaniel)
Mason, Nick 1945- .... **CLC 35**
Mason, Tally
　　See Derleth, August (William)
Mass, Anna .... **CLC 59**
Mass, William
　　See Gibson, William
Massinger, Philip 1583-1640 .... **LC 70**
　　See also BRWS 11; DLB 58; RGEL 2
Master Lao
　　See Lao Tzu
Masters, Edgar Lee 1868-1950 ..... **PC 1, 36;
　　TCLC 2, 25; WLCS**
　　See also AMWS 1; CA 104; 133; CDALB
　　1865-1917; DA; DAC; DAM MST,
　　POET; DLB 54; EWL 3; EXPP; MAL 5;
　　MTCW 1, 2; MTFW 2005; RGAL 4;
　　TUS; WP
Masters, Hilary 1928- .... **CLC 48**
　　See also CA 25-28R; 217; CAAE 217;
　　CANR 13, 47, 97; CN 6, 7; DLB 244
Mastrosimone, William 1947- .... **CLC 36**
　　See also CA 186; CAD; CD 5, 6
Mathe, Albert
　　See Camus, Albert
Mather, Cotton 1663-1728 .... **LC 38**
　　See also AMWS 2; CDALB 1640-1865;
　　DLB 24, 30, 140; RGAL 4; TUS
Mather, Increase 1639-1723 .... **LC 38**
　　See also DLB 24
Mathers, Marshall
　　See Eminem
Mathers, Marshall Bruce
　　See Eminem
Matheson, Richard (Burton) 1926-
　　.. **CLC 37**
　　See also AAYA 31; CA 97-100; CANR 88,
　　99; DLB 8, 44; HGG; INT CA-97-100;
　　SCFW 1, 2; SFW 4; SUFW 2
Mathews, Harry (Burchell) 1930- .... **CLC 6,
　　52**
　　See also CA 21-24R; CAAS 6; CANR 18,
　　40, 98; CN 5, 6, 7
Mathews, John Joseph 1894-1979 . **CLC 84;
　　NNAL**
　　See also CA 19-20; 142; CANR 45; CAP 2;
　　DAM MULT; DLB 175; TCWW 1, 2

Mathias, Roland (Glyn) 1915- .... **CLC 45**
　　See also CA 97-100; CANR 19, 41; CP 1,
　　2, 3, 4, 5, 6, 7; DLB 27
Matsuo Basho 1644(?)-1694 .... **LC 62; PC 3**
　　See Basho, Matsuo
　　See also DAM POET; PFS 2, 7, 18
Mattheson, Rodney
　　See Creasey, John
Matthews, (James) Brander 1852-1929
　　.. **TCLC 95**
　　See also CA 181; DLB 71, 78; DLBD 13
Matthews, Greg 1949- .... **CLC 45**
　　See also CA 135
Matthews, William (Procter III) 1942-1997
　　.. **CLC 40**
　　See also AMWS 9; CA 29-32R; 162; CAAS
　　18; CANR 12, 57; CP 2, 3, 4, 5, 6; DLB
　　5
Matthias, John (Edward) 1941- .... **CLC 9**
　　See also CA 33-36R; CANR 56; CP 4, 5, 6,
　　7
Matthiessen, F(rancis) O(tto) 1902-1950
　　.. **TCLC 100**
　　See also CA 185; DLB 63; MAL 5
Matthiessen, Peter 1927- .. **CLC 5, 7, 11, 32,
　　64**
　　See also AAYA 6, 40; AMWS 5; ANW;
　　BEST 90:4; BPFB 2; CA 9-12R; CANR
　　21, 50, 73, 100, 138; CN 1, 2, 3, 4, 5, 6,
　　7; DA3; DAM NOV; DLB 6, 173, 275;
　　MAL 5; MTCW 1, 2; MTFW 2005; SATA
　　27
Maturin, Charles Robert 1780(?)-1824
　　.. **NCLC 6, 169**
　　See also BRWS 8; DLB 178; GL 3; HGG;
　　LMFS 1; RGEL 2; SUFW
Matute (Ausejo), Ana Maria 1925- . **CLC 11**
　　See also CA 89-92; CANR 129; CWW 2;
　　DLB 322; EWL 3; MTCW 1; RGSF 2
Maugham, W. S.
　　See Maugham, W(illiam) Somerset
Maugham, W(illiam) Somerset 1874-1965
　　......... **CLC 1, 11, 15, 67, 93; SSC 8, 94;
　　WLC 4**
　　See also AAYA 55; BPFB 2; BRW 6; CA
　　5-8R; 25-28R; CANR 40, 127; CDBLB
　　1914-1945; CMW 4; DA; DA3; DAB;
　　DAC; DAM DRAM, MST, NOV; DFS
　　22; DLB 10, 36, 77, 100, 162, 195; EWL
　　3; LAIT 3; MTCW 1, 2; MTFW 2005;
　　NFS 23; RGEL 2; RGSF 2; SATA 54;
　　SSFS 17
Maugham, William Somerset
　　See Maugham, W(illiam) Somerset
Maupassant, (Henri Rene Albert) Guy de
　　1850-1893 ...... **NCLC 1, 42, 83; SSC 1,
　　64; WLC 4**
　　See also BYA 14; DA; DA3; DAB; DAC;
　　DAM MST; DLB 123; EW 7; EXPS; GFL
　　1789 to the Present; LAIT 2; LMFS 1;
　　RGSF 2; RGWL 2, 3; SSFS 4, 21; SUFW;
　　TWA
Maupin, Armistead 1944- .... **CLC 95**
　　See also CA 125; 130; CANR 58, 101;
　　CPW; DA3; DAM POP; DLB 278; GLL
　　1; INT CA-130; MTCW 2; MTFW 2005
Maupin, Armistead Jones, Jr.
　　See Maupin, Armistead
Maurhut, Richard
　　See Traven, B.
Mauriac, Claude 1914-1996 .... **CLC 9**
　　See also CA 89-92; 152; CWW 2; DLB 83;
　　EWL 3; GFL 1789 to the Present
Mauriac, Francois (Charles) 1885-1970
　　................................ **CLC 4, 9, 56; SSC 24**
　　See also CA 25-28; CAP 2; DLB 65; EW
　　10; EWL 3; GFL 1789 to the Present;
　　MTCW 1, 2; MTFW 2005; RGWL 2, 3;
　　TWA

McKay, Festus Claudius 1889-1948
See McKay, Claude
See also BW 1, 3; CA 104; 124; CANR 73;
DA; DAC; DAM MST, MULT, NOV,
POET; MTCW 1, 2; MTFW 2005; TUS

McKuen, Rod 1933- .... **CLC 1, 3**
See also AITN 1; CA 41-44R; CANR 40;
CP 1

McLoughlin, R. B.
See Mencken, H(enry) L(ouis)

McLuhan, (Herbert) Marshall 1911-1980
.... **CLC 37, 83**
See also CA 9-12R; 102; CANR 12, 34, 61;
DLB 88; INT CANR-12; MTCW 1, 2;
MTFW 2005

McManus, Declan Patrick Aloysius
See Costello, Elvis

McMillan, Terry 1951- . **BLCS; CLC 50, 61,
112**
See also AAYA 21; AMWS 13; BPFB 2;
BW 2, 3; CA 140; CANR 60, 104, 131;
CN 7; CPW; DA3; DAM MULT, NOV,
POP; MAL 5; MTCW 2; MTFW 2005;
RGAL 4; YAW

McMurtry, Larry 1936- ..... **CLC 2, 3, 7, 11,
27, 44, 127**
See also AAYA 15; AITN 2; AMWS 5;
BEST 89:2; BPFB 2; CA 5-8R; CANR
19, 43, 64, 103; CDALB 1968-1988; CN
2, 3, 4, 5, 6, 7; CPW; CSW; DA3; DAM
NOV, POP; DLB 2, 143, 256; DLBY
1980, 1987; EWL 3; MAL 5; MTCW 1,
2; MTFW 2005; RGAL 4; TCWW 1, 2

McMurtry, Larry Jeff
See McMurtry, Larry

McNally, Terrence 1939- .. **CLC 4, 7, 41, 91;
DC 27**
See also AAYA 62; AMWS 13; CA 45-48;
CAD; CANR 2, 56, 116; CD 5, 6; DA3;
DAM DRAM; DFS 16, 19; DLB 7, 249;
EWL 3; GLL 1; MTCW 2; MTFW 2005

McNally, Thomas Michael
See McNally, T.M.

McNally, T.M. 1961- .... **CLC 82**
See also CA 246

McNamer, Deirdre 1950- .... **CLC 70**

McNeal, Tom .... **CLC 119**

McNeile, Herman Cyril 1888-1937
See Sapper
See also CA 184; CMW 4; DLB 77

McNickle, (William) D'Arcy 1904-1977
.... **CLC 89; NNAL**
See also CA 9-12R; 85-88; CANR 5, 45;
DAM MULT; DLB 175, 212; RGAL 4;
SATA-Obit 22; TCWW 1, 2

McPhee, John 1931- .... **CLC 36**
See also AAYA 61; AMWS 3; ANW; BEST
90:1; CA 65-68; CANR 20, 46, 64, 69,
121; CPW; DLB 185, 275; MTCW 1, 2;
MTFW 2005; TUS

McPherson, James Alan 1943-
.... **BLCS; CLC 19, 77; SSC 95**
See also BW 1, 3; CA 25-28R; CAAS 17;
CANR 24, 74, 140; CN 3, 4, 5, 6; CSW;
DLB 38, 244; EWL 3; MTCW 1, 2;
MTFW 2005; RGAL 4; RGSF 2; SSFS
23

McPherson, William (Alexander) 1933-
.... **CLC 34**
See also CA 69-72; CANR 28; INT
CANR-28

McTaggart, J. McT. Ellis
See McTaggart, John McTaggart Ellis

McTaggart, John McTaggart Ellis 1866-1925
.... **TCLC 105**
See also CA 120; DLB 262

Mead, George Herbert 1863-1931
.... **TCLC 89**
See also CA 212; DLB 270

Mead, Margaret 1901-1978 .... **CLC 37**
See also AITN 1; CA 1-4R; 81-84; CANR
4; DA3; FW; MTCW 1, 2; SATA-Obit 20

Meaker, Marijane 1927-
See Kerr, M. E.
See also CA 107; CANR 37, 63, 145; INT
CA-107; JRDA; MAICYA 1, 2; MAIC-
YAS 1; MTCW 1; SATA 20, 61, 99, 160;
SATA-Essay 111; YAW

Medoff, Mark (Howard) 1940- ... **CLC 6, 23**
See also AITN 1; CA 53-56; CAD; CANR
5; CD 5, 6; DAM DRAM; DFS 4; DLB
7; INT CANR-5

Medvedev, P. N.
See Bakhtin, Mikhail Mikhailovich

Meged, Aharon
See Megged, Aharon

Meged, Aron
See Megged, Aharon

Megged, Aharon 1920- .... **CLC 9**
See also CA 49-52; CAAS 13; CANR 1,
140; EWL 3; RGHL

Mehta, Deepa 1950- .... **CLC 208**

Mehta, Gita 1943- .... **CLC 179**
See also CA 225; CN 7; DNFS 2

Mehta, Ved 1934- .... **CLC 37**
See also CA 1-4R, 212; CAAE 212; CANR
2, 23, 69; DLB 323; MTCW 1; MTFW
2005

Melanchthon, Philipp 1497-1560 .... **LC 90**
See also DLB 179

Melanter
See Blackmore, R(ichard) D(oddridge)

Meleager c. 140B.C.-c. 70B.C. ..... **CMLC 53**

Melies, Georges 1861-1938 .... **TCLC 81**

Melikow, Loris
See Hofmannsthal, Hugo von

Melmoth, Sebastian
See Wilde, Oscar (Fingal O'Flahertie Wills)

Melo Neto, Joao Cabral de
See Cabral de Melo Neto, Joao
See also CWW 2; EWL 3

Meltzer, Milton 1915- .... **CLC 26**
See also AAYA 8, 45; BYA 2, 6; CA 13-
16R; CANR 38, 92, 107; CLR 13; DLB
61; JRDA; MAICYA 1, 2; SAAS 1; SATA
1, 50, 80, 128; SATA-Essay 124; WYA;
YAW

Melville, Herman 1819-1891 ... **NCLC 3, 12,
29, 45, 49, 91, 93, 123, 157; SSC 1, 17,
46, 95; WLC 4**
See also AAYA 25; AMW; AMWR 1;
CDALB 1640-1865; DA; DA3; DAB;
DAC; DAM MST, NOV; DLB 3, 74, 250,
254; EXPN; EXPS; GL 3; LAIT 1, 2; NFS
7, 9; RGAL 4; RGSF 2; SATA 59; SSFS
3; TUS

Members, Mark
See Powell, Anthony

Membreno, Alejandro .... **CLC 59**

Menand, Louis 1952- .... **CLC 208**
See also CA 200

Menander c. 342B.C.-c. 293B.C. .. **CMLC 9,
51; DC 3**
See also AW 1; CDWLB 1; DAM DRAM;
DLB 176; LMFS 1; RGWL 2, 3

Menchu, Rigoberta 1959- . **CLC 160; HLCS
2**
See also CA 175; CANR 135; DNFS 1;
WLIT 1

Mencken, H(enry) L(ouis) 1880-1956
.... **TCLC 13**
See also AMW; CA 105; 125; CDALB
1917-1929; DLB 11, 29, 63, 137, 222;
EWL 3; MAL 5; MTCW 1, 2; MTFW
2005; NCFS 4; RGAL 4; TUS

Mendelsohn, Jane 1965- .... **CLC 99**
See also CA 154; CANR 94

Mendoza, Inigo Lopez de
See Santillana, Inigo Lopez de Mendoza,
Marques de

Menton, Francisco de
See Chin, Frank (Chew, Jr.)

Mercer, David 1928-1980 .... **CLC 5**
See also CA 9-12R; 102; CANR 23; CBD;
DAM DRAM; DLB 13, 310; MTCW 1;
RGEL 2

Merchant, Paul
See Ellison, Harlan

Meredith, George 1828-1909 .... **PC 60;
TCLC 17, 43**
See also CA 117; 153; CANR 80; CDBLB
1832-1890; DAM POET; DLB 18, 35, 57,
159; RGEL 2; TEA

Meredith, William (Morris) 1919- ... **CLC 4,
13, 22, 55; PC 28**
See also CA 9-12R; CAAS 14; CANR 6,
40, 129; CP 1, 2, 3, 4, 5, 6, 7; DAM
POET; DLB 5; MAL 5

Merezhkovsky, Dmitrii Sergeevich
See Merezhkovsky, Dmitry Sergeyevich
See also DLB 295

Merezhkovsky, Dmitry Sergeevich
See Merezhkovsky, Dmitry Sergeyevich
See also EWL 3

Merezhkovsky, Dmitry Sergeyevich
1865-1941 .... **TCLC 29**
See Merezhkovsky, Dmitrii Sergeevich;
Merezhkovsky, Dmitry Sergeyevich
See also CA 169

Merimee, Prosper 1803-1870 .. **NCLC 6, 65;
SSC 7, 77**
See also DLB 119, 192; EW 6; EXPS; GFL
1789 to the Present; RGSF 2; RGWL 2,
3; SSFS 8; SUFW

Merkin, Daphne 1954- .... **CLC 44**
See also CA 123

Merleau-Ponty, Maurice 1908-1961
.... **TCLC 156**
See also CA 114; 89-92; DLB 296; GFL
1789 to the Present

Merlin, Arthur
See Blish, James (Benjamin)

Mernissi, Fatima 1940- .... **CLC 171**
See also CA 152; FW

Merrill, James 1926-1995 .... **CLC 2, 3, 6, 8,
13, 18, 34, 91; PC 28; TCLC 173**
See also AMWS 3; CA 13-16R; 147; CANR
10, 49, 63, 108; CP 1, 2, 3, 4; DA3; DAM
POET; DLB 5, 165; DLBY 1985; EWL 3;
INT CANR-10; MAL 5; MTCW 1, 2;
MTFW 2005; PAB; PFS 23; RGAL 4

Merriman, Alex
See Silverberg, Robert

Merriman, Brian 1747-1805 .... **NCLC 70**

Merritt, E. B.
See Waddington, Miriam

Merton, Thomas (James) 1915-1968
.... **CLC 1, 3, 11, 34, 83; PC 10**
See also AAYA 61; AMWS 8; CA 5-8R;
25-28R; CANR 22, 53, 111, 131; DA3;
DLB 48; DLBY 1981; MAL 5; MTCW 1,
2; MTFW 2005

Merwin, W.S. 1927- ... **CLC 1, 2, 3, 5, 8, 13,
18, 45, 88; PC 45**
See also AMWS 3; CA 13-16R; CANR 15,
51, 112, 140; CP 1, 2, 3, 4, 5, 6, 7; DA3;
DAM POET; DLB 5, 169; EWL 3; INT
CANR-15; MAL 5; MTCW 1, 2; MTFW
2005; PAB; PFS 5, 15; RGAL 4

Metastasio, Pietro 1698-1782 .... **LC 115**
See also RGWL 2, 3

Metcalf, John 1938- .... **CLC 37; SSC 43**
See also CA 113; CN 4, 5, 6, 7; DLB 60;
RGSF 2; TWA

Metcalf, Suzanne
See Baum, L(yman) Frank

Mew, Charlotte (Mary) 1870-1928 . TCLC 8
See also CA 105; 189; DLB 19, 135; RGEL
2

Mewshaw, Michael 1943- .... CLC 9
See also CA 53-56; CANR 7, 47, 147;
DLBY 1980

Meyer, Conrad Ferdinand 1825-1898
.... NCLC 81; SSC 30
See also DLB 129; EW; RGWL 2, 3

Meyer, Gustav 1868-1932
See Meyrink, Gustav
See also CA 117; 190

Meyer, June
See Jordan, June

Meyer, Lynn
See Slavitt, David R(ytman)

Meyers, Jeffrey 1939- .... CLC 39
See also CA 73-76, 186; CAAE 186; CANR
54, 102; DLB 111

Meynell, Alice (Christina Gertrude
Thompson) 1847-1922 .... TCLC 6
See also CA 104; 177; DLB 19, 98; RGEL
2

Meyrink, Gustav .... TCLC 21
See Meyer, Gustav
See also DLB 81; EWL 3

Michaels, Leonard 1933-2003 .... CLC 6, 25;
SSC 16
See also AMWS 16; CA 61-64; 216; CANR
21, 62, 119; CN 3, 45, 6, 7; DLB 130;
MTCW 1; TCLE 1:2

Michaux, Henri 1899-1984 .... CLC 8, 19
See also CA 85-88; 114; DLB 258; EWL 3;
GFL 1789 to the Present; RGWL 2, 3

Micheaux, Oscar (Devereaux) 1884-1951
.... TCLC 76
See also BW 3; CA 174; DLB 50; TCWW
2

Michelangelo 1475-1564 .... LC 12
See also AAYA 43

Michelet, Jules 1798-1874 .... NCLC 31
See also EW 5; GFL 1789 to the Present

Michels, Robert 1876-1936 .... TCLC 88
See also CA 212

Michener, James A. 1907(?)-1997 .... CLC 1,
5, 11, 29, 60, 109
See also AAYA 27; AITN 1; BEST 90:1;
BPFB 2; CA 5-8R; 161; CANR 21, 45,
68; CN 1, 2, 3, 4, 5, 6; CPW; DA3; DAM
NOV, POP; DLB 6; MAL 5; MTCW 1, 2;
MTFW 2005; RHW; TCWW 1, 2

Mickiewicz, Adam 1798-1855 .... NCLC 3,
101; PC 38
See also EW 5; RGWL 2, 3

Middleton, (John) Christopher 1926-
.... CLC 13
See also CA 13-16R; CANR 29, 54, 117;
CP 1, 2, 3, 4, 5, 6, 7; DLB 40

Middleton, Richard (Barham) 1882-1911
.... TCLC 56
See also CA 187; DLB 156; HGG

Middleton, Stanley 1919- .... CLC 7, 38
See also CA 25-28R; CAAS 23; CANR 21,
46, 81, 157; CN 1, 2, 3, 4, 5, 6, 7; DLB
14, 326

Middleton, Thomas 1580-1627 .... DC 5; LC
33, 123
See also BRW 2; DAM DRAM, MST; DFS
18, 22; DLB 58; RGEL 2

Migueis, Jose Rodrigues 1901-1980
.... CLC 10
See also DLB 287

Mikszath, Kalman 1847-1910 .... TCLC 31
See also CA 170

Miles, Jack .... CLC 100
See also CA 200

Miles, John Russiano
See Miles, Jack

Miles, Josephine (Louise) 1911-1985
.... CLC 1, 2, 14, 34, 39
See also CA 1-4R; 116; CANR 2, 55; CP 1,
2, 3, 4; DAM POET; DLB 48; MAL 5;
TCLE 1:2

Militant
See Sandburg, Carl (August)

Mill, Harriet (Hardy) Taylor 1807-1858
.... NCLC 102
See also FW

Mill, John Stuart 1806-1873 ... NCLC 11, 58
See also CDBLB 1832-1890; DLB 55, 190,
262; FW 1; RGEL 2; TEA

Millar, Kenneth 1915-1983 .... CLC 14
See Macdonald, Ross
See also CA 9-12R; 110; CANR 16, 63,
107; CMW 4; CPW; DA3; DAM POP;
DLB 2, 226; DLBD 6; DLBY 1983;
MTCW 1, 2; MTFW 2005

Millay, E. Vincent
See Millay, Edna St. Vincent

Millay, Edna St. Vincent 1892-1950 ... PC 6,
61; TCLC 4, 49, 169; WLCS
See Boyd, Nancy
See also AMW; CA 104; 130; CDALB
1917-1929; DA; DA3; DAB; DAC; DAM
MST, POET; DLB 45, 249; EWL 3;
EXPP; FL 1:6; MAL 5; MBL; MTCW 1,
2; MTFW 2005; PAB; PFS 3, 17; RGAL
4; TUS; WP

Miller, Arthur 1915-2005 ... CLC 1, 2, 6, 10,
15, 26, 47, 78, 179; DC 1; WLC 4
See also AAYA 15; AITN 1; AMW; AMWC
1; CA 1-4R; 236; CABS 3; CAD; CANR
2, 30, 54, 76, 132; CD 5, 6; CDALB
1941-1968; DA; DA3; DAB; DAC; DAM
DRAM, MST; DFS 1, 3, 8; DLB 7, 266;
EWL 3; LAIT 1, 4; LATS 1:2; MAL 5;
MTCW 1, 2; MTFW 2005; RGAL 4;
RGHL; TUS; WYAS 1

Miller, Henry (Valentine) 1891-1980
.... CLC 1, 2, 4, 9, 14, 43, 84; WLC 4
See also AMW; BPFB 2; CA 9-12R; 97-
100; CANR 33, 64; CDALB 1929-1941;
CN 1, 2; DA; DA3; DAB; DAC; DAM
MST, NOV; DLB 4, 9; DLBY 1980; EWL
3; MAL 5; MTCW 1, 2; MTFW 2005;
RGAL 4; TUS

Miller, Hugh 1802-1856 .... NCLC 143
See also DLB 190

Miller, Jason 1939(?)-2001 .... CLC 2
See also AITN 1; CA 73-76; 197; CAD;
CANR 130; DFS 12; DLB 7

Miller, Sue 1943- .... CLC 44
See also AMWS 12; BEST 90:3; CA 139;
CANR 59, 91, 128; DA3; DAM POP;
DLB 143

Miller, Walter M(ichael, Jr.) 1923-1996
.... CLC 4, 30
See also BPFB 2; CA 85-88; CANR 108;
DLB 8; SCFW 1, 2; SFW 4

Millett, Kate 1934- .... CLC 67
See also AITN 1; CA 73-76; CANR 32, 53,
76, 110; DA3; DLB 246; FW; GLL 1;
MTCW 1, 2; MTFW 2005

Millhauser, Steven 1943- .. CLC 21, 54, 109;
SSC 57
See also CA 110; 111; CANR 63, 114, 133;
CN 6, 7; DA3; DLB 2; FANT; INT CA-
111; MAL 5; MTCW 2; MTFW 2005

Millhauser, Steven Lewis
See Millhauser, Steven

Millin, Sarah Gertrude 1889-1968 . CLC 49
See also CA 102; 93-96; DLB 225; EWL 3

Milne, A. A. 1882-1956 .... TCLC 6, 88
See also BRWS 5; CA 104; 133; CLR 1,
26, 108; CMW 4; CWRI 5; DA3; DAB;
DAC; DAM MST; DLB 10, 77, 100, 160;
FANT; MAICYA 1, 2; MTCW 1, 2;
MTFW 2005; RGEL 2; SATA 100; WCH;
YABC 1

Milne, Alan Alexander
See Milne, A. A.

Milner, Ron(ald) 1938-2004 .... BLC 3; CLC
56
See also AITN 1; BW 1; CA 73-76; 230;
CAD; CANR 24, 81; CD 5, 6; DAM
MULT; DLB 38; MAL 5; MTCW 1

Milnes, Richard Monckton 1809-1885
.... NCLC 61
See also DLB 32, 184

Milosz, Czeslaw 1911-2004 ... CLC 5, 11, 22,
31, 56, 82; PC 8; WLCS
See also AAYA 62; CA 81-84; 230; CANR
23, 51, 91, 126; CDWLB 4; CWW 2;
DA3; DAM MST, POET; DLB 215; EW
13; EWL 3; MTCW 1, 2; MTFW 2005;
PFS 16; RGHL; RGWL 2, 3

Milton, John 1608-1674 .... LC 9, 43, 92; PC
19, 29; WLC 4
See also AAYA 65; BRW 2; BRWR 2; CD-
BLB 1660-1789; DA; DA3; DAB; DAC;
DAM MST, POET; DLB 131, 151, 281;
EFS 1; EXPP; LAIT 1; PAB; PFS 3, 17;
RGEL 2; TEA; WLIT 3; WP

Min, Anchee 1957- .... CLC 86
See also CA 146; CANR 94, 137; MTFW
2005

Minehaha, Cornelius
See Wedekind, Frank

Miner, Valerie 1947- .... CLC 40
See also CA 97-100; CANR 59; FW; GLL
2

Minimo, Duca
See D'Annunzio, Gabriele

Minot, Susan (Anderson) 1956- ..... CLC 44,
159
See also AMWS 6; CA 134; CANR 118;
CN 6, 7

Minus, Ed 1938- .... CLC 39
See also CA 185

Mirabai 1498(?)-1550(?) .... PC 48
See also PFS 24

Miranda, Javier
See Bioy Casares, Adolfo
See also CWW 2

Mirbeau, Octave 1848-1917 .... TCLC 55
See also CA 216; DLB 123, 192; GFL 1789
to the Present

Mirikitani, Janice 1942- .... AAL
See also CA 211; DLB 312; RGAL 4

Mirk, John (?)-c. 1414 .... LC 105
See also DLB 146

Miro (Ferrer), Gabriel (Francisco Victor)
1879-1930 .... TCLC 5
See also CA 104; 185; DLB 322; EWL 3

Misharin, Alexandr .... CLC 59

Mishima, Yukio ... CLC 2, 4, 6, 9, 27; DC 1;
SSC 4; TCLC 161; WLC 4
See Hiraoka, Kimitake
See also AAYA 50; BPFB 2; GLL 1; MJW;
RGSF 2; RGWL 2, 3; SSFS 5, 12

Mistral, Frederic 1830-1914 .... TCLC 51
See also CA 122; 213; GFL 1789 to the
Present

Mistral, Gabriela
See Godoy Alcayaga, Lucila
See also DLB 283; DNFS 1; EWL 3; LAW;
RGWL 2, 3; WP

Mistry, Rohinton 1952- .. CLC 71, 196; SSC
73
See also BRWS 10; CA 141; CANR 86,
114; CCA 1; CN 6, 7; DAC; SSFS 6

Mitchell, Clyde
See Ellison, Harlan

Mitchell, Emerson Blackhorse Barney 1945-
.... NNAL
See also CA 45-48

Mitchell, James Leslie 1901-1935
See Gibbon, Lewis Grassic
See also CA 104; 188; DLB 15
Mitchell, Joni 1943- .... **CLC 12**
See also CA 112; CCA 1
Mitchell, Joseph (Quincy) 1908-1996
.... **CLC 98**
See also CA 77-80; 152; CANR 69; CN 1,
2, 3, 4, 5, 6; CSW; DLB 185; DLBY 1996
Mitchell, Margaret (Munnerlyn) 1900-1949
.... **TCLC 11, 170**
See also AAYA 23; BPFB 2; BYA 1; CA
109; 125; CANR 55, 94; CDALBS; DA3;
DAM NOV, POP; DLB 9; LAIT 2; MAL
5; MTCW 1, 2; MTFW 2005; NFS 9;
RGAL 4; RHW; TUS; WYAS 1; YAW
Mitchell, Peggy
See Mitchell, Margaret (Munnerlyn)
Mitchell, S(ilas) Weir 1829-1914 .. **TCLC 36**
See also CA 165; DLB 202; RGAL 4
Mitchell, W(illiam) O(rmond) 1914-1998
.... **CLC 25**
See also CA 77-80; 165; CANR 15, 43; CN
1, 2, 3, 4, 5, 6; DAC; DAM MST; DLB
88; TCLE 1:2
Mitchell, William (Lendrum) 1879-1936
.... **TCLC 81**
See also CA 213
Mitford, Mary Russell 1787-1855 .. **NCLC 4**
See also DLB 110, 116; RGEL 2
Mitford, Nancy 1904-1973 .... **CLC 44**
See also BRWS 10; CA 9-12R; CN 1; DLB
191; RGEL 2
Miyamoto, (Chujo) Yuriko 1899-1951
.... **TCLC 37**
See Miyamoto Yuriko
See also CA 170, 174
Miyamoto Yuriko
See Miyamoto, (Chujo) Yuriko
See also DLB 180
Miyazawa, Kenji 1896-1933 .... **TCLC 76**
See Miyazawa Kenji
See also CA 157; RGWL 3
Miyazawa Kenji
See Miyazawa, Kenji
See also EWL 3
Mizoguchi, Kenji 1898-1956 .... **TCLC 72**
See also CA 167
Mo, Timothy (Peter) 1950- ...... **CLC 46, 134**
See also CA 117; CANR 128; CN 5, 6, 7;
DLB 194; MTCW 1; WLIT 4; WWE 1
Modarressi, Taghi (M.) 1931-1997 .. **CLC 44**
See also CA 121; 134; INT CA-134
Modiano, Patrick (Jean) 1945- ...... **CLC 18,
218**
See also CA 85-88; CANR 17, 40, 115;
CWW 2; DLB 83, 299; EWL 3; RGHL
Mofolo, Thomas (Mokopu) 1875(?)-1948
.... **BLC 3; TCLC 22**
See also AFW; CA 121; 153; CANR 83;
DAM MULT; DLB 225; EWL 3; MTCW
2; MTFW 2005; WLIT 2
Mohr, Nicholasa 1938- .... **CLC 12; HLC 2**
See also AAYA 8, 46; CA 49-52; CANR 1,
32, 64; CLR 22; DAM MULT; DLB 145;
HW 1, 2; JRDA; LAIT 5; LLW; MAICYA
2; MAICYAS 1; RGAL 4; SAAS 8; SATA
8, 97; SATA-Essay 113; WYA; YAW
Moi, Toril 1953- .... **CLC 172**
See also CA 154; CANR 102; FW
Mojtabai, A(nn) G(race) 1938- .... **CLC 5, 9,
15, 29**
See also CA 85-88; CANR 88
Moliere 1622-1673 .... **DC 13; LC 10, 28, 64,
125, 127; WLC 4**
See also DA; DA3; DAB; DAC; DAM
DRAM, MST; DFS 13, 18, 20; DLB 268;
EW 3; GFL Beginnings to 1789; LATS
1:1; RGWL 2, 3; TWA

Molin, Charles
See Mayne, William (James Carter)
Molnar, Ferenc 1878-1952 .... **TCLC 20**
See also CA 109; 153; CANR 83; CDWLB
4; DAM DRAM; DLB 215; EWL 3;
RGWL 2, 3
Momaday, N. Scott 1934- ..... **CLC 2, 19, 85,
95, 160; NNAL; PC 25; WLCS**
See also AAYA 11, 64; AMWS 4; ANW;
BPFB 2; BYA 12; CA 25-28R; CANR 14,
34, 68, 134; CDALBS; CN 2, 3, 4, 5, 6,
7; CPW; DA; DA3; DAB; DAC; DAM
MST, MULT, NOV, POP; DLB 143, 175,
256; EWL 3; EXPP; INT CANR-14;
LAIT 4; LATS 1:2; MAL 5; MTCW 1, 2;
MTFW 2005; NFS 10; PFS 2, 11; RGAL
4; SATA 48; SATA-Brief 30; TCWW 1,
2; WP; YAW
Monette, Paul 1945-1995 .... **CLC 82**
See also AMWS 10; CA 139; 147; CN 6;
GLL 1
Monroe, Harriet 1860-1936 .... **TCLC 12**
See also CA 109; 204; DLB 54, 91
Monroe, Lyle
See Heinlein, Robert A.
Montagu, Elizabeth 1720-1800 ...... **NCLC 7,
117**
See also FW
Montagu, Mary (Pierrepont) Wortley
1689-1762 .... **LC 9, 57; PC 16**
See also DLB 95, 101; FL 1:1; RGEL 2
Montagu, W. H.
See Coleridge, Samuel Taylor
Montague, John (Patrick) 1929- .... **CLC 13,
46**
See also CA 9-12R; CANR 9, 69, 121; CP
1, 2, 3, 4, 5, 6, 7; DLB 40; EWL 3;
MTCW 1; PFS 12; RGEL 2; TCLE 1:2
Montaigne, Michel (Eyquem) de 1533-1592
.... **LC 8, 105; WLC 4**
See also DA; DAB; DAC; DAM MST;
DLB 327; EW 2; GFL Beginnings to
1789; LMFS 1; RGWL 2, 3; TWA
Montale, Eugenio 1896-1981 . **CLC 7, 9, 18;
PC 13**
See also CA 17-20R; 104; CANR 30; DLB
114; EW 11; EWL 3; MTCW 1; PFS 22;
RGWL 2, 3; TWA; WLIT 7
Montesquieu, Charles-Louis de Secondat
1689-1755 .... **LC 7, 69**
See also DLB 314; EW 3; GFL Beginnings
to 1789; TWA
Montessori, Maria 1870-1952 ..... **TCLC 103**
See also CA 115; 147
Montgomery, (Robert) Bruce 1921(?)-1978
See Crispin, Edmund
See also CA 179; 104; CMW 4
Montgomery, L(ucy) M(aud) 1874-1942
.... **TCLC 51, 140**
See also AAYA 12; BYA 1; CA 108; 137;
CLR 8, 91; DA3; DAC; DAM MST; DLB
92; DLBD 14; JRDA; MAICYA 1, 2;
MTCW 2; MTFW 2005; RGEL 2; SATA
100; TWA; WCH; WYA; YABC 1
Montgomery, Marion H., Jr. 1925- .. **CLC 7**
See also AITN 1; CA 1-4R; CANR 3, 48;
CSW; DLB 6
Montgomery, Max
See Davenport, Guy (Mattison, Jr.)
Montherlant, Henry (Milon) de 1896-1972
.... **CLC 8, 19**
See also CA 85-88; 37-40R; DAM DRAM;
DLB 72, 321; EW 11; EWL 3; GFL 1789
to the Present; MTCW 1
Monty Python
See Chapman, Graham; Cleese, John
(Marwood); Gilliam, Terry; Idle, Eric;
Jones, Terence Graham Parry; Palin,
Michael (Edward)
See also AAYA 7

Moodie, Susanna (Strickland) 1803-1885
.... **NCLC 14, 113**
See also DLB 99
Moody, Hiram 1961-
See Moody, Rick
See also CA 138; CANR 64, 112; MTFW
2005
Moody, Minerva
See Alcott, Louisa May
Moody, Rick .... **CLC 147**
See Moody, Hiram
Moody, William Vaughan 1869-1910
.... **TCLC 105**
See also CA 110; 178; DLB 7, 54; MAL 5;
RGAL 4
Mooney, Edward 1951-
See Mooney, Ted
See also CA 130
Mooney, Ted .... **CLC 25**
See Mooney, Edward
Moorcock, Michael 1939- ...... **CLC 5, 27, 58**
See Bradbury, Edward P.
See also AAYA 26; CA 45-48; CAAS 5;
CANR 2, 17, 38, 64, 122; CN 5, 6, 7;
DLB 14, 231, 261, 319; FANT; MTCW 1,
2; MTFW 2005; SATA 93, 166; SCFW 1,
2; SFW 4; SUFW 1, 2
Moorcock, Michael John
See Moorcock, Michael
Moore, Alan 1953- .... **CLC 230**
See also AAYA 51; CA 204; CANR 138;
DLB 261; MTFW 2005; SFW 4
Moore, Brian 1921-1999 .. **CLC 1, 3, 5, 7, 8,
19, 32, 90**
See Bryan, Michael
See also BRWS 9; CA 1-4R; 174; CANR 1,
25, 42, 63; CCA 1; CN 1, 2, 3, 4, 5, 6;
DAB; DAC; DAM MST; DLB 251; EWL
3; FANT; MTCW 1, 2; MTFW 2005;
RGEL 2
Moore, Edward
See Muir, Edwin
See also RGEL 2
Moore, G. E. 1873-1958 .... **TCLC 89**
See also DLB 262
Moore, George Augustus 1852-1933
.... **SSC 19; TCLC 7**
See also BRW 6; CA 104; 177; DLB 10,
18, 57, 135; EWL 3; RGEL 2; RGSF 2
Moore, Lorrie .... **CLC 39, 45, 68**
See Moore, Marie Lorena
See also AMWS 10; CN 5, 6, 7; DLB 234;
SSFS 19
Moore, Marianne (Craig) 1887-1972
.... **CLC 1, 2, 4, 8, 10, 13, 19, 47; PC 4,
49; WLCS**
See also AMW; CA 1-4R; 33-36R; CANR
3, 61; CDALB 1929-1941; CP 1; DA;
DA3; DAB; DAC; DAM MST, POET;
DLB 45; DLBD 7; EWL 3; EXPP; FL 1:6;
MAL 5; MBL; MTCW 1, 2; MTFW 2005;
PAB; PFS 14, 17; RGAL 4; SATA 20;
TUS; WP
Moore, Marie Lorena 1957- .... **CLC 165**
See Moore, Lorrie
See also CA 116; CANR 39, 83, 139; DLB
234; MTFW 2005
Moore, Michael 1954- .... **CLC 218**
See also AAYA 53; CA 166; CANR 150
Moore, Thomas 1779-1852 ..... **NCLC 6, 110**
See also DLB 96, 144; RGEL 2
Moorhouse, Frank 1938- .... **SSC 40**
See also CA 118; CANR 92; CN 3, 4, 5, 6,
7; DLB 289; RGSF 2
Mora, Pat 1942- .... **HLC 2**
See also AMWS 13; CA 129; CANR 57,
81, 112; CLR 58; DAM MULT; DLB 209;
HW 1, 2; LLW; MAICYA 2; MTFW
2005; SATA 92, 134

Author Index

Norman, Marsha (Williams) 1947-
.... **CLC 28, 186; DC 8**
See also CA 105; CABS 3; CAD; CANR
41, 131; CD 5, 6; CSW; CWD; DAM
DRAM; DFS 2; DLB 266; DLBY 1984;
FW; MAL 5

Normyx
See Douglas, (George) Norman

Norris, (Benjamin) Frank(lin, Jr.) 1870-1902
.... **SSC 28; TCLC 24, 155**
See also AAYA 57; AMW; AMWC 2; BPFB
2; CA 110; 160; CDALB 1865-1917; DLB
12, 71, 186; LMFS 2; MAL 5; NFS 12;
RGAL 4; TCWW 1, 2; TUS

Norris, Leslie 1921-2006 .... **CLC 14**
See also CA 11-12; 251; CANR 14, 117;
CAP 1; CP 1, 2, 3, 4, 5, 6, 7; DLB 27,
256

North, Andrew
See Norton, Andre

North, Anthony
See Koontz, Dean R.

North, Captain George
See Stevenson, Robert Louis (Balfour)

North, Captain George
See Stevenson, Robert Louis (Balfour)

North, Milou
See Erdrich, Louise

Northrup, B. A.
See Hubbard, L. Ron

North Staffs
See Hulme, T(homas) E(rnest)

Northup, Solomon 1808-1863 ..... **NCLC 105**

Norton, Alice Mary
See Norton, Andre
See also MAICYA 1; SATA 1, 43

Norton, Andre 1912-2005 .... **CLC 12**
See Norton, Alice Mary
See also AAYA 14; BPFB 2; BYA 4, 10,
12; CA 1-4R; 237; CANR 2, 31, 68, 108,
149; CLR 50; DLB 8, 52; JRDA; MAI-
CYA 2; MTCW 1; SATA 91; SUFW 1, 2;
YAW

Norton, Caroline 1808-1877 .... **NCLC 47**
See also DLB 21, 159, 199

Norway, Nevil Shute 1899-1960
See Shute, Nevil
See also CA 102; 93-96; CANR 85; MTCW
2

Norwid, Cyprian Kamil 1821-1883
.... **NCLC 17**
See also RGWL 3

Nosille, Nabrah
See Ellison, Harlan

Nossack, Hans Erich 1901-1977 .... **CLC 6**
See also CA 93-96; 85-88; CANR 156;
DLB 69; EWL 3

Nostradamus 1503-1566 .... **LC 27**

Nosu, Chuji
See Ozu, Yasujiro

Notenburg, Eleanora (Genrikhovna) von
See Guro, Elena (Genrikhovna)

Nova, Craig 1945- .... **CLC 7, 31**
See also CA 45-48; CANR 2, 53, 127

Novak, Joseph
See Kosinski, Jerzy

Novalis 1772-1801 .... **NCLC 13**
See also CDWLB 2; DLB 90; EW 5; RGWL
2, 3

Novick, Peter 1934- .... **CLC 164**
See also CA 188

Novis, Emile
See Weil, Simone (Adolphine)

Nowlan, Alden (Albert) 1933-1983 . **CLC 15**
See also CA 9-12R; CANR 5; CP 1, 2, 3;
DAC; DAM MST; DLB 53; PFS 12

Noyes, Alfred 1880-1958 .... **PC 27; TCLC 7**
See also CA 104; 188; DLB 20; EXPP;
FANT; PFS 4; RGEL 2

Nugent, Richard Bruce 1906(?)-1987
.... **HR 1:3**
See also BW 1; CA 125; DLB 51; GLL 2

Nunn, Kem .... **CLC 34**
See also CA 159

Nussbaum, Martha Craven 1947-
.... **CLC 203**
See also CA 134; CANR 102

Nwapa, Flora (Nwanzuruaha) 1931-1993
.... **BLCS; CLC 133**
See also BW 2; CA 143; CANR 83; CD-
WLB 3; CWRI 5; DLB 125; EWL 3;
WLIT 2

Nye, Robert 1939- .... **CLC 13, 42**
See also BRWS 10; CA 33-36R; CANR 29,
67, 107; CN 1, 2, 3, 4, 5, 6, 7; CP 1, 2, 3,
4, 5, 6, 7; CWRI 5; DAM NOV; DLB 14,
271; FANT; HGG; MTCW 1; RHW;
SATA 6

Nyro, Laura 1947-1997 .... **CLC 17**
See also CA 194

Oates, Joyce Carol 1938- . **CLC 1, 2, 3, 6, 9,
11, 15, 19, 33, 52, 108, 134; SSC 6, 70;
WLC 4**
See also AAYA 15, 52; AITN 1; AMWS 2;
BEST 89:2; BPFB 2; BYA 11; CA 5-8R;
CANR 25, 45, 74, 113, 129, 228; CDALB
1968-1988; CN 1, 2, 3, 4, 5, 6, 7; CP 5,
6, 7; CPW; CWP; DA; DA3; DAB; DAC;
DAM MST, NOV, POP; DLB 2, 5, 130;
DLBY 1981; EWL 3; EXPS; FL 1:6; FW;
GL 3; HGG; INT CANR-25; LAIT 4;
MAL 5; MBL; MTCW 1, 2; MTFW 2005;
NFS 8, 24; RGAL 4; RGSF 2; SATA 159;
SSFS 1, 8, 17; SUFW 2; TUS

O'Brian, E. G.
See Clarke, Arthur C.

O'Brian, Patrick 1914-2000 .... **CLC 152**
See also AAYA 55; BRWS 12; CA 144; 187;
CANR 74; CPW; MTCW 2; MTFW 2005;
RHW

O'Brien, Darcy 1939-1998 .... **CLC 11**
See also CA 21-24R; 167; CANR 8, 59

O'Brien, Edna 1932- .... **CLC 3, 5, 8, 13, 36,
65, 116; SSC 10, 77**
See also BRWS 5; CA 1-4R; CANR 6, 41,
65, 102; CDBLB 1960 to Present; CN 1,
2, 3, 4, 5, 6, 7; DA3; DAM NOV; DLB
14, 231, 319; EWL 3; FW; MTCW 1, 2;
MTFW 2005; RGSF 2; WLIT 4

O'Brien, Fitz-James 1828-1862 ...... **NCLC 21**
See also DLB 74; RGAL 4; SUFW

O'Brien, Flann .... **CLC 1, 4, 5, 7, 10, 47**
See O Nuallain, Brian
See also BRWS 2; DLB 231; EWL 3;
RGEL 2

O'Brien, Richard 1942- .... **CLC 17**
See also CA 124

O'Brien, Tim 1946- ...... **CLC 7, 19, 40, 103,
211; SSC 74**
See also AAYA 16; AMWS 5; CA 85-88;
CANR 40, 58, 133; CDALBS; CN 5, 6,
7; CPW; DA3; DAM POP; DLB 152;
DLBD 9; DLBY 1980; LATS 1:2; MAL
5; MTCW 2; MTFW 2005; RGAL 4;
SSFS 5, 15; TCLE 1:2

Obstfelder, Sigbjoern 1866-1900 .. **TCLC 23**
See also CA 123

O'Casey, Sean 1880-1964 ... **CLC 1, 5, 9, 11,
15, 88; DC 12; WLCS**
See also BRW 7; CA 89-92; CANR 62;
CBD; CDBLB 1914-1945; DLB 10; DAB;
DAC; DAM DRAM, MST; DFS 19; DLB
10; EWL 3; MTCW 1, 2; MTFW 2005;
RGEL 2; TEA; WLIT 4

O'Cathasaigh, Sean
See O'Casey, Sean

Occom, Samson 1723-1792 ... **LC 60; NNAL**
See also DLB 175

Occomy, Marita (Odette) Bonner
1899(?)-1971
See Bonner, Marita
See also BW 2; CA 142; DFS 13; DLB 51,
228

Ochs, Phil(ip David) 1940-1976 ...... **CLC 17**
See also CA 185; 65-68

O'Connor, Edwin (Greene) 1918-1968
.... **CLC 14**
See also CA 93-96; 25-28R; MAL 5

O'Connor, (Mary) Flannery 1925-1964
.... **CLC 1, 2, 3, 6, 10, 13, 15, 21, 66,
104; SSC 1, 23, 61, 82; TCLC 132;
WLC 4**
See also AAYA 7; AMW; AMWR 2; BPFB
3; BYA 16; CA 1-4R; CANR 3, 41;
CDALB 1941-1968; DA; DA3; DAB;
DAC; DAM MST, NOV; DLB 2, 152;
DLBD 12; DLBY 1980; EWL 3; EXPS;
LAIT 5; MAL 5; MBL; MTCW 1, 2;
MTFW 2005; NFS 3, 21; RGAL 4; RGSF
2; SSFS 2, 7, 10, 19; TUS

O'Connor, Frank .... **CLC 23; SSC 5**
See O'Donovan, Michael Francis
See also DLB 162; EWL 3; RGSF 2; SSFS
5

O'Dell, Scott 1898-1989 .... **CLC 30**
See also AAYA 3, 44; BPFB 3; BYA 1, 2,
3, 5; CA 61-64; 129; CANR 12, 30, 112;
CLR 1, 16; DLB 52; JRDA; MAICYA 1,
2; SATA 12, 60, 134; WYA; YAW

Odets, Clifford 1906-1963 .... **CLC 2, 28, 98;
DC 6**
See also AMWS 2; CA 85-88; CAD; CANR
62; DAM DRAM; DFS 3, 17, 20; DLB 7,
26; EWL 3; MAL 5; MTCW 1, 2; MTFW
2005; RGAL 4; TUS

O'Doherty, Brian 1928- .... **CLC 76**
See also CA 105; CANR 108

O'Donnell, K. M.
See Malzberg, Barry N(athaniel)

O'Donnell, Lawrence
See Kuttner, Henry

O'Donovan, Michael Francis 1903-1966
.... **CLC 14**
See O'Connor, Frank
See also CA 93-96; CANR 84

Oe, Kenzaburo 1935- . **CLC 10, 36, 86, 187;
SSC 20**
See Oe Kenzaburo
See also CA 97-100; CANR 36, 50, 74, 126;
DA3; DAM NOV; DLB 182; DLBY 1994;
LATS 1:2; MJW; MTCW 1, 2; MTFW
2005; RGSF 2; RGWL 2, 3

Oe Kenzaburo
See Oe, Kenzaburo
See also CWW 2; EWL 3

O'Faolain, Julia 1932- ... **CLC 6, 19, 47, 108**
See also CA 81-84; CAAS 2; CANR 12,
61; CN 2, 3, 4, 5, 6, 7; DLB 14, 231, 319;
FW; MTCW 1; RHW

O'Faolain, Sean 1900-1991 .... **CLC 1, 7, 14,
32, 70; SSC 13; TCLC 143**
See also CA 61-64; 134; CANR 12, 66; CN
1, 2, 3, 4; DLB 15, 162; MTCW 1, 2;
MTFW 2005; RGEL 2; RGSF 2

O'Flaherty, Liam 1896-1984 ...... **CLC 5, 34;
SSC 6**
See also CA 101; 113; CANR 35; CN 1, 2,
3; DLB 36, 162; DLBY 1984; MTCW 1,
2; MTFW 2005; RGEL 2; RGSF 2; SSFS
5, 20

Ogai
See Mori Ogai
See also MJW

Ogilvy, Gavin
See Barrie, J(ames) M(atthew)

O'Grady, Standish (James) 1846-1928
.... **TCLC 5**
See also CA 104; 157

Pinsky, Robert 1940- ...... **CLC 9, 19, 38, 94, 121, 216; PC 27**
See also AMWS 6; CA 29-32R; CAAS 4; CANR 58, 97, 138; CP 3, 4, 5, 6, 7; DA3; DAM POET; DLBY 1982, 1998; MAL 5; MTCW 2; MTFW 2005; PFS 18; RGAL 4; TCLE 1:2

Pinta, Harold
See Pinter, Harold

Pinter, Harold 1930- . **CLC 1, 3, 6, 9, 11, 15, 27, 58, 73, 199; DC 15; WLC 4**
See also BRWR 1; BRWS 1; CA 5-8R; CANR 33, 65, 112, 145; CBD; CD 5, 6; CDBLB 1960 to Present; CP 1; DA; DA3; DAB; DAC; DAM DRAM, MST; DFS 3, 5, 7, 14; DLB 13, 310; EWL 3; IDFW 3, 4; LMFS 2; MTCW 1, 2; MTFW 2005; RGEL 2; RGHL; TEA

Piozzi, Hester Lynch (Thrale) 1741-1821
.... **NCLC 57**
See also DLB 104, 142

Pirandello, Luigi 1867-1936 . **DC 5; SSC 22; TCLC 4, 29, 172; WLC 4**
See also CA 104; 153; CANR 103; DA; DA3; DAB; DAC; DAM DRAM, MST; DFS 4, 9; DLB 264; EW 8; EWL 3; MTCW 2; MTFW 2005; RGSF 2; RGWL 2, 3; WLIT 7

Pirsig, Robert M(aynard) 1928- .. **CLC 4, 6, 73**
See also CA 53-56; CANR 42, 74; CPW 1; DA3; DAM POP; MTCW 1, 2; MTFW 2005; SATA 39

Pisan, Christine de
See Christine de Pizan

Pisarev, Dmitrii Ivanovich
See Pisarev, Dmitry Ivanovich
See also DLB 277

Pisarev, Dmitry Ivanovich 1840-1868
.... **NCLC 25**
See Pisarev, Dmitrii Ivanovich

Pix, Mary (Griffith) 1666-1709 .... **LC 8**
See also DLB 80

Pixerecourt, (Rene Charles) Guilbert de 1773-1844 .... **NCLC 39**
See also DLB 192; GFL 1789 to the Present

Plaatje, Sol(omon) T(shekisho) 1878-1932
.... **BLCS; TCLC 73**
See also BW 2, 3; CA 141; CANR 79; DLB 125, 225

Plaidy, Jean
See Hibbert, Eleanor Alice Burford

Planche, James Robinson 1796-1880
.... **NCLC 42**
See also RGEL 2

Plant, Robert 1948- .... **CLC 12**

Plante, David 1940- .... **CLC 7, 23, 38**
See also CA 37-40R; CANR 12, 36, 58, 82, 152; CN 2, 3, 4, 5, 6, 7; DAM NOV; DLBY 1983; INT CANR-12; MTCW 1

Plante, David Robert
See Plante, David

Plath, Sylvia 1932-1963 .... **CLC 1, 2, 3, 5, 9, 11, 14, 17, 50, 51, 62, 111; PC 1, 37; WLC 4**
See also AAYA 13; AMWR 2; AMWS 1; BPFB 3; CA 19-20; CANR 34, 101; CAP 2; CDALB 1941-1968; DA; DA3; DAB; DAC; DAM MST, POET; DLB 5, 6, 152; EWL 3; EXPN; EXPP; FL 1:6; FW; LAIT 4; MBL; MTCW 1, 2; MTFW 2005; NFS 1; PAB; PFS 1, 15; RGAL 4; SATA 96; TUS; WP; YAW

Plato c. 428B.C.-347B.C. .... **CMLC 8, 75; WLCS**
See also AW 1; CDWLB 1; DA; DA3; DAB; DAC; DAM MST; DLB 176; LAIT 1; LATS 1:1; RGWL 2, 3; WLIT 8

Platonov, Andrei
See Klimentov, Andrei Platonovich

Platonov, Andrei Platonovich
See Klimentov, Andrei Platonovich
See also DLB 272

Platonov, Andrey Platonovich
See Klimentov, Andrei Platonovich
See also EWL 3

Platt, Kin 1911- .... **CLC 26**
See also AAYA 11; CA 17-20R; CANR 11; JRDA; SAAS 17; SATA 21, 86; WYA

Plautus c. 254B.C.-c. 184B.C. ..... **CMLC 24; DC 6**
See also AW 1; CDWLB 1; DLB 211; RGWL 2, 3; WLIT 8

Plick et Plock
See Simenon, Georges (Jacques Christian)

Plieksans, Janis
See Rainis, Janis

Plimpton, George 1927-2003 .... **CLC 36**
See also AITN 1; AMWS 16; CA 21-24R; 224; CANR 32, 70, 103, 133; DLB 185, 241; MTCW 1, 2; MTFW 2005; SATA 10; SATA-Obit 150

Pliny the Elder c. 23-79 .... **CMLC 23**
See also DLB 211

Pliny the Younger c. 61-c. 112 ..... **CMLC 62**
See also AW 2; DLB 211

Plomer, William Charles Franklin 1903-1973
.... **CLC 4, 8**
See also AFW; BRWS 11; CA 21-22; CANR 34; CAP 2; CN 1; CP 1, 2; DLB 20, 162, 191, 225; EWL 3; MTCW 1; RGEL 2; RGSF 2; SATA 24

Plotinus 204-270 .... **CMLC 46**
See also CDWLB 1; DLB 176

Plowman, Piers
See Kavanagh, Patrick (Joseph)

Plum, J.
See Wodehouse, P(elham) G(renville)

Plumly, Stanley (Ross) 1939- .... **CLC 33**
See also CA 108; 110; CANR 97; CP 3, 4, 5, 6, 7; DLB 5, 193; INT CA-110

Plumpe, Friedrich Wilhelm
See Murnau, F.W.

Plutarch c. 46-c. 120 .... **CMLC 60**
See also AW 2; CDWLB 1; DLB 176; RGWL 2, 3; TWA; WLIT 8

Po Chu-i 772-846 .... **CMLC 24**

Podhoretz, Norman 1930- .... **CLC 189**
See also AMWS 8; CA 9-12R; CANR 7, 78, 135

Poe, Edgar Allan 1809-1849 .... **NCLC 1, 16, 55, 78, 94, 97, 117; PC 1, 54; SSC 1, 22, 34, 35, 54, 88; WLC 4**
See also AAYA 14; AMW; AMWC 1; AMWR 2; BPFB 3; BYA 5, 11; CDALB 1640-1865; CMW 4; DA; DA3; DAB; DAC; DAM MST, POET; DLB 3, 59, 73, 74, 248, 254; EXPP; EXPS; GL 3; HGG; LAIT 2; LATS 1:1; MSW; PAB; PFS 1, 3, 9; RGAL 4; RGSF 2; SATA 23; SCFW 1, 2; SFW 4; SSFS 2, 4, 7, 8, 16; SUFW; TUS; WP; WYA

Poet of Titchfield Street, The
See Pound, Ezra (Weston Loomis)

Poggio Bracciolini, Gian Francesco 1380-1459 .... **LC 125**

Pohl, Frederik 1919- .... **CLC 18; SSC 25**
See also AAYA 24; CA 61-64, 188; CAAE 188; CAAS 1; CANR 11, 37, 81, 140; CN 1, 2, 3, 4, 5, 6; DLB 8; INT CANR-11; MTCW 1, 2; MTFW 2005; SATA 24; SCFW 1, 2; SFW 4

Poirier, Louis 1910-
See Gracq, Julien
See also CA 122; 126; CANR 141

Poitier, Sidney 1927- .... **CLC 26**
See also AAYA 60; BW 1; CA 117; CANR 94

Pokagon, Simon 1830-1899 .... **NNAL**
See also DAM MULT

Polanski, Roman 1933- .... **CLC 16, 178**
See also CA 77-80

Poliakoff, Stephen 1952- .... **CLC 38**
See also CA 106; CANR 116; CBD; CD 5, 6; DLB 13

Police, The
See Copeland, Stewart (Armstrong); Summers, Andrew James

Polidori, John William 1795-1821
.... **NCLC 51**
See also DLB 116; HGG

Poliziano, Angelo 1454-1494 .... **LC 120**
See also WLIT 7

Pollitt, Katha 1949- .... **CLC 28, 122**
See also CA 120; 122; CANR 66, 108; MTCW 1, 2; MTFW 2005

Pollock, (Mary) Sharon 1936- .... **CLC 50**
See also CA 141; CANR 132; CD 5; CWD; DAC; DAM DRAM, MST; DFS 3; DLB 60; FW

Pollock, Sharon 1936- .... **DC 20**
See also CD 6

Polo, Marco 1254-1324 .... **CMLC 15**
See also WLIT 7

Polonsky, Abraham (Lincoln) 1910-1999
.... **CLC 92**
See also CA 104; 187; DLB 26; INT CA-104

Polybius c. 200B.C.-c. 118B.C. ..... **CMLC 17**
See also AW 1; DLB 176; RGWL 2, 3

Pomerance, Bernard 1940- .... **CLC 13**
See also CA 101; CAD; CANR 49, 134; CD 5, 6; DAM DRAM; DFS 9; LAIT 2

Ponge, Francis 1899-1988 .... **CLC 6, 18**
See also CA 85-88; 126; CANR 40, 86; DAM POET; DLBY 2002; EWL 3; GFL 1789 to the Present; RGWL 2, 3

Poniatowska, Elena 1932- ... **CLC 140; HLC 2**
See also CA 101; CANR 32, 66, 107, 156; CDWLB 3; CWW 2; DAM MULT; DLB 113; EWL 3; HW 1, 2; LAWS 1; WLIT 1

Pontoppidan, Henrik 1857-1943 ... **TCLC 29**
See also CA 170; DLB 300

Ponty, Maurice Merleau
See Merleau-Ponty, Maurice

Poole, Josephine .... **CLC 17**
See Helyar, Jane Penelope Josephine
See also SAAS 2; SATA 5

Popa, Vasko 1922-1991 .... **CLC 19; TCLC 167**
See also CA 112; 148; CDWLB 4; DLB 181; EWL 3; RGWL 2, 3

Pope, Alexander 1688-1744 ..... **LC 3, 58, 60, 64; PC 26; WLC 5**
See also BRW 3; BRWC 1; BRWR 1; CD-BLB 1660-1789; DA; DA3; DAB; DAC; DAM MST, POET; DLB 95, 101, 213; EXPP; PAB; PFS 12; RGEL 2; WLIT 3; WP

Popov, Evgenii Anatol'evich
See Popov, Yevgeny
See also DLB 285

Popov, Yevgeny .... **CLC 59**
See Popov, Evgenii Anatol'evich

Poquelin, Jean-Baptiste
See Moliere

Porete, Marguerite (?)-1310 .... **CMLC 73**
See also DLB 208

Porphyry c. 233-c. 305 .... **CMLC 71**

Porter, Connie (Rose) 1959(?)- .... **CLC 70**
See also AAYA 65; BW 2, 3; CA 142; CANR 90, 109; SATA 81, 129

Porter, Gene(va Grace) Stratton .. **TCLC 21**
See Stratton-Porter, Gene(va Grace)
See also BPFB 3; CA 112; CWRI 5; RHW

Porter, Katherine Anne 1890-1980 .. **CLC 1, 3, 7, 10, 13, 15, 27, 101; SSC 4, 31, 43**
See also AAYA 42; AITN 2; AMW; BPFB 3; CA 1-4R; 101; CANR 1, 65; CDALBS; CN 1, 2; DA; DA3; DAB; DAC; DAM MST, NOV; DLB 4, 9, 102; DLBD 12; DLBY 1980; EWL 3; EXPS; LAIT 3; MAL 5; MBL; MTCW 1, 2; MTFW 2005; NFS 14; RGAL 4; RGSF 2; SATA 39; SATA-Obit 23; SSFS 1, 8, 11, 16, 23; TCWW 2; TUS

Porter, Peter (Neville Frederick) 1929-
.... **CLC 5, 13, 33**
See also CA 85-88; CP 1, 2, 3, 4, 5, 6, 7; DLB 40, 289; WWE 1

Porter, William Sydney 1862-1910
See Henry, O.
See also CA 104; 131; CDALB 1865-1917; DA; DA3; DAB; DAC; DAM MST; DLB 12, 78, 79; MTCW 1, 2; MTFW 2005; TUS; YABC 2

Portillo (y Pacheco), Jose Lopez
See Lopez Portillo (y Pacheco), Jose

Portillo Trambley, Estela 1927-1998
.... **HLC 2**
See Trambley, Estela Portillo
See also CANR 32; DAM MULT; DLB 209; HW 1

Posey, Alexander (Lawrence) 1873-1908
.... **NNAL**
See also CA 144; CANR 80; DAM MULT; DLB 175

Posse, Abel .... **CLC 70**

Post, Melville Davisson 1869-1930
.... **TCLC 39**
See also CA 110; 202; CMW 4

Potok, Chaim 1929-2002 .. **CLC 2, 7, 14, 26, 112**
See also AAYA 15, 50; AITN 1, 2; BPFB 3; BYA 1; CA 17-20R; 208; CANR 19, 35, 64, 98; CLR 92; CN 4, 5, 6; DA3; DAM NOV; DLB 28, 152; EXPN; INT CANR-19; LAIT 4; MTCW 1, 2; MTFW 2005; NFS 4; RGHL; SATA 33, 106; SATA-Obit 134; TUS; YAW

Potok, Herbert Harold -2002
See Potok, Chaim

Potok, Herman Harold
See Potok, Chaim

Potter, Dennis (Christopher George) 1935-1994 .... **CLC 58, 86, 123**
See also BRWS 10; CA 107; 145; CANR 33, 61; CBD; DLB 233; MTCW 1

Pound, Ezra (Weston Loomis) 1885-1972
.... **CLC 1, 2, 3, 4, 5, 7, 10, 13, 18, 34, 48, 50, 112; PC 4; WLC 5**
See also AAYA 47; AMW; AMWR 1; CA 5-8R; 37-40R; CANR 40; CDALB 1917-1929; CP 1; DA; DA3; DAB; DAC; DAM MST, POET; DLB 4, 45, 63; DLBD 15; EFS 2; EWL 3; EXPP; LMFS 2; MAL 5; MTCW 1, 2; MTFW 2005; PAB; PFS 2, 8, 16; RGAL 4; TUS; WP

Povod, Reinaldo 1959-1994 .... **CLC 44**
See also CA 136; 146; CANR 83

Powell, Adam Clayton, Jr. 1908-1972
.... **BLC 3; CLC 89**
See also BW 1, 3; CA 102; 33-36R; CANR 86; DAM MULT

Powell, Anthony 1905-2000 . **CLC 1, 3, 7, 9, 10, 31**
See also BRW 7; CA 1-4R; 189; CANR 1, 32, 62, 107; CDBLB 1945-1960; CN 1, 2, 3, 4, 5, 6; DLB 15; EWL 3; MTCW 1, 2; MTFW 2005; RGEL 2; TEA

Powell, Dawn 1896(?)-1965 .... **CLC 66**
See also CA 5-8R; CANR 121; DLBY 1997

Powell, Padgett 1952- .... **CLC 34**
See also CA 126; CANR 63, 101; CSW; DLB 234; DLBY 01

Powell, (Oval) Talmage 1920-2000
See Queen, Ellery
See also CA 5-8R; CANR 2, 80

Power, Susan 1961- .... **CLC 91**
See also BYA 14; CA 160; CANR 135; NFS 11

Powers, J(ames) F(arl) 1917-1999 ... **CLC 1, 4, 8, 57; SSC 4**
See also CA 1-4R; 181; CANR 2, 61; CN 1, 2, 3, 4, 5, 6; DLB 130; MTCW 1; RGAL 4; RGSF 2

Powers, John J(ames) 1945-
See Powers, John R.
See also CA 69-72

Powers, John R. .... **CLC 66**
See Powers, John J(ames)

Powers, Richard 1957- .... **CLC 93**
See also AMWS 9; BPFB 3; CA 148; CANR 80; CN 6, 7; MTFW 2005; TCLE 1:2

Pownall, David 1938- .... **CLC 10**
See also CA 89-92, 180; CAAS 18; CANR 49, 101; CBD; CD 5, 6; CN 4, 5, 6, 7; DLB 14

Powys, John Cowper 1872-1963 .. **CLC 7, 9, 15, 46, 125**
See also CA 85-88; CANR 106; DLB 15, 255; EWL 3; FANT; MTCW 1, 2; MTFW 2005; RGEL 2; SUFW

Powys, T(heodore) F(rancis) 1875-1953
.... **TCLC 9**
See also BRWS 8; CA 106; 189; DLB 36, 162; EWL 3; FANT; RGEL 2; SUFW

Pozzo, Modesta
See Fonte, Moderata

Prado (Calvo), Pedro 1886-1952 .. **TCLC 75**
See also CA 131; DLB 283; HW 1; LAW

Prager, Emily 1952- .... **CLC 56**
See also CA 204

Pratchett, Terry 1948- .... **CLC 197**
See also AAYA 19, 54; BPFB 3; CA 143; CANR 87, 126; CLR 64; CN 6, 7; CPW; CWRI 5; FANT; MTFW 2005; SATA 82, 139; SFW 4; SUFW 2

Pratolini, Vasco 1913-1991 .... **TCLC 124**
See also CA 211; DLB 177; EWL 3; RGWL 2, 3

Pratt, E(dwin) J(ohn) 1883(?)-1964
.... **CLC 19**
See also CA 141; 93-96; CANR 77; DAC; DAM POET; DLB 92; EWL 3; RGEL 2; TWA

Premchand .... **TCLC 21**
See Srivastava, Dhanpat Rai
See also EWL 3

Prescott, William Hickling 1796-1859
.... **NCLC 163**
See also DLB 1, 30, 59, 235

Preseren, France 1800-1849 .... **NCLC 127**
See also CDWLB 4; DLB 147

Preussler, Otfried 1923- .... **CLC 17**
See also CA 77-80; SATA 24

Prevert, Jacques (Henri Marie) 1900-1977
.... **CLC 15**
See also CA 77-80; 69-72; CANR 29, 61; DLB 258; EWL 3; GFL 1789 to the Present; IDFW 3, 4; MTCW 1; RGWL 2, 3; SATA-Obit 30

Prevost, (Antoine Francois) 1697-1763
.... **LC 1**
See also DLB 314; EW 4; GFL Beginnings to 1789; RGWL 2, 3

Price, Reynolds 1933- .... **CLC 3, 6, 13, 43, 50, 63, 212; SSC 22**
See also AMWS 6; CA 1-4R; CANR 1, 37, 57, 87, 128; CN 1, 2, 3, 4, 5, 6, 7; CSW; DAM NOV; DLB 2, 218, 278; EWL 3; INT CANR-37; MAL 5; MTFW 2005; NFS 18

Price, Richard 1949- .... **CLC 6, 12**
See also CA 49-52; CANR 3, 147; CN 7; DLBY 1981

Prichard, Katharine Susannah 1883-1969
.... **CLC 46**
See also CA 11-12; CANR 33; CAP 1; DLB 260; MTCW 1; RGEL 2; RGSF 2; SATA 66

Priestley, J(ohn) B(oynton) 1894-1984
.... **CLC 2, 5, 9, 34**
See also BRW 7; CA 9-12R; 113; CANR 33; CDBLB 1914-1945; CN 1, 2, 3; DA3; DAM DRAM, NOV; DLB 10, 34, 77, 100, 139; DLBY 1984; EWL 3; MTCW 1, 2; MTFW 2005; RGEL 2; SFW 4

Prince 1958- .... **CLC 35**
See also CA 213

Prince, F(rank) T(empleton) 1912-2003
.... **CLC 22**
See also CA 101; 219; CANR 43, 79; CP 1, 2, 3, 4, 5, 6, 7; DLB 20

Prince Kropotkin
See Kropotkin, Peter (Aleksieevich)

Prior, Matthew 1664-1721 .... **LC 4**
See also DLB 95; RGEL 2

Prishvin, Mikhail 1873-1954 .... **TCLC 75**
See Prishvin, Mikhail Mikhailovich

Prishvin, Mikhail Mikhailovich
See Prishvin, Mikhail
See also DLB 272; EWL 3

Pritchard, William H(arrison) 1932-
.... **CLC 34**
See also CA 65-68; CANR 23, 95; DLB 111

Pritchett, V(ictor) S(awdon) 1900-1997
.... **CLC 5, 13, 15, 41; SSC 14**
See also BPFB 3; BRWS 3; CA 61-64; 157; CANR 31, 63; CN 1, 2, 3, 4, 5, 6; DAM NOV; DLB 15, 139; EWL 3; MTCW 1, 2; MTFW 2005; RGEL 2; RGSF 2; TEA

Private 19022
See Manning, Frederic

Probst, Mark 1925- .... **CLC 59**
See also CA 130

Procaccino, Michael
See Cristofer, Michael

Proclus c. 412-c. 485 .... **CMLC 81**

Prokosch, Frederic 1908-1989 ..... **CLC 4, 48**
See also CA 73-76; 128; CANR 82; CN 1, 2, 3, 4; CP 1, 2, 3, 4; DLB 48; MTCW 2

Propertius, Sextus c. 50B.C.-c. 16B.C.
.... **CMLC 32**
See also AW 2; CDWLB 1; DLB 211; RGWL 2, 3; WLIT 8

Prophet, The
See Dreiser, Theodore

Prose, Francine 1947- .... **CLC 45, 231**
See also AMWS 16; CA 109; 112; CANR 46, 95, 132; DLB 234; MTFW 2005; SATA 101, 149

Protagoras c. 490B.C.-420B.C. .... **CMLC 85**
See also DLB 176

Proudhon
See Cunha, Euclides (Rodrigues Pimenta) da

Proulx, Annie
See Proulx, E. Annie

Proulx, E. Annie 1935- .... **CLC 81, 158**
See also AMWS 7; BPFB 3; CA 145; CANR 65, 110; CN 6, 7; CPW 1; DA3; DAM POP; MAL 5; MTCW 2; MTFW 2005; SSFS 18, 23

Proulx, Edna Annie
See Proulx, E. Annie

Ragni, Gerome 1942-1991 .... **CLC 17**
See also CA 105; 134

Rahv, Philip .... **CLC 24**
See Greenberg, Ivan
See also DLB 137; MAL 5

Raimund, Ferdinand Jakob 1790-1836
.... **NCLC 69**
See also DLB 90

Raine, Craig (Anthony) 1944- .... **CLC 32, 103**
See also CA 108; CANR 29, 51, 103; CP 3, 4, 5, 6, 7; DLB 40; PFS 7

Raine, Kathleen (Jessie) 1908-2003 . **CLC 7, 45**
See also CA 85-88; 218; CANR 46, 109; CP 1, 2, 3, 4, 5, 6; DLB 20; EWL 3; MTCW 1; RGEL 2

Rainis, Janis 1865-1929 .... **TCLC 29**
See also CA 170; CDWLB 4; DLB 220; EWL 3

Rakosi, Carl .... **CLC 47**
See Rawley, Callman
See also CA 228; CAAS 5; CP 1, 2, 3, 4, 5, 6, 7; DLB 193

Ralegh, Sir Walter
See Raleigh, Sir Walter
See also BRW 1; RGEL 2; WP

Raleigh, Richard
See Lovecraft, H. P.

Raleigh, Sir Walter 1554(?)-1618 ...... **LC 31, 39; PC 31**
See Ralegh, Sir Walter
See also CDBLB Before 1660; DLB 172; EXPP; PFS 14; TEA

Rallentando, H. P.
See Sayers, Dorothy L(eigh)

Ramal, Walter
See de la Mare, Walter (John)

Ramana Maharshi 1879-1950 .... **TCLC 84**

Ramoacn y Cajal, Santiago 1852-1934
.... **TCLC 93**

Ramon, Juan
See Jimenez (Mantecon), Juan Ramon

Ramos, Graciliano 1892-1953 .... **TCLC 32**
See also CA 167; DLB 307; EWL 3; HW 2; LAW; WLIT 1

Rampersad, Arnold 1941- .... **CLC 44**
See also BW 2, 3; CA 127; 133; CANR 81; DLB 111; INT CA-133

Rampling, Anne
See Rice, Anne
See also GLL 2

Ramsay, Allan 1686(?)-1758 .... **LC 29**
See also DLB 95; RGEL 2

Ramsay, Jay
See Campbell, (John) Ramsey

Ramuz, Charles-Ferdinand 1878-1947
.... **TCLC 33**
See also CA 165; EWL 3

Rand, Ayn 1905-1982 ..... **CLC 3, 30, 44, 79; WLC 5**
See also AAYA 10; AMWS 4; BPFB 3; BYA 12; CA 13-16R; 105; CANR 27, 73; CDALBS; CN 1, 2, 3; CPW; DA; DA3; DAC; DAM MST, NOV, POP; DLB 227, 279; MTCW 1, 2; MTFW 2005; NFS 10, 16; RGAL 4; SFW 4; TUS; YAW

Randall, Dudley (Felker) 1914-2000
.... **BLC 3; CLC 1, 135**
See also BW 1, 3; CA 25-28R; 189; CANR 23, 82; CP 1, 2, 3, 4, 5; DAM MULT; DLB 41; PFS 5

Randall, Robert
See Silverberg, Robert

Ranger, Ken
See Creasey, John

Rank, Otto 1884-1939 .... **TCLC 115**

Ransom, John Crowe 1888-1974 . **CLC 2, 4, 5, 11, 24; PC 61**
See also AMW; CA 5-8R; 49-52; CANR 6, 34; CDALBS; CP 1, 2; DLB 45, 63; EWL 3; EXPP; MAL 5; MTCW 1, 2; MTFW 2005; RGAL 4; TUS

Rao, Raja 1908-2006 .... **CLC 25, 56**
See also CA 73-76; CANR 51; CN 1, 2, 3, 4, 5, 6; DAM NOV; DLB 323; EWL 3; MTCW 1, 2; MTFW 2005; RGEL 2; RGSF 2

Raphael, Frederic (Michael) 1931- .. **CLC 2, 14**
See also CA 1-4R; CANR 1, 86; CN 1, 2, 3, 4, 5, 6, 7; DLB 14, 319; TCLE 1:2

Ratcliffe, James P.
See Mencken, H(enry) L(ouis)

Rathbone, Julian 1935- .... **CLC 41**
See also CA 101; CANR 34, 73, 152

Rattigan, Terence (Mervyn) 1911-1977
.... **CLC 7; DC 18**
See also BRWS 7; CA 85-88; 73-76; CBD; CDBLB 1945-1960; DAM DRAM; DFS 8; DLB 13; IDFW 3, 4; MTCW 1, 2; MTFW 2005; RGEL 2

Ratushinskaya, Irina 1954- .... **CLC 54**
See also CA 129; CANR 68; CWW 2

Raven, Simon (Arthur Noel) 1927-2001
.... **CLC 14**
See also CA 81-84; 197; CANR 86; CN 1, 2, 3, 4, 5, 6; DLB 271

Ravenna, Michael
See Welty, Eudora

Rawley, Callman 1903-2004
See Rakosi, Carl
See also CA 21-24R; 228; CANR 12, 32, 91

Rawlings, Marjorie Kinnan 1896-1953
.... **TCLC 4**
See also AAYA 20; AMWS 10; ANW; BPFB 3; BYA 3; CA 104; 137; CANR 74; CLR 63; DLB 9, 22, 102; DLBD 17; JRDA; MAICYA 1, 2; MAL 5; MTCW 2; MTFW 2005; RGAL 4; SATA 100; WCH; YABC 1; YAW

Ray, Satyajit 1921-1992 .... **CLC 16, 76**
See also CA 114; 137; DAM MULT

Read, Herbert Edward 1893-1968 .... **CLC 4**
See also BRW 6; CA 85-88; 25-28R; DLB 20, 149; EWL 3; PAB; RGEL 2

Read, Piers Paul 1941- .... **CLC 4, 10, 25**
See also CA 21-24R; CANR 38, 86, 150; CN 2, 3, 4, 5, 6, 7; DLB 14; SATA 21

Reade, Charles 1814-1884 .... **NCLC 2, 74**
See also DLB 21; RGEL 2

Reade, Hamish
See Gray, Simon (James Holliday)

Reading, Peter 1946- .... **CLC 47**
See also BRWS 8; CA 103; CANR 46, 96; CP 5, 6, 7; DLB 40

Reaney, James 1926- .... **CLC 13**
See also CA 41-44R; CAAS 15; CANR 42; CD 5, 6; CP 1, 2, 3, 4, 5, 6, 7; DAC; DAM MST; DLB 68; RGEL 2; SATA 43

Rebreanu, Liviu 1885-1944 .... **TCLC 28**
See also CA 165; DLB 220; EWL 3

Rechy, John 1934- .... **CLC 1, 7, 14, 18, 107; HLC 2**
See also CA 5-8R, 195; CAAE 195; CAAS 4; CANR 6, 32, 64, 152; CN 1, 2, 3, 4, 5, 6, 7; DAM MULT; DLB 122, 278; DLBY 1982; HW 1, 2; INT CANR-6; LLW; MAL 5; RGAL 4

Rechy, John Francisco
See Rechy, John

Redcam, Tom 1870-1933 .... **TCLC 25**

Reddin, Keith 1956- .... **CLC 67**
See also CAD; CD 6

Redgrove, Peter (William) 1932-2003
.... **CLC 6, 41**
See also BRWS 6; CA 1-4R; 217; CANR 3, 39, 77; CP 1, 2, 3, 4, 5, 6, 7; DLB 40; TCLE 1:2

Redmon, Anne .... **CLC 22**
See Nightingale, Anne Redmon
See also DLBY 1986

Reed, Eliot
See Ambler, Eric

Reed, Ishmael 1938- ... **BLC 3; CLC 2, 3, 5, 6, 13, 32, 60, 174; PC 68**
See also AFAW 1, 2; AMWS 10; BPFB 3; BW 2, 3; CA 21-24R; CANR 25, 48, 74, 128; CN 1, 2, 3, 4, 5, 6, 7; CP 1, 2, 3, 4, 5, 6, 7; CSW; DA3; DAM MULT; DLB 2, 5, 33, 169, 227; DLBD 8; EWL 3; LMFS 2; MAL 5; MSW; MTCW 1, 2; MTFW 2005; PFS 6; RGAL 4; TCWW 2

Reed, John (Silas) 1887-1920 .... **TCLC 9**
See also CA 106; 195; MAL 5; TUS

Reed, Lou .... **CLC 21**
See Firbank, Louis

Reese, Lizette Woodworth 1856-1935
.... **PC 29; TCLC 181**
See also CA 180; DLB 54

Reeve, Clara 1729-1807 .... **NCLC 19**
See also DLB 39; RGEL 2

Reich, Wilhelm 1897-1957 .... **TCLC 57**
See also CA 199

Reid, Christopher (John) 1949- ...... **CLC 33**
See also CA 140; CANR 89; CP 4, 5, 6, 7; DLB 40; EWL 3

Reid, Desmond
See Moorcock, Michael

Reid Banks, Lynne 1929-
See Banks, Lynne Reid
See also AAYA 49; CA 1-4R; CANR 6, 22, 38, 87; CLR 24; CN 1, 2, 3, 7; JRDA; MAICYA 1, 2; SATA 22, 75, 111, 165; YAW

Reilly, William K.
See Creasey, John

Reiner, Max
See Caldwell, (Janet Miriam) Taylor (Holland)

Reis, Ricardo
See Pessoa, Fernando (Antonio Nogueira)

Reizenstein, Elmer Leopold
See Rice, Elmer (Leopold)
See also EWL 3

Remarque, Erich Maria 1898-1970
.... **CLC 21**
See also AAYA 27; BPFB 3; CA 77-80; 29-32R; CDWLB 2; DA; DA3; DAB; DAC; DAM MST, NOV; DLB 56; EWL 3; EXPN; LAIT 3; MTCW 1, 2; MTFW 2005; NFS 4; RGHL; RGWL 2, 3

Remington, Frederic S(ackrider) 1861-1909
.... **TCLC 89**
See also CA 108; 169; DLB 12, 186, 188; SATA 41; TCWW 2

Remizov, A.
See Remizov, Aleksei (Mikhailovich)

Remizov, A. M.
See Remizov, Aleksei (Mikhailovich)

Remizov, Aleksei (Mikhailovich) 1877-1957
.... **TCLC 27**
See Remizov, Alexey Mikhaylovich
See also CA 125; 133; DLB 295

Remizov, Alexey Mikhaylovich
See Remizov, Aleksei (Mikhailovich)
See also EWL 3

Renan, Joseph Ernest 1823-1892
.... **NCLC 26, 145**
See also GFL 1789 to the Present

Renard, Jules(-Pierre) 1864-1910 . **TCLC 17**
See also CA 117; 202; GFL 1789 to the Present

Rivera, Tomas 1935-1984 .... **HLCS 2**
See also CA 49-52; CANR 32; DLB 82; HW 1; LLW; RGAL 4; SSFS 15; TCWW 2; WLIT 1

Rivers, Conrad Kent 1933-1968 .... **CLC 1**
See also BW 1; CA 85-88; DLB 41

Rivers, Elfrida
See Bradley, Marion Zimmer
See also GLL 1

Riverside, John
See Heinlein, Robert A.

Rizal, Jose 1861-1896 .... **NCLC 27**

Roa Bastos, Augusto 1917-2005 ..... **CLC 45; HLC 2**
See also CA 131; 238; CWW 2; DAM MULT; DLB 113; EWL 3; HW 1; LAW; RGSF 2; WLIT 1

Roa Bastos, Augusto Jose Antonio
See Roa Bastos, Augusto

Robbe-Grillet, Alain 1922- ... **CLC 1, 2, 4, 6, 8, 10, 14, 43, 128**
See also BPFB 3; CA 9-12R; CANR 33, 65, 115; CWW 2; DLB 83; EW 13; EWL 3; GFL 1789 to the Present; IDFW 3, 4; MTCW 1, 2; MTFW 2005; RGWL 2, 3; SSFS 15

Robbins, Harold 1916-1997 .... **CLC 5**
See also BPFB 3; CA 73-76; 162; CANR 26, 54, 112, 156; DA3; DAM NOV; MTCW 1, 2

Robbins, Thomas Eugene 1936-
See Robbins, Tom
See also CA 81-84; CANR 29, 59, 95, 139; CN 7; CPW; CSW; DA3; DAM NOV, POP; MTCW 1, 2; MTFW 2005

Robbins, Tom .... **CLC 9, 32, 64**
See Robbins, Thomas Eugene
See also AAYA 32; AMWS 10; BEST 90:3; BPFB 3; CN 3, 4, 5, 6, 7; DLBY 1980

Robbins, Trina 1938- .... **CLC 21**
See also AAYA 61; CA 128; CANR 152

Roberts, Charles G(eorge) D(ouglas) 1860-1943 .... **SSC 91; TCLC 8**
See also CA 105; 188; CLR 33; CWRI 5; DLB 92; RGEL 2; RGSF 2; SATA 88; SATA-Brief 29

Roberts, Elizabeth Madox 1886-1941
.... **TCLC 68**
See also CA 111; 166; CLR 100; CWRI 5; DLB 9, 54, 102; RGAL 4; RHW; SATA 33; SATA-Brief 27; TCWW 2; WCH

Roberts, Kate 1891-1985 .... **CLC 15**
See also CA 107; 116; DLB 319

Roberts, Keith (John Kingston) 1935-2000
.... **CLC 14**
See also BRWS 10; CA 25-28R; CANR 46; DLB 261; SFW 4

Roberts, Kenneth (Lewis) 1885-1957
.... **TCLC 23**
See also CA 109; 199; DLB 9; MAL 5; RGAL 4; RHW

Roberts, Michele (Brigitte) 1949- .. **CLC 48, 178**
See also CA 115; CANR 58, 120; CN 6, 7; DLB 231; FW

Robertson, Ellis
See Ellison, Harlan; Silverberg, Robert

Robertson, Thomas William 1829-1871
.... **NCLC 35**
See Robertson, Tom
See also DAM DRAM

Robertson, Tom
See Robertson, Thomas William
See also RGEL 2

Robeson, Kenneth
See Dent, Lester

Robinson, Edwin Arlington 1869-1935
.... **PC 1, 35; TCLC 5, 101**
See also AMW; CA 104; 133; CDALB 1865-1917; DA; DAC; DAM MST; POET; DLB 54; EWL 3; EXPP; MAL 5; MTCW 1, 2; MTFW 2005; PAB; PFS 4; RGAL 4; WP

Robinson, Henry Crabb 1775-1867
.... **NCLC 15**
See also DLB 107

Robinson, Jill 1936- .... **CLC 10**
See also CA 102; CANR 120; INT CA-102

Robinson, Kim Stanley 1952- .... **CLC 34**
See also AAYA 26; CA 126; CANR 113, 139; CN 6, 7; MTFW 2005; SATA 109; SCFW 2; SFW 4

Robinson, Lloyd
See Silverberg, Robert

Robinson, Marilynne 1944- ..... **CLC 25, 180**
See also AAYA 69; CA 116; CANR 80, 140; CN 4, 5, 6, 7; DLB 206; MTFW 2005; NFS 24

Robinson, Mary 1758-1800 .... **NCLC 142**
See also DLB 158; FW

Robinson, Smokey .... **CLC 21**
See Robinson, William, Jr.

Robinson, William, Jr. 1940-
See Robinson, Smokey
See also CA 116

Robison, Mary 1949- .... **CLC 42, 98**
See also CA 113; 116; CANR 87; CN 4, 5, 6, 7; DLB 130; INT CA-116; RGSF 2

Roches, Catherine des 1542-1587 .... **LC 117**
See also DLB 327

Rochester
See Wilmot, John
See also RGEL 2

Rod, Edouard 1857-1910 .... **TCLC 52**

Roddenberry, Eugene Wesley 1921-1991
See Roddenberry, Gene
See also CA 110; 135; CANR 37; SATA 45; SATA-Obit 69

Roddenberry, Gene .... **CLC 17**
See Roddenberry, Eugene Wesley
See also AAYA 5; SATA-Obit 69

Rodgers, Mary 1931- .... **CLC 12**
See also BYA 5; CA 49-52; CANR 8, 55, 90; CLR 20; CWRI 5; INT CANR-8; JRDA; MAICYA 1, 2; SATA 8, 130

Rodgers, W(illiam) R(obert) 1909-1969
.... **CLC 7**
See also CA 85-88; DLB 20; RGEL 2

Rodman, Eric
See Silverberg, Robert

Rodman, Howard 1920(?)-1985 ...... **CLC 65**
See also CA 118

Rodman, Maia
See Wojciechowska, Maia (Teresa)

Rodo, Jose Enrique 1871(?)-1917 ... **HLCS 2**
See also CA 178; EWL 3; HW 2; LAW

Rodolph, Utto
See Ouologuem, Yambo

Rodriguez, Claudio 1934-1999 .... **CLC 10**
See also CA 188; DLB 134

Rodriguez, Richard 1944- .. **CLC 155; HLC 2**
See also AMWS 14; CA 110; CANR 66, 116; DAM MULT; DLB 82, 256; HW 1, 2; LAIT 5; LLW; MTFW 2005; NCFS 3; WLIT 1

Roelvaag, O(le) E(dvart) 1876-1931
See Rolvaag, O(le) E(dvart)
See also CA 117; 171

Roethke, Theodore (Huebner) 1908-1963
...... **CLC 1, 3, 8, 11, 19, 46, 101; PC 15**
See also AMW; CA 81-84; CABS 2; CDALB 1941-1968; DA3; DAM POET; DLB 5, 206; EWL 3; EXPP; MAL 5; MTCW 1, 2; PAB; PFS 3; RGAL 4; WP

Rogers, Carl R(ansom) 1902-1987
.... **TCLC 125**
See also CA 1-4R; 121; CANR 1, 18; MTCW 1

Rogers, Samuel 1763-1855 .... **NCLC 69**
See also DLB 93; RGEL 2

Rogers, Thomas Hunton 1927- .... **CLC 57**
See also CA 89-92; INT CA-89-92

Rogers, Will(iam Penn Adair) 1879-1935
.... **NNAL; TCLC 8, 71**
See also CA 105; 144; DA3; DAM MULT; DLB 11; MTCW 2

Rogin, Gilbert 1929- .... **CLC 18**
See also CA 65-68; CANR 15

Rohan, Koda
See Koda Shigeyuki

Rohlfs, Anna Katharine Green
See Green, Anna Katharine

Rohmer, Eric .... **CLC 16**
See Scherer, Jean-Marie Maurice

Rohmer, Sax .... **TCLC 28**
See Ward, Arthur Henry Sarsfield
See also DLB 70; MSW; SUFW

Roiphe, Anne 1935- .... **CLC 3, 9**
See also CA 89-92; CANR 45, 73, 138; DLBY 1980; INT CA-89-92

Roiphe, Anne Richardson
See Roiphe, Anne

Rojas, Fernando de 1475-1541 .. **HLCS 1, 2; LC 23**
See also DLB 286; RGWL 2, 3

Rojas, Gonzalo 1917- .... **HLCS 2**
See also CA 178; HW 2; LAWS 1

Roland (de la Platiere), Marie-Jeanne 1754-1793 .... **LC 98**
See also DLB 314

Rolfe, Frederick (William Serafino Austin Lewis Mary) 1860-1913 .... **TCLC 12**
See Al Siddik
See also CA 107; 210; DLB 34, 156; RGEL 2

Rolland, Romain 1866-1944 .... **TCLC 23**
See also CA 118; 197; DLB 65, 284; EWL 3; GFL 1789 to the Present; RGWL 2, 3

Rolle, Richard c. 1300-c. 1349 ...... **CMLC 21**
See also DLB 146; LMFS 1; RGEL 2

Rolvaag, O(le) E(dvart) .... **TCLC 17**
See Roelvaag, O(le) E(dvart)
See also DLB 9, 212; MAL 5; NFS 5; RGAL 4

Romain Arnaud, Saint
See Aragon, Louis

Romains, Jules 1885-1972 .... **CLC 7**
See also CA 85-88; CANR 34; DLB 65, 321; EWL 3; GFL 1789 to the Present; MTCW 1

Romero, Jose Ruben 1890-1952 ... **TCLC 14**
See also CA 114; 131; EWL 3; HW 1; LAW

Ronsard, Pierre de 1524-1585 ...... **LC 6, 54; PC 11**
See also DLB 327; EW 2; GFL Beginnings to 1789; RGWL 2, 3; TWA

Rooke, Leon 1934- .... **CLC 25, 34**
See also CA 25-28R; CANR 23, 53; CCA 1; CPW; DAM POP

Roosevelt, Franklin Delano 1882-1945
.... **TCLC 93**
See also CA 116; 173; LAIT 3

Roosevelt, Theodore 1858-1919 .... **TCLC 69**
See also CA 115; 170; DLB 47, 186, 275

Roper, William 1498-1578 .... **LC 10**

Roquelaure, A. N.
See Rice, Anne

Rosa, Joao Guimaraes 1908-1967 . **CLC 23; HLCS 1**
See Guimaraes Rosa, Joao
See also CA 89-92; DLB 113, 307; EWL 3; WLIT 1

Rose, Wendy 1948- ..... CLC 85; NNAL; PC 13
See also CA 53-56; CANR 5, 51; CWP; DAM MULT; DLB 175; PFS 13; RGAL 4; SATA 12

Rosen, R. D.
See Rosen, Richard (Dean)

Rosen, Richard (Dean) 1949- .... CLC 39
See also CA 77-80; CANR 62, 120; CMW 4; INT CANR-30

Rosenberg, Isaac 1890-1918 .... TCLC 12
See also BRW 6; CA 107; 188; DLB 20, 216; EWL 3; PAB; RGEL 2

Rosenblatt, Joe .... CLC 15
See Rosenblatt, Joseph
See also CP 3, 4, 5, 6, 7

Rosenblatt, Joseph 1933-
See Rosenblatt, Joe
See also CA 89-92; CP 1, 2; INT CA-89-92

Rosenfeld, Samuel
See Tzara, Tristan

Rosenstock, Sami
See Tzara, Tristan

Rosenstock, Samuel
See Tzara, Tristan

Rosenthal, M(acha) L(ouis) 1917-1996
.... CLC 28
See also CA 1-4R; 152; CAAS 6; CANR 4, 51; CP 1, 2, 3, 4, 5, 6; DLB 5; SATA 59

Ross, Barnaby
See Dannay, Frederic; Lee, Manfred B.

Ross, Bernard L.
See Follett, Ken

Ross, J. H.
See Lawrence, T(homas) E(dward)

Ross, John Hume
See Lawrence, T(homas) E(dward)

Ross, Martin 1862-1915
See Martin, Violet Florence
See also DLB 135; GLL 2; RGEL 2; RGSF 2

Ross, (James) Sinclair 1908-1996 .. CLC 13; SSC 24
See also CA 73-76; CANR 81; CN 1, 2, 3, 4, 5, 6; DAC; DAM MST; DLB 88; RGEL 2; RGSF 2; TCWW 1, 2

Rossetti, Christina 1830-1894 . NCLC 2, 50, 66; PC 7; WLC 5
See also AAYA 51; BRW 5; BYA 4; CLR 115; DA; DA3; DAB; DAC; DAM MST, POET; DLB 35, 163, 240; EXPP; FL 1:3; LATS 1:1; MAICYA 1, 2; PFS 10, 14; RGEL 2; SATA 20; TEA; WCH

Rossetti, Christina Georgina
See Rossetti, Christina

Rossetti, Dante Gabriel 1828-1882
.... NCLC 4, 77; PC 44; WLC 5
See also AAYA 51; BRW 5; CDBLB 1832-1890; DA; DAB; DAC; DAM MST, POET; DLB 35; EXPP; RGEL 2; TEA

Rossi, Cristina Peri
See Peri Rossi, Cristina

Rossi, Jean-Baptiste 1931-2003
See Japrisot, Sebastien
See also CA 201; 215

Rossner, Judith 1935-2005 ...... CLC 6, 9, 29
See also AITN 2; BEST 90:3; BPFB 3; CA 17-20R; 242; CANR 18, 51, 73; CN 4, 5, 6, 7; DLB 6; INT CANR-18; MAL 5; MTCW 1, 2; MTFW 2005

Rossner, Judith Perelman
See Rossner, Judith

Rostand, Edmond (Eugene Alexis)
1868-1918 .... DC 10; TCLC 6, 37
See also CA 104; 126; DA; DA3; DAB; DAC; DAM DRAM, MST; DFS 1; DLB 192; LAIT 1; MTCW 1; RGWL 2, 3; TWA

Roth, Henry 1906-1995 ... CLC 2, 6, 11, 104
See also AMWS 9; CA 11-12; 149; CANR 38, 63; CAP 1; CN 1, 2, 3, 4, 5, 6; DA3; DLB 28; EWL 3; MAL 5; MTCW 1, 2; MTFW 2005; RGAL 4

Roth, (Moses) Joseph 1894-1939 .. TCLC 33
See also CA 160; DLB 85; EWL 3; RGWL 2, 3

Roth, Philip 1933- .. CLC 1, 2, 3, 4, 6, 9, 15, 22, 31, 47, 66, 86, 119, 201; SSC 26; WLC 5
See also AAYA 67; AMWR 2; AMWS 3; BEST 90:3; BPFB 3; CA 1-4R; CANR 1, 22, 36, 55, 89, 132; CDALB 1968-1988; CN 3, 4, 5, 6, 7; CPW 1; DA; DA3; DAB; DAC; DAM MST, NOV, POP; DLB 2, 28, 173; DLBY 1982; EWL 3; MAL 5; MTCW 1, 2; MTFW 2005; RGAL 4; RGHL; RGSF 2; SSFS 12, 18; TUS

Roth, Philip Milton
See Roth, Philip

Rothenberg, Jerome 1931- .... CLC 6, 57
See also CA 45-48; CANR 1, 106; CP 1, 2, 3, 4, 5, 6, 7; DLB 5, 193

Rotter, Pat ed. .... CLC 65

Roumain, Jacques (Jean Baptiste) 1907-1944
.... BLC 3; TCLC 19
See also BW 1; CA 117; 125; DAM MULT; EWL 3

Rourke, Constance Mayfield 1885-1941
.... TCLC 12
See also CA 107; 200; MAL 5; YABC 1

Rousseau, Jean-Baptiste 1671-1741 ...... LC 9

Rousseau, Jean-Jacques 1712-1778 .. LC 14, 36, 122; WLC 5
See also DA; DA3; DAB; DAC; DAM MST; DLB 314; EW 4; GFL Beginnings to 1789; LMFS 1; RGWL 2, 3; TWA

Roussel, Raymond 1877-1933 .... TCLC 20
See also CA 117; 201; EWL 3; GFL 1789 to the Present

Rovit, Earl (Herbert) 1927- .... CLC 7
See also CA 5-8R; CANR 12

Rowe, Elizabeth Singer 1674-1737 .... LC 44
See also DLB 39, 95

Rowe, Nicholas 1674-1718 .... LC 8
See also DLB 84; RGEL 2

Rowlandson, Mary 1637(?)-1678 .... LC 66
See also DLB 24, 200; RGAL 4

Rowley, Ames Dorrance
See Lovecraft, H. P.

Rowley, William 1585(?)-1626 . LC 100, 123
See also DFS 22; DLB 58; RGEL 2

Rowling, J.K. 1965- .... CLC 137, 217
See also AAYA 34; BYA 11, 13, 14; CA 173; CANR 128, 157; CLR 66, 80, 112; MAICYA 2; MTFW 2005; SATA 109; SUFW 2

Rowling, Joanne Kathleen
See Rowling, J.K.

Rowson, Susanna Haswell 1762(?)-1824
.... NCLC 5, 69
See also AMWS 15; DLB 37, 200; RGAL 4

Roy, Arundhati 1960(?)- .... CLC 109, 210
See also CA 163; CANR 90, 126; CN 7; DLB 323, 326; DLBY 1997; EWL 3; LATS 1:2; MTFW 2005; NFS 22; WWE 1

Roy, Gabrielle 1909-1983 .... CLC 10, 14
See also CA 53-56; 110; CANR 5, 61; CCA 1; DAB; DAC; DAM MST; DLB 68; EWL 3; MTCW 1; RGWL 2, 3; SATA 104; TCLE 1:2

Royko, Mike 1932-1997 .... CLC 109
See also CA 89-92; 157; CANR 26, 111; CPW

Rozanov, Vasilii Vasil'evich
See Rozanov, Vassili
See also DLB 295

Rozanov, Vasily Vasilyevich
See Rozanov, Vassili
See also EWL 3

Rozanov, Vassili 1856-1919 .... TCLC 104
See Rozanov, Vasilii Vasil'evich; Rozanov, Vasily Vasilyevich

Rozewicz, Tadeusz 1921- ..... CLC 9, 23, 139
See also CA 108; CANR 36, 66; CWW 2; DA3; DAM POET; DLB 232; EWL 3; MTCW 1, 2; MTFW 2005; RGHL; RGWL 3

Ruark, Gibbons 1941- .... CLC 3
See also CA 33-36R; CAAS 23; CANR 14, 31, 57; DLB 120

Rubens, Bernice (Ruth) 1923-2004
.... CLC 19, 31
See also CA 25-28R; 232; CANR 33, 65, 128; CN 1, 2, 3, 4, 5, 6, 7; DLB 14, 207, 326; MTCW 1

Rubin, Harold
See Robbins, Harold

Rudkin, (James) David 1936- .... CLC 14
See also CA 89-92; CBD; CD 5, 6; DLB 13

Rudnik, Raphael 1933- .... CLC 7
See also CA 29-32R

Ruffian, M.
See Hasek, Jaroslav (Matej Frantisek)

Ruiz, Jose Martinez .... CLC 11
See Martinez Ruiz, Jose

Ruiz, Juan c. 1283-c. 1350 .... CMLC 66

Rukeyser, Muriel 1913-1980 ...... CLC 6, 10, 15, 27; PC 12
See also AMWS 6; CA 5-8R; 93-96; CANR 26, 60; CP 1, 2, 3; DA3; DAM POET; DLB 48; EWL 3; FW; GLL 2; MAL 5; MTCW 1, 2; PFS 10; RGAL 4; SATA-Obit 22

Rule, Jane (Vance) 1931- .... CLC 27
See also CA 25-28R; CAAS 18; CANR 12, 87; CN 4, 5, 6, 7; DLB 60; FW

Rulfo, Juan 1918-1986 . CLC 8, 80; HLC 2; SSC 25
See also CA 85-88; 118; CANR 26; CD-WLB 3; DAM MULT; DLB 113; EWL 3; HW 1, 2; LAW; MTCW 1, 2; RGSF 2; RGWL 2, 3; WLIT 1

Rumi, Jalal al-Din 1207-1273 ..... CMLC 20; PC 45
See also AAYA 64; RGWL 2, 3; WLIT 6; WP

Runeberg, Johan 1804-1877 .... NCLC 41

Runyon, (Alfred) Damon 1884(?)-1946
.... TCLC 10
See also CA 107; 165; DLB 11, 86, 171; MAL 5; MTCW 2; RGAL 4

Rush, Norman 1933- .... CLC 44
See also CA 121; 126; CANR 130; INT CA-126

Rushdie, Salman 1947- .... CLC 23, 31, 55, 100, 191; SSC 83; WLCS
See also AAYA 65; BEST 89:3; BPFB 3; BRWS 4; CA 108; 111; CANR 33, 56, 108, 133; CN 4, 5, 6, 7; CPW 1; DA3; DAB; DAC; DAM MST, NOV, POP; DLB 194, 323, 326; EWL 3; FANT; INT CA-111; LATS 1:2; LMFS 2; MTCW 1, 2; MTFW 2005; NFS 22, 23; RGEL 2; RGSF 2; TEA; WLIT 4

Rushforth, Peter 1945-2005 .... CLC 19
See also CA 101; 243

Rushforth, Peter Scott
See Rushforth, Peter

Ruskin, John 1819-1900 .... TCLC 63
See also BRW 5; BYA 5; CA 114; 129; CD-BLB 1832-1890; DLB 55, 163, 190; RGEL 2; SATA 24; TEA; WCH

Russ, Joanna 1937- .... **CLC 15**
    See also BPFB 3; CA 25-28; CANR 11, 31,
    65; CN 4, 5, 6, 7; DLB 8; FW; GLL 1;
    MTCW 1; SCFW 1, 2; SFW 4
Russ, Richard Patrick
    See O'Brian, Patrick
Russell, George William 1867-1935
    See A.E.; Baker, Jean H.
    See also BRWS 8; CA 104; 153; CDBLB
    1890-1914; DAM POET; EWL 3; RGEL
    2
Russell, Jeffrey Burton 1934- .... **CLC 70**
    See also CA 25-28R; CANR 11, 28, 52
Russell, (Henry) Ken(neth Alfred) 1927-
    .... **CLC 16**
    See also CA 105
Russell, William Martin 1947-
    See Russell, Willy
    See also CA 164; CANR 107
Russell, Willy .... **CLC 60**
    See Russell, William Martin
    See also CBD; CD 5, 6; DLB 233
Russo, Richard 1949- .... **CLC 181**
    See also AMWS 12; CA 127; 133; CANR
    87, 114
Rutherford, Mark .... **TCLC 25**
    See White, William Hale
    See also DLB 18; RGEL 2
Ruysbroeck, Jan van 1293-1381 . **CMLC 85**
Ruyslinck, Ward .... **CLC 14**
    See Belser, Reimond Karel Maria de
Ryan, Cornelius (John) 1920-1974 ... **CLC 7**
    See also CA 69-72; 53-56; CANR 38
Ryan, Michael 1946- .... **CLC 65**
    See also CA 49-52; CANR 109; DLBY
    1982
Ryan, Tim
    See Dent, Lester
Rybakov, Anatoli (Naumovich) 1911-1998
    .... **CLC 23, 53**
    See Rybakov, Anatolii (Naumovich)
    See also CA 126; 135; 172; SATA 79;
    SATA-Obit 108
Rybakov, Anatolii (Naumovich)
    See Rybakov, Anatoli (Naumovich)
    See also DLB 302; RGHL
Ryder, Jonathan
    See Ludlum, Robert
Ryga, George 1932-1987 .... **CLC 14**
    See also CA 101; 124; CANR 43, 90; CCA
    1; DAC; DAM MST; DLB 60
Rymer, Thomas 1643(?)-1713 .... **LC 132**
    See also DLB 101
S. H.
    See Hartmann, Sadakichi
S. S.
    See Sassoon, Siegfried (Lorraine)
Sa'adawi, al- Nawal
    See El Saadawi, Nawal
    See also AFW; EWL 3
Saadawi, Nawal El
    See El Saadawi, Nawal
    See also WLIT 2
Saba, Umberto 1883-1957 .... **TCLC 33**
    See also CA 144; CANR 79; DLB 114;
    EWL 3; RGWL 2, 3
Sabatini, Rafael 1875-1950 .... **TCLC 47**
    See also BPFB 3; CA 162; RHW
Sabato, Ernesto 1911- . **CLC 10, 23; HLC 2**
    See also CA 97-100; CANR 32, 65; CD-
    WLB 3; CWW 2; DAM MULT; DLB 145;
    EWL 3; HW 1, 2; LAW; MTCW 1, 2;
    MTFW 2005
Sa-Carneiro, Mario de 1890-1916
    .... **TCLC 83**
    See also DLB 287; EWL 3
Sacastru, Martin
    See Bioy Casares, Adolfo
    See also CWW 2

Sacher-Masoch, Leopold von 1836(?)-1895
    .... **NCLC 31**
Sachs, Hans 1494-1576 .... **LC 95**
    See also CDWLB 2; DLB 179; RGWL 2, 3
Sachs, Marilyn 1927- .... **CLC 35**
    See also AAYA 2; BYA 6; CA 17-20R;
    CANR 13, 47, 150; CLR 2; JRDA; MAI-
    CYA 1, 2; SAAS 2; SATA 3, 68, 164;
    SATA-Essay 110; WYA; YAW
Sachs, Marilyn Stickle
    See Sachs, Marilyn
Sachs, Nelly 1891-1970 .... **CLC 14, 98**
    See also CA 17-18; 25-28R; CANR 87;
    CAP 2; EWL 3; MTCW 2; MTFW 2005;
    PFS 20; RGHL; RGWL 2, 3
Sackler, Howard (Oliver) 1929-1982
    .... **CLC 14**
    See also CA 61-64; 108; CAD; CANR 30;
    DFS 15; DLB 7
Sacks, Oliver 1933- .... **CLC 67, 202**
    See also CA 53-56; CANR 28, 50, 76, 146;
    CPW; DA3; INT CANR-28; MTCW 1, 2;
    MTFW 2005
Sacks, Oliver Wolf
    See Sacks, Oliver
Sackville, Thomas 1536-1608 .... **LC 98**
    See also DAM DRAM; DLB 62, 132;
    RGEL 2
Sadakichi
    See Hartmann, Sadakichi
Sa'dawi, Nawal al-
    See El Saadawi, Nawal
    See also CWW 2
Sade, Donatien Alphonse Francois
    1740-1814 .... **NCLC 3, 47**
    See also DLB 314; EW 4; GFL Beginnings
    to 1789; RGWL 2, 3
Sade, Marquis de
    See Sade, Donatien Alphonse Francois
Sadoff, Ira 1945- .... **CLC 9**
    See also CA 53-56; CANR 5, 21, 109; DLB
    120
Saetone
    See Camus, Albert
Safire, William 1929- .... **CLC 10**
    See also CA 17-20R; CANR 31, 54, 91, 148
Sagan, Carl 1934-1996 .... **CLC 30, 112**
    See also AAYA 2, 62; CA 25-28R; 155;
    CANR 11, 36, 74; CPW; DA3; MTCW 1,
    2; MTFW 2005; SATA 58; SATA-Obit 94
Sagan, Francoise .... **CLC 3, 6, 9, 17, 36**
    See Quoirez, Francoise
    See also CWW 2; DLB 83; EWL 3; GFL
    1789 to the Present; MTCW 2
Sahgal, Nayantara (Pandit) 1927- .. **CLC 41**
    See also CA 9-12R; CANR 11, 88; CN 1,
    2, 3, 4, 5, 6, 7; DLB 323
Said, Edward W. 1935-2003 .... **CLC 123**
    See also CA 21-24R; 220; CANR 45, 74,
    107, 131; DLB 67; MTCW 2; MTFW
    2005
Saint, H(arry) F. 1941- .... **CLC 50**
    See also CA 127
St. Aubin de Teran, Lisa 1953-
    See Teran, Lisa St. Aubin de
    See also CA 118; 126; CN 6, 7; INT CA-
    126
Saint Birgitta of Sweden c. 1303-1373
    .... **CMLC 24**
Sainte-Beuve, Charles Augustin 1804-1869
    .... **NCLC 5**
    See also DLB 217; EW 6; GFL 1789 to the
    Present
Saint-Exupery, Antoine de 1900-1944
    .... **TCLC 2, 56, 169; WLC**
    See also AAYA 63; BPFB 3; BYA 3; CA
    108; 132; CLR 10; DA3; DAM NOV;
    DLB 72; EW 12; EWL 3; GFL 1789 to
    the Present; LAIT 3; MAICYA 1, 2;
    MTCW 1, 2; MTFW 2005; RGWL 2, 3;
    SATA 20; TWA

Saint-Exupery, Antoine Jean Baptiste Marie
    Roger de
    See Saint-Exupery, Antoine de
St. John, David
    See Hunt, E(verette) Howard, (Jr.)
St. John, J. Hector
    See Crevecoeur, Michel Guillaume Jean de
Saint-John Perse
    See Leger, (Marie-Rene Auguste) Alexis
    Saint-Leger
    See also EW 10; EWL 3; GFL 1789 to the
    Present; RGWL 2
Saintsbury, George (Edward Bateman)
    1845-1933 .... **TCLC 31**
    See also CA 160; DLB 57, 149
Sait Faik .... **TCLC 23**
    See Abasiyanik, Sait Faik
Saki .... **SSC 12; TCLC 3; WLC 5**
    See Munro, H(ector) H(ugh)
    See also BRWS 6; BYA 11; LAIT 2; RGEL
    2; SSFS 1; SUFW
Sala, George Augustus 1828-1895
    .... **NCLC 46**
Saladin 1138-1193 .... **CMLC 38**
Salama, Hannu 1936- .... **CLC 18**
    See also CA 244; EWL 3
Salamanca, J(ack) R(ichard) 1922- . **CLC 4,**
    15
    See also CA 25-28R; 193; CAAE 193
Salas, Floyd Francis 1931- .... **HLC 2**
    See also CA 119; CAAS 27; CANR 44, 75,
    93; DAM MULT; DLB 82; HW 1, 2;
    MTCW 2; MTFW 2005
Sale, J. Kirkpatrick
    See Sale, Kirkpatrick
Sale, John Kirkpatrick
    See Sale, Kirkpatrick
Sale, Kirkpatrick 1937- .... **CLC 68**
    See also CA 13-16R; CANR 10, 147
Salinas, Luis Omar 1937- . **CLC 90; HLC 2**
    See also AMWS 13; CA 131; CANR 81,
    153; DAM MULT; DLB 82; HW 1, 2
Salinas (y Serrano), Pedro 1891(?)-1951
    .... **TCLC 17**
    See also CA 117; DLB 134; EWL 3
Salinger, J.D. 1919- ...... **CLC 1, 3, 8, 12, 55,**
    56, 138; SSC 2, 28, 65; WLC 5
    See also AAYA 2, 36; AMW; AMWC 1;
    BPFB 3; CA 5-8R; CANR 39, 129;
    CDALB 1941-1968; CLR 18; CN 1, 2, 3,
    4, 5, 6, 7; CPW 1; DA; DA3; DAB; DAC;
    DAM MST, NOV, POP; DLB 2, 102, 173;
    EWL 3; EXPN; LAIT 4; MAICYA 1, 2;
    MAL 5; MTCW 1, 2; MTFW 2005; NFS
    1; RGAL 4; RGSF 2; SATA 67; SSFS 17;
    TUS; WYA; YAW
Salisbury, John
    See Caute, (John) David
Sallust c. 86B.C.-35B.C. .... **CMLC 68**
    See also AW 2; CDWLB 1; DLB 211;
    RGWL 2, 3
Salter, James 1925- . **CLC 7, 52, 59; SSC 58**
    See also AMWS 9; CA 73-76; CANR 107;
    DLB 130
Saltus, Edgar (Everton) 1855-1921
    .... **TCLC 8**
    See also CA 105; DLB 202; RGAL 4
Saltykov, Mikhail Evgrafovich 1826-1889
    .... **NCLC 16**
    See also DLB 238:
Saltykov-Shchedrin, N.
    See Saltykov, Mikhail Evgrafovich
Samarakis, Andonis
    See Samarakis, Antonis
    See also EWL 3
Samarakis, Antonis 1919-2003 .... **CLC 5**
    See Samarakis, Andonis
    See also CA 25-28R; 224; CAAS 16; CANR
    36

Author Index

Schelling, Friedrich Wilhelm Joseph von
1775-1854 .... **NCLC 30**
See also DLB 90
Scherer, Jean-Marie Maurice 1920-
See Rohmer, Eric
See also CA 110
Schevill, James (Erwin) 1920- .... **CLC 7**
See also CA 5-8R; CAAS 12; CAD; CD 5,
6; CP 1, 2, 3, 4, 5
Schiller, Friedrich von 1759-1805 .... **DC 12;
NCLC 39, 69, 166**
See also CDWLB 2; DAM DRAM; DLB
94; EW 5; RGWL 2, 3; TWA
Schisgal, Murray (Joseph) 1926- ...... **CLC 6**
See also CA 21-24R; CAD; CANR 48, 86;
CD 5, 6; MAL 5
Schlee, Ann 1934- .... **CLC 35**
See also CA 101; CANR 29, 88; SATA 44;
SATA-Brief 36
Schlegel, August Wilhelm von 1767-1845
.... **NCLC 15, 142**
See also DLB 94; RGWL 2, 3
Schlegel, Friedrich 1772-1829 ...... **NCLC 45**
See also DLB 90; EW 5; RGWL 2, 3; TWA
Schlegel, Johann Elias (von) 1719(?)-1749
.... **LC 5**
Schleiermacher, Friedrich 1768-1834
.... **NCLC 107**
See also DLB 90
Schlesinger, Arthur M(eier), Jr. 1917-
.... **CLC 84**
See also AITN 1; CA 1-4R; CANR 1, 28,
58, 105; DLB 17; INT CANR-28; MTCW
1, 2; SATA 61
Schlink, Bernhard 1944- .... **CLC 174**
See also CA 163; CANR 116; RGHL
Schmidt, Arno (Otto) 1914-1979 ..... **CLC 56**
See also CA 128; 109; DLB 69; EWL 3
Schmitz, Aron Hector 1861-1928
See Svevo, Italo
See also CA 104; 122; MTCW 1
Schnackenberg, Gjertrud 1953- .... **CLC 40;
PC 45**
See also AMWS 15; CA 116; CANR 100;
CP 5, 6, 7; CWP; DLB 120, 282; PFS 13
Schnackenberg, Gjertrud Cecelia
See Schnackenberg, Gjertrud
Schneider, Leonard Alfred 1925-1966
See Bruce, Lenny
See also CA 89-92
Schnitzler, Arthur 1862-1931 ... **DC 17; SSC
15, 61; TCLC 4**
See also CA 104; CDWLB 2; DLB 81, 118;
EW 8; EWL 3; RGSF 2; RGWL 2, 3
Schoenberg, Arnold Franz Walter 1874-1951
.... **TCLC 75**
See also CA 109; 188
Schonberg, Arnold
See Schoenberg, Arnold Franz Walter
Schopenhauer, Arthur 1788-1860
.... **NCLC 51, 157**
See also DLB 90; EW 5
Schor, Sandra (M.) 1932(?)-1990 .... **CLC 65**
See also CA 132
Schorer, Mark 1908-1977 .... **CLC 9**
See also CA 5-8R; 73-76; CANR 7; CN 1,
2; DLB 103
Schrader, Paul (Joseph) 1946- .... **CLC 26,
212**
See also CA 37-40R; CANR 41; DLB 44
Schreber, Daniel 1842-1911 .... **TCLC 123**
Schreiner, Olive (Emilie Albertina)
1855-1920 .... **TCLC 9**
See also AFW; BRWS 2; CA 105; 154;
DLB 18, 156, 190, 225; EWL 3; FW;
RGEL 2; TWA; WLIT 2; WWE 1

Schulberg, Budd (Wilson) 1914- ...... **CLC 7,
48**
See also BPFB 3; CA 25-28R; CANR 19,
87; CN 1, 2, 3, 4, 5, 6, 7; DLB 6, 26, 28;
DLBY 1981, 2001; MAL 5
Schulman, Arnold
See Trumbo, Dalton
Schulz, Bruno 1892-1942 ..... **SSC 13; TCLC
5, 51**
See also CA 115; 123; CANR 86; CDWLB
4; DLB 215; EWL 3; MTCW 2; MTFW
2005; RGSF 2; RGWL 2, 3
Schulz, Charles M. 1922-2000 .... **CLC 12**
See also AAYA 39; CA 9-12R; 187; CANR
6, 132; INT CANR-6; MTFW 2005;
SATA 10; SATA-Obit 118
Schulz, Charles Monroe
See Schulz, Charles M.
Schumacher, E(rnst) F(riedrich) 1911-1977
.... **CLC 80**
See also CA 81-84; 73-76; CANR 34, 85
Schumann, Robert 1810-1856 .... **NCLC 143**
Schuyler, George Samuel 1895-1977
.... **HR 1:3**
See also BW 2; CA 81-84; 73-76; CANR
42; DLB 29, 51
Schuyler, James Marcus 1923-1991 . **CLC 5,
23**
See also CA 101; 134; CP 1, 2, 3, 4, 5;
DAM POET; DLB 5, 169; EWL 3; INT
CA-101; MAL 5; WP
Schwartz, Delmore (David) 1913-1966
.... **CLC 2, 4, 10, 45, 87; PC 8**
See also AMWS 2; CA 17-18; 25-28R;
CANR 35; CAP 2; DLB 28, 48; EWL 3;
MAL 5; MTCW 1, 2; MTFW 2005; PAB;
RGAL 4; TUS
Schwartz, Ernst
See Ozu, Yasujiro
Schwartz, John Burnham 1965- ..... **CLC 59**
See also CA 132; CANR 116
Schwartz, Lynne Sharon 1939- .... **CLC 31**
See also CA 103; CANR 44, 89; DLB 218;
MTCW 2; MTFW 2005
Schwartz, Muriel A.
See Eliot, T(homas) S(tearns)
Schwarz-Bart, Andre 1928-2006 ... **CLC 2, 4**
See also CA 89-92; CANR 109; DLB 299;
RGHL
Schwarz-Bart, Simone 1938- ... **BLCS; CLC
7**
See also BW 2; CA 97-100; CANR 117;
EWL 3
Schwerner, Armand 1927-1999 .... **PC 42**
See also CA 9-12R; 179; CANR 50, 85; CP
2, 3, 4, 5, 6; DLB 165
**Schwitters, Kurt (Hermann Edward Karl
Julius)** 1887-1948 .... **TCLC 95**
See also CA 158
Schwob, Marcel (Mayer Andre) 1867-1905
.... **TCLC 20**
See also CA 117; 168; DLB 123; GFL 1789
to the Present
Sciascia, Leonardo 1921-1989 . **CLC 8, 9, 41**
See also CA 85-88; 130; CANR 35; DLB
177; EWL 3; MTCW 1; RGWL 2, 3
Scoppettone, Sandra 1936- .... **CLC 26**
See Early, Jack
See also AAYA 11, 65; BYA 8; CA 5-8R;
CANR 41, 73, 157; GLL 1; MAICYA 2;
MAICYAS 1; SATA 9, 92; WYA; YAW
Scorsese, Martin 1942- ...... **CLC 20, 89, 207**
See also AAYA 38; CA 110; 114; CANR
46, 85
Scotland, Jay
See Jakes, John

Scott, Duncan Campbell 1862-1947
.... **TCLC 6**
See also CA 104; 153; DAC; DLB 92;
RGEL 2
Scott, Evelyn 1893-1963 .... **CLC 43**
See also CA 104; 112; CANR 64; DLB 9,
48; RHW
Scott, F(rancis) R(eginald) 1899-1985
.... **CLC 22**
See also CA 101; 114; CANR 87; CP 1, 2,
3, 4; DLB 88; INT CA-101; RGEL 2
Scott, Frank
See Scott, F(rancis) R(eginald)
Scott, Joan .... **CLC 65**
Scott, Joanna 1960- .... **CLC 50**
See also CA 126; CANR 53, 92
Scott, Paul (Mark) 1920-1978 ..... **CLC 9, 60**
See also BRWS 1; CA 81-84; 77-80; CANR
33; CN 1, 2; DLB 14, 207, 326; EWL 3;
MTCW 1; RGEL 2; RHW; WWE 1
Scott, Ridley 1937- .... **CLC 183**
See also AAYA 13, 43
Scott, Sarah 1723-1795 .... **LC 44**
See also DLB 39
Scott, Sir Walter 1771-1832 ... **NCLC 15, 69,
110; PC 13; SSC 32; WLC 5**
See also AAYA 22; BRW 4; BYA 2; CD-
BLB 1789-1832; DA; DAB; DAC; DAM
MST, NOV, POET; DLB 93, 107, 116,
144, 159; GL 3; HGG; LAIT 1; RGEL 2;
RGSF 2; SSFS 10; SUFW 1; TEA; WLIT
3; YABC 2
Scribe, (Augustin) Eugene 1791-1861
.... **DC 5; NCLC 16**
See also DAM DRAM; DLB 192; GFL
1789 to the Present; RGWL 2, 3
Scrum, R.
See Crumb, R.
Scudery, Georges de 1601-1667 .... **LC 75**
See also GFL Beginnings to 1789
Scudery, Madeleine de 1607-1701 . **LC 2, 58**
See also DLB 268; GFL Beginnings to 1789
Scum
See Crumb, R.
Scumbag, Little Bobby
See Crumb, R.
Seabrook, John
See Hubbard, L. Ron
Seacole, Mary Jane Grant 1805-1881
.... **NCLC 147**
See also DLB 166
Sealy, I(rwin) Allan 1951- .... **CLC 55**
See also CA 136; CN 6, 7
Search, Alexander
See Pessoa, Fernando (Antonio Nogueira)
Sebald, W(infried) G(eorg) 1944-2001
.... **CLC 194**
See also BRWS 8; CA 159; 202; CANR 98;
MTFW 2005; RGHL
Sebastian, Lee
See Silverberg, Robert
Sebastian Owl
See Thompson, Hunter S.
Sebestyen, Igen
See Sebestyen, Ouida
Sebestyen, Ouida 1924- .... **CLC 30**
See also AAYA 8; BYA 7; CA 107; CANR
40, 114; CLR 17; JRDA; MAICYA 1, 2;
SAAS 10; SATA 39, 140; WYA; YAW
Sebold, Alice 1963(?)- .... **CLC 193**
See also AAYA 56; CA 203; MTFW 2005
Second Duke of Buckingham
See Villiers, George
Secundus, H. Scriblerus
See Fielding, Henry
Sedges, John
See Buck, Pearl S(ydenstricker)

Sedgwick, Catharine Maria 1789-1867
.... **NCLC 19, 98**
See also DLB 1, 74, 183, 239, 243, 254; FL
1:3; RGAL 4
Sedulius Scottus 9th cent. -c. 874
.... **CMLC 86**
Seelye, John (Douglas) 1931- .... **CLC 7**
See also CA 97-100; CANR 70; INT CA-
97-100; TCWW 1, 2
Seferiades, Giorgos Stylianou 1900-1971
See Seferis, George
See also CA 5-8R; 33-36R; CANR 5, 36;
MTCW 1
Seferis, George .... **CLC 5, 11; PC 66**
See Seferiades, Giorgos Stylianou
See also EW 12; EWL 3; RGWL 2, 3
Segal, Erich (Wolf) 1937- .... **CLC 3, 10**
See also BEST 89:1; BPFB 3; CA 25-28R;
CANR 20, 36, 65, 113; CPW; DAM POP;
DLBY 1986; INT CANR-20; MTCW 1
Seger, Bob 1945- .... **CLC 35**
Seghers, Anna .... **CLC 7**
See Radvanyi, Netty
See also CDWLB 2; DLB 69; EWL 3
Seidel, Frederick (Lewis) 1936- ...... **CLC 18**
See also CA 13-16R; CANR 8, 99; CP 1, 2,
3, 4, 5, 6, 7; DLBY 1984
Seifert, Jaroslav 1901-1986 ...... **CLC 34, 44,
93; PC 47**
See also CA 127; CDWLB 4; DLB 215;
EWL 3; MTCW 1, 2
Sei Shonagon c. 966-1017(?) .... **CMLC 6**
Sejour, Victor 1817-1874 .... **DC 10**
See also DLB 50
Sejour Marcou et Ferrand, Juan Victor
See Sejour, Victor
Selby, Hubert, Jr. 1928-2004 ... **CLC 1, 2, 4,
8; SSC 20**
See also CA 13-16R; 226; CANR 33, 85;
CN 1, 2, 3, 4, 5, 6, 7; DLB 2, 227; MAL
5
Selzer, Richard 1928- .... **CLC 74**
See also CA 65-68; CANR 14, 106
Sembene, Ousmane
See Ousmane, Sembene
See also AFW; EWL 3; WLIT 2
Senancour, Etienne Pivert de 1770-1846
.... **NCLC 16**
See also DLB 119; GFL 1789 to the Present
Sender, Ramon (Jose) 1902-1982 ..... **CLC 8;
HLC 2; TCLC 136**
See also CA 5-8R; 105; CANR 8; DAM
MULT; DLB 322; EWL 3; HW 1; MTCW
1; RGWL 2, 3
Seneca, Lucius Annaeus c. 4B.C.-c. 65
.... **CMLC 6; DC 5**
See also AW 2; CDWLB 1; DAM DRAM;
DLB 211; RGWL 2, 3; TWA; WLIT 8
Senghor, Leopold Sedar 1906-2001 . **BLC 3;
CLC 54, 130; PC 25**
See also AFW; BW 2; CA 116; 125; 203;
CANR 47, 74, 134; CWW 2; DAM
MULT, POET; DNFS 2; EWL 3; GFL
1789 to the Present; MTCW 1, 2; MTFW
2005; TWA
Senior, Olive (Marjorie) 1941- .... **SSC 78**
See also BW 3; CA 154; CANR 86, 126;
CN 6; CP 6, 7; CWP; DLB 157; EWL 3;
RGSF 2
Senna, Danzy 1970- .... **CLC 119**
See also CA 169; CANR 130
Serling, (Edward) Rod(man) 1924-1975
.... **CLC 30**
See also AAYA 14; AITN 1; CA 162; 57-
60; DLB 26; SFW 4
Serna, Ramon Gomez de la
See Gomez de la Serna, Ramon
Serpieres
See Guillevic, (Eugene)

Service, Robert
See Service, Robert W(illiam)
See also BYA 4; DAB; DLB 92
Service, Robert W(illiam) 1874(?)-1958
.... **PC 70; TCLC 15; WLC 5**
See Service, Robert
See also CA 115; 140; CANR 84; DA;
DAC; DAM MST, POET; PFS 10; RGEL
2; SATA 20
Seth, Vikram 1952- .... **CLC 43, 90**
See also BRWS 10; CA 121; 127; CANR
50, 74, 131; CN 6, 7; CP 5, 6, 7; DA3;
DAM MULT; DLB 120, 271, 282, 323;
EWL 3; INT CA-127; MTCW 2; MTFW
2005; WWE 1
Seton, Cynthia Propper 1926-1982 . **CLC 27**
See also CA 5-8R; 108; CANR 7
Seton, Ernest (Evan) Thompson 1860-1946
.... **TCLC 31**
See also ANW; BYA 3; CA 109; 204; CLR
59; DLB 92; DLBD 13; JRDA; SATA 18
Seton-Thompson, Ernest
See Seton, Ernest (Evan) Thompson
Settle, Mary Lee 1918-2005 ...... **CLC 19, 61**
See also BPFB 3; CA 89-92; 243; CAAS 1;
CANR 44, 87, 126; CN 6, 7; CSW; DLB
6; INT CA-89-92
Seuphor, Michel
See Arp, Jean
Sevigne, Marie (de Rabutin-Chantal)
1626-1696 .... **LC 11**
See Sevigne, Marie de Rabutin Chantal
See also GFL Beginnings to 1789; TWA
Sevigne, Marie de Rabutin Chantal
See Sevigne, Marie (de Rabutin-Chantal)
See also DLB 268
Sewall, Samuel 1652-1730 .... **LC 38**
See also DLB 24; RGAL 4
Sexton, Anne (Harvey) 1928-1974 ... **CLC 2,
4, 6, 8, 10, 15, 53, 123; PC 2; WLC 5**
See also AMWS 2; CA 1-4R; 53-56; CABS
2; CANR 3, 36; CDALB 1941-1968; CP
1, 2; DA; DA3; DAB; DAC; DAM MST,
POET; DLB 5, 169; EWL 3; EXPP; FL
1:6; FW; MAL 5; MBL; MTCW 1, 2;
MTFW 2005; PAB; PFS 4, 14; RGAL 4;
RGHL; SATA 10; TUS
Shaara, Jeff 1952- .... **CLC 119**
See also AAYA 70; CA 163; CANR 109;
CN 7; MTFW 2005
Shaara, Michael 1929-1988 .... **CLC 15**
See also AAYA 71; AITN 1; BPFB 3; CA
102; 125; CANR 52, 85; DAM POP;
DLBY 1983; MTFW 2005
Shackleton, C. C.
See Aldiss, Brian W.
Shacochis, Bob .... **CLC 39**
See Shacochis, Robert G.
Shacochis, Robert G. 1951-
See Shacochis, Bob
See also CA 119; 124; CANR 100; INT CA-
124
Shadwell, Thomas 1641(?)-1692 .... **LC 114**
See also DLB 80; IDTP; RGEL 2
Shaffer, Anthony 1926-2001 .... **CLC 19**
See also CA 110; 116; 200; CBD; CD 5, 6;
DAM DRAM; DFS 13; DLB 13
Shaffer, Anthony Joshua
See Shaffer, Anthony
Shaffer, Peter 1926- .. **CLC 5, 14, 18, 37, 60;
DC 7**
See also BRWS 1; CA 25-28R; CANR 25,
47, 74, 118; CBD; CD 5, 6; CDBLB 1960
to Present; DA3; DAB; DAM DRAM,
MST; DFS 5, 13; DLB 13, 233; EWL 3;
MTCW 1, 2; MTFW 2005; RGEL 2; TEA

Shakespeare, William 1564-1616 ..... **WLC 5**
See also AAYA 35; BRW 1; CDBLB Be-
fore 1660; DA; DA3; DAB; DAC; DAM
DRAM, MST, POET; DFS 20, 21; DLB
62, 172, 263; EXPP; LAIT 1; LATS 1:1;
LMFS 1; PAB; PFS 1, 2, 3, 4, 5, 8, 9;
RGEL 2; TEA; WLIT 3; WP; WS; WYA
Shakey, Bernard
See Young, Neil
Shalamov, Varlam (Tikhonovich) 1907-1982
.... **CLC 18**
See also CA 129; 105; DLB 302; RGSF 2
Shamloo, Ahmad
See Shamlu, Ahmad
Shamlou, Ahmad
See Shamlu, Ahmad
Shamlu, Ahmad 1925-2000 .... **CLC 10**
See also CA 216; CWW 2
Shammas, Anton 1951- .... **CLC 55**
See also CA 199
Shandling, Arline
See Berriault, Gina
Shange, Ntozake 1948- . **BLC 3; CLC 8, 25,
38, 74, 126; DC 3**
See also AAYA 9, 66; AFAW 1, 2; BW 2;
CA 85-88; CABS 3; CAD; CANR 27, 48,
74, 131; CD 5, 6; CP 5, 6, 7; CWD; CWP;
DA3; DAM DRAM, MULT; DFS 2, 11;
DLB 38, 249; FW; LAIT 4, 5; MAL 5;
MTCW 1, 2; MTFW 2005; NFS 11;
RGAL 4; SATA 157; YAW
Shanley, John Patrick 1950- .... **CLC 75**
See also AMWS 14; CA 128; 133; CAD;
CANR 83, 154; CD 5, 6; DFS 23
Shapcott, Thomas W(illiam) 1935- . **CLC 38**
See also CA 69-72; CANR 49, 83, 103; CP
1, 2, 3, 4, 5, 6, 7; DLB 289
Shapiro, Jane 1942- .... **CLC 76**
See also CA 196
Shapiro, Karl 1913-2000 .. **CLC 4, 8, 15, 53;
PC 25**
See also AMWS 2; CA 1-4R; 188; CAAS
6; CANR 1, 36, 66; CP 1, 2, 3, 4, 5, 6;
DLB 48; EWL 3; EXPP; MAL 5; MTCW
1, 2; MTFW 2005; PFS 3; RGAL 4
Sharp, William 1855-1905 .... **TCLC 39**
See Macleod, Fiona
See also CA 160; DLB 156; RGEL 2
Sharpe, Thomas Ridley 1928-
See Sharpe, Tom
See also CA 114; 122; CANR 85; INT CA-
122
Sharpe, Tom .... **CLC 36**
See Sharpe, Thomas Ridley
See also CN 4, 5, 6, 7; DLB 14, 231
Shatrov, Mikhail .... **CLC 59**
Shaw, Bernard
See Shaw, George Bernard
See also DLB 10, 57, 190
Shaw, G. Bernard
See Shaw, George Bernard
Shaw, George Bernard 1856-1950 ... **DC 23;
TCLC 3, 9, 21, 45; WLC 5**
See Shaw, Bernard
See also AAYA 61; BRW 6; BRWC 1;
BRWR 2; CA 104; 128; CDBLB 1914-
1945; DA; DA3; DAB; DAC; DAM
DRAM, MST; DFS 1, 3, 6, 11, 19, 22;
EWL 3; LAIT 3; LATS 1:1; MTCW 1, 2;
MTFW 2005; RGEL 2; TEA; WLIT 4
Shaw, Henry Wheeler 1818-1885 . **NCLC 15**
See also DLB 11; RGAL 4
Shaw, Irwin 1913-1984 .... **CLC 7, 23, 34**
See also AITN 1; BPFB 3; CA 13-16R; 112;
CANR 21; CDALB 1941-1968; CN 1, 2,
3; CPW; DAM DRAM, POP; DLB 6,
102; DLBY 1984; MAL 5; MTCW 1, 21;
MTFW 2005

Shaw, Robert (Archibald) 1927-1978
.... **CLC 5**
See also AITN 1; CA 1-4R; 81-84; CANR
4; CN 1, 2; DLB 13, 14

Shaw, T. E.
See Lawrence, T(homas) E(dward)

Shawn, Wallace 1943- .... **CLC 41**
See also CA 112; CAD; CD 5, 6; DLB 266

Shaykh, al- Hanan
See al-Shaykh, Hanan
See also CWW 2; EWL 3

Shchedrin, N.
See Saltykov, Mikhail Evgrafovich

Shea, Lisa 1953- .... **CLC 86**
See also CA 147

Sheed, Wilfrid (John Joseph) 1930-
.... **CLC 2, 4, 10, 53**
See also CA 65-68; CANR 30, 66; CN 1, 2,
3, 4, 5, 6, 7; DLB 6; MAL 5; MTCW 1,
2; MTFW 2005

Sheehy, Gail 1937- .... **CLC 171**
See also CA 49-52; CANR 1, 33, 55, 92;
CPW; MTCW 1

Sheldon, Alice Hastings Bradley
1915(?)-1987
See Tiptree, James, Jr.
See also CA 108; 122; CANR 34; INT CA-
108; MTCW 1

Sheldon, John
See Bloch, Robert (Albert)

Sheldon, Walter J(ames) 1917-1996
See Queen, Ellery
See also AITN 1; CA 25-28R; CANR 10

Shelley, Mary Wollstonecraft (Godwin)
1797-1851 .... **NCLC 14, 59, 103, 170;**
SSC 92; WLC 5
See also AAYA 20; BPFB 3; BRW 3;
BRWC 2; BRWS 3; BYA 5; CDBLB
1789-1832; DA; DA3; DAB; DAC; DAM
MST, NOV; DLB 110, 116, 159, 178;
EXPN; FL 1:3; GL 3; HGG; LAIT 1;
LMFS 1, 2; NFS 1; RGEL 2; SATA 29;
SCFW 1, 2; SFW 4; TEA; WLIT 3

Shelley, Percy Bysshe 1792-1822 . **NCLC 18,**
93, 143, 175; PC 14, 67; WLC 5
See also AAYA 61; BRW 4; BRWR 1; CD-
BLB 1789-1832; DA; DA3; DAB; DAC;
DAM MST, POET; DLB 96, 110, 158;
EXPP; LMFS 1; PAB; PFS 2; RGEL 2;
TEA; WLIT 3; WP

Shepard, James R. .... **CLC 36**
See also CA 137; CANR 59, 104; SATA 90,
164

Shepard, Jim
See Shepard, James R.

Shepard, Lucius 1947- .... **CLC 34**
See also CA 128; 141; CANR 81, 124;
HGG; SCFW 2; SFW 4; SUFW 2

Shepard, Sam 1943- ... **CLC 4, 6, 17, 34, 41,**
44, 169; DC 5
See also AAYA 1, 58; AMWS 3; CA 69-72;
CABS 3; CAD; CANR 22, 120, 140; CD
5, 6; DA3; DAM DRAM; DFS 3, 6, 7,
14; DLB 7, 212; EWL 3; IDFW 3, 4;
MAL 5; MTCW 1, 2; MTFW 2005;
RGAL 4

Shepherd, Jean (Parker) 1921-1999
.... **TCLC 177**
See also AAYA 69; AITN 2; CA 77-80; 187

Shepherd, Michael
See Ludlum, Robert

Sherburne, Zoa (Lillian Morin) 1912-1995
.... **CLC 30**
See also AAYA 13; CA 1-4R; 176; CANR
3, 37; MAICYA 1, 2; SAAS 18; SATA 3;
YAW

Sheridan, Frances 1724-1766 .... **LC 7**
See also DLB 39, 84

Sheridan, Richard Brinsley 1751-1816
.... **DC 1; NCLC 5, 91; WLC 5**
See also BRW 3; CDBLB 1660-1789; DA;
DAB; DAC; DAM DRAM, MST; DFS
15; DLB 89; WLIT 3

Sherman, Jonathan Marc 1968- ..... **CLC 55**
See also CA 230

Sherman, Martin 1941(?)- .... **CLC 19**
See also CA 116; 123; CAD; CANR 86;
CD 5, 6; DFS 20; DLB 228; GLL 1;
IDTP; RGHL

Sherwin, Judith Johnson
See Johnson, Judith (Emlyn)
See also CANR 85; CP 2, 3, 4, 5; CWP

Sherwood, Frances 1940- .... **CLC 81**
See also CA 146, 220; CAAE 220

Sherwood, Robert E(mmet) 1896-1955
.... **TCLC 3**
See also CA 104; 153; CANR 86; DAM
DRAM; DFS 11, 15, 17; DLB 7, 26, 249;
IDFW 3, 4; MAL 5; RGAL 4

Shestov, Lev 1866-1938 .... **TCLC 56**

Shevchenko, Taras 1814-1861 .... **NCLC 54**

Shiel, M(atthew) P(hipps) 1865-1947
.... **TCLC 8**
See Holmes, Gordon
See also CA 106; 160; DLB 153; HGG;
MTCW 2; MTFW 2005; SCFW 1, 2;
SFW 4; SUFW

Shields, Carol 1935-2003 . **CLC 91, 113, 193**
See also AMWS 7; CA 81-84; 218; CANR
51, 74, 98, 133; CCA 1; CN 6, 7; CPW;
DA3; DAC; MTCW 2; MTFW 2005; NFS
23

Shields, David 1956- .... **CLC 97**
See also CA 124; CANR 48, 99, 112, 157

Shiga, Naoya 1883-1971 .. **CLC 33; SSC 23;**
TCLC 172
See Shiga Naoya
See also CA 101; 33-36R; MJW; RGWL 3

Shiga Naoya
See Shiga, Naoya
See also DLB 180; EWL 3; RGWL 3

Shilts, Randy 1951-1994 .... **CLC 85**
See also AAYA 19; CA 115; 127; 144;
CANR 45; DA3; GLL 1; INT CA-127;
MTCW 2; MTFW 2005

Shimazaki, Haruki 1872-1943
See Shimazaki Toson
See also CA 105; 134; CANR 84; RGWL 3

Shimazaki Toson .... **TCLC 5**
See Shimazaki, Haruki
See also DLB 180; EWL 3

Shirley, James 1596-1666 ...... **DC 25; LC 96**
See also DLB 58; RGEL 2

Sholokhov, Mikhail (Aleksandrovich)
1905-1984 .... **CLC 7, 15**
See also CA 101; 112; DLB 272; EWL 3;
MTCW 1, 2; MTFW 2005; RGWL 2, 3;
SATA-Obit 36

Shone, Patric
See Hanley, James

Showalter, Elaine 1941- .... **CLC 169**
See also CA 57-60; CANR 58, 106; DLB
67; FW; GLL 2

Shreve, Susan
See Shreve, Susan Richards

Shreve, Susan Richards 1939- .... **CLC 23**
See also CA 49-52; CAAS 5; CANR 5, 38,
69, 100; MAICYA 1, 2; SATA 46, 95, 152;
SATA-Brief 41

Shue, Larry 1946-1985 .... **CLC 52**
See also CA 145; 117; DAM DRAM; DFS
7

Shu-Jen, Chou 1881-1936
See Lu Hsun
See also CA 104

Shulman, Alix Kates 1932- .... **CLC 2, 10**
See also CA 29-32R; CANR 43; FW; SATA
7

Shuster, Joe 1914-1992 .... **CLC 21**
See also AAYA 50

Shute, Nevil .... **CLC 30**
See Norway, Nevil Shute
See also BPFB 3; DLB 255; NFS 9; RHW;
SFW 4

Shuttle, Penelope (Diane) 1947- .... **CLC 7**
See also CA 93-96; CANR 39, 84, 92, 108;
CP 3, 4, 5, 6, 7; CWP; DLB 14, 40

Shvarts, Elena 1948- .... **PC 50**
See also CA 147

Sidhwa, Bapsi 1939-
See Sidhwa, Bapsy (N.)
See also CN 6, 7; DLB 323

Sidhwa, Bapsy (N.) 1938- .... **CLC 168**
See Sidhwa, Bapsi
See also CA 108; CANR 25, 57; FW

Sidney, Mary 1561-1621 .... **LC 19, 39**
See Sidney Herbert, Mary

Sidney, Sir Philip 1554-1586 .... **LC 19, 39,**
131; PC 32
See also BRW 1; BRWR 2; CDBLB Before
1660; DA; DA3; DAB; DAC; DAM MST,
POET; DLB 167; EXPP; PAB; RGEL 2;
TEA; WP

Sidney Herbert, Mary
See Sidney, Mary
See also DLB 167

Siegel, Jerome 1914-1996 .... **CLC 21**
See Siegel, Jerry
See also CA 116; 169; 151

Siegel, Jerry
See Siegel, Jerome
See also AAYA 50

Sienkiewicz, Henryk (Adam Alexander Pius)
1846-1916 .... **TCLC 3**
See also CA 104; 134; CANR 84; EWL 3;
RGSF 2; RGWL 2, 3

Sierra, Gregorio Martinez
See Martinez Sierra, Gregorio

Sierra, Maria de la O'LeJarraga Martinez
See Martinez Sierra, Maria

Sigal, Clancy 1926- .... **CLC 7**
See also CA 1-4R; CANR 85; CN 1, 2, 3,
4, 5, 6, 7

Siger of Brabant 1240(?)-1284(?)
.... **CMLC 69**
See also DLB 115

Sigourney, Lydia H.
See Sigourney, Lydia Howard (Huntley)
See also DLB 73, 183

Sigourney, Lydia Howard (Huntley)
1791-1865 .... **NCLC 21, 87**
See Sigourney, Lydia H.; Sigourney, Lydia
Huntley
See also DLB 1

Sigourney, Lydia Huntley
See Sigourney, Lydia Howard (Huntley)
See also DLB 42, 239, 243

Siguenza y Gongora, Carlos de 1645-1700
.... **HLCS 2; LC 8**
See also LAW

Sigurjonsson, Johann
See Sigurjonsson, Johann

Sigurjonsson, Johann 1880-1919 .. **TCLC 27**
See also CA 170; DLB 293; EWL 3

Sikelianos, Angelos 1884-1951 .... **PC 29;**
TCLC 39
See also EWL 3; RGWL 2, 3

Silkin, Jon 1930-1997 .... **CLC 2, 6, 43**
See also CA 5-8R; CAAS 5; CANR 89; CP
1, 2, 3, 4, 5, 6; DLB 27

Skelton, John 1460(?)-1529 ... **LC 71; PC 25**
See also BRW 1; DLB 136; RGEL 2
Skelton, Robin 1925-1997 .... **CLC 13**
See Zuk, Georges
See also AITN 2; CA 5-8R; 160; CAAS 5;
CANR 28, 89; CCA 1; CP 1, 2, 3, 4, 5, 6;
DLB 27, 53
Skolimowski, Jerzy 1938- .... **CLC 20**
See also CA 128
Skram, Amalie (Bertha) 1847-1905
.... **TCLC 25**
See also CA 165
Skvorecky, Josef 1924- .... **CLC 15, 39, 69,**
152
See also CA 61-64; CAAS 1; CANR 10,
34, 63, 108; CDWLB 4; CWW 2; DA3;
DAC; DAM NOV; DLB 232; EWL 3;
MTCW 1, 2; MTFW 2005
Slade, Bernard 1930- .... **CLC 11, 46**
See Newbound, Bernard Slade
See also CAAS 9; CCA 1; CD 6; DLB 53
Slaughter, Carolyn 1946- .... **CLC 56**
See also CA 85-88; CANR 85; CN 5, 6, 7
Slaughter, Frank G(ill) 1908-2001 .. **CLC 29**
See also AITN 2; CA 5-8R; 197; CANR 5,
85; INT CANR-5; RHW
Slavitt, David R(ytman) 1935- .... **CLC 5, 14**
See also CA 21-24R; CAAS 3; CANR 41,
83; CN 1, 2; CP 1, 2, 3, 4, 5, 6, 7; DLB
5, 6
Slesinger, Tess 1905-1945 .... **TCLC 10**
See also CA 107; 199; DLB 102
Slessor, Kenneth 1901-1971 .... **CLC 14**
See also CA 102; 89-92; DLB 260; RGEL
2
Slowacki, Juliusz 1809-1849 .... **NCLC 15**
See also RGWL 3
Smart, Christopher 1722-1771 ..... **LC 3; PC**
13
See also DAM POET; DLB 109; RGEL 2
Smart, Elizabeth 1913-1986 .... **CLC 54**
See also CA 81-84; 118; CN 4; DLB 88
Smiley, Jane (Graves) 1949- ..... **CLC 53, 76,**
144
See also AAYA 66; AMWS 6; BPFB 3; CA
104; CANR 30, 50, 74, 96; CN 6, 7; CPW
1; DA3; DAM POP; DLB 227, 234; EWL
3; INT CANR-30; MAL 5; MTFW 2005;
SSFS 19
Smith, A(rthur) J(ames) M(arshall)
1902-1980 .... **CLC 15**
See also CA 1-4R; 102; CANR 4; CP 1, 2,
3; DAC; DLB 88; RGEL 2
Smith, Adam 1723(?)-1790 .... **LC 36**
See also DLB 104, 252; RGEL 2
Smith, Alexander 1829-1867 .... **NCLC 59**
See also DLB 32, 55
Smith, Anna Deavere 1950- .... **CLC 86**
See also CA 133; CANR 103; CD 5, 6; DFS
2, 22
Smith, Betty (Wehner) 1904-1972 ... **CLC 19**
See also BPFB 3; BYA 3; CA 5-8R; 33-
36R; DLBY 1982; LAIT 3; RGAL 4;
SATA 6
Smith, Charlotte (Turner) 1749-1806
.... **NCLC 23, 115**
See also DLB 39, 109; RGEL 2; TEA
Smith, Clark Ashton 1893-1961 .... **CLC 43**
See also CA 143; CANR 81; FANT; HGG;
MTCW 2; SCFW 1, 2; SFW 4; SUFW
Smith, Dave .... **CLC 22, 42**
See Smith, David (Jeddie)
See also CAAS 7; CP 3, 4, 5, 6, 7; DLB 5
Smith, David (Jeddie) 1942-
See Smith, Dave
See also CA 49-52; CANR 1, 59, 120;
CSW; DAM POET

Smith, Iain Crichton 1928-1998 ...... **CLC 64**
See also BRWS 9; CA 21-24R; 171; CN 1,
2, 3, 4, 5, 6; CP 1, 2, 3, 4, 5, 6; DLB 40,
139, 319; RGSF 2
Smith, John 1580(?)-1631 .... **LC 9**
See also DLB 24, 30; TUS
Smith, Johnston
See Crane, Stephen (Townley)
Smith, Joseph, Jr. 1805-1844 .... **NCLC 53**
Smith, Kevin 1970- .... **CLC 223**
See also AAYA 37; CA 166; CANR 131
Smith, Lee 1944- .... **CLC 25, 73**
See also CA 114; 119; CANR 46, 118; CN
7; CSW; DLB 143; DLBY 1983; EWL 3;
INT CA-119; RGAL 4
Smith, Martin
See Smith, Martin Cruz
Smith, Martin Cruz 1942- . **CLC 25; NNAL**
See also BEST 89:4; BPFB 3; CA 85-88;
CANR 6, 23, 43, 65, 119; CMW 4; CPW;
DAM MULT, POP; HGG; INT CANR-
23; MTCW 2; MTFW 2005; RGAL 4
Smith, Patti 1946- .... **CLC 12**
See also CA 93-96; CANR 63
Smith, Pauline (Urmson) 1882-1959
.... **TCLC 25**
See also DLB 225; EWL 3
Smith, Rosamond
See Oates, Joyce Carol
Smith, Sheila Kaye
See Kaye-Smith, Sheila
Smith, Stevie 1902-1971 ... **CLC 3, 8, 25, 44;**
PC 12
See also BRWS 2; CA 17-18; 29-32R;
CANR 35; CAP 2; CP 1; DAM POET;
DLB 20; EWL 3; MTCW 1, 2; PAB; PFS
3; RGEL 2; TEA
Smith, Wilbur 1933- .... **CLC 33**
See also CA 13-16R; CANR 7, 46, 66, 134;
CPW; MTCW 1, 2; MTFW 2005
Smith, William Jay 1918- .... **CLC 6**
See also AMWS 13; CA 5-8R; CANR 44,
106; CP 1, 2, 3, 4, 5, 6, 7; CSW; CWRI
5; DLB 5; MAICYA 1, 2; SAAS 22;
SATA 2, 68, 154; SATA-Essay 154; TCLE
1:2
Smith, Woodrow Wilson
See Kuttner, Henry
Smith, Zadie 1975- .... **CLC 158**
See also AAYA 50; CA 193; MTFW 2005
Smolenskin, Peretz 1842-1885 ...... **NCLC 30**
Smollett, Tobias (George) 1721-1771 .. **LC 2,**
46
See also BRW 3; CDBLB 1660-1789; DLB
39, 104; RGEL 2; TEA
Snodgrass, W.D. 1926- ..... **CLC 2, 6, 10, 18,**
68; PC 74
See also AMWS 6; CA 1-4R; CANR 6, 36,
65, 85; CP 1, 2, 3, 4, 5, 6, 7; DAM POET;
DLB 5; MAL 5; MTCW 1, 2; MTFW
2005; RGAL 4; TCLE 1:2
Snorri Sturluson 1179-1241 .... **CMLC 56**
See also RGWL 2, 3
Snow, C(harles) P(ercy) 1905-1980 .. **CLC 1,**
4, 6, 9, 13, 19
See also BRW 7; CA 5-8R; 101; CANR 28;
CDBLB 1945-1960; CN 1, 2; DAM NOV;
DLB 15, 77; DLBD 17; EWL 3; MTCW
1, 2; MTFW 2005; RGEL 2; TEA
Snow, Frances Compton
See Adams, Henry (Brooks)
Snyder, Gary 1930- .... **CLC 1, 2, 5, 9, 32,**
120; PC 21
See also AMWS 8; ANW; BG 1:3; CA 17-
20R; CANR 30, 60, 125; CP 1, 2, 3, 4, 5,
6, 7; DA3; DAM POET; DLB 5, 16, 165,
212, 237, 275; EWL 3; MAL 5; MTCW
2; MTFW 2005; PFS 9, 19; RGAL 4; WP

Snyder, Zilpha Keatley 1927- .... **CLC 17**
See also AAYA 15; BYA 1; CA 9-12R;
CANR 38; CLR 31; JRDA; MAICYA 1,
2; SAAS 2; SATA 1, 28, 75, 110, 163;
SATA-Essay 112, 163; YAW
Soares, Bernardo
See Pessoa, Fernando (Antonio Nogueira)
Sobh, A.
See Shamlu, Ahmad
Sobh, Alef
See Shamlu, Ahmad
Sobol, Joshua 1939- .... **CLC 60**
See Sobol, Yehoshua
See also CA 200; RGHL
Sobol, Yehoshua 1939-
See Sobol, Joshua
See also CWW 2
Socrates 470B.C.-399B.C. .... **CMLC 27**
Soderberg, Hjalmar 1869-1941 .... **TCLC 39**
See also DLB 259; EWL 3; RGSF 2
Soderbergh, Steven 1963- .... **CLC 154**
See also AAYA 43; CA 243
Soderbergh, Steven Andrew
See Soderbergh, Steven
Sodergran, Edith (Irene) 1892-1923
See Soedergran, Edith (Irene)
See also CA 202; DLB 259; EW 11; EWL
3; RGWL 2, 3
Soedergran, Edith (Irene) 1892-1923
.... **TCLC 31**
See Sodergran, Edith (Irene)
Softly, Edgar
See Lovecraft, H. P.
Softly, Edward
See Lovecraft, H. P.
Sokolov, Alexander V(sevolodovich) 1943-
See Sokolov, Sasha
See also CA 73-76
Sokolov, Raymond 1941- .... **CLC 7**
See also CA 85-88
Sokolov, Sasha .... **CLC 59**
See Sokolov, Alexander V(sevolodovich)
See also CWW 2; DLB 285; EWL 3; RGWL
2, 3
Solo, Jay
See Ellison, Harlan
Sologub, Fyodor .... **TCLC 9**
See Teternikov, Fyodor Kuzmich
See also EWL 3
Solomons, Ikey Esquir
See Thackeray, William Makepeace
Solomos, Dionysios 1798-1857 ...... **NCLC 15**
Solwoska, Mara
See French, Marilyn
Solzhenitsyn, Aleksandr I. 1918- . **CLC 1, 2,**
4, 7, 9, 10, 18, 26, 34, 78, 134; SSC 32;
WLC 5
See Solzhenitsyn, Aleksandr Isayevich
See also AAYA 49; AITN 1; BPFB 3; CA
69-72; CANR 40, 65, 116; DA; DA3;
DAB; DAC; DAM MST, NOV; DLB 302;
EW 13; EXPS; LAIT 4; MTCW 1, 2;
MTFW 2005; NFS 6; RGSF 2; RGWL 2,
3; SSFS 9; TWA
Solzhenitsyn, Aleksandr Isayevich
See Solzhenitsyn, Aleksandr I.
See also CWW 2; EWL 3
Somers, Jane
See Lessing, Doris
Somerville, Edith Oenone 1858-1949
.... **SSC 56; TCLC 51**
See also CA 196; DLB 135; RGEL 2; RGSF
2
Somerville & Ross
See Martin, Violet Florence; Somerville,
Edith Oenone
Sommer, Scott 1951- .... **CLC 25**
See also CA 106

Sommers, Christina Hoff 1950- .... **CLC 197**
See also CA 153; CANR 95

Sondheim, Stephen (Joshua) 1930-
.... **CLC 30, 39, 147; DC 22**
See also AAYA 11, 66; CA 103; CANR 47,
67, 125; DAM DRAM; LAIT 4

Sone, Monica 1919- .... **AAL**
See also DLB 312

Song, Cathy 1955- .... **AAL; PC 21**
See also CA 154; CANR 118; CWP; DLB
169, 312; EXPP; FW; PFS 5

Sontag, Susan 1933-2004 . **CLC 1, 2, 10, 13,
31, 105, 195**
See also AMWS 3; CA 17-20R; 234; CANR
25, 51, 74, 97; CN 1, 2, 3, 4, 5, 6, 7;
CPW; DA3; DAM POP; DLB 2, 67; EWL
3; MAL 5; MBL; MTCW 1, 2; MTFW
2005; RGAL 4; RHW; SSFS 10

Sophocles 496(?)B.C.-406(?)B.C. ... **CMLC 2,
47, 51, 86; DC 1; WLCS**
See also AW 1; CDWLB 1; DA; DA3;
DAB; DAC; DAM DRAM, MST; DFS 1,
4, 8; DLB 176; LAIT 1; LATS 1:1; LMFS
1; RGWL 2, 3; TWA; WLIT 8

Sordello 1189-1269 .... **CMLC 15**

Sorel, Georges 1847-1922 .... **TCLC 91**
See also CA 118; 188

Sorel, Julia
See Drexler, Rosalyn

Sorokin, Vladimir .... **CLC 59**
See also Sorokin, Vladimir Georgievich

Sorokin, Vladimir Georgievich
See Sorokin, Vladimir
See also DLB 285

Sorrentino, Gilbert 1929-2006 ..... **CLC 3, 7,
14, 22, 40**
See also CA 77-80; 250; CANR 14, 33, 115,
157; CN 3, 4, 5, 6, 7; CP 1, 2, 3, 4, 5, 6,
7; DLB 5, 173; DLBY 1980; INT
CANR-14

Soseki
See Natsume, Soseki
See also MJW

Soto, Gary 1952- .. **CLC 32, 80; HLC 2; PC
28**
See also AAYA 10, 37; BYA 11; CA 119;
125; CANR 50, 74, 107, 157; CLR 38;
CP 4, 5, 6, 7; DAM MULT; DLB 82;
EWL 3; EXPP; HW 1, 2; INT CA-125;
JRDA; LLW; MAICYA 2; MAICYAS 1;
MAL 5; MTCW 2; MTFW 2005; PFS 7;
RGAL 4; SATA 80, 120; WYA; YAW

Soupault, Philippe 1897-1990 .... **CLC 68**
See also CA 116; 147; 131; EWL 3; GFL
1789 to the Present; LMFS 2

Souster, (Holmes) Raymond 1921- .. **CLC 5,
14**
See also CA 13-16R; CAAS 14; CANR 13,
29, 53; CP 1, 2, 3, 4, 5, 6, 7; DA3; DAC;
DAM POET; DLB 88; RGEL 2; SATA 63

Southern, Terry 1924(?)-1995 .... **CLC 7**
See also AMWS 11; BPFB 3; CA 1-4R;
150; CANR 1, 55, 107; CN 1, 2, 3, 4, 5,
6; DLB 2; IDFW 3, 4

Southerne, Thomas 1660-1746 .... **LC 99**
See also DLB 80; RGEL 2

Southey, Robert 1774-1843 .... **NCLC 8, 97**
See also BRW 4; DLB 93, 107, 142; RGEL
2; SATA 54

Southwell, Robert 1561(?)-1595 .... **LC 108**
See also DLB 167; RGEL 2; TEA

Southworth, Emma Dorothy Eliza Nevitte
1819-1899 .... **NCLC 26**
See also DLB 239

Souza, Ernest
See Scott, Evelyn

Soyinka, Wole 1934- . **BLC 3; CLC 3, 5, 14,
36, 44, 179; DC 2; WLC 5**
See also AFW; BW 2, 3; CA 13-16R;
CANR 27, 39, 82, 136; CD 5, 6; CDWLB
3; CN 6, 7; CP 1, 2, 3, 4, 5, 6 ,7; DA;
DA3; DAB; DAC; DAM DRAM, MST,
MULT; DFS 10; DLB 125; EWL 3;
MTCW 1, 2; MTFW 2005; RGEL 2;
TWA; WLIT 2; WWE 1

Spackman, W(illiam) M(ode) 1905-1990
.... **CLC 46**
See also CA 81-84; 132

Spacks, Barry (Bernard) 1931- .... **CLC 14**
See also CA 154; CANR 33, 109; CP 3, 4,
5, 6, 7; DLB 105

Spanidou, Irini 1946- .... **CLC 44**
See also CA 185

Spark, Muriel 1918-2006 ..... **CLC 2, 3, 5, 8,
13, 18, 40, 94; PC 72; SSC 10**
See also BRWS 1; CA 5-8R; 251; CANR
12, 36, 76, 89, 131; CDBLB 1945-1960;
CN 1, 2, 3, 4, 5, 6, 7; CP 1, 2, 3, 4, 5, 6,
7; DA3; DAB; DAC; DAM MST, NOV;
DLB 15, 139; EWL 3; FW; INT CANR-
12; LAIT 4; MTCW 1, 2; MTFW 2005;
NFS 22; RGEL 2; TEA; WLIT 4; YAW

Spark, Muriel Sarah
See Spark, Muriel

Spaulding, Douglas
See Bradbury, Ray

Spaulding, Leonard
See Bradbury, Ray

Speght, Rachel 1597-c. 1630 .... **LC 97**
See also DLB 126

Spence, J. A. D.
See Eliot, T(homas) S(tearns)

Spencer, Anne 1882-1975 .... **HR 1:3**
See also BW 2; CA 161; DLB 51, 54

Spencer, Elizabeth 1921- .. **CLC 22; SSC 57**
See also CA 13-16R; CANR 32, 65, 87; CN
1, 2, 3, 4, 5, 6, 7; CSW; DLB 6, 218;
EWL 3; MTCW 1; RGAL 4; SATA 14

Spencer, Leonard G.
See Silverberg, Robert

Spencer, Scott 1945- .... **CLC 30**
See also CA 113; CANR 51, 148; DLBY
1986

Spender, Stephen 1909-1995 .... **CLC 1, 2, 5,
10, 41, 91; PC 71**
See also BRWS 2; CA 9-12R; 149; CANR
31, 54; CDBLB 1945-1960; CP 1, 2, 3, 4,
5, 6; DA3; DAM POET; DLB 20; EWL
3; MTCW 1, 2; MTFW 2005; PAB; PFS
23; RGEL 2; TEA

Spengler, Oswald (Arnold Gottfried)
1880-1936 .... **TCLC 25**
See also CA 118; 189

Spenser, Edmund 1552(?)-1599 .... **LC 5, 39,
117; PC 8, 42; WLC 5**
See also AAYA 60; BRW 1; CDBLB Be-
fore 1660; DA; DA3; DAB; DAC; DAM
MST, POET; DLB 167; EFS 2; EXPP;
PAB; RGEL 2; TEA; WLIT 3; WP

Spicer, Jack 1925-1965 .... **CLC 8, 18, 72**
See also BG 1:3; CA 85-88; DAM POET;
DLB 5, 16, 193; GLL 1; WP

Spiegelman, Art 1948- .... **CLC 76, 178**
See also AAYA 10, 46; CA 125; CANR 41,
55, 74, 124; DLB 299; MTCW 2; MTFW
2005; RGHL; SATA 109, 158; YAW

Spielberg, Peter 1929- .... **CLC 6**
See also CA 5-8R; CANR 4, 48; DLBY
1981

Spielberg, Steven 1947- .... **CLC 20, 188**
See also AAYA 8, 24; CA 77-80; CANR
32; SATA 32

Spillane, Frank Morrison .... **CLC 3, 13**
See Spillane, Mickey
See also BPFB 3; CMW 4; DLB 226; MSW

Spillane, Mickey 1918-2006
See Spillane, Frank Morrison
See also CA 25-28R; CANR 28, 63, 125;
DA3; MTCW 1, 2; MTFW 2005; SATA
66

Spinoza, Benedictus de 1632-1677 ...... **LC 9,
58**

Spinrad, Norman (Richard) 1940- . **CLC 46**
See also BPFB 3; CA 37-40R, 233; CAAE
233; CAAS 19; CANR 20, 91; DLB 8;
INT CANR-20; SFW 4

Spitteler, Carl 1845-1924 .... **TCLC 12**
See also CA 109; DLB 129; EWL 3

Spitteler, Karl Friedrich Georg
See Spitteler, Carl

Spivack, Kathleen (Romola Drucker) 1938-
.... **CLC 6**
See also CA 49-52

Spofford, Harriet (Elizabeth) Prescott
1835-1921 .... **SSC 87**
See also CA 201; DLB 74, 221

Spoto, Donald 1941- .... **CLC 39**
See also CA 65-68; CANR 11, 57, 93

Springsteen, Bruce 1949- .... **CLC 17**
See also CA 111

Springsteen, Bruce F.
See Springsteen, Bruce

Spurling, Hilary 1940- .... **CLC 34**
See also CA 104; CANR 25, 52, 94, 157

Spurling, Susan Hilary
See Spurling, Hilary

Spyker, John Howland
See Elman, Richard (Martin)

Squared, A.
See Abbott, Edwin A.

Squires, (James) Radcliffe 1917-1993
.... **CLC 51**
See also CA 1-4R; 140; CANR 6, 21; CP 1,
2, 3, 4, 5

Srivastava, Dhanpat Rai 1880(?)-1936
See Premchand
See also CA 118; 197

Stacy, Donald
See Pohl, Frederik

Stael
See Stael-Holstein, Anne Louise Germaine
Necker
See also EW 5; RGWL 2, 3

Stael, Germaine de
See Stael-Holstein, Anne Louise Germaine
Necker
See also DLB 119, 192; FL 1:3; FW; GFL
1789 to the Present; TWA

**Stael-Holstein, Anne Louise Germaine
Necker** 1766-1817 .... **NCLC 3, 91**
See Stael; Stael, Germaine de

Stafford, Jean 1915-1979 . **CLC 4, 7, 19, 68;
SSC 26, 86**
See also CA 1-4R; 85-88; CANR 3, 65; CN
1, 2; DLB 2, 173; MAL 5; MTCW 1, 2;
MTFW 2005; RGAL 4; RGSF 2; SATA-
Obit 22; SSFS 21; TCWW 1, 2; TUS

Stafford, William (Edgar) 1914-1993
.... **CLC 4, 7, 29; PC 71**
See also AMWS 11; CA 5-8R; 142; CAAS
3; CANR 5, 22; CP 1, 2, 3, 4, 5; DAM
POET; DLB 5, 206; EXPP; INT CANR-
22; MAL 5; PFS 2, 8, 16; RGAL 4; WP

Stagnelius, Eric Johan 1793-1823
.... **NCLC 61**

Staines, Trevor
See Brunner, John (Kilian Houston)

Stairs, Gordon
See Austin, Mary (Hunter)

Stalin, Joseph 1879-1953 .... **TCLC 92**

Stampa, Gaspara c. 1524-1554 . **LC 114; PC
43**
See also RGWL 2, 3; WLIT 7

Tate, Nahum 1652(?)-1715 .... **LC 109**
See also DLB 80; RGEL 2

Tauler, Johannes c. 1300-1361 ..... **CMLC 37**
See also DLB 179; LMFS 1

Tavel, Ronald 1940- .... **CLC 6**
See also CA 21-24R; CAD; CANR 33; CD 5, 6

Taviani, Paolo 1931- .... **CLC 70**
See also CA 153

Taylor, Bayard 1825-1878 .... **NCLC 89**
See also DLB 3, 189, 250, 254; RGAL 4

Taylor, C(ecil) P(hilip) 1929-1981 ... **CLC 27**
See also CA 25-28R; 105; CANR 47; CBD

Taylor, Edward 1642(?)-1729 ..... **LC 11; PC 63**
See also AMW; DA; DAB; DAC; DAM MST, POET; DLB 24; EXPP; RGAL 4; TUS

Taylor, Eleanor Ross 1920- .... **CLC 5**
See also CA 81-84; CANR 70

Taylor, Elizabeth 1912-1975 .... **CLC 2, 4, 29**
See also CA 13-16R; CANR 9, 70; CN 1, 2; DLB 139; MTCW 1; RGEL 2; SATA 13

Taylor, Frederick Winslow 1856-1915
.... **TCLC 76**
See also CA 188

Taylor, Henry (Splawn) 1942- .... **CLC 44**
See also CA 33-36R; CAAS 7; CANR 31; CP 6, 7; DLB 5; PFS 10

Taylor, Kamala 1924-2004
See Markandaya, Kamala
See also CA 77-80; 227; MTFW 2005; NFS 13

Taylor, Mildred D. 1943- .... **CLC 21**
See also AAYA 10, 47; BW 1; BYA 3, 8; CA 85-88; CANR 25, 115, 136; CLR 9, 59, 90; CSW; DLB 52; JRDA; LAIT 3; MAICYA 1, 2; MTFW 2005; SAAS 5; SATA 135; WYA; YAW

Taylor, Peter (Hillsman) 1917-1994 . **CLC 1, 4, 18, 37, 44, 50, 71; SSC 10, 84**
See also AMWS 5; BPFB 3; CA 13-16R; 147; CANR 9, 50; CN 1, 2, 3, 4, 5; CSW; DLB 218, 278; DLBY 1981, 1994; EWL 3; EXPS; INT CANR-9; MAL 5; MTCW 1, 2; MTFW 2005; RGSF 2; SSFS 9; TUS

Taylor, Robert Lewis 1912-1998 ..... **CLC 14**
See also CA 1-4R; 170; CANR 3, 64; CN 1, 2; SATA 10; TCWW 1, 2

Tchekhov, Anton
See Chekhov, Anton (Pavlovich)

Tchicaya, Gerald Felix 1931-1988
.... **CLC 101**
See Tchicaya U Tam'si
See also CA 129; 125; CANR 81

Tchicaya U Tam'si
See Tchicaya, Gerald Felix
See also EWL 3

Teasdale, Sara 1884-1933 ... **PC 31; TCLC 4**
See also CA 104; 163; DLB 45; GLL 1; PFS 14; RGAL 4; SATA 32; TUS

Tecumseh 1768-1813 .... **NNAL**
See also DAM MULT

Tegner, Esaias 1782-1846 .... **NCLC 2**

Teilhard de Chardin, (Marie Joseph) Pierre
1881-1955 .... **TCLC 9**
See also CA 105; 210; GFL 1789 to the Present

Temple, Ann
See Mortimer, Penelope (Ruth)

Tennant, Emma (Christina) 1937- . **CLC 13, 52**
See also BRWS 9; CA 65-68; CAAS 9; CANR 10, 38, 59, 88; CN 3, 4, 5, 6, 7; DLB 14; EWL 3; SFW 4

Tenneshaw, S. M.
See Silverberg, Robert

Tenney, Tabitha Gilman 1762-1837
.... **NCLC 122**
See also DLB 37, 200

Tennyson, Alfred 1809-1892 .. **NCLC 30, 65, 115; PC 6; WLC 6**
See also AAYA 50; BRW 4; CDBLB 1832-1890; DA; DA3; DAB; DAC; DAM MST, POET; DLB 32; EXPP; PAB; PFS 1, 2, 4, 11, 15, 19; RGEL 2; TEA; WLIT 4; WP

Teran, Lisa St. Aubin de .... **CLC 36**
See St. Aubin de Teran, Lisa

Terence c. 184B.C.-c. 159B.C. .... **CMLC 14; DC 7**
See also AW 1; CDWLB 1; DLB 211; RGWL 2, 3; TWA; WLIT 8

Teresa de Jesus, St. 1515-1582 .... **LC 18**

Teresa of Avila, St.
See Teresa de Jesus, St.

Terkel, Louis .... **CLC 38**
See Terkel, Studs
See also AAYA 32; AITN 1; MTCW 2; TUS

Terkel, Studs 1912-
See Terkel, Louis
See also CA 57-60; CANR 18, 45, 67, 132; DA3; MTCW 1, 2; MTFW 2005

Terry, C. V.
See Slaughter, Frank G(ill)

Terry, Megan 1932- .... **CLC 19; DC 13**
See also CA 77-80; CABS 3; CAD; CANR 43; CD 5, 6; CWD; DFS 18; DLB 7, 249; GLL 2

Tertullian c. 155-c. 245 .... **CMLC 29**

Tertz, Abram
See Sinyavsky, Andrei (Donatevich)
See also RGSF 2

Tesich, Steve 1943(?)-1996 .... **CLC 40, 69**
See also CA 105; 152; CAD; DLBY 1983

Tesla, Nikola 1856-1943 .... **TCLC 88**

Teternikov, Fyodor Kuzmich 1863-1927
See Sologub, Fyodor
See also CA 104

Tevis, Walter 1928-1984 .... **CLC 42**
See also CA 113; SFW 4

Tey, Josephine .... **TCLC 14**
See Mackintosh, Elizabeth
See also DLB 77; MSW

Thackeray, William Makepeace 1811-1863
.... **NCLC 5, 14, 22, 43, 169; WLC 6**
See also BRW 5; BRWC 2; CDBLB 1832-1890; DA; DA3; DAB; DAC; DAM MST, NOV; DLB 21, 55, 159, 163; NFS 13; RGEL 2; SATA 23; TEA; WLIT 3

Thakura, Ravindranatha
See Tagore, Rabindranath

Thames, C. H.
See Marlowe, Stephen

Tharoor, Shashi 1956- .... **CLC 70**
See also CA 141; CANR 91; CN 6, 7

Thelwall, John 1764-1834 .... **NCLC 162**
See also DLB 93, 158

Thelwell, Michael Miles 1939- .... **CLC 22**
See also BW 2; CA 101

Theobald, Lewis, Jr.
See Lovecraft, H. P.

Theocritus c. 310B.C.- .... **CMLC 45**
See also AW 1; DLB 176; RGWL 2, 3

Theodorescu, Ion N. 1880-1967
See Arghezi, Tudor
See also CA 116

Theriault, Yves 1915-1983 .... **CLC 79**
See also CA 102; CANR 150; CCA 1; DAC; DAM MST; DLB 88; EWL 3

Theroux, Alexander (Louis) 1939- ... **CLC 2, 25**
See also CA 85-88; CANR 20, 63; CN 4, 5, 6, 7

Theroux, Paul 1941- ... **CLC 5, 8, 11, 15, 28, 46, 159**
See also AAYA 28; AMWS 8; BEST 89:4; BPFB 3; CA 33-36R; CANR 20, 45, 74, 133; CDALBS; CN 1, 2, 3, 4, 5, 6, 7; CP 1; CPW 1; DA3; DAM POP; DLB 2, 218; EWL 3; HGG; MAL 5; MTCW 1, 2; MTFW 2005; RGAL 4; SATA 44, 109; TUS

Thesen, Sharon 1946- .... **CLC 56**
See also CA 163; CANR 125; CP 5, 6, 7; CWP

Thespis fl. 6th cent. B.C.- .... **CMLC 51**
See also LMFS 1

Thevenin, Denis
See Duhamel, Georges

Thibault, Jacques Anatole Francois
1844-1924
See France, Anatole
See also CA 106; 127; DA3; DAM NOV; MTCW 1, 2; TWA

Thiele, Colin 1920-2006 .... **CLC 17**
See also CA 29-32R; CANR 12, 28, 53, 105; CLR 27; CP 1, 2; DLB 289; MAICYA 1, 2; SAAS 2; SATA 14, 72, 125; YAW

Thistlethwaite, Bel
See Wetherald, Agnes Ethelwyn

Thomas, Audrey (Callahan) 1935- .. **CLC 7, 13, 37, 107; SSC 20**
See also AITN 2; CA 21-24R, 237; CAAE 237; CAAS 19; CANR 36, 58; CN 2, 3, 4, 5, 6, 7; DLB 60; MTCW 1; RGSF 2

Thomas, Augustus 1857-1934 .... **TCLC 97**
See also MAL 5

Thomas, D.M. 1935- .... **CLC 13, 22, 31, 132**
See also BPFB 3; BRWS 4; CA 61-64; CAAS 11; CANR 17, 45, 75; CDBLB 1960 to Present; CN 4, 5, 6, 7; CP 1, 2, 3, 4, 5, 6, 7; DA3; DLB 40, 207, 299; HGG; INT CANR-17; MTCW 1, 2; MTFW 2005; RGHL; SFW 4

Thomas, Dylan (Marlais) 1914-1953 .. **PC 2, 52; SSC 3, 44; TCLC 1, 8, 45, 105; WLC 6**
See also AAYA 45; BRWS 1; CA 104; 120; CANR 65; CDBLB 1945-1960; DA; DA3; DAB; DAC; DAM DRAM, MST, POET; DLB 13, 20, 139; EWL 3; EXPP; LAIT 3; MTCW 1, 2; MTFW 2005; PAB; PFS 1, 3, 8; RGEL 2; RGSF 2; SATA 60; TEA; WLIT 4; WP

Thomas, (Philip) Edward 1878-1917
.... **PC 53; TCLC 10**
See also BRW 6; BRWS 3; CA 106; 153; DAM POET; DLB 19, 98, 156, 216; EWL 3; PAB; RGEL 2

Thomas, Joyce Carol 1938- .... **CLC 35**
See also AAYA 12, 54; BW 2, 3; CA 113; 116; CANR 48, 114, 135; CLR 19; DLB 33; INT CA-116; JRDA; MAICYA 1, 2; MTCW 1, 2; MTFW 2005; SAAS 7; SATA 40, 78, 123, 137; SATA-Essay 137; WYA; YAW

Thomas, Lewis 1913-1993 .... **CLC 35**
See also ANW; CA 85-88; 143; CANR 38, 60; DLB 275; MTCW 1, 2

Thomas, M. Carey 1857-1935 ...... **TCLC 89**
See also FW

Thomas, Paul
See Mann, (Paul) Thomas

Thomas, Piri 1928- .... **CLC 17; HLCS 2**
See also CA 73-76; HW 1; LLW

Thomas, R(onald) S(tuart) 1913-2000
.... **CLC 6, 13, 48**
See also CA 89-92; 189; CAAS 4; CANR 30; CDBLB 1960 to Present; CP 1, 2, 3, 4, 5, 6, 7; DAB; DAM POET; DLB 27; EWL 3; MTCW 1; RGEL 2

Thomas, Ross (Elmore) 1926-1995 . **CLC 39**
   See also CA 33-36R; 150; CANR 22, 63;
   CMW 4
Thompson, Francis (Joseph) 1859-1907
   .... **TCLC 4**
   See also BRW 5; CA 104; 189; CDBLB
   1890-1914; DLB 19; RGEL 2; TEA
Thompson, Francis Clegg
   See Mencken, H(enry) L(ouis)
Thompson, Hunter S. 1937(?)-2005 . **CLC 9,**
   17, 40, 104, 229
   See also AAYA 45; BEST 89:1; BPFB 3;
   CA 17-20R; 236; CANR 23, 46, 74, 77,
   111, 133; CPW; CSW; DA3; DAM POP;
   DLB 185; MTCW 1, 2; MTFW 2005;
   TUS
Thompson, James Myers
   See Thompson, Jim (Myers)
Thompson, Jim (Myers) 1906-1977(?)
   .... **CLC 69**
   See also BPFB 3; CA 140; CMW 4; CPW;
   DLB 226; MSW
Thompson, Judith (Clare Francesca) 1954-
   .... **CLC 39**
   See also CA 143; CD 5, 6; CWD; DFS 22
Thomson, James 1700-1748 ... **LC 16, 29, 40**
   See also BRWS 3; DAM POET; DLB 95;
   RGEL 2
Thomson, James 1834-1882 .... **NCLC 18**
   See also DAM POET; DLB 35; RGEL 2
Thoreau, Henry David 1817-1862
   .. **NCLC 7, 21, 61, 138; PC 30; WLC 6**
   See also AAYA 42; AMW; ANW; BYA 3;
   CDALB 1640-1865; DA; DA3; DAB;
   DAC; DAM MST; DLB 1, 183, 223, 270,
   298; LAIT 2; LMFS 1; NCFS 3; RGAL
   4; TUS
Thorndike, E. L.
   See Thorndike, Edward L(ee)
Thorndike, Edward L(ee) 1874-1949
   .... **TCLC 107**
   See also CA 121
Thornton, Hall
   See Silverberg, Robert
Thorpe, Adam 1956- .... **CLC 176**
   See also CA 129; CANR 92; DLB 231
Thubron, Colin (Gerald Dryden) 1939-
   .... **CLC 163**
   See also CA 25-28R; CANR 12, 29, 59, 95;
   CN 5, 6, 7; DLB 204, 231
Thucydides c. 455B.C.-c. 395B.C.
   .... **CMLC 17**
   See also AW 1; DLB 176; RGWL 2, 3;
   WLIT 8
Thumboo, Edwin Nadason 1933- .... **PC 30**
   See also CA 194; CP 1
Thurber, James (Grover) 1894-1961
   .... **CLC 5, 11, 25, 125; SSC 1, 47**
   See also AAYA 56; AMWS 1; BPFB 3;
   BYA 5; CA 73-76; CANR 17, 39; CDALB
   1929-1941; CWRI 5; DA; DA3; DAB;
   DAC; DAM DRAM, MST, NOV; DLB 4,
   11, 22, 102; EWL 3; EXPS; FANT; LAIT
   3; MAICYA 1, 2; MAL 5; MTCW 1, 2;
   MTFW 2005; RGAL 4; RGSF 2; SATA
   13; SSFS 1, 10, 19; SUFW; TUS
Thurman, Wallace (Henry) 1902-1934
   .... **BLC 3; HR 1:3; TCLC 6**
   See also BW 1, 3; CA 104; 124; CANR 81;
   DAM MULT; DLB 51
Tibullus c. 54B.C.-c. 18B.C. .... **CMLC 36**
   See also AW 2; DLB 211; RGWL 2, 3;
   WLIT 8
Ticheburn, Cheviot
   See Ainsworth, William Harrison
Tieck, (Johann) Ludwig 1773-1853
   .... **NCLC 5, 46; SSC 31**
   See also CDWLB 2; DLB 90; EW 5; IDTP;
   RGSF 2; RGWL 2, 3; SUFW

Tiger, Derry
   See Ellison, Harlan
Tilghman, Christopher 1946- .... **CLC 65**
   See also CA 159; CANR 135, 151; CSW;
   DLB 244
Tillich, Paul (Johannes) 1886-1965
   .... **CLC 131**
   See also CA 5-8R; 25-28R; CANR 33;
   MTCW 1, 2
Tillinghast, Richard (Williford) 1940-
   .... **CLC 29**
   See also CA 29-32R; CAAS 23; CANR 26,
   51, 96; CP 2, 3, 4, 5, 6, 7; CSW
Tillman, Lynne ? .... **CLC 231**
   See also CA 173; CANR 144
Timrod, Henry 1828-1867 .... **NCLC 25**
   See also DLB 3, 248; RGAL 4
Tindall, Gillian (Elizabeth) 1938- ..... **CLC 7**
   See also CA 21-24R; CANR 11, 65, 107;
   CN 1, 2, 3, 4, 5, 6, 7
Tiptree, James, Jr. .... **CLC 48, 50**
   See Sheldon, Alice Hastings Bradley
   See also DLB 8; SCFW 1, 2; SFW 4
Tirone Smith, Mary-Ann 1944- ...... **CLC 39**
   See also CA 118; 136; CANR 113; SATA
   143
Tirso de Molina 1580(?)-1648 .... **DC 13;**
   HLCS 2; LC 73
   See also RGWL 2, 3
Titmarsh, Michael Angelo
   See Thackeray, William Makepeace
Tocqueville, Alexis (Charles Henri Maurice
   Clerel Comte) de 1805-1859 . **NCLC 7,**
   63
   See also EW 6; GFL 1789 to the Present;
   TWA
Toer, Pramoedya Ananta 1925-2006
   .... **CLC 186**
   See also CA 197; 251; RGWL 3
Toffler, Alvin 1928- .... **CLC 168**
   See also CA 13-16R; CANR 15, 46, 67;
   CPW; DAM POP; MTCW 1, 2
Toibin, Colm 1955- .... **CLC 162**
   See also CA 142; CANR 81, 149; CN 7;
   DLB 271
Tolkien, J(ohn) R(onald) R(euel) 1892-1973
   .... **CLC 1, 2, 3, 8, 12, 38; TCLC 137;**
   WLC 6
   See also AAYA 10; AITN 1; BPFB 3;
   BRWC 2; BRWS 2; CA 17-18; 45-48;
   CANR 36, 134; CAP 2; CDBLB 1914-
   1945; CLR 56; CN 1; CPW 1; CWRI 5;
   DA; DA3; DAB; DAC; DAM MST, NOV,
   POP; DLB 15, 160, 255; EFS 2; EWL 3;
   FANT; JRDA; LAIT 1; LATS 1:2; LMFS
   2; MAICYA 1, 2; MTCW 1, 2; MTFW
   2005; NFS 8; RGEL 2; SATA 2, 32, 100;
   SATA-Obit 24; SFW 4; SUFW; TEA;
   WCH; WYA; YAW
Toller, Ernst 1893-1939 .... **TCLC 10**
   See also CA 107; 186; DLB 124; EWL 3;
   RGWL 2, 3
Tolson, M. B.
   See Tolson, Melvin B(eaunorus)
Tolson, Melvin B(eaunorus) 1898(?)-1966
   .... **BLC 3; CLC 36, 105**
   See also AFAW 1, 2; BW 1, 3; CA 124; 89-
   92; CANR 80; DAM MULT, POET; DLB
   48, 76; MAL 5; RGAL 4
Tolstoi, Aleksei Nikolaevich
   See Tolstoy, Alexey Nikolaevich
Tolstoi, Lev
   See Tolstoy, Leo (Nikolaevich)
   See also RGSF 2; RGWL 2, 3
Tolstoy, Aleksei Nikolaevich
   See Tolstoy, Alexey Nikolaevich
   See also DLB 272

Tolstoy, Alexey Nikolaevich 1882-1945
   .... **TCLC 18**
   See Tolstoy, Aleksei Nikolaevich
   See also CA 107; 158; EWL 3; SFW 4
Tolstoy, Leo (Nikolaevich) 1828-1910
   ...... **SSC 9, 30, 45, 54; TCLC 4, 11, 17,**
   28, 44, 79, 173; WLC 6
   See Tolstoi, Lev
   See also AAYA 56; CA 104; 123; DA; DA3;
   DAB; DAC; DAM MST, NOV; DLB 238;
   EFS 2; EW 7; EXPS; IDTP; LAIT 2;
   LATS 1:1; LMFS 1; NFS 10; SATA 26;
   SSFS 5; TWA
Tolstoy, Count Leo
   See Tolstoy, Leo (Nikolaevich)
Tomalin, Claire 1933- .... **CLC 166**
   See also CA 89-92; CANR 52, 88; DLB
   155
Tomasi di Lampedusa, Giuseppe 1896-1957
   See Lampedusa, Giuseppe (Tomasi) di
   See also CA 111; DLB 177; EWL 3; WLIT
   7
Tomlin, Lily 1939(?)-
   See Tomlin, Mary Jean
   See also CA 117
Tomlin, Mary Jean .... **CLC 17**
   See Tomlin, Lily
Tomline, F. Latour
   See Gilbert, W(illiam) S(chwenck)
Tomlinson, (Alfred) Charles 1927- .. **CLC 2,**
   4, 6, 13, 45; PC 17
   See also CA 5-8R; CANR 33; CP 1, 2, 3, 4,
   5, 6, 7; DAM POET; DLB 40; TCLE 1:2
Tomlinson, H(enry) M(ajor) 1873-1958
   .... **TCLC 71**
   See also CA 118; 161; DLB 36, 100, 195
Tonna, Charlotte Elizabeth 1790-1846
   .... **NCLC 135**
   See also DLB 163
Tonson, Jacob fl. 1655(?)-1736 .... **LC 86**
   See also DLB 170
Toole, John Kennedy 1937-1969 .... **CLC 19,**
   64
   See also BPFB 3; CA 104; DLBY 1981;
   MTCW 2; MTFW 2005
Toomer, Eugene
   See Toomer, Jean
Toomer, Eugene Pinchback
   See Toomer, Jean
Toomer, Jean 1894-1967 . **BLC 3; CLC 1, 4,**
   13, 22; HR 1:3; PC 7; SSC 1, 45;
   TCLC 172; WLCS
   See also AFAW 1, 2; AMWS 3, 9; BW 1;
   CA 85-88; CDALB 1917-1929; DA3;
   DAM MULT; DLB 45, 51; EWL 3; EXPP;
   EXPS; LMFS 2; MAL 5; MTCW 1, 2;
   MTFW 2005; NFS 11; RGAL 4; RGSF 2;
   SSFS 5
Toomer, Nathan Jean
   See Toomer, Jean
Toomer, Nathan Pinchback
   See Toomer, Jean
Torley, Luke
   See Blish, James (Benjamin)
Tornimparte, Alessandra
   See Ginzburg, Natalia
Torre, Raoul della
   See Mencken, H(enry) L(ouis)
Torrence, Ridgely 1874-1950 .... **TCLC 97**
   See also DLB 54, 249; MAL 5
Torrey, E(dwin) Fuller 1937- .... **CLC 34**
   See also CA 119; CANR 71
Torsvan, Ben Traven
   See Traven, B.
Torsvan, Benno Traven
   See Traven, B.
Torsvan, Berick Traven
   See Traven, B.

Twain, Mark .... **SSC 6, 26, 34, 87; TCLC 6, 12, 19, 36, 48, 59, 161; WLC 6**
See Clemens, Samuel Langhorne
See also AAYA 20; AMW; AMWC 1; BPFB 3; BYA 2, 3, 11, 14; CLR 58, 60, 66; DLB 11; EXPN; EXPS; FANT; LAIT 2; MAL 5; NCFS 4; NFS 1, 6; RGAL 4; RGSF 2; SFW 4; SSFS 1, 7, 16, 21; SUFW; TUS; WCH; WYA; YAW

Tyler, Anne 1941- ...... **CLC 7, 11, 18, 28, 44, 59, 103, 205**
See also AAYA 18, 60; AMWS 4; BEST 89:1; BPFB 3; BYA 12; CA 9-12R; CANR 11, 33, 53, 109, 132; CDALBS; CN 1, 2, 3, 4, 5, 6, 7; CPW; CSW; DAM NOV, POP; DLB 6, 143; DLBY 1982; EWL 3; EXPN; LATS 1:2; MAL 5; MBL; MTCW 1, 2; MTFW 2005; NFS 2, 7, 10; RGAL 4; SATA 7, 90, 173; SSFS 17; TCLE 1:2; TUS; YAW

Tyler, Royall 1757-1826 .... **NCLC 3**
See also DLB 37; RGAL 4

Tynan, Katharine 1861-1931 .... **TCLC 3**
See also CA 104; 167; DLB 153, 240; FW

Tyndale, William c. 1484-1536 .... **LC 103**
See also DLB 132

Tyutchev, Fyodor 1803-1873 .... **NCLC 34**

Tzara, Tristan 1896-1963 .. **CLC 47; PC 27; TCLC 168**
See also CA 153; 89-92; DAM POET; EWL 3; MTCW 2

Uchida, Yoshiko 1921-1992 .... **AAL**
See also AAYA 16; BYA 2, 3; CA 13-16R; 139; CANR 6, 22, 47, 61; CDALBS; CLR 6, 56; CWRI 5; DLB 312; JRDA; MAI-CYA 1, 2; MTCW 1, 2; MTFW 2005; SAAS 1; SATA 1, 53; SATA-Obit 72

Udall, Nicholas 1504-1556 .... **LC 84**
See also DLB 62; RGEL 2

Ueda Akinari 1734-1809 .... **NCLC 131**

Uhry, Alfred 1936- .... **CLC 55**
See also CA 127; 133; CAD; CANR 112; CD 5, 6; CSW; DA3; DAM DRAM, POP; DFS 11, 15; INT CA-133; MTFW 2005

Ulf, Haerved
See Strindberg, (Johan) August

Ulf, Harved
See Strindberg, (Johan) August

Ulibarri, Sabine R(eyes) 1919-2003
.... **CLC 83; HLCS 2**
See also CA 131; 214; CANR 81; DAM MULT; DLB 82; HW 1, 2; RGSF 2

Unamuno (y Jugo), Miguel de 1864-1936
... **HLC 2; SSC 11, 69; TCLC 2, 9, 148**
See also CA 104; 131; CANR 81; DAM MULT, NOV; DLB 108, 322; EW 8; EWL 3; HW 1, 2; MTCW 1, 2; MTFW 2005; RGSF 2; RGWL 2, 3; SSFS 20; TWA

Uncle Shelby
See Silverstein, Shel

Undercliffe, Errol
See Campbell, (John) Ramsey

Underwood, Miles
See Glassco, John

Undset, Sigrid 1882-1949 . **TCLC 3; WLC 6**
See also CA 104; 129; DA; DA3; DAB; DAC; DAM MST, NOV; DLB 293; EW 9; EWL 3; FW; MTCW 1, 2; MTFW 2005; RGWL 2, 3

Ungaretti, Giuseppe 1888-1970 .. **CLC 7, 11, 15; PC 57**
See also CA 19-20; 25-28R; CAP 2; DLB 114; EW 10; EWL 3; PFS 20; RGWL 2, 3; WLIT 7

Unger, Douglas 1952- .... **CLC 34**
See also CA 130; CANR 94, 155

Unsworth, Barry (Forster) 1930- ... **CLC 76, 127**
See also BRWS 7; CA 25-28R; CANR 30, 54, 125; CN 6, 7; DLB 194, 326

Updike, John 1932- ...... **CLC 1, 2, 3, 5, 7, 9, 13, 15, 23, 34, 43, 70, 139, 214; SSC 13, 27; WLC 6**
See also AAYA 36; AMW; AMWC 1; AMWR 1; BPFB 3; BYA 12; CA 1-4R; CABS 1; CANR 4, 33, 51, 94, 133; CDALB 1968-1988; CN 1, 2, 3, 4, 5, 6, 7; CP 1, 2, 3, 4, 5, 6, 7; CPW 1; DA; DA3; DAB; DAC; DAM MST, NOV, POET, POP; DLB 2, 5, 143, 218, 227; DLBD 3; DLBY 1980, 1982, 1997; EWL 3; EXPP; HGG; MAL 5; MTCW 1, 2; MTFW 2005; NFS 12, 24; RGAL 4; RGSF 2; SSFS 3, 19; TUS

Updike, John Hoyer
See Updike, John

Upshaw, Margaret Mitchell
See Mitchell, Margaret (Munnerlyn)

Upton, Mark
See Sanders, Lawrence

Upward, Allen 1863-1926 .... **TCLC 85**
See also CA 117; 187; DLB 36

Urdang, Constance (Henriette) 1922-1996
.... **CLC 47**
See also CA 21-24R; CANR 9, 24; CP 1, 2, 3, 4, 5, 6; CWP

Urfe, Honore d' 1567(?)-1625 .... **LC 132**
See also DLB 268; GFL Beginnings to 1789; RGWL 2, 3

Uriel, Henry
See Faust, Frederick (Schiller)

Uris, Leon 1924-2003 .... **CLC 7, 32**
See also AITN 1, 2; BEST 89:2; BPFB 3; CA 1-4R; 217; CANR 1, 40, 65, 123; CN 1, 2, 3, 4, 5, 6; CPW 1; DA3; DAM NOV, POP; MTCW 1, 2; MTFW 2005; RGHL; SATA 49; SATA-Obit 146

Urista (Heredia), Alberto (Baltazar) 1947-
.... **HLCS 1**
See Alurista
See also CA 182; CANR 2, 32; HW 1

Urmuz
See Codrescu, Andrei

Urquhart, Guy
See McAlmon, Robert (Menzies)

Urquhart, Jane 1949- .... **CLC 90**
See also CA 113; CANR 32, 68, 116, 157; CCA 1; DAC

Usigli, Rodolfo 1905-1979 .... **HLCS 1**
See also CA 131; DLB 305; EWL 3; HW 1; LAW

Usk, Thomas (?)-1388 .... **CMLC 76**
See also DLB 146

Ustinov, Peter (Alexander) 1921-2004
.... **CLC 1**
See also AITN 1; CA 13-16R; 225; CANR 25, 51; CBD; CD 5, 6; DLB 13; MTCW 2

U Tam'si, Gerald Felix Tchicaya
See Tchicaya, Gerald Felix

U Tam'si, Tchicaya
See Tchicaya, Gerald Felix

Vachss, Andrew 1942- .... **CLC 106**
See also CA 118; 214; CAAE 214; CANR 44, 95, 153; CMW 4

Vachss, Andrew H.
See Vachss, Andrew

Vachss, Andrew Henry
See Vachss, Andrew

Vaculik, Ludvik 1926- .... **CLC 7**
See also CA 53-56; CANR 72; CWW 2; DLB 232; EWL 3

Vaihinger, Hans 1852-1933 .... **TCLC 71**
See also CA 116; 166

Valdez, Luis (Miguel) 1940- .... **CLC 84; DC 10; HLC 2**
See also CA 101; CAD; CANR 32, 81; CD 5, 6; DAM MULT; DFS 5; DLB 122; EWL 3; HW 1; LAIT 4; LLW

Valenzuela, Luisa 1938- .... **CLC 31, 104; HLCS 2; SSC 14, 82**
See also CA 101; CANR 32, 65, 123; CD-WLB 3; CWW 2; DAM MULT; DLB 113; EWL 3; FW; HW 1, 2; LAW; RGSF 2; RGWL 3

Valera y Alcala-Galiano, Juan 1824-1905
.... **TCLC 10**
See also CA 106

Valerius Maximus fl. 20- .... **CMLC 64**
See also DLB 211

Valery, (Ambroise) Paul (Toussaint Jules) 1871-1945 .... **PC 9; TCLC 4, 15**
See also CA 104; 122; DA3; DAM POET; DLB 258; EW 8; EWL 3; GFL 1789 to the Present; MTCW 1, 2; MTFW 2005; RGWL 2, 3; TWA

Valle-Inclan, Ramon (Maria) del 1866-1936
.... **HLC 2; TCLC 5**
See del Valle-Inclan, Ramon (Maria)
See also CA 106; 153; CANR 80; DAM MULT; DLB 134; EW 8; EWL 3; HW 2; RGSF 2; RGWL 2, 3

Vallejo, Antonio Buero
See Buero Vallejo, Antonio

Vallejo, Cesar (Abraham) 1892-1938
.... **HLC 2; TCLC 3, 56**
See also CA 105; 153; DAM MULT; DLB 290; EWL 3; HW 1; LAW; RGWL 2, 3

Valles, Jules 1832-1885 .... **NCLC 71**
See also DLB 123; GFL 1789 to the Present

Vallette, Marguerite Eymery 1860-1953
.... **TCLC 67**
See Rachilde
See also CA 182; DLB 123, 192

Valle Y Pena, Ramon del
See Valle-Inclan, Ramon (Maria) del

Van Ash, Cay 1918-1994 .... **CLC 34**
See also CA 220

Vanbrugh, Sir John 1664-1726 .... **LC 21**
See also BRW 2; DAM DRAM; DLB 80; IDTP; RGEL 2

Van Campen, Karl
See Campbell, John W(ood, Jr.)

Vance, Gerald
See Silverberg, Robert

Vance, Jack 1916-
See Queen, Ellery; Vance, John Holbrook
See also CA 29-32R; CANR 17, 65, 154; CMW 4; MTCW 1

Vance, John Holbrook .... **CLC 35**
See Vance, Jack
See also DLB 8; FANT; SCFW 1, 2; SFW 4; SUFW 1, 2

Van Den Bogarde, Derek Jules Gaspard Ulric Niven 1921-1999 .... **CLC 14**
See Bogarde, Dirk
See also CA 77-80; 179

Vandenburgh, Jane .... **CLC 59**
See also CA 168

Vanderhaeghe, Guy 1951- .... **CLC 41**
See also BPFB 3; CA 113; CANR 72, 145; CN 7

van der Post, Laurens (Jan) 1906-1996
.... **CLC 5**
See also AFW; CA 5-8R; 155; CANR 35; CN 1, 2, 3, 4, 5, 6; DLB 204; RGEL 2

van de Wetering, Janwillem 1931- . **CLC 47**
See also CA 49-52; CANR 4, 62, 90; CMW 4

Van Dine, S. S. .... **TCLC 23**
See Wright, Willard Huntington
See also DLB 306; MSW

Vivekananda, Swami 1863-1902 ... **TCLC 88**

Vizenor, Gerald Robert 1934- ...... **CLC 103; NNAL**
See also CA 13-16R, 205; CAAE 205; CAAS 22; CANR 5, 21, 44, 67; DAM MULT; DLB 175, 227; MTCW 2; MTFW 2005; TCWW 2

Vizinczey, Stephen 1933- .... **CLC 40**
See also CA 128; CCA 1; INT CA-128

Vliet, R(ussell) G(ordon) 1929-1984
.... **CLC 22**
See also CA 37-40R; 112; CANR 18; CP 2, 3

Vogau, Boris Andreyevich 1894-1938
See Pilnyak, Boris
See also CA 123; 218

Vogel, Paula A. 1951- .... **CLC 76; DC 19**
See also CA 108; CAD; CANR 119, 140; CD 5, 6; CWD; DFS 14; MTFW 2005; RGAL 4

Voigt, Cynthia 1942- .... **CLC 30**
See also AAYA 3, 30; BYA 1, 3, 6, 7, 8; CA 106; CANR 18, 37, 40, 94, 145; CLR 13, 48; INT CANR-18; JRDA; LAIT 5; MAICYA 1, 2; MAICYAS 1; MTFW 2005; SATA 48, 79, 116, 160; SATA-Brief 33; WYA; YAW

Voigt, Ellen Bryant 1943- .... **CLC 54**
See also CA 69-72; CANR 11, 29, 55, 115; CP 5, 6, 7; CSW; CWP; DLB 120; PFS 23

Voinovich, Vladimir 1932- .... **CLC 10, 49, 147**
See also CA 81-84; CAAS 12; CANR 33, 67, 150; CWW 2; DLB 302; MTCW 1

Voinovich, Vladimir Nikolaevich
See Voinovich, Vladimir

Vollmann, William T. 1959- .... **CLC 89, 227**
See also CA 134; CANR 67, 116; CN 7; CPW; DA3; DAM NOV, POP; MTCW 2; MTFW 2005

Voloshinov, V. N.
See Bakhtin, Mikhail Mikhailovich

Voltaire 1694-1778 .... **LC 14, 79, 110; SSC 12; WLC 6**
See also BYA 13; DA; DA3; DAB; DAC; DAM DRAM, MST; DLB 314; EW 4; GFL Beginnings to 1789; LATS 1:1; LMFS 1; NFS 7; RGWL 2, 3; TWA

von Aschendrof, Baron Ignatz
See Ford, Ford Madox

von Chamisso, Adelbert
See Chamisso, Adelbert von

von Daeniken, Erich 1935- .... **CLC 30**
See also AITN 1; CA 37-40R; CANR 17, 44

von Daniken, Erich
See von Daeniken, Erich

von Eschenbach, Wolfram c. 1170-c. 1220
.... **CMLC 5**
See Eschenbach, Wolfram von
See also CDWLB 2; DLB 138; EW 1; RGWL 2

von Hartmann, Eduard 1842-1906
.... **TCLC 96**

von Hayek, Friedrich August
See Hayek, F(riedrich) A(ugust von)

von Heidenstam, (Carl Gustaf) Verner
See Heidenstam, (Carl Gustaf) Verner von

von Heyse, Paul (Johann Ludwig)
See Heyse, Paul (Johann Ludwig von)

von Hofmannsthal, Hugo
See Hofmannsthal, Hugo von

von Horvath, Odon
See von Horvath, Odon

von Horvath, Odon
See von Horvath, Odon

von Horvath, Odon 1901-1938 ..... **TCLC 45**
See von Horvath, Oedoen
See also CA 118; 194; DLB 85, 124; RGWL 2, 3

von Horvath, Oedoen
See von Horvath, Odon
See also CA 184

von Kleist, Heinrich
See Kleist, Heinrich von

Vonnegut, Kurt, Jr.
See Vonnegut, Kurt

Vonnegut, Kurt 1922- .. **CLC 1, 2, 3, 4, 5, 8, 12, 22, 40, 60, 111, 212; SSC 8; WLC 6**
See also AAYA 6, 44; AITN 1; AMWS 2; BEST 90:4; BPFB 3; BYA 3, 14; CA 1-4R; CANR 1, 25, 49, 75, 92; CDALB 1968-1988; CN 1, 2, 3, 4, 5, 6, 7; CPW; DA; DA3; DAB; DAC; DAM MST, NOV, POP; DLB 2, 8, 152; DLBD 3; DLBY 1980; EWL 3; EXPN; EXPS; LAIT 4; LMFS 2; MAL 5; MTCW 1, 2; MTFW 2005; NFS 3; RGAL 4; SCFW; SFW 4; SSFS 5; TUS; YAW

Von Rachen, Kurt
See Hubbard, L. Ron

von Sternberg, Josef
See Sternberg, Josef von

Vorster, Gordon 1924- .... **CLC 34**
See also CA 133

Vosce, Trudie
See Ozick, Cynthia

Voznesensky, Andrei (Andreievich) 1933-
.... **CLC 1, 15, 57**
See Voznesensky, Andrey
See also CA 89-92; CANR 37; CWW 2; DAM POET; MTCW 1

Voznesensky, Andrey
See Voznesensky, Andrei (Andreievich)
See also EWL 3

Wace, Robert c. 1100-c. 1175 ...... **CMLC 55**
See also DLB 146

Waddington, Miriam 1917-2004 ..... **CLC 28**
See also CA 21-24R; 225; CANR 12, 30; CCA 1; CP 1, 2, 3, 4, 5, 6, 7; DLB 68

Wagman, Fredrica 1937- .... **CLC 7**
See also CA 97-100; INT CA-97-100

Wagner, Linda W.
See Wagner-Martin, Linda (C.)

Wagner, Linda Welshimer
See Wagner-Martin, Linda (C.)

Wagner, Richard 1813-1883 ... **NCLC 9, 119**
See also DLB 129; EW 6

Wagner-Martin, Linda (C.) 1936- .. **CLC 50**
See also CA 159; CANR 135

Wagoner, David (Russell) 1926- .. **CLC 3, 5, 15; PC 33**
See also AMWS 9; CA 1-4R; CAAS 3; CANR 2, 71; CN 1, 2, 3, 4, 5, 6, 7; CP 1, 2, 3, 4, 5, 6, 7; DLB 5, 256; SATA 14; TCWW 1, 2

Wah, Fred(erick James) 1939- .... **CLC 44**
See also CA 107; 141; CP 1, 6, 7; DLB 60

Wahloo, Per 1926-1975 .... **CLC 7**
See also BPFB 3; CA 61-64; CANR 73; CMW 4; MSW

Wahloo, Peter
See Wahloo, Per

Wain, John (Barrington) 1925-1994
.... **CLC 2, 11, 15, 46**
See also CA 5-8R; 145; CAAS 4; CANR 23, 54; CDBLB 1960 to Present; CN 1, 2, 3, 4, 5; CP 1, 2, 3, 4, 5; DLB 15, 27, 139, 155; EWL 3; MTCW 1, 2; MTFW 2005

Wajda, Andrzej 1926- .... **CLC 16, 219**
See also CA 102

Wakefield, Dan 1932- .... **CLC 7**
See also CA 21-24R, 211; CAAE 211; CAAS 7; CN 4, 5, 6, 7

Wakefield, Herbert Russell 1888-1965
.... **TCLC 120**
See also CA 5-8R; CANR 77; HGG; SUFW

Wakoski, Diane 1937- .... **CLC 2, 4, 7, 9, 11, 40; PC 15**
See also CA 13-16R, 216; CAAE 216; CAAS 1; CANR 9, 60, 106; CP 1, 2, 3, 4, 5, 6, 7; CWP; DAM POET; DLB 5; INT CANR-9; MAL 5; MTCW 2; MTFW 2005

Wakoski-Sherbell, Diane
See Wakoski, Diane

Walcott, Derek 1930- .. **BLC 3; CLC 2, 4, 9, 14, 25, 42, 67, 76, 160; DC 7; PC 46**
See also BW 2; CA 89-92; CANR 26, 47, 75, 80, 130; CBD; CD 5, 6; CDWLB 3; CP 1, 2, 3, 4, 5, 6, 7; DA3; DAB; DAC; DAM MST, MULT, POET; DLB 117; DLBY 1981; DNFS 1; EFS 1; EWL 3; LMFS 2; MTCW 1, 2; MTFW 2005; PFS 6; RGEL 2; TWA; WWE 1

Waldman, Anne (Lesley) 1945- .... **CLC 7**
See also BG 1:3; CA 37-40R; CAAS 17; CANR 34, 69, 116; CP 1, 2, 3, 4, 5, 6, 7; CWP; DLB 16

Waldo, E. Hunter
See Sturgeon, Theodore (Hamilton)

Waldo, Edward Hamilton
See Sturgeon, Theodore (Hamilton)

Walker, Alice 1944- ..... **BLC 3; CLC 5, 6, 9, 19, 27, 46, 58, 103, 167; PC 30; SSC 5; WLCS**
See also AAYA 3, 33; AFAW 1, 2; AMWS 3; BEST 89:4; BPFB 3; BW 2, 3; CA 37-40R; CANR 9, 27, 49, 66, 82, 131; CDALB 1968-1988; CN 4, 5, 6, 7; CPW; CSW; DA; DA3; DAB; DAC; DAM MST, MULT, NOV, POET, POP; DLB 6, 33, 143; EWL 3; EXPN; EXPS; FL 1:6; FW; INT CANR-27; LAIT 3; MAL 5; MBL; MTCW 1, 2; MTFW 2005; NFS 5; RGAL 4; RGSF 2; SATA 31; SSFS 2, 11; TUS; YAW

Walker, Alice Malsenior
See Walker, Alice

Walker, David Harry 1911-1992 ..... **CLC 14**
See also CA 1-4R; 137; CANR 1; CN 1, 2; CWRI 5; SATA 8; SATA-Obit 71

Walker, Edward Joseph 1934-2004
See Walker, Ted
See also CA 21-24R; 226; CANR 12, 28, 53

Walker, George F(rederick) 1947- . **CLC 44, 61**
See also CA 103; CANR 21, 43, 59; CD 5, 6; DAB; DAC; DAM MST; DLB 60

Walker, Joseph A. 1935-2003 .... **CLC 19**
See also BW 1, 3; CA 89-92; CAD; CANR 26, 143; CD 5, 6; DAM DRAM, MST; DFS 12; DLB 38

Walker, Margaret 1915-1998 . **BLC; CLC 1, 6; PC 20; TCLC 129**
See also AFAW 1, 2; BW 2, 3; CA 73-76; 172; CANR 26, 54, 76, 136; CN 1, 2, 3, 4, 5, 6; CP 1, 2, 3, 4, 5, 6; CSW; DAM MULT; DLB 76, 152; EXPP; FW; MAL 5; MTCW 1, 2; MTFW 2005; RGAL 4; RHW

Walker, Ted .... **CLC 13**
See Walker, Edward Joseph
See also CP 1, 2, 3, 4, 5, 6, 7; DLB 40

Wallace, David Foster 1962- .. **CLC 50, 114; SSC 68**
See also AAYA 50; AMWS 10; CA 132; CANR 59, 133; CN 7; DA3; MTCW 2; MTFW 2005

Wallace, Dexter
See Masters, Edgar Lee

Willard, Nancy 1936- .... **CLC 7, 37**
See also BYA 5; CA 89-92; CANR 10, 39,
68, 107, 152; CLR 5; CP 2, 3, 4, 5; CWP;
CWRI 5; DLB 5, 52; FANT; MAICYA 1,
2; MTCW 1; SATA 37, 71, 127; SATA-
Brief 30; SUFW 2; TCLE 1:2
William of Malmesbury c. 1090B.C.-c.
1140B.C. .... **CMLC 57**
William of Ockham 1290-1349 .... **CMLC 32**
Williams, Ben Ames 1889-1953 .... **TCLC 89**
See also CA 183; DLB 102
Williams, Charles
See Collier, James Lincoln
Williams, Charles (Walter Stansby)
1886-1945 .... **TCLC 1, 11**
See also BRWS 9; CA 104; 163; DLB 100,
153, 255; FANT; RGEL 2; SUFW 1
Williams, C.K. 1936- .... **CLC 33, 56, 148**
See also CA 37-40R; CAAS 26; CANR 57,
106; CP 1, 2, 3, 4, 5, 6, 7; DAM POET;
DLB 5; MAL 5
Williams, Ella Gwendolen Rees
See Rhys, Jean
Williams, (George) Emlyn 1905-1987
.... **CLC 15**
See also CA 104; 123; CANR 36; DAM
DRAM; DLB 10, 77; IDTP; MTCW 1
Williams, Hank 1923-1953 .... **TCLC 81**
See Williams, Hiram King
Williams, Helen Maria 1761-1827
.... **NCLC 135**
See also DLB 158
Williams, Hiram Hank
See Williams, Hank
Williams, Hiram King
See Williams, Hank
See also CA 188
Williams, Hugo (Mordaunt) 1942- . **CLC 42**
See also CA 17-20R; CANR 45, 119; CP 1,
2, 3, 4, 5, 6, 7; DLB 40
Williams, J. Walker
See Wodehouse, P(elham) G(renville)
Williams, John A(lfred) 1925- .... **BLC 3;**
CLC 5, 13
See also AFAW 2; BW 2, 3; CA 53-56, 195;
CAAE 195; CAAS 3; CANR 6, 26, 51,
118; CN 1, 2, 3, 4, 5, 6, 7; CSW; DAM
MULT; DLB 2, 33; EWL 3; INT CANR-6;
MAL 5; RGAL 4; SFW 4
Williams, Jonathan (Chamberlain) 1929-
.... **CLC 13**
See also CA 9-12R; CAAS 12; CANR 8,
108; CP 1, 2, 3, 4, 5, 6, 7; DLB 5
Williams, Joy 1944- .... **CLC 31**
See also CA 41-44R; CANR 22, 48, 97
Williams, Norman 1952- .... **CLC 39**
See also CA 118
Williams, Roger 1603(?)-1683 .... **LC 129**
See also DLB 24
Williams, Sherley Anne 1944-1999 .. **BLC 3;**
CLC 89
See also AFAW 2; BW 2, 3; CA 73-76; 185;
CANR 25, 82; DAM MULT, POET; DLB
41; INT CANR-25; SATA 78; SATA-Obit
116
Williams, Shirley
See Williams, Sherley Anne
Williams, Tennessee 1911-1983 .... **CLC 1, 2,**
5, 7, 8, 11, 15, 19, 30, 39, 45, 71, 111;
DC 4; SSC 81; WLC 6
See also AAYA 31; AITN 1, 2; AMW;
AMWC 1; CA 5-8R; 108; CABS 3; CAD;
CANR 31, 132; CDALB 1941-1968; CN
1, 2, 3; DA; DA3; DAB; DAC; DAM
DRAM, MST; DFS 17; DLB 7; DLBD 4;
DLBY 1983; EWL 3; GLL 1; LAIT 4;
LATS 1:2; MAL 5; MTCW 1, 2; MTFW
2005; RGAL 4; TUS

Williams, Thomas (Alonzo) 1926-1990
.... **CLC 14**
See also CA 1-4R; 132; CANR 2
Williams, William C.
See Williams, William Carlos
Williams, William Carlos 1883-1963
.... **CLC 1, 2, 5, 9, 13, 22, 42, 67; PC 7;**
SSC 31; WLC 6
See also AAYA 46; AMW; AMWR 1; CA
89-92; CANR 34; CDALB 1917-1929;
DA; DA3; DAB; DAC; DAM MST,
POET; DLB 4, 16, 54, 86; EWL 3; EXPP;
MAL 5; MTCW 1, 2; MTFW 2005; NCFS
4; PAB; PFS 1, 6, 11; RGAL 4; RGSF 2;
TUS; WP
Williamson, David (Keith) 1942- .... **CLC 56**
See also CA 103; CANR 41; CD 5, 6; DLB
289
Williamson, Ellen Douglas 1905-1984
See Douglas, Ellen
See also CA 17-20R; 114; CANR 39
Williamson, Jack .... **CLC 29**
See Williamson, John Stewart
See also CAAS 8; DLB 8; SCFW 1, 2
Williamson, John Stewart 1908-2006
See Williamson, Jack
See also CA 17-20R; CANR 23, 70, 153;
SFW 4
Willie, Frederick
See Lovecraft, H. P.
Willingham, Calder (Baynard, Jr.)
1922-1995 .... **CLC 5, 51**
See also CA 5-8R; 147; CANR 3; CN 1, 2,
3, 4, 5; CSW; DLB 2, 44; IDFW 3, 4;
MTCW 1
Willis, Charles
See Clarke, Arthur C.
Willy
See Colette, (Sidonie-Gabrielle)
Willy, Colette
See Colette, (Sidonie-Gabrielle)
See also GLL 1
Wilmot, John 1647-1680 .... **LC 75; PC 66**
See Rochester
See also BRW 2; DLB 131; PAB
Wilson, A.N. 1950- .... **CLC 33**
See also BRWS 6; CA 112; 122; CANR
155; CN 4, 5, 6, 7; DLB 14, 155, 194;
MTCW 2
Wilson, Andrew Norman
See Wilson, A.N.
Wilson, Angus (Frank Johnstone) 1913-1991
.... **CLC 2, 3, 5, 25, 34; SSC 21**
See also BRWS 1; CA 5-8R; 134; CANR
21; CN 1, 2, 3, 4; DLB 15, 139, 155;
EWL 3; MTCW 1, 2; MTFW 2005; RGEL
2; RGSF 2
Wilson, August 1945-2005 .... **BLC 3; CLC**
39, 50, 63, 118, 222; DC 2; WLCS
See also AAYA 16; AFAW 2; AMWS 8; BW
2, 3; CA 115; 122; 244; CAD; CANR 42,
54, 76, 128; CD 5, 6; DA; DA3; DAB;
DAC; DAM DRAM, MST, MULT; DFS
3, 7, 15, 17; DLB 228; EWL 3; LAIT 4;
LATS 1:2; MAL 5; MTCW 1, 2; MTFW
2005; RGAL 4
Wilson, Brian 1942- .... **CLC 12**
Wilson, Colin (Henry) 1931- .... **CLC 3, 14**
See also CA 1-4R; CAAS 5; CANR 1, 22,
33, 77; CMW 4; CN 1, 2, 3, 4, 5, 6; DLB
14, 194; HGG; MTCW 1; SFW 4
Wilson, Dirk
See Pohl, Frederik
Wilson, Edmund 1895-1972 . **CLC 1, 2, 3, 8,**
24
See also AMW; CA 1-4R; 37-40R; CANR
1, 46, 110; CN 1; DLB 63; EWL 3; MAL
5; MTCW 1, 2; MTFW 2005; RGAL 4;
TUS

Wilson, Ethel Davis (Bryant) 1888(?)-1980
.... **CLC 13**
See also CA 102; CN 1, 2; DAC; DAM
POET; DLB 68; MTCW 1; RGEL 2
Wilson, Harriet
See Wilson, Harriet E. Adams
See also DLB 239
Wilson, Harriet E.
See Wilson, Harriet E. Adams
See also DLB 243
Wilson, Harriet E. Adams 1827(?)-1863(?)
.... **BLC 3; NCLC 78**
See Wilson, Harriet; Wilson, Harriet E.
See also DAM MULT; DLB 50
Wilson, John 1785-1854 .... **NCLC 5**
Wilson, John (Anthony) Burgess 1917-1993
See Burgess, Anthony
See also CA 1-4R; 143; CANR 2, 46; DA3;
DAC; DAM NOV; MTCW 1, 2; MTFW
2005; NFS 15; TEA
Wilson, Lanford 1937- . **CLC 7, 14, 36, 197;**
DC 19
See also CA 17-20R; CABS 3; CAD; CANR
45, 96; CD 5, 6; DAM DRAM; DFS 4, 9,
12, 16, 20; DLB 7; EWL 3; MAL 5; TUS
Wilson, Robert M. 1941- .... **CLC 7, 9**
See also CA 49-52; CAD; CANR 2, 41; CD
5, 6; MTCW 1
Wilson, Robert McLiam 1964- .... **CLC 59**
See also CA 132; DLB 267
Wilson, Sloan 1920-2003 .... **CLC 32**
See also CA 1-4R; 216; CANR 1, 44; CN
1, 2, 3, 4, 5, 6
Wilson, Snoo 1948- .... **CLC 33**
See also CA 69-72; CBD; CD 5, 6
Wilson, William S(mith) 1932- .... **CLC 49**
See also CA 81-84
Wilson, (Thomas) Woodrow 1856-1924
.... **TCLC 79**
See also CA 166; DLB 47
Wilson and Warnke eds. .... **CLC 65**
Winchilsea, Anne (Kingsmill) Finch
1661-1720
See Finch, Anne
See also RGEL 2
Winckelmann, Johann Joachim 1717-1768
.... **LC 129**
See also DLB 97
Windham, Basil
See Wodehouse, P(elham) G(renville)
Wingrove, David 1954- .... **CLC 68**
See also CA 133; SFW 4
Winnemucca, Sarah 1844-1891 ... **NCLC 79;**
NNAL
See also DAM MULT; DLB 175; RGAL 4
Winstanley, Gerrard 1609-1676 .... **LC 52**
Wintergreen, Jane
See Duncan, Sara Jeannette
Winters, Arthur Yvor
See Winters, Yvor
Winters, Janet Lewis .... **CLC 41**
See Lewis, Janet
See also DLBY 1987
Winters, Yvor 1900-1968 .... **CLC 4, 8, 32**
See also AMWS 2; CA 11-12; 25-28R; CAP
1; DLB 48; EWL 3; MAL 5; MTCW 1;
RGAL 4
Winterson, Jeanette 1959- .... **CLC 64, 158**
See also BRWS 4; CA 136; CANR 58, 116;
CN 5, 6, 7; CPW; DA3; DAM POP; DLB
207, 261; FANT; FW; GLL 1; MTCW 2;
MTFW 2005; RHW
Winthrop, John 1588-1649 .... **LC 31, 107**
See also DLB 24, 30
Wirth, Louis 1897-1952 .... **TCLC 92**
See also CA 210
Wiseman, Frederick 1930- .... **CLC 20**
See also CA 159

Wylie, Elinor (Morton Hoyt) 1885-1928
.... **PC 23; TCLC 8**
See also AMWS 1; CA 105; 162; DLB 9, 45; EXPP; MAL 5; RGAL 4

Wylie, Philip (Gordon) 1902-1971 .. **CLC 43**
See also CA 21-22; 33-36R; CAP 2; CN 1; DLB 9; SFW 4

Wyndham, John .... **CLC 19**
See Harris, John (Wyndham Parkes Lucas) Beynon
See also DLB 255; SCFW 1, 2

Wyss, Johann David Von 1743-1818
.... **NCLC 10**
See also CLR 92; JRDA; MAICYA 1, 2; SATA 29; SATA-Brief 27

Xenophon c. 430B.C.-c. 354B.C. .. **CMLC 17**
See also AW 1; DLB 176; RGWL 2, 3; WLIT 8

Xingjian, Gao 1940-
See Gao Xingjian
See also CA 193; DFS 21; DLB 330; RGWL 3

Yakamochi 718-785 .... **CMLC 45; PC 48**

Yakumo Koizumi
See Hearn, (Patricio) Lafcadio (Tessima Carlos)

Yamada, Mitsuye (May) 1923- .... **PC 44**
See also CA 77-80

Yamamoto, Hisaye 1921- .... **AAL; SSC 34**
See also CA 214; DAM MULT; DLB 312; LAIT 4; SSFS 14

Yamauchi, Wakako 1924- .... **AAL**
See also CA 214; DLB 312

Yanez, Jose Donoso
See Donoso (Yanez), Jose

Yanovsky, Basile S.
See Yanovsky, V(assily) S(emenovich)

Yanovsky, V(assily) S(emenovich) 1906-1989
.... **CLC 2, 18**
See also CA 97-100; 129

Yates, Richard 1926-1992 .... **CLC 7, 8, 23**
See also AMWS 11; CA 5-8R; 139; CANR 10, 43; CN 1, 2, 3, 4, 5; DLB 2, 234; DLBY 1981, 1992; INT CANR-10; SSFS 24

Yau, John 1950- .... **PC 61**
See also CA 154; CANR 89; CP 4, 5, 6, 7; DLB 234, 312

Yearsley, Ann 1753-1806 .... **NCLC 174**
See also DLB 109

Yeats, W. B.
See Yeats, William Butler

Yeats, William Butler 1865-1939 .... **PC 20, 51; TCLC 1, 11, 18, 31, 93, 116; WLC 6**
See also AAYA 48; BRW 6; BRWR 1; CA 104; 127; CANR 45; CDBLB 1890-1914; DA; DA3; DAB; DAC; DAM DRAM, MST, POET; DLB 10, 19, 98, 156; EWL 3; EXPP; MTCW 1, 2; MTFW 2005; NCFS 3; PAB; PFS 1, 2, 5, 7, 13, 15; RGEL 2; TEA; WLIT 4; WP

Yehoshua, A(braham) B. 1936- . **CLC 13, 31**
See also CA 33-36R; CANR 43, 90, 145; CWW 2; EWL 3; RGHL; RGSF 2; RGWL 3; WLIT 6

Yellow Bird
See Ridge, John Rollin

Yep, Laurence Michael 1948- .... **CLC 35**
See also AAYA 5, 31; BYA 7; CA 49-52; CANR 1, 46, 92; CLR 3, 17, 54; DLB 52, 312; FANT; JRDA; MAICYA 1, 2; MAICYAS 1; SATA 7, 69, 123; WYA; YAW

Yerby, Frank G(arvin) 1916-1991 ... **BLC 3; CLC 1, 7, 22**
See also BPFB 3; BW 1, 3; CA 9-12R; 136; CANR 16, 52; CN 1, 2, 3, 4, 5; DAM MULT; DLB 76; INT CANR-16; MTCW 1; RGAL 4; RHW

Yesenin, Sergei Aleksandrovich
See Esenin, Sergei

Yevtushenko, Yevgeny (Alexandrovich) 1933-
.... **CLC 1, 3, 13, 26, 51, 126; PC 40**
See Evtushenko, Evgenii Aleksandrovich
See also CA 81-84; CANR 33, 54; DAM POET; EWL 3; MTCW 1; RGHL

Yezierska, Anzia 1885(?)-1970 .... **CLC 46**
See also CA 126; 89-92; DLB 28, 221; FW; MTCW 1; RGAL 4; SSFS 15

Yglesias, Helen 1915- .... **CLC 7, 22**
See also CA 37-40R; CAAS 20; CANR 15, 65, 95; CN 4, 5, 6, 7; INT CANR-15; MTCW 1

Yokomitsu, Riichi 1898-1947 .... **TCLC 47**
See also CA 170; EWL 3

Yonge, Charlotte (Mary) 1823-1901
.... **TCLC 48**
See also CA 109; 163; DLB 18, 163; RGEL 2; SATA 17; WCH

York, Jeremy
See Creasey, John

York, Simon
See Heinlein, Robert A.

Yorke, Henry Vincent 1905-1974 .... **CLC 13**
See Green, Henry
See also CA 85-88; 49-52

Yosano, Akiko 1878-1942 . **PC 11; TCLC 59**
See also CA 161; EWL 3; RGWL 3

Yoshimoto, Banana .... **CLC 84**
See Yoshimoto, Mahoko
See also AAYA 50; NFS 7

Yoshimoto, Mahoko 1964-
See Yoshimoto, Banana
See also CA 144; CANR 98; SSFS 16

Young, Al(bert James) 1939- .. **BLC 3; CLC 19**
See also BW 2, 3; CA 29-32R; CANR 26, 65, 109; CN 2, 3, 4, 5, 6, 7; CP 1, 2, 3, 4, 5, 6, 7; DAM MULT; DLB 33

Young, Andrew (John) 1885-1971 ..... **CLC 5**
See also CA 5-8R; CANR 7, 29; CP 1; RGEL 2

Young, Collier
See Bloch, Robert (Albert)

Young, Edward 1683-1765 .... **LC 3, 40**
See also DLB 95; RGEL 2

Young, Marguerite (Vivian) 1909-1995
.... **CLC 82**
See also CA 13-16; 150; CAP 1; CN 1, 2, 3, 4, 5, 6

Young, Neil 1945- .... **CLC 17**
See also CA 110; CCA 1

Young Bear, Ray A. 1950- . **CLC 94; NNAL**
See also CA 146; DAM MULT; DLB 175; MAL 5

Yourcenar, Marguerite 1903-1987 . **CLC 19, 38, 50, 87**
See also BPFB 3; CA 69-72; CANR 23, 60, 93; DAM NOV; DLB 72; DLBY 1988; EW 12; EWL 3; GFL 1789 to the Present; GLL 1; MTCW 1, 2; MTFW 2005; RGWL 2, 3

Yuan, Chu 340(?)B.C.-278(?)B.C.
.... **CMLC 36**

Yurick, Sol 1925- .... **CLC 6**
See also CA 13-16R; CANR 25; CN 1, 2, 3, 4, 5, 6, 7; MAL 5

Zabolotsky, Nikolai Alekseevich 1903-1958
.... **TCLC 52**
See Zabolotsky, Nikolay Alekseevich
See also CA 116; 164

Zabolotsky, Nikolay Alekseevich
See Zabolotsky, Nikolai Alekseevich
See also EWL 3

Zagajewski, Adam 1945- .... **PC 27**
See also CA 186; DLB 232; EWL 3

Zalygin, Sergei -2000 .... **CLC 59**

Zalygin, Sergei (Pavlovich) 1913-2000
.... **CLC 59**
See also DLB 302

Zamiatin, Evgenii
See Zamyatin, Evgeny Ivanovich
See also RGSF 2; RGWL 2, 3

Zamiatin, Evgenii Ivanovich
See Zamyatin, Evgeny Ivanovich
See also DLB 272

Zamiatin, Yevgenii
See Zamyatin, Evgeny Ivanovich

Zamora, Bernice (B. Ortiz) 1938- . **CLC 89; HLC 2**
See also CA 151; CANR 80; DAM MULT; DLB 82; HW 1, 2

Zamyatin, Evgeny Ivanovich 1884-1937
.... **SSC 89; TCLC 8, 37**
See Zamiatin, Evgenii; Zamiatin, Evgenii Ivanovich; Zamyatin, Yevgeny Ivanovich
See also CA 105; 166; SFW 4

Zamyatin, Yevgeny Ivanovich
See Zamyatin, Evgeny Ivanovich
See also EW 10; EWL 3

Zangwill, Israel 1864-1926 .. **SSC 44; TCLC 16**
See also CA 109; 167; CMW 4; DLB 10, 135, 197; RGEL 2

Zanzotto, Andrea 1921- .... **PC 65**
See also CA 208; CWW 2; DLB 128; EWL 3

Zappa, Francis Vincent, Jr. 1940-1993
See Zappa, Frank
See also CA 108; 143; CANR 57

Zappa, Frank .... **CLC 17**
See Zappa, Francis Vincent, Jr.

Zaturenska, Marya 1902-1982 .... **CLC 6, 11**
See also CA 13-16R; 105; CANR 22; CP 1, 2, 3

Zayas y Sotomayor, Maria de 1590-c. 1661
.... **LC 102; SSC 94**
See also RGSF 2

Zeami 1363-1443 .... **DC 7; LC 86**
See also DLB 203; RGWL 2, 3

Zelazny, Roger 1937-1995 .... **CLC 21**
See also AAYA 7, 68; BPFB 3; CA 21-24R; 148; CANR 26, 60; CN 6; DLB 8; FANT; MTCW 1, 2; MTFW 2005; SATA 57; SATA-Brief 39; SCFW 1, 2; SFW 4; SUFW 1, 2

Zhang Ailing
See Chang, Eileen
See also CWW 2; DLB 328; RGSF 2

Zhdanov, Andrei Alexandrovich 1896-1948
.... **TCLC 18**
See also CA 117; 167

Zhukovsky, Vasilii Andreevich
See Zhukovsky, Vasily (Andreevich)
See also DLB 205

Zhukovsky, Vasily (Andreevich) 1783-1852
.... **NCLC 35**
See Zhukovsky, Vasilii Andreevich

Ziegenhagen, Eric .... **CLC 55**

Zimmer, Jill Schary
See Robinson, Jill

Zimmerman, Robert
See Dylan, Bob

Zindel, Paul 1936-2003 .... **CLC 6, 26; DC 5**
See also AAYA 2, 37; BYA 2, 3, 8, 11, 14; CA 73-76; 213; CAD; CANR 31, 65, 108; CD 5, 6; CDALBS; CLR 3, 45, 85; DA; DA3; DAB; DAC; DAM DRAM, MST, NOV; DFS 12; DLB 7, 52; JRDA; LAIT 5; MAICYA 1, 2; MTCW 1, 2; MTFW 2005; NFS 14; SATA 16, 58, 102; SATA-Obit 142; WYA; YAW

Zinn, Howard 1922- .... **CLC 199**
See also CA 1-4R; CANR 2, 33, 90

Zinov'Ev, A.A.
See Zinoviev, Alexander

Zinov'ev, Aleksandr
See Zinoviev, Alexander
See also DLB 302

Zinoviev, Alexander 1922-2006 .... **CLC 19**
See Zinov'ev, Aleksandr
See also CA 116; 133; 250; CAAS 10

Zinoviev, Alexander Aleksandrovich
See Zinoviev, Alexander

Zizek, Slavoj 1949- .... **CLC 188**
See also CA 201; MTFW 2005

Zoilus
See Lovecraft, H. P.

Zola, Emile (Edouard Charles Antoine)
1840-1902 . **TCLC 1, 6, 21, 41; WLC 6**
See also CA 104; 138; DA; DA3; DAB;
DAC; DAM MST, NOV; DLB 123; EW
7; GFL 1789 to the Present; IDTP; LMFS
1, 2; RGWL 2; TWA

Zoline, Pamela 1941- .... **CLC 62**
See also CA 161; SFW 4

Zoroaster 628(?)B.C.-551(?)B.C. .. **CMLC 40**

Zorrilla y Moral, Jose 1817-1893 .. **NCLC 6**

Zoshchenko, Mikhail (Mikhailovich)
1895-1958 .... **SSC 15; TCLC 15**
See also CA 115; 160; EWL 3; RGSF 2;
RGWL 3

Zuckmayer, Carl 1896-1977 .... **CLC 18**
See also CA 69-72; DLB 56, 124; EWL 3;
RGWL 2, 3

Zuk, Georges
See Skelton, Robin
See also CCA 1

Zukofsky, Louis 1904-1978 .. **CLC 1, 2, 4, 7,**
11, 18; PC 11
See also AMWS 3; CA 9-12R; 77-80;
CANR 39; CP 1, 2; DAM POET; DLB 5,
165; EWL 3; MAL 5; MTCW 1; RGAL 4

Zweig, Paul 1935-1984 .... **CLC 34, 42**
See also CA 85-88; 113

Zweig, Stefan 1881-1942 .... **TCLC 17**
See also CA 112; 170; DLB 81, 118; EWL
3; RGHL

Zwingli, Huldreich 1484-1531 .... **LC 37**
See also DLB 179

Literary Criticism Series
Cumulative Topic Index

This index lists all topic entries in Thompson Gale's *Children's Literature Review* (CLR), *Classical and Medieval Literature Criticism* (CMLC), *Contemporary Literary Criticism* (CLC), *Drama Criticism* (DC), *Literature Criticism from 1400 to 1800* (LC), *Nineteenth-Century Literature Criticism* (NCLC), *Short Story Criticism* (SSC), and *Twentieth-Century Literary Criticism* (TCLC). The index also lists topic entries in the Gale Critical Companion Collection, which includes the following publications: *The Beat Generation* (BG), *Feminism in Literature* (FL), *Gothic Literature* (GL), and *Harlem Renaissance* (HR).

Topic Index

Topic Index

NCLC Cumulative Nationality Index

Nationality Index

NCLC-177 Title Index

ISBN-13: 978-0-7876-9848-5
ISBN-10: 0-7876-9848-2